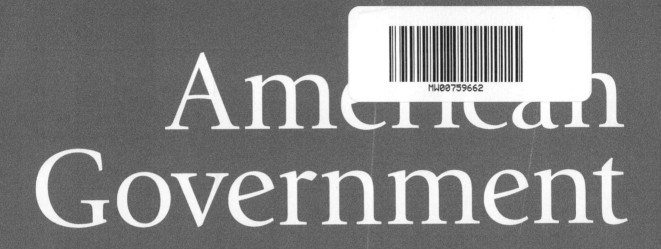

American Government

IN **BLACK** AND **WHITE:**
DIVERSITY AND DEMOCRACY

Third Edition

Paula D. McClain
Duke University

Steven C. Tauber
University of South Florida

New York Oxford
OXFORD UNIVERSITY PRESS

Oxford University Press is a department of the University of Oxford.
It furthers the University's objective of excellence in research,
scholarship, and education by publishing worldwide.
Oxford is a registered trademark of Oxford University Press
in the UK and certain other countries.

Published in the United States of America by
Oxford University Press
198 Madison Avenue, New York, NY 10016,
United States of America.

Library of Congress Cataloging-in-Publication Data

Names: McClain, Paula Denice, author. | Tauber, Steven C., author.
Title: American government in Black and White : diversity and democracy /
    Paula D. McClain, Duke University, Steven C. Tauber, University of South Florida.
Description: Third edition. | New York : Oxford University Press, [2017]
    | Includes index.
Identifiers: LCCN 2016042631 (print) | LCCN 2016047624 (ebook) | ISBN
    9780190298791 (pbk.) | ISBN 9780190298807
Subjects: LCSH: United States--Politics and government.
    | Minorities--Political activity--United States. | United States--Race
    relations--Political aspects.
Classification: LCC JK275 .M333 2017 (print) | LCC JK275 (ebook)
    | DDC 320.473--dc23
LC record available at https://lccn.loc.gov/2016042631

Printing number: 9 8 7 6 5 4 3

Printed in Canada by Webcom

To my husband, Paul C. Jacobson, daughters Kristina and Jessica and grandsons, Jackson and Sterling, whose love and support continued to sustain me throughout this long and continuing project.

Paula D. McClain

Dedicated to my wife Meghan and the memory of her sister Kathleen Hogan (1971–2013)

Steven C. Tauber

Contents

Brief Contents

To the Student

Alexis de Tocqueville, who was an early French visitor to the United States and wrote *Democracy in America* (1835), believed that the essence of America was in the uniquely free and egalitarian ideas that abounded at its founding. Yet, Tocqueville noted that the treatment and situation of Blacks and Indians in the United States contradicted the American passion for democracy. He saw slavery and the denial of constitutional rights and protections to Blacks as the principal threat to the American democratic system. From his perspective, Blacks would never be included in America's democracy; even the American Revolution's egalitarian principles would never change Whites' negative views of Blacks. Indians, he felt, would resist being civilized, and in so doing would be wiped out. Tocqueville believed that the institution of slavery should be abolished, but he also felt that the aftermath would be catastrophic because Blacks, Whites, and Indians would not be able to live together, so White genocidal violence against Blacks and Indians would follow.

For much of the history of the United States, the issues of race and the place of Blacks and American Indians, and later other racial or ethnic minority groups such as Asians and Latinos have been enduring threads in the American political fabric. Although they are still threads that can be pulled to generate angst and divisions, a great deal has changed since Tocqueville made his observations in 1835.

In 2008, Senator Barack Obama (D-IL) became the Democratic nominee for President of the United States and the first Black person to represent a major political party in the presidential race in the history of the United States. On November 4, 2008, Obama was elected the first African American president of the United States, with a wide margin in both the popular and electoral votes. He was reelected to a second term in 2012 by a substantial, albeit somewhat reduced, margin in the popular and electoral votes.

Many Americans view the historic election of a Black as president as a signal that issues of racism and inequality have been resolved and that there is no need for more or new public policies to address racial inequalities. They assert that any remaining inequalities are the result of a lack of individual initiative, not societal barriers. On the contrary, we believe that the election of Barack Obama brought into sharp relief the centrality of issues of race to American politics. In fact, President Obama's success might make it more difficult, not less, to address some of the issues of inequality that continue to exist in the United States.

In this book, we are concerned with the complexities of the American political system and inequalities that continue to exist within it. If you read and understand the text, we believe you will benefit in four ways.

First, government is more than just a set of institutions, rules, and procedures by which those institutions operate. Government exists also in our perceptions about and our experiences with government. Every American might perceive government differently, and each of us behaves somewhat differently based on these perceptions. Describing government in this sense is not something that is feasible here, but we can report on the perceptions of different peoples grouped by shared characteristics. The United States is not "one nation . . . indivisible" but, instead, something different to each of us based on our citizenship status, socioeconomic class, religion, age, place of residence, race, ethnicity, gender, and many other factors.

Second, we offer a practical view of American government supported by empirical analysis. By using hard evidence to support our views, we hope to avoid a naive "how government should work" approach and give you a firm base for developing informed opinions. For example, we list the powers of the president, but in reality these powers are limited and the president is much less powerful than a simple list of official powers would suggest.

Third, you will have a sense of how race has played out in the American governmental system and its politics. Although some historical events present a sad and painful look at the American system, recent events such as the election of President Obama show a more hopeful albeit cautious look at the American political system and its politics.

Finally, reading this book will give you a more holistic and realistic perspective on American government. You will have a sense of what government can do and what American citizens must do to help government achieve its objectives. Regardless of whether that help comes through social movements, voting, or participation in other types of political activity, people—individually and collectively—are central to the American governmental system.

New to the Third Edition

- A sleek and modern four-color design and revamped photo program bring enhanced visual interest to this award-winning text.
- Updates and analysis place the 2016 election and its results into political and cultural context for students.
- Expanded coverage of Latinos highlights the importance and complexities of the political influence wielded by this growing demographic and voting group.
- Enhanced discussion of political science research in relevant chapters provides insights into both the scholarly debates and consensus of the discipline. Many of the tables in the chapters have been updated with the most recent data available.

Revisions to the 2016 Election Update

- Updated coverage on voter purges in Florida (p. 63).
- Updated voter ID discussion (p. 143).
- Updated Equal Rights Amendment discussion (p. 155).
- Updated same-sex marriage discussion (p. 157).
- Updated discussion of the Congressional Black Caucus (p.179).
- Updated discussion of minorities in the cabinet (p. 217).
- Updated discussion of clashes between President Obama and Congress (p. 221).
- Updated caseload data (pp. 255–266).
- Updated minority state party chairs (p. 424).
- Updated information on policy enactment and affirmative action (p. 491).
- More citations added to all chapters.
- Updated opening vignette for Chapters 2, 4, 5, 6, 7, 8, 10, 11, 13, 14, and 15.
- Post-election updates made to Chapter 15, Campaigns and Elections.
- Updated coverage in Chapter 12, including: Chicano Movement; Asian American Movement; Anti-Nuclear Movement; added material to the last paragraph on page 370 on Tea Party and Black Lives Matter.
- Updates to seventeen tables, three figures, and "Measuring Equality" features.

Organization of This Book

Chapter 1, "American Government and Politics in a Racially Divided World," introduces the concept of government in its general and various forms. It also shows that the choices the Framers of the Constitution made in structuring the new governments were neither accidental nor unconnected. The structures of these governments had theoretical and philosophical foundations in classical liberalism, republicanism, and a tradition of exclusion.

Chapter 2, "The Constitution: Rights and Race Intertwined," introduces the basic government documents—the Declaration of Independence and the Constitution. It addresses the events and problems under the Articles of Confederation that led to the drafting of the 1787 Constitution and focuses on the overt and tacit role that slavery played throughout the constitutional process.

Chapter 3, "Federalism: Balancing Power, Balancing Rights," explains the concept of federalism—the balance of power between the national government and the states. It also discusses how that power has ebbed and flowed since the founding of the republic.

Chapter 4, "Civil Liberties: Freedom and Government Authority in Tension," addresses the tension between government authority and the civil liberties afforded citizens under the Bill of Rights. We pay particular attention to how each amendment also offers protections against state governments.

Chapter 5, "Civil Rights: Inequality and Equality," focuses on the increased legal protection afforded various racial and ethnic minorities and women over time and how the reality of this protection has varied across levels of government. We also discuss the differences in timing of the extensions of these protections to the various groups, including the LGBT community, the elderly, and disabled people.

Chapter 6, "Congress: Representation and Lawmaking," outlines the general functions of and influences on Congress, as well as the nature of representation in our democratic system.

Chapter 7, "The Presidency: Conventional Wisdom Redefined," looks at the Office of the President. We outline the roles, powers, and limitations of the president of the United States and the Office of the President, with the purpose of presenting a realistic view of what can and cannot reasonably be expected of presidents. We pay particular attention to the presidential selection process.

Chapter 8, "The Bureaucracy: Career Government Employees, Accountability, and Race," addresses the important topic of government agencies. We examine and assess the relative size and range of functions of the national bureaucracy, and the racial, ethnic, and gender composition of these bureaucracies.

Chapter 9, "The Judiciary: Blending Law and Politics," describes the structure, selection processes, and decision-making dynamics of the national courts. The influence of these factors on the operation of these important institutions highlights the differences among various levels of courts.

Chapter 10, "Public Opinion: Divided By Race?" listens to the voice of the people. We explore the complexities of public opinion by examining the views of the many publics that exist in the American political system, including their racial, gender, and regional differences. A second focus is the role public opinion plays in the American political process.

Chapter 11, "The Media: Reinforcing Racial Stereotypes?" focuses on the role of the media in the American political process. We examine the media's influence on the formation of public opinion, policy agenda setting, and campaigns. We also consider the importance of symbols and symbolism and the "parallel press."

Chapter 12, "Social Movements: Civil Rights as a Movement Model," looks at how opinions are mobilized into efforts to address grievances. Preconditions and timing are of key interest. Drawing from illustrations of several populations, we examine why groups coalesce into social movements at certain points in time and not at others when conditions are perhaps even worse.

Chapter 13, "Interest Groups: Good Outcomes with Few Resources," flows from the discussion of social movements. This chapter distinguishes between social movements and interest groups and examines the ways in which interest groups affect the policy process and influence political outcomes. We note that interest groups are not only those organizations or racial and ethnic minorities and women who have been excluded from the political process, but also are far more likely to include strong majority-dominated organizations whose influence and access are generally much greater than those of the so-called special interests of disadvantaged groups.

Chapter 14, "Political Parties: Linking Voters and Governing Institutions," provides a history of the development of the national two-party system in the United States. We discuss the pros and cons of a two-party system as well as the strengths and weaknesses of the current Democratic and Republican parties. The history of the experiences of Blacks, Latinos, American Indians, and Asian Americans is discussed to provide a context for the current placement of these groups within the two political parties.

Chapter 15, "Voting and Elections: From Obama to Clinton," discusses the voting behaviors of the American public. Voting at the national level for the president commands the most attention. We also consider the factors of race and gender in the examination of voting patterns.

Chapter 16, "The Making of Domestic and Foreign Policy," outlines the public policymaking process, summarizing how all institutions and processes converge to help explain what government does and does not do. It focuses on the differences and the relationship between both domestic and foreign policy.

Note about Terminology

Before proceeding, it is important to define the terms used throughout the book.[1] First, the terms *Black* and *African American* are used interchangeably. Recent research suggests that among Americans of African descent, slightly more than 1 percent difference exists in those who prefer to be called Black (48.1 percent) and those who prefer to be called African American (49.2 percent).[2] Our own preference is for the term *Black* because it concisely describes an identity and a status in American society that are based on color. The Black experience in the United States differs markedly from that of White ethnics, and the use of *African American* might convey the impression that Blacks are just another ethnic group similar to Italian Americans, Irish Americans, or Polish Americans.

Similarly, we use *Latino* and *Hispanic* interchangeably as umbrella terms when we cannot distinguish among subgroups of the nation's Spanish-origin population. Many academics reject the term *Hispanic* because it was devised by the U.S. Census Bureau to classify individuals and is devoid of any connection to the people to which it refers in the United States. The term comes from the Latin word for Spain and is associated with people from the Iberian Peninsula in Europe. It refers to people of Spain, Portugal, Gibraltar, and Andorra, and clearly does not technically include individuals of Mexican, Puerto Rican, Cuban, and Central and South American descent. We most often use *Latino* in recognition of this distinction because this term refers more exclusively to persons of Mexican and Latin American origin.

Third, we use the term *Indian peoples* or *American Indians* rather than the population term *Native American*. Scholars of American Indian politics dislike the term *Native American* because it can be applied literally to any person born in the Americas. Although the terms *Indian peoples* and *American Indians* ignore geographical differences and cultural diversity among Indian groupings, they are the preferred terms of scholars working in the area.[3]

Fourth, the term *Asian American* is an umbrella term for a number of ethnic origin groups—Japanese, Koreans, Chinese, Filipinos, Southeast Asians, and East Indians. We use the term when we or the data we use do not allow us to differentiate among these various ethnic origin groups.

At times, we use the term *ethnicity* in a specific sense of the term—generally meaning the groupings of people on the basis of learned characteristics, often associated with national origin. Issues of ethnicity are particularly pertinent in the Latino, Asian, and Indian groups and are becoming more important in the Black population as the number of Black immigrants from Africa and the Caribbean increases.

We also use the terms *racial minority* or *racial and ethnic minorities* as a shorthand method of identifying Blacks, Latinos, Asian Americans, and American Indians collectively based on their proportion of the population vis-à-vis the majority White population.

We also use the generic term *women* at times, but most often we specify which group of women to which we are referring. Women as a category have been excluded from participation in many segments of American society, but we do not consider the generic category of women as a numerical minority of the population.

Significantly, we use the capitalized form for all of the various racial and ethnic groups—White, Black, Asian American, American Indian, and Latino—as well as for the various ethnic origin groups, such as Mexican American.

Finally, a word about the concept of *equality* that we examine and apply throughout this book. There are many ongoing debates about the kinds of equality and which should be embraced and pursued by governmental policies. Political philosophers pitch "equality of opportunity" against "equality of outcome" and weigh in on their relative benefits. Measures of fairness or justice are overlaid on top of these categories in an attempt to moderate their disparate results. In this book, we look at all these values through the lens of racial and ethnic disparity. Thus, some of the measures and evaluations of equality we suggest apply only to those who have suffered or benefited from racial and ethnic inequality. Other lessons we draw about equality can be applied across the spectrum of public policy—to the poor White woman in Appalachia, the auto worker who just lost his job, the gay person being taunted at work, or the disabled person who cannot go where she wants because there is no wheelchair access. We do not take on these inequalities in as great a depth as we do racial and ethnic inequality, but many of the measures and evaluations of equality we make can be extended to them as well—and we encourage students to read the text with that in mind.

Chapter Features

Each chapter has a set of features that highlight the main themes of the chapter and provide information important to understanding many of the points raised in the chapter. Each feature plays a specific role in the text in support of our approach to American government:

- Chapter opening **vignettes**, drawn from actual events, that highlight the theme of complex inequalities. These vignettes are intended to help make concrete concepts that might appear abstract.
- **Glossary** definitions in the text when the term is first encountered, making it easier to find the definitions and understand their meaning in context.
- **Measuring Equality boxes** provide empirical, quantitative data that support a conclusion or underscore an argument we make to provide you with information on a topic that might be unfamiliar.
- **Our Voices boxes** contain excerpts from the writings of important people or organizations to allow you to "hear" their voices and excerpts from original documents important to the development and workings of the American political system.
- **Evaluating Equality boxes** contain a scenarios that ask you to use the central points of the chapter as a basis for thinking critically about aspects of our political system. These are framed in terms of questions for debate or discussion.
- **Chapter conclusions** tie the chapter content into the opening vignette and draw the themes together.
- **Review questions** at the end of each chapter that are also tied to the theme. By focusing on the review questions, you will be able to distill the main issues from each chapter.
- **Additional readings** with short annotations for each reference.

In all, we hope these features add to your interest in the story of American government that we tell through the lens of race and ethnicity.

Ensuring Student Success

Oxford University Press offers instructors and students a comprehensive ancillary package for qualified adopters of *American Government in Black and White: Diversity and Democracy*:

- **Ancillary Resource Center (ARC):** This convenient, instructor-focused website provides access to all of the up-to-date teaching resources for this text while guaranteeing the security of grade-significant resources.

In addition, it allows Oxford University Press to keep instructors informed when new content becomes available. Register for access and create your individual user account by visiting **www.oup.com/us/mcclain**.

The following items are available on the ARC:

- **Instructor's Manual and Test Bank:** includes chapter objectives, detailed chapter outlines, lecture suggestions and activities, discussion questions, and video and web resources. The test bank includes multiple-choice, short answer, and essay questions.
- **Computerized Test Bank:** utilizes Diploma, a test authoring and management tool. Diploma is designed for both novice and advanced users and enables instructors to create and edit questions, compose randomized quizzes and test with an intuitive drag-and-drop tool, post quizzes and tests to online courses, and print quizzes and tests for paper-based assessments.
- **Downloadable and customizable PowerPoint slides:** including one set for in-class presentations and the other for text images
- **Access to thirty CNN videos** correlated to the chapter topics of the text. Each clip is approximately five to ten minutes long, offering a great way to launch your lecture
- **Companion website at www.oup.com/us/McClain:** This open access companion website includes a number of learning tools to help students study and review key concepts presented in the text including learning objectives, key-concept summaries, quizzes, essay questions, web activities, and web links.

Interactive Media Activities - Available on the free open access Companion Website (www.oup.com/us/mcclain) are designed to reinforce key concepts with real world situations. Each activity:

- Takes 15 to 20 minutes to complete, and produce unique results for each student
- Enables students to experience how politics works, seeing the trade-offs required to produce meaningful policies and outcomes
- Is optimized to work on any mobile device or computer
- Ends with Assessments to connect the activity to classroom discussions

Interactive Media Activities include:

- NEW – Individualism vs. Solidarity
- Passing Immigration Reform
- Electing Cheryl Martin
- Building the USS Relief
- Intervening in Bhutan
- The Fight Against Warrantless Wiretapping
- Balancing the Budget
- NEW – Redistricting in "Texachusetts"
- NEW – Saving the Electric Car
- Election Reform

- NEW – Fact-checking the Media
- NEW – Passing the Thirteenth Amendment
- NEW – Negotiating with China

NEW *A Closer Look* **Media Tutorials** – Available on the *American Government: Diversity and Democracy* free, open access Companion Website (**www.oup. com/us/McClain**) these activities are designed to teach key concepts and help students master important class material. Each tutorial runs 3–5 minutes and ends with assessment opportunities for student to test what they know. Topics include:

- The Constitution: A Brief Tour
- Civil Rights: How does the 14th Amendment ensure equal right for all Citizens?
- Federalism: What does it mean to Incorporate the Bill of Rights?
- Political Participation: What affects voter turnout?
- Media: How the news is shaped by agenda setting, framing, and profit bias?
- Interest Groups: What is a Political Action Committee, and what makes some PACs Super PACs?
- Congress: Why do we hate Congress but keep electing the same representatives?
- The Judiciary: How do judges interpret the Constitution?
- Polling: How do we know what people know?
- Campaigns and Elections: How does Gerrymandering work?

Course Cartridges containing student and instructor resources are available through Angel, Blackboard, Canvas, D2L, Moodle, Respondus, or whatever course management system you prefer.

- *Now Playing: Learning American Government Through Film*
  Through documentaries, feature films, and YouTube videos, *Now Playing: Learning American Government Through Film* provides a variety of suggested video examples that illustrate concepts covered in the text. Each video is accompanied by a brief summary and discussion questions. It is available in both a student and an instructor version and can be packaged with *American Government: Diversity and Democracy* for free.

- **Format Choices**: Oxford University Press offers cost-saving alternatives to meet the needs of all students. This text offered in a Loose Leaf format at a 30% discount off the list price of the text; and in an eBook format, thought CourseSmart for a 50% discount. You can also customize our textbooks to create the course material you want for your class. For more information, please contact your Oxford University Press sales representative, call 800.280.0280, or visit us online at **www.oup.com/us/mcclain**.

Packaging Options

Adopters of *American Government in Black and White: Diversity and Democracy* can package any Oxford University Press book with the text for a 20 percent savings off the total package price. See our many trade and scholarly offerings at www.oup.com, then contact your local OUP sales representative to request a package ISBN.

Acknowledgments

This text has been long in the making even though it was published at an auspicious time in U.S. political history. Many reviewers, editors, colleagues, and friends have given advice and offered help while we developed the text. It is impossible to thank everyone individually who contributed to our efforts, but it is important to acknowledge the vast collective effort that resulted in such a mold-breaking text. We accept responsibility for any errors and shortcomings reflected in the text but share full credit for its strengths with the people who joined us in making this book possible.

The reviewers for the first edition deserve special credit for combining content expertise with pedagogical concern and an eye on late-breaking 2008 election developments:

Russell G. Brooker, *Alverno College*

Michael S. Rodriguez, *Richard Stockton College of New Jersey*

Bilal Dabir Sekou, *University of Hartford*

Sherri L. Wallace, *University of Louisville*

We would also like to thank the reviewers of the second edition:

Damien Arthuer, *West Virginia State University*

Robert Ballinger, *South Texas College*

Geoff Bowden, *Savannah State University*

Meigan M. Fields, *Fort Valley State University*

Nicole Krassas, *Eastern Connecticut State University*

Anthony A. Maalouf, *Delaware County Community College*

Linda McKinstry, *Delaware County Community College*

Nathan K. Mitchell, *Prairie View A&M University*

Billy Monroe, *Prairie View A&M University*

Megan Ostbur, Xavier *University of Louisiana*

Mordu Serry-Kamal, *Winston-Salem State University*

James Daniel Steele, *North Carolina Agricultural and Technical State University*

Richard W. Waterman, *University of Kentucky*

S. Ife Williams, *Delaware County Community College*

Zaphon Wilson, *Saint Augustine's University*

Ahmed Y. Zohny, *Coppin State University*

We would also like to thank the reviewers of the third edition:

Rosalind Blanco Cook, *Tulane University*
Jeffrey Bloodworth, *Gannon University*
Joseph Romance, *Fort Hays State University*
Alec Ewald, *University of Vermont*
Edward Larsen, *Delaware County Community College*
Lenore VanderZee, *State University of New York at Canton*
Raymond Sandoval, *Dallas County Community College*
Ervin Kallfa, Hostos *Community College*

On the third edition we are deeply indebted to the excellent staff at Oxford University Press. In particular, we would like to thank Marissa Dadiw for expert photo research, marketing, and editorial assistance. We would also like to thank Lori Bradshaw, Elizabeth Bortka, and Susan Brown for their outstanding editorial notes, which have undoubtedly improved this text. We are also grateful to Jennifer Carpenter for her guidance and leadership in our revisions. Finally, we would like to thank the thousands of students we have taught over the years.

—**Paula D. McClain and Steven C. Tauber**

The third edition has also been a collective effort. Duke University graduate students, Gloria Ayee, Nura Sediqe, and Taneisha Means spent countless hours gathering new data and updating older material. Jessica Johnson Carew completed the Instructor's Manual and Test Bank and I am appreciative that she agreed to take on that arduous task. I also want to thank Steve Tauber for signing on as a coauthor on a project that had many fits and starts, and lots of twists and turns. It has been a pleasure working with Steve on the first, second and third editions of this book, and I anticipate that this will be a long-term co-authorship.

On a personal note, I could not have achieved much of what I have accomplished professionally without the love and support of my husband, Paul C. Jacobson. We have developed into quite a team over the decades, pursuing both our careers (Paul is a lawyer) while raising two daughters—Kristina and Jessica. We are now the proud grandparents of two grandsons, Jackson B. Ragland and Sterling A. Ragland (Kristina's sons), and find that we enjoy being grandparents almost as much as we enjoy being parents. Paul has been involved in this project in more ways than he had anticipated, or appreciated. I thank him for his unconditional support and continuing love. This book is dedicated to them with much love and appreciation.

—**Paula D. McClain**

Numerous conversations with my colleagues in the School of Interdisciplinary Global Studies (formerly the Department of Government & International Affairs) at the University of South Florida, especially Mark Amen, Cheryl Hall, Rachel May, Susan MacManus, Bernd Reiter, Cheryl Rodriguez, and Scott Solomon, have been invaluable. I would also like to thank Paula McClain, one of my mentors from graduate school, for inviting me to be a coauthor. I have enjoyed working with her on both editions of this book and look forward to future collaborations.

On a personal level, I would like to thank my friends in the Tampa Bay area, as well as those scattered throughout the nation, for their support and friendship. I am thankful for the love and support of my in-laws Red and Ellen Hogan. I am especially grateful to my parents, Richard and Barbara Tauber, for their love, support, and encouragement throughout my life. Finally and most important, I am indebted to my wife, Meghan Tauber. I would not have been able to complete this book without her love, support, humor, and friendship through all the ups and downs that come with a project of this magnitude.

—**Steven C. Tauber**

About the Authors

 Paula D. McClain is professor of political science and public policy and Dean of the Graduate School and Vice Provost for Graduate Education at Duke University. She directs the American Political Science Association's Ralph Bunche Summer Institute, hosted by Duke University and funded by the National Science Foundation and Duke University. She was formerly the cofounding director of the Center for the Study of Race, Ethnicity and Gender in the Social Sciences at Duke University. A Howard University PhD, her primary research interests are in racial minority group politics, particularly minority political and social competition, and urban politics. Her articles have appeared in numerous journals, and she is author of many books, including the popular, award-winning classroom supplement, *"Can We All Get along?": Racial and Ethnic Minorities in American Politics*, co authored with Joseph Stewart, Jr., and the seventh edition will be published in early 2017. Jessica Johnson Carew will be joining her as a new co-author. Professor McClain has won many awards for scholarship and teaching and has served the discipline in many capacities. She was elected to the American Academy of Arts and Sciences in 2014. She is particularly valued for her commitment to mentoring students from every background.

 Steven C. Tauber entered the University of California–San Diego with the goal of becoming a doctor and then a lawyer. By his junior year, however, he found his political science courses so intellectually stimulating that he decided to pursue a career as a political science professor. He entered the PhD program in government at the University of Virginia, receiving his PhD in 1995, and started teaching at the University of South Florida in Tampa, where he is now an associate professor with tenure. He is also currently serving a stint as department chair. Professor Tauber enjoys teaching classes in introduction to American government, constitutional law, judicial politics, research methods and statistics, and American political thought. He has published refereed journal articles and book chapters on interest group use of the federal judiciary, minority group politics, and the effect of animal advocacy groups. In 2016 he published *Navigating the Jungle: Law, Politics, and the Animal Advocacy Movement* (Routledge). His current research focuses primarily on animal rights in a global context. Just as some of his undergraduate political science classes sparked his interest in political science, he hopes that this book will have the same effect on the current generation of undergraduate students.

CHAPTER 1

American Government and Politics in a Racially Divided World

In 2016, Gov. Jack Markell signed a long-awaited resolution officially apologizing for the state's role in slavery. The apology for slavery illustrates the long and sometimes painful history of the United States' struggle with race, from the time of Thomas Jefferson, a slave owner, to President Barack Obama, the first Black president of the United States.

December 6, 2015, marked the 150th anniversary of the abolishment of slavery, when the U.S. Congress ratified the Thirteenth Amendment to the Constitution. There were numerous events recognizing the end of slavery, including an official White House event presided over by President Obama. On February 11, 2016, Delaware joined eight other states to formally apologize for slavery when Governor Jack Markell (D) signed the state's joint resolution. Delaware's resolution acknowledged its participation in 226 years of slavery first of both Native Americans and Africans in the mid-1600s; by the close of the 1700s its entire slave population was of African descent. The resolution also included acknowledgments that Delaware criminalized humanitarian attempts to assist slaves and that in later times Delaware passed and enforced Jim Crow laws to deny the rights of African American citizens for much of the twentieth century.[1]

On July 29, 2008, the U.S. House of Representatives passed a nonbinding resolution, introduced and championed by Representative Steven Cohen (D-TN), which offered a formal apology for the government's participation in African American slavery and the establishment of Jim Crow laws. The resolution said, in part, "African Americans continue to suffer from the consequences of slavery and Jim Crow—long after both systems were formally abolished—through enormous damage and loss, both tangible and intangible, including the loss of human dignity and liberty, the frustration of careers and professional lives, and the long-term loss of income and opportunity."[2]

On June 18, 2009, the U.S. Senate unanimously passed a similar resolution apologizing to African Americans for slavery and Jim Crow. The Senate resolution said explicitly that the apology could not be used in support of reparations (or compensation for past wrongs).[3]

Reparations A concept or tool for providing monetary payments to members of aggrieved groups based on past wrongful actions against them or their ancestors.

intro *The story of apologies for slavery is a complex one that highlights some of the underlying dilemmas that face the U.S. political system—how to reconcile its stated principles of how individuals should be treated with how the government actually treats and has treated individuals. The apologies are intended to acknowledge the nation's complicity in a destructive and immoral institution, at the same time avoiding any discussion of reparations for the descendants of those enslaved.*

Both sides criticize the apologies for slavery. Arkansas Governor Mike Beebe (D) questioned whether Arkansas should join the other Southern states in apologizing for slavery: "I think Arkansas has as good a feel for folks working together as any Southern state or any other state, so I think we've moved past that."[4] In Georgia, which also debated the issue, former speaker of the house Glen Richardson (R) expressed the views of many of his constituents when he said, "I'm not sure what we ought to be apologizing for. I think slavery was wrong—absolutely. But no one here was in office then."[5]

On the other side, John Hope Franklin (now deceased), a prominent historian of African American history, was also not a fan of apologies. Referring to North Carolina's issuance of an apology on April 12, 2007, by a unanimous vote of the House and the Senate, Franklin said:

> *It's going to become an epidemic now. People are running around apologizing for slavery. What about that awful period since slavery—Reconstruction, Jim Crow and all the rest? What about the enormous wealth that was built up by Black labor? If I was sitting on a billion dollars that someone had made when I sat on them, I probably would not be slow to apologize, if that's all it takes. I think that's little to pay for the gazillions that Black people built up—the wealth of this country—with their labor, and now you're going to say I'm sorry I beat the hell out of you for all these years? That's not enough.[6]*

On May 31, 2007, Alabama governor Bob Riley (R) signed a resolution expressing the state's "profound regret" for Alabama's participation in slavery and apologizing for slavery's wrongs and their lingering aftereffects.[7] With his signature, Alabama became the fourth Southern state to issue an apology for slavery, following apologies issued by the legislatures of Maryland, Virginia, and North Carolina. Riley said, "Slavery was evil and is a part of American history. I believe all Alabamians are proud of the tremendous progress we have made and continue to make."[8] Florida issued an apology in March 2008. In the North, New York was the first state to issue an apology, in June 2007, followed by New Jersey in January 2008, and Tennessee and Connecticut in 2009.

Despite apologies by several states, apologies by the federal government and on behalf of the American people for mistreatment of a segment of its population are rare. It was not until 1988 that Congress passed legislation issuing an apology and providing reparations for Japanese Americans interned during World War II. In 1993, the United States apologized to native Hawaiians for providing military assistance to the White businessmen who in 1893 had overthrown Queen Liliuokalani, placed her under house arrest, and seized the islands of Hawaii for the United States.

These actions and the controversy surrounding them raise several questions and concerns about the American political system. Why did a government founded on the concepts of freedom and equality engage in actions and put in place policies that were inequitable and unjust? Why is it so difficult for this government to make amends for the inequities and inequalities it created? Who benefits from inequalities? When inequalities are created, those who have access to an arena such as voting, employment, political office, and education, gain at the expense of those who are denied opportunities. When government moves to correct the inequalities it created, those

In 1893, the United States military, at the behest of White businessmen, overthrew Queen Liliuokalani and seized the islands of Hawaii for the United States. On July 4, 1894, the Republic of Hawaii was declared with Sanford B. Dole as president. Queen Liliuokalani was eventually arrested in 1895 and held until 1896.

who have gained a privileged position might perceive a lessening of opportunities for themselves. Is it possible to correct inequalities for those aggrieved without creating the belief that the government is reducing opportunities for others? These are difficult questions, but ones that the American political system has struggled with since its inception.

The U.S. government is built on a foundation with values that are expressed in phrases such as "All men are created equal"; "life, liberty, and the pursuit of happiness"; and "government by the people." These phrases, many Americans believe, convey the essence of the United States. Yet these simple phrases do not convey the complexities of government, the reality that government treats people differently, or the continual struggle necessary to ensure that the values expressed in those phrases apply equally to all Americans.

All of these questions illustrate the complicated and conflicted nature of American government and politics in our time. Yet the sources of these complexities and conflicts are rooted in the history of government in general and of the United States in particular. Only by exploring that history can we understand these issues more fully. To that end, this opening chapter begins by examining what government is, what it does, and what forms it can take. This information serves as the context for understanding the ideas that influenced the creation of the American political system and continue to this day to shape its political debates.

The Nature of Government

Can you imagine a situation in which all people could do whatever they wanted without regard for how their actions could affect others? If you wanted to drive 100 miles per hour through your neighborhood streets, or launch a rocket from your backyard, you could do so without concern for the safety of your neighbors or airline passengers overhead. It is difficult to imagine living in a country without some mechanism for controlling the behaviors and managing the conflicts that arise when people interact. The mechanism that does this is government.

When you think of government, some of you might think of the president and the White House, others think of senators and representatives and the U.S. Capitol, and still others think of the Internal Revenue Service, the people down at city hall, or the postal service. Each of these thoughts recognizes a part of government. In the simplest sense, **government** is a social institution that controls the behavior of people. It does this by managing conflicts, establishing order, and devising rules and regulations. More concretely, government is the entity that has the authority to make decisions for you and all those who live in a political unit, such as a country, a state, or a city. When we speak of the government, we refer to those individuals who make up that political and administrative hierarchy.

Government A social institution that controls the behavior of people; the political and administrative hierarchy of an organized state.

The Functions of Government

Government serves several essential functions, including providing security, serving the public good, managing and resolving conflicts, and offering services. A first function of government is the provision of security. National governments maintain armed forces to protect their countries from attack from other countries; for example, the United States maintains an armed force that consists of the U.S. Army, Navy, Air Force, Marines, and Coast Guard. The United States is estimated to have from 700 to 1,000 bases around the world that range from small drone sites in Afghanistan to large permanent military bases, such as Ramstein Air Force Base in Germany.[9]

Government provides security in other ways as well. It tries to protect citizens from such harms as unfair business practices, discrimination, and denial of constitutional rights. In the United States laws have been passed to correct those harms, such as the 1968 Fair Housing Act aimed at protecting African Americans and other racial minorities from discrimination in the purchase of a home and the renting of an apartment or house. In addition, Title IX of the Education Amendments of 1972, as amended, prohibits discrimination on the basis of sex in federally assisted education programs. The latter has had a tremendous effect on the ability of women to participate in sports. In 1971, women made up 7 percent of high school athletes; in 2008, women made up 41 percent of all high school athletes. At the university level, women were 15 percent of all college athletes in 1971, but 43 percent of all college athletes by 2008.[10] In 2012, at the collegiate level, there were 8.73 women's varsity teams per school, up from 2.5 in 1970.[11]

A second function of government is to provide for the **public good**, a policy or action that benefits society as a whole rather than a specific individual. Government has the responsibility to address issues and problems in terms of how they affect the well-being of the larger society. Even though you also might think about issues and problems that affect society, you, like most individuals, are likely to make decisions for your own benefit. Thus, government is the entity charged with making decisions that will reflect broad, rather than narrow, interests in society.

Public Good A government policy or action that benefits society as a whole rather than a specific individual.

One way government ensures the public good is through laws and regulations. For example, legislation to protect the environment, such as the Clean Air Act of 1963, and its amendments over the years, has the broader interests of society as its objective and is therefore a public good. National defense is also a public good because it provides security for the entire nation, not a particular individual. The Civil Rights Act of 1964 made it illegal to discriminate against African Americans and other racial minorities in the use of public accommodations, such as restaurants, movie theaters, and hotels, thereby outlawing segregation and serving the interests of all citizens.

The process of determining what is best for the well-being of society, however, generates debate and controversy, which leads to a third function of government: managing and resolving conflict. The give-and-take in a governmental

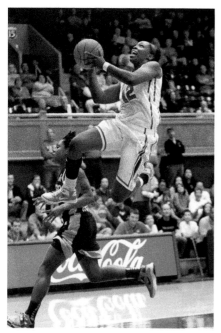

Title IX has expanded opportunities for female athletes and has resulted in the development of major women's sports teams. Chelsea Gray (12) of Duke University drives to the basket against Dawnn Maye of Georgia Tech in an NCAA women's college basketball game on December 6, 2012. Duke won the game 85–52.

Politics The conflict, competition, and compromise that occur within a political system.

Democracy A system of government in which political power is exercised by the people.

Direct Democracy A democracy in which the people are able to participate directly in decision making.

system, and the resolution of the problems that arise in that system through the process of discussion, bargaining, and competition, are called **politics**. Bargaining could occur among groups that want different outcomes on the same issue or among individuals who want to occupy positions in government. Government serves as the arbitrator of this compromise process. Congress balances the arguments from groups of people who will be affected by specific legislation and tries to balance those interests in compromises struck in the final bill.

Governments also offer services, a fourth function, many of which would not be had if government did not provide them. In the United States, our government supports the postal system, education, hospitals, transportation, and Social Security for elderly citizens, among other things. Although some private entities might build a toll highway, it is unlikely that the national interstate highway system that runs from east to west and north to south in the country would have been built without the federal government. Likewise, large public universities, such as the University of California–Berkeley, Ohio State University, or the University of Maryland–College Park, would not have been established without the land grants of the federal government's Morrill Acts of 1862 and 1890.[12]

Although most governments participate in these functions, not all governments do so in the same way. For example, in Denmark health care is universal and basically free to patients. In the United States, despite the passage of the Affordable Care Act of 2010 that will provide health care for many of the currently uninsured, people must pay something for physician and hospital services.[13] The differences in how governments approach these functions are rooted in the type of government in question, its philosophical foundations, and its source of authority.

The Types of Government

Some form of government oversees every country in the world, but those governments differ in form and structure. The United States is a **democracy**, a system of government in which the people exercise political power. The word *democracy* derives from the Greek words *demos* (the people) and *kratos* (authority). The way in which people participate in a democracy may be direct or indirect (representative). **Direct democracy** exists when people make decisions themselves rather than electing individuals to make decisions on their behalf. The democracy of the ancient Greeks was direct in that everyone who was eligible to participate in government had a say in the decision-making process in an open forum. In the United States, the town meeting format found today in some New England towns serves as a form of direct democracy. Every resident of the town is eligible to participate in the town meeting and to vote on the resolution of issues taken up in the meeting.

Indirect (or **representative) democracy** exists when people do not make governmental decisions themselves but elect individuals to represent their interests. Indirect, or representative, democracy is the most common form of government found in the world today; individuals elect officials to represent them in the political process and to participate on their behalf. The United States is a representative democracy. Americans elect people to represent them at all levels of government—U.S. Congress, state legislatures, city councils, school boards, and mayors' offices, among others. Most countries that are democracies are representative; no pure direct democracies exist among the governments of the world today.

Indirect (or **Representative) Democracy** A democracy in which people do not participate directly in decision making and instead elect individuals to represent their interests.

Most democracies derive their governmental authority from a written **constitution**, which is a set of formal written rules and principles governing the country. In a **constitutional democracy**, authority for government stems from the constitution. In such democracies, all actions by government must conform to the constitution, and officials who make and enforce the law are themselves subject to the law.

Constitution A set of formal written rules and principles governing a state.

Constitutional Democracy A government that derives its authority from a constitution.

Constitutional democracies share several characteristics.

1. There are free elections in which candidates compete with each other, and the political opposition (those not in power) is free to criticize the government.
2. The press and other media are free, meaning they operate independently of the government, and censorship is rare.
3. Elections are held at regular intervals; elected officials serve for a prescribed length of time, never for life; and the transition of power from one elected official to the next is a peaceful process.
4. Personal and civil rights, such as freedom of speech and religion, are protected.[14]

The United States, Great Britain, Canada, Australia, Iceland, the Netherlands, South Africa, and a host of other countries that exhibit these characteristics are constitutional democracies. Although Great Britain does not have a single written constitution similar to that of the United States, its governing principles stem from numerous legislative acts, common law, and conventions that provide a constitutional framework.

Principles of Constitutional Democracies

Even though the structures of constitutional democracies may differ—for instance, certain countries have presidents and other countries have prime ministers and parliaments—they all share several common principles. These principles provide a common basis for understanding some of the values present in constitutional democracies. These principles are the rule of law, natural law, and natural rights. Understanding the principles common to constitutional democracies provides a window through which to view the essential features of the American political system.

The Rule of Law

Rule of Law The predominance of law over discretionary authority.

A first element of constitutional democracy is a belief in the **rule of law**, the idea that laws should take precedence over the arbitrary governance of people. According to the rule of law, all citizens, including the government and government officials, must obey the law. This principle prohibits constitutional democracies from acting in an arbitrary and capricious manner. For example, the U.S. government cannot take your property without following a prescribed legal process. By law and constitutional authority, the government cannot detain you without telling you the charges and allowing you to obtain legal counsel. Government's actions must adhere to authority granted in a constitution or in laws passed by the legislature.

The rule of law is a core principle of the American political system. Laws passed by a legislative body such as the U.S. Congress, a state legislature, or a city council are intended to bring order and fairness to the political system. By the rule of law, everyone is supposed to be equal before the law, and the law is supposed to apply equally to all. No person—rich, poor, official, or ordinary—is supposed to be above the law. In reality, the United States has a history of treating its citizens differently based on race, gender, and sexual orientation. Paula D. McClain and Joseph Stewart, Jr. argue that for much of the nation's history, Blacks were subject to a "separate system of laws."[15]

Natural Law

Natural Law Law that comes from nature and is superior to statutory law.

A second principle underlying a constitutional democratic government is **natural law**, law that comes from nature and is superior to written law passed by legislatures. The theory of natural law holds that a system of right or justice comes from nature rather than from rules of society and that it applies to all persons. Human beings have the ability to reason ("right reason") and through the use of reason are able to determine the proper and correct thing to do. Cicero (106–43 BCE), a political philosopher in ancient Rome and one of the earliest to discuss the concept, provided a definition of natural law:

> There is in fact a true law—namely, right reason—which is in accordance with nature, applies to all men, and is unchangeable and eternal. By its commands this law summons men to the performance of their duties; by its prohibitions it restrains them from doing wrong. Its commands and prohibitions always influence good men, but are without effect on the bad. To invalidate this law by human legislation is never morally right, nor is it permissible ever to restrict its operation, and to annul it wholly impossible.[16]

Statutory Law A type of law pertaining to rules made by legislatures, especially Congress.

Natural law theory argues that if **statutory law**, or the laws passed by legislative bodies, conflicts with natural law—for example, the correct thing to do—it need not be obeyed. The U.S. Declaration of Independence invokes natural law in its first paragraph:

> When in the course of human events it becomes necessary for one people to dissolve the political bands which have connected them with another, and to assume among the powers of the earth, the *separate and equal station to which the Laws of Nature and of Nature's God entitle them*, a decent respect to the opinions of mankind requires that they should declare the causes which impel them to the separation.

The clause emphasized here in italics argues that natural law entitled the colonists to break away from Great Britain.

Natural Rights

A third and last common principle of constitutional democratic governments is that of **natural rights**, those rights to which every person is entitled and that exist apart from and are not dependent on government, such as life and liberty. Natural rights stem from natural law and belong to individuals from birth. The concept of natural rights is drawn primarily from the work of John Locke (1632–1704), an English political theorist. Locke argued that natural law endowed people with natural rights, which for Locke were "life, liberty, and property." In the Declaration of Independence, Thomas Jefferson adapted Locke's natural rights of life, liberty, and property to "Life, Liberty, and the pursuit of Happiness."

Natural Rights Rights to which every person is entitled, such as life and liberty; rights that are not dependent on government.

Foundations of American Government

Given that constitutional democracies share similar principles of government, yet might differ in structure, why does the United States have the political system that it does? What are the theoretical and philosophical underpinnings of the system, and from where did they come?

The American system of government draws on several theories of government and governing in Western European political thought and is the product of multiple political traditions. These traditions include (1) **classical liberalism**, a name now applied to a body of Western European political philosophy that is concerned with the freedom of the individual and the role of government in protecting that freedom; (2) **classical republicanism**, a theory that says rule by the people ought to be indirect through representatives; and (3) **inegalitarianism**, a tradition of excluding large segments of the American population from participation in the political system despite the universal language of equality, liberty, and freedom.[17] These traditions are central to an understanding of the American political system.

Classical Liberalism A body of Western European political philosophy that is concerned with the freedom of the individual and the role of government in protecting that freedom.

Classical Republicanism A theory that rule by the people ought to be indirect through representatives.

Inegalitarianism A tradition of excluding large segments of the American population from participation in the political system despite the language of equality, liberty, and freedom.

Classical Liberalism

The founders of American government, particularly Thomas Jefferson, author of the Declaration of Independence, were familiar with contemporary Western European political thought. They were especially influenced by the ideas

Feudalism A system of landholding involving a network of allegiances and obligations.

of classical liberalism, a body of thought aimed at liberating the individual from the oppressive restraints of feudalism and monarchial rule.

Under **feudalism**, a system of landholding practiced widely in Medieval Europe, peasants, called serfs, pledged their loyalty and a portion of their income to a lord in exchange for protection. Rather than protect the serfs, however, lords too often abused their power over their dependents.

By the fifteenth century, feudalism had begun to die out in England, France, and other countries in Western Europe, only to be replaced by monarchical rule. Although the change brought serfdom to an end, people in these countries were still subject to the seemingly arbitrary authority of their rulers. In time, political thinkers began to challenge this authority and collectively their ideas came to define what we now call classical liberalism.

Thomas Hobbes (1588–1679), a British political philosopher, believed, as expressed in his work *Leviathan* (1651), that by nature men are aggressive and, therefore, are afraid of being attacked. To protect themselves from attack, men contract with each other to form a civil society and to create a mechanism, government, for resolving these fears. Men create government by entering into a **social contract** in which people give up a little bit of their independence for the safety and peace that government creates. Hobbes stated that without government, life would be extremely difficult and possibly very "nasty, brutish, and short," to use his oft-quoted words.

Social Contract Individuals creating government by entering into a contract with it.

The work of English political theorist John Locke best exemplifies classical liberalism, particularly his *Two Treatises of Government* (1689). In these works, Locke argued that the responsibility of government is to protect an individual's right to own property. If the government fails in this responsibility, then the people have the right to overturn the government and establish a new one.

Locke proposed several mechanisms for limiting government's power. First, the powers of government should be divided among several branches. Locke distrusted executive power (the monarch) and believed that the executive should be subordinate and accountable to the legislature (parliament). But he believed that controls needed to be placed on the legislature as well. These controls include a belief in the rule of law, a view that laws should not be arbitrary but should be designed for the good of the people, and an argument that taxes should not be raised without the consent of the people or their representatives.

Although liberal theorists might differ on some key ideas, such as their notions of natural law, individualism, and self-interest, all liberal theories share these four characteristics:[18]

1. *Liberalism is optimistic.* This optimism is expressed in the belief that society works better if individuals are left to themselves without government interference. Liberalism places great faith in the behavior and motivations of individuals unrestrained by coercive restrictions.

2. *Liberalism favors the individual over the group*. Liberalism gives individual self-determination or individualism priority over societal good. Individual freedom is paramount, and government should not infringe on that freedom.

3. *Liberalism supports free-market economics*. Liberalism holds that the role of government is to protect and facilitate economic development. Government should not enact legislation or regulations that hamper economic development. This tenet is exemplified in the work of eighteenth-century Scottish philosopher Adam Smith (1723–1790), whose book *An Inquiry into the Nature and Causes of the Wealth of Nations* (1776) is considered the first modern work of economics and the primer for free-market economics, what he called self-interested competition. He argued against the development of monopolies.

4. *Liberalism places reason before faith*. Liberalism seeks to "liberate" the human mind from unquestioned acceptance of religious dogma by focusing on those things that can be proved or demonstrated. The widespread belief at the time, known as the divine right of kings, held that the monarch derived his or her right to rule from the will of God. Thus, the monarch was not subject to any authority other than that of God.

The influence of classical liberalism is evident in the early documents of the nation—the Declaration of Independence, the state constitutions developed after independence, and the U.S. Constitution. Thomas Jefferson drew substantially from John Locke in writing the Declaration of Independence. Locke's natural rights—"life, liberty, and property"—became Jefferson's "Life, Liberty, and the pursuit of Happiness." Jefferson adapted Locke's statement on equality—"men being by nature all free, equal, and independent"—to "All men are created equal." According to the Declaration, "To secure these [natural] rights, Governments are instituted among Men."

Classical liberal theory is also prominent in *The Federalist Papers* (1787), essays written by Alexander Hamilton of New York, James Madison of Virginia, and John Jay of New York, in support of ratification of the Constitution. One fundamental liberal principle central to several of the essays is government's responsibility to protect private property and to provide an environment in which people can use private property as a basis for commerce. Arguing in favor of limited government, the authors stated that the political system of the new United States would be one in which the national government and state governments shared power, but that the powers given to the national government would be "few and defined." The writers also wanted to assure the states that the scope of the national government's role would be limited primarily by a checks-and-balances system that would prevent any one of the three branches of the national government from acquiring too much power.

Classical liberal theory has exerted other influences as well. The American political values of religious toleration, separation of church and state, freedom of expression, restrictions on police behavior, free elections, and an economic policy aimed at sustained growth on the basis of private ownership derive from the theory of classical liberalism.[19]

It would be a mistake to confuse classical liberalism with the way we use the term *liberal* (political liberalism) in our contemporary political world. In contemporary politics, a **liberal** is someone who believes that government has a role to play in the lives of individuals and that government should be looked to for solutions to problems. Political liberals support programs aimed at job creation, universal health care, elimination of discrimination in American society, and support for the poor, among others. Liberals are also interested in protecting individual civil rights and liberties and believe that government has a responsibility to protect citizens' rights.

We juxtapose this definition of contemporary political liberalism against the definition of the contemporary political term *conservative*. **Conservatives** are individuals who believe in a limited role for government and do not believe that government should be turned to for solutions to some problems. Conservatives believe that too much government regulation hinders the ability of the free market to function unfettered; conservatives are strong believers in a free-market economy. They are not in favor of governmental expansion of individual rights and liberties. Conservatives do believe, however, that the government has a major role to play in defense, and they are more likely to support increases in defense spending while opposing spending in social program areas. In many ways, contemporary conservatism resembles classical liberalism more than today's political liberalism does.

Classical Republicanism

Whereas classical liberalism emphasizes individualism and self-interest, classical republicanism concerns itself with **civic virtue**, the subordination of individualism and individual self-interest to the interest of society. Civic virtue is demanded both of those who govern and those who are governed. Classical republicanism, with its origins in ancient Rome, views government as divided into different branches with a checks-and-balances system preventing any one branch from gathering too much power.[20] Direct democracy is unworkable, in this view, because it is unwieldy to have everyone participating in government's decision-making process. Thus, republicans argue for representative democracy—individuals elect other individuals to represent them in government's affairs.

English political theorists such as James Harrington, Algernon Sidney, and French jurist Baron de Montesquieu wrote on aspects of republicanism. James Harrington (1611–1677) in *The Commonwealth of Oceana* (1656) argued that, although the government is accountable to the people, direct democracy is impossible because it is chaotic, with everyone trying to participate in decision making. Thus, government should be a representative democracy in which the people elect officials to represent them. Algernon Sidney (1622–1683) also

---

Liberal An individual who believes that government has a role to play in the lives of individuals and that government can provide solutions to policy problems.

Conservative Individual who believes that government should play a limited role in the lives of individuals and that government is not the source of solutions for problems.

Civic Virtue The subordination of individualism and individual self-interest to the interest of society.

rejected direct democracy and argued in *Discourses Concerning Government* (1698, published after his death) that people would delegate their authority to the legislature.

Charles-Louis de Secondat, Baron de Montesquieu (1689–1755), a French observer of British government, in his work *Spirit of the Laws* (1748), further refined the idea of the division of power among several branches of government in what he called the balanced constitutions. Montesquieu believed that if legislative, executive, and judicial powers were all held by the same person or body it would signal the end of liberty. He saw the principle of separation of powers as a guarantee on the restraint of government and the assurance that individuals would retain their liberty.[21]

Five characteristics, common to all republican theories, define the essence of classical republicanism:

Thomas Hobbes (1588–1679), a British political philosopher, believed that government was necessary, but that individuals enter into a social contract with government in which they give up a little bit of their independence for the safety and peace that government creates.

1. *Republicanism believes in a virtuous citizenry.* Classical republicanism defines a virtuous citizenry as a public-spirited, self-sacrificing people devoted to the general good of the community. Both leaders and followers will subordinate private interests to the public good. Virtuous citizens will participate in government with the public good in mind.

2. *Republicanism is concerned with property.* Like classical liberalism, classical republicanism is concerned with property. In classical republicanism, property ownership is a primary criterion for holding political office and for voting for those who run for office.

3. *Republicanism sees the people as the ultimate authority but believes they must be kept at a distance.* Government governs with the consent of the people. The people, however, delegate their authority to representatives who then run the government on behalf of the people. Government works best when the masses of people are kept far from the levers of power.

4. *Republicanism advocates a distribution of power across branches of government.* No one person should be able to control all the levers of power. To avoid such singular control, power must be distributed among the branches of government. This arrangement has become known as the doctrine of separation of powers. Also, a system of checks and balances exists to prevent any one branch from garnering too much power.

5. *Republicanism believes that the rights of individuals must be protected.* Even though individuals delegate their authority to elected

John Locke (1632–1704), an English philosopher, argued that government's responsibility is to protect an individual's right to own property, and if government fails, then the people have the right to overturn the government and establish a new one.

Charles-Louis de Secondat de Montesquieu (1689–1755), a French philosopher and jurist, was considered a classical republican theorist. He saw the principle of separation of powers as a guarantee on the restraint of government and the assurance that individuals would retain their liberty.

representatives, they must have their rights protected from the government. This protection occurs through a bill of rights.

The influence of classical republicanism is evident in the state constitutions and the U.S. Constitution, particularly in the government values associated with republicanism: the rule of law, a sovereign people, elected representatives, separation of powers, and a system of checks and balances on the branches of government. As with liberal ideas, republican ideas also ran throughout *The Federalist Papers*. In the papers, the authors discussed in detail the reasons that the new government would be a **republican form of government** rather than a direct democracy. Citizens would elect people to represent them in government, and the views of the people would be filtered through these individuals. Those elected individuals would administer the government. Yet, other voices spoke out at the time, voices arguing that classical republicanism required the abolition of slavery. See the remarks of the Rev. Lemuel Haynes in "Our Voices: Lemuel Haynes—Republicanism and Slavery" on page 17.

Republican Form of Government A government whose powers are exercised by elected representatives who are directly or indirectly accountable to the people governed.

It is important not to confuse classical republicanism with the contemporary Republican Party. In some ways, contemporary Democrats (who are often liberals) espouse philosophies and support policies closer to those of classical republicanism than to those of classical liberalism. Both the Democratic and Republican parties, although differing in philosophy and policy preferences, are grounded in the classical liberal and classical republican foundations undergirding the U.S. political system.

Tradition of Exclusion (Inegalitarianism)

The American Founders created a system based on liberal and republican ideals. They believed that individual freedoms and liberties were fundamental values. They were passionate in their arguments defending these beliefs. Despite the inclusive and egalitarian principles embodied in such words as *equality*, *liberty*, and *freedom*, however, the Founders did not intend for such principles to be universally applied. Instead, they followed a **tradition of exclusion** (or inegalitarianism) that denied to large segments of the American population the protections promised in the Declaration of Independence and the Constitution. This exclusionary tradition, which many would argue is consistent with some of the tenets of liberalism, accepted the notion that not all people are equal and that inequalities are acceptable and need not be corrected. Moreover, the Founders did not see this tradition of exclusion as being inconsistent with the notion that "all men are created equal." In other words, liberalism provides room for the development of inegalitarianism. The inequality of treatment under this tradition was often based on characteristics such as race, gender, ethnicity, and religion.[22] (Table 1.1 provides a comparison of the elements of classical liberalism, classical republicanism, and the tradition of exclusion.)

Tradition of Exclusion
A tradition that excludes groups from the political system based on their ascribed traits, such as race, gender, and religion.

The origins of this tradition are many and varied. In some instances, the origins are rooted in practice and culture. In others, they are anchored in the works of political philosophers. At the time of the founding of the United States, gender, ethnic, racial, and religious hierarchies were worldwide phenomena.

White Women. Many of the attitudes toward women and their place in society can be traced to a global or philosophical context, but some aspects of the attitudes were uniquely American. The subordination of White women during colonial times created cultural and economic discrimination against them.[23]

In addition, Western political philosophy during the Enlightenment (the Age of Reason in the eighteenth century), with which the Founders were familiar, rarely considered the role of women in the civic and political arenas. When political philosophers did mention women, they were considered in subservient roles to men in not only physical but mental and moral capabilities as well. French philosopher Jean-Jacques Rousseau (1712–1778) argued that the world of women was separate from the empire of men. Women were not to be members of the political world.[24] Rousseau wrote in *Emile* (1762): "In

TABLE 1.1 Key Points of Comparison of Classical Liberalism, Classical Republicanism, and the Tradition of Exclusion

Classical Liberalism Optimism	Classical Republicanism Pessimism	Tradition of Exclusion Oppression
Government by consent	Government based on popular sovereignty	Government based on the consent of White males
Direct democracy	Elected representatives	People defined narrowly in terms of race (White), gender (male), and religion (Protestant)
Limited government	Separation of powers and checks and balances	Limited government, but force of government used to exclude non-Whites and White women
Majority rule but with minority protection	Barriers to majority rule	Minority rights nonexistent
Market economy	Market economy	Non-Whites and White women excluded from economy
Individual/equal rights paramount	Property ownership/natural rights central	Property ownership rights denied to most, but not all, non-Whites and some women; a majority of Blacks were considered property
Rule of law	Rule of law	Law used to oppress non-Whites and, to a lesser extent, White women
Religious freedom	Religious freedom	White Protestants considered superior to all others

the union of the sexes each alike contributes to the common end, but in different ways. From this diversity springs the first difference which may be observed between man and woman in their moral relations. The man should be strong and active; the woman should be weak and passive; the one must have both the power and the will; it is enough that the other should offer little resistance."[25]

Aspects of English common law—law derived from custom and practice rather than legislative statutes—that governed the relations between husbands and wives also played a major role in defining the role of women in the new nation. That law included the doctrine of **coverture**, which transferred a woman's civic identity to her husband at marriage, giving him use and direction of her property. Thus, married women had no identity apart from that of their husbands.[26] Coverture's influence on the role of women carried over to the American colonies.

Coverture A doctrine and system in British common law according to which marriage merged a woman's legal identity with that of her husband.

our voices

Lemuel Haynes—Republicanism and Slavery

Between 1776 and 1820, Lemuel Haynes, a Black New England Congregational minister and patriot of the Revolution, wrote a series of essays and sermons setting his opposition to slavery and his insistence on equal rights for Black Americans in the context of the two great influences on his thinking: republican ideology and New Divinity theology, a movement away from the Calvinist theology of the New England Puritans. Drawing from republican ideology, Haynes argued that because liberty was a natural right, slavery was unlawful. Republican liberty, he continued, was threatened by slavery and oppression, which undermined the virtue that led individuals to promote and defend liberty.

Here are excerpts from "Liberty Further Extended: Or Free thoughts on the illegality of Slave-keeping; Wherein those arguments that Are used in its vindication Are plainly confuted. Together with a humble Address to such as are Concearned in the practise" (1776):

It is not my Business to Enquire into Every particular practise, that is practised in this Land, that may come under this Odeus Character; But, what I have in view, is humbly to offer som[e] free thoughts, on the practise of Slave-keeping. Opression, is not spoken of, nor ranked in the sacred oracles, among the Least of those sins, that are the procureing Caus of those signal Judgments, which god is pleas'd to bring upon the Children of men. Therefore let us attend. I mean to white [write] with freedom, yet with the greatest Submission.

And the main proposition, which I intend for some Breif illustration is this, Namely, That an *African, or, in other terms, that a Negro may Justly Chalenge, and has*

an undeniable right to his ["freed(om)" is blotted out] *Liberty: Consequently, the practise of Slave-keeping, which so much abounds in this Land is illicit.*

Why do you think that Haynes felt that slavery threatened the republican notion of liberty?

Lemuel Haynes (1753–1833) was an influential African American religious leader who argued against slavery. Haynes's arguments against slavery were grounded in classical republican theory.

Blacks. In the case of Blacks, American colonists' views stemmed not from English common law, but from attitudes and behaviors the colonists had brought with them. For the English, Blacks' skin color set them apart from White colonists. Because Blacks were from a continent that was not Christian, they were also, in this view, defective in religion. For many Whites, these two aspects made Blacks something less than human beings. Therefore, many Whites did not consider owning Blacks as slaves to be wrong.[27]

The first Africans arrived at Jamestown, Virginia, in 1619 as indentured servants, individuals who contracted themselves to work as servants for a specified period of time for people who often had paid their passage to the American colonies. By 1641, Massachusetts had incorporated slavery into colonial law. Slavery was instituted on a broad scale in Virginia in 1661 as the need for labor increased and Whites found Indian servitude and slavery inadequate and the supply of White indentured servants insufficient. The permanent enslavement of Africans and African Americans became the answer to the labor problem. The supply of Blacks appeared to be endless, and their color made them easily identifiable.[28]

Rogers Smith, a University of Pennsylvania political theorist, argues that these negative attitudes toward Blacks were given a uniquely American character when political figures at the time of the founding began to use a fascination with the science of the Enlightenment to explain the differences between Blacks and Whites.[29] Thomas Jefferson was one of those individuals. Jefferson's original draft of the Declaration of Independence included an indictment of King George for his participation in the Black slave trade, but the language was struck from the final version. Jefferson, while a member of the Virginia House of Burgesses, also pushed for the abolition of slavery in Virginia.

Jefferson, however, did not believe that Blacks should be citizens. Nor did his antislavery sentiments prevent him from owning slaves himself (see "Evaluating Equality: Thomas Jefferson and Sally Hemings". In his *Notes on the State of Virginia* (1785), a book in which Jefferson sought to use the scientific methodology of the Enlightenment to study everything from foliage to Blacks, Jefferson was uncompromising in his belief that Blacks were innately inferior to Whites. He advocated removing free Blacks from the nation and colonizing them somewhere away from the United States.[30] Some scholars argue that Jefferson helped to inaugurate the historical tendency in America to legitimize racial prejudice with the gloss of pseudoscience—fake science utterly lacking supporting evidence.[31]

Social Construction of Race The construction of a group of people of various phenotypes, skin colors, and physical characteristics for political and social purposes such as enslavement and exclusion.

Race is a prominent thread in the American political fabric and is part of the original tapestry of the American political system. Yet race is a social and political, rather than a biological, construction. The **social construction of race** in the United States evolved directly from government's interest in defining and expanding the boundaries of Blackness for purposes of enslavement initially and for purposes of exclusion later. Many states went to great lengths to define the amount of "Negro" blood (e.g., one-eighth, one-sixteenth, "any ascertainable amount of Negro blood") that legally classified an individual as Black.[32] The state-supported and legally codified definition of who was Black resulted in the construction of a group that varied widely in phenotype, skin color, and physical characteristics.

American Indians. The arguments used for the inferiority of Blacks were applied to American Indians as well. Many colonists felt that because American Indians, like Blacks, were not Christian and their skin color was dark, they were

evaluating equality

Thomas Jefferson and Sally Hemings

Is it possible to reconcile Thomas Jefferson's views on slavery with his actions?

Thomas Jefferson is often characterized as being opposed to slavery. Yet he continued to own slaves. Is it possible to reconcile these seemingly contradictory elements?

Jefferson's Views

Jefferson's original draft of the Declaration of Independence contained a sharp attack on King George III for his support and facilitation of the slave trade and the enslavement of Africans. This attack, however, was unacceptable to both Northern and Southern delegates and was removed from the final document. In later years, Jefferson would write passionately of the evils of slavery and the need to abolish the institution.

Despite his antislavery views, Jefferson did not believe that the United States should attempt to incorporate Blacks into the nation. In his *Notes on the State of Virginia*, Jefferson was uncompromising in his belief that Blacks were innately inferior to Whites. He advocated removing free Blacks from the nation and colonizing them outside the United States. He also found Blacks physically offensive and argued against the intermixing of White and Black blood.

Jefferson's Actions

Despite Jefferson's writings on the evils of slavery, he did not free his own slaves. Even on his death, he freed only five of his approximately 130 slaves. In addition, during his life,

Jefferson was said to have fathered children by his slave Sally Hemings, although Jefferson and his supporters denied that this was true. Some Jefferson historians have pointed to his disdain for Blacks as proof that he would not have fathered children with his slave.

In 1998, however, DNA testing confirmed, within a certain degree of probability, that Thomas Jefferson had fathered at least one of Hemings's children.[1] Meticulous research by Annette Gordon-Reed, a law professor at Harvard University, is now acknowledged to provide additional proof that Jefferson indeed fathered all of Sally Hemings's children.[2]

- Is it possible to reconcile Jefferson's public pronouncements and his belief in liberal and republican ideals with his private behavior of owning slaves, including his own children? Why or why not?

- Does the contradiction between Jefferson's public writings and private behavior have any parallels with contemporary politicians and government or public figures today? Explain your answer.

[1] E. A. Foster et al., "Jefferson Fathered Slave's Last Child," *Nature* 196 (November 1998): 27–28.

Historical research and DNA evidence showed that Thomas Jefferson fathered Sally Hemings's six children. Yet, many of Jefferson's White descendants refused to accept the evidence. Shay Banks-Young, a descendant of Sally Hemings's son, Madison, is shown with Lucian Truscott IV, a White descendant of Jefferson, after the Monticello Association voted not to extend membership to the descendants of Hemings on May 5, 2002. Banks-Young holds a copy of a photo of a Black man with a zipper across his mouth that Truscott said was sent to him in an e-mail by former association president John Works, Jr. Works said he regretted sending the photo.

[2] Annette Gordon-Reed, *Thomas Jefferson and Sally Hemings: An American Controversy* (Charlottesville: University of Virginia Press, 1997).

not quite human and were culturally and intellectually inferior to Europeans. The colonists felt that if Indians were to live near or among White settlements, they needed to be transformed into "civilized" human beings.[33] Massachusetts divided its Indian population into wild tribes and converted tribes.[34]

Because the colonists perceived Indians to be unfamiliar with European ways of thinking and to have vastly different conceptions of property than they themselves did, the colonists developed the notion that Indians were similar to children and needed to be directed in all aspects of life. The colonists then decided that Indian lands should be sold to settlers at reduced prices as an exercise in the colonists' trusteeship of Indians and their lands.[35] With the takeover of their lands, many tribes went to war with settlers as they moved west. Whites came to look on Indians as alien enemies who should be and needed to be destroyed.[36]

The tradition of exclusion and denial of rights and privileges to certain groups shaped the definition of who was an "American" in the new nation.[37] "True" Americans were those who possessed morally and intellectually superior traits often associated with race and gender. Thus, many Americans believed that non-Whites and women should be governed as subjects or second-class citizens and be excluded from participation in the nation.[38] The tradition of exclusion was based on several assumptions:

> *Men were naturally suited to rule over women.* Women were inferior to men in physical as well as mental and moral capabilities. Therefore, women were not suited to participate in public life.
>
> *White northern Europeans were superior, culturally and biologically, to southern, darker-skinned Europeans, African Americans, American Indians, and all other races and civilizations.* Non-White peoples were inferior in every aspect, and many Whites questioned whether darker-skinned people were even human.
>
> *Protestant Christianity was superior to any other form of religion.* Protestant Christians were superior to those who practiced other religions.

Exclusion and the Founding

Under the tradition of exclusion, groups of Americans were excluded from full participation in the new nation, and that exclusion was hierarchical. It ranged from the initial denial of the vote to unpropertied White males, to the denial of the vote and participation in the formal structures of government to White women, to the denial of citizenship and suffrage to African Americans and American Indians (see "Measuring Equality: Who Was Eligible to Be Included in 'We the People'" on page 22).

Although the Founders intended the rights and guarantees of the Constitution to extend to all free White males, not all free White males were eligible to participate in the affairs of government. In the early days of the nation, only propertied White males were eligible to vote. Property ownership was thought to give people a stake in the political system and allow them to have a say in how it was run. Those who owned no property, therefore, had no stake in the system and thus no right to a voice in government decision making.

It is true that White women were citizens of the United States from the beginning of the new nation,[39] but the relationship of White women to the new nation was different in substantial and important respects from the relationship of White males to their nation. The political exclusion of White women from the Constitution did not originate with that document. State constitutions written after 1776 explicitly or implicitly denied White women the limited political rights they had enjoyed before the Revolution, such as the ability to vote in local elections. None of the new state constitutions, except that of New Jersey, granted women the right to vote.

The primary reasoning behind not giving the vote to women was the continued reliance, present since colonial times, on coverture, which (as explained earlier) held that on marriage a woman's legal identity merged into that of her husband. Thus, to give women in the new nation the right to vote would be synonymous with giving their husbands two votes.

The Founders did not intend the Constitution to apply to Blacks and Indians.[40] Following the ratification of the Constitution, Congress passed the Naturalization Act of 1790 in response to its new constitutional power to legislate a uniform rule to deal with the process by which foreigners could be "admitted to the rights of citizens." The act stated, as did all naturalization legislation from 1790 through 1854, that only a "free White person" was eligible to become a citizen of the United States. Because, according to prevailing belief, Indians and slaves did not understand the European way of life and political system, they were not free and were, therefore, not suited to be members of the political system or to exercise the duties and responsibilities of citizenship, and they were justifiably excluded from all this legislation.[41]

The issue of what to do with Black slaves in the new nation was central to several of the compromises struck on the Constitution. In the end, an African American's right to liberty conflicted with a White master's right to property. In keeping with the classical liberal foundations of the nation, the right of property took precedence.[42] Many of the Founders viewed Blacks as property, not citizens of the new republican nation.

Under the Articles of Confederation, the country's first constitution, the Continental Congress established a committee to address the question of Indian inclusiveness. The initial committee report recommended that Congress urge the states to make it easy for Indians to become citizens. Most

Portrait of Mrs. John Stevens (Judith Sargent, later Mrs. John Murray) 1751–1820, by John Singleton Copley. Judith Sargent, like Lemuel Haynes, was a voice of those excluded from the original conception of those eligible to participate in the new nation. White women, like slaves, freed Blacks, and American Indians, were not originally considered a part of the political system.

measuring equality

Who Was Eligible to Be Included in "We the People"?

The pie chart provides a visual illustration of the number of people present at the founding of the United States and, of those, how many were eligible to participate in the new nation. Indians were not counted, so the population number was actually greater than the 3.9 million shown here. The chart shows that 20.7 percent of the population were White males over the age of sixteen. The actual number of people eligible to participate in the new nation was even smaller than 20.7 percent because the requirements were "a White male, twenty-one years of age and over, and a property owner." According to National Archives estimates, as few as 6 percent of the counted population were White male property owners. What picture of the new nation do these data present? Who was included in the phrase "We the People"?

Total population: 3,893,874
Total does not add up to 100 due to rounding.

Figure 1.1

American Indians traded with, protected, and supported European settlers until conflict erupted over control of land. This report, however, was tabled by the Congress. A subsequent report by a different committee "referred to Indians, not as potential citizens, but as possible allies."[43] This categorization meant that Indians were not to be included as citizens in the new nation. They were foreign aliens outside the nation despite their living physically within it.

Despite the Founders' notions about the place of American Indians in the new nation, they drew on many of the concepts practiced by them. American Indians exercised democratic norms and behaviors before contact with Europeans. The most famous Indian confederation was the League of the Iroquois, located in what is now upper New York State. Although there is disagreement over the date of the establishment of the League of the Iroquois, it existed

The map shows the land of the six Iroquois nations that covered what is now the states of New York and Pennsylvania.

prior to contact with Europeans. Many scholars suggest that the League of the Iroquois influenced the shaping of the U.S. Constitution. Benjamin Franklin used the league as the basis for the Albany Plan of Union in 1754.[44] In October 1988, the U.S. Congress passed Concurrent Resolution 331 to recognize the influence of the Iroquois Constitution on the U.S. Constitution and Bill of Rights.

The Iroquois Confederacy initially consisted of five tribes—the Mohawk, Onondaga, Oneida, Cayuga, and Seneca—with the Tuscarora joining in 1722. This loose group of tribes formed an organized government based on several democratic principles. The league was governed by a constitution, the Great Law of Peace. Under the constitution, the chiefs of the tribes were appointed by the female leaders of the tribes, who also had the authority to remove the chiefs for misconduct, sickness, or other reasons causing them to be ineffective. When a chief died, the women chose a new one.[45]

The governing council of the initial Five Nation Confederation consisted of fifty representatives divided proportionally among the tribes, with the Onondagas having fourteen delegates; the Cayugas, ten; the Mohawks and Oneidas, nine delegates each; and the Senecas, eight. (Initially, the Tuscarora had no voting rights.) Warriors were prohibited from being council representatives because they might adopt warlike positions and attempt to promote warlike policies. All delegates were chosen by their tribes in accordance with tribal governance rules. The council was obliged to meet every five years, more often if necessary.[46]

The Great Law of Peace was initially recorded with beads on wampum belts, as were records of meetings and decisions reached by the Council of the

Five Nations. Concern about possible loss or destruction of the belts prompted translation of the document into English in 1880 by Seth Newhouse, a Mohawk.[47]

Conclusion

The opening vignette about the various apologies for slavery and later segregation illustrates how central race was to the development of the American political system. As was demonstrated throughout the chapter, race intertwined intimately with the liberal and republican theories at the foundation of this system.

Aspects of classical liberalism include the notion of limited government, the rule of law, and the primacy of private property. Concepts associated with the classical republican tradition include a sense of civic virtue, a belief that institutions derive their authority from the people, and support for elected representation. The tradition of exclusion subscribes to the notion of inequality among people. According to this tradition, true Americans are drawn only from a certain group of people, a group that excludes non-Whites and women. The Founders of the American system of government blended inegalitarian beliefs with the principles of classical liberalism and classical republicanism.[48]

The classical liberal and republican foundations of the American political system remain embodied in American government. Strains of the traditions of exclusion endure as well. Inequalities abound in our political system, many stemming directly from this tradition. We still struggle with the paradox of a commitment to democratic and egalitarian principles and a continued conflict between these principles and the experiences of many citizens who have been and are treated differently by the American government.

REVIEW QUESTIONS

1. What are the three principles underlying constitutional democracy?
2. How and where are these three principles evident in the American system of government?
3. What were the three theoretical traditions at the foundation of the American political system?
4. How did elements of the tradition of exclusion influence who was covered by the Constitution?
5. Please explain this statement: One cannot truly be a student of American government and politics without understanding the role that race played in the development of the American political system.

KEY TERMS

Civic Virtue p. 12
Classical Liberalism p. 9
Classical Republicanism p. 9
Conservatives p. 12
Constitution p. 7

Constitutional Democracy p. 7
Coverture p. 16
Democracy p. 6
Direct Democracy p. 6
Feudalism p. 10

Government p. 4
Indirect (or Representative)
Democracy p. 7
Inegalitarianism p. 9
Liberal p. 12

readings

ADDITIONAL READINGS

Bruce E. Johansen, *Forgotten Founders: How the American Indian Helped Shape Democracy.* Boston: Harvard Common Press, 1982.

This study investigates the use of democratic principles by American Indians prior to contact with Europeans and how Indian use of these principles helped shape the American democratic system.

Alan Ray Gibson, *Interpreting the Founding: Guide to the Enduring Debates over the Origins and Foundations of the American Republic,* 2nd ed. revised and expanded. Lawrence: University Press of Kansas, 2009.

This book provides summaries and analyses of the leading interpretive frameworks that have guided the study of the Founding.

M. N. S. Sellers, *American Republicanism: Interpretation of the Constitution of the United States.* New York: New York University Press, 1994.

This book examines the influence of the Roman republic on the U.S. Constitution.

Linda K. Kerber, *Women of the Republic: Intellect and Ideology in Revolutionary America.* Chapel Hill: University of North Carolina Press, 1980.

This book studies the political views of American women during the founding of the nation.

Sidney Kaplan, *The Black Presence in the Era of the American Revolution, 1770–1800.* Washington, DC: National Portrait Gallery, Smithsonian Institution, 1973.

This book chronicles Black American speaking and writing during the Revolutionary period.

CHAPTER 2

The Constitution: Rights and Race Intertwined

The University of Maryland gained national attention in 2015 when an email from a fraternity member resurfaced. The email was from 2014 and included racial slurs and offensive language about women and sexual consent. The resulting investigation spurred a contentious debate about the difference between free speech and hate speech.

In March 2015, a January 2014 email written during rush week by a white University of Maryland member of Kappa Sigma fraternity surfaced and was posted on social media. The email uses the word "n****r," as well as racist epithets against people of Middle Eastern and Asian descent. He says "Don't invite any n****r gals or curry monsters or slanted eye chinks, unless they're hot." After discussing his plans for sexual intercourse, the writer adds, "f*** consent."[1] The University launched an investigation and the fraternity immediately suspended the undergraduate author and sender of the email pending an investigation. The individual submitted a letter of resignation from Kappa Sigma, but the fraternity said that it was in the process of formally expelling the person from the fraternity.[2]

President Wallace Loh immediately issued a statement saying that the vulgar language and sentiment of the email were reprehensible to the University of Maryland community. He then took to Twitter to express his views as a person and not as the university president.

The January 2014 email that emerged a few days ago has shaken me. The utter disregard for decency, the racist invective, the mindless disparaging of sexual consent, has left me angry and profoundly saddened. And quite honestly, I am struggling with justifying this email as free speech. It has hurt and offended members of our campus family. Including me. Where does free speech and hate speech collide? What should prevail? What justification can we have that tacitly condones this kind of hate? I want to engage in a conversation with you. Are some of you feeling the same way? Post your thoughts, your point of view.

Many of the responses indicated that they felt the student who wrote the email and the students who received it should be expelled. Others called out the fraternity and asked why they did not do something about the sender before the email became public, as the email was sent more than a year before it was exposed.

In the end, to the shock of many, after the investigation, the university found that the email did not violate university policy and thus, there was no basis on which to discipline the student. The university concluded that the message in the email, despite its reprehensible denigrating of various groups of people, was protected speech. The student, along with his parents, apologized to the campus community for the hurt and offense his message caused in a message sent through President Loh. While the university did not find any grounds for disciplinary action, the student agreed to withdraw from the university and to leave campus.[3]

intro *This vignette highlights one aspect of the U.S. Constitution that is central to our system of government—freedom of speech. In this instance, and on many university campuses around the country, there is growing debate about whether hate speech is, in fact, free speech. This is an ongoing controversy and legal scholars come down on both sides of the argument—hate speech is not free speech, and hate speech is free speech. This is a complex debate because as precious as the right to free speech is, it is not automatic and it is not absolute. Constitutional rights are far more nuanced and complicated than most Americans realize.*

This chapter examines how the Founders of the nation went about making the Constitution the basic governing document of the United States. The story of the Constitution is one that describes guarantees of liberty and freedom for some, while simultaneously excluding large segments of the population that were present in the new United States at the time of ratification. Moreover, issues of race were central to the debates about the Constitution and played a major role in the distribution of power in the new nation. Race and the construction of the new nation were intertwined and woven into the political fabric of the United States.

A Revolution for Independence

The path to the American Revolution was long and winding. The buildup to the Revolution consisted of many events, some that pushed the colonists away from Britain and others that gave the colonists pause and pulled them back. The decision to declare independence and go to war was not an easy one, and it was carefully considered by all those involved.

The Road to Revolution

The issues of colonial autonomy and monarchial rule were central questions that fueled the American Revolution. The colonists were upset with what they perceived to be unfair acts by King George III and Parliament. Between 1739 and 1763, Great Britain engaged in several wars in Europe and in the Americas that generated a tremendous debt. Faced with this debt and the expense of maintaining troops in the Americas, Great Britain decided to raise revenue from the colonies. Up to that point, the colonies had not been expected to generate revenue, and they historically paid very little tax to the Crown.

In 1764, Parliament passed the American Revenue Act, commonly referred to as the Sugar Act, which required the colonies to pay a heavy tariff on sugar and other raw materials and on manufactured products imported to the colonies from foreign countries. That act was followed in the same year by the Currency Act, which prohibited the colonies from issuing currency. In 1765, Parliament passed the Quartering Act, which required local governments in the colonies to provide barracks and supplies for British troops. In the same year, it also passed the Stamp Act, which placed a tax on everything printed or written on paper—newspapers, pamphlets, insurance policies, playing cards, legal documents, ships' documents, licenses, and so forth.

The Stamp Act was the first legislation to impose a direct tax on the colonists themselves, and they feared that this would be the first of many direct taxes to come.[4] The colonists had resented earlier legislation, but now they organized to protest the latest act. The Massachusetts Assembly called for a general meeting on Britain's revenue-raising tactics. Nine colonies sent representatives to this meeting, the Stamp Act Congress, which met in New York City in October 1765. The congress declared that taxation without representation was a violation of the colonists' rights as British subjects and argued that only the colonial government, not Parliament, could levy taxes on the colonists. The colonists backed up their protests with a boycott against goods made in Britain.

Faced with the dramatic drop in exports to the colonies, Parliament eventually repealed the Stamp Act in 1766, but at the same time it passed the Declaratory Act, which stated that Parliament had supremacy over the colonies "in all cases whatsoever." Another series of acts in 1767, named the Townshend Acts after Charles Townshend, the British chancellor of the Exchequer, instituted heavy taxes on all vessels entering colonial ports and placed duties on all manufactured goods. Colonial resentment and opposition continued to mount as pamphleteers and newspapers fanned the fires of protest against Parliament's actions.[5]

In 1773, Parliament passed the Tea Act as a means of bailing out the East India Company, which was on the verge of bankruptcy. The act not only imposed a tax on tea imported into America, but also gave the East India Company exclusive rights to sell tea to the colonies. Protests against the Tea Act took place in several colonies, but the most dramatic incident occurred in Boston. On the night of December 16, 1773, colonists disguised as American Indians boarded ships docked in Boston harbor and threw chests of tea overboard. The infamous Boston Tea Party destroyed 340 chests of tea worth nearly £10,000. Parliament responded with the Coercive Acts, which closed Boston Harbor, revoked Massachusetts's colonial charter, sent British officials charged with crimes to England or Canada for trial, and again legalized the housing of British troops in unoccupied buildings in the colonies.

Opposition to Britain continued to build, particularly in Massachusetts. In May 1774, participants in a Boston town meeting called for a general colonial congress to deal collectively with the colonies' problems with Britain. In September 1774, twelve colonies sent delegates, fifty-six in all, to the meeting of the First Continental Congress in Philadelphia. The Congress denounced the

On December 16, 1773, the Sons of Liberty boarded ships in Boston Harbor and threw three crates of tea overboard in protest of the British government and the East India Company's tax policy on tea and the Tea Act, which the colonists considered unfair.

Coercive Acts as cruel and illegitimate, arguing that Parliament had no authority over the colonies because the colonies owed allegiance to the king only. The delegates drafted a resolution addressed to King George and the British and American peoples stating their opposition to the acts and calling for another boycott of British goods.[6] Before the Congress dispersed at the end of the month, it laid plans for the Second Continental Congress to meet in May 1775.

To King George III, the actions and resolution of the First Continental Congress meant that the colonies were now in a state of rebellion. The winter of 1774–1775 passed without major incidents, but on April 18, 1775 (some sources say April 19), British troops and Massachusetts militiamen exchanged gunfire at the battles of Lexington and Concord, two small farm villages in eastern Massachusetts. The American Revolution had begun. The Second Continental Congress, meeting in May 1775, in Philadelphia, took control of the war and in June, named George Washington as chief of the Continental Forces and charged him with raising an army to fight the British.

Declaring Independence

Although the Second Continental Congress authorized the raising of an army to fight the British, it issued no formal call for independence from Britain. The congress believed that Massachusetts and the rest of the colonies had the right to resist Britain's oppressive behavior, but it was not yet convinced that severing ties with Britain was the correct step. As the fighting continued, however,

Crispus Attucks (c. 1723–1770), a former slave, merchant, and seaman, was the first person killed on March 5, 1770, by British soldiers in what has become known as the Boston Massacre. The British soldiers who fired the fatal shots were tried and defended by John Adams, who used Attucks's race and supposed terrifying looks as a justification for the soldiers killing him. The soldiers were acquitted.

many colonists began to consider independence from Britain. Thomas Paine, a British journalist and political philosopher who came to the colonies in 1774 at the request of Benjamin Franklin, helped sway that opinion. In January 1776, Paine wrote *Common Sense*, a pamphlet that argued strongly for the immediate declaration of independence for the colonies. *Common Sense* was wildly popular, selling between 300,000 and 500,000 copies.

By the spring of 1776, sentiment was running high for breaking with Britain.[7] North Carolina was the first colony to authorize its delegates to the Second Continental Congress to vote for independence, with Virginia a close second. Richard Henry Lee of Virginia, a representative to both Continental Congresses and an ardent advocate of independence, offered a resolution that the colonies declare themselves independent of Great Britain.

After much debate, the Second Continental Congress decided to appoint a committee to draft a declaration of independence. The committee consisted of Thomas Jefferson of Virginia, Benjamin Franklin of Pennsylvania, John Adams of Massachusetts, Robert R. Livingston of New York, and Roger Sherman of Connecticut. Jefferson drafted the document, which cataloged the abuses of King George and drew on several Western European political traditions, principally liberalism and republicanism (see Chapter 1), as justification for the colonies to declare their independence. (See Table 2.1 for a list of selected events leading up to the Declaration of Independence.)

TABLE 2.1 Selected Legislation/Events Leading to the Declaration of Independence

Legislation/Events	Date	Provisions	Colonial Reaction
Sugar Act	April 5, 1764	Revises duties on sugar, coffee, tea, wine, other imports; expands jurisdiction of vice-admiralty courts	Protest in several assemblies of taxation for revenue
Stamp Act	March 22, 1765; repealed March 18, 1766	Requires that printed documents (deeds, newspapers, marriage licenses, etc.) be issued only on special stamped paper purchased from stamp distributors	Riots in cities; collectors forced to resign; Stamp Act Congress (October 1765)
Quartering Act	May 1765	Requires colonists to supply British troops with housing and other items (candles, firewood, etc.)	Protest in assemblies; New York Assembly punished for failure to comply (1767)
Declaratory Act	March 18, 1766	Declares Parliament's sovereignty over the colonies "in all cases whatsoever"	Celebration over repeal of the Stamp Act blotting out effect of this act
Townshend Revenue Acts	June 26, June 29, July 2, 1767; all repealed except duty on tea	Imposes new duties on glass, lead, paper, paints, tea; tightens customs collections in America	Nonimportation of British goods; protest in assemblies; newspaper attacks on British policy
Boston Massacre	March 1770	Five men were killed by British soldiers. Crispus Attucks, a runaway slave from Framingham, MA, and subsequent sailor, was the first to die in the attack and thus became the first person to die in the American Revolution.	The British soldiers were defended by John Adams, the future second president of the United States, who used Attucks's race in his defense of the British soldiers, referring to Attucks as "a stout Molatto fellow, whose very looks, was enough to terrify any person." The soldiers were acquitted.
Tea Act	May 10, 1773	Gives East India Company right to sell tea directly to Americans; reduces some duties on tea	Protests against favoritism shown to monopolistic company; tea destroyed in Boston (December 16, 1773)
Coercive Acts (Intolerable Acts)	March–June 1774	Closes port of Boston; restructures Massachusetts government; restricts town meetings; quarters troops in Boston; sends British officials accused of crimes to England or Canada for trial	Boycott of British goods; convening of First Continental Congress (September 1774)
Prohibitory Act	December 22, 1775	Declares British intention to coerce Americans into submission; imposes embargo on American goods; seizes American ships	Movement of Continental Congress closer to decision for independence

Thomas Jefferson, third president of the United States, was the author of the Declaration of Independence and a slave holder. He fathered six children with his slave, Sally Hemings, freeing the children in his lifetime but not freeing their mother in his will. His children were the only slaves that Jefferson ever freed.

Although he was a slave owner himself, Jefferson's original draft of the Declaration of Independence included an indictment of King George for engaging in and perpetuating slavery: "violating the most sacred rights of life and liberty in the persons of a distant people who never offended him, captivating and carrying them into slavery in another hemisphere or to incur miserable death in their transportation hither to." Both Southern and Northern delegates objected to the clause. Southerners argued that slavery was fundamental to the economy of the new nation, and Northerners viewed slavery merely as a business that needed regulating.[8] The debate over removing this indictment foreshadowed the difficulties that the issue of slavery would present the new nation and for the nation moving forward. The way the nation handled issues of race at the beginning continue to influence how the nation deals with issues of race today.

On July 4, 1776, the Continental Congress voted on a declaration of independence and announced, with these words, the colonies' independence from Britain:

We, therefore, the Representative of the United States of America, . . . do, in the Name, and by the Authority of the good People of these Colonies, solemnly publish and declare, That these United Colonies are, and of Right ought to be Free and Independent States; that they are Absolved from all Allegiance to the British Crown, and that all political connection between them and the State of Great Britain, is and ought to be totally dissolved.

The story of the road to independence can be placed under the broad category of inequitable treatment. The colonists felt that Britain was not treating them fairly on a number of dimensions—taxing the colonies to pay debts in Britain when the colonists were not allowed to have representatives in Parliament, removing power from the colonial governments, and trampling on what the colonists perceived to be their rights to govern themselves. Debates about equality and inequality were central to the concerns that brought about independence from Britain and the founding of the United States of America.

The meaning of equality was posited within their colonial experiences and the influence of the Enlightenment, and was within the context of the basic principle of freedom. Scholars have argued that the equality spoken of in the Declaration of Independence was not one of human equality as we think about it now, but the position of man in the state of nature.[9] The Founders held no illusions that all people were born with equality of intellect or virtue; in fact, Thomas Jefferson and John Adams, in a series of letters, both identified a group of individuals who were to be entrusted with running the new nation and the common man. They saw no conflict between the idea that all men are created equal and what they saw as natural inequalities between human beings.[10]

Given the belief in inequalities among human beings, the Founders made assumptions about who was and who was not to be included in this new government. Despite the language of equality and inclusion, many people who lived in the new nation—White women, free Blacks, enslaved Blacks, and American Indians—were not to be included as participants in the new nation.

First Attempt at National Government: The Articles of Confederation

When Richard Henry Lee offered his resolution for independence, he also proposed a plan for a new form of government for the nation. Britain, with which the colonies were now at war, had a **unitary form of government**, a system in which the central government exercises complete control and authority over its states or governmental units. Lee proposed a **confederation**, a system in which states or other types of government units organize a weak central government with limited scope and powers while reserving ultimate power for themselves. In such a government, each state retains its power, sovereignty, and independence.

A Limited National Government

Shortly after the appointment of the committee to draft the Declaration of Independence, another committee was established, chaired by John Dickinson of Delaware, to devise a plan for the new governmental structure.[11] On July 12, 1776, Dickinson's committee submitted the "Articles of Confederation and Perpetual Union" to the Second Continental Congress. Whereas the Continental Congress had swiftly passed the Declaration of Independence, the delegates debated for more than a year before voting on the Articles of Confederation. On November 15, 1777, the Congress formally adopted the Articles and sent them to the thirteen states for ratification. Final ratification of the Articles of Confederation did not occur until 1781 when Maryland, the last of the states to do so, finally ratified.[12]

The Articles of Confederation set up a central government with very limited powers. The states were used to operating independently and were not keen on ceding power to a central government. The Articles established a **unicameral form of government**, a system with a legislative body of one house only, and named their legislature the Congress. As the central government, Congress could enact legislation, but it had little power to enforce the laws it passed. Real power resided in the states. Members of Congress were appointed annually by the state legislatures, which also paid their salaries. Each state, regardless of population size, had one vote in Congress. There was also no executive branch and no national judicial system.

Congress was given the authority to declare war and to negotiate peace, to coin and borrow money, to make treaties and alliances, to regulate trade with

Unitary Form of Government A system in which the central government exercises complete control and authority over subunits of government, which means that states or other governmental units do not have autonomous powers.

Confederation A system in which states or other types of government units organize a weak central government with limited scope and powers while reserving ultimate power for themselves.

Unicameral Form of Government A government system that consists of only one legislative body (rather than two or more).

American Indians, and to appoint military officers. Congress also could not enact taxes or control trade among the states. States were free to compete with each other for trade with foreign countries, and the competition was fierce.

Weaknesses of the Articles of Confederation

Economic conditions in the new nation were depressed during the early years of the new republic. Imports from and exports to Britain had dropped significantly, and farm income had fallen. Under the Articles, each state issued its own currency, and the shortage of revenue led residents in many states to call on their state governments to issue more currency so that people could pay their debts.

In Massachusetts, many farmers faced the loss of their property or imprisonment because they were unable to pay their debts and taxes. In 1786–1787, dissident farmers, who attempted to shut down courthouses, clashed several times with local militias, which were defending the courts. The most serious rebellion was led by Daniel Shays, a Revolutionary War veteran. In September 1786, Shays and his followers marched on Springfield, where the state supreme court was meeting, and surrounded the courthouse, thereby forcing the court to adjourn. In December, Shays and his forces again marched on Springfield in an attempt to capture an arsenal (see "Our Voices: Prince Hall [1748–1807]"). Although their attempt to take the arsenal was unsuccessful and Shays's forces were eventually defeated, the uprising highlighted the level of discontent with state government, particularly the legislature and the courts.

Shays's Rebellion exposed the weakness of the Articles of Confederation. The national government was unable to support Massachusetts during the rebellion. Congress authorized the raising of troops, but it had no authority to raise money to support them. Under the Articles, Congress could only ask states for the money it needed to carry out its functions. Clearly, Congress required revenue to send and receive ambassadors, manage domestic and foreign affairs, establish post offices, staff and equip military forces, and handle the few other limited functions delegated to the national government. Lacking the authority to force either the states or the people to pay taxes (a power reserved solely to the states) led to predictable and devastating results.

The mechanisms for adopting and changing the Articles presented problems. Both processes required all thirteen states to agree. Thus, it was not until four years after the national Congress adopted the Articles in 1777 that the last state, Maryland, finally ratified them. Changes were also unlikely under the rule of unanimity; each state, in effect, had the power of veto. Thus, any revision or alteration of the Articles could have been blocked by the disapproval of one state. In all, the problems manifested in the Articles of Confederation seemed to suggest that the people who had successfully revolted against the world's greatest military power might not be able to figure out how to govern themselves. It was against this backdrop that the Congress, in February 1787, called a convention to meet in Philadelphia to revise the Articles of Confederation.

our voices

Prince Hall (1748–1807)

In September 1786, during the uprising known as Shays's Rebellion, Governor James Bowdoin issued a call for volunteers to head west to help put down the rebellion. Prince Hall, a former slave who, having been initially denied membership in White Freemason organizations, founded the African American Freemasons, the African Lodge No. 1, in Boston, wrote a letter to Governor Bowdoin offering the services of seven hundred Black troops. Historians contend that Hall made this offer in an effort to show the loyalty of Black Americans to the state of Massachusetts and, although they were denied citizenship, to demonstrate the desire of Blacks to be citizens of the state and, by extension, citizens of the United States. Historians also suggest that Bowdoin rejected the offer because, although slavery had been abolished in Massachusetts, hostility to Blacks in general and fear of armed Black men in particular were high.

In his letter, Hall drew on his group's organization as Freemasons to make his argument for the willingness of these men to volunteer on behalf of the state of Massachusetts.

Here is an excerpt from Hall's letter to Governor James Bowdoin in November 1786:

> We, by the Providence of God, are members of a fraternity that not only enjoins upon us to be peaceable subjects to the civil powers where we reside, but it also forbids our having any concern in any plot or conspiracies against the state where we dwell; and as it is the unhappy lot of this state at the present date, and as the meanest of its members must feel that want of a lawful and good government, as we have been protected for many years under this once happy Constitution, so we hope, by the blessing of God, we may long enjoy that blessing; therefore, we, though unworthy members of this Commonwealth, are willing to help and support, as far as our weak and feeble abilities may become necessary in this time of trouble and confusion, as you in your wisdom shall direct us. That we may, under just

Prince Hall, a former slave, founded the African American Freemasons. During Shays's Rebellion in 1786, Hall wrote to Massachusetts' Governor Bowdoin to volunteer seven hundred Black troops to fight on behalf of the State of Massachusetts.

> and lawful authority, live peaceable lives in all godliness and honesty, is the hearty wish of your humble servants, the members of the African Lodge.

Sources: Corey D. B. Walker, *A Noble Fight: African American Freemasonry and the Struggle for Democracy in America* (Urbana: University of Illinois Press, 2008), 77–79; Sidney Kaplan, *The Black Presence in the Era of the American Revolution, 1770–1800* (Greenwich, CT: New York Graphic Society, 1973).

Second Attempt at National Government: The Constitution

When the fifty-five men we now know as the Framers of the Constitution met in Philadelphia in the summer of 1787, their purpose was to deal with an economic and political crisis and to address problems with the governmental system established by the Articles of Confederation. The convention delegates faced a balancing problem. The most obvious course of action was to shift some power from the state governments to the national government. But if they gave too much power to the national government, they would create a unitary form of government. Most delegates wanted to avoid this solution because such a government might too closely resemble the system under the British. Thus, the convention delegates established a government in which some powers remained at the state level, some were vested in the national government, and some were shared, an arrangement also known as **concurrent powers**. In so doing, the delegates established a **national government**, the central government under a federal system.

The Convention Delegates

The idea of a federal government did not appear out of thin air to the convention delegates as they sat sweating through the summer heat of Philadelphia. The Framers drew on the political philosophies of liberalism and republicanism as they set about revising the government. They also drew on their own experience. More than 70 percent of the members of the convention held high state offices. Many of these men had participated in the formation of a government at the state level. Three of the twelve states represented at the Constitutional Convention sent their governors. (Rhode Island's legislature, controlled by those sympathetic to Shays, did not send any delegates.) Four-fifths of the delegates had served in the Continental Congress established under the Articles; eight others had signed the Declaration of Independence.[13]

In addition to their government experience, the Framers shared other characteristics. All of the delegates who convened in Philadelphia were male and White, as White males were the only ones with political power in the early republic. They were well educated; more than half of them had attended college. They were also wealthy. Although the forms of wealth varied—including land, businesses, slaves, cash, credit, or bonds—most of the delegates had amassed sizable fortunes. Thus, the Framers were hardly representative of the new nation's overall population (see "Measuring Equality: Whom did the Framers Represent?").

Forming a New Government

The delegates to the Philadelphia convention quickly made three procedural decisions that would ultimately prove crucial to the success of their efforts. First, they chose George Washington to preside over the sessions. It is hard to overestimate Washington's stature at the time. He had headed the army that had defeated the British for the new country's independence and had taken no pay for his efforts. He had paid the revolutionary soldiers who served under him out of his own pocket. One-fifth of the attendees had served as officers under Washington's command. In addition, he owned a good bit of the country—thousands of acres of land in Kentucky, Maryland, the Northwest Territory (the area between the Ohio and Mississippi Rivers that eventually

Concurrent Powers Powers shared by the national government and state governments, such as the power to tax and borrow money.

National Government A system of government in which powers are distributed between the central government (federal government) and subunits, such as states.

measuring equality

Whom Did the Framers Represent?

The language of the Constitution guarantees equality and freedom to all men. Yet we know that the Framers of the Constitution intended the guarantees and protections to apply only to a small segment of the population in the United States at the time. Who were the Framers really (see Table 2.A)? How representative of the rest of the population were they (see Table 2.B)? What do the data here on the characteristics of the Framers suggest to you about the strata of the population that they represented?

TABLE 2.A Characteristics of the Fifty-Five Framers[a]

White: 100% (55)
Male: 100% (55)

Occupation
Lawyer only: 47.3% (26)
Lawyer and another profession: 16.3% (9)

Education
University educated: 56.4% (31)

Institutions attended
Princeton University (10)
University of Pennsylvania (2)
Columbia College (2)
William and Mary College (3)
Harvard University (3)
Scottish universities (3)
Yale University (4)
Middle and Inner Temple, London (6)

Government Experience
Colonial/military official: 94.5% (52)
Member of Continental Congress: 74.5% (41)

Property Ownership
Owned their residences: 100% (55)
Owned lands used for farming: 56.4% (31)
Owned slaves: 31% (17)

Economic Level[b]
Wealthy: 10.9% (6)
Middle class/comfortable: 76.3% (42)
Poor: 12.7% (7)

TABLE 2.B Characteristics of the General Population According to the 1790 Census[c]

Race
White: 80.40% (3,140,531)
Slave Blacks: 17.83% (694,207)
Free Blacks: 1.52% (59,196)

Gender (White population only)
Males: 50.92% (1,599,213)
Females: 49.08% (1,541,318)

Education Level[d]
"Most" White male children in the North attended school for 4 to 6 months a year from age 4 to 14.
"Substantial amount" of White male children in the South attended school for 4 to 6 months a year from age 4 to 14.
"Few" White male children in the West attended school or were literate.
"Very few" White male children attended college or university.[e]
"Very few" White female children received any formal classroom instruction.

Significant Colonial Occupations[f]
Farming
Lumbering
Fishing
Iron mining
Trading in furs and skins
Producing naval stores

(Continued)

measuring equality *(Continued)*

TABLE 2.B *(Continued)*

Property Ownership
White slave-owning families: 11.6% (47,664)
Land owners: 13% (of 1774 population)
People associated with slave owning: 7.2% (of White population in 1790); 6.13% (in 1774)

Economic Level (in 1774) (category classifications determined from the distribution of wealth)[g]
High wealth: Top 2% held 24.6% of the wealth.
Middle wealth: Top 20% held 73.2% of the wealth.
Low wealth: 70% held only 28.6% of the wealth.
Very low wealth: Bottom 10% owned 1.7% of the wealth (in other words, they were in debt).
No wealth: 81.53% had no measurable wealth.

a "The U.S. Constitution: The Delegates," National Archives and Records Administration, http://www.gov/exhall/charters/constitution/confath. html; Forrest McDonald, We the People: The Economic Origins of the Constitution (Chicago: University of Chicago Press, 1958), chaps. 1–3.
b Information on economic levels was drawn from the "Biographical Index of Our Founding Fathers," National Archives and Record Administration, Washington, DC. The category classifications were determined from language in the biographies. Actual dollar figures of wealth and income are not readily available.
c Unless otherwise indicated, data are taken from the 1790 census, which mainly surveyed population characteristics.
d Carl F. Kaestle, Pillars of the Republic (New York: Hill and Wang, 1983); Genealogical Publishing Company, A Century of Population Growth (Baltimore: GPC, 1989).
e The 1790 census indicated that there were 807,312 White males over the age of sixteen in the country. A listing of the most prominent colleges and universities at the same time shows a combined enrollment of 1,122 students (White males).
f Stella H. Sutherland, Population Distribution in Colonial America (New York: Columbia University Press, 1936), xi.
g Alice Hanson Jones, Wealth of a Nation to Be (New York: Columbia University Press, 1980); Alice Hanson Jones, American Colonial Wealth (New York: Arno Press, 1977).

became the states of Ohio, Indiana, Illinois, Michigan, Wisconsin, and part of Minnesota), Pennsylvania, and Virginia.

Second, the group decided to hold secret sessions. No information emerged from the meetings until the final announcement. This secrecy was important because the third major decision the conventioneers quickly reached was to scrap their mandate merely to "revise the Articles of Confederation." They decided instead to draft a new document. Thus, the Constitution came into being only because the Framers chose to ignore the instructions they had been given by their state legislatures and to draft a new national governing document.

In one sense, this decision was as revolutionary as the decision to break from England, but in this case the Framers were, quite literally, revolting against themselves. In essence, the Framers were threatening their own privileged status by deciding to replace the government in which many of them served and to shift power away from the states they represented. Nevertheless, without the secrecy, the opposition to creating a new national government would have had the chance to mobilize.

The Great Compromise

Edmund Randolph of Virginia introduced the plan that proposed adopting a new national government rather than amending the Articles of Confederation. The **Virginia Plan**, drafted by fellow Virginian James Madison, called for the establishment of a strong central government with three branches: legislative, executive, and judicial. The legislature would consist of two houses—that is, it would be a **bicameral legislature**—with the number of representatives for each state based on population size or money contributions to the national government.

Representatives to the lower house would be elected by the people, and members of the upper chamber would be elected by the lower house from nominations submitted by the state legislatures. The legislature would select the national chief executive. The judicial branch would consist of a supreme court and subordinate national courts whose judges would be selected by the legislature. The plan also proposed the creation of a committee of revision to consist of a chief executive and several members of the judiciary. This committee would have veto power over legislative acts.

The Virginia Plan's proposal for proportional representation in the legislature favored the more populous states of the time—Virginia, Massachusetts, and Pennsylvania. Needless to say, the smaller states of New Jersey and Georgia were opposed to the Virginia Plan. Under the Articles of Confederation, each state had equal representation. Proportional representation of the Virginia Plan would give more power to the more populous states.

William Paterson of New Jersey introduced an alternative plan that aimed to amend the Articles of Confederation. The **New Jersey Plan** sought to maintain the confederation's unicameral legislature wherein each state was represented equally with one representative per state. Representatives would be elected by state legislatures. The plan also called for the creation of a supreme court. To address problems that had surfaced under the Articles of Confederation, Congress would be given more power. The New Jersey Plan proposed shifting the power to tax and regulate foreign and interstate commerce from the individual states to the national legislature. Congress could also name more than one person to a chief executive committee—a plural executive that would have no veto power.

The delegates debated differences between the Virginia and New Jersey plans but decided to move in the direction suggested by the Virginia Plan, because they wanted to create a new national government, not merely amend the Articles of Confederation. A committee was appointed to resolve the differences between the two plans and forge them into one document. The most significant problem continued to be the issue of equal versus proportional representation. Finally, Roger Sherman of Connecticut offered a compromise.

Sherman's plan, known as the **Connecticut Compromise**, or the **Great Compromise**, proposed that each state would have equal representation in the upper house of the legislature, the Senate, and proportional representation in the lower House of Representatives. Representation in the House would be based on a state's population, with one elected representative for every thirty

Virginia Plan Drafted by James Madison of Virginia at the 1787 Constitutional Convention; a proposal for a system of government that called for the establishment of a strong central government with three branches: a bicameral legislature, a chief executive chosen by the legislature, and a powerful judiciary.

Bicameral Legislature A legislature with two bodies, usually referred to as the upper and lower chambers, or, as is most common in the United States, the House and the Senate.

New Jersey Plan Drafted by William Paterson of New Jersey at the 1787 Constitutional Convention; a proposal for a system of government that called for the maintenance of a confederation with a unicameral legislature in which all states were represented equally, a multimember executive without the power to veto legislation, and a supreme court.

Great Compromise (or **Connecticut Compromise**) Worked out by a committee at the 1787 Constitutional Convention, a compromise that called for membership in the House of Representatives based on population, with states having equal representation in the Senate.

Slavery was a cruel and harsh institution that paid little to no attention to familial relations. This woodcut from the 1800s is a rarity in that it depicts the auctioning of an entire family. Nevertheless, there was no guarantee that a family would be able to stay together.

thousand persons. There would be a total of fifty-six representatives. The lower house would have the power to originate legislation for raising and spending money. In the Senate, each state would have equal representation, with two senators for each state selected by the state's legislature.[14] (In the end, the size of the House of Representatives was set at sixty-five in the original Constitution from 1787 until the first census in 1790, at which point the size of the House grew to 105.[15])

The question of how to determine the population base for representation in the lower house required additional debate and compromise. Slavery was at the heart of the debate, although the issue was not the abolition of slavery. Delegates from slaveholding states considered slaves property, not people. Nevertheless, for the sake of greater power in the national government, they wanted slaves counted as free persons to determine representation in the lower house. This would give the slaveholding states added votes in the House of Representatives, despite the fact that the slaves being counted for purposes of representation would not be represented by those who were elected. Delegates from nonslaveholding states, however, did not want the slaves counted.

The debate was resolved, at least until the Civil War, by the **Three-Fifths Compromise**, which counted each slave as three-fifths of a person for representational purposes in the House of Representatives (see "Evaluating Equality: The Effect of the Three-Fifths Compromise on the Political Power of the South" on page 44). The delegates finally voted on and passed the Great

Three-Fifths Compromise
A compromise reached at the Constitutional Convention over how state populations were to be counted for purposes of allocating seats in the House of Representatives; each slave was to be counted as three-fifths of a person for representational purposes.

Compromise, and the document was given to a committee charged with organizing and refining the draft constitution. Members of the committee included Alexander Hamilton of New York and James Madison of Virginia.

Debate over Ratification

On September 17, 1787, the convention passed the draft constitution and forwarded it to the Continental Congress to be passed on to the states. For the Constitution to become the new national governing document, it had to be ratified by three-fourths of the states, or nine of the thirteen. Ratification was not an easy process, as there was significant opposition to the Constitution. Those in favor of ratification called themselves **Federalists**, leaving those against it to identify themselves as Antifederalists. The Federalists favored a strong central government with a bicameral national legislature, whereas the **Antifederalists** preferred a weaker federal government with a unicameral national legislature.

On September 28, 1787, the Continental Congress sent the Constitution to the states without making any specific recommendation for or against ratification. Several states were not pleased with the new document, especially New York, which was concerned about an erosion of state authority. To counter opposition, the Federalists decided to conduct a concerted campaign for ratification. Three of the signers of the proposed Constitution—James Madison of Virginia and Alexander Hamilton and John Jay of New York—wrote a series of anonymous letters to the public laying out the arguments in favor of immediate ratification. Many leaders of the thirteen states were terrified that a strong national government would infringe on their sovereign powers. *The Federalist Papers*, as the letters became known when they were collected and published as a volume, sought to show that the states and the national government would share powers and that most of the powers already held and exercised by the states would remain as such.

Prominent opponents of the Constitution were Richard Henry Lee, Patrick Henry, and George Mason of Virginia; Sam Adams of Massachusetts; and George Clinton of New York. The Antifederalists, who believed the proposed Constitution would fail and anarchy and despotism would ensue, insisted on the addition of a bill of rights, feared a consolidated government, opposed unlimited taxing power, and were opposed to standing armies in peacetime.[16]

Ratification took some time because many states had specific concerns. The absence of a bill of rights to protect civil liberties troubled many states, especially North Carolina. Delaware was the first state to ratify, on December 7, 1787, but the Constitution was not finally approved until New Hampshire, the ninth state to do so, ratified on June 21, 1788. Rhode Island, which refused to send a delegation to the Philadelphia convention, rejected the Constitution in March 1788, and stayed out of the new nation until 1790, when it ratified the Constitution by just two votes at a state convention. (Rhode Island's state legislature was so fractionalized that it could not function.) (See

Federalists Proponents of the Constitution during the ratification process.

Antifederalists Opponents of the Constitution during the ratification process.

The Federalist Papers A collection of the eighty-five articles written by James Madison, Alexander Hamilton, and John Jay in support of the ratification of the Constitution.

evaluating equality

The Effect of the Three-Fifths Compromise on the Political Power of the South

This congressional compromise, which counted each slave as three-fifths of a person for representational purposes in the House of Representatives, resolved the debate on how to apportion representatives in the House. Although not what the Southern delegates wanted, the Three-Fifths Compromise nevertheless tilted political power in the House of Representatives and in the new government to the South. Table 2.C, derived from the 1790 census (the first census after ratification of the Constitution), shows the

TABLE 2.C   1790 Census Population Statistics[a]

	Total Population	White Males 16 Years and Over	White Males Under 16 Years	All Other White Females	Free Persons	Slaves
Connecticut	237,655	60,739 [25.56%]	54,289 [22.84%]	117,208 [49.32%]	2,771 [1.17%]	2,648 [1.11%]
Delaware	59,096	11,783 [19.94%]	12,143 [20.55%]	22,384 [37.88%]	3,899 [6.60%]	8,887 [15.04%]
Georgia	82,548	13,103 [15.87%]	14,044 [17.01%]	25,739 [31.18%]	398 [0.48%]	29,264 [35.35%]
Maryland	319,728	55,915 [17.49%]	51,339 [16.06%]	101,395 [31.71%]	8,043 [2.52%]	103,036 [32.23%]
Massachusetts	378,556	95,433 [25.21%]	87,279 [23.06%]	190,475 [50.32%]	5,369 [1.42%]	0
New Hampshire	141,899	36,074 [25.42%]	34,855 [24.56%]	70,183 [49.46%]	630 [0.44%]	157 [0.11%]
New Jersey	184,139	45,251 [24.57%]	41,416 [22.49%]	83,287 [45.23%]	2,762 [1.50%]	11,423 [6.20%]
New York	340,241	83,815 [24.63%]	78,258 [23.00%]	152,293 [44.76%]	4,682 [1.38%]	21,193 [6.23%]
North Carolina	395,005	70,172 [17.76%]	77,653 [19.66%]	141,356 [35.79%]	5,041 [1.28%]	100,783 [25.51%]
Pennsylvania	433,611	110,559 [25.50%]	106,928 [24.66%]	205,886 [47.48%]	6,531 [1.51%]	3,707 [0.85%]
Rhode Island	69,112	16,506 [23.23%]	15,745 [22.78%]	32,869 [47.56%]	3,484 [5.04%]	958 [1.39%]
South Carolina	249,073	35,576 [14.28%]	37,722 [15.14%]	66,880 [26.85%]	1,801 [0.72%]	107,094 [43.00%]
Virginia	747,550	110,936 [14.84%]	116,135 [15.54%]	215,046 [28.77%]	12,866 [1.72%]	292,627 [39.13%]

[a] The facts and assertions listed here are attributable to Gary Wills and are taken from his text as well as lectures and roundtable discussions conducted at the Hoover Institute at Stanford University. Both video and audio files as well as a transcript of the latter discussion can be found at http://www.hoover.org/multimedia/uk/2993311.html

population distributions in the thirteen original states.

Here are some of the effects of the Three-Fifths Compromise:

- In 1793, the size of the House of Representatives was 105 members; Southern states received forty-seven seats, rather than the thirty-three they would have received if slaves had not been counted.

- In 1812, the size of the House of Representatives was 143 members and slaveholding states had seventy-six seats, instead of the fifty-nine they would have had.
- In 1833, the size of the House was 240 members and Southern states had ninety-eight seats, instead of the seventy-three they would have had.

- By 1850, the North had twice the population of the South, but Southerners had held the presidency for fifty of sixty-two years and had occupied eighteen of thirty-one Supreme Court seats.

Source: U.S. Census, 1790; http://www.hoover.org/multimedia/uk/2993311.html

Table 2.2 for a comparison of the Articles of Confederation with the Constitution.)

The Bill of Rights

The new government took office in January 1789. Presidential electors were chosen in the states as they were electing their representatives to the House and as the state legislatures were appointing senators. The Constitution provided for the president to be elected by electors, rather than by popular vote. How states chose their electors was up to them, with most electors chosen by the state legislatures, but a small number were chosen through an election. The first Congress met in New York in March, and in April, the Senate counted the presidential electors' ballots for president. George Washington was elected unanimously with 69 electoral votes, but each elector had two votes and John Adams received the second highest number of votes and was chosen as vice president. One of Congress's first acts was to send to the states twelve amendments to the Constitution that had grown out of the state ratifying conventions. Of these, the last ten were ratified by the states and, in 1791, they became a part of the U.S. Constitution. These first ten amendments are called the **Bill of Rights**. The two amendments that were not ratified dealt with establishing a ratio of the number of people to be represented by one member of the House of Representatives and forbidding the Senate and House from raising their own salaries.

The Bill of Rights, pushed by the Antifederalists and proposed by James Madison of Virginia, spells out individual rights and liberties. As with other elements of the Constitution, the Bill of Rights was not original to that document. Many state constitutions, in particular the Constitution of Virginia (1776), had such protections. The language of the Virginia Declaration of Rights, written by George Mason and adopted by the Virginia Constitutional Convention on June 12, 1776, became the basis for the Bill of Rights.

Bill of Rights The first ten amendments to the Constitution, which focus primarily on individual liberties and basic rights.

TABLE 2.2 The Articles of Confederation versus the Constitution

Political Challenge	Articles of Confederation	Constitution
Process for ratification or amendment	Consent of every state legislature	Consent of three-fourths of state conventions or legislatures
Number of houses in legislature	One	Two
Type of representation	One to seven delegates for each state; each state with only one vote in Congress	Two senators for each state in upper house (Senate); each senator with one vote. One representative to lower house (House of Representatives) for every 30,000 people (in 1788) in a state; each representative with one vote
Process of election and term of office	Delegates appointed annually by state legislatures	Senators chosen by state legislatures for six-year term (direct election after 1913); representatives chosen by vote of citizens for two-year term
Executive	No separate executive; delegates annually electing one of their number president, who possesses no veto, no power to appoint officers or to conduct policy; administration of government carried out by a committee of states	Separate executive branch; president elected by electoral college to four-year term; president granted veto, power to conduct policy and to appoint ambassadors, judges, and officers of executive departments established by legislation
Judiciary	Most adjudication left to state and local courts; Congress the final court of appeal in disputes between states	Separate branch consisting of Supreme Court and inferior courts established by Congress to enforce federal law
Taxation	Taxes levied only by states; congressional funding of the Common Treasury through requests for state contributions	Federal government granted powers of taxation
Regulation of commerce	Foreign commerce regulated by treaty made by Congress but with no check on conflicting state regulations	Regulation of all foreign commerce by Congress through treaty; congressional consent required for all state regulations
Slavery	Makes no specific reference to slavery, but refers to "free inhabitants" in various sections. Also, the notion of counting slaves as three-fifths of a person actually originated during debates about how to establish a property foundation for taxation purposes of the new states. The measure was never passed, but the assumption is that slavery was to be allowed.	Slavery was to be allowed, although not stated explicitly, prohibited Congress from outlawing slave trade for twenty years, slaves were to count as three-fifths of a person for representation purposes, and runaway slaves were to be returned to their masters

National Government Under the Constitution

Government under the Articles of Confederation had been in existence for only seven years when the Framers decided to replace it with something else. For these men to repudiate so quickly a system that many of them had participated in creating indicated that the problems with the system were numerous and widespread.

National Supremacy

An important part of the Constitution that separates it so fundamentally from the Articles of Confederation is the **supremacy clause**, which states that the Constitution and the laws of the United States are the law of the land and supreme to all other laws passed by state and local governments. By this assertion the Framers dealt with the overarching problem of the Articles. As long as a national law was made under authority granted in the Constitution, it superseded state law when the two came into conflict.

Supremacy Clause A clause in Article 6 of the Constitution stipulating that the Constitution and national laws are "supreme," meaning that when state laws are in conflict with national laws, the latter supersede and take precedence.

The Legislative Branch

Under the Articles, state legislatures had appointed delegates to Congress and the appointees were expected to vote as their states' legislatures wished. Delegates who violated their instructions could be recalled. This arrangement allowed state legislatures to exercise power in the national government. The new Constitution set fixed terms of office for members of Congress and provided that at least some members of Congress would be directly elected by the people. These provisions allowed national legislators to act independently of their states' legislatures.

The Framers also assigned the legislative branch responsibility for dealing with specific problems denied it under the Articles. Table 2.3 lists the **enumerated powers**, which consist of seventeen specific grants of power to Congress. This was the first time our national government granted power in this way. With the supremacy clause and the listing of the enumerated powers, the Framers were changing how the new nation was governed, because they were granting supreme power to the national government but also clearly specifying, and thereby limiting, its power.

Enumerated Powers Powers of the federal government specifically stated in the Constitution.

Under the Articles of Confederation, the national government did not have the power to levy taxes. Only the states had the power to tax. Thus, the first power they granted the new Congress dealt with the power to tax. Congress could "lay and collect taxes, duties, imposts and excises."

The Constitution grants Congress explicit powers to regulate the instruments of commerce. Such authority includes the following:

- the power to borrow money
- the power to regulate interstate and foreign commerce and trade with Indian tribes

TABLE 2.3 **Enumerated Powers of Congress in Article 1, Section 8 of the Constitution**

Congress has the following powers:
1. to collect taxes, duties, imposts, and excises
2. to provide for defense and general welfare
3. to borrow money
4. to regulate commerce with foreign nations, states, and Indian tribes
5. to establish naturalization and bankruptcy laws
6. to coin money and determine standards of weights and measures
7. to provide for punishment of securities and money counterfeiting
8. to establish post offices and post roads
9. to devise copyright and patent laws
10. to define and punish pirates and felonies committed on the high seas and crimes against the law of nations
11. to declare war
12. to raise and support armies
13. to provide and maintain a navy
14. to make rules for governing and regulating land and naval forces
15. to organize, arm, and discipline the militia
16. to exercise exclusive control of the seat of government of the United States
17. to make laws necessary to carry out the other sixteen powers

- the power to establish bankruptcy laws, standards of weights and measures, post offices and post roads, and patent and copyright laws
- the power to coin money
- the power to punish counterfeiters and pirates

The Framers also gave Congress a set of powers of authority for a national military. Congress is explicitly empowered to declare war, to provide for and regulate an army and a navy, and to do the same for the militia.

The Framers could not anticipate every situation that might call for a response from national government. Rather than try to specify every power Congress might need, they added a clause dealing with **implied powers**—those powers exercised by the government that are not specifically mentioned in the Constitution. The first clause of Article 1, Section 8, of the Constitution states that Congress shall have the power "to make all Laws which shall be necessary and proper for carrying into execution the foregoing powers, and all other powers vested by this Constitution in the government of the United States, or in any Department or officer thereof."

This clause, known as the **necessary and proper clause**, gives Congress the authority to make whatever laws are necessary and proper to carry out its enumerated responsibilities. The clause is sometimes called the elastic clause because it allows the meaning of the Constitution to be stretched. It is the basis of the implied powers of the national government. For example, nowhere in the Constitution does it say that Congress should establish an internal revenue service. But Congress is empowered to collect taxes and, after the Sixteenth Amendment, to do so on the basis of income. Thus, the necessary and proper clause of the Constitution allows Congress to create an agency to

Implied Powers Government powers that are inferred from the powers expressly enumerated in the Constitution.

Necessary and Proper Clause A clause in Article 1 of the Constitution giving Congress the authority to make whatever laws are necessary and proper to carry out its enumerated responsibilities (sometimes called the elastic clause).

execute its expressed power to tax. How the courts interpret the necessary and proper clause determines the scope of the national government's authority. In 1819, Chief Justice of the Supreme Court John Marshall articulated a broad interpretation of the word "necessary" in the context of the necessary and proper clause. In the landmark case of *McCulloch v. Maryland* (1819), Marshall ruled that the Bank of the United States was constitutional under the "necessary and proper clause" even though the bank was not imperative for Congress to carry out its enumerated powers.[17]

The Executive Branch

Under the Articles, there was only one branch of government, the legislative branch, that had no concrete power to execute any of the decisions it made. For example, if Congress asked the states to contribute troops to a national army and one state decided not to do so, who would enforce Congress's request? The Articles did not specify. The Framers addressed this problem by creating an executive branch of government. In so doing, they vested "the executive Power" in a president, elected indirectly by the voters, whose job, among other duties, was to "take Care that the Laws be faithfully executed."

The decision to have a president was a compromise. The Virginia Plan proposed a single executive, whereas the New Jersey Plan provided for a plural executive. The Founders decided on a single executive called a president, having already explicitly ruled out any possibility of the use of titles of nobility and having prohibited any person holding any office in the new nation from accepting, without the consent of Congress, any title or office from "any King, Prince or Foreign State."

The Judicial Branch

Just as there had been no executive under the Articles, there had been no judicial system. Laws passed by the national Congress were enforced in state courts by judges selected in the individual states. This arrangement led to a great deal of variation in how laws were enforced across states.

To resolve this issue, the Framers created a third branch of government. Article 3, Section 1, of the Constitution states that the judicial power of the United States is to be vested in "one Supreme Court and in such inferior courts as the Congress may from time to time ordain and establish." This article established a federal court system with the U.S. Supreme Court at the top of the system having final authority over all lower courts, and with Congress granted the power to create lower-level national courts.

Liberalized Amendment Rules

The requirement under the Articles that all states agree to an amendment gave each state a veto power over any change in government. Attaining unanimity on any nontrivial proposal was virtually impossible. Thus, the Framers relaxed the rules on formally amending the Constitution. Article 5 specifies that three-fourths of the states must ratify a proposed amendment to the

Constitution before it can become law. By giving the power to block fundamental changes to a small minority of states rather than to any one state, the Framers made changing the Constitution difficult enough to ensure stable government, but not so difficult as to completely thwart improvement or modification.

Since the passage of the first ten amendments, the Constitution has been amended seventeen times. These amendments have dealt with a variety of issues. For instance, the Twelfth Amendment (ratified in 1804) established the mechanism for presidential elections, the Thirteenth Amendment (ratified in 1865) abolished slavery, the Nineteenth Amendment (ratified in 1920) granted voting rights to women, and the Twenty-Sixth Amendment (ratified in 1971) lowered the voting age to eighteen. Many of the amendments have extended constitutional protections to segments of the American population left out of the original Constitution. It has been estimated that more than 10,000 amendments to the Constitution have been proposed in Congress, many of them several times, since ratification in 1789.[18] (See Table 2.4 for a complete listing and description of the amendments.)

Planning for Potential Pitfalls

Just because the Framers thought the national government should be stronger than it was under the Articles of Confederation does not mean that they were in favor of a powerfully centralized government. In fact, the federal form of government they adopted attempted to balance powers evenly between the national and state governments rather than concentrate powers at any one level. The Framers went to extraordinary lengths to try to prevent any one part of government, any one group, or any one official from wielding too much power. The general rule seems to have been this: When in doubt, divide power.

Separating Powers

The possibility of an all-powerful chief executive, legislature, or judiciary that could exercise unlimited power was an essential concern of the Framers. To prevent such a possibility, they decided on a **separation of powers** among the branches of government. (See Chapter 1 discussion on classical republicanism, which advocated dispersing power among several branches of government.)

Separation of Powers The manner in which the Constitution divides power among the three branches of government—the legislature, the executive, and the judiciary.

Varying Terms of Office

The Constitution sets the terms of office for members of each branch of the national government. Terms of office vary to prevent any one person from gathering unlimited power by being able to stay in office indefinitely. Members of the House of Representatives serve two-year terms, and all members of the House come up for reelection at the same time. Senators are elected for six-year terms, with one-third of the Senate up for reelection every two years. The president and vice president are elected for four-year terms, and, since the

TABLE 2.4 AMENDMENTS TO THE CONSTITUTION

Amendment 1 (1791)
Freedom of religion, speech, the press, assembly, and petition

Amendment 2 (1791)
Right to bear arms

Amendment 3 (1791)
Right of a person not to have to house (quarter) soldiers without the person's consent

Amendment 4 (1791)
Right of a person to not be subject to unreasonable searches and seizures; no warrants without probable cause

Amendment 5 (1791)
Right to a grand jury for capital and infamous crimes, to avoid double jeopardy, against self-incrimination, to due process, and to compensation for public appropriation of private property

Amendment 6 (1791)
Right to a speedy and public trial, to a jury, to be informed of the nature of one's crime, to be confronted with the witnesses against one, to aid in obtaining witnesses, and to assistance of counsel

Amendment 7 (1791)
Right to a jury in common lawsuits if controversy exceeds $20 and the right not to have the facts of a jury trial reexamined by any court other than according to the rules of the common law

Amendment 8 (1791)
Right to be free of cruel or unusual punishment or excessive bail

Amendment 9 (1791)
Right to all fundamental rights in addition to those listed in first eight amendments

Amendment 10 (1791)
The powers not delegated to the federal government by the Constitution, or prohibited by it to the states, reserved for the states or the people

Amendment 11 (1798)
Limitation of jurisdiction of the federal judiciary: does not extend to suits brought by citizens of one state against another state or foreign citizens against a state within the United States

Amendment 12 (1804)
Electoral College and process of electing the president and vice president

Amendment 13 (1865)
Abolition of slavery

Amendment 14 (1868)
Definition of a citizen of the United States and right to due process of law and to equal protection; prevention of states from interfering in the rights of citizens
Representation in House according to all persons in each state
Loss of right to run for office if one has engaged in insurrection or rebellion
Public debt of the United States

Amendment 15 (1870)
Extension of the right to vote to Black males; no denial of this right based on "race, color, or previous condition of servitude"

Amendment 16 (1913)
Income tax

Amendment 17 (1913)
Popular election of senators

Amendment 18 (1919)
Prohibition

Amendment 19 (1920)
Women's suffrage

Amendment 20 (1933)
Beginning and end of the terms of president, vice president, and Congress
What transpires if president dies before inauguration, if no one gets enough votes to be president by time new term should begin, and if there is neither a president nor a vice president

Amendment 21 (1933)
Repeal of Prohibition

Amendment 22 (1951)
Term limits of presidency

Amendment 23 (1961)
Appointment of Washington, DC, electors to Electoral College

Amendment 24 (1964)
Right to vote without being subjected to a poll or any other tax

Amendment 25 (1967)
Succession and process for removal of the president

Amendment 26 (1971)
Right to vote lowered to eighteen years of age

Amendment 27 (1992)
Congressional compensation/remuneration

ratification of the Twenty-Second Amendment in 1951, no person can be elected more than twice or serve for more than ten years as president of the United States. Judges of national courts are the only officials who have unlimited terms once appointed and confirmed.

Selecting National Government Officials

Each national government official originally had, and largely continues to have, a different method of selection. Members of the House of Representatives are directly elected by the people. Under the original Constitution, U.S. senators were selected by the legislatures in their respective states. The Seventeenth Amendment, adopted in 1913, changed the method of selection so that U.S. senators are now directly elected by the people of the state in which they reside.

Electoral College The entity that selects the president and vice president, consisting of 538 electors chosen from the fifty states and the District of Columbia.

Although citizens vote for the president every four years, the United States does not have direct election of the president. The president is, in fact, officially selected by the **Electoral College**—a collection of individuals nominated by political parties who are pledged to support the party's candidate in the official presidential election. When voters go to the polls to vote for the president, they are actually voting for a set of electors, whose names, in some states, are listed beside the names of the presidential candidate from each political party.

The Electoral College consists of 538 electors; their number is equal to the total number of senators and House members from the fifty states plus three electors from the District of Columbia. Forty-eight states have a winner-take-all electoral vote distribution, and two states, Nebraska and Maine, have a system of proportional allocation of their electoral votes. A presidential candidate must receive a majority (270 votes) of the Electoral College votes to be elected. Although Americans usually know which candidate received the majority of the popular vote and Electoral College vote on election night, the president is not officially elected until December when the electors for the winning candidate travel to their respective state capitals to cast the official votes and certify the election. There have been three instances where the individual elected president won the Electoral College vote, but lost the national popular vote—in 1876 Democrat Samuel Tilden won the popular vote but lost the Electoral College vote to Republican Rutherford B. Hayes; in 1880 Democrat Grover Cleveland won the popular vote, but lost the electoral votes to Republican Benjamin Harrison; and in 2000, Democrat Al Gore won the national popular vote, but Republican George W. Bush won the Electoral College vote.

Members of the national judiciary are selected by the president, and their appointments must be approved by the Senate. The two-stage process is another aspect of separation of powers: One branch cannot act unilaterally to appoint individuals to lifetime appointments to the judiciary. The president may nominate judges, but the Senate must actually make the appointments by approving the nominations. Since 1789, of the 160 nominations to the U.S.

Supreme Court, twelve were not confirmed by the Senate, eleven nominees withdrew, ten were not acted on by the Senate, and three nominees' hearings were postponed (http://www.senate.gov/pagelayout/reference/nominations/Nominations.htm).

Qualifying for National Office

The formal qualifications for holding a position in each branch of government differ. Even though these differences might appear small, they are worth noting because they highlight the view the Framers had of the qualities and maturity of the people that could hold office in each branch. Each representative must be at least twenty-five years old, hold U.S. citizenship for at least seven years, and be a resident of the state from which he or she is elected at the time of election. U.S. senators must be at least thirty years of age, have a minimum of nine years of citizenship, and reside in the state from which elected. The president must be a natural-born citizen, at least thirty-five years old, and a resident of the United States for no less than fourteen years. The Constitution prescribes no such age, citizenship, or residential requirements for judges in national courts.

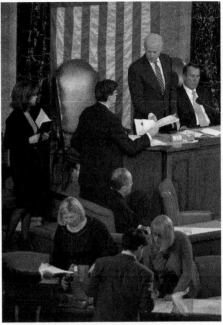

U.S. Vice President Joe Biden (2nd R, top) takes part in the count of the Electoral College votes for the 2012 presidential election as Speaker John Boehner (R, top) looks on during a joint session at the Capitol in Washington on January 4, 2013. U.S. President Barack Obama was officially declared the winner of the 2012 presidential election after the counting session—a constitutionally mandated requirement.

Instituting Checks and Balances

In addition to the structural separations of powers, the Framers built a system of functional checks by which each branch can influence outcomes in one or both of the other branches. Congress has certain powers that it can use to check the power of both other branches of government. For example, Congress controls appropriations, "the power of the purse," and thus it determines how much money is available for officials in the other two branches to carry out their duties. Likewise, Congress can impeach, convict, and remove from office both executive and judicial officials. Yet within Congress, checks on its own powers are present. Both houses of Congress must pass legislation before it can become law, thereby providing for a check of one legislative body on the other.

The Supreme Court has the power to review acts of Congress and declare legislation unconstitutional, a power not contained in the Constitution but one that evolved through the process of judicial review. This authority of the Supreme Court means that Congress cannot pass legislation that violates the Constitution. The Court has a check on the authority of the president because the actions of a president can be brought before the Court through suit filed by Congress.

Both the executive and legislative branches have the power to check the judiciary. The president appoints federal judges and justices of the Supreme

Court. Congress can then pass legislation or propose constitutional amendments that override Supreme Court decisions. In addition, Congress has the power to impeach federal judges and Supreme Court justices.

The president can veto legislation passed by Congress. This power ensures that legislation passed by Congress must clear an additional hurdle before it becomes law. Congress can override a presidential veto, but the vote required to override—two-thirds of each house—is much higher than the simple majority, or one more than half, required to pass legislation. The president is commander in chief of the armed forces, but only Congress has the power to declare war. The president negotiates treaties with foreign governments and nominates members for the cabinet and other governmental posts; the Senate must approve treaties and confirm the president's nominees.

Conclusion

The opening vignette about the University of Maryland student's email raised the tension between an individual's First Amendment free-speech right to write racist messages and the university's concern about the environment where all students feel welcome and safe. This example is illustrative of how issues about race can become intertwined with constitutional rights and guarantees. Discussions about race and the role it would play in the founding of the new nation were front and center for the Founders and for many of the people who were excluded from the protections and guarantees provided in the governing document, the Constitution, that provides the framework for our system of government.

REVIEW QUESTIONS

1. Why did the colonies decide to declare their independence from Britain?

2. What were the reasons the drafters of the Articles of Confederation chose the type of governmental structure that they did?

3. In what ways were the Framers of the Constitution not representative of the population of the United States?

4. What were the differences between the Virginia Plan and the New Jersey Plan? How were these differences reconciled?

5. What did the Three-Fifths Compromise say about the role of slaves in the new nation?

KEY TERMS

Antifederalists p. 43
Bicameral Legislature p. 41
Bill of Rights p. 45
Concurrent Powers p. 38

Confederation p. 35
Electoral College p. 52
Enumerated Powers p. 47
Federalist Papers, The p. 43

Federalists p. 43
Great Compromise p. 41
Implied Powers p. 48
National Government p. 38

ADDITIONAL READINGS

Jack P. Greene, *Understanding the American Revolution: Issues and Actors*. Charlottesville: University Press of Virginia, 1995.

This book approaches the American Revolution by examining how the shape and nature of colonial politics and the backgrounds of specific individuals led to the American Revolution.

Sylvia R. Frey, *Water from the Rock: Black Resistance in a Revolutionary Age*. Princeton, NJ: Princeton University Press, 1991.

This book explores the role of slavery and slave resistance during the period of the American Revolution.

Gordon S. Wood, *The Creation of the American Republic*. Chapel Hill: University of North Carolina Press, 1969.

This study focuses on the motives of the Founders and identifies social divisions as the source of opposition to or support for ratification of the Constitution.

Akhil Reed Amar, *America's Constitution: A Biography*. New York: Random House, 2006.

This book examines not only what the Constitution says, but also why it says what it does.

Annette Gordon-Reed, *Thomas Jefferson and Sally Hemings: An American Controversy*. Charlottesville: University of Virginia Press, 1998.

This book brings the complicated relationships between slaves and slaveholders to light with a focus on Thomas Jefferson and Sally Hemings.

CHAPTER 3

Federalism: Balancing Power, Balancing Rights

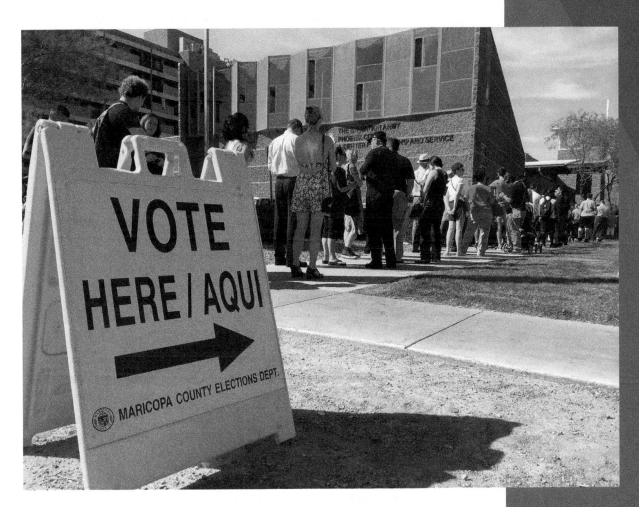

Hopeful voters wait in long lines at a polling place in downtown Phoenix to cast a vote in Arizona's presidential preference election on March 22, 2016 Initially, Maricopa County officials blamed the long lines on more Independents voting than expected, but they eventually conceded that severely slashing the number of polling sites caused the long waits. The United States Justice Department is investigating the county government's actions.

On March 22, 2016, the state of Arizona held its vote for the presidential primary, and although voting proceeded smoothly in most of the state, voters in Maricopa County—the largest county in the state because it contains the Greater Phoenix Metropolitan Area—waited in line for several hours, with many people denied the opportunity to vote. Initially county officials blamed the long lines on the fact that Independent voters were voting in the Democratic and Republican primaries, but they later conceded that the problem was that the county sharply reduced the number of voting sites compared to previous elections. In fact, the number of polling sites in Maricopa County dwindled from 400 in 2008 to 200 in 2012 to 60 in 2016. Maricopa County had 1.25 million eligible voters in 2016, which means that with 60 polling stations, the county provided one polling station for every 20,000 voters. The ratio was nowhere near as stark in other Arizona counties. Pima County, which contains the major city of Tucson, provided one polling station for every 1,200 voters. The rural counties of Navajo and Apache supplied one voting station for about every 1,000 eligible voters. Maricopa County officials justified the severe cutbacks on voting sites as a way to save money.[1]

Although these long lines inconvenienced all voters in Maricopa County, there is a race and ethnicity component to this story because Maricopa County is more than 30 percent Latino,[2] which means that Maricopa County's decision to cut polling places heavily influenced Latinos. In fact, had the county made this decision to cut voting sites prior to 2013, it would have been required to seek approval from the United States government—specifically the Department of Justice—because the *Voting Rights Act of 1965* required the state of Arizona to preclear any changes in voting procedures with the U.S. Department of Justice. Arizona was one of the states designated as having a history of discrimination, which means that its reduction of polling sites would have needed the approval of the federal government, and given the negative impact on Latino voters, it is unlikely that the Justice Department would have allowed the county to cut so many polling places. However, in 2013 the United States Supreme Court ruled that the section of the Voting

Voting Rights Act of 1965
A federal law that has significantly curtailed disenfranchisement of racial and ethnic minorities by banning literacy tests, empowering the federal government to investigate voting discrimination based on race and ethnicity, and requiring federal supervision of jurisdictions with a history of voting discrimination (the U.S. Supreme Court has sharply limited the last provision).

Rights Act identifying certain states as having a history of voting discrimination was unconstitutional,[3] which effectively ended the need for Arizona localities to preclear changes in voting procedures, such as closing polling places. Still, the United States Justice Department did announce that it would investigate Maricopa County's actions based on its still intact authority under the Voting Rights Act to investigate any state or local government actions that limit racial and ethnic minorities' right to vote.[4]

intro *In addition to describing how Maricopa County's action caused frustration for many voters, this story illustrates the importance of voting as an issue of federalism. **Federalism** refers to the balance of power between the national government and the state and local governments. Each level of government serves a distinct function and affects Americans' daily lives. Central to federalism is the concept of **sovereignty**, which means complete political power and authority. Therefore, the question of federalism concerns the extent to which the national government has sovereignty over the entire nation compared to the state and local governments' sovereignty over their respective regions.*

The issue of control over voting procedures is a prime example of federalism's significance. Specifically, the Constitution and national laws regulate voting to make it fairer, especially for racial and ethnic minorities; yet, states and local governments exercise tremendous discretion over voting procedures, such as where to place polling stations, voter identification requirements, and early voting rules. However, the U.S. Constitution, specifically the Fifteenth Amendment (ratified in 1870) gave the national government control over voting, and under the authority of this amendment Congress passed the Voting Rights Act in 1965 to ensure that racial and ethnic minorities would fully realize the right to vote. In other words, the national government exerted authority over the states to protect voting rights. However, in 2013, the U.S Supreme Court returned much of that power back to the states by effectively ending the preclearance requirement for certain jurisdictions.

The balance of power among the three levels of government, but especially between the national government on one hand and the state and local governments on the other, has been controversial throughout American political history. Recall from Chapter 2 that under the Articles of Confederation virtually all authority resided in the state and local governments, whereas the national government was extremely weak. The ratification of the Constitution, however, represented a major power shift in favor of the national government. Since then, federalism has evolved considerably. Moreover, as the story of Maricopa County's voting problems shows, the balance of power between the national government and the states significantly affects racial and ethnic minorities.

In this chapter, we examine the role of federalism in American government, paying special attention to how federalism affects racial and ethnic minorities. Before

Federalism The balance of power between the national government on one side and the state and local governments on the other side.

Sovereignty Complete political power and authority.

understanding the relationship among the levels of government, one must first understand the structures of and actors in state and local governments; therefore, we begin the chapter with an explanation of state and local governments. We then shift the discussion to federalism under the Constitution, which provides the framework for federalism. Finally, we turn our attention to the development and evolution of federalism over the course of American history.

Federalism and State and Local Governments

Federalism concerns state and local governments, so it is important to understand how the state and local governments function. In many significant ways, state and local governments mirror the national government, although there is some variation. In this section, we cover the structure of state legislatures, governors, and courts, focusing on the similarities and differences among the states. We then examine the unique issues involving local government.

State and local governments make policies that affect their residents' daily lives, and so they also influence the politics of race and ethnicity. As a general, albeit not exclusive rule, the higher the concentration of racial and ethnic minority population in a state or local area, the greater the influence racial and ethnic minorities exert on their government. Moreover, the concentration of key minority groups (Blacks, Latinos, Asian Americans, and American Indians) varies throughout the United States. Figures 3.1, 3.2, 3.3, and 3.4 show

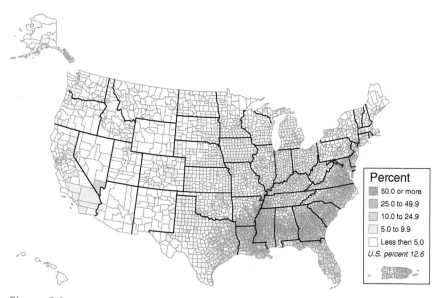

Figure 3.1 African American Population as a Percentage of County Population: 2010.

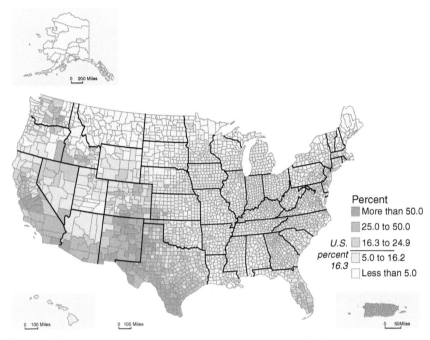

Figure 3.2 Latino Population as a Percentage of Total Population by County: 2010.

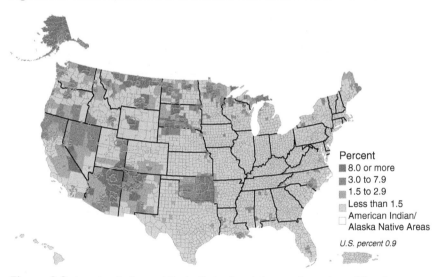

Figure 3.3 American Indian and Alaska Native Population as a Percentage of County Population: 2010.

the population concentrations of Blacks, Latinos, Asian Americans, and American Indians, respectively. We see that African Americans tend to be concentrated in the South and East, whereas Latinos are more concentrated in the Southwest. Asian Americans generally live on the West coast, and American Indians are more scattered.

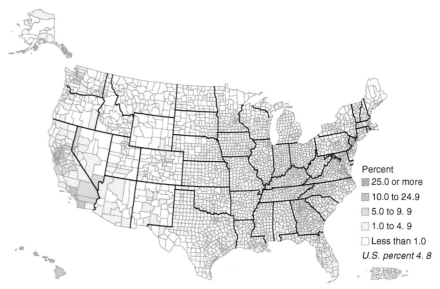

Figure 3.4 Asian Population as a Percentage of County Population: 2010.

State Legislatures

Similar to the U.S. Congress, state legislatures represent the citizens of the states and make laws governing the states. Forty-nine states have a **bicameral legislature**, which means there are two distinct houses of the legislature. The only exception is Nebraska, which has a **unicameral form of government**, or one-house, legislature. Despite this similarity in structure, state legislatures vary in terms of how frequently they meet. For example, in 2016, the state legislatures in Montana, Nevada, North Dakota, and Texas will not formally meet, and the legislature in New Mexico will formally meet for only one month. Conversely, the legislatures in Illinois, Massachusetts, Michigan, New Jersey, New York, Ohio, Pennsylvania, and Wisconsin will be in session throughout most of the year.[5]

Given state legislatures' power to make policies within the state, representation is a key issue. After the census every ten years, each state government carves the state into districts representing distinct geographic regions, and each district sends representatives to the state legislature based on population. In some states, such as Florida, only one legislator represents each district, but in other states, such as Washington, multiple legislators represent a single district. Prior to the 1960s, state legislative districts had wild deviations in population within a state, with rural, unpopulated areas having the same number of representatives as heavily populated urban areas, many of which contained large minority populations. Thus, rural interests dominated state legislatures, and urban areas were underrepresented relative to their population. In 1964, the U.S. Supreme Court in *Reynolds v. Sims* ruled that within each state, the legislative districts must be roughly equal in population,[6] which resulted in fairer representation, but minorities remained concentrated in certain districts.

Bicameral Legislature
A legislature with two bodies, usually referred to as the upper and lower chambers, or, as is most common in the United States, the House and the Senate.

Unicameral Form of Government A government system that consists of only one legislative body (rather than two or more).

In most states, after each census, the political party that controls the state legislature or governorship redraws legislative districts in ways that maximize its chances of winning seats in the legislature and thus retaining its majority control. This process is known as **gerrymandering**, and we discuss it in more detail in Chapter 6.

Gerrymandering The practice in which a group, usually a political party, uses redistricting to maximize its chances of winning elections.

Gerrymandering can also affect racial and ethnic minorities. After the passage of the Voting Rights Act of 1965—see the opening story—more racial and ethnic minorities were able to vote; therefore, to diminish minorities' electoral power, many state governments, particularly although not exclusively in the South, gerrymandered districts in a way that divided minority populations among multiple districts. This had the effect of limiting the number of Blacks and Latinos elected to state legislatures, because Whites rarely voted for minority candidates.

To prevent states from drawing legislative districts that discriminated against minorities, the U.S. Congress amended the Voting Rights Act in 1982. Then, in 1986 the U.S. Supreme Court ruled that the amended Voting Rights Act prohibited districts that diminished minorities' ability to elect minority legislators, even if the state did not purposely intend to discriminate.[7] As a result of these developments, gerrymandering began in favor of minority interests. Since the 1990s, state legislatures have drawn more **majority-minority districts**, meaning districts in which more than half of the residents belong to a single minority group. With more majority-minority districts, the number of minority legislators, especially Blacks and Latinos, has increased dramatically (see "Measuring Equality: Black and Latino Representation in State Legislatures").

Majority-Minority Districts Legislative districts that contain a population made up of more than 50 percent of a racial or ethnic minority group.

Governors

Just as state legislatures are in many ways similar to the U.S. Congress, state executives, known as governors, share similar responsibilities with respect to their states as the U.S. president has with respect to the country as a whole. Governors enforce laws made by the state legislatures, but they vary considerably in terms of their power.

Similar to the president, governors have the power to veto or reject laws passed by state legislatures, but many governors exercise more veto authority than the president enjoys. For example, most governors possess the power of a **line-item veto**, which means that they can reject specific expenditures and taxes, while allowing the remainder of a law to prevail. The line-item veto essentially gives governors the power to change legislation, not just to veto bills. The president of the United States lacks such line-item veto authority.[8]

Line-Item Veto Governors' power to reject specific expenditures and taxes, while allowing the remainder of a bill to stand.

Additionally, governors exert authority by appointing the leaders of the state agencies that administer laws, including agencies dealing with law enforcement, transportation, prison management, education (including public colleges and universities), financial regulation, and emergency management. By appointing the key agency leaders, governors influence policymaking in

measuring equality

Black and Latino Representation in State Legislatures

Black and Latino representation in state legislatures is important to ensure that policies reflect the interests of these groups. The Voting Rights Act and U.S. Supreme Court decisions resulted in state legislatures drawing majority-minority districts, which helped Blacks and Latinos increase their representation in state legislatures, particularly in states that have sizable Black and Latino populations.

Initially, minority representation can be understood as the percentage of each group in the legislature; however, that figure alone is not sufficient because it does not account for the size of the group's population in the

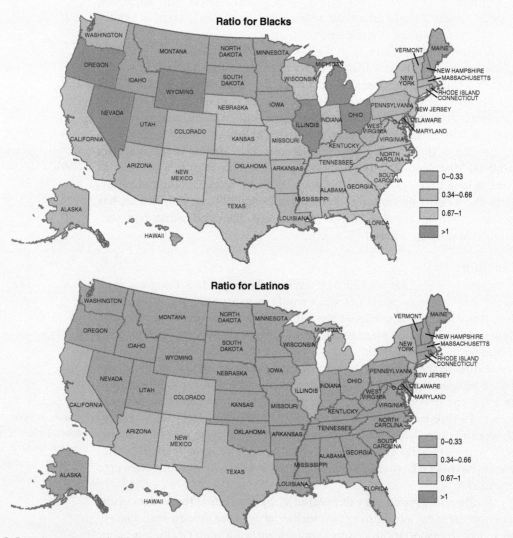

Figure 3.5 Ratio of Black and Latino Representation in State Legislatures Over Population.

(Continued)

measuring equality *(Continued)*

state. For example, if Blacks constitute 15 percent of a state legislature, then one would assume that they are well represented, and in many states this figure would demonstrate high representation. However, if the state is 25 percent Black, then the 15 percent figure would reflect underrepresentation. Therefore, it is useful to consider minority representation as a ratio of the percentage of the group in the state legislature divided by the percentage of the group in the population of the state. A ratio less than one indicates underrepresentation, and a ratio greater than one indicates overrepresentation.

The maps in Figure 3.5 show the ratio of the percentage of Blacks and Latinos in each state legislature over the percentage of Blacks and Latinos in each state. States in green have a ratio between 0 and 0.33; states in blue have a ratio between 0.34 and 0.66; states in orange have a ratio between 0.67 and 1; and states in red have a ratio over 1.

When evaluating these maps, consider Figures 3.1 and 3.2, which show population concentrations of Blacks and Latinos. Can you see any patterns? Notice that African American ratios are higher than Latino ratios in most states. What are some possible reasons for this discrepancy?

these areas. There is variation, however, across states in terms of which positions governors appoint and which are elected separately.

Given the power that governors wield, they can exert a tremendous influence on racial and ethnic minorities within the state, particularly in voting. The story of Maricopa County that we recounted at the beginning of the chapter is only one of numerous examples of voting problems in states and localities that disproportionately affect minorities. For example, during the 2012 election Floridians experienced long lines, which a recent study confirms affected racial and minority voters more than white voters.[9] One of the reasons for the long lines was the reduction of early voting days, in which the government opens poll site for several weeks before the actual election day. Although Florida's state legislature passed the initial bill to reduce the number of early voting days, Governor Rick Scott signed the legislation—he could have vetoed it. Furthermore, when local election officials petitioned the governor to extend early voting days because of anticipated Election Day turnout, the governor refused. Secretary of State Ken Detzner, an appointee of Governor Scott's, was responsible for certifying the state's official results. Detzner admitted to significant problems with the state's voting procedures and claimed that he would lead the investigation into the problems that occurred.[10] In early 2013, after initially denying the state's responsibility for the election problems, Governor Scott announced his preference for restoring early voting days and increasing the number of early voting sites.[11] In 2014, the state tried to purge ineligible voters, but reversed course after county election officials protested that doing so would mistakenly remove too many eligible minority voters.[12]

Actions by governors influence the lives of all citizens in a state, including racial and ethnic minorities, and yet few racial and ethnic minority members have served as governors. Governors must be elected by the entire state, which makes it less likely that a racial or ethnic minority can win. Although it is

New Mexico Governor Susana Martinez speaks during the third day of the Republican National Convention at the *Tampa Bay Times* Forum (now called Amalie Arena) on August 29, 2012, in Tampa, FL. Although Latinos, especially in New Mexico, overwhelmingly vote Democratic, Governor Martinez is a Republican who presides over a reliably Democratic state. As chief executive, Governor Martinez, like all governors, exerts significant authority over the government of New Mexico.

obviously not true that people will only vote for a candidate who shares their race or ethnicity, as evidenced by the election and reelection of President Barack Obama, political science research has established the existence of racially polarized voting; that is, the general tendency of voters to vote for members of their own racial or ethnic group. Yet, there is also research that evidences the lack of polarized voting.[13]

Currently, no minority group constitutes a majority of a state's population, although Latinos come close in New Mexico, where they make up 47.7 percent of the population.[14] In fact, the governor of New Mexico, Susana Martinez, is the first Hispanic female governor in the United States. Table 3.1 provides the short list of current and former minority governors. Examine that table in light of the concentrations of Blacks, Latinos, and Asians (as seen in Figures 3.1, 3.2, and 3.3).

State Courts

The third branch of state government is the state judiciary. Both national and state governments have judicial systems, but the bulk of cases that transpire in court on a daily basis, such as most criminal prosecutions and lawsuits for monetary damages, take place in state trial courts. Even most criminal cases that receive national and even international attention, such as the Casey Anthony and George Zimmerman murder trials, take place in state courts.

TABLE 3.1 Current and Former Minority Governors

Name	State	Race/Ethnicity	Party	Term
Current				
Nikki Haley	South Carolina	South Asian	R	2011–present
David Ige	Hawaii	Japanese American	D	2014–present
Susanna Martinez	New Mexico	Mexican American	R	2011–present
Brian Sandoval	Nevada	Mexican American	R	2011–present
Former				
Raul Castro	Arizona	Mexican American	D	1975–1977
Ben Cayetano	Hawaii	Filipino	D	1994–2002
Bobby Jindal	Louisiana	South Asian	R	2007–2016
Gary Locke	Washington	Chinese American	D	1996–2005
Robert Martinez	Florida	Cuban American	R	1987–1991
Miguel Otero	New Mexican Terr.	Mexican American	R	1897–1906
Romulado Pacheco	California	Mexican American	R	1875
David Paterson	New York	African American	D	2008–2010
Deval Patrick	Massachusetts	African American	D	2007–2015
P.B.S. Pinchback	Louisiana	African American	R	1872–1873
Bill Richardson	New Mexico	Mexican American	D	2003–2011
John D. Waihe'e	Hawaii	Native Hawaiian	D	1986–1994
Douglas Wilder	Virginia	African American	D	1989–1993

Source: Data adapted from Paula D. McClain and Joseph Stewart, Jr., "Can We All Get Along?": Racial and Ethnic Minorities in American Politics (Boulder, CO: Westview Press, 2010), p. 161, updated by the authors.

State courts are hierarchical systems with different levels ranked in order of authority. At the bottom rung are state trial courts, which decide criminal and civil cases, ranging from petty to major concerns. Juries determine the outcome of most of the more important cases, and the judge acts as a referee to ensure that the trial proceeds fairly. About forty states have intermediate appellate courts that hear appeals, which are reviews of the legal decisions made in lower court cases. All states also have a court of last resort, usually, but not always, called a state supreme court. These courts of last resort have the final say on appeals within their respective states.

Although juries play a key role in state judiciaries, judges are the most important actors in these institutions, and states vary considerably in how they select judges. Recall from Chapter 2 that federal judges are nominated by the president, confirmed by the Senate, and serve for a term of good behavior (i.e., they serve life terms as long as they are not removed from office after impeachment). However, states use a variety of methods for selecting their judges.

Merit System A system of selecting state judges in which a nonpartisan commission presents the governor with a short list of judicial candidates, out of which the governor selects one name; that judge later appears before the voters in a retention election.

Retention Election A type of judicial election in which voters decide only whether to keep the judge in office; there are no opposition candidates.

In Virginia the state legislature selects judges, whereas in two others—New Jersey and California (for appellate judges only)—the governor makes the decision. Many states hold elections, and in some of these states, such as Pennsylvania, Texas, and West Virginia, the judges run with political party labels, whereas in other states, such as Arkansas, Minnesota, and Washington, they run in nonpartisan elections. Since the twentieth century many states, including Alaska, Missouri, Utah, Vermont, and Wyoming, have employed the **merit system**, in which an unelected, nonpartisan commission provides a short list of potential judges to fill a vacancy. The governor (or in South Carolina the legislature) then must select one name from that list to serve a term as a judge. When the term ends in most merit selection states, the voters decide whether to keep the judge in a **retention election**; there is no opponent. If the voters decide to retain the judge, then he or she serves another term; if not, there is a vacancy and the process starts anew.[15]

Political scientists study whether the type of judicial selection system influences legal policy within a state. Many observers are concerned that elected judges act more as politicians than as judges; they worry more about pleasing the voters than serving the law. In fact, scholars have found that judicial elections are beginning to resemble elections for legislative and executive branch offices, with an increased amount of campaign spending, money raising (primarily from attorneys who might appear before the judges), and more negative advertisements. One expert notes that judicial elections have become "nastier, noisier, and costlier."[16] Another criticism of elected judiciaries is that judges will make decisions according to public opinion, instead of what the law requires. Empirical evidence shows that judges facing imminent election do alter their opinions to comport with voters' attitudes.[17] Despite these criticisms of judicial elections, however, some scholars defend elections, arguing that the critics' indictments are overblown and elections preserve accountability by allowing voters to remove unfit judges.[18]

Because state courts have the power to overturn laws that violate the state constitution, establish rules of criminal procedure, and set parameters governing civil suits, they are clearly important policymakers. Therefore, the number of minority state judges is a key issue in racial and ethnic politics. The U.S. Supreme Court ruled in 1991 that the Voting Rights Act requires the drawing of majority-minority districts in judicial elections that occur in districts.[19] The empirical evidence on whether the type of selection system influences minority representation is mixed, however. One study showed that historically states with partisan election systems were among the first states to include a Black justice on the state court of last resort.[20] However, other studies demonstrate that the type of formal selection system does not affect minority representation in state courts.[21] Additionally, despite isolated instances of minority judges losing retention elections, such as Latino California Supreme Court Justice Cruz Reynoso in 1986, empirical evidence shows that race plays no role in retention voting.[22]

Local Governments

Federalism not only involves the relationship between the national government and state governments, it also entails the relationship between state and local governments. The Constitution does not explicitly mention local governments (except for Washington, DC). **Dillon's Rule**, articulated in an 1868 case by Judge John Dillon, stipulates that municipal governments may only draw power from what state governments grant them; they lack independent authority. Dillon's Rule dominated municipal governance until the twentieth century when more states began adopting **home rule** for their local governments to give them more autonomy in carrying out daily operations. The question of home rule is especially complex concerning the status of Washington, DC.

The Constitution created Washington, DC, to be the nation's capital and house the federal government, but it has now evolved into a vibrant city with more than 650,000 residents, over 50 percent of whom are Black and almost 10 percent of whom are Latino.[23] The Washington, DC metropolitan area is even larger, extending into southern Maryland and northern Virginia. In many respects, Washington, DC is like all other major American cities, except for one key difference—it does not belong to a state. Instead, it is controlled by the U.S. Congress and president, although it does possess some home rule. As a result there are often clashes between Congress and the residents of Washington, DC. For example, in 2015 Washington, DC, officially decriminalized personal possession of marijuana after residents overwhelmingly voted for this policy in 2014. However, Republicans in Congress oppose decriminalization; therefore, they have threatened to use their authority to undermine this policy. In fact, two House members—Jason Chaffetz (R-UT) and Mark Meadows (R-NC)—threatened to imprison Washington, DC, mayor Muriel Bowser for defying Congress's authority.[24] Many residents of Washington, DC, are so resentful of living under congressional authority that they want Washington DC, to become a state, or at the very least send voting members to the United States House of Representatives and Senate, where they currently lack representation. However, at this point, they still remain under Congress's control.

All states are divided into political units known as counties (in Louisiana they are known as parishes), and except in Connecticut and Rhode Island counties have their own government, often called **county commissions**, which makes policies that apply to the county. **Municipalities** are the incorporated districts—cities and towns—that exist within counties. County and municipal governments handle local issues, such as sewage treatment, waste management, snow removal, neighborhood maintenance, economic development, police and fire protection, and parks and recreation. In some states, county governments share these responsibilities with municipal governments, but in other states the tasks are separated. **School districts** are local government entities that create policies for public schools from kindergarten through high school.

Dillon's Rule A principle of local governance in which municipal governments lack independent authority; they can only draw power from their state governments.

Home Rule A principle of local governance in which local governments can govern themselves independently of the state governments.

County Commissions Representative bodies that make policies that apply to the county.

Municipalities The incorporated districts, usually cities or towns, that comprise the local government.

School Districts Local government entities that create policies for public schools.

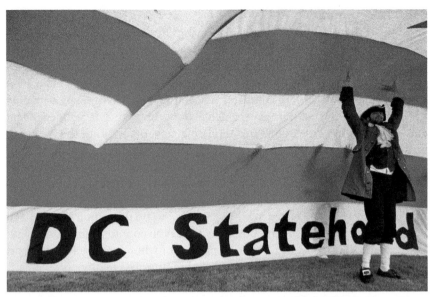

Nikolas Schiller of the DC Statehood Green Party helps fly a giant DC Statehood flag on the West Lawn of the Capitol following the DC voting rights march on Monday, April 16, 2007.
Washington, DC, occupies a unique place in American federalism. Although more than 650,000 people, most of whom are racial or ethnic minorities, live in DC, the national government still controls some of the governance of the city, and DC voters have no representation in Congress. Many DC residents believe that DC should achieve full statehood, which would allow it to control its own sovereignty and enjoy representation in Congress.

Municipal governments, which are at the heart of local governments, consist of elected legislative bodies, usually known as city councils or city commissions, and executive figures, known as mayors. In some cities the council selects the mayor, but in other cities voters separately elect the mayor. Mayors' powers also vary tremendously across different localities. Some cities have mayors who are essentially figureheads, with no real power, while appointed city managers handle most of the executive functions. Conversely, in other cities mayors exert significant executive authority, similar to the U.S. president and many governors.

Given their vast powers, municipal governments are obviously influential in the daily lives of racial and ethnic minorities, especially in the areas of law enforcement, neighborhood maintenance, and economic development. As a result, minority representation in municipal government is an important factor shaping how the governments affect minorities' lives. At one time, cities with large minority populations lived under White mayors, but since the 1970s, minority mayors have been far more common in cities with high minority populations.

Federalism and the Constitution

As the architecture of American government, the Constitution sets the framework for the balance of power between the national and state and local

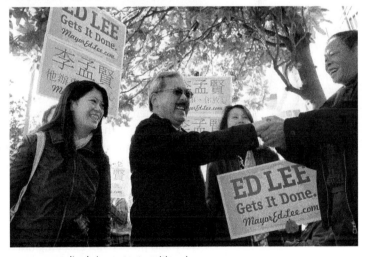

As chief executives of their municipalities, mayors occupy exceedingly important positions in urban politics and within the American federal system. Pictured here are three significant minority mayors: Stephanie Rawlings-Blake (Baltimore, MD), who is African American; Tomás Regalado (Miami, FL), who is Latino; Edwin Lee (San Francisco, CA), who is Asian American.

governments. As discussed in Chapter 2, the U.S. Constitution was designed primarily to create a stronger national government in response to the weaknesses of the Articles of Confederation, which placed virtually all power with the states. Therefore, key parts of the Constitution expand the power of the national government, even as other sections protect state authority. In this section, we examine how national power expanded through both the Constitution and its amendments, and also how the Constitution preserves state autonomy.

The Constitution and National Government Power

For the most part, Article I, Section 8 of the Constitution enumerates the powers of the national government. As discussed in Chapter 2, Article I, Section 8 powers are vast, giving the national government the power to tax, borrow on the credit of the United States, coin money, conduct foreign affairs, and maintain the armed forces to protect the security of the United States, among many others. In times of national disasters, federalism often requires national and state and local governments to work together. For example, after Hurricane Sandy struck the Northeast in Fall 2012, the Federal Emergency Management Agency, part of the national government, worked with state and local governments in New Jersey, New York, and Connecticut to help people evacuate and then recover after the storm had passed. At other times, however, conflict marks the relationship between the different levels of government, as in the aftermath when Hurricane Katrina struck the Gulf Coast in August 2005. At that time, state and local governments bemoaned the national government's failure to provide sufficient assistance.[25]

Commerce Clause
A constitutional provision that gives the national government the authority to regulate commerce among the states, foreign nations, and Indian tribes; it has been used to expand the power of the national government.

One extremely significant enumerated power is the **commerce clause**, which gives the national government the authority to regulate commerce among the states, foreign nations, and Indian tribes. Under the Articles of Confederation the national government lacked the authority to regulate interstate commerce, which led to economic chaos during that period. The Framers understood that the nation is stronger with a national economy regulated by the national government. As we discuss later in this chapter, the commerce clause was instrumental in expanding national power in terms of economic regulation, and also in areas of civil rights.

Necessary and Proper Clause A clause in Article I of the Constitution giving Congress the authority to make whatever laws are necessary and proper to carry out its enumerated responsibilities (sometimes called the elastic clause).

Another crucial clause in Article I, Section 8 is the **necessary and proper clause** (or elastic clause), which gives the national government the authority to enact laws implied by the enumerated powers, as long as the laws are "necessary and proper" for carrying out one of the enumerated powers. The elastic clause provides the national government with the opportunity to expand its authority as long as it can show that the implied power is plausibly connected to an enumerated power.

Article I also grants Congress the authority to "establish uniform Rule of Naturalization," which has been significant for minority group politics because it gives the national government the power to set immigration and citizenship policy. Under this authority, Congress passed the Naturalization Act of 1790, which limited the possibility of citizenship only to free Whites. Since then, Congress has passed numerous bills that have both restricted and expanded the ability of immigrants, especially racial and ethnic minorities, to become American citizens. In addition, the national government has clashed with states over immigration policy (see Chapter 5).

The **supremacy clause**, Article VI, stipulates that the Constitution and national laws and treaties created under constitutional authority are "the supreme law of the land." The Constitution authorizes the national government to make laws and treaties and prevents state and local governments from enacting policies that contradict them. If there is a conflict between a state law and a constitutionally legitimate national one, then the national law supersedes the state law every time. For example, because the Constitution and national civil rights laws prohibit racial discrimination, states cannot validly enact laws that allow for such discrimination.

Article IV establishes national rules directing how states must relate to each other. The **extradition clause** (Article IV, Section 2, Clause 2) stipulates that if a person is charged with a crime in one state and flees to another state, then the second state must transport the accused criminal back to the first state. The **full faith and credit clause** (Article IV, Section I) requires states to recognize official documents and records from other states. For example, a driver's license issued in New York is also valid in Wyoming.

The **privileges and immunities** clause prevents states from discriminating against citizens of other states. Therefore, if a citizen of North Carolina travels to South Carolina, then South Carolina cannot hold the North Carolinian to a different legal standard simply because he or she is from a different state. However, through their power to grant licenses in certain professions, states can prevent out-of-state residents, such as doctors and lawyers, from practicing their profession in the state. This power emanates from the fact that the nonresidents lack a license, not solely because they are from another state.

Finally, it is worth noting that prior to the end of slavery, Article IV also included the **fugitive slave clause**, which stipulated that if slaves escaped from a slave state to a free state, then they were not considered free. The free state was required to return the escaped slaves to their owners in the slave state.

Article I, Section 10 lists specific powers that the Constitution denies to states. Most notably, states are forbidden from entering into treaties with other nations and coining money. Furthermore, the **interstate compact clause** requires the approval of Congress when states enter into official agreements with one another, for instance to manage transportation facilities, waterways, and environmental concerns that transverse state lines. Other provisions in this section protect individual liberties against state governments. States cannot pass a **bill of attainder**—a law that punishes specific people who have not first been convicted in a court. Moreover, states are forbidden from enacting **ex post facto laws**, which are criminal sanctions that apply retroactively and could result in governments charging people for acts committed before they were outlawed.

Supremacy Clause A clause in Article VI of the Constitution stipulating that the Constitution and national laws are supreme, meaning that when state laws conflict with national laws, national laws take precedence.

Extradition Clause A provision in the Constitution stipulating that if a person is charged with a crime in one state and flees to another state, then the second state must transport the accused criminal back to the first state.

Full Faith and Credit Clause A constitutional provision requiring states to recognize official documents and records from other states.

Privileges and Immunities Clause A provision in Article IV of the Constitution that prevents states from discriminating against citizens of other states.

Fugitive Slave Clause A clause in the Constitution stipulating if slaves escaped from a slave state to a free state the free state must return them to their owners in the slave state. The Thirteenth Amendment invalidated this clause.

Interstate Compact Clause A clause in Article I, Section 10 of the Constitution that requires the approval of Congress when states enter into official agreements with one another.

Bill of Attainder A law passed by a legislative body that punishes specific people without convicting them in a court.

Ex Post Facto Law A criminal sanction that applies retroactively and could result in governments charging people for acts committed before they were outlawed.

Thirteenth Amendment An amendment to the Constitution that prohibits slavery throughout the United States.

Fourteenth Amendment An amendment to the Constitution that prevents states from denying on the basis of race full citizenship to their residents.

Due Process Clause A specific provision of the Fourteenth Amendment that requires states to use normal judicial and criminal procedures before denying a citizen life, liberty, or property.

Equal Protection Clause A specific provision of the Fourteenth Amendment that prevents states from passing laws that treat people differently on account of race or ethnicity.

Fifteenth Amendment An amendment to the Constitution that prevents states from denying the right to vote on the basis of race or ethnicity.

Nineteenth Amendment An amendment to the Constitution that prevents states from denying women the right to vote because of their sex.

Poll Taxes Fees that states charged citizens to vote and that disenfranchised the poor and minority citizens.

Police Power A general, unwritten power to regulate health, safety, and morals.

Constitutional Amendments and National Power

The Constitution of 1787 bestows significant authority on the national government, and several amendments have further expanded the national government's power, especially in the area of civil rights. Prior to the Civil War, states determined the civil rights status of their residents. Many states, especially Southern and border states, relegated Blacks to the status of slaves, and even most states that banned slavery denied Blacks basic rights, such as voting, owning property, and serving on juries. A small number of states conferred civil rights on African Americans, but they did not always stop discrimination by private entities.

After the end of the Civil War, however, three major constitutional amendments shifted the balance of power in favor of the national government to determine civil rights policies. The **Thirteenth Amendment** (1865) banned slavery throughout the United States; thus, states were no longer free to decide whether to allow slavery. The **Fourteenth Amendment** (1868) prevented states from denying on the basis of race full citizenship to their residents, and two clauses in this amendment are especially significant for setting national civil rights policy. The **due process clause** requires states to use normal judicial and criminal procedures before denying a citizen the right to life, liberty, or property. The **equal protection clause** prevents states from passing laws that treat citizens differently on the basis of race. Finally, the **Fifteenth Amendment** (1870) prevents states from denying citizens the right to vote because of their race or ethnicity. Of course, as we discuss later in this chapter and in Chapter 5, states circumvented the requirements of these amendments until the middle of the twentieth century.

During the twentieth century, three constitutional amendments expanded national authority over states concerning the question of voter eligibility. The **Nineteenth Amendment** prevents states from denying women the right to vote because of their sex. The Twenty-Fourth Amendment ends the practice of **poll taxes**, which were fees that states charged citizens as a condition of being able to vote. Because many racial and ethnic minorities tended to be poorer than Whites, poll taxes disproportionately hurt racial and ethnic minority voters. Finally, the Twenty-Sixth Amendment set a nationwide voting eligibility age of eighteen. Prior to the ratification of the amendment, many states had set voting eligibility at twenty-one years old.

The Constitution and State Power

Although much of the Constitution expands national power, some provisions preserve state authority. Whereas the national government is restricted solely to powers enumerated in the Constitution or implied by those enumerated powers, state governments enjoy much broader **police powers**—general and unwritten powers to regulate health, safety, and morals. This principle is enshrined in the **Tenth Amendment**, which is part of the Bill of Rights. Specifically, the Tenth Amendment provides that "the powers not delegated to the United States by the Constitution, nor prohibited by it to the States, are reserved to the States respectively, or to the people." In other words, the amendment stipulates that the states are the default possessors of power; powers belong to the states unless the Constitution expressly grants them to the national government or expressly denies them to the states.

Although the Tenth Amendment is the most important constitutional guardian of state power, other aspects of the Constitution preserve state authority as well. The Eleventh Amendment prevents citizens of one state (or foreigners) from suing another state in federal court, unless the state consents. Furthermore, the nature of representation in the national government enhances state authority. Article I establishes that each state, regardless of population, sends two senators to the U.S. Senate; therefore, the U.S. Senate represents states more than it represents people. For example, Wyoming, which as of 2015 has a population of only 586,107, enjoys the same representation in the Senate as California, which as of 2015 has 39,144,818 people.[26] Similarly, the Electoral College selects the president based on results in individual states, which elevates the importance of states in presidential selection (see Chapter 7).

Tenth Amendment An amendment to the Constitution that guarantees states powers not given to the national government or forbidden to the states.

The Evolution of American Federalism

Although the Constitution establishes the balance of power between states and the national government, federalism is not a static concept; it has changed considerably over the course of American history. Depending on the dominant ideology in the government and varying economic and social concerns, different versions of federalism have emerged as power has shifted between the national government and the states. As we explain this evolution of federalism and the debates that surround it, we emphasize Congressional legislation and U.S. Supreme Court decisions that have been instrumental. In addition, we look at how the changing dynamics of federalism have influenced racial and ethnic minorities.

Federalism in the Early Republic and Industrialization

After the ratification of the Constitution, the United States faced a choice between adopting an agricultural economy dominated by local farms and interests or an industrial economy promoted by the national government. By the 1790s, the national government embraced industrialization and promoted industrial manufacturing. To accomplish these goals, the U.S. government sought major improvements in roads, railroads, and canals to transport raw materials to manufacturing facilities and the finished products to consumers. These massive projects, which extended across state lines, required a tremendous amount of funding, which the national government raised through private banks and through its power to borrow money, tax, and spend.

McCulloch v. Maryland. To facilitate these financial goals, in 1791 Congress chartered the Bank of the United States, also known as the "national bank." As noted federalism scholar Daniel Elazar observed, the bank "served as the fiscal and banking arm of the federal government and manager of the federal deposits."[27] Given this scope, the bank was able to control a considerable amount of economic activity in the United States. Some political leaders, notably Thomas Jefferson and James Madison, opposed the national bank and argued that the national government lacked the constitutional authority to establish a bank. However, supporters, led by Treasury Secretary Alexander Hamilton, disagreed with that claim, maintaining that the national bank was constitutional and important to achieving economic success. Although the bank charter expired in 1811, it was revived in 1817, which regenerated the controversy.

As a means of opposing the re-chartered Bank of the United States, the Maryland legislature voted to tax the branch of the United States Bank located in Baltimore. When the bank cashier refused to pay the tax, the controversy went to the U.S. Supreme Court. In the 1819 U.S. Supreme Court case *McCulloch v. Maryland*, Chief Justice John Marshall upheld the bank and overruled the tax. Marshall, a fervent nationalist, argued that even though the Constitution does not explicitly grant Congress the power to establish a bank, the bank is a "necessary and proper" way for the national government to carry out its explicit powers to tax, spend, borrow money, and regulate commerce.[28] In addition to upholding the bank, this case established a loose interpretation of the word "necessary" in the necessary and proper clause, so that the **implied power** need only facilitate the execution of an enumerated power, rather than being required for it. Marshall's broad interpretation of "necessary" still stands today and has allowed the national government to expand its power in other areas.

Implied Power Government powers that are inferred from the powers expressly enumerated in the Constitution.

Gibbons v. Ogden. The Marshall Court expanded the power of the national government in other areas as well. In the 1824 *Gibbons v. Ogden* decision, the Supreme Court instituted a broad definition of the commerce clause. The case arose from a conflict between two companies competing for shipping business in the waterways between New York and New Jersey. One company, owned by Aaron Ogden, possessed exclusive rights granted by the national government to the entire area between the two states, whereas the other company, owned by Thomas Gibbons, possessed exclusive rights granted by the state of New York to New York's waterways.

When this dispute arrived at the Supreme Court, Chief Justice John Marshall ruled that the national government controls all stages of commerce that extend across state lines. As a result, even when the instrument of commerce occurs within a state's border at a particular time, the national government retains authority as long as the goods or services extend into another state. Moreover, the Court ruled that commerce is not restricted to the mere trading of goods and services; it also includes navigation across state lines.[29] This case established a precedent of broadly interpreting the commerce clause.

Civil Rights Issues. Despite this expansion of national authority in the service of industrialization and economic growth, states still retained authority when it came to questions about slavery and civil rights for Blacks and American Indians. When the national government set civil rights policy, it was generally concerned with preserving slavery. In 1793, Congress passed the Fugitive Slave Act, which established the process for capturing and returning slaves who escaped to free states—recall that Article IV of the Constitution protected slave owners' ability to secure their escaped slaves' return. When Pennsylvania, a free state, enacted laws forbidding the return of slaves who escaped to Pennsylvania, the Supreme Court overturned that policy as a violation of Article IV and the Fugitive Slave Act.[30]

The Supreme Court expanded state control over civil rights in the 1857 *Dred Scott v. Sandford* case. This case concerned a slave who had lived in free territory and returned to the slave state of Missouri, where he sued for his freedom. By this time Chief Justice Roger Taney had replaced John Marshall, and Taney did not share Marshall's enthusiasm for the supremacy of national authority. In Chapter 5 we discuss in more detail the renowned civil rights impact of Chief Justice Taney's decision in *Dred Scott*, but Taney's opinion also had bearing on federalism because he declared the Missouri Compromise to be unconstitutional. The Missouri Compromise was a federal law that determined which American territories could allow slavery and which ones could not. Taney ruled that Congress lacked the authority to regulate slavery in the territories; therefore, territories could determine basic civil rights questions for themselves.[31]

Latinos and American Indians also felt federalism's affects. For example, the Treaty of Guadalupe Hidalgo, which settled the Mexican-American War in 1848, granted citizenship to the conquered Mexicans who elected to stay in the newly annexed portions of the United States. However, western states, most notably California, still mistreated Mexican Americans, even taking their property.[32] With respect to American Indians, the Constitution suggests that Indian tribes are separate entities, and the commerce clause includes the national government's power to regulate commerce with them. However, during the early American Republic the national and state governments subjugated Indians by removing them from their tribal lands and in many cases committing genocide against them. See "Our Voices: John Marshall and the Status of Indian Tribes" for excerpts from two early 1830s U.S. Supreme Court cases that articulate the status of Indian Tribes in our federal system.

Dual Federalism and the Ascendency of State Autonomy

Although the Civil War represented a victory for national unity over state autonomy, the period after the Civil War is best characterized as one in which state governments enjoyed increased independence from the national government. The type of federalism that dominated during the late nineteenth and early twentieth centuries is known as **dual federalism**, in which state governments and the national government ruled only in their own spheres. Federalism scholar Martin Grodzins referred to dual federalism as "layer cake federalism," because of the clear lines between national and state government authority.[33] The national government was limited to a strict interpretation of the powers granted in the Constitution, and states enjoyed broad police powers to rule within their own territory.[34] Accordingly, states were able to decide for themselves policies concerning economic regulation and civil rights—an idea often referred to as "states' rights."

Dual Federalism A view of federalism in which the national government is limited to a strict interpretation of the powers granted in the Constitution, while states enjoy broad police power to rule within their own territory.

Monopolies. After the Civil War, a primary economic issue concerned regulating against the excesses of the industrialized economy, including the development of **monopolies**, which exist when one company controls an entire industry. With one dominant company, there is no competition, and without competition workers and consumers suffer. Other economic problems concerned exploiting labor by making workers toil long hours in unsafe and uncomfortable conditions for little pay. Industrial corporations frequently employed children in these positions. Although state governments and the national government allowed many of these economic problems to persist, the national government by the late nineteenth century and in the early twentieth century attempted to regulate the most severe excesses. However, the U.S. Supreme Court, which was dominated by justices who advocated states' rights, significantly curtailed the national government's authority to regulate the economy.

Monopoly A situation in which one company controls an entire industry.

To address the problem of monopolies, Congress passed the Sherman Antitrust Act of 1890, which gave the national government the authority to break up monopolies into different companies. The national government based its power on the commerce clause, under the view that monopolies are vast, interstate entities that affect the national economy. However, in the 1895 *United States v. E.C. Knight Company* case the Supreme Court limited the national government's authority. In this case, the U.S. government wanted to prevent one company from owning 98 percent of sugar refining in the nation. The Supreme Court ruled, however, that sugar production was manufacturing, which is

our voices

John Marshall and the Status of Indian Tribes

Prior to the ratification of the Constitution in 1787, Indian tribes were considered foreign nations that could individually enter into treaties with colonial governments and states under the Articles of Confederation. The Constitution gave the national government the authority to engage with different tribes, and the Indian Commerce Clause gives the national government the authority to regulate commerce with Indian tribes; however, state governments also sought to exert authority over the tribes located within their borders.

Indians were initially highly independent in their relations with the American government, but the tradition of exclusion dominating American politics during the early nineteenth century produced policies that usurped tribal lands and even led to genocide in many cases. In the early 1830s, the U.S. Supreme Court, particularly Chief Justice John Marshall, settled disputes over the status of Indians in the American federal system. Although Marshall was an ardent nationalist, when it came to the status of Indian tribes his view was more nuanced.

Cherokee Nation v. Georgia, 30 U.S. 1 (1831)

After the state of Georgia sought to seize the Cherokee land within its borders, the Cherokee Nation challenged these actions as a violation of treaties in which the U.S. government formally recognized Cherokee lands as belonging to the tribe. The supremacy clause places the provisions of national treaties over state laws; therefore, the Cherokee petitioned the Court to overturn Georgia's policy. The outcome of this case depended on the status of Indian tribes in the American federal system. If Cherokee were analogous to an independent nation, then they had grounds to seek recompense in federal court. However, if the Cherokee lacked the status of an independent nation, then they could not use the federal judiciary to secure their rights. In patronizing language, Chief Justice Marshall ruled that Indian tribes were not similar to independent nations and that the Indian tribes were subordinate to American government. Marshall wrote:

> Though the Indians are acknowledged to have an unquestionable, and heretofore, unquestioned right to the lands they occupy, until that right should be extinguished by a voluntary cession to our government, yet it may well be doubted whether those tribes which reside within those acknowledged boundaries of the United States can, with strict accuracy, be denominated foreign nations. They may, more correctly, perhaps, be denominated domestic dependent nations. They occupy a territory to which we assert a title independent of their will, which must take effect in point of possession when their right of possession ceases. Meanwhile they are in a state of pupillage. Their relation to the United States resembles that of a ward to his guardian.
>
> They look to our government for protection; rely upon its kindness and its power; appeal to it for the relief of their wants; and address their President as their Great Father. They and their country are considered by foreign nations, as well as by ourselves, as being so completely under the sovereignty and dominion of the United States that any attempt to acquire their lands, or to form a political connection to them, would be considered by all as an invasion of our territory and an act of hostility.

Worcester v. Georgia, 31 U.S. 515 (1832)

The following year, the Supreme Court decided the case of *Worcester v. Georgia*, which involved Samuel Worcester, a northern White missionary who lived with the Cherokee and supported their struggle against oppression. In response to Worcester's influence with the Cherokee, the state of Georgia enacted a law that banned Whites from living in Cherokee areas unless they secured a license from the state. Worcester was arrested for violating this law and sentenced to four years in prison. He appealed his conviction, arguing that the Constitution, treaties between the U.S. Government and Cherokee, and federal statutes determine who is allowed to reside in Indian tribal lands; therefore, state governments lack the authority to proscribe who could live in Cherokee territory. This time, Chief Justice Marshall sided in favor of tribal authority, ruling that Indian tribes are independent entities that can control their own territory. In this opinion, Marshall more readily accepts the notion that Indian

(Continued)

our voices *(Continued)*

tribes exert sovereignty over their own affairs, and are in many ways equal to other nations, particularly in their dealings with the national government. He wrote:

The Indian nations had always been considered as distinct, independent political communities, retaining their original natural rights as the undisputed possessors of the soil from time immemorial, with the single exception of that imposed by irresistible power, which excluded them from intercourse with any other European potentate than the first discoverer of the coast of a particular region claimed: and this was a restriction which those European potentates imposed on themselves, as well as on the Indians. The very term "nation," so generally applied to them, means "a people distinct from others." The Constitution, by declaring treaties already made, as well as those to be made, as supreme law of the land,

has adopted and sanctioned the previous treaties with the Indian nations, and consequently admits their rank among those powers who are capable of making treaties. The words "treaty" and "nation" are words of our own language, selected in our diplomatic and legislative proceedings, by ourselves, having each a definite and well understood meaning. We have applied them to Indians, as we have applied them to other nations of the earth. They are applied to all in the same sense.

- Why do you think Justice Marshall ruled so differently in these two cases?
- How has the national government's regard for the status of American Indians changed since the time of these rulings?

Sources: Adapted from *Cherokee Nation v. Georgia*, 30 U.S. 1, 17–18 (1831) and *Worcester v. Georgia*, 31 U.S. 515, 559–560 (1832).

distinct from commerce and that the Tenth Amendment gave states the sole authority to regulate monopolies in the manufacturing sector.[35] The Court's creation of this distinction between manufacturing and commerce and its reading of the Tenth Amendment limited the national government's authority to regulate most monopolies.

Child Labor. The Supreme Court also used this commerce versus manufacturing distinction to prevent the national government from addressing the problem of child labor. Many companies exploited poor children by paying them low wages for long hours and dangerous work. The Keating-Owen Child Labor Act of 1916 forbade the interstate shipment of any good that was produced with child labor. The 1918 case of *Hammer v. Dagenhart* overturned this law, however, because a narrow majority of the justices held that it regulated child labor at the manufacturing stage, not the commerce stage; accordingly, the national government lacked the authority to issue regulations under the commerce clause. The Tenth Amendment gave states sole authority to regulate child labor,[36] but few states enacted meaningful regulations, and child labor persisted throughout the early twentieth century.

Grants-in-Aid. Despite these restraints, the national government exerted some limited authority. For example, in the 1860s the national government sought to improve education and research in agriculture, mining, and engineering to expand technology and economic growth. It lacked the power, though, even under the commerce clause, to charter national universities or compel states to shift their universities' missions toward these technological fields. To address this problem, Congress passed the Morrill Land Grant Act of 1862, in which the national government donated federally owned property to the states, conditioned on the states establishing agricultural, mining, or technological universities on that property. This law was an early example of a **grant-in-aid**—the national government providing money or property to the states to accomplish a policy goal. In the Second Morrill Land Grant Act, which was passed in 1890, the national government donated property to create technological universities for African Americans because many states denied them admission to their public universities. This law established historically Black colleges and universities (HBCUs), which helped educate millions of African Americans during the height of segregation—and still do today.[37]

Civil Rights Issues. In addition to controlling economic policy, states continued to determine civil rights policies during the late nine-

Graduates are pictured at Florida A&M University, which is a historically Black college and university. In the late nineteenth century, the national government provided states with the land to establish universities designed to educate African Americans, who were explicitly denied admission to White state schools in Southern and border states. The creation of HBCUs is an example of the national government using its funding power to influence public policy.

teenth and early twentieth centuries. Recall that the Thirteenth, Fourteenth, and Fifteenth Amendments expanded national authority to regulate civil rights policy; however, by the late nineteenth century it became clear that the U.S. Supreme Court's interpretation of the Fourteenth and Fifteenth Amendments allowed states to deny rights and treat people differently because of race. Southern states required that Blacks and Whites be separated in all public facilities, including schools. In *Plessy v. Ferguson* (1896), the U.S. Supreme Court established the legal principle of **separate but equal**, which meant that under the Fourteenth Amendment equal protection clause the states could segregate by race, as long as they provided facilities for both races.[38] Aside from the fact that separate but equal allowed dominant White elites to separate themselves from Blacks in the South and Mexican Americans in the Southwest, the reality is that the facilities were nowhere near equal. For example, White schools in the South received far more funds and had much better facilities compared to Black schools.

Despite the Fifteenth Amendment ban on racial discrimination in voting, states enacted passing literacy tests as a condition for registering to vote. Although literacy tests appear to be race-neutral, they were administered in a

Grants-in-Aid National government expenditures that provide money or property to the states to accomplish a policy goal.

Separate but Equal A legal principle that allowed states to segregate the races in public facilities, as long as the state provided each race with basic access to the public facility in question.

way that allowed Whites to pass and Blacks to fail. Recall, as well, that during this period states were allowed to levy poll taxes, which disproportionately affected African Americans. Finally, the U.S. Supreme Court invalidated the national government's ability to prosecute state officials who denied Blacks the right to vote[39] and to prosecute violent terrorist organizations, such as the Ku Klux Klan, for intimidating Blacks attempting to vote.[40] With these restraints on the national government, it was left to the states to decide whether or not to prosecute individuals who prevented Blacks from voting, and Southern states and many Northern states refused to do so. In short, during the late nineteenth and early twentieth century, the Fifteenth Amendment provided no real limitations on states' abilities to disenfranchise people on account of race.

Cooperative Federalism and the Growth of the National Government

The period of dual federalism ended in the 1930s when the national government successfully exerted control over the national economy and ushered in a new period known as **cooperative federalism**. Unlike dual federalism, in which there were clear distinctions between state and national authority, cooperative federalism entailed greater shared powers between the national and state governments, and as a result the national government increased its authority. Federalism scholar Martin Grodzins referred to cooperative federalism as "marble cake federalism," because the distinctions between national and state authority were blurred rather than reflecting separate spheres as in dual federalism.[41]

Cooperative Federalism
A view of federalism in which the national government expands its power and blurs the lines between national and state authority.

Incorporation. Since the 1930s, one way the national government's authority has increased relative to the states is through the process of **incorporation**— the application of the Bill of Rights (see Chapter 2) to state and local governments. Before the twentieth century the Supreme Court repeatedly held that the Bill of Rights was intended to apply only to the national government and not the states; therefore, states were free to enact policies that violated the liberties contained in the Bill of Rights, such as freedom of speech, freedom of religion, freedom from warrantless searches, and trial by jury. However, in *Palko v. Connecticut* (1937), the Court announced the principle of selective incorporation, which stipulates that the most important provisions of the Bill of Rights apply to the states as well.[42] Since 1937 virtually all of the provisions in the Bill of Rights have been considered essential and thus incorporated. States are no longer able to deny their residents basic liberties. We discuss incorporation in more detail in Chapter 4.

Incorporation The application of the Bill of Rights to state and local governments.

Economic Regulation. Another way in which the national government has increased its authority relative to the states was in the area of economic regulation. The impetus behind this change in federalism was the Great Depression and President Franklin Roosevelt's New Deal. During the Great Depression,

Under the principle of "separate but equal" the U.S. Supreme Court allowed states to segregate their facilities, including public schools, as long they provided facilities for both races. They did this despite the Fourteenth Amendment to the Constitution, which requires that states treat Blacks and Whites equally. As these photos demonstrate, however, the facilities were not remotely equal. The White school children are in comfortable, spacious facilities, whereas Black children are in primitive, crowded conditions. In 1954 the U.S. Supreme Court overturned the "separate but equal" principle.

which began in 1929, the economy stagnated, unemployment skyrocketed, financial institutions failed, the agricultural industry declined, and the country experienced a host of other economic and social problems. To combat these economic troubles, the New Deal, which President Roosevelt proposed when he entered office in 1933, consisted of national policies that took unprecedented control over the economy by creating work for the unemployed, regulating banks and the stock market, controlling agricultural production, and protecting labor unions. During President Roosevelt's first term, however, the U.S. Supreme Court overturned New Deal programs, arguing that they exceeded the national government's authority to regulate commerce, again relying on the distinction between manufacturing and commerce as well as the Court's belief that the Tenth Amendment gave states sole authority to regulate the economy.[43]

In 1937, however, Supreme Court Justice Owen Roberts, who voted to overturn New Deal legislation in the past, changed his view and voted to uphold economic regulation. The landmark case *National Labor Relations Board v. Jones & Laughlin Steel Company* concerned the constitutionality of the Wagner Act, which protected workers' rights to unionize. The Court ruled that even though Jones & Laughlin engaged in manufacturing, its vast steel enterprise was interstate and commercial in scope.[44] In 1941, after President Roosevelt replaced anti–New Deal justices, who had retired or died, with New Deal supporters, the Supreme Court unanimously rejected the distinction between commerce and manufacturing, giving the national government the authority to regulate the economy.[45]

Moreover, in the 1942 *Wickard v. Filburn* case, the Supreme Court upheld an even more expansive view of the national government's commerce power. This case concerned the Agricultural Adjustment Act of 1938, which sought to stabilize farm prices by setting quotas limiting individual farmers' crop production. Roscoe Filburn was fined under this act because he exceeded his allotted wheat quota, but he claimed that because he used the excess wheat to feed his own livestock, his activity was not interstate and was thus outside the scope of national regulation. The Supreme Court disagreed and unanimously upheld the fine against Filburn, arguing that even if the activity was confined within Filburn's Ohio farm, it still had a "substantial effect" on interstate commerce.[46] Accordingly, the national government could now regulate any economic endeavor, as long as it could show a substantial effect on interstate commerce.

During the 1960s, President Lyndon Johnson's Great Society Program and "War on Poverty" further increased the power of the national government. Johnson sought to combat poverty through government programs designed to improve education, housing, transportation, and health care for the poor. However, the national government lacks the constitutional authority to simply mandate programs to improve the welfare of the poor. Instead, the national government employed **categorical grants**, which are grants-in-aid that contain numerous, detailed provisions on how the states and

Categorical Grants Grants-in-aid that contain numerous, detailed provisions on how the states and local governments use the money.

local governments must use the money. For example, in the Medicaid program the national government gives money to the states with strict regulations dealing with how health care coverage should be provided to poor people.[47] Another example of a categorical grant is Head Start, which was established in the 1960s to provide states with money to create early childhood education programs for poor children. By accepting the money of categorical grants, states agree to numerous requirements dictated by the national government.[48]

The national government has also expanded its power through the use of **unfunded mandates**—directives the national government issues to state and local governments without compensating them for complying. For example, environmental legislation, such as the Clean Air Act (passed in 1970) and the Clean Water Act (passed in 1972), require state and local governments to limit pollution in the air and water, but the states and localities are responsible for paying the cost of the environmental cleanup that these laws require. Additionally, in 1974 Congress required states and local governments to pay their employees minimum wage and extra compensation for overtime. In 1976, the U.S. Supreme Court ruled that this unfunded mandate violated states' Tenth Amendment rights,[49] but in 1985 the Court reversed itself and upheld this mandate.[50] Although unfunded mandates have accomplished important policy goals, they place considerable financial burden on states and localities; accordingly, they are quite controversial.[51]

Unfunded Mandates Directives the national government issues to state and local governments without compensating them for complying.

Civil Rights Policies. In addition to economic concerns, changes in civil rights policies since the 1950s have also exerted a strong impact on federalism. In the landmark 1954 *Brown v. Board of Education* case, the U.S. Supreme Court ended the principle of "separate but equal" and ruled that the Fourteenth Amendment prevents states from segregating races.[52] In other words, the Court created a national policy that prohibited states from separating races in public facilities. Although Southern states resisted desegregation, by the late 1950s and 1960s Presidents Eisenhower and Kennedy dispatched the military to forcibly integrate public schools.

Brown v. Board of Education addressed direct discrimination by the states, but it did not address racial discrimination committed by private businesses, which often refused to hire or promote racial minorities (as well as women). Many private businesses, such as restaurants and hotels, refused to serve minorities or forcibly separated them from Whites. In 1964, Congress and President Johnson passed the landmark **Civil Rights Act of 1964**, which addressed private mistreatment of minorities. The national government drew its authority to ban racial discrimination in the private sector from the commerce clause because racial discrimination substantially affected interstate commerce— recall the substantial effect language from the *Wickard v. Filburn* case. Although Southern hotel and restaurant owners challenged the constitutionality of the Civil Rights Act based on the view that regulating racial discrimination exceeds the national government's constitutional authority, in 1964 the

Civil Rights Act of 1964 A federal law that prevents private businesses from discriminating in service and personnel policies.

Supreme Court unanimously upheld the Civil Rights Act, ruling that racial discrimination substantially affects interstate commerce.[53]

During the 1960s and 1970s, the national government also assumed more authority over voting. The Fifteenth Amendment prevents states from discriminating on the basis of race when it comes to voting, but as we discussed earlier, states used devices such as literacy tests to prevent Blacks from voting. To address these problems, Congress passed the Voting Rights Act of 1965, which banned states from using literacy tests. Moreover, Sections 4 and 5 of the Voting Rights Act nationalized voting procedures. Section 4 identifies states and localities that have a history of voting discrimination against Blacks or Latinos, and these jurisdictions are reported in Table 3.2. Section 5 then stipulates that those covered jurisdictions cannot alter any voting procedure unless the U.S. Justice Department or a federal judge ensures that the change does not negatively affect minority voting rights. However, in early 2013 the U.S. Supreme Court ruled in the case of *Shelby County, AL v. Holder* that the formula used in Section 4 of the Voting Rights Act was unconstitutional, arguing that national government supervision over those jurisdictions is no longer necessary because vestiges of discrimination have been removed. Some justices, such as Justice Sonya Sotomayor, indicated that this provision was still necessary, but Justice Antonin Scalia referred to it as a "racial entitlement."[54] Although Congress could revise Sections 4 and 5 of the Voting Rights Act, it has not done so, and experts indicate that it is unlikely that it will.[55] Amendments to the Voting Rights Act also require states to print bilingual or trilingual ballots in areas that have significant populations of people who are not native English speakers. In sum, the Voting Rights Act represented a major shift in national authority over voting to protect racial and ethnic minorities, although problems still persist in many states. In the "Evaluating Equality Box" we discuss in more detail the controversies over the *Shelby County, AL v. Holder* decision and its impact on federalism.

The relationship among the national government, state governments, and American Indian tribes has also changed extensively since the early twentieth century. Beginning in the 1930s, the national government expanded tribal sovereignty for the Indians living on reservations. The 1975 Indian Self-Determination and Education Act enhanced tribal governments' ability to govern themselves. Yet federal laws have expanded individual rights of Indians living on tribal land, thus restricting tribal authority. Most notably, the Indian Civil Rights Act of 1968 granted individual Indians the same constitutional rights vis à vis their tribal governments that other Americans have with respect to their state and local governments. Therefore, tribal governments must respect freedom of speech, freedom of the press, freedom of religion, and procedural guarantees in criminal justice.[56]

Additionally, U.S. Supreme Court decisions that have increased the rights of women have also limited state authority. The landmark case *Reed v. Reed* (1971) overturned state policies that arbitrarily favored one sex over the other. This case specifically concerned an Idaho law that explicitly preferred males

Evaluating Equality

Shelby County (AL) v. Holder and Section 4 of Voting Rights Act

The Voting Rights Act of 1965 and its subsequent amendments have significantly curbed racial discrimination in voting. Section 2 of the act prevents any state or locality from denying someone the right to vote based on race or ethnicity, and it gives the national government and citizens the authority to sue any state or local government that violates the act. Since the passage of the act, federal courts have used Section 2 to expand voting rights for racial and ethnic minorities. Sections 4 and 5 of the Act work differently. Section 4 articulated a formula to identify states and localities with a history of disenfranchising racial and ethnic minorities, and Section 5 requires that these "covered" jurisdictions cannot change any voting procedure without the advanced permission of the United States Justice Department. The Justice Department must make sure that the proposed changes will not depress minority voting. Although Sections 4 and 5 were initially intended to be temporary, Congress actually expanded the range of covered jurisdictions since the Voting Rights Act's passage in 1965.

Students should understand that the Voting Rights Act is not only important for civil rights (see Chapter 5), but it is also important for federalism, particularly Sections 4 and 5. These parts of the act single out specific jurisdictions and place them under the control of the national government. Although all states and localities can be sued under Section 2, only some states and localities must endure the additional supervision of the national government.

Most states and localities are permitted to change polling places or the times during which polls are open, but the covered jurisdictions must seek the Justice Department's permission to make the same changes.

Alabama has been covered under Section 4 since the Act was first passed in 1965, and in 2011 Shelby County, AL challenged the constitutionality of Sections 4 and 5. Specifically, Shelby County argued that this portion of the Act violated state sovereignty because it treated states unequally, whereas the national government argued that the "covered" jurisdictions' history of disenfranchisement necessitated disparate treatment. In its *Shelby County, AL v. Holder* decision, the U.S. Supreme Court sided with Shelby County and ruled that Section 4 was unconstitutional because the historic voting discrimination that initially justified the formula was no longer present in the "covered" jurisdictions; therefore, Congress lacks the authority to treat states unequally.

The Supreme Court was sharply divided in this decision. Writing for the majority Chief Justice John Roberts noted that Sections 4 and 5 of the Voting Rights represented a radical change in the principles of federalism and that national governments should treat the sovereign states equally. He states, "While one state waits months or years and expends funds to implement a validly enacted law, its neighbor can typically put the same law immediately through the normal legislative process." However, he recognizes that the extensive minority

disenfranchisement in the covered areas warranted "these departures from the basic features of our system of government." The problem for Roberts was that "Nearly fifty years later, things have changed dramatically." Roberts cites statistics showing that minority voter registration is just as high in the covered jurisdictions as in the non-covered jurisdictions. The extent of minorities elected to office is also as high, if not higher, in the covered jurisdictions than in the non-covered jurisdictions. Therefore, the infringements on state authority were no longer warranted.

Conversely, Justice Ruth Bader Ginsburg wrote for the four dissenting justices. Justice Ginsburg argues that the Fifteenth Amendment, the constitutional basis of the Voting Rights Act, gives Congress the "power to enforce [the amendment] by appropriate legislation." This authority gives Congress wide discretion to prevent racial disenfranchisement, even if it infringes on state sovereignty. Justice Ginsburg agreed with the majority that there have been tremendous improvements in minority voting rights and access since the passage of the Act. In fact, she credits Sections 4 and 5 for creating these improvements; therefore, Congress should have the authority to keep these provisions in place—to preserve and expand on voting rights success. Justice Ginsburg cited numerous recent examples of the preclearance provision preventing covered jurisdictions from enacting policies that would have depressed minority voting. She stated, "Throwing out preclearance

(Continued)

Evaluating Equality *(Continued)*

when it has worked and is continuing to work to stop discriminatory changes is like throwing away your umbrella in a rainstorm because you are not getting wet."

Although there is no debate over the importance of protecting minority voting rights, this case presents interesting contrasts on views of federalism—the conflict between state autonomy on one side and the national government's authority on the other side. Review the full opinion from the official U.S. Supreme Court website, http://www.supremecourt. gov/opinions/12pdf/12-96_6k47.pdf. Debate among yourselves the merits of the different arguments, and for the purposes of this chapter, focus the debate on the principles of federalism that this case represents, as well as the intersection between federalism and racial equality. At what point should the national government be allowed to treat states differently based on historic discrimination? Is Justice Ginsburg's umbrella analogy correct—will the covered jurisdictions revert to practices that diminish minority voting? How should the story of the long lines in Maricopa, Arizona, shape opinions on this issue?

TABLE 3.2 **Jurisdictions Previously Covered under Section 5 of the Voting Rights Act**

States Completely Covered
Alabama
Alaska
Arizona
Georgia
Louisiana
Mississippi
South Carolina
Texas
Virginia
States Partially Covered by County
California: 4 out of 58 counties
Florida: 5 out of 67 counties
New York: 4 out of 62 counties
North Carolina: 40 out of 100 counties
South Dakota: 2 out of 66 counties
States Partially Covered by City/Town
Michigan: 2 towns
New Hampshire: 10 towns

Source: Adapted from The United States Department of Justice, "Jurisdictions previously covered by Section 5," https://www.justice.gov/crt/jurisdictions-previously-covered-section-5#note1, accessed April 22, 2016.

over females in determining who would control estates in inheritance cases.[57] Another federalism and women's issue relates to abortion. In the 1973 historic *Roe v. Wade* case, the U.S. Supreme Court overturned state laws that banned abortion, ruling that pregnant women have a constitutional right to abortion.[58] We cover abortion in more detail in Chapters 4 and 5, but the fact that the *Roe* decision created a national policy on abortion rights reflects a significant shift in favor of national authority.

The Era of Devolution

By the 1970s, the dominant thinking among political leaders, especially, but not exclusively, Republicans, was that the national government had assumed too much authority during the 1960s. Critics argued that states and local governments better understand their own problems, so they should be able to control their own policies without too much interference from the national government. The national government should set general policies, but state and local governments should decide the details. As a result of this shift in thinking, the national government began to pursue a policy of **devolution**—a partial return of power to state and local governments.

Devolution A view of federalism that advocates partially returning power to state and local governments.

The Role of Presidents and Congress. Devolution began in 1969 under President Richard Nixon, who used the term "New Federalism" to promote his priorities of taking power away from the national government and returning it to the state and local governments. President Ronald Reagan expanded devolution in the 1980s, and most presidents since that time, including Democratic President Bill Clinton, have advocated devolution policies in some form or another. In fact, in his 1996 State of the Union Address, President Clinton famously stated, "The era of big government is over. But we cannot go back to the time when our citizens were left to fend for themselves."[59] The primary method of promoting devolution is through **block grants**—grants-in-aid from the national government that are general, contain minimal regulations, and give state and local governments considerable discretion on how the money should be used. Unlike categorical grants, in which the national government strongly controls how states use the money, block grants enable states to spend the money as they best see fit to accomplish a general policy goal.

Block Grants Grants-in-aid from the national government that are general, contain minimal regulations, and give state and local governments considerable discretion on how the money should be used.

For example, in 1974 the national government created the Community Development Block Grant Program, which allowed states and local governments to provide housing for the poor and help improve neighborhoods.[60] Another, more controversial, block grant was the Personal Responsibility and Work Opportunity Act of 1996, also known as welfare reform. The Republican-controlled Congress and Democratic President Bill Clinton passed this bill, which replaced categorical grant welfare programs, most notably Aid to Families with Dependent Children (AFDC), with Temporary Assistance for Needy Families (TANF). TANF provides money to states with minimal regulation, except the direction that the states use the money to help recipients find meaningful employment.[61] Critics of TANF argue that it has not provided adequate funds for the poor and has caused many people, especially children and minorities, to suffer in extreme poverty.[62] Although the U.S. government has touted it as a success, the National Association of Black Social Workers has argued that TANF has not helped Black families and that under the law, White recipients have been more likely than Black recipients to find meaningful employment.[63]

Despite the dominance of devolution since 1980, the national government has still exerted its authority over states when it comes to certain policy goals. For example, the national government lacks the constitutional authority to mandate a minimum drinking age, which falls under the state police power. However, when a majority of political leaders desired to establish a national twenty-one-year-old drinking age, Congress passed, and usually pro-devolution president Ronald Reagan signed, the National Minimum Drinking Age Act of 1984, which withholds highway funds to states that do not adopt a twenty-one-year-old drinking age. The U.S. Supreme Court upheld this act, ruling that Congress did not exceed its authority.[64] Furthermore, the Americans with Disabilities Act (ADA) of 1990 (which we discuss in more detail in Chapter 5) requires that businesses and state and local governments update their facilities so that people with disabilities can access them. Because the national government did not fully fund these improvements, the ADA has amounted to an unfunded mandate.

Questions of federalism have been less clear under the Obama administration. During the first two years of the Obama presidency, with the help of a Democratic Congress, the national government enacted significant policies that favored national authority. The American Recovery and Reinvestment Act of 2009, also better known as the Stimulus Act, gave $787 billion to the states, with specific instructions that the funds be used for policies, such as hiring teachers, building infrastructure projects, and extending unemployment benefits. However, because the national government lacks the authority to mandate that states follow these rules, or even take the money, states are not required to enact these policies. In fact, initially some Republican governors refused to take any stimulus money, and even though they eventually relented, some states did not accept all of the money.[65]

The Patient Protection and Affordable Care Act of 2010, also known as Affordable Care Act or ObamaCare, gives the national government a considerable amount of control over states' ability to provide health insurance. The Affordable Care Act also requires that individuals purchase health insurance or pay a penalty, and the U.S. Supreme Court upheld this provision, despite challenges that it exceeds the national government's power.[66]

Conversely, the Obama administration has deferred to states in some areas. For example, since 2013 a few states have legalized cannabis, even allowing the legal sale of marijuana. Because the national government still bans the sale of marijuana, the Obama administration possesses the authority to use federal law enforcement to arrest marijuana sellers in these states regardless of state law.[67] Nevertheless, the Obama administration announced that it would allow states to operate legalized marijuana sales as long as states regulated them.[68]

Whereas some 2016 presidential candidates (e.g., Chris Christie and Marco Rubio) would have used the national government to overrule state marijuana legalization, and president-elect Donald Trump has indicated his support of medical marijuana and opposition to legalizing marijuana for recreation use. Still, he has also suggested that states should make their own policies.[69]

In short, despite many critics of the Obama administration who have charged that his policies have given too much authority to the national government, there is anecdotal evidence showing both his willingness to use national authority and to defer to states. A recent scholarly analysis of the federalism impact of President Obama's policies substantiates this more nuanced view. It shows that the national government has increased its authority under the Obama administration, but it has also provided creative flexibility to the states.[70]

The Role of the Supreme Court. Since 1980, the U.S. Supreme Court has been a significant institution in devolving power back to the states. Notably, the Court has restricted the national government's use of the commerce clause to expand its authority. For example, the Gun Free School Zones Act of 1990 criminalized possession of a firearm within 1,000 feet of a school. Normally, states control questions of gun possession and education, but in this instance the national government justified its authority under the commerce clause because guns in schools devalue education and cause additional crime that spreads across state lines, both of which substantially affect interstate commerce. However, in the 1995 case *United States v. Lopez* the U.S. Supreme Court narrowly overturned this law because it did not accept the national government's justification of a "substantial effect." Chief Justice Rehnquist wrote, "To uphold the government's contentions here, we would have to pile inference upon inference in a manner that would bid fair to convert congressional authority under the Commerce Clause to a general police power of the sort retained by the states."[71]

Additionally, in 2000, in *United States v. Morrison*, the U.S. Supreme Court overturned the portion of the Violence Against Women Act of 1994 that allowed victims of gender-based violence to sue their attackers in federal court. Although states normally decide questions of gender-based violent crimes, the national government argued that violence against women costs the national economy over $3 billion per year; therefore, gender-based violence substantially affects interstate commerce. However, the Supreme Court rejected that argument.[72]

Despite the Supreme Court's willingness to reign in the national government, it has upheld the national government's use of the commerce clause to override state authority in particular policy areas. The concept of **preemption**, which is based on the supremacy clause, permits the national government to overturn state and local laws that conflict with national policies, and preemption has been especially controversial in drug enforcement policies. Beginning in the 1990s many states decriminalized marijuana for medicinal use. However, the national government banned any use of marijuana under the Controlled Substances Act, and the Drug Enforcement Agency enforced the law

Preemption A concept that permits the national government to overturn state and local laws.

against people who had permission in their states to use marijuana for medical uses. These patients challenged the national government's policy, arguing that the marijuana they used did not cross state lines and so the national government lacked power to regulate it under the commerce clause. In the 2005 *Gonzales v. Raich* case, a majority of the Supreme Court relied on the *Wickard v. Filburn* case to show that marijuana use exerts a "substantial effect" on interstate commerce.[73]

Although the Supreme Court has upheld preemption in cases related to drug enforcement, it has declined to preempt state laws in other areas. For example, in the 1991 *Gregory v. Ashcroft* case, the Court ruled that a state's Tenth Amendment right to determine qualifications for political office supersedes the federal Age Discrimination in Employment Act, which prohibits employment discrimination based on age (see Chapter 5). In this case, a Missouri state judge unsuccessfully challenged a state law requiring judges to retire at the age of 70.[74]

Since the 1980s, devolution has occurred with respect to the issue of abortion as well. Recall, that in 1973 the U.S. Supreme Court declared that women have a right to an abortion, which nationalized the issue. States were no longer able to outlaw the procedure. Since then, the Supreme Court has upheld the general right to an abortion, but it has allowed states to institute restrictions on abortion, such as mandatory waiting periods before an abortion can be performed, requirements that physicians show the patient photographs of the fetus, and parental consent for minors seeking an abortion.[75]

The U.S. Supreme Court has also weighed in on the issue of devolution with respect to civil rights, particularly over how to integrate public schools. By the late 1960s, many public schools were still segregated not because of state government action, but rather because of geography. Blacks, Latinos, and Whites tended to live in different neighborhoods, and therefore went to different schools. In 1971, the U.S. Supreme Court upheld the practice of court-ordered busing White and minority students to schools farther from their home to achieve full integration.[76] However, twenty years later the U.S. Supreme Court gave permission for local areas to cease busing if they could show they made a genuine effort to achieve integration.[77]

In 2007, the Court actually interfered with state and local government efforts to integrate schools. The City of Seattle assigned children to public schools to ensure that schools were racially mixed, even if children were required to attend schools far from their homes. The Court ruled that this use of race as a criterion of school assignment violated the Fourteenth Amendment's equal protection clause (see Chapter 5).[78]

Finally, the Supreme Court has reinterpreted the Eleventh Amendment in a way that influences federalism in general and racial politics in particular. Recall that the Eleventh Amendment prevents states from being sued in federal court by citizens of another state, but it is silent on the issue of states being sued by their own citizens. In the 1996 case of *Seminole Tribe of*

Florida v. Florida, the Supreme Court expanded the Eleventh Amendment to shield states. Under its power to regulate commerce with Indian tribes, the national government passed the Indian Gaming Regulatory Act of 1988, which recognized tribes' rights to run casinos, even if the state in which they are located bans casino gambling. The law required the state government and tribe to enter into negotiations on establishing casinos, and if the state failed to negotiate in good faith, then the tribe could sue the state in federal court. However, the U.S. Supreme Court ruled that the Eleventh Amendment contains protections for states that extend beyond the strict language of the amendment; therefore, states could be exempt from being sued in federal court by their own citizens.[79]

Since the early republic the U.S. Supreme Court has been instrumental in drawing the lines between state power and national power, ruling in favor of both. Table 3.3 lists the key Supreme Court cases that have expanded the power of the national government at the expense of state and local governments, and Table 3.4 lists the key U.S Supreme Court cases that have given more .power to state and local governments.

TABLE 3.3 **Key U.S. Supreme Court Cases Expanding the Power of the National Government at the Expense of State and Local Governments in the Areas of Economics and Civil Rights**

Case Name	Year	Issue area
Brown v. Board of Education	1954	Civil Rights
Chisom v. Roemer	1991	Civil Rights
Garcia v. San Antonio Metropolitan Transit Authority	1985	Economics
Gibbons v. Ogden	1824	Economics
Heart of Atlanta Motel v. United States	1965	Civil Rights
Katzenbach v. McClung	1965	Civil Rights
McCulloch v. Maryland	1819	Economics
National Federation of Independent Business v. Sebelius	2012	Economics
National Labor Relations Bd. v. Jones & Laughlin Steel	1937	Economics
Reed v. Reed	1971	Civil Rights
Roe v. Wade	1973	Civil Rights
Swann v. Charlotte-Mecklenburg Board of Education	1971	Civil Rights
Thornburg v. Gingles	1986	Civil Rights
United States v. Darby Lumber	1941	Economics
Wickard v. Filburn	1942	Economics

TABLE 3.4 Key U.S. Supreme Court Cases Limiting National Authority and Giving Power to State and Local Governments in the Areas of Economics and Civil Rights

Case Name	Year	issue area
Board of Education, Oklahoma City v. Dowell	1991	Civil Rights
Carter v. Carter Coal Company	1936	Economics
Dred Scott v. Sandford	1857	Civil Rights
Gregory v. Ashcroft	1991	Civil Rights
Hammer v. Dagenhart	1819	Economics
National League of Cities v. Usery	1976	Economics
Planned Parenthood v. Casey	1992	Civil Rights
Plessy v. Ferguson	1896	Civil Rights
Prigg v. Pennsylvania	1842	Civil Rights
Schechter Poultry Corporation v. United States	1935	Economics
Seminole Tribe of Florida v. Florida	1996	Civil Rights
Shelby County, AL v. Holder	2013	Civil Rights
United States v. Butler	1936	Economics
United States v. Cruikshank	1875	Civil Rights
United States v. E.C. Knight Company	1895	Economics
United States v. Morrison	2000	Civil Rights
United States v. Reese	1876	Civil Rights

Conclusion

The controversies over mishaps during the 2016 presidential primary in Arizona and during the 2012 presidential election typify the significance of federalism in American government. To ensure fair elections and prevent racial discrimination, the national government exerts considerable control over voting procedures. The Fifteenth Amendment and the Voting Rights Act limit states' abilities to disenfranchise racial and ethnic minorities. However, states still decide questions of where to locate polling places, how long to allow voting, and what kind of authority voting officials have over voters. When Maricopa County slashed the number of polling sites, there were frustratingly long lines, particularly in areas with heavy minority populations.

The U.S. federal government consists of three distinct levels (national, state, and local), and each level performs key policymaking functions and affects people's daily lives in different ways. Moreover, there is tremendous competition for power among the three levels of government, especially between the national government on one side and state and local governments on the other. The balance of power among the levels of government is called federalism, and it is a central component of American government and politics. Federalism influences all aspects of American government, but it plays an especially significant role in minority group politics.

State and local governments are key components of our federal system. Although they share many similarities, individual states and localities structure their governments differently from the legislatures that make the laws, to the governors and mayors that execute them, and the courts that settle disputes. Although racial and ethnic minorities have been traditionally excluded from positions of power in state and local government, since the late twentieth century, many minority groups are better represented in state legislatures, courts, and even as governors.

The Constitution forms the framework for the balance of power between the national government and the state and local governments. The Framers of the Constitution sought to strengthen the national government; therefore, many constitutional provisions expand national authority. However, parts of the Constitution, most notably the Tenth Amendment, preserve state power. The original Constitution allowed states to determine their own civil rights policies, even to the point of allowing slavery. However, constitutional amendments have restricted states' abilities to deny people rights, especially in voting. The Fifteenth Amendment bars states from denying people the right to vote on account of race; the Nineteenth Amendment prohibits states from denying people the right to vote on account of sex; and the Twenty-Fourth Amendment prevents states from enacting poll taxes, which disproportionately hurt poor and minority populations.

During the early years of the Republic the national government expanded power to promote industrialization and economic development. After the Civil War, the period of dual federalism dominated. State governments and the national government governed within their own spheres, and the Supreme Court sharply curtailed the authority of the national government. Despite the passage of the post–Civil War constitutional amendments, states were still free to mistreat racial and ethnic minorities until the middle of the twentieth century. States required facilities to be segregated and cleverly circumvented the Fifteenth Amendment.

After the Great Depression, the period of cooperative federalism emerged, and the lines between state and national authority blurred. Cooperative federalism was characterized by significant increases in the power of the national government, often at the expense of state and local governments. Supreme Court decisions such as *Brown v. Board of Education*, and federal statutes such as the Civil Rights Act of 1964 and the Voting Rights Act of 1965, nationalized civil rights policies and advanced equality.

Since the 1970s, a period of devolution has occurred. Although the national government has given some power back to the states, it still retains considerable authority over policymaking. Moreover, although previous

Democratic Presidents Jimmy Carter and Bill Clinton endorsed devolution, President Barack Obama appears more willing to assert the authority of the national government. Yet even the policies of the Obama administration respect the autonomy of state governments when compared to President Johnson's Great Society Era.

REVIEW QUESTIONS

1. To what extent are Blacks and Latinos represented in state legislatures, and how does this minority representation vary by region?

2. How specifically did the original Constitution expand national authority but enable states to maintain slavery?

3. Compare and contrast civil rights outcomes in the eras of dual federalism, cooperative federalism, and devolution. In which era have civil rights advances been most apparent? Why?

4. How did the controversies over access to voting and long lines at the polls during the 2012 and 2016 elections reflect issues of federalism?

5. How has federalism influenced the status of Indian tribes in American government?

KEY TERMS

Bicameral Legislature p. 62
Bill of Attainder p. 73
Block Grants p. 89
Categorical Grants p. 84
Civil Rights Act of 1964 p. 85
Commerce Clause p. 72
Cooperative Federalism p. 82
County Commissions p. 69
Devolution p. 89
Dillon's Rule p. 69
Dual Federalism p. 78
Due Process Clause p. 74
Equal Protection Clause p. 74
Ex Post Facto Law p. 73
Extradition Clause p. 73
Federalism p. 59

Fifteenth Amendment p. 74
Fourteenth Amendment p. 74
Fugitive Slave Clause p. 73
Full Faith and Credit Clause p. 73
Gerrymandering p. 63
Grants-in-Aid p. 81
Home Rule p. 69
Implied Power p. 76
Incorporation p. 82
Interstate Compact Clause p. 73
Line Item Veto p. 63
Majority-Minority Districts p. 63
Merit System p. 68
Monopoly p. 78
Municipalities p. 69
Necessary and Proper Clause p. 72

Nineteenth Amendment p. 74
Police Power p. 74
Poll Taxes p. 74
Preemption p. 91
Privileges and Immunities Clause p. 73
Retention Election p. 68
School Districts p. 69
Separate but Equal p. 81
Sovereignty p. 59
Supremacy Clause p. 73
Tenth Amendment p. 75
Thirteenth Amendment p. 74
Unfunded Mandates p. 85
Unicameral Form of Government p. 62
Voting Rights Act of 1965 p. 58

ADDITIONAL READINGS

Christopher P. Banks and John C. Blakeman, *The U.S. Supreme Court and New Federalism: From the Rehnquist to the Roberts Court* (Lanham, MD: Rowman & Littlefield, 2012).

This book offers a thorough account of the Supreme Court's federalism jurisprudence over the past quarter-century, particularly its deference to state governments. Although Banks

and Blakeman focus on national security and religious liberty, the book chronicles decisions concerning race and ethnicity.

Charles S. Bullock III, Ronald Keith Gaddie, and Justin J. Wert, *The Rise and Fall of the Voting Rights Act* (Norman, OK: University of Oklahoma Press, 2016).

This book traces Black access to voting from Reconstruction through the present, and their extensive data demonstrate that the Voting Rights Act and its amendments have improved minority voting participation and representation. They also analyze how the politics of the federal judiciary led to the recent landmark decision in *Shelby County (AL) v. Holder*.

W. Dale Mason, *Indian Gaming: Tribal Sovereignty and American Politics* (Norman: University of Oklahoma Press, 2000).

This is one of the leading analyses of how casino gambling on American Indian reservations has influenced the position of tribal governments in the larger context of American federalism.

Tyson King Meadows and Thomas F. Schaller, *Devolution and Black State Legislators: Challenges and Choices in the Twenty-First Century* (Albany: SUNY Press, 2006).

As devolution has given more power to state governments, state legislatures have become a more important public policy force. As a result, African American state legislators now play a significant role in shaping policy in the states, and this book offers a thorough analysis of the more than six hundred African Americans who serve in state legislatures.

Ruth P. Morgan, *Governance by Decree: The Impact of the Voting Rights Act in Dallas* (Lawrence: University Press of Kansas, 2004).

This book carefully examines the impact of the Voting Rights Act on one particular local area—Dallas, Texas. The author demonstrates that although the Voting Rights Act initially improved minority participation and representation in Dallas local government, subsequent amendments, judicial decisions, and the actions of the U.S. Department of Justice have resulted in negative unintended consequences.

CHAPTER 4

Civil Liberties: Freedom and Government Authority in Tension

Taken from the cell phone video of the incident, this picture depicts North Charleston, SC, Police Officer Michael T. Slager shooting unarmed Walter Scott on April 4, 2015. Clearly, Scott is unarmed and fleeing Slager. Based on this video evidence, Slager was arrested and charged with murder, and he was released from jail in January of 2016 after a judge granted him bail. He is currently awaiting trial.

North Charleston, South Carolina, is a large suburb of Charleston, and about 47 percent of its slightly more than 100,000 residents are African American.[1] In early April of 2015 North Charleston became the focus of national media attention after a white police officer shot an unarmed African American North Charleston resident. Initially, Officer Michael Slager claimed that after he stopped Walter Scott for a broken taillight, Scott grabbed his stun gun; therefore, Slager had no choice but to shoot Scott. However, a bystander took a cell phone video of the incident, and ultimately the video was released to the *New York Times*, which aired the video of the shooting to the American public. This video contradicted Slager's account, and showed Scott running away from Slager, who then shot Scott in the back several times. After Scott fell, Slager approached him and appeared to yell at him, but Slager was unresponsive. Slager then handcuffed Scott, walked approximately 30 feet from Scott's body, picked up an object, returned to Scott's body, and subsequently dropped the object. Family members indicated that Scott probably ran from Slager because he owed child support payments and feared arrest. After the video was aired Slager was arrested and charged with murder.[2]

Slager was initially denied bail, which meant that he would remain in jail until his trial, which would not start until about eighteen months after his arrest. However, in January of 2016, a judge reversed that decision and released Slager from jail on a $500,000 bond. The judge ordered Slager to house arrest, meaning that Slager will not be able to leave his residence, barring exceptions dealing with medical issues or legal matters pertaining to his case. The judge ruled that Slager was not dangerous and was unlikely to flee; therefore house arrest was appropriate. Slager's trial is set for October 31, 2016.[3]

The shooting of Walter Scott is also important because since 2014 there have been a large number of instances in which police officers have killed unarmed Black males, including among others the shooting of Michael Brown in Ferguson, Missouri; the strangling of Eric Garner in Staten Island, New York; and the shooting of twelve-year-old Tamir Rice

chapter outline

features

in Cleveland, Ohio. **Many Americans regard this problem as stemming from racial profiling—a law enforcement technique that targets racial and ethnic minorities because of their race or ethnicity. Police officers who engage in racial profiling, most of whom are white, assume that African Americans or Latinos are violent; therefore, they use lethal force when it is clearly not warranted. Unlike Michael Slager's case, most of the officers involved in these shootings escape prosecution.**

Racial Profiling A law enforcement technique that singles out suspects on the basis of their race or ethnicity.

intro *The controversy over police shootings in general and the shooting of Walter Scott in particular is an example of the politics surrounding* **civil liberties**—*the constitutional freedoms that Americans enjoy and on which governments may not encroach. The term* civil liberties *is often confused with the term* civil rights, *which concerns the protections against unequal treatment that the government guarantees all groups. We discuss civil rights in the next chapter. Here we focus on the issue of civil liberties, which concerns the individuals' freedom from governmental control.*

Civil Liberties The constitutional freedoms that Americans enjoy and on which the government may not encroach.

The Bill of Rights guarantees a variety of civil liberties, which are shown in Table 4.1, and the story of Walter Scott's shooting involves a number of these important liberties. By targeting African Americans and Latinos, police arbitrarily and unequally use their power to invade people's freedoms without any suspicion of wrongdoing, which implicates key civil liberties contained in the Fourth and Fifth Amendments. It is equally important to realize that despite the nefarious nature of Slager's criminal charge of murder, civil liberties also protect him. He has a Sixth Amendment right to a fair trial with effective assistance of counsel, and if he is convicted, then the Eighth Amendment prevents him from enduring "cruel and unusual punishment." As Slager's story also shows, the Eighth Amendment's ban on excessive bail ultimately allowed Slager to be freed from jail while awaiting trial.

This chapter focuses on the politics of civil liberties. Table 4.1 lists a vast number of civil liberties; however, there are too many to discuss in a single chapter. For our purposes, four aspects of civil liberties merit extended discussion: freedom of expression, freedom of religion, criminal justice, and privacy. The story also demonstrates that, although the amendments in the Bill of Rights spell out Americans' civil liberties, the language of the amendments is ambiguous; therefore, civil liberties are not absolutes. Often, the ambiguity of the Bill of Rights is manifested in debates between the government's perceived need to exert authority in the name of regulating public morals and safety and those who place a greater value on individual liberty and autonomy. Some argue that racial profiling is unacceptable in a society based on constitutional liberties, whereas others support the government's need to take these kinds of measures to preserve public safety.

Additionally, civil liberties controversies have a racial and ethnic component. As the opening story indicates, many African Americans, such as Walter Scott, are targeted for different treatment by law enforcement officers because of their race. This chapter demonstrates a number of other ways in which race plays a key role the politics of civil liberties.

TABLE 4.1 Liberties Contained in the Bill of Rights

Amendment	Status of Liberty	Incorporation Status
First	No government establishment of a religion	1947
First	Free exercise of religion	1940
First	Freedom of speech	1927
First	Freedom of the press	1931
First	Freedom to peacefully assemble	1937
First	Freedom to petition the government for redress	1937
Second	Right to bear arms	2010
Third	Protection against quartering of soldiers in private homes during times of peace	Not incorporated
Fourth	Protection against search of a home or business without a warrant issued by a neutral third party and based on probable cause	1949
Fifth	Protection against trial for major crimes without a grand jury indictment	Not incorporated
Fifth	Guarantee of no trial twice for the same offense (double jeopardy clause)	1969
Fifth	Protection against being forced to testify against oneself	1964
Fifth	Protection against denial of life, liberty, or property without due process of law	Specified in the Fourteenth Amendment
Fifth	Protection against taking of private property (eminent domain clause)	1896
Sixth	Right of defendants to have a speedy, public trial	1967
Sixth	Right of defendants to have a trial by jury	1968
Sixth	Right of defendants to be informed of their charges	1965
Sixth	Right of defendants to confront their accusers and compel witnesses to testify on their behalf	1965
Sixth	Right of counsel for criminal defendants	1963
Seventh	Right of defendants to have a trial by jury in civil suits	Not incorporated
Eighth	Protection against the imposition of excessive bail or fines	Not incorporated
Eighth	Protection against imposition of "cruel and unusual punishment"	1962
Ninth	Guarantee of unwritten rights retained by the people	N/A[a]
Tenth	Granting to states powers not reserved to the national government or prohibited to the states	Not incorporated[b]

a The Ninth Amendment itself cannot be incorporated because it does not enumerate a specific right; however, the Ninth Amendment was used to incorporate the unwritten right to privacy in 1965.
b Because the Tenth Amendment grants rights to states and not to people, it is not relevant to incorporation.
Source: Adapted from David O'Brien, Constitutional Law and Politics, Vol. 2: Civil Rights and Civil Liberties, 8th ed. (New York: Norton, 2011), 330–332.

The Bill of Rights

As already mentioned, civil liberties are an important part of the Bill of Rights. Before discussing specific civil liberties, let us consider how the Bill of Rights affects American government.

Origins of the Bill of Rights

Chapter 2 explained that the Bill of Rights was not part of the original Constitution. After the initial Constitution was drafted, many political leaders contended that a bill of rights was necessary to protect against government encroachments on civil liberties. These leaders feared that a centralized national government would become tyrannical, similar to the tyranny the colonists experienced when ruled by the English king and Parliament; that is, the centralized government in London. Supporters of a bill of rights believed that state governments would protect liberties because, unlike the national government, they were close to the governed. Furthermore, many states already had enumerated protections, such as those in the Virginia Declaration of Rights, which we also discussed in Chapter 2. Supporters of the Bill of Rights maintained that, without similar specified limitations, the national government could become too powerful.

Despite this push for a bill of rights, many Framers, most notably Alexander Hamilton and James Madison, opposed including a bill of rights in the Constitution. This group argued that separation of powers and checks and balances would be sufficient to protect individual liberty and prevent the national government from becoming tyrannical. In "Federalist Paper No. 84," Alexander Hamilton predicted that specifically listing individual rights could actually lessen liberty because the government would adhere only to those rights listed and would not respect any equally important unlisted rights.[4]

Nevertheless, there was enough support for a bill of rights that its absence threatened to prevent the ratification of the Constitution. To increase support for ratification, James Madison agreed to propose a bill of rights as constitutional amendments after the Constitution was ratified. In 1791, the first ten amendments became the Bill of Rights.[5]

Incorporation of the Bill of Rights

Initially, the Bill of Rights applied only to the national government. Although people feared that the national government would trounce civil liberties, they were less concerned about the states and localities. By the early nineteenth century, however, it was clear that state and local governments were violating civil liberties, even those contained in the Bill of Rights. As a result, the question of **incorporation**—whether the Bill of Rights should apply to the states as well as to the national government—arose.

An example of the incorporation problem occurred during the early nineteenth century when the city of Baltimore conducted internal improvements

Incorporation The application of the Bill of Rights to state and local governments.

Eminent Domain A provision in the Fifth Amendment to the Constitution that requires the government to provide compensation when it takes private property for public use.

Fourteenth Amendment An amendment to the Constitution that prevents states from denying on the basis of race full citizenship to its residents.

Due Process Clause A specific provision in the Fourteenth Amendment to the Constitution that requires states to use normal judicial and criminal procedures before denying a citizen life, liberty, or property.

Selective Incorporation The process by which the Supreme Court has gradually incorporated specific liberties deemed absolutely necessary in a free society.

on its pier. In doing so, the city caused John Barron, a wharf owner, to lose money after the improvements diverted water away from his wharf. A trial court awarded Barron compensation in accordance with the Fifth Amendment **eminent domain** clause, which requires the government to provide compensation when it takes private property for public use. However, in 1833 the U.S. Supreme Court ruled that Baltimore did not need to compensate Barron because the Fifth Amendment did not apply to the states and localities. In other words, the Supreme Court refused to incorporate the Bill of Rights.[6]

The ratification of the **Fourteenth Amendment** in 1868 reinvigorated the question of incorporation. The Fourteenth Amendment was added to the Constitution after the Civil War to ensure that states gave former slaves full citizenship rights. Specifically, the amendment's **due process clause** prevents states from denying any resident life, liberty, or property without following normal criminal and judicial procedures. Many legal thinkers at the time, such as U.S. Supreme Court Justice John Marshall Harlan, argued that the protections contained in the Bill of Rights were inherent in the concept of "due process of law" and therefore the due process clause should incorporate the entire Bill of Rights. However, in the 1884 case of *Hurtado v. California*, the Supreme Court refused to use the due process clause to incorporate the Bill of Rights after the state of California indicted Hurtado for a capital crime without a grand jury, an action that the Fifth Amendment prevents.[7] We discuss the Fourteenth Amendment in more detail in Chapter 5.

In the twentieth century, the Supreme Court moderated its stance on incorporation by adopting the concept of **selective incorporation**, the incorporation of only some of the liberties in the Bill of Rights. The selective incorporation principle was first announced in the 1937 case of *Palko v. Connecticut*. After the state of Connecticut tried Frank Palko twice for the same crime, he argued that the state had violated his Fifth Amendment right against double jeopardy. Although the U.S. Supreme Court ruled that the Fifth Amendment double jeopardy clause should not be incorporated, Justice Benjamin Cardozo established that the due process clause of the Fourteenth Amendment incorporates only those liberties deemed to be essential for a free society.[8] Thus, Cardozo created a distinction within the Bill of Rights between more important liberties, which should be incorporated, and less important liberties, which should not be incorporated. Since 1937, especially during the 1950s and 1960s, the Supreme Court gradually incorporated most of the liberties contained in the Bill of Rights, and currently only a few liberties remain unincorporated. Table 4.1 indicates when each liberty has been incorporated or if it has not been.

Because of selective incorporation, most civil liberties are now uniformly applied throughout the United States. As a result, many of the liberties we discuss throughout this chapter apply at all levels of government: nation, state, and local. Recall from Chapter 3 how incorporation increased the power of the national government and decreased the power of states and localities.

Freedom of Expression

The First Amendment of the Constitution states, "Congress shall make no law . . . abridging the freedom of speech, or of the press; or of the right of the people to peacefully assemble, and to petition the government for redress." Although the language of the First Amendment seems clear, the issue of free expression is quite nebulous. There are a number of instances in which the government has restrained free expression out of concern for security, civility, and morality. Moreover, debates over freedom of expression often intersect minority-group politics. This section discusses the key freedom-of-expression topics of political dissent, pornography, and offensive speech, and freedom of the press.

Political Dissent

An essential ingredient of free expression is the right to political dissent, which entails advocating fundamental changes in our form of government, even calling for its overthrow, or joining a group that promotes those subversive ideas. During the early twentieth century, fears of a communist revolution compelled the national and state governments to outlaw views perceived to be anti-American. For example, in 1917, following the entry of the United States into World War I and the communist takeover of Russia, the federal government passed the Espionage Act, which outlawed interference with the nation's war effort. Thousands of people who actively opposed America's policy in World War I and expressed support for communism, socialism, and other left-wing causes were convicted and sentenced to lengthy prison terms—even death—for violating this law. States passed similar statutes as well.

Emma Goldman was a Jewish Russian immigrant anarchist who advocated overthrowing the government in the early twentieth century. Because political dissent was not protected at the time, she was imprisoned and eventually deported for expressing her views, which would be constitutionally protected today.

Despite the First Amendment, the U.S. Supreme Court upheld these laws by using the **clear and present danger test**, which allowed the government to criminalize expression that is "used in such circumstances and are of such a nature as to create a clear and present danger that they will bring about the substantial evils that Congress has a right to prevent."[9] Although the clear and present danger test seemingly protected civil liberties and restricted government control, the Supreme Court from the 1920s through the 1950s usually interpreted the mere advocacy of communism or socialism as a clear and present danger. Therefore, numerous Americans, many of whom were immigrants, were punished for political dissent. For example, Emma Goldman was a Russian immigrant and anarchist who advocated overthrowing the U.S. government. She was imprisoned several times throughout her life for advocacy of

Clear and Present Danger Test A guideline that requires the government to demonstrate that banned expression poses a definite and immediate threat to peace or national security.

her ideas, most notably opposing American entry into World War I. She was eventually deported.[10] By the late 1960s, however, the Supreme Court fully protected the right of political dissent by reinterpreting the clear and present danger test to protect dissent unless it directly encourages lawless actions.[11]

Another form of political dissent is flag desecration, in which an individual or group burns or otherwise defiles the American flag. Flag desecration is a method of expressing opposition to American policies and even the American system of government itself, and many people consider it to be extremely offensive. Consequently, most states and the federal government outlawed it. However, in 1989 the U.S. Supreme Court included flag desecration as a form of political dissent protected under the First Amendment.[12] On numerous occasions, Congress has attempted to propose a constitutional amendment to overturn the Supreme Court's decision and allow the government to criminalize flag desecration, but despite always passing comfortably in the House, the proposal has failed to garner the necessary two-thirds vote in the Senate.

Pornography and Offensive Speech

Pornography is a form of expression with limited First Amendment protection. National, state, and local governments contend that to protect the safety and morals of their citizens, they possess the authority to ban sexually explicit material. When deciding the level of protection to afford sexually explicit material, the U.S. Supreme Court has distinguished between obscene material, which is not protected, and non-obscene material, which is protected.

Prior to the 1950s, the federal and state governments heavily regulated explicit material based on a standard of what could be harmful to the most vulnerable in society. Therefore, state and local governments were allowed to ban literature, including classics, because merely a few passages could harm children. In a series of pornography cases between the 1950s and 1970s, the Supreme Court developed a more permissive definition of obscenity. Most important, the *Miller* standard (from the 1973 Supreme Court case *Miller v. California*) stipulates that material is protected under the First Amendment if the work as a whole is not excessively sexual or if it has political, literary, artistic, or scientific value. However, states and local communities have tremendous leeway in defining prurience and determining whether the questionable material possesses redeeming value.[13] Under the *Miller* standard, local communities can regulate the dissemination or display of sexually explicit material, including the sale of pornographic magazines and the establishment of adult entertainment businesses. States and localities, however, can no longer ban literature and cinema.

Other government regulations have limited speech that is offensive even if it is not sexual in nature. In 1942, the Supreme Court established the **fighting words** exception to the First Amendment, which stipulates that some forms of expression can damage other people or create a breach of the peace. Fighting words are essentially not speech; thus, they are not protected under the First Amendment.[14]

Fighting Words Derisive, insulting, or offensive words that inflict damage on other people and are therefore not protected by the First Amendment.

By the late 1960s, however, American culture had become more tolerant of derisive, insulting, and coarse language. This trend was reflected in the Supreme Court's constriction of the fighting words exception, which increased protection for speech that many deem to be offensive. In the 1971 landmark case of *Cohen v. California*, the Supreme Court significantly limited states' ability to criminalize the public display of curse words.[15]

Regulations on offensive speech intersect with minority-group politics in debates over **hate speech**, or expression that is hostile toward racial or ethnic minorities (as well as expression directed toward those of a particular gender, sexual orientation, or religious preference). During the late 1980s and early 1990s, many states, localities, and public universities adopted regulations prohibiting hate speech. However, in 1992, the U.S. Supreme Court struck down bans on hate speech, ruling that, although governments can ban fighting words, they cannot prohibit fighting words specifically directed toward minority groups. By singling out fighting words directed against minority groups, the laws discriminate against people who hold a particular viewpoint, the holding of which the First Amendment protects.[16]

Still, the Supreme Court has upheld restrictions on hate speech. For example, in 1993 the U.S. Supreme Court unanimously upheld state laws that allow for increased criminal penalties when victims are purposely selected because of their race, ethnicity, national origin, gender, religion, or sexual orientation.[17] In addition, states are permitted to ban burning a cross as a means of expressing anti-Black views because the specific act of cross-burning is

Hate Speech A form of expression that is hostile toward a particular race, ethnicity, gender, religion, nationality, or sexual orientation.

Members of the Ku Klux Klan attend a cross burning ceremony. Although the First Amendment protects the Klan's expression of their hateful views, the Supreme Court has ruled that cross burning is not protected because it is a form of violent intimidation. Consequently, states are able to outlaw cross burning.

inextricably linked with Ku Klux Klan terrorist actions; thus it is exempted from First Amendment protections.[18] In 2015 the Supreme Court upheld Texas's policy of preventing offensive messages on state-issued specialty license plates. Like many states, Texas allows private organizations to place messages on license plates, which automobile owners can then obtain by paying an additional fee. In 2009 the Texas Division of the Sons of Confederate Veterans applied to create a specialty license plate that displayed the Confederate flag, but the state denied the application because the Confederate flag was deemed offensive, particularly to racial and ethnic minorities. The U.S. Supreme court ruled that the state had the authority to prevent the impression that it endorses offensive views.[19]

Freedom of the Press

The First Amendment also explicitly protects freedom of the press, but the press is a broad term that encompasses a variety of media, including print media (newspapers, pamphlets, and magazines), broadcast radio and television, cable and satellite radio and television, and the Internet. The extent of First Amendment protection varies considerably among these media. The First Amendment protects print media by limiting **prior restraint**, which is a government attempt to prevent or impede the publication and distribution of printed material. Consequently, the American government cannot prevent the publication of material that is highly critical of its policies, even during times of war.[20]

Prior Restraint A usually impermissible government regulation that prevents the publication of printed material.

Likewise, protections against prior restraint can protect media outlets that maliciously attack racial and ethnic minorities. During the 1920s, the state of Minnesota closed Jay Near's newspaper, the *Saturday Press*, because its anti-Black, anti-Jewish, and anti-Catholic prejudice violated a state law banning the publication of "malicious, scandalous, or defamatory" material. The state threatened to fine Near if he continued to publish his paper. However, the U.S. Supreme Court overturned this law as a prior restraint in violation of the First Amendment.[21]

Similar to preventing bans on most hate speech, the First Amendment freedom of the press prevents prior restraints on racist publications. It is important to contrast American protection for hate speech with other constitutional democracies that protect civil liberties. For example, as a means of preventing another rise of the Nazi Party, Germany bans neo-Nazi and other hateful publications.

Libel The publication of written material that damages a person's reputation.

Another freedom of the press issue concerns **libel**, which is the publication of written material that damages a person's reputation. Individuals who are libeled can sue the publication for monetary damages; thus, libel presents a financial burden on the freedom of the press. Newspapers and magazines would censor themselves from printing controversial stories out of fear that they would have to pay significant damages to victims of libel. However, the U.S. Supreme Court ruled that the First Amendment requires that public figures suing for libel must show not only that the information in question is untrue, but also that the publication deliberately intended to be malicious, false, and damaging.[22] If a public figure suing for libel cannot prove that the publication intended to inflict harm, then the publication is protected under the First Amendment.

In contrast to the strong First Amendment protection that print media enjoy, broadcast radio and television are subject to considerable government regulation. The different standard results from the availability of outlets for expression. With print media, anyone with enough means can publish and distribute his or her views. But there are a finite number of frequencies on which broadcast radio and television stations can transmit their signal. Therefore, stations may not broadcast unless the federal government, specifically the Federal Communications Commission (FCC), grants a license. Based on its authority to issue these licenses, the FCC can regulate the content of the broadcasts. For example, because children can be easily exposed to radio and television broadcasts, the FCC prohibits the airing of "indecent material."[23]

Like print media, cable and satellite television and radio, the Internet, and streaming services, such as Netflix, enjoy strong First Amendment protection. Cable and satellite subscribers voluntarily decide to purchase their system and can choose which channels are transmitted into their homes; therefore, cable and satellite subscribers enjoy much more control over what their children could unwittingly watch compared to broadcast radio and television listeners. Because the Internet can be used easily to access pornography, the federal government has sought to regulate sexually explicit material on the Internet; however, the Supreme Court has invalidated these laws as a violation of the First Amendment.[24] The federal judiciary still limits governmental attempts to censor pornography on the Internet.

The cast of the Netflix original series *Orange Is the New Black* receive a Screen Actors Guild Award. The show depicts life in a female federal prison. It emphasizes issues of race, sexual orientation, political corruption, and problems associated with mass incarceration. Because *Orange Is the New Black* is shown on a streaming service it is able to depict sexually explicit scenes and mature subject matter, which would not be permitted on broadcast television.

Freedom of Religion

The debate over the relationship between religion and government is a critical civil liberties issue. As with freedom of expression, freedom of religion draws on the First Amendment. Specifically, the First Amendment states that "Congress shall make no law respecting an establishment of religion, or prohibiting the free exercise thereof." The establishment clause prevents the government from sponsoring or favoring religion. The free exercise clause ensures that all Americans are free to worship as they choose. Because these clauses are worded so broadly, their interpretation is ambiguous when applied to political controversies surrounding religio. Furthermore, the interpretation of both clauses has affected minority-group politics.

Establishment of Religion

Establishment Clause
A provision in the First Amendment to the U.S. Constitution that prevents the government from endorsing religion.

Separation of Church and State A constitutional principle that prevents the government (federal, state, or local) from interfering with or advancing religion or religious activity.

The **establishment clause** prohibits state sponsorship of religion, which since 1947 the U.S. Supreme Court has interpreted to mean a separation of church and state.[25] **Separation of church and state** prevents the government (state, federal, or local) from interfering with or advancing any religion or religious activity. For example, since the 1960s the U.S. Supreme Court has consistently ruled that all forms of organized prayer in public school violate the establishment clause even though a vast majority of Americans favor voluntary prayer in public schools.[26]

However, the Supreme Court has recently interpreted the establishment clause to allow some government mixing with religion, especially when a government provides funds that can aid religious institutions. Several states and localities have provided parents of children in poorly performing public schools with vouchers to apply toward tuition at private schools. Because the vast majority of voucher recipients use the money for parochial schools, many people argue that the voucher programs violate the establishment clause, but the Supreme Court has ruled that vouchers do not directly aid religion and are thus constitutional.[27] A similar establishment clause controversy concerns government expenditures to religious charities to handle social welfare duties, which has been the practice in both the George W. Bush and Barack Obama administrations and is handled in the Executive Branch by the Office of Faith-Based and Neighborhood Partnerships.[28]

Minority-group politics intersects issues of government funding of religious schools and social services because low-income Blacks and Latinos are often the beneficiaries of such policies. Although many racial and ethnic minorities oppose vouchers, a significant number of Blacks and Latinos are willing to overlook the establishment clause concerns and push for any program that addresses poverty in minority communities. A 2015 survey shows that Blacks and Latinos favor school vouchers for low-income families significantly more than the national average—58 percent for Latinos and 66 percent for African Americans versus 42 percent of the national average.[29]

Free Exercise of Religion

Although the **free exercise clause** clearly prevents laws that directly prohibit the practice of religion, it is less clear whether it protects against neutral, secular laws that indirectly and unintentionally hinder religion. Prior to the 1960s, laws that disadvantaged religious worship were permitted as long as they were designed with a neutral, nonreligious intent. As a result, adherents to uncommon religions often suffered unintentional discrimination at the hands of those who adhered to the more mainstream religions.[30]

By the 1960s, the free exercise clause was expanded to emphasize an individual's ability to worship regardless of the intent of a law. If a neutral law adversely affected religious worship, then the government was required to show a compelling reason for enforcing the law. Thus, Americans were exempt from following laws that hindered the practice of their religion, unless the government could show a compelling justification to require obedience to those laws.[31]

Although this standard allowed for religious exemptions from secular laws, the Supreme Court would not exempt religious groups if the government could show a compelling justification for requiring them to adhere to these laws. Two controversial examples of compelling justification involve race and ethnicity. During the 1970s, Bob Jones University, a Christian college, lost its tax-exempt status because its ban on interracial dating and marriage violated federal civil rights laws. The school claimed that the free exercise clause allowed it to discriminate, but the Supreme Court ruled that the government's interest in preventing racial discrimination overrode the free exercise clause.[32] In 1987, the Supreme Court ruled that New Jersey prison security regulations were a compelling justification for denying Islamic prisoners, many of whom were Black, permission to congregate for prayer during a lockdown.[33]

In 1990, the U.S. Supreme Court reinterpreted the free exercise clause in favor of government authority over individual religious liberty. In the landmark case of *Employment Division v. Smith* (1990), two Native American drug counselors were fired for ingesting the hallucinogenic substance peyote as part of an ancient religious ceremony. The state of Oregon denied them unemployment benefits, arguing that the counselors had been dismissed for "disciplinary" reasons, and the U.S. Supreme Court upheld this policy, refusing to overturn neutral, secular laws even if they hinder the practice of religion.[34] By shifting the emphasis back to the intent of the law, this ruling diminished religious liberty for adherents to nontraditional religions, particularly American Indian Peoples. "Our Voices: The Right to Practice Nontraditional Religions (*Employment Division v. Smith*)," on page 114, discusses in more detail the issue of religious liberty for Native Americans.

Despite the Supreme Court's more recent tilt toward government authority in free exercise cases, the free exercise clause has protected Americans, especially racial and ethnic minorities, from laws that directly prevent them from practicing their religion. In 1993, the Supreme Court struck down a city

Free Exercise Clause
A provision in the First Amendment to the U.S. Constitution that prevents the government from prohibiting people from practicing their religion.

of Hialeah, FL, ordinance that banned the ritualistic sacrifice of animals within the city limits. This policy was intended to prevent Santeria worshippers,[35] most of whom are Latino or Afro-Caribbean, from practicing their religion. Because the ordinance was specifically directed at Santeria, the Court ruled that it was not a neutral, secular law.[36] In 2006, the U.S. Supreme Court overturned a criminal ban on a hallucinogenic tea used in tribal religious ceremonies because outlawing the sacred tea violated American Indians' free exercise of religion.[37]

Recently, free exercise of religion has become an issue for American Muslims. Unlike some countries, such as France, the United States has not banned certain Muslim practices, such as women wearing a veil (or *hijab*), but there have been conflicts concerning Islamic religious practices. For example, the clothing store Abercrombie & Fitch did not hire Samantha Elauf, a Muslim woman who wears the hijab, because her hijab conflicted with the store's dress code policy. The Equal Employment Opportunity Commission (EEOC), a government agency that protects individuals' civil rights (see Chapter 8), sued Abercrombie & Fitch on Elauf's behalf because the company's religious discrimination violated Title VII of the Civil Rights Act (see Chapter 5). The U.S. Supreme Court ruled overwhelmingly that the company cannot refuse to hire someone for wearing the religious garment, even if that person does not explicitly ask for an accommodation.[38] Similarly, in 2015 the Supreme Court ruled against an Arkansas prison that prevented Muslim inmates from growing beards. The state argued that this regulation was necessary because inmates could hide contraband in their beards, but the U.S. Supreme Court unanimously ruled in favor of Muslim prisoners' religious liberty.[39]

Criminal Justice

Civil liberties are also relevant for criminal justice issues. Several amendments in the Bill of Rights protect individuals and limit government law enforcement at each stage of the criminal justice process: investigation (Fourth and Fifth), trial (Sixth), and punishment (Eighth). Because the language of these amendments is broadly worded, their application to criminal justice issues varies considerably. The unequal application of civil liberties to criminal justice has led to less protection for racial and ethnic minorities, especially as a result of the "War on Drugs" and the "War on Terror."

Investigation

The Fourth Amendment to the Constitution states that "The right of the people to be secure in their persons, houses, papers, and effects, against unreasonable searches and seizures shall not be violated, and no Warrants shall issue, but upon probable cause, supported by oath or affirmation, and particularly describing the place to be searched, and the persons or things to be seized." Therefore, before law enforcement officers search people, homes, or businesses, they are required by the Fourth Amendment to secure a **search warrant**,

Search Warrant A legal document that allows law enforcement to search someone's person, home, or business.

which is a legal document issued by a judge or a magistrate that specifically authorizes police to enter into a private area and search for and seize evidence of criminal activity. The Fourth Amendment stipulates that the judge or magistrate cannot issue a warrant unless the law enforcement officer has shown **probable cause**—the majority of the evidence must support the existence of criminal activity. This amendment protects individuals because the police must prove to a neutral third party—the judge or magistrate—that there is sufficient reason to violate the sanctity of someone's property or person. To enforce the provisions of the Fourth Amendment, the **exclusionary rule** mandates that any evidence gathered in violation of the Fourth Amendment may not be used in court against the defendant unless the law enforcement officers in question are able to demonstrate that they acted in good faith.[40]

Despite these clear civil liberties guarantees embodied in the Fourth Amendment, there have been exceptions to the warrant requirement, especially as technological advancements have allowed law enforcement to uncover evidence inside a person's home or business without physically entering the structure. In 1967, the Supreme Court ruled that law enforcement agents needed a warrant before listening to private telephone conversations with a wiretap device.[41] However, in the name of fighting terrorism since the September 11, 2001, attacks, the U.S. government has conducted electronic wiretap investigations of suspected terrorists without warrants. In 2006, a federal judge ruled that the government needed to get a warrant even for terrorism investigations. However, that decision was overturned on appeal, and the U.S. Supreme Court declined to review that appeal.[42]

Conversely, civil liberties organizations have successfully stopped another data collection process in which the National Security Agency (NSA), an intelligence gathering agency in the national government, collected everyone's telephone "meta-data," without any suspicion of terrorist activity. The NSA did not record conversations, but it did record who made the calls, who received the calls, and the length of the calls. The American Civil Liberties Union (ACLU) challenged this practice in federal court arguing that it violated the Fourth Amendment and even the USA PATRIOT Act (this is an acronym for Uniting and Strengthening America by Providing Appropriate Tools Required to Intercept and Obstruct Terrorism), which authorized more extensive surveillance after the September 11 attacks. In 2015 the Second Circuit Court of Appeals sided with the ACLU and invalidated the mass, suspicionless "meta" searches.[43] Soon after this decision, Congress passed the USA Freedom Act, which replaced the expired USA PATRIOT Act, and this new bill explicitly banned these searches of phone records.[44]

The concept of racial profiling, or singling out suspects for searches because of their race or ethnicity, also presents important concerns about the application of the Fourth Amendment. Many citizens and political leaders have charged that law enforcement officers are considerably more likely to stop and search vehicles driven by minorities compared to vehicles driven by Whites. As we discussed in this chapter's opening vignette, racial profiling

Probable Cause A legal requirement that there be more evidence indicating guilt than indicating innocence before a law enforcement officer can act.

Exclusionary Rule A judicially created civil liberties protection that prohibits the use of evidence gathered in violation of the Fourth Amendment.

our voices

The Right to Practice Nontraditional Religions (*Employment Division v. Smith*)

Although the First Amendment clearly protects an individual's right to pursue a chosen religion, American laws and policies often discriminate against people who adhere to nontraditional religions. Laws that have the effect of discriminating against religious minorities are drafted to be neutral and to have no explicit intent to hinder religious practice, but they still harm nontraditional worshippers. For example, Alfred Smith and Galen Black were two drug and alcohol rehabilitation counselors who belonged to the Native American Church. As part of their religion, Smith and Black participated in a sacred ceremony involving the ingestion of peyote, which is an illegal substance that induces a psychedelic effect. Even though drug laws exempted American Indian religions from prosecution, Smith and Black were still dismissed from their jobs because they had violated a policy forbidding the consumption of a controlled substance. The state of Oregon then denied Smith and Black unemployment benefits because they had been dismissed for disciplinary reasons. They took their case to

the Supreme Court, arguing that Oregon's secular, neutral policy still hindered the practice of their religion in violation of the First Amendment.

The excerpts here come from an exchange between Craig A. Dorsay, who argued Smith and Black's case before the U.S. Supreme Court, and Associate Justice Antonin Scalia. Much of Dorsay's argument focused on the importance of protecting a nontraditional, even unpopular, religious practice. His use of the term *ethnocentric* to describe Oregon's policy is particularly interesting. An ethnocentric view evaluates other cultures according to the preconceived notions of one's own culture. In other words, the dominant Judeo-Christian viewpoint in Oregon was unwilling to go beyond its own religious precepts to understand the importance of peyote in American Indian religion. Note also how Dorsay compared the practice of ingesting peyote to the consumption of sacramental wine. The late Justice Scalia was clearly skeptical and assumed that peyote was necessarily harmful.

Native Americans engage in a peyote ceremony. Although peyote is generally a banned substance, the First Amendment's free exercise clause allows Native Americans to use it as part of a religious ceremony that they have been practicing for thousands of years.

our voices *(Continued)*

DORSAY: If you looked at this situation and Indian people were in charge of government, and you look at the devastating impact that alcohol has had on Indian people . . . you might well find that alcohol was the Schedule 1 substance and peyote was not listed at all. And we are getting here to the heart of the ethnocentric view . . . of what constitutes religion in the United States. And I think that needs to be looked at very hard before determining what is a dangerous substance and what is not.

SCALIA: Your pointing to the traditional use of wine at religious services would not make any difference. I don't assume that the states would be compelled to allow excessive use of alcohol, drunken parties on grounds of religion. . . . I don't see a correlation between the wine and the peyote. I mean, it is acknowledged that . . . the whole purpose of the ingestion of peyote is its hallucinogenic effect.

DORSAY: I don't disagree with that. What I disagree with is the fact that the ingestion is harmful. There is no documented evidence that the use of peyote in these carefully circumscribed ceremonials has any harm to the individual, to the society . . . , or to . . . law enforcement.

Ultimately, the majority of the Supreme Court did not accept Dorsay's argument and upheld Oregon's policy. In his opinion, Scalia recognized that this ruling "will place at a relative disadvantage those religious practices that are not widely engaged in; but that is an unavoidable consequence of democratic government."*

* *Employment Division v. Smith*, 494 U.S. 872 (1990), 893.

Source: Adapted from Peter Irons, ed., *May It Please the Court: The First Amendment* (New York: New Press, 1997), 91–92. The entire oral argument can be heard at Oyez.org, sponsored by the Illinois Institute of Technology Chicago, Kent School of Law, http://www.oyez.org/cases/1980-1989/1989/1989_88_1213.

searches are based on race or ethnicity and not suspicion of specific wrongdoing; thus, they represent an arbitrary, unequal application of the Fourth Amendment.

Because the September 11, 2001, attacks on the World Trade Center and the Pentagon were carried out by people smuggling weapons onto commercial airliners, the government has greatly intensified security at airports. All passengers, regardless of suspicion, are subject to hand searches of their luggage and x-ray searches of their person. However, because all September 11 hijackers were Middle Eastern men, passengers who fit that profile are most likely to be searched. Soon after September 11, survey evidence indicated that numerous Americans favored more extensive security procedures for people who appeared to be Middle Eastern. Even liberals such as then–Democratic senator from New York (and subsequent Secretary of State and unsuccessful candidate for President in 2008 and 2016) Hillary Clinton suggested she would favor racial profiling to enhance security at airports.[45] In fact, a poll conducted a couple of weeks after the September 11 attacks showed that a similar number of Blacks (71 percent) and Whites (66 percent) believed that authorities should regard Middle Easterners with more suspicion.[46] Conversely, there are others who argue that racial profiling serves no law enforcement purpose and denies citizens their basic constitutional rights. Regardless of one's views on racial profiling, its use clearly creates an unequal application of the Fourth Amendment. "Evaluating Equality: Recognizing and Debating Conflicting Values in Political Cartoons on Racial Profiling in Fighting Terrorism" on page 117 explores this controversy in more detail from the perspective of political cartoons.

Among other guarantees, The Fifth Amendment to the Constitution provides that "No person . . . shall be compelled in any criminal case to be a witness against himself." This provision clearly guarantees that defendants cannot be forced to furnish information that could be used against them in a trial. However, the language does not obviously apply to police interrogations, and, before the 1960s states were able to determine their own police interrogation procedures, which often included physical and psychological means of extracting confessions. In 1964, the U.S. Supreme Court expanded the scope of the Fifth Amendment when it ruled that confessions would not be admissible at trial if the police refused a suspect's request that an attorney be present during the interrogation.[47] With an attorney present, the suspect is able to counter the various confession-inducing techniques that police employ.

The Supreme Court expanded legal protections against forced confessions when it issued its landmark ruling in *Miranda v. Arizona* (1966). In this case, police in Phoenix, Arizona, suspected that Ernesto Miranda, a twenty-three-year-old illiterate indigent, had kidnapped and raped an eighteen-year-old woman. While in police custody and without an attorney, Miranda confessed to the crime, and prosecutors used that confession to convict him of rape and kidnapping. Miranda appealed his conviction, and the U.S. Supreme Court extended its control over the way in which police officers question suspects. In addition to allowing attorneys to be present during interrogation, the ruling stated that law enforcement agents are required to inform suspects of what have come to be called **Miranda rights**.[48] This ruling advanced civil liberties by ensuring that citizens' ignorance of their rights does not preclude enjoyment of those rights.

Miranda Rights The Supreme Court's requirement that law enforcement must inform criminal suspects of the following: (1) that they have the right to remain silent, (2) that anything they say can be used against them in court, (3) that they have the right to the presence of an attorney, and (4) that if they cannot afford an attorney, then the court will appoint one before the interrogation takes place.

Trial

The Sixth Amendment to the Constitution guarantees that "In all criminal prosecutions, the accused shall enjoy the right to a speedy trial, by an impartial jury . . . and to have the Assistance of Council in his defence." Although the Constitution explicitly guarantees both liberties, they are not applied equally throughout the United States. For most of the nation's history, state governments did not provide defense attorneys for defendants who could not afford legal counsel. In the early 1960s, the Supreme Court ruled that the Sixth Amendment requires states to appoint attorneys for defendants who cannot afford them.[49] As a result, states and localities now provide the needy with legal counsel through public defenders, who are government-employed attorneys charged with the task of advocating on behalf of criminal defendants who cannot afford legal fees. The requirement that courts must provide counsel for poor defendants has equalized the application of a critical civil liberty.

Despite the requirement that states and localities appoint counsel for the indigent, class inequities in legal representation for criminal defendants still exist. With limited financial support, public defenders are not able to devote

evaluating equality

Recognizing and Debating Conflicting Values in Political Cartoons on Racial Profiling in Fighting Terrorism

The Fourth Amendment guarantees that law enforcement cannot stop, search, or harass Americans without reasonable suspicion of wrongdoing. However, many Americans, especially in times of crisis, are willing to forgo this right to enhance security. After the September 11, 2001, attacks, airline passengers surrendered more of their Fourth and Fifth Amendment civil liberties. Everyday items have been banned from airplanes, air travelers are required to submit to xray searches, and they and their luggage can be stopped and searched at any time. Because of the threat of terrorism, airline passengers do not enjoy the same rights as if they are in a car, on the street, or in their homes.

The issue of airport searches becomes more complex because searches are not conducted uniformly. Because the September 11 hijackers were all Middle Eastern men, people who appear to be of the same ethnic background are far more likely to be searched. Supporters of this form of racial profiling argue that it is a sensible way to ensure the safety of all Americans. They value security above all else. Conversely, opponents of racial profiling at airports argue that civil liberties need to be applied equally for all people regardless of race or national origin. They emphasize the values of equality and a uniform application of civil liberties.

Through the use of visual and verbal humor, the two political cartoons here typify the values underlying both views. The Wayne Stayskal cartoon from the *Tampa Tribune* (June 10, 2002) (top) endorses the value of security. By ignoring what is "obvious" before their eyes, these security personnel, who refuse to profile, are compromising security as symbolized by the extraterrestrial being's security threat. The 2002 Lalo Alcaraz cartoon from the *LA Weekly* (bottom) supports the value that individual liberties must be applied universally if they are to mean anything. This cartoon depicts racial profiling not as a safety measure, but

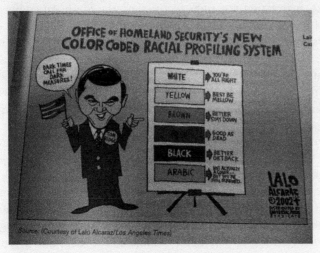

Source: (Courtesy of Lalo Alcaraz/Los Angeles Times)

(Continued)

evaluating equality *(Continued)*

instead as an arbitrary and discriminatory practice.

Although the cartoons use humor to illustrate their opinions, racial profiling is a serious issue. Nobody should condone blatant racial or ethnic profiling, but the issue does present important debates about the balance between security and liberty. To what extent should airport security use physical appearance in making decisions to

investigate terrorist activities? Should individuals have less civil liberties protection in airports, which are more vulnerable to a terrorist attack? Do more recent terrorist attacks, such as the Boston Marathon bombing, the Pulse Nightclub shooting in Orlando, or the San Bernardino shootings, merit additional scrutiny in public, i.e., outside of airports? As the opening story, as well as the numerous other instances of police

shooting unarmed Blacks, demonstrates, racial profiling also occurs in everyday law enforcement that is not related to terrorism. To what extent should national, state, and local governments use their authority to prevent this form of racial profiling? Is prosecuting police officers, such as Michael Slager, an appropriate remedy? Debate these issues among your classmates.

---

sufficient time and resources to defending their many clients. The indigent might get a defense, but it is probably not the best possible defense. Conversely, wealthy clients are able to afford highly skilled lawyers who can devote full attention to their cases.

This disparity affects racial and ethnic minorities, who are often in need of public defenders. To accommodate racial and ethnic minority clients, many states have sought to improve the diversity of their public defender offices. For example, Colorado recently required state criminal justice agencies, including public defenders' offices, to report the number of racial and ethnic minorities on staff and to "actively recruit minority candidates" for key positions.[50]

In addition to mandating the right to counsel, the Sixth Amendment grants an accused person the right to trial by an impartial jury. The size of juries varies across states, ranging from six to twelve members. Whereas a trial judge rules on matters of law, a jury decides whether the evidence proves beyond a reasonable doubt that a defendant is guilty. Although all states are required to try criminal defendants with a jury, the impartiality of juries is less clear. The process of convening juries allows each side to manipulate the type of jury that is empaneled.

Prior to the commencement of a trial, prosecutors and defense attorneys submit questions to a pool of possible jurors to eliminate potentially prejudiced jurors. Judges will dismiss any potential juror deemed unable to decide the case fairly and objectively. Additionally, the prosecution and the defense are each allotted a set number of **peremptory challenges**, which allow them to dismiss a potential juror without providing a reason. Both sides strategically use their given number of peremptory challenges to eliminate people who would be most predisposed against their side.

Peremptory Challenges The right of each side in a legal case to discard a set number of potential jurors without needing to express a reason for doing so.

This jury selection process has led to the underrepresentation of racial and ethnic minorities on juries. Since the end of the Civil War, the U.S. Supreme Court has consistently prevented states from actively prohibiting Blacks from serving on juries.[51] Nevertheless, prosecutors routinely used their peremptory challenges to remove African Americans from specific juries, particularly in cases with an African American defendant.

Although the U.S. Supreme Court in 1986 ruled that it is unconstitutional for prosecutors to use their peremptory challenges to eliminate Blacks or other racial minorities from a specific jury,[52] there is still some controversy over whether discrimination still exists. Legal experts have found that prosecutors are still able to get away with racial discrimination by using racially neutral terms to justify excluding racial minorities. For example, in Alabama 85 percent of Blacks in a jury pool were dismissed for vague reasons, such as they "were unkempt and gruff," "resembled the [Black] defendant," or "were unemployed."[53] However, a recent empirical study has found that peremptory challenges do not affect the racial and ethnic composition of juries throughout the United States, but juries with only six members are less racially diverse than juries with twelve members.[54]

A death row inmate at the Lieber Correctional Institution near Ridgeville, SC, February 19, 2003. The death penalty is a controversial issue of civil liberties, with some people arguing that it violates the Eighth Amendment ban on cruel and unusual punishment and discriminates against racial and ethnic minorities. However, a majority of the country supports capital punishment.

Punishment

The Eighth Amendment to the Constitution states, "Excessive bail shall not be required, nor excessive fines imposed, nor cruel and unusual punishments inflicted"; however, the amendment provides no clear definition of "cruel." The Eighth Amendment prevents brutal or wantonly negligent treatment of prisoners. As a result, prisoners who are victims of excessive force can recover monetary damages.[55] But the Eighth Amendment does not apply to questions concerning the magnitude of a criminal sentence or whether the "sentence fits the crime." In fact, in 1991 the U.S. Supreme Court ruled that it was not cruel and unusual for Michigan to sentence a man to life in prison without parole for possessing 672 grams of cocaine, even though murderers in Michigan received the same sentence (Michigan has no death penalty) and the equivalent crime in other states carried significantly lower penalties.[56] Although some states have relaxed these mandatory life without parole sentences for drug crimes, the Supreme Court's interpretation of the Eighth Amendment persists today.

There is also evidence that criminal sentences are disproportionate according to race and ethnicity. Since the 1970s, African American and Latino incarceration rates have increased at a much faster rate than the incarceration rate of Whites. According to the most recent data available in 2014, the African American incarceration rate in the United States is 1,451 per 100,000 people, compared to 405 per 100,000 Latinos and 276 per 100,000 whites. Overall, Blacks are 5.3 times more likely than Whites to be incarcerated, and Latinos are 1.5 times more likely.[57]

Table 4.2 demonstrates that, despite a few exceptions, states with the highest Black incarceration rates have low Black populations and states with the lowest Black incarceration rates have high Black populations. Table 4.3 shows that similar patterns do not exist for Latinos. We discuss racial disparities in sentencing in more detail in Chapter 16, focusing especially on the racial impact of inequities between sentencing for crack cocaine versus powder cocaine.

The Eighth Amendment has been significant in the issue of the death penalty. Although many Americans regard capital punishment as "cruel and unusual," the Eighth Amendment does not prevent death sentences. Each state sets its own policies on capital punishment, including whether to use it at all. The Supreme Court has also upheld states' authority to choose their method of execution, despite claims that they cause immense suffering before killing the inmate.[58] Currently, thirty-one states have the death penalty, and seventeen states plus the District of Columbia do not. Since 2007 six states that had capital punishment (Connecticut, Illinois, Maryland, Nebraska, New Jersey, New Mexico, and New York) have abolished it. Governors in four states with capital punishment (Colorado, Oregon, Pennsylvania, and Washington) have imposed moratoriums on executions, but capital punishment still exists in those states, and future governors could reinstitute executions.[59]

TABLE 4.2 States with the Highest and Lowest Black Incarceration Rates (per 100,000 Population) and Percent Black Population (2014 Data)

Highest Black Incarceration Rate			Lowest Black Incarceration Rate		
State	Rate	Percent Black	State	Rate	Percent Black
Oklahoma	2,625		Hawaii	585	2.6
Wisconsin	2,542	6.6	Massachusetts	605	8.4
Vermont	2,357	1.3	Maine	839	1.4
Iowa	2,349	3.5	Maryland	862	30.5
Idaho	2,160	0.8	North Dakota	888	2.4
Arizona	2,126	4.8	New York	896	17.6
Oregon	2,061	2.1	Rhode Island	934	7.9
Montana	1,985	0.6	North Carolina	951	22.1
Colorado	1,891	4.5	South Carolina	1,030	27.6
Texas	1,844	12.5	Mississippi	1,052	37.6

Sources: Adapted from The Sentencing Project, "State-By-State Data: State Data Map," http://www .sentencingproject.org/the-facts#map?dataset-option=SIR; U.S. Census, "Quick Facts," https://www .census.gov/quickfacts/table/PST045215/00, both accessed April 29, 2016. Washington, DC, was not included in this analysis.

TABLE 4.3 States with the Highest and Lowest Latino Incarceration Rates (per 100,000 Population) and Percent Latino Population (2014 Data)

Highest Latino Incarceration Rate			Lowest Latino Incarceration Rate		
State	Rate	Percent Latino	State	Rate	Percent Latino
Arizona	842	30.7	Louisiana	34	5.0
Pennsylvania	668	6.8	Hawaii	75	10.4
Idaho	619	12.2	Florida	85	24.5
Colorado	587	21.3	Michigan	93	4.9
Connecticut	583	15.4	Maine	104	1.6
Wisconsin	563	6.6	Virginia	116	9.0
Texas	541	38.8	Alaska	148	7.0
Oklahoma	530	10.1	South Carolina	172	5.5
Wyoming	495	9.9	West Virginia	167	1.5
South Dakota	480	3.6	Tennessee	180	5.2

Sources: Adapted from The Sentencing Project, "State-By-State Data: State Data Map," http://www .sentencingproject.org/the-facts#map?dataset-option=SIR; U.S. Census, "Quick Facts," https://www.census.gov/ quickfacts/table/PST045215/00, both accessed April 29, 2016. Washington, DC, was not included in this analysis.

There is evidence that capital punishment is administered in a racially discriminatory fashion. In the late 1980s, social scientists uncovered evidence of two specific forms of racial discrimination in capital punishment. With all else held constant, Black defendants were more likely than White defendants to receive capital punishment, and prosecutors were far more likely to seek and receive death sentences in cases where the victim was White than in cases where the victim was Black.[60] However, the U.S. Supreme Court has ruled that statistical evidence of racial discrimination in capital punishment generally is insufficient by itself to invalidate the death sentence of any individual.[61] "Measuring Equality: Discrimination, Death Row Population, and Executions in States with the Death Penalty" addresses this issue in more detail.

Privacy

All the civil liberties discussed up to this point are mentioned specifically in one of the amendments in the Bill of Rights. However, the U.S. Supreme Court has extended protection to a civil liberty that is not explicitly mentioned in the Constitution: the right to privacy. This right refers to an individual's general right to be left alone, and although this right is not specifically mentioned

measuring equality

Discrimination, Death Row Population, and Executions in States with the Death Penalty

Many activists and scholars have uncovered evidence of racial disparities in capital sentencing patterns, in which minorities are more likely than Whites to receive a death sentence. These disparities could be the result of different crime patterns, disparate rates of arrest, prosecutorial discretion in seeking the death penalty, and the behavior of juries and judges in deciding sentences. Although we do not conclusively test these competing explanations here, we do address geographical variations in these disparities for Blacks and Latinos. Table 4.4 displays by state the percentage of the overall population that is Black, the percentage of the death row population that is Black, and the ratio of Blacks on death row to Blacks in the population. A ratio greater than 1:1 means that Blacks are sentenced to death in a proportion larger than their presence in the population, and a ratio less than

1:1 demonstrates that Blacks are sentenced to death in a proportion that is lower than their presence in the population. Additionally, Figure 4.1 shows for each region (North, South, Midwest, and West) the average ratio of Black composition on death row to Black population percentage.

What are some patterns among the different states? Is there significant variation among regions? Considering the regional history of discrimination against Blacks, are you surprised by those results?

We have conducted the same analysis for Latinos (see Table 4.5). Again, examine whether there is significant variation among the states and regions. Considering the regional history of discrimination against Latinos, are you surprised by those results? Do you notice any stark differences between the sentencing disparities for Blacks and the disparities for Latinos?

measuring equality (Continued)

TABLE 4.4 **Blacks on Death Row**

State	Percent of State Black	Percent of Death Row Black	Ratio Death Row/Population
North			
Delaware	22.2	61.1	2.75:1
Pennsylvania	11.6	53.3	4.59:1
Midwest			
Indiana	9.6	23.1	2.41:1
Kansas	6.3	30.0	4.76:1
Missouri	11.8	31.0	2.63:1
Nebraska	4.9	20.0	4.08:1
Ohio	12.6	53.1	4.21:1
Oklahoma	7.7	42.9	5.57:1
South			
Alabama	26.7	53.1	1.99:1
Arkansas	15.6	55.6	3.56:1
Florida	16.8	38.9	2.32:1
Georgia	31.5	50.0	1.59:1
Kentucky	8.2	17.6	2.15:1
Louisiana	32.5	66.7	2.05:1
Mississippi	37.5	54.2	1.45:1
North Carolina	22.1	51.6	2.33:1
South Carolina	27.8	53.5	1.92:1
Tennessee	17.0	46.5	2.74:1
Texas	12.5	41.4	3.31:1
Virginia	19.7	42.8	2.17:1
West			
Arizona	4.7	12.8	2.72:1
California	6.5	36.2	5.57:1
Colorado	4.5	100.0	22.22:1
Idaho	0.8	0.0	0.00:1
Montana	0.6	0.0	0.00:1
Nevada	9.1	36.7	4.03:1
New Mexico	2.1	0.0	0.00:1
Oregon	2.0	8.8	4.40:1
South Dakota	1.9	0.0	0.00:1
Utah	1.3	11.1	8.54:1
Washington	4.1	44.4	10.83:1
Wyoming	1.6	0.0	0.00:1

(Continued)

measuring equality *(Continued)*

TABLE 4.5 **Latinos on Death Row**

State	Percent of State Latino	Percent of Death Row Latino	Ratio Death Row/ Population
North			
Delaware	8.9	16.7	1.88:1
Pennsylvania	6.6	9.4	1.42:1
Midwest			
Indiana	6.6	0.0	0.00:1
Kansas	11.4	0.0	0.00:1
Missouri	4.0	0.0	0.00:1
Nebraska[a]	10.2	50.0	4.90:1
Ohio	3.5	2.1	0.60:1
Oklahoma	9.8	4.1	0.42:1
South			
Alabama	4.1	1.0	0.24:1
Arkansas	7.0	0.0	0.00:1
Florida	24.1	7..8	0.32:1
Georgia	9.3	3.8	0.41:1
Kentucky	3.4	0.0	0.00:1
Louisiana	4.8	3.7	0.77:1
Mississippi	3.0	0.0	0.00:1
North Carolina	9.0	2.8	0.31:1
South Carolina	5.4	2.3	0.43:1
Tennessee	4.8	1.4	0.29:1
Texas	38.6	27.8	0.72:1
Virginia	8.9	0.0	0.00:1
West			
Arizona	30.5	22.4	0.73:1
California	38.6	24.9	0.65:1
Colorado	21.2	0	0.00:1
Idaho	12.0	0.0	0.00:1
Montana	3.5	0.0	0.00:1
Nevada	27.8	11.4	0.41:1
New Mexico[a]	47.7	0.0	0.00:1
Oregon	12.5	8.8	0.70:1
South Dakota	3.6	0.0	0.00:1
Utah	13.5	22.2	1.64:1
Washington	12.2	0.0	0.00:1
Wyoming	9.8	0.0	0.00:1

[a] *Although these states have abolished capital punishment, people sentenced to death prior to the change in the law currently remain on death row.*

measuring equality *(Continued)*

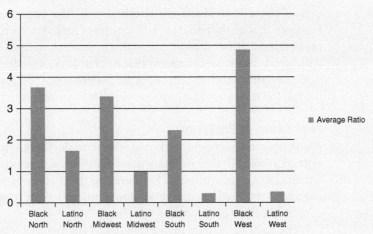

Figure 4.1 Average Ratio of Group Composition on Death Row to Group Composition of Population by Region (North, Midwest, South, and West) and Race (Black and Latino).

Sources: Adapted from Deborah Fins, Criminal Justice Project of the NAACP Legal Defense Fund, *Death Row, USA: Winter 2016*, 36–37, http://www.naacpldf.org/files/publications/DRUSA_Winter_2016.pdf, accessed April 30, 2016; U.S. Census Bureau, "State and County Quick Facts," https://www.census.gov/quickfacts/table/PST045215/00, accessed April 30, 2016.

in the Constitution, it is considered just as fundamental as the rights enumerated in the Constitution.

The right to privacy gives Americans a zone of control over personal life decisions, and this zone of control is immune from government intrusion. Because the legal definition of privacy is so vague, however, there is little agreement on how far this zone should extend. The debates over the right to privacy have been most acute regarding decisions affecting a person's own autonomy and reproductive freedom. These debates have also affected minority-group politics.

Personal Autonomy

One aspect of privacy concerns personal autonomy, the ability of individuals to control significant life decisions without government interference. Personal autonomy includes sexual relations between consenting adults, particularly same-sex couples. For most of American history, states were permitted to ban sexual activity between people of the same sex, and in the 1984 case of *Bowers v. Hardwick*, the U.S. Supreme Court upheld these laws as constitutional.[62]

After 1984, many states overturned such laws on their own, and those that kept the laws rarely enforced them. Nevertheless, in 1998 the state of Texas fined two males $200 each for engaging in sexual activity with each other. In the landmark 2003 *Lawrence v. Texas* decision, the U.S. Supreme Court overturned *Bowers v. Hardwick*, holding that laws banning consensual sexual activity between adults infringe on the individual's right to privacy.[63]

Right to Die An extension of the right to privacy that includes an individual's right to refuse life-saving medical treatment but does not include the right to commit suicide.

Another personal autonomy issue concerns the **right to die**. Most states possess some authority to prevent individuals from taking their own lives, even if those individuals are terminally ill. The Supreme Court has ruled, however, that an individual's right to privacy includes the right to refuse medical treatment either directly, through a spouse, or indirectly, through a living will, which is a legal document that directs doctors to discontinue treatment under certain circumstances when the patient is unconscious. Absent prior approval, the state's interest in preserving life outweighs the right to privacy.[64]

Reproductive Freedom

Challenges to state laws interfering with reproductive choice are crucial to the right to privacy. In the landmark case of *Griswold v. Connecticut* (1965), the U.S. Supreme Court overturned a law banning the dissemination of birth control because it violated an unwritten constitutional right to privacy that allows couples access to birth control.[65]

The right to privacy then extended to the issue of abortion. In the early 1970s, most states, including Texas, outlawed abortion. So when Jane Roe, a poor woman residing in Texas, was pregnant, she could not obtain an abortion. With the help of lawyers interested in legalizing abortion, Roe sued the state of Texas for the right to an abortion, and in the landmark case *Roe v. Wade* (1973), the U.S. Supreme Court extended the unwritten constitutional right of privacy to include a woman's control over her pregnancy. The right to an abortion is segmented into three trimesters (periods of three months each). In the first trimester, states have no authority to regulate abortions, but in the second trimester, states can regulate abortions to protect the mother's health. In the third trimester, when the fetus is most able to live outside the woman's womb, states are free to ban abortions in most instances.[66]

This decision generated tremendous controversy between the "pro-choice" view, which supports extending the right to privacy to a woman's control over her pregnancy, and the "pro-life" view, which believes that the government has the authority to protect the fetus in the womb. Pressured by influential groups that bill themselves as "pro-life," many states enacted laws that restricted abortions and made them more difficult to obtain. For example, many states require women to receive counseling before getting an abortion, impose a waiting period (up to twenty-four hours) before a woman can receive an abortion, and order minors to notify their parents or even seek parental consent before getting an abortion. Although the Supreme Court consistently upheld the right to an abortion, it allowed states to enact restrictions that limit that right.[67] Significant controversy continues to exist over attempts to enact restrictions on abortions. For example, in 2015 the United States House of Representatives passed a bill that would ban abortions after twenty weeks of pregnancy, but Democrats in the Senate prevented passages in that chamber.[68] Moreover, under the auspices of ensuring the safety of the procedures, about half of American states regulate abortion providers by: requiring abortions to be performed by clinics that have admitting privileges to hospitals, forcing

Abortion is a controversial political issue that generates considerable passion on both sides. Many people believe that life begins at conception; therefore, abortion is tantamount to murder. Others believe that the constitutional right to privacy protects a woman's decision to control her pregnancy.

clinics to be located within a prescribed distance from a hospital, and specifying the length and width of rooms and corridors in abortion clinics. Abortion rights supporters argue that these provisions are unnecessary for safety and are instead subtle ways to limit or eliminate access to abortion.[69] In late June of 2016 the U.S. Supreme Court overturned by a 5–3 vote Texas' restrictions on abortion, including a requirement that doctors have admitting privileges at a nearby hospital and regulations on the building. The majority ruled that these restrictions amounted to an "undue burden" on the right to abortion.[70]

Many of these restrictions accomplished their goals of reducing abortion access within states. For example, in the early 1990s Mississippi had twelve abortion clinics, but by 2005 only one clinic, in Jackson, remained.[71] The lack of abortion access adversely impacts low-income women, many of whom are racial or ethnic minorities, because it is more difficult for them to travel far distances to get an abortion. One study demonstrates that travel distance is more likely to decrease abortion access for Latina women compared to Black and White women.[72]

Attitudes about abortion also differ among different racial and ethnic groups. About half of women receiving abortions in the United States are white, and about 41 percent of women receiving abortions are African Americans.[73] Moreover, as Figure 4.2 shows, Latinos support abortion far less than do Whites and Blacks. The figure also demonstrates that White mainline

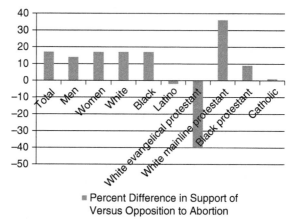

- Percent Difference in Support of
  Versus Opposition to Abortion

Figure 4.2 Differences in Support for Abortion by Group.
Source: Data adapted from the Pew Forum on Religion and Public Life, Public Opinion on Abortion: Views on Abortion, 1995–2016, April 8, 2016, http://www.pewforum.org/2016/04/08/public-opinion-on-abortion-2/, accessed May 1, 2016.

Protestants are more supportive of abortion rights than are Black Protestants, and men are slightly more supportive of abortions than are women. Additionally, a recent study shows that support for abortion varies among Latinos depends on religious identification. Catholic Latinos support abortion rights more than Fundamentalist Protestant Latinos do.[74]

Conclusion

Civil liberties are the constitutional freedoms that individuals enjoy and on which the government may not encroach, and they are a central component of the relationship between individuals and their government. The Bill of Rights specifies liberties, such as freedom of expression, freedom of religion, and freedom in the criminal justice process, and most provisions of the Bill of Rights apply to all levels of government. Additionally, since the 1960s the U.S. Supreme Court has read a right to privacy into the Bill of Rights.

Although civil liberties are spelled out in the Bill of Rights, their language is vague, ambiguous, and subject to individual interpretation. This chapter examined the specific civil liberties issues of political dissent, pornography and offensive speech, freedom of the press, separation of church and state, freedom to worship, protections for those accused of crimes, including right to counsel and right to jury trial, criminal sentencing policies, personal autonomy, and reproductive freedom.

The politics of race and ethnicity shapes controversies over civil liberties. Occasionally, civil liberties and racial equality can clash. Issues concerning the regulation of hate speech and cross burnings demonstrate the complexity of this conflict.

Racial and ethnic minorities have received less civil liberties protection than have Whites. Undoubtedly, civil liberties have been applied more equally since the founding of the American Republic, but key U.S. Supreme Court rulings, especially since the 1980s, have afforded federal, state, and local governments considerable discretion to decide civil liberties questions. As a result, many government actions have resulted in lower civil liberties for racial and ethnic minorities. For example, although American Indians' religious activities that involve illegal drug use are immune from prosecution, the group's religious practices are not fully protected. States are free to deny unemployment benefits to American Indians who are fired for engaging in religious ceremonies involving illegal drug use. Additionally, in some states the lack of abortion access affects minority women more than it affects White women.

Racial inequality in civil liberties is most pronounced in issues of criminal justice. Higher incarceration rates for minorities than for Whites and racial discrimination in capital punishment demonstrate that civil liberties are not uniformly applied across racial and ethnic groups. In many states, racial and ethnic minorities are underrepresented in public defender offices and on juries.

The story of racial profiling and the police shootings of African Americans, such as Walter Scott, clearly illustrate the intersection between race and ethnicity and civil liberties. For the protections of the Fourth and Fifth Amendments to have any meaning, they must be applied equally. Yet, law enforcement officers arbitrarily violated African Americans' civil liberties because of their ethnicity. In short, racial and ethnic politics greatly influences the extent to which civil liberties are fully enjoyed in the United States.

review
REVIEW QUESTIONS

1. To what extent does the First Amendment protect hate speech in general and cross burnings in particular?

2. How does the current interpretation of the free exercise clause affect Native Americans' freedom of worship?

3. What is racial profiling, and what Fourth Amendment questions does it raise?

4. To what extent are the fair trial guarantees of the Sixth Amendment fully applied to racial and ethnic minority groups? Focus specifically on limits on peremptory challenges and the measures some states have taken to ensure that public defenders are more responsive to the needs of minority defendants.

5. To what extent are there disproportionate criminal sentences for racial and ethnic minorities? Do those disparities also exist for capital punishment?

terms
KEY TERMS

Civil Liberties p. 101
Clear and Present Danger Test p. 105
Due Process Clause p. 104
Eminent Domain p. 104
Establishment Clause p. 110
Exclusionary Rule p. 113
Fighting Words p. 106

Fourteenth Amendment p. 104
Free Exercise Clause p. 111
Hate Speech p. 107
Incorporation p. 103
Libel p. 108
Miranda Rights p. 116
Peremptory Challenges p. 118

Prior Restraint p. 108
Probable Cause p. 113
Racial Profiling p. 101
Right to Die p. 126
Search Warrant p. 112
Selective Incorporation p. 104
Separation of Church and State p. 110

readings

ADDITIONAL READINGS

Jon B. Gould, *Speak No Evil: The Triumph of Hate Speech Regulation*. Chicago: University of Chicago Press, 2005.

This thorough study provides an empirical analysis of the reasons behind the adoption and continuation of hate speech regulation on college campuses.

Steve Holbert and Lisa Rose, *The Study of Guilt and Innocence: Racial Profiling and Police Practices in America*. San Ramon, CA: Page Marque Press, 2004.

This clearly argued and thoroughly researched book examines the issue of racial profiling and its long history in American law enforcement.

Carolyn N. Long, *Religious Freedom and Indian Rights: The Case of Oregon v. Smith*. Lawrence: University Press of Kansas, 2000.

This is a scholarly analysis of the Supreme Court's landmark ruling limiting religious liberty.

John Tehranian, *Whitewashed: America's Invisible Middle Eastern Minorities*. New York: New York University Press, 2009.

This book addresses racial profiling and discrimination against Middle Easterners in the United States, especially after the attacks of September 11, 2001.

Tram Nguyen, *We Are All Suspects Now: Untold Stories from Immigrant Communities After 9/11*. Boston: Beacon Press, 2005.

This book presents stories of immigrant families who were targeted by law enforcement after the attacks of September 11, 2001.

CHAPTER 5

Civil Rights: Inequality and Equality

Zaira Garcia hugs her father, who is an undocumented immigrant, despite the fact that Zaira is an American citizen because she was born in the United States. In 2014 President Obama issued an order that would have allowed Mr. Garcia to work in the United States without fear of deportation, but a federal judge halted the president's order. In 2016 the Supreme Court split 4–4 on the question of the legality of President Obama's order, which meant that the lower court ruling is upheld. Therefore, Mr. Garcia's legal status is still uncertain.

Z aira Garcia is a female college graduate who lives in Austin, Texas, and similar to many people her age, she has a close relationship with her parents. However, unlike most other Americans her age, Ms. Garcia's relationship with her parents is in jeopardy because of a legal issue. In the late 1980s her parents entered the United States illegally, and despite the barriers that he faced as an undocumented immigrant, Mr. Garcia was able to use his carpentry skills to build a home and provide for his family, which includes Zaira and her three sisters. Because Zaira and her sisters were born in Texas, they are American citizens and enjoy all the benefits that citizenship provides. However, her parents' presence in the United States is illegal; therefore, they face deportation and separation from their children at any time. In fact, Mr. Garcia was deported in 1995, but he was able to illegally reenter the United States again. However, undocumented immigrants who illegally reenter the United States are subject to lengthy prison terms if they are recaptured. Therefore, now Mr. Garcia fears a fate worse than deportation. In the meantime, because he is undocumented, Mr. Garcia has been exploited by some of the people who have hired him. If a client fails to pay the agreed fee for Mr. Garcia's work, then because of his undocumented status, Mr. Garcia has no legal recourse to seek recompense.[1]

For many years immigration activists wanted Congress to amend the nation's immigration laws to allow undocumented parents with American citizen children the ability to stay in the United States legally. However, Congress failed to address this issue; therefore, in November of 2014 President Obama issued an executive order entitled Deferred Action for Parental Accountability (DAPA). Under DAPA, undocumented immigrants who have children legally living in the United States and have not been convicted of a crime are permitted to apply to work legally in the United States. In short, DAPA provided help for more than four million people in the same situation as Zaira Garcia's parents.[2] However, soon after President Obama announced his plan twenty-six states (all with Republican governors) challenged the act in federal court, arguing that the president lacks the authority to create the DAPA policy and is instead required to enforce the immigration laws that currently exist. In February 2015 a federal district court judge issued a preliminary injunction preventing President Obama from implementing DAPA, which was later upheld by a federal appeals court. In 2016 the U.S. Supreme Court agreed to hear the case, but only eight justices were able to rule because of the death of Justice Antonin Scalia. The Court's ruling was split evenly 4–4, and because tie votes uphold the lower court's decision, the Court prevented President Obama from implementing DAPA.[3]

intro

The issue of undocumented immigrants has emerged as one of the most controversial civil rights issues in recent years. In 2014, there were an estimated 11.3 million unauthorized immigrants living in the United States, and about 49 percent of them are from Mexico. While the number of undocumented immigrants in the United States had grown from 8.4 million in 2000, it had actually shrunk from a record high of 12.2 million in 2007.[4] Many of these undocumented immigrants work in menial jobs in the hotel, restaurant, construction, and agricultural industries, and although they are valuable to the economy, a considerable number of Americans resent their presence in the United States because of their unauthorized status; they believe illegal immigrants take jobs from legal workers and cause violence. Presidential candidate Donald Trump based much of his 2016 presidential campaign stoking the anti-illegal immigration feelings that many Americans hold. The fact that families like the Garcias have undocumented parents with American citizen children complicates this debate.

*The story of Zaira Garcia and controversies over undocumented immigrants typify the politics of **civil rights**, which are the protections against unequal treatment that the government guarantees to all groups. Throughout American history, many people have been, and in some cases still are, treated unfairly because of their race, national origin, gender, or sexual orientation. Improvement in civil rights has been gradual and intermittent for many groups, with some groups receiving more protections than others.*

Civil rights progress is initiated when the victims of the discrimination form organizations that actively seek equality through social change, and governments respond by gradually protecting those victims from unfair treatment. The extent of civil rights success varies across different groups. The politics of civil rights is dynamic and complex in terms of defining discrimination and determining the ultimate outcome. Moreover, as this story demonstrates, various institutions of government—the president, Congress, and the federal courts, and state governments—play a key role in shaping civil rights policy, often in conflict with each other.

Although we address issues of race and ethnicity throughout this book, this chapter focuses specifically on the politics of civil rights. First, we define terms and explain concepts that are essential to understanding civil rights. Then we address the civil rights struggles of African Americans, Latinos, Asian Americans, American Indians, women, the lesbian, gay, bisexual, and transgendered (LGBT) community, the elderly, and people with disabilities.

Civil Rights The protections against unequal treatment that the government guarantees to all groups.

Civil Rights Terms and Concepts

Prior to our discussion of civil rights, we must first define the terms and concepts that frame civil rights politics. Although many of the terms appear familiar, their meanings are subtle and demand precise explanation. Three concepts especially relevant to civil rights are group designation, forms of inequality, and segregation.

Group Designation

Group designation, or the classification of a set of people based on defined criteria, is a fluid concept that is particularly relevant in the examination of civil rights. A significant group demarcation is **race**, which is the classification of people based on physical characteristics, especially skin color. People often mistakenly believe that race is determined biologically, but, in fact, it is socially constructed. The designation of a person's race in the United States has historically been decided by American society's desire to exclude groups of people from participation in the social and political life of the nation. For example, until the middle of the twentieth century, many states wrote laws designating the degree of Black ancestry necessary to be legally classified as Black. Louisiana and North Carolina used the one-sixteenth criterion (one great-great-grandparent), but most states used a one-eighth standard (if at least one great-grandparent was Black, a person was legally considered to be Black).[5]

> **Race** A socially constructed classification of people based on their physical characteristics, especially skin color.

Determining precise racial classification can be difficult because an increasing number of people identify themselves as belonging to more than one race. For example, musician Bruno Mars, whose birth name is Peter Gene Hernandez, has a father who is Puerto Rican and European and a mother who is Filipino and Puerto Rican.[6] Table 5.1 demonstrates the fluid categorizations for race used by the U.S. Census throughout American history.

> **Ethnicity** A socially constructed classification of people based on national origin or culture.

Another concept used to indicate group status is **ethnicity**, or classification based on national origin or culture. Although many people use the terms race and ethnicity interchangeably, the two words are distinct. People of different ethnicities are often members of the same race. For example, Italian Americans and Irish Americans are White in terms of race but are of different ethnicities. Likewise, people of different races may be of the same ethnicity. Some Latinos, a classification based on ethnicity, are White, whereas others are Black, Asian, or American Indian. The 2010 U.S. Census blurred the distinction between race and ethnicity by designating White, Black, Asian American, Indian or Alaskan Native, Chinese, Japanese, and Hawaiian, and other Pacific islanders as different racial categories, but it considered Latino an ethnicity. Some argue that Judaism is an ethnicity because there is a shared immigrant-based culture, but others maintain that Judaism is a religion, not an ethnicity, especially because there are different ethnic groups that adhere to the religion.[7] As with race, classifications based on ethnicity have been a significant basis for unequal treatment throughout American history.

TABLE 5.1 Racial Categories Used by the U.S. Census, 1790–2010

Year	Categories
1790	Free Whites, other free persons, and slaves
1800, 1810	Free Whites, other free persons (except Indians not taxed), and slaves
1820	Free Whites, slaves, free colored persons, and other persons (except Indians not taxed)
1830, 1840	Free White persons, slaves, and free colored persons
1850	White, Black, and mulatto
1860	White, Black, mulatto, and Indian
1870, 1880	White, Black, mulatto, Chinese, and Indian
1890	White, Black, mulatto, quadroon, octaroon, Chinese, Japanese, and Indian
1900	White, Black, Chinese, Japanese, and Indian
1910	White, Black, mulatto, Chinese, Japanese, Indian, and other
1920	White, Black, mulatto, Indian, Chinese, Japanese, Filipino, Hindu, Korean, and other
1930	White, Negro, Mexican, Indian, Chinese, Japanese, Filipino, Hindu, Korean, and other
1940	White, Negro, Indian, Chinese, Japanese, Filipino, Hindu, Korean, and other
1950	White, Negro, Indian, Japanese, Chinese, Filipino, and other
1960	White, Negro, American Indian, Japanese, Chinese, Filipino, Hawaiian, part Hawaiian, Aleut, and Eskimo
1970	White, Negro or Black, American Indian, Japanese, Chinese, Filipino, Hawaiian, Korean, and other
1980	White, Negro, Japanese, Chinese, Filipino, Korean, Vietnamese, American Indian, Asian Indian, Hawaiian, Guamanian, Samoan, Eskimo, Aleut, and other
1990	White, Black, American Indian, Eskimo, Aleut, Chinese, Filipino, Hawaiian, Korean, Vietnamese, Japanese, Asian Indian, Guamanian, other Pacific Islander, and other
2000	White, Black/African American/Negro, American Indian or Alaskan Native, Asian Indian, Chinese, Filipino, other Asian, Hawaiian, Guamanian or Chomorro, Samoan, other Pacific Islander, other, and some other race (individuals who consider themselves multiracial can choose two or more races)
2010	White, Black/African American/Negro, American Indian or Alaskan Native, Asian Indian, Japanese, Native Hawaiian, Chinese, Korean, Guamanian or Chomorro, Filipino, Vietnamese, Samoan, Other Asian, Other Pacific Islander, Some other race

Sources: Adapted from National Research Council, Measuring Racial Discrimination: Panel on Methods for Assessing Discrimination *(Washington, DC: National Academies Press, 2004), 31; United States Census 2010, "Census Form: Question 6, What is this person's race?" http://www.censusquestions.com/2010-us-census-form.pdf, accessed May 22, 2016.*

Gender Social relations between the sexes and attitudes about how the sexes interact and the roles that society assumes they will play.

Another group demarcation is **gender**, which refers to social classifications based on sex. Whereas sex is determined biologically (i.e., one is born male or female), gender refers to the social ramifications of distinctions between male and female. Students learning a foreign language, such as French or Spanish, are familiar with the concept of gender whereby some words are designated masculine and others are designated feminine. Gender has legal and political connotations because governments and private entities have denied women the same opportunities as men. Additionally, gender identity plays a significant role in civil rights politics because people who are transgender identify with a different gender than what they were assigned at birth. Transgendered people can often be subject to humiliating forms of discrimination, which we discuss later in the chapter.

Forms of Inequality

Inequality The extent to which one group enjoys more political, social, or economic benefits than another group.

Inequality of Opportunity A form of inequality in which laws or official actions deny specific groups social, political, or economic benefits that are available to other groups.

Inequality of Outcome A form of inequality in which social and demographic forces, not official laws or policies, cause one group to enjoy more political, social, or economic benefits than another group.

At the core of civil rights politics is the concept of **inequality**—that is, the extent to which one group enjoys more political, social, or economic benefits than another group. **Inequality of opportunity** exists when laws or official government actions deny specific groups social, political, and economic benefits that are available to other groups. With inequality of opportunity a dominant group controls the government and uses that authority to mistreat subordinate groups based on their characteristics. For example, until the twentieth century, many state laws, written by exclusively male lawmakers, discriminated against women by denying them the opportunity to pursue certain professions, vote, or own property. Conversely, **inequality of outcome** is a form of inequality in which social and demographic forces, not laws or official actions, cause one group to enjoy more political and economic benefits than another group. Because the dominant group does not explicitly use governmental authority to discriminate or deny opportunities to the subordinate group, redressing inequality of outcome is murky and controversial. For example, as we discuss later in this chapter, women on average earn less money than men for the same jobs. This inequality does not stem from official government policies; in fact, there are laws that prevent some types of salary discrimination against women.

Segregation

Segregation Physical separation of a dominant group from a subordinate group.

Another concept important for civil rights is **segregation**, in which a dominant group physically separates itself from a subordinate group. Some religious groups, such as the Amish or Hasidic Jews, choose to segregate themselves, but the vast majority of segregation results from the dominant group seeking to separate itself from the subordinate group. For example, when Southern White society insisted on segregating public schools through the 1960s, they operated on the belief that Black children were inferior and should not associate with their White children. Many Southern Whites even expressed fears that Blacks and Whites going to school together could lead to them dating and even procreating with one another. Segregation almost

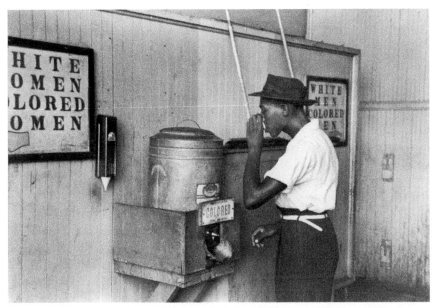

During the era of Jim Crow segregation and before the Civil Rights Act, Blacks and Whites were forced to use different restrooms and drink from different fountains.

always results in unequal enjoyment of political, social, and economic benefits. In the segregated South, Black schools received far less public money and were provided with lower quality facilities compared to White schools.

Segregation that occurs as the result of law or official government action is known as **de jure segregation**. An example of de jure segregation existed when state laws mandated separate schools for Black children and White children, which, as we explain later in this chapter, wrought terrible hardships on African Americans.

Segregation that occurs through natural forces or results from social practice is called **de facto segregation**. Thus, de facto segregation is neither legally sanctioned nor government imposed. For example, despite the elimination of laws and policies establishing segregated schools, many schools today are still overwhelmingly White, Black, or Latino because economic forces and individual preferences have resulted in housing patterns that separate people by race or ethnicity.

De Jure Segregation Physical separation of groups that results from laws or official government actions.

De Facto Segregation Physical separation of groups that is not legally sanctioned or imposed by the government but instead stems from individual preferences and economic forces.

Race, Ethnicity, and Civil Rights

Although civil rights encompasses a wide variety of groups, the plurality of civil rights issues concern race and ethnicity. A vast number of racial and ethnic groups have experienced discrimination and segregation, but a single chapter cannot adequately cover them all. Therefore, this section focuses on the most significant—African Americans, Latinos, Asian Americans, and

American Indians. Each story involves inequality and segregation, the formation of political movements to improve civil rights, and significant, yet incomplete, civil rights progress.

Blacks

Because Blacks have traditionally suffered the most from discrimination, their struggle has exerted the most significant impact on civil rights in the United States throughout the entire course of American history. The story of Black civil rights is one marked by extreme mistreatment with a slow, gradual increase in the enjoyment of civil rights. Currently, the vestiges of *de jure* discrimination and segregation have vanished, but civil rights issues still remain for African Americans.

Enslavement of Blacks. Africans were first brought to the Western Hemisphere as slaves during the 1600s to meet labor shortages in the burgeoning agricultural industries. Enslaved Africans living in the American colonies enjoyed no civil rights, and although some Blacks did become free, colonial governments did not regard free Blacks as equal to Whites.

Even during the American Revolution, when political leaders espoused principles of liberty and equality for all, the tradition of exclusion, which was based on Whites' views that Blacks were inferior, denied Blacks fundamental rights. An original draft of the Declaration of Independence reprimanded the King of England for his role in the slave trade, but the authors struck this

One of the most despicable aspects of the slave trade was dividing families, even separating parents from their children.

clause from the final document because many of the delegates to the Continental Congress, including Thomas Jefferson, owned slaves.[8]

After the establishment of the American Republic, the U.S. Constitution did not give any rights to slaves or free Blacks; each state determined its own policy on civil rights. By the early nineteenth century, Northern states had abolished slavery, and some laws in Northern states actually protected Blacks' civil rights. For example, in the early 1780s courts in Massachusetts no longer recognized the legality of slavery, and as a result slaves successfully sued for freedom.

But it was still the case that free Blacks were denied basic civil rights in Northern states. In fact, free Blacks could vote only in the states of New York, Rhode Island, Massachusetts, Maine, Vermont, and New Hampshire, and even in those states Blacks were subject to segregation and unequal treatment. Because the economies of Southern states still relied heavily on slave labor, their laws explicitly recognized the existence of slavery and the property rights of slaveholders. Blacks had absolutely no civil rights in the South.[9]

Although slavery was not controversial during the founding era, by the early nineteenth century slavery had emerged as a contentious issue. A growing number of people concentrated in the Middle Atlantic and New England states where slavery was not central to the economy, known as **abolitionists**, morally opposed slavery. Abolitionists advocated laws to end or restrict slavery, and many of them actively helped to free slaves.

Abolitionists Nineteenth-century political activists who sought to end slavery.

Nineteenth-century laws in Northern states reflected the abolitionists' hostility toward slavery. For example, many Northern states criminally banned Southern slaveholders from entering their boundaries to capture runaway slaves. However, the U.S. Supreme Court in 1842 ruled in *Prigg v. Pennsylvania* that the U.S. Constitution, federal laws, and slaveholders' property rights superseded the authority of states seeking to protect runaway slaves and punish slave catchers.[10]

As the nation expanded westward during the nineteenth century, debates over slavery in the new territories exacerbated the rancor between pro- and antislavery forces. The Northwest Ordinance of 1787 banned slavery in newly annexed territory, which eventually became the states of Ohio, Indiana, Illinois, Michigan, Wisconsin, and parts of Minnesota. By the early nineteenth century, conflicts between Northerners and Southerners arose over whether to admit new states as slave states or free states. The Missouri Compromise of 1820 allowed Missouri to enter as a slave state as long as Maine could enter as a free state, and the compromise set a latitudinal boundary, north of which slavery was prohibited and south of which slavery was permitted. However, in 1854 the Kansas and Nebraska Act allowed the citizens (i.e., White males) of the territories of Kansas and Nebraska to determine for themselves whether to allow slavery, even though both territories were north of the boundary where slavery should have been prohibited.

Dred Scott v. Sandford
A controversial 1857 Supreme Court decision that ruled Congress lacked power to regulate slavery and Blacks had no civil rights.

By the late 1850s, debates over slavery had become too intractable to reconcile. The 1857 U.S. Supreme Court case of **Dred Scott v. Sandford** concerned a Missouri slave (Dred Scott) who tried to sue for his freedom in Illinois—a free state. Chief Justice Roger Taney ruled that Congress had no authority to ban slavery in the territories and that because Blacks were not citizens of the United States, they could not sue in federal court.[11] This controversial decision prevented Congress from regulating slavery, and it denied fundamental civil rights to Blacks. The *Dred Scott* decision was a leading contributing factor to the Civil War.

The Civil War and Reconstruction. The Civil War initiated minor and usually unenforced improvements in civil rights for African Americans. In 1862, President Abraham Lincoln established the **Emancipation Proclamation** as the first federal policy offering civil rights for Blacks. This executive order freed all slaves in the Confederacy as of January 1, 1863. Of course, because the war still raged, the federal government did not have jurisdiction over the rebellious states, and the proclamation did not affect the few Union states that retained vestiges of slavery (Maryland, Delaware, Kentucky, West Virginia, and Missouri). After the South lost the Civil War, the ratification of the **Thirteenth Amendment** to the U.S. Constitution in 1865 officially forbade slavery throughout the United States.

Although the Thirteenth Amendment ended slavery, discrimination against African Americans still existed. Most notably, former Confederate states passed **Black Codes**, which singled out African Americans for mistreatment and discrimination. See "Our Voices: South Carolina's Black Codes" for a more complete discussion of this issue. In response to these codes, Congress proposed the **Fourteenth Amendment**, which was ratified in 1868. This amendment was designed to ensure that states gave former slaves full citizenship rights.

In Chapter 4, we discussed the due process clause of the Fourteenth Amendment, which prevents states from denying any resident life, liberty, or property without following normal criminal and judicial procedures. The Fourteenth Amendment contains an analogous clause: the **equal protection clause**, which requires state laws to treat all people equally regardless of their race or ethnicity. Additionally, to address voting discrimination, the **Fifteenth Amendment**, ratified in 1870, prohibited voting discrimination on account of race.

Immediately following the Civil War, the period of Reconstruction provided hope for supporters of Black civil rights. **Reconstruction** refers to the period from 1865 to 1877 in which a set of policies brought the former rebellious Confederate states back into the Union. Congress directed Reconstruction, and because former abolitionists and Republican supporters of civil rights controlled Congress, Reconstruction initially punished White Southerners and insisted on civil rights for African Americans. For example, Congress sought to ensure a livelihood for former slaves by creating the Freedman's Bureau, which provided former slaves with land, food, and education.[12]

More important, Congress passed the Civil Rights Act of 1870, the Civil Rights Act of 1871, and the Civil Rights Act of 1875, which enforced the

Emancipation Proclamation An executive order issued by President Abraham Lincoln during the Civil War that freed the slaves in the Confederacy.

Thirteenth Amendment An amendment to the Constitution that prohibits slavery throughout the United States.

Black Codes Laws passed in Southern states during the immediate aftermath of the Civil War that singled out African Americans for mistreatment and discrimination.

Fourteenth Amendment An amendment to the Constitution that prevents states from denying on the basis of race full citizenship to their residents.

Equal Protection Clause A specific provision in the Fourteenth Amendment that prevents states from passing laws that treat people differently on account of race or ethnicity.

Fifteenth Amendment An amendment to the Constitution that prevents states from denying the right to vote on the basis of race or ethnicity.

Reconstruction The period from 1865 to 1877 in which former Confederate states were brought back into the Union, often characterized by a military presence in the South and civil rights progress for Blacks.

our voices

South Carolina's Black Codes

Although the Thirteenth Amendment ended slavery throughout the United States, Southern states passed laws, known as Black Codes, to regulate the conduct of newly freed African Americans. Black Codes regulated many aspects of African Americans' lives, including terms of employment and personal relationships, and they were based on the view that the former slaves were inherently inferior to Whites. Specifically, Black Codes mandated that any orphaned, homeless, or unemployed Black person could be forced to work as an apprentice. They required that any African American choosing to own a business or pursue a career as an artisan had to pay a fee, seek a license, and serve as an apprentice.

Supporters of Black Codes claimed that they were necessary to integrate the former slaves into a postwar society, but opponents challenged that claim, arguing that the imposed apprenticeship reestablished a system of servitude. The Fourteenth Amendment to the Constitution overturned all Black Codes.

Here are excerpts from South Carolina's Black Code. Note the difference between the rules for males versus females, which reflect the blatant gender discrimination of the time period.

> Be it enacted by the Senate and House of Representatives . . .
>
> VII. . . . Marriage between a white person and a person of color, shall be illegal and void. . . .
>
> IX. The marriage of an apprentice shall not, without consent of the master, be lawful. . . .
>
> XV. A child over the age of two years, born of a colored parent, may be bound by the father, if he is living in the District, or in the case of his death or his absence from the District, by the mother, as an apprentice, to any respectable white or colored person, who is competent, to make a contract—a male until he shall attain the age of twenty-one years and a

female until she shall attain the age of eighteen years. . . .

XXIII. The master shall have authority to inflict moderate chastisement and impose reasonable restraint upon his apprentice, and to recapture him if he departs from his service.

XLV. On farms or in out-door service, the hours of labor, except on Sunday, shall be from sun-rise to sun-set, with a reasonable interval for breakfast and dinner. . . . The servant shall be careful of all the animals and instruments used by him, shall protect the same from injury by other persons, and shall be answerable for all property lost, destroyed or injured by his negligence, dishonesty or bad faith. . . .

XLVI. . . . Servants shall be quiet and orderly in their quarters . . . and retire to rest at reasonable hours. . . .

LXXII. No person of color shall pursue or practice the art, trade or business of an artisan, mechanic or shopkeeper, or any other trade of employment or a business (besides that of husbandry, or that of a servant under contract for services or labor) on his own account or for his own benefit . . . until he shall have obtained a license therefore from the Judge of the District Court. . . .

XCVII. . . . The District Judge or a Magistrate shall issue a warrant for the arrest of any person of color known or believed to be a vagrant. . . . On conviction, the defendant shall be liable to imprisonment, and to hard labor. . . .

XCVIII. The defendant, if sentenced to labor after conviction, may, by order of the District Judge or Magistrate, before whom he was convicted, be hired for such wages as can be obtained for his services. . . .

Source: Adapted from Albert P. Blaustein and Robert L. Zangrando, *Civil Rights and the Black American: A Documentary History* (New York: Clarion, 1970), 217–225.

Fourteenth and Fifteenth Amendments by criminalizing interference with the lawful exercise of civil rights, such as voting and using public accommodations. Because the Union Army maintained a strong presence in the South during Reconstruction, these laws were strictly enforced. As a result of Reconstruction, African Americans voted, whereas former Confederate soldiers could not. Consequently, many Blacks were elected to local, state, and federal offices.

The Era of Segregation and Discrimination. Despite the promise of Reconstruction, the initial progress toward full civil rights for African Americans was short-lived. The disputed election of 1876 marked the beginning of the end of Reconstruction when Republican presidential candidate Rutherford B. Hayes promised some Southern states that if he received their electoral votes, he would withdraw federal troops from the South. When Hayes assumed office in 1877, he fulfilled his promise to remove troops and effectively ended Reconstruction.[13] Without the military presence enforcing civil rights laws, states were free to discriminate against Blacks. States passed **Jim Crow laws**, which segregated all public facilities, such as transportation, schools, libraries, hotels, hospitals, theaters, parks, and cemeteries. The name Jim Crow came from a figure in a well-known nineteenth-century traveling minstrel show, in which a White actor depicted extremely offensive stereotypes of African Americans.[14]

Black leaders sought to challenge segregation in federal court. In 1892, Homer Plessy, who was one-eighth Black, refused to sit in the "colored only" section of a train leaving New Orleans, Louisiana. He was arrested, convicted, and fined for violating Louisiana's segregation law. Plessy then appealed to the Supreme Court, arguing that Jim Crow laws violated the Fourteenth Amendment. In the infamous *Plessy v. Ferguson* case of 1896, the Court ruled against Plessy and upheld Jim Crow laws, arguing that the Fourteenth Amendment equal protection clause permitted segregation as long as the facilities provided for each race were equal. The Court thereby established the **separate but equal principle**, which sanctioned segregating African Americans as long as they were given the same facilities granted to Whites.[15]

By the beginning of the twentieth century, Blacks were treated as second-class citizens. In addition to living under a strictly segregated system, African Americans suffered severe economic discrimination. Despite the claims of the "equal" in "separate but equal," states spent three times more per capita on education for White students than for Black students, and as a result Black schools were overcrowded, unsanitary, and staffed with poorly trained and underpaid teachers. Only rarely would White-owned companies hire Blacks, and even Black professionals, such as doctors, found limited opportunities. To make matters worse, terrorist organizations such as the Ku Klux Klan intimidated Blacks with violence. Between 1900 and 1920, an average of sixty-seven African Americans were lynched per year.[16]

Another form of discrimination against African Americans concerned **disenfranchisement**, or denial of the right to vote. In 1876, the U.S. Supreme Court ruled that Congress lacked jurisdiction to regulate state and local elections,[17] which allowed states to enact policies intended to disenfranchise African Americans in those elections. Blacks attempting to register to vote in Southern states faced **literacy tests**, which were seemingly race-neutral but were administered in a blatantly discriminatory fashion. For example, Whites

Jim Crow Laws The southern practice of racially segregating all public facilities, such as transportation, schools, libraries, hotels, hospitals, theaters, parks, and cemeteries.

Plessy v. Ferguson
A controversial 1896 Supreme Court decision that ruled that under the Fourteenth Amendment, states were allowed to segregate by race.

Separate but Equal Principle A legal principle that allowed states to segregate the races in public facilities, as long as the state provided each race with basic access to the public facility in question.

Disenfranchisement
A government denying a group the right to vote.

Literacy Tests A form of disenfranchisement in which potential voters need to demonstrate the ability to read as a condition for registering to vote.

would be given simple reading tests, whereas Blacks were required to read and understand complicated provisions in the state constitution. Moreover, White local government officials graded Blacks much more harshly than they graded Whites. **Grandfather clauses** exempted people from literacy tests who had been able to vote at the end of the Civil War, which obviously applied only to Whites and not to Blacks. **Poll taxes**—fees assessed on people registering to vote—contributed to African American disenfranchisement because Blacks were less likely than Whites to be able to afford those fees. African Americans even suffered from Ku Klux Klan terrorist intimidation when they attempted to register to vote.

Grandfather Clauses A policy designed to disenfranchise Blacks by exempting Whites, but not Blacks, from literacy tests.

Poll Taxes Fees that states charged citizens to vote and that disenfranchised the poor and minority citizens.

As a result of these disenfranchisement techniques, Black voter registration in the South was extremely low. As late as 1962, only 13.4 percent of African Americans in Alabama and 6.7 percent in Mississippi were registered to vote, despite the fact that 30.0 percent of the total population of Alabama and 42.0 percent of the total population of Mississippi were Black.[18] Because Blacks made up such a small percentage of the electorate, they could not elect political leaders who would address their political, social, and economic concerns.

The Civil Rights Era. By the middle of the twentieth century, civil rights prospects for Blacks improved. A key turning point in civil rights history was World War II. First, the war highlighted the contradiction between the American war against racial, ethnic, and religious hatred in Europe on the one hand and the atrocious treatment of African Americans in the United States on the other hand.[19] In addition, an economic perspective emphasizes the fact that during the war the government's need for massive increases in industrial production improved Black employment in factories, but Black employees soon clashed with White business leaders and employees. To prevent these conflicts from disrupting the war effort, the government enacted policies that protected African American workers. For example, the government banned defense companies receiving federal money from employment discrimination based on race, and it created the Fair Employment Practices Committee to enforce this order.[20]

Interest groups and social movements were extremely critical in establishing more significant civil rights progress. In the early twentieth century, civil rights activists formed groups to lobby the national government to end de jure segregation, terrorist violence, and inequality of opportunity. The most significant group was the National Association for the Advancement of Colored People (NAACP), which was established in 1909 to pressure national, state, and local governments to increase political and economic equality, end segregation, and ensure voting rights.[21]

NAACP leaders recognized that because legislatures and executives were accountable only to the White electorate, those branches of government would be unreceptive to NAACP claims. Accordingly, the NAACP concentrated its resources on providing the financial and intellectual sponsorship of litigation in the federal judiciary, where legal argument, not the will of the majority, influences outcomes. The organization was successful in the 1915 case of *Guinn and Beal v. United States*, in which the Supreme Court ruled that grandfather clauses violated the Fifteenth Amendment.[22] Sponsoring litigation became such an integral part of the NAACP that in 1940 the NAACP formed an entirely separate litigating organization known as the NAACP Legal Defense and Education Fund (LDF) to focus solely on litigating, while the main NAACP would concentrate more on lobbying.[23]

The most significant of the cases that the LDF litigated is ***Brown v. Board of Education***, the 1954 U.S. Supreme Court decision that overruled the principle of "separate but equal" and prohibited states from segregating schools on account of race. In the Court's opinion, Chief Justice Earl Warren wrote: "We conclude that in the field of public education the doctrine of 'separate but equal' has no place. Separate educational facilities are inherently unequal."[24] For the first time since the 1870s, the national government imposed on the states meaningful civil rights requirements. Despite the significance of the *Brown v. Board of Education* ruling, segregation and discrimination persisted. Most Southern school districts continued to segregate schools until the late 1950s and early 1960s when Presidents Dwight Eisenhower and John Kennedy deployed armed forces to ensure the safety of African American students entering formerly segregated schools. The *Brown v. Board of Education* decision was limited in expanding civil rights because it did not address

Brown v. Board of Education A landmark 1954 Supreme Court case that prohibited government-sponsored segregation as a violation of the Fourteenth Amendment equal protection clause.

Rosa Parks sitting on a bus in Montgomery, Alabama. In 1955, Ms. Parks refused to relinquish her seat to a White rider, despite the city rule that Blacks needed to sit in the back of the bus. Her arrest sparked a boycott of the Montgomery bus system, which ultimately was a catalyst for the Civil Rights Movement of the 1950s and 1960s.

discrimination by private businesses, such as transportation facilities, hotels, and restaurants.

Civil rights leaders recognized that litigation alone would not be a successful strategy for dealing with those forms of discrimination, and they organized a variety of protest strategies, including boycotts of the facilities that discriminated against African Americans. The most notable boycott was the Montgomery bus boycott, which was spawned by the arrest of Rosa Parks for her refusal to relinquish her seat to a White passenger in 1955. Instead of riding the bus, Blacks in Montgomery walked, carpooled, or found other means of transportation in the hopes of depriving the bus company of the critical revenue it earned from African American patrons.

Sit-ins, where Black patrons refused to move from the White section of restaurants and other public accommodations, were another form of nonviolent resistance. The most significant sit-in took place in 1960, when four Black college students refused to disperse from a Whites-only lunch counter in Greensboro, North Carolina. The national press publicized the protest, and over the next month sit-ins were launched throughout the country.

Sit-in A form of protest against segregated restaurants in which Black patrons refused to move from Whites-only sections.

Large marches were another form of nonviolent protest. They enabled civil rights leaders to show the American public and the country's political leaders the extent of intense opposition to discrimination. The most significant march was the August 1963 March on Washington, which drew more than 200,000 Americans of all races and ethnicities; numerous civil rights organizations, labor unions, and religious groups participated as well. At the culmination of the march, civil rights leader Dr. Martin Luther King, Jr. delivered his famous and inspirational "I Have a Dream" speech. Television coverage of the March on Washington introduced Americans to the Civil Rights Movement and helped to shift public opinion in favor of meaningful federal civil rights legislation.

As a result of the protests, increasing public pressure, and the political skills of President Lyndon Johnson, Congress passed the landmark **Civil Rights Act of 1964** to end segregation and discrimination in the private sector. Specifically, the law prohibited discrimination and segregation in public accommodations, even privately owned hotels and restaurants; allowed the president to deny funds to federal agencies, states, and localities that discriminated on account of race or ethnicity; and required the Justice Department to bring legal action against school districts that still resisted desegregation. The law also prevented employers from discriminating on account of race or ethnicity in hiring, firing, or promotion decisions.

Civil Rights Act of 1964 A federal law that prevented private businesses from discriminating in service and personnel policies.

Congress also passed the **Voting Rights Act of 1965**, which empowered the federal government to supervise voting in states and localities to guarantee voting rights for African Americans. As discussed in Chapter 3, the law invalidated voting procedures designed to discriminate, including literacy tests. The law allowed federal officials to assume control over voter registration in jurisdictions where there had been voting discrimination, and the act required any locality with a history of voting discrimination to obtain

Voting Rights Act of 1965 A federal law that significantly curtailed disenfranchisement of racial and ethnic minorities by banning literacy tests and requiring federal supervision of jurisdictions with a history of voting discrimination.

This photo from the historic 1963 March on Washington exemplifies the goals of the Civil Rights Movement during the 1960s. Media coverage of this march demonstrated to the American public and political leaders the seriousness of racial discrimination and the widespread support to end it.

permission from the U.S. Department of Justice before changing any aspect of their voting practices. The Justice Department would ensure that the changes were not intended to weaken minority voting. However, as we discussed in Chapter 3, the 2013 Supreme Court decision in *Shelby County v. Holder* invalidated the formula used to determine which jurisdictions were subject to preclearance.[25]

The Voting Rights Act of 1965 quickly increased Black voting participation. Black voter registration in the South increased from 38 percent in 1965 to 65 percent by 1969, and in Mississippi alone Black voting registration jumped from 7 to 67 percent.[26] The Voting Rights Act was expanded in the 1980s and 1990s to require states to draw legislative districts with more Blacks and Latinos (we discuss this in more detail in Chapter 6). See "Measuring Equality: Voter Registration and the Voting Rights Act of 1965" for a more detailed discussion of the results of the Voting Rights Act.

Busing. Although civil rights progress erased much of the inequality of opportunity facing Blacks since the colonial period, they still encountered inequality of outcome and de facto desegregation. For example, in the late 1960s federal courts required school districts to bus Black students into predominately White schools and White students into predominately Black schools to integrate public schools that were de facto segregated. Many White, and even some Black, parents objected strenuously to school district busing of their

measuring equality

Voter Registration and the Voting Rights Act of 1965

Voting is crucial to political power, and therefore disenfranchisement is a severe form of discrimination. From the beginning of the American Republic, states solely determined eligibility for voting. At the time, most states, even ones that had abolished slavery, denied Blacks the right to vote. States were even free to disenfranchise Whites who did not own a sufficient amount of property. The Fifteenth Amendment to the Constitution, ratified in 1870, was designed to prevent racial discrimination in voting, but it was unsuccessful in achieving that goal. States, mainly in the South, disenfranchised Blacks through poll taxes, literacy tests (as well as grandfather clauses), and failure to prosecute terrorist intimidation against African Americans attempting to vote. The Voting Rights Act of 1965 sought to end disenfranchisement by banning literacy tests and, more important, placing jurisdictions with a history of racial disenfranchisement under federal supervision.

Although this book focuses on the national government, state government is still important because, as discussed in Chapter 3, it enacts policies on criminal justice, education, welfare, and civil rights. State legislatures generally draw districts for the U.S. House of Representatives. Accordingly, civil rights advocates are extremely concerned about minority representation in state legislatures, and the Voting Rights Act was designed to address this concern.

We compiled data from the eleven states of the former Confederacy, and the results are shown in Figures 5.1 and 5.2. Figure 5.1 illustrates for each year the combined percentage of African Americans in the eleven state legislatures. Figure 5.2 displays the increase (in percentage units) from the previous time. The percentage of Black legislators has consistently increased since the passage of the Voting Rights Act, but the rate of increase has varied considerably. What factors could explain the overall increase in Black legislators?

What factors could explain the different rates of increase?

Figure 5.1 Percentage of Southern State Legislators Who Are Black, from Prior to the Voting Rights Act through 2007. The States are Alabama, Arkansas, Georgia, Florida, Louisiana, Mississippi, North Carolina, South Carolina, Tennessee, Texas, and Virginia.

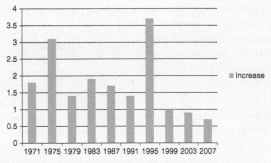

Figure 5.2 Increase (from the Previous Time) in the Percentage of Southern State Legislators Who Are Black, 1971–2007. The States are Alabama, Arkansas, Georgia, Florida, Louisiana, Mississippi, North Carolina, South Carolina, Tennessee, Texas, and Virginia.

children to schools, often located far away from their homes, but in 1971 the U.S. Supreme Court upheld mandatory busing as an acceptable means of achieving integrated schools.[27]

There is empirical evidence that busing helped to end de facto segregation. During the late 1950s and early 1960s, almost no Black schoolchildren attended majority White schools in the South, but by the 1970s and 1980s about 45 percent of Black schoolchildren attended majority White schools in the South.[28]

In 1991, the Supreme Court allowed school districts to end busing even if de facto segregation still existed as long as the school district showed a federal judge that it had made a good faith effort to integrate schools.[29] During the 1990s, school districts throughout the country ended two decades of busing. However, many communities, such as Seattle, Washington, still made their public school assignments to ensure a racial balance. In 2007, though, the U.S. Supreme Court ruled that assigning students to public school based on race violates the Constitution, even if the policy is designed to help racial or ethnic minorities.[30]

Empirical evidence shows that since the early 1990s, there have been increases in de facto segregation. Between the middle of the 1980s and the early 2000s, the percentage of Blacks attending majority White schools in the South declined from about 45 percent to about 30 percent.[31] Figure 5.3 demonstrates that between the early 1990s and 2009–2010 there was a clear increase in Black schoolchildren attending segregated schools—schools containing more than 50 percent minority students. Figure 5.4 reveals a slight increase in Black students attending heavily segregated schools—those containing more than 90 percent minority students. A 2016 study by the Government Accountability Office, a federal government research agency, found not only an increasing number of predominately Black and Latino schools, but it also found that these schools had higher levels of poverty and offered far fewer classes in math, science, and college preparation than schools with a larger percentage of white students.[32]

Affirmative Action. Another civil rights controversy is **affirmative action**, which refers to policies that attempt to help racial and ethnic minorities (as

Affirmative Action Corrective policies that attempt to help racial and ethnic minorities (as well as women) achieve equality in education and the workforce by providing them with advantages in college admission, hiring, promotion, and the awarding of contracts.

Figure 5.3 Percentage of Black Schoolchildren Attending Schools with More Than 50 Percent Minority Students, 1991–1992 and 2009–2010, by Region.

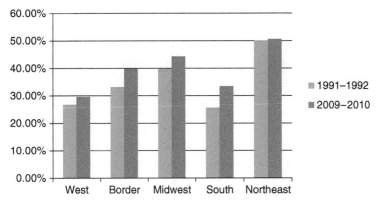

Figure 5.4 Percentage of Black Schoolchildren Attending Schools with More Than 90 Percent Minority Students, 1991–1992 and 2009–2010, by Region.

well as women) achieve equality in education and employment by providing them with advantages in college admission, hiring, promotion, and the awarding of contracts. Although controversial when applied to women and Latinos, affirmative action is especially contentious for Black civil rights. During the 1960s and early 1970s, public and private universities reserved a number of undergraduate and graduate admission slots for minorities. Many private companies gave hiring and promotion advantages to minorities, and recipients of federal, state, and local government contracts were required to subcontract to a minimum number of minority-owned businesses.

Supporters of affirmative action argue that it helps to remedy past discrimination because the preferences give racial and ethnic minorities opportunities they previously lacked. Additionally, supporters contend that affirmative action increases minorities in universities and businesses, which ensures diversity in education and the workplace. Opponents of affirmative action maintain that the preferences amount to discrimination against Whites, which violates the prohibition against racial inequality embodied in the equal protection clause of the Fourteenth Amendment. African American law professor Stephen Carter, who received some benefits from affirmative action, criticizes racial preferences because they stigmatize minority professionals as being admitted to universities or hired for jobs solely because of affirmative action. Carter also maintains that affirmative action mainly helps middle- and upper-class minorities and allows the government to ignore expensive policies that genuinely address problems experienced by poor minorities.[33] In state university systems, some states, such as Texas and Michigan, still use affirmative action, whereas other states, such as Florida and California, do not.

Thus far, the U.S. Supreme Court has struck a middle ground on affirmative action. In cases such as *Regents of the University of California v. Bakke* (1978)[34] and *Grutter v. Bollinger* (2003),[35] the Supreme Court invalidated quota systems that reserved allotted spaces for racial and ethnic minorities in college and graduate school admissions. However, the Court did allow state universities to consider minority status as an asset when considering admissions. In 2012, the Supreme Court agreed to rehear the issue of granting preferences in the case of *Fisher v. University of Texas*. The Texas university system guarantees admission to its public universities for high school students who graduate in the top 10 percent of their class, which helps bolster minority enrollment because many schools are overwhelmingly Black or Latino. The remaining students are then considered based on other factors, which can include race. When Abigail Fisher, a White student, was not admitted to the University of Texas under this system, she sued, arguing that the state policy discriminated against her on account of race. However, in 2013 the U.S. Supreme Court declined to issue a substantive decision on affirmative action; instead, it sent the case back to the lower court for further analysis.[36] In 2016 the Supreme Court upheld the University of Texas' policy of considering race as one of many factors in its admissions decisions.[37]

Recent Changes in Voting Laws. Another civil rights controversy concerns newly enacted voting laws that are racially neutral on their face but disproportionally harm Blacks and Latinos. As we mentioned in Chapter 3, voter ID laws require voters to show a government-issued picture identification, such as a driver's license or passport, to cast a vote.

Since 2011, some states have passed voter ID laws arguing that this policy will prevent people from fraudulently impersonating others when voting. These laws have been enacted by Republican-controlled state governments. Opponents claim that the instances of voter fraud by one person impersonating another are so rare that these laws are not necessary. In addition, opponents argue that these laws will disproportionally harm poor, urban, and elderly voters, many of whom are Black or Latino, because they are unlikely to drive or possess the means to travel abroad and thus have passports.

Voter ID opponents have challenged the laws in court, arguing that they are discriminatory, but the results have been mixed. In October 2012 and again in January 2014, Pennsylvania courts invalidated the state's voter ID law, ruling that too many legitimate voters would be disenfranchised.[38] In 2013 the U.S. Justice Department challenged North Carolina's ID strict voter ID law as a violation of the Voting Rights Act, arguing that the laws discriminate against voters on account of race.[39] In April of 2016 a federal judge upheld the law, but in July the appeals court overturned the law, ruling that the North Carolina legislature had intended to discriminate against minority voters when it passed the Voter ID law.[40]

Another change concerns the shortening of the early voting period. Early voting allows people to vote by mail or in person for up to two weeks prior to Election Day, and since 2000 many states have instituted early voting to increase voter turnout and limit long lines on Election Day. Analysts believe that early voting stimulates minority voting because it makes voting less cumbersome and allows voting organizations to mobilize minority voters. However, since 2011 some states have limited the amount of time available for early voting, arguing that it would be easier to administer elections if there were a gap between the early voting period and Election Day.

Initially, the federal government limited states' ability to constrict early voting days. The U.S. Justice Department was skeptical of the changes in Florida—recall that at the time, the Voting Rights Act required Justice Department approval of voting changes in five Florida counties. Ultimately, the state and federal government agreed to a compromise in which the state would have fewer early voting days but extend the hours for each of those days. Ohio's early voting reductions applied only to in-state voters, not to voters living abroad or serving in the military, but a federal judge ruled that all voters in Ohio needed to be treated equally, which forced the state to reinstitute the longer early voting period.[41]

Latinos

Like African Americans, Latinos have experienced discrimination and segregation. Since 2003, Latinos have been now the largest minority group in the United States,[42] but this statistic is deceiving because there are a variety of subgroups classified as Latino. The term **Latino** refers to those of Spanish or Portuguese colonial ancestry, including Mexican Americans (also called Chicanos), Puerto Ricans, Cuban Americans, and Central and South American immigrants. Recall from the Prologue our preference for the term *Latino* over the term *Hispanic*.

Latino An ethnic category describing people of Spanish or Portuguese colonial ancestry from the Caribbean, Central America, and South America.

Mexican Americans. As a result of the American conquest of Mexico during the Mexican American War (1846–1848) and the Treaty of Guadalupe Hidalgo, which was signed at its conclusion in 1848, Mexico ceded its northern portion to the United States (the area encompassing the present states [or portions thereof] of California, Nevada, Utah, Arizona, New Mexico, Texas, Oklahoma, Kansas, Colorado, and Wyoming). The treaty gave Mexicans living in the ceded land the choice of returning to Mexico or living in American territory, where they could become American citizens. However, despite being citizens, the Mexican Americans who elected to stay in the United States and their descendants experienced the same kinds of discrimination, segregation, and violent intimidation that African Americans faced. As more Mexicans immigrated to the United States during the nineteenth century, they, too, were subjected to unequal treatment and segregation.

The Mexican American Civil Rights Movement did not begin until the late nineteenth century. Disparate organizations throughout the Southwest concentrated on providing Mexican Americans with economic opportunities, organizing voter registration drives, and fighting against discrimination. In 1929, several Latino groups in Texas, loosely following the model of the NAACP, united to form the League of United Latin American Citizens (LULAC). During the 1940s and 1950s, LULAC, like the NAACP, sponsored federal and state litigation that ended segregation of Mexican-American schoolchildren and allowed Mexican Americans to be included on juries. Notably, in the late 1940s, before the landmark *Brown v. Board of Education* decision, LULAC sponsored a case that resulted in a lower federal court halting the practice of Orange County, California, segregating White and Mexican-American schoolchildren. LULAC has also focused on improving the lives of Latinos by registering Latinos to vote, establishing Mexican-American education programs, teaching English, and assisting in economic development.[43]

By the 1960s, Mexican Americans, like Blacks, had secured legal protections for civil rights, although inequality of outcome remained. The Civil Rights Act of 1964 and Voting Rights Act of 1965 applied to Mexican Americans, but during the late 1960s and early 1970s Mexican-American civil rights activists organized protests and boycotts to address social and economic issues specific to Chicanos. In 1968, Mexican-American high school students in Los Angeles staged a walkout to protest the racist portrayal of Mexican Americans in their classes. During the 1960s and 1970s, César Chávez, a labor leader who founded the United Farm Workers Union, fought for better wages for Chicano agricultural workers by organizing strikes and boycotts of the agricultural products of growers who exploited Mexican farmworkers. In the late 1960s, Chávez convinced consumers to boycott California grapes because of the poor working conditions the mainly Chicano farmworkers endured. The boycott was successful when grape growers agreed to bargain with farmworkers and provide better pay and working conditions.[44]

Mexican Americans achieved a major victory in 1975 when Congress expanded the Voting Rights Act to cover "language minorities." This new policy stipulated that if at least 5 percent of a county did not speak English and less than 50 percent of eligible citizens registered to vote in the previous election did not, then the county was required to print bilingual ballots. A large number of Mexican Americans who spoke only Spanish no longer faced linguistic barriers to voting.[45]

Puerto Ricans. Puerto Ricans are another sizable Latino population in the United States. Puerto Rico was originally a Spanish colony, but the United States assumed control over it after the Spanish-American War in 1899. Puerto Rico then became a territory of the United States, but the Jones Act of 1917 allowed Puerto Ricans to move freely to the mainland United States and conferred American citizenship on all Puerto Ricans who chose to move here. Since 1952, the island of Puerto Rico has been an American commonwealth, which means that its inhabitants do not enjoy the full extent of rights that U.S. citizens enjoy. Puerto Ricans living on the island were eligible for the draft before the shift to an all-volunteer army in 1973, and they do not pay federal income taxes. Puerto Rico falls under the jurisdiction of federal courts (see Chapter 8), but inhabitants on the island are not represented in American government. Puerto Rico sends a resident commissioner to the House, and this person can serve and vote on committees, but he or she is not eligible to vote on legislation. Puerto Rico has no representative to the U.S. Senate, and Puerto Ricans do not vote in the presidential election.[46]

On Election Day in 2012, residents of Puerto Rico voted on their status in a two-part ballot question. The first question asked if residents of the island wanted to change Puerto Rico's current status, and 54 percent voted to reject commonwealth status. The second part then asked voters to choose among three options: becoming a state, becoming an independent nation, or becoming more independent but still linked to the United States. On this question, 61 percent voted for statehood. This vote marked the first time Puerto Ricans expressed support for statehood, although many voters left these questions blank. Of course, the process of Puerto Rican statehood is not complete because Congress must decide whether to admit Puerto Rico as the fifty-first state. Although President Obama has announced his willingness to respect the outcome of the vote, the outcome in Congress is less certain. Some Republicans might oppose Puerto Rican statehood because the state would most likely elect Democrats to the House and Senate and vote Democratic for president. Other members of Congress might object to the fact that Spanish is an official language in Puerto Rico. Moreover, in the same election Puerto Ricans voted to oust their pro-statehood governor in favor of a governor who opposes statehood.[47] In 2016, Puerto Rico suffered a serious financial crisis that made it difficult for it to pay creditors. The United States Congress and the Obama Administration are working on a plan to bail out Puerto Rico, but the plan would place greater controls on the Puerto Rican budget and economy.[48]

Although Puerto Ricans living on the mainland United States are full American citizens, like Mexican Americans and Blacks they have faced discrimination and segregation. However, they attained legal protection against discrimination through the Civil Rights Act of 1964 and the Voting Rights Act of 1965. As a result, Puerto Rican Americans have legal recourse if they are subjected to political and economic discrimination. Nevertheless, as with other racial or ethnic minorities, Puerto Ricans still suffer from inequality of outcome and de facto segregation.[49]

Cuban Americans. As a result of American foreign policy concerns, the Cuban American civil rights experience has been unique compared to that of other Latino groups. After Fidel Castro instituted a communist takeover of Cuba in 1959, professional and elite Cubans, who stood to lose their wealth under Castro's redistributive policies and faced political persecution, defected to the nearby United States. The United States, which ideologically opposed Castro's rule, readily accepted these immigrants. As a result, Cuban Americans have not always shared the civil rights concerns of the other Latino groups, although Cuban Americans have been victims of discrimination. Like other racial and ethnic minorities, Cuban Americans benefited from civil rights legislation such as the Civil Rights Act of 1964 and the Voting Rights Act of 1965. Cuban Americans can now sue if they are not hired or promoted because of their ethnicity.

In 1980, Cuban president Fidel Castro expelled thousands of political and criminal prisoners to the United States. Keeping with the practice of welcoming Cuban immigrants, President Jimmy Carter allowed them to enter the United States. These immigrants, known as the *Marielitos*, were poorer and tended to have darker skin color compared to earlier Cuban immigrants. Moreover, not all of the *Marielitos* were political prisoners; some were common criminals. As a result, the U.S. government abandoned its policy of open immigration for Cuban immigrants and detained the *Marielitos* for months before allowing them to enter American society. Since the early 1980s, *Marielitos* and their offspring have become American citizens.[50]

Immigration. Despite the differences among Latino groups, the issue of legal and illegal immigration affects all Latino subgroups. Historically, American law employed a quota system to reduce the number of Latinos (as well as other ethnicities and races) living in the United States. Although immigration quotas were relaxed during the 1960s, many impoverished residents of Mexico, South America, and Central America lack the resources to immigrate legally. They, therefore, have illegally entered the United States to work in agricultural, manual labor, and custodial jobs that pay poorly by American standards, but not by the standards of the immigrants' home countries.

To combat illegal immigration, the federal, state, and local governments have adopted policies denying government services to and banning the employment of illegal immigrants. The Obama administration's immigration policy prioritizes deporting criminals, and a record number of deportations have occurred under the Obama administration.[51] However, as the opening story shows, President Obama has also used his authority to attempt to give some undocumented immigrants the ability to work in the United States.

Although illegal immigration has been a vibrant political issue for many years, it has recently become more salient. Opponents of illegal immigration argue that the rule of law should be paramount and that the government should prosecute employers who violate the law by hiring undocumented immigrants and deport people who violate the law by entering the United States illegally. Some Latinos who legally immigrated to the United States might also resent that they had to endure an arduous process, whereas immigrants who came to the United States illegally bypassed those difficulties. Opponents of illegal immigration also contend that undocumented immigrants take jobs that would have gone to legal residents and citizens, which is a powerful argument during difficult economic times. Moreover, others note that the rise in drug and gun violence occurring along the American border with Mexico has been partially caused by undocumented immigrants. The issue of opposition to illegal immigrants reached a high point during the 2016 presidential election campaign, particularly after Republican presidential candidate Donald Trump stated when he announced his candidacy that "When Mexico sends its people, they're not sending their best . . . They're bringing drugs. They're bringing crime. And some, I assume, are good people."[52]

Advocates for undocumented immigrants, however, contend that economic downturns notwithstanding, people who come to the United States illegally take jobs that no legal resident would consider performing, such as working in agricultural fields, washing dishes in restaurants, and cleaning hotel rooms. These advocates contend that the enforcement mechanisms should focus on the companies that hire undocumented immigrants, particularly because they take advantage of their workers' undocumented status by paying extremely low wages, forcing long hours, and providing no benefits. Moreover, many Americans believe in strong border enforcement but argue that the people who are already here and are productive residents should be given an opportunity to become legal residents, instead of disrupting their lives by deporting them. As the opening story shows, many of these advocates focus on undocumented parents who have children who were born in the United States and are thus American citizens. "Evaluating Equality: Terminology and Support for Illegal Immigration Reform" explores in more detail how wording affects perceptions of the illegal immigration controversy.

Since 2010, illegal immigration has been especially controversial in state politics. Arizona enacted SB 1070, which requires law enforcement officers to arrest anyone suspected of being in the country illegally who cannot provide proper documentation. The law also criminalizes any immigrant, even legal ones, who fails to possess the paperwork verifying that they are legally entitled to be in the United States, and the law empowers citizens to sue government officials if they believe the law is not being enforced. Supporters of the law argue that it is an effective way to combat a grave legal, economic, and social problem. However, opponents of the law fear that the paperwork requirements could result in the improper detention of legal immigrants, as well as the harassment and targeting of all Latinos, including U.S. citizens. Many businesses also worry that the law will cause Latinos to leave the state, which would damage the economy. President Obama said that the law would "undermine basic notions of fairness that we cherish as Americans."[53]

Opponents of the law immediately pursued strategies to overturn it. They staged massive protests in Arizona and in other states, and many activists called for professional organizations, including sports associations, to boycott the state. These efforts were designed to increase public opposition to the law, in hopes that the state would rescind the law or elect new politicians who would. In 2011, Arizona voters held a special recall election, which successfully replaced Republican State Senator Russell Pearce—the primary author of the law—with another Republican who has a more moderate view of illegal immigration laws.[54]

In addition, the Obama administration and antidiscrimination groups filed federal lawsuits seeking to overturn the law. In 2012, in *Arizona v. United States*, the U.S. Supreme Court overturned the portions of SB 1070 that enacted criminal penalties on immigrants because it said those provisions interfered with the federal government's authority to enforce immigration laws. However, the Court left intact the provision of SB 1070 that directed law

evaluating equality

Terminology and Support for Illegal Immigration Reform

The debate over illegal immigration has been central to civil rights politics since the 1960s. The U.S. government liberalized immigration during the 1960s by ending stringent ethnic quotas and giving high priority to keeping families together. But it was still difficult for low-skilled Latinos, especially Mexican Americans, to immigrate to the United States. Spurred by poverty in their home country and a demand for cheap labor in the United States, millions of people immigrated to the United States illegally from across the Mexican border. In 1986, Congress passed the Immigration Reform and Control Act (IRCA), which increased scrutiny on employers who hire illegal immigrants. The IRCA did, however, give illegal immigrants living in the United States for at least five years the opportunity to become American citizens. Despite the act's efforts, the IRCA did not lessen the controversy over illegal immigration, and during the early part of the twenty-first century the debate over illegal immigration has become an extremely contentious issue. In 2007, Congress and President Bush again sought a comprehensive immigration law that would have increased border enforcement and provided a way for existing undocumented immigrants to become legal residents and even citizens. However, the bill never passed. Since then there has been no significant progress on the passage of a meaningful immigration bill.

Americans are split over the issue of immigration reform, particularly the opportunity for undocumented immigrants to become U.S. citizens. To create the impression that this provision would reward people who broke American laws, opponents of

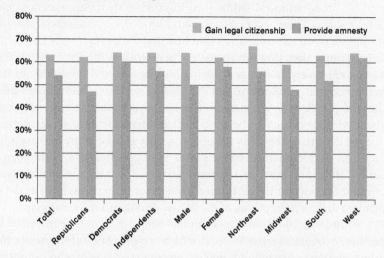

Figure 5.5 Percentage Supporting "Gain Legal Citizenship" for Illegal Immigrants Versus "Provide Amnesty" for Illegal Immigrants.

the bill couched it in terms of "amnesty," which connotes rewarding lawbreakers. However, supporters of the bill argued that this provision did not grant amnesty; instead, they said it created a path to citizenship for illegal immigrants who had lived and worked in the United States for a long time.

Throughout much of this chapter, we have covered both sides of the arguments over illegal immigration, but here we are interested in how the wording used in the debate affects people's perceptions of it. A 2007 survey conducted by the respected Pew Research Center illustrates how wording can influence public attitudes toward immigration. One question asked whether the respondent agreed with an illegal immigration policy that would "provide a way to gain legal citizenship if they [illegal immigrants] meet certain conditions," and another question asked whether the respondent agreed with a policy that would

"provide amnesty if they meet certain conditions." For each question, Figure 5.5 shows the percentage of different groups that claimed they favored the proposal.

Try an experiment with your friends, family, or coworkers by asking them about their views on whether the government should provide a way for undocumented workers to become legal residents or citizens. However, use the different wordings from the survey with different people. Do you notice different responses? Even when debating the issue among classmates, try to determine if supporters of immigration reform are likely to use different language than opponents do.

Source: Data adapted from Andrew Kohut, "Democratic Leaders Face Growing Opposition on Iraq, Mixed Views on Immigration Bill," *Pew Research Center for the People and the Press,* June 7, 2007, 3, http://www.people-press.org/files/legacy-pdf/335.pdf accessed September 19, 2016.

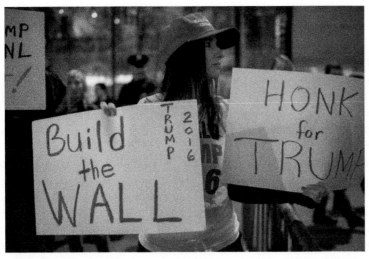

One of Donald Trump's plans to stop illegal immigration is to build a wall between Mexico and the United States, and force the Mexican government to pay for the wall. Here we see a Donald Trump supporter advocating for this wall. This woman held this sign while Latino groups were protesting Trump's rhetoric.

enforcement officers to require people they suspect of being illegal immigrants to show proof of legal residence. The majority of the Court argued that there was not enough evidence that this provision would be applied in a racially discriminatory manner, but the justices kept open the possibility that they would be willing to reconsider that ruling in the future if evidence of racial discrimination under the law emerged.[55]

Regardless of the substantive arguments over illegal immigration policies, many advocates for minorities are concerned about the anti-Latino rhetoric that pervades the debate. In some cases, the anti-illegal immigration rhetoric has focused on all immigrants, regardless of legal status, and at times this rhetoric has employed prejudiced stereotypes of Latinos. For example, in May 2012, U.S. Representative Steve King (R-IA) compared immigrants to dogs when he addressed constituents on the issue of immigration and remarked, "You want a good birddog? You want the one that is going to be aggressive? Pick the one that's the friskiest, not the one that's over there sleeping in the corner."[56] Additionally, the notion of an immigrant "sleeping in the corner" references a long-held stereotype of Latinos—Mexican Americans in particular—as being lazy. As discussed above, from the beginning of his campaign, Donald Trump has made stereotypical statements about Mexican immigrants. The Anti-Defamation League (ADL), an organization that monitors hate groups, notes that odious immigration rhetoric was once confined to hate groups, such as the Ku Klux Klan and Neo-Nazis. However, the ADL discovered that now this rhetoric comes from mainstream politicians and media outlets. The ADL report even shows that some groups claiming to be pro-environment proffer discredited claims that legal and illegal immigration harm the environment.[57]

Asian Americans

From the founding of the republic through the early twentieth century, federal laws discriminated against Asian immigrants, a racial minority group with origins in southern and eastern Asia, including Korea, China, Japan, Southeast Asia, and the Indian subcontinent. Recall from Chapter 1 that based on the tradition of exclusion, the Naturalization Act of 1790 only allowed free White immigrants to become citizens; therefore, Asian immigrants were not eligible to become citizens. During the 1800s, many Chinese immigrants came to the United States to provide cheap labor to build railroads, and subsequently other Asian immigrants moved to the West Coast of the United States to seek economic opportunities.

As Asian immigration continued, individual states and the national government responded to growing anti-Asian prejudice by passing legislation that discriminated against Asian Americans. For example, based on the premise that the influx of Chinese immigrants "endangers the good order of certain localities,"[58] the federal government passed the Chinese Exclusion Act in 1882, which virtually eliminated Chinese immigration. Likewise, the 1913 California Alien Land Act expressly prohibited aliens, mainly Asian immigrants, from owning land or leasing it for more than three years. These laws applied only to the immigrants themselves, not to their children born on American soil, who automatically received citizenship. Similar to African Americans, Asian Americans were also subjected to state-sponsored segregation prior to *Brown v. Board of Education.*[59]

The most severe example of discrimination against Asian Americans occurred during World War II. After the Japanese government bombed Pearl Harbor, the military and many Americans feared Japanese American disloyalty. Consequently, in February 1942, President Roosevelt issued Executive Order 9066, which empowered the U.S. military to relocate all Japanese Americans, many of them citizens, residing on the West Coast to internment camps, which were stark, inhospitable prison camps located in the desert. The order also allowed the U.S. government to seize Japanese Americans' property. Despite this blatant and cruel discrimination, in the infamous 1944 *Korematsu v. United States* case, the U.S. Supreme Court upheld the internments, ruling that the government's need to protect national security from Japanese espionage was a compelling enough justification.[60]

Legislation passed after World War II extended civil rights to Asian Americans. The 1952 McCarran–Walter Immigration Act increased immigration quotas for Asian immigrants, and it allowed the immigrants to become naturalized citizens. The Civil Rights Act of 1964 and the Voting Rights Act of 1965 (and its extension to language minorities in 1975) applied to Asian Americans as it did to other minority groups. These laws protected Asian Americans' civil rights and guaranteed their right to vote.[61]

Unlike Black and Latino civil rights activism, Asian American activism has not been sustained. There have been limited protest movements, and much of the interest group activity has focused on a single ethnic background. For example, the Japanese American Citizens League (JACL) was founded in 1930 to fight for civil rights for Japanese Americans. The JACL's most significant accomplishment was successfully lobbying for the Civil Liberties Act of 1988, which provided an apology and $20,000 in compensation to each surviving Japanese American who had been interned during World War II.[62] Similar to LULAC, the Chinese American Citizens Alliance focuses on registering Chinese Americans to vote and teaching the English language to recent immigrants.[63] The group Chinese for Affirmative Action has advocated in support of immigrants' rights and access to bilingual education.[64]

American Indians

American Indian is the term used to describe the racial category of the indigenous people who lived in the geographic area of the United States before European settlers arrived. Recall that the term *American Indian* is preferable to the term *Native American*, which could apply to any person born in the United States. The relationship between Indian tribes and the federal government is unique compared to that of other groups because the U.S. government has treated Indian tribes as separate nations within the United States, even negotiating through treaties. Throughout American history, American Indians have experienced genocide, harsh treatment, discrimination, and segregation at the hands of the U.S. government, but they have gradually gained civil rights.

To create room for White settlers on Indian-occupied land, the federal government forcibly and harshly removed Indian peoples and segregated them on **reservations** in the Western territories during the early nineteenth century. Among the Cherokee Tribe alone, 17,000 people were removed from Georgia to the Oklahoma Territory during the late 1830s and 1840s, and almost 4,000 people did not survive the brutal journey, known as the Trail of Tears.[65]

During the late nineteenth century, discrimination against American Indians took the form of forced assimilation in which the federal government sought to bring Indian peoples off the reservations and into White society. The Dawes Severalty Act, passed in 1887, granted a 160-acre homestead and citizenship to any indigenous person who renounced his or her tribal holdings and heritage. Touted as a way to promote integration of Indian peoples into White society, the law instead undermined

Reservations Portions of land set aside for American Indians removed from their ancestral lands by the federal government.

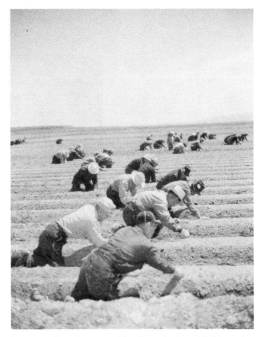

Japanese Americans working in agricultural fields at the Tule Lake internment camp in northeastern California. Despite the Constitution's prohibition against racial discrimination, during World War II the U.S. government mistrusted the loyalty of Japanese Americans and confined many of them, including native-born citizens, in harsh internment camps like this one.

Omaha boys at the Carlisle Indian Industrial School in Carlisle, PA, circa 1880. This boarding school was one of many throughout the United States that sought to assimilate American Indians into White culture. In addition to receiving education and training, students were forced to cut their hair and were punished for speaking their native language.

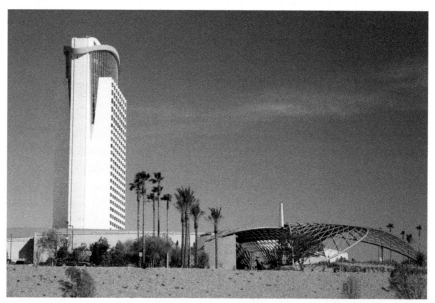

Because American Indian tribes enjoy considerable sovereignty, they are able to own gambling casinos, like the one pictured here, even if the state in which the tribe is located bans or heavily regulates gambling. These casinos have generated significant revenue for Native American tribes, but many critics argue that the profits are not fairly distributed among all tribal members.

tribal culture. Tribal governments lost their authority, and Indians remaining with their tribes were not eligible for American citizenship.[66]

In the twentieth century, the federal government extended civil rights protections to American Indians, although these advances occurred gradually and suffered setbacks. The Indian Citizenship Act of 1924 conferred American citizenship, including the right to vote, on all Indian peoples regardless of where they lived. In 1934, Congress overturned the Dawes Severalty Act with the passage of the Indian Reorganization Act, which, despite some setbacks, eventually restored sovereignty to tribal governments.[66] The Civil Rights Act of 1964 and Voting Rights Act of 1965 increased political and economic equality for American Indians.

Despite this civil rights progress, inequality of opportunity and outcome still existed for American Indians. As a result, American Indian protest movements intensified during the late 1960s and early 1970s. The most significant American Indian civil rights organization is the American Indian Movement (AIM), which was founded in 1968.

Initially, AIM focused on offering legal assistance to Indians and fighting police brutality, but in the early 1970s, the organization shifted its focus to protests and marches to demand civil rights. In 1973, members of AIM organized an armed occupation of Wounded Knee in South Dakota (the historic site of an 1890 massacre of Indians), and they claimed the land as the property of the Lakota people. AIM members argued that they were reclaiming historic land, but the FBI and federal marshals confronted the occupying force, and an armed battle ensued. The federal government and members of AIM were at an armed standoff for more than two months before reaching an agreement. One AIM member was killed, but the federal government still charged AIM leaders for the occupation. A federal judge subsequently dismissed the charges.[67]

In the late twentieth century, the federal government established the policy of **sovereignty**, giving each tribe freedom to regulate its own people and allowing tribes to operate according to their own customs. Most notably, sovereignty has benefited Indian tribes economically by permitting them to operate gambling casinos on their lands. The 1988 Indian Gaming Regulatory Act required any state that allows gambling, even in the form of a lottery, to negotiate agreements with Indian tribes to delineate rules for operating casinos. As a result, many Indian tribes have been permitted to build profitable casinos on their reservation lands, which have allowed these tribes to amass considerable wealth. But many Indian activists, including leaders of AIM, have criticized tribal leaders for not equitably distributing gambling profits among all Indians, especially those who do not reside on tribal lands.[68]

Sovereignty A government policy toward American Indians that allows each tribe to regulate its own people and operate according to its own customs.

Nonracial and Ethnic Struggles for Civil Rights

The Fourteenth Amendment protects racial and ethnic minorities, but it does not specify protections for discrimination on the basis of gender and sexual orientation. Nevertheless, women, members of the LGBT community, the elderly, and the disabled have experienced discrimination. Over the course of the twentieth century, each group has engaged in political activism and gradually achieved civil rights, although inequality still exists.

Women

Discrimination against women has been rampant throughout most of the history of the United States. During the early nineteenth century, most states prevented married women from signing contracts, abused wives from leaving their husbands, and widows from inheriting property. Other laws prevented all adult women, regardless of marital status, from pursuing prestigious occupations. By the early 1800s, every state denied women the right to vote. Because of this discrimination, female civil rights activists initiated their struggle for equal rights during the nineteenth century. In 1848, about two hundred women and men attended a conference in Seneca Falls, New York, to discuss discrimination against women. The conference produced the Seneca Falls Declaration of Sentiments and Resolutions, which called for equal treatment and voting rights for women. Interestingly, the organizers of the conference initially met in other social movements, particularly the abolitionist movement, where they recognized that women were also victims of discrimination despite being highly capable.

Suffrage Movement Large-scale efforts of organizations and activists during the late nineteenth and early twentieth centuries to secure the right to vote for women.

During the late nineteenth century, the **suffrage movement**, led by activists such as Susan B. Anthony and Elizabeth Cady Stanton, sought to secure the right to vote for women. Members of this movement objected strenuously when the Fifteenth Amendment prohibited denial of suffrage on the basis of race, color, or previous servitude, but not on the basis of sex. As a result of continued activism, some states eventually granted women the right to vote, although by 1918 most had not. The suffrage movement finally achieved its goal in 1920 with the ratification of the **Nineteenth Amendment** to the Constitution, which gave women the right to vote by prohibiting states from discriminating on account of sex when determining voter eligibility.

Nineteenth Amendment An amendment to the Constitution that prevents states from denying women the right to vote because of their sex.

Despite the adoption of the Nineteenth Amendment, state and federal laws continued to treat women unequally. New Deal programs, which created numerous federal jobs during the Great Depression, were not available to women. Although women had worked factory jobs because of labor shortages during World War II, after the war women were subjected to severe employment discrimination. During the 1960s, the federal government passed modest civil rights laws for women, and the Civil Rights Act of 1964 applied to gender discrimination as well as to discrimination based on race, color, and national origin. But the federal government did not enforce laws against gender discrimination as stringently as it did for race. During the 1970s, the U.S. Supreme Court applied the Fourteenth Amendment to women, but only partially, and not with the same force as it did for racial and ethnic minorities.[69]

Dissatisfied with the weak and poorly enforced federal laws, women's civil rights groups mobilized for stronger protections. The National Organization for Women (NOW), which was founded in 1967 to ensure legal equality for women and abortion rights, led an effort to lobby both houses of Congress to propose an **equal rights amendment** to the U.S. Constitution. Although activists had been seeking such an amendment since the 1920s, NOW and its allies achieved an initial victory in 1972 when both houses of Congress proposed an amendment that read, "Equality of rights under the law shall not be denied or abridged by the United States or any state on account of sex."

If ratified, this amendment would have required the Supreme Court to view gender discrimination cases exactly as it viewed racial discrimination and to strike down virtually all state laws discriminating against women unless the government could show a compelling justification. During the ratification process, however, conservative groups organized to oppose the Equal Rights Amendment, arguing that it would undermine women's roles as wives and mothers and would ultimately erode the traditional family. By the time the deadline for ratification had passed in 1982, the amendment fell short of the requisite three-fourths of the states needed for ratification, even though survey evidence indicated that a majority of Americans supported the amendment.[70] Subsequent Congresses have reintroduced the amendment, but it has not been passed. In 2015, Representative Jackie Speier (D-CA) introduced a bill that would end the time limit on the Equal Rights Amendment so that more states would be able to ratify it. Although her bill had 163 cosponsors, it has not passed the House.[71]

Women also suffer from inequality of outcome because they are paid less than men. Until the twentieth century, women were relegated to performing housework and raising children, and they were not paid for those efforts. During World War II, high demand for munitions and a labor shortage brought women into the workforce for the first time. Nevertheless, women were paid less than their male counterparts, and after the war ended women were dismissed from their jobs. In 1963, Congress passed the Equal Pay Act, which required that women be paid the same as men for the same work.[72] Business can circumvent the law by giving men and women different job classifications, despite performing the same tasks. Since the 1970s, the federal government has strengthened equal pay requirements, but inequities still exist. As Figure 5.6 shows, there is still an income gap between men and women, although that gap has narrowed over the past fifty years.

During the late 1980s and 1990s, **sexual harassment** emerged as an important gender equality issue. Sexual harassment refers to any unwelcome sexual comments or treatment in the workplace or in an education institution. It can include a supervisor's offer to a subordinate to exchange favorable treatment for sex, an employer's failure to prevent a sexually hostile work environment, or a professor's offer to a student to exchange good grades for sex.

Even though both men and women can be victims of sexual harassment, this form of discrimination affects women disproportionately. In 1986, the U.S. Supreme Court ruled in the case *Meritor Savings Bank v. Vinson* that any sexual harassment creating a hostile work environment violates the

Equal Rights Amendment
A proposed, but unratified, constitutional amendment that would have prevented gender discrimination to the same extent that the Fourteenth Amendment prevents racial and ethnic discrimination.

Sexual Harassment
Unwelcome sexual comments or treatment in the workplace or an educational institution.

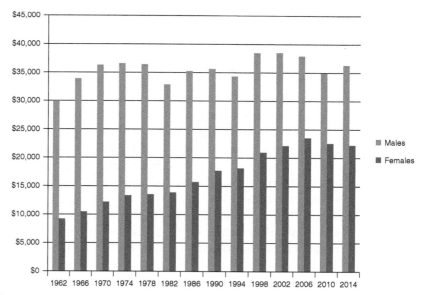

Figure 5.6 Median Income of Male and Female Workers, 1962–2014 (All figures in 2014 dollars).

Source: Adapted from United States Census, "Historical Income Tables: People: Table P-2. Race and Hispanic Origin by Median income and Sex, 1947–2014: All Races," https://www.census.gov/hhes/www/income/data/historical/people/, accessed May 27, 2016.

employment discrimination provisions of the Civil Rights Act, and a voluntary sexual relationship is not a suitable defense.[73]

Lesbians, Gays, Bisexuals, and the Transgendered

LGBT people have been subjected to discrimination and violent attacks, and although there has been some civil rights progress, they still face exclusion. Prior to the 1970s, most states criminalized homosexual activity, police often harassed establishments that catered to gays and lesbians, and being gay or lesbian was often considered an acceptable reason to fire or refuse to hire someone.

Beginning in the 1970s, gays and lesbians organized marches to protest unfair treatment and demonstrate to Americans that they represented a significant political force. Interest groups lobbied state and local governments and sponsored litigation to overturn discriminatory policies. When the AIDS epidemic first broke in the early 1980s, groups such as ACT-UP emerged to lobby for more federal money devoted to AIDS treatment.

In recent years, there has been progress in ending discrimination based on sexual orientation, but this progress has been intermittent and incomplete. As we discussed in Chapter 3, the U.S. Supreme Court invalidated state laws banning homosexual activity.[74] Additionally, in 2011 the Obama Defense Department officially ended the "Don't Ask, Don't Tell" policy that discharged homosexuals from the military, therefore allowing openly gay and lesbian

At the turn of the twenty-first century, no states allowed same-sex marriage, but since then states gradually allowed same-sex marriage. In 2015, the U.S Supreme Court ruled that laws banning same-sex marriage were unconstitutional, which legalized it throughout the United States. However, some local judges and government officials have steadfastly refused to sanction same-sex marriages, citing religious objections.

soldiers to continue serving.[75] Moreover, many states and localities have passed ordinances prohibiting economic and housing discrimination based on sexual orientation.

Another LGBT issue concerns government recognition of same-sex marriage. For many years, LGBT rights organizations have argued that the failure to recognize same-sex marriages denied those couples civil rights because they were not able to enjoy the benefits that opposite-sex couples enjoy, such as inheritance and hospital visitation. Initially, some states adopted **civil unions**, which afforded same-sex couples the same legal rights as opposite-sex married couples without sanctioning the marriage. However, beginning in the late 2000s, states legalized same-sex marriage on their own, although most states still banned it. In 2015 the U.S Supreme Court issued its landmark decision in *Obergefell v. Hodges*, which ruled that laws banning same-sex marriage violated the Fourteenth Amendment Due Process Clause; therefore, the Court legalized same-sex marriage throughout the nation.[76] Despite the ruling many state and local officials still refused to sanction same-sex marriages, citing religious objections. For example, Rowan County (Kentucky) Clerk Kim Davis, who is responsible for issuing marriage licenses, refused to issue any marriage licenses in order to avoid sanctioning same-sex marriage, citing religious objections. Therefore, a federal judge jailed Davis for contempt of court because she refused to do her job as required by law. Davis was released a few days later, and she agreed not to prevent her employees from issuing marriage licenses to all couples. Eventually, the judge agreed to allow Davis to keep her

Civil Unions Government policies that provide official legal recognition of same-sex couples without sanctioning marriage.

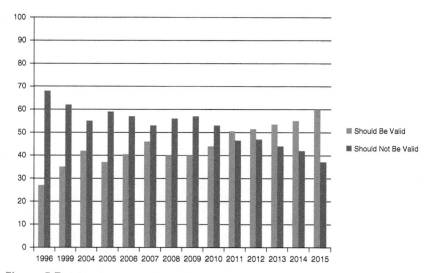

Figure 5.7 Public Opinion on Whether Same-Sex Marriage Should Be Valid (Percentage Saying It Should Be Valid Versus Percentage Saying It Should Not Be Valid), 1996–2015. Results were averaged over the year when the poll was taken more than once in a calendar year.
Source: Adapted from Gallup, "In Depth: Topics A to Z: Marriage," http://www.gallup.com/poll/117328/marriage. aspx, accessed May 28, 2016.

name off all marriage licenses.[77] Despite this heated opposition, as Figure 5.7 shows, a majority of Americans support same-sex marriage.

Notwithstanding these advances, there are minimal federal protections for sexual orientation, and as a result many places throughout the United States permit employment, economic, and housing discrimination based on sexual orientation. Additionally, violent crimes based on the victim's LGBT status are on the rise. Sexual orientation now ranks second in hate crime characteristics—behind only race and ahead of religion, national origin, and disability.[78] Since 2009, federal law has contained provisions against hate crimes based on sexual orientation, but only thirty states have hate crime laws that include sexual orientation. Only fifteen of those states include gender identity.[79]

Even more recently the issue of transgender discrimination has emerged as a civil rights issue. Some states and localities have laws protecting transgendered people from discrimination in areas such as housing and employment, but many places do not protect transgendered people from discrimination. Recently, there has been a controversy over whether transgendered people should be able to use public restrooms that correspond to the gender with which they identify. For example, the city of Charlotte, North Carolina, passed an ordinance allowing transgendered people to use the public restroom that corresponds to their gender identity, but this policy prompted the state of

North Carolina to pass a law that required everyone to use the bathroom that corresponds to the sex on their birth certificate, regardless of their gender identity. In response to this discriminatory law, corporations, such as PayPal, refused to open facilities in the state; other corporations, such as the National Basketball Association, threatened similar boycotts; and entertainers, such as Bruce Springsteen, cancelled events in North Carolina.[80]

In May of 2016, the Obama administration issued a statement to state and local officials that transgendered students in public schools have the right to use the bathroom that corresponds to their gender identity. In this statement the government contended that "the desire to accommodate others' discomfort cannot justify a policy that singles out or disadvantages a particular class of students." In response, a number of states, led by Texas, have sued the Obama administration in federal court arguing that the president cannot deny states and localities the ability to set their own bathroom-use policies.[81]

Elderly and Disabled

A number of other groups have experienced discrimination and civil rights progress, including the elderly and disabled. To combat workplace discrimination based on age, the Age Discrimination in Employment Act (ADEA), passed in 1967, prohibits employers from discriminating in hiring, promoting, compensating, or laying off employees on account of age. The American Association for Retired Persons, an organization that represents people over the age of fifty, devotes efforts to litigating against age discrimination in employment.[82]

Likewise, the Americans with Disabilities Act (ADA), passed in 1990, prohibits employers from discriminating against employees because of physical disability. In fact, the ADA requires employers to provide reasonable accommodations, such as sign language interpreters for the hearing impaired and Braille facilities for visually impaired employees or job applicants. The ADA also requires all public accommodations, places where the public should reasonably be able to access, to provide facilities for people with disabilities. Therefore, buildings were required to build wheelchair ramps, install electric doors, and add Braille for the elevators. The ADA has been especially prevalent in colleges and universities, which are now required to provide the aforementioned facilities for people with physical disabilities. Additionally, colleges and universities must offer services that assist students with learning disabilities. Similar to other civil rights organizations, the Disability Rights Education & Defense Fund advocates on behalf of disabled Americans.[83]

Conclusion

This entire book focuses on the politics of race and ethnicity, but this chapter concentrated specifically on the history of discrimination and civil rights progress for a select few groups. First, we explained the precise meaning of key terms relevant to civil rights politics. We then focused on different groups' civil rights histories. We devoted a significant portion of this chapter to the Black civil rights struggle because it has been the most active and is the most well-known. However, Blacks are not the only racial or ethnic group with a vibrant civil rights history. Accordingly, this chapter addressed the civil rights struggles of Latinos, Asian Americans, and American Indians. Because civil rights politics is not exclusive to racial and ethnic minorities, we also traced the history of civil rights concerning gender, sexual orientation, age, and disability.

Although there are obvious differences among the groups we covered, all the civil rights stories share important similarities. Each group experienced severe forms of unequal treatment, segregation, or both, but each group also engaged in various forms of political activism, such as lobbying legislatures, sponsoring litigation, and protesting. This activism yielded significant civil rights victories for each group, but this progress has not been complete, and important civil rights issues remain.

In addition to discussing the civil rights histories of each group, this chapter addressed political controversies affecting civil rights in general. For example, one controversial issue concerns the policies intended to redress past discrimination. Affirmative action policies are designed to give minorities assistance in hiring, promotion, and admission to education institutions, but critics point out that these policies violate principles against racial discrimination by favoring racial and ethnic minorities over Whites. Busing promotes more integration of schools, but it places hardships on the children who are bused, as well as their parents. New voter ID laws and shorter early voting periods could hinder minority turnout, but several state governments assert that these measures are necessary to administer elections. **Hate crime legislation** seeks to prevent violent crimes committed out of prejudice, but opponents of these laws believe that violent actions should be punished equally, regardless of the motive.

Hate Crime Legislation Laws that enhance criminal penalties for crimes committed out of prejudice toward certain groups.

Immigration is one of the most interesting and controversial civil rights issues. From the founding of the nation, the U.S. government has crafted immigration policies as a means of excluding certain races and ethnicities from coming to the United States. Since the twentieth century, however, immigration law has been overtly used as a means of racial and ethnic exclusion. Today, the controversy centers on illegal immigration. Debate has centered on the federal government's immigration policies and state laws, such as Arizona SB 1070, which target undocumented residents within state borders. Moreover, as the story of Zaira Garcia and her father demonstrates, policies concerning undocumented immigrants significantly affect the lives of millions of people. This chapter illustrated in depth the arguments on all sides of the immigration debate, as well as how issues of wording can affect public perception over the debate. In short, the vexing controversies over illegal immigration illustrate the complex and dynamic nature of civil rights policy.

review
REVIEW QUESTIONS

1. Why is President Obama's DAPA policy so controversial?
2. What are the similarities and differences among the civil rights stories for different racial and ethnic groups?
3. How has the policy of sovereignty influenced equality of outcome for American Indian peoples?
4. What civil rights gains did women make during the twentieth century, and where does inequality still exist?
5. What are some of the key current controversies over civil rights concerning sexual orientation?

terms
KEY TERMS

Abolitionists p. 139
Affirmative Action p. 148
Black Codes p. 140
Brown v. Board of Education p. 144
Civil Rights p. 133
Civil Rights Act of 1964 p. 145
Civil Unions p. 165
De Facto Segregation p. 137
De Jure Segregation p. 137
Disenfranchisement p. 142
Dred Scott v. Sandford p. 139
Emancipation Proclamation p. 140
Equal Protection Clause p. 140
Equal Rights Amendment p. 163

Ethnicity p. 134
Fifteenth Amendment p. 140
Fourteenth Amendment p. 140
Gender p. 136
Grandfather Clauses p. 143
Hate Crime Legislation p. 168
Inequality p. 136
Inequality of Opportunity p. 136
Inequality of Outcome p. 136
Jim Crow Laws p. 142
Latino p. 151
Literacy Tests p. 142
Nineteenth Amendment p. 162
Plessy v. Ferguson p. 142

Poll Taxes p. 143
Race p. 134
Reconstruction p. 140
Reservations p. 159
Segregation p. 136
Separate but Equal Principle p. 142
Sexual Harassment p. 163
Sit-in p. 145
Sovereignty p. 161
Suffrage Movement p. 162
Thirteenth Amendment p. 140
Voting Rights Act of 1965 p. 145

readings
ADDITIONAL READINGS

Marisa Abrajano and Zoltan L. Hajnal, *White Backlash: Immigration, Race, and American Politics*, Princeton, NJ: Princeton University Press, 2015.

This book uses extensive data analysis to demonstrate how debates over immigration have moved whites toward the Republican Party while racial and ethnic minorities have moved toward the Democrats.

Daniel Kryder, *Divided Arsenal: Race and the American State During World War II*. New York: Cambridge University Press, 2000.

This book shows how the government's need for economic production during World War II led to policies that advanced civil rights for African Americans.

Paula D. McClain and Joseph Stewart, Jr., *"Can We All Get along?": Racial and Ethnic Minorities in American Politics*, 6th ed. Boulder, CO: Westview Press, 2014.

This book analyzes the politics surrounding the most prominent racial and ethnic minorities in the United States—Blacks, Latinos, Asian Americans, and American Indian peoples—from historical, legal, institutional, behavioral, and policy perspectives.

Nancy E. McGlen, Karen O'Connor, Laura Van Assendelft, and Wendy Gunther-Canada, *Women, Politics, and American Society*, 5th edition. New York: Longman, 2010.

This book explicates the theoretical, historical, and contemporary aspects of the issue of women's rights, including a global perspective on those rights.

Jami K. Taylor and Donald T. Haider-Markel, eds., *Transgender Rights and Politics: Groups, Issue Framing, and Policy Adoption*. Ann Arbor, MI: University of Michigan Press, 2014.

This edited volume examines the role of political messaging and interest groups in shaping transgender rights policies in the United States and in other nations.

Richard M. Valelly, *The Two Reconstructions: The Struggle for Black Enfranchisement*. Chicago: University of Chicago Press, 2004.

This book compares the failed attempts to secure genuine voting rights for African Americans during the late nineteenth century to the more successful enfranchisement efforts of the late twentieth century.

CHAPTER 6

Congress: Representation and Lawmaking

Representative Will Hurd (R-TX) at a committee hearing. Representative Hurd defeated a Democratic incumbent in 2014, which was a bad year for congressional Democrats. Moreover, he is an anomaly in Congress because he is an African American Republican who represents a majority-Latino district. Although, Donald Trump's anti-Latino rhetoric was an issue in Hurd's 2016 reelection campaign, Hurd still won reelection.

The 23rd Congressional District of Texas is a sprawling district that stretches along the Mexican border from the outskirts of San Antonio all the way to the outskirts of El Paso, with numerous small towns contained within. It is the largest district in the state of Texas, according to landmass; in fact, it is one of the largest in the United States. Given its location, the 23rd District is largely Latino—67.7 percent according to latest estimates—and has only a small African American population—3.4 percent according to the latest estimate.[1] Given its large Latino population, this region has been represented by a Latino member of the House since the 1980s after the Voting Rights Act (see Chapters 3 and 5) was amended to ensure more minority representation in the U.S. House and state legislatures. Moreover, given its vast landscape, the district has actually been fairly competitive between Republicans and Democrats, with Latino representatives from both parties, which is why the election result in 2014 was so unique. Because 2014 was an unfavorable year for Democrats, it was not surprising that Democratic Representative Pete Gallego, who is Latino, narrowly lost his seat to a Republican. However, it was surprising that he was defeated by Republican Will Hurd, who is African American.

In many respects Representative Hurd's background is typical of a member of Congress. He graduated with a degree in computer science from Texas A&M University, where he served as student body president. He then went on to serve as an intelligence officer in the Middle East, and after leaving the CIA, he worked at a cybersecurity firm.[2] Nevertheless, African American Republicans in Congress are rare. He is only one of two Black Republican House members (the other is Mia Love from Utah), and there is only one African American Republican Senator—Tim Scott from South Carolina. Because of the Democratic Party's progressive views on economic and social issues, African American elected officials tend to be Democrats, but Representative Hurd is one of the few exceptions. Additionally, Hurd's victory is surprising because he is a non-Latino who represents an overwhelmingly Latino district. Since the 1980s states have created **majority-minority districts**, which are legislative districts that contain more than 50 percent of a minority group. Although

Majority-Minority Districts Legislative districts that contain a population made up of more than 50 percent of a racial or ethnic minority group.

creating a majority-minority district does not guarantee a minority representative, most majority-minority districts are represented by a racial or ethnic minority. It is even rarer for a representative of a *majority-minority* district to belong to a different racial or ethnic minority group than the majority race or ethnicity in the district. In short, Representative Hurd's presence in Congress is exceptional.

Given the competitiveness of the district, Representative Hurd's first term in office was non-controversial. He has focused primarily on national security issues, particularly border security, which is not surprising because much of his district runs along the border between Mexico and the United States, and cybersecurity, which is not surprising given his background. He has focused on issues of concern to his largely Latino constituency, and part of his website appears in both English and Spanish.[3]

However, the racial composition of Hurd's district is playing a major role in his reelection campaign in 2016. Pete Gallego is challenging Representative Hurd in a rematch, and because the race was so close in 2014 and because the district is so balanced between Democrats and Republicans, the race is one of the most competitive in 2016. More interestingly, the anti-Latino rhetoric of Republican presidential nominee Donald Trump is significantly influencing the race. Despite being a loyal Republican, Representative Hurd has not endorsed Donald Trump, citing his statements about women and minorities. In other words, Hurd is favoring his constituency over his party. Nevertheless, Gallego ran attack ads against Hurd that associate him with Trump.[4] Still, Representative Hurd narrowly won reelection in 2015.[5]

intro

Will Hurd's story demonstrates several aspects of how Congress works that we address in this chapter. First, the electoral history of the 23rd District represents the importance of elections in determining the functioning of Congress. As we discuss later in the chapter most U.S House districts are not very competitive between Republicans and Democrats, but Hurd's district is an exception. When there are significant partisan shifts in these competitive districts the party control of the House can change, which has happened twice in the past decade—Democrats gained control in 2006 and Republicans regained control in 2010. As we will show, the party that controls the House of Representatives significantly influences the type of legislation that is passed or not passed. Like Representative Hurd, many endangered Republican House members retained their seats. The Democrats picked up only six additional seats in 2016, which means that the Republicans will control the House in the 115th Congress.

Finally, Representative Hurd exemplifies the important role that race plays in congressional politics. Most Black legislators represent districts that are majority Black, but

Hurd is an exception because his district contains only a small fraction of African Americans. In fact, the 23rd District of Texas is actually a majority-Latino district that has been represented by a Mexican American for the past thirty years. Additionally, most African American representatives are liberal and Democratic, but Representative Hurd is a conservative Republican. In short, he is the exception to the rule that African American representatives tend to be liberal Democrats. Finally, although many observers expected that Donald Trump's racially charged rhetoric against Latinos would significantly affect Congressional races, the outcome demonstrated that the Trump's affect was minor.

Article 1, Section 1, of the U.S. Constitution vests "all legislative power . . . in a Congress of the United States." As such, Congress is the primary policymaking institution in American government. Article 1, Section 1, also divides Congress into two houses: the Senate and the House of Representatives. The House was designed to closely represent the people. It is apportioned by state population, and all 435 members are up for reelection every two years. The Senate, which was designed to be somewhat removed from the public, contains one hundred senators, with each state represented by two senators, who serve six-year, staggered terms.

But the Constitution does not, and cannot, specify congressional politics, which is a complex undertaking. This chapter introduces these complexities by analyzing the nature of congressional representation, the importance of congressional organization and leadership, the lawmaking process, and the competing influences on members' decisionmaking. Throughout the chapter, we pay close attention to the role of race and ethnicity in congressional politics.

The Nature of Congressional Representation

Representative A person chosen to make policy decisions on behalf of a defined group of people.

Constituency The people who choose a representative to act on their behalf.

Congressional representation has two components: the constituents and their representatives. The **representative** is the person chosen to make laws on behalf of a defined group of people, and the **constituency** comprises the people who choose the representative to act on their behalf. For the most part, constituencies are determined by geographic region, and each region possesses a particular character in terms of the constituents' dominant political views, economic interests, cultural values, and racial and ethnic breakdown. These regional socioeconomic and ideological characteristics are reflected in the type of person who serves as a representative. Here we address the complex relationship between geography and representation by focusing on unrepresented areas, the process of drawing legislative districts, and the characteristics of American members of Congress. We pay special attention to the representation of racial and ethnic minorities.

The Unrepresented

Even though the United States is a representative democracy, a significant portion of people living under American control are denied any representation in Congress. The Commonwealth of Puerto Rico[6] and the territories of American Samoa, Guam, Northern Mariana Islands, and Virgin Islands are subject to

American laws, but people living there, most of whom are racial or ethnic minorities, do not send voting members to the U.S. House or Senate. Instead, each region sends a nonvoting delegate to the House, but not to the Senate. These delegates are able to speak on the floor, offer bills, and participate fully in committees (even as committee leaders), but they lack the most essential power—voting for or against proposed legislation.

Washington, DC, which, unlike a commonwealth or territory, is fully a part of the United States, also sends only a nonvoting delegate to the House. This arrangement is especially controversial because full-fledged American citizens reside in Washington, DC, which has almost 675,000 residents, more than 60 percent of whom are non-White.[7] Yet, DC residents are still denied any representation in Congress. For many years, the current nonvoting delegate, Eleanor Holmes Norton (D-DC), has actively advocated the allocation of a voting representative for Washington, DC, which we discuss in "Our Voices: Nonvoting Delegate Eleanor Holmes Norton and Representation for Washington, DC."

When the Democrats took control of Congress in 2007, there was some progress toward giving Washington, DC, a voting representative. In 2007, the

Gerrymandering often results in bizarrely shaped districts that connect disparate parts of states. Ohio's 2012 congressional districts are an example of gerrymandering. Although some districts are compact, others clearly are not. The 6th District travels from the northeast part of the state to southern Ohio. The 4th District extends from the urban areas on Lake Erie to rural farmland.

our voices

Nonvoting Delegate Eleanor Holmes Norton and Representation for Washington, DC

When introducing legislation, members of Congress usually provide opening remarks to specify the purpose of their bill and thus set the terms for debate on the bill. Following is an excerpt of Delegate Eleanor Holmes Norton's speech to the House floor on January 9, 2007, announcing that she would introduce HR 328, which would grant Washington, DC, a vote in the House of Representatives. These words eloquently express the frustration of Americans denied representation in their government and demonstrate how Washington, DC's lack of a voting representative in Congress amounts to racial discrimination.

Ms. Norton: Mr. Speaker, I come to the House to inform the House that I have today filed a bill to give full voting rights in this House to the people of the District of Columbia, who are second per capita in the Federal income tax they pay to support this government, this House and this Senate, and who have fought and died

in every war since the creation of a Republic, including the outrageous war where we now serve.

I come in gratitude that the House is now governed by my own party, which for decades has supported not only what my bill today would afford, a vote in the House, but a vote in both Houses, and I come to thank my own caucus for that support. But I also come in some frustration and with some impatience. I come in frustration that I am still a second-class citizen in my own House. . . .

I had hoped to be able to vote on the bills we all ran on that are now before the House. I came to speak today, but once again, when the vote came, I could not vote. I couldn't vote because I was not even allowed the vote in the Committee of the Whole that I won when the Democrats were last in power.

. . . I have tried everything, I have tried statehood, I have tried Committee of the Whole. It is time to try

Delegate Eleanor Holmes Norton (D-DC), holds a news conference in late 2012. Because Washington, DC does not have representation in the House, Delegate Norton is not able to vote on legislation, but she can fully serve on committees. Delegate Norton has pushed to provide Washington, DC with voting representation.

our voices *(Continued)*

the real thing, Mr. Speaker, when there are 650,000 people who pay their taxes and have met every obligation, and are not recognized as citizens in their own House and send somebody to the House that is not even recognized to vote on this House, not even in the Committee of the Whole.

I come to express their frustration, to say I am leaving all that behind. I have introduced the bill they want. . . . We want our votes. We want it in the 110th Congress, and we want it now. I speak for them as a woman who knows what it means to be a second-class citizen, and who, once she left the District and went to law school, said, "I shall never again be a second-class citizen." Yes, I grew up in segregated schools in this town, in segregated Washington. That is what it meant to be a second-class

citizen. Now to be a second-class civics citizen, after 200 years, has become too much to bear.

So I have introduced a bill to make it absolutely clear, as my people have said I must do today, that there is boiling determination among the people of the District of Columbia to get this vote. . . .

This is the 110th, Mr. Speaker. This is the moment of truth. This is the moment when the Democrats have not only the opportunity, but the obligation to give a vote in the 110th Congress to the people of the District of Columbia.

Source: Adapted from *Congressional Record*, 110th Congress, H231–H232, https://www.congress.gov/crec/2007/01/09/CREC -2007-01-09-pt1-PgH231-2.pdf accessed August 17, 2016.

House passed a measure that would add a vote in the House for DC and an at-large seat for Utah (until the next census),[8] thus bringing the total number of House members to 437. However, this bill did not pass in the Senate for reasons we discuss later in this chapter. After Democrats expanded their House and Senate majorities in the 2008 elections, the chances of giving DC a voting representative seemingly increased. In early 2009, the Senate passed the same bill it had rejected in 2007, but the bill stalled in the House.[9] When the Republicans regained control of the House in 2011 the prospects of a voting representative for the District ended, and, in fact, the House further limited the power of nonvoting delegates.[10]

Districts

Because members of Congress represent people living within specifically defined boundaries, Congress is a geographically based institution. Senators represent people living in states, and House members represent people living in parts of states or, in a few cases, the entire state. **Reapportionment** is the process of allotting states a number of representatives based on population figures determined after each official decennial census. Because every state regardless of size has two senators, reapportionment is not necessary for the Senate.

As the U.S. population increased and more states were added to the union during the nineteenth century, the House increased its number of members until 1930, when the size of the House was capped at 435.[11] Since then, states that gain the most people after the previous census increase their representation in the House, whereas states that lose population or do not grow as much as other states decrease their representation in the House. As a result, in the

Reapportionment The process of assigning states a number of representatives to the House of Representatives after each decennial census.

past two decades many states in the South and the West have added representatives, whereas states in the Northeast and Midwest have lost representatives.

Once a state receives its allotment of representatives, the state legislature then draws geographical boundaries delineating the area that each member will represent. This process is known as **redistricting**, and it determines the geography of districts for the U.S. House. For example, if a state receives ten representatives to the House, then the legislature divides the state into ten geographical regions, each one represented by a single member.

Because of political motivations, state legislatures do not necessarily redistrict to reflect distinct communities within the state. Instead, **gerrymandering**, which is a group's use of redistricting to maximize its chances of winning seats in a legislative body, is prevalent during the redistricting process. Usually, the political party that controls the state legislature gerrymanders to maximize its chances of winning seats to the U.S. House. Although gerrymandering does not guarantee that one party will represent a particular seat, it does maximize the odds that the majority party in the state legislature will enhance its representation in the House.

State legislatures enjoy considerable discretion in redistricting, but there are some significant restrictions. First, the district must be contiguous; that is, its geographical shape must be a complete entity. A district cannot be divided into two separate parts of a state, and the U.S. Supreme Court requires that all House districts within a state be equal in population.[12] In fact, the Supreme Court has overturned redistricting plans with population deviations as small as 0.7 percent.[13]

State legislatures are also required to pay close attention to race and ethnicity when drawing legislative districts. To prevent state legislatures from gerrymandering to fragment areas of minority concentration and, in turn, decrease the numbers of minorities in the House, Congress amended the Voting Rights Act in 1982, and since then state legislatures have created majority-minority districts (districts in which a racial or ethnic minority composes a majority of the population) wherever possible.

As a direct result of majority-minority districts, the number of Black and Latino House members increased significantly after the 1992 election. But in the mid-1990s, the Supreme Court invalidated some majority-minority districts, ruling that state legislatures could use race as one factor in drawing legislative district but that the Constitution prevents them from using race as the predominant factor.[14] As a result, even after the 2010 census many majority-minority districts still favored Blacks and Latinos, although the number is lower than it was during the 1990s. Nevertheless, as Figure 6.1 demonstrates, the number of Blacks elected to the U.S. House has generally gradually increased since 1992 and the number of Latinos has increased more sharply.

Members of Congress

Ultimately, the composition of a district helps to determine the type of representative elected. The Constitution imposes only age, citizenship, and residency requirements for serving in the House and Senate (see Chapter 2). There

Redistricting The process by which a state is divided into geographical regions, with each region electing a member of the House of Representatives.

Gerrymandering The practice in which a group, usually a political party, uses redistricting to maximize its chances of winning elections.

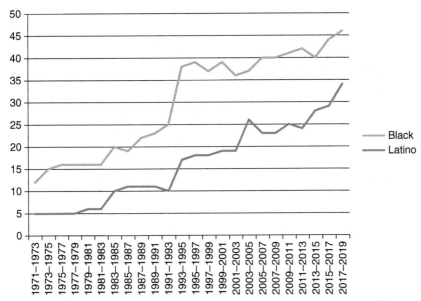

Figure 6.1 Number of Black and Latino Representatives Serving in the U.S. House of Representatives, 1971–1973 through 2017–2019.

are no requirements concerning occupation or education. Nevertheless, most members are college educated and are socioeconomically well off.

For most of the nation's history, racial minorities were extremely underrepresented in the House and Senate, but in recent years they have closed the gap. In the 115th Congress (2017–2019), African Americans constitute 10.6 percent of the voting members of the House of Representatives, Latinos are 7.8 percent, Asian Americans are 3.0 percent, and American Indians are 0.5 percent. As a result of the creation of majority-minority districts, in 1992 the Southern states of Virginia, North Carolina, South Carolina, Florida, Mississippi, and Alabama elected African Americans to the U.S. House for the first time since Reconstruction. Table 6.1 lists the racial and ethnic minority voting members of the 115th Congress.

Although the drawing of majority-minority districts has undoubtedly increased the number of minority representatives, opponents contend that increased minority representation does not necessarily result in better policies for minority constituents. This debate centers on the tension among competing views concerning the nature of representation. We can divide these views into three types. **Descriptive representation** concentrates on whether the characteristics of representatives match the characteristics of their constituents. **Symbolic representation** emphasizes the feelings of confidence and acceptance that the constituents have for their representative and the legislative institution as a whole. **Substantive representation** concerns whether representatives advocate policies that benefit their constituents.[15]

Majority-minority districts usually elect a minority representative, which satisfies descriptive representation concerns. A minority representative can

Descriptive Representation The extent to which the characteristics of a representative correspond with the general characteristics of his or her constituency.

Symbolic Representation The extent to which constituents trust and accept their representative and the legislative institution as a whole.

Substantive Representation The extent to which representatives advocate policies that benefit their constituents.

TABLE 6.1 Racial and Ethnic Minority Voting Members of the 115th Congress (2017–2019)

African Americans in the House of Representatives

Alma Adams (D-NC)
Karen Bass (D-CA)
Joyce Beatty (D-OH)
Sanford Bishop (D-GA)
Anthony Brown (d-MD)
G. K. Butterfield (D-NC)
Andre Carson (D-IN)
Yvette Clarke (D-NY)
William Lacy Clay III (D-MO)
Emmanuel Cleaver (D-MO)
James Clyburn (D-SC)
John Conyers (D-MI)
Elijah Cummings (D-MD)
Danny Davis (D-IL)
Val Demmings (D-FL)
Keith Ellison (D-MN)

Dwight Evans (D-PA)
Marcia L. Fudge (D-OH)
Al Green (D-TX)
Alcee Hastings (D-FL)
Will Hurd (R-TX)
Sheila Jackson-Lee (D-TX)
Hakeem Jeffries (D-NY)
Eddie Bernice Johnson (D-TX)
Hank Johnson (D-GA)
Robin Kelly (D-IL)
Al Lawson (D-FL)
Brenda Lawrence (D-MI)
Barbara Lee (D-CA)
John Lewis (D-GA)
Mia Love (R-UT)

Donald McEachin (D-VA)
Gregory Meeks (D-NY)
Gwen Moore (D-WI)
Donald Payne, Jr. (D-NJ)
Cedric Richmond (D-LA)
Lisa Blunt Rochester (D-DE)
Bobby Rush (D-IL)
David Scott (D-GA)
Robert Scott (D-VA)
Teri Sewell (D-AL)
Bennie Thompson (D-MI)
Marc Veasey (D-TX)
Maxine Waters (D-CA)
Bonnie Watson-Coleman (D-NJ)
Frederica Wilson (D-FL)

African Americans in the Senate

Cory Booker (D-NJ)
Kamala Harris (D-CA)
Tim Scott (R-SC)

Latinos in the House of Representatives

Pete Aguilar (D-CA)
Nanette Barragan (D-CA)
Xavier Becerra (D-CA)
Salud Carbajal (D-CA)
Tony Cárdenas (D-CA)
Joaquín Castro (D-TX)
Lou Correa (D-CA)
Henry Cuellar (D-TX)
Carlos Curbelo (R-FL)
Mario Diaz-Balart (R-FL)
Adriano Espaillat (D-NY)
Bill Flores (R-TX)

Ruben Gallego (D-AZ)
Vincente Gonzalez (D-TX)
Raúl Grijalva (D-AZ)
Luis Gutierrez (D-IL)
Jaime Herrera-Beutler (R-WA)
Ruben Kihuen (D-NV)
Raul Labrador (R-ID)
Ben Ray Luján (D-NM)
Michelle Lujan Grisham (D-NM)
Alex Mooney (R-WV)
Grace Napolitano (D-CA)

Ileana Ros-Lehtinen (R-FL)
Lucille Roybal-Allard (D-CA)
Raul Ruiz (D-CA)
Linda Sánchez (D-CA)
José Serrano (D-NY)
Alberto Sires (D-NJ)
Darren Soto (D-FL)
Norma Torres (D-CA)
Juan Vargas (D-CA)
Filemon Vela (D-TX)
Nydia Velázquez (D-NY)

Latinos in the Senate

Ted Cruz (R-TX)

Catherine Cortez Masto (D-NV)
Robert Menendez (D-NJ)

Marco Rubio (R-FL)

Asian Americans in the House of Representatives

Ami Bera (D-CA)
Judy Chu (D-CA)
Tulsi Gabbard (D-HI)
Colleen Hanabasa (D-HI)
Ro Khanna (D-CA)

Raja Krishnamoorthi (D-IL)
Pramila Jayapal (D-WA)
Ted Lieu (D-CA)
Doris Matsui (D-CA)

Grace Meng (D-NY)
Stephanie Murphy (D-FL)
Robert Scott (D-VA)[a]
Mark Takano (D-CA)

Asian Americans in the Senate

Tammy Duckworth (D-IL)
Mazie Hirono (D-HI)

American Indians in the House of Representatives

Tom Cole (R-OK)

Markwayne Mullin (R-OK)

[a] Representative Scott is both African American and Filipino.
Sources: Data compiled from the U.S. House website (www.house.gov) and the U.S. Senate website (www.senate.gov), accessed May 8, 2014. The authors updated this with 2016 election results.

evaluating equality

Should the Race or Ethnicity of a Representative Matter?

As this section has discussed, political leaders pay considerable attention to the race and ethnicity of elected representatives, especially in the United States House of Representatives. Consequently, civil rights leaders have focused on the creation of majority-minority districts, which since the 1990s have increased the number of Black and Latino representatives. However, many critics argue that focusing on the race or ethnicity of the elected representative is inappropriate and that White representatives can advocate for their minority constituents equally as well just as minority representatives can. For example Steve Cohen (D-TN), who is white, represents the 9th District of Tennessee (Memphis and the surrounding area), which

according to the U.S. Census is 65.7 percent Black.[*] Yet, Representative Cohen receives the highest marks from civil rights organizations on issues of importance to African Americans (as well as Latinos), and he is consistently reelected.[**] Moreover, as this chapter's opening vignette shows, Representative Will Hurd (R-TX) is African American but represents a majority-Latino district, and he will continue to do so for the 115th Congress.

Students should debate the question over whether it is necessary for a minority representative to represent a majority-minority district. When framing this debate, focus on the differences among descriptive, symbolic, and substantive representation. Does the amount

of overall minority representation in the U.S. House affect the kinds of legislation the institution will pass, or not pass? If, as the research we cited in the chapter demonstrates, the creation of majority-minority districts has increased overall Republican representation, then has the increase of minority representatives been a benefit for Blacks and Latinos? Research the careers of Representatives Cohen and Hurd. What do they add to this debate?

[*] United States Census, "My Congressional District: 114th Congress," http://www.census.gov/mycd/, accessed June 12, 2016.

[**] Congressman Steve Cohen, "Congressman Cohen's Vote Ratings," https://cohen.house.gov/about/vote-ratings, accessed June 12, 2016.

help to increase the trust that racial and ethnic minorities place in their representative, Congress, and the American government as a whole. As a result, majority-minority districts can enhance symbolic representation.

But in terms of substantive representation, minority-majority districts can be problematic. The creation of these districts often renders the surrounding districts devoid of minority voters, and those districts are not likely to elect a representative who would advocate on behalf of policy issues important to racial or ethnic minorities. In other words, a majority-minority district creates one minority representative and one (or more) representative(s) in surrounding districts who would not be concerned with the plight of racial and ethnic minorities. If the residents of the majority-minority district were to be divided in half and put into larger White districts, then no minority representative would be elected, but there would be two White representatives who would need to advocate on behalf of the policy preferences of the substantial minority populations in their districts because those minority populations could still determine the outcome of an election. These White representatives would provide substantive representation to their racial and ethnic minority constituents.[16]

Because senators represent entire states, it is more difficult for racial and ethnic minorities to win Senate seats. However, there have been some successes, especially in states with larger minority populations. There are nine minority senators at the start of the 115th Congress, which is the most in

American history. Mazie Hirono (D-HI) and Tammy Duckworth (D-IL) are the two Asian American senators. Catherine Cortez Masto (D-NV), Robert Menendez (D-NJ), Marco Rubio (R-FL), and Ted Cruz (R-TX) are four Latino senators. Kamala Harris (D-CA), Tim Scott (R-SC), and Corey Booker (D-NJ) are the three African American senators. In 2012 South Carolina Governor Nikki Haley appointed Scott to replace Jim DeMint, who resigned his seat, and in 2013 Booker won a special election to replace Frank Lautenberg, who died in office. Booker and Scott were easily reelected to full terms in 2014. The history of minorities who have served in the Senate is given in Table 6.2.

Overall, the 113th Congress also became more diverse in other ways. Tammy Baldwin (D-WI) became the first openly gay senator; Kyrsten Sinema (D-AZ) became the first openly bisexual member elected to Congress; and Mark Takano (D-CA) became the first openly gay minority elected to Congress. The 115th Congress has the most minority senators in history (nine), and the House has three Indian Americans, including the first female Indian American (Pramila Jayapal (D-WA)).

Congressional Organization and Leadership

Every two years, American voters elect the entire House of Representatives and one-third of the Senate, and a new Congress is seated the following January. To conduct legislative business effectively, the two houses must organize themselves, and the most important organizing principle is **political party** (see Chapter 14 for more details on political parties). In each chamber, either the Democratic or Republican Party wins a majority of the seats. If the partisan split in the Senate is 50–50, then the vice president of the United States, who casts deciding votes in the Senate, will cast the vote in favor of his or her

Political Party Mass organizations that seek to elect candidates to public office and influence policymaking.

House Minority Leader Nancy Pelosi (D-CA), center, with Democratic women of the House for a group photo on the first day of the 113th Congress in Washington, January 3, 2013. After the 2012 election more women won House and Senate seats than in any time in U.S. history. In fact, White males are now a minority of Democratic House members.

TABLE 6.2 Minorities Who Have Served in the United States Senate

Name	State	Party	Race	Dates of Service
Daniel Akaka	Hawaii	Democrat	Asian American	1990–2013
Edward W. Brooke	Massachusetts	Republican	African American	1967–1979
Blanche K. Bruce	Mississippi	Republican	African American	1875–1881
Corey Booker	New Jersey	African American	Democrat	2013–present
Roland Burris	Illinois	Democrat	African American	2009–2010
Ben Nighthorse Campbell	Colorado	Republican	American Indian	1993–2005
Dennis Chavez	New Mexico	Democrat	Latino	1935–1962
Ted Cruz	Texas	Republican	Latino	2013–present
William Cowan	Massachusetts	African American	Democrat	2013
Charles Curtis	Kansas	Republican	American Indian	1907–1913, 1915–1929
Tammy Duckworth	Illinois	Democrat	Asian American	2017–present
Hiram K. Fong	Hawaii	Republican	Asian American	1959–1977
Kamala Harris	California	Democrat	African American	2017–present
Samuel I. Hayakawa	California	Republican	Asian American	1977–1983
Mazie Hirono	Hawaii	Democrat	Asian American	2013–present
Daniel Inouye	Hawaii	Democrat	Asian American	1963–2012
Octaviano Larrazolo	New Mexico	Republican	Latino	1928–1929
Melquiades R. Martinez	Florida	Republican	Latino	2005–2009
Catherine Cotez	Masto Nevada	Democrat	Latino	2017–present
Spark M. Matsunaga	Hawaii	Democrat	Asian American	1977–1990
Robert Menendez	New Jersey	Democrat	Latino	2006–present
Joseph M. Montoya	New Mexico	Democrat	Latino	1964–1977
Carol Moseley-Braun	Illinois	Democrat	African American	1993–1999
Barack Obama	Illinois	Democrat	African American	2005–2008
Robert Owen	Oklahoma	Democrat	American Indian	1907–1925
Hiram R. Revels	Mississippi	Republican	African American	1870–1871
Marco Rubio	Florida	Republican	Latino	2011–present
Ken L. Salazar	Colorado	Democrat	Latino	2005–2009
Tim Scott	South Carolina	Republican	African American	2012–present

Source: United States Senate, "Ethnic Diversity in the Senate," http://www.senate.gov/artandhistory/history/common/briefing/minority_ senators.htm, accessed May 8, 2014 and updated by authors.

party. This situation occurred during the first half of 2001 when Vice President Richard Cheney gave his support to the Republicans. In June 2001, however, former Republican senator Jim Jeffords (VT) left the Republican Party, thus giving Democrats outright control of the Senate.

Majority Party The political party in the House or the Senate that has more than half of the seats and therefore controls the leadership, rules, and outcome of legislation.

Minority Party The political party in the House or the Senate that has fewer than half of the seats and therefore does not control the leadership, rules, or outcome of legislation.

Speaker of the House The most powerful position in the House of Representatives; the leader of the majority party; the person who articulates the House's legislative priorities and ensures their passage.

The party with more seats is known as the **majority party**, and the party with fewer seats is the **minority party**. In the House and Senate, the majority party controls the organizational structure and occupies the most important leadership positions. Although the House and Senate are similarly organized, there are key differences between the two bodies, and in both congressional organization is interwoven with the politics of race and ethnicity.

Leadership in the House

Because the House of Representatives contains 435 members, it must be tightly organized to function. Accordingly, the majority party selects the important House leaders, who exert significant control over the procedures and outcomes of legislation. Most notably, in the House of Representatives, the majority party controls the agenda throughout the legislative process. As a result, majority party leaders are able to ensure the passage of legislation that they favor and prevent the passage of legislation that they oppose.[17]

The most important position in the House of Representatives is the **Speaker of the House**. Before each Congress commences in the January following the election, the majority party selects its candidate for Speaker, and at the beginning of the congressional term the entire House chooses its Speaker. All members of the majority party are expected to support their party's choice for Speaker; thus, the majority party's Speaker candidate is guaranteed to be elected.

The Speaker of the House is the leader of the entire House of Representatives, but the primary function of the Speaker is to be the leader of the majority party. Thus, the Speaker will articulate the majority party's legislative priorities and work to ensure that the House passes them. Likewise, Speakers use their authority to prevent the minority party's legislative priorities from being passed into law. Speakers of the House oversee legislative business, refer bills to committees, control debates, act as House spokespeople, and apply rules of parliamentary procedure—in short, they control the fate of the bills that are introduced.

Speakers are also extremely influential in determining the membership and leaders of committees. Consequently, they tremendously influence the power and prestige of the majority party members. Although personal leadership styles vary, the Speakers all use their authority over majority party members to ensure that there is enough support for the bills they want passed. No racial or ethnic minorities have been speaker, and from 2007 until 2011 Nancy Pelosi (D-CA) was the only woman to serve in this powerful position.

House Majority Leader The second most powerful leader in the House of Representatives; the person who assists the Speaker in passing the majority party's legislative priorities.

Whip A legislative leader who assists the party by counting votes and persuading members to vote according to the party leaders' wishes.

Administering the House is far too extensive a responsibility to handle alone; Speakers use deputies to help accomplish their goals. The **House majority leader** is the second most powerful position in the House of Representatives, and his or her function is to assist in articulating, planning, and implementing the Speaker's legislative agenda and strategy. Following the Speaker and majority leader in the party hierarchy is the majority **whip**, who is the vote counter for the majority party. The majority whip surveys the majority party members to determine their views on pending legislation and then persuades them to vote according to the party leadership's wishes.

The majority party alone chooses its majority leader and whip through a secret ballot, although the Speaker, who is selected first, can influence party members' subsequent choices. Like the Speaker, the majority leader and the majority whip occupy extremely powerful positions in the House, and they often use that power on behalf of their constituents. Therefore, racial and ethnic minorities can benefit when they serve in one of these powerful positions, but their influence depends on partisan control of the House. After Democrats took control of the House in 2007 Black Representative James Clyburn (D-SC) became the majority whip. When Republicans took control of the House, Clyburn had to settle for the less powerful and less prestigious position of assistant Democratic (minority) leader, with the primary function of communicating between the House Democrats and the president. Moreover, when he was majority whip, Clyburn had twenty staff members and a $2 million budget, but his staff was reduced to six and his budget decreased sharply after he lost that position.[18]

U.S. Representative James E. Clyburn (D-SC) speaks on stage during the final day of the Democratic National Convention on September 6, 2012, in Charlotte, NC. When Democrats were the majority party in the House from 2007–2011, Representative Clyburn held the powerful position of majority whip. However, after Democrats lost the majority, Clyburn was relegated to the less powerful position of assistant democratic leader.

The minority party has leaders as well, but they are typically unable to significantly affect the legislative outcomes of the House. The **House minority leader** is in charge of the minority party, and like the Speaker, she or he articulates the minority party's legislative priorities and keeps the minority party unified behind those priorities. The minority leader helps determine minority party committee assignments and acts as a national spokesperson for the minority party. The minority whip is the second in command for the minority party, serves as a party spokesperson, and is responsible for counting votes and persuading members of the minority party to vote as their leadership wishes.

House Minority Leader The leader of the minority party in the House of Representatives; the person who articulates the legislative priorities of the minority party and opposes the majority party's priorities but exerts minimal control over the outcome of legislation.

The minority leaders, despite their leadership roles, are unable to push their party's legislative program through the House. Instead, they offer opposition to the majority's legislative agenda in the hopes that their party will capture a majority of the seats in the next election. For example, in January 2011, the newly empowered House Republican majority voted to repeal the controversial Affordable Care Act, a health care reform law passed in 2010. Although Democratic minority leaders opposed repealing the law, they were powerless to stop the majority Republicans, or even slow the passage of the bill and force some concessions from the Republican majority. At best, the Democratic leaders were able to secure virtually universal opposition to the Republican bill. Since Republicans took control in 2011, the House has passed more than fifty bills designed to repeal or significantly alter the Affordable Care Act, but these bills did not pass the Senate until 2016, after Republicans took control of the Senate. Still President Obama successfully vetoed the repeal.[19]

Leadership in the Senate

Compared to House leaders, leaders in the Senate exert less influence over their members. The vice president of the United States is the president of the

Senate, but this designation is largely formal. The vice president votes only to break a tie and presides over the Senate only on special occasions, such as the State of the Union address or an address to the Senate by a foreign dignitary. The president pro tempore is the presiding officer of the Senate when the vice president declines to serve in that role, which is usually the case. Nevertheless, this position is largely honorary, going to the longest serving member of the majority party. Usually, the president pro tempore does not even preside over Senate meetings, instead appointing junior members of the majority party to perform that duty.

The most important leader of the Senate is the **Senate majority leader**, who is elected by the majority party in the Senate. The majority leader's position is roughly analogous to that of the Speaker of the House, except that it wields far less power. Senate majority leaders articulate the majority party's legislative priorities, determine the legislative calendar, influence majority party members' committee assignments, and schedule debates and votes. Similar to the Speaker of the House, the majority leader uses his or her power to secure majority party support for the party's legislative agenda. The **Senate majority whip**, also known as the assistant majority leader, counts votes and persuades members to vote according to the leadership's wishes. Similar to the House of Representatives, the minority party in the Senate has leaders, but unlike their counterparts in the House, the Senate minority leaders consult with the majority leaders when scheduling debates and votes. The leader of the minority party in the Senate is known as the **Senate minority leader**.

Committees

Like any other large institution that performs a variety of functions, Congress divides its labor into specialized units known as committees. Most committees are further split into subcommittees, which work on bills in an even more specialized fashion. Once a bill is introduced in either house, the Speaker or the Senate majority leader refers it to the appropriate committees, and then those committees conduct hearings at which experts testify on the bill's merits. In the Senate, committees also conduct hearings when the Senate is deciding whether to ratify treaties and approve presidential nominees to the executive branch and the federal judiciary.

After conducting hearings and collecting other information, the committee amends the original bill at a markup session. Some of these changes can be minor, such as a slight adjustment in spending, but other amendments completely change the bill's nature. Because the majority party enjoys a majority of members on the committee, it controls which amendments are passed. The final product to emerge from the markup session rarely resembles the original bill.

Finally, the committee recommends passage or rejection of the bill. Generally, bills (and nominations in the Senate) that are not reported favorably from committees will not be scheduled for a vote and thus do not pass. The majority party leadership and the majority members on the committees dominate the decisions that the committees make. Table 6.3 lists the standing

Senate Majority Leader The most powerful position in the Senate; the person who articulates the majority party's legislative priorities and works to pass them.

Senate Majority Whip (also called the assistant majority leader) A majority party leader in the Senate who counts votes, persuades members to vote according to the leadership's wishes, and assists the majority leader in passing the majority party's legislation.

Senate Minority Leader The leader of the minority party of the Senate; the person who articulates the legislative priorities of the minority party and opposes the majority party's priorities but exerts limited control over the outcome of legislation.

TABLE 6.3 Standing Committees of the House and Senate, 114th Congress (2015–2017)

HOUSE		
Committee	Size (Party)	Percent of Committee That Is a Racial or Ethnic Minority[a]
Agriculture	45 (26R/19D)	15.6
Appropriations	51 (30R/21D)	21.6
Armed Services	63 (36R/27D)	14.3
Budget	36 (22R/14D)	19.4
Education and the Workforce	38 (22R/16D)	27.8
Energy and Commerce	54 (31R/23D)	16.6
Ethics	10 (5R/5D)	20.0
Financial Services	60 (34R/26D)	21.3
Foreign Affairs	44 (25R/19D)	20.5
Homeland Security	30 (18R/12D)	30.0
House Administration	9 (6R/3D)	11.1
Intelligence	21 (12R/9D)	14.3
Judiciary	39 (23R/16D)	25.6
Natural Resources	47 (26R/21D)	21.3
Oversight and Government Reform	43 (25R/18D)	25.6
Rules	13 (9R/4D)	15.4
Science, Space, and Technology	37 (21R/16D)[b]	13.5
Small Business	22 (12R/10D)	45.5
Transportation and Infrastructure	59 (34R/25D)	15.3
Veterans' Affairs	24 (14R/10D)	16.7
Ways and Means	39 (24R/15D)	12.8
SENATE		
Agriculture, Nutrition, and Forestry	20 (11R/9D)	0.0
Appropriations	30 (16R/14D)	0.0
Armed Services	26 (14R/12D)	7.7
Banking, Housing, and Urban Affairs	22 (12R/10D)	9.1
Budget	22 (12R/10D)	0.0
Commerce, Science, and Transportation	24 (13R/11D)	12.5
Energy and Natural Resources	22 (12R/10D)	4.5
Environment and Public Works	20 (11R/9D)	5.0

(continued)

TABLE 6.3 (*Continued*)

Committee	Size (Party)	Percent of Committee That Is a Racial or Ethnic Minority[a]
Ethics	6 (3R/3D)	0.0
Finance	26 (14R/12D)	7.7
Foreign Relations	19 (10R/9D)	5.3
Health, Education, Labor, and Pensions	22 (12R/10D)	4.5
Homeland Security and Govt. Affairs	16 (9R/7D)	6.3
Indian Affairs	14 (8R/6D)	0.0
Intelligence	15 (8R/7D)	13.3
Judiciary	20 (11R/9D)	11.1
Rules and Administration	18 (10R/8D)	5.6
Small Business and Entrepreneurship	19 (10R/9D)	21.1
Veterans' Affairs	15 (8R/7D)	6.7

Note: Although Angus King (I-ME) and Bernard Sanders (I-VT) are technically Independents, they both support the Democratic leadership and are organizationally part of the Democratic Party in the Senate.
[a] *Because nonvoting delegates can vote in committee, they are included in both the size counts and the percentage of the committee that is a racial or ethnic minority.*
[b] *There are vacancies on this committee as of June 10, 2016; therefore, these numbers might change.*
Sources: Data compiled from the U.S. House website (http://www.house.gov/committees/) and U.S. Senate website (http://www.senate.gov/committees/committees_home.htm), accessed June 11, 2016.

committees, their partisan composition, and the percentage of racial and ethnic minorities that serve on them in the 114th Congress.

Committee and subcommittee chairs, who are members of the majority party, possess the authority to call meetings, set agendas for meetings, decide which witnesses testify at hearings, and preside over meetings and markup sessions. By refusing to schedule a bill for committee action, the chair can defeat a bill unilaterally because it cannot proceed to the House or Senate floor for a vote. During the 1950s, conservative White Southern committee chairs used this power to prevent the passage of civil rights bills. A majority (218) of the House can sign a discharge petition to dislodge a bill from a committee's jurisdiction, but a successful discharge petition requires the signature of members of the majority party, who are wary of opposing powerful committee chairs or party leadership. Successful discharge petitions are therefore a rare occurrence.

Long-term service on a committee, known as seniority, is a requirement for becoming a committee chair, but the leadership has the final say on naming committee chairs. After the Democrats won control of Congress in 2006, many Black, Latino, and Asian American Democratic representatives and senators were senior enough to chair powerful committees, but when Republicans regained control of the House in 2010 the number of minority committee

THE GOP'S COMMITTEE CHAIRMEN

SPEAKER JOHN BOEHNER HAS ANNOUNCED CHAIRMEN APPOINTMENTS IN 19 OF THE 21 MAJOR COMMITTEES SO FAR:

NO WOMEN. NO MINORITIES. NINETEEN WHITE MEN.
WELCOME TO THE NEW REPUBLICAN PARTY, SAME AS THE OLD REPUBLICAN PARTY.

THINK PROGRESS

After Republicans maintained control of the House of Representatives in the 2012 election, the majority party leadership presented the American people with their list of committee chairs, all of whom are White males. After this list generated negative publicity, Speaker John Boehner named Representative Candice Miller (R-MI), a White female, as the chair of the House Administration Committee—one of the least powerful committees in the House.

chairs sharply decreased. At the start of the 113th Congress, Senator Robert Menendez (D-NJ) became the only minority committee chair in either house of Congress when he assumed control of the Senate Foreign Relations Committee, but he lost that position in 2015 when the Democrats become the minority party in the Senate. The 114th Congress has no minority committee chairs.

Informal Organizations

In addition to parties, leaders, and committees, members of Congress organize themselves informally into special **caucuses**, which focus on common geographical, economic, or cultural issues or concerns. Some examples include the Congressional Wine Caucus, the Congressional Sportsmen Caucus, the Congressional Human Rights Caucus, and the Congressional Animal Protection Caucus. These caucuses are bicameral and bipartisan, and they try to publicize issues to focus attention on their members' key priorities.

Three caucuses advocate on behalf of racial and ethnic minorities. Since 1971, the **Congressional Black Caucus** (CBC) has promoted African

Caucuses Informal organizations within Congress.

Congressional Black Caucus An informal organization consisting of African Americans elected to the United States Congress.

Members of the Congressional Black Caucus, including current chair G. K. Butterfield, Andre Carson, William Lacy Clay, Shelia Jackson Lee, and Karen Bass, seated at the Wellspring Methodist Church in Ferguson, MO. After a Ferguson police officer killed African American teenager Michael Brown in 2014, the city has become a focal point for the question of how law enforcement officers treat minorities. As the primary organization in Congress that advocates on behalf of African Americans, the Congressional Black Caucus highlights issues of importance for African Americans.

American members for leadership positions and has pushed for legislation beneficial to African Americans. For example, the Congressional Black Caucus has recently fought against changes to voter eligibility laws, which can depress minority turnout.[20] In the 114th Congress, all of the African American Democratic members of Congress are members of the CBC, but Mia Love (R-UT) is the only African American Republican member—Senator Tim Scott (R-SC) and Representative Will Hurd (R-TX) are not.[21] Likewise, the Congressional Hispanic Caucus (CHC) advocates on behalf of issues of importance to Latinos, such as immigration.[22] The CHC consists of Democratic members of Congress who are Latino, in addition to Representative Jim Costa, who is of Portuguese descent but does not meet the definition of Latino that we use in this book. None of the Latino Republican House and Senate members has joined the CHC.[23] The Congressional Asian Pacific American Caucus advocates on behalf of issues relevant to Asian Americans, and it consists of Asian American members of Congress, as well as members who do not have an Asian background.[24]

The Lawmaking Process

The lawmaking process in Congress is extremely complex, and there are major differences between the House and Senate. The different rules in each chamber influence policymaking in that chamber. The majority party in the House dominates the lawmaking process without consulting with the minority, whereas the majority party in the Senate exerts far less control over the process of lawmaking. It is also true that Congress has nonlegislative functions, and these functions influence minority-group politics.

Activity on the House Floor

After the applicable committee in the House of Representatives approves a bill, the House Rules Committee decides how the bill will be considered by the full House. The Rules Committee develops a rule that specifies the additional amendments that can be considered, the amount of time for debate, and the schedule for voting on final passage of the bill. The chair of the Rules Committee works closely with majority party leaders to craft a rule that gives the majority party a legislative advantage. In fact, until the early twentieth century, the Speaker actually chaired the Rules Committee.[25]

When the majority party leadership wants to see a bill passed quickly, the chair of the Rules Committee will not allow the minority party to offer amendments that could change the nature of a bill or delay its passage. The Rules Committee will schedule little time for debate and call for a quick vote to prevent opponents from building opposition to the bill. Rules Committee chairs can prevent the passage of bills they oppose by refusing to schedule those bills for debate and vote. For example, during the 1950s the segregationist chair of the Rules Committee, Howard W. Smith (D-VA), used his authority to prevent civil rights bills from moving to the House floor for a vote.[26]

Once the Rules Committee schedules a rule (i.e., a date and time for voting, time allotted for debate, and amendments that can be considered), the bill proceeds to the House floor; that is, it is put before consideration of all 435 members of the institution. The House first votes on the Rules Committee's rule, which is virtually guaranteed to pass. Once the House approves the rule, it then considers the amendments that the Rules Committee allowed, and amendments that receive a majority vote become part of the bill.

The Rules Committee's allotted time for debate is then divided evenly between the majority and minority parties, and each side designates a floor manager to control the debate. Usually, the floor manager for the majority party is the committee or subcommittee chair and the floor manager for the minority party is the ranking minority member who was most active in developing (or usually opposing) the bill. Each floor manager then organizes the speakers for his or her side. For the most part, there is little actual debate; instead, each speaker reads a prepared statement and then is able to enter a longer statement with attachments into the official proceedings of Congress, known as the *Congressional Record*. House members vote at the time and date that the rule provides. In short, the majority party in the U.S. House of Representatives dominates the content of legislation and the speed at which it passes. The minority party has very little influence over either.

Congressional Record The published record of the official proceedings of Congress.

Action on the Senate Floor

Although the procedures in the Senate generally mirror those in the House, there are crucial differences. Because the Senate has far fewer members than the House, the rules are far less formal. The rules in the Senate allow for more individual freedom and for minority party input. As in the House, Senate bills must pass through committees, although the committees, subcommittees, and the chairs exert far less authority over the outcome of legislation. However, unlike the House Rules Committee, the Senate Committee on Rules and Administration lacks the power to schedule bills on the Senate floor. Instead, the majority and minority leaders try to negotiate a unanimous consent agreement in which every member agrees to which amendments can be considered, the allotment of debate time, and the vote schedule. However, if one senator objects, then he or she can derail the proceedings. Consequently, Senate leaders usually accommodate individual senators' requests to introduce amendments or speak on a bill.

The Senate majority leader must also take into account the minority party's concerns when drafting legislation and unanimous consent agreements. Senators who oppose a bill are free to speak as long they want, employing a tactic known as a **filibuster**. Because a vote cannot occur as long as a senator holds the floor, filibusters are a strategy for the minority party to block further consideration of a bill. Senators can end debate only through a **cloture vote**, which requires the support of three-fifths of the Senate (sixty senators). If the minority party has the support of at least forty-one senators (the minimum number to block a cloture vote), then it can prevent the majority party from passing its desired legislation. As we discuss in later chapters, filibusters had been used to block presidential nominations to the executive and judicial branches.

Unlike the minority party in the House, the minority party in the Senate can use the filibuster to force the majority party to allow the minority party's amendments to be considered, add more time to the debate, and postpone final considerations of the bill. The minority party can also force the majority party to compromise on the substance of the bill. Consequently, although Senate Republicans enjoy a majority in the 114th Congress, majority leader Mitch McConnell (R-KY) needs to consult with the minority leader on his high-priority bills to avoid a Democratic filibuster.

The filibuster has also affected civil rights policy. For example, as we mentioned earlier, the House passed by a significant margin the bill to give Washington, DC (and its large African-American population) a voting member of the House. But when the bill arrived in the Senate, Minority Leader McConnell staged a filibuster because he claimed Congress lacked the constitutional authority to give Washington, DC, a voting member in the House. The cloture vote was 57–42,[27] which was not sufficient to end the filibuster. Consequently, even though a considerable majority of the House and Senate supported the bill, the rules of the Senate prevented it from becoming law.

Filibuster A parliamentary technique in the Senate that allows senators to delay or block votes by talking endlessly.

Cloture vote A procedure in the Senate to stop a filibuster that requires three-fifths of the senators (sixty) agreeing to end debate.

Reconciling Differences Between House and Senate Bills

The Constitution requires that bills emerging from the House and Senate must be identical to become law. But as we have already made clear, bills undergo many changes in both houses, and in the Senate, but not in the House, the majority party compromises with the minority party. As a result, major legislation passed in the House is rarely identical to the same legislation passed in the Senate.

Congress reconciles different bills through the use of a **conference committee**, whose members are selected by the majority and minority leaders in both houses. As with other committees, the majority party enjoys a majority on conference committees. When naming members to the conference committee, party leaders usually defer to the committee chairs and ranking minority members who worked on the bill. Conference committee members attempt to reconcile the different versions of the bill through compromise. A majority of all the conferees must agree to the compromise for it to take effect. Then the compromise must be approved by a majority of both houses. In short, lawmaking procedures are extremely complex. To clarify this complexity, Figure 6.2 diagrams the process of lawmaking.

Conference Committee A committee composed of members of the House and the Senate that reconciles different versions of the same bill.

Nonlawmaking Functions of Congress

A significant portion of the work that Congress does is not legislative, and these nonlawmaking functions are important for American government, including the politics of race and ethnicity. One nonlegislative congressional function is the Senate's role in confirming presidential appointments. Although most presidential nominees are confirmed, the Senate and the president have occasionally clashed over appointments.

For example, in 1999 President Bill Clinton nominated Ronnie White to be a federal district court judge for the Eastern District of Missouri. Justice White was the first African American to serve on the Missouri State Supreme Court, and most people expected the Senate to confirm him easily. However, Republican Senator John Ashcroft (R-MO) pressured his colleagues to oppose the nomination because he argued that Justice White had reversed too many criminal convictions and death sentences. Senator Ashcroft convinced his Republican colleagues to oppose the nomination, and because the Republicans were then the majority party, White's nomination failed. Democratic Senators, Democratic politicians in Missouri, and civil rights leaders maintained that Justice White's record on criminal matters was the same as that of other justices in Missouri. Despite Republican denials, White's supporters charged that racism was the real reason for the opposition to White, and this controversy affected Senator Ashcroft's 2000 reelection bid,[28] which he eventually lost.

Another nonlawmaking function of Congress is the impeachment and removal power. **Impeachment** refers to the power to charge the president, vice president, or a federal judge with "treason, bribery, or other high crimes and misdemeanors." The Constitution gives the impeachment power to the House

Impeachment The process by which the House of Representatives charges a president, vice president, or federal judge with a high crime or misdemeanor; the Senate can then decide to remove that official from office with a two-thirds vote.

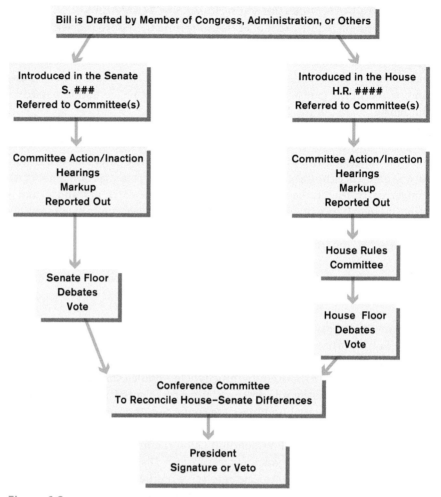

Figure 6.2 How a Bill Becomes a Law.

of Representatives. When a member of the House introduces impeachment charges, the Judiciary Committee conducts hearings featuring testimony from constitutional experts, those making the charges, and those defending the public official. The Judiciary Committee decides whether to recommend impeachment, and the final impeachment decision is determined by a majority of the House of Representatives.

If someone is impeached, then a committee in the Senate investigates whether there is enough evidence to convict and remove the official, which requires support of two-thirds of the Senate. Only two presidents—Andrew Johnson in 1868 and Bill Clinton in 1998—have been impeached, but they were not removed from office. Several federal judges have been impeached and removed from office. In 1989, Black federal judge Alcee Hastings was impeached and removed from office for accusations of bribery, but in 1992 he was elected to the House from a district in south Florida, and he still serves today in a district that is slightly more than 50 percent African American.[29]

Because impeachments are rarely used, Congress generally polices the executive branch and the bureaucracy through its oversight power, which allows Congress to investigate apparent problems in an executive (see Chapter 7) or bureaucratic (see Chapter 8) agency that it created. Inherent in the lawmaking power of Congress is the authority to make sure that its laws are enforced according to its intentions and to prevent waste, fraud, or abuse in government. Generally, committees and subcommittees handle oversight, usually in the form of hearings, which not only provide evidence, but also generate publicity for a cause.

Although oversight often features interbranch disputes, it is largely a partisan process. Committee chairs have tremendous discretion in determining whether to conduct oversight investigations. As a result, Congress is less likely to exercise its oversight power in periods of **unified government**, when the president's party is the same as that in the majority of both houses, than in periods of **divided government**, when one or both houses of Congress are controlled by the party opposite the president's. This partisanship was evident when the Republicans assumed control of the House in 2011 and announced that they would sharply increase investigations of the Obama administration on issues such as its perceived failure to enforce immigration laws. House Democrats argued that Republicans were motivated by a partisan desire to embarrass President Obama.[30] In 2107 there will be a Republican President and Republican controlled Congress; therefore, one would predict that there will be fewer investigations of the executive branch.

Unified Government
A period in which both houses of Congress are controlled by the same party as the president.

Divided Government
A period in which the president is of one political party and the majority of one or both houses of Congress is of the other party.

Influences on Congressional Decision-Making

There are various influences on legislators' voting behavior, including constituents, party leaders, colleagues, interest groups, and staff. These competing influences are further shaped by minority-group politics.

Constituents

A fundamental basis of representative government is that representatives act on behalf of their constituents. Partisan gerrymandering creates numerous districts that are overwhelmingly Democratic or Republican, and representatives of those districts are easily able to vote according to the preferences of a large majority of their constituents. Likewise, racial and ethnic minority members of the House who represent majority-minority districts are usually able to vote in accordance with their constituents' preferences, especially on civil rights issues. However, states, and even many House districts, have heterogeneous populations, and the political views and policy preferences of these constituents are less clear to their representatives in Congress.

The relationship between members of Congress and their constituents is complex and has been the subject of political science research. David

Mayhew's classic study *Congress: The Electoral Connection* is based on the fundamental assumption that members of Congress are primarily motivated by reelection. Consequently, much of their behavior aims more to enhance their prestige than to craft meaningful public policy. For example, members of Congress devote considerable effort to "advertising," in which they generate a favorable image by sending information and working with the local media. Furthermore, when communicating with their constituents, members of Congress "credit claim," whereby they create the impression that their actions have influenced the government in a positive direction.[31] Additionally, Richard Fenno spent time with a small number of selected members of the House of Representatives both in Washington, DC, and in their districts. He found that representatives adopt a "home style" in how they relate to their different types of constituencies—the entire geographic region they represent, the people they expect to vote for them, the politically engaged supporters who will work on their behalf, and their close political associates.[32]

Casework Favors and other forms of assistance that members of Congress provide to their constituents.

Building off the work of Mayhew, political scientist Morris Fiorina emphasizes how members of Congress also act on behalf of constituents and secure a reelection advantage through "constituency service" or **casework**.[33] Casework entails members of Congress advocating on behalf of constituents who need assistance in dealing with the federal government, such as finding a lost Social Security check, settling conflicts with the Internal Revenue Service, or appointing students to a military academy. Because members of Congress have influence over government employees, casework requires minimal staff time; in return, members win grateful constituents. A recent study demonstrates that Black representatives have been extremely instrumental in providing casework and funding to their African-American constituents.[34]

Franking Privilege The ability of members of Congress to send noncampaign material to their constituents free of charge.

To represent constituents adequately and enhance reelection chances, members of Congress must communicate frequently with their constituents. Senators and representatives who live close to Washington, DC, live in their districts and commute to the Capitol. Others frequently travel back to their districts on the weekends and during recesses. Members of Congress also advertise to their constituents through the mail. The **franking privilege** allows senators and representatives to send newsletters and surveys to their constituents without paying postage fees. Although franked mail cannot be used for campaign material (which must come from the congressperson's campaign account) and cannot be used within 90 days of an election,[35] members of Congress are able to use the franking privilege to promote their accomplishments, which can help them to get reelected.

All members maintain websites that contain text, audio, and visual information about the member, the district, committee work, votes, and casework. Senators and representatives who are concerned about their Latino constituents provide Spanish-language versions of their websites. Some representatives who have a large number of Latino and Asian American constituents even offer multilingual versions of their websites.

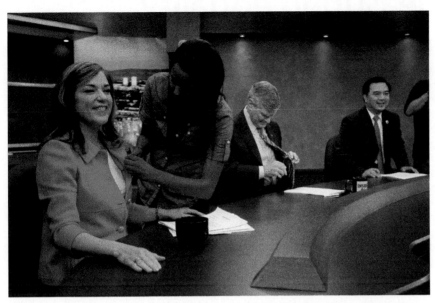

Representative Loretta Sanchez (D-CA) getting ready to debate her Republican opponent Van Tran in the 2010 election. Sanchez's district contains sizable populations of Latinos and Asian Americans. With Sanchez being Latino and Tran being Vietnamese American, the race drew national attention, but Sanchez won handily. Representative Sanchez still needs to communicate with all of her constituents; therefore, her House website (http://lorettasanchez.house.gov/) is available in over 100 different languages, but as of 2017 she will no longer serve in Congress.

Party Leaders

It should be quite evident by now that political party is extremely important in determining members' votes, particularly in the House of Representatives. The party leadership strongly influences committee assignments, allocation of campaign resources, and power within the legislative institution. But at times members go against their party leaders because their constituents' interests clash with those leaders' goals. For example, when the Republicans controlled the House in 1996, Speaker Newt Gingrich (R-GA) pushed for a bill that would have allowed states to deny education to the children of undocumented immigrants. Although Republican representative Ileana Ros-Lehtinen (R-FL) usually votes with her party, she opposed the bill because the large Latino population in her district vehemently opposed it.[36] "Measuring Equality: The Influence of Race and Political Party on Congressional Voting," explores in more detail the tension between race and ethnicity and party in congressional voting.

Colleagues

Because Congress is a collegial institution (unlike the executive), senators and representatives often influence each other's behavior. Many legislators develop friendships with colleagues, and these friendships can affect votes. However, **logrolling**, or the trading of votes, is the most common means by

Logrolling The practice by members of Congress of trading votes or other favors to enhance members' mutual interests.

measuring equality

The Influence of Race and Political Party on Congressional Voting

Students of Congress investigate the competing influences on members' voting behavior, and one key debate concerns the influence of race and ethnicity versus that of political party. Throughout this chapter, we have demonstrated the importance of both party and racial and ethnic background, and here we quantitatively test the influence of both factors by using congressional voting scorecards.

Many interest groups rate members of Congress according to how they voted on a selection of bills that the group identifies as high priority. In this example, we focus on the National Hispanic Leadership Agenda (NHLA), which has rated members of the House of Representatives of the 113th Congress (2013–2015, the most recent data available). The NHLA is concerned with economic, social, and political issues that affect all racial and ethnic minorities, but its main focus is on Latino concerns. The NHLA scores each House member with a percentage between 0 and 100 for support of its priority bills. To simplify the presentation, we classify House members who support at least two-thirds of the NHLA's bills as "high supporters," those who support between one-third and two-thirds as "moderate supporters," and those who support less than one-third of the NHLA's priorities as "low supporters." We are specifically interested in comparing the extent to which race and political party influence the likelihood that a House member will be

classified as a high supporter, moderate supporter, or low supporter.

Figure 6.3 displays the results for the percent of House members in each racial and ethnic group (White, Black, and Latino) that rank high, moderate, or low on the NHLA scores. The figure shows that all African American House members were in the high category (keep in mind that these data predate the addition of two African American Republicans in the U.S. House); therefore, being an African American is clearly related to a House member's support for the NHLA's priorities. Interestingly, support for the NHLA is lower among Latinos than it is for Blacks, with 75.0 percent of Latinos in the high category, 14.3 percent in the moderate, and 10.7 percent in the low category. Figure 6.3 also shows that support for the NHLA among White representatives is the lowest, with 34.6 percent in the high category, 10.7 percent in the moderate category, and 63.7 percent in the low category. There were not enough Asian American or American Indian representatives to analyze separately.

These results suggest that race matters because Black and Latino representatives are far more supportive of the NHLA than White representatives are. However, a similar analysis based on political party yields significant information as well. Figure 6.4 shows that 97.0 percent of House Democrats are in the high category, but no Republicans are in the high category. No Democrats are in

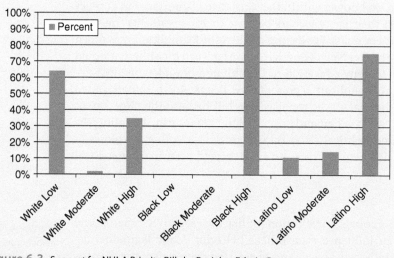

Figure 6.3 Support for NHLA Priority Bills by Racial or Ethnic Group.

measuring equality *(Continued)*

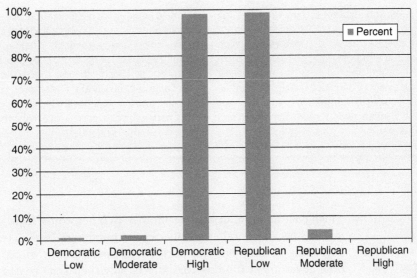

Figure 6.4 Support for NHLA Priority Bills by Political Party.

the low category, but 97.4 percent of Republicans are. Additionally, 2.6 percent of Republicans are moderate supporters, and 2.0 percent of Democrats are rated as moderate. The most significant finding here is that Democrats of any race support the NHLA more than do Whites and even Latinos, which suggests that political party matters more than ethnicity.

Finally, Latino support of the NHLA could be lower than the Black or Democratic support because there were conservative Republican Latinos in the 108th

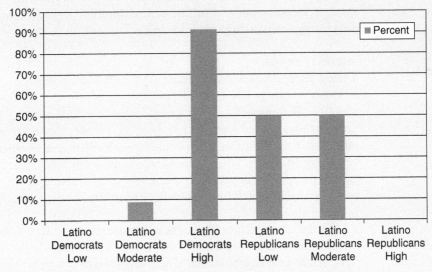

Figure 6.5 Support for NHLA Priority Bills among Latinos by Political Party.

Source: Data adapted from National Hispanic Leadership Agenda, Congressional Scorecard, First and Second Session, 113th Congress. August 2014, pp. 4–5, https://nationalhispanicleadership.org/images/Scorecards/ NHLA_2014scorecard_090915_forweb_2.pdf, accessed June 12, 2016.

(continued)

measuring equality *(Continued)*

Congress. We test this hypothesis by comparing the scores of Latino Republicans to those of Latino Democrats (see Figure 6.5). Whereas 91.3 percent of Latino Democrats are in the high category (8.7 percent are in the moderate category and there are no Latino Democrats in the low category), none of the Latino Republicans are, as can be seen in Figure 6.5. Instead, 50 percent of Latino Republicans are rated as moderate and 50 percent are rated as low.

Latino Republicans are more supportive of the NHLA than are Republicans as a whole, and they are more supportive than Whites; therefore, their ethnicity does matter. However, Latino Democrats and even Democrats of any race are much more supportive of the NHLA than Latino Republicans are. Moreover, Latino Democrats are closely matched with Democrats of any race. In short, party seems to matter more than ethnicity in supporting the NHLA's priorities.

Pork Barrel Spending Federal money spent on projects that benefit only a specific member's district or state.

which colleagues influence one another. In other words, legislators vote a certain way because another member agreed to support them in a particular vote. Logrolling is common with **pork barrel spending**, in which members propose government funding that affects only their state or district.[37] Because pork barrel projects are crucial to reelection, members are loath to vote against their colleagues' pork barrel spending out of fear of losing those colleagues' votes. The classic example of pork barrel spending is the case of the so-called "Bridge to Nowhere," in which Congress voted in 2005 to appropriate $233 million to build a massive bridge from Ketchikan, Alaska (with a population of about 8,000 people) to Gravina Island (with a population of 50 people). Although many commenters decried the need for this bridge, the chair of the House Transportation and Infrastructure Committee—Don Young (R-AK)—used his authority to help his home state.[38]

Interest Groups

Interest groups, organized collections of individuals who come together to influence public policy (see Chapter 13), are also important influences on members of Congress. Interest groups provide information to members of Congress who tend to support the positions of these groups. Those legislators can use that information when debating with colleagues or when justifying votes to constituents. These groups try to convince as many members of Congress as possible to support their desired legislation. Interest groups also influence legislators' votes by mobilizing constituents to contact members of Congress about public policy issues.

Groups advocating on behalf of racial and ethnic minorities have actively lobbied Congress in support of congressional legislation. The Japanese American Citizens League lobbied individual members of Congress to pass the Civil Liberties Act of 1988, which apologized to and provided reparations for Japanese Americans who had been interned during World War II.[39] The League of United Latin American Citizens, an interest group that advocates on behalf of Latinos, organized a campaign for supporters to contact their representatives and senators about including children of legal immigrants in government-funded children's health insurance.[40]

Staff

Legislators require staff to assist them with their daily responsibilities. Staffers conduct research, correspond with constituents, summarize bills, and write speeches. At times, staff members will actually write a bill that a member introduces. Although legislators are in charge of their offices, they rely heavily on staff. Members of Congress also employ staff to work in their districts or states on local concerns, casework, and promotion of the legislator's accomplishments. Each committee has a majority and a minority party staff, and, as one would expect, the majority staff is larger and has more resources. Although one might believe that congressional staff focus primarily on assisting in policymaking, political scientist Morris Fiorina finds otherwise. He writes, "when given . . . employees to allocate as they see fit, congressmen . . . put the lion's share to work on the most important thing, reelection, while reserving a few for secondary matters such as formulating our country's laws."[41]

Conclusion

As we discussed in Chapter 2, Congress is the primary lawmaking branch of the U.S. government, but the Constitution is vague on how Congress should operate. The Constitution lays out the membership requirements and powers of the House and Senate, but the actual functioning of the two institutions is far more complex. Although state boundaries determine the composition of the Senate, creating districts for House seats is more complicated.

The Constitution does not consider political parties in its design for Congress, but political party dominates. Party leaders exert tremendous influence over the outcome of legislation. The committee system divides labor into smaller units, and the committee chairs, who are members of the majority party, use their power to control the work of the committees.

The procedures in the House and Senate differ. The House Rules Committee allows the majority party to determine the fate of legislation that the House considers. Conversely, the Senate filibuster gives the minority party much more influence over the speed at which legislation passes and the content of the legislation.

Finally, there are a variety of influences on the behavior of members of Congress. Some of these influences, such as party leaders, colleagues, and staff, are internal to the institution of Congress. Other influences, such as constituents and interest groups, exist outside Congress.

This chapter emphasized the importance of race and ethnicity in congressional politics. People who live in Washington, DC, Puerto Rico, and the American territories, many of whom are members of a racial or ethnic minority group, currently lack any representation in Congress. The creation of majority-minority districts has increased the number of Black and Latino members of the House. Informal congressional caucuses have been useful for minorities to improve their clout in Congress. Historically, the leadership structure and committee system, especially the power of the chair, were used to subjugate racial and ethnic minorities. But now Black, Latino, and Asian American members of Congress have amassed enough seniority to be able to assume positions of power in the House and Senate, although racial and ethnic minority legislators are more powerful when Democrats control the House or Senate than when Republicans are in charge. The filibuster in the Senate has prevented the passage of progressive civil rights legislation, but it has also prevented the passage of legislation detrimental to civil rights.

Representative Will Hurd's (R-TX) story clearly reveals the intersection between race and congressional politics. Most Black and Latino representatives represent districts that contain a majority of their race or ethnicity and are liberal Democrats, but Representative Hurd is Black and comes from a majority-Latino district. Although he has focused on more nonpartisan issues concerning homeland security, he is still a conservative, and he is only one of two African American members of Congress who has not joined the Congressional Black Caucus. In short, Congress is a complex governing institution that has offered racial minority groups both disappointment and promise.

REVIEW QUESTIONS

1. How do majority-minority districts increase minority representation in the House?

2. How do issues of descriptive representation, symbolic representation, and substantive representation affect the impact of racial and ethnic minorities in Congress?

3. How can congressional leaders, committee chairs, and informal organizations influence racial and ethnic politics?

4. What are the nonlawmaking functions of Congress, and how can they influence the politics of race and ethnicity?

5. What are the important influences on the voting behavior of racial and ethnic minority members of Congress?

KEY TERMS

Casework p. 196

Caucuses p. 189

Cloture Vote p. 192

Conference Committee p. 193

Congressional Black Caucus p. 189

Congressional Record p. 191

Constituency p. 174

Descriptive Representation p. 179

Divided Government p. 195

Filibuster p. 192

Franking Privilege p. 196

Gerrymandering p. 178

House Majority Leader p. 184

House Minority Leader p. 185

Impeachment p. 193

Logrolling p. 197

Majority-Minority Districts p. 172

Majority Party p. 182

Minority Party p. 182

Political Party p. 182

Pork Barrel Spending p. 200

Reapportionment p. 177

Redistricting p. 178

Representative p. 174

Senate Majority Leader p. 186

Senate Majority Whip p. 186

Senate Minority Leader p. 186

Speaker of the House p. 184

Substantive Representation p. 179

Symbolic Representation p. 179

Unified Government p. 195

Whip p. 184

ADDITIONAL READINGS

Richard F. Fenno, *Going Home: Black Representatives and Their Constituents*. Chicago: University of Chicago Press, 2003.

> This book updates Fenno's classic work by analyzing the representation styles of four African American members of the House—Louis Stokes (D-OH), Barbara Jordan (D-TX), Chaka Fattah (D-PA), and Stephanie Tubbs Jones (D-OH)—and paying close attention to the issue of race.

Christian R. Grose, *Congress in Black and White: Race and Representation in Congress and at Home*. New York: Cambridge University Press, 2011.

> This book uses a variety of sophisticated methodologies to examine the debate between descriptive and substantive representation for Black members of Congress. The author finds that although Black representatives are not influential on legislative outputs, they are extremely important for constituent services, such as casework and bringing money to Black communities.

Stephen Middleton, ed, *Black Congressmen During Reconstruction: A Documentary Sourcebook*. Westport, CT: Greenwood Press, 2002.

> This book examines the contribution of each of the twenty-two African American representatives and senators who served from 1870 to 1901.

Robert Singh, *The Black Congressional Caucus: Racial Politics in the U.S. Congress*. Thousand Oaks, CA: Sage, 1998.

> A European political scientist offers a comprehensive, systematic, and balanced analysis of the impact of the Congressional Black Caucus.

Katherine Tate, *Black Faces in the Mirror: African Americans and Their Representatives in the U.S. Congress*. Princeton, NJ: Princeton University Press, 2003.

> This is a comprehensive, rigorous, empirical study of the extent to which Black representatives work on behalf of their Black constituents and of Black constituents' perceptions of their representatives.

CHAPTER 7

The Presidency: Conventional Wisdom Redefined

Donald Trump rides down an escalator at Trump Tower in New York City immediately before announcing his candidacy for the presidency. During that speech Trump referred to Mexican immigrants as "criminals," "rapists," and "drug dealers." Throughout the campaign Trump's comments about racial and ethnic minorities, Muslims, women, and the disabled generated considerable controversy. Still, despite losing the popular vote, Donald Trump was bale to win the presidency by securing more electoral votes.

B arack Obama's election to the presidency in 2008 was undoubtedly one of the most significant events in U.S. history because he was the first non-White to assume the highest office in American politics. During his campaign, candidate Obama focused on issues such as ending the Iraq War, refocusing the War on Terrorism on al Qaida, stimulating the lagging economy, reforming the health care system, addressing illegal immigration, and regulating the finance industry. He clearly had an ambitious agenda when he entered office, most of which transcended race. Nevertheless, President Obama's election as the first non-White American president was undoubtedly a momentous event. Some analysts interpreted President Obama's election to mean that racism in the United States had been eradicated. Even before President Obama was elected, conservative commentator Dinesh D'Souza, who is of South Asian descent, argued that Obama's success indicated that racism was no longer a significant problem in the United States. D'Souza wrote in September 2008 that "there could not be a better sign that America has left behind its racist past.... Don't get me wrong: I'm not saying that racism does not exist. This is a big country, and surely one can find several examples of it. But racism, which used to be systemic, is now only episodic."[1]

By the end of President Obama's two terms in office, it was clear that most of the issues during his presidency did not involve race, but the idea that President Obama's election and subsequent reelection signified an end to racism, turned out to be wishful thinking at best. As we discuss several times throughout this book, incidents of law enforcement agents assaulting unarmed African Americans continue to occur. Moreover, a recent study demonstrates that on average, Black and Latino households have less than 10 percent the amount of wealth of the average White household.[2] Furthermore, despite the fact that President Obama handily won two elections, many people were openly disrespectful to him because of his race. Protestors against the president's policies carried signs depicting racist images; members of Congress were openly disrespectful to him; and a "Birther" conspiracy contends that Barack Obama was born in Kenya (despite clear evidence that he was born in Hawaii), which would mean that he was not even a legitimate president.

Interestingly one of the leading "Birthers" was real estate mogul and reality television star Donald Trump, who in 2016 became the Republican Party nominee for president. Throughout his campaign, Trump made number of racially offensive statements and engaged in behavior that was prejudiced against racial and ethnic minorities, women, Muslims, and the disabled. Most notable among Donald Trump's controversial statements and actions were: accusing Mexico of sending immigrants who are rapists; calling for the banning of Muslim immigrants; suggesting that Muslims should be profiled; referring to African Americans as "the Blacks"; suggesting that President Obama was sympathetic to terrorists; refusing to disavow the support of a Ku Klux Klan leader; making misogynist comments about female journalists; criticizing the Muslim faith of the parents of an American soldier killed in Iraq; and openly mocking a disabled reporter. In short, issues of race and ethnicity, as well as gender and disability prejudice, have been central to the 2016 presidential election. Despite extremely low approval ratings and losing the popular vote, Donald Trump was able to win the presidency by eking out narrow victories in the normally Democratic states of Michigan, Pennsylvania, and Wisconsin, largely because of overwhelming support from White voters.

intro *The story of Barack Obama and Donald Trump's presidential campaigns highlights key elements of the American presidency. American presidents are obvious leaders in American politics, holding what most regard as the most powerful position in the world; therefore, the selection process is arguably an extremely significant aspect of American politics. However, merely occupying the office of the president does not guarantee that presidents are able to accomplish their goals. Presidents need to convince Congress to pass their legislative priorities, which requires a tremendous amount of political skill. For example, although President Obama was successful in accomplishing many other legislative goals, he failed to persuade Congress to pass meaningful immigration reform legislation. Despite these limitations of the office, presidents do have some authority entirely over the executive branch, which means that they can influence policy, and they spend a significant amount of time managing an extensive federal workforce. Finally, the historic election of our first non-White president in 2008, his reelection in 2012, the racially-charged tone of Donald Trump's successful campaign, and the defeat of the first female major party nominee demonstrate that race (and gender) are central to the politics of the American presidency.*

In this chapter, we discuss the politics of the presidency. We first explain the presidential selection process, and we then discuss the president's formal powers. The latter half of the chapter examines the vast structure of the executive branch, the relationship between the president and Congress, and the importance of the president as a public figure. Throughout this chapter, we demonstrate how the presidency intersects with racial and ethnic politics.

Becoming President

Article 2, Section 1, of the U.S. Constitution requires that the president of the United States be at least thirty-five years old, a natural-born citizen of the United States, and a resident of the United States for at least fourteen years. All presidents have been over forty at the time of their inauguration, with most over the age of fifty. Barack Obama was forty-seven when he was inaugurated, which makes him one of the youngest presidents, and Bill Clinton was even younger at forty-six. Donald Trump will be seventy at his inauguration, making him the oldest president in American history at the time of his inauguration. Despite the antiquated origins of the citizenship and residency provisions, they are still in effect. These fairly lax requirements notwithstanding, becoming president is extremely difficult and complex.

Diversity

Before explaining the presidential selection process itself, we want to examine the diversity among those who compete for the presidency. Put simply, American presidents have not been diverse. Until 2009, all presidents were White, male, and Christian. In fact, except for John F. Kennedy, who was Catholic, all other presidents have been Protestant. Some females and non-Whites ran for president prior to 2008. In 1872, Victoria Woodhull became the first woman to run for president. She ran with former slave Frederick Douglass as her vice presidential candidate. In 1972, Shirley Chisholm, who in 1968 had been the first African American female elected to the House of Representatives, sought the Democratic Party nomination for president. Although unsuccessful, she was the first African American to seek the presidency on a major party ticket. In 1984, civil rights activist Jesse Jackson finished third in the battle for the Democratic Party nomination for president. In 1988, Jackson won more votes and delegates than he had won in 1984 and finished second.[3]

Of course, the 2008 presidential election was historic because for the first time Americans elected a non-White candidate to be president. Notwithstanding President Obama's election, the 2008 presidential election featured a highly diverse group of candidates. Former first lady and then-senator Hillary Rodham Clinton (D-NY) was the first female candidate to launch a significant campaign. In fact, she was the early favorite to win the Democratic nomination and narrowly lost it to Barack Obama. New Mexico governor Bill Richardson (D-NM) became the first major Latino candidate. President Obama ended up winning handily in 2008, earning 52.9 percent of the popular vote and 67.8 percent of the Electoral College vote.[4] See "Our Voices: Barack Obama's First Inaugural Address" on page 210 for excerpts from Barack Obama's 2009 inauguration speech.

In his 2012 reelection campaign, President Obama was the only Democratic candidate, but the Republican field was more diverse than it had been in the past. Representative Michele Bachmann (R-MN) was the second female presidential candidate on the Republican side (Elizabeth Dole was the first in 2000). In the fall of 2011, African-American businessman Herman Cain emerged as a leading Republican candidate, but reports of sexual harassment and extramarital affairs, as well as poor performances on nationally televised interviews, doomed his candidacy. Cain withdrew from the race before the Iowa caucus in January 2012. In the spring of 2012 Mitt Romney clinched the Republican nomination, becoming the first Mormon—a member of a nontraditional religion founded in the U.S.—to win the nomination of a major political party. Again, President Obama won with a smaller but still significant popular vote margin (51.0 percent to 47.2 percent) and a robust Electoral College margin of 332 to 206.[5] President Obama is one of only three Democrats in American history who won two elections with more than 50 percent of the popular vote each time (Andrew Jackson and Franklin Roosevelt are the other two).

The 2016 campaign has also featured a diverse set of candidates. Two Cuban Americans—Senator Ted Cruz (R-TX) and Senator Marco Rubio (R-FL)—ran competitive races for the Republican nomination, but they both lost to the eventual nominee Donald Trump. Additionally, Republican candidates also included an African American, retired neurosurgeon Dr. Ben Carson, and a female candidate, former business executive Carly Fiorina. However, both of those candidates dropped out of the race in early 2016. The Democratic field was initially less diverse; but Democrats made history in 2016 because they nominated Hillary Clinton as the first female nominee of either major party. Hillary Clinton picked Senator Tim Kaine (D-VA), who is a White male, as her running mate. However, they lost the election, despite winning the popular vote.[6]

The Presidential Selection Process

Despite Obama's success, the process a potential nominee must follow to become president has contributed to the lack of diversity among presidents. The presidential selection process is divided into two stages, both of which eliminate many candidates. In the first stage, candidates vie for the Democratic or Republican Party nomination by competing for delegates in each state and the several territories. The candidate who receives a majority of the party's delegates is selected as the party's nominee. Then, in the second stage, the two nominees face each other in the general election.

The Nomination Battle. There are a variety of ways that states select their delegates for each party's presidential nomination contest. Some states award delegates through **caucuses**, in which party activists attend local meetings to pick delegates who are attached to certain candidates. Most states hold primaries, in which voters decide how the state will award its delegates. In closed primaries, only registered members of the party can vote in their party's **primary**, and in open primaries, any registered voter, regardless of party registration, can receive one of the two major party ballots when she or he shows up at the polls. We discuss these processes in more detail in Chapters 14 and 15.

Caucus A method for political parties to select their candidates for office whereby party members convene at local meetings.

Primary A method for political parties to select their candidates for office whereby people vote in an election.

our voices

Barack Obama's First Inaugural Address, January 20, 2009

The inauguration of a president is a momentous occasion in American political life. In addition to the formal swearing in of a president and the official start of a presidential term, presidents deliver speeches that outline their plans for the following four years. President Obama's inauguration in 2009 was especially historic because it marked the first time that a non-White became president. At the same time, President Obama was entering office at a time of national crisis. The nation was engaged in two wars (Iraq and Afghanistan), and the economy was in serious trouble, with hundreds of thousands of jobs being lost each month, a collapsing financial system and stock market, a record number of foreclosures, and plummeting home values. There was also severe political division. President Obama did not have the luxury of focusing on the historic nature of his election; instead, his address focused on the troubles facing the United States. Nevertheless, when discussing the divisions that plague American politics and international affairs, President Obama struck a hopeful tone, promoting cultural, racial, and religious diversity.

> My fellow citizens: I stand here today humbled by the task before us, grateful for the trust you have bestowed, mindful of the sacrifices borne by our ancestors. . . .
>
> Forty-four Americans have now taken the presidential oath. The words have been spoken during rising tides of prosperity and the still waters of peace. Yet, every so often, the oath is taken amidst gathering clouds and raging storms. . . .
>
> That we are in the midst of crisis is now well understood. Our nation is at war against a far-reaching network of violence and hatred. Our economy is badly weakened, a consequence of greed and irresponsibility on the part of some, but also our collective failure to make hard choices and prepare the nation for a new age. Homes have been lost, jobs shed, businesses shuttered. Our health care is too costly, our

schools fail too many. And each day brings further evidence that the ways we use energy strengthen our adversaries and threaten our planet. . . .

> On this day we gather because we have chosen hope over fear, unity of purpose over conflict and discord. On this day we come to proclaim an end to the petty grievances and false promises, the recriminations and worn-out dogmas that for far too long have strangled our politics. . . .
>
> For we know that our patchwork heritage is a strength, not a weakness. We are a nation of Christians and Muslims, Jews and Hindus, and nonbelievers. We are shaped by every language and culture, drawn from every end of this Earth. And because we have tasted the bitter swill of civil war and segregation and emerged from that dark chapter stronger and more united, we cannot help but believe that the old hatreds shall someday pass; that the lines of tribe shall soon dissolve; that as the world grows smaller, our common humanity shall reveal itself, and that America must play its role in ushering in a new era of peace. . . .
>
> This is the price and the promise of citizenship. This is the source of our confidence, the knowledge that God calls on us to shape an uncertain destiny. This is the meaning of our liberty and our creed; why men and women and children of every race and faith can join in celebration across this magnificent Mall, and why a man whose father less than sixty years ago might not have been served at a local restaurant can now stand before you to take a most sacred oath. . . .
>
> Thank you. God bless you, and God bless the United States.

Source: Adapted from Barack Obama, "Inaugural Address," January 20, 2009. Online by Gerhard Peters and John T. Woolley, *The American Presidency Project,* http://www.presidency.ucsb .edu/ws/index.php?pid=44, accessed June 27, 2016.

Traditionally, Iowa holds the first caucus and New Hampshire holds the first primary. Candidates generally need to do well in these states to emerge as a serious contender for the nomination. But neither state is diverse—as of 2015 New Hampshire is 93.9 percent White, and Iowa is 91.8 percent White.[7] It can be difficult, then, for racial minority candidates to attract voters in these key states and thus start their campaigns in a strong position. However, minority candidates have recently fared well in the Iowa caucus, with President Obama winning in 2008 and Senator Ted Cruz winning in 2016.

The General Election. The winners of the Democratic and Republican nominations then face each other in the general election. This election determines the president through the **Electoral College**, in which each state is given a number of electoral votes equal to the number of representatives it sends to the House of Representatives plus two. The presidential election is thus decided by separate elections in each of the fifty states, plus the District of Columbia, which receives three electoral votes.

Electoral College The entity that selects the president and vice president, consisting of 538 electors chosen from the states and the District of Columbia.

In fact, it is possible for a candidate to win more overall votes than his or her opponent but lose in the Electoral College and not become president. A well-known example of this problem occurred in 1876, and it is especially important because the outcome of this election affected African American civil rights history. In 1876, Democratic candidate Samuel Tilden won 51.5 percent of the popular vote, thus beating his Republican opponent, Rutherford B. Hayes, by 254,235 votes. Moreover, the initial Electoral College tally gave Tilden a 184 to 165 favorable margin. The results were disputed in the former Confederate states of Florida, Louisiana, and South Carolina, which early results showed had voted for Tilden. Republicans claimed that widespread election fraud, including the disenfranchisement of reliably Republican Black voters, meant that those states had actually voted for Hayes. To settle the dispute, Congress created the Federal Election Commission, consisting of members of the Senate, the House, and the Supreme Court, and this commission ruled in favor of Hayes, giving him the electoral votes for all three states. Many argue that this dispute was settled by a compromise that stipulated if Hayes received the votes of those three states, then the federal government would withdraw troops from the former Confederate states, effectively ending Reconstruction.[8] Chapter 5 discussed how ending Reconstruction led to serious civil rights violations for Black Southerners.

The problems of 1876 were echoed in the presidential election of 2000. The results from the state of Florida were disputed because of problems with ballots, as well as widespread reports of difficulties that minorities had faced when voting. The Florida Supreme Court required a hand recount of votes in counties with disputed ballots, but the U.S. Supreme Court then halted that recount, arguing that the Equal Protection Clause of the Fourteenth Amendment requires that the recount rules be uniform for all counties throughout the state.[9] This decision ultimately gave the electors of the state of Florida, and the presidency, to Republican George W. Bush. Regardless of the disputed outcome in Florida, Al Gore received more overall votes nationally than George Bush (48.4 percent of the popular vote went for Gore, and 47.9 percent of the popular vote went for Bush). Because Bush was declared the narrow winner in such pivotal states as Florida and Ohio, he was able to eke out the Electoral College victory even though Gore's popular vote totals stemmed from wide victories in large, populous states including California, New York, and Massachusetts.[10]

During the 2008 presidential election, the Electoral College might have worked to Obama's disadvantage because a Black candidate could have experienced difficulty winning states that were overwhelmingly White. Because Obama's appeal cut across racial and ethnic boundaries, he was able to win predominantly White states, such as Iowa, Vermont, New Hampshire, Maine, and Minnesota. These results were essentially repeated in 2012, with President Obama still winning many overwhelmingly White states. Hillary Clinton actually did worse in largely White states, losing Iowa and one electoral vote from Northern Maine. "Measuring Equality: Scatterplots of Obama and Trump Vote and Minority Populations," shows in more detail how racial and ethnic characteristics of the states correlate to Obama's success in 2012, while comparing how race and ethnicity factored into the 2016 election, which featured two White candidates.

Financing Presidential Campaigns

The process of running for president, including both the nomination process and the general election, is extremely expensive. Once a candidate announces a bid for the presidency, he or she is first required to raise considerable sums of money to pay for the extensive costs of travel, polling, advisers, and advertising. Previous minority candidates had been disadvantaged in raising money, but in his 2008 campaign President Obama significantly out-raised all of his rivals in both the primary and general elections. In 2012, President Obama still out-raised his Republican opponents, including his general election rival Mitt Romney, but the margin was closer. A significant reason for President Obama's successful fundraising was his campaign's ability to use high-tech data mining techniques that target individual contributors according to each person's online activity, social media use, and purchases. The Obama campaign also used these techniques to target people to encourage them to vote.[11]

In 2016, Hillary Clinton and her allies raised far more money than Donald Trump and his allies – $1.3 billion to $795 million. Still, Clinton's monetary advantage was not enough to secure victory. In fact, she was not as successful as Obama in generating turnout because overall voter turnout in 2016 was the lowest in terms of percentage since 1996.

A significant difference between the 2008 and subsequent elections was the rise of **Super PACs**. Super PACs are allowed to raise an unlimited amount of money from any source, including individuals, corporations, labor unions, and interest groups, and they are then allowed to spend this money in support of or opposition to any political candidate, including people running for president, as long as their activities are not directly coordinated with a campaign. After the Supreme Court formally allowed for the existence of Super PACs in 2010, these groups became extremely influential in elections because unlike campaigns, which are restricted in how much money they can raise from individuals or corporations, Super PACs are able to raise unlimited sums. Furthermore, because individuals or corporations can donate an unlimited amount of money to Super PACs, they can dominate political campaigns. A total of 1,283 Super PACs raised more than $833 million and spent over $641 million in the 2012 election.[13] Because many corporations and extremely wealthy individuals opposed President

Super PACs Political action committees allowed to raise an unlimited amount of money from any source, including individuals, corporations, labor unions, and interest groups. These committees are then allowed to spend this money in support of or opposition to any political candidate, including people running for president, so long as their activities are not directly coordinated with a campaign.

measuring equality

Scatterplots of Obama and Trump Vote and Minority Populations

Because presidents are elected by the Electoral College, candidates need to focus their campaigns on winning key states. As a result, the Electoral College has traditionally been viewed as detrimental to minority candidates because most states are majority White. Barack Obama's 2012 and Donald Trump's 2016 general election victories, however, provide evidence rejecting the hypothesis that the Electoral College disadvantages minority candidates. We demonstrate this with the two sets of three graphs in Figures 7.1, 7.2, and 7.3 depicting the relationship of the percentage of the state that is Black, Latino, and White with the percentage of the vote that Obama received in the state. Social scientists refer to these graphs as scatterplots. For each scatterplot, the x-axis reports the percentage of the state that is Black, Latino, or White and the y-axis shows the percentage of the vote Obama received in the 2012 general election. Each data point on the scatterplot represents each state (and one represents the District of Columbia, which has three electoral votes). As a basis of comparison, we provide

the same information in Figures 7.4, 7.5, and 7.6 for Donald Trump, a White candidate.

If the data points in the scatterplot appear to coalesce around a line that trends upward, then there is evidence that the greater the proportion of the group living in a state, the higher the percentage of the vote Obama or Trump received. That is, there is a positive relationship between the presence of the group in a state's population and support for Obama or Trump. If there is a clear pattern of a line trending downward, then the greater the proportion of the group living in a state, the lower the percentage of the vote Obama or Trump received. That is, there is a negative relationship between the presence of the group in a state's population and support for Obama or Trump. If there is no line that discernibly trends upward or downward, then there is no relationship between the percentage of the group living in a state and the vote Obama or Clinton received.

In the three scatterplots for Obama, there does not appear to be any clear noticeable pattern. In other words,

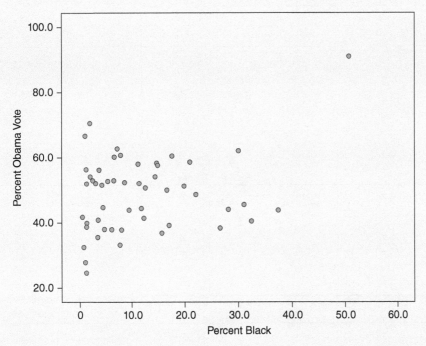

Figure 7.1 Scatterplot of Black Population and Obama 2012 Vote.

(Continued)

measuring equality *(Continued)*

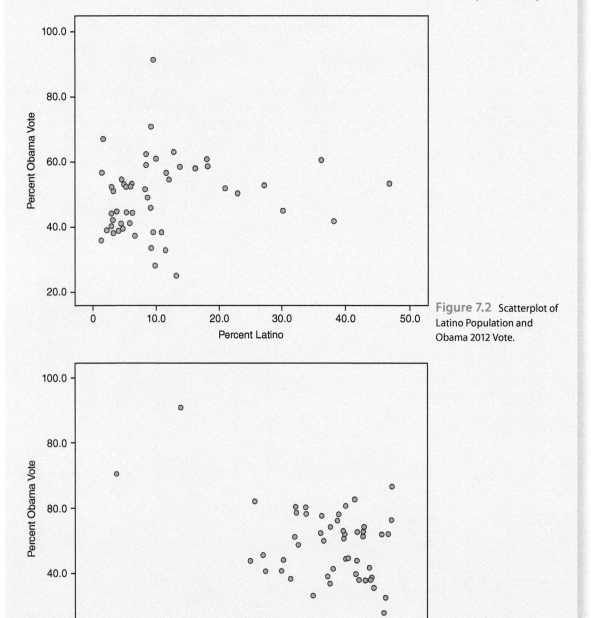

Figure 7.2 Scatterplot of Latino Population and Obama 2012 Vote.

Figure 7.3 Scatterplot of White Population and Obama 2012 Vote.

measuring equality

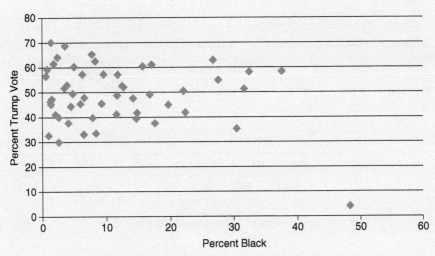

Figure 7.4 Scatterplot of Black Population and Trump 2016 Vote.

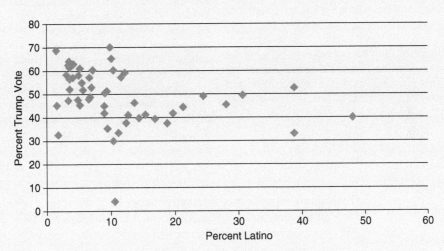

Figure 7.5 Scatterplot of Latino Population and Trump 2016 Vote.

(Continued)

measuring equality *(Continued)*

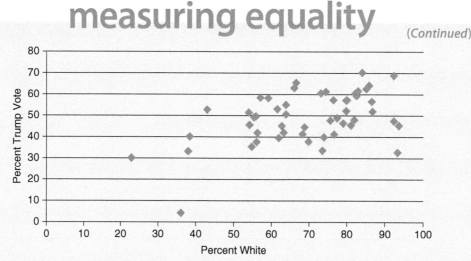

Figure 7.6 Scatterplot of White Population and Trump 2016 Vote.

Obama did just as well in states with high Black, Latino, and White populations as he did in states with low populations of each group. Although Obama did better among Blacks and Latinos than he did among Whites, his appeal clearly crossed racial boundaries. He was quite successful in largely White states such as Iowa, Maine, Vermont, and New Hampshire. This appeal among White voters meant that the Electoral College did not present a barrier to the minority candidate. The patters are generally similar for Donald Trumps's results. Despite the fact that Blacks and Latinos overwhelmingly voted for Clinton, There does not appear to be a relationship between the percent of Blacks and Latinos living in a state and Trump's electoral success. However, there does appear to be a slight relationship between a state's White composition and its support for Trump—he tended to do better in states with a higher conentration of Whites.

Sources: Vote result data from John Woolley and Gerhard Peters, "Election of 2012," *The American Presidency Project* (Santa Barbara, CA: University of California at Santa Barbara, 1999–2014), http://www.presidency.ucsb.edu/showelection.php?year=2012, accessed January 18, 2013. Population data from U.S. Census, "State and County Quick Facts," http://quick-facts.census.gov/qfd/index.html, accessed January 18, 2013; CNN, "Presidential Results," http://www.cnn.com/election/results/president and United States Census Bureau, "Quick Facts," https://www.census.gov/quickfacts/table/SEX255215/00, both accessed November 13, 2016.

Obama and his policies, conservative Super PACs dominated over liberal Super PACs in general, and Super PACs devoted to Mitt Romney far outspent Super PACs devoted to President Obama. Although in 2016 Hillary Clinton got morre support than Donald Trump did from from Super PACs and outside groups, overall Super PACS spent more money advocating for conservatives than they did advocating for liberals. Figure 7.7 shows the amount of money that the top ten Super PACs and other outside groups spent on major presidential candidates in 2016. Figure 7.8 shows the general amount of money that that the Super PACs spent on liberal and conservative messages in 2012.

Presidential Power

Although the Framers of the Constitution recognized the necessity of a national executive branch, they were wary of executive power. As a result, the

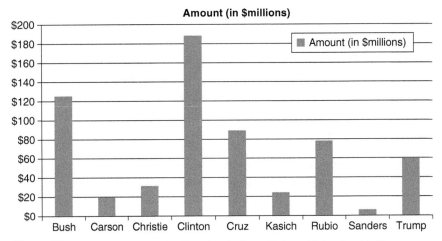

Figure 7.7 Amount in Millions of Dollars that the Super PACs and Other Outside Groups Spent on Leading Presidential 2016 Candidates.

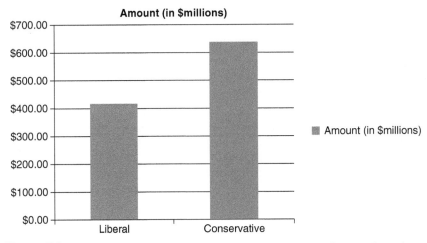

Figure 7.8 Amount in Millions of Dollars that the Super PACs Spent on Conservative and Liberal Messages During the 2016 Election Cycle.

U.S. Constitution provides for only limited presidential powers. The Framers designed the presidency primarily to exert minimal influence on policymaking; instead, the president should focus on protecting the nation and administering policies enacted by Congress. As Alexander Hamilton wrote in *Federalist No. 70*, "Energy in the executive is a leading character in the definition of good government. It is essential to the protection of the community against foreign attacks . . . to the steady administration of the laws . . . to the security of liberty against the enterprises and assaults of ambition, of faction, and of anarchy."[14] Nineteenth- and early-twentieth-century presidents kept to this limited role. Clearly, there were exceptions, such as Abraham Lincoln, who increased his authority to fight the Civil War, but for the most part early presidents followed the lead of Congress.

Modern Presidency Since
Franklin Roosevelt in 1933, the
conception of the presidency,
which is characterized by a
powerful president who seeks
to lead Congress, connects with
the American public, and
presides over an enormous
executive branch.

That focus changed with Franklin Roosevelt in 1933. His presidency was
the beginning of the **modern presidency**, in which the president shares
policy-making power with Congress and often leads Congress. Consequently, presidents can use this power to shape civil rights policy making.
Many scholars see a mixed record on the presidents' use of their power to
advance civil rights, depending on the president. For example, they consider
President Lyndon Johnson as a strong advocate of civil rights policies,
whereas Ronald Reagan sought policies that minority groups generally opposed. However, scholar Russell Riley shows that both premodern and
modern presidents, including Johnson, avoided taking the lead on civil rights
action unless public opinion and social movements sufficiently pressured
them to do so.[15]

In this section, we analyze presidential power by looking at the administrative, foreign, and domestic powers of the modern president. We explain how
presidential power is broad and yet has limitations. In doing so, we address how
presidential power affects racial and ethnic minorities. In subsequent sections,
we then focus on executive branch organization in the modern presidency and
the presidents' success and failure in leading Congress in policymaking.

Administrative Powers of the President

The administrative power of the president refers to the president's authority to
enforce laws and ensure that policies take effect. Although administrative
power entails presidents carrying out the will of Congress, it often provides
presidents with the ability to shape public policy because they enjoy wide discretion when enforcing laws. For example, the Obama administration has
emphasized enforcement of civil rights laws in an effort to limit housing discrimination, racial profiling, and hate crimes and has even challenged state
policies, such as Arizona's immigration law (see Chapter 5).[16] President-Elect
Donald Trump's rhetoric as a candidate suggests that he will not use administrative power to enforce civil rights as vigorously as President Obama did.

Signing Statements
Presidential declarations issued
along with legislative bill
signings that express
reservations about parts of a bill
or announce an unwillingness
to enforce aspects of the bill.

Presidents have also exercised discretion in enforcing laws through the
use of **signing statements**, in which presidents submit a proclamation concerning their interpretation of a bill when they sign it into law. Many signing
statements merely comment on the benefits of the law, but they can be more
controversial when the president expresses reservations about aspects of a bill.
At times a signing statement can even indicate areas that the president intends
not to enforce. Presidents have used signing statements since the administration
of James Monroe, but their use has increased tremendously since the 1980s.[17]

Under President George W. Bush, the use of signing statements became
more controversial because he used signing statements to ignore aspects of
laws requiring better treatment of detainees captured in Iraq and Afghanistan.
At the end of 2007 and in early 2008, President Bush angered many civil rights
leaders, as well as members of Congress, when he issued a signing statement
indicating that he could ignore some of the sanctions that Congress had imposed on the government of Sudan for egregious human rights violations it

was committing in Darfur.[18] As a candidate, Barack Obama criticized President Bush's use of signing statements, but as president, he issued thirty-four signing statements from 2009 through 2015. Although this figure seems large, it pales in comparison to the 155 signing statements that George W. Bush issued during his first seven years in office.[19] Although most of President Obama's signing statements have not been controversial, on December 31, 2011, he issued one on a defense bill that included a provision preventing the transfer of suspected terrorists to foreign governments. President Obama claimed that the provision would hamper his ability to fight terrorism.[20]

Presidents also exert administrative power by issuing **executive orders**, which are directives to executive branch employees to carry out specific actions. Executive orders are administrative in nature because they entail the president's commanding a subordinate. Some executive orders also affect public policy, especially in the area of racial and ethnic discrimination. For example, in 1943, Franklin Roosevelt signed Executive Order 9088, which forcibly relocated more than 100,000 Japanese Americans from the West Coast to internment camps in the desert. However, in 1941, Roosevelt advanced racial and ethnic equality by issuing Executive Order 8802, which banned racial, ethnic, and religious discrimination in the federal government and in defense companies under contract with the federal government.[21] In 1965, President Lyndon Johnson issued Executive Order 11246, which required that businesses contracting with the federal government "take affirmative action to ensure that applicants are employed and that employees are treated during employment, without regard to their race, color, religion, sex, or national origin."[22] This executive order was significant in establishing affirmative action and accelerating the economic and social progress of racial and ethnic minorities. Executive orders also affect foreign policy. In July 2012, President Obama issued Executive Order 13620, which allows the federal government to impose trade and economic sanctions on groups and individuals in the African nation of Somalia who steal money, employ children as soldiers, or commit violence against women or girls.[23]

President Obama's executive orders have been especially significant in the area of immigration. As we discussed in Chapter 5, there are numerous undocumented immigrants living in the United States who have children who were born in the United States and are therefore citizens. This disparity of legal status among family members has been extremely trying especially because undocumented parents are unable to find stable work and support their families. Because Congress was unable to address this problem, President Obama issued an executive order that ended deportation for undocumented parents with children who are legal residents or citizens, and it created a process for these undocumented immigrants to obtain official permission to work in the United States. However, a federal appeals court overturned this action because it exceeded executive authority—the president was engaged in lawmaking, which is the function of Congress. In June of 2016 the U.S. Supreme Court was divided 4–4 on this question because Justice Antonin Scalia,

Executive Orders Directives that the president issues to subordinates in the executive branch and that have the force of law.

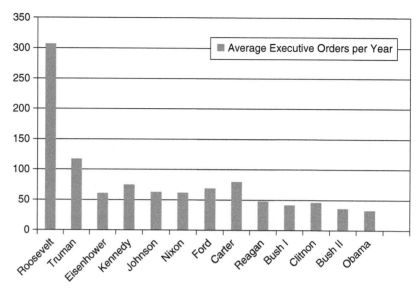

Figure 7.9 Average Number of Executive Orders Issued per Year, Roosevelt Through Obama
Source: Adapted from Gerhard Peters and John T. Woolley, "Executive Orders." The American Presidency Project. Ed. John T. Woolley and Gerhard Peters. Santa Barbara, CA. 1999–2016. Available from the World Wide Web: http://www.presidency.ucsb.edu/data/orders.php., accessed June 27, 2016.

who passed away in February, was not replaced (see Chapter 9 for more on the controversy over replacing Justice Scalia). Consequently, as of the publication of this book, President Obama's executive action is not in effect.[24] Despite the controversy over President Obama's executive orders on immigration, the reality is, as Figure 7.9 shows, President Obama has issued fewer executive orders than many of his predecessors.

Article 2 of the Constitution grants presidents the power to nominate executive branch officials (we discuss the executive branch personnel in the next section), ambassadors, and federal judges. In the private sector, the hiring of personnel is a key administrative task; similarly, the president's appointment power is an essential part of the presidential administrative function. There is, however, a check on the presidential appointment power because most appointments are subject to Senate confirmation. For the most part, the Senate approves presidents' executive branch nominations, but it has occasionally rejected nominees for character-related reasons, such as dishonest financial dealings or display of inappropriate behavior. In fact the last time a cabinet member was rejected was in 1989 when the Senate rejected President George H. W. Bush's choice of former Texas Senator John Tower to be secretary of defense because of Tower's reputation for overuse of alcohol and mistreatment of women, as well as his financial dealings with defense contractors.[25] Occasionally, presidents will withdraw cabinet nominees who generate controversy and are unlikely to be confirmed. Still, throughout the history of the Republic, there have been over five hundred cabinet nominations, but only a total of twenty-one have been rejected or withdrawn.[26]

Foreign Powers of the President

The Constitution gives the president three basic foreign policymaking powers: (1) receiving ambassadors from other nations, (2) negotiating treaties, and (3) serving as commander-in-chief of the armed forces. Modern presidents have tremendously expanded their power over foreign policy. In fact, in 1936 the U.S. Supreme Court recognized the president as the "sole organ" in foreign affairs.[27] As we will soon see, even when Congress has constitutional authority over foreign affairs in areas such as treaty ratification (for the Senate) and declaration of war, the office of the president has usurped Congress's foreign policy powers.

Article 2 of the Constitution gives the president the authority to negotiate treaties, but it requires that two-thirds of the Senate ratify a treaty for it to take effect. Occasionally, the Senate has rejected treaties that presidents negotiated. Most notably, it rejected the Treaty of Versailles at the end of World War I because too many senators opposed the requirement that the United States commit military troops to European conflicts. Despite the ratification requirement, presidents possess the authority to withdraw from treaties without seeking the Senate's consent. For instance, in 2002 President George W. Bush unilaterally withdrew the United States from the Anti-Ballistic Missile Treaty with Russia to pursue a space-based missile defense system.[28]

As an alternative to treaties, presidents have enhanced their foreign policy authority by negotiating with foreign nations through **executive agreements**. These are pacts between presidents and foreign nations that do not require the Senate's approval. The U.S. Supreme Court has upheld the legitimacy of executive agreements and has ruled that they enjoy the same legal status as treaties.[29] As a result, modern presidents have increasingly relied on executive agreements as a way to avoid the Senate's check on their authority to negotiate with other nations. During the first fifty years of the American Republic (1789–1839), presidents negotiated twice as many treaties as executive agreements. However, since 1990 presidents have used executive agreements nine times more often than treaties.[30]

Executive Agreements Agreements between the president and foreign nations that, because they are not treaties, do not need the approval of the Senate.

The president's commander-in-chief power gives him considerable influence over foreign policy. The Framers of the Constitution intended for Congress to declare war—granting what are called **Congressional War Powers**—and then, in the role of commander-in-chief, the president assumes the responsibility for fighting the war. This arrangement is consistent with the Constitution's basic design that the president carries out the policies that Congress makes.

Congressional War Powers The power granted by the Constitution (in Article 1, Section 8) to Congress to decide when the United States goes to war.

Prior to the 1950s, either Congress declared war or presidents only sent troops into limited engagements without congressional authorization. In 1950, however, President Harry Truman dispatched U.S. forces into the Korean conflict without any congressional authorization Congress declaring war. The Korean War, as it came to be called, was different from previously undeclared hostilities in that it required U.S. citizens to be drafted, which meant that ordinary citizens were forced into military service, and it resulted in heavy

American casualties. Subsequently, presidents dispatched troops into major conflicts including Vietnam, the first Persian Gulf War, the Iraq War, the war in Afghanistan, and combat operations against ISIS without a congressional declaration of war, although Congress did authorize funding for those wars.

From the time of the attacks of September 11, 2001, when terrorists led by Osama bin Laden killed almost three thousand Americans by hijacking airliners and crashing them into buildings, President George W. Bush expanded the president's commander-in-chief power. In the immediate response to the attacks, President Bush sent U.S. troops to Afghanistan to search for members of al Qaida—the terrorist group responsible for the attacks—and to topple the Taliban government in Afghanistan because it supported and harbored al Qaida terrorists. President Bush ordered that many of the people captured in this operation be sent to Guantánamo Bay, a naval facility in Cuba that the United States operates.

Enemy Combatants The status given to individuals captured in battle who do not belong to any national military force.

Because these detainees were not part of any national military force, President Bush classified them as **enemy combatants** instead of prisoners of war, who must be afforded internationally recognized humanitarian protections guaranteed under the Geneva Conventions—a set of treaties and international agreements that control the treatment of civilians and prisoners of war during armed conflict. As a result, the Bush administration claimed it could bypass

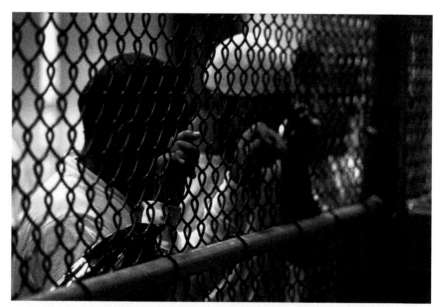

In this photo, Guantánamo detainees are pictured inside a common area at Camp 6 high-security detention facility at Guantánamo Bay U.S. Naval Base, Cuba, March 30, 2010. The vast majority of the detainees are people from the Middle East and South Asia, who were captured in the War on Terror launched after the attacks of September 11, 2011. Upon entering office in 2009, President Obama signed an executive order closing Guantánamo, but as of 2016 it still remains open.

the Geneva Conventions in its treatment of these detainees. Furthermore, President Bush argued that these enemy combatants would be processed outside the normal U.S. criminal justice system and be held indefinitely without trial. Congress passed the Detainee Treatment Act and Military Commissions Act, which essentially codified into law President Bush's policy. However, the Supreme Court ruled that the Geneva Conventions do apply to the detainees and that the U.S. government cannot deny the detainees their habeas corpus rights.[31] Although throughout most of his presidency Barack Obama has indicated his desire to close Guantánamo, it remains open as of 2016.

President Bush took other extraordinary powers in the name of fighting terrorism after 2001. He allowed "enhanced interrogation techniques" to be used on people captured in Afghanistan and in the subsequent war in Iraq. He claimed that these techniques were legal, but critics charged that they amounted to torture, which is illegal. The most controversial of these techniques was "waterboarding," an ancient method of eliciting information in which an interrogator ties down the victim, puts a cloth in his mouth, and pours water on him. This technique simulates drowning and instills in the victim an intense sense of panic. President Obama announced early in his presidency that the United States would no longer use enhanced interrogation techniques, including waterboarding.[32]

President Bush also authorized the use of unmanned drones to attack suspected terrorists, despite the fact that these drones often killed civilians. However, unlike the case with torture, President Obama did not end the use of drones—in fact he significantly expanded the drone program. According to a recent estimate, President Obama ordered ten times more drone strikes than President Bush did. He also authorized the killing ten times more suspected terrorists and about twice as many civilians as President Bush did.[33]

Although Donald Trump was somewhat vague on his overall foreign policy objectives, he did state specific goals, such as ending the nuclear deal with Iran, ending international agreements and treaties designed to fight climate change, and renegotiating or ending trade deals with other nations. He also stated that he wants to defeat ISIS, as did candidate Hillary Clinton, but he never offered specific details on how we plans to accomplish this important goal. As of press time for this book, President-Elect Trump has not offered specific foreign policy measures he plans to take as president.

Domestic Powers of the President

Although the Framers did not intend for the president to participate actively in making domestic policy, much of the modern president's activities are geared toward influencing domestic policy. Presidents influence the making of domestic policy through their constitutional power (in Article 1, Section 7) to **veto** bills passed by Congress. The Framers gave the president the veto power to prevent Congress from passing ill-considered laws, but they prevented the president from using the veto in a tyrannical fashion by stipulating that Congress can override a veto by a two-thirds vote in each chamber. If the president neither signs nor vetoes a law after a ten-day period has passed (excluding

Veto The president's ability to cancel legislation passed by Congress.

Pocket Veto A way for the president to overturn a bill passed by Congress when the president does not act on a bill within ten days of passage (excluding Sundays) and Congress adjourns in the meantime.

Sundays), then the bill automatically becomes law. The president can defeat a bill through a **pocket veto**, which occurs if the president does not sign or veto a bill and Congress adjourns before the requisite ten days have elapsed. Pocket vetoes have become increasingly rare, but they can have important policy implications, even in the area of civil rights. For example, in 1990 President George H. W. Bush pocket vetoed the Indian Preference Act, which would have provided advantages for American Indian–owned companies bidding for federal contracts.[34]

Modern presidents influence domestic policy mainly by suggesting to Congress which laws to pass. Although presidents lack the constitutional authority to introduce bills in Congress, they can suggest legislation, which a member of the House or the Senate then formally introduces. The U.S. Constitution gives the president an opportunity to recommend policy in Article 2, Section 3, which states that the president "shall from time to time give to the Congress Information on the State of the Union, and recommend to their Consideration such Measures as he shall judge necessary and expedient." The advent of television has allowed presidents to use the **State of the Union address** as an opportunity to build public support for their policy objectives. In 1947, President Harry Truman delivered the first televised State of the Union address during the daytime,[35] and in 1965 President Lyndon Johnson moved the State of the Union address to the evening to draw a larger audience.[36] President Johnson took advantage of his audience to promote his policy goals, including civil rights. He specifically promised to improve opportunities for African Americans "through the enforcement of the civil rights laws and elimination of barriers to the right to vote."[37]

State of the Union Address An annual occasion in which the president speaks before Congress to suggest laws that Congress should pass.

However, modern presidents do not restrict themselves to the State of the Union address; they constantly urge Congress to pass their legislative priorities. Specifically, presidents propose an annual budget, which determines how much money the government spends in various sectors (e.g., defense, infrastructure, welfare, education, scientific research, and the arts). Presidents suggest other important economic and social policies that they want Congress to enact.

The types of programs that presidents advocate depend on their ideology and political party. Generally, Republican presidents, such as Ronald Reagan and George W. Bush, propose to cut domestic spending on social welfare programs (although overall domestic spending did increase under their administrations), restrict abortion rights, lessen business regulations, and decrease taxes. Conversely, Democratic presidents, such as Bill Clinton and Barack Obama, seek to increase federal domestic spending on education, expand health insurance coverage, and preserve the environment. In his first term, President Obama articulated an active agenda, including a massive proposal to stimulate the ailing economy, reform of health care, development of alternative energy sources, deficit reduction, and improvement of the environment. President Obama was able to ensure the passage of the economic stimulus and health care reform legislation, but he had little success in environmental policy and deficit reduction. For much of his presidency, Obama proposed legislation that would fix the immigration system by allowing

President Obama delivers his final State of the Union Address to Congress on January 12, 2016. The Constitution requires that the president report on the state of the union, but modern presidents have used this opportunity to set Congress's legislative agenda and take advantage of free media attention. President Obama used this opportunity to highlight what he believed were the achievements of his presidency in the areas of job creation, deficit reduction, environmental protection, health care, and foreign policy.

undocumented immigrants to remain and work in the United States, particularly when doing so keeps families together. However, Congress has not enacted any immigration legislation during his presidency, which is why President Obama resorted to executive actions (see discussion above).[38] Later in this chapter, we address in more detail the resources and strategies presidents use to accomplish their goals in Congress.

Executive Branch Organization

Because the tasks of administering the federal government are too extensive for the president to handle alone, a vast executive branch is necessary. Article 2 of the Constitution creates the office of the vice president and alludes to "public ministers and consuls" but does not specify how presidents should organize their administrations. During the eighteenth and nineteenth centuries, executive branch organization was fairly simple, but as the modern president's powers and responsibilities expanded during the twentieth century, executive branch organization became exceedingly more complex.

In fact, a large, complex executive branch is a defining characteristic of the modern presidency. There are many divisions within the executive branch. The closest circle comprises the vice president and the president's spouse. The circle then extends out to include the cabinet, the Executive Office of the President,

Vice President Charles Curtis (1929–1933) throws out a baseball before a game. Although he exerted little influence over policy while serving as vice president, Curtis is important because he is the only minority thus far to be vice president.

and the White House staff. In this section we cover the various aspects of the executive branch, and we raise issues concerning racial and ethnic diversity throughout the executive branch.

The Vice President

The Framers intended for the vice president to assume the presidency in case of a vacancy and break tie votes in the Senate. Initially, Article 2, Section 1, of the U.S. Constitution stipulated that the person who received the second highest number of electoral votes would serve as vice president, but the Twelfth Amendment and the development of political parties allowed voters to select the president and vice president as a team. In Chapter 12, we discuss in more detail how the problems of the election of 1800 led to the Twelfth Amendment, as well as the amendment's impact on the development of political parties.

Until the middle of the twentieth century, vice presidents performed mainly ceremonial and official functions, and they had minimal impact on policymaking, except for the rare opportunities to break tie votes in the Senate. In the late twentieth century, vice presidents became more active policy advisers. President Jimmy Carter was the first president to make his vice president, Walter Mondale, an important policy adviser who led numerous projects. Subsequent vice presidents provided their bosses with counsel on important issues. For example, Dick Cheney, who served under President George W. Bush, was instrumental in shaping energy policy and foreign affairs, especially the Iraq War. Barack Obama's vice president, Joe Biden, has been an important adviser, especially in the area of foreign affairs and defense policy.[39]

As with presidents, there has been little diversity among vice presidents. All vice presidents have been male, Christian, and, with one exception, White. President Herbert Hoover's (1929–1933) vice president, Charles Curtis, was a member of the Kaw tribe and thus was the only non-White vice president.[40] There are three instances of major party vice presidential candidates who were neither male nor Christian. In 1984, Democratic presidential nominee Walter Mondale chose Geraldine Ferraro as the first female running mate on a major party ticket, but they lost the election to the all-male Republican ticket of Ronald Reagan and George H. W. Bush. In 2000, Democratic presidential candidate Al Gore chose Senator Joseph Lieberman (D-CT), who is Jewish, as his running mate, but that ticket lost to Republicans George Bush and Dick Cheney, both Protestants. In 2008, Republican candidate John McCain selected Alaska Governor Sarah Palin as his running mate, but they lost to the all-male Democratic ticket of Barack Obama and Joe Biden. Both major party running mates in 2016—Tim Kaine for the Democrats and Mike Pence for the Republicans—are white males.

The President's Spouse

Because all presidents thus far have been male, the president's spouse is called the "first lady," and most first ladies have not publicly influenced their husbands' decisions. Until the middle of the twentieth century, cultural norms frowned on women participating in civic life outside the home, so first ladies could be active only behind the scenes. Eleanor Roosevelt (wife of President Franklin Delano Roosevelt) greatly expanded the role of first lady. She was deeply interested in politics and often publicly urged her husband to take positions favoring racial and ethnic minorities, women, and laborers.

As social mores regarding the role of women evolved during the 1960s and 1970s, expectations of the first lady changed as well. As the first presidential spouse born after World War II, Hillary Clinton revolutionized the position of first lady. With a law degree and an impressive career in public service and private practice, she was as qualified to serve in a formal capacity as other members of the executive branch. None of her predecessors, even Eleanor Roosevelt, could have made that claim. As a result, President Clinton relied extensively on her advice, and he was the first president to appoint his wife to an official position besides that of first lady when in 1993 he named her as co-chair of the Health Care Task Force. In 2000, Hillary Clinton won election to the U.S. Senate from the state of New York, thereby becoming the first presidential spouse to serve in government completely in her own right. In 2008, she vied for the Democratic nomination for president, but she lost narrowly to Barack Obama. Then, in 2009, President Obama named her secretary of state, and she served in that capacity until February 2013. After Donald Trump is inaugurated, the First Lady will be Melania Trump, who is Donald Trump's third wife. She was born in Slovenia (then Yugoslavia) and will be 46 at the time of her husband's inauguration. Therefore she will be one of the youngest First Ladies and only the second one who was not born in the United States.

In 2009, Michelle Obama became the first African American first lady. Like Hillary Clinton, Obama is an Ivy League–educated lawyer who had earned a six-figure income. She has publicly expressed support for her husband's policy proposals, but, unlike Hillary Clinton, Michelle Obama has not taken an active policy role. Instead, she has emphasized more family-oriented issues, such as childhood obesity and assisting spouses and children of active military personnel. In 2012, Michelle Obama became increasingly active in her husband's re-election campaign by appearing at campaign stops, delivering a rousing speech at the

Eleanor Roosevelt (left) and Autherine Lucy smile as they appear together on the speaker's stand during a civil rights rally held in Madison Square Garden. Ms. Roosevelt's predecessors as first ladies, and even most of her successors, focused predominately on ceremonial duties, but Ms. Roosevelt was deeply engaged in policy, particularly in the area of civil rights.

Democratic National Convention, and working on "grassroots" efforts, such as registering voters and recruiting volunteers.[41]

The Cabinet

Cabinet The key presidential aides, each of whom heads an executive branch department, as well as others that the president designates.

A significant part of the executive branch is the **cabinet**, which consists of the heads of each executive department and other officials presidents deem worthy of cabinet-level status. The executive branch is divided into various departments that specialize in a particular policy area. Table 7.1 lists the current executive departments and information on each department's cabinet secretary (as of June 2016). Cabinet officials are responsible for managing their departments and advising the president, especially in their specific policy areas. Although not directly members of the cabinet, deputy secretaries, undersecretaries, and assistant secretaries assist cabinet members in the performance of their duties, and all are important executive branch figures as well.

Although the cabinet members are part of the executive branch, Congress actually creates executive departments. In 1789, Congress created four cabinet positions—Secretary of State, Secretary of the Treasury, Secretary of War, and Attorney General—and these are currently considered the most important cabinet positions, often referred to as the "inner cabinet." Starting in the

TABLE 7.1 The Cabinet, 2016

Department	Name	Race	Gender
State	John Kerry	White	Male
Treasury	Jack Lew	White	Male
Defense	Ashton Carter	White	Male
Justice	Loretta E. Lynch	Black	Female
Interior	Sally Jewell	White	Female
Agriculture	Thomas J. Vilsack	White	Male
Commerce	Penny Pritzker	White	Female
Labor	Thomas Perez	Latino	Male
Health and Human Services	Sylvia Mathews Burwell	White	Female
Housing and Urban Development	Julián Castro	Latino	Male
Transportation	Anthony Foxx	Black	Male
Energy	Ernest Moniz	White	Male
Education	John King	Black	Male
Veterans Affairs	Robert McDonald	White	Male
Homeland Security	Jeh Johnson	Black	Male

Source: Adapted from White House, "The Cabinet," https://www.whitehouse.gov/administration/cabinet, accessed June 25, 2016.

nineteenth century, as the federal government assumed more responsibilities, Congress added relevant executive departments. The first such department was the Department of the Interior, which Congress established in 1849 to manage expanding American land, as well as to control the native peoples who inhabited that land. Initially, the Interior Department was largely responsible for discriminating against American Indians, but since the late twentieth century, it has provided them with increased civil rights by promoting economic development, education, and health care for Indian tribes.[42]

Although the cabinet was designed to advise the president on policy matters, modern presidents have deemphasized the cabinet's advisory function. Presidents rarely convene meetings of their entire cabinet to consult on policy issues, and those meetings do not involve substantive policy discussions. One member of President Clinton's cabinet described the meetings this way: "Clinton cabinet meetings are informational, not deliberative. They occur when all the members need to be briefed on a particular initiative and told how much and how they will support it."[43] President Obama, especially during his second term, has ignored his cabinet even more than his predecessors. As presidential staff scholar Kathryn Dunn Tenpas notes, "While President Obama is not the first to keep his cabinet members at arm's length, the degree to which this administration has marginalized the critical role of the executive branch is stunning."[44]

Additionally, although each cabinet member deals with a specialized area, presidents rarely consult with their cabinet when seeking advice on a specific policy. Usually, each president calls on a select few cabinet members for advice on substantive issues. For example, when prosecuting the wars in Afghanistan and Iraq, George W. Bush relied more extensively on the advice of Secretary of Defense Donald Rumsfeld than on the advice of Secretary of State Colin Powell.[45] Although President Obama does not rely on many of his cabinet members, he does solicit advice from his secretaries of defense and of state in national security matters. When planning the mission to kill Osama bin Laden in 2011, President Obama relied heavily on his then secretaries of defense and state Robert Gates and Hillary Clinton, respectively.[45]

Instead of relying on the cabinet for policy advice, presidents usually use cabinet officials to build political and public support for policies. For example, President Obama's Labor Secretary, Tom Perez, has publically defended President Obama's executive actions on immigration reform, most notably allowing undocumented immigrants with American citizen children to work legally in the United States. In addition to being Latino, Perez's position as labor secretary means that his job entails persuading Americans to support President Obama's policies that relate to workplace issues, such as his immigration actions.[47]

For most of American history, cabinets consisted solely of White males, but starting in the twentieth century, diversity in the cabinet became more salient. Over a decade after women won the right to vote, Franklin Delano Roosevelt chose the first woman cabinet secretary (Frances Perkins, Secretary

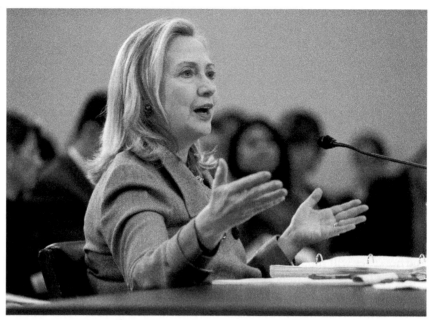

Secretary of State Hillary Rodham Clinton testifies on February 29, 2012, before the House Subcommittee on State, Foreign Operations, and Related Programs concerning North Korea. Secretary Clinton is the only first lady who was later elected to political office on her own. After President Obama narrowly defeated her for the Democratic Party nomination and became president, he named Ms. Clinton as his secretary of state, where she dealt with difficult issues, such as the wars in Iraq and Afghanistan, Iran, and North Korea. She received the Democratic Party nomination in 2016 but lost the general election.

of Labor, 1933–1945). Women did not lead one of the four major executive departments (Treasury, State, Defense, and Justice) until the Clinton administration, when women served as attorney general (Janet Reno, 1993–2001) and secretary of state (Madeleine Albright, 1997–2001).

Racial and ethnic diversity on the cabinet did not become an issue until the 1960s. In addition to the symbolic importance of a diverse executive branch, bringing the experience of minorities into the cabinet gives those groups a voice in executive branch politics. Secretary Perez's experience as a child of immigrants from the Dominican Republic enhances his ability to act on behalf of the president's immigration actions. With pivotal appointments, several modern presidents advanced the diversity of the cabinet. Lyndon B. Johnson chose the first African American (Robert C. Weaver, Secretary of Housing and Urban Development, 1966–1968); Ronald Reagan chose the first Latino (Lauro Cavazos, Secretary of Education, 1988–1990);[48] and Bill Clinton chose the first Asian American (Norman Mineta, Secretary of Commerce, 2000–2001).

Since the 1990s, presidential cabinets have become even more diverse. During the 1992 campaign, Clinton promised to appoint "an administration that looks like America,"[49] and his cabinet was considerably more diverse than that of any of his predecessors. President George W. Bush's cabinet was fairly diverse as well. He was also the first president to appoint minorities to key cabinet positions. Colin Powell and Condoleezza Rice, both African Americans, served as Secretary of State from 2001 to 2005 and 2005 to 2009, respectively, and Alberto Gonzalez, a Latino, served as Attorney General from 2005 to 2007. Condoleezza Rice was the first Black woman to serve in a major cabinet position. In 2009, President Obama appointed the first African American Attorney General, Eric Holder, and he replaced Holder with Loretta Lynch, the first African American female to serve as Attorney General.

As President Obama embarked on his second term, several of his key cabinet officials decided to resign, including Secretary of State Hillary Clinton, Secretary of Defense Leon Panetta, and Secretary of the Treasury Timothy Geithner. In January 2013, President Obama decided to nominate Senator John Kerry (D-MA) as Secretary of State, former Senator Chuck Hagel (R-NE) as Secretary of Defense, and his Chief of Staff Jacob Lew as Secretary of the Treasury. At the same time, President Obama nominated John Brennan to fill a vacancy as the CIA Director. Because all three nominees are White males, many observers criticized the lack of diversity among President Obama's initial second-term cabinet nominees, especially because he was considering nominating United Nations Ambassador Susan Rice, who is an African American female, as Secretary of State. The Obama administration disagreed with these critics, arguing that the president appointed more women and minorities than its predecessors and that it should not be judged solely according to these four appointments.[50] Since then, the diversity of President Obama's cabinet has changed as well. In January of 2013 Latino Secretary of the Interior Ken Salazar announced that he was leaving the cabinet, and President Obama replaced him with Sally Jewell, a White female. Asian American Secretary of Energy Steven Chu also stepped down, and President Obama nominated Ernest Moniz, who is White, to succeed him. President Obama did appoint Latino Thomas Perez to replace Latina departing Energy Secretary Hilda Solis and Julian Castro, who is Latino, to replace Shaun Donovan as Secretary of Housing and Urban Development. Additionally, in his second term President Obama replaced two White cabinet secretaries with two African Americans—Anthony Foxx as Secretary of Transportation and John King as Secretary of Education. Table 7.1 lists the members of President Obama's cabinet, as well as their race/ethnicity and gender.

The Executive Office of the President

Because modern presidents do not rely heavily on their cabinet for advice, they use the **Executive Office of the President (EOP)** for expert, reliable counsel. The EOP is divided into different departments (see Table 7.2), each of which provides the president with expert advice. Unlike cabinet officers, who are selected for political reasons, EOP officials are selected for their expertise, which is why presidents prefer to consult with the EOP instead of the cabinet. However, cabinet officers do serve in EOP departments (e.g., the Secretaries of

Executive Office of the President (EOP) A part of the executive branch that is divided into specific offices and contains key advisers who assist the president in managing the executive branch and developing policies.

Early in President Barack Obama's second term he named a number of new key administration officials, most of whom were White males. This photo emerged after public criticism of the president for his lack of diverse appointments. The photo depicts the president in a staff meeting without any women present; however, Senior Advisor Valerie Jarrett was in the room, although she was not visible in the photo.

State, Defense, and Treasury are part of the National Security Council).[51] Many EOP members also serve political roles, such as defending the president's proposals; therefore, presidents want to ensure that members of the EOP share their views on relevant public policy issues. For example, the Director of the Office of Management and Budget not only prepares the budget but also makes statements and issues press releases in support of the president's fiscal policies.[52]

Racial, ethnic, and gender diversity in the EOP is important because it influences public policies that affect the lives of racial minorities, but there has been little diversity in the top echelons of the EOP. One notable exception was Franklin Raines, an African American who served as the director of the Office of Management and Budget under President Clinton from 1996 to 1998. The only minority who served in a high-ranking position in the EOP under President George W. Bush was Claude Allen, who was the director of the Domestic Policy Council from 2005 to 2006. In his first term, President Obama appointed minorities to serve in key positions in the EOP, including United States Trade Representative Ron Kirk (who is Black and resigned in 2013).[53] As of 2016 the one high profile member of the Executive Office of the President is Susan Rice, who serves as President Obama's National Security Advisor (see below) and thus sits on the National Security Council.

TABLE 7.2 Executive Office of the President

Department	Year Established
Council of Economic Advisers	1946
Council on Environmental Quality	1969
Domestic Policy Council	1993
Homeland Security Council	2001
National Economic Council	1993
National Security Council	1947
Office of Administration	1977
Office of Faith-Based and Community Initiatives	2001
Office of Management and Budget	1970
Office of National AIDS Policy	2001
Office of National Drug Control Policy	1988
Office of Science and Technology Policy	1976
Office of the First Lady	Traditional
President's Foreign Intelligence Advisory Board	1956
Privacy and Civil Liberties Board	2004
United States Trade Representative	1963
USA Freedom Corps	2002
White House Fellows Office	1964
White House Military Office	Traditional

Source: Adapted from White House, "Executive Office of the President," http://www.whitehouse.gov /government/eop.html, accessed July 22, 2008.

The White House Staff

The **White House staff** includes the president's personally selected advisers, in whom he places considerable trust when seeking counsel. Whereas Congress creates executive departments and offices in the Executive Office of the President, and the Senate approves presidential nominees to those positions, the president solely determines the positions that exist on his White House staff, and White House staff members do not require the Senate's approval. Because the president is not required to consult with Congress concerning the White House staff, he can trust that those individuals have only his interests in mind.

The White House staff contains key advisers on domestic policy, foreign policy, legal counsel, and communication with the public. A fundamental White House staff position is the **Press Secretary**, who communicates directly with the members of the press who cover the White House. The Press Secretary

White House Staff The president's personal advisers, who do not need senatorial approval when appointed and provide critical political and policy advice to the president.

Press Secretary A member of the president's staff who conducts daily briefings with members of the media.

Chief of Staff A key assistant to the president who coordinates executive branch employees and serves as a link between other presidential advisers and the president.

conducts daily briefings with the media to answer questions and explain the actions of the president. Presidents also employ a **Chief of Staff**, who oversees executive branch personnel and filters all information from executive branch employees to the president. The Chief of Staff often determines which executive branch individuals meet with the president and for how long.

As with other key presidential advisers, racial and ethnic diversity is a key issue with the White House staff. As we discussed earlier, minority representation is important for symbolic reasons as well as for bringing a racial minority perspective into policymaking (see "Evaluating Equality: Racial and Ethnic Representation in the Executive Branch" for more on this issue). In 1955, President Eisenhower appointed E. Frederic Morrow as White House Administrative Officer for special projects; he was the first African American to have a key position on the White House staff. Even so, racial and ethnic minorities have continued to be underrepresented in important White House staff positions. All Press Secretaries and Chiefs of Staff have been White. Condoleezza Rice (2001–2005) and Susan Rice (2013–present) are the only minorities (and minority females) who served as the National Security Advisor.

Presidents and Congress

A key aspect of presidential politics concerns the relationship between the executive branch and Congress. In our system of checks and balances (see Chapter 2), the president does not act alone—he must be concerned with Congress. Presidents seek to set Congress's agenda, but they are not necessarily guaranteed success. Accordingly, an important element of the president's policymaking role entails persuading Congress to enact his legislative proposals. Renowned presidency scholar Richard Neustadt explains that presidents are forced to persuade members of Congress by bargaining with congressional leaders.[54] Conversely, leading political scientist Samuel Kernell demonstrates that since the 1970s bargaining has not been a viable strategy for presidents and they, instead, take their case directly to the public.[55] This section addresses both how presidents negotiate with members of Congress and how presidents try to mobilize public support. In addition, this section covers how executive-congressional relations often influence minority group politics.

Negotiating with Congress

When dealing with Congress, presidents employ a variety of strategies to impel Congress to agree to support their policies, including the threat of a veto. Presidents must exercise caution when threatening a veto because Congress could put the president in the undesirable position of having to choose between vetoing popular legislation and surrendering to Congress. For example, the Civil Rights Act of 1990 was designed to make it easier for minority employees to sue employers for discrimination. President George H. W. Bush threatened to veto the bill because he believed that technical legal language in the bill would lead to racial quotas, and he tried to convince Congress to

evaluating equality

Racial and Ethnic Representation in the Executive Branch

The modern executive branch is vast and tremendously important to the success of the presidency. It consists of the cabinet, subcabinet, Executive Office of the President, and White House staff. Moreover, race and ethnicity are central to American politics and to the presidency in particular. Therefore, racial and ethnic representation in the executive branch is a key debate in American politics.

Supporters of diversity in the executive branch argue that a diverse cabinet is important for symbolic reasons. Diverse cabinets represent the progress the United States has made in its treatment of racial minorities. Furthermore, presidents who can show the public that their cabinets reflect the background of the nation are able to claim more legitimacy for their actions, especially when those actions affect racial and ethnic minorities. Recall candidate Bill Clinton's 1992 pledge to appoint a cabinet that "looks like America." Additionally, racial and ethnic minorities in the executive branch can bring their unique experiences and perspectives into presidential decision making. Accordingly, there are substantive reasons to insist that presidents have diverse executive branches.

Critics argue, however, that race and ethnicity should not factor into presidential decisions to appoint executive branch officials. Presidents should be concerned solely with nominating individuals based on their qualifications, regardless of race or ethnicity. Moreover, many observers argue that a White executive branch official is just as capable as a minority official to represent, or even promote, minority interests. Others note that now that we have a Black president, symbolic diversity is less of a concern in the executive branch because it already exists at the top.

Debate among your classmates the importance of racial and ethnic diversity in presidential administrations. Does the need for diversity vary among the different executive branch divisions—the cabinet versus the Executive Office of the President or the White House staff? Does the fact that President Obama is Black influence the need for diversity?

change the law so that employers would have a better chance of defending their practices. When Congress refused, the president vetoed the act, despite public support for it and the fact that it had passed by a vote of 273–154 in the House and 62–34 in the Senate.[56] The following year, however, the president negotiated with congressional leaders to fashion the Civil Rights Act of 1991, which included language that made it clear that racial quotas were not required.[57] President Bush signed this bill.

Because presidents are the highest ranking elected officials within their political party, they are leaders of their political party, and they use that position to win support in Congress. The importance of party leadership depends on whether the president governs in times of divided government or unified government. **Divided government** occurs when the president is of one party and one or both houses of Congress is controlled by the other party. Presidents face difficulty persuading Congress to adopt their proposals during periods of divided government. **Unified government** occurs when the president and the majority of both houses of Congress are of the same political party; the president's chances of legislative success improve during periods of unified government.

During most of his presidency, Barack Obama was faced with divided government; therefore, he has needed to negotiate with Republicans to

Divided Government
A period in which the president is of one political party and the majority of one or both houses of Congress is of the other party.

Unified Government
A period in which both houses of Congress are controlled by the same party as the president.

accomplish his ambitious second-term agenda. Some of the more intractable issues have included reviving a still sluggish economy, tax reform, spending cuts, immigration, and gun control. However, he has not been successful in persuading Congress to adopt his policies. In late September 2013, clashes between President Obama (and Democrats in Congress) and the Republicans in Congress exploded when the two sides fought over continued funding for the government. More conservative House and Senate Republicans would not agree to provide funding for any nonessential government operations unless Congress defunded the Affordable Care Act, which Republicans overwhelmingly oppose. President Obama and the Democrats in Congress refused to accept that decision; therefore, the federal government shut down for two weeks in October. As the shutdown continued, the public increasingly blamed Republicans for the problems that the shutdown caused, and on October 16, 2013, enough Republicans agreed to fund the government without defunding the Affordable Care Act.[58]

Even in periods of unified government, however, presidents cannot always rely on support from other party members in Congress, as constituent pressures could lead members of Congress to oppose the president's proposals. Consequently, presidents must negotiate with individual members of Congress to secure favorable outcomes. In exchange for congressional support, presidents offer political rewards, such as an invitation to dine at the White House, campaign appearances on behalf of a member of Congress, or federal

President Obama and former Speaker of the House John Boehner (R-OH) met in the White House on July 23, 2011, to discuss how to avert a debt default. As both men's forced smiles indicate, those negotiations were extremely fractious. In periods of divided government, the president and congressional leaders of the opposite party must find ways to compromise for laws to be passed.

appointments to a senator's or representative's friends and political supporters. Even personal visits and phone calls to individual members of Congress
help presidents persuade members of Congress. President Lyndon B. Johnson
was exceptionally skilled at these kinds of negotiations. Johnson convinced
Southern senators and representatives to stop obstructing civil rights bills,
and he ultimately succeeded in securing the passage of the landmark Civil
Rights Act of 1964 and Voting Rights Act of 1965 (see Chapter 5). Johnson's
predecessor John F. Kennedy lacked Johnson's negotiation skills; he could not
convince Congress to pass these civil rights bills.[59]

Presidents and the Public

Noted political science scholar Samuel Kernell maintains that bargaining directly with congressional leaders is unlikely to yield success; therefore, presidents "go public," which means that they take their case directly to the
American people, hoping that increased support for their policies will force
Congress to pass them. Presidents deliver these messages to the American
people through the media.[60]

Presidents often use their popular support when trying to persuade Congress to pass their policy agenda. Because members of Congress want to please
their constituents, they do not want to oppose a popular president. Some presidents have been able to claim a **mandate**, in which they argue that a solid
election victory should translate into support for their policy priorities. For
example, Lyndon Johnson used his landslide victory in 1964 to push for passage of civil rights laws and his War on Poverty programs, and Ronald Reagan
used his solid victory in 1980 to convince Congress to pass tax cuts. Conversely, two recent presidents—Bill Clinton and George W. Bush—tried to
claim mandates, but their popular vote totals were low relative to those of
other presidents. As a result, Clinton and Bush could not rely on their election
victories to convince Congress to pass their policy programs.

Mandate A president's claim to Congress that his election victory signifies the public's support for his policy preferences.

Initially, President Obama's sizable margin in the 2008 election and high
public approval after his inauguration in 2009 helped him to convince Congress to enact key programs, such as the economic stimulus bill. However, as a
result of the slow and anemic economic recovery, his public support dropped.
After the Republican successes in the 2010 congressional election, President
Obama's mandate appeared to have dissipated, but his solid reelection victory
might have revived his mandate. As we mentioned earlier, President Obama
has contended with divided government throughout his second term, which
has made it difficult for him to achieve his goals.

Public approval of a president varies by president and during different periods of his presidency. Most presidents' public support peaks early in their
presidency, and then as presidents serve into their second term (if they have
one), their popularity declines. Shortly after the attacks of September 11,
2001, President Bush enjoyed approval ratings in the upper 80 percent range,
and during the early months of the Iraq War, his approval rating was in the
70 percent range. After his close reelection in 2004, President Bush's approval

continuously dropped because of rising opposition to the Iraq War, ethical scandals in the administration, and the administration's failure to respond to the devastating effects of Hurricane Katrina. By summer 2008, his approval rating was in the upper 20 percent range. President Obama started in the mid-60 percent range, but opposition to his health care bill and a sluggish economic recovery caused his approval to decrease to the mid-40 percent range by early 2012. As President Obama commenced his reelection campaign in 2012 his approval rose to about 50 percent, and by Election Day his approval was over 50 percent. However, after the botched implementation of the health care bill in late 2013, President Obama's approval ratings fell throughout 2014. Nevertheless, by 2016 President Obama's approval rating reached above 50 percent.[61]

Race and ethnicity often influence how members of the public perceive the president. As a Black candidate, Barack Obama strongly appealed to African Americans, Latinos, and Asian Americans, and his approval has consistently been higher among Blacks and Latinos than it has been with Whites. Figure 7.10 demonstrates that although Bush had much lower overall approval compared

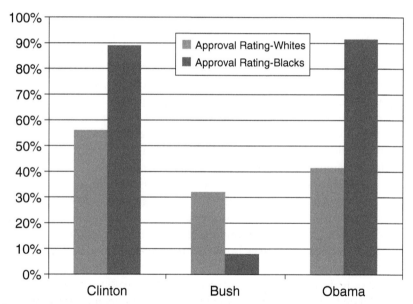

Figure 7.10 Approval Rating Among Whites and Blacks for Presidents Clinton, Bush, and Obama at the End of Their Second Terms

Sources: Clinton: Frank Newport, "Blacks and Whites Continue to Differ Sharply on Obama—Graph: President Clinton's Job Approval Averages By Race," Gallup, August 3, 2010, http://www.gallup.com/poll/141725/blacks -whites-continue-differ-sharply-obama.aspx, accessed June 26, 2016.

Bush: "Bush Job Approval Rating: Little Difference Among Whites, Hispanics," Gallup, June 29, 2007, http://www .gallup.com/poll/28009/bush-job-approval-rating-little-difference-among-whites-hispanics.aspx, accessed June 26, 2016.

Obama: "Obama Weekly Job Approval by Demographic Groups" (averaged), Gallup, March 2016, http://www .gallup.com/poll/121199/obama-weekly-job-approval-demographic-groups.aspx, accessed June 26, 2016.

to Obama and Clinton, Bush is the only president who had greater support among Whites than he did from Blacks. Both Clinton and Obama have extremely high—90 percent—support from African Americans. However, Clinton had higher White support than Obama does.

Congressional Investigations of the Executive Branch

Because the Framers feared executive tyranny, they wanted to ensure that Congress could prevent the executive branch from becoming too powerful. As a result, congressional committees investigate corruption or incompetence within the executive branch. Congressional investigations can even lead to **impeachment** of the president. Impeachment occurs when the U.S. House officially charges the president, vice president, or a federal judge with a serious violation. Once an official is impeached, the Senate decides whether to remove that person from office, which requires a two-thirds vote. Thus far, only Andrew Johnson and Bill Clinton have been impeached by the House of Representatives. President Johnson was impeached in 1868 because he dismissed Secretary of War Edwin Stanton in violation of the Tenure of Office Act. President Clinton was impeached in late 1998, charged with perjury and obstruction of justice because he lied to investigators about an extramarital affair. Neither Johnson nor Clinton was convicted in the Senate, and each president remained in office until the end of his term. Even if congressional investigations do not lead to impeachment, they can reveal embarrassing or incriminating information and inflict political damage on presidents.

> **Impeachment** The process by which the House of Representatives charges a president, vice president, or federal judge with a high crime or misdemeanor; the Senate can then decide to remove that official from office with a two-thirds vote.

Although Congress can compel executive branch officials to testify, presidents can, in response, invoke **executive privilege**, in which they shield confidential communications among executive branch officials to preserve national security or to ensure the integrity of the executive branch. In 1974, President Richard Nixon declared executive privilege to prevent a special prosecutor investigating Watergate from listening to audiotapes of his conversations with executive branch officials. In the case *United States v. Nixon* (1974), the Supreme Court officially recognized the existence of executive privilege but also limited its scope. The Court ruled that presidents can use executive privilege to protect information related to the official functioning of the executive branch, but they cannot use it to shield themselves from investigation of wrongdoing.[62]

> **Executive Privilege** Presidential authority to keep some of the communications among executive branch personnel private and free from Congress, the courts, and the public.

Executive privilege was especially controversial during the Bush administration. Private organizations even sued the vice president for information concerning a task force that proposed energy policies, but the Supreme Court ruled that the vice president did not need to submit those documents.[63] President Obama first invoked executive privilege in June 2012 over a congressional investigation into "Fast and Furious," a botched federal sting operation that allowed illegal guns to enter Mexico. Mexican gangs then used these weapons to kill a federal agent. Although the Obama administration answered many questions and submitted thousands of pages of documents to congressional investigators, President Obama cited executive privilege and directed his Attorney

General Eric Holder to withhold some information. The Republican-controlled House found Holder in contempt of Congress and sought to challenge the use of executive privilege in federal court. Democrats boycotted that vote, arguing that Republicans were motivated by partisanship. The Democratic-controlled Senate did not vote to find Holder in contempt or challenge the use of executive privilege.[64] Once Holder resigned in 2015 this issue was no longer salient.

Conclusion

The presidency is undoubtedly a crucial position in U.S. government, and in this chapter we discussed key aspects of presidential politics and power. The presidential selection process puts serious demands on anyone who wants to become president. As the chief law enforcer, the president enjoys considerable discretion in how policies affect people's everyday lives, and since the 1930s the president has even been a leader in shaping foreign and domestic policies. Presidents preside over an expansive executive branch, and they possess considerable resources when dealing with Congress, including mobilizing public support. However, their influence can be limited. In short, the president is the single most important figure in American politics.

Given its political importance, the presidency features prominently in the politics of race and ethnicity. The president's discretion in enforcing laws greatly influences the extent to which civil rights laws actually limit discrimination, and there have been significant variations among different presidents in their willingness to enforce civil rights laws. Moreover, the president's ability to shape the diversity of the executive branch has been instrumental in the symbolic and substantive politics of race and ethnicity.

Barack Obama's election and presidency are obviously momentous in terms of minority group politics because he is the first non-White president. Although other minorities, such as Shirley Chisholm, Jesse Jackson, Al Sharpton, Bill Richardson, and Herman Cain, have vied for a major party nomination, Obama is the only minority to win a major party nomination and two general elections.

Despite the significance of Obama's election and reelection for minority-group politics, it is important to understand that race was not the only relevant factor. White presidents have affected the lives of racial and ethnic minorities. President Lyndon B. Johnson, for example, boldly used his powers to ensure that civil rights laws were vigorously enforced, skillfully worked with Congress to ensure the passage of landmark civil rights bills, and appointed more racial and ethnic minorities to key positions than any of his predecessors. Additionally, Americans of all races voted for Obama because of his opposition to the war in Iraq, his foreign policy views, his plans to improve the U.S. economy, and his stances on other issues such as health care, the environment, and gun control—none of which pertain to race and ethnicity. In fact, during his first term, President Obama devoted the bulk of his time and effort to foreign and domestic issues that transcend race.

Finally, as the opening story demonstrates, Barack Obama will be leaving office in 2017; therefore his replacement will exert a significant impact on the politics of race or ethnicity. Given the racially charged tone of Donald Trump's campaign, we do not know how his presidency will shape the politics of race and ethnicity.

review
REVIEW QUESTIONS

1. How can presidential powers influence civil rights?
2. Is diversity in the executive branch important? Why or why not?
3. How has the presidential selection process disadvantaged racial minority candidates, and why was Barack Obama able to overcome these disadvantages in 2008 and 2012?
4. Does Barack Obama's success mean that those disadvantages are no longer present? Why or why not?
5. What do President Obama's failure to secure immigration reform and his subsequent executive actions on immigration reveal about the presidency?

terms
KEY TERMS

Cabinet p. 228
Caucus p. 209
Chief of Staff p. 234
Congressional War Powers p. 221
Divided Government p. 235
Electoral College p. 211
Enemy Combatants p. 222
Executive Agreements p. 221

Executive Office of the President (EOP) p. 231
Executive Orders p. 219
Executive Privilege p. 239
Impeachment p. 239
Mandate p. 237
Modern Presidency p. 218
Pocket Veto p. 224

Press Secretary p. 233
Primary p. 209
Signing Statements p. 218
State of the Union Address p. 224
Super PACs p. 212
Unified Government p. 235
Veto p. 223
White House Staff p. 233

readings
ADDITIONAL READINGS

Jesse Jackson, Frank Clemente, and Frank Watkins, *Keep Hope Alive: Jesse Jackson's 1988 Presidential Campaign* (Boston: South End Press, 1989).

    This book, a collection of primary source documents related to Jesse Jackson's 1988 run for the presidency, focuses specifically on Jackson's ideal of "hope," his views on economic policy, his national security ideas, and his call for justice for racial and ethnic minorities, women, gays and lesbians, the elderly, the disabled, and the poor.

Nicholas Laham, *The Reagan Presidency and the Politics of Race: In Pursuit of Colorblind Justice and Limited Government* (Westport, CT: Praeger, 1998).

    This book objectively chronicles President Reagan's attempts to reverse civil rights policies enacted during the 1960s and 1970s and focuses specifically on Reagan's goals of ending affirmative action and willingness to allow private institutions receiving any federal funding, even indirectly, to discriminate on account of race, gender, age, or health.

E. Frederic Morrow, *Black Man in the White House: A Diary of the Eisenhower Years by the Administrative Officer for Special Projects, the White House, 1955–1961* (New York: Coward-McCann, 1963).

    The first African American to serve in the White House staff recounts his experiences, provides an honest assessment of Eisenhower's civil rights record, and describes the daily life of White House staffers and the critical role they play in serving their presidents.

Russell L. Riley, *The Presidency and the Politics of Racial Inequality: Nation Keeping from 1831 to 1965* (New York: Columbia University Press, 1999).

    This book historically analyzes presidents' impact on civil rights policies from Andrew Jackson through Lyndon Johnson. Riley argues that presidents are so concerned with "nation keeping" that they do not pursue policies of racial equality, unless there is sufficient public will or social movement pressure.

James A. Thurber, ed., *Obama in Office* (Boulder, CO: Paradigm, 2011).

This is an edited volume in which leading political scientists contribute scholarly chapters that analyze different elements of President Obama's first two years in office.

Richard Wolffe, *Renegade: The Making of a President* (New York: Crown, 2009).

This book reveals some of the highs and lows of Obama's personal and political life prior to his national political career as well as providing a glimpse into the daily life of a presidential campaign.

CHAPTER 8

The Bureaucracy: Career Government Employees, Accountability, and Race

A Flint, Michigan, resident holds a sample of the city's tap water. The brown water demonstrates how Flint's water supply was contaminated. The problems began when government bureaucrats switched the water supply for the city's residents, and the new water caused the pipes to corrode, which contaminated the water. Although residents had been complaining about their water for a couple of years, state and local government bureaucrats ignored the problem until the media reported that the water was contaminated with lead, a poison that can cause brain damage in children.

Flint is a city in south-central Michigan with about 100,000 residents, a majority (56 percent) of whom are African American. Although it was once a thriving manufacturing center, Flint is an economically slumping city, with more than 40 percent of its residents living below the poverty line.[1]

In 2012 the financially strapped city sought to save money by ceasing to use water from Detroit, with the intention of hooking up to the Karegnondi Water Authority (KWA), which uses Lake Huron as its source. However, when Flint disconnected from the Detroit water system, it was not able to connect to the KWA; therefore, it needed to temporarily use water from the Flint River. The water in the Flint River contains corrosive elements, which after interacting with the pipes caused lead and other poisonous heavy metals to seep into Flint's water supply. Nevertheless, city officials assured the residents that their water was safe for drinking and bathing, citing Michael Prysby—an official with the Michigan Department of Environmental Quality (MDEQ). In fact, the city did not even treat the water to limit the corrosion. By the summer of 2014, residents complained about the quality of their water, even bringing the brown-colored water samples to public meetings. City and state official responsible for ensuring a safe water supply did not respond to these complaints. As the problems with Flint's water supply continued through late 2014 and early 2015, General Motors, which operates a local plant, stopped using Flint water because it was corroding the machines, and even more importantly, state and local government offices provided bottled water for their employees.

By the spring and summer of 2015, scientists had demonstrated that Flint's water supply was severely contaminated, and a city test revealed significant amounts of lead in the water. Lead is especially dangerous because it can cause brain damage in children. Still, the MDEQ denied the severity of the problem, indicating that its tests showed that Flint's water was safe. An MDEQ official even told the residents to "relax." However, in August of 2015, the press showed that the MDEQ tampered with the evidence used in their test, and by September of 2015 independent scientists found that not only was Flint's water supply severely contaminated with lead, but also that children in the area had high levels of lead in their blood.

By the end of 2015, Flint had switched back to the Detroit water system, but the story did not end. The mayor of Flint, governor of Michigan, and president of the United States all declared a "state of emergency" in Flint and surrounding areas because of the lack of safe water. In early 2016 the United States Environmental Protection Agency (EPA), a federal agency in charge of environmental quality, issued an "emergency order" that allowed it to control the process of bringing safe water to the Flint residents. The EPA cited the state and city's failures as its reason for taking control of the situation. In February of 2016 the United States House of Representatives Committee on Oversight and Government Reform investigated the failures in Flint. City and state officials, including Michigan governor Rick Snyder and the head of the EPA Gina McCarthy testified before the committee. A separate independent probe blamed city officials and the governor of Michigan, but it put the bulk of the blame on the Michigan Department of Environmental Quality. In April of 2016, the Michigan attorney general, which is an elected position, announced that he was filing criminal charges for neglect of duty and tampering with evidence against Michael Prysby and Stephen Busch, of the Michigan Department of Environmental Quality, and Michael Glasgow, the Flint official in charge of water quality. As of this edition's press time, these criminal cases remain unresolved.[2]

intro *The story of the failures* of Flint and the Michigan Department of Environmental Quality demonstrate the importance of the **bureaucracy** in American government. A bureaucracy is a large, complex organization in which people work within specified levels of rank and authority to carry out the policies of that organization. Bureaucracies exist in corporations, universities, and governments. In the case of the Flint Water Crisis, as it has become known, the state and city bureaucracies were responsible for the contaminated water, but in this chapter, we are interested in the federal government bureaucracy, which carries out federal policies and provides services to the American public. In fact, the Environmental Protection Agency, part of the federal bureaucracy, was instrumental in responding to this crisis.

The Flint Water Crisis illustrates key aspects of bureaucratic politics. First, the effectiveness of a bureaucracy depends on the competence and experience of its leaders. The MDEQ and City of Flint bureaucrats were supposed to ensure that people had access to safe water, but because of their negligence and unethical behavior,

> **Bureaucracy** A large, complex organization in which employees work within specific levels of rank and authority to carry out the policies of that organization.

they clearly failed in this regard. Second, the fact that the U.S. House of Representatives and Michigan attorney general responded to the crisis by investigating and even bringing criminal charges against the bureaucrats who were most at fault reveals the issue of oversight of the bureaucracy. Although, as we show in this chapter, the bureaucracy is supposed to be free from politics, elected officials supervise the bureaucracy's functioning in American government. Third, a bureaucracy influences racial and ethnic minorities. The residents of Flint, Michigan, are overwhelmingly non-White, and they are the ones who have suffered the most because of the failure of bureaucratic government.

We begin this chapter by examining the organizational structure of the federal bureaucracy and then discuss the bureaucrats, who are the employees of the bureaucracy. In the latter part of the chapter we explore bureaucratic power. We discuss what bureaucracies do, the sources of bureaucratic power, and ways to limit the federal bureaucracy. Throughout the chapter, we emphasize how the bureaucracy affects racial and ethnic minorities.

Bureaucratic Organization

A key aspect of the federal bureaucracy is its organization. The federal bureaucracy is divided into four separate categories: (1) cabinet departments, (2) independent regulatory commissions, (3) independent executive agencies, and (4) government corporations. Each of these sections is further divided and subdivided into units responsible for more specialized functions.

Determining bureaucratic structure is often politically controversial. The president and Congress establish and eliminate sections of the bureaucracy based on the importance that they place on those sections' functions. As we discuss in this section, the organization of the bureaucracy influences the ability of agencies to perform their functions, which, in turn, affects racial and ethnic minorities.

Cabinet Departments

Cabinet Departments The major divisions within the executive branch, with each performing a specific function.

Cabinet departments are major divisions of the executive branch and perform a wide range of executive functions (see Table 8.1). Each executive department contains several divisions, which are then subdivided into specialized functions. In Chapter 7, we discussed the role the cabinet plays in executive politics, but in this chapter we focus more on the cabinet departments as bureaucratic agencies. In other words, we are less concerned now with the cabinet secretaries and undersecretaries, the positions at the top of the departments. Rather, we are interested in the middle- and lower-level positions that carry out the daily, detailed activities necessary for governing.

Many of these specialized units within cabinet departments focus on racial and ethnic political issues. For example, the Department of Justice is in charge of enforcing federal laws, including civil rights laws. Specifically, the Civil Rights Division of the Department of Justice enforces laws that protect against racial and ethnic discrimination, as well as unequal treatment of the

TABLE 8.1 **Federal Cabinet Departments**

Department	Year Established	Number of Full-Time Civilian Employees (Fiscal Year 2014)
State	1789	10,068
Treasury	1789	86,049
Defense	1789/1947[a]	89,547[b]
Justice	1789/1870[c]	110,427
Interior	1849	49,052
Agriculture	1889	72,889
Commerce	1903/1913[d]	34,857
Labor	1903/1913[d]	15,077
Health and Human Services	1953/1980[e]	62,099
Education	1953/1980[e]	3,815
Housing and Urban Development	1965	8,255
Transportation	1967	53,684
Veterans' Affairs	1989	308,176
Energy	1977	14,341
Veterans' Affairs	1989	308,176
Homeland Security	2003	167,422

[a] The Defense Department was renamed from the War Department, created in 1789.

[b] This figure does not include employees in the Department of the Army or Department of the Navy.

[c] The attorney general position was created in 1789, but the Justice Department was created in 1870.

[d] The Commerce Department and Labor Department were originally merged together as the Department of Commerce and Labor, which was created in 1903.

[e] The Department of Health, Education, and Welfare, created in 1953, was split into two separate departments in 1980.

Sources: Adapted from White House, "President's Cabinet" (with links to each department), http://www.whitehouse.gov/administration/cabinet/, accessed February 17, 2012; United States Office of Personnel Management, "Table 3: NSFTP Federal Executive Branch Employment by Cabinet Level Agency," Sizing Up the Executive Branch, Fiscal Year 2014, https://www.opm.gov/policy-data-oversight/data-analysis-documentation/federal-employment-reports/reports-publications/sizing-up-the-executive-branch.pdf, accessed July 2, 2016.

disabled, the elderly, and members of nontraditional religions. The division was created in 1957,[3] and it is divided into various sections (see Table 8.2), each of which specializes in different aspects of civil rights enforcement. The Civil Rights Division is run by an assistant attorney general, who is appointed by the president and confirmed by the Senate, but the majority of the attorneys and nonattorneys who carry out the everyday tasks necessary for enforcing civil rights laws are not political appointees. Instead, they are hired based on their qualifications.

Although the cabinet bureaucracy are staffed by career employees who focus mainly on performing their jobs and not serving the president, the

TABLE 8.2 **Sections of the Civil Rights Division of the Department of Justice**

Section	Function(s)
Appellate	Manages appeals for civil rights cases the U.S. government litigates in the U.S. Courts of Appeals and U.S. Supreme Court
Criminal	Investigates and prosecutes parties charged with criminal violations of federal civil rights laws
Disability Rights	Enforces Americans with Disabilities Act (ADA) and assists federal agencies with ADA compliance
Educational Opportunities	Enforces antidiscrimination laws pertaining to education; represents Department of Education in federal court
Employment Litigation	Enforces antidiscrimination laws pertaining to employment
Federal Coordination and Compliance	Enforces antidiscrimination policies for any entity that receives federal and compliance funds
Housing and Civil Enforcement	Enforces laws preventing discrimination in housing, credit, and public accommodations on account of citizenship or immigrant status
Office of Special Counsel for Immigration-Related Unfair Employment Practices	Enforces laws banning employment discrimination on account of citizenship or status; offers educational outreach for employers
Policy and Strategy	Coordinates with other federal agencies to analyze and propose policies and regulations pertaining to civil rights
Special Litigation	Enforces civil rights laws protecting "institutionalized persons, conduct of law enforcement agencies, access to reproductive health clinics and places of religious worship, and religious exercise of institutionalized persons"
Voting	Enforces the Voting Rights Act of 1965 and other laws protecting against voting discrimination

Source: Adapted from U.S. Department of Justice, Civil Rights Division, "About the Division," https://www.justice.gov/crt/about-division, accessed July 2, 2016.

president still exercises control over the cabinet bureaucracy. The case of the Federal Emergency Management Agency (FEMA) illustrates how placing an agency in the cabinet bureaucracy affects its performance. FEMA was first created in 1979 to coordinate the government's responses to natural disasters, such as floods, earthquakes, and hurricanes.[4] It was initially established as an independent agency, which, as we discuss below, operates independently of the president. By most accounts FEMA was successful when it was an independent agency, especially during the 1990s.[5]

However, after the attacks of September 11, 2001, the federal government reorganized its disaster response apparatus, and in 2003 FEMA was placed under the jurisdiction of the newly created Department of Homeland Security. This change in FEMA's status diminished the federal government's ability to respond to natural disasters. FEMA's funding decreased under this new arrangement. The Bush administration reduced FEMA's independence and reoriented FEMA's mission toward responding to terror attacks and away from responding to natural disasters. Furthermore, unlike his predecessors who appointed emergency management professionals to lead FEMA, President George W. Bush appointed a political supporter named Michael Brown, who had no experience with emergency management. Consequently, when Hurricane Katrina struck southeastern Louisiana in August of 2005 and subsequently flooded the city of New Orleans, FEMA was completely unprepared to deal with the disaster. Essentially the poor residents of New Orleans, most of whom were African Americans, were unable to evacuate the city, and they were stranded for days without food and water. Many of these evacuees died. Most observers cite FEMA's lack of independence and Michael Brown's incompetence as the source of this failure.[6] Moreover, this bureaucratic failure disproportionately affected African Americans, who were twice as likely as Whites to lack the means to evacuate.[7]

Independent Regulatory Commissions

Independent regulatory commissions are established by Congress to regulate a specific economic or social interest. When Congress deems that legislation alone cannot adequately address an important regulatory need, it creates an independent regulatory commission to perform that function. Independent

Independent Regulatory Commissions Government bodies that issue and enforce regulations on specified economic and social interests.

New Orleans police officers escort flood victims who were rescued after Hurricane Katrina. Most observers believe that FEMA's incompetent leadership and lack of preparation contributed immensely to the suffering of numerous low-income and Black residents of New Orleans and surrounding areas. Since this fiasco, FEMA has been managed by emergency management experts. President Obama in particular has stressed expertise, professionalism, and rigorous training for all FEMA employees, including the agency leaders.

regulatory commissions make rules, enforce them by conducting investigations of violations, and then adjudicate disputes arising from the enforcement of those rules (although those decisions can be appealed to the federal judiciary). In short, they act as legislature, executive, and judiciary, albeit in a narrowly defined policy area.

Each commission consists of commissioners who are appointed by the president and subject to the Senate's confirmation, and each commission relies on career staff people, who are hired instead of appointed. Unlike other presidential appointees, the commissioners serve for fixed terms, and the president cannot remove them if he disagrees with their decisions.[8] The statutes that create regulatory commissions require that there be a close balance of Democratic and Republican commissioners. This means that a Republican president could at times be forced to appoint a Democrat, and vice versa. Nevertheless, presidents have opportunities to shape the effect of regulatory commissions through appointments, with Republican presidents generally preferring commissioners who favor less regulation and Democratic presidents generally preferring commissioners who favor more regulation.

Independent regulatory commissions affect public policies, including issues of racial and ethnic discrimination. For example, since 1964 the Equal Employment Opportunity Commission (EEOC) has been responsible for investigating discrimination complaints that employees bring against their employers. After listening to the complaints, the EEOC commissioners try to mediate the conflict, or they can decide to bring a federal civil suit against the employer.[9] Therefore, the EEOC is extremely important in the everyday details of the fight against racial and ethnic (as well as gender, age, and disability) discrimination.

Although EEOC commissioners are appointed to fixed terms, presidents can still influence the vigor with which the commission pursues discrimination claims (assuming the Senate confirms their nominees). For example, in 1982 President Ronald Reagan appointed Clarence Thomas (who now serves on the U.S. Supreme Court) as the chair of the EEOC. Reagan sought to limit the number of civil rights suits that the EEOC initiated, and according to a congressional study, under Thomas's leadership the EEOC was less effective in enforcing civil rights laws than it had been prior to his leadership.[10] Conversely, in 2012, President Barack Obama designated Jenny Yang, an Asian American woman who had previously worked as an attorney for the U.S. Justice Civil Rights Division (see above), to be the chair of the EEOC.[11] In addition to ensuring that workplace discrimination laws are enforced, Yang has focused on how technological advances can both increase and limit workplace discrimination on account of race, gender, sexual orientation, and disability.[12] Presidents are therefore able to influence the political direction of the EEOC with key appointments.

Independent Executive Agencies

Independent Executive Agencies Parts of the federal bureaucracy with specified functions that are independent from cabinet departments, do not regulate, and do not charge fees for their services.

Independent executive agencies are bureaucratic agencies that focus on narrow areas, but they are independent from cabinet departments, do not regulate, and do not earn revenue. Some of the more well-known independent agencies are the Central Intelligence Agency, which was created in 1947 to gather information necessary for national security,[13] and the National Aeronautics and Space Administration, which was created in 1958 to conduct scientific research on the earth's atmosphere and explore outer space.[14]

The U.S. Commission on Civil Rights is a key independent agency involved in racial and ethnic politics. Unlike the EEOC, the U.S. Commission on Civil Rights does not actually enforce civil rights laws. Instead, it gathers qualitative and quantitative evidence and holds hearings to determine the extent to which discrimination exists. It also evaluates the effectiveness of civil rights laws and writes reports on its findings. The commission consists of eight commissioners, each of whom serves a six-year term. The president appoints four commissioners, who are not subject to Senate confirmation, and Congress appoints the other four commissioners. Staff people conduct the everyday, detailed work of the commission.[15]

Similar to the EEOC, the ability of the U.S. Commission on Civil Rights to affect civil rights policy depends on the ideology of its

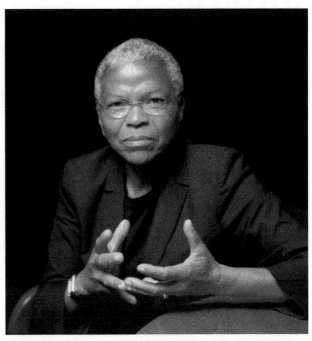

Dr. Mary Frances Berry was a former chair of the U.S. Commission on Civil Rights. As an independent executive agency, the U.S. Committee on Civil Rights does not exert direct authority over policymaking, but Dr. Berry used her position to emphasize issues important to racial and ethnic minorities, such as voting irregularities in Florida during the 2000 election. After she left the commission in 2004, Dr. Berry concentrated her efforts in academia. She is professor of history at the University of Pennsylvania, and she frequently comments on civil rights issues pertaining to minorities and women.

commissioners, especially the chair. One of the most notable chairs of the commission was Dr. Mary Frances Berry, a historian and academic leader by training. During the 1970s, President Jimmy Carter appointed her to the commission, and in 1993 President Bill Clinton promoted her to chair. During her tenure as chair, she aggressively investigated systematic police brutality against minorities and the conditions on Indian reservations.[16] She is best known for her extensive investigation of whether racial discrimination occurred in Florida during the 2000 presidential election. In fact, over the objection of two conservative commissioners, she issued a strongly worded statement arguing that Florida had committed numerous violations of the Voting Rights Act.[17] "Our Voices: The U.S. Commission on Civil Rights and the Controversy over Florida and the 2000 Election" has more detail on her actions.

President George W. Bush replaced Dr. Berry with Gerald Reynolds, who is also African American, but he is a conservative Republican who pursued a more conservative course. For example, in 2007 Reynolds launched an investigation of affirmative action in law schools with the purpose of exposing

our voices

The U.S. Commission on Civil Rights and the Controversy over Florida and the 2000 Election

The delayed reporting of the results of the 2000 presidential election outcome in Florida was undoubtedly notorious, but racial discrimination in the state's conduct of the election was especially controversial. Critics charged that (1) Florida's method of purging invalid voters unfairly targeted Blacks, (2) there was an inordinate police presence at polling places in areas with high Black populations, (3) polling places in areas with high Black populations mysteriously changed locations, and (4) the systematic unequal distribution of voting resources unfairly affected minority voters.

As a result of these problems, the U.S. Commission on Civil Rights conducted a thorough investigation of irregularities in Florida's 2000 vote. Here we provide excerpts from a letter that the chair, Dr. Mary Frances Berry, wrote to Florida governor Jeb Bush (R). The letter highlights the problems the commission uncovered. It also reveals how this crucial bureaucratic agency operates and specifically demonstrates the commission's investigative and subpoena powers.

Dear Governor Bush:

I am writing to express my deep disappointment with your statement of priorities that was presented during the opening of the Florida legislative session, in which you did not address the most serious problems. . . . As you know, the Commission has undertaken a formal investigation into allegations by Floridians of voting irregularities arising out of the November 7, 2000, Presidential election. The Commission has held two fact-finding hearings in Florida to examine whether eligible voters faced avoidable barriers that undermined their ability to cast ballots and have their ballots counted in a closely contested election. . . .

. . . Over 100 witnesses testified under oath before the commission, including approximately 65 scheduled witnesses who were scheduled for the two hearings due to their knowledge of and/or expertise with the issues under investigation. The Commission heard testimony from top elected and appointed state officials, including your own testimony, that of the Secretary of State, the Attorney General, the Director of the Florida Division of Elections, and other Florida state and county officials. A representative of . . . a firm involved in the controversial, state-sponsored removal of felons from the voter registration rolls also testified.

We also heard the sworn testimony of registered voters and experts on election reform issues, election laws and procedures, and voting rights. Also, the Chair and Executive Director of the Select Task Force on Election Reforms that you established testified before the Commission. Testimony was received from the supervisors of elections for several counties, county commission officials, law enforcement personnel, and a state's attorney. In addition to the scheduled witnesses, the Commission extended an opportunity for concerned persons, including Members of Congress and members of the Florida State Legislature, to submit testimony under oath that was germane to the issues under investigation. Significantly, the Commission subpoenaed scores of relevant documents to assist with the investigation.

. . . These problems cry out for solutions, for example, a process for ensuring equitable allocation of resources to ensure that poor and/or people-of-color areas are not disproportionally affected. They also include a better process for identifying felons who are ineligible to vote, ensuring coordination between the DMV and election boards to make sure registrations are actually filed and on a timely basis, funds for better training of poll workers, improved and updated communication systems, funds for voter education, and clarifications in the law to permit provisional ballots to be cast, when appropriate. . . .

Because I believe the need to address these problems is serious, I have determined that the commission should hold additional hearings in Florida . . . to assess what changes have been legislated or enacted at the state and local level and to report to the public what progress has been made. . . .

Respectfully,

Mary Frances Berry

Chairperson

Source: Adapted from U.S. Commission on Civil Rights, "Letter to Governor Bush from Chairperson Berry," March 1, 2001, http://www.usccr.gov/pubs/vote2000/Berry.htm, accessed July 2, 2016.

problems with affirmative action programs.[18] After Reynolds's term expired in 2011, President Barack Obama appointed Martin Castro, a Latino Democrat, to be chair. In January 2013, Castro and the commission investigated incidents of sexual assault in the military, after male soldiers were not punished for assaulting female soldiers. Castro even posed the idea of having a civilian agency handle the sexual assault cases instead of the military.[19]

Government Corporations

Government corporations perform tasks similar to those in the private sector, charge for those services, and keep the revenue they generate, but unlike private-sector corporations, government corporations are run by the federal government and receive a significant portion of their operating funds from government expenditures. The oldest government corporation is the U.S. Post Office, which Article 1, Section 8, of the U.S. Constitution specifically authorizes Congress to establish. These corporations often assume such responsibilities because disadvantaged citizens cannot afford those services without government involvement and funding.

Government Corporations Parts of the federal bureaucracy that charge fees for the services that they provide to the American public.

The National Railroad Passenger Corporation, better known as Amtrak, provides passenger rail service to more than five hundred U.S. cities, and it has been a particularly controversial government corporation. Many citizens use Amtrak because they cannot afford airline or personal automobile travel, which means that Amtrak cannot charge expensive rates. As a result, it loses money, and the federal government subsidizes those losses. During congressional debates over funding Amtrak, Democrats usually advocate higher funding and Republicans usually advocate cutting funding or turning passenger rail service completely over to the private sector.[20]

The Bureaucrats

In addition to bureaucratic organization, **bureaucrats**—the employees who work in the federal bureaucracy—are an important part of American government. After all, people administer laws on a daily basis; organizational charts do not. The size of the federal bureaucracy has grown immensely since 1940 when there were fewer than one million executive branch civilian employees (excluding the post office) until now (2014) where there are over two million executive branch civilian employees.[21] Given the enormous number of employees, it is important to examine who these bureaucrats are and how and why they are hired. The opening vignette exposed the problems with incompetent and unethical bureaucrats in Flint, Michigan, and the story of FEMA's response to Hurricane Katrina demonstrates the difference between a political appointee managing FEMA and an experienced professional managing FEMA. There are also issues of racial and ethnic diversity among the bureaucrats to be discussed.

Bureaucrats The employees who work in a bureaucracy.

Politics versus Merit

During the early years of the American Republic, when the bureaucracy was small, government leaders were not overly concerned with the competence and skill of federal bureaucrats. Initially, federal bureaucrats were exclusively from the upper classes of American society, but Andrew Jackson's presidential victory in 1828 drastically changed the process of hiring bureaucrats. Jackson expanded the **patronage** system, also known as the "spoils system," in which government bureaucrats were hired based on political and partisan support of the winning candidate, not based on their training, education, experience, or demonstrated ability. Jackson believed that the federal bureaucracy could function only if bureaucrats supported his principles. He also used patronage to give commoners a greater stake in the federal bureaucracy, which he regarded as elitist. As the two-party system emerged in the 1840s and 1850s, patronage became more entrenched. Those who supported the political party of the winning candidate were hired to fill federal bureaucratic positions. The incumbent party then demanded continued support from federal employees, and if they refused, they could be fired. If the incumbent party lost, then existing employees were fired and replaced with the supporters of the winning party.[22] Although the patronage system bred corruption and incompetence in the bureaucracy, it did provide immigrants, and even ethnic minorities, with bureaucratic jobs when the private sector would not hire them. Nevertheless, there is considerable debate over the extent to which patronage actually helped immigrants and ethnic minorities.[23]

After the Civil War, many high-level bureaucrats in the Grant administration were involved in corruption scandals, which engendered calls for reform of the patronage system. With the government expanding its authority over social and economic policy, reformers argued that the patronage system was too corrupt and inefficient to meet the needs of the changing federal government. In 1881, newly inaugurated president James Garfield adhered to these reformist views and refused to staff federal bureaucratic positions based on patronage. Charles Guiteau, who unsuccessfully sought a position from Garfield, assassinated the president so that Vice President Chester Arthur, who opposed reform, could become president. But Garfield's assassination martyred the cause for reforming the federal bureaucracy, and in 1883 Congress passed the Civil Service Reform Act of 1883, better known as the **Pendleton Act**, which transformed the federal bureaucracy from a patronage system into a merit system. It required career bureaucrats, known as **civil servants**, to be hired based on their performance on a competitive examination. It also guaranteed job security to those employees hired through the examination process, and it banned supervisors from compelling political support from their employees. The Pendleton Act created the Civil Service

Patronage A system of hiring bureaucrats because they supported the winning political candidate, not because they had the skill, training, and experience for their jobs.

Pendleton Act A federal law passed in 1883 that required bureaucrats to be hired and retained according to their demonstrated skill, not their political affiliation.

This Thomas Nast cartoon depicts President-elect Grover Cleveland as the Hercules of civil service reform, opposing the Tammany tiger of patronage. Patronage was a system that gave federal jobs to people based on their support of the winning candidate, and not on merit. Because patronage led to corruption and incompetence, reformers sought to replace the patronage system with a merit system.

Commission, now known as the Office of Personnel Management, to ensure fair treatment of civil servants.[24]

Politicization of the bureaucracy reemerged during the New Deal, and in response Congress passed the **Hatch Act** in 1939 to forbid federal employees from engaging in virtually all political activities. For example, federal government employees could not run for any political office, even local nonpartisan ones, or work for a political party, or manage an election campaign. By removing employees from political participation, this law clearly depoliticized the federal bureaucracy, but it also limited the freedom of federal employees. In 1993, at the urging of President Clinton, Congress passed the Hatch Act Amendments of 1993, which liberalized the Hatch Act to allow federal employees to participate in campaigns on behalf of other candidates. Federal bureaucrats are still forbidden, however, from displaying blatant partisanship, soliciting campaign contributions, or working on political campaigns while on the job. Under the new regulations, civil servants still cannot run for partisan offices, but they can run for local, nonpartisan offices.[25]

Diversity

Similar to private-sector companies, government bureaucracies have historically discriminated against women and minorities in hiring and promotion. The Civil Rights Act prohibits federal, state, and local governments from discriminatory hiring practices. However, there has been considerable controversy over how to determine the existence of discrimination. Clearly, if plaintiffs (the parties bringing the discrimination complaint) can show that a government agency intentionally discriminated against them, then courts would find a violation and order equitable hiring practices.

Determining that discrimination exists becomes more contentious when government agencies do not intentionally discriminate, but their hiring or promotion procedures wind up disproportionately hurting minorities. For example, racial minorities traditionally score lower on hiring examinations compared to Whites; consequently, some government agencies hire Whites at a greater rate than Blacks or Latinos. In one case, African Americans sued the city of Washington, DC, because their lower scores on an examination to become police officers resulted in lower hiring rates. In 1976, the U.S. Supreme Court ruled that disparate performance on an examination does not by itself constitute a violation of antidiscrimination law.[26] Because of this decision, civil rights plaintiffs experience greater difficulty challenging government hiring practices that are not intentionally discriminatory but that disproportionately harm racial and ethnic minorities.

The federal government has actively tried to increase women and minority employment through affirmative action (see Chapter 5). As early as 1971, the Civil Service Commission (now called the Office of Personnel Management) required federal government agencies to set numerical goals, but not binding quotas, to ensure that women and minorities were represented fairly

Civil Servants Federal bureaucrats who are not political appointees, but instead are hired according to their education and performance on an examination.

Hatch Act A federal law passed in 1939 and amended in 1993 that restricts federal employees' partisan political activities.

evaluating equality

Diversity in the Bureaucracy: The Case of the Bureau of Indian Affairs

As we have seen throughout this chapter bureaucratic performance greatly affects racial and ethnic minorities; therefore minority representation in the bureaucracy is a significant issue. As we show, particularly in the Measuring Equality box, racial and ethnic minorities are not well represented in the federal bureaucracy, especially at the higher levels. Given how the work of the bureaucracy affects racial and ethnic minorities, e.g., FEMA and the U.S. Customs and Border Protection, how important is racial and ethnic diversity in the bureaucracy?

One particularly interesting aspect of diversity in federal bureaucracy concerns the Bureau of Indian Affairs, which was created in 1824 and is the oldest federal bureaucratic department to handle Indian affairs. Because the American government then sought to subjugate Indians through military force, the BIA was initially part of the Department of War. Over the next two decades, the federal government removed Indians from their tribal lands and placed them on reservations in the interior regions of the United States. When

Command post of the Police of the Bureau of Indian Affairs after wildfires burned 60,000 acres and dozens of homes on August 6, 2012, in Creek County, Oklahoma. The Bureau of Indian Affairs (BIA) Police is a bureaucratic agency in the Department of Interior that provides law enforcement assistance to reservations that lack their own tribal police forces and partially oversees tribal police forces.

the Department of the Interior was established in 1849, the BIA was moved from the War Department to the Interior Department.

To get a sense of how this bureaucratic organization shapes the daily lives of American Indians, explore in detail the Bureau of Indian Affairs website, which can be linked from the Department of the Interior site or accessed directly at http://www.bia.gov/. Then, debate among your classmates over the importance of diversity in the BIA workforce, particularly for American Indians.

in the federal workforce. To compensate for past discrimination and achieve a representative workforce, most agencies accorded preferential treatment to minority and female applicants.[27] Disgruntled White male employees argued that this form of affirmative action discriminated against them. However, in 1987 the U.S. Supreme Court ruled that the Civil Rights Act did not prevent governments, even those without a history of discrimination, from employing affirmative action to eliminate gender employment disparities.[28]

There is mixed evidence that antidiscrimination laws and affirmative action programs have significantly increased the proportion of racial and ethnic minorities serving in the federal bureaucracy. Although women and minorities are represented in the federal bureaucracy in a proportion equal to their proportion of the population, both groups tend to occupy lower level positions. Minorities are not as well represented in the upper echelons of the federal bureaucracy. "Measuring Equality: Minority Representation in the Federal Civilian Workforce" on page 259 explores in more detail the racial and ethnic composition of the federal bureaucracy.

Bureaucratic Policymaking and Power

Despite being unelected and unaccountable, bureaucrats are important policymakers. In addition to executing orders and statutes, bureaucracies actually make rules and regulations for implementing those decrees. Implementation includes rulemaking and administrative adjudication. These activities provide bureaucracies with considerable power, which they seek to maintain through internal and external means, and bureaucratic power exerts a clear impact on racial and ethnic minorities.

Implementation

Bureaucracies are charged with the function of **implementation**; that is, bureaucracies conduct the daily activities that put into effect the laws passed by legislatures and orders issued by executives. There are several aspects of implementation that we discuss in this section: enforcement, rulemaking, and administrative adjudication.

Implementation The day-to-day process by which bureaucrats enforce laws and carry out policies.

Enforcement. By enforcement of the policies made in the popularly accountable branches of government, bureaucracies influence the lives of racial and ethnic minorities. For example, U.S. Customs and Border Protection (CBP) is part of the Department of Homeland Security, and it enforces laws preventing illegal contraband and persons from entering the United States. Given the importance of immigration for Latinos and other racial and ethnic minorities, the CBP plays a key role in racial and ethnic politics, not because it shapes relevant policies, but because it carries them out on an everyday basis. Table 8.3 provides a glimpse into the daily activities of the CBP.

The way in which laws should be enforced is defined by the policymaking institutions of government, but the bureaucrats carrying out the daily enforcement functions enjoy considerable discretion. Even though Congress writes the policies and expresses its intent on how laws should be enforced, executive branch leaders set clear guidelines on how enforcement should proceed, and bureaucrats receive considerable training and guidance on how to carry out enforcement duties, the daily decisions that bureaucrats make when implementing policies greatly influence how a policy is carried out.

For example, agents who work for the CPB follow strict rules set by Congress and the president, their training is similar, and they must follow the directives issued from CPB leaders and the Department of Homeland Security. In short,

TABLE 8.3 A Typical Day in U.S. Customs and Border Protection (Based on Fiscal Year 2015 Data)

Processed	
1,048,632 passengers and pedestrians	72,179 truck, rail, and sea containers
Conducted	
22 arrests of wanted criminals at ports of entry	367 refusals of inadmissible persons at U.S. ports of entry
Seized	
9,435 pounds of narcotics	$356,396 undeclared or illegal currency
Deployed	
807 canine teams	379 horse patrols
Employed	
52,472 total employees	2,413 agricultural specialists
33,947 CPB officers	691 air interdiction agents (pilots)
20,183 border patrol agents	
Conducted Operations	
328 ports of entry	136 border patrol stations within 20 sectors, with 35 permanent checkpoints

Source: Adapted from Department of Homeland Security, U.S. Customs and Border Protection, "On a Typical Day in Fiscal Year 2015, CPB...,"
https://www.cbp.gov/newsroom/stats/typical-day-fy2015, accessed July 2, 2016.

border patrol agents are under strict control when performing their jobs. Nevertheless, the typical agent deals with millions of individuals and vehicles coming across the border, and the actual decision to further investigate a specific person or a particular vehicle is up to the person at the border checkpoint who is making the assessment. Of course, those decisions greatly influence how border laws are actually implemented.

Rulemaking The process by which bureaucrats issue regulations that have the force of law.

Rulemaking. Bureaucracies implement laws by **rulemaking**, which is more complex than simply enforcing laws. Rulemaking occurs when bureaucratic agencies issue regulations that apply to other government agencies or to private citizens, and these regulations have the force of law. Starting during the New Deal, Congress delegated much of its complex economic and social regulatory authority to bureaucratic agencies, because it did not have the time and staff necessary to write the necessary rules. As a result, unelected, unaccountable bureaucrats have come to influence policy, sometimes greatly.

The Administrative Procedure Act of 1946 requires that bureaucratic rules first be publicly proposed in the *Federal Register*, which is the official collection of U.S. government documents published on a daily basis. The public can comment on each proposed rule for a period of at least thirty days, and then the rule is officially promulgated. In some cases, an agency is even required to

measuring equality

Minority Representation in the Federal Civilian Workforce

As we have discussed throughout this book, minority representation in government is a crucial issue in racial and ethnic politics, and, as this chapter shows, minority representation in the bureaucracy is a key issue as well. In the text, we provide basic information about minority underrepresentation, but here we explore this question in more detail by examining minority representation at different levels of the federal bureaucracy.

White-collar civilian federal bureaucrats are ranked according to the General Schedule (GS). There are fifteen rankings, with GS-1 being the lowest and GS-15 being the highest, and within each rank there are ten gradations. Jobs are defined according to rank, and good job performance and seniority allow employees to move up within each rank, but employees do not necessarily move up a GS level unless they change jobs. Additionally, as we discuss later in this chapter, the Senior Executive Service (SES) contains top-level administrators whom the president could place in any agency to ensure that the agency or department functions efficiently. The SES is the highest rank of the federal civilian civil service.

Not only does the GS indicate rank and prestige, but its rankings are also tied to employees' salaries. In 2015, the salary ranges were as follows: (1) GS1–GS4 was $18,161–$32,517; (2) GS5–GS8 was $27,982–$49,907;

(3) GS9–GS12 was $42,399–$79,936; (4) GS13–GS15 was $73,115–$132,122; and (5) SES (2016) is $150,200–$205,700.

To determine the extent of minority representation in the federal civilian workforce, we present graphical data concerning minority representation at different GS levels. Figure 8.1 shows the percentage of each minority group at these levels. Blacks are the best represented minority group at each level. At the lower levels (through GS12) Latinos are the next best represented, but at the higher levels (GS13–GS15 and SES) Asian Americans are the next best represented. American Indians have the lowest level of representation. Note that Black, Latino, and Indian representation decreases

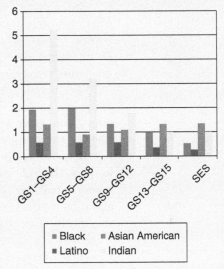

Figure 8.2 Minority Representation in the General Schedule Compared with Minority Representation in the Population.
Sources: Bureaucracy statistics are adapted from Office of Personnel Management, Annual Report to the Congress: Federal Equal Opportunity Recruitment Program, Fiscal Year 2010, 15, 25, 35, 45, http://www.opm.gov/About_OPM/Reports/FEORP/2010/feorp2010 .pdf, accessed February 13, 2012. GS salary data are from "Salary Table 2015-GS," https://www.opm.gov/policy-data-oversight/pay -leave/salaries-wages/salary-tables/pdf/2015/GS.pdf; and from "Salary Table No. 2016-EX," https://www.opm.gov/policy-data -oversight/pay-leave/salaries-wages/salary-tables/pdf/2016/EX.pdf, both accessed July 2, 2016. 2010 population data are from U.S. Census, "Quick Facts: USA 2010," http://quickfacts.census.gov/qfd/states /00000.html, accessed February 14, 2012.

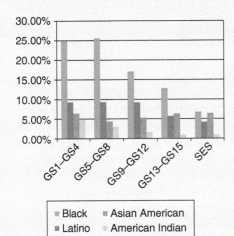

Figure 8.1 Minority Representation in the General Schedule.

(Continued)

measuring equality *(Continued)*

with higher rankings, but Asian American representation remains relatively constant throughout the GS levels.

Figure 8.2 factors the extent to which each group is represented in the population. We divided the percentage of each group in the different GS categories by the percentage of that group in the population (according to 2010 census figures). A score above 1 signifies that the group is overrepresented, and a score below 1 signifies that the group is underrepresented. As a percentage of the population, American Indians are the best represented in the lower GS levels (through GS12), but Asian Americans are the best represented in the higher levels (GS13–GS15 and SES). Blacks are overrepresented in the lower categories and underrepresented in the higher categories. As a percentage of population, Latinos are the most underrepresented. They are underrepresented in each category and have the lowest level of representation in each category.

hold public hearings on certain proposed rules. Agencies can modify rules in response to feedback from the public.[29]

The impact of bureaucratic rules varies. Some rules, such as the Federal Aviation Administration's (part of the Department of Transportation) regulations governing passenger behavior on commercial airliners, have a narrow focus.[30] Other rules, such as the Environmental Protection Agency's (EPA) regulations governing auto emissions or wetlands preservation, enjoy a wide scope.[31]

Bureaucratic rules might not be as significant as congressional statutes or major presidential actions, but they can affect the daily lives of racial and ethnic minorities. For example, in 2010 the Federal Housing Finance Agency (FHFA), which supports and regulates the mortgage industry, issued a final rule that clarified procedures for ensuring fair treatment of women and minorities. This rule was designed to implement the Housing and Economic Recovery Act of 2008, which was designed to address the mortgage crisis brought about by malfeasance in the banking and finance industries. The rule was specifically concerned with preventing these industries from preying on women and minorities. After the initial rule was proposed, the FHFA revised aspects of the rule in response to public comments.[32]

Administrative Adjudication
The quasi-judicial process by which a bureaucratic agency resolves a dispute between the agency and a private citizen.

Administrative Adjudication. Bureaucracies also implement policies through **administrative adjudication**, in which a bureaucratic agency resolves a dispute between a private party and a governmental entity through a quasi-judicial process. Administrative law judges, who work for the various bureaucratic agencies, hear the disputes and offer solutions. Administrative adjudication decisions can be appealed to the federal judiciary, usually to the DC Circuit Court of Appeals and ultimately to the U.S. Supreme Court.

Some bureaucratic agencies try to avoid administrative adjudication by providing for alternative dispute resolution, or mediation. For example, after an employee brings a discrimination complaint to the EEOC, the EEOC provides for a neutral third party to hear both sides of the dispute. This mediation is purely voluntary, and the mediator's goal is to encourage both sides to reach a solution that eliminates the need for further government action.[33]

Sources of Bureaucratic Power

Understanding bureaucratic power requires knowing more than how bureaucracies enforce laws, make rules, or adjudicate disputes; it also requires knowing how bureaucracies gain and keep power. Much bureaucratic power emanates from sources internal to the bureaucracies themselves. One internal source of power is expertise. Generally, bureaucrats know their substantive area better than members of Congress and even political appointees in the executive branch do. For example, the Division of Civil Rights in the Department of Justice can be a powerful force in civil rights policy because it is staffed with attorneys who are experts in civil rights and antidiscrimination law. However, as we saw with the opening story on the Flint Water Crisis or the failures after Hurricane Katrina, bureaucrats are not always competent, and their bungling affects people's everyday lives, including racial and ethnic minorities.

Because bureaucratic agencies do not make policy in isolation, they derive power by relying on alliances with other parts of the federal government. Many people view these alliances as an **iron triangle** consisting of a bureaucratic agency, corresponding congressional committees (and subcommittees), and corresponding client interest groups (see Figure 8.3).[34] According to the iron triangle metaphor, these three sides control policymaking over their substantive issue area, and it is difficult for outside forces to penetrate this triangle. Bureaucrats foster good relations with congressional committees and subcommittees to ensure that their agencies are well funded and laws are crafted in a way that is advantageous for the agency. Bureaucrats use interest groups to enhance public support for their actions. In turn, both congressional committee members and interest groups benefit from their relationship with bureaucrats because they can influence how the agencies carry out their functions. A classic example of an iron triangle is in defense policy, which tends to be dominated by the defense contractors (corporate interests), members of the House and Senate Armed Service Committees, and officials in the U.S. Department of Defense.

Another view of bureaucratic policymaking uses an **issue networks** metaphor, which perceives the relationships among bureaucracies and other actors more informally. In addition to the three components of the iron triangle, issue networks contain the following: a variety of opposing interest groups, law firms, think tanks, academics, the media, public relations experts, political consultants, courts, and legislative staff. Moreover, unlike the stable iron triangles, issue networks are dynamic and constantly evolving as the nature of an issue changes.[35]

For example, immigration policy is not dominated by a monolithic coalition of bureaucratic agencies, congressional committees, and a dominant

Iron Triangle A conception of bureaucratic policymaking in which policymaking is dominated by congressional committees, interest groups, and bureaucratic agencies.

Issue Networks A conception of policymaking as dynamic and not controlled by any particular set of groups or institutions.

Executive Branch Agencies

Congressional Committees and Subcommittees

Interest Groups

Figure 8.3 The Iron Triangle.

client interest group. Instead, many bureaucratic agencies and congressional committees (and subcommittees) are involved in immigration policy. Some interest groups—e.g., Latino civil rights groups—support expanded immigration and amnesty for illegal immigrants, whereas other citizen groups hold opposite views. The media, think tanks, academics, the agriculture industry, the high-tech industry, immigration attorneys, and courts all participate in making immigration policy.

Controlling Bureaucracies

Thus far, we have shown that bureaucracies exert tremendous influence on the daily lives of American citizens. Because in the age of the merit system most bureaucrats are hired, not elected or even appointed by elected officials, bureaucracies are not directly accountable to the people whose lives they influence. This system is problematic in a representative democracy. To check bureaucracies, the three branches of government have attempted to limit bureaucratic power.

Executive Control over Bureaucracies

Just because the president is the chief of the bureaucracy does not mean that presidents and key administration officials, such as the chief of staff, are always able to manage the federal bureaucracy without worrying about dissent. The same situation holds true for bureaucratic supervisors and their subordinates. In some bureaucracies, such as the armed forces, the president and military supervisors control their subordinates with minimal difficulty. In other bureaucratic arenas, conflicts exist between career bureaucrats and higher level political appointees, including the president.

For example, the Department of Justice criminally prosecuted two Latino U.S. Border Patrol agents—Jose Compean and Ignacio Ramos—for firing on an unarmed drug suspect and concealing evidence in 2005. After the two men were convicted and sentenced each to more than a decade in prison, the 13,000 career Border Patrol agents unanimously and publicly expressed their lack of confidence in U.S. Border Patrol chief David Aguilar, whom President George W. Bush had appointed. On President Bush's last day in office, he commuted Compean's and Ramos's sentences, which allowed them to leave prison and be placed on three years of probation.[36] Likewise, in 2012, the union representing Border Patrol agents protested the two-year prison sentence given to Latino Border Patrol agent Jesus Diaz for violating the constitutional rights of a fifteen-year-old suspected of marijuana smuggling.[37]

Presidents can control such embarrassing bureaucratic conflicts by reorganizing bureaucracies to suit their ideology and personal management styles. In this way, presidents can ensure that bureaucrats act in accordance with their wishes. As we discussed earlier in this chapter, after the attack of September 11, 2001, President Bush put FEMA under the control of the Department of Homeland Security because he thought states should bear more of the emergency response duties and FEMA should concentrate on responding to terrorist attacks. However, it bears mentioning that presidents have found that their authority to reorganize the bureaucracy is limited by the requirement that Congress must actually pass the reorganization as a bill.

During the late 1970s, President Jimmy Carter was especially concerned about controlling the bureaucracy. As a result, he persuaded Congress to pass the Civil Service Reform Act of 1978, which imposed modern management principles on the federal bureaucracy. This law created the **Senior Executive Service**, consisting of trained administrators the president could place in any agency to ensure compliance with his orders.[38] Figure 8.2 in "Measuring Equality: Minority Representation in the Federal Civilian Workforce" (page 260) showed that racial and ethnic minorities, especially Blacks and Latinos, are underrepresented in the Senior Executive Service.

U.S. Border Patrol agents escort an illegal immigrant to a holding area prior to deportation. As federal bureaucrats, border patrol agents carry out the daily tasks necessary to enforce immigration policies made by Congress and the president.

Presidents can control the bureaucracy through **central clearance**, which requires that all budget requests and legislative proposals coming from a federal agency be approved by the Office of Management and Budget (OMB) before the president submits them to Congress.[39] Presidents fear that agencies' budget requests and legislative proposals are based more on the selfish interests of the agencies and client groups than on concern for the administration or the American public. Because the OMB is under presidential control, central clearance allows presidents to ensure that the budget requests they submit to Congress serve solely their interests.

At times, bureaucrats sidestep central clearance and go directly to members of Congress to achieve objectives. Bureaucrats and their client groups try to curry favor with specific members of congressional committees who might be receptive to their proposals. In other words, bureaucrats rely on their alliances with groups and other institutions as a way to limit presidential control over their jobs.

Whistleblowers are another concern of presidents, administration officials, and even senior-level bureaucrats. A **whistleblower** is a bureaucrat who publicly exposes incompetence, mismanagement, or corruption within his or her agency. Whistleblowers are considered vital to the national interest because by exposing problems in the federal bureaucracy, they make the government more responsive and accountable to its citizens. But whistleblowers often face reprisals from their supervisors, and at times they have even been fired. The Civil Service Reform Act of 1978 and the Whistleblower Protection Act of 1989 prevent bureaucratic supervisors from retaliating against whistleblowers

Senior Executive Service High-level bureaucrats the president places in different agencies to ensure compliance with his directives.

Central Clearance A requirement that all agency budget requests receive approval from the Office of Management and Budget before the president submits them to Congress.

Whistleblowers Bureaucrats who publicly expose waste, fraud, or abuse in their agency.

by firing them or subjecting them to adverse consequences.[40] One of the most famous recent whistleblowers is Edward Snowden—a former contractor for the Central Intelligence Agency who leaked information about American surveillance programs throughout the world. In order to escape prosecution, Snowden moved to Russia, where he currently resides.

Whistleblowers have occasionally exposed racial and ethnic discrimination in the federal bureaucracy. For example, during the 1990s, Marsha Coleman-Adebayo, an African American female, worked for the U.S. Environmental Protection Agency in South Africa. She discovered that a multinational company's mining of vanadium, which is a dangerous chemical, had caused numerous deaths in South Africa. However, the EPA refused to do anything about it; therefore, Coleman-Adebayo publicized what was happening. EPA officials retaliated against her in ways that she describes as sexist and racist. For example, they referred to her as "uppity," which is a term that has usually been used against African Americans who do not accept unequal treatment. They also referred to her as an "honorary White person" and sarcastically called her "Rosa Parks." Several years later Coleman-Adebayo won a discrimination suit against the EPA.[41]

Legislative Control over Bureaucracies

Despite the close connection between Congress and the federal bureaucracy, the two institutions conflict when Congress tries to control the bureaucracy. Congress creates, alters, or eliminates bureaucratic agencies and positions, and it can use that power to exert control over bureaucrats. Congress also controls bureaucracies through budgeting. Because bureaucrats desire optimal funding for their agencies, they often adhere to the wishes of congressional leaders, particularly those serving on committees relevant to the bureaucrats' work. Congress can reduce budgets for bureaucratic agencies that refuse to submit to its control, although often the mere threat of a budget reduction is sufficient to influence bureaucratic behavior.

Furthermore, as we discussed in the opening vignette, Congress supervises the bureaucracy through its oversight power (see Chapters 6 and 7), in which relevant committees conduct investigations and hearings to maintain control over the executive branch and the federal bureaucracy. Congress uses these investigations to determine whether bureaucracies execute laws according to congressional intent and to evaluate the effectiveness of a law or policy. Congress also conducts investigations into bureaucratic fraud and wasteful practices. As the story of the Flint Water Crisis demonstrates, oversight is an important legislative check against bureaucratic abuses, although members of Congress have often used oversight to inflate their image with constituents at the expense of hardworking, albeit unpopular, federal bureaucrats.

Congressional oversight of the bureaucracy was also critical after Hurricane Katrina. In addition to investigating FEMA's failure in planning to deal with intense flooding in New Orleans, Congress probed problems with the long-term aftermath of the storm. For example, FEMA was responsible for providing displaced persons, including a large number of African Americans, with trailers to be used as temporary residences. After residents complained that the trailers contained noxious fumes, FEMA field workers recommended testing all the trailers for poisonous gas, but FEMA leaders refused to accept responsibility and would not conduct the tests. Some residents were sickened, and one even died from formaldehyde exposure. In 2007, the House Oversight and Government Reform Committee investigated the incident. After uncovering FEMA's attempt to cover up its failure to address the problem, the committee held a public hearing at which then FEMA director R. David Paulison apologized and promised to monitor more closely the safety of the trailers.[42]

Congress also conducts oversight through the **Government Accountability Office (GAO)**. The GAO is an independent, nonpartisan part of the legislative branch that audits the executive branch's expenditures and supervises how bureaucracies actually spend money appropriated by Congress. The head of the GAO, known as the **comptroller general**, is appointed to a fixed fifteen-year term by the president from a list of names provided by a bipartisan panel of congressional leaders.[43] The GAO has been instrumental in helping congressional committees investigate FEMA's immediate and long-term handling of Hurricane Katrina.[44]

Until the 1980s, Congress used a legislative veto to control the bureaucracy. The **legislative veto** was a provision in a law that allowed one or both houses to overturn bureaucratic actions. However, the U.S. Supreme Court overturned the legislative veto in the 1983 case of *Immigration and Naturalization Service v. Chadha*, a ruling that also affected racial and ethnic minority politics.

Jagdish Chadha was a Kenyan of Indian descent who held a British passport; he was admitted to the United States on a student visa, as are numerous international students who study today at U.S. colleges and universities. Because neither Kenya nor India would allow him to return, Chadha and his family continued to stay in the United States past the expiration date of his visa. The Immigration and Naturalization Service (INS) began the process of deporting Chadha, but after the attorney general intervened because of Chadha's hardship case, the INS suspended the deportation. Because the INS was subject to a legislative veto, the House of Representatives overturned the INS suspension and ordered Chadha to be deported. The Supreme Court then ruled that the legislative veto amounted to congressional interference with the executive branch and therefore violated the Constitution.[45] As a result, Chadha was not deported, and he is currently a U.S. citizen.

Government Accountability Office (GAO) The part of the legislative branch that is responsible for auditing how bureaucratic agencies spend money appropriated by Congress.

Comptroller General The head of the Government Accountability Office.

Legislative Veto An act of one or both houses of Congress that overturns an administrative action. The Supreme Court invalidated such acts in 1983.

Jagdish Rai Chadha sits with his wife Terry Lorentz and daughter Sashi. Bowling Green State University student Chadha, born of Indian parents in Kenya, won a U.S. Supreme Court battle that prevented his deportation when his visa expired and the Kenyan and British governments refused to acknowledge his citizenship. The Supreme Court ruled that the legislative veto, which was the process used to deport Chadha, violated the Constitution. Chadha eventually became an American citizen.

Judicial Control over Bureaucracies

Courts also possess authority to control bureaucracies by ruling that bureaucratic actions violate the U.S. Constitution or a federal statute. Because much of the Constitution deals with race and ethnicity, judicial control over the bureaucracy can affect the lives of racial and ethnic minorities. For example, prior to the mid-1970s, U.S. Border Patrol agents would stop automobiles near, but not at, the Mexican border merely because the occupants appeared to be of Latino descent. The Supreme Court ruled in 1975 that this bureaucratic practice violated the Fourth Amendment guarantee against unreasonable search and seizures.[46]

Despite the occasions when the judiciary overturns bureaucratic practices, its effectiveness as a control is limited. Whereas executives and legislators are free to act of their own accord to control bureaucracies, courts can act only when an aggrieved party initiates a case challenging a bureaucratic decision or action. Judicial rules require that an aggrieved party be able to demonstrate that the bureaucratic agency directly caused injury, and if the judiciary enforces these rules strictly, then it can restrict access to the courts. As we discuss in Chapter 9, the political composition of the Supreme Court determines whether the federal judiciary will employ open or restrictive rules of access. The more conservative Court of the 1990s and 2000s has limited the ability of groups to challenge bureaucratic procedures.

The high cost of litigation designed to contest bureaucratic decisions also limits courts' ability to control bureaucracies. Because of the complex and expensive nature of administrative litigation, specialized attorneys require extensive legal fees. The Equal Access to Justice Act, passed in 1980, authorizes federal courts to award attorneys' fees to successful plaintiffs litigating in the public interest. Although attorneys' fees presumably offset some of the costs of litigation, judges still enjoy tremendous discretion in awarding fees, which means that challenging bureaucracies in the courts is still a difficult task. As a result, many racial and ethnic minority activists have established public interest groups that litigate, often against bureaucracies, to achieve the desired political results. For example, the Mexican American Legal Defense and Education Fund litigates on behalf of immigrants who face adverse actions at the hands of federal bureaucrats.[47]

Conclusion

Although often out of the limelight, the federal bureaucracy is undoubtedly an important part of the federal government. The bureaucracy and the bureaucrats who work for it perform the detailed work of governing by providing services and implementing policies, the latter of which entails enforcing laws, making rules, and adjudicating disputes. Bureaucracies perform a wide variety of essential tasks, such as regulating the economy, preserving the environment, exploring outer space, and delivering the mail. This chapter covered the basics of bureaucratic politics by explaining the structure of the federal bureaucracy, the bureaucrats who work for it, the activities of the bureaucracy, sources of bureaucratic power, and attempts to limit bureaucracies.

Most important, this chapter emphasized how the federal bureaucracy affects racial and ethnic politics. For example, moving FEMA from an independent agency to a cabinet department hurt its ability to respond to Hurricane Katrina, which adversely affected African Americans. Additionally, the daily activities of border patrol agents and employees who work for the Bureau of Indian Affairs greatly affect the lives of Latinos and American Indians respectively. Furthermore, as with other aspects of American government, minority representation is a significant issue in the bureaucracy. Government policies to ensure more minority representation have certainly improved diversity, but racial and ethnic minorities are not well represented at the upper echelons. We also showed that bureaucratic organization and bureaucratic power (as well as attempts to limit it) are crucial in the everyday lives of racial and ethnic minorities. Throughout this chapter, we demonstrated that the federal bureaucracy influences specific issues in racial and ethnic politics such as immigration, voting rights violations, enforcement of civil rights laws, public awareness of racial profiling, and help for minority-owned businesses.

A recent glaring bureaucratic concern for racial and ethnic politics is the failure of the Michigan state bureaucracy in addressing the Flint Water Crisis. Similar to FEMA's failures before, during, and after Hurricane Katrina, different aspects of bureaucratic politics led to the MDEQ's poor performance. Although the officials were supposed to be experts in their field, their negligence and incompetence led contaminating the water supply and poisoning children, many of whom are African Americans. Still, a federal bureaucratic agency— the Environmental Protection Agency—took control of the situation to distribute safe drinking water to residents of Flint. We also saw how legislative oversight of the bureaucracy has been a key aspect of investigations into the wrongdoing surrounding the Flint Water Crisis. At the state level, the officials who were most to blame have been criminally charged for their negligence, although the outcome of these cases remains unresolved as of press time for this book. The story of the Flint Water Crisis surely demonstrates some of the ways in which the bureaucracy greatly affects racial and ethnic minorities.

review
REVIEW QUESTIONS

1. How does the professionalism of bureaucratic employees affect their ability to function effectively?

2. What are some examples of federal cabinet departments (and subunits), independent regulatory commissions, independent executive agencies, and government corporations that are important for racial and ethnic minorities?

3. What are some of the measures that the federal government has used to increase diversity in the federal bureaucracy? To what extent have those measures been successful?

4. How can implementation, especially rulemaking and administrative adjudication, affect the daily lives of racial and ethnic minorities?

5. How effective is the judiciary in preventing bureaucrats from discriminating on account of race or ethnicity?

KEY TERMS

Administrative Adjudication p. 260
Bureaucracy p. 245
Bureaucrats p. 253
Cabinet Departments p. 246
Central Clearance p. 263
Civil Servants p. 254
Comptroller General p. 265
Government Accountability Office p. 265

Government Corporations p. 253
Hatch Act p. 255
Implementation p. 257
Independent Executive
    Agencies p. 250
Independent Regulatory
    Commissions p. 249
Iron Triangle p. 261

Issue Networks p. 261
Legislative Veto p. 265
Patronage p. 254
Pendleton Act p. 254
Rulemaking p. 258
Senior Executive Service p. 263
Whistleblowers p. 263

ADDITIONAL READINGS

Marsha Coleman-Adebayo, *No Fear: A Whistleblower's Triumph over Corruption and Retaliation at the EPA* (Chicago: Chicago Review Press, 2011).

> The author recounts her experience as a whistleblower while working at the Environmental Protection Agency. The book discusses the deleterious effects of the mining operation that caused numerous deaths in South Africa, the EPA's initial refusal to act, her public exposure of the problem, the sexist and racist retaliation she endured; her successful court victory, and her establishment of an organization dedicated to protecting whistleblowers.

Christopher Cooper and Robert Block, *Disaster: Hurricane Katrina and the Failure of Homeland Security* (New York: Times Books, 2006).

> In this book, two reporters for the *Wall Street Journal* closely examine the bureaucratic reasons for FEMA's failure to respond adequately to Hurricane Katrina.

Steven P. Erie, *Rainbow's End: Irish Americans and the Dilemmas of Urban Machine Politics, 1840–1985* (Berkeley and Los Angeles: University of California Press, 1988).

> This book contends that Asian Americans, Blacks, Latinos, and even many Irish Americans did not benefit from patronage as much as others have claimed.

Kelly Lytle Hernández, *Migra! A History of the U.S. Border Patrol* (Berkeley: University of California Press, 2010).

> This book carefully chronicles the history of border patrol and immigration enforcement in the United States, concentrating specifically on how the U.S. Border Patrol came to exclusively focus on Mexican immigrants.

Brian K. Landsberg, *Enforcing Civil Rights: Race Discrimination and the Department of Justice* (Lawrence: University Press of Kansas, 1997).

> The author, a former career attorney for the Civil Rights Division of the Department of Justice, provides an insider's account of how this key bureaucratic division has enforced civil rights laws.

Robert Lee Maril, *Patrolling Chaos: The U.S. Border Patrol in Deep South Texas* (Lubbock: Texas Tech University Press, 2004).

> This work examines the daily activities of border patrol agents from the perspective of the agent on the front lines.

CHAPTER 9

The Judiciary: Blending Law and Politics

California law professor Goodwin Liu is sworn in on Capitol Hill in Washington, April 16, 2010, prior to testifying before the Senate Judiciary Committee hearing on his nomination to be U.S. Circuit Judge for the Ninth Circuit. Liu was never confirmed because Senate Republicans filibustered his nomination, arguing that he was too liberal. He now serves on the Supreme Court of California.

Goodwin Liu was born in 1970 in Georgia to parents who immigrated to America from Taiwan. As a child, Liu moved to Sacramento, California, where he was an extremely successful student. Liu graduated from Stanford University, earned a Rhodes Scholarship, helped found the AmeriCorps national service organization, and then graduated from Yale Law School in 1998. After law school, Liu clerked for U.S. Supreme Court Justice Ruth Bader Ginsburg and subsequently worked in the private sector. He soon joined the faculty of Boalt Law School at the University of California–Berkeley, one of the top American law schools. He quickly developed a reputation as a prolific and groundbreaking scholar, and he was promoted to associate dean.[1]

In early 2010, President Barack Obama nominated Liu to be a judge on the Ninth Circuit Court of Appeals. This court is extremely important in the U.S. judicial system because it handles appeals in federal cases originating in Alaska, Hawaii, Washington, Oregon, California, Arizona, Nevada, Idaho, Montana, and Pacific territories. Liu's nomination was especially important because Asian Americans have been underrepresented in the federal judiciary, and President Obama sought to rectify that problem by nominating more Asian American judges than any of his predecessors. Additionally, Liu was a well-known liberal legal scholar, who had written books and articles advocating that the Constitution be interpreted by contemporary standards, instead of in accordance with the intention of its authors. Consequently, Democratic senators and many in the legal community praised Liu's nomination, but archconservatives and Republican senators immediately complained that Liu would be an activist judge who would not rule according to legal precepts. Liu's Republican critics pointed to his vast legal writings and the fact that in 2005 Liu testified before the Senate Judiciary Committee against the confirmation of Supreme Court Justice Samuel Alito. Senate Democrats, the Obama administration, and legal scholars (including some conservatives) countered that Liu's nontraditional roots and scholarly achievements merited his confirmation. Moreover, they noted that the Senate had previously confirmed conservative judges with controversial publications. In May 2010, the Senate Judiciary Committee approved Liu's nomination by a 12–7 vote, with all Democrats voting in favor of him and all Republicans opposing him.[2]

After a year-long delay, Liu finally came to the full Senate for a vote, but Republicans launched a filibuster (see Chapter 6) against the nomination. The final cloture vote was 52 to 43; therefore, even though a majority of the Senate supported Liu's nomination, he did not get a sufficient number of votes to end the filibuster and was not seated on the bench. Senate Democrats and the Obama administration were outraged. Senator Dianne Feinstein (D-CA) said that "to prevent an up-or-down vote for Professor Liu is to keep us from fulfilling our responsibility as senators."[3] However, we should note that in 2003, when the Republicans controlled the Senate, Democrats successfully filibustered Republican President George Bush's appeals court nomination of conservative Latino Miguel Estrada. Many of the same Democratic senators who criticized the Republican filibuster of Liu, including Senator Feinstein, voted to filibuster Estrada.[4] Although Liu would not serve on the federal bench, in September 2011, California Governor Jerry Brown named Liu to be a justice on the California Supreme Court.[5] Moreover, in 2013, the Democratically controlled Senate changed the rules to prevent filibusters from obstructing lower-court nominees who enjoy the support of the majority of the Senate.[6]

intro

Justice Liu's story reveals important aspects of the federal judiciary, particularly the significance of the lower courts, such as the Ninth Circuit Court of Appeals. Although the U.S. Supreme Court is the most important and most well-known court in the federal judiciary, there are a vast number of federal courts and federal judges that significantly influence American politics. Liu's story also demonstrates the political nature of the appointment of federal judges, despite the notion that law and judging are considered by many to be above politics. As we discuss later in this chapter, the political fight over filling the vacancy left by the death of Supreme Court Justice Antonin Scalia has been extremely controversial, but it is important to recognize that the same political forces influence nomination battles in the lower courts as well. Finally, although Liu's race did not directly affect his rejection, this story emphasizes the importance of racial and ethnic representation on the federal bench.

This chapter discusses the politics of the federal judiciary. It examines the complexity of judicial politics by first defining law and explaining how the federal judiciary is organized. Then we examine the powers and limitations of the federal judiciary, especially concerning issues of civil rights. The chapter proceeds to a detailed *discussion of the judicial selection process, which as the story of Goodwin Liu demonstrates, evidences the highly political nature of the federal courts. We then explain judicial decision-making. Throughout this chapter, we emphasize the importance of race and ethnicity in judicial politics.*

Law and Courts

The primary task of the judicial branch is to interpret the law, but the concept of "law" is multifaceted and complex. Because the law cannot administer itself, courts are the political institutions that interpret the law and apply it to everyday situations. American courts exist under a dual system of authority, with state courts responsible for interpreting state law and federal courts responsible for interpreting federal law. Both systems operate simultaneously, but because we focus on the national government in this chapter, here we concentrate primarily on the structure of the federal court system. We addressed state courts in Chapter 3.

Dimensions of Law

Many Americans intuitively understand the meaning of the word *law*, but furnishing a workable definition is more difficult. Henry Abraham, an esteemed political scientist, defines law as "the rules of conduct that pertain to a given political order in society, rules that are backed by the organized force of the community."[7] Although generally helpful, this definition does not cover the many types of law that are relevant to American government. Most of this chapter deals with **public law**, which refers to legal matters that concern the government, at least as one of the parties to a legal dispute. Conversely, **private law** generally concerns disputes that rise between individuals—the government acts only as a referee.

There are a variety of types of public law, including constitutional law, statutory law, and administrative law. **Constitutional law** refers to the rules for our government expressed in the Constitution. This kind of law is relevant for questions concerning separation of powers, federalism, civil rights, and civil liberties. **Statutory law** concerns laws that are made by the U.S. Congress and by state legislatures. **Administrative law** encompasses the rules and regulations made by bureaucrats and administrative agencies (see Chapter 8), which are not directly accountable to the public. The federal judiciary's power to interpret law gives it tremendous authority in shaping constitutional, statutory, and administrative politics.

American law is also divided into criminal law and civil law. **Criminal law** is law that pertains to violations of a code of behavior specified by local, state, or federal statutes; therefore it falls under the category of public law. Serious crimes, such as homicide, rape, and armed robbery, are classified as felonies, and they often receive stiff sentences, including the death penalty for some homicides. The less serious crimes are known as misdemeanors, which are punishable by no more than one year in jail, a modest fine, or both; in

Public Law A type of law in which the government is a party to the case.

Private Law A type of law that concerns disputes between individuals.

Constitutional Law A type of law pertaining to the rules for our government expressed in the Constitution.

Statutory Law A type of law pertaining to rules made by legislatures, especially Congress.

Administrative Law A type of law pertaining to the rules made by bureaucrats and administrative agencies.

Criminal Law A type of law that pertains to violations of a code of behavior specified in local, state, and federal statutes.

some cases, there is no penalty. Criminal cases involve a government prosecutor, who argues that a defendant is guilty of a crime, and a defense attorney, who argues that the evidence against the defendant is insufficient to prove guilt beyond a reasonable doubt.

Civil law refers to disputes between private parties; therefore, legal experts consider it to be private law. Most civil cases involve disputes over a monetary value, such as alimony in a divorce case, compensation for negligent actions, and contract disputes. Some civil actions involve non-monetary issues, such as custody battles in divorce cases. Regardless of whether monetary damages are sought, civil cases do not result in prison time or fines. Civil law cases feature a plaintiff (the party litigating the claim) and a defendant (the party against whom the claim is brought). Unlike criminal cases, civil cases do not always involve the government, although a government agency can be a plaintiff or a defendant in a civil case.

Civil Law A type of law that pertains to a dispute between two parties, at least one of which is a nongovernmental private party.

Organization of the Federal Judiciary

The American judiciary consists of two simultaneously operating tracks—state courts and federal courts. The bulk of cases take place at the state court level, and the federal judiciary does not rule on a case unless it falls under federal jurisdiction. In criminal law, federal jurisdiction involves accusations of breaking federal statutes (e.g., abetting international terrorists, engaging in counterfeiting, kidnapping across state lines, and committing crimes on federal property). Civil law cases become federal only when the plaintiff and defendant are from different states and the value of the suit exceeds $75,000. The federal judiciary also exercises jurisdiction over controversies arising from the U.S. Constitution.

Article 3 of the U.S. Constitution creates "one Supreme Court and . . . such inferior courts as Congress may from time to time ordain and establish." In 1789, Congress fulfilled this obligation by passing the Judiciary Act, which created the federal judiciary's three-tiered structure. It consists of U.S. District Courts, U.S. Circuit Courts of Appeals, and the U.S. Supreme Court.[8] Each level of the federal judiciary performs a distinct task (see Figure 9.1).

The U.S. District Courts serve primarily as the federal trial courts for both criminal and civil cases. Congress establishes each district, which is determined by geography. During the 2015 fiscal year, the ninety-four districts in the United States contained 677 authorized judgeships and 359,105 cases were filed, for an average of 530.4 cases per judge.[9] In federal criminal trials and civil suits, the district courts serve as the fact-finding institution, with judges presiding over trials and juries usually deciding if defendants are guilty (in criminal cases) or negligent (in civil cases). District courts also rule on constitutional cases. When people challenge government actions as unconstitutional, the case is often first heard in a district court, but the judge renders the decision without a jury.

Each district court is responsible for applying Supreme Court decisions to its specific geographic area. After the Supreme Court ruled in the second

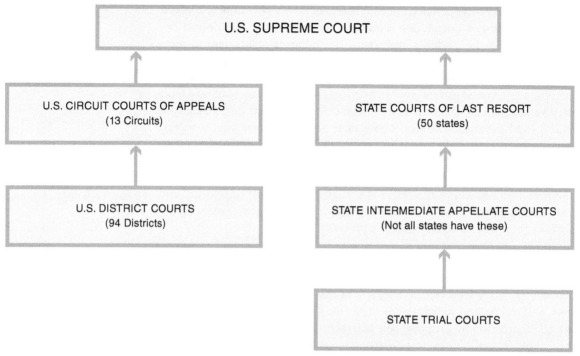

Figure 9.1 Ladder of Authority of American Courts.

Brown v. Board of Education decision in 1955 that Southern states had to deseg-regate their schools with "all deliberate speed,"[10] federal district court judges in the South were responsible for deciding exactly how much time schools in their districts would be given to integrate. The geographic concentration of the federal district courts put these judges in a difficult position because they lived in their districts and faced intense pressure from their neighbors, friends, and associates to delay integration. Some of these judges were even victims of harassment.[11]

The federal judiciary also contains an intermediate level of appeals, known as the U.S. Circuit Courts of Appeals. An appeal reviews legal ques-tions arising from a district court trial or a district court ruling on a specific legal matter. During fiscal year 2015, there were 167 authorized circuit court judgeships and 52,698 appeals were filed. Additionally, in 2015 there was an average of approximately 947 cases filed per panel.[12]

A panel of three judges decides most appeals, and the side that earns the vote of at least two of the judges prevails. The nation is divided into eleven geographical circuits, each of which consists of a combination of neighboring states. The U.S. Court of Appeals for the Federal Circuit handles customs and patent cases, and the Circuit Court of Appeals for the District of Columbia hears appeals from cases involving federal government agencies and many administrative law cases.

At the top of the judicial hierarchy ladder is the U.S. Supreme Court, which currently consists of nine justices. Article 3 of the Constitution grants the Supreme Court **original jurisdiction** "in all cases affecting ambassadors, other public ministers and consuls, and those in which a state shall be a party." In those rare instances, a case avoids the lower courts and starts at the Supreme Court. The vast majority of the Supreme Court's cases are **appellate jurisdiction** in which the Supreme Court hears cases on appeal. The Supreme Court hears appeals from both the U.S. Circuit Courts of Appeals and from state supreme courts if the case concerns a federal constitutional or statutory issue.

Original Jurisdiction
A defined set of cases that avoids a lower court and goes directly to the Supreme Court.

Appellate Jurisdiction
The types of cases in which the Supreme Court reviews legal issues decided by a lower court.

Judicial Powers and Limitations

Although the Constitution clearly defines the functions of the president and Congress, it is vague on the powers of the judiciary. Nevertheless, through the power of **judicial review**, whereby a court can nullify a law, policy, or government action by deeming it to be unconstitutional, the federal judiciary plays a critical role in shaping policy. Because it is not mentioned in the Constitution, the Supreme Court took the power of judicial review. This power is important, particularly in advancing civil rights. Legal scholars and political scientists propose a variety of philosophies on how judges should use the power of judicial review and on the limits of judicial review. These different views also interact with minority-group politics.

Judicial Review The power of a court to overturn a law or official government action because it is deemed unconstitutional.

The Origins and Development of Judicial Review

A major facet of the federal judiciary is that the Framers designed it to be independent from popular control; that is, it was designed to go against the will of the majority. Article III of the U.S. Constitution states that once confirmed, federal judges serve a term of "good behavior"—that is, they can be removed from office only through the impeachment process. Impeachment of federal judges has generally been reserved for judges who commit ethical violations, not for judges who make unpopular decisions. Thus, Americans and their elected representatives lack recourse to remove federal judges who issue unpopular decisions, which allows federal judges to follow the law instead of public opinion.

Although judicial review is not specifically mentioned in the Constitution, there is evidence that many Framers wanted the federal judiciary to possess this power. That the judiciary was designed to be independent from public opinion indicates that the Framers intended for the judiciary to check the popularly accountable branches of government, which is the basis of judicial review. After the Revolution, many state courts invalidated statutes that violated state constitutions.[13] Nevertheless, the early Supreme Court did not use the power of judicial review until the 1803 case of *Marbury v. Madison*.[14]

The controversy that led to judicial review began after the presidential election of 1800, in which Thomas Jefferson defeated incumbent John Adams.

At the end of his presidency, Adams nominated and the Senate approved a number of new federal judges, including William Marbury, who was named the Justice of the Peace for the District of Columbia. Although duly appointed and confirmed by the end of Adams's term, Marbury did not receive his official paperwork by the time Jefferson was inaugurated. Incoming Secretary of State James Madison was required to deliver Marbury's paperwork, but, because of residual bitterness from the 1800 election and resentment over Adams's late appointments, Jefferson ordered Madison not to deliver Marbury's paperwork, thus denying him the judicial position. Marbury sued Madison and argued that a provision in the Judiciary Act of 1789 required the Court to order Madison to deliver the paperwork.

In 1803, Chief Justice John Marshall decided this seemingly insignificant case. Since assuming the position of chief justice in 1801, Marshall had sought to establish judicial review to increase the power of the federal judiciary and the national government. But Marshall knew that Jefferson and congressional leaders opposed judicial review. He therefore needed to act carefully. Marshall shrewdly saw the *Marbury v. Madison* case as his perfect opportunity. He ruled that the portion of the Judiciary Act on which Marbury staked his claim was unconstitutional; thus, he could not order Madison to deliver the paperwork. Although the outcome of the decision favored Madison (and Jefferson), Marshall was the real winner. Because Jefferson and Madison won the case, they felt vindicated and did not vigorously challenge Marshall's use of judicial review. The Supreme Court has retained the power of judicial review since the *Marbury v. Madison* ruling.[15]

Judicial Review and Constitutional Interpretation

By striking down many important laws, judicial review plays a critical role in policymaking. Since 1803, the U.S. Supreme Court has used judicial review to overturn laws and official actions at the national, state, and local levels. Given its extraordinary power, the way in which justices approach judicial review and interpret the Constitution becomes extremely important.

Judicial Restraint
A conception of judicial review that believes courts should not overturn laws or government actions unless there is a clear directive in the Constitution.

There are different views on the extent to which judges should use judicial review to interfere with the elected branches of government. The **judicial restraint** view argues that the courts should defer to the will of the elected branches of government unless there is a blatant violation of the Constitution. Advocates of judicial restraint believe that because federal judges are unelected and unaccountable to the public, they should rarely be involved in policymaking. That task belongs to the popularly accountable branches of government—executives and legislatures.

Judicial Activism
A conception of judicial review that believes courts should overturn laws or government actions even if there is no clear constitutional directive.

Conversely, the doctrine of **judicial activism** holds that the courts should vigorously check the other branches of government, even if the Constitution has not been explicitly violated. Advocates of judicial activism believe that the role of the judiciary is to correct injustices, especially for groups and individuals who are disadvantaged in the popularly elected branches of government.

A related issue concerns the proper way to interpret the Constitution. Because judicial review entails judges' deciding whether laws or actions violate the Constitution, the way in which judges interpret the Constitution shapes how they perform the task of judicial review. The doctrine of **original intent** argues that the Constitution should be interpreted strictly according to the intention of the people who wrote it, mainly the delegates to the Constitutional Convention, the Congresses that proposed the amendments, and the state legislatures that ratified the amendments. Advocates of original intent believe that unelected and unaccountable judges should not substitute their personal views of the Constitution for the views of the Framers.

Original Intent A belief that the Constitution should be interpreted only according to the intent of its authors.

Conversely, the doctrine of a **Living Constitution** argues that judges should update the meaning of the Constitution to fit contemporary controversies and social mores. Advocates of the Living Constitution believe that the meaning of the Constitution and its amendments should not be frozen in past eras that are no longer relevant.[16]

Living Constitution A belief that the Constitution should be interpreted to reflect contemporary times.

Judicial Review and Civil Rights

Judicial review has been especially important in advancing civil rights. In the 1950s, many state legislatures and governors—predominantly but not exclusively in the South—were insensitive or even hostile to the claims of African Americans seeking equal treatment and an end to segregation. Because Blacks were disenfranchised (see Chapter 5), these elected institutions were not responsive to their concerns. In fact, most politicians were responsive to the prejudice that existed among Whites. The U.S. Congress was also unresponsive to issues of racial and ethnic discrimination, and although Presidents Truman and Eisenhower contributed to the expansion of civil rights, they did not consistently support minority groups' efforts against discrimination.

The Supreme Court's use of judicial review was the only recourse at the time for racial and ethnic minority groups combating inequality and segregation. In the landmark 1954 case *Brown v. Board of Education*,[17] the U.S. Supreme Court employed judicial review to declare state segregation laws to be a violation of the Fourteenth Amendment to the Constitution, thereby invalidating those segregation laws. This use of judicial review resulted in a shifting policy in relation to federalism. Prior to the *Brown* decision, states believed that it was their "right" to discriminate on account of race, but the Supreme Court's use of judicial review made the issue of racial discrimination a national one. There are other ways (discussed in this chapter) in which the federal judiciary's use of judicial review (or refusal to overturn laws or actions) has affected civil rights.

The debates between judicial activism and judicial restraint and between original intent and the Living Constitution have therefore affected civil rights. Because most of the people involved in drafting the Fourteenth Amendment did not intend for it to prohibit segregation, and the same Congress that proposed the Fourteenth Amendment also voted to segregate schools in the District of Columbia, a strict original-intent approach to interpreting the Fourteenth

evaluating equality

Judicial Review, Legal Interpretation, and Civil Rights

Although it is an accepted aspect of our political system, judicial review is still controversial. Because federal judges are unelected and unaccountable, judicial review gives them the authority to thwart the will of the majority, which is undemocratic. In his classic book, *The Least Dangerous Branch: The Supreme Court and the Bar of Politics,** legal scholar Alexander Bickel created the term "counter-majoritarian difficulty" to describe how judicial review conflicts with democratic government and majority rule. However, most legal scholars support judicial review, even if they disagree with specific decisions, because it prevents the majority from violating the rights of the minority. Judicial review preserves the Constitution as the supreme law of the land.

Judicial review is also important for civil rights. As we discussed above, it was responsible for landmark civil rights cases, such as *Brown v. Board of Education*. However, it was also responsible for cases that infringed on civil rights, such as *Dred Scott v. Sandford* (see Chapter 5). Moreover, as we discuss in Chapter 5, judicial review has been used to limit affirmative action. In addition to judicial review itself, the way in which courts interpret the Constitution can affect civil rights. As we discussed above, an original intent method of constitutional interpretation usually results in limiting civil rights.

Debate among your classmates the merit of judicial review in general and how it could influence civil rights outcomes in particular. Then debate the relative virtues of original intent versus the living Constitution and the virtues of judicial activism and judicial restraint. Again, focus the debate on how each method of interpretation can influence civil rights outcomes.

*Alexander M. Bickel, *The Least Dangerous Branch: The Supreme Court at the Bar of Politics* (Indianapolis and New York: The Bobbs-Merrill Company, 1962).

Amendment would rule that the amendment does not prevent segregation. Consequently, civil rights advocates have preferred judicial activism and a Living Constitution interpretation. The justices deciding *Brown v. Board of Education* updated the meaning of the Fourteenth Amendment—taking a Living Constitution approach—by using recently published social science data demonstrating that segregation greatly harmed Black schoolchildren.[18] The Evaluating Equality box explores in more detail how judicial review and legal interpretation influence civil rights.

Limitations on the Courts

Because judicial review provides the federal judiciary with considerable power, limitations on judicial authority are important. One limitation is that courts cannot enforce their own rulings; to implement these rulings, judges must rely on other branches. This limitation was evident when President Andrew Jackson refused to enforce a Supreme Court decision that protected the sovereignty of the Cherokee Nation and supremacy of the national government against the state of Georgia.[19] Conversely, Presidents Dwight Eisenhower and John Kennedy deployed the military to enforce federal court orders to integrate public schools in the South.[20]

The constitutional amendment process can also check Supreme Court decisions. If enough members of Congress and states disagree with the way that the Supreme Court interprets the Constitution, then a constitutional amendment can change the Constitution according to the preferences of that majority. One reason that Congress proposed the Fourteenth Amendment (1868), which confers full citizenship on all citizens regardless of race, was to reverse the holding of the infamous 1857 *Dred Scott v. Sandford* decision. In that case, the Court ruled that Blacks, whether free or slave, were not citizens under the Constitution, and it invoked judicial review to invalidate the Missouri Compromise, in which Congress demarcated where slavery would be allowed. The Court held that Congress lacked the authority to decide which states and territories could be free or slave states.[21]

Congress can also constrain the Court's power to interpret statutes by clarifying or rewriting a law in response to a Court decision. For example, in the 1989 case *Wards Cove Packing, Inc. v. Atonio*, the Supreme Court ruled that the Civil Rights Act of 1964 required plaintiffs claiming discrimination to prove that the employer practices in question intended to discriminate,[22] which made it more difficult for racial and ethnic minorities to win employment discrimination cases. In response to these decisions, Congress passed the Civil Rights Act of 1991, which explicitly placed the burden of proof on the employer to show that hiring practices were related to nondiscriminatory business necessities.[23] In short, Congress explicitly changed the language of the statute to reverse the Court's interpretation of the Civil Rights Act.

The federal judiciary also places internal restraints on itself by requiring that cases be **justiciable**. That is, the Court will only hear cases that feature two real parties requesting review to resolve an existing dispute. One key aspect of justiciability is **standing**. It requires litigants to demonstrate that they have actually been injured; one party may not sue on another party's behalf. Determining whether the litigants bringing suit have actually been injured can be extremely ambiguous, and the outcome of standing cases often reflects the prevailing ideology on the Court. For example, in the early 1970s the Supreme Court granted standing to environmentalists by ruling that environmental or aesthetic damage constituted sufficient injury to a person challenging a government policy that causes environmental damage.[24] The more conservative Supreme Court during the 1990s limited environmental suits by restricting standing for environmentalists.[25]

Another aspect of justiciability is **mootness**, which requires that a case still be germane; it cannot have resolved itself. Sometimes, the Supreme Court is able to postpone deciding a particularly controversial issue if it deems a case to be moot. For instance, in 1974, the Supreme Court would not entertain a White student's claim that the University of Washington Law School's use of affirmative action unconstitutionally discriminated against him because he was denied admission, whereas minorities with lower grades and LSAT scores were admitted. The district court ordered that the student be admitted, and the state appealed. By the time the case reached the Supreme Court in 1974, the student was about to graduate. Thus, the case was deemed moot,[26] and the Court was able to postpone ruling on the controversial issue of affirmative action.

Justiciable The requirement that there must be an actual case or controversy between two parties for the federal judiciary to decide a case.

Standing An aspect of justiciability that requires the party bringing the case to show that the policy in question has caused it an injury.

Mootness An aspect of justiciability that requires that the conflict causing the case must still be germane; it could not have resolved itself on its own.

Precedent A principle articulated in a previous case that judges use to decide current cases.

Precedent is a legal concept that checks judicial power. Precedent means that when ruling on a case, judges should use the principles established in similar cases that were previously decided. In the American legal tradition, judges are expected to adhere to precedent because it makes the law stable and predictable. But strict adherence to precedent can stifle progressive legal change, especially with cases concerning racial and ethnic discrimination. For example, in 1896 the U.S. Supreme Court issued its first interpretation of the extent to which the Fourteenth Amendment equal protection clause banned segregation. In the *Plessy v. Ferguson* decision, the Supreme Court allowed states to segregate facilities by race through its now discredited principle of "separate but equal."[27]

A strict adherence to precedent would have required future courts to use that principle when deciding segregation cases. However, *Brown v. Board of Education* overturned the "separate but equal" precedent, with Chief Justice Earl Warren writing: "In approaching this problem, we cannot turn the clock back . . . to 1896 when *Plessy v. Ferguson* was written. We must consider public education in light of its full development."[28] By recognizing that the *Plessy* precedent was no longer relevant, the Court advanced civil rights.

Precedents are occasionally overturned because of personnel changes on the Court. The issue of affirmative action (see Chapter 5) illustrates this point. In 1990, the U.S. Supreme Court upheld by a 5–4 vote a federal policy that gave racial minorities a preference when seeking broadcasting licenses, ruling that the government need to ensure diversity in broadcasting outweighed possible discrimination suffered by nonminorities.[29] In 1991, Justice Clarence Thomas, who opposes affirmative action, replaced Justice Thurgood Marshall, who supported it. Consequently, in 1995 the Supreme Court reversed the 1990 precedent and overruled government policies that favored minorities.[30]

Thurgood Marshall—the first non-White Supreme Court Justice—was appointed in 1967. When he retired in 1991, he was replaced by Clarence Thomas who, like Marshall, is African American, but Thomas holds different views than Marshall. In 2009, for the first time in American history, the Supreme Court included two non-Whites: Clarence Thomas and Sonia Sotomayor, the first Latina justice.

Judicial Selection

Given the federal judiciary's power and the fact that once confirmed, judges serve as long as they want, unless they are impeached for ethical violations, we want to focus on the characteristics of federal judges and the process by which they are selected. This selection process is the only time the elected branches of government (and the people) have any influence over the composition of the federal judiciary. The process in turn influences the racial and ethnic composition of the federal bench.

Nominating Judges

When selecting federal judges, presidents, with the help of staff, look for qualified candidates, but not necessarily for the top legal minds. Technically, there is no requirement that a federal judge have a formal legal education, and until 1957 there was always at least one justice on the Supreme Court who did not possess a law degree.[31] There is now an expectation that federal judges not only have a law degree, but also have experience in the federal legal system; many believe that Supreme Court justices should have appellate judicial experience. In fact, Elena Kagan is the only current justice who never served as a judge before being nominated, but she was the Dean of Harvard Law School and U.S. Solicitor General.[32]

Even though merit is important, presidents are more concerned about satisfying political considerations when filling judicial vacancies. For lower court appointments, presidents rely on **senatorial courtesy**, by which they consult with senators in their party who represent the states where the vacancy occurs. Those senators often select qualified individuals, but they are generally more concerned with rewarding political supporters. There is even evidence that political service is relevant for Supreme Court nominations. For example, when nominating Earl Warren to be chief justice of the Supreme Court in 1953, Republican president Dwight Eisenhower strongly considered Warren's past service to the Republican Party, including running as the Republican nominee for vice president in 1948.[33]

Senatorial Courtesy The practice whereby a president consults with senators in his party to find potential lower court vacancies that occur in the senators' states.

Presidents are primarily concerned that their judicial appointees share their ideology. Republican presidents tend to support advocates of judicial restraint and original intent in controversial civil rights and civil liberties cases; Democratic presidents tend to back judicial activists and supporters of a living Constitution. As a result, most judicial nominees come from the same party as the nominating president. Since 1977, at least 80 percent of district and appeals court appointments have been of the same party as the appointing president.[34]

Supreme Court appointments are extremely important and receive considerable attention. (See Table 9.1 for a list of current justices and see the photo to the right.) It follows, then, that presidents are especially concerned about ideological compatibility. Candidates

The U.S. Supreme Court Justices in their robes. Front row, left to right: Clarence Thomas, Antonin Scalia (who has since died), Chief Justice John Roberts, Anthony Kennedy, and Ruth Bader Ginsburg. Back row, left to right: Sonia Sotomayor, Stephen Breyer, Samuel Alito, and Elena Kagan.

TABLE 9.1 Justices of the U.S. Supreme Court, 2016[a]

Name	Race	Born	Year Appt.	Appt. Pres.	Party
John Roberts, Chief Justice	White	1955	2005	G. W. Bush	R
Anthony Kennedy	White	1936	1987	Reagan	R
Clarence Thomas	Black	1948	1991	G. H. W. Bush	R
Ruth Bader Ginsburg	White	1933	1993	Clinton	D
Stephen Breyer	White	1938	1994	Clinton	D
Samuel Alito	White	1955	2006	G. W. Bush	R
Sonia Sotomayor	Latina	1954	2009	Obama	D
Elena Kagan	White	1960	2010	Obama	D

[a]As of the press time for this edition, there is still an unfilled vacancy on the U.S. Supreme Court.

Source: Adapted from U.S. Supreme Court, "Biographies of Current Justices of the Supreme Court," http://www.supremecourt.gov/about/biographies.aspx, accessed July 11, 2016.

for president even campaign on the kinds of justices they would appoint to the Supreme Court if elected. Although presidents usually have succeeded in appointing ideologically compatible justices, sometimes they are disappointed. President George H. W. Bush appointed Justice David Souter from New Hampshire based on the advice of his White House Chief of Staff John Sununu, who had been governor of New Hampshire. Bush wrongly expected Souter to be conservative and restrained on civil rights and civil liberties issues, but Justice Souter emerged as more liberal than expected (see Table 9.2).[35]

Confirming Judges

The appointment process does not end with the president's nomination, because ultimately the Senate decides whether to confirm the nominee. The Judiciary

TABLE 9.2 Average Ideology Score of U.S. Justices Supreme Court Justices Appointed since 1937 (Arranged from Most Liberal to Most Conservative)

Justice	Appointing President and Party	Average Ideology
William Douglas	Franklin Roosevelt, Democrat	−4.12
Thurgood Marshall	Lyndon Johnson, Democrat	−2.83
William Brennan	Dwight Eisenhower, Republican	−1.94
Sonia Sotomayor[a]	Barack Obama, Democrat	−1.93
Hugo Black	Franklin Roosevelt, Democrat	−1.76
John Paul Stevens	Gerald Ford, Republican	−1.72
Elena Kagan[a]	Barack Obama, Democrat	−1.66

Justice	Appointing President and Party	Average Ideology
Ruth Ginsburg	[a]William Clinton, Democrat	−1.60
Frank Murphy	Franklin Roosevelt, Democrat	−1.59
Wiley Rutledge	Franklin Roosevelt, Democrat	−1.40
Stephen Breyer[a]	William Clinton, Democrat	−1.27
Abraham Fortas	Lyndon Johnson, Democrat	−1.20
Earl Warren	Dwight Eisenhower, Republican	−1.17
David Souter	George H. W. Bush, Republican	−0.93
Arthur Goldberg	John F. Kennedy, Democrat	−0.79
James Byrnes	Franklin Roosevelt, Democrat	−0.20
Harry Blackmun	Richard Nixon, Republican	−0.12
Stanley Reed	Franklin Roosevelt, Democrat	0.36
Byron White	John F. Kennedy, Democrat	0.44
Tom Clark	Harry Truman, Democrat	0.49
Felix Frankfurter	Franklin Roosevelt, Democrat	0.54
Potter Stewart	Dwight Eisenhower, Republican	0.56
Anthony Kennedy[a]	Ronald Reagan, Republican	0.68
Robert Jackson	Franklin Roosevelt, Democrat	0.73
Sandra D. O'Connor	Ronald Reagan, Republican	0.88
Lewis Powell	Richard Nixon, Republican	0.93
Fred Vinson	Harry Truman, Democrat	1.00
Harold Burton	Harry Truman, Democrat	1.02
Sherman Minton	Harry Truman, Democrat	1.10
Charles Whitaker	Dwight Eisenhower, Republican	1.26
John Roberts[a]	George W. Bush, Republican	1.30
John Harlan II	Dwight Eisenhower, Republican	1.63
Warren Burger	Richard Nixon, Republican	1.85
Samuel Alito[a]	George W. Bush, Republican	1.88
Antonin Scalia[a]	Ronald Reagan, Republican	2.45
William Rehnquist	Richard Nixon, Republican	2.84
Clarence Thomas[a]	George H. W. Bush, Republican	3.47

Source: Data adapted from, Andrew D. Martin and Kevin M. Quinn, Martin-Quinn Scores: Measures, *http://mqscores.berkeley.edu/measures.php, accessed July 13, 2016. For each justice, the authors averaged the mean scores for each year provided by Martin and Quinn.*

[a]*Data available only through 2014.*

Committee conducts hearings at which the nominee and any other interested parties testify. Then the committee issues a recommendation, and the entire Senate votes on the nomination. With more recent nominations, the Judiciary Committee hearings last for days, often involving extensive questioning of nominees themselves in addition to hours of testimony from groups and individuals supporting and opposing the nominee.

The majority of judicial nominations are approved with little opposition, even in periods of divided government (see Chapters 6 and 7), but there have been some exceptions. Lower court nominations can be rejected if a president fails to abide by senatorial courtesy. If a senator in that president's party who represents the state where the vacancy occurs opposes the nomination, then the Senate Judiciary Committee will most likely refuse to act on the nomination, thus preventing that person from being confirmed.

Supreme Court nominees have also been rejected because of accusations of character flaws. For example, in 1969 the Senate rejected appeals court judge Clement Haynsworth when President Richard Nixon nominated him to the U.S. Supreme Court because Haynsworth had ruled in cases where he had a financial conflict of interest.[36] Clarence Thomas was almost rejected in 1991 because he was accused of sexually harassing a female employee. Law professor Anita Hill claimed that while she worked for Clarence Thomas at the Department of Education and Equal Employment Opportunity Commission, Thomas

Supreme Court nominee Elena Kagan testifies during her confirmation hearings before the Senate Judiciary Committee at the U.S. Capitol in Washington, June 29, 2010. Many Republicans opposed her nomination, believing that she is too liberal. Nevertheless, she was confirmed, and for the first time in American history three women serve simultaneously on the U.S. Supreme Court.

had frequently made sexually suggestive comments to her. Although this allegation was initially part of a confidential FBI background investigation, it was publically disclosed, and the Senate Judiciary Committee subsequently required Hill to testify. Hill's testimony provided graphic detail about the sexual harassment, and because the proceedings were televised millions of Americans viewed Hill's testimony. When Clarence Thomas was called to testify, he commented that the hearing was "a high-tech lynching for uppity Blacks who deign to think for themselves." Thomas was contending that he was being persecuted for being a Black conservative. Thomas was confirmed by a narrow 52–48 margin, and his confirmation generated a long-lasting impact by putting the issue of sexual harassment on the national stage and prompted many women to run for political office in 1992.[37]

The Senate has also rejected Supreme Court nominees who are perceived to be ideologically extreme. This means that a nominee who advocates extreme restraint is less likely to be confirmed in a Democratic-controlled Senate and a nominee who advocates extreme activism is less likely to be confirmed in a Republican-controlled Senate. In 1987, the Democratic Senate rejected Ronald Reagan's nomination of Robert Bork because Bork had cultivated a reputation as a proponent of extreme restraint and original intent views, such as the unwillingness to recognize a constitutional right to privacy (see Chapter 4) or to extend Fourteenth Amendment protections to women (see Chapter 5). Moreover, Bork's rejection changed the nomination process because the Senate, the media, and the public have paid closer attention to the nomination process, particularly the ideology of the nominee.[38] Nevertheless, to date there have not been any Senates votes that have resulted in a rejection.

When Justice Antonin Scalia unexpectedly died in February of 2016, President Obama had an opportunity to appoint his third Supreme Court justice. However, immediately upon Justice Scalia's passing—before President Obama nominated anybody—Senate Majority Leader Mitch McConnell announced that the Senate would not even vote on a nomination, arguing that because President Obama's presidency was almost concluded, the next president should name the replacement. Regardless, President Obama nominated DC Appeals Court Judge Merrick Garland as Scalia's replacement. Garland is generally regarded as a centrist who was overwhelmingly approved for the appeals court and earned praise from many Republicans.[39] Yet, as of press time for this book, the Senate Judiciary Committee has yet to schedule a hearing on the nomination, and given Republican Donald Trump's election as president, Garland will not be confirmed.

Recently, lower court nominees have not been confirmed because of procedural maneuvering in the Senate. Beginning in the 1990s, the Republican-controlled Senate thwarted some of President Bill Clinton's nominees because the Judiciary Committee Chair, Orrin Hatch (R-UT), refused to act on lower court nominees deemed too activist. Those nominees would have most likely been confirmed by the Senate if there had been a vote, but Senator Hatch used his powers as chair to prevent that vote from occurring. When the Democrats controlled the Senate (2001–2002 and 2007–2008), the Judiciary Committee chair, Patrick Leahy (D-VT), held up President Bush's nominees who advocated extreme restraint. Furthermore, when the Republicans controlled the Senate from 2003 through 2006, Senate Democrats filibustered some of President Bush's more extreme restraint nominees, such as Miguel Estrada, and, as the opening vignette shows, Republicans have been willing to filibuster President Obama's nominees. Despite these more controversial procedural rejections, a significant majority of judicial nominees are confirmed.[40]

Race and Ethnicity and Judicial Nominations

For much of American history, many aspects of representativeness have influenced federal court appointments. Because Supreme Court decisions affect particular regions, presidents have used region as a key criterion for selecting nominees. Presidents have also been concerned with religious representativeness, particularly ensuring that Catholic and Jewish justices serve on the Supreme Court. For the first time in American history, the Supreme Court contains no Protestants—five are Catholic (Roberts, Kennedy, Thomas [who converted], Alito, and Sotomayor) and three are Jewish (Ginsburg, Breyer, and Kagan). However, no other religious minorities have ever served on the Supreme Court.

Gender is a concern as well. In 1981, President Reagan appointed Sandra Day O'Connor as the first female justice, and in 1994 President Clinton appointed Ruth Bader Ginsburg as the second female justice. Justice O'Connor's retirement in 2005 left only one woman serving on the Supreme Court, but both of President Obama's Supreme Court appointments thus far (Sonia Sotomayor and Elena Kagan) have been female; consequently, since 2010 there have been three women on the Supreme Court—the most ever. As of 2014, about 24.9 percent of all federal court judges are female.[41]

Race and ethnicity have also emerged as a significant factor in lower court appointments. Presidents John Kennedy, Lyndon Johnson, and Richard Nixon appointed a few members of racial and ethnic minority groups, primarily to the district courts, but it was not until the Carter administration that presidents became more concerned with representing minorities. "Measuring Equality: Presidents' Records of Minority Judicial Appointments to the Lower Federal Courts" discusses in more detail presidents' records on appointing minorities to the federal district and appeals courts, and it demonstrates how President Obama has significantly outpaced his predecessors in terms of nominating minorities to the federal judiciary, especially Asian Americans, which we discussed in the opening vignette.

Unlike nominations to the lower courts, however, race and ethnicity have not been a crucial factor with Supreme Court nominations. In 1967, President Johnson appointed Thurgood Marshall as the first African American to serve on the Court, and this was undoubtedly a historic appointment. When Justice Marshall retired in 1991, President George H. W. Bush was faced with the prospect of an all-White Supreme Court; he therefore placed a high priority on appointing another racial minority member. At the same time, President Bush

measuring equality

Presidents' Records of Minority Judicial Appointments to the Lower Federal Courts

This chapter has shown that the federal district courts and courts of appeals are important institutions in American government. These lower courts shape policies that affect racial and ethnic minorities. The extent to which racial and ethnic minorities are represented on these courts often translates into the legal protections those groups receive.

Presidential nomination is crucial to minority representation on the federal judiciary, but, as we discuss in this chapter, presidents did not pay attention to race or ethnicity when nominating federal judges until the 1960s. Only presidents Lyndon Johnson and George H. W. Bush appointed African Americans to the U.S. Supreme Court, and Barack Obama appointed the only Latina to the Supreme Court. To date, no Asian American or American Indian has ever served on the Supreme Court. There are considerably more opportunities, however, to appoint racial and ethnic minorities to the lower courts. President Jimmy Carter (1977–1981) was the first president to emphasize expanding racial minority representation on the federal bench. When it comes to appointing minorities in general and Blacks and Asian Americans in particular, President Barack Obama has far surpassed his predecessors.

Figure 9.2 examines the minority appointment records of Presidents Jimmy Carter, Ronald Reagan, George H. W. Bush, Bill Clinton, George W. Bush, and Barack Obama (through the end of his first term). We display the data in the form of a bar chart, or histogram, which visually shows for each president the proportion of nominees according to race (White, Black, Latino, and Asian American). We have combined the data for the two courts.

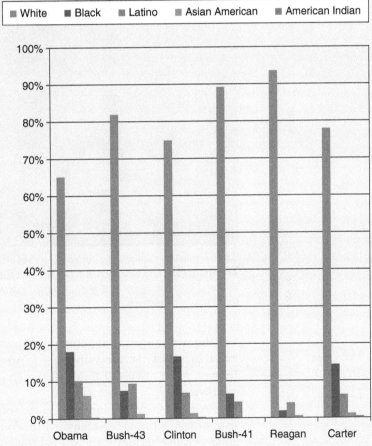

Figure 9.2 Race/Ethnicity of Judges in the Lower Federal Courts Selected during the Carter, Reagan, G. H. W. Bush, Clinton, G. W. Bush, and Obama (through the end of 2014) presidencies.

Sources: Data adapted from Sheldon Goldman, Elliot Slotnick, and Sara Schiavoni, "Writing the Book of Judges: Part 1 Obama's Judicial Appointment Record After Six Years," Journal of Law and Courts, vol. 3 (2015): 331–367: 356, 364; Jennifer Segal Diascro and Rorie Spill Solberg, "George W. Bush's Legacy on the Federal Bench: Policy in the Face of Diversity," Judicature 92, 6 (2009): 294–295.

(Continued)

measuring equality *(Continued)*

- As you examine the data, try to ascertain whether presidents over time have been more likely to nominate minorities.
- To what extent does a president's political party (Carter, Clinton, and Obama are the three Democratic presidents here) influence this minority appointment record?
- Are there variations among the different minority groups?

U.S. Supreme Court judge Sonia Sotomayor arrives in San Juan, December 16, 2009. Sotomayor was visiting Puerto Rico for the first time since becoming the U.S. Supreme Court's first Latino justice, on the invitation of local and U.S. federal judges for a few private engagements and to spend time with relatives.

was also determined to appoint a supporter of judicial restraint and original intent, so he picked conservative African American appeals court judge Clarence Thomas. As we discussed above, Justice Thomas's confirmation was extremely controversial.

President Obama nominated Judge Sotomayor not only as a female, but also as the first Latina representative to serve on the Supreme Court. Judge Sotomayor is Puerto Rican, and she became the first Supreme Court justice who is both a member of an ethnic minority group and a woman. As of yet, there have been no American Indians or Asian Americans on the Supreme Court, although we should expect such nominations in the future.

Race and ethnicity can also play a role in the Senate confirmation of judicial nominees. In Chapter 6 we discussed the Senate's rejection of President Clinton's district court nomination of African American Ronnie White. Furthermore, as the opening vignette demonstrated, Republican Senators successfully filibustered President Obama's nomination of Goodwin Liu. Goodwin Liu was not the only Asian American judicial nominee who faced a Republican filibuster. In 2009, President Obama nominated Edward Chen to the U.S. District Court for the Northern District of California, and Republicans delayed his confirmation, also claiming that he was too liberal. Judge Chen was eventually confirmed, but the process took more than 600 days, and only four Republican senators supported him.[42] As the opening vignette indicated, in 2013 the Senate amended its rules to prevent filibusters for lower-court nominees.

The confirmation battle over President Obama's nomination of Sonia Sotomayor to the Supreme Court also centered on race and ethnicity. As the first Latina nominated to the Supreme Court, she had tremendous support from Latinos and Latino groups. Latino activists were not only pleased about the possibility of the first Latina representative on the Supreme Court, but they also emphasized her personal story of growing up poor and being raised by a single mother. Similar to other successful Latinos, she worked hard and earned scholarships to prestigious schools (Princeton and Yale Law School in her case) and distinguished herself with a successful career. She serves as an inspiration to Puerto Ricans and other Latinos throughout the United States.[43] Even Florida senator Mel Martinez, then the lone Latino Republican senator, who normally takes conservative positions on legal matters, was happy with Judge Sotomayor. Senator Martinez commented that he was "very impressed with her, not only her personal qualities, but her understanding of the role of the judiciary and the role of the judge."[44]

Vocal opponents of Sotomayor's confirmation, mainly Republicans and conservative activists, also focused on aspects of race and ethnicity. Some critics attacked her ruling in the case of *Ricci v. DeStefano*, which she decided as a judge on the U.S. Second Circuit Court of Appeals. This case concerned the affirmative action policy of the city of New Haven, Connecticut, which promoted African American firefighters over Whites who scored higher on an examination. Judge Sotomayor sided with the city in this case. Before her confirmation vote, the U.S. Supreme Court sided with the White firefighters by a 5–4 vote, which provided more fodder for Sotomayor's critics.[45]

Additionally, critics attacked a previous statement that Judge Sotomayor had made. Specifically, she was quoted as saying, "A wise Latina woman with the richness of her experience would, more often than not, reach a better conclusion than a White male who hasn't lived that life." Even though her decision in *Ricci v. DeStefano* was consistent with the rulings of White justices and her statement was clearly meant to emphasize the importance of diversity in the federal judiciary, critics attacked her views on race. Most notably, former Republican Speaker of the House of Representatives Newt Gingrich and talk radio host Rush Limbaugh referred to her as "racist" or a "reverse racist." Although other Republican leaders refused to use the word *racist*, they still criticized her views on race and the law.[46] Despite these controversies, Sonia Sotomayor was easily confirmed by a 68–31 vote, with nine Republicans and all Democrats voting in her favor.[47]

Decision-Making on the Supreme Court

Because the Supreme Court is a critical policymaking institution, we will look now at how the justices arrive at decisions. There are procedures by which the Supreme Court arrives at decisions, as well as influences on that decision-making. The decision-making process in turn affects minority-group politics.

Decision-Making Procedures

When a party loses in the U.S. court of appeals or a state supreme court, then that party can appeal its case to the U.S. Supreme Court. For more than a century, the Supreme Court automatically heard the appeals that came before it, but by the early twentieth century its caseload had become too burdensome. In response, Congress passed the Judiciary Act of 1925, which gave the Supreme Court the authority to decide whether to hear a case.

Now virtually all litigants seeking to appeal a case to the U.S. Supreme Court must file a **writ of *certiorari***, which asks the Court to hear the case. *Certiorari* is a Latin word meaning "to be informed of, or to be made certain in regard to." The so-called "Rule of Four" requires that four of the nine justices must agree to grant certiorari for the Court to hear the case, but the Court annually rejects approximately 99 percent of the certiorari petitions it receives.[48] When a certiorari petition is denied, the lower court opinion stands. Thus, the circuit courts of appeals and state supreme courts are extremely important in our judicial system.

For the few cases in which the Court grants certiorari, the justices solicit briefs, which are written legal arguments, from the attorneys for the two parties involved in the case. These briefs must follow a specified legal format and argue the legal merits of their clients' position. Justices read these briefs and often use them as a guide in reaching a decision and writing an opinion. Additionally, the justices read ***amicus curiae***—Latin for "friend of the court"—**briefs**, which are filed by parties who are not direct litigants in the case but have a vested interest in the outcome. Just like regular briefs, amicus curiae briefs can influence how the justices decide both certiorari decisions and case outcomes.[49]

The justices also listen to the litigants' oral arguments. Usually, the Court grants an hour total of oral argument for each case—each side is allotted one-half hour. In rare exceptions, the Court grants each side an hour. During the oral argument, justices are free to interrupt the litigants with questions, which are charged to the lawyers' time. Justices intend for questions to point out flaws in litigants' arguments or to help them make their case.

After oral argument, the justices then confer privately in conference to discuss each case. The chief justice establishes rules for and presides over the conference discussion. The conference also includes a vote on the issue, with

Writ of *Certiorari* A formal legal document filed by the losing party in a lower court case that asks the Supreme Court to hear an appeal.

Amicus Curiae (Friend of the Court) Briefs Briefs filed by parties that have an interest in the outcome of a case but are not directly involved in it.

the side garnering at least five votes constituting the majority. If the chief justice is in the majority, then he assigns one of the justices (or himself) to write the opinion for the majority, known as the **majority opinion**. If the chief justice is not in the majority, then the most senior justice in the majority assigns the opinion. The justice assigned to write the majority opinion circulates a rough draft to the other justices, who can opt to endorse it or write their own opinions. A **concurring opinion** agrees with the outcome of the case but for reasons different from those expressed in the majority opinion. If a justice does not agree with the outcome of a case, then he or she writes a **dissenting opinion** arguing why the majority opinion was incorrect.

Because dissenting opinions represent the "losing" viewpoint, they have no legal validity, but they might ultimately prove useful. When the Supreme Court allowed racial segregation in *Plessy v. Ferguson* (1896), Justice John Marshall Harlan dissented, arguing that the Constitution prevents racial segregation.[50] Although Justice Harlan was the lone dissenter, his opinion was adopted more than fifty years later when the Supreme Court declared segregation to be unconstitutional in *Brown v. Board of Education* (1954).[51] "Our Voices: Opinions of African American Supreme Court Justices" on page 293 examines in more detail the importance of dissenting opinions in civil rights cases.

Majority Opinion The opinion reflecting the winning outcome of a Supreme Court case that is signed by at least a plurality of the justices.

Concurring Opinion An opinion that agrees with the outcome of a Supreme Court case but for reasons different from those expressed in the majority opinion.

Dissenting Opinion An opinion that disagrees with the winning side of a Supreme Court case and explains why.

The Influence of a Judge's Background on Judicial Decision-Making

Since the middle of the twentieth century political scientists have recognized that judges' backgrounds influence how they decide cases. We discussed above the importance of race and gender in the selection process. In addition to the issue of representation in an important branch of government, the race and gender of judges could also influence how they decide cases. However the empirical research on the influence of race on judicial decision-making for federal and state judges is mixed. Many studies demonstrate that race exerts no effect on judges' decisions in criminal and civil rights cases.[52] Nevertheless, others have argued that minority judges bring the perspective of their community to their work as judges,[53] and there is some evidence that minority judges are more "even-handed" than White judges when sentencing Black and White defendants.[54] There is also considerable debate over the extent that gender directly affects judicial decision-making in civil rights cases. Some studies have shown that gender exerts no impact on judicial decision-making,[55] whereas, other studies have found that women judges tend to rule in a more liberal fashion compared to male judges.[56] The bulk of empirical research has uncovered mixed evidence that gender influences judicial decision-making.[57]

Despite the lack of clarity on the influence of race and gender on judges' decision-making, there is overwhelming evidence that judges' personal beliefs also influence judicial decision-making. As we discussed above, there are different philosophies of legal interpretation—judicial activism versus judicial restraint and original intent versus the living Constitution—and judges' personal beliefs shape which philosophy they embrace. Political Scientists Jeffrey Segal and Harold Spaeth wrote a groundbreaking book entitled *The Supreme Court and the Attitudinal Model*,[58] which argues that in deciding key cases Supreme Court justices are in fact policymakers—similar to members of Congress and the executive branch. Moreover, the justices make decisions based on their policy preferences, with liberal justices desiring liberal rulings on civil rights, civil liberties, and economic regulation cases, whereas conservative justices desire conservative outputs in those cases. Segal and Spaeth's book is especially interesting because they do not merely advocate for the importance of judicial ideology as a factor in judicial decision-making; they argue that ideology is by far the best explanation of judicial decision-making. Table 9.2 reports the ideology of recent Supreme Court justices, using scores developed by legal scholars Andrew Martin and Kevin Quinn, which are based on how the justices actually vote, with negative numbers indicating a more liberal justice and positive numbers indicating a more conservative justice. Notice the pattern whereby Democratic presidents appoint more liberal justices and Republican presidents appoint more conservative justices. However, there are notable exceptions.

Attorney Influence on Court Decision-Making

Judges do not constitute the entirety of the American judicial system. Different types of attorneys also influence judicial decision-making. The **Solicitor General** is an executive branch attorney who argues the U.S. government's position, particularly the views of the president, before the U.S. Supreme Court. The Supreme Court allows the solicitor general to file amicus curiae briefs in any case he or she chooses. Because the solicitor general appears so frequently before Court, he or she not only gains litigation experience; he or she also develops a close relationship with the justices. This helps to increase the solicitor general's chances of success in the federal judiciary, and empirical evidence demonstrates that the solicitor general is more likely than other parties to succeed in the Supreme Court at both the certiorari and merit stages.[59]

Federal judges are assisted by law clerks, who are recent law school graduates, and they also influence judicial decision-making. Law clerks research cases and write drafts of opinions, and Supreme Court clerks also issue recommendations on certiorari petitions. Law clerks at the federal level start in the lower courts, usually right out of law school. After one year of experience at the lower court level, a select few clerks then move on to the Supreme Court. Law clerks generally serve for a period of one year and then often use their clerkships to obtain teaching positions at prestigious law schools or lucrative work in private practice.

Many Supreme Court justices once served as law clerks. The current chief justice, John Roberts, clerked for Associate Justice William Rehnquist in the early 1980s, who, in turn, had clerked for Justice Robert Jackson during the 1950s. Law clerks generally hail from elite law schools and tend to be White and male. Since the early 1980s, 5 percent of law clerks have been Asian American, but fewer than 2 percent have been Black or Latino.[60]

Solicitor General A high-ranking lawyer in the Justice Department who argues cases before the Supreme Court on behalf of the U.S. government.

our voices

Opinions of African American Supreme Court Justices

Opinions are an essential part of the judicial process. In addition to merely rendering a decision, judges write lengthy opinions that explain the reasons for their rulings, and these opinions are responsible for the development of American law. Opinions generally contain legal analysis that discusses the key precedents that led the author to his or her decision. Occasionally, opinions reveal the personal values and experiences of the authors.

The values and experiences reflected in opinions written by racial minority judges sometimes emphasize the relevance of race in American law in a way that few other government words or actions can. Following we excerpt opinions from the two African American Supreme Court justices—Thurgood Marshall and Clarence Thomas. Justice Marshall's opinion is from his dissent in *University of California v. Bakke*, in which a majority of the Court required that a White applicant be admitted to the University of California–Davis Medical School. Marshall argued that the Court should not interfere with a state university's use of a quota system that favors minority candidates as a way to compensate for past discrimination. Justice Thomas's opinion is from *Virginia v. Black*, which concerned the constitutionality of Virginia's ban on cross burning. Black argued that cross burning should be protected under the First Amendment's freedom of speech. The Supreme Court upheld the ban, but it ruled that the First Amendment does offer some protection to cross burning. Justice Thomas disagreed with that view, declaring that cross burning is different from mere speech because of its close ties to Ku Klux Klan terrorism. Notice how both justices use race in their dissenting opinions even though one is identified as a liberal judge and the other as a conservative.

> Marshall Dissent: . . . For it must be remembered that, during most of the past 200 years, the Constitution as interpreted by this Court did not prohibit the most ingenious and pervasive forms of discrimination against the Negro. Now when a state acts to remedy the effects of that legacy of discrimination, I cannot believe that the same Constitution stands as a barrier. . . . The position of the Negro today in America is the tragic, but inevitable, consequence of centuries of unequal treatment. Measured by any benchmark of comfort or achievement, meaningful equality remains a distant dream for the Negro. . . . At every point from birth to death the impact of the past is reflected in the still disfavored position of the Negro. In light of the sorry history of discrimination and its devastating impact on the lives of Negroes, bringing the Negro into the mainstream of American life, should be state interest of the highest order. To fail to do so will ensure that America will forever remain a divided society.

Thomas Dissent: I believe that the majority errs in imputing an expressive component to the activity in question [cross burning]. . . . In my view, whatever expressive value cross burning has, the legislature simply wrote it out by banning only intimidating conduct undertaken by a particular means. A conclusion that the statute prohibiting cross burning with an intent to discriminate sweeps beyond a prohibition on certain conduct into the zone of expression overlooks not only the words of the statute but also reality. . . . Indeed, the connection between cross burning and violence is well-ingrained. . . . To me, the majority's brief history of the Ku Klux Klan only reinforces the common understanding of the Klan as a terrorist organization, which, in its endeavor to intimidate, or even eliminate those it dislikes, uses the most brutal of methods. . . . In our culture, cross burning has almost invariably meant lawlessness and understandably instills in its victims well-grounded fear of physical violence.

Sources: Regents of the University of California v. Bakke, 438 U.S. 235 (1978), 387, 395–396; *Virginia v. Black*, 538 U.S. 343 (2003), 388–391.

Many attorneys who litigate before the Supreme Court work for interest groups (see Chapter 13) that use litigation as a means to affect public policy. **Interest group litigation** refers to litigation by organized groups on behalf of clients to influence public policy, and such litigation has been especially

Interest Group Litigation
The practice of interest groups arguing cases before the judiciary as a means of influencing public policy.

NAACP Legal Defense Fund attorneys George E. C. Hayes, left, Thurgood Marshall, center, and James Nabrit, right, outside of the U.S. Supreme Court building after their historic victory in *Brown v. Board of Education*. This victory underscores the importance of interest groups in the judicial process because these attorneys carefully planned a strategy that revolutionized education for racial and ethnic minorities. However, the NAACP Legal Defense Fund and other civil rights interest groups argue that education has been resegregating in recent years.

useful for racial and ethnic minority interest groups. Because prior to the 1970s the elected branches of government were usually not receptive to the claims of racial and ethnic minority groups, the politically independent federal courts, where success depends on skillful legal argument and not on political support, became an attractive option.

The most significant example of an interest group that litigates is the National Association for the Advancement of Colored People and its offshoot, the NAACP Legal Defense and Education Fund (LDF). The NAACP won landmark Supreme Court cases that ended racial discrimination in housing and voting.[61] The LDF carefully planned the litigation campaign for the extremely crucial case of *Brown v. Board of Education*.[62] In the process, the group has contributed immensely to ending racial discrimination. The LDF still uses litigation to advance civil rights in issues related to voting, criminal law, education, employment, and public accommodations.[63]

Based on the LDF's success, other interest groups advocating on behalf of racial and ethnic minorities have employed a litigation strategy to improve the civil rights of the people they represent. The Mexican American Legal Defense and Education Fund argues cases on behalf of Latinos to influence policies concerning education and employment discrimination, immigration, and voting rights.[64] The Native American Rights Fund litigates civil rights issues for American Indians, such as protecting tribal identity and resources, ending discrimination against Indians, and negotiating with the federal and state governments on behalf of tribes and individuals.[65] Asian Americans Advancing Justice (formerly the Asian American Justice Center) argues cases for Asian Americans concerning discrimination, voting rights, anti-Asian violence, language barriers, and immigration.[66]

Conclusion

Despite the political independence of the federal judiciary, there is no doubt that it is a highly political institution. Congress creates the organization of the federal judiciary, and because the certiorari process prevents the Supreme

Court from hearing most appeals, lower courts serve a vital function in the federal judiciary. Moreover, debates over the extent to which federal judges should use judicial review manifest themselves along political lines, especially during the process of appointing judges. When selecting judicial nominees, presidents generally employ political and ideological criteria, and the Senate considers political ramifications when it decides whether to confirm those nominees. Finally, interest groups and executive branch officials play an important role in the judicial process.

Throughout this chapter, we have demonstrated the important connection between the judiciary and the politics of race and ethnicity. The federal judiciary interprets constitutional, statutory, and administrative law, all of which pertain to civil rights. Because federal judges are not accountable to the public, they are able to act on behalf of racial and ethnic minority groups, which often lack political support for their goals. Additionally, the organization of the federal judiciary and the judiciary's decision-making procedures, especially on the Supreme Court, greatly affect the extent of legal protections for racial and ethnic minorities.

Debates over the power of judicial review also affect racial and ethnic minorities. Most groups advocating on behalf of civil rights rely on judicial activism and the notion of a living Constitution more than on judicial restraint and original intent. The president's willingness to enforce judicial decisions and Congress's reaction to key rulings can also affect the advancement of civil rights. Constraints on the judiciary, such as justiciability and strict adherence to precedent, can stifle civil rights progress.

The story of President Obama's appointment of Goodwin Liu emphasizes the relevance of race and ethnicity in judicial politics. Although 109 of the 112 individuals who have served on the U.S. Supreme Court have been White, recent presidents, especially President Obama, have sought to increase the presence of African Americans, Latinos, and Asian Americans on the lower courts. In other words, minority representation is a key issue in the judicial system as a whole.

Goodwin Liu's story and the confirmation battle over Judge Sotomayor also reveal that the issue of the presence of racial and ethnic minorities on the federal bench extends beyond descriptive and symbolic representation. Minority representation affects the substance of the decisions reached. Because most racial and ethnic minority judges have experienced firsthand the harmful effects of discrimination, they embrace judicial activism on civil rights and civil liberties cases. But there are exceptions, such as Supreme Court Justice Clarence Thomas and President Bush's appeals court appointment of conservative Black female Judge Janice Rogers Brown.[67] In sum, there is no doubt that the nomination and confirmation of racial and ethnic minorities to the federal judiciary are crucial issues in minority group politics.

REVIEW QUESTIONS

1. What was the role of federal district court judges in enforcing desegregation laws?

2. How do debates about judicial activism versus judicial restraint and about a living Constitution versus original intent relate to minority group politics?

3. How does the judicial nomination and confirmation process influence racial and ethnic minority representation on the federal bench?

4. What proportion of lower court judges are Black, Latino, Asian American, and American Indian, and what impact do these proportions have on civil rights decisions?

5. How has interest group activity led to judicial decisions that have advanced civil rights?

KEY TERMS

Administrative Law p. 272

Amicus Curiae (Friend of the Court) Briefs p. 290

Appellate Jurisdiction p. 275

Civil Law p. 273

Concurring Opinion p. 291

Constitutional Law p. 272

Criminal Law p. 272

Dissenting Opinion p. 291

Interest Group Litigation p. 293

Judicial Activism p. 276

Judicial Restraint p. 276

Judicial Review p. 275

Justiciable p. 279

Living Constitution p. 277

Majority Opinion p. 291

Mootness p. 279

Original Intent p. 277

Original Jurisdiction p. 275

Precedent p. 280

Private Law, p. 272

Public Law, p. 272

Senatorial Courtesy p. 281

Solicitor General p. 292

Standing p. 279

Statutory Law p. 272

Writ of *Certiorari* p. 290

ADDITIONAL READINGS

Ken Foskett, *Judging Thomas: The Life and Times of Clarence Thomas* (New York: Morrow, 2004).

This book offers an objective and personal account of Justice Thomas's life and career.

Anna O. Law, *The Immigration Battle in American Courts* (New York: Cambridge University Press, 2010).

This book examines the historic role of the federal judiciary in shaping immigration law. The author's careful analysis demonstrates that immigrants fare better in the U.S. Circuit Courts of Appeals than in the U.S. Supreme Court.

Carl T. Rowan, *Dream Makers, Dream Breakers: The World of Justice Thurgood Marshall* (New York: Welcome Rain, 2002).

This is a rerelease of the distinguished journalist Carl T. Rowan's classic biography of the nation's first non-White U.S. Supreme Court justice.

Carlos R. Soltero, *Latinos and the American Law: Landmark Supreme Court Cases* (Austin: University of Texas Press, 2006).

This book provides a chronological account of key U.S. Supreme Court cases that have affected Latino civil rights since the nineteenth century.

Alexander Tsesis, *We Shall Overcome: A History of Civil Rights and the Law* (New Haven, CT: Yale University Press, 2008).

This book carefully traces the history of the extent to which law and courts have affected discrimination, particularly against African Americans, in the United States.

CHAPTER 10

Public Opinion: Divided By Race?

Protesters march against police shootings during a rally in Washington, DC, on December 13, 2014.

n July 2014, Eric Garner was killed by a New York City police officer, Daniel Panteleo, on a sidewalk where he was selling loose cigarettes. In August 2014, an unarmed Black teenager, Michael Brown, was shot and killed by a White police officer, Darren Wilson, in Ferguson, Missouri. In Cleveland, Ohio, in November of that year, a police officer killed Tamir Rice, a twelve-year-old boy with a toy gun. In April 2015, three Black men were killed by police. Freddie Gray in Baltimore died as a result of a broken neck suffered when not secured in a police van and officers were alleged to have given him a "rough ride" that caused his injuries. Walter Scott was shot in the back while running away from a police officer after a traffic stop in North Charleston, South Carolina. Eric Harris was killed by a volunteer reserve sheriff's deputy, Robert Bates, in Tulsa, Oklahoma, who stepped in after police had subdued Harris and had him on the ground and pulled his gun and shot him. Bates said he thought he was pulling out his taser, but pulled out his gun instead. These events led to demonstrations across the country, some disruptive, and raised the issue of police treatment of Blacks and relations among police departments and Black communities around the nation.

A national poll conducted by the Associated Press and NORC between July 17 and 19, 2015, identified deep racial divides on the issue of law enforcement and violence. Overall, the nation was split on whether police violence against the public was a problem—32 percent said it was an extremely or very serious problem, 35 percent viewed it as a moderately serious problem and 33 percent said it was not a problem at all or not too serious a problem. When these national numbers are divided by race, the divergent views are striking. Among Blacks, 73 percent thought that police violence against citizens was a very or extremely serious problem, as well as did 51 percent of Latinos, while only 20 percent of Whites felt the same way. An overwhelming majority—81 percent—of Blacks believe that police use deadly force too quickly against Blacks in most communities, as do 61 percent of Latinos, compared to just 33 percent of Whites.[1]

intro *These events highlight the delicate nature of race and racial issues in the country and how different populations view events with racial overtones. This also highlights the complexity of public opinion and how demographic differences affect how individuals perceive and see them. In this instance, Blacks, Latinos and Whites see these events through starkly different lenses. So race and what it represents in the United States has an influence on the attitudes people have on events and issues. Attitudes are also affected by gender, partisan, economic, and regional differences, among others. What people think about political events, how they behave, and the opinions they hold are influenced by these as well as other factors. What individuals think about government policies and the politicians who formulate them, how individuals vote, and how they view the political system are all influenced by public opinion. Yet the formation of public opinion arises out of a complex set of factors that affect individuals differently. Whereas some factors might be universal, other factors are related to the complex inequalities in the American political system. These are questions that arise when we talk about Americans' attitudes toward social and political issues.*

Public Opinion Overview

Public opinion is the collective opinion of large segments of the population on an issue, candidate, or public policy on which the public might be much divided and lack a consensus. Concern about public opinion is as old as the nation. As the Framers drafted the Constitution, they realized that acceptance of the document would require convincing the American public of the importance of ratification. To this end, Alexander Hamilton, James Madison, and John Jay wrote a series of newspaper columns now called the *Federalist Papers* to convince the American public that the new Constitution should be ratified. Through these columns, Hamilton, Madison, and Jay were trying to influence public opinion because they recognized that the support of the majority of the people for this new document was essential if the document was to be considered legitimate.

> **Public Opinion** The collective opinions of large segments of the population on an issue, candidate, or public policy on which the public might be much divided and lack a consensus.

Likewise, during the Civil War, Abraham Lincoln was keenly aware of the importance of cultivating public opinion and maintaining public support for the Union's war effort and for the Union's efforts to secure help from foreign countries. Lincoln sent a commission to Europe for the purpose of influencing "the two great governments [England and France] by bringing the press and the clergy, and then the people, to an understanding of the causes and purposes of the Civil War."[2] President Lincoln himself did as much as he could through speeches and open letters published in the newspapers to influence public opinion. Perhaps the best testament to his concern with public opinion is exemplified in this statement: "In this age, in this country, public sentiment is everything. With it, nothing can fail; against it, nothing can succeed. Whoever moulds public sentiment, goes deeper than he who enacts statutes or pronounces judicial decisions."[3]

A century later, President John F. Kennedy found himself in the midst of a public opinion imbroglio. On September 10, 1962, the Supreme Court ruled that the University of Mississippi had to admit James Meredith, a Black Mississippi resident, to the University of Mississippi. Mississippi Governor Ross Barnett refused to obey the Supreme Court's decision, setting up an inevitable conflict with President Kennedy and the federal government.

Kennedy had paid little attention to civil rights up to this point in his presidency and had not followed through on his promise to issue an executive order banning housing discrimination in federally funded agencies. His explanation for this lack of follow-through, given in an interview, was that the order would be issued "in a way which will maintain a consensus [national public opinion]," and he expressed concern about not getting too far ahead of public opinion.[4] The situation in Mississippi, however, required action that would put Kennedy ahead of public opinion on integration in general and school integration in particular.

After negotiations with Governor Barnett failed, and Barnett reneged on a proposed solution, Attorney General Robert F. Kennedy told the governor that President Kennedy was going to give an address to the nation (see "Our Voices: Transcript of Conversation between Attorney General Robert F. Kennedy and Governor Ross Barnett of Mississippi"). If Barnett did not agree to a plan to register Meredith, President Kennedy would reveal to the nation, and to Barnett's supporters in Mississippi, that Barnett had struck a deal to allow Meredith to register and then had reneged. Barnett finally agreed to a plan, and on Sunday, September 30, James Meredith was moved onto the campus of the University of Mississippi under the protection of federal marshals, and President Kennedy addressed the nation to say that the Supreme Court decision was being enforced.

At the same time that President Kennedy was speaking, however, thousands of White students and other individuals were rioting in Oxford, Mississippi, over the admission of James Meredith.[5] As a result of the violence, public opinion actually started to reflect a belief that President Kennedy was moving too fast on civil rights.[6] Nevertheless, Kennedy became more committed to civil rights after the University of Mississippi crisis, and he realized that civil rights was an issue about which government would have to take action and public opinion would simply have to catch up.

A few years later, during the Vietnam War, the U.S. military, under the command of General William Westmoreland, tried to mislead the American public about U.S. success in the war so as to maintain support for the war. General Westmoreland and the officers under his command began to release daily body counts of the North Viet Cong killed by U.S. and South Vietnamese forces in an effort to portray the United States and its South Vietnamese allies as winning the war. Later investigations revealed that these figures had been false and had been doctored to portray the United States as winning a war that it had actually been losing.

In the fall of 1967, the Johnson administration began a public relations campaign to sell the increasingly unpopular war to the American people and the press. In so doing, General Westmoreland went on tour to declare to the

our voices

Transcript of Conversation between Attorney General Robert F. Kennedy and Governor Ross Barnett of Mississippi (Sunday, September 20, 1962)

RFK: I don't think that will be very pleasant, Governor. I think you are making a mistake handling it in that fashion. I suppose that if you feel it is helpful to you politically. It is not helping the people of Mississippi or the people of the United States. But I gather that is secondary in your judgment. I think it is silly going through this whole facade of your standing there; our people drawing guns; your stepping aside; to me it is dangerous and I think this has gone beyond the stage of politics, and you have a responsibility to the people of that state and to the people of the United States. This is a real disservice. . . .

RB: I'm not interested in politics personally. I have said so many times—we couldn't have integration and I have got to do something. I can't just walk back. . . .

RFK: The President is going on TV tonight. He is going through the statement [he] had with you last night. He will have to say why he called up the National Guard; that you had an agreement to permit Meredith to go to Jackson to register, and your lawyer, Mr. Watkins, said this was satisfactory; and you would let him fly in by helicopter.

RB: That won't do at all.

RFK: You broke your word to him.

RB: You don't mean the President is going to say that tonight?

RFK: Of course he is; you broke your word; now you suggest we send in troops, fighting their way through a barricade. You gave your word. Mr. Watkins gave him his word. You didn't keep it.

RB: Where didn't I keep it, in what particular?

RFK: When you said you would make an agreement and that Meredith would come into Jackson; send everybody to Oxford.

RB: Don't say that. Please don't mention it.

RFK: The President has to say that. You said we would fly him into Jackson and register him while you had everyone at Oxford. Then you would say he has been registered and you would permit him to come to Oxford by helicopter on Tuesday and go to school. Mr. Watkins pledged his word to the President; we

have it all down. You talk to Mr. Watkins and reach an agreement between the two of you, and how you are going to handle this.

Mississippi Governor Ross Barnett, left, enjoys a laugh with former Mississippi Governor Hugh White (back to camera) prior to the Ole Miss–Kentucky football game on September 29, 1962, in Jackson, Mississippi. Barnett obviously was unaware the president ordered troops assembled in Memphis to use in Ole Miss integration if necessary. Students waved Rebel flags as Barnett arrived.

James Meredith (right), the first Black student to enroll in the University of Mississippi, visits Attorney General Robert F. Kennedy at the Justice Department. The meeting was arranged by Kennedy after Meredith appeared on a nationwide TV show. Meredith urged the attorney general to press for stronger civil rights.

public that American armed forces were wearing down the communist enemy and winning the war of attrition. Westmoreland, among others, was very concerned with the public's perception of the war. Public support for the war had been deteriorating at a steady rate throughout the conflict, and as the war dragged on, that support declined even further.[7]

Thirty-four years later, after the devastating terrorist attacks on the World Trade Center in New York and on the Pentagon in Washington, DC, the United States began an air attack on Afghanistan and later initiated ground operations. Afghanistan was the country from which attackers, led by Osama bin Laden, planned the September 11, 2001, attack on the United States, although all of the attackers but one were Saudi Arabian. Despite overwhelming public support for retaliatory action, President George W. Bush and his advisers knew that to sustain a "war" effort against terrorism, they would have to continue molding public opinion to this cause. So the Bush administration hired a former Madison Avenue advertising executive to develop strategies to get its message across to the country's allies and to the American people in an effort to maintain support for the war effort.[8]

The administration, however, decided to use the September 11 attacks as a pretext for invading Iraq and removing from power Saddam Hussein, its leader at the time. Members of the administration used a variety of mechanisms to convince the domestic and international communities that Hussein had weapons of mass destruction. For example, Secretary of State Colin Powell made a presentation to the United Nations, putting his reputation on the line, in which he stated that Iraq did indeed have weapons of mass destruction. U.S. forces invaded Iraq on March 20, 2003. As time wore on and more information was revealed, it became clear that the Bush administration had misled the American public on the reasons for the invasion of Iraq. Over the years, the administration was unable to maintain public support for a war that most Americans came to view as unwarranted.

Political Culture and Public Opinion

How are opinions formed? What makes some people fervently support a particular policy position or candidate whereas others oppose the position or candidate with equal passion? Public opinion is not formed in a vacuum. Life experiences, environment, family background, education, race, gender, and the intersection of the two and the political culture of the United States all contribute to the formation of public opinion. Here we want to explore these factors to identify how they contribute to the formation of public opinion.

Political Culture The attitudes, beliefs, and values that undergird or are at the foundation of a political system.

Political culture is the attitudes, beliefs, and values that undergird or are at the foundation of a political system.[9] America's political culture is grounded in the founding principles of the country—freedom, equality, representative government, and the conflicting tradition of exclusion of segments of American citizens, among others—and encompasses how people view government and its role. As Chapter 1 demonstrated, the theoretical foundations on which the country was built were varied; thus, people can have different opinions on what government should and should not do. Despite differences of opinion on the role of government, however, most Americans view the American system of government as legitimate and support the country's political process. There are many aspects of political culture that influence how people think and why they think the way they do.

Public opinion provides indications of the current thinking and direction of American culture.[10] Public opinion on certain issues provides the lens through which to view current trends in American life (see "Measuring Equality: Donald Trump, Barack Obama and the "Birthers" on page 320). For example, growing public support for the belief that people should be more self-sufficient could mean declining tolerance or sympathy for welfare recipients. This changing belief could signal public support for overhaul and reform of the welfare system.

Political Socialization

One major influence on public opinion is **political socialization**, the process through which a person gains political understanding and forms a set of political beliefs. The early influences in political socialization are the family and the school. Conversations about politics at the dinner table, overheard by children when parents, older siblings, or relatives are talking, play a major role in the development of political opinions and attitudes. Children often adopt the political positions and support for particular candidates of their parents. As children form new friendships, however, and expand their sphere of activities, their political views and attitudes might change to reflect these new experiences.

Political Socialization The process through which a person gains political understanding and forms a set of political beliefs.

Schools are essential to political socialization because governments, including that of the United States, use schools to develop students' civic values. If a political system is to continue to exist and thrive, it must have citizens who believe in its ideals and support its political institutions. Children say the Pledge of Allegiance and learn that the United States is the principal democracy in the world. They learn democracy through election for class officers, express their preferences in mock presidential elections, and, as they enter higher grades, study civics, social studies, and history.

Political socialization continues throughout a person's life as political understanding deepens and political beliefs and values shift over time. Later influences include work experience and changing family circumstances. The views that a person holds as a young adult might be very different from the views he or she holds after marriage and children and could be different still when the person retires and sees the political system from the view of someone on a fixed income who is concerned about whether the Social Security system is financially sound.

Expressions of Public Opinion

People express their opinions about government, politics, and politicians in several ways. Clearly, election results reflect public opinion. Citizens express their opinions by voting for candidates who share some of their political and policy preferences. Winning candidates invariably interpret their victories as mandates for their policy preferences. Even though such interpretations offer a very simplistic view of voters' preferences, most politicians assume that a vote cast for a candidate means the voter supports the candidate's positions.

Writing letters or sending electronic messages to elected officials and newspapers is another expression of public opinion. Elected officials pay attention to these communications and assume, rightly or wrongly, that they represent public opinion on a particular subject. Newspapers use letters to the editor as a measure of public support or discontent with an official policy, issue, or program. Television news programs often use "person-on-the-street" interviews to represent public opinion on an issue.

Participation in demonstrations is another form of public opinion. Large events can attract considerable attention and might influence decision-makers to take some action. On March 25, 2006, an estimated 500,000 people gathered in downtown Los Angeles to protest proposed legislation in Congress

Immigration activists hold signs as they protest in front of Freedom Tower in downtown Miami, January 28, 2013. The Florida Immigrant Coalition, together with other immigrant families and community organizations, have initiated the "Di Que Si!" campaign, which translates into "Say yes!" in English, demanding immigration reform that creates a system that keeps families united. Activists and immigrants also asked for the suspension of deportations as lawmakers work on immigration reform, and announced they would join a national mobilization in favor of immigration reform in Washington, DC, on April 10, 2013.

that would have placed restrictions on immigrants in the United States and would have addressed aspects of illegal immigration into the country. As a result of the Los Angeles demonstration, in April of that year rallies for immigrant rights were held in numerous cities across the country and drew millions of people in support of immigrant rights.[11]

The increasing uses of the Internet and email have made it easier for individuals to express their opinions to network and cable news organizations, talk shows, national public affairs programs, and elected officials. It is commonplace for these entities to invite people to log on and "vote" for a particular policy option or to express their favorable or unfavorable view of a politician who has become controversial. Organizations conducting electronic polls will always preface their comments about the results with the phrase "in our nonscientific poll" because the technique by which the data were gathered is not representative of the American public. The opinions are representative only of those individuals who choose to log on and respond to the survey. Illustrative of this point is the notice that ABCNews.com posts explaining the nonrepresentative nature of its online polls:

> ABCNews.com posts online ballots as a way of encouraging users to express their views and participate in our community. These ballots, however, are not polls. They are not based on scientific, representative samples and their results are vulnerable to manipulation by individuals or groups with an interest in the outcome. They are for entertainment only. To avoid confusion and discourage manipulation, we do not offer percentaged results of online ballots—only vote totals. We do not refer to them as "polls" or "surveys," words that indicate the use of a representative sample. These ballots do not constitute a reliable sounding of public opinion.[12]

Each of these responses is an expression of public opinion, but not one of them measures the opinion of the entire American public. They represent the views—sometimes very effectively—of only those who vote, write letters, send email messages, participate in mass demonstrations, or complete online surveys. Individuals who participate in demonstrations, write letters, and send email messages are those who are the most active and committed to a particular issue. If none of these activities reflects the views of the entire American public, is there any way to discover the opinion of the entire U.S. population on some issue or on a candidate for the presidency? The answer to this question is survey research.

Measuring Public Opinion

Survey research, the administration of questionnaires to a sample of respondents selected from some population, is particularly useful for making descriptive and explanatory studies of large populations. Survey research takes a number of forms. One form of survey research is the questionnaire we complete after purchasing a computer or appliance or the customer satisfaction survey we are given after we have used a service or filed a complaint. The most

Survey Research
Administration of questionnaires to a sample of respondents selected from a particular population, useful for making descriptive and explanatory studies of large populations.

common form of survey research is public opinion polling. Public opinion polls assess the attitudes, opinions, and behaviors of a population, for example, U.S. voters' views of policy issues and electoral candidates.

Survey research and public opinion polling as it now exists were developed almost exclusively in the United States by academics and commercial polling organizations. Businesses use public opinion polling to determine their markets or assess the quality of their service. Today public opinion polls are conducted by universities, commercial polling organizations, and news organizations. The American National Election Study (ANES) is conducted by the University of Michigan, and now in partnership with Stanford University, during presidential election years in an effort to understand why people voted the way they did and what factors influenced their votes.[13] The General Social Survey, collected by the National Opinion Research Center at the University of Chicago, gathers data on social aspects of the U.S. population.

The most prominent commercial polling organizations are the Gallup organization, Harris Polls, and Roper Center for Public Opinion Research. These organizations conduct surveys on a variety of topics ranging from attitudes toward the economy to whether people watched a particular sporting event to how people feel about a particular political event or a political candidate. Unlike university surveys done once a year or every election cycle, commercial polling organizations might conduct a survey each week. Many of the major newspapers, such as the *New York Times*, the *Washington Post*, and the *Los Angeles Times*, have polling directors and staff.

Newspapers are interested in how people feel about issues and candidates nationally as well as locally. For national polls, many news organizations have formed partnerships with commercial polling organizations or with other news organizations to conduct national polls. Some of the pairings are CNN/*Time*/Opinion Research Corporation, ABC News/*Washington Post*, *New York Times*/CBS News, and NBC News/*Wall Street Journal*.

The Mechanics of Polling

Sample A small set of people carefully drawn from a larger population to reflect its overall characteristics.

The mechanics of conducting a poll determine how much confidence we should have in the survey's results. The mechanics include how the **sample**, a small set of people gathered from a larger population, is drawn; how the questions are worded; in what order they appear; when (time) the data are gathered; and how the data are gathered. When the mechanics are done incorrectly or sloppily, the results could be suspect or completely wrong.

How the Sample Is Drawn

The *Literary Digest*, published between 1890 and 1938, was a respected news magazine that had predicted correctly the elections of 1924, 1928, and 1932. In 1936, it predicted that Alf Landon would defeat Franklin D. Roosevelt in a landslide. Culling names from telephone books and auto registration lists across the country, the *Literary Digest* sent out 10 million ballots asking people to check their preferences for president.[14] More than 2 million ballots were returned, and the results predicted Republican Alf Landon would win with a stunning 57 percent to 43 percent landslide over the incumbent Democratic president, Franklin Roosevelt.[15] In actuality, Roosevelt beat Landon in a landslide with 61 percent of the vote.[16] Although the process by which the *Literary Digest* sampled public opinion had worked in the past, it failed miserably in the midst of the Depression, when only the wealthy had telephones and automobiles. Thus, the sample was not representative of the extraordinarily large proportion of the population that was poor and turned out in large numbers at the polls.

George Gallup predicted that Roosevelt would win by a substantial margin. In conducting his poll, Gallup used a method called **quota sampling**, a procedure in which interviewers choose people to be interviewed based on their proportion or quota in the general population being polled. In a quota sample, the number of women polled, for example, would be proportionate to the number of women in the general population. Gallup's sample, then, was more representative of the population of the United States than was the *Literary Digest* sample, which was biased toward wealthy and Republican voters.

Although Gallup correctly predicted the outcome of the 1936 presidential election, in the presidential election of 1948, all of the pollsters, including

Quota Sampling A type of sample in which individuals to be interviewed are selected based on their proportion or quota in the general population being polled.

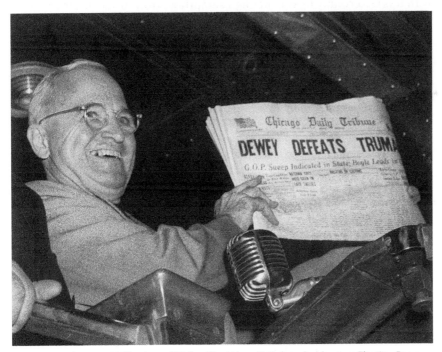

In this November 4, 1948 file photo, U.S. President Harry S. Truman holds up an Election Day edition of the *Chicago Daily Tribune*, which, based on early results, mistakenly announced "Dewey Defeats Truman."

Probability Sampling
A general term for a sample selected in accordance with probability theory, which ensures that every person in the population has an equal chance of being selected for the sample.

Sampling Error The degree of expected error in sampling results that comes from estimating the responses of the population from a sample.

Gallup, predicted that Republican candidate Thomas Dewey would beat Democratic president Harry Truman. But Truman beat Dewey 49.5 percent to 45.1 percent. This election showed that, even though quota sampling had been accurate in the past, new ways of drawing samples were necessary. At the time, a number of academic statisticians, particularly Leslie Kish of the University of Michigan, were experimenting with **probability sampling** methods, ways of drawing a sample that use probability theory to ensure that every person in the population has an equal chance of being selected for the sample. A basic principle of probability sampling is that a sample will be representative of the population from which it is drawn if all members of the population have an equal chance of being selected in the sample.[17]

Statistically drawn samples tend to have respondents who are representative of the target population. Such a sample will approximate the gender, racial, and regional distribution of the population under study. Additionally, the development of probability sampling took the decision of whom to interview out of the hands of the interviewer, which had led to bias in the results because interviewers tended to select people like themselves. Using probability sampling techniques, Kish and his associates had correctly predicted that Truman would prevail in the election. Yet even samples drawn using probability methods cannot be assumed to reflect the opinions and behaviors of the entire U.S. population with absolute accuracy. Probability sampling deals with this uncertainty by calculating a **sampling error**, the degree of expected error in the results that comes from estimating the responses of the population from a sample. Sampling error is expressed as plus or minus a certain percentage rate, depending on the size of the sample for the results of the survey. Often survey results will note a sampling error of "plus or minus three percentage points" (+/−3). For example, for the results indicating that 48 percent of the people support Candidate A, and 44 percent of the people support Candidate B, the actual range for Candidate A is 51 percent (+3) to 45 percent (−3), and the range for Candidate B is 47 percent (+3) to 41 percent (−3). When political races are described as being a statistical dead heat, which this example is, even though it looks like one candidate is leading, it means that the results fall within the sampling error, thereby making the differences not significant.

How a Question Is Worded

Sampling is the most important mechanic in assuring a poll's accuracy, but other factors have been shown to have significant effects in certain circumstances. As we saw in the chapter opening vignette, the way in which a question is worded can make a difference.

Table 10.1 shows the difference in responses people gave to questions on support for affirmative action. When the question was worded using the phrase "designed to help Blacks, women and other minorities to get better jobs and education," more than three-fourths of the respondents (77 percent) favored affirmative action programs. When the question was phrased "which

TABLE 10.1 Different Wording for Questions Measuring Support for Affirmative Action Programs

To overcome past discrimination, do you favor or oppose affirmative action programs designed to help Blacks, women, and other minorities to get better jobs and education?

Favor	77
Oppose	17
Don't know/refused	6

To overcome past discrimination, do you favor or oppose affirmative action programs that give special preferences to qualified Blacks, women, and other minorities in hiring and education?

Favor	61
Oppose	26
Don't know/refused	13

We should make every possible effort to improve the positions of Blacks and other minorities, even if it means giving them preferential treatment.

Agree	31
Disagree	65

Note: Responses are in percentages.

Source: Pew Research Center for the People and the Press, "Public Backs Affirmative Action, But Not Minority Preferences," June 2, 2009. http://www.pewresearch.org/2009/public-backs-affirmative-action-but-not-minority-preferences.

give special preferences to qualified Blacks and other minorities in hiring and education," a lesser number of respondents (61 percent), but still a majority, supported affirmative action programs. But when the phrasing was "We should make every possible effort to improve the position of Blacks and other minorities, even if it means giving them preferential treatment," support dropped significantly (to 31 percent). The questions were trying to get at the same thing, but clearly the use of "preferential treatment" triggered negative responses to affirmative action.

When a Question Is Asked within the Survey

The order in which questions are asked can also affect responses. The response to a question at the beginning of a survey can affect the answers to later questions, for instance.[18] For example, in 1980 a poll conducted by the Harris organization asked respondents at the beginning of the survey if they intended to vote for President Jimmy Carter or Senator Edward Kennedy (D-MA), who was challenging Carter in the Democratic primaries. This question was followed by a series of questions about domestic and foreign policy. Toward the end of the survey, the respondents were asked again for whom they would vote. By the end of the survey, support for Carter had declined sharply, as the domestic and foreign policy questions related to President Carter's performance in office. Clearly, putting these questions in between the questions about candidate preference primed negative feelings about President Carter as respondents moved through the questionnaire.

With the popularity of online surveys, researchers have begun to explore whether question ordering makes a difference. If all the questions are on the same page and respondents can see all the questions and pick the order in which they answer questions, then the order of the questions does not change how people respond. But, if questions are put on separate pages and respondents cannot move forward without providing a response and cannot go back to a previous page to change an answer, then question ordering does make a difference.[19]

When Data Are Gathered

The time at which a poll is taken can also dramatically affect the accuracy of the poll results. Polls taken very early in a political race are usually poor predictors of the eventual outcome. Nowhere is this more evident than in presidential races. The presidential election cycle usually begins about eighteen to twenty-four months before the actual election, but except for the news media, few Americans are focused on the election until after Labor Day of the election year. For that reason, public opinion polls taken far in advance of the election tell us little about who is going to win the election.

In the 2008 presidential primaries, early polls in 2007 indicated that Senator Hillary Rodham Clinton was going to be the presidential nominee for the Democrats and former New York City mayor Rudy Giuliani was going to be the nominee for the Republicans. By January 2008, pollsters were collecting data on a head-to-head matchup between Clinton and Giuliani in the November presidential general election, so convinced were they of the accuracy of their early polling data. Not only did the pollsters believe the data, both Giuliani and Clinton also believed the poll numbers and made strategy decisions based on those early numbers.

But Giuliani's campaign failed to gain traction, and he dropped out, and Senator Clinton battled Senator Barack Obama for the nomination until summer 2008. The inevitability of Clinton's nomination, based on early polling, fell short, and she was not able to gain the Democratic presidential nomination.

During the 2016 presidential primaries, in early 2015, even before former governor Jeb Bush entered the race, pollsters were predicting that he would be the Republican nominee and were polling on the eventual matchup between Bush and Hillary Clinton, the presumed Democratic nominee. Unlike 2008, Clinton did not assume the mantel of inevitability in 2016 and this time did not believe the polling and ran a successful campaign to become the Democratic nominee. Jeb Bush, on the other hand, did not gain traction after he announced his candidacy in June 2015 and dropped out on February 20, 2016. Assuming that polls taken a year before or even months before a presidential election are meaningful misses the shifting nature of public opinion.

How Data Are Gathered

The way in which data are gathered also makes a difference in poll results. Most of the public opinion polls conducted by news organizations, commercial pollsters, politicians, and political campaigns are telephone interviews. One complicating factor for telephone surveys is the growing prevalence of cell phones as the primary phone for many Americans. Survey researchers have begun to develop techniques that will sample cell phone numbers to see if the attitudes of cell phone users are different from those of landline users. A recent report found that these two populations do not differ substantively in their attitudes on key political measures such as presidential approval, Iraq policy, presidential primary voter preference, and party affiliation, but that the cost of interviewing a cell phone user is about three times more than the cost of interviewing a landline user.[20] Another challenge to telephone interviewing is the increasing use of caller ID and respondents' resistance to being interviewed.

Since the 2000 presidential election, online Internet polling has become much more prevalent. As previously discussed, Internet polls are not scientifically grounded and cannot be trusted to yield accurate results. There are many reasons for this, including the fact that only a portion of the total electorate has access to the Internet (even though these numbers have been growing) and Internet poll respondents tend to be self-selected rather than scientifically constructed according to good sampling techniques.

The unreliability of Internet polling and daily tracking polls is part of the reason that the 2012 presidential nomination and election processes were difficult to follow with any accuracy. The differences in results were directly related to how the samples were drawn, the size of the sample, how the poll was conducted, and how the questions were worded, all the factors we have been exploring. Table 10.2 shows the final Gallup Tracking Poll for the 2012

TABLE 10.2 2012 Pre-Election Presidential Ballot

Gallup Final 2012 Pre-Election Presidential Ballot November 1–4, 2012

	Mitt Romney/ Paul Ryan %	Barack Obama/ Joe Biden %	Other (vol.) %	No Opinion %
Likely voters	49	48	1	3
Final allocated estimate[a]	50	49	1	—
Registered voters	46	49	1	4

[a]*The allocated estimate represents the vote choice of likely voters with undecided voters removed from the sample. Undecided votes were allocated proportionally; due to rounding this resulted in one-percentage-point increases in the final result for each candidate.*

(vol.) = volunteered response

Source: Gallup Daily tracking, GALLUP.

presidential election. Gallup's Daily Tracking Polls favored Mitt Romney and were considered an outlier from the other tracking polls. Gallup had Romney up by as much as seven points during the final week of the election. The poll Gallup released the day before the election gave Romney a one-point lead over President Obama. Analysis suggests that Gallup's sampling frame was biased toward Republican voters, overestimated the size of the White portion of the electorate, and that its formula for the likely-voter screen not only overestimated White voters, but underestimated younger voters.[21] President Obama won the election 51 to 47 percent. As you can see from Table 10.2 the registered voter sample was closer to the final vote total than was the likely voter sample. Virtually all of the 2016 pre-election polls predicted that Hillary Clinton would win the presidency. As in 2012, the polls were off. and Donald Trump won the Electoral College vote, but lost the popular vote. The Association of Public Opinion Research (APOR) together a committee to try to figure out what went wrong in both 2012 and 2016.

Race, Gender, and Public Opinion

The U.S. population is a multiracial one, and increasingly so, yet many generalizations about American public opinion were developed from survey data coming largely from White respondents. Race influences public opinion because the historically disparate treatment of racial minorities in American society has an effect on public opinion. The effects of race on public opinion, in particular, take on added significance as the demographics of the U.S. population continue to change. These demographic shifts are likely to influence changes in public opinion that will, in turn, lead to changes in the U.S. political system.

For example, the 2014 census population update indicated that Latinos were 17.4 percent of the population, up from 12.5 percent in 2000, and non-Latino Whites were 62.2 percent of the population, down from 69.1 percent in 2000. Estimates based on the 2010 census predict that by 2060, Latinos will constitute 28.6 percent of the U.S. population, African Americans will be 14.3 percent of the population, Asian Americans will make up 9.3 percent of the population, and non-Latino Whites will be only 43.6 percent of the population.[22] California was a majority-minority state, with Blacks, Latinos, and Asians making up the majority.[23]

Gender differences in public opinion have also been identified, but they are much less dramatic than racial differences. Nevertheless, the changing nature of the role of women in American society has resulted in some public opinion differences. The intersection of race and gender for Black women and other women of color adds an additional dynamic and complexity to the examination of public opinion. For these reasons, the effects of race and gender on the formation of public opinion merit special attention.

Race

From its inception, the United States has had tremendous difficulties in dealing with issues of race. Black Americans were officially enslaved beginning about 1641, the date that slavery was incorporated into colonial law by the colony of Massachusetts, until after the Civil War.[24] Notwithstanding emancipation, Blacks endured continued segregation, discrimination, and denial of political freedoms and constitutional guarantees until the Civil Rights Movement of the 1950s and 1960s began to break down those barriers.

Despite tremendous advancements in diminishing inequalities between Blacks and Whites, many realities of life suggest that Black Americans live in a different world and have different life chances from those of White Americans. A study published in 2001 by economist and law professor Ian Ayers found that there were continued inequalities between Blacks and Whites but that these were often more subtle. For instance, car dealers regularly charged Blacks more for cars than White men. Blacks had more difficulty than Whites getting kidney transplants, and Black defendants were frequently required to post higher bail bonds than their White counterparts.[25]

The history of racism and discrimination and the continuing inequalities between the races are the context in which public opinion held by Blacks and other racial minorities is formed. Political scientist Paul Abramson suggests that Blacks and Whites experience different political realities, the extent to which each group can participate in the political system results in differences in political attitudes and in different beliefs about how much influence each group has on the system. He argues that many of the attitudes of Black Americans reflect an accurate response to the realities of Black political life in the United States.[26]

This difference in political realities is reflected in the opinions and attitudes held by different racial groups in the United States. For example, in a June 15 to July 10, 2015, Gallup Poll, 72 percent of Whites believed that Blacks had as good a chance as Whites to get any kind of job for which they were qualified; a majority (63 percent) of Blacks disagreed. Given that Blacks believe they do not have an equal chance to get any kind of job, 69 percent of Blacks felt that new civil rights laws were needed to reduce discrimination, whereas only 31 percent of Whites believed new laws were needed. Additionally, 58 percent of Whites believed that a solution to relations between Blacks and Whites would eventually be worked out, whereas 59 percent of Blacks felt that relations between Blacks and Whites will always be a problem.[27]

These differences in opinion are rooted in the reality that Blacks have experienced numerous forms of discrimination, particularly racial profiling (being targeted by police on the basis of race alone and not behavior), from the police.[28] Whites by and large have not experienced discriminatory treatment. As a result, they have a different perspective on equality of opportunity and on treatment by the police than do Blacks, who have experienced and continue to experience discrimination (see "Evaluating Equality: Differences in Perception of Racism against Black Americans").[29]

evaluating equality

Differences in Perception of Racism against Black Americans

Blacks and Whites experience life differently, and that difference results in differences in perceptions of issues. Figure 10.1 shows differences in perception about whether racism against Black Americans is or is not widespread.

Figure 10.1

Differences in Perceptions of Racism Against Blacks.
Source: Gallup Poll,
June 15–July 10, 2015.

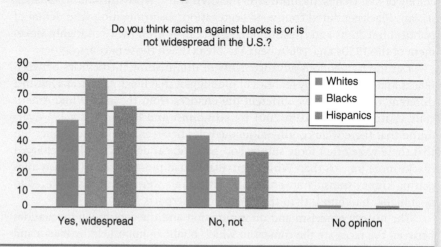

Do you think racism against blacks is or is not widespread in the U.S.?

During every election cycle, the news media conflate Black support for the Democratic Party with the belief that this means that Blacks are politically liberal. But those who study Black and Latino political attitudes argue that it is inappropriate to use the standard political ideology labels of "liberal," "moderate," and "conservative"—which were developed through national studies that contained few non-Whites—and apply them to the Black and Latino populations. Describing all racial minorities in general as liberal overlooks the complexity and variability of attitudes within the various racial communities. Moreover, the application of such labels implies that there is an agreed-on definition of their meaning and that individuals who identify themselves by these labels are able to define what they mean.[30]

Beliefs that the federal government should take an active role in reducing unemployment, providing services for the poor, and improving the socioeconomic position of Blacks or other racial minorities are generally regarded as representing liberal attitudes. Support for prayer in public schools is considered a conservative attitude. Yet these two positions—support for an active role for government and for prayer in schools—are found within African-American public opinion, which raises doubts about the assignment of such labels as liberal and conservative. According to all of the available data, Blacks identify themselves across the ideological spectrum, with just as many Blacks self-identifying as some variant of liberal as identifying as some variant of conservative.[31] Regardless of self-identified ideological labels, Blacks' policy preferences are generally liberal across a variety of issues, such as increased government spending on food stamps, Medicare, crime, and employment and jobs. But with the exception of capital punishment, Blacks are relatively conservative on a range of social policy issues, such as abortion, school prayer, and same-sex marriage.[32]

The designations of liberal and conservative do not accurately reflect the attitudes of various Latino groups.[33] The 2006 Latino National Survey reported that Mexican Americans are more likely to describe themselves as some variant of conservative than as liberal. But more identify themselves as moderate than as conservative or liberal. Puerto Ricans and Cubans, however, are more likely to self-describe as some degree of conservative than as liberal or moderate. Regardless of self-identified ideological labels, large majorities of all three groups support what could be characterized as liberal domestic policy issues, such as increased spending for public education, child care services, the environment, and public assistance and welfare.[34]

On the surface and according to the standard political science explanations, there appears to be a conflict between the varied ideological orientations among these groups and their support for a policy agenda that calls for active federal government in solving problems (a liberal position). If, however, we take into account the social and political realities of these groups, it is not difficult to understand how Blacks and Latinos can call themselves conservatives but still feel strongly that the government has a role to play in creating an equal playing field, expanding opportunities, and enforcing antidiscrimination laws. Historical context has a forceful explanatory power, and we must recognize that it is the lens through which the public opinion held by racial minorities is formed, which differs substantively from the historical perspective of Whites.

Table 10.3 illustrates racial differences on two important policy issues—the death penalty and gun regulation—that are connected to different political realities for Blacks and Whites. As Table 10.3 illustrates, there is a dramatic difference in support for the death penalty among Blacks and Whites, with about one-half (54.56 percent) of Blacks supporting the death penalty compared to more than three-fourths (76.86 percent) of Whites; Latinos anchor the middle of the continuum (65.71 percent in favor).

These differences in opinion are rooted in the reality that Blacks have less confidence in the equal application of the law and are more critical of police tactics.[35] Whites are less likely to believe that the criminal justice system is biased, and their interactions with police, for the most part, have been cordial.[36] As we demonstrated in Chapter 5, the presence of racial and ethnic minorities on death row is disproportionate to their numbers in the population and contributes to differences in such perceptions.

Racial differences are also present on the issue of gun regulation. Two-thirds (63.82 percent) of Blacks, compared to slightly more than two-fifths (42.59 percent) of Whites, think the federal government should make it more difficult for people to purchase a gun. Blacks are more likely to be victims of violent crimes than are Whites and to live in neighborhoods with higher levels of crime.[37] For example, 2013 data collected by the United Nations on homicide across the world showed that a Black American is eight times more likely to be a homicide victim than a White American is.[38] Thus, Blacks exhibit a

TABLE 10.3 Racial Differences on Social Policy Issues

Do you favor or oppose the death penalty for persons convicted of murder?

	Percent		
	Blacks	Latinos	Whites
Favor	54.56	65.71	76.86
Oppose	45.44	34.29	23.14
	n = 964	*n* = 974	*n* = 3,436

More than half of Black Americans are opposed to the death penalty, while more than three fourths of Whites are in favor.

Do you think the federal government should make it more difficult for people to buy a gun than it is now, make it easier for people to buy a gun, or keep these rules about the same as they are now?

	Percent		
	Blacks	Latinos	Whites
More difficult	63.82	58.70	42.59
Easier	1.59	5.40	6.36
The same	34.59	35.90	51.05
	n = 1,006	*n* = 1,000	*n* = 3,487

Source: 2012 American National Election Study.

heightened fear of crime and concern about crime compared with Whites. As such, Blacks are more likely to be supportive of gun regulation than are Whites. Latino support for more difficulty in purchasing guns (58.70 percent) is similar to that of Blacks.

Gender

Gender Social relations between the sexes and attitudes about how the sexes interact and the roles that society assumes they will play.

The effect of gender on the formation of public opinion was not recognized as an important factor until the 1980s.[39] Before then, public opinion studies focused on other factors that influenced public opinion formation, such as race, religion, and social class.[40] The belief at the time was that women's public opinion was identical to men's.[41]

In discussing **gender**, political science literature makes a distinction between sex, which refers to biological characteristics, and gender, which refers to social relations between the sexes and attitudes about how the sexes interact and the roles that society assumes they will play. The use of the term gender in public opinion refers to how the social roles assigned to women and the nature of their interaction with men affect how they perceive issues. This is different from the ascriptive category of sex—male and female.

Gender Gap The difference between men and women on such crucial issues as partisan identification and voting for certain candidates.

In politics, differences between men and women on partisan identification and voting are referred to as the **gender gap**.[42] The date of the emergence of the gender gap is debated by scholars. The common date given is the 1980 presidential election, when women were less likely than men to support Ronald Reagan. Female support for Reagan was 6 to 9 percent less than male support.[43] Yet others suggest that the earliest emergence of the contemporary gender gap was in the 1964 election of Lyndon B. Johnson, when women were more aligned with the Democratic Party than men were.[44]

The 1990s saw an increase in the gender gap. The 1992 and 1996 presidential elections showed a new increase in the gender gap at levels above those during the Reagan era.[45] Bill Clinton received 8 percent more votes from women in 1992 than did George H. W. Bush and a whopping 16 percent more votes from women in 1996. In the 2000 election, Al Gore's margin with female voters was 11 percentage points higher than George W. Bush's, but the gap narrowed considerably in 2004, when John Kerry's margin with women was only 3 percentage points over George W. Bush's.[46]

The gap widened again in 2008. Despite the presence of Alaska governor Sarah Palin as the vice presidential nominee on the Republican ticket, women voted for Senator Barack Obama by 7 percentage points over Senator John McCain. What is interesting about the 2008 presidential contest is that the gender gap appears to be the result of support for Obama among Black women (96 percent for Obama), Latina women (68 percent), and women of other races (64 percent). The majority of White women (53 percent) voted for McCain, as did the majority of White men (57 percent).[47]

The gender gap was still present in the 2012 elections. Exit polling showed that President Obama took the majority of the female vote (55 percent), but only 46 percent of the White female vote. His margin of victory among women came from the votes of Black women (96 percent), Latina women (68 percent), and Asian and other non-White women (64 percent). These groups voted in similar proportions for President Obama in 2008. It is therefore important, where possible, to break out various groups of women to get a better sense of which women contribute to the gender gap.

As in 2012, the gender gap was present in the 2016 elections.[48] Exit poll data showed that Hillary Clinton received 54 percent of the female vote compared to Donald Trump, who received 42 percent. But the majority of White women (53 percent) voted for Trump, so Clinton's margin among female voters once again came from women of color—94 percent of Black women voted for Clinton as did 68 percent of Latinas.

Political science research has found that as more women went to work, they came to view themselves as being limited by their gender in the labor market. The research has also shown that women became more gender conscious between 1972 and 1983.[49] The view that their gender limited their employment opportunities, coupled with increasing gender consciousness, began to move women's public opinion preferences in a direction opposite that of men's. Notably, the gender gap generally was attributed to women's liberal preferences on policy issues such as abortion and equal rights, social welfare, women's rights, and the environment.[50] The largest gender differences appeared on policies related to aid to the unemployed and war and peace issues.[51] The most enduring differences surrounded the latter, with women consistently less approving of policies that involve the use of violence, either domestically or internationally, than are men.[52]

Yet the gender gap is not the result of women's changing attitudes alone. Another contributor to the gender gap is attitudinal changes in male party identification and voting. From 1952 to 1996, men were more conservative than women were on social welfare questions. Also, men were more conservative across social spending issues.[53] From 1952 to 2004, the percentage of women identifying with the Republican Party declined by 5 percentage points, from 58 to 53 percent. Yet during this same period, the percentage of men identifying with the Democratic Party dropped 16 percent, from 59 to 43 percent.[54] Thus, men's political behavior was a major contributor to the gender gap.

The social and political context in which women have existed in American society contributes to the formation of public opinion. Although all women are not influenced in the same way, for many the recognition of gender limitations contributes to the development of attitudes that differ from those of men. Table 10.4 shows gender differences on the same two social policy issues—the

TABLE 10.4 Gender Differences on Social Policy Issues

Do you favor or oppose the death penalty for persons convicted of murder?

	Percent	
	Men	**Women**
Favor	73.50 (2,047)	68.52 (2,033)
Oppose	26.50 (738) n = 2,785	31.48 (934) n = 2,967

Do you think the federal government should make it more difficult for people to buy a gun than it is now, make it easier for people to buy a gun, or keep these rules about the same as they are now?

	Percent	
	Men	**Women**
More difficult	40.37 (1,145)	57.39 (1,752)
Easier	8.15 (231)	2.98 (91)
The same	51.48 (506) n = 2,836	39.63 (491) n = 3,053

A majority of women feel that it should be more difficult to buy a gun, while only two-fifths of men think the same way. About half of men think that the rules should be kept about the same.

Source: 2012 American National Election Study.

death penalty and gun regulation. As Table 10.4 demonstrates, women favor the death penalty in smaller proportions than do men, and women are far more likely to favor making it more difficult to buy a gun than are men.

Even with both racial and gender differences present, we want to look within those categories to see if the intersection of race and gender makes even more of a difference on these policy preferences. As Table 10.5 indicates, there are differences among White men and women and Black men and women in these two policy areas. Of all of the race and gender groups, Black women

TABLE 10.5 Support for the Death Penalty and Gun Control by Race and Gender

Do you favor or oppose the death penalty for persons convicted of murder?

Race and Gender	Death Penalty	
	Favor	Oppose
White men	78.46	21.54
White women	75.30	24.70
Black men	61.28	38.72
Black women	49.36	50.64
Latino men	64.53	35.47
Latino women	66.80	33.20
Other men	77.30	22.70
Other women	64.74	35.26

Do you think the federal government should make it more difficult for people to buy a gun than it is now, make it easier for people to buy a gun, or keep these rules about the same as they are now?

Race and Gender	Gun Control		
	More Difficult	Easier	The Same
White men	34.07	9.65	56.28
White women	50.88	3.17	45.95
Black men	55.12	1.86	43.02
Black women	70.31	1.39	28.30
Latino men	50.31	7.22	42.47
Latino women	66.60	3.69	29.71
Other men	40.10	10.70	49.20
Other women	54.14	3.87	41.99

Note: Column numbers are percentage of total number of people responding in the category.

Source: 2012 American National Election Study.

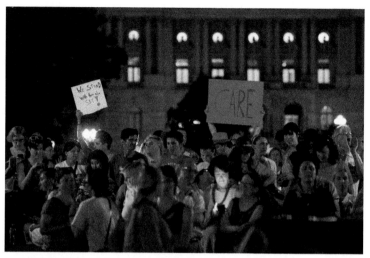

Protesters gather outside the Capitol during the Democrat sit-in, June 22, 2016. The Democratic members of the House of Representatives, led by Congressman John Lewis, staged a sit-in to protest the House's failure to hold a vote on gun control legislation after the mass murder of forty-nine people at a gay bar in Orlando, Florida.

measuring equality

Donald Trump, Barack Obama, and the "Birthers"

In 2011, Donald Trump, the 2016 Republican presidential nominee, talked incessantly about his questions of whether President Obama was actually born in Hawaii. He even said that he had sent private investigators to Hawaii to see what they could find, and that no one seemed to remember him in school or any other place. President Obama then released his Hawaiian long-form birth certificate proving that he was, indeed, born in Hawaii and is a natural born United States citizen. But Trump's "Birther" campaign did become a talking point in the 2012 election because of Trump's support for Mitt Romney, the 2012 Republican nominee. In the 2016 Republican primaries, one of the presidential contenders Senator Ted Cruz *was* born in Alberta, Canada, to a United States citizen mother and a Cuban-born father. Yet, an August 28 to 30, 2015 survey by Public Policy Poll of Republican voters found that, despite the evidence to the contrary, only 29 percent of Republicans believed that President Obama was born in the United States, while 40 percent believed Senator Cruz was born in the United States.

What factors might explain this difference?

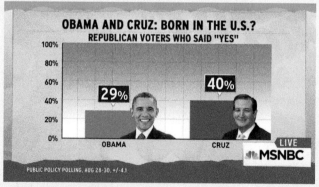

Figure 10.2 Obama and Cruz: Born in the United States? Republican voters who said "yes."

are the least supportive of the death penalty (49.36 percent) and White men are the most supportive (78.46 percent). White women are closer to White men on support for the death penalty than they are to Black women, who are overwhelmingly opposed. A slightly higher percentage of Latino women favor the death penalty than do Latino men, but the difference is marginal (66.80 percent to 64.53 percent).

On the issue of gun control, Black women again are the most supportive of the federal government making it more difficult to purchase a gun (70.31 percent), with Latino women close behind (66.60 percent). Majorities or half of White women, Black men, and Latino men also favor making it more difficult to purchase a gun, but there is a 15 to 20 percentage point difference in their support from that of Black women. The difference between these groups' support and that of Latino women ranges from 11 to 15 percentage points. What these figures suggest is that race, gender, and the intersection between the two have significant influences on public opinion.

Demographic Factors

Educational level affects a person's opinions and attitudes, as do income, region, and urban, suburban, or rural location. Political science research has found that persons with higher incomes, education levels, professional occupations, and suburban residence are more inclined to identify with the Republican Party, whereas those with lower incomes, lower education levels, labor and blue-collar jobs, and urban residence are more inclined to identify with the Democratic Party.[55]

Regional location and urban versus rural environments also influence public opinion. People living in different parts of the country often have different political views. For example, people in the Northeast are generally more liberal on social issues than are people in the South. Even within the same section of the country, however, the views of people living in rural areas might be markedly different from those of people living in urban areas. Those living in suburban areas might hold views different from those living in rural or urban areas. The social and political environments of rural, urban, and suburban locales differ, and consequently, the issues that are significant to residents of each type of area also vary.[56]

Table 10.6 shows the differences in attitudes toward the federal government making it more difficult to obtain a gun, by selected demographic characteristics. People who live in the Northeast (58.14 percent) are significantly more supportive of making it more difficult to obtain a gun than are those who live in the West (48.58 percent). In general, individuals making less than $40,000 and those at the upper end of the income scale are more supportive of making it more difficult to purchase a gun than are those in the middle income ranges. Based on broad religious categories, although the sample size is small, Jewish individuals are far more likely to support efforts to make it more difficult to purchase a gun than are Protestants.

TABLE 10.6 **Differences in Support for Gun Control by Selected Characteristics—Region, Income, and Religion**

Do you think the federal government should make it more difficult for people to buy a gun than it is now, make it easier for people to buy a gun, or keep these rules about the same as they are?

	More Difficult	Easier	The Same
Region			
Northeast	58.14	5.12	36.74
n = 958	*n* = 557	*n* = 49	*n* = 352
Midwest	45.54	4.86	49.60
n = 1,256	*n* = 572	*n* = 61	*n* = 623
South	47.82	4.71	47.47
n = 2,269	*n* = 1,085	*n* = 107	*n* = 1,077
West	48.58	7.47	43.95
n = 1,406	*n* = 683	*n* = 105	*n* = 618
Income			
<$19,999	49.13	4.05	46.82
n = 346	*n* = 170	*n* = 14	*n* = 162
$20,000–$39,999	54.64	4.49	40.87
n = 646	*n* = 353	*n* = 29	*n* = 264
$40,000–$59,999	47.42	3.92	48.66
n = 485	*n* = 230	*n* = 19	*n* = 236
$60,000–$74,999	44.39	5.34	50.27
n = 187	*n* = 83	*n* = 10	*n* = 94
$75,000–$89,999	40.00	0.87	59.13
n = 115	*n* = 46	*n* = 1	*n* = 68
$90,000–$99,999	61.29	6.45	32.26
n = 31	*n* = 19	*n* = 2	*n* = 10
$100,000–$124,999	39.39	6.06	54.55
n = 66	*n* = 26	*n* = 4	*n* = 36
$125,000–$149,999	45.16	0.00	54.84
n = 31	*n* = 14	*n* = 0	*n* = 17
$150,000+	53.85	3.84	42.31
n = 52	*n* = 28	*n* = 2	*n* = 22
Religion			
Protestant	46.07	6.06	47.87

TABLE 10.6 Differences in Support for Gun Control by Selected Characteristics—Region, Income, and Religion (*continued*)

	More Difficult	Easier	The Same
$n = 1,502$	$n = 692$	$n = 91$	$n = 719$
Catholic	56.07	4.55	39.37
$n = 988$	$n = 554$	$n = 45$	$n = 389$
Jewish	72.16	5.15	22.68
$n = 97$	$n = 70$	$n = 5$	$n = 22$
Other	44.7	7.69	47.61
$n = 1,235$	$n = 552$	$n = 95$	$n = 588$

Note: Column numbers are percentage of total number of people responding in the category.

Source: 2012 American National Election Study.

Partisan Identification

Another influence is **partisan identification**, or which political party an individual most identifies with. A person who identifies with the Democratic Party is more likely to favor Democratic policy positions and candidates. A person who identifies with the Republican Party will favor Republican positions and candidates. There is also a relationship between ideology and partisan identification. If a person feels that government should be used to resolve societal problems, then she might be drawn to the Democratic Party. If a person feels that government should have a limited role in society, then he might be attracted to the Republican Party.

> **Partisan Identification** The political party an individual most identifies with.

Research further suggests that positions on racial policies are also a defining difference between Republicans and Democrats. On issues of race, the current Republican Party is viewed by Blacks and other individuals as hostile to Blacks and other non-White groups, and the party has had a tortured history with race throughout most of the twentieth century. Republican presidents and presidential candidates from Herbert Hoover forward have employed a Southern strategy—using issues of race to bring former Southern White Democrats into the Republican Party—to move the party away from its image as the party of Lincoln (read as the party of Blacks) and to win elections.[57] Political scientist Tasha Philpot argues that modern Republican presidents from Ronald Reagan onward extended the Southern strategy past the Mason-Dixon line to exploit racial divisions among working- and middle-class White Democrats, pulling them into the Republican Party.[58]

The Democratic Party, in contrast, is perceived by Blacks and others as being more welcoming to and supportive of Blacks, although it has been criticized for taking Black voters for granted in past elections. The nomination and election of Barack Obama have reinforced the view of the Democrats as being more amenable and open to Blacks. President Lyndon B. Johnson's push for civil rights legislation during the 1960s resulted in another kind of "push": of White Democrats into the Republican Party. Even though not every Republican or Democrat fits these particular characterizations, the overall perception exists. Moreover, the perceptions were reinforced by the tenor and tone of the 2016 presidential election and the visual pictures presented by the national conventions of both parties. The Republican Party sent fewer Black delegates to the convention in 2016 than it had "at any point in the past century."[59] Less than one percent of delegates at the RNC were African American (only 18 out of 2,472).[60] Hispanic delegates made up a slightly higher percentage of delegates than African Americans.[61] There were at least 133 Hispanic delegates at the RNC.[62] In direct contrast to the 2016 Republican National Convention, half of the delegates at the Democratic National Convention were non-White. Twenty-five percent of delegates were Black, 16 percent Latino, and nine percent Asian American or Native American. According to the Clinton campaign, 1,182 delegates were Black, 747 were Latino, 292 were Asian America, and 147 were Native American.[63]

To recap, children initially adopt the political party identification and political views of their parents, and many will stick with those initial identifications. As people grow older, they might be attracted to the party opposite their parents' for a number of reasons. Political science research reports that some people will gravitate toward one party or another based on such factors as income, education, occupation, and place of residence. The factors mentioned earlier concerning which people are more likely to be Democrats and which are more likely to be Republicans are generalizations based on political science research. Clearly, there are individuals from high socioeconomic categories who are Democrats and from lower socioeconomic categories who are Republicans, but political science research has identified broad generalizations of which individuals are more likely to be attracted to one party or the other.[64]

The Media

The media strongly influence public opinion. Television, in particular, has become increasingly important in transmitting information. A Gallup poll taken in April 1937 reported that 91 percent of Americans said they read a newspaper daily. When questioned in April 1981 about their major source of news, 70 percent of respondents reported getting their news from daily newspapers. By July 1998, the percentage of Americans reporting that they got their news from daily newspapers had dropped to 50 percent.[65] A January 1999 survey by the Media Studies Center reported that 65 percent of those in the sample received most of their news from television and only 21 percent received their news from newspapers.[66] A 2012 survey of news consumption by the Pew Research Center found that 55 percent of their sample received their news from television and 50 percent indicated that they also got their news from online and digital sources, whereas only 29 percent read a newspaper for their news.[67] A 2013 Gallup survey also found that television was the main place Americans turned to for news about current events (55 percent), significantly ahead of the Internet at 18 percent. Television was the primary source of news for all age groups, although those aged 18 to 29 and 30 to 49 had lower percentages (50 percent), than those aged 50 to 64 (58 percent) and 65 and older (68 percent).[68]

Even though most people report getting their news from television, they do not always mean television news programs. Many indicate that they receive their news from entertainment shows such as *Saturday Night Live, Entertainment Tonight,* and *Inside Hollywood*.[69] It has also been suggested that young voters, eighteen to twenty-four years old, get their news from the late-night television talk shows such as *The Tonight Show Starring Jimmy Fallon, The Late Show with Stephen Colbert, Last Week Tonight with John Oliver* and *Politically Incorrect with Bill Maher*. A 2014 study from the University of Delaware found that on the issue of net neutrality, those who watched *The Daily Show, Colbert* and *Last Week Tonight with John Oliver* were more informed about the issue than those that watched cable news, read news online, or read newspapers.[70] In a 2014 Public Religion Research Institute and the Brookings Institution survey, Jon Stewart was viewed as a more trusted source of news than MSNBC.[71]

A 2016 survey by the Pew Research Center: Journalism and Media found that only 2 and 3 percent of respondents regularly learned something about the 2016 candidates and campaign from national or local daily newspapers, respectively, and 11 percent received their campaign news from the radio. Although more people received their news about the campaign from cable news programs (24 percent) than from nightly network news programs (10 percent), the percentage of people getting their campaign news from either cable or the network news programs had dropped significantly since 2000, when 48 percent of Americans got their campaign news from the local news programs and 45 percent got it from the networks. The number of people (27 percent) getting their campaign news from the Internet (combined social media and news website/app) in 2016 increased significantly from the 9 percent who had indicated the Internet was their main source of campaign news in 2000. Republicans are twice as likely as Democrats to say cable news is the most helpful with 2016 campaign news, while Democrats are slightly more likely to identify local news as their source. Late night comedy shows also have a partisan bent—three in ten Democrats indicate that these shows are one source of their political knowledge, but only 16 percent of Republicans and 25 percent of Independents identified them as such. About a third, 34 percent, of those aged eighteen to twenty-nine learned about the candidates and campaigns from late night comedy shows, the highest percentage of any group.[72]

What is interesting, however, especially in light of the emphasis placed on young voters during the 2008, 2012, and 2016 presidential elections, is that six in ten, 61 percent, of millennials (individuals born between 1981 to 1996) report getting political news on Facebook in a given week, a much larger percentage than mentioned any other news source. This is a major shift from the 2012 election when only 29 percent of people under age thirty were going

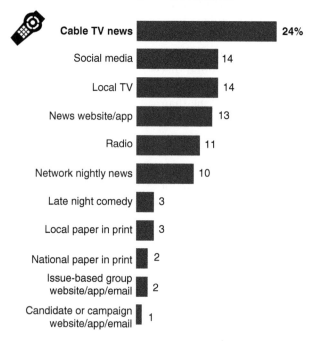

Vast majority of Americans learning about 2016 presidential election; cable news seen as most helpful source type

91% of U.S. adults learned about the 2016 presidential election in the past week

*Among those who learned about the election, % who name each source type as **most helpful***

- Cable TV news — **24%**
- Social media — 14
- Local TV — 14
- News website/app — 13
- Radio — 11
- Network nightly news — 10
- Late night comedy — 3
- Local paper in print — 3
- National paper in print — 2
- Issue-based group website/app/email — 2
- Candidate or campaign website/app/email — 1

Source: Survey conducted Jan 12–27, 2016

PEW RESEARCH CENTER

Figure 10.3 Where People Get Their Campaign News.
Source: Pew Research Center, January 12–27, 2016. http://www.journalism. org/2016/02/04/the-2016-presidential-campaign-a-news -event-thats-hard-to-miss/

Bradley Effect The difference between how Black candidates poll and how they perform at the ballot box (also called the Wilder effect).

online to get campaign news. This also stands in stark contrast to baby boomers (individuals born between 1946 to 1964) for whom local TV news, 60 percent, tops the list of sources for political news. Generation X, individuals born between 1965 and 1980, bridge the gap between millennials and baby boomers with about half (51 percent) indicating that they get political and government news on Facebook in a given week and a little less than half (46 percent) saying they do so from local TV.[73] Figure 10.3 shows data from the Pew Research Center indicating where people said they got their campaign news. We explore the role of media in political attitudes and effects much more in the following chapter.

The Bradley Effect

Throughout the 2008 presidential election, many journalists and even more political pundits began to speculate about whether the poll numbers for Senator Obama were an accurate reflection of how people felt or whether the **Bradley effect**—the difference between how Black candidates poll and how they perform at the ballot box—was in play. The term stems from the 1982 run of Los Angeles mayor Tom Bradley for governor of California. The polls indicated that Bradley was significantly ahead of his opponent heading into the election, and even exit polling indicated that Bradley was going to win. Yet Bradley lost by a narrow margin, which raised the question of a subtle anti-Black bias among White voters who were unwilling to tell pollsters that they would not vote for a Black man.

The Bradley effect, sometimes also called the Wilder effect, was present in the 1989 gubernatorial race in Virginia, in which L. Douglas Wilder, a Black candidate, was fifteen percentage points ahead two weeks before the election, but won by just 6,582 votes out of the 1.7 million cast.[74] Once again, the explanation for Wilder's underperformance in actual ballots versus people who said they were going to vote for him was the anti-Black bias of some White voters and their unwillingness to admit it to pollsters.

The influence of racial attitudes on White voting patterns is one that political scientists grapple with and the question that news media hyped during the 2008 election. Were the poll numbers for Barack Obama real? Or were they an artifact of some White voters not wanting to say that they would not vote for a Black candidate? Political scientist Daniel J. Hopkins explored the question of the Bradley/Wilder effect on elections with Black candidates running against White candidates to see if it was still present in electoral races. His results suggested that the Bradley/Wilder effect was present in a number of political contests throughout the 1980s and 1990s, but that since then, it appears to be dissipating in some instances or disappearing altogether in others.[75]

Until more research is conducted, we will not know if the Bradley/Wilder effect is truly gone, as race is still a potent factor in American politics. In the case of President Obama, evidence suggests that the Bradley/Wilder effect was not in play. The final average of all of the tracking polls reported by RealClear Politics had Senator Obama at 52.1 percent to Senator McCain's 44.5 percent. The final results of the presidential election were Senator Obama at 52.9 percent and Senator McCain at 45.6 percent. In this instance, Obama's vote total tracked very close to his standing in the polls on the day of the election.

The 2012 exit polls did show a racial dimension in voting. Romney took the majority of the White vote (59 percent), Obama took 93 percent of the Black vote, 71 percent of the Latino vote, and 73 percent of the Asian vote. These numbers coupled with the smaller portion of the White vote (39 percent) secured Obama's clear and substantive victory over Romney. Obama had a higher proportion of the White vote in 2008 (43 percent) than he did in 2012 (39 percent).

Public Opinion and Politics

Public opinion is a central element of politics in the American political system and serves many purposes. First, it reflects the degree of public support for government actions. Public officials recognize that some government actions need the support of the public to succeed. Moreover, the loss of public support for a government action might signal declining political fortunes for elected officials. For example, as a result of negative public opinion, President Ronald Reagan's administration had to back off of a proposal to classify catsup as a vegetable so that it could cut funding for the federal school lunch program in 1981. In 2008, President George W. Bush's administration backed away from its decision to allow increased levels of arsenic in drinking water.[76]

Second, public opinion serves as an effective check on political leadership because it can often keep politicians from gathering too much political power or from making decisions or policies that are contrary to the public will.[77] Public opinion can influence politicians who show poor judgment or who are incompetent or corrupt to resign their offices.[78] For example, President Richard Nixon's presidential approval ratings declined steadily from his highest rating of 67 percent in the last week of January 1973 to a low of 24 percent in the second week of August 1974 when he resigned.[79] Although public opinion was not the only influential factor in Nixon's decision to resign, it played a key role because it indicated that Nixon could not survive the Watergate scandal and his involvement in covering it up.

Although not necessarily leading to resignation, falling approval ratings can severely curtail a president's political influence. Such was the case with President George W. Bush. President Bush's approval ratings were in the high 80s right after the terrorist attack on September 11, 2001. They declined somewhat in early 2003, but spiked again with the invasion of Iraq. Unfortunately, as the Iraq war dragged on and more information was revealed about the administration's manipulation of the American public with false claims of Iraqi stockpiles of weapons of mass destruction, President Bush's approval rating sank to almost 25 percent. As his term ended, his approval ratings dipped below that of President Nixon twenty-seven years earlier.

Third, during elections candidates and political parties do extensive polling to find out which candidates are running ahead and which policy positions taken by the candidates resonate with voters. Few politicians today will embark on major public policy initiatives without first knowing how the public might react to them. Critics often charge that "governing by polls" reduces innovativeness in public policy and diminishes a political leader's willingness to make difficult and unpopular decisions.[80] In response, those in public office say that knowing how the public will react to a decision, particularly an unpopular one, provides them with advance warning and allows them to prepare the public for an unfavorable decision.

Candidates for political office, especially for president, rely heavily on polling to fine-tune or retool their campaign message and strategies. In the 2008 presidential race, Senator McCain changed campaign strategies and messages in the face of polling data indicating that Americans wanted change and therefore that he would have to appeal to that sentiment if he were going to be successful.

But sometimes polls can be misleading. Late in the campaign, McCain, in an October 26, 2008, appearance on *Meet the Press*, confidently indicated that his campaign was doing fine and that he was going to win. This statement resulted from internal campaign polling that indicated he was only 4 percentage points behind Senator Obama in the presidential campaign.[81] Public opinion polling is now a staple of political campaigns and has fluctuated from year to year in its accuracy and predictive capacity.

Finally, in a representative democracy like the United States, public opinion provides a gauge of how people feel about their government and their institutions. Public opinion might reflect support for the actions of government or a distrust of government and those who run it. Public opinion is also a way for the American public to influence the issues and the behaviors of elected officials.[82]

Conclusion

Public opinion is an essential part of the U.S. political process. On the one side, it is used by politicians to gauge public support for or disapproval of particular policies and to gauge their own standing with the public. It also serves as a barometer of how well candidates' campaigns are faring. On the other side, individuals see public opinion polls as a measure of how well their politicians are doing or as a mechanism for the collective public to let politicians know how the electorate feels about policy issues. Yet the factors that help form public opinion are complex and varied. The opening vignette highlighted racial differences on the question of affirmative action.

This chapter has explored the importance of public opinion to democracy and how concern about public opinion has been a part of the U.S. political system since the beginning of the nation. The measuring of public opinion is a precise and scientific process, and much of what are called public opinion surveys are really only the opinions of individuals who are willing to participate in online ballots. The material presented in this chapter has given a broad overview of public opinion and the process of gathering data and identifying attitudes and behaviors of the American public.

As the opening vignette illustrated, racial dimensions and divisions exist on important issues within the American electorate. Race, gender, and the intersection of the two produce differences in public opinion that are often not identified in general discussions and presentations of public opinion. Yet race, gender, and other factors play a major role in the formation of what people think and why they feel the way they do. Taking those differences into account presents a broader picture of the variety of public opinion in the American political system and how those varied factors affect what people think about issues.

REVIEW QUESTIONS

1. Why is public opinion important to a representative democracy?
2. What factors influence the formation of public opinion?
3. How do race and gender affect the formation of public opinion, and why do different groups have such different opinions on key issues?

4. What is survey research?
5. What is the Bradley effect?

KEY TERMS

Bradley Effect p. 326
Gender p. 316
Gender Gap p. 316
Partisan Identification p. 323

Political Culture p. 302
Political Socialization p. 303
Probability Sampling p. 308
Public Opinion p. 299

Quota Sampling p. 307
Sample p. 306
Sampling Error p. 308
Survey Research p. 305

readings

ADDITIONAL READINGS _____

Herbert Asher, *Polling and the Public: What Every Citizen Should Know,* 7th ed. (Washington, DC: Congressional Quarterly Press, 2007).

> This book is an introduction to the philosophy, mechanics, and interpretation of public opinion polling and polls.

Carroll J. Glynn, Susan Herbst, Mark Lindeman, Garrett J. O'Keefe, and Robert Y. Shapiro, *Public* (Boulder, CO: Westview Press, 2004).

> This book is a comprehensive and interdisciplinary examination of public opinion formation and change. It analyzes the nature of political and social attitudes in the United States.

Melissa Harris-Lacewell, *Barbershops, Bibles, and BET: Everyday Talk and Black Political Thought* (Princeton, NJ: Princeton University Press, 2004).

> This book examines the multiple venues and influences that shape African American political and social opinions.

Virginia Sapiro and Shauna L. Shames, "The Gender Basis of Public Opinion," in *Understanding Public Opinion*, 3rd edition, ed. Barbara Norrander and Clyde Wilcox (Washington, DC: Congressional Quarterly Press, 2009).

> This chapter provides an excellent overview of the role of gender in public opinion formation, the gender gap, and how gender roles, gender identities, and gender stereotyping affect public opinion.

Howard Schumann, Charlotte Steeh, Lawrence Bobo, and Maria Krysan, *Racial Attitudes in America: Trends and Interpretations* (Cambridge, MA: Harvard University Press, 1997).

> This book examines the trends in Black and White public opinion from the 1940s through the late 1990s.

CHAPTER 11

The Media: Reinforcing Racial Stereotypes?

Comedian and television host Larry Wilmore waves after he was introduced as the main speaker at the White House Correspondents' Association Dinner on April 30, 2016, as First Lady Michelle Obama looks on. This event often features comedians who make fun of presidents, the media, and politics. Wilmore's presentation was especially controversial because of his blunt language on race, including calling President Obama "my ni**a."

Since the early 1900s, the White House Correspondents' Association (WHCA) has represented the journalists who cover the White House, and it now numbers approximately 250 people. Beginning in May of 1921 the WHCA has held the annual White House Correspondents' Dinner as a social event. In 1924 President Calvin Coolidge became the first president to attend the dinner. Since then, the dinner has grown tremendously, with 2,600 people attending. Each year a famous entertainer performs at the dinner, and the entire nation can view the event on C-SPAN.[1]

Frequently the entertainment at the dinner features comedians who make fun of the president, the media, and politics in general. In 2016, comedian Larry Wilmore was the main speaker at the WHCA dinner. Wilmore, who is African American, hosted the late night political comedy show *The Nightly Show*, which at the time aired on the cable channel Comedy Central—it was recently cancelled. On *The Nightly Show* Wilmore made fun of political issues, focusing extensively on issues of race and ethnicity.[2] Wilmore's speech at the 2016 WHCA featured typical jokes that made fun of President Obama's failure to close Guantanamo prison and his use of drone strikes to combat terrorists (see Chapters 4 and 6 respectively). However, much of Wilmore's speech addressed issues of race in an especially controversial manner. He opened his speech by saying. "Welcome to 'Negro Night' here at the Washington Hilton, or as FOX News will report, 'Two Thugs Disrupt Elegant Dinner in D.C.'" Wilmore was referring to the fact that both he and President Obama are Black and that Fox News, a conservative cable news channel, reports the news in a manner that paints racial and ethnic minorities, particularly President Obama, in a negative light. Later in the presentation, Wilmore referenced the fact that former Republican presidential candidate Ben Carson, who is Black, had praised former President Andrew Jackson, who had owned slaves. Wilmore stated, "From the grave, Andrew Jackson replied 'What did that j**aboo say?'" The word Wilmore used is an offensive term applied to African Americans. Wilmore closed his speech, stating, "Words alone do me no justice. So, Mr. President, if I'm going to keep it 100: Yo, Barry, you did it, my ni**a. You did it." Wilmore's choice of words and blunt discussion of race was extremely controversial. The attendees generally did not laugh at Wilmore's jokes, and, in fact, many of them groaned and booed.[3]

The bulk of the reaction to Wilmore's presentation focused on his use of the word "ni**a" in reference to and in front of the nation's first Black president. Many people of all races found it to be offensive, but others viewed it as a commentary on how the media and politicians have treated President Obama. After his performance, Wilmore distinguished between the use of the "N word" ending in "a" versus ending in "er." The "er" usage was the term Whites had used for many years to denigrate African Americans, whereas the "a" usage is common among African Americans because, according to Wilmore, it "takes the power out of the word."[4]

intro

The controversy over Larry Wilmore's WHCA Dinner speech demonstrates the importance of the mass media in American politics. The **mass media** *are those sources of information, including print, radio, television, and the Internet, that reach a significant number of people. Although the scope of the media includes nonpolitical news, entertainment, and sports, it also focuses on politics. The mass media's coverage of politics influences how the public perceives political events, which, in turn can influence how political leaders view those events.*

The media's ability to shape how viewers perceive political events and issues is known as **framing**.[5] *One of Larry Wilmore's jokes focused on how conservative cable news channel Fox News frames stories about race and ethnicity in a negative light. One notable example, among numerous examples, of where Fox News framed stories about race occurred in 2011 after President Obama invited hip-hop artist Common to a White House poetry reading. Fox News claimed that the nation's first Black president had inappropriately invited a "vile rapper" who hates law enforcement to the White House. However, Common's music generally fosters a positive social message, including speaking out against police brutality. In fact, a couple of years before president Obama invited Common to the White House, Fox News had actually praised him.[6]*

Moreover, this story reveals the significance of newer media and the conflation of media and entertainment. Traditionally, newspapers covered politics, and during the twentieth century broadcast radio and television emerged as important. However, by the turn of the twenty-first century, politically biased cable news stations, such as Fox, which advocates a conservative view, and MSNBC, which advocates a liberal view, as well as entertainment shows, such as Wilmore's The Nightly Show, *became major sources from which people receive political information. Moreover, entertainers such as Larry Wilmore, Jon Stewart, John Oliver, and Stephen Colbert, have engaged in serious journalism and affected the news. Wilmore's use of the "N word" itself became a significant focus of the news. Additionally, new social media, such as Facebook and Twitter, have emerged in the twenty-first century as key sources of information, especially for young people. Social media sites featured heavy coverage of Wilmore's speech.[7]*

Mass Media Sources of information, including print, radio, television, and the Internet, that reach a large number of people.

Framing The media's ability to shape how viewers interpret political events and issues.

Finally, this story also reveals the key role that race and ethnicity plays in the mass media. Although President Obama's agenda has centered on nonracial issues, such as health care, economic stimulus, and foreign policy, the fact remains that as the nation's first Black president, issues of race are still extremely relevant. Larry Wilmore sought to point out how other politicians have treated—and how the media has covered—President Obama's race, and he chose to employ the controversial use of a severe racial epithet to make his point.

This chapter covers the mass media and politics. We begin by tracing the history of the media's coverage of politics, focusing on the different types of media that have emerged. Then we address the media industry, examining the owners of media outlets and the profession of journalism. The chapter then discusses the media's coverage of elections and government officials and institutions. Throughout this chapter, we examine how the politics of race and ethnicity intersects with the politics of the mass media.

A History of Media and Politics

The relationship between government and the media has continually changed throughout American history, especially as technological advancements have altered the way in which the media transmit information to the public. Here we look at the evolution of print media from the early years of the Republic through the twenty-first century, and we discuss the impact that newspapers, radio, broadcast television, cable television, the Internet, and social media have exerted on politics.

Agenda Setting The media's power to influence the importance that the public places on issues.

We also investigate the key role the media play in **agenda setting**.[8] That is, the media are powerful because when the press chooses to focus on particular issues, the public tends to think those issues are important. Thus, the media's power of agenda setting, as well as of framing, affects minority-group politics.

Print Media

During the early years of the American Republic, newspapers were highly biased and opinionated; they made no pretense of reporting the news and political issues in an objective fashion. As a result, newspapers were instrumental in shaping public opinion during the American Revolution and during debates over ratification of the Constitution. As political parties developed during the early nineteenth century (see Chapter 14), each political party controlled at least one newspaper that exclusively contained favorable coverage of its own politicians and unfavorable coverage of the opposition. Moreover, interest groups and religious organizations of that era published newspapers to expound their political and social views. In contrast, another kind of newspaper, known as the **penny press**, covered human interest stories, rather than political issues, in an attempt to attract readers.

Penny Press Nineteenth-century newspapers that eschewed coverage of politics and instead focused on human interest stories.

The early nineteenth-century media covered issues of race and ethnicity. Penny presses were especially interested in the Mexican-American War, and much of their coverage perpetuated negative stereotypes of Mexicans. The penny press and popular novels of the late 1840s depicted Mexicans as inferior to Whites and in need of Whites to civilize them, a portrayal that increased public support for the Mexican-American War and fomented anti-Mexican prejudice.[9]

During this era, abolitionists relied heavily on the use of the media to advocate an end to slavery. In 1821, Quaker abolitionist Benjamin Lundy founded a newspaper called *The Genius of Universal Emancipation*, which recounted the horrors of slavery and the slave trade. The paper advocated for gradual abolition and recolonization of the slaves. William Lloyd Garrison, another abolitionist, joined Lundy's paper, but Garrison assumed the more radical position of immediate abolition and integration of the former slaves into American society. Garrison later formed his own newspaper, *The Liberator*, which was the most influential abolitionist periodical. *The Liberator* published accounts of the horrors of slavery, as well as morally persuasive pieces that convinced many Americans to join the abolitionist cause (see "Our Voices: *The Liberator* and Abolitionism" on page 337). When emancipating the slaves, President Abraham Lincoln cited the influence of Garrison.[10]

Garrison's paper also inspired former slave and antislavery advocate Frederick Douglass to start his own abolitionist newspaper, called the *North Star*, out of Rochester, New York. Like *The Liberator*, the *North Star* advocated abolition, but it took more radical positions for the time, such as suggesting that Blacks arm themselves, and supporting women's rights. The *North Star* was especially important because it was the first major U.S. newspaper operated by an African American. In fact, not only did free Blacks in the North read Douglass's paper, but also many Whites read it. Douglass's success set a crucial example that Blacks were capable of significant intellectual achievement.[11]

By the late nineteenth century, many newspapers were engaging in **yellow journalism**, which consisted of sensationalist reports intended to titillate the masses to sell papers and advertising space. Yellow journalism papers focused on crime and vice stories, perpetuated scientific hoaxes, and offered bogus "miracle cures." They often distorted facts to make stories more enticing, especially when perpetuating stereotypes and influencing public opinion about issues of race and ethnicity. For example, William Randolph Hearst's *San Francisco Examiner*, an early yellow journalism paper, often referred to Chinese and Japanese immigrants in highly unflattering terms. Hearst suggested that Asian immigrants stole jobs from hard-working, honest White laborers. The paper also falsely claimed that Chinese and Japanese immigrants caused crime, gambling, prostitution, and opium addiction.[12]

Other newspapers such as *The New York Times* pursued a different type of journalism by focusing primarily on disseminating accurate information. This more objective press relegated opinion to the editorial pages and eschewed crass gossip or human interest stories. Yet even these so-called objective newspapers still perpetuated stereotypes of racial and ethnic minorities. For example, *The New York Times* referred to Indian tribes that tried to assimilate into

Yellow Journalism A form of journalism popular during the late eighteenth and early nineteenth centuries that sensationalized stories and distorted facts to sell more papers.

Nineteenth-century newspapers were instrumental in perpetuating racial and ethnic stereotypes. This picture, from an 1880 edition of *Frank Leslie's Illustrated*, depicts a Chinese "heathen" laughing at another person's misfortune. These types of images created the unfair stereotype of Chinese immigrants as alien and untrustworthy.

Parallel Press Newspapers and other forms of media geared toward specific racial and ethnic minority groups.

White culture as "semi-civilized" and tribes that did not assimilate as "wild and predatory."[13]

By the turn of the twentieth century, journalism had become a major industry, with the print media expanding tremendously throughout the United States. Every city, every town, and even many rural areas had their own daily newspaper, and many cities had two major daily newspapers. Technological advances such as the telephone and photography enhanced newspapers' ability to report events and the quality of their presentation. Moreover, during this print media explosion, weekly news magazines such as *Time* and *Newsweek* emerged. These periodicals summarized the events of the week and offered editorial opinions through syndicated columnists.

Part of the twentieth-century print media explosion consisted of the growth of the **parallel press**, or newspapers that advocated on behalf of specific racial or ethnic minority groups. Minorities who published parallel press newspapers sought to counteract the stereotypical portrayal of minorities in the White press. The parallel press traced its roots to the nineteenth century, but these publications proliferated during the twentieth century. Many White newspapers and journalists dismissed the parallel press as inferior to the White newspapers, but during the twentieth century the parallel press was instrumental in inspiring activism on behalf of Blacks, Latinos, Asian Americans, and American Indians.

There are too many examples of the parallel press to recount all of them here, but some leading publications stand out. Ida Wells-Barnett published the *Memphis Free Speech*, which spoke out against the lynching of African Americans and pushed for anti-lynching legislation. The *Chicago Defender*, established by Robert Abbott in 1905, became a leading force in journalism. Whereas other Black newspapers included human interest stories, Abbott sought to raise the intellectual level of his newspaper, and he wanted it to be an instrument for improving the lives of Blacks. Most notably, the *Chicago Defender*'s circulation reached the South, and Abbott explicitly encouraged Black Southerners to migrate to Northern cities, where they would face less discrimination and enjoy more economic opportunity. To this day, the *Chicago Defender* is still a leading African American newspaper in the United States.[14]

Latino newspapers during the nineteenth century focused on issues pertaining to Latino immigrants. The earliest Spanish-language newspapers were founded in San Francisco in the 1850s after many Mexicans immigrated to northern California in search of gold and the United States had conquered

our voices

The Liberator and Abolitionism

William Lloyd Garrison is one of the most well-known abolitionists, and he spread his views by publishing *The Liberator*. Like many of the partisan presses of the early nineteenth century, Garrison's *The Liberator* convinced people to support the immediate abolition of slavery. Garrison's publication often took radical stances on abolition, chastising both the slave trade and moderate abolitionists.

The excerpt here comes from the first edition of *The Liberator*, published on January 1, 1831. Garrison was fined for libel because of an earlier depiction of the slave trade, and the court would have waived the penalty if Garrison had apologized to the ship's owner, Francis Todd. However, Garrison refused to apologize. Instead, he devoted his first edition of *The Liberator* to justifying his actions by reprinting his depiction of the slave trade. Although Garrison started his newspaper with no subscribers, the power of this account garnered 450. The writing style is different from that of contemporary media, but the tone of this piece is similar to that of many opinionated blogs of the contemporary era.

> The ship . . . sailed a few weeks since from this port with a cargo of slaves for the New Orleans market. . . . I am determined to cover with thick infamy all who are concerned in this nefarious business. I have stated that the ship *Francis* hails from my native place, Newburyport (Massachusetts), is commanded by a Yankee captain, and owned by a townsman named Francis Todd. . . . It is no worse to fit out practical cruisers, or to engage in the foreign slave trade, than to pursue a similar trade along our coast; and the men who have the wickedness to participate therein, for the purpose of heaping up wealth, should be sentenced to solitary confinement for life;

they are the enemies of our own species—highway robbers and murderers; and their final doom will be, unless they speedily repent, to occupy the lowest depths of perdition. I know that the man who is allowed to freight his vessel with slaves at home, for a distant market, would be thought worthy of death if he should take a similar freight on the coast or Africa; but I know, too, that this distinction is absurd, and at war with the common sense of mankind, and that God and good men regard it with abhorrence. I recollect that it was always a mystery in Newburyport how Mr. Todd contrived to make profitable voyages to New Orleans and other places, when other merchants, with as fair an opportunity to make money, and sending at the same ports at the same time, invariably made fewer speculations. The mystery seems to be unraveled. Any man can gather up riches, if he does not care by what means they are obtained. The *Francis* carried off seventy-five slaves, chained in a narrow place between decks. Captain Brown originally intended to take one hundred and fifty of these unfortunate creatures; but another hard-hearted ship-master underbid him in the piece of passage for the remaining moiety. Captain B., we believe, is a mason. Where was his charity or brotherly kindness? I respectfully request the editor of the *Newburyport Herald* to copy this article, or publish a statement of the facts contained herein—not for the purpose of giving information to Mr. Todd, for I shall send him a copy of this number, but in order to enlighten the public mind in that quarter.

Source: Adapted from Truman Nelson, ed., *Documents of Upheaval: Selections from William Lloyd Garrison's* The Liberator, *1831–1865* (New York: Hill and Wang, 1966), 1–3.

what is now the southwestern portion of the United States (see Chapter 5). These papers, such as *Sud Americano*, reported the news from the immigrants' home countries. Other Spanish-language papers were concerned with issues facing immigrants in the United States. In the Los Angeles area, *El Heraldo de México* focused on the rights of immigrant laborers, whereas *El Espectador* argued that immigrants should assimilate into White society. Asian American parallel press publications concentrated mainly on news relevant to the

A stack of *Diario Las Américas* newspapers as they are prepared for delivery in Miami, FL. *Diario Las Américas* is one of multiple examples of the media explosion of the parallel press.

immigrants' country of origin, but during the twentieth century they also examined issues pertaining to life in the United States.[15]

Tribal newspapers report on the news relating to each tribe. Most were sponsored by tribal governments, but more recent independent papers criticized tribal governments and institutions, as well as the U.S. government. Pan-Indian newspapers dealt with issues affecting American Indians throughout the United States. Some Indian parallel press publications advocated assimilation with Whites, whereas others more stridently called for preserving tribal identity.[16]

Broadcast Radio and Television

The invention of broadcast technology greatly changed the influence of the media. Although first invented in 1906, radio broadcasting did not flourish until the 1920s, when the economy boomed and the price of radios dropped significantly. Impressed by radio's ability to transmit voices across the nation in seconds, political leaders used the medium to communicate with the American public. President Franklin Delano Roosevelt shrewdly recognized the importance of radio for building public support. During the Great Depression, Roosevelt's radio addresses, known as fireside chats, calmed a nervous population.[17]

Although television began as an entertainment medium, by the 1950s it had become a major factor in political journalism. Not only could Americans hear the news while it occurred; they also could see it. The 1952 election demonstrated television's importance in politics. Presidential candidate Dwight D. Eisenhower aired catchy advertisements on television stations,[18] and television stations covered the campaign and election results. Television's importance in the 1952 election prompted networks to launch fifteen-minute nightly newscasts, which were later expanded to thirty minutes.

Television's ability to bring moving pictures into people's living rooms influenced Americans' attitudes on major political issues during the 1960s, such as the Vietnam War, cultural changes, and, most notably, civil rights for racial and ethnic minorities. Many White Americans were not familiar with the extent of the oppression that minorities, especially Southern Blacks, endured. Television coverage of key civil rights events, such as sit-ins and integration of schools, introduced Whites to the salience of the issue.

Two televised events in particular were instrumental in shaping public opinion about the Civil Rights Movement. Television stations widely covered the 1963 March on Washington. Millions of Americans witnessed the widespread support for civil rights among Blacks and Whites, as well as Dr. Martin Luther King, Jr.'s historic "I Have a Dream" speech. Furthermore, televised coverage of the police brutality inflicted on civil rights protesters in Alabama alerted previously uninformed Americans to the severe injustices that Blacks suffered. Civil rights activist and current member of the U.S. House of Representatives John Lewis (D-GA), who was beaten by police and Klansmen numerous times during the early 1960s, credits televised coverage of that police brutality with increasing public support for the Voting Rights Act of 1965.[19]

There are, however, systematic studies that dispute the notion that the media helped the cause of civil rights. The Kerner Commission, which

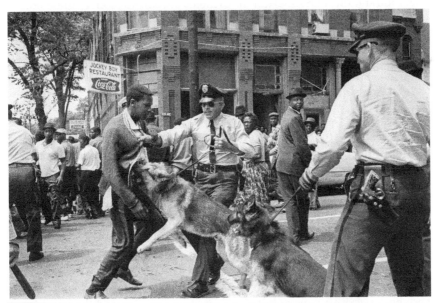

This 1963 picture of police attacking a peaceful civil rights protestor made the front page of major national newspapers, such as *The New York Times*. As a result, the American public, as well as President Kennedy, recognized the brutal treatment of African Americans in the South, thus demonstrating the media's agenda-setting power.

investigated the causes of racially oriented civil unrest during the late 1960s, blamed the media for their failure to report on the problems of discrimination against Blacks and for their reinforcement of negative stereotypes. Scholarly research further shows that in some non-Southern cities, such as Los Angeles, the coverage of civil rights actually declined during the 1960s— at the height of the Civil Rights Movement. Other research has found that when Northern newspapers and television stations did cover civil rights, the tone of the reporting was not positive toward the movement. Newspapers often referred to the protesters as "outside agitators" or "communists," and some media coverage even reinforced stereotypes of Blacks as angry and uncivilized.[20]

Similar to the parallel press in the print media, there are minority-owned radio and television stations that can influence the coverage of minority-group politics. Black Entertainment Television (BET) is primarily an entertainment-oriented television network that since 1980 has emphasized cultural issues, but it also covers news events that are important to Blacks. However, in 2000 BET was sold to media corporation Viacom.[21] Likewise, Univision is a Spanish-language television network that appeals to Latinos, and it provides its own Spanish-language news program, *Noticiero Univision.*[22]

Cable and Satellite

Technological advances during the late twentieth century generated an expansion of media outlets. The use of satellites has greatly expanded the number of television stations that American households are able to receive. Some households have their own satellite receivers, and others subscribe to cable companies that transmit through cable hookups. Cable and satellite television can provide a wide variety of channels, including news channels, to the American public along with expanded news coverage. Conversely, broadcast media have limited space for news stations.

Cable and satellite television have tremendously altered the way in which the media cover politics. Launched in 1980, CNN provides nonstop news coverage and public affairs programming. Whereas network news stations usually wait until the evening to report the day's events, CNN broadcasts stories as they happen and provides continual coverage. Other cable and satellite news stations, such as MSNBC and Fox, followed CNN's lead, thus expanding the number of cable news channels. Recent evidence demonstrates that people who view cable news spend twice as much time watching the news as do people who view broadcast news stations.[23]

Another important cable and satellite station is C-SPAN, which provides live coverage of the U.S. House and U.S. Senate. Three C-SPAN stations carry floor debates, committee hearings, markup sessions, and press conferences, and the network also airs public affairs programming beyond the activities of Congress. C-SPAN is most significant because Americans have an opportunity to follow the activities of their elected representatives, and it lets representatives communicate directly with their constituents.[24]

Since the late twentieth century, cable and satellite television have been instrumental in framing of issues relevant to minority-group politics. Because there are a large number of cable news outlets, each channel (even each program) has specific ideological slants and political focuses. Accordingly, there is ample space for programming that deals with issues pertaining to minority-group politics.

For example, former CNN and current Fox Business News television host Lou Dobbs focuses on illegal immigration. According to the Fox Business News website, the host of the program is an award-winning journalist who is supported by a wide variety of groups across the political spectrum.[25] But according to the Southern Poverty Law Center (SPLC), an organization that tracks the activities of racists and hate groups, a number of Lou Dobbs's guests on his CNN show made overtly prejudiced claims about Latinos, as well as about Blacks and other minorities. The SPLC reports that some of Dobbs's guests are connected to White supremacist groups, such as the Council of Conservative Citizens. Dobbs never divulged these guests' racist views and treated these individuals as heroes of the working class.[26]

More remarkably, as the opening vignette demonstrates, cable and satellite television entertainment shows, such as *The Nightly Show*, have provided some of the most serious news coverage. Although he was not the first host of Comedy Central's *The Daily Show*, comedian Jon Stewart advanced the idea of mixing late-night comedy entertainment with news. Stewart offered a humorous take on the news that has provided some of the most significant analysis of key events in the 2000s and 2010s, such as the war in Iraq, the economic collapse of 2008, and the Obama presidency. In 2015 Stewart left the show and was replaced with Trevor Noah, a South African comedian who is half Black and half White. At the same time, Comedy Central also

Robert Johnson, the founder of Black Entertainment Television (BET). Johnson started BET in 1980 as the first Black-owned and Black-themed television station. Over the next two decades Johnson oversaw BET's tremendous growth, as the station expanded beyond entertainment to cover matters of political and social importance to African Americans and other minority groups. Johnson served as a rare exception to the White dominance of the media industry. In 2000, Johnson sold BET to media conglomerate Viacom, and as a result he became the first African American billionaire. Since then, he has branched into other ventures, such as hotel management and co-owning the Charlotte Bobcats of the National Basketball Association.

aired *The Colbert Report*, featuring comedian and actor Stephen Colbert's portrayal of an obnoxious right-wing pundit, but it offered an ironic twist on key news events. Colbert ended the *Colbert Report* in 2015 to become the host of *The Late Show* on CBS, replacing the venerable David Letterman. Colbert continues to provide humorous accounts of key news events, particularly the 2016 election, but he no longer plays the conservative media pundit character. Comedy Central replaced the *Colbert Report* with Larry Wilmore's *The Nightly Show*; Wilmore had previously been the "Senior Black Correspondent" on the *Daily Show*. In 2016 the Comedy Central canceled *The Nightly Show*.

These late night comedy shows have heavily criticized the "legitimate" media for their failure to report accurately or deeply on current events. Moreover, the presence of these two shows on cable and satellite television means that viewers, especially younger ones, have access to as much insightful analysis of current events as the serious media outlets offer. In October 2010 both Stewart and Colbert organized a "Rally to Restore Sanity," where about 200,000 people converged on the Mall in Washington, DC. Their rally was held in response to conservative media personality Glen Beck's "Rally to Restore Honor," and it criticized media sensationalism of political differences and urged people to engage in reasoned political discourse.[27] A humorist offering insightful commentary on politics is not a new phenomenon in American culture, and scholars regard Stewart and Colbert as contemporary versions of Benjamin Franklin and Mark Twain.[28]

The Internet and Social Media

Because an increasing number of Americans, especially younger ones, rely on the Internet, it has become a significant medium for transmitting news. Internet news sites such as Politico.com are now competitive with major cable and broadcast television news stations for reporting and analyzing political news. In fact, even traditional media outlets, such as magazines, newspapers, broadcast television networks, and cable channels, have their own websites. Since 2000 the Internet has evolved and produced innovative ways to influence politics. For example, YouTube allows people to upload videos, and then any user

Trevor Noah as host of *The Daily Show*. Noah, who is multiracial, replaced Jon Stewart as host of this late night comedy show. Noah provides a humorous take on news events, especially those concerning race and ethnicity, such as police shootings of unarmed African Americans and Republican presidential candidate Donald Trump's bigoted statements against Latinos and Muslims.

can access those videos. Since Barack Obama was elected president, he has delivered a weekly radio address through YouTube, and the White House has its own YouTube channel.[29]

The importance of YouTube for minority-group politics became evident during the 2006 Virginia Senate election, which featured Republican incumbent George Allen against Democratic challenger Jim Webb. Allen was heavily favored for reelection, and he was even touted as a leading candidate for the 2008 Republican presidential nomination. However, in summer 2006 Allen confronted a Webb volunteer named S. R. Siddarth who was videotaping one of Allen's rallies. Siddarth was a college student born in the United States, but Allen emphasized Siddarth's Indian heritage during their confrontation. Allen referred to Siddarth as "macaca," which is an archaic pejorative applied to people of South Asian descent, and Allen "welcomed" the native-born Siddarth to America. Siddarth videotaped Allen's offensive, prejudiced tirade, and the Webb campaign downloaded the video to YouTube. After the video of Allen spread throughout the Internet, the mainstream news channels reported the story, and as a result of the negative publicity, Allen narrowly lost the election and never launched a campaign for the presidency.[30]

A specific kind of Internet site known as a **Blog**, short for "web log," has also influenced politics during the past few years. A blog is a web diary that provides other content, such as videos and links to other websites and blogs, and the authors (or bloggers) update their site frequently and allow other users to post comments. Many blogs are politically oriented, such as the DailyKos, which expresses liberal views, and Redstate.com, which expresses conservative views.[31]

The parallel press also uses the Internet to communicate with the public. For example, the *Chicago Defender*, a venerated parallel press newspaper, now has a website that covers local (Chicago), state (Illinois), national, and international news important to African Americans. Unlike the newspaper version, the *Chicago Defender* website is updated frequently, and readers are able to provide their opinions on key news events.[32] Furthermore, there are a number of blogs dedicated to minority-group politics, such as Afro-Netizen (http://afronetizen.blogs.com), LatinoPoliticsBlog (http://latinopoliticsblog.com), and the Asian American Action Fund (http://www.aaa-fund.com/?page_id=9769).

Not all Internet news comes from professional media outlets. Much of the Internet is not professionally supervised, and any person possesses the ability to broadcast his or her often uninformed opinion as news. Unlike the more professional media sources (e.g., newspapers, broadcast, and cable), websites, blogs, and even purveyors of email rumors do not necessarily check the accuracy of their stories. Many unsubstantiated Internet stories have affected politics, especially on matters of race and ethnicity. Racially motivated, baseless Internet rumors concerning President Obama have been prevalent since he commenced his presidential campaign. These rumors claim, for example, that he is a secret Muslim; that he is not a legitimate president because he was born

Blog A website in which the operator states his or her opinion, allows readers to post comments, and provides links to news stories and other blogs.

in Kenya; and that he even appeared in the 1993 video for the hip-hop hit, "Whoomp! (There It Is)."[33]

Social media, such as Facebook and Instagram, are extremely relevant in American politics. These Internet sites allow people with similar interests or even groups of friends to share information, photographs, games, and videos with one another. A similar site is Twitter, which allows someone to post small messages (up to 140 characters long). Interested people can follow that person's messages throughout the course of the day. Many ordinary citizens have used this newest form of media to express their political views. Moreover, President Obama, presidential candidates, members of Congress, interest groups, and even mainstream media outlets are on Facebook and Twitter. Social media, as well as cell phones and YouTube, were instrumental communication tools among the youth activists in the Arab Spring, grassroots revolts against longtime dictators in Arab nations Egypt, Libya, Tunisia, and others.[34]

By the 2010s social media has emerged as a significant source of news for Americans. According to a recent survey 10 percent of American adults receive their news from Twitter, and over 40 percent of American adults receive their news from Facebook. The same survey shows that younger people are considerably more likely than middle-age and older adults to receive their news from social media. Interestingly, there is no difference in social media news consumption between Whites and minorities.[35] Another survey reveals that for the 2016 election, 24 percent of the public receive their information from cable television, and 14 percent receive their information from social media. Only 2 percent reported getting information from a newspaper, which is actually less than the percent who stated they obtain information from late night comedy—3

Republican Presidential nominee Donald Trump often used Twitter to communicate his views, especially about race. In this tweet, Trump accuses the federal judge, Gonzalo Curiel, presiding over a fraud claim against him of exhibiting bias because the judge ruled against Trump. Trump later complained that the judge was biased against him because he is a "Mexican," despite the fact that Judge Curiel was born and raised in the United States. Republicans and Democrats rebuked Trump for exhibiting racial bias against Latinos.

percent. For eighteen- to twenty-nine-year-olds social media was by far the highest source of news on the 2016 election—35 percent. For other age groups (30–49, 50–64, and 65 and older) cable television is the most common source. Only 1 percent of seniors receive 2016 election news from social media.[36]

The impact of social media on civil rights is mixed. Civil rights groups can use social media to promote their ideas and organize events. For example, Black Lives Matter uses social media to promote their ideas and plan protests.[37] However, social media also allows people to advance racist and other hateful ideas. In fact, a recent study shows that one percent of all Twitter messages in Louisiana contained hateful expression towards racial and ethnic minorities, women, or the LGBT community.[38] Republican presidential candidate Donald Trump has used Twitter extensively to promote his campaign, and many of his "tweets" have expressed inflammatory messages about racial and ethnic minorities. For example, in late 2015 Trump claimed on Twitter that 81 percent of Whites who are murdered are killed by African Americans, despite the fact that the real number is closer to 15 percent. The fact-checking organization PolitiFact rated his claim "Pants on Fire," which is the lowest rating on its "Truth-O-Meter."[39]

The Media Industry

The news media are a major industry and for that reason deserve close attention. The media industry has become increasingly more concentrated, and there is a lack of diversity in professional journalism.

A veiled woman takes pictures with her cell phone during clashes with Egyptian riot police near Tahrir Square in Cairo, Egypt, November 22, 2011. Cell phones and social media were instrumental communication tools among activists in the Arab Spring.

The Media Business

Until the middle of the twentieth century, newspapers, radio stations, and network affiliates were separately owned enterprises that thrived economically. Beginning in the 1990s, however, many newspapers began to lose their profitability, and by 2000 the newspaper business was in severe decline. Newspapers found it increasingly difficult to compete with cable television and Internet-based media, especially among younger people. Many newspapers completely folded or switched to an Internet-only delivery system. For example, in March 2009 the *Seattle Post-Intelligencer*, a venerated newspaper in existence since 1863, announced that it was ceasing its print newspaper production and providing only Internet content. The *Post-Intelligencer* had lost about half of its readership during the previous few years, and in 2008 it lost $14 million. By 2009, there was no money to support a newspaper. Although the *Post-Intelligencer* retained its Internet site, the vast majority of the newspaper's employees lost their jobs. Additionally, in 2012 the *New Orleans Times-Picayune*, which had been a daily newspaper for 175 years, reduced its publications to only three times per week.[40]

Formerly independent newspapers have tried to survive by allowing large media holding companies such as Gannett and the McClatchy Company[41] to purchase them. Although these companies have in some cases been able to preserve the newspapers' solvency, their centralized authority can stifle the independence of the press coverage of events, especially political campaigns and governance.

The radio and television industries have recently experienced a similar trend. Larger companies, such as iHeartMedia, Inc., formerly known as Clear Channel,[42] have bought local radio stations. Again, consolidation has kept radio stations financially stable, but it has also decreased their independence. Currently, broadcast networks and cable stations are owned by major corporations. For example, Comcast Cable owns NBC Universal (including cable stations CNBC and MSNBC), and Disney owns ABC.[43] In fact, six large corporations (Comcast, News Corp, Disney, Viacom, Time Warner, and CBS) own a substantial majority of American media outlets.[44] This degree of corporate involvement in the media can undermine the objectivity and credibility of the news, especially because these large corporations are often embroiled in financial, labor, and environmental controversies.

Media Personnel

The people who work for the media, especially professional journalists and editors, are among the elites in American society. Although journalists during the eighteenth and nineteenth centuries were not educated or considered to be intellectual, by the twentieth century journalism had become an intellectual occupation. Overall, journalists today are more educated than average Americans are, and their socioeconomic status is closer to that of the politicians they cover than to that of their readers. In fact, many journalists and columnists move back and forth between working for the press and pursuing political careers. For example, current MSNBC commentator Michael Steele was the former chair of the Republican National Committee (see Chapter 14).

Despite an intention to report political events objectively, journalists are human beings whose biases and personal experiences undoubtedly influence their reporting. Political leaders and the American public often accuse journalists of exhibiting a liberal bias. Indeed, surveys of members of the media reveal that journalists lean more toward the Democratic Party than the American public does.[45] But the increasingly more corporate character of media organizations and reliance on advertisements suggest a conservative bias in the media. As we discussed earlier, Fox News's coverage of Common's appearance at the White House demonstrates that media bias concerning issues of race and ethnicity greatly affects how politics is covered.

This emphasis on liberal and conservative biases in the news media disregards a more significant form of media bias. All members of the media—journalists and publishers—share the goal of increasing newspaper circulation, ratings, website hits, or Twitter followers. This commonly shared goal results in a bias toward negative coverage of virtually all political leaders, regardless of their ideology. Specifically, the media exhibit a bias toward reporting scandals, which is a lucrative endeavor.[46]

Given that media professionals are at least somewhat biased, diversity of the profession is a critical issue. If the news media are dominated by White men, then issues pertaining to women and minority groups might not get the attention they would if the media were more diverse.

Prior to the women's liberation movement of the 1960s, Americans considered journalism to be one of the few acceptable occupations for women. But this has not translated into gender equity in the newsroom. In 2015, women accounted for 37.1 percent of all newspaper employees, and only 35.3 percent of supervisors were women.[47]

Racial and ethnic minorities are also underrepresented in the media. Figure 11.5 demonstrates that racial and ethnic minorities are not well represented as newspaper employees. The data shown also demonstrate that minority representation has grown since the late 1970s, most likely as a result of greater attention paid to diversity, but there has been a slight decline since the mid-2000s. Overall, representation of racial and ethnic minorities in newspapers has remained extremely low. "Measuring Equality: Racial and Ethnic Minority Representation in the Media" addresses in more detail minority group presence in broadcast radio and television.

Press Coverage of Politics and Government Officials and Institutions

Given the media's influence on politics, the relationship between the media and the government is worth examining closely. Not only do the media provide information that voters use when making electoral decisions, the media also are a tool for candidates seeking office. In addition, the press covers

measuring equality

Racial and Ethnic Minority Representation in the Media

The extent to which racial and ethnic minorities are represented in the media undoubtedly can influence the way in which the media frame issues of race and ethnicity. Just as the presence of minorities in political institutions affects the way in which those institutions treat minorities, the presence of minorities in the media should influence how the media cover racial and ethnic minority politics. As we discussed in previous chapters, minority representation in government institutions has improved since the 1980s. Therefore, we would expect that minority representation in media would have increased as well. Likewise, the number of minorities in supervisory positions, the ones that exert the most control over coverage, should also increase.

Here, we measure Black, Latino, Asian American, and American Indian representation in broadcast radio and television news jobs, and compare those results from 2000 to 2016. Given the emphasis on minority representation during this time frame, we would expect that minority representation has grown since 2000. We therefore must test this hypothesis.

But raw percentages of minority-group representation alone will not provide a complete picture because Black, Latino, and Asian American populations have grown since 2000. To elaborate further, we use ratios to compare minority representation between 2000

and 2016. Specifically, the ratios measure the percentage of the group in the position divided by the percentage of the group in the population. A ratio of 1 means that the group is as well represented in the position as it is in the population. A ratio above 1 indicates overrepresentation, and a ratio below 1 indicates underrepresentation. Each figure examines Black, Latino, Asian American, and American Indian representation on four levels: total workforce in broadcast television (Figure 11.1), total workforce in broadcast radio (Figure 11.2), news directors in broadcast television (Figure 11.3), and news directors in broadcast radio (Figure 11.4).

These results are interesting because, despite increased attention to minority recruitment, Black representation, Latino representation, and Asian American representation have generally, albeit not exclusively, decreased since 2000. Yet, American Indian representation has increased significantly. Different groups fare better in different settings. Blacks are currently best represented in television employment, whereas American Indians are best represented in radio employment. Moreover, Blacks, Latinos, and Asian Americans are better represented in television than in radio, but American Indians are better represented in radio than in television.

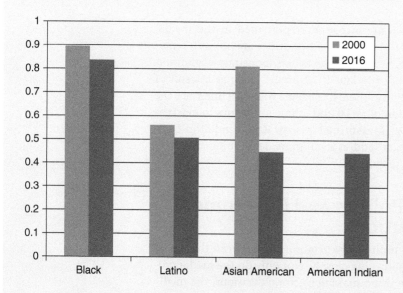

Figure 11.1 Minority Group Presence in Broadcast Television Workforce 2000 and 2016

(Continued)

measuring equality *(Continued)*

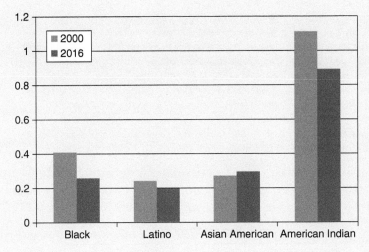

Figure 11.2 Minority Group Presence in Broadcast Radio Workforce 2000 and 2016

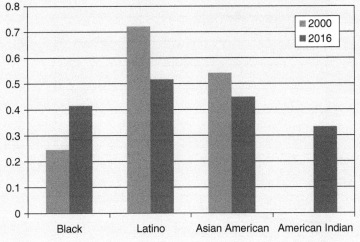

Figure 11.3 Minority Group Presence as Broadcast Television News Directors 2000 and 2016

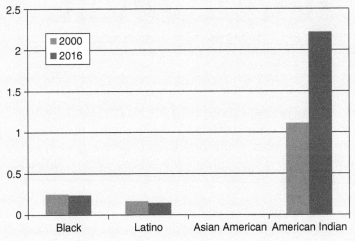

Figure 11.4 Minority Group Presence as Broadcast Radio News Directors 2000 and 2016

(Continued)

measuring equality *(Continued)*

Among television news directors, all groups' level of representation is about the same, although it is worth mentioning that Latino representation has shrunk precipitously since 2000. Blacks, Latinos, and Asian Americans are severely underrepresented as radio news directors, but American Indians are extremely overrepresented. Blacks, Latinos, and Asian Americans enjoy higher representation as television news directors compared to radio news directors. American Indians are better represented in radio.

Sources: Data adapted from Bob Papper, "RTDNA Research: Women and Minorities in Newsrooms," Radio-Television News Directors Association, July 11, 2016, http://www.rtdna.org/article/rtdna_research_women_and_minorities_in_newsrooms, accessed July 20, 2016; United States Census Bureau, "Table 1: Population by Hispanic or Latino Origin and by Race for the United States," Overview of Race and Hispanic Origin: 2000, https://www.census.gov/prod/2001pubs/c2kbr01-1.pdf, accessed July 20, 2016; United States Census, "Quick Facts: United States," https://www.census.gov/quickfacts/table/PST045215/00, accessed July 20, 2016.

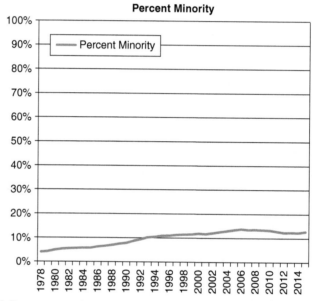

Figure 11.5 Percentage of Minorities Employed in Daily Newspapers, 1978–2014
Source: American Society for Newspaper Editors, "Table A: Minority Employment in Daily Newspapers," Newsroom Diversity Survey: 2015 Census, July 28, 2015, http://asne.org/content.asp?pl=140&sl=129&contentid=129, accessed July 19, 2016.

government institutions, and this coverage influences how citizens perceive these institutions. In turn, the government tries to regulate the media, which is a significant aspect of media politics. Media coverage of minority candidates and government officials is especially important in minority-group politics.

Reporting of Elections

Major political campaigns have a symbiotic relationship with the media. The media report on elections because of the public's interest, and the campaigns need the media to communicate their message and appeal to voters. Elections often entail vigorous and complex debates over competing visions of public policies, yet media outlets tend to focus their coverage on the aspects of elections that attract more readers and viewers. During elections, the press covers key campaign events on a daily basis, and it devotes considerable prime-time coverage to major events, such as national party conventions and televised debates.

Media coverage often extends beyond mere reporting of the events. Most newspaper, radio, television, and Internet sources also feature commentators who offer analyses on the races they cover. Most media stations, except for rare exceptions such as C-SPAN and PBS, often focus on the personalities of the candidates and the poll numbers of the race, instead of on the relevant issues.

The media affect political campaigns through the power of **priming**, in which the press's evaluation of a candidate influences how the public perceives the candidate.[48] For example, during the 2016 presidential election campaign the media has generally primed Donald Trump undisciplined, erratic, and boorish and Hillary Clinton as untrustworthy and insincere. Of course, conservative news outlets, especially Fox News, prime Donald Trump more positively and Hillary Clinton negatively, whereas liberal news outlets, especially MSNBC, prime Hillary Clinton positively and Donald Trump negatively.

Priming The media's ability to influence how the public perceives politicians and candidates.

There is considerable debate about media coverage of minority candidates, especially about whether minority candidates receive less coverage than White candidates and whether minority candidates receive less favorable coverage than White candidates. Although the parallel press provides considerable positive coverage of minority candidates, empirical studies of the mainstream press have shown that there is mixed evidence as to whether minority candidates receive more coverage than their White opponents and whether coverage of minority candidates is favorable, unfavorable, or neutral. Anecdotally, minority candidates claim that their coverage is unfavorable, White opponents claim that the coverage of minority candidates is favorable, and the media claim that the coverage is neutral. When different racial and ethnic minority candidates run against each other, particularly Blacks against Latinos, then the coverage of the race increases compared to when a minority candidate runs against a White opponent.[49]

The issue of media coverage of Black candidates became more salient during Barack Obama's historic candidacy in 2008. Both of Obama's main opponents (Democrat Hillary Rodham Clinton during the primary and Republican John McCain in the general election) claimed that the media were far more favorable to Obama than to them. Neither campaign claimed that the media were acting out of racial favoritism, but their charges were quite evident. The McCain campaign website even sponsored a contest entitled, "The Media is in LOVE with Barack Obama" and asked supporters to select a song that best characterized the media's favoritism toward Obama. Although the media devoted more coverage to Obama than to his opponents, media coverage is always more extensive for the newer candidates.[50] It bears noting that the media did emphasize negative aspects of Obama's campaign, such as his association with Rev. Jeremiah Wright, who was recorded making incendiary comments suggesting that the United States deserved some blame for the attacks of September 11, 2001.[51]

Questions of media bias and race were particularly relevant during the 2012 campaign. After Black Republican presidential candidate Herman Cain emerged as a leading candidate, media coverage of his background naturally intensified. When the media reported that Cain had engaged in extramarital affairs and sexual harassment, Cain's conservative and Tea Party supporters claimed that the media was against Cain because he is a Black conservative who attacked a liberal Black president.[52] After Cain faded from public view, issues of racial bias in the media still persisted, largely because of President Obama's presence in the race. For example, less than two weeks before the election, former Republican vice-presidential candidate and Fox News contributor Sarah Palin criticized President Obama's response to a terrorist attack on the U.S. Embassy in Libya that resulted in the deaths of four Americans, including Ambassador Chris Stevens. Believing that the President was covering up his culpability, she employed the term "shuck and jive," which is a racist term dating back to the slavery era that depicts African Americans as disingenuous. Palin denied that her use of the term was racist, stating that others, including liberals, had used the term before.[53]

There were minority candidates during the 2016 Republican presidential nominating process—including Latinos Marco Rubio and Ted Cruz and African American Ben Carson. Interestingly, the coverage focusing on Ben Carson's race has also included President Obama because had Carson won the presidency, then he would have followed as the second Black president. In October of 2015, News Corporation (which owns Fox News) CEO Rupert Murdoch said that Ben Carson would be the first Black president, implying that President Obama is not really Black.[54]

Coverage of Government Officials and Institutions

Media coverage of politicians once they are elected is important because elected politicians require the media to communicate their message, especially if they plan to run for reelection, and the media need to cover elected politicians to satisfy the public's interest. Because the president is the single most powerful person in American government, press coverage of the president is even more important. This coverage is carried out by the **White House press corps**, which include the print, radio, television, and Internet reporters who cover presidents and their administrations. This is an elite assignment in professional journalism, and as we discussed in the opening vignette, the organization representing the press corps is the White House Correspondents' Association, which hosted the dinner in which Larry Wilmore delivered his controversial presentation. With varying degrees of success, presidents cultivate friendly relations with the White House press corps to elicit better coverage and, ultimately, a positive public image.

White House Press Corps Those elite journalists responsible for covering the president and key executive branch officials.

The **press secretary** is a member of the White House staff who handles the bulk of the president's press relations. He or she holds daily briefings with the members of the White House press corps, who then use the information they gather to report on the presidency. Some cable channels, such as C-SPAN, air the full briefings. Press secretaries shape significantly how the press and ultimately the public view the president's performance. Presidents also communicate with the media through **press conferences**, which are formal question-and-answer sessions that the press secretary, and occasionally the president himself, holds with members of the White House press corps.[55]

Press Secretary A member of the president's staff who conducts daily briefings with members of the media.

The White House press corps and the position of press secretary have been dominated by White men. To date, there have been no minority press secretaries, and only two press secretaries have been female (Dee Dee Meyers for Bill Clinton and Dana Perino for George W. Bush). Even Barack Obama's press secretaries, Robert Gibbs, Jay Carney, and Josh Earnest, have been White men. The vast majority of the White House press corps is also White, but there are some leading minorities who cover or have covered the White House. April Ryan is an African American who works for American Urban Radio Network,[56] Kristen Welker is an African American who works at NBC News,[57] and Myles Miller is an African American who works at *The Daily*, which is News Corporation's iPad news outlet.[58]

Press Conferences Formal question-and-answer sessions that the president or the press secretary holds with the White House press corps.

Media coverage is also crucial for members of the U.S. Congress because they must continually communicate with their constituents. House and Senate party leaders schedule weekly press briefings when Congress is in session, and many individual members appear on national television broadcasts. Members of Congress also use C-SPAN to generate exposure to their constituents.

Just as the White House press corps specializes in covering the president, journalists for major national news organizations specialize in covering Congress. This coverage tends to be negative, emphasizing partisan gridlock and scandals plaguing individual members. Because the national media coverage is negative and scandal-driven, members of Congress prefer to communicate with their constituents through their hometown media. Local television and print journalists benefit from interviews with members of Congress and tend to provide more favorable coverage.

There is mixed evidence as to whether coverage of minority members of Congress differs from coverage of White members. Systematic comparisons of coverage have been conducted for Black and White members of Congress. These studies have shown that Black representatives are portrayed as more compassionate but less honest than their White counterparts. Another study has found that, although the majority of coverage of both races is neutral, there have been instances in which White members of Congress are shown in a better light than Black members are.[59]

Government Regulation

The relationship between the media and government is also characterized by government attempts to regulate the press. The First Amendment to the

Constitution stipulates that "Congress shall make no law . . . abridging the freedom . . . of the press." This amendment has provided newspapers, radio broadcasts, television, cable, and the Internet with a significant amount of protection from government regulation.

Prior Restraint A usually impermissible governmental regulation that prevents the publication of written material.

One type of government attempt to regulate the press is known as **prior restraint**, in which the government prevents publication of material it deems objectionable. Since the early twentieth century, the Supreme Court has clearly prevented most forms of prior restraint. In 1931, the Supreme Court overturned a Minnesota law that empowered judges to enjoin the publication of malicious, scandalous, and defamatory newspapers. The state used this law to stop the publication of the *Saturday Press*, which was a highly racist and anti-Jewish newspaper. The U.S. Supreme Court ruled that Minnesota's form of prior restraint violated the First Amendment.[60] The military is able to prevent the publication of certain materials that could jeopardize national security, but even in those cases the government must present clear evidence that a genuine national security issue is at stake, or the Court will protect the press against prior restraint. In the 1971 case *New York Times v. United States*, the executive branch sought to prevent the *New York Times* from publishing the Pentagon Papers, which were leaked government documents that revealed the U.S. government's serious mistakes during the Vietnam War, which was still being waged at the time. The Supreme Court ruled that the government lacked a sufficient national security justification to engage in prior restraint, even though publication of the Pentagon Papers would undermine public support for the Vietnam War.[61]

The U.S. Supreme Court has also prevented state and local governments from censoring the media even if the government possessed noble intentions. For example, to protect the privacy of rape victims, Georgia prevented the publication or broadcast of their names, but in 1975 the U.S. Supreme Court overturned that law, ruling that any legal obstacle to publishing public information violated the First Amendment.[62] The Supreme Court has even overturned state laws preventing the publication of names of juveniles involved in crimes as either offenders or victims.[63] The Supreme Court has ruled in favor of freedom of the press when it conflicts with other constitutional liberties. The Court overturned a Nebraska trial court judge who stopped press coverage of a trial based on a fear that the publicity would endanger the defendant's Sixth Amendment right to a fair trial.[64]

There are some exceptions to the Court's absolutist stance. For example, the Court has ruled that trial judges can hold journalists in contempt and even jail them for refusing to reveal their sources. In other words, journalists do not have a First Amendment right to withhold their sources.[65] Another exception to the Court's absolutist stance on freedom of the press concerns broadcast radio and television. Because the airwaves are a publicly owned scarce resource, the federal government, primarily through the **Federal Communications Commission (FCC)**, has assumed authority to regulate the content of these broadcasts. The Supreme Court has allowed the FCC to prohibit sexually

Federal Communications Commission (FCC) An independent regulatory commission that licenses and regulates the content of broadcast radio and television.

explicit content on broadcast radio or television, even if that material would have been protected if it appeared in print, on cable, or on the Internet. The Supreme Court justifies this distinction because the broadcast media are more intrusive on unwitting consumers, especially children.[66] However, it is important to recognize that the FCC only regulates the "decency" content on broadcast television and radio; it does not regulate sexually explicit content on cable or satellite television and radio or the Internet.[67]

Conclusion

There is no question that the media play an extremely important role in American politics, and this chapter covered the significant aspects of media and politics. The media can set the political agenda, and through the power of framing and priming, they can influence how the public interprets events and political actors. During the nineteenth century, the press took the form of partisan and interest group propaganda newspapers or penny presses and yellow journalism newspapers that appealed to the masses. During the twentieth century, a more professional press boomed, and new technologies, such as radio, television, cable television, and the Internet, changed the way in which Americans received their political news. Currently, the media are a form of big business, and journalism is a respected profession. The press influences not only the coverage of political campaigns, but also the institutions of government.

The press has affected many aspects of American government, including minority-group politics. Throughout American history, most forms of the media perpetuated stereotypes against racial and ethnic minorities, and because the media influence public opinion, this biased coverage shaped Americans' attitudes toward minorities (see "Evaluating Equality: Racial Bias in the Press Coverage of Hurricane Katrina?").

evaluating equality

Racial Bias in the Press Coverage of Hurricane Katrina?

On August 29, 2005, Hurricane Katrina made landfall in southeastern Louisiana and triggered considerable flooding throughout New Orleans and other Gulf Coast communities. Low-income residents of New Orleans who lacked the means to evacuate were forced to remain in their homes during the storm and the ensuing flooding. While they were stranded, they had no access to electricity, money, or food. Moreover, there was a shortage of public safety officials, which increased the possibility of civil disorder. Because people were enduring such hardships, journalists, photographers, and television cameras descended on New Orleans and the surrounding areas.

A considerable amount of media attention focused on the racial aspects of Hurricane Katrina. On the one hand, media coverage alerted many

(Continued)

evaluating equality *(Continued)*

Americans to the horrendous living conditions that the low-income, and largely Black, residents of New Orleans endured. On the other hand, most of the journalists and photographers covering the hurricane and its aftermath were White, and at times the coverage was racially prejudiced. The media exaggerated reports of looting and lawlessness among the mainly Black residents. David Wellman, a leading American sociologist, suspected that the media's depiction of Blacks as criminals reinforced society's belief that Blacks are predisposed to criminal behavior, which could have "delayed relief" to the victims.

The racial bias was most notable when Yahoo! News, an Internet news website, showed two photographs of people carrying groceries after the storm. One photograph showed a young Black male wading through water and carrying a case of soda and a bag, and the caption read that the man was "looting." A

Actual photo caption: "A young man walks through chest-deep flood water after looting a grocery store in New Orleans on August 30, 2005."

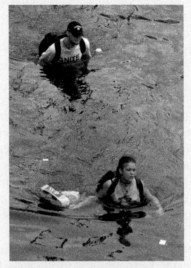

Actual photo caption: "Residents wade through chest-deep water after finding bread and soda from a local grocery store after Hurricane Katrina came through the area on August 29, 2005 in New Orleans."

second photograph depicted a White couple, who were also wading through water carrying food, but this caption said that the couple was "finding" groceries.

Racial and ethnic minorities, as well as many Whites, regarded this double standard as evidence of racial bias in the media, and because news on the Internet travels quickly, many Americans were aware of it within one day. African American hip-hop artist Kanye West stated during a concert he promoted to raise money for hurricane relief, "I hate the way they portray us in the media. You see a Black family, it says they are looting. You

see a White family, it says they're looking for food."* Despite this controversy, a survey showed that about three-quarters of both Blacks and Whites regarded media coverage of Katrina as "responsible."**

Closely examine both photographs and captions shown here.

- Debate among your classmates over the extent that racial bias influenced the juxtaposition of these photographs and captions.
- Based on everything you have learned in this chapter debate the extent of racial bias in the media overall. Has coverage of racial and ethnic minorities improved over the years?
- Pay close attention to how arguments in this debate vary according to one's race and ethnicity.

* Carrie Peyton Dahlberg, "Images of Disaster Bring Race Issue to the Fore," *Sacramento Bee*, September 3, 2005, A1.

** CNN/USA Today/Gallup Poll cited in Mike McDaniel, "Katrina's Aftermath: Racial Bias Comes to the Forefront; Terms, Pictures Used by the Media Prompt Debate," *Houston Chronicle*, September 19, 2005, 1.

Sources: Carrie Peyton Dahlberg, "Images of Disaster Bring Race Issue to the Fore," *Sacramento Bee*, September 3, 2005, A1; Mike McDaniel, "Katrina's Aftermath: Racial Bias Comes to the Forefront; Terms, Pictures Used by the Media Prompt Debate," *Houston Chronicle*, September 19, 2005, 1; Tania Rulli, "Who's a Looter? In Storm's Aftermath, Pictures Kick Up a Different Kind of Tempest," *New York Times*, September 5, 2005, C1.

There is no doubt that the media bear responsibility for mistreatment of Blacks, Latinos, Asian Americans, and American Indians. Nevertheless, the media have also helped minorities overcome discrimination. The parallel press helped to mobilize minorities to fight for civil rights, and there is even some evidence that the mainstream media's coverage of the 1960s Civil Rights Movement increased Americans' support for civil rights legislation. Despite clear improvements, it is still the case that racial and ethnic minorities are underrepresented in employment in the media.

Finally, the media's coverage of minority-group politics became extremely salient during President Obama's election, first term, reelection campaign, and second term. Barack Obama's critics and vanquished opponents claim that the media were overly favorable toward him, but there is evidence that the largely White conservative media have been overly critical of Obama throughout his presidency.

The story about Larry Wilmore's presentation at the White House Correspondents' Dinner illustrates the significance of the media in politics and government. Wilmore's controversial use of the "N Word" set off a national debate, which demonstrates the media's ability to shape public discourse and opinion. The fact that this story played out on social media and was initiated by an entertainer evidences the dominance of newer media over traditional media. Finally, this story dealt with a Black political comedian roasting the first Black president exemplifies the role of race in the media coverage of politics. In short, the issue of the media and minority politics is complex and dynamic.

review REVIEW QUESTIONS

1. What were abolitionist newspapers, and how did they influence the controversies over slavery?

2. What is the parallel press, and what are key examples of it in print, radio, television, and the Internet?

3. How much did television influence the success of the Civil Rights Movement?

4. How have new media influenced the coverage of issues of race and ethnicity?

5. How well is each minority group (Blacks, Latinos, Asian Americans, and American Indians) represented in the media, and to what extent is each group represented in the top echelons of the media?

terms KEY TERMS

Agenda Setting p. 334

Blog p. 343

Federal Communications Commission (FCC) p. 354

Framing p. 333

Mass Media p. 333

Parallel Press p. 336

Penny Press p. 334

Press Conferences p. 353

Press Secretary p. 353

Priming p. 351

Prior Restraint p. 354

White House Press Corps p. 352

Yellow Journalism p. 335

readings
ADDITIONAL READINGS

Arnold Gibbons, *Race, Politics, and the White Media: The Jesse Jackson Campaigns* (Lanham, MD: University Press of America, 1993).

This book looks at Jesse Jackson's campaigns for president in 1984 and 1988 and the function of race in press treatments of those campaigns.

Stephanie Greco Larson, *Media and Minorities: The Politics of Race in News and Entertainment* (Lanham, MD: Rowman and Littlefield, 2006).

This book demonstrates how the media's portrayal of racial and ethnic minorities in news and entertainment has perpetuated stereotypes, which, in turn, has hindered civil rights progress.

Truman Nelson, ed., *Documents of Upheaval: Selections from William Lloyd Garrison's* The Liberator, *1831–1865* (New York: Hill and Wang, 1966).

This volume, containing key excerpts from *The Liberator*, provides primary source evidence of the media's influence on public opinion.

Gene Roberts and Hank Klibanoff, *The Race Beat: The Press, the Civil Rights Struggle, and the Awakening of a Nation* (New York: Knopf, 2006).

This meticulously researched book examines the history of the media's coverage of racial discrimination in the South and the civil rights struggle that followed.

Patrick S. Washburn, *The African American Newspaper: Voice of Freedom* (Evanston, IL: Northwestern University Press, 2006).

This book traces the history of Black newspapers from their founding as abolitionist tracts during the early 1800s, through their growth after the Civil War, to their height in the first half of the twentieth century, as well as to their decline (along with all newspapers) during the early twenty-first century.

CHAPTER 12

Social Movements: Civil Rights as a Movement Model

Group portrait of some of the more than 100 students named in the legal case *Dorothy Davis, et al. v. County School Board of Prince Edward County, Virginia*, a lawsuit filed to seek, initially, repairs for Robert Moton High School, a segregated school in Farmville, VA, March 1953. The case was later, on appeal, attached to the landmark *Brown v. Board of Education* case. Among those pictured is Dorothy E. Davis (center, with glasses), for whom the suit was named.

On April 23, 1951, M. Boyd Jones, the Black principal of the segregated Robert R. Moton High School in Farmville, Virginia, received an anonymous call saying that two of his students were about to encounter trouble with police at the Greyhound bus station. After Jones left the building, notes, supposedly from Jones, were delivered to each classroom calling an emergency assembly. When students and teachers arrived, instead of Jones, they saw Barbara Rose Johns, a sixteen-year-old junior, standing at the lectern.

Johns demanded that the teachers leave and pounded her shoe on the lectern for effect. The teachers left. Barbara then gave an impassioned speech about the numerous problems at the school: tar-paper additions that served as overflow classrooms, used and outdated textbooks, no science labs, and broken-down buses, among other complaints. She implored her classmates to go on strike until the county's White supervisors met student demands for a new school. The students marched out of school to the county courthouse and confronted the school superintendent with their demands.

The students then contacted a National Association for the Advancement of Colored People (NAACP) lawyer in Richmond, Oliver W. Hill, who expressed an interest in taking the students' case. But he had one crucial stipulation: The students would have to agree to challenge segregation outright and not just ask for a new segregated school. The strike continued to the end of the school year.

White officials responded by firing Jones, but at the same time they did appropriate $875,000 to build a new high school for Blacks. On May 23, 1951, after hundreds of Black parents signed a petition of support, Hill and his associates filed suit in federal court in Richmond on behalf of the 117 Moton students, demanding that the Virginia law enforcing segregated schools be voided. This case was combined with three others from Kansas, South Carolina, and Delaware on appeal to the Supreme Court, which issued its unanimous decision on May 17, 1954, in the famous *Brown v. Board of Education of Topeka* ruling. The Court affirmed that "in the field of public education the doctrine of 'separate but equal' has no place."[1]

intro *The 1951 strike by Black high* school students in Virginia is just one example of numerous protest activities by Black Americans in many communities around the nation. According to historian John Hope Franklin, beginning shortly after the end of Reconstruction in the late 1870s and then gathering speed and intensity in the 1880s, many states and localities passed laws segregating Black Americans in almost every aspect of their daily lives. In addition, many states rewrote their state constitutions to remove as many Blacks as possible from the voting rolls and make it almost impossible for them to register to vote.[2]

Over time, these local protests aimed at local governments and local segregation ordinances grew into a national movement for Black civil rights aimed at the federal government. From early local protests in the 1950s, the Civil Rights Movement (CRM) gained momentum and supporters. It presented to the nation and the world the determination of Black Americans to dismantle the separate system of laws under which Blacks were forced to live. Despite fierce violence, murders, and reprisals from those who wanted to maintain segregation, the CRM's goals of the removal of the legal structures of racial inequality and political rights would become realities. The CRM is among the most prominent and successful social movements to have occurred in the United States. The promise of political inclusion that resulted in the election to the presidency of Barack Obama is directly related to the CRM and all of those Americans who risked life and limb to force the United States to live up to its ideals.

Social movements play an important role in democracies. They are one mechanism through which changes are brought about. In representative democracies such as the United States, change can come through legislation passed by city councils, state legislatures, and the national Congress. It also can occur through decisions by the courts at all levels of government. All of these methods of change, however, are achieved through individuals working within government structures.

What mechanisms are available to those outside of government to influence change? A first mechanism is individuals expressing their opinion to elected officials to push those officials, where possible, to make changes in the system. A second mechanism is electing individuals who are sympathetic to making those changes. A third mechanism is mounting a social movement.

A Social Movement Defined

A **social movement** is a sustained challenge to those in power put forth by individuals, acting in concert with others, who have been excluded from the political process or who consider themselves political outsiders. Social movements provide a way for those without a voice in the political system to make their concerns known to decision makers. Those inside government or with access through interest groups, political action committees, wealth, or position have no need for social movements as they already have the ability to get the attention of decision makers. Those involved in social movements are usually a minority of the population, but over time their activities might change the attitudes of the majority and garner their support. Social movements can pressure decision makers to make changes.[3]

Social Movement A sustained challenge to those in power put forth by individuals, acting in concert with others, who have been excluded from the political process or who consider themselves political outsiders.

In the United States, a number of successful social movements, such as the Civil Rights Movement, the women's suffrage movement, and later the women's rights movement, the labor movement, and the gay rights movement, have brought about significant changes.

There have also been social movements that failed to maintain their momentum and achieve their goals, such as the poor people's campaign, a campaign to push for economic opportunities for Blacks that was begun shortly after the assassination of Dr. Martin Luther King Jr. in 1968. Other campaigns were repressed by federal, state, or, in a few instances, private authority, such as the Bisbee miners' strike.[4] The Bisbee, Arizona, Mexican and Mexican-American miners' strike in July 1917, which was part of a larger movement by Mexican and Mexican-American miners demanding wage equity and the ability to organize into unions, was ended when private police for Phelps-Dodge Mining Company rounded up striking miners, put them in railroad boxcars, and sent them to New Mexico, where the miners were imprisoned for two months in an army stockade.[5]

Participation in social movements can be dangerous, as often those who disagree with the movement's demands might retaliate against the participants and threaten them with violence or loss of employment. Many participants in the Civil Rights Movement, for example, were beaten, and some were even murdered.

Conditions That Give Rise to Social Movements

Scholars have identified several conditions necessary for the rise of social movements. First, these movements arise from **shared grievances**, complaints against the political system (national, state, or local) by a group of people who agree generally on the causes of the complaints and the possible means of resolving them. This discontent is produced by some combination of structural conditions; for example, government laws and governmental action, coupled with a shared belief by those affected that something should be done, cause people to come together in collective action to push the system to resolve the grievances.[6] The aggrieved provide the necessary resources and labor to support the movement. In the United States, the Civil Rights Movement arose from shared grievances and drew support from existing social organizations with experienced leaders, potential followers, communication networks, money, and labor.

Second, the formation of social movements requires a **supportive environment**. This is an environment that is receptive to the ideals and demands of the social movement, even though the entire political system might not be willing to listen to its concerns. Events in the larger society might provide an opportunity for a social movement to evolve, enlarge its base of support, or make significant headway in its goals. Society as a whole might have become more tolerant of or receptive to the concerns espoused by the movement. For example, during the Vietnam War, as the U.S. public grew increasingly concerned about the large number of casualties, and despite government

Shared Grievances Complaints against the political system (national, state, or local) by a group of people who agree generally on the causes of the complaints.

Supportive Environment An environment receptive to the ideals and demands of a social movement.

assertions that the United States and its South Vietnamese allies were winning the war, more and more people came to believe the war was being lost and thus began to support the antiwar movement. Recently, public opinion data show that Americans are becoming more supportive of gay and lesbian rights and more comfortable with same-sex marriage. Polls suggest that the public is evolving on the question of rights and protections for gay and lesbian citizens. In the 2012 elections, voters in Maine and Maryland legalized same-sex marriage, and in Minnesota voters rejected a ban on same-sex marriage.

Third, a **catalyst**, an event or events that push an issue to the forefront and galvanize people to action, will spark a social movement. On Friday, June 27, 1969, New York City police raided a Greenwich Village gay bar called the Stonewall Inn.[7] Police raids on gay bars in New York were not unusual; police routinely raided these bars, ostensibly looking for liquor law and other violations. What was unusual about this night was the reaction of the patrons to the raid. They confronted the police "first with jeers, then a hail of coins, paving stones, and parking meters."[8] This spontaneous resistance continued throughout the weekend. Out of the Stonewall "uprising," the modern phase of the gay liberation movement arose. In the wake of Stonewall, demonstrations in response to the events there were held in New York as well as many other cities across the country. Gay liberation groups organized in the summer of 1969 in cities as diverse as New York, San Francisco, and Minneapolis.[9] Within two years of what was now referred to as the Stonewall rebellion, gay liberation groups operated in every major city and on almost every campus in the United States, Canada, Australia, and Western Europe.[10]

> **Catalyst** An event that energizes and coalesces a social movement.

Fourth, sometimes **catalytic leadership**, social activists who create or recognize opportunities to protest a group's concerns, can be a trigger. Catalytic leadership can help create a social movement when the leaders highlight and draw on deep-rooted feelings of injustice.[11] César Chávez of the National Farm Workers Association, later the United Farm Workers Union, is an example. Chávez was executive director of the Community Service Organization, a civil rights organization of urban Mexican Americans. Beginning in 1962, Chávez, along with Dolores Huerta, founder of the Agricultural Workers Association, began organizing Mexican grape workers in Delano, California. He created a program of services for the workers that included a credit union, a consumer co-op, welfare and citizenship counseling, and programs that addressed community issues such as racism in the local schools and rental price gouging.[12] His National Farm Workers Association grew from three hundred members in 1962 to more than one thousand by 1964.

> **Catalytic Leadership** Social activists who create or recognize opportunities to galvanize people to organized action.

A strike by Filipino grape workers in 1965 reluctantly forced Chávez's organization to participate in the strike because the Mexicans and Filipinos worked side by side in the same fields. The strike was broken within a week, and Chávez knew that he had to mobilize outside support for his efforts. He toured the country speaking at universities, church gatherings, and union meetings. The response was overwhelming. He not only raised money for his

Dolores Huerta, a labor leader and civil rights activist, co-founded the United Farm Workers with César Chávez.

union, but also recruited volunteers to come to California to help organize the farm workers.[13]

A hallmark of social movement activity is the use of unconventional methods, like mass demonstrations, sit-ins, and marches, to push the agenda and draw attention to the cause. A single demonstration, however, does not constitute a social movement. For example, the Million Man March on October 16, 1995, in Washington, DC, was a political demonstration to promote African American unity and family values. The National Park Service estimated the crowd at somewhere between 400,000 and 600,000, but that estimate was disputed, as Washington, DC, officials estimated the crowd at more than 1 million.[14] The hope was that it would spark a social movement, but it turned out to be a demonstration with little lasting effect.

Another more recent example is the October 16, 2011, the Right2Know March for Genetically Engineered Foods (GMO), a coalition of organizations, businesses, and individuals concerned about labeling of genetically engineered food in the United States. The march began in New York City, continued 313 miles to Washington, DC, and then demonstrated in front of the White House. The number of marchers is estimated to have been around five hundred. Social movements are sustained activities that occur over long periods of time, and the Right2Know March does not qualify.

In final sections of the chapter, we discuss the broader reasons why some social movements flounder or actually fail, and why other social efforts do not become formal movements.

Social Movements and Democracy

The United States has seen a number of successful social movements that have enriched its democracy by bringing previously excluded groups into the political process or by highlighting conditions that called for government intervention. Social movements play a valuable role in American democracy. Many of the changes that have occurred in the American political system would not have happened without a social movement.[15]

Despite the democratic foundation of the United States, throughout the nation's history many groups—Blacks, Mexican Americans, American Indians, and women—have been excluded from the political process. The political system treated these citizens differently and inequitably. They were designated as "second-class" citizens based solely on their physical characteristics. These excluded groups used social movements as one of the mechanisms to bring about their inclusion in the political process and to achieve legal and political rights. These social movements forced the United States to ensure that the rights and guarantees expressed in the Constitution were extended to all Americans.

Social movements, which are most often organized by a minority of the populace, may, by changing public opinion, sway a majority of the public to accept and embrace the movement's cause. Changing public opinion is a powerful force in moving decision makers to grapple with the concerns of a movement. The environmental movement has produced fundamental changes in Americans' attitudes toward nature and the environment. In 1965, when questions about the environment first appeared on public opinion surveys, only about one in ten Americans considered the issue to be very serious. By 1970, however, approximately seven in ten Americans believed that air pollution and water pollution were very or somewhat serious problems.[16] By 2012, Americans were concerned with environmental issues beyond air and water. When questioned about how much individuals worried about specific environmental issues, majorities indicated that they worried a great deal or a fair amount about global warming, the loss of tropical rain forests, and contamination of soil and water from toxic wastes.[17]

Changing public policy is a principal objective of a social movement. Once a social movement has brought its concerns to the attention of decision makers, changes in public policy are possible. The modern women's rights movement produced profound changes in public law, social policy, basic economic relationships, and social and cultural attitudes toward women.[18]

Social movements can bring about increased participation in the political process on the part of those who are directly affected by an issue and those who have sympathy with the affected. Increases in voter registration and voter turnout might result from increased attention to issues of concern to a social movement.

Social movements can bring about changes in the structures of political institutions. Many participants in social movements might choose careers in government—national, state, and local—to ensure that the issues of concern to them continue to receive attention from multiple levels of government.[19] As "outsiders" become "insiders" in government, they can change the way governments operate. Research on the effect of minority mayors shows that the appointment of minorities in leadership positions, such as police chief or department heads, changes the demographic character of the personnel in those departments and how those departments operate.[20]

Not all social movements have had a positive effect on American democracy—for example, the various phases of what sociologists Betty Dobratz and Stephanie Shanks-Meile call the White supremacy/separatist movement.[21] The founding of the Ku Klux Klan in 1865 by former Confederate soldiers upset with the South's loss and the abolition of slavery was the beginning of a movement whose basis for organization was hatred of Blacks and loss of a slave-based economic system. Over time, the movement spawned multiple hate groups, such as the White Aryan Resistance, the National Socialist White People's Party, and the National Alliance, which hate not only Blacks, but also Catholics, Jews, gays, and lesbians. Many of the activities of these groups are aimed at denying individuals their rights to participate in the political process and, in some extreme instances, their right to live.

Another element of the White supremacy/separatist movement is a hatred of the U.S. government.[22] The groups whose dominant theme is antigovernment hatred are referred to as "patriot" or militia groups. They include the John Birch Society, the Sons of Liberty, the Police against the New World Order (Idaho), and the Constitution Party. Militia groups, such as the Illinois State Militia, also exist in many states.[23]

These groups define themselves as opposed to the "New World Order," what they see as the emergence of a unified worldwide global government. They claim that the federal government is illegitimate because its policies— gun control, affirmative action, legalization of abortion for White women, tolerance of illegal immigration—have declared war on the White race.[24] According to these groups, the federal government should be destroyed. Timothy McVeigh, who bombed the Alfred P. Murrah Federal Building in Oklahoma City on April 19, 1995, killing 168 people, was a part of this movement, which sees the federal government as the enemy. Until his execution, McVeigh maintained that his action was justified.

The Southern Poverty Law Center (SPLC) of Montgomery, Alabama, estimates that there were approximately 892 organized hate groups in 2015, with the most active being the Ku Klux Klan, neo-Nazis, and racist skinhead groups.[25] Although not an overwhelming force, the White supremacy/separatist movement has many active members. These groups were particularly active in cyberspace in attacking candidate Obama during the 2008 presidential election and predicting doom for the United States if a Black man was elected

Cowart   Schlesselman

Two neo-Nazi skinheads, Daniel Gregory Cowart (left), 20, and Paul Michael Schlesselman (right), 18, shown in their police booking photos, were arrested on October 22, 2008, on charges of planning to rob a gun dealer to get guns to shoot Democratic presidential candidate Barack Obama. In addition, they planned to shoot as many other Blacks as possible.

president. Although not all threats to President Obama come from hate groups, news reports have indicated that the Secret Service investigates about ten threats per day against him, which is a reduction from the fifty per day just after his election in 2008.[26]

Successful American Social Movements

Some of the most successful social movements in the United States have been the Civil Rights Movement, the women's suffrage movement and later the women's rights movement, the labor movement, the environmental movement, and the anti–Vietnam War movement. Most recently the LGBT movement is having success at both the national and state levels. The objective of social movements is change, and change, in many instances, does not come about quickly. Many social movements therefore persist for a long time, and some social movements take a long time to mature.[27]

The Civil Rights Movement

The Civil Rights Movement was not one overall movement led from the top; rather, it was a collection of local movements that, when added together, constituted a national social movement and produced massive social change. Although the movement was most active in the 1950s and 1960s, its roots extend back to the nineteenth century. As discussed in Chapter 5, in the 1896 *Plessy v. Ferguson* decision, the U.S. Supreme Court upheld as constitutional "separate but equal" facilities for Blacks and Whites.[28] The ruling, which gave the stamp of constitutionality to racial segregation, allowed the states, especially in the South, to continue the system of social segregation that became known as **Jim Crow laws**. The *Plessy* decision also provided the constitutional cover for Southern states to change their state constitutions or pass laws that removed the vote from Blacks.

Jim Crow Laws The Southern practice of racially segregating all public facilities such as transportation, schools, libraries, hotels, hospitals, theaters, parks, and cemeteries.

Start of the Movement: 1900–1920. The Court decision in *Plessy* and the removal of the franchise sparked an immediate response from Black Americans. In at least twenty-five Southern cities between 1900 and 1906, Blacks organized boycotts to protest new laws enforcing segregation in streetcars. At the same time, violence and terrorism against Blacks increased as Whites sought to reinforce the legal structures that ensured their dominance.[29]

The struggle against Jim Crow continued into the twentieth century. The National Association for the Advancement of Colored People (NAACP) was formed in 1909, and in later years its legal arm, the NAACP Legal Defense and Education Fund, began to go to court to challenge segregation in, initially, higher education and other aspects of daily life. Blacks returning from military service in World War I, the war that had promised "to make the world safe for democracy," argued that the democracy they had fought for in Europe should be extended to Blacks at home. Black Americans became more vocal in their opposition to racial discrimination and segregation through demonstrations, newspaper articles, and meetings and discussions held at activist Black churches, barber shops, beauty salons, and other venues.[30] Whites responded to this increased activity with anti-Black campaigns, increased **lynchings**, and more than twenty-five riots in the summer of 1919. Little change occurred in the legal and political life of Blacks during the 1920s.

Movement Spurred by New Deal and World War II: 1930–1950. President Franklin Delano Roosevelt's New Deal included a number of programs intended to provide relief and recovery during the Great Depression of the 1930s. Although the New Deal programs were not aimed specifically at Blacks, a number of Black leaders, such as Ralph Bunche, Mary McLeod Bethune, Robert Weaver, and William Hastie, became informal advisers to Roosevelt and pushed for the creation of commissions, executive orders, government programs, and changes in policy intended to break down legal and social barriers for Blacks. In 1939, the Supreme Court ruled in *Missouri ex rel Gaines v. Canada* that Lloyd L. Gaines, a Black who had been denied admission to the University of Missouri Law School because of his race, had to be admitted.[31] The Gaines decision marked the first major break in the wall of segregation that had been established after *Plessy*.[32]

More than one million Black men and women served in the armed forces in World War II. Black civil rights activity increased significantly during the war years as many Black leaders linked the fight against fascism in Europe with the fight against racial discrimination and segregation in the United States.[33] By the end of the war, returning veterans and Blacks at home were determined to eliminate the Jim Crow laws governing life for Black Americans in the United States. It was out of this increased commitment and the changes wrought by World War II that the modern phase of the Civil Rights Movement emerged.

Modern Phase Begins: 1950–1960. A bus boycott in Baton Rouge, Louisiana, began on June 19, 1953. The boycott sought to have the city enforce an ordinance that allowed Black riders to be seated in city buses on a first-come, first-served basis. The city refused to discipline drivers who failed to enforce the ordinance, and Blacks staged a mass boycott of the bus system. Within days, the White political and business leaders of Baton Rouge offered a compromise that would make most of the seats on the bus open on a first-come, first-served basis. At a mass meeting of more than 8,000 Black Americans, the compromise was approved and the boycott called off.[34]

In December 1955, Rosa Parks, a seamstress and NAACP activist, refused to give her seat on a bus in Montgomery, Alabama, to a White man. A local segregation ordinance required Blacks to sit in the back, but if all of the White seats in the front were filled, Blacks were supposed to give up their seats to Whites and stand. Parks was arrested for violating the segregation ordinance, and her arrest energized the Black citizens of Montgomery to mobilize and boycott the bus system. The Montgomery bus boycott, initially organized by

Lynching The practice of killing people by mob action outside of the formal judicial process. In the United States, lynching was used as an intimidation tactic against Black Americans.

the Women's Political Council, a group of women who were faculty members at Alabama State College or teachers in the Montgomery school system, founded by Mary Fair Burks in 1946 and headed at that time by Jo Ann Gibson Robinson, enlisted the young Reverend Martin Luther King Jr. to lead the protest. It lasted 381 days. The Montgomery Improvement Association, the group formed to guide the bus boycott, filed suit in February 1956 in U.S. district court challenging the constitutionality of bus segregation. The boycott ended when the Supreme Court declared Alabama's state and local laws requiring segregation on buses unconstitutional in December 1956.[35]

The success of the Montgomery Improvement Association launched a national movement for Black civil rights by motivating other communities to engage in local protests against local and state governments. Although the Baton Rouge boycott had occurred earlier, it did not launch a national movement for several reasons. It lasted only a couple of days because concessions were offered relatively quickly. In contrast, the extended length of the Montgomery boycott required dynamic leadership and extensive organization and generated local and national publicity. The Baton Rouge boycott did not lead to a court case, whereas the Montgomery boycott took its petition all the way to the Supreme Court, whose ruling affected all Alabama state and local bus segregation ordinances.

In 1957, King, along with civil rights activists Bayard Rustin and Ella Baker, formed the **Southern Christian Leadership Conference (SCLC),** which was designed to be the umbrella organization that would link church-based affiliates throughout the South in the nonviolent struggle for racial justice. King was elected SCLC's president, and Ella Baker was its first executive director.[36]

While Blacks were coming together to protest for their rights, White Southerners were organizing in opposition to the growing Civil Rights Movement. In 1956, Alabama passed a law that banned the NAACP from operating in the state, as did several other states. In Mississippi, the **White Citizens' Council**, formed in 1954, used economic reprisals and legal repression to intimidate and repress civil rights activists and supporters.[37]

Nonviolent Civil Disobedience Increases: 1960–1965. The Civil Rights Movement in the 1960s focused on two primary objectives—eliminating segregation and discrimination and removing barriers to Black voter registration and participation. To achieve these goals, movement participants engaged in actions of nonviolent civil disobedience. A primary tactic was the sit-in. On February 1, 1960, in Greensboro, North Carolina, four freshmen from North Carolina A&T University sat down at a Whites-only lunch counter in Woolworth's. They were refused service, but remained all day at the counter. The next day, twenty students occupied the lunch counter. Some White students from a local women's college joined the sit-in on the third day, and the number of students at the lunch counter swelled to eighty-five.[38] By the end of the week, sit-ins had spread to other cities in North Carolina, and by the end of

Southern Christian Leadership Conference (SCLC) Group designed to be the umbrella organization that would link church-based affiliates throughout the South in the nonviolent struggle for racial justice.

White Citizens' Council Formed in 1954 in Mississippi to prevent the implementation of *Brown v. Board of Education*, the White Citizens' Council's membership consisted of plantation owners, bankers, doctors, legislators, and others opposed to Black civil rights and determined to maintain segregation.

Student Non-Violent Coordinating Committee (SNCC) Organization of college students dedicated to continuing the campaign for social justice started by the North Carolina A&T students.

the month sit-ins were happening in other towns and cities in the South. In April 1960, college students, with Ella Baker in attendance, formed the **Student Non-Violent Coordinating Committee (SNCC)** to continue directing the campaign started by the North Carolina A&T students.

In spring 1961, the Congress of Racial Equality (CORE) decided to test the enforcement of the Supreme Court's decision outlawing segregation in interstate transportation by having interracial groups ride buses from Washington, DC, to various Southern cities. One bus was firebombed outside of Birmingham, another ran into a vicious mob assault at the bus station in Montgomery, and bus riders were arrested in Jackson, Mississippi. CORE and SNCC continued to send individuals to replace those arrested until Attorney General Robert F. Kennedy finally directed the Interstate Commerce Commission to enforce regulations barring segregation in interstate terminals.[39]

Martin Luther King Jr. emerged as the national leader of this growing protest movement. King was an eloquent and powerful speaker able to articulate the ideals of the movement and the power of the principles of nonviolent protest. In 1963, at the invitation of local Blacks who were organizing against segregation and demanding the right to vote, King and some members of SCLC went to Birmingham, Alabama. SCLC, in concert with local groups, organized a boycott of downtown businesses during the height of the Easter season to protest the stores' refusal to hire Black sales clerks. Demonstrators marched to city hall to protest the city's segregation laws.

Many people were arrested, including King. While in jail, King wrote to the White clergy of Birmingham who condemned the demonstrations, explaining to them in his famous "Letter from Birmingham Jail" why the protests and demonstrations were occurring in Birmingham (see "Our Voices: Excerpt from Martin Luther King Jr.'s Letter from Birmingham Jail" on page 372). Eight White Alabama clergy had issued a statement critical of King and the demonstrations, saying that protests and demonstrations were not the right approach to addressing grievances. King chastised these clergymen for criticizing the demonstrations but not the conditions that had led to the demonstrations.[40]

Birmingham police commissioner Eugene "Bull" Connor was determined to stop the civil rights demonstrators. As the protesters, including a great many Black schoolchildren and teenagers, marched, sang, and prayed, Connor and his forces turned on them with night sticks, snarling attack dogs, and high-pressure water hoses. Millions of television viewers watched in horror at the images of the young demonstrators being blown off their feet by water hoses and attacked by dogs.[41]

With the assistance of negotiators sent by the Kennedy administration, the city's businesses began to negotiate with the demonstrators. After three days of meetings, the two sides reached an agreement to desegregate downtown stores and employ Black clerks. Whites responded to the compromise agreement with numerous bombings, which ignited further rioting. Finally, under pressure from the federal government, the mayor ratified the agreement and repealed the city's segregation laws.[42] The Birmingham demonstrations touched off similar demonstrations throughout the South and pushed Black civil rights to the forefront of national policy.[43]

On June 11, 1963, President John Kennedy addressed the nation in the wake of Governor George Wallace's unsuccessful attempt to block the admission of two Black students to the University of Alabama. Wallace stood in the door of the Registrar's Office in an attempt to keep the students from registering. A representative of Attorney General Robert Kennedy announced that he had a proclamation from President Kennedy ordering Wallace "to cease his illegal resistance to the federal court order on integration."[44] In the address, Kennedy pledged that he would urge Congress to act on legislation that he would be sending forward, and on June 19 he submitted his civil rights bill.[45]

Firefighters turn their hoses full force on civil rights demonstrators, July 15, 1963, in Birmingham, Alabama, one of the focal points of the desegregation movement.

On August 28, 1963, between 200,000 and 500,000 people (estimates varied depending on who was doing the counting) marched on Washington, DC, to lobby for the civil rights bill. The March on Washington for Jobs and Freedom was organized by a coalition of civil rights organizations—the NAACP, SCLC, CORE, SNCC, and the National Urban League—and a Black union active in civil rights, the Brotherhood of Sleeping Car Porters and Maids. The principal organizer, however, was Bayard Rustin, an important behind-the-scenes organizer and civil rights activist and a confidant of A. Philip Randolph, the organizer and founder of the Brotherhood of Sleeping Car Porters and Maids. (Both Rustin and Randolph had called for a march on Washington in 1941 to protest discrimination in the defense industry, but they called it off after President Franklin Roosevelt issued Executive Order 8802 [Fair Employment Act], which banned discrimination in the defense industry and in federal bureaus. Rustin was also gay and became an advocate for gay and lesbian issues toward the end of his life.)

It was the largest political demonstration the United States had ever seen. Hundreds of thousands of participants gathered at the Washington Monument and at noon began marching toward the Lincoln Memorial. Once at the memorial, many people spoke on the steps of the monument, but the most memorable was Martin Luther King, who delivered what became known as his "I Have a Dream" speech.[46] His words rang out over the crowd and were carried live on national television: "I say to you today, my friends, so even though we face the difficulties of today and tomorrow, I still have a dream. It is a dream deeply rooted in the American dream. I have a dream that one day this nation will rise up and live out the true meaning of its creed: 'We hold these truths to be self-evident that all men are created equal.'"[47]

our voices

Excerpt from Martin Luther King Jr.'s Letter from Birmingham Jail

April 16, 1963

MY DEAR FELLOW CLERGYMEN,

While confined here in the Birmingham city jail, I came across your recent statement calling my present activities "unwise and untimely." Seldom do I pause to answer criticism of my work and ideas. If I sought to answer all the criticisms that cross my desk, my secretaries would have little time for anything other than such correspondence in the course of the day, and I would have no time for constructive work. But since I feel that you are men of genuine good will and that your criticisms are sincerely set forth, I want to try to answer your statements in what I hope will be patient and reasonable terms. . . .

You deplore the demonstrations taking place in Birmingham. But your statement, I am sorry to say, fails to express a similar concern for the conditions that brought about the demonstrations. I am sure that none of you would want to rest content with the superficial kind of social analysis that deals merely with effects and does not grapple with underlying causes. It is unfortunate that demonstrations are taking place in Birmingham, but it is even more unfortunate that the city's white power structure left the Negro community with no alternative. . . .

I must make two honest confessions to you, my Christian and Jewish brothers. First, I must confess that over the past few years I have been gravely disappointed with the white moderate. I have almost reached the regrettable conclusion that the Negro's great stumbling block in his stride toward freedom is not the White Citizen's Counciler or the Ku Klux Klanner, but the white moderate, who is more devoted to "order" than to justice; who prefers a negative peace which is the absence of tension to a positive peace which is the presence of justice; who constantly says: "I agree with you in the goal you seek, but I cannot agree with your methods of direct action"; who paternalistically believes he can set the timetable for another man's freedom; who lives by a mythical concept of time and who constantly advises the Negro to wait for a "more convenient season." Shallow understanding from people of good will is more frustrating than absolute misunderstanding from people of ill will. Lukewarm acceptance is much more bewildering than outright rejection.

I had also hoped that the white moderate would reject the myth concerning time in relation to the struggle for freedom. I have just received a letter from a white brother in Texas. He writes: "All Christians know that the colored people will receive equal rights eventually, but it is possible that you are in too great a religious hurry. It has taken Christianity almost two thousand years to accomplish what it has. The teachings of Christ take time to come to earth." Such an attitude stems from a tragic misconception of time, from the strangely rational notion that there is something in the very flow of time that will inevitably cure all ills. Actually, time itself is neutral; it can be used either destructively or constructively. More and more I feel that the people of ill will have used time much more effectively than have the people of good will. We will have to repent in this generation not merely for the hateful words and actions of the bad people but for the appalling silence of the good people. Human progress never rolls in on wheels of inevitability; it comes through the tireless efforts of men willing to be co-workers with God, and without this hard work, time itself becomes an ally of the forces of social stagnation. We must use time creatively, in the knowledge that the time is always ripe to do right. Now is the time to make real the promise of democracy and transform our pending national elegy into a creative psalm of brotherhood. Now is the time to lift our national policy from the quicksand of racial injustice to the solid rock of human dignity. . . .

I hope this letter finds you strong in the faith. I also hope that circumstances will soon make it possible for me to meet each of you, not as an integrationist or a civil rights leader but as a fellow clergyman and a Christian brother. Let us all hope that the dark clouds of racial prejudice will soon pass away and the deep fog of misunderstanding will be lifted from our fear-drenched communities, and in some not too distant tomorrow the radiant stars of love and brotherhood will shine over our great nation with all their scintillating beauty.

Yours for the cause of Peace and Brotherhood,

MARTIN LUTHER KING JR.

Source: Reprinted by arrangement with the Heirs to the Estate of Martin Luther King Jr., c/o Writers House as agent for the proprietor New York, NY.

Increasing organized protest activity in the South fueled the Civil Rights Movement in 1964 and 1965, as did the commitment of President Lyndon B. Johnson to see strong civil rights legislation enacted. Despite opposition from Southern legislators, Johnson was able to persuade Congress to pass the Civil Rights Act of 1964, which banned discrimination in public facilities and employment. The next year, Johnson convinced Congress to pass the Voting Rights Act of 1965, which provided federal supervision of voter registration practices and elections. The act effectively opened the polls to Black Americans for the first time since the end of Reconstruction.[48]

The Women's Suffrage and Women's Rights Movements

Many White women were involved in the abolitionist movement that sought to end slavery. As these women became skilled at organizing, and became aware not only of the inequities of slavery, but also of the inequities in women's status, they began to voice their own grievances.[49] Thus, the impetus for the early origins of the movement sprang from two main sources—women's growing awareness of their common conditions and grievances and the growth of the antislavery movement.[50]

The First Wave of the Women's Rights Movement. The first wave of the women's rights movement developed in the twelve years preceding the Civil War. In July 1848, antislavery activists Elizabeth Cady Stanton and Lucretia Mott organized a convention to be held in Seneca Falls, New York, which would call for the extension of political, legal, and social rights to women. The convention aimed to improve the nation by making it guarantee equal rights to all its citizens.

One of the few men present at Seneca Falls was former slave and prominent abolitionist Frederick Douglass. Of the convention and women's rights, he wrote in an editorial in his newspaper the *North Star* on July 28, 1848, "We hold woman to be justly entitled to all we claim for man. We go farther, and express our conviction that all political rights which it is expedient for man to exercise, it is equally so for woman."[51]

Using the Declaration of Independence as a framework, Stanton wrote a "declaration of sentiments" in which she connected the emerging women's rights movement to the principles in the declaration.[52] Convention delegates unanimously approved the Declaration of Sentiments

Frederick Douglass (1818–1895) was one of the few men at the Seneca Falls Convention and remained committed to women's rights throughout his life.

and most of the resolutions proposed to address women's grievances. The only resolution that did not pass unanimously was the call for women's suffrage, but opposition dissipated after the convention.[53] As a result of the Seneca Falls convention, women's rights conventions were held regularly from 1850 until the start of the Civil War.

Sojourner Truth was among a small group of free, Black, feminist-abolitionists in the North in the early nineteenth century. This group also included Maria Stewart (1803–1879), born a free Black but later became an indentured servant until she was sixteen and later became an abolitionist and lecturer, and Frances E. Watkins Harper (1825–1911), a free Black abolitionist, suffragist, author and poet.[54] Sojourner Truth, born Isabella Baumfree, as a slave in Ulster County, New York is recognized as the individual who was most responsible for connecting the abolition of slavery and women's rights during the nineteenth century. At a time when most people thought of slaves as male and women as White, Sojourner Truth was particularly concerned with highlighting the complexities of Black women's race and gender identities.[55] Sojourner Truth attended her first women's right's convention in Worcester, Massachusetts in 1850, where Frederick Douglass was also present. The two had first met in 1842 in Northampton, Massachusetts, at the Northampton Association. Beyond their race, Frederick Douglass and Sojourner Truth had little in common. Douglass "saw himself as a statesman-in-the-making and modeled his comportment on the well-educated antislavery leaders with whom he worked."[56] Douglass had a condescending attitude toward Truth and viewed her as a "genuine specimen of the uncultured Negro."[57]

In 1851, Sojourner Truth (1797–1883) addressed the audience at the Women's Rights Convention in Akron, Ohio, and emphasized the important difference between White women and Black women in terms of their relationships to White men.[58] Truth's legendary "Ain't I a Woman" speech was recorded by presiding officer Frances D. Gage and was published in *Truth's Narrative* (1875) and *History of Woman Suffrage* (vol. I, 115–117).[59]

One problem that developed for the women's movement after the Civil War was that because it had been closely tied to the antislavery movement, it also continued to be closely tied to the debate and ratification of the Thirteenth, Fourteenth, and Fifteenth Amendments. Some of those who had been members of the abolitionist movement focused their efforts solely on Black male suffrage, but others who had been involved in the abolitionist movement felt that Black men should not get the vote before White women did.

Sojourner Truth (1797–1883), born a slave in Ulster County, New York, and escaped with her child in later years, was among a small group of free, Black, feminist-abolitionists active in both the abolitionist and early wave of the women's rights movement.

In 1866, Frederick Douglass and Charles Remond (1810–1873), a free Black abolitionist activists and lecturer, were among the vice presidents chosen to helm the leadership of the newly established Equal Rights Association (ERA) in 1866 after the American Anti-Slavery Association disbanded. Douglass was concerned that the ERA would become an organization that focused solely on women's rights.[60]

Sojourner Truth played an active role in the Equal Rights Association (ERA) along with Francis Watkins Harper. While both women were nationally-renowned orators, they did not hold positions of power within the ERA.[61] By comparison, Black women's involvement in the ERA was as limited as Black men's involvement had been in the prewar Anti-Slavery Society. Over the course of the ERA's three-year history, the organization had over fifty national officers and speakers participate at its conventions, but of that number, there were only five Black women and five Black men.[62]

In debates over Black and women's suffrage that were directly connected to the ratification of the Fourteenth Amendment that added "male" to the discussion of denying the right to vote and connecting that to representation, Truth opposed Frederick Douglass and other Black abolitionists, including Frances Harper, who were against removing "male" from the amendment. Instead she sided with White feminists on the issue. In a speech delivered at the annual meeting of the American Equal Rights Association, in New York in 1867, Truth talked about her fear that Black men would ignore the plight of Black women once they got the vote.[63]

As a result, the women's movement splintered into two groups over the Fifteenth Amendment, which explicitly prohibited denial of the franchise because of race, color, or previous condition of servitude. Stanton and Susan B. Anthony formed the National Woman Suffrage Association (NWSA), which focused on all-inclusive suffrage at the national level. Lucy Stone and her daughter, Alice Stone Blackwell, formed the American Woman Suffrage Association (AWSA), which supported the Fifteenth Amendment even though it excluded women. They argued that women's suffrage would best be achieved at the state level.[64]

At this point, Frederick Douglass publicly broke with Stanton and Anthony over their increasing opposition to the Fifteenth Amendment and Stanton's increasingly racist rhetoric.[65] While Sojourner Truth was actively involved in the issue of women's suffrage, she also split from Susan B. Anthony and Elizabeth Cady Stanton due to conflicting positions on the Fifteenth Amendment to the U.S. Constitution after Stanton had stated that she would not support the Black vote over women's suffrage.

After the Fifteenth Amendment was ratified, Black women began organizing for the right to vote even though they had been largely excluded by White women from their push for the franchise for women.[66] The emergence of the Black women's club movement in the late 1890s was the result of Black women forming organizations to contribute to the "uplift" of Black America and to address problems facing Black communities, such as health, education, and women's suffrage. Douglass's and Truth's break with the early founders of the women's suffrage movement and the exclusion of Black women from the agenda of White women in later years created a tension between Black and White women that has remained in the contemporary women's rights movement.

In 1890, NWSA and AWSA were reunited in the National American Woman Suffrage Association (NAWSA), with Elizabeth Cady Stanton as its president.[67] NAWSA began to petition and lobby states where women could vote, such as Kansas, Wyoming, and North Dakota, for passage of an amendment to the U.S. Constitution. Women, both White and Black, demonstrated, lobbied, and protested for women's suffrage, with one of the largest marches of women and their supporters, five thousand strong, taking place in Washington, DC, on March 3, 1913. The National Woman's Party also formed during this time.

In 1920, the Nineteenth Amendment, which granted women the right to vote, was finally ratified. After ratification, Black women who tried to vote were met with resistance from the National Woman's Party and were excluded from its efforts.[68] In 1923, Alice Paul, the leader of the National Woman's Party, drafted an equal rights amendment for the Constitution. The text of the amendment was simple: "Men and women have equal rights throughout the United States."[69] Paul's amendment was introduced into both the Senate and the House of Representatives, but it was not passed by either body at the time.

The Second Wave of the Women's Rights Movement. From the 1920s through the late 1950s, no national women's movement existed that was devoted to the issue of women's rights. Two events in the 1960s triggered the second wave of the women's rights movement. President Kennedy appointed Esther Peterson, a labor and consumer activist, head of the Department of Labor's Women's Bureau, and she convinced Kennedy to appoint a presidential commission on the status of women. Its 1963 report documented discrimination against women in virtually every area of American life, which ultimately resulted in the Equal Pay Act of 1963.[70] This, in turn, set the stage to extend Title 7 of the Civil Rights Act of 1964, the amendment that outlaws discrimination in employment, to include sex.[71]

Pauli Murray (1910–1985), civil rights and feminist activist, lawyer, university professor and college president, and one of the first females to be ordained an Episcopal priest, was a co-founder of the National Organization of Women (NOW) in 1966.

The second event was the publication in 1963 of *The Feminine Mystique* by journalist Betty Friedan, which documented the emotional and intellectual oppression that White middle-class educated women were experiencing because of limited life options.[72] In 1966, the National Organization for Women was founded. Its goal was to bring women into full participation in the mainstream of American society immediately in true equal partnership with men.[73]

Each of these events sparked a large increase in protests, demonstrations, and lobbying and renewed interest in an equal rights amendment. Like Alice Paul's earlier proposal, the new Equal Rights Amendment (ERA) was simple and direct: "Equality of rights under the law shall not be denied or abridged by the United States or by any state on account of sex." Congress approved the amendment on March 22, 1972, and sent it to the states for ratification. The campaign for ratification drew millions of women of all races to pressure their state legislatures to ratify the amendment. By the end of the year, twenty-two of the required thirty-eight states had ratified the amendment. Women's rights activists thought that ratification was a foregone conclusion.[74]

Not all women supported the ERA, however. A STOP ERA campaign led by the late Phyllis Schlafly was particularly effective in mounting opposition to the amendment. Schlafly and her group argued that the ERA would decriminalize rape, legitimize homosexuality, integrate public restrooms, guarantee abortion rights, lead men to abandon their families, and subject women to the military draft.[75] For a discussion of the arguments on both sides of the ERA, see "Evaluating Equality: What Arguments Did Supporters and Opponents of the ERA Put Forth?"

The STOP ERA forces persuaded some male legislators in several states to reject ratification. As the 1982 deadline for ratification approached, the ERA was just three states short of the thirty-eight states needed for ratification. Seventy-five percent of female legislators in the three states that were still considering the measure—Virginia, Illinois, and Arkansas—supported the ERA (which meant that some female legislators voted against the measure), but only 46 percent of male legislators voted to ratify.[76] In the end, the three states failed to ratify and the amendment went down to defeat. Despite the loss of the ERA, the second wave of the Women's Rights Movement accomplished a number of goals: It pushed through the passage of numerous pieces of legislation to protect women in the workplace and equalize funding for women's sports, it opened up doors for women in almost all professional fields, and it raised the consciousness of millions of American women.

Third Wave of the Women's Rights Movement. Some argue that a third wave of the Women's Rights Movement began in the early 1990s. Women's issues are still central to political debates, as we saw in the 2012 and 2016 elections, although scholars might debate whether the women's rights movement is still as prominent and as active as it once was. Nevertheless, the first piece of legislation signed by President Obama after he took office was the Lilly Ledbetter Fair Pay Act of 2009. The Ledbetter Act, amending the Civil Rights Act of 1964, states that the 180-day statute of limitations for filing an equal pay lawsuit resets with each paycheck that continues to result in unequal pay. Ledbetter had worked as a supervisor for Goodyear Tire and Rubber Company for twenty years. Shortly before she retired she found that she was being paid significantly less per month than the three male supervisors doing the same job. She sued, but the U.S. Supreme Court ruled that she had not filed within the 180-day requirement. The Ledbetter Act remedied this, as it is unlikely that many women will know within 180 days that they are being paid less than their male counterparts for the same work. Some activists have argued that the attack on women's rights over contraception and the funding of Planned Parenthood especially present in the 2012 and 2016 elections calls for a renewed women's rights movement.[77] The question of whether the women's rights movement is in a fourth wave or a continuation of the third is an open question that scholars will have to address.

evaluating equality

What Arguments Did Supporters and Opponents of the ERA Put Forth?

On March 22, 1971, the U.S. Senate passed the Equal Rights Amendment by a vote of 84–8 and sent it to the states to be ratified.* The entire amendment consisted of three sections:

Section 1. Equality of Rights under the law shall not be denied or abridged by the United States or any state on account of sex.

Section 2. The Congress shall have the power to enforce, by appropriate legislation, the provisions of this article.

Section 3. This amendment shall take effect two years after the date of ratification.

In Support of the ERA

The pro-ERA forces contended that the amendment would accomplish the following:

- Invalidate pay schemes called dual pay schedules for men and women being paid differently when they performed the same job.
- Eliminate state statutes that automatically exempted women from serving on a jury.
- Abolish restrictions on the legal capacity of married women, such as their right to establish a domicile, hold a driver's license in their own names, or go into business for themselves; on provisions in

family law giving greater responsibility to a husband and presuming dependence in a wife; and on the presumptions in divorce that a wife should care for any children and receive alimony.

- Eliminate gender differences in state and federal pension and Social Security benefits.
- Eliminate laws establishing different sentences for the same crime (in some states, Georgia, for example, men convicted of a crime would be given fixed sentences, whereas women convicted of the same crime would be given indeterminate sentences).
- Abolish restrictions on women entering and advancing in the armed forces.**

In Opposition to the ERA

The anti-ERA forces argued that the amendment would result in the following:

- Hurt homemakers and the family because it would abolish a husband's duty to support his wife.
- Mean that women had to be admitted to West Point in numbers equal to those of men.
- Subject women to the draft.
- Make girls eligible for the same athletic teams as boys in public schools and state universities.
- Render separate athletic competitions for men and women illegal.

- Reduce certain Social Security retirement benefits for women to the same level as those available to similarly situated men.
- Abolish freedom of choice among boys' schools, girls' schools, and coed schools (individuals would no longer be able to choose the type of educational setting they wanted for their children).
- Eliminate separate physical education classes for girls and boys in public schools.
- Abolish separate prison cells for men and women.
- Make separate public bathrooms for men and women illegal.***

Read the text of the amendment and then examine the claims of the pro- and anti-ERA forces.

- What effect do you think the proposed amendment would have actually had on the legal and social aspects of women's lives?
- What is your assessment of the validity of the claims of both sides?

*Mary Frances Berry, *Why the ERA Failed: Politics, Women's Rights, and the Amending Process of the Constitution* (Bloomington: Indiana University Press, 1986), 64.

**Jane J. Mansbridge, *Why We Lost the ERA* (Chicago: University of Chicago Press, 1986), 56–59.

***Ibid., 90–117.

The Labor Movement

In the years following the Civil War, the United States experienced phenomenal industrial expansion and tremendous economic changes. Manufacturing became increasingly mechanized, and corporations with nationwide scope controlled many industries, including mining, transportation, and steel. At the same time, massive immigration provided a large labor supply for the new factories and mines. Conditions in these new factories, mines, and steel plants were often unhealthy and frequently dangerous. Wages were low, and in many instances entire families, including children as young as six, worked twelve to sixteen hours a day just to earn enough money to subsist.[78]

Craft-based unions for skilled workers such as bricklayers, carpenters, and shoemakers had existed for some time in the United States, but these unions were usually local in character and concerned primarily with maintaining the standards of a particular craft. The nationalization of American business convinced labor leaders that labor had to organize on a nationwide basis to meet the challenge of industry.[79] One early attempt at national union organization occurred in 1866 with the creation of the National Labor Union (NLU). One of the NLU's objectives was the establishment of an eight-hour workday. The NLU's emphasis on this goal bore fruit in 1868 when Congress established an eight-hour day for federal workers, but the union dissolved in 1872.

In 1869, the Noble and Holy Order of the Knights of Labor was started in Philadelphia. On January 1, 1878, the Knights of Labor held a national convention and adopted a national structure and platform. By 1883, the union had grown from 9,000 to nearly 60,000 members.[80] The Knights of Labor's first strike against the telegraph companies in 1883 failed, but a year later its strike against the railroad companies succeeded in forcing them to rescind their attempt to reduce workers' wages. This was the first major victory of a union against a monopolistic giant, and workers flocked to join.[81]

In 1881, the Federation of Organized Trades and Labor Unions (FOTLU) was established to unite independent trade unions of skilled workers into a single federation. By 1886, FOTLU had evolved into the American Federation of Labor (AFL), whose aim was to protect skilled labor, such as carpenters, cigar makers, printers, iron and steelworkers, and iron molders. The AFL convinced these skilled workers that craft organizations could represent their interests better than could an organization that included millions of unskilled workers.[82]

The power of unions and the labor movement itself waxed and waned during the late 1800s and early 1900s, making gains on some fronts and losing ground in others. A horrific tragedy on March 25, 1911, pushed the issue of worker safety to the forefront. The Triangle Shirtwaist Company in New York City, a sweatshop that employed primarily immigrant women, caught fire. The exits had been locked by the company to prevent theft and the workers had no way out. Many of the women scrambled onto a fire escape that collapsed because of the excess weight. The fire department's ladders only reached to the

On March 25, 1911, 146 immigrant garment workers were killed after they were trapped on the upper floors of the Asch Building after the Triangle Shirtwaist Factory caught fire. The owners of the factory had chained shut the exit doors, and the workers, who were mostly young women, perished in the fire or died after jumping from the ten-story building. This photo shows the gutted remains of the tenth floor, with only the floors and walls intact.

sixth floor of the building, but the fire was on the top two floors. Many women jumped to their death trying to escape the flames, and others perished in the fire. All told, 146 people died in the fire. This tragic event pushed various levels of government to begin to do something about the health and safety of workers, including instituting fire codes and child labor laws.

In 1925, the first labor union organized by Blacks, the Brotherhood of Sleeping Car Porters and Maids, came into existence. The union was headed by A. Philip Randolph and organized by Black porters and maids who worked for the Pullman Company. Blacks were excluded from certain jobs, such as conductor, worked many hours without pay, and were charged for items stolen by their White passengers.[83] The Pullman Company fought the union and even cultivated many members of the Black press, particularly the Chicago *Defender* and its publisher, Robert Abbott, who joined with the company in denouncing the union.[84] It won a charter from the AFL in 1935, and the Pullman Company finally recognized the union in 1937. The union negotiated a landmark contract with the Pullman Company, winning $2 million in pay increases, a shorter work week, and overtime pay.

At the time, more than 20,000 Blacks worked for the railroads, the largest category of Black labor in the United States and Canada.[85] Many of the members of the Brotherhood of Sleeping Car Porters and Maids became major players in the later phases of the Civil Rights Movement. They included A. Philip Randolph, one of the organizers of the 1963 March on Washington; E. D. Nixon, who played a key role in the Montgomery bus boycott; Thurgood Marshall, the lead attorney on *Brown v. Board of Education of Topeka* in 1954 and the first Black Supreme Court justice; and Malcolm X, a civil rights activist whose approach was at odds with that of Martin Luther King and other mainstream civil rights leaders.[86]

Despite opposition to and repression of various aspects of the labor movement, it achieved a number of benefits for workers, including the standards of an eight-hour workday (1916) and a forty-hour workweek. Labor movement activities led to other accomplishments as well, such as prohibitions against child labor (1916, 1938), creation of the Department of Labor (1913), workplace safety rules and regulations (1938), a minimum wage (1938), and collective bargaining (1933, 1935).

Scholars view the 1930s and 1940s as the "glory" years for organized labor,[87] as it had a friendly national government in the administration of Franklin Roosevelt. One major piece of labor legislation that passed early in

Roosevelt's administration was the Wagner Act (1935), more commonly known as the National Labor Relations Act. The act allowed the right to strike and the right to choose a union and imposed a number of prohibitions on the behavior of management.[88]

At the conclusion of World War II in 1945, organized labor had a membership of more than 14 million workers, but labor had lost an ally in the White House with Franklin Roosevelt's death, and coalitions to fight labor reemerged. In 1947, Congress passed the Taft-Hartley Bill, which amended the Wagner Act by defining a set of unfair labor practices for labor in response to the Wagner Act's setting of unfair acts by management.[89]

In 1955, the Congress of Industrial Organizations (CIO), headed by Walter Reuther, and the AFL, headed by George Meany, merged to form a new union, the AFL-CIO. At the time, the new union covered one-third of all nonagricultural workers in the United States. Traditionally, the day-to-day practices of unions across the country discriminated heavily against Black and female workers, but once these two organizations became one, George Meany, the new head of the AFL-CIO, pushed the labor movement to actively support the Civil Rights Movement and was influential in helping to pass the Civil Rights Act of 1964, the Voting Rights Act of 1965, and the 1972 amendments to the Voting Rights Act.[90] Scholars suggest that Meany's interest was increasing membership in the AFL-CIO, and Black workers were a ready source of new members. Yet the merger did not remove the discrimination Black workers and female workers of all races experienced from the unions.

In the late 1970s, the first signs of union decline became apparent when President Jimmy Carter could not win congressional approval, in a Democrat-controlled Congress, to reform the National Labor Relations Act. President Ronald Reagan actively pursued aggressive antiunion policies, and in 1981 he broke a strike by the Professional Air Traffic Controllers Organization by firing all 11,000-plus members when they refused an order to return to work.[91] The union was decertified by the Federal Labor Relations Board in 1981. This strike is seen as pivotal in undermining the ability of unions, both private and public, to bargain and to use strikes as leverage.

If we look at union membership, we see that the labor movement does not have the strength and influence that it once had. Union membership fell from a high of 20.1 percent of the workforce in 1983 to just above the all-time low at 11.1 percent in 2015 (see "Measuring Equality: Unions and Wages"). Much of the growth in the U.S. economy over the last several decades has been in the service industry or in manufacturing jobs in nonunion businesses.

Yet other indicators suggest that labor still plays a major role in the U.S. economy. Although membership is down, belonging to a labor union is still beneficial to workers. In 2015, members of unions made approximately 21 percent more in wages per week than nonunion members did (as shown in "Measuring Equality"). Evidence also suggests that unions are beneficial to the wage structure for Blacks and female workers of all colors. Black workers

measuring equality

Unions and Wages

Unions grew out of the labor movement and have had a significant effect on the wages and working conditions of its members. Union membership is on the decline, but workers who are members of unions still earn higher wages than workers who are not members of unions. Figures 12.1 and 12.2 display the percentage of union members in the workforce and the higher wages earned by that decreasing share of the workforce.

Sources: U.S. Bureau of Labor Statistics, "Union Membership, 1983–2012," Table 1, "Union Affiliation of Employed Wage and Salary Workers by Selected Characteristics" (calculated from data), and Table 2, "Median Weekly Earnings of Full-Time Wage and Salary Workers by Union Affiliation and Selected Characteristics"; Bureau of Labor Statistics, U.S. Department of Labor, *The Editor's Desk,* "Union Membership Declines in 2012," http://www.bls.gov/opub/ted/2013/ted_20130124.htm, accessed February 14, 2013. Union affiliation data from Current Population Survey available at: http://www.bls.gov/cps/cpslutabs.htm accessed July 1, 2016.

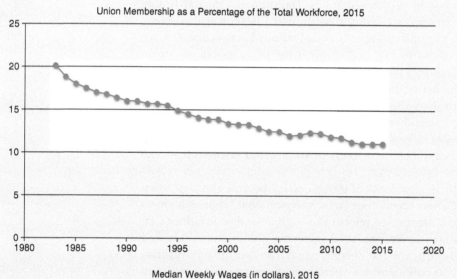

Union Membership as a Percentage of the Total Workforce, 2015

Figure 12.1
Union Membership as a Percentage of the Total Workforce, 2015.

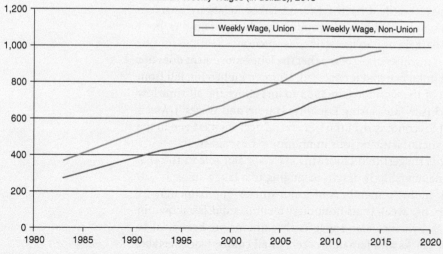

Median Weekly Wages (in dollars), 2015

Weekly Wage, Union — Weekly Wage, Non-Union

Figure 12.2
Median Weekly Wages (in dollars), 2015.

are more likely to belong to a union than White workers are, and the gap between women and men on this same dimension has narrowed considerably in the last thirty years. So even though the argument that the labor movement is dead is a popular one, working in jobs backed by a union still carries benefits for workers that are not matched in nonunion jobs.

The Environmental Movement

In 1962, biologist Rachel Carson published *Silent Spring*, which identified and highlighted the negative effects of pesticides on the environment and on human health. Carson's book spawned the modern environmental movement. Public attention shifted from land preservation and resource management, the predominant concerns of the conservation movement, to the effects of pollution and the environment on public health and quality of life.[92] Americans began to view their environment through the lenses of technology and its side effects—smog and petrochemicals such as plastics, solvents, pesticides, abrasives, and fuel additives—along with increases in environmentally triggered diseases. The public became cognizant of the toxins in waterways that killed fish, polychlorinated biphenyl in the Hudson River, high mercury levels in fish, and oil spills off the various coasts of the United States. This awareness pushed individuals to act, and the 1970s were a decade of intense environmental activity.

In 1969, Wisconsin Democratic Senator Gaylord Nelson announced that in spring 1970 there would be a national grassroots demonstration on the environment. Nelson wanted to push the issue of the environment, which had been building since 1962, onto the national agenda. On April 22, 1970, throngs of Americans celebrated the first Earth Day. The environmental movement tapped into the social activism swirling on college campuses from the civil rights and the anti–Vietnam War movements. As the environmental movement took hold, membership in older conservation organizations grew, as did the formation of new environmental organizations, such as the League of Conservation Voters, an organization dedicated to lobbying Congress for environmental legislation, in 1970.

The movement was successful in pushing the federal government to do more to protect the environment. Legislation included the Environmental Policy Act of 1970, the creation of the Environmental Protection Agency, the establishment of the Occupational Safety and Health Administration, and the Comprehensive Environmental Response, Compensation, and Liability Act, or "Superfund," to finance the cleaning up of thousands of abandoned toxic waste sites around the country. Yet issues of race were also intimately intertwined with issues of the environment, and out of the environmental movement grew the environmental justice movement.

Sociologist Robert Bullard is considered the "father of environmental justice," as his early research revealed that impoverished communities with high numbers of racial minorities disproportionately suffered from hazardous toxins in their neighborhood and workplaces. The situation of increased

Environmental Racism Intentional or unintentional racial discrimination in the enforcement of environmental laws and regulations and in the targeting of racial minority communities for the siting of pollution-producing industries or hazardous waste sites and other related environmentally hazardous entities.

exposure to environmental hazards in Black rural and urban communities has been called **environmental racism**.

Bullard began his work in this area in the late 1970s, right after he had finished graduate school, when he was asked by his wife to collect data for a lawsuit filed against the city of Houston over its plans to locate a landfill in the middle of a predominately Black, middle-class suburban neighborhood where 85 percent of the people owned their homes. Through his research, he discovered that 100 percent of all the city-owned landfills in Houston were in Black neighborhoods, although Blacks were only 25 percent of the city's population.[93] His book *Dumping in Dixie: Race, Class, and Environmental Quality* (first published in 1990) grew out of his initial work in Houston.[94] Bullard was one of the organizers of the first National People of Color Environmental Leadership Summit in 1991, which developed the organizing principles for the environmental justice movement.

Despite early successes, the broader environmental movement suffered setbacks during the administrations of Ronald Reagan and George W. Bush. Industries and conservatives pushed back on environmental regulations, pushed to open federal lands to logging, and lobbied successfully to have national parks opened to snowmobiles. Funds were cut for enforcement of environmental laws and regulations, and questions were raised about the existence of global warming. Each of these decisions was aimed at retarding the federal government's efforts to protect or clean up the environment and, in some instances, allowed people, businesses, and industries to continue behaving in ways that contributed to the destruction of the environment. President Obama's administration has tried to roll back some of these Bush-era regulations, but he has run into resistance from Republican members of Congress. Congress continued to resist his environmental policies throughout the remainder of his term.

The Anti–Vietnam War Movement

The Vietnam War (1959–1975) was a nationalist struggle between forces in North Vietnam that wanted to unify the country under a communist regime and forces in South Vietnam, who, along with the United States, did not want that unification to occur. Vietnam had been a French colony for more than sixty years and tensions between the Vietnamese and French existed as a result. In 1945, the Viet Minh, the group that lead the struggle for independence from French colonialism, established a new government, calling it the Democratic Republic of Vietnam. The French, with military aid from the United States, fought against what amounted to independence for the French colony. The French were defeated at the battle of Dien Bien Phu in spring 1954 and pulled out of Vietnam.[95]

A convention in Geneva that same year partitioned the country into two governments—the Democratic Republic of Vietnam in the North (communist) and the Republic of Vietnam (anticommunist) in the south. The United

States was concerned about a communist takeover of the entire country, so President Eisenhower sent in military advisors to assist the South Vietnamese in 1959, with President Kennedy increasing the number of advisors in 1961 and 1962 to 11,300 U.S. troops. Kennedy had planned to begin to withdraw the advisors, but his assassination brought Lyndon Johnson into the presidency and he, based on more optimistic military advice about a U.S. victory, increased the number of U.S. advisors to 21,000. Combat troops were committed in early 1965, rising from 3,500 to 184,000 by the end of 1965 and to 429,000 by the end of 1966.[96]

The first glimpse of opposition to U.S. involvement in Vietnam occurred in 1963 on a small number of college campuses in reaction to what was perceived as religious intolerance in Vietnam when Buddhist monks set themselves on fire in protest of the treatment of Buddhists by the South Vietnamese. Shortly after Lyndon B. Johnson's inauguration in early 1965, the United States began bombing and moving troops into North Vietnam, and in response the antiwar movement began to take form. College students were concerned about increased draft call-ups as the number of ground troops in Vietnam increased and the differential draft deferments given to those seeking them. The first antiwar organization was the National Committee to End the War in Vietnam.[97] At first, this movement sought to change policy by educating the nation and its leaders in Washington. The first "teach-in" discussion about the merits of the war began in March, and a priority was put on explaining to the public and members of Congress the folly of beginning military engagement.[98]

On April 17, 1965, the recently formed student activist movement called Students for a Democratic Society, along with the SNCC, organized what was then the largest antiwar demonstration march in Washington, with 25,000 people attending. As the year progressed, more demonstrations occurred, with some attracting hundreds of thousands, even millions, of protesters.[99] Early protesters also expressed their discontent through the burning of draft cards. The practice caught on in the summer of 1965 and became such a popular form of protest that Congress passed, and President Johnson signed, a law making it a federal crime to willfully destroy one's card.[100]

As the antiwar movement grew in visibility and popularity, some celebrities took public antiwar stances and suffered severe consequences. In 1967, heavyweight champion Muhammad Ali, declaring himself a conscientious objector, refused three times to step forward when his name was called to be inducted into the military. He was arrested and later that year convicted. The public response to Ali's actions was largely negative, and he was stripped of his license to box in every state in the United States and stripped of his World Boxing Association title. These actions prevented him from fighting for more than three years until the Supreme Court unanimously overturned his conviction in 1971. At that time, the backlash against Blacks and other members of racial groups who opposed the war was swift and ferocious.[101]

The biggest demonstration in Boston's history happened on Vietnam Moratorium Day as an estimated 100,000 persons shouted in cadence on Boston Common that they wanted the Vietnam War ended "Now!" The Moratorium to End the War in Vietnam was a peace rally held on the Boston Common, October 15, 1969.

One of the most well-known demonstrations occurred at the 1968 Democratic National Convention. When President Johnson decided not to run for reelection, his vice president, Hubert Humphrey, became the de facto front-runner. Senator Eugene McCarthy of Minnesota entered the race first on an antiwar platform, with Senator Robert F. Kennedy of New York entering later, also with an antiwar stance. Kennedy eclipsed McCarthy and was considered the most likely challenger to Humphrey for the nomination. Tragically, Kennedy was assassinated, and the nomination campaign culminated at the Democratic National Convention in Chicago, pitting Humphrey, again the front-runner, against McCarthy and Senator George McGovern of South Dakota, another opponent of the war.[102]

Meanwhile, several thousand members of the antiwar movement had converged on the city to protest the convention. Chicago Mayor Richard Daley had promised that law and order would be maintained. Demonstrators gathered in parks and in the streets to engage in various protest activities. The police used tear gas in an attempt to disband the crowds, and a major rally in Grant Park turned ugly when police resorted to violence and protesters responded in kind.[103] Several other confrontations between protesters and the Chicago police and Illinois National Guard occurred, with one conflict escalating into a massive brawl on Michigan Avenue that received extensive local and national coverage.[104] Humphrey gave his acceptance speech to an amphitheater full of Daley's patronage workers and loyalists, who chanted, "We want Daley; we want Daley," as the melee stormed outside.[105]

For much of this period, the civil rights and antiwar movements were happening concurrently, but not in concert. At first, the issues appeared separate and the interests involved not necessarily aligned. As the movements matured, however, activists in both groups recognized that there was at least some degree of overlap between the goals of each group and that forging a common cause could be mutually beneficial.

Dr. Martin Luther King Jr., the most visible leader of the Civil Rights Movement, was initially hesitant to speak in opposition to the war, for fear of alienating President Johnson. As the war developed, however, King began to express increasingly strong opposition. He first spoke out in a speech at Howard University in March 1965, claiming that the war was "accomplishing nothing" and calling for a negotiated settlement. Other mainstream civil rights groups followed suit shortly thereafter. The Mississippi Freedom Democratic Party, a political party organized primarily by Black Mississippians that challenged the seating of the all-White Mississippi delegation to the 1964 Democratic National Convention in Atlantic City, argued against Black participation in the war, citing as absurd the request for Blacks to risk their lives and to kill so that White Americans could get richer. SNCC adopted an antiwar stance, claiming that the government had been deceptive in the war effort, just as it had been in its concern for the freedom of minorities, both at home and abroad.[106]

Another argument for opposition to the war was that Black youths were disproportionately likely to be drafted and disproportionately likely to see combat. Deferment options allowed by the Selective Service favored middle- and upper-class men and male college students, who were generally more likely to be White.[107] As such, Blacks were carrying an overlarge share of the burden of the war on behalf of a country that would not fully recognize their rights.

In 1967, at New York's Riverside Church, Dr. King gave one of his most stirring speeches, arguing passionately against the war. King enumerated his reasons for advocating an end to U.S. involvement in Vietnam. He was dismayed at how the expense of the war drew funds away from the antipoverty programs started only a few years before, and he noted that such conflicts were a drain on the lives, productivity, and finances of the country. King made explicit the connection between the civil rights and peace movements.

Reaction to this speech was largely negative. *The New York Times* published an editorial claiming that the two problems of the war and of equality were separate and distinct, and that by addressing the war, King was diffusing the efforts of his movement, as well as undermining the appeal of the Civil Rights Movement to those not opposed to the war. Despite the backlash, King continued to participate in the antiwar movement until his assassination in 1968.

Lesbian, Gay, Bisexual, and Transgender Movement

Social movements by lesbian, gay, bisexual, and transgender (LGBT) people share the goal of social acceptance of homosexuality, bisexuality, and transgenderism. The communities have collaborated and worked separately to organize for gay liberation, lesbian feminism, the queer movement, and transgender activism. LGBT activists work through political and cultural avenues—organizing lobbying and street marches, support groups, community events, magazines, film, literature, academic research and writing, and business activity, for example—to challenge the dominance of heterosexual norms and constructions of femininity and masculinity and to combat homophobia. Political goals include extending civil and legal rights and protections.[108]

The LGBT movement dates back to the eighteenth and nineteenth centuries. In 1924, the Society for Human Rights was established in Chicago. This was the first recorded gay rights organization in the United States. The organization was founded by Henry Gerber, a World War I veteran, who had experienced relative freedom as a gay male in Europe. The organization disbanded soon after its founding because of a police raid of Gerber's home and the arrest of the small group of members of the organization. Although all charges were dropped, the raid doomed the organization. The modern movement was launched immediately following World War II with the word "homophile," which emphasized love instead of sex.[109]

In 1950, The Mattachine Society, the first national gay rights organization, was formed in Los Angeles by Harry Ray and a group of his male friends. The Mattachine Society was an activist organization whose primary goal was to protect and improve the rights of homosexuals. The Daughters of Bilitis, a lesbian organization, was formed in San Francisco in 1956. The organization, the first lesbian civil rights and political rights organization in the United States, was conceived as an alternative to lesbian bars, which were subjected to frequent raids and police harassment. In 1962, Illinois became the first U.S. state to de-criminalize homosexual acts between consenting adults done in private. On July 4, 1965, picketers at Independence Hall in Philadelphia staged the first Reminder Day to call public attention to the lack of civil rights for LGBT people. The gatherings continued annually for five years.[110]

In 1966, gay bars were technically legal in New York but the State Liquor Society had a regulation against serving LGBT people in bars because they were assumed to be disruptive. This refusal to serve gays had no basis in law. As such, agents used their internal regulation to raid gay bars and other bars refused to serve gay individuals. On April 21, 1966, the Mattachine Society, drawing from the civil rights sit-ins, decided to stage a "sip-in"—several men would go into a bar, identify themselves as gay, then wait to be served or

In April 1966, these men walked into Julius' and announced that they were gay; the bartender put his hand over the glass and refused to serve them.

denied service and then file suit if denied service. On that day, three young men set out to test whether they would be served. The first set of bars they tried to enter had been tipped off and closed to avoid the protesters. At the next couple of restaurants, the group handed the waitress a note that said, "We are homosexuals. We believe that a place of public accommodation has an obligation to serve an orderly person, and that we are entitled to service as long as we are orderly." At both of these restaurants, they were served drinks. They then went to Julius', knowing that they would be denied service. They walked in, the bartender put glasses down, they announced that they were gay and the bartender put his hand over the glass. The picture was captured by a photographer from *The Village Voice*. (In April 2016, Julius' marked the Sip-In's fiftieth anniversary.)[111]

Out of the gay liberation movement of the 1970s arose the gay rights movement, a reformist movement that sees gays and lesbians as a minority group demanding civil rights. On June 28, 1970, the first gay pride march was held a year after the Stonewall riots. The riots spurred this group into activism, and served, as mentioned earlier, as a catalyst for the modern phase of the movement. The marchers traveled up a single lane of traffic on New York's Sixth Avenue.

Lesbian feminism also arose in the 1970s to emphasize the male dominance of the LGBT movement. In the 1970s and 1980s, gay rights organizations proliferated throughout the United States. Prominent among them were the National Gay and Lesbian Task Force, the Human Rights Campaign, and ACT UP (AIDS Coalition to Unleash Power). The 1980s, in particular, launched a new era with the emergence of AIDS and the decimation of leaders. Gay activists were able to garner significant support from the Democratic Party, when the party added a nondiscrimination clause on sexual orientation to its platform in 1980. Additionally, campaigns urging gay men and women to "come out of the closet" (e.g., National Coming Out Day) were critical factors that enabled openly gay individuals to run for public office and work to promote gay rights.[112]

More militant groups focusing on direct action also emerged such as ACT UP (1987), Queer Nation (1990), and Lesbian Avengers (1992). "Queer" became the referential term for younger activists who saw "gay and lesbian" as too normatively and politically conservative; conversely, the acronym LGBT has also become a commonplace descriptor in an effort to unify the various communities.

Slowly, some members of mainstream civil rights groups began to see solidarity with the goals of the LGBT movement, albeit slowly. In 1998, Coretta Scott King, the widow of Martin Luther King Jr., called on the civil rights community to join the struggle against homophobia. She received criticism from members of the Black Civil Rights Movement for comparing civil rights to gay rights. But in 2012 the NAACP came out in support of same-sex marriage, much to the consternation of some Black ministers.

Also in 1998, Matthew Shepard, a student at the University of Wyoming, was attacked and tortured near Laramie, Wyoming. He was lured from a bar by

Aaron McKinney and Russell Henderson, taken to a remote site, beaten, and killed. Shepard was murdered because he was gay and his death ignited demonstrations across the United States and highlighted hate crimes against LGBT individuals. Henderson pleaded guilty to murdering Shepard and is serving life in prison. McKinney was convicted of second-degree murder and felony robbery and kidnapping that made him eligible for the death penalty.[113] McKinney was spared the death penalty when Shepard's parents asked the court to show mercy on McKinney, saying, "This is the time to begin the healing process, to show mercy to someone who refused to show any mercy." McKinney was sentenced to two consecutive life sentences.

In 2009, President Obama signed the Matthew Shepard and James Byrd Jr. Hate Crimes Prevention Act, named for Shepard and James Byrd, Jr., a Black man who was chained to a pickup truck in Jasper, Texas, and dragged to his death, also in 1998. It took more than a decade to get this legislation through Congress, but it was finally accomplished with support from more than three hundred national law enforcement, professional, education, civil rights, religious, and civic organizations, and more than twenty-six state attorneys general. Among the organizations were the Gay and Lesbian Alliance Against Defamation, the Human Rights Campaign, the NAACP, the National Association of Latino Elected and Appointed Officials (NALEO), the Sikh American Legal Defense and Education Fund (SALDEF), and the National Organization of Women, among others.[114] The champion within the U.S. Senate was the late Senator Edward M. Kennedy (D-MA) and among those pushing the legislation were the Gay and Lesbian Alliance Against Defamation and the Human Rights Campaign.

Support of civil unions and same-sex marriage began to gain strength in 2000, when Vermont became the first state to recognize civil unions between gay and lesbian couples and the Massachusetts Supreme Court ruled that only full marriage rights are consistent with the state constitution.[115]

Same-sex marriages became legal in Massachusetts in 2004. Nineteen states and the District of Columbia followed suit making same-sex marriages legal. As this book goes to press, same-sex marriage is legal in thirty-two states and the District of Columbia. But court battles continue in those states with legislative and state constitutional prohibitions and in those states where the courts struck down restrictive legislation.

Successes for the movement continued to come with President Obama pushing Congress to repeal the "Don't Ask, Don't Tell" policy banning gay and lesbian soldiers from serving openly in the military in 2011. The policy came into being in 1993, when President Clinton tried to lift the ban on gays and lesbians serving openly in the military. The compromise was that they could serve as long as they did not tell anyone or openly declare their sexual orientation. The lifting of the ban, a tremendous accomplishment, was followed in 2012 when President Obama declared his support for same-sex marriage. He had previously supported civil unions, but this was the first time he expressed his support for same-sex marriage. In his January 21, 2013, inaugural address,

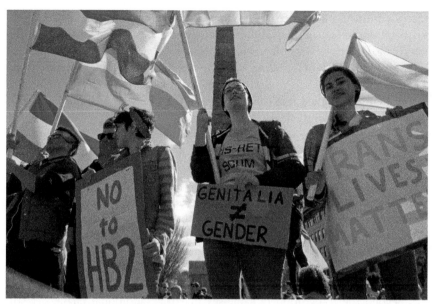

People in Asheville, North Carolina, protest the state's Public Facilities Privacy & Security Act, or HB2, that restricts the rights of those who are transgender.

President Obama mentioned the gay rights movement and the Stonewall uprising, placing the rights of LGBT citizens in the forefront of the struggle for civil rights.

The public attitude toward issues related to LGBT issues is also changing, suggesting a more supportive environment for the goals of the LGBT movement. According to a 2014 report by the Williams Institute at UCLA, the shift in support is something that is not only due to younger generation's support, but they find that a "broader cultural shift affects people of all ages."[116] A 2015 Gallup poll showed that 60 percent of Americans now support same-sex marriage. What is interesting from their finding is that this is the highest level of support found by Gallup polls since they first asked the question in 1996.[117] In 1996, only 27 percent asked were in support, so the marked change within the last two decades is an important implication to consider.

In addition to a shifting tide in public opinion, the LGBT movement has had very important successes and challenges occur in recent years that has pushed the conversation forward in public discourse. The movement to gain legal recognition of same-sex marriages has become one of the most recent areas where LGBT rights is being pushed forward. In 2015, thirty-seven states had made same-sex marriage legal. This shifted to becoming legal nationally with the landmark case of *Obergefell v. Hodges*. June 26, 2015, served to be a historic day of victory for advocates and supporters of the LGBT movement. The court voted 5–4 in in the case of *Obergefell v. Hodges*.

In a 5–4 majority, led by Justice Anthony Kennedy, the Supreme Court ruled that the U.S. Constitution provided the right for same-sex couples to marry within the U.S. In the Supreme Court's opinion, Justice Anthony M. Kennedy wrote for the majority. Justice Kennedy said, "No longer may this liberty be denied . . . No union is more profound than marriage, for it embodies the highest ideals of love, fidelity, devotion, sacrifice and family. In forming a marital union, two people become something greater than once they were." Justice Kennedy argued that the plaintiffs in the case were seeking for, "equal dignity in the eyes of the law."[118]

The decision came upon the second anniversary of the *United States v. Windsor* ruling, whereby the U.S. Supreme Court had struck down Section 3 of the Defense of Marriage Act (DOMA). This ruling, which had occurred in 2013, had previously denied federal recognition to same-sex marriages, and the striking down of the law provided federal benefits to same-sex couples, in the same manner afforded heterosexual couples.[119]

While the 2015 ruling has served to be an important historic moment that has gained public support, as the 2015 public opinion polls highlight, challenges still persist. In the state of Alabama, for example, eleven counties refused to comply with the law.[120]

Beyond the recognition of same-sex marriage, additional challenges still remain for LGBT communities and advocates to address. In 2016, the state of North Carolina passed into law "House Bill 2." Better known as HB 2, it was passed into law by the Republican-dominated General Assembly in a special one-day session in March 2016. This law requires transgender people to utilize restrooms that correspond to the sex on their birth certificate.[121] Moreover, the legislation prevents cities from passing their own ordinances that would be more accommodating to the transgender people's accommodations and preferences.[122]

The passage of the law has caused national uproar and calls for boycotts. Major musicians, including Bruce Springsteen, Demi Lovato, and the bands Pearl Jam and Maroon 5, canceled concerts in the state. Moreover, companies such as PayPal and Deutsche Bank USA announced they are canceling plans to expand within the state of North Carolina.[123] The NBA has also expressed serious concern and has been outspoken against the law. The 2017 All-Star Games were scheduled to occur in Charlotte, but since the passage of the law, the NBA moved the games to New Orleans.[124] The Atlantic Coast Conference (ACC) and the NCCA moved play-off and championship games out of North Carolina.

The U.S. Department of Justice has filed a lawsuit against the state, as have civil rights organizations including the ACLU, Equality North Carolina, among others. Attorney General Loretta Lynch said this has put the state of North Carolina in "direct opposition to federal laws prohibiting discrimination on the basis of sex and gender identity. More to the point, they created state-sponsored discrimination against transgender individuals who simply seek to engage in the most private of functions in a place of safety and security, a right taken for granted by most of us."[125]

According to a 2016 poll of North Carolina registered voters conducted by Elon University, 39 percent were in support of the state lawmakers allowing cities to pass transgender-friendly rules, and 49 percent of the population were in opposition to the HB 2 proposal.[126] The poll highlights how this issue has become divisive among registered voters in the state of North Carolina.

North Carolina is not the only state that has tried to push forward legislation that has disparate effect on LGBT communities. In the state of Mississippi, HB 1523 was signed into law, allowing court clerks the right to refuse wedding licenses to same-sex couples.[127] On July 1, 2016, Judge Carlton W. Reeves struck down that part of the law, reinforcing the Supreme Court ruling on same-sex marriage. Interestingly, Reeves is an African American judge, and tied the potential discrimination this law has back to the racist past of the state. Reeves also noted, "In physics, every action has its equal and opposite reaction. In politics, every action has its predictable overreaction. . . . The Supreme Court's same-sex marriage decision, *Obergefell v. Hodges*, has led to HB 1523. The next chapter of this back-and-forth has begun."[128]

Other Important U.S. Social Movements

The Chicano Civil Rights Movement

The Chicano civil rights movement, otherwise known as *"El Movimiento,"* extended the Mexican American civil rights movement, which began in the 1940s, to counteract negative stereotypes of Mexicans in mass media and culture; assert economic and political rights around the restoration of land grants, farm workers' rights, and voting; address discrimination; and cultivate an awareness of collective history. "Chicano" was originally a derogatory reference to migrants' children, who were seen by the culture at large as neither "American" nor "Mexican." Mexican Americans adopted the term in the 1960s as a symbol of ethnic pride and self-determination. Despite the emergence of national groups such as the American G. I. Forum and the Mexican American Legal Defense and Educational Fund (1968), the movement remained limited in scope and was focused on the Southwest region, and did not become pan-Hispanic.

The movement was influenced by the Black Civil Rights Movement both in the general activism the latter inspired and in the involvement of Chicano student leaders. Student organizers, concerned about the conservatism of the earlier Civil Rights Movement, created mass walkouts and sit-ins to call awareness to the movement. The 1964 "Crystal City Revolt," in which the Political Association of Spanish-Speaking Organizations was formed and collaborated with the predominantly Mexican American local chapter of the Teamsters Union, elected Mexican Americans over White candidates for the city council. In 1968, mass walkouts of high school students were organized in Denver and East Los Angeles. The Chicano movement's focus on local economic and political control generated solidarity and established Chicano institutions.[129]

Farm workers' rights became an important issue in the second half of the twentieth century, with one of the most prominent leaders being César E. Chávez, a notable Chicano national leader in the Civil Rights Movement. With Dolores Huerta, he cofounded the United Farm Workers Movement, which galvanized a lot of attention around farm workers' rights, with activism occurring as early as 1957 well into the 1980s. The movement helped generate the creation of such present-day Latino organizations as the National Council of La Raza (NCLR) and the Mexican American Legal Defense and Educational Fund (MALDEF).

American Indian Movement

American Indians, after a seventy-year hiatus following the Wounded Knee massacre of 1890, started agitating for greater political, cultural, and economic rights in the 1960s and 1970s.[130] American Indians did not receive U.S. citizenship until 1924 and did not gain suffrage until the Voting Rights Act of 1965. The American Indian Religious Freedom Act (1978) was vital in securing religious rights, and American Indians continued to press for other rights, including those concerning tribal sovereignty, hunting and fishing, travel, and land.

Dennis Banks, George Mitchell, Herb Powless, Clyde Bellecourt, Eddie Benton-Banai, and others founded the American Indian Movement (AIM), an activist organization modeled on Black protest groups, in 1968. AIM organized several mass demonstrations in the 1970s to call attention to the American Indian plight, including the takeover of the Bureau of Indian Affairs (1972), the occupation of Wounded Knee on the Pine Ridge reservation (1973), and the Longest Walk (1978) from San Francisco to Washington, DC.

AIM and other groups continue to advocate for American Indian interests, renew their diverse heritages, assist in urban and rural employment programs, and monitor police activity. They are also involved in fighting symbolic degradation or marginalization of American Indians by protesting national holidays such as Thanksgiving or Columbus Day. In 2007, a delegation of Lakota Sioux declared secession from the United States, citing broken treaties and loss of territory. The group declared its intention to the State Department to form a separate nation, the Republic of Lakotah.

Asian American Movement

The Black Civil Rights Movement inspired student leadership and activism on several fronts, and Asian Americans were one such minority group that walked this path. Although each ethnic group had litigated, organized, and participated politically when able and necessary, a national panethnic coalition had not transpired. The Civil Rights Movement intensified awareness about racism and discrimination. Like the Black Civil Rights Movement, the Asian American movement developed from local actions. In 1968, Chinese Americans in San Francisco organized to get the city government to pay attention to the problems in Chinatown. They eventually organized a protest march down Grant Avenue, the main street that runs through Chinatown. In 1968 and 1969, Asian American college students at San Francisco State and the University of California–Berkeley expressed their displeasure with their treatment at the institutions. The anti–Vietnam War movement, particularly prevalent on college campuses, placed middle-class Asian Americans in a unique position to consider the cultural, political, and military implications of being "Asian" and the racial implications of U.S. military policy.[131]

A number of organizations grew out of this movement, such as the Asian American Legal Defense Fund and Asian Americans Advancing Justice (AAJC). These groups represent Asian American interests at the national level. At present, Asian American groups are tackling issues such as equitable wages for immigrant workers, language access programs for voting rights, and post-9/11 civil liberties.

The Antinuclear Movement

Opponents of nuclear technology and power have been active since the 1960s in organizing against nuclear technology, the use of depleted uranium in warfare, and the practice of food irradiation or radiation. The environmental movement's emergence and the use of atomic weapons in Japan during World War II coalesced with a cultural suspicion of technology and radioactivity.

At one point, there were fifty loosely affiliated grassroots antinuclear organizations in the United States. These organizations and individual activists engage in public education via the Internet, demonstrations, and concerts; in nonviolent direct action such as demonstrations, picketing, or blockages; or in violent confrontation through sabotage or demonstrations. Campaigns involving the Calvert Cliffs Nuclear Power Plant, Seabrook Station Nuclear Power Plant, Diablo Canyon Power Plant, Shoreham Nuclear Power Plant, and Three Mile Island captured public attention in the 1970s. The movement has also been successful in delaying construction or stopping commitments to build new nuclear plants. Concerned with nuclear accidents and waste, activists advocate nuclear-free energy alternatives such as biomass, wind and solar power, and geothermal power.[132]

The movement includes not only grassroots organization but also scientists, including Nobel laureates such as Linus Pauling and Hermann Joseph Muller. The Committee for Nuclear Responsibility, the Federation of American Scientists, and the Union of Concerned Scientists are notable national organizations that have been very influential in advocating for this issue.

Religious Fundamentalist Movement

In the United States, Christian fundamentalism is rooted in the Niagara Bible Conference (1878–1897), which sought to define the fundamentals of belief. The movement quickly moved beyond the conservative Presbyterian academics and theologians who originated the movement to other denominations such as the Baptists. The original meaning of fundamentalism has changed over time, and fundamentalism is now associated with a particular segment of evangelical Protestantism that looks to separate and distance itself from modernity and modern culture. Yet, there are variants of fundamentalism that see one way of distancing themselves from modernity and modern culture is to participate in politics to assert their views and influence government in their direction.[133]

Rob Grant and Jerry Falwell are among the fundamentalist clergy who advocated Christian intervention in U.S. politics in the 1970s. Now known as the Christian Right, religious fundamentalists have been instrumental in shaping policy and determining elections through organizations such as the Christian Coalition and the Family Research Council. By the mid-1990s, the Republican Party had gained control of the White House, Congress, and some seats on the Supreme Court, through the activism of the Christian Right.

Recently, the Religious Right has focused on preventing the passage of same-sex marriage legislation as part of their agenda. In February 2014, they pushed forward a bill in Arizona to give restaurants the right to refuse service to gay couples; the legislation passed with a 33 to 27 vote. Jan Brewer, the governor of Arizona, vetoed the bill.

Why Some Social Movements Decline and Some Fail

Social movements are not permanent entities. They arise out of specific conditions and even successful movements find it difficult to sustain themselves over time. Moreover, some movements that have a major presence in society might fail in their efforts to bring about changes. A number of factors account for both outcomes.

Factors That Contribute to Social Movement Decline

Social movements do not go on forever and the reasons for their decline are varied. Some social movements decline because members have difficulty maintaining a commitment to the movement over long periods of time. Activists who have worked hard for a long time may grow weary and believe that it is time for others to take the lead. Sometimes a new generation of leaders is not available or their view of the goals of the movement might be different from those of the previous generation.

Factionalism Divisions that develop within a movement that may weaken it or cause its demise.

Another factor that contributes to the decline of social movements is **factionalism**, divisions that develop within the movement. Participants in social movements might disagree about goals and strategies for achieving those goals. During the early years of the Civil Rights Movement, participants generally adhered to tactics of nonviolent civil disobedience and recognized that progress might be slow. By the late 1960s, however, some participants, especially college students, felt progress was too slow and that nonviolent methods were no longer effective. More militant groups emerged, such as the SNCC and the Black Panthers, as part of the Black Power movement, to press for faster action and more radical tactics. Black power advocates argued for separation from Whites rather than integration, which was the goal of older civil rights organizations. The gulf between the newer and older groups was too great to be repaired and the factionalism severely affected the ability of the CRM to remain unified.

Changes in public opinion can also contribute to the decline of social movements. A supportive environment is important not only for the development of a social movement, but for the maintenance of a movement as well. The public might begin to feel that the movement's grievances have all been addressed or solved and thus is no longer receptive to the continued or further demands. This change in public opinion might signal that issues related to the movement's goals no longer have the support of the majority of the public. When a social movement begins to lose favorable public opinion, the movement can begin to decline. The ability of the CRM to continue pushing for Black advancement was affected by the shift in public opinion on the importance of civil rights as the most important issue facing the country. In January 1965, 52 percent of Americans saw race relations as the most important issue, but by January 1967 close to 55 percent saw the war in Vietnam as the most important issue.[134]

Sometimes social movements generate counter-movements that organize in opposition to the goals and objectives of the social movement. Counter-movements can be very effective in working against the ideals of the social movement. A good example is the organization of the major tobacco companies—Philip Morris, R. J. Reynolds, Brown and Williamson, American Tobacco, and Lorillard—to unsuccessfully fight the antismoking movement's success in banning smoking in workplaces in California.[135]

Success itself may contribute to the decline of a social movement. Once a social movement has achieved its objectives, some participants might feel that there is nothing left to do. For example, once the war in Vietnam ended, the antiwar movement dissolved. The main issue around which the movement arose no longer existed.

Factors That Contribute to Social Movement Failure

Not all social movements succeed. First, a social movement might fail if its goals are too broad or unrealistic. Social movements with limited objectives have a higher probability of success than those whose goals are very broad and not well defined, such as the early 1900s goal of the International Workers of the World (the Wobblies) to restructure the entire U.S. government. That objective was clearly impossible to achieve.

Second, the inability to organize effectively is another contributor to failure. Groups seeking policy changes within existing political structures must organize to negotiate with the political system.[136] Failure to organize doomed the poor people's campaign in 1968.

Third, suppression, the use of physical, legal, and violent force against a social movement might lead to failure. For example, in the late nineteenth century large corporations fought labor unions' efforts to unionize employees, and in many instances the struggles between the unions and corporations involved considerable violence. One example is the 1892 violent struggle between the Amalgamated Association of Iron and Steel Workers, an AFL affiliate, and the steel industry, especially steel baron Andrew Carnegie.[137] Carnegie hired a private army from the Pinkerton Company that, with the help of 6,000 federal and state troops, violently put down the strike and left ten dead.[138]

Historically, more social movements probably fail than succeed. Yet failure to achieve social movement goals does not mean that participants did not take away valuable lessons from the experience. Movement participants can learn from their mistakes and bring increased knowledge and experience to other social movements. Failed social movements can also raise issues that American society will focus on in the future.

The populist movement and its resultant Populist Party of the 1890s were not successful in changing public policy at the time, but later, during the Progressive Era (1900–1916), many of their goals were achieved. These achievements included the adoption of the Australia ballot (or secret ballot) system, enforcement of the eight-hour workday, introduction of initiative and referendum techniques (forms of legislative input from the electorate), and direct election of U.S. senators.

As a more recent example, in 1968 the SCLC had planned to erect a tent city, Resurrection City, on the mall in Washington, DC, to house Black, White, American Indian, and Latino poor. Residents of Resurrection City were to demonstrate daily to focus attention on the plight of the poor in the United States. The assassination of Martin Luther King Jr. in April of that year threw the SCLC and the Civil Rights Movement in general into turmoil. Despite King's death, the SCLC decided to move forward with the poor people's

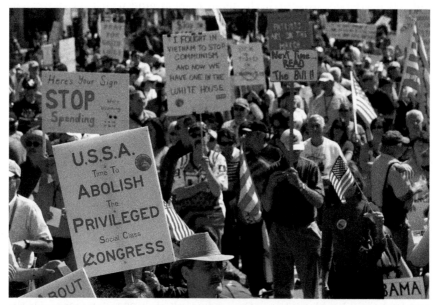

People hold signs during a Tea Party protest in Freedom Plaza April 15, 2010 in Washington, DC. The event, titled the People's Tax Revolt, coincided with the day that American citizens are required to file their national income tax.

campaign. Resurrection City was muddy from rain, its inadequate sanitation facilities created an unhealthy environment, and those leading the campaign did not possess the necessary leadership and organization skills. The result was failure of the movement.

Social movements spring from a variety of sources, often from grievances by groups that have been excluded from the political process. Social movements are important to democracy because they push the system to be more responsive to the needs of a portion of its citizens. Social movement activity also enriches democracy because, in some instances, it brings people into the system and expands participation. Social movement activity, however, is not easy, and those who participate can suffer financially and, sometimes, physically. Both successful and failed social movements contribute to and strengthen democracy by changing public policies and opening up the system to individuals previously excluded.

Social Movement or Political Activism?

As you have seen, social movements are difficult to launch and even harder to sustain. Many span decades of activity from multitudes of people, and for some, the loss of life before seeing any glimmer of success. Some people assume that if people organize and hold large rallies or even support candidates, this constitutes a social movement. As you can see from this chapter, social movements are more than rallies and support for candidates. Two recent groups, Black Lives Matter and the Tea Party, are organizations of people who are politically active, but do not constitute social movements as discussed in this chapter. Only time will tell if they grow into new social movements.

Black Lives Matter

The Black Lives Matter movement began in 2012, after the death of seventeen-year-old Trayvon Martin.[139] The suspect, George Zimmerman, was recorded and verified for having shot Trayvon, but said he had done so under Florida's "Stand Your Ground" law.[140] Extensive discussion occurred about the racial profiling of a young Black teenager. Zimmerman went to trial and was acquitted. Trayvon's death and the release of the suspect created national uproar as individuals perceived that justice was not served in the death of Trayvon.[141]

Patrisse Cullors, Opal Tometi, and Alicia Garza, three community organizers, began discussing whether Black lives matter.[142] Cullors developed the hashtag #BlackLivesMatter, in an effort to assert that there should be accountability when unarmed African Americans are murdered. These three organizers began a national conversation via social media on the disparate effect of violence toward Black Americans, particularly at the hands of law enforcement.[143] As the deaths of unarmed Black Americans continued, the movement began to gain national popularity. The death of Michael Brown in Ferguson, Missouri, on August 9, 2014, became an important moment for the movement.[144] The movement began to include more vocal leaders, including DeRay Mckesson, a public school administrator who became a vocal activist within the movement, providing strong critique of the police response that occurred within Ferguson, Missouri. Protest demonstrations began increasing, as more deaths at the hands of the police continued with the high profile case of the death of Freddie Gray in Baltimore and Sandra Bland in Texas. Within the one-year span of August 2014 to 2015, over 950 protest demonstrations occurred nationwide.[145]

The movement's influence has two points that need to be kept in mind. One, the founders of the movement include members of the Black American community that are typically within the margins, providing a strong platform for queer Black women, and members of the African American community from other marginalized communities—such as undocumented people, the working poor, and agnostics and atheists. They emphasize that the struggle is meant to include and uplift traditionally marginalized experiences. In a magazine interview, co-founder Opal Tometi emphasized, "It's not just about Black heterosexual lives . . . It's about all Black lives."[146]

Secondly, this is not just a national movement, but has spread internationally, with chapters now in Canada and Ghana. In Canada, activists in Toronto shut down a major highway to protest the death of two Black Canadians at the hands of police.[147] Additional international campaigns included the #Palestine2Ferguson campaign, where protestors in Ferguson began conversation with Palestinians residing in Gaza, later resulting in an international convening between organizers in Ferguson with activists in Gaza.[148]

In addition to protesting the death of unarmed Black men and women, Black Lives Matter activists have utilized nonviolent protest mechanisms to bring issue to police brutality by protesting Black Friday and organizing protest movements during the 2015–16 campaign cycle.[149] They have particularly brought attention to the 2016 Democratic campaign process, pressuring Bernie Sanders and Hillary Clinton, as the majority of Black American voters vote for the Democratic ticket. They have utilized different tactics at specific campaign rallies as a means to ensure that the Black vote is not taken for granted by the Democratic Party. As a result of these efforts, both Sanders and Clinton have incorporated more conversations around the issues that Black Lives Matter is pointing out. The movement has decided not to endorse any presidential candidate for the elections, but is seeking to continue holding individuals within government accountable through their organizing strategies. Events during the summer of 2016—the police shootings of Alton Sterling in Baton Rouge, Louisiana, and Philando Castile in Minneapolis, Minnesota, and the shooting death of five police officers in Dallas by a lone Black Army veteran shooter after a peaceful march to protest the deaths of Sterling and Castile—have raised the issue of police killing of Black men and support for police officers front and center. We will see if the two sides are able to find common ground moving forward. At this point, Black Lives Matters is an activist group, not a social movement.

Tea Party

The origins of the Tea Party are in dispute. One view is that the Tea Party began in 2009 in protest of the economic stimulus package and bank bailout that was implemented by President Obama's administration.[150] According to Goldstein, "The Tea Party is a nationalist movement that uses originalist rhetoric to advance a narrow conception of what America is, what ideas are American, and who is truly American."[151] Tea Party supporters believe that the fundamental values on which America was founded—limited government, free market, and libertarian principles of individualism—are embodied in the Constitution. "The Tea Party movement's constitutional rhetoric is built around a narrative of golden age of the nation's founding, in which the nation's fundamental principles were established fully formed and eternal by the Founders and embodied in the Constitution."[152] In February 2009, Keli Carendar, a blogger, organized a protest in Seattle, Washington. This protest is considered to be the first Tea Party–type protest.[153] That same month, CNBC Business News editor Rick Santelli made mention of the existence of a Tea Party movement in the United States in a rant against President Obama signing the $787 billion stimulus bill into law. Also in February, the Nationwide Tea Party Coalition held a conference call with conservative activists to plan a series of protests, which occurred on February 27 with thousands of demonstrators protesting in fifty-one cities.[154]

Another view is that it is not grassroots organized protest activity, but is an example of corporate "astroturfing"—"defined as a movement that 'appears to be grassroots, but is either funded, created, or conceived by a corporation or industry trade association, political interest group or public relations firm.'"[155] A 2013 study found that national organizations funded by corporations, for example, Americans for Prosperity and FreedomWorks, played pivotal roles in structuring, organizing, and supporting the Tea Party in its early stages. These organizations provided training, communication, and materials for the earliest Tea Party activities, including the February 27, 2009, demonstrations. The study identifies that Americans for Prosperity and FreedomWorks have their origins in the tobacco industries' organization of smokers' rights groups in the 1980s to fight control of tobacco. Citizens for a Sound Economy, a Koch Industry funded group organized in 1984, split into Americans for Prosperity and FreedomWorks in 2004. Koch Industry and other companies created these third-party groups for decades and Tea Party strategy and leadership came out of these groups.[156] If this second view is accurate, then the origins of the groups would not be in keeping with the theory of how social movements arise.

Regardless of which history of the origins of the Tea Party is correct, the fact is that it has been extremely active in the electoral politics arenas. Supporters of the Tea Party had "vowed to purge the Republican Party of officials they [considered to be] not sufficiently conservative and to block the Democratic agenda on the economy, the environment, and health care."[157] Their activities have had a profound effect on the internal politics of the Republican Party, and on the electoral fortunes of the Democratic Party in the 2010 midterm elections. Their influence in the 2012 presidential elections was considerably less than in 2010 and the question has been raised as to whether it is on the decline. There are varying views about the long-term sustainability of the Tea Party, as prominent candidates that ran for office in 2012, from Alaska to Indiana to Delaware, failed to win primaries and elections, and, in 2014, many of the Tea Party candidates lost in Republican primaries. Nevertheless, six Tea Party candidates won open senate seats—Dan Sullivan (Alaska), Tom Cotton (Arkansas), Cory Gardner (Colorado), Joni Ernst (Iowa), Steve Daines (South Dakota), and Ben Sasse (Nebraska), which was a major accomplishment.

In the 2016 Republican presidential primary, of the seventeen contenders, six—Senators Ted Cruz, Rand Paul and Marco Rubio, former Senator Rick Santorum, and former governors Rick Perry and Mike Huckabee—were considered Tea Party candidates. Of the six, only Cruz, Paul and Rubio, were considered serious contenders. In the end, only Cruz's campaign survived to the end of the primary season, but lost out to Donald J. Trump, who became the Republican presidential nominee. Many of the Tea Party candidates that challenged Republican incumbents or vied for open seats lost. For example, in Indiana, the Republican establishment candidate, Todd Young, overwhelmingly bested Tea Party candidate Marlin Stuztman for the Republican nomination for an open senate seat. Speaker of the House Paul Ryan drew a Tea Party challenger, but easily won his primary contest. Time will tell if the Tea Party's influence is on the demise, particularly with the unlikely rise of Donald Trump as the GOP 2016 presidential nominee, but what is not in dispute is that the Tea Party is not a social movement, but a politically active collective of individuals.

Conclusion

This chapter has explored the important phenomenon of social movements. Social movements spring from a variety of sources, often from grievances by groups that have been excluded from the political process. Social movements are important to democracy because they push the system to be more responsive to the needs of a portion of its citizens. Social movement activity also enriches democracy because, in some instances, it brings people into the system and expands participation. But social movement activity is not easy, and those who participate often suffer, financially and sometimes physically. Both successful and failed social movements contribute to and strengthen democracy by raising issues that are then debated in the political arena.

We have explored several successful social movements and the positive effects they have had in bringing previously excluded groups into the political life of the United States. Each of these movements used different tactics to achieve their results, and for many the results were achieved over long periods of time. Yet not all social movement activity makes positive contributions to democratic systems. Those social movements that intend to deprive some citizens of their rights and that use domestic terrorism to push their agenda act contrary to the principles of representative government. Nevertheless, the strength of the American government system is such that these social movements have little effect on its overall structure.

When Barbara Rose Johns stood at the lectern in her segregated high school in Farmville, Virginia, in 1951 and led a boycott against the unequal conditions Blacks experienced under segregation, she and others involved in what became known as the Civil Rights Movement opened the door and laid the path for the election of former Senator Barack Obama to the presidency. Without the CRM pushing open the doors of access to millions of Black Americans and knocking down barriers to political participation for Blacks, as well as other disenfranchised groups, Barack Obama's successful campaign for the highest office in the United States would not have been possible.

In fact, the election of President Obama in 2008 and his reelection in 2012 saw the participation of several historical social movements in his victory—labor, women, and Blacks and Latinos. Even though young voters, particularly Black young voters, were mobilized in support of his candidacy, as is clear from the discussion in this chapter their mobilization does not fit the definition of a social movement. But their mobilization, combined with the mobilization of several historical social movements, propelled him to victory. In a sense, President Obama is a product of a number of America's successful social movements.

Hillary Clinton's nomination as the first woman presidential candidate for one of the two major political parties is also a product of the waves of the women's movement, as well as other historical social movements. Unfortunately, Hillary Clinton was not successful in being elected the first female President of the United States. Her election, like that of President Obama, would have the product of a number of successful social movements and would have been a major prize for the various waves of the women's movement.

Most of the social movements discussed have waned or are weakened as they have had success and achieved their goals. But the LGBT movement is still pushing forward and gaining steam. Its struggle, like those of other social movements, has taken place over decades and it is possible that it still has decades of struggle ahead before it achieves all of its objectives. But, like other movements, time is on its side and the American public is moving in its direction.

review
REVIEW QUESTIONS

1. What is a social movement, and why are social movements important in general? Why are social movements important to democracies?

2. What conditions give rise to social movements?

3. What are the similarities among the successful social movements discussed in this chapter?

4. What role does a supportive environment play in the success or failure of social movements?

5. Why do social movements fail?

KEY TERMS

Catalyst p. 363
Catalytic Leadership p. 363
Environmental Racism p. 384
Factionalism p. 396
Jim Crow Laws p. 367

Lynching p. 368
Shared Grievances p. 362
Social Movement p. 361
Southern Christian Leadership Conference
(SCLC) p. 369

Student Non-Violent Coordinating
Committee (SNCC) p. 370
Supportive Environment p. 362
White Citizens' Council p. 369

ADDITIONAL READINGS

Lee Ann Banaszak, *Why Movements Succeed or Fail: Opportunity, Culture, and the Struggle for Woman Suffrage* (Princeton, NJ: Princeton University Press, 1996).

> This is a comparison of the movement for women's suffrage in the United States and in Switzerland.

Foster Rhea Dulles and Melvyn Dubofsky, *Labor in America: A History*, 7th ed. (Arlington Heights, IL: Harlan Davidson, 2004).

> This history of labor in the United States focuses on organization, leaders, and strikes, but is also a good general history of the labor movement.

Charles C. Euchner, *Extraordinary Politics: How Protest and Dissent Are Changing American Democracy* (Boulder, CO: Westview Press, 1996).

> This book is a study of the effect of American social movements on the structures of government.

Sidney Tarrow, *Power in Movement: Social Movements and Contentious Politics*, 3rd ed. (Cambridge, UK: Cambridge University Press, 2011).

> This is a good summary of the resource mobilization and cultural interpretations approaches to the study of social movements.

Robert Weisbrot, *Freedom Bound: A History of America's Civil Rights Movement* (New York: Norton, 1990).

> This book covers the origins of the Civil Rights Movement and highlights the peak years of the struggle for racial equality.

Jeff Goodwin and James M. Jasper, eds., *The Social Movements Reader: Cases and Concepts* (Oxford, UK: Wiley, 2009).

> This edited book includes essays on various aspects of social movements from their origins, their organization, who participates, why people drop out, and case studies of several social movements.

CHAPTER 13

Interest Groups: Good Outcomes with Few Resources

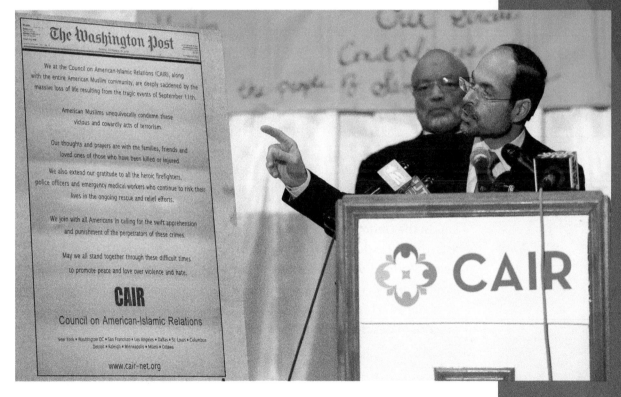

Nihad Awad, right, national executive director of the Council on American-Islamic Relations, talks about an advertisement his organization ran in the Washington Post during a news conference with religious members and local politicians on Thursday, December 3, 2015, in Jersey City, NJ. The advertisement was responding to comments made by Republican presidential candidate Donald Trump, who claimed people celebrated the September 11 terrorist attacks in Jersey City.

A nti-Muslim rhetoric was a hallmark of the presidential campaign of the 2016 Republican nominee Donald Trump. Trump went as far as to accuse the Muslim-American community of sheltering terrorists and of being complicit in attacks such as the ones in San Bernardino, California, and Orlando, Florida, since the perpetrators in both incidents had pledged allegiance to the Islamic State (ISIS).[1] In March 2016, a senior law enforcement official revealed the FBI's plans to implement the *Shared Responsibility Committee* program, which aims to counter violent extremism and confront radicalization in Muslim American communities.[2] Many Muslim-Americans are already subject to a certain degree of government surveillance. The Council on American-Islamic Relations is an Islamic advocacy group founded in 1994 and headquartered in Washington, DC, with regional offices throughout the country. The organization works to challenge negative stereotypes about Muslims, and is "dedicated to providing an Islamic perspective on issues of importance to the American public."[3] In April 2016, the Michigan Chapter of CAIR filed two federal lawsuits in response to the U.S. government's use of secret watch lists that target thousands of Muslim Americans.[4] One class-action lawsuit sought damages on behalf of Muslims in the United States who had been included on government watch lists that branded them as "known or suspected terrorists" without being afforded due process under the law.[5] In the second lawsuit, CAIR asked a district judge in Alexandria, Virginia, for an injunctive and declaratory relief in order to challenge the U.S. government's continued practice of designating Muslim Americans as potential terrorists.[6]

intro

The lawsuits against the terror watch lists will continue for a long time. But groups like the Council on American-Islamic Relations (CAIR) take on issues and practices that disadvantage and discriminate against Muslim Americans. These groups also provide a counternarrative of American Muslims to the one presented by Donald Trump and others such as Representative Peter King (R) of New York, who in 2011 as House Chairman of the Homeland Security Committee, called a set of hearings to address what he termed the growing threat of Islamic radicalism in the United States. The ability of interest groups to initiate action is significant and important. Interest

groups are players in American politics and can wield a great deal of influence in poli-
cymaking at all levels of government—local, state, and national.

This chapter explores the role of interest groups in American politics. It examines
not only the role of interest groups in general, but also the role of interest groups whose
agendas and activities focus on non-White populations or whose membership con-
sists primarily of various non-White groups. We begin by exploring interest groups—
what they are, what they do, and the influence they wield. We look at interest groups
through the theoretical lens of pluralism because it views the political system as a
competition among groups. We then discuss the various types of interest groups, their
strategies, and why some interest groups are successful.

Moreover, we discuss the significance of interest groups to the politics and policy
preferences of Black Americans and other racial and ethnic groups.

Interest Groups and Their Functions

Interest groups (also known as pressure groups) are private (i.e., nongovern-ment) organizations whose members act together to influence public policy to promote their interests. These groups act as intermediaries, representing the public's and private group's interests and preferences to policymakers at all levels of government—federal, state, and local—with the intent of influencing decisions on public policy.[7] The members of interest groups can be individuals or institutions, such as corporations, nonprofit groups, or associations. What binds members of interest groups together is a common interest, which might be an economic issue, a social issue, or a particular policy issue.

For example, the NAACP is concerned with civil rights issues for African Americans, but it takes up issues related to other non-White groups as well. It was founded in 1909 by sixty Blacks and Whites partly in response to the con-tinued and increasing practice of lynching and the 1908 race riots in Spring-field, Illinois. Among those who founded the NAACP were W. E. B. Du Bois, Ida B. Wells-Barnett, Mary Church Terrell, and Oswald Garrison Villard (see "Our Voices: Ida B. Wells-Barnett").[8]

The National Urban League, originally named the Committee on Urban Conditions among Negroes, founded in 1910, grew out of concerns for the new Black migrants from the South moving into the urban areas of the North in the early 1900s. The organization was spearheaded by a White woman, Ruth Standish Baldwin, a wealthy widow with a strong social conscience, and a Black man, Dr. George Edmund Haynes, a graduate of Fisk University, who became the organization's first executive secretary. In 1911, the National League on the Urban Conditions among Negroes was created through the merger of the committee with the Committee for the Improvement of Indus-trial Conditions among Negroes in New York (founded in New York in 1906) and the National League for the Protection of Colored Women (founded in 1905). In 1920, the name was shortened to the National Urban League.[9]

Interest groups are not the same as social movements. The latter arise from specific circumstances that galvanize people to action to pressure

Interest Groups Organizations whose members act together to influence public policy to promote their common interests (also known as pressure groups).

our voices

Ida B. Wells-Barnett (1862–1931)

Ida B. Wells-Barnett was one of the first anti-lynching activists in the early 1890s. She traveled to lynching sites, gathering details and publishing pamphlets about the horrors of mob violence. She was also a suffragist, women's rights advocate, and journalist. She was co-owner of the *Memphis Free Speech and Headlight* in Memphis, Tennessee. It was burned out in 1892 as a result of her articles on lynching and other injustices, and she was forced to leave town. She settled in Chicago and continued her journalism career, was a central figure in the Negro clubwoman movement, and was a founding member of many organizations that she believed would work to eliminate the injustices experienced by African Americans.

Wells-Barnett was acutely aware of the importance of interest groups. We can see that in the following letter she wrote to the *Chicago Defender*, a prominent Black newspaper, on March 19, 1910. In this letter, she discusses the Original Rights Society, a short-lived group in New York committed to the basic civil rights stated in the Declaration of Independence and the Constitution, but not protected for many citizens.

> Editor Defender:
>
> In last week's issue you spoke of the sign in the State street car which advertised a certain cemetery that sold lots exclusively to white people. . . . Every one seems indignant and feels that something should be done, but no one seems to know just what may be done to have the objectionable sign removed.
>
> Two things occur to me that might be tried, but both of them require what our people have not—effective organization in the race for civic and racial purposes.

> In the disorganized condition in which we stand to-day, we could not bring pressure enough to bear perhaps to have those objectionable signs removed, but if we could count on the entire race for moral and financial support unitedly, the mayor, the city council, the aldermen of the ward would find a way to have these signs removed. . . .
>
> And right here comes the need of organization that would take in every Negro, man, woman and child, in Chicago, especially the Second ward. If the Negroes would join the Original Rights Society, they would have their organization for themselves, and they would have the moral and active support of others in the movement. For the Original Rights Society is not composed alone of colored people. It is an organization established in New York City, and with growing branches throughout the country, composed largely of white people. They are fighting for the original rights of every American citizen, and that means us, too. . . .
>
> If we should join the Original Rights Society in large numbers here in Chicago, we would not only be organized ourselves to do effective combined work along any line needed for our benefit, but we would have the help of the white members in any fight for our rights. Who knows but it might help us win the aldermanic victory. . . .
>
> Ida B. Wells-Barnett, 3234 Rhodes Ave., Tel. Douglas 2960

Source: Ida B. Wells-Barnett, "The Original Rights Society," *Chicago Defender*, March 19, 1910.

Ida B. Wells-Barnett (1862–1931), Mary Church Terrell (1863–1954), and Anna Julia Cooper (1858–1964) were important figures in the Black Women's Club Movement, whose purpose was to "uplift" Black America. All three were also active in numerous other Black social and political organizations and women's rights organizations, and all were accomplished authors.

government to make changes. Many of these movements are short-lived, and no permanent organization emerges. Some successful social movements, however, have led to the formation of interest groups. For example, the American Federation of Labor–Congress of Industrial Organizations, a labor union, evolved into an interest group for labor interests, and the women's rights movement generated the National Organization for Women (NOW).

A Group-Based View of American Politics

James Madison envisioned the United States as a society in which conflict, rather than consensus, would predominate. In "Federalist No. 10," he warned that the United States would be subject to the development of factions. For Madison, a faction was a number of citizens united by some common impulse or passion that might adversely affect the rights of other citizens or the interests of the larger community.[10] He believed that the most common and durable sources of factions were economic differences among people. Madison explained, "Those who hold and those who are without property have ever formed distinct interests in society. Those who are creditors, and those who are debtors, fall under a like discrimination. A landed interest, a manufacturing interest, a mercantile interest, a moneyed interest, with many lesser interests, grow up of necessity in civilized nations, and divide them into different classes, actuated by different sentiments and views."[11]

Madison saw these factions as potential dangers for democracy if they gained too much political power. But Madison also believed that because individuals would have numerous interests and move in and out of factions, no one faction would dominate and control political outcomes. In political science, this view of American politics as dominated by interest groups is called pluralism, or interest group theory.

Pluralism

Pluralism, or interest group theory, is a theory of politics that contends that power is group-based and that political outcomes are the result of competition among groups. Early in the twentieth century, sociologist Arthur Bentley discussed the influence of political interest groups in American politics. In *The Process of Government* (1908), he argued that the "stuff of politics and government were not structures and laws but interest groups and their activity."[12] Bentley contended that Madison's conception of factions formed the basis for a theory of democratic government that views competition among groups as the foundation for policymaking and political outcomes. Bentley stressed the benefit to representative government of the struggle among a "plurality" of interest groups, and he believed that political preferences grew out of group affiliation and identifications. For Bentley, American politics was group politics.[13]

David Truman applied Bentley's interest group theory to political science in his work *The Governmental Process* (1951).[14] Truman studied interest group

Pluralism A theory of politics that contends that power is group-based and that, because there are multiple points of access within American government, each group possesses an equality of opportunity when competing with other groups for power and resources (also known as interest group theory).

formation and viewed the number and existence of interest groups as a measure of the stability of a democratic system. He assumed that all interest groups would adopt a democratic perspective, that they would produce alliances and coalitions that were in the best interest of the public good. For Truman, the prime objective of interest groups is to influence the making of public policy. Policy outcomes, for Truman, are the result of pressure from interest groups at various points in the political process.[15]

Truman's work influenced other scholars, among them political scientist Robert Dahl, who is considered the founding influence on pluralism and is identified as the most influential of the pluralist scholars. Dahl first stated the fundamentals of pluralism in his 1961 book, *Who Governs? Democracy and Power in an American City.*[16]

Pluralism makes several assumptions about politics and the political system:

1. Politics is group-based. The distribution of power and policy formation comes through competition among groups.
2. Although groups might differ in the political resources they hold, the process of competition will balance out these differences.
3. Government will act as a neutral arbiter of the competition, but groups will try to influence government at various points.
4. Many centers of power exist, and different groups have access to a variety of power centers. Thus, if a group is blocked from one center of power, it will always have access to another.
5. Change in a pluralistic system is gradual or incremental, primarily because of the bargaining that occurs among interest groups.
6. Every group has equal access to the political process. Even though not every group will win all of the time, each group will win or lose depending on the issue and on the group's ability to use political resources.

Criticisms of Pluralism

Critics of pluralism contest several of these assumptions. In *The Semisovereign People* (1960), E. E. Schattschneider argued that, despite the positive benefits to the political system that Bentley and Truman saw from interest groups, the majority of Americans do not have any interest group representation.[17] Schattschneider saw interest group representation skewed in the direction of those who have political resources and influence, particularly the wealthy. He stated that "the flaw in the pluralist heaven is that the heavenly chorus sings with a strong upper-class accent."[18]

Theodore J. Lowi, in *The End of Liberalism* (1969),[19] agreed with Schattschneider that most Americans are not represented by interest groups and are shut out of the policymaking process, which has been captured by a wide array of interest groups. These groups influence not only the formation of legislation through pressure on legislators, but also the implementation of legislation through pressure on the executive agencies responsible for policy implementation.

Lowi described this process as the **iron triangle**, the interlocking three-way relationship among a well-financed interest group, a congressional committee or subcommittee that makes the laws, and bureaucratic agencies that administer the law.[20] Lowi coined the phrase "interest group liberalism" to refer to the perversion of pluralism by the dominance of private interests in the policymaking process. The effect of interest group liberalism is that Congress, which has the constitutional responsibility to determine broad goals for American society, has abdicated its responsibility to interest groups.[21] Nevertheless, pluralism assumes that what happens in the political system is the result of the contest among groups, and interest groups play an important role in this contestation.

Iron Triangle A conception of bureaucratic policymaking in which policymaking is dominated by congressional committees, interest groups, and bureaucratic agencies.

Interest Group Formation

Why do interest groups form, and why do people join? The early group theory of politics scholars assumed that interest groups would form automatically once a group of individuals identified their common interests or recognized a threat to their interests. Later research failed to support this assumption. Economist Mancur Olson argues that individuals who have an interest in a particular policy might share that interest with others who will also be affected.[22] Yet they will not necessarily organize to achieve those policies. Individuals do not necessarily act in their common interest, particularly if they feel that their participation in a large group makes little difference to the eventual outcome. It is the proverbial "I am one person, so my participation does not count for much" syndrome. In addition, if people feel that benefits will go to more people than participated in pushing for the policy, that feeling also serves as a deterrent to joining an interest group.[23] Consequently, the incentive for any one individual to become involved in an interest group is very low. This view is known as the **logic of collective action**.

Olson further argues that the rational individual (an individual who is interested in what is best for her- or himself) will seek to become a **free rider**; that is, she or he will benefit from a policy without having contributed to its formulation or paying for the advantages it confers. In other words, if someone else works to provide a collective good that will also benefit me without my having to work for it, then I, as a rational individual, will choose to become a free rider. For example, if I live in a place where it snows and all owners are responsible for clearing the snow from their garages in the alley, the neighbors might band together to hire someone to come plow out the alley every time it snows. But my house is at the end of the alley, and I figure that my neighbors in the middle of the block will pay for the service and I will get the snow from my garage removed anyway because a path has to be made for my neighbors to get out. So, I choose not to pay. Olson would say that I am a "rational individual." This cleared alleyway would be considered a **collective good**, which

Logic of Collective Action The view that the costs of large groups collectively organizing are high and the benefits to individual members are relatively low; thus the appeal to rational members is one of deterrence to organizing collectively.

Free Rider A person who profits from the activities of others without participating in those activities.

Collective Good Any benefit that if available to one member of the community cannot be denied to any other, regardless of whether he or she bore any of the costs of providing it.

is any benefit that if available to one member of the community cannot be denied to any other, regardless of whether the individual bore any of the costs of providing it.[24]

Scholars have tested Olson's theories and have concluded that in some respects Olson is correct. Many organizations, such as environmental and consumer groups, have few members but provide collective goods that the majority of people "free ride" on. Indeed, the difficulties that political actors have in stimulating voters and policymakers to address key challenges such as global warming and health care reform are examples of the continued relevance of the free rider syndrome.

According to Olson's theory, no one would ever get involved in an interest group, yet lots of people do. James Q. Wilson argues that people join organizations and interest groups in exchange for particular benefits.[25] AARP is an interest group that works on behalf of senior citizens and tries to influence public policies that will benefit them. One factor in the organization's influence is a large membership base and the ability to say that AARP represents 38 million senior citizens.[26] Even though AARP works on behalf of seniors, however, many join not for that reason, but for the tangible benefits the organization offers in the form of reduced insurance rates (auto, health), senior discounts for services and products such as prescription drugs, investment advice, and a host of other programs. Some people join for the benefits even if they disagree with the political work the organization does.

Social organizations, such as sororities, fraternities, and social clubs, might have larger public service goals than the social scene with which they are associated. Yet they know that many people will want to become members because they perceive the organizations as prestigious and believe that becoming a member will add to their own self-esteem or professional résumé.

Other organizations, such as the American Red Cross and the American Cancer Society, do not offer material or other incentives, but they know that many people will want to be involved because they believe in the long-range objectives of the organization. These members might also have had personal experiences that compel them to be involved. These types of organizations push their objectives to the broader public in an effort to attract people who believe in what the organizations are doing.

Types of Interest Groups

A French visitor to the new United States in 1831–1832, Alexis de Tocqueville, commented on the ability of citizens of the new nation to organize into groups to participate in the political system. Tocqueville stated, "As soon as several inhabitants of the United States have taken up an opinion or a feeling which they wish to promote in the world, they look out for mutual assistance; and as soon as they have found each other out, they combine. From that moment they are no longer isolated men, but a power seen from afar, whose actions serve for an example, and whose language is listened to."[27] It is as true now as in the 1830s that the United States is a nation in which people participate in organizations. A recent survey found that there are approximately 23,891 national organizations (see Table 13.1 for a categorization of some of them).

Interest groups are political organizations formed principally for the purpose of representing the groups' interests in government decision-making and policy formation. As already noted, there are a great many interest groups, and they cover a wide range of issues. Despite the great numbers of interest groups, it is possible to classify them.

H. R. Mahood has developed a typology that divides interest groups into two broad categories: economic and noneconomic.[28] Mahood places business

TABLE 13.1 Total Number of National Interest Groups and Associations, 2015

Category	National	%[a]
Athletic and Sports Organizations	900	3.76
Chambers of Commerce and Trade and Tourism Organizations	126	.53
Cultural Organizations	1,611	6.74
Educational Organizations	1,345	5.63
Engineering, Technological, and Natural and Social Science Organizations	1,508	6.31
Environmental and Agricultural Organizations	1,422	5.95
Fan Clubs	119	.49
Fraternal, Nationality, and Ethnic Organizations	399	1.67
Greek and Non-Greek Letter Societies, Associations, and Federations	295	1.23
Health and Medical Organizations	4,070	17.04
Hobby and Avocational Organizations	1,288	5.4
Labor Unions, Associations, and Federations	163	0.68
Legal, Governmental, Public Administration, and Military Organizations	895	3.75
Public Affairs Organizations	1,585	6.63
Religious Organizations	965	4.04
Social Welfare Organizations	3,167	13.23
Trade, Business, and Commercial Organizations	3,487	14.60
Veterans', Hereditary, and Patriotic Organizations	546	2.29
Total	**23,891**	

[a] Percentages might not add to 100 because of rounding.

Source: Encyclopedia of Associations: National Organizations of the U.S., 54th ed. (2015). Accessed using Gale Directory Library, Duke University Library.

Note: The information for this table was found using the advanced search function in the Gale Directory Library. I selected "Encyclopedia of Associations—National Organizations of the U.S." under select directories. Then, I used the drop box in the advanced search field and clicked "section heading(sh)," and typed each interest group category in the box to the right.

(Walmart stores), labor (AFL-CIO), professional (American Bar Association), and agriculture (National Cattlemen's Association) interest groups in the economic category. In the noneconomic category, he lists civil rights (National Council of La Raza, or NCLR), government (American Federation of State, County, and Municipal Employees, or AFSCME), ideological (American Conservative Union), public interest (League of Women Voters), and single-issue (National Abortion Rights Action League) groups. Mahood does not mention religious interest groups, but they constitute another subcategory of noneconomic groups (National Council of Churches, or NCC).

Economic Interest Groups

These are interest groups whose primary concern is the economic well-being of their members. We can look at four broad categories of economic interest groups: agriculture, business, labor, and professions.

Agriculture. A wide variety of interest groups represent agriculture, including groups that represent farmers and groups that represent particular crops and commodities.[29] In direct reaction to the increasing influence of business, particularly railroad barons, American farmers were among the first to organize as an interest group to promote and protect their interests. They did this through the Grange, which was organized in Minnesota in 1867. The National Grange, as it is called today, is still a very active interest group that pushes for legislation and policies that benefit agriculture.

Farming has become a more complex sector in the twenty-first century. Most of the family farms that existed in the days of the Grange have been replaced by big agribusinesses. Farming interests are now more diverse, and agriculture does not speak with a united voice. Agriculture also consists of food export businesses, farm equipment dealers, pesticide and fertilizer manufacturers, and a myriad of other interests.[30]

Business. Business interest groups form to protect the ability of businesses to sell their products and services and make a profit with as little government oversight and regulation as possible.[31] Whereas agriculture interests began to organize in the 1860s, business interests began to organize in the early twentieth century. The U.S. Chamber of Commerce, founded in 1912, is the world's largest business federation and represents 3 million businesses of all sizes, sectors, and regions, as well as state and local chambers and industry associations. Its core function, according to its website, "is to fight for free enterprise before Congress, the White House, regulatory agencies, the courts, the court of public opinion, and governments around the world."[32] The Business Roundtable, established in 1972, is an association of chief executive officers of leading U.S. companies.[33] Like the Chamber of Commerce, the Business Roundtable provides an authoritative voice on business to pressure decision makers to make business-friendly public policy.[34]

The economic crisis of 2008 and 2009 saw business groups organize even more intensely to push policies favorable to business. The Obama administration proposed regulations to regulate the derivatives (a generic name for a variety of financial investments) market and sent bills to Congress in 2009. Seven large trade associations, including the Business Roundtable, the National Association of Manufacturers, and the U.S. Chamber of Commerce, recently formed the Coalition of Derivatives End-Users to oppose new regulations.[35] Congress eventually passed the Dodd-Frank Wall Street Reform and Consumer Protection Act in July 2010. The act seeks to regulate financial markets, so that the financial meltdown experienced in 2008 and 2009 will not happen again. It establishes a Consumer Financial Protection Agency that will oversee credit reporting agencies, debit and credit cards, payday and consumer loans, and credit card fees, among other things. It also creates the Financial Stability Oversight Council that will identify risks that might bring about another financial collapse. There is continuing controversy surrounding Dodd-Frank, but it appears to be working.

Labor. Labor interest groups represent a wide variety of workers, from miners (United Mine Workers of America), teamsters (Teamsters), and steelworkers (United Steel Workers of America), to teachers (National Education Association), professional football players (National Football League Players Association), and Hollywood screenwriters (Writers Guild of America). Thus, labor interests span a broad segment of the employment arena.

All of these groups represent unionized workers. Like agriculture interests, labor interests are also diverse and do not speak with a united voice. Each labor interest group works to push its specific interests. Labor unions are not as powerful today as in past decades. In 2015, only 11.1 percent of the U.S. workforce was unionized, down from 20.1 percent in 1983.[36]

Even though older unions are losing members, others in new job arenas are growing. As the service industries expand, the Service Employees International Union (SEIU) is growing at a fast pace. SEIU represents workers in three sectors—health care, property services, and public employment. SEIU is also active in lobbying for specific public policies. For example, as of October 16, 2016, the union, its PAC, and its members contributed about $5.7 million to political candidates for the 2016 election.[37] (Table 13.2 provides a list of the various types of labor unions in the United States.)

Professions. Numerous professions have organized into professional associations, many of which also function as interest groups on issues that affect their profession. An example of a well-known professional interest group is the American Medical Association (AMA), an association of medical professionals and medical doctors, founded in 1847. Since its formation, the AMA has worked to advance the art and science of medicine. It is the premier association involved with health care in the United States, and no other health-related

TABLE 13.2 Selection of Different Types of Labor Unions

Labor Union	Inception	Website
Actors' Equity Association	1913	http://www.actorsequity.org
AFL-CIO	1955	http://www.aflcio.org
American Federation of Television and Radio Artists (AFTRA)	1937	www.sagaftra.org
Alliance of Canadian Cinema, Television and Radio Artists (ACTRA)	1943	http://www.actra.ca/actra/control/main
American Federation of State, County and Municipal Employees (AFSCME)	1932	http://www.afscme.org
Association of Flight Attendants (AFA)	1930	www.afacwa.org
American Federation of Teachers (AFT)	1916	http://www.aft.org/about
American Postal Workers Union, AFL–CIO (APWU)	1970	http://www.apwu.org
Bakery, Confectionery, Tobacco Workers and Grain Millers International Union	1886	http://www.bctgm.org
Brotherhood of Locomotive Engineers and Trainmen	1863	http://www.ble.org
Brotherhood of Maintenance of Way Employees Division–International Brotherhood of Teamsters (BMWE-IBT)	1887	http://www.bmwe.org
Chicago Federation of Labor, AFL-CIO	1852	http://www.chicagolabor.org
Coalition of Graduate Employee Unions (CGEU)	1992	http://thecgeu.org
Communications Workers of America (CWA)	1938	http://www.cwa-union.org
Directors Guild of America	1936	http://www.dga.org
Electronic and Space Technicians (EAST) Local 1553	1953	http://www.east1553.com
Exotic Dancers Union SEIU Local 790 (San Francisco)	1993	http://www.bayswan.org/eda-sf
Fraternal Order of Police	1915	http://www.fop.net
Glass, Molders, Pottery, Plastics & Allied Workers International Union (GMP)	1842	http://www.gmpiu.org
Graphic Communications International Union (GCIU)	2005	https://teamster.org/divisions/graphic-communications.
Industrial Workers of the World	1905	http://www.iww.org
International Alliance of Theatrical Stage Employees	1893	http://www.iatse-intl.org
International Association of Fire Fighters (IAFF)	1918	http://www.iaff.org
International Association of Machinists and Aerospace Workers (IAMAW)	1888	http://www.goiam.org
International Brotherhood of Electrical Workers (IBEW)	1891	http://www.ibew.org
International Longshoremen's Association AFL-CIO (ILA)	1892	http://www.ilaunion.org/
International Union of Bricklayers and Allied Craft Workers (BAC)	1865	http://www.bacweb.org
International Union of Industrial and Independent Workers	1997	http://iuiiw.us/

TABLE 13.2 (*Continued*)

Labor Union	Inception	Website
International Union of Operating Engineers (IUOE)	1896	http://www.iuoe.org
International Union of Painters and Allied Trades	1887	http://www.iupat.org
International Union of Police Associations (IUPA)	1954	http://www.iupa.org
Laborers' International Union of North America (LIUNA)	1903	http://www.liuna.org
Major League Baseball Players Association	1885	http://www.mlbplayers.com
National Air Traffic Controllers Association (NATCA)	1987	http://www.natca.org
National Education Association (NEA)	1857	http://www.nea.org
National Association of Catholic School Teachers (NACST)	1978	http://www.nacst.com
National Association of Letter Carriers (NALC)	1889	http://www.nalc.org
National Football League Players Association	1956	http://www.nflpa.com
National Hockey League Players' Association	1967	http://www.nhlpa.com
Office & Professional Employees International Union (OPEIU)	1936	http://www.opeiu.org
Pride@Work	1905	http://prideatwork.org
Screen Actors Guild (SAG)	1933	http://www.sag.org
Seafarers International Union of North America (SIU)	1938	http://www.seafarers.org
Security, Police and Fire Professionals of America (SPFPA), International Union	1938	http://www.spfpa.org
International Brotherhood of Teamsters	1903	http://www.teamster.org
Newspaper Guild	1933	http://www.newsguild.org
United Electrical, Radio & Machine Workers of America	1936	http://www.ueunion.org
United Association of Journeymen and Apprentices of the Plumbing and Pipe Fitting Industry of the United States and Canada (UA)	1889	http://www.ua.org
United Automobile, Aerospace and Agricultural Implement Workers of America International Union (UAW)	1935	http://www.uaw.org
United Farm Workers of America, AFL-CIO (UFW)	1962	http://www.ufw.org

Source: Unions.org (http://www.unions.org/home/).

organization can match it in terms of political access or influence on decision makers. Despite its prominence, however, in 2012, the latest year for which figures are available, only 224,503 of 878,194 physicians with active licenses in the United States were members of the AMA (see "Evaluating Equality: The AMA Apologizes to Black Physicians").[38]

Another example of a professional interest group is the American Bar Association (ABA), founded in 1878. Its stated mission is "to serve equally our members, our profession and the public by defending liberty and delivering

evaluating equality

The AMA Apologizes to Black Physicians

The American Medical Association is a powerful interest group, but it historically excluded Black physicians from membership. In 1870, the integrated National Medical Society (an organization of primarily Black doctors) delegation was excluded from the AMA annual meeting in Washington, DC. In 1874, the AMA adopted a system of governance that allowed each state medical society to decide which local societies would be recognized by the AMA. In the face of exclusion from the AMA, the National Medical Association (NMA) was founded in 1895 as an association for Black physicians. The NMA still remains the collective voice for more than 25,000 Black physicians in the United States.

In addition to refusing Black physicians membership, the AMA worked to restrict opportunities for the education of Black physicians. In 1910, the AMA undertook a review of Black medical schools and forced all but two, Meharry Medical College and Howard University, to shut their doors. As a result, only two medical schools remained in the entire nation for the training of Black physicians.

In July 2008, the AMA officially apologized for having excluded Black physicians from membership, for listing Black doctors as "colored" in its national physician directories for decades, and for failing to speak against federal funding of segregated hospitals and in favor of civil rights legislation. The apology came as a response to an AMA-sponsored report on the historical racial divide

Daniel Hale Williams (1856–1931) was a famous cardiologist and surgeon who performed the first successful open heart surgery in the United States. A graduate of Chicago Medical School, he was not allowed to practice in Chicago hospitals because of his race. He founded Provident Hospital and Training School for Nurses, which employed a racially integrated staff. Williams was one of the founders of the National Medical Association (NMA) in 1895 as an alternative to the American Medical Association that did not allow Blacks to join.

in organized medicine. The AMA report indicated that racism in medicine created and perpetuated poor health outcomes for America's Black citizens. As a result, the United States continues to face severe health disparities based on race in the twenty-first century.

Sources: "AMA Apologizes for Past Inequality Against Black Doctors," amednews.com, July 28, 2008, http://www.ama-assn.org/amednews/2008/07/28/prsb0728.htm, accessed July 15, 2009; "History of the National Medical Association," http://www.medpagetoday.com/publichealthpolicy/publichealth/10094, accessed July 15, 2009.

justice as the national representative of the legal profession."[39] In 2016, the ABA had more than 400,000 members.[40]

Noneconomic Interest Groups

Noneconomic interest groups are concerned about issues of benefit to society as a whole or to large groups of individuals even if they are not members of the group. We can divide these groups into six broad categories: civil rights, government, ideology, public interest, single issue, and religion.

Civil Rights. Civil rights interest groups are concerned with issues such as equal opportunity, voting rights, civil liberties, and race and gender discrimination. Examples of civil rights interest groups are the National Association for the Advancement of Colored People, the National Council of La Raza, and the National Organization for Women.

The NAACP, founded in 1909, is the nation's oldest and largest civil rights organization. The NAACP has over 2,000 branches and chapters, and more than 300,000 members. The NAACP is made up of hundreds of thousands of volunteer activists in some 2,200 NAACP Adult, Youth, and College Units across the United States, as well as in the organization's overseas branches in Japan, Germany, and Korea. The NAACP's principle mission "is to ensure the political, educational, social, and economic equality of rights of all persons and to eliminate race-based discrimination." The NAACP is active at the national, state, and local levels addressing problems, lobbying for legislation, and protesting racial injustices. The NAACP also has a significant online and social media presence. As of July 2016, the organization had 555,893 Facebook fans, 144,300 Twitter followers, and 177,717 followers on NAACPConnect on Google Plus.[41]

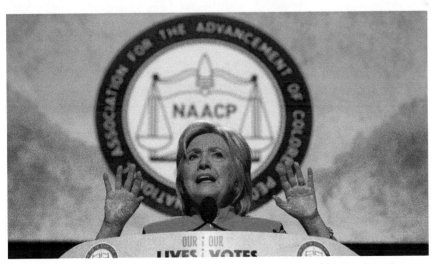

Hillary Clinton speaks at the National Association for the Advancement of Colored People (NAACP) 107th Annual Convention in July, 2016.

The NCLR, founded in 1968, is the largest Latino organization serving all Latino groups—Mexican Americans, Puerto Ricans, Cubans, and South and Central Americans—in all regions of the country. The organization has more than three hundred affiliates in forty-one states, Puerto Rico, and the District of Columbia. Its objective is to work to improve opportunities for Latino Americans. As a nonpartisan organization, NCLR partners with its affiliates across the country "to serve millions of Latinos in the areas of civic engagement, civil rights and immigration, education, workforce and the economy, health and housing."[42] Like the NAACP, NCLR works at all levels of government.

The National Organization for Women (NOW), established in 1966, is the largest feminist organization in the United States, with over 500,000 contributing members. The organization describes itself as "an intersectional, multi-issue, multi-strategy organization that takes a holistic approach to women's rights." NOW has more than 500 chapters, including local chapters and Campus Action Networks, in all fifty states and the District of Columbia. Through intersectional grassroots activism, NOW works "to promote feminist ideals, lead societal change, eliminate discrimination, and achieve and protect the equal rights of all women and girls in all aspects of social, political, and economic life."[43]

Government. Most government interest groups are state or local organizations that push their interests with the federal government. The National

Rep. Patricia Roybal Caballero, D-Albuquerque, speaks in Santa Fe at a New Mexico House Business and Employment Committee on January 29, 2015. Caballero has been elected to the board of the nation's oldest Latino civil rights group despite concerns over partisanship and bylaw violations. Caballero became national treasurer for the League of United Latin American Citizens at the group's convention in Salt Lake City.

League of Cities (NLC) is an American advocacy organization that is dedicated to helping city leaders build better communities. The organization, which works in partnership with forty-nine municipal leagues, represents over 19,000 cities, towns, and villages. The mission of the NLC is to strengthen and promote cities as centers of opportunity, leadership, and governance by advocating in Washington, DC, for cities and towns through lobbying efforts and grassroots campaigns. The organization also provides educational programs and training, networking opportunities, and other services to local officials. More than 2,000 municipalities around the country are members of the National League of Cities.[44]

A government interest group that functions like a union for public employees is the American Federation of State, County, and Municipal Employees. AFSCME has more than 1.6 million members, and they include nurses, corrections officers, child care providers, emergency medical technicians, and sanitation workers. Over the years, it has lobbied for collective bargaining for public employees and actively supports political candidates in national, state, and local elections. When Dr. Martin Luther King Jr. was assassinated in 1968, he was in Memphis to support the Memphis AFSCME sanitation workers.[45]

Ideology. Ideological interest groups are groups that adhere to a particular belief system or ideal about how society and government should be structured and what public policies are most desirable.[46] Ideological interest groups range along the political continuum from the far left to the extreme right and include organizations such as the American Civil Liberties Union (ACLU), the American Conservative Union, the Cato Institute, and People for the American Way (PFAW).

The Cato Institute, for example, is a Washington, DC–based public policy research organization established in 1977. Its name derives from the *Cato Letters*, libertarian pamphlets disseminated in the American colonies prior to the Revolutionary War. A libertarian organization,[47] the institute's mission is to increase the understanding of public policies based on the principles of limited government, free markets, individual liberty, and peace. Cato's goal is to push public

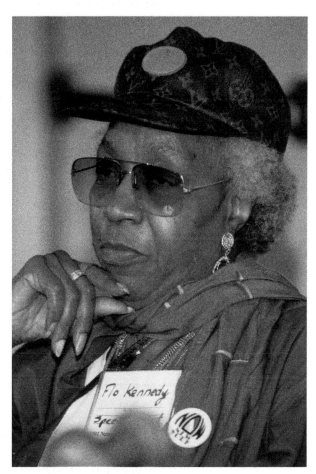

Florynce (Flo) Kennedy, a feminist lawyer and civil rights activist, was a founding member of the National Organization for Women in 1966, but she left in 1971 because of the organization's inability to tackle head-on issues she considered important. She was one of the few Black women involved in a White feminist organization. She went on to found the Feminist Party, which supported Shirley Chisholm's bid for president in 1972.

policies that are consistent with the principles of limited government, individual liberty, and peace.[48] The institute's key research foci include education and child policy, law and civil liberties, government and politics, energy and the environment, trade policy, health care and welfare, foreign policy and national security, and social security.

A counter to the Cato Institute is the liberal advocacy group People for the American Way. Founded in 1981 by Hollywood television and movie producer Norman Lear, the original mission of PFAW was to counter the growing clout and divisive message of right-wing televangelists, popular in the 1980s. Its objectives today are to push public policies that embrace America's diversity, respect Americans' rights, and defend liberty, democracy, and the American way.[49]

Public Interest. Public interest groups aim to speak for broad groups of citizens, such as consumers, environmentalists, and political reformers. An example of a public interest group is Public Citizen, founded in 1971 by Ralph Nader. The nonprofit organization views itself as representing "consumer interests in Congress, the executive branch and the courts."[50] Headed most recently by Robert Weissman, Public Citizen has more than 400,000 members and supporters and fights for "openness and democratic accountability in government, for the right of consumers to seek redress in the courts; for clean, safe and sustainable energy sources; for social and economic justice in trade policies; for strong health, safety and environmental protections; and for safe, effective and affordable prescription drugs and health care."[51] Among its accomplishments are the following: (1) pushing the U.S. Occupational Safety and Health Administration to adopt safety measures that protect workers from exposure to crystalline silica dust; (2) urging Congress to adopt standards that would protect consumers' First Amendment right to post anonymous reviews of products and services online; (3) protecting students from exploitative practices of for-profit colleges and universities; (4) ensuring that airbags are now standard in automobiles; and (5) urging the removal of dangerous drugs and dietary supplements such as Rezulin and ephedra from the market. (Public Citizen also pushed congressional legislation that would have limited damage awards in medical malpractice and product defect cases, but it was defeated.)[52]

Single Issue. Single-issue interest groups focus solely on one specific issue, such as abortion or gun control. The issues usually generate a great deal of emotion, and these groups are able to marshal enormous resources and energy in their quest to achieve their single objective.[53] Mothers Against Drunk Driving (MADD) is an example of a single-issue interest group. Candace Lightner founded MADD in 1980 after her thirteen-year-old daughter was killed by a hit-and-run driver in California. MADD has more than three hundred affiliates with approximately 3 million members.[54] MADD is one of the largest and most influential nonprofit organizations in the United States working to address issues related to drunk driving. MADD's mission is "to end drunk driving, help fight drugged driving, support the victims of these violent crimes and prevent underage drinking." Since its founding, MADD, according to its own publicity, was instrumental in the passage of the national minimum drinking age (of twenty-one) law in 1984 and has helped pass more than 2,300 anti–drunk driving and underage drinking laws.[55] In 2006, MADD launched the Campaign to Eliminate Drunk Driving. The campaign focuses on high visibility enforcement to catch drunk drivers and discourage individuals from driving drunk, requiring ignition interlock devices (in-car breathalyzers) for anyone who has had a past conviction for drunk driving, and supporting the development of advanced vehicle technology that can determine if a driver is drunk.[56]

Religion. Religious interest groups represent a particular denomination or a coalition of several denominations. Their objective is to push a particular set of policy issues that conform to their religious beliefs or to speak out on issues that they feel reflect those beliefs. An example of a religious interest group is the Christian Coalition of America, commonly referred to as the Christian Coalition, founded by Pat Robertson in 1989 to "give Christians a voice in government."[57] The Coalition is one of the largest conservation grassroots political organizations in the United States, and is associated with evangelical and fundamentalist Christians. The Coalition describes its mission as representing the pro-family point of view before local councils, school boards, state legislatures, and Congress; training leaders for effective social and political action; and defending the rights of Christians.

The National Council of Churches (NCC), formed in 1950, is a cooperative agency of thirty-eight Protestant, Evangelical, Orthodox, Anglican, and historic African American denominations. Its activities include working for peace and justice in the United States and addressing issues ranging from poverty and racism to the environment and family ministries. The NCC makes the views of the worldwide Christian community known to government and keeps its constituents informed of legislative and other developments of interest to the churches.[58]

Techniques of Interest Groups

Interest groups participate in the political process in a variety of ways to make sure that their interests are pushed and will benefit favorably from government decisions. To achieve this outcome, interest groups use a number of techniques: lobbying; electioneering, which includes the use of political action committees (PACs); education; litigation; and media campaigns to influence public opinion.

The choice of techniques by an interest group is related to the particular goals of the group and the intended targets of the group's efforts. For example, if the goal is to pass a particular piece of legislation, then an interest group might choose lobbying. If the goal is to elect more public officials sympathetic to the objectives of the group, it might choose some form of electioneering.

Lobbying

Lobbying The process by which an individual, a group, or an organization seeks to influence government policymakers.

Lobbying is the communication of data or opinions to a government decision maker in an effort to influence a specific decision.[59] Lobbying is typically done by an individual working for or representing an interest group. The word originated from the behavior of people who waited in the lobbies of government buildings to talk with legislators. Mythology has it that the word "lobby" originated during the administration of President Ulysses S. Grant, who, it is said, would drink brandy and smoke cigars in the lobby of the Willard Hotel in Washington, DC, and people who wanted something from the government would meet Grant in the lobby. The term, however, most likely originated with the British Parliament, specifically the House of Lords, in the first half of the nineteenth century.[60] Whatever the origins, lobbying and lobbyists are important players in the political process.

Lobbying strategies are either direct or indirect. Direct lobbying consists of personal contact between a lobbyist and a public official. Lobbyists who participate in direct lobbying are often former public officials, former members of Congress, or members of past presidential administrations. Because these individuals have personal relationships with current members of Congress and have contacts in other branches of the government, they can be particularly effective lobbyists. Direct lobbying is also done by law firms in Washington, DC, that work for specific business sectors, such as oil or tobacco industries. Special interest groups also hire public relations firms to engage in lobbying activities.[61]

Indirect lobbying involves the use of more roundabout techniques to communicate with decision makers. One aspect of indirect lobbying is the

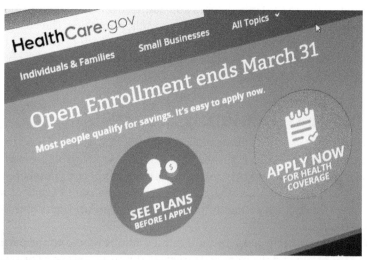

The rollout of the Affordable Care Act (Obamacare) Website Healthcare.gov on October 1, 2013 was fraught with problems: the site could not handle the volume of people trying to sign up, the system crashed when some people were almost done signing up, and some of the links to the various policy options did not work. Despite the horrendous rollout, the number of enrollees in various healthcare plans exceeded the target of 7 million people.

orchestrating of what might appear to be a groundswell of support for a particular issue from the constituents of the policymaker. Organized letter writing campaigns, phone calls, email messages, text messages, and other types of "grassroots" activity are forms of indirect lobbying. AARP has been very successful with indirect lobbying techniques on behalf of its members on issues related to middle-aged and senior citizens.

Electioneering

Another technique of interest groups is **electioneering**, working actively on behalf of a political candidate or political party. There are a number of electioneering activities. One is endorsement, a public declaration of support, of political candidates. Interest groups give their public support to candidates in the expectation that if the candidate is elected, her or his decisions and policies will be favorable to the interest group. Every national, state, and local election finds interest groups supporting different candidates in the hopes of gaining favorable consideration once they are elected.

Electioneering Working actively on behalf of a political candidate or political party with activities that might include publicly endorsing a candidate, making a campaign contribution, or making phone calls.

Another aspect of electioneering is campaign donations. Because many interest groups are prohibited by law from using their own funds to contribute to political candidates, they establish political action committees through which they can funnel contributions to political candidates. Since 1907, Congress has periodically passed legislation aimed at controlling contributions to political campaigns.

In 1971, Congress consolidated its earlier reform efforts into the Federal Campaign Act, which authorized corporations and interest groups to set up political action committees or PACs that could raise and spend money, and pool campaign contributions to elect or defeat political candidates. PACs are able to contribute more money to political candidates than individual donors. PACs are nevertheless limited to contributions of $5,000 per candidate each election cycle. Each primary, general, or runoff election is considered a separate election. This $5,000 limit was preserved in the Bipartisan Campaign Reform Act of 2002.

Yet PACs can also give $15,000 per calendar year to a national party committee; $5,000 per year to state, district, and local party committees; and $5,000 per year to any other political committee. PACs are able to spread money around to lots of different political entities during an election year and in the years leading up to an election year.[62]

The limits on individual contributions ($2,700 per candidate per election in 2015–2016) make PACs important sources of campaign money for political candidates.[63] Table 13.3 lists the top twenty PACs (according to the Federal Election Commission) with the largest campaign contributions in 2015–2016. Table 13.4 shows the top ten corporate PACs by contributions to candidates, from January 2015 to June 30, 2015. According to information released by the FEC, as of January 1, 2016 there were a total of 5,819 PACs in the United States, with 1,621 of that number having corporate interests.[64]

In addition to PACs, another set of campaign actors are groups called 527s, independent political groups named for the section of the IRS tax code

TABLE 13.3 Top 20 PAC Contributors to Candidates, 2015–2016

Rank	Contribution	Percent to Democrats	Percent to Republicans
Honeywell International	$1,633,664	36%	64%
AT&T	$1,551,750	40%	60%
Lockheed Martin	$1,513,750	35%	65%
National Beer Wholesalers Assn.	$1,383,700	40%	60%
Intl. Brotherhood of Electrical Workers	$1,292,750	98%	2%
Northrop Grumman	$1,282,700	40%	60%
Blue Cross and Blue Shield	$1,253,400	33%	66%
Credit Union National Assn.	$1,252,850	47%	53%
National Assn. of Realtors	$1,246,580	37%	63%
American Bankers Assn.	$1,149,458	20%	79%
Boeing	$1,094,000	41%	59%
PricewaterhouseCoopers	$1,088,849	35%	65%
National Rural Electric Cooperative Assn.	$1,078,375	23%	77%
New York Life Insurance	$1,066,700	44%	56%
American Crystal Sugar	$1,060,500	45%	55%
Comcast	$1,048,900	40%	60%
Air Line Pilots Assn.	$1,041,250	51%	49%
Majority Cmte. PAC	$1,035,000	0 %	100%
American Assn. for Justice	$1,016,000	97%	3%
Union of Operating Engineers	$974,330	63%	37%

Note: For ease of identification, the names used in this section are those of the organizations connected with the PACs, rather than the official PAC names.

Based on data released by the FEC on July 21, 2016.

Source: Open Secrets.org, 2016, www.opensecrets.org/pacs/toppacs.php

that regulates the financial activities of all political groups whose purpose is to influence elections.[65] In the 2004 election, both George W. Bush and Senator John Kerry were targeted by 527 groups. The 527 Swift Boat Veterans for Truth went after Senator Kerry by challenging his service in Vietnam and attacking his patriotism.

The activities of the Swift Boat group caused a great deal of controversy and called into question the role of 527s. Although the Bipartisan Campaign Reform Act (commonly known as the McCain-Feingold Act) prohibits

political parties and campaigns from accepting unlimited, unregulated donations from corporations, unions, and individuals, the law does not mention
527s. If the 527s do not coordinate their activities with candidates or political
parties, they can raise unlimited amounts of money and run political ads as
long as they do not explicitly endorse a particular candidate. This latter requirement is easy to get around because the focus in 527 ads makes clear
which candidate is favored.[66]

The Bipartisan Campaign Reform Act was challenged in the Supreme
Court. In early September 2009, the Supreme Court heard arguments in the
case *Citizens United v. Federal Election Committee*. The case involves an anti–
Hillary Clinton movie, *Hillary: The Movie* that the commission said was a campaign attack ad regulated under the act. The conservative group that made the
film, Citizens United, said the movie was a documentary and not a political
advertisement. The central question put before the Court was whether corporations and labor unions have the same protected First Amendment free
speech rights as individuals to participate in elections without facing censorship. The questions from the justices suggested that a majority might be inclined to declare that corporations have a First Amendment right to spend
their money and express views during elections just as individuals do.[67] On
January 21, 2010, the Supreme Court did, indeed, rule that corporations and
labor unions have the same protected First Amendment rights as individuals
and that they could give unlimited amounts of money to PACs. This decision
opened the floodgates for corporate donations to PACs and the creation of
Super PACs in the 2012 presidential election. In some instances, the Super
PACs were funded by one individual, a practice raising the specter that individuals and corporations are able to "buy" elections.

Education

Almost every interest group feels that it must educate the public on the issues
that it wants resolved by government. One way to educate the public is to dis-
seminate information about the issue in the hopes that the "facts" will persuade the public to support the interest group's position.[68] If a group is able to
generate public support or sympathy for its position, then the group is able to
cite that support when presenting arguments to decision makers.

Most interest groups do not have the resources and staff to do extensive
research, so what they do produce might be limited. Nevertheless, every day
in Washington and in state capitols around the country, interest groups inun-
date the public and politicians with the results of studies that support their
position. It is essential to the success of their overall objectives that interest
groups be viewed as experts in the area in which they have an interest.
High-quality research reports go a long way toward establishing that credibility. The Union of Concerned Scientists, an antinuclear public interest group,
has been able to establish this credibility and is viewed by news organizations
and legislators as a credible source on nuclear energy matters, despite their
own views.[69]

Litigation

The goals that interest groups pursue through litigation are varied, but some of the main objectives are establishing principles of constitutional right and challenging the constitutionality or legitimacy of legislative and executive actions.[70] Using the courts as a venue to pursue interest group aims might seem counterintuitive, but courts are important policymaking institutions that have the power to settle disputes and to make sweeping changes to or initiate new policies.[71]

For interest groups, one direct approach to litigation is to sponsor individuals who want to go to court to challenge an issue. This particular approach can be time consuming and very expensive, so many interest groups avoid it. But a successful suit can bring big rewards to the interest group and its members.

In 2002, individuals at the Cato Institute filed suit challenging Washington, DC's Firearms Control Regulations Act of 1975, which restricted Washington residents from owning handguns. The district court originally dismissed the suit, but the U.S. Court of Appeals for the DC Circuit overturned the dismissal and struck down some provisions of the law as unconstitutional. On June 26, 2008, the Supreme Court ruled in a 5–4 decision in *District of Columbia et al. v. Heller* that the District of Columbia cannot ban a citizen from keeping a handgun at home. The Court thereby threw out one of the nation's most restrictive gun control laws.[72] The day after the U.S. Supreme Court ruling that affirmed the rights of individuals to own handguns,[73] the NRA filed suit against the city of San Francisco (*Guy Montag Doe v. San Francisco Housing Authority*) to overturn the ban on handguns in public housing.[74] In 2009, the San Francisco Housing Authority reached a settlement with the NRA, allowing residents to legally possess firearms within public housing facilities.

In December 2012, the United States experienced the deadliest mass shooting at a grade school or high school when twenty children and six adults were murdered at Sandy Hook Elementary School in Newtown, Connecticut. Following that shooting, there was a significant push for legislation on gun control and ammunition legislation. In January 2013, the Obama administration introduced a proposal that included twenty-three executive actions designed to curb gun violence. Congress has been unable to pass any gun control legislation, except for renewing a ban against firearms that can pass undetected through metal detectors (Undetectable Firearms Act of 1988) in 2013.[75] In a CNN/ORC poll conducted in December 2015, 48 percent of Americans said they were in favor of stricter gun control laws, while 51 percent said they were opposed to stricter gun control laws.[76] The NRA, which represents the business interests of gun manufacturers and distributors,[77] has vehemently opposed any form of gun and ammunition regulation.

In 2015, the U.S. Supreme Court rejected the NRA's appeal over two San Francisco gun control measures in *Jackson v. City and County of San Francisco*, 14–704. The NRA was challenging a 2007 law that required people who store handguns at home to put them in a lockbox or disable them with a trigger lock.[78]

Another direct approach is to file *amicus curiae* (friend of the court) briefs on cases that will have an effect on the interest group. In the *Heller* case, amicus briefs were filed by the NRA and the Institute for Justice, among forty-seven others, against the handgun ban. Briefs in favor of upholding the ban were filed by the NAACP Legal Defense and Education Fund (LDF), the American Bar Association, and the American Academy of Pediatrics, among twenty others.[79]

Because the courts are highly attuned to the articulation of political interests, interest groups also use indirect, nonlitigation approaches to influence juridical outcomes. Although the techniques and tactics for influencing the courts are more limited, one tactic is to try to influence the judicial selection process so that judges favorable to an interest groups' aims are nominated to the bench. At the federal level, all judges are appointed by the president, and interest groups can exercise a great deal of influence on a president who shares their objectives.

Interest groups can also be influential in blocking a nomination to the court. President Ronald Reagan's nomination of Robert Bork in 1987 to the Supreme Court was blocked with the help of strong opposition from interest groups, such as the ACLU, the NAACP, the Gay and Lesbian Alliance, NOW, the Nation Institute (a liberal think tank), and the National Urban League.[80]

Another indirect tactic is to educate judges, lawyers, and other members of the legal community on issues of concern to the interest group to establish that there is growing support for a particular viewpoint. This particular tactic is expressed through law review articles that advocate an approach that the interest groups feel the courts should take. The NAACP has used this tactic in its push to eliminate racial discrimination in all aspects of American society. As part of the organization's efforts to outlaw restrictive covenants in real estate (language in deeds that forbade the property from being sold to Blacks and, in some instances, Jews), between 1946 and 1948 the NAACP coordinated the appearance of more than thirty books and law review articles urging the Supreme Court to reverse itself on restrictive covenants. The Court finally did in 1948 in *Shelly v. Kramer*, a decision that has been attributed to the legal educational work of the NAACP.[81]

Media Campaigns

Interest groups use mass media to influence public opinion, but because media campaigns are very expensive, not all interest groups have the resources to engage in them. As a result, media campaigns are usually undertaken by trade or business interest groups or well-financed groups such as the NRA and health care associations such as the Health Insurance Association of America.[82]

There are three types of media campaigns: goodwill, offensive, and defensive. A goodwill campaign attempts to create a favorable image for the interest group. To create such an image, a group might sponsor cultural programs on public broadcasting or underwrite a public service campaign.[83] For example, the tobacco industry—specifically Lorillard Tobacco Co., Philip Morris USA, and R. J. Reynolds Tobacco Co.—has been the primary force behind the Coalition for Responsible Tobacco Retailing, an organization of retailers, wholesalers, and manufacturers whose objective is "to educate and train retailers on preventing underage tobacco sales."[84] The coalition sponsors a series of "We Card" public service announcements.[85] This program encourages retail stores to display the "We Card" sign, to require identification from individuals wanting to buy cigarettes who appear younger than twenty-seven, and to train salesclerks to comply with state laws on the sale of tobacco to minors. The coalition and its "We Card" program attempt to portray the tobacco industry as trying to do its part to combat teenage smoking.

In an offensive media campaign, an interest group tries to generate public support for a specific positive policy objective. For example, when the Chrysler Corporation almost went bankrupt in 1979 and asked the federal government to bail it out, the company placed full-page ads in leading newspapers under the broad headline "Would America be better off without Chrysler?"[86] The implication was that if Chrysler went under, that would be the end of an American institution and would be bad for the country. The campaign was successful.

The question of the survival of the U.S. auto industry arose again in late 2008 and early 2009. The U.S. government provided billions of dollars in bailout money to General Motors (GM) and Chrysler (Ford did not require bailout money at the time). In an effort to build support for the bailout and change public perceptions of the automakers, GM and Chrysler developed Internet ads and videos aimed at individuals searching the web for information on the bailout or a specific automaker. GM, for example, created the GM "Facts and Fiction" campaign, which gave GM's perspective and asked people to "Support the U.S. Auto Industry."[87]

In another example, forty-five scientists in 2002 accused the publishers of an academic journal of being influenced by the tobacco industry and of not upholding the normal academic process of peer-reviewed articles. The editor of the journal was paid $30,000 by the Tobacco Institute to write an article for the journal that dismissed the dangers of secondhand smoke.[88]

Defensive media campaigns are designed to rally the public behind an interest group's position to prevent a change or a bill from being enacted.[89] In early 2009, the U.S. Chamber of Commerce was one of the major opponents of the Employee Free Choice Act (EFCA), a bill supported by organized labor that would make it easier for unions to organize workers. EFCA would amend the National Labor Relations Act to require the National Labor Relations Board to certify a union as the employees' bargaining representative without an election if a majority of employees sign cards indicating that they want to be represented by a specific union. These cards, referred to as card checks, are authorizations from the signatories that they want to form a union or be represented by a specific union.

Under current law, workers can select union representation either through an election process or through a majority sign-up card check. The National Labor Relations Board will certify a union as an exclusive representative only if the union is chosen through a secret ballot process or if the employer agrees to accept the card check results. The employer is not required to honor the card checks and can insist on a secret ballot election.[90]

Supporters of EFCA want more control in the hands of the workers, whereas opponents want more control in the hands of employers. As part of the campaign against EFCA, the Chamber of Commerce has run a number of television ads, which have been replayed numerous times on YouTube, characterizing the issue as a voting rights issue. According to the ads, EFCA would strip workers of their secret ballot right. The ads even have a union "boss" named Bill who posts the names and pictures of those who support or oppose the union, underscoring the chamber's argument that workers' voting rights would be removed if EFCA passed. After the Democrats lost control of the House of Representatives in 2010, the bill has stalled in Congress.

Factors That Make Interest Groups Effective

A study asking legislators to identify the factors that make one interest group more effective than another determined that the most influential factors are the following:

1. The size, wealth, and cohesion of the group and the amount of information and services it can provide the legislator.
2. The importance and reliability of the group as perceived by the legislator.
3. The type of interests that the group represents, with legislators more likely to give more credence to business and economic interest groups than to consumer groups.
4. The interest group's position on pending legislation (lobbyists are often more successful at preventing legislation than at pushing a bill through the legislative maze).
5. The strength and cohesion of the political parties within a legislator's state or within Congress on the issue in question.
6. The degree of competition among the interest groups on either side of the issue.[91]

These criteria help explain why some interest groups have more power and access than others. Many business and labor interest groups are large and well financed and can employ full-time lobbyists to provide information to legislators.[92] These groups can also provide legislators with the perks associated with lobbying; these range from minor perks such as social engagements and dinners to major perks such as international trips.

Groups without size, wealth, and full-time lobbyists find it difficult to compete. If, as the saying goes, money talks, how can interest groups with fewer financial resources influence decision makers? Can these less wealthy groups ever be on an equal footing with wealthier groups?

Political and Financial Inequalities

Pluralism assumes that all groups have equal access to the political system and its decision makers. Although the theory acknowledges that some interest groups will have more of one type of resource than other groups do, it concludes that resources of one type will counterbalance resources of another type. For example, an interest group with more money will be checked by another that has better organizational skills, or an interest group with large numbers will be checked by another that has more media access. Critics of these assumptions charge that this kind of equilibrium does not exist.

Pluralism has also been criticized for obscuring the role that race has played and continues to play in American society. For example, pluralism assumes that interests will become diversified across economic, social, and political issues; thus, there will be little need for racial and ethnic groups to organize around group-based issues. Race and ethnicity will be eclipsed as these other issues take precedence.

Pluralism also contends that once groups realize their subjective interests, they will become incorporated into the political system. This view would suggest that once the NAACP had legal successes, such as *Brown v. Board of Education of Topeka* in 1954, its focus would have broadened beyond issues related to Black Americans. Indeed, there would have no longer been a need for the NAACP to exist as an interest group.

Also, pluralism's notion that all groups have equal access to the political process assumes that there are no legal or structural barriers that might keep some groups from gaining access. The sustained history of the denial of the vote to Black Americans in the past, and in some instances present, hurdles to registration and voting make it difficult to maintain that interest groups such as the NAACP have had equal access to the political process.

Although in theory the political system might be open to everyone, all groups do not have the same access to decision makers. In a political world that is more and more dependent on money, groups with more financial resources are going to have an edge. To paraphrase a line from George Orwell's *Animal Farm*, all interest groups are created equal, but some groups are more equal than others. Less well-financed groups must use different tactics to get the attention of decision makers. These tactics, such as mobilizing the membership, as the environmental movement has done through grassroots lobbying, are more difficult to organize and manage successfully. "Measuring Equality: Selected Racial and Ethnic Interest Groups and Their Resources" on page 433 lists a number of interest groups that focus on issues of concern to racial and ethnic groups. As Table 13.4 demonstrates, the resources they have available to them are quite modest. For example, in 2015 the NAACP Legal Defense Fund (LDF) had a total revenue of approximately $17.5 million, and

measuring equality

Selected Racial and Ethnic Interest Groups and Their Resources

Racial and ethnic interest groups compete with other interest groups from a position of constrained resources. This resource deficit suggests that for these groups to bring issues to the fore and to be successful they must rely on their organizational, litigation, and political activity rather than on a foundation of healthy budgets to support their work. The text discusses the difference between the budgets of the NAACP Legal Defense and Educational Fund and the American Civil Liberties Union. Both are successful interest groups, but the LDF has done so from an incredibly smaller resource base, as shown in Table 13.4.

TABLE 13.4 **Selected Racial and Ethnic Interest Groups and Their Resources**

Name of Group	Year of Founding	Revenue*	Current Concerns
African Americans			
Congress of Racial Equality (CORE)	1942	2014: <$1 million[1]	Self-determination, equality, equal access to information, technology and healthcare
Joint Center for Political and Economic Studies	1970	2012: $7.1 million[†]	Black economic studies and minority economic advancement, Black voter registration and participation, business development, civil rights, education, health policy, welfare and poverty
NAACP Legal Defense and Educational Fund, Inc. (LDF)	1940	2015: $17.5 million[2]	Affirmative action (education and workplace), civil rights, fair employment, housing reform, felon disenfranchisement, voting rights
National Association for the Advancement of Colored People (NAACP)	1909	2014: $27.9 million[†]	Affirmative action, environmental racism, economic opportunities, equal access to education, Supreme Court
National Urban League	1910	2014: $51.1 million[†]	Civic engagement, civil rights, economic self-sufficiency, education and career development, employment and job training, health and quality of life
Latinos			
LatinoJustice PRLDEF	1972	2015: $3.9 million[†]	Immigrant discrimination, rights of Latina immigrant workers, redistricting
League of United Latin American Citizens (LULAC)	1929	$0.8 million[†] (unlisted year)	Economic conditions, educational attainment, political influence, housing, health and civil rights
Mexican American Legal Defense and Education Fund (MALDEF)	1968	2016: $5 million[3]	Education, employment, immigrants' rights, political access, public resource equity
National Council of La Raza (NCLR)	1968	2015: $47.8 million[4]	Assets/investments, civil rights, immigration, education, employment, economic status, health, census policy

measuring equality *(Continued)*

Name of Group	Year of Founding	Revenue*	Current Concerns
Asian Americans			
Asian American Legal Defense and Education Fund	1974	2014: $1.4 million[5]	Immigrant rights, civic participation, and voting rights, economic justice for workers, language access, census policy, affirmative action, educational equity, elimination of anti-Asian violence, police misconduct, human trafficking
American Indians			
National Congress of American Indians	1944	2015: $4.3 million[†]	Tribal governance, community development, health and human services, land and natural resources, cultural protection, federal recognition
Native American Rights Fund (NARF)	1970	2014: $6.7 million[†]	Tribal existence/sovereignty, tribal natural resources, religious freedom, voting rights

The most recent financial data available is provided in this table.

Sources:

† Avention, Inc. 2016. OneSource, accessed August 4, 2016.

[1] GuideStar. 2016. "GuideStar Report Generated for Congress of Racial Equality." http://www.guidestar.org/ViewPdf.aspx?PdfSource=0&ein=30-0454763, accessed August 4, 2016.

[2] NAACP Legal Defense and Education Fund. 2015. "Consolidated Financial Statements and Supplementary Information for the Year Ended June 30, 2015." http://www.naacpldf.org/files/about-us/Audited-Financial-Statement-NAACP-LDF-2015.pdf, accessed July 30, 2016.

[3] The Leadership Conference. 2016. "Mexican American Legal Defense and Education Fund (MALDEF)." http://www.civilrights.org/equal-opportunity/about/maldef.html, accessed July 30, 2016.

[4] National Council of La Raza. 2016. 2015 NCLR Annual Report. http://publications.nclr.org/bitstream/handle/123456789/1532/2015nclrannualreport_web.pdf?sequence=1&isAllowed=y, accessed August 4, 2016.

[5] Asian American Legal Defense and Education Fund. 2016. Annual Report 2014. http://aaldef.org/2014AnnualReport-final.pdf, accessed August 4, 2016.

in 2016 the Mexican American Legal Defense and Education Fund (MALDEF) had a budget of $5 million. In contrast, the well-funded ACLU had more than $137 million in total financial support and revenue in 2015.[93]

All three of these organizations use litigation as their strategy, but the ACLU has far more resources at its disposal to battle in court than do MALDEF and the LDF. Most of the interest groups that represent the concerns of racial and ethnic groups do not have substantial budgets. These groups cannot afford many of the amenities that allow them to gain access to decision makers on the same footing as other better financed interest groups do.

There is an additional element of complexity for organizations that represent the interests of what political scientist Dara Z. Strolovitch refers to as "marginalized groups": How well do these interest groups represent the concerns of members within their groups who are further marginalized? Strolovitch suggests that within each of these larger groups are issues that affect the group's population as a whole, issues that affect the majority of the members equally, issues that affect an advantaged subgroup within the group, and issues that are related to an economically, socially, or politically disadvantaged subgroup within the broader membership group. What she finds is that, even though the relevant interest groups provide some representation for their disadvantaged members, they are substantially less active when it comes to issues affecting disadvantaged subgroups than they are when it comes to issues affecting more advantaged subgroups.[94]

For example, Black and Latino interest groups are more likely to highlight majority issues such as racial profiling (Black) and census undercount (Latino) than either is to emphasize welfare (disadvantaged-subgroup issue). Both interest groups address universal issues, such as Social Security, and advantaged-subgroup issues of affirmative action in government contracting and higher education. In the past, general civil rights organizations address the majority issue of hate crimes, but shy away from disadvantaged-subgroup issues such as discrimination against lesbian, gay, bisexual, or transgender individuals.[95] But recently, the NAACP has come out in support of same-sex marriages and support for antidiscrimination laws to protect lesbian, gay, bisexual, or transgender individuals. What Strolovitch's research reveals is that within the broader system of inequalities among the interest groups representing Blacks and other racial and ethnic groups, there are further inequalities within those groups over which issues and which segments of their constituents are addressed.

Conclusion

This chapter has explored what interest groups are and what role they play in a democratic society. There are many different types of interest groups, with differing objectives, and these groups vary in many substantive ways. The various techniques interest groups use to influence political leaders on issues of importance to them have been discussed, along with some of the constraints that interest groups face in contributing money to politicians they feel will be important to their policy positions.

The common assumptions about interest groups are that "special interests" are code words for forces that operate against the public good and that the only special interests that matter are those funded by big money. In contrast, the story of racial and ethnic interest groups reveals that some special interests are very important for protecting and asserting the rights of groups often pushed to the margins of American society.

Even though the NAACP, the Urban League, and other interest groups that operate on behalf of racial and ethnic minorities are not the best funded, they can be effective. When they are effective, it is because their message or cause catches the attention and spirit of the general public or a significant portion of the public. In this instance, numbers can be as important as dollars. These interest groups are also effective when they employ strategies that do not rely entirely on money or numbers; for example, when they file specifically chosen and carefully researched lawsuits. Interest groups have been pivotal in American politics in the struggle for civil, political, and constitutional protections and rights for racial and ethnic groups. The vignette at the beginning of the chapter demonstrated how one Muslim civil rights group organized to oppose what they perceived to be an attack on Muslim Americans. This is not the only Muslim civil rights group and they have joined forces to protect the rights of Muslim Americans in many different arenas.

REVIEW QUESTIONS

1. What are interest groups, and what do they do?
2. Why do interest groups form, and who belongs to interest groups?
3. What tactics and strategies do interest groups use?
4. How do racial and ethnic interest groups differ from other types of interest groups?
5. What factors contribute to the success of racial and ethnic interest groups?

KEY TERMS

Collective Good p. 411
Electioneering p. 425
Free Rider p. 411

Interest Groups p. 407
Iron Triangle p. 411
Lobbying p. 424

Logic of Collective Action p. 411
Pluralism p. 409

ADDITIONAL READINGS

Theodore J. Lowi, *The End of Liberalism* (New York: Norton, 1979).
This book contains a classic analysis of the extent to which interest groups have captured various parts of the American political process.

E. E. Schattschneider, *The Semisovereign People* (New York: Random House, 1960).
This critique of pluralism identifies the elitist nature of interest groups and their effect on the political system.

Kay Lehman Schlozman and John T. Tierney, *Organized Interests and American Democracy* (New York: Harper and Row, 1986).
The authors present a thorough examination of interest groups, their tactics and techniques, and their activities.

Dara Strolovitch, *Affirmative Advocacy: Race, Class, and Gender in Interest Group Politics* (Chicago: University of Chicago Press, 2007).
This book explores how interest groups concerned with racial, ethnic, and gender issues have difficulty addressing the concerns of the most marginalized among their constituencies.

Patricia Sullivan, *Lift Every Voice: The NAACP and the Civil Rights Movement* (New York: New Press, 2009).
This book is the first major history of the NAACP.

Political Parties: Linking Voters and Governing Institutions

Donna Brazile addresses the 2016 Democratic National Convention in Philadelphia, PA, on July 26, 2016. Brazile, who has over 30 years of experience working for the Democratic Party, was named the Interim Chair of the Democratic National Committee after former chair Debbie Wasserman-Schultz resigned when hacked emails revealed that she and other party leaders exhibited bias against Democratic Party presidential candidate Bernie Sanders. Democrats were not successful in 2016, and they will select a new party chair.

Donna Brazile was born on December 15, 1959, in Kenner, Louisiana. She was the third of nine children in a working class family—her mother a maid and her father a janitor. Brazile first became involved in politics at the young age of nine when she worked for a city council candidate who promised to build a playground in her neighborhood. That candidate won, and he kept his promise by building that playground. While in high school and college at Louisiana State University, Brazile worked for Jimmy Carter's 1976 and 1980 presidential campaigns. After graduating college Brazile worked with Dr. Martin Luther King Jr.'s widow Coretta Scott King to organize the twentieth anniversary of the March on Washington in 1983, and in 1984 she worked on Jesse Jackson's campaign for the Democratic Party nomination for the presidency (see Chapter 6). Since then, she has been active in Democratic Party politics, becoming Democratic presidential candidate Al Gore's campaign manager in 2000—the first African American female to manage the presidential campaign for a major party's nominee. After Gore's defeat in 2000, Brazile stayed active in politics, taught college classes, wrote books, and served as a commentator for CNN. She worked on President Obama's 2008 and 2012 campaigns, and in 2011 she briefly served as the chair of the Democratic National Committee (DNC).[1]

In late July 2016 as the Democratic National Convention was about to commence, the group WikiLeaks, which leaks sensitive information hacked from government computers, publicized emails from Democratic Party leaders who had disparaged candidate Bernie Sanders. As a result, the chair of the DNC Debbie Wasserman Schultz resigned, and once again Donna Brazile stepped in as the chair of the DNC. As chair of the DNC, Brazile is an integral part of the Democratic Party election for the Presidency, as well as for U.S. House and Senate seats. She was active on the campaign trail, and has specifically focused building support for Democratic candidates, especially Hillary Clinton, among key groups, particularly African Americans.[2] However, her brief term was controversial, especially after the press discovered that while she worked for CNN, she had given the Clinton campaign advance notice of questions that would be asked during a debate with Bernie Sanders.[3] The Democrats under-performed in 2016; therefore, despite her lifelong achievements, Brazile was not successful as the party chair.

intro

This story illustrates the importance of political parties in American politics. ***Political parties*** *are mass organizations that seek to elect candidates to public office and ultimately influence public policy by linking voters with governing institutions. Consequently, the position of a national committee chair, such as the one that Donna Brazile holds, plays a key role in American politics. Because political parties seek to win elections and influence public policy, they need to develop political strategies to attract as many voters as possible, especially among America's growing racial and ethnic minority populations. It is important to note that Brazile is only the fourth racial or ethnic minority to chair a major political party—the others are Ron Brown, who is African American and chaired the Democratic National Committee in the 1990s; Mel Martinez, who is Latino and chaired the Republican National Committee in the 2000s; and Michael Steele, who is African American and chaired the Republican National Committee in the early 2010s.*

This chapter focuses on the important aspects of political parties. We begin by tracing the development of the American two-party system. Then we examine how parties are organized at the national, state, and local levels. We also address voters' connections to political parties and group attachments to political parties. Although the political parties also function in government, we covered this aspect of political parties in Chapters 6, 7, and 9; therefore in this chapter we pay less attention to the role of political parties in governing. This chapter emphasizes throughout the relationship between political parties and minority-group politics.

Political Parties Mass organizations that seek to elect candidates to public office and influence policymaking.

The Development of the Two-Party System

The United States currently has a **two-party system** in which only the Republican Party and the Democratic Party realistically compete for most elected offices. For that reason, we begin by looking at the development of our two-party system. We first discuss the history of early political parties, specifically focusing on the formation of the Republican Party and the Democratic Party. We then address how the Republican Party and the Democratic Party have changed in terms of balance of power and ideology. We also discuss the important **minor parties**—that is, political parties other than the Democrats and Republicans—that still can influence American politics. We emphasize how political party development has intersected with the politics of race and ethnicity.

Two-Party System A government system in which only two political parties realistically compete for elected offices.

Minor Parties Political parties in a two-party system that are not one of the dominant two political parties.

The Early Parties

President George Washington, like most of the Framers, vociferously opposed the formation of political parties. In fact, he included within his administration people who held divergent political views. His vice president, John Adams, and his secretary of the treasury, Alexander Hamilton, favored increasing national power, borrowing money on the credit of the national government, using the national government to promote an industrial economy, and supporting England in its war with France. Conversely, Washington's secretary of state, Thomas Jefferson, opposed a national debt and supported

Democratic-Republicans
An early political party that
Thomas Jefferson formed to
oppose the nationalist policies
of John Adams and Alexander
Hamilton.

Federalist Party An early
political party led by John
Adams and Alexander Hamilton
that supported nationalizing the
economy.

Sedition Act A 1798 law that
criminalized harsh criticism of
President John Adams and his
policies.

Twelfth Amendment An
amendment to the Constitution
that requires the president and
vice president to be elected on
separate ballots.

preserving state power, expanding westward to build an agricultural economy,
and siding with France in conflicts with England.

When President Washington declined to run for a third term in 1796,
Jefferson and Adams faced each other in the presidential election. The supporters of Jefferson became known as the **Democratic-Republicans** (or Jef-
fersonian-Republicans), and the supporters of Adams were known as the
Federalist Party. Despite the similar name, the Federalist Party is not necessarily the same as the Federalists who supported ratification of the Constitution. This development marked the beginning of the American two-party
system.

After Adams's narrow Electoral College victory, Jefferson's supporters continued to attack Adams, especially in the press. In response, the Federalists,
who controlled Congress, passed the **Sedition Act**, which criminalized harsh
criticism of Adams and his policies. Many of Jefferson's supporters were severely punished under this act. In response, Jefferson used his opposition to
the Sedition Act to organize against Adams and the Federalists.

The election of 1800 featured a rematch between John Adams, the Federalist candidate, and Thomas Jefferson, the Democratic-Republican candidate.
In preparation for that election, Jefferson organized Democratic-Republicans
throughout the country at the local level. In addition to focusing on his own
campaign, Jefferson seeded Democratic-Republican candidates to run for the
U.S. House of Representatives and state offices.[4]

The Democratic-Republicans won handily in races throughout the nation,
and the party won a majority of electoral votes. However, Jefferson and another Democratic-Republican, Aaron Burr, actually received the same number
of electoral votes. Ultimately, the House of Representatives selected Jefferson
as president. As a result of the confusion over the election of 1800, the **Twelfth
Amendment** to the Constitution was ratified in 1804 to require that the presidential and vice presidential selections take place on separate ballots. This
change allowed political parties to flourish because it ensured that a party's
presidential and vice presidential candidates could run as a team representing
the party.

The election of 1800 also brought about the demise of the Federalists and
in essence created a one-party system in the United States. Throughout the
early nineteenth century, Democratic-Republicans dominated national, state,
and local governments. Despite the one-party government, political, geographical, and social cleavages persisted. Northerners clashed with Southerners over the issue of slavery, class differences were widening, and the coastal
cities conflicted with the interior region over economic development.

By the election of 1824, these factions could no longer coexist in the same
political party, and four significant candidates were running for president as
Democratic-Republicans. Although Andrew Jackson, who represented commoners and Western settlers, won a plurality of the electoral votes, he did not
win a majority. Speaker of the House Henry Clay finished fourth in the election, but he used his power to give the presidency to John Quincy Adams

(recall that the House selects the president when no candidate secures a majority of the Electoral College), who represented the Northern elite and finished second to Jackson in the Electoral College and popular votes. Adams then appointed Henry Clay to be secretary of state. Andrew Jackson and his supporters referred to this arrangement as a "corrupt bargain," and they organized at the local level throughout the nation to oppose the Adams administration. This organization became the **Democratic Party**. Unlike previous party organizations, which revolved around political elites, Jackson used common people to organize campaigns. In 1828, Jackson and his Democrats challenged John Quincy Adams, and the Democratic Party's superior organizing ability gave Jackson a solid victory.[5]

Democratic Party One of the two major political parties, established by Andrew Jackson in the 1820s to champion the interests of commoners.

The Democrats, unlike the Framers, extolled political parties as essential to preserving the democratic republic and checking abuses of power. Additionally, Jackson used his authority over federal appointments and federal contracts to reward Democratic Party activists who brought voters to the polls; that is, he instituted the patronage system, which we discussed in detail in Chapter 8.

Although patronage had existed previously, Jackson greatly expanded it to cover most federal workers, and he established local patronage organizations, known as machines, to bring in voters at the local level. Undoubtedly, the exchange of votes for jobs and contracts was corrupt. Nevertheless, Jackson argued that patronage was the right of the victor, and it made the bureaucracy more responsive and democratic by giving commoners government jobs. The patronage machines were also inclusive of immigrants who faced ethnic discrimination in the private sector. As long as party activists produced votes, patronage machines would provide them with jobs regardless of their ethnic background. However, there is considerable debate over the extent to which patronage actually helped immigrants and ethnic minorities.[6]

Opposition parties soon developed over disagreement with Jackson's policies and his aggressive use of presidential power. Henry Clay, who in 1832 had failed to unseat Jackson for the presidency, unified a diverse group of Jackson's opponents into a political party known as the **Whigs**. Although there was a diversity of beliefs among the Whigs, all party members shared an antipathy toward Andrew Jackson. By 1840, Whigs had won twenty gubernatorial elections spanning the nation, and Whig candidate William Henry Harrison had won the presidency.

Whigs A political party founded in the 1830s to oppose the politics and policies of President Andrew Jackson.

The Whigs and the Democrats competed for national, state, and local positions throughout the 1840s, thus reestablishing a two-party system. However, both parties suffered from internal factional strife, primarily over the issue of slavery in the expanding territories. During the 1850s, internal disagreements over slavery permanently destroyed the Whig Party. In 1854, antislavery Whigs, unaligned abolitionists, and even some antislavery Northern Democrats formed the **Republican Party**. The party opposed expanding slavery, insisted that the Union remain united, and promoted industrialization. In 1860, slavery divided the Democratic Party to the point that it named two

Republican Party One of the two major political parties, founded in the 1850s by former Whigs who opposed slavery.

Immigrants are naturalized in Tammany Hall in New York City. During the nineteenth century, Tammany Hall was the most important political party machine and exerted a significant influence over American politics. Because party organizations were most concerned about winning elections, they were more open to immigrants than were most other segments of American life. Although immigrants are undoubtedly treated better today than they were during the nineteenth century, the issue of immigration is still central to party politics.

presidential candidates, which allowed Republican Abraham Lincoln to win the presidential election.[7]

Realignment and Republican Party Dominance

Immediately following the Civil War, there was competition between the two parties, but the Republicans tended to be more successful. From the end of the Civil War until 1896, the Republicans controlled the presidency, with only one Democrat—Grover Cleveland—serving as president during that period. However, it is worth noting that Democratic presidential candidates won the popular vote in 1876 (Samuel Tilden) and 1888 (Grover Cleveland), but they lost in the Electoral College. During this period, control of the House of Representatives was fairly evenly split, but Republicans controlled the Senate for all but two terms.

By the election of 1896, groups of voters in the United States had shifted their support to the Republican Party. The upper class, middle class, farmers, Northerners, Midwesterners, Westerners, and even the few African Americans who could vote supported Republicans; Democratic support came only from the South and some parts of Northern urban areas, although most urban areas voted Republic during this time. Moreover, this shift in support in favor of the Republican Party lasted for an extended period; it was not a one-time phenomenon. Between 1897 and 1933, the only Democratic president was Woodrow Wilson (1913–1921). Republicans also controlled the House and Senate for the majority of that period. During this period, the Republican Party was successful in every region of the nation, except for the South, where the Democrats dominated. The election of 1904 best illustrates this regional divide. Although the Democratic candidate, Alton Parker, was from New York, he won only in the eleven former Confederate states plus Kentucky and Maryland. Theodore Roosevelt—the Republican—won in every other state.[8]

Political scientists use the term **realignment** to refer to periods when voter allegiances toward the political parties shift for an extended period of time, resulting in one party's emerging as dominant.[9] (See Table 14.1 for a view of party domination and demise.) There is some disagreement among political scientists concerning which elections initiated a realignment, especially because some of the early examples coincided with the initial development of the two-party system (e.g., 1800, 1828, and 1860). Nevertheless, 1896 is commonly regarded as the beginning of a realignment in favor of the Republican Party. However, David Mayhew, an eminent political scientist, doubts the validity of the realignment concept.[10]

During this period of Republican dominance, there were key policy differences between the Republicans and the Democrats. The Democratic Party generally represented the interests of laborers; it supported breaking up

Realignment Periods when voter allegiances toward the political parties shift for an extended period of time, resulting in one party emerging as dominant.

TABLE 14.1 Major Political Parties in the United States

Political Party	Year Founded	Successes
Federalist	1796	Competitive with Democratic-Republicans until 1816 No longer exists
Democratic-Republican	1796	Competitive with Federalists Dominant until 1824 No longer exists
Democratic	Late 1820s	Competitive with Whigs until 1852 Competitive with Republicans until 1896 Weaker party until 1932 Dominant party until 1968 Competitive with Republicans through present
Whigs	Early 1830s	Competitive with Democrats until 1852 No longer exists
Republican	1854	Competitive with Democrats until 1896 Dominant party until 1932 Weaker party until 1968 Competitive with Democrats through present

monopolies, ensuring legal protections for workers, and lowering tariffs. Republicans represented wealthy and middle-class voters in the North, Midwest, and West; the party favored less government intervention in the economy.

The issue of extending federal protections for Blacks also separated the two parties. Although the Northern urban Democratic machines incorporated ethnic immigrants, they were not concerned about Blacks. The Southern wing of the Democratic Party, which dominated throughout the South, was adamantly opposed to civil rights and sought to preserve segregation.

The Republican Party during this period was split on the issue of civil rights. The party had been founded on its opposition to slavery, and during Reconstruction many "Radical Republicans" in Congress used the power of the federal government to secure civil rights for the former slaves. However, in 1877 Republican president Rutherford B. Hayes formally ended Reconstruction and abandoned the Republican Party's commitment to civil rights.[11] Consequently, the Republican Party fractured into two wings: **Black and Tan Republicans** supported federal enforcement of civil rights for African Americans, whereas **Lily White Republicans** did not.[12]

Black and Tan Republicans
A wing of the Republican Party that supported civil rights for African Americans.

Lily White Republicans
A wing of the Republican Party that opposed civil rights for African Americans.

The New Deal Coalition and Democratic Party Dominance

The Republican Party's domination of American politics ended with the 1932 election, which initiated a realignment in favor of the Democrats. In 1932, during the height of the Great Depression, Democratic presidential candidate Franklin Roosevelt promised that, unlike the actions of incumbent Republican president Herbert Hoover, his New Deal would use the federal government to alleviate suffering, stimulate the economy, and prevent similar problems from recurring. This message, coupled with Roosevelt's unique ability to bring optimism to a gloomy electorate, gave him, as well as House and Senate Democrats, a landslide victory that made the Democrats into the majority party for the first time since the Civil War.

New Deal Coalition The groups that supported President Franklin Roosevelt's policies and as a result made the Democrats the dominant party during the 1930s and 1940s.

Democratic control persisted throughout the 1930s and 1940s because Roosevelt assembled a **New Deal coalition** consisting of traditional Democratic supporters in the South and in Northern cities, as well as farmers, the middle class, and even African Americans. All of these groups allied with the Democrats because they viewed the New Deal as the best solution to their economic problems.[13] From 1933 through 1968, only one Republican served as president (Dwight Eisenhower, from 1953–1961) and the Democrats controlled Congress almost 90 percent of the time.

Despite the dominance of the Democratic Party during this period, there were conflicts within the party over foreign policy. After World War II, the United States was primarily concerned with containing communism, especially after the Soviet Union and China obtained nuclear weapons. Democratic president Harry Truman sought a hardline stance against communism by building up the U.S. arsenal and fighting communists in Korea. Other Democrats wanted a less bellicose stance toward communist nations.

A more significant division in the Democratic Party occurred over the issue of civil rights. Traditionally, the Democratic Party had vigorously opposed civil rights legislation, whereas Republicans had been divided over the issue. However, after Roosevelt brought more African Americans into the Democratic Party, many party leaders advocated federal enforcement of civil rights laws.

This controversy erupted during the Democratic National Convention in 1948 when presidential nominee Harry Truman insisted that the Democrats support civil rights. Under the leadership of South Carolina governor Strom Thurmond, Southern delegates walked out of the convention and formed the States' Rights Party. The fledgling party nominated Thurmond as their presidential candidate. Despite the fact that Truman was reelected, Thurmond won the states of South Carolina, Louisiana, Alabama, and Mississippi, which had voted Democratic in every other election since Reconstruction.[14]

White Southerners' ties to the Democratic Party weakened again in 1964. Democratic president Lyndon Johnson successfully pushed for key civil rights legislation, but Republican presidential nominee Barry Goldwater vigorously opposed the federal government's involvement in civil rights. Although Johnson won a landslide victory, Goldwater did extremely well in the South. The 1964 election was the first time since Reconstruction that Georgia, Alabama, Mississippi, Louisiana, and South Carolina supported a Republican presidential candidate.

The End of Party Dominance and the Rise of Party Competition

With the election of 1968, conflicts within the Democratic Party resulted in a loss of its dominance. That is to say, the 1968 election began a period of **dealignment**, a period in which voters abandon their ties to the political parties; consequently, there has been balance between the two parties since 1969.[15] During the period between 1968 and 2014, Republicans won seven presidential elections and Democrats won five, although Democrat Al Gore did win the popular vote in 2000, despite losing the Electoral College and thus the election. Democrats completely controlled Congress slightly more than half the time during that same period, and Republicans completely controlled Congress about one-fifth of the time. There was a split in the control of Congress slightly more than one-fourth of the time. Presidential elections since 2000 have been close in the popular vote, and, although 2000 and 2004 were close in the Electoral College, Democratic President Barack Obama scored sizable Electoral College victories in 2008 and 2012, but in 2016 Republican Donald Trump won the Electoral College while losing the popular vote by over one million voters.

The Democrats fractured during the late twentieth century because of continued policy disputes among party members. Foreign policy disagreements contributed to the loss of the party's dominance. In 1968, the Democrats were extremely divided over the Vietnam War, which President Lyndon Johnson had perpetuated, and during the 1980s many people who had generally voted Democratic supported Republican presidential candidate Ronald Reagan because of his hardline stance against communism.

Dealignment A period in which voters abandon their ties to the political parties, resulting in a balance of power between Republicans and Democrats

Social issues such as abortion, gay rights, and prayer in school also splintered the Democratic Party. Socially conservative working-class voters, who had been voting Democratic for economic reasons, began supporting the Republican Party because of its conservative positions on social issues. Likewise, many wealthy and suburban voters, who had traditionally voted Republican because of economic issues, switched to the Democratic Party because the Republicans' conservative stance on social issues alienated them.

Race has been a major cause of changes in party balance. By the 1960s, Democratic Party leaders fully embraced civil rights, which earned them the support of most African Americans. In 1968, segregationist Alabama governor George Wallace left the Democratic Party and ran for the presidency on the American Independent Party ticket. Wallace won the states of Arkansas, Louisiana, Mississippi, Alabama, and Georgia. Except for President Johnson's home state of Texas, all other Southern states supported Republican candidate Richard Nixon.[16] Nixon and his strategists, particularly Kevin Phillips, employed what is known as the *Southern Strategy*, in which Republicans would

A pin supporting the candidacy of Alabama Governor George Wallace (1919–1998) for president. Originally a Democrat, Wallace ran as an Independent in 1968 because he was dissatisfied with the Democratic Party's support for civil rights policies. Although he lost the election, Wallace performed well for a minor party candidate, winning 9 million votes and 46 electoral votes (all from the South). Moreover, his actions split the Southern states from the Democratic Party and ensured a period of Republican domination in the region. In 1972, Wallace rejoined the Democratic Party and again ran for president, but he was crippled in an assassination attempt during the primary. He then returned to Alabama to serve three more terms as governor. Later in life he sought the forgiveness of Alabama's Black population and their votes were crucial to maintaining him in office.

espouse conservative positions, especially on race, in order to win in the South and be more competitive nationally with the Democrats.[17]

Since then, the South has tilted Republican, with Whites largely supporting the Republicans and Blacks overwhelmingly supporting the Democrats. Barack Obama did narrowly win in Florida, North Carolina, and Virginia in 2008 and in Florida and Virginia in 2012, which indicates slight improvement from the 2000 and 2004 elections, when Democrats were shut out in the South. Nevertheless, in 2016 Hillary Clinton only won in Virginia, and as of November 2016 there are only two Democratic governors in the former Confederacy (Terry McAuliffe in Virginia and John Bel Edwards of Louisiana). All eleven state legislatures are controlled by Republicans.

Minor Parties

Although American political party development has been characterized by the two major parties, there have been important minor parties throughout American history. Minor parties have focused on specific issues, such as the Prohibition Party, which seeks to ban alcohol,[18] or the United States Marijuana Party, which pursues decriminalization of currently illegal drugs, especially marijuana.[19] Other minor parties represent socioeconomic groups that the two parties have ignored. For example, during the late nineteenth century the People's Party (also known as the Populist Party) represented small farmers.

Minor parties have also been ideologically based. During the early twentieth century, the Progressive Party was concerned with political and electoral reform, and in 1912 former Republican president Theodore Roosevelt ran as the Progressive Party candidate. Although Democrat Woodrow Wilson won that race, Roosevelt performed better than incumbent Republican president William Howard Taft.[20]

Some minor parties have emphasized race and ethnicity (see "Evaluating Equality: Minor Parties and Racial and Ethnic Minorities"). During the late nineteenth century, the Equal Rights Party sought civil rights for Blacks and women's suffrage. Unfortunately, most minor parties dealing with race and ethnicity have been based on maintaining prejudice, not on advancing civil rights. The American Party (also known as the Know Nothing Party), which emerged in the mid-1850s, contained former Whigs who espoused anti-immigration and anti-Catholic views. The States' Rights Party and the American Independent Party both supported segregation and decried federal involvement in enforcing civil rights laws, and they were successful in the South in the 1948 and 1968 elections, respectively.[21]

Party Organization

To organize voters, win elections, and influence public policy, political parties require complex organizations to articulate a coherent set of policy goals and run campaigns. Although government leaders, such as members of Congress and of the executive branch, are important to political party organizations,

evaluating equality

Minor Parties and Racial and Ethnic Minorities

As we have demonstrated in this chapter, the United States has a two-party system in which the Republican Party and the Democratic Party dominate politics and government. Minor parties, albeit occasionally important, rarely win elections to major federal and state offices.

Our election system is one reason that the two major parties continue to dominate elections, especially in the House of Representatives. All House seats are single-member districts, with winner-take-all elections. Thus, each state is divided into geographical regions, known as districts, and each district is represented by a single representative. The candidate who gets the most votes in that district wins the election, even if he or she has not received a majority of the votes and has finished only a few votes ahead of the second-place finisher. As a result, it is virtually impossible for a minor party candidate to finish first in any district. Therefore, minor party candidates are unlikely to serve in representative institutions.

An alternative system, known as proportional representation, has multimember districts. In this system, as seen in nations such as Israel, Italy, and Germany, a state is not divided into single-member districts. Instead, the entire state, or a region of the state, selects several representatives, and the top vote-getters are awarded seats. For example, if a region sends five representatives to a legislative chamber, then the region is not divided into five separate districts. Instead, the top five vote-getters are sent to the chamber. Therefore, minor party candidates have a decent chance of finishing in the top five and being elected. In some nations, such as Israel, there are no districts; legislative seats are awarded by party proportional to the outcome of the vote. As long as a party receives 2 percent of the vote, it is guaranteed seats in the legislature.

There has been considerable debate over whether the United States should adopt a proportional representation system to give minor parties more of a voice, and this debate is especially relevant for minority-group politics. On the one hand, if the United States adopts a proportional representation system, then racial and ethnic minority groups can form political parties specifically geared to their needs, and those parties could win seats in the U.S. House and in state legislatures. Alternatively, minority groups could coalesce to form a political party that focuses on the general needs of racial and ethnic minority groups. Even if minority groups do not form their own political parties, other minor parties could be an attractive alternative for minority voters. For example, in in 2016 the Green Party ticket features Ajamu Baraka, an African American, as its Vice Presidential candidate.*

Conversely, proportional representation could result in the election of overtly prejudiced parties or other people whose views are contrary to the goals of racial and ethnic minorities. In some proportional representation nations, such as Germany, outright racist political parties are banned. However, because the First Amendment guarantees free speech and free association rights (see Chapters 2 and 4), it is difficult to ban prejudice-based parties in the United States.

Debate among your classmates the merits of a proportional representation system for the United States, which would give more power to minor political parties. In doing so, investigate the following websites of the minor parties that are currently active in the United States: the Libertarian Party (http://www.lp.org), the Green Party (http://www.gp.org), the Constitution Party (http://www.constitutionparty.com), the Peace and Freedom Party (http://peaceandfreedom.org/home/), and the Socialist Party (http://socialistparty-usa.net/). Which system is better for American politics overall? Which system is better for racial and ethnic minorities in the United States? For a more in-depth analysis of the effect of the type of voting system, see Douglas J. Amy, *Behind the Ballot Box: A Citizen's Guide to Voting Systems* (Westport, CT: Praeger, 2000).

* Jill2016, "Meet Ajamu," http://www.jill2016.com/meet_ajamu, accessed September 22, 2016.

much of the work of political parties is conducted by party activists, who operate away from public view. There are different components of political party organization: the party conventions, the national committees, and state and local organizations. In each component, there is a relationship between minority-group politics and party organization.

National Party Conventions

The national party conventions are held every four years (during the summer of election years), and they are important features of political party organizations. At these national conventions, delegates nominate their presidential and vice presidential candidates, offer a statement of the party's principles and beliefs, and make rules to govern the party. Each state sends a number of delegates proportional to the size of its population. These delegates are party activists who are usually attached to a specific candidate for the presidential nomination.

The method for selecting delegates to the convention has been extremely controversial. Early in our nation's history, party members in Congress nominated presidential and vice presidential candidates, but in 1832 the Democrats moved to the caucus-convention system in which party members met in local meetings called **caucuses** to select convention delegates. By taking away the nomination decision from elite government leaders and giving it to local party activists, the caucus-convention system increased commoners' political access. However, local party leaders used power that they amassed through patronage to direct the outcome of the caucuses and thus influence presidential and vice presidential nominations.

To limit the control of local party leaders, many states switched from caucuses to **primaries**, in which party members select nominees through elections. Registered members of the political party vote for candidates in the primary, and the state awards delegates based on the outcome of that vote. The Democratic Party generally awards delegates proportionally to the outcome in each state, whereas the Republican Party often gives all or most delegates to the winner of the state primary, regardless of the closeness of the result.[22]

The clash between primaries and caucuses exploded during the Democratic Party Convention in 1968. Despite winning numerous primaries, Minnesota senator Eugene McCarthy did not capture the nomination because Vice President Hubert Humphrey, who did not win any primaries, secured the nomination through party leaders and delegates selected in caucuses. After the Democrats lost that presidential election, the party changed its rules to better represent regular party members and encourage states to use primaries instead of caucuses.

Since the 1970s, many states have switched from caucuses to primaries. Although these reforms increased public access to the party, the Democrats also established the use of **superdelegates**, or party leaders who are automatically selected as delegates and vote to nominate the candidate they prefer regardless of the results of primaries and caucuses. The Republican Party

Caucuses A method for political parties to select their candidates for office whereby party members convene at local meetings.

Primaries A method for political parties to select their candidates for office whereby people vote in an election.

Superdelegates Delegates to the Democratic National Convention who are not selected by primaries or caucuses but instead are established party leaders.

encouraged its states to use primaries, but it did not adopt all of the Democratic reforms. The use of superdelegates was extremely controversial during the 2016 Democratic Party nomination. Because most superdelegates (as well as a majority of the pledged delegates) supported Hillary Clinton, Bernie Sanders and his supporters complained that the superdelegates give an unfair advantage to candidates who have the support of the party leader but not necessarily the Democratic Party voters. During the Democratic National Convention in 2016 the party agreed to establish a commission that would create a new rule for 2020 that requires many of the superdelegates to be awarded according to the vote in their states.[23]

Party Platform A statement a political party produces at its national convention that summarizes the basic policy principles of the party.

The Democratic reforms of the 1970s also increased the number of racial and ethnic minorities, women, and young people serving as delegates to the national conventions. The Republicans have not adopted these reforms, which is one reason that the delegates to the Democratic National Convention are far more diverse than the delegates to the Republican National Convention. Figure 14.1 reports Black representation at the Democratic and Republican National Conventions from 1932 through 2012. Black representation at the Democratic National Convention increased after 1968 and especially in 2008 and 2012, when Barack Obama was the nominee. Black representation at the Republican National Convention remained low, especially in 2008 and 2012.

Conventions produce a **party platform**, which delineates the party's basic principles (see "Our Voices: Political Party Platforms and Civil Rights" on page 453). Initially, a committee drafts a platform, which convention delegates must then approve. Because platforms define the party for a particular election, they are important. But they are nonbinding; in fact, when convenient, candidates oppose parts of their own party's platform. The 2016 Republican Party Platform contains some extremely controversial positions, including allowing states to require transgender people to use the bathroom that corresponds with the sex indicated on their birth certificate, seeking to overturn the U.S. Supreme Court decision that legalized same-sex marriage, claiming that children raised by an opposite-sex married couple are least likely to experience emotional and psychological difficulties (despite the lack of scientific evidence supporting this claim), and declaring pornography to be a public health problem.[24]

Keynote address by Representative Barbara Jordan, Democratic National Convention, July 12, 1976. In 1972, Jordan became the first African American woman elected to the U.S. House of Representatives from a Southern state. The speech she delivered at this convention is regarded as one of the most rousing convention speeches in American history. In addition to being groundbreaking as a Black female leader, Representative Jordan, who died in 1996, suffered from multiple sclerosis and was confined to a wheelchair for much of her adult life. Moreover, although she never publically announced it, Representative Jordan was a lesbian.

Senator Ted Cruz (R-TX) addresses the Republican National Convention in Cleveland, Ohio, on July 20, 2016, with his image on video in the background. Cruz was the eventual nominee Donald Trump's main opponent during the nominating process. It is common for former opponents to speak during a national convention, but Cruz's speech was extremely controversial because after strongly advocating for conservative principles, Senator Cruz refused to endorse the nominee Donald Trump. The crowd reacted with boos. Cruz later stated that during the nominating contests Trump had harshly attacked Cruz's wife Heidi. Trump also suggested that Cruz's father, who was born in Cuba, had been part of the plot to assassinate President John F. Kennedy. There was absolutely no evidence to support this claim, and Cruz did not forgive Trump for these allegations, although he eventually endorsed Trump in the fall.

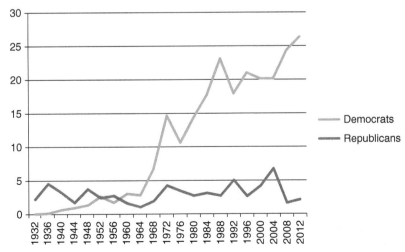

Figure 14.1 Percentage of Convention Delegates Who Are African Americans.

National Party Committees

Because national conventions meet only once every four years, the everyday work of running a national party falls to the national committee—the Republican National Committee or the Democratic National Committee (DNC). **National committees** determine the national parties' policy goals, devise electoral strategies, make rules and regulations to govern the party, and raise money to be used by the party and its candidates.

National Committee The organization responsible for making rules and regulations for a party when the conventions are not in session, raising money for the party, and directing the party's electoral strategy.

The two parties structure their committees quite differently from one another. Because the Republican Party values state sovereignty, the RNC contains three representatives from each state, the District of Columbia, American Samoa, Guam, Puerto Rico, and the Virgin Islands. At least one of those three representatives must be a woman. The Democratic Party is less concerned with state sovereignty and favors diversity. As a result, state representation on the DNC is proportional to population, and the DNC contains at-large positions designed to increase the representation of minorities and women.[25]

In the 1980s and 1990s, the RNC and the DNC increased their power through their control over fundraising. The Federal Election Campaign Act of 1974 had limited the amount of donations of **hard money**, through which individuals and groups give money directly to candidates. But the law had not limited the amount of contributions of **soft money**, unregulated campaign donations that go to support the infrastructure of the party but cannot be used directly on campaigns.

Hard Money The heavily regulated money that is directly raised by political candidates.

Soft Money The less regulated money that is raised by a political party to support and maintain the party.

By the 1990s, both national committees were using soft money to fund advertisements that did not explicitly suggest voting for a particular candidate but nevertheless greatly influenced how people voted. To correct the problems that these advertisements posed, the Bipartisan Campaign Reform Act (BCRA) of 2002 prohibited parties from using soft money for political advertisements; they could use only hard money for that purpose. Political leaders challenged the act as a violation of the First Amendment guarantee of free speech, but the U.S. Supreme Court upheld the constitutionality of the ban.[26] The BCRA limited the ability of the RNC and DNC to raise funds for elections, but both national committees still raise a substantial amount of money through hard-money donations.

National Committee Chair The head of each party's national committee, who is most responsible for directing the party's electoral strategies.

Because both national committees meet only several times per year, they leave the primary operations of the party to the **national committee chair**. For the party that controls the presidency, the president recommends a committee chair, whom the national committee automatically approves. As the opening vignette shows, the national committee selects the chair on its own for the party that does not control the presidency. The national committee chair and a staff of permanent advisers work behind the scenes to develop the party's political positions, devise electoral strategies, raise money, and coordinate national party goals with those of state and local parties. When a party controls the presidency, its national chair avoids upstaging the president by assuming a less public role than the national committee chair for the party that does not control the presidency.

our voices

Political Party Platforms and Civil Rights

Political party platforms are significant aspects of party politics. They state the party's basic principles, but candidates and elected officials are not bound to them. A committee consisting of party leaders drafts the platforms, a practice that can mean they do not necessarily represent the views of a majority of party members or even party leaders. Nevertheless, because platforms are statements of fundamental party principles, they are a vital way to understand the views of the political parties and predict the type of policies that candidates in that party would seek to enact if elected.

Throughout American history, the issue of race has been crucial in certain party platforms, and here we provide excerpts from different party platforms pertaining to race. Some excerpts represent advancements in civil rights, such as the 1856 Republican Party platform calling for an end to slavery in the territories and the 1948 Democratic Party platform embracing civil rights. Conversely, some excerpts represent a retreat from civil rights, such as the States' Rights Party platform in 1948 and the American Independent Party platform in 1968, both of which emphatically opposed civil rights.

> Republican Party Platform, 1856: As our Republican forefathers, when they abolished Slavery in all our National Territory, ordained that no person shall be deprived of life, liberty, or property without due process of law, it becomes our duty to maintain this provision of the Constitution against all attempts to violate it for the purpose of establishing Slavery in the Territories of the United States . . . , prohibiting its existence or extension therein. . . . We deny the authority of Congress, of a Territorial Legislation, of any individual, or association of individuals, to give legal existence of Slavery in any Territory of the United States. . . . [t]he Constitution confers upon Congress sovereign powers over the Territories of the United States for their government; and that in the exercise of this power, it is both the right and the imperative duty of Congress to prohibit in the Territories those twin relics of barbarism—Polygamy and Slavery.

Democratic Party Platform, 1948: The Democratic Party commits itself to continuing its efforts to eliminate all racial, religious, and economic discrimination. We again state our belief that racial and religious minorities must have the right to live, the right to work, the right to vote, the full and equal protection of the laws, on a basis of equality with all citizens as guaranteed by the Constitution. We highly commend President Harry S. Truman on his courageous stand on the issue of civil rights. . . . We pledge ourselves to legislation to admit . . . displaced persons found eligible for citizenship without discrimination as to race or religion.

States' Rights Party, 1948: We stand for the segregation of the races and the integrity of each race. . . . We oppose the elimination of segregation, the repeal of miscegenation statutes, the control of private employment by Federal bureaucrats called for by the misnamed civil rights program. . . . We oppose and condemn the action of the Democratic Convention in sponsoring a civil rights program calling for the elimination of segregation, social equality by Federal fiat, regulations of private employment practices, voting, and local law enforcement.

American Independent Party, 1968: The Federal Government has adopted so-called "Civil Rights Acts," particularly the one adopted in 1964, which have set race against race and class against class, all of which we condemn. It shall be our purpose to take such steps and pursue such courses as may be necessary and required to restore to the states the power and authority which rightfully belong to state and local governments, so that each state shall govern and control its internal affairs without interference or domination of the Federal Government.

Source: Adapted from John Woolley and Gerhard Peters, "Political Party Platforms," *American Presidency Project* (Santa Barbara: University of California, Santa Barbara, 1999–2016)," http://www.presidency.ucsb.edu/platforms.php, accessed July 27, 2016.

National committee chairs often influence election outcomes. For example, after the Democratic defeat in the 2004 election, DNC chair Howard Dean instituted the "Fifty State Strategy," in which Democrats would compete in all parts of the country instead of concentrating only on large urban areas and the coastal regions of the United States where Democrats traditionally do well. Dean's strategy was instrumental in the Democrats' success in the 2006 elections when the party won control of the House and Senate, doing exceptionally well in areas where Republicans traditionally win. The Democrats' continued triumphs in 2008, including Barack Obama's comfortable victory, are further evidence of the success of Dean's strategy.[27]

As the opening vignette further indicates, racial and ethnic minorities are not well represented in national party leadership. Ron Brown, who was African American, was the first non-White who chaired the Democratic National Committee. Brown was a key leader of Jesse Jackson's 1988 presidential campaign, and in 1989 the DNC elected him to be chair. Brown's service as DNC chair is credited with paving the way for Bill Clinton's 1992 presidential victory.[28]

Two minorities have chaired the RNC. In 2006, the RNC named Florida senator Mel Martinez, a Cuban American, as its co-chair, largely to reach out to Latinos. However, Martinez clashed with Republican leaders over his moderate stance on undocumented immigration, and he could not balance his duties as senator and RNC chair; in 2007 Martinez resigned the RNC position.[29] In 2009, after President Obama handily defeated Senator John McCain (R-AZ) to become the first Black president, the Republican National Committee elected Michael Steele, the African American former lieutenant governor of Maryland, as the RNC chair.[30] Although Steele was successful during the 2010 midterm elections, the Republicans returned to a White male national committee chair in 2011 when Reince Priebus defeated Michael Steele. Despite the Republican losses in the 2012 election, the Republican National Committee reelected Priebus as the committee chair, citing his fundraising prowess. In fact, Priebus's support was so solid that he ran unopposed.[31]

There is slightly more minority representation at lower levels of national party leadership. As we have mentioned, the DNC reserves positions for racial and ethnic minorities, and the DNC makes an explicit effort on its website to reach out to Blacks, Latinos, Asian Americans, and American Indians, as well as seniors, LGBT communities, and the disabled.[32] Also, several DNC officers, in addition to Donna Brazile, are minorities, including vice chair Maria Elena Durazo (who is Latina), National Finance Committee Chair Henry Muñoz (who is Latino) and Secretary Stephanie Rawlings-Blake (who is Black).[33] The RNC currently has no minorities in its leadership,[34] but its website does explicitly reach out to Latinos, Blacks, and Asian Amercians.[35]

State and Local Organizations

State and local party organizations are important in American politics. The bottom level of local party organization consists of the elected committee members for the smallest political district in the state, usually called a ward or a precinct. Wards or precincts are generally the size of neighborhoods. All interested party members living in the ward select committee members at caucus meetings or through primaries. Each ward committee selects a chairperson.

At the next level are the local committees, which cover the geographic region of an urban area, county, or congressional district. Depending on the state, local committee members are chosen at county party conventions or by candidates for office. Local party organizations coordinate election volunteers, telephone local residents, campaign door-to-door, and place campaign signs throughout the area. Additionally, local party committees run candidates in local elections, although many cities and counties are nonpartisan.

The state party central committee is the highest level of state party organization. State central committees perform a variety of important functions, including organizing state conventions, writing state party platforms, raising money, overseeing how the party spends money, selecting the state party's presidential electors, representing the state in national committees, recruiting candidates, and providing candidates with funds, public opinion polling, and media services. Although the state party establishes the rules and regulations for the local parties, the local parties select the members to the state committee; thus, local parties are able to influence the state party's policies.[36]

State and local party organizations used to be extremely powerful, but that power has eroded during the twentieth century. State and local party leaders historically used their positions to control patronage, and as a result they amassed great wealth and power. One of the most renowned local party leaders was William M. Tweed, known as "Boss Tweed," who ran the Tammany Hall Democratic Party organization in New York City. Beginning in the late nineteenth century, reforms limited their influence. Because precinct bosses could dominate their local area by knowing how many votes each party worker

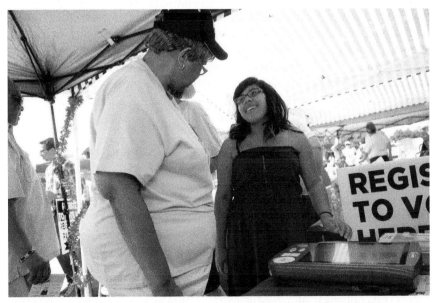

Shelba Richardson, left, explains an electronic voting machine to Brenda Carillo, right. Richardson works for the Montgomery County (Texas) Democratic Party, and she is seeking to ensure that Latinos register and vote in upcoming elections. County party officials, such as Richardson, often interface directly with individuals to increase their party's chance of success in local, state, and national elections.

brought, states moved to a secret ballot, which prevented party leaders from knowing who voted for which candidate. Many cities moved to nonpartisan elections, which further limited the power of state and local party leaders.[37]

National policies have also limited the power of state and local parties. In 1976 and again in 1990, the U.S. Supreme Court overturned patronage practices in state and local governments. Specifically, the Court ruled that hiring government employees based on partisan affiliation punishes applicants from nonfavored political parties, which violates their First Amendment right to freedom of association.[38] Without the ability to promise employment in exchange for party service, state and local parties cannot always easily attract volunteers to work for the party. Despite their decreased influence, state political parties still exert significant authority within their respective states.

White Primary A practice by Southern state Democratic parties in the late nineteenth and early twentieth centuries intended to disenfranchise Blacks by preventing them from voting in the crucial Democratic Party primary elections.

The politics of race and ethnicity is relevant in state and local parties. State parties historically perpetrated discrimination by adopting **White Primary** rules, which prevented Blacks from voting in primaries. Southern state Democratic Party organizations claimed that as private groups they were free to prohibit Blacks from voting in primary elections. In the early twentieth century, because the Democrats were the only viable party in the South, primaries effectively determined who would win office. By prohibiting Blacks from voting in the primaries, the state parties effectively disenfranchised all Black voters. In 1944, the U.S. Supreme Court ruled that state party organizations were government institutions, not private organizations, and thus they were constitutionally prohibited from disenfranchising Blacks in primaries.[39]

Since then, racial and ethnic minorities have not only been able to participate in state party primaries, but they have also been better represented in state and local party organizations. Although most state party chairs have been White, there have been some minorities leading state parties. For example, James Evans, the Chair of the Utah Republican Party, is African American,[40] and the current chair of the Colorado Democratic Party is Latino Rick Palacio.[41]

Parties and Voters

Ultimately, political parties are concerned with winning elections, which means that understanding how parties function in the electoral process adds to a more complete view of American politics. As we have shown in this chapter, parties recruit and nominate candidates, raise money, and provide election strategies. Because we cover elections in detail in Chapter 15, here we focus more on how the parties function in the minds of the voters: how voters connect with the major political parties and how groups attach to those parties.

Party Identification

Voters' psychological attachment to the political parties can be measured through party identification. As we saw in Chapter 10, party identification is ascertained though public opinion surveys. It is usually expressed on a seven-point scale where a respondent characterizes his or her party

Michael Steele bangs the gavel shortly after being elected as Chair of the Republican National Committee in January 2009. Steele was the first African American to serve as the RNC chair, and despite engineering a successful 2010 election campaign for Republicans, the RNC selected Reince Priebus to replace Steele in 2011. Steele is now a commentator on MSNBC.

identification as Strong Democrat, Weak Democrat, Independent-Leaning Democrat, Independent, Independent-Leaning Republican, Weak Republican, or Strong Republican. Again, party identification measures a voter's psychological attachment to the party; it is different from that voter being a registered party member or voting a particular way in elections.

It seems intuitively correct that voters' views of the parties' candidates and stances on the issues would influence party identification. This is certainly the case, but political scientists have also shown that individuals establish their party identification because of their upbringing, race and ethnicity, religion, and social class. Therefore, party identification explains how people view the candidates and ultimately how they vote. People who identify as Democrats are likely to vote Democratic, and people who identify as Republicans are likely to vote Republican. The Independents and leaners tend to split their votes between the two parties or vote for minor party candidates.[42]

Parties and Group Attachments

Because party identification is so closely tied to social background, it is also tied to geography, a connection we have already discussed. The South used to be solidly Democratic, but it now leans Republican. The Northeast used to be solidly Republican, but now it is much more Democratic. Although region is still important, group attachment to political parties is more complex and includes religious affiliation, income, gender, and race and ethnicity.

There is some relationship between partisanship and age. Recently, voters under thirty have identified more as Democratic and Independent versus

Republican, largely because the Republican Party's conservative stances on social issues, such as abortion and LGBT rights, repel many younger voters. Whereas 33 percent of people born before 1945 identify as Republican, only 22 percent of Generation Xers (people born between 1965 and 1980) and 18 percent of Millennials (people born between 1981 and 1996) identify as Republican. However, Millennials are far more likely to identify as Independent compared to the older generations.[43] The candidacy of Barack Obama has moved younger voters further away from the Republican Party. In 2012, President Obama won 60 percent of voters under thirty, which was only a five-point decrease from 2008.[44] Both political parties try to court the younger voters. The Democratic National Committee website devotes a specific section to young voters and students, and the Republican National Committee website devotes a section to millennials.[45]

Because of the two parties' stances on economic issues, such as taxes and welfare spending, wealthier people tend to identify with Republicans, whereas poorer people are more Democratic. In 2014, party identification for people with annual incomes under $30,000 was 17 percent Republican, 35 percent Democratic, and 42 percent Independent. Conversely, for people with annual incomes over $150,000 the party identification breakdown was 29 percent Republican, 29 percent Democratic, and 38 percent Independent. There is a similar split after counting Independents who lean towards the Democrats or Republicans. People who make over $150,000 are still split fairly evenly— 47 percent Republican and 45 percent Democratic. However, 54 percent of people who make less than $30,000 identify or lean as Democrats, compared to only 31 percent who identify and lean as Republicans.[46]

Party identification also corresponds to religious groups. Protestants have traditionally identified with Republicans, and Catholics, many of whom were immigrants and labor union members, tended to be Democrats. But because Protestantism is so vast, the connection between party and Protestantism is less clear. Adherents to fundamentalist or evangelical Protestant sects are more Republican than are adherents to mainstream or liberal sects of Protestantism. White Protestants slightly identify with the Republicans, whereas Black Protestants overwhelmingly identify with the Democrats. Moreover, some Catholics, particularly religious conservatives, have moved away from the Democratic Party because of its liberal stance on social issues, especially abortion and LGBT rights. Still, White Catholics tilt slightly Democratic, whereas Latino Catholics are more than twice as likely to identify with Democrats than with Republicans. Jewish voters of all age groups have overwhelmingly identified as Democratic.[47]

Soon after women earned the right to vote, there was no relationship between party and gender, but the feminist revolution of the 1960s spawned a gender gap in which women identify with and vote for candidates of the Democratic Party more than men do. In Chapter 10, we discussed the gender gap in terms of differences between male and female opinion on policy issues; here we focus more on the gap's impact on party identification.

Since the 1970s, the Democratic Party has reserved leadership spots for women and adopted positions favoring equal rights. Consequently, women have gravitated toward the Democratic Party. In 2015, there was an eleven-point gap between men and women who identified with the Democratic Party (37 percent for women and 26 percent for men).[48] The gender gap in party identification helps explain different voting patterns between men and women. During the 2012 election, Mitt Romney won 52 percent of the male vote, whereas Barack Obama won 55 percent of the female vote.[49]

Patterns exist for party attachment and racial minority status,[50] which Table 14.2 shows in detail. Because the Republican Party was founded as an abolitionist party, the few African Americans who could vote in 1856 naturally gravitated toward the Republicans. During Reconstruction, Republican leaders in Congress insisted on federal protections for the civil rights of African Americans. Southern Blacks were active in Republican Party organizations, and all African American politicians were Republicans.

TABLE 14.2 Partisan Identification by Race and Ethnicity (in Percent)

Group	Democrat	Independent	Republican	Nonpartisan
African American	76	14	10	N/A
Mexican American	56	29	15	N/A
Puerto Rican	64	16	20	N/A
Cuban American	32	20	48	N/A
Dominican	73	17	9	N/A
Salvadoran	57	30	13	N/A
Other Central American	50	28	22	N/A
Other Latino	60	23	17	N/A
Japanese American	42	17	14	28
Chinese American	25	28	7	40
Korean American	38	6	18	39
Filipino American	35	18	19	28
Asian Indian	39	21	7	33
Vietnamese American	22	15	29	34
Other Asian	36	15	14	35
American Indian	47	12	41	N/A

Note: All numbers are rounded to the nearest percent. Leaners are included with Democrats and Republicans; therefore, Independents are those who would not indicate even a preference for either political party.

Source: Data adapted from Paula D. McClain and Joseph Stewart Jr., "Can We All Get along?": Racial and Ethnic Minorities in American Politics, 6th ed. (Boulder, CO: Westview Press, 2014), 93, 95, 99, 100.

Franklin Roosevelt's presidency caused many African Americans to support the Democratic Party. Not only did African Americans benefit from Roosevelt's economic policies, but also Roosevelt consulted Black intellectuals, such as Robert Weaver, Ralph Bunche, and Mary McLeod Bethune. First Lady Eleanor Roosevelt's outspoken support of civil rights also endeared African Americans to the Democratic Party.

As Blacks migrated to Northern cities, such as Detroit and Chicago, they found a far more welcoming Democratic Party than the segregationist Democratic Party they had known in the South. Lyndon Johnson's strong civil rights record brought most African Americans to the Democratic Party, whereas Republican opposition to the goals of Black civil rights leaders, especially since the 1980s, drove many Blacks away from the Republican Party. Now African Americans overwhelmingly identify as Democrats.

Even though African Americans overwhelmingly identify with Democrats, many observers argue that the Democratic Party takes Blacks for granted. The party actively seeks Black support during elections, but when the election is over, Democrats abandon Blacks by failing to elevate Blacks to leadership positions and ignoring policy issues central to many Blacks. Of course, much of this criticism stems from Black Republicans who seek to draw Blacks to the Republican Party.

Even Black leaders who argue that the Democratic Party takes Blacks for granted still promote voting for the Democratic Party. For example, in 2004 Jesse Jackson, who has frequently clashed with White Democratic leaders, quipped, "While some Democrats take Blacks for granted, Republicans take Blacks for fools."[51] In Chapter 15, we discuss in more detail how the Obama presidency may alter the perception that Democrats take Blacks for granted.

Because Latinos are composed of a variety of ethnicities, Latino partisan identification is not uniform. Mexican Americans and Puerto Ricans tend to be Democratic, primarily because of the party's strong commitment to civil rights and economic policies that benefit the working and middle classes. Cuban Americans, however, are more Republican than Democratic because the Republican Party had been strongly and consistently opposed to the communist regime of Fidel Castro in Cuba. Moreover, many of the Cuban refugees who came to the United States between 1960 and 1980 were from the upper classes, and as we demonstrated earlier, wealthier people tend to identify with the Republican Party.

There is recent evidence of a slight shift of Cubans toward the Democrats. Many of the post-1980 Cuban immigrants and second- and even third-generation Cuban Americans are less concerned with Fidel (and Raúl) Castro and more concerned with civil rights and economic equality. Moreover, Republican politicians' anti-immigration rhetoric has alienated some Cuban Americans from the Republican Party.

A growing proportion of Latinos come from the Dominican Republic, Central America, and South America. Because they are emerging Latino groups, there is not extensive research on their party identification trends.

Nevertheless, Table 14.2, which reflects the most recent analysis of Latino party identification, shows that Central Americans, Dominicans, Salvadorans, and other Latinos are overwhelmingly Democratic.

In addition to national origin, Latino party identification differs according to religious intensity. "Measuring Equality: Latinos, Religious Preference, and Party Support" demonstrates that evangelical Latinos are far more likely to identify with Republicans than are other Latino religious groups.

measuring equality

Latinos, Religious Preference, and Party Support

As the text, especially Table 14.2, demonstrates, Latino party identification is a complex issue. Mexican Americans and Puerto Ricans are much more likely to identify with Democrats than with Republicans, but Cuban Americans lean toward the Republicans. In other words, Latino political party identification depends on nation of origin. Here we explore another layer of how Latinos view the political parties—religion. We are interested not in national origin, but in the extent to which religious preference influences political party identification among Latinos. We use data from a 2007 survey of Latinos (the most recent figures that are available) in the United States conducted by the Pew Hispanic Center, which is a leading public opinion researcher of Latinos in America.

We compare results among four different religious preferences. First, we examine Catholics, who practice the traditional religion of Latinos because it is the primary religion in Spain. As we discuss in this chapter, Catholics have traditionally identified with the Democrats, but because of issues such as abortion, many Catholics have moved to the Republican Party. Second, we investigate mainline Protestants, the traditional sects of Protestantism (e.g., Baptist, Episcopalian, Lutheran, Methodist, and Presbyterian). Party identification among mainline Protestants generally varies considerably. Third, we look at evangelical Protestants, or born-again Christians. Evangelicals are adherents to newer sects of Protestantism, such as Pentecostals and Assembly of God, and they are extremely religious. They hold conservative views on social issues such as abortion and sexual orientation rights. Consequently, evangelicals in general tend to identify with the Republican Party. Fourth, we examine seculars; that is, Latinos who are not

religious. Because nonreligious people tend to be more liberal than religious people, seculars in general tend to identify with the Democrats.

In addition to looking at Latino party identification among religions, we divide our analysis among different issues. The Pew Hispanic Center asked Latinos to identify which party is better at handling a wide variety of issues, and we selected five issues that are relevant to minority-group politics in general and to Latino politics in particular: (1) the economy, (2) education, (3) immigration, (4) morality, and (5) civil rights. Figure 14.2 reports the results that the Pew Hispanic Center found. Each graph shows the percentage of Latinos in each religious preference category who identify with Democrats and the percentage of Latinos who identify with Republicans. We report only the Democratic and Republican identifiers, not those who answered "independents," "both," or "neither." Consequently, the percentages do not add up to 100 percent.

Although there is some variation in the responses among the different religious groups and across the different issues, there is a clear pattern. On all five issues, Catholic Latinos, mainline Protestant Latinos, and secular Latinos are considerably (two to three times) more likely to identify with the Democrats than with the Republicans. Conversely, on all five issues, evangelical Latinos split fairly evenly between the Democrats and the Republicans. These findings indicate that, in addition to national origin, religious preference influences Latino party identification.

Source: Data adapted from Roberto Suro et al., *Changing Faiths: Latinos and the Transformation of American Religion* (Washington, DC: Pew Research Center, 2007), 82–83, http://www.pewhispanic .org/files/reports/75.pdf, accessed February 29, 2012.

(Continued)

measuring equality

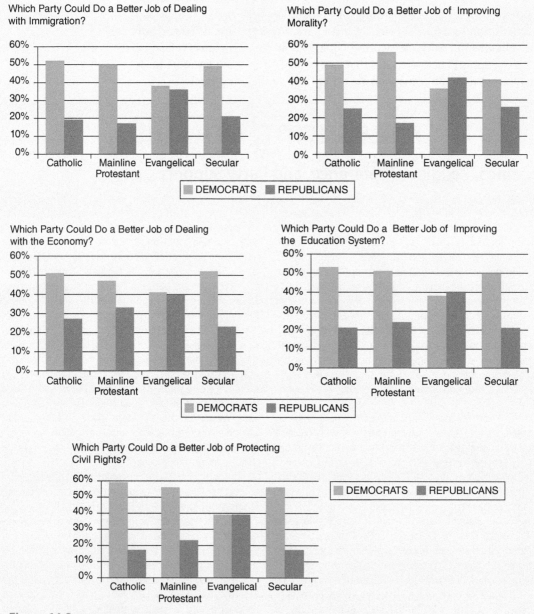

Figure 14.2 Which Party Could Do a Better Job?

Asian Americans identify with the Democrats, most likely as a result of the Democratic Party's more favorable immigration and civil rights stances. Nevertheless, for many Asian Americans, particularly Chinese Americans, party affiliation has been fleeting. In the 1970s and 1980s, Chinese Americans and Vietnamese immigrants supported the Republican Party because of its staunch opposition to communism, but more recently Asian Americans of all ethnicities have favored the Democrats.

There has been scant research conducted on the party affiliation of American Indians. Generally, American Indians identify with the party that exhibits more pro-Indian policies. For example, during the 1970s many Navajos supported the Republicans because the Nixon administration conferred more sovereignty to the Navajos over their land. However, by the 1980s American Indians had shifted to the Democrats.

Conclusion

Although political parties are not official governing institutions recognized by the U.S. Constitution, they play a crucial role in American politics because they link voters with elected governmental positions. This chapter covered the key aspects of political parties. We examined the complex development of our two-party system, and although the Republicans and the Democrats currently dominate our government, minor parties have occasionally played an important role. We also looked at the organizational structure of political parties, examining the significance of national conventions, national committees, and state and local organizations. The chapter concluded with a discussion of the concept of party identification, as well as group attachments to political parties.

The politics of race and ethnicity has also been quite relevant in political party politics. The issue of slavery divided the Democratic Party, destroyed the Whig Party, and created the Republican Party. After the Civil War, the Democratic Party was staunchly segregationist, whereas the Republicans were split over civil rights. Since the 1940s, the Democratic Party has supported civil rights and attracted African Americans, as well as other racial and ethnic minorities. At the same time, the Democratic Party's support of civil rights has alienated many White southerners, who have drifted to the Republicans.

Issues of race and ethnicity are also relevant to party organization. The Democratic Party actively sought to increase the representation of racial and ethnic minorities (as well as women and young people) at its national convention and on the DNC. As a result, Democratic Party leadership has more racial and ethnic minorities than Republican Party leadership does. Both parties have had minorities serve as committee chair (Mel Martinez and Michael Steele for the Republicans and Ron Brown and Donna Brazile for the Democrats), but there have been no other racial or ethnic minorities running political parties.

Party identification also has a racial and ethnic component because group attachments to political parties are evident. African Americans, Mexican Americans, Puerto Ricans, Central Americans, Asian Americans, and American Indians tend to identify with the Democratic Party. Cuban Americans tend to identify with the Republican Party. Interestingly, differing religious preference influences party identification for Latinos.

Our opening story about Donna Brazile's selection and lack of success in 2016 reveals key information about party politics in general and racial and ethnic elements of parties in particular. It illustrates the power and relevance of the national committee chair position. Brazile's term as DNC chair in 2016 was controversial, and ultimately the Democrats under-performed in the election. They were successful with minority voters, at least this who turned out, but White voters significantly favored Donald Trump, giving him the victory in the Electoral College.

review
REVIEW QUESTIONS

1. What impact did debates over slavery have on the Whig Party, Democratic Party, and Republican Party?

2. How did issues of race influence the loss of Democratic Party dominance during the late twentieth century?

3. How representative are delegates to the Democratic and the Republican national conventions?

4. What are some examples of racial and ethnic minorities who have led party organizations?

5. What are the party identification breakdowns for Blacks, Mexican Americans, Puerto Ricans, Cuban Americans, Central Americans, Asian Americans, and American Indians? Why does each group tend to identify with a certain party?

terms
KEY TERMS

Black and Tan Republicans p. 444
Caucuses p. 449
Dealignment p. 445
Democratic Party p. 441
Democratic-Republicans p. 440
Federalist Party p. 440
Hard Money p. 451
Lily White Republicans p. 444

Minor Parties p. 439
National Committee Chair p. 452
National Committee p. 451
New Deal Coalition p. 444
Party Platform p. 450
Political Parties p. 439
Primaries p. 449
Realignment p. 443

Republican Party p. 441
Sedition Act p. 440
Soft Money p. 452
Superdelegates p. 449
Twelfth Amendment p. 440
Two-Party System p. 439
Whigs p. 441
White Primary p. 456

readings
ADDITIONAL READINGS

Robert Bruns, *Jesse Jackson: A Biography* (Westport, CT: Greenwood Press, 2005).

This book examines Reverend Jesse Jackson's life and career, including his run for the Democratic Party nomination in 1984 and 1988.

Steven P. Erie, *Rainbow's End: Irish-Americans and the Dilemmas of Urban Machine Politics, 1840–1985* (Berkeley and Los Angeles: University of California Press, 1988).

In this book, Erie shows that racial and ethnic minorities, immigrants, and even Irish Americans did not benefit from patronage as much as others have claimed.

Keli Goff, *Party Crashing: How the Hip-Hop Generation Declared Political Independence* (New York: Perseus Books, 2008).

In this informative and highly readable book, Goff surveys a sample of four hundred African Americans from the post–baby boom generations (those born between 1963 and 1990) and finds that, although these generations of Blacks still have ties to the Democratic Party, these are not as strong as the ties held by their parents and grandparents.

Steven A. Holmes, *Ron Brown: An Uncommon Life* (New York: Wiley, 2000).

This book chronicles the life and career of Ron Brown, the first Black chair of the Democratic National Committee.

David Lublin, *The Republican South: Democratization and Partisan Change* (Princeton, NJ: Princeton University Press, 2004).

This book examines why the Republican Party has transformed itself from a moribund party in the South into the majority party in that region.

CHAPTER 15

Voting and Elections: The End of the Obama Era

Presidential candidate Hillary Clinton delivers her concession speech Wednesday, from the New Yorker Hotel's Grand Ballroom in New York City, NY, on November 9, 2016. This was a painful defeat, as she won the popular vote by several million votes, but lost the Electoral College.

F or the second time in sixteen years, the presidential candidate who received the largest share of the popular vote did not receive the necessary electoral votes. Hillary Clinton received 48.1% (64,469,963) to Donald Trump's 46.5% (62,379,366) of the votes cast (totals as the book goes to press). But Trump received 290 electoral votes to Clinton's 232. This is the fifth time in U.S. election history that a candidate who lost the popular vote became president—John Quincy Adams in 1824, Rutherford B. Hayes in 1976 and Benjamin Harrison in 1888.[1] The fourth and most recent time this happened was in 2000, when vice president Al Gore received 500,000 more popular votes than George W. Bush, but after a recount and the Supreme Court intervention stopping that recount, Florida's electoral votes went to Bush and he became president.

Hillary Clinton was the first woman to be the presidential nominee of a major political party and the polls all suggested that she would win the presidency and break one of the remaining glass ceilings for women in the United States. On November 9, 2016, Hillary Clinton gave her concession speech to a great deal of disappointment on the part of her supporters and, as she said, a great deal of pain for her. Here are excerpts from her speech.

Thank you so very much for being here. I love you all, too. Last night I congratulated Donald Trump and offered to work with him on behalf of our country.

I hope that he will be a successful president for all Americans. This is not the outcome we wanted or we worked so hard for, and I'm sorry we did not win this election for the values we share and the vision we hold for our country.

But I feel pride and gratitude for this wonderful campaign that we built together. This vast, diverse, creative, unruly, energized campaign. You represent the best of America, and being your candidate has been one of the greatest honors of my life.

I know how disappointed you feel, because I feel it too. And so do tens of millions of Americans who invested their hopes and dreams in this effort. This is painful, and it will be for a long time. But I want you to remember this.

Our campaign was never about one person, or even one election. It was about the country we love and building an America that is hopeful, inclusive, and big-hearted. We have seen that our nation is more deeply divided than we thought. But I still believe in America, and I always will. And if you do, then we must accept this result and then look to the future. Donald Trump is going to be our president. We owe him an open mind and the chance to lead. Our constitutional democracy enshrines the peaceful transfer of power.

We don't just respect that. We cherish it. It also enshrines the rule of law; the principle we are all equal in rights and dignity; freedom of worship and expression. We respect and cherish these values, too, and we must defend them.

Let me add: Our constitutional democracy demands our participation, not just every four years, but all the time. So let's do all we can to keep advancing the causes and values we all hold dear. Making our economy work for everyone, not just those at the top, protecting our country and protecting our planet.

And breaking down all the barriers that hold any American back from achieving their dreams. We spent a year and a half bringing together millions of people from every corner of our country to say with one voice that we believe that the American dream is big enough for everyone.

For people of all races, and religions, for men and women, for immigrants, for LGBT people, and people with disabilities. For everyone.

. . .

This loss hurts, but please never stop believing that fighting for what's right is worth it.

It is, it is worth it.

And so we need—we need you to keep up these fights now and for the rest of your lives. And to all the women, and especially the young women, who put their faith in this campaign and in me: I want you to know that nothing has made me prouder than to be your champion.

Now, I know we have still not shattered that highest and hardest glass ceiling, but someday someone will—and hopefully sooner than we might think right now. [Cheers and applause]

And to all of the little girls who are watching this, never doubt that you are valuable and powerful and deserving of every chance and opportunity in the world to pursue and achieve your own dreams.[2]

intro

Chapter 1 detailed the political philosophies undergirding the U.S. political system. In that discussion, we noted that the representative democracy structure of the United States is based on the principle that individuals elect representatives to present their views and make informed choices on their behalf. This also implies another principle—that individuals have the ability to hold their representatives accountable by voting them out of office if they prove dissatisfactory.

Given these dual principles, and hence dual responsibilities, elections and the electoral process are central to the workings of the Republic. Although elections are at the core of the system, there are many different electoral systems within the United States. By law, every U.S. citizen eighteen years of age and older is eligible to vote. (Exceptions to this include convicted felons in some states, prisoners in correctional facilities in most states, and other people prohibited by state laws.) Yet the rates at which various groups of U.S. citizens register to vote and then actually do vote vary by race, gender, ethnicity, and region of the country. The reasons for the differences are not simply reasons of personal preference. In many cases, historical and structural barriers account for some of the disparity.

Understanding the role of elections and how and why people vote is essential to comprehending the core principles of representative democracy. This chapter explores the electoral process of the United States, and voting is one of the key ingredients of that process. We also look at the 2016 election in detail to provide, at the presidential level, a context for many of the concepts and issues discussed in the chapter.

The Electoral Process: Nominating a Candidate

Elections The process by which individuals make political choices by voting.

Elections are the process by which individuals make political choices by voting. In representative democracies such as the United States, elections provide legitimacy to the system by implying that individuals have a say in who runs their government and what policies are initiated.

The nomination process in the United States is not uniform across offices or levels of government. The nomination procedure depends on the office being sought, and nomination rules vary depending on whether the office is at the national, state, or local level. No matter what the level of the office being sought, however, states and local governments control the election process. The three procedures for nomination are caucuses, primary elections, and party conventions.

Caucuses

As introduced in the previous chapter, a caucus is a private meeting or gathering of individuals or representatives of political parties who choose delegates standing for or pledged to candidates running for particular offices. The early caucuses were composed of private citizens who were prominent and active in politics in their communities. As political parties developed, they assumed control of the caucus process. By the late 1790s, they used caucuses to choose congressional, state, and local candidates.

In addition, caucuses of congressional members of a political party would choose the party's presidential nominees.[3] The election of Andrew Jackson in 1828 and his renomination in the first national political party convention in 1832 signaled the end of the congressional caucus method of selecting parties' presidential nominees.[4] The caucus system is still a part of the presidential selection process, but it functions much differently from the congressional caucuses of the nineteenth century.

During the presidential election season, Americans hear a lot about the Iowa presidential caucuses, the first presidential selection contest in the country for both Democrats and Republicans since 1972,[5] as the news media cover the multitude of visits that presidential hopefuls from both parties make to that state. These caucuses, however, do not directly choose the presidential candidate; they are used to elect delegates committed to a particular candidate at each political party's sequence of conventions from the local to the state to the national level. These delegates are called **pledged delegates**. In 2016, fourteen states, including Alaska, Colorado, Iowa, Maine, Washington, and Hawaii, held Democratic caucuses, and twelve others (including the District of Columbia and Kentucky, which were not caucused by Democrats) held Republican caucuses.[6] Both parties held caucuses in American Samoa, Guam, the Northern Mariana Islands, and the U.S. Virgin Islands.

Pledged Delegates Party members elected or chosen at the state and local levels to support a particular candidate at the party's national convention.

The 2016 presidential party nomination process produced an interesting and unexpected rise of unlikely candidates in both the Democratic and the Republican parties. During the 2016 presidential primary season, Iowa's caucuses for both Democrats and Republicans were held on February 1, 2016. At the beginning of the 2016 Democratic presidential primaries, several

The nine remaining Republican presidential candidates participated in a debate in Las Vegas, Nevada on Tuesday, December 15, 2015. From left, John Kasich, Carly Fiorina, Marco Rubio, Ben Carson, Donald Trump, Ted Cruz, Jeb Bush, Chris Christie, and Rand Paul.

individuals seriously considered running for office. These included Rhode Island's former governor, Lincoln Chafee, Maryland's former governor, Martin O'Malley, Harvard law professor Lawrence Lessig, and senators Hillary Clinton and Bernie Sanders.[7] Another name floated was that of Massachusetts senator Elizabeth Warren, who some thought would make a bid for the presidency.[8] Heading into the Iowa caucuses, however, the only two candidates who stepped forward to run for the nomination were Hillary Clinton and Bernie Sanders.

Hillary Clinton was considered the front-runner and the odds-on favorite to become the Democratic nominee.[9] Bernie Sanders was considered a very long shot because he was not a Democrat, but an independent senator from Vermont, who caucused with the Democrats in the Senate but was not a member of the party. He also identified himself as a democratic socialist, a label not usually associated with U.S. politicians. As such, his challenge to Clinton was not taken seriously.[10] Clinton won the Iowa caucus; however, she won it by the closest margin within the history of the Iowa caucus. This slim margin of victory generated debate about the popularity of Sanders's bid for the position and Clinton's potential vulnerabilities.

The road to the Republican nominee went through twelve primary debates beginning on August 6, 2015. Republican primary voters tend to be far more conservative than the general voting population and the more or extreme conservative portions of the primary voting populations pushed the primary candidates to the extreme right on many public policy issues, including immigration, contraception, abortion, revenues, and taxes.

The wide range of individuals running for the Republican nomination made the 2016 Republican primary process particularly newsworthy. At the beginning of the process, it remained unclear as to who the favorite was for the Republican Party. When the primary season began, early in 2015, seventeen candidates were considering running for the Republican ticket—reality star and businessman Donald Trump; former governors Jeb Bush (Florida), Rick Perry (Texas), George Pataki (New York), Jim Gilmore (Virginia), and Mike Huckabee (Arkansas); senators Rand Paul (Kentucky), Marco Rubio (Florida), Ted Cruz (Texas), and Lindsey Graham (South Carolina); former senator Rick Santorum; governors John Kasich (Ohio), Scott Walker (Wisconsin), Chris Christie (New Jersey), and Bobby Jindal (Louisiana); Carly Fiorina, the former chief executive officer of Hewlett Packard, the only woman in the field; and retired neurosurgeon Ben Carson, the only black candidate.[11] The Iowa caucus was the first place where voting began, on February 1, 2016. Ted Cruz won, with Marco Rubio and Donald Trump following narrowly behind. The former governor of Arkansas, Mike Huckabee, dropped out after the Iowa caucus, as did the former senator of Pennsylvania, Rick Santorum. (Santorum had won the Iowa caucus against Mitt Romney in 2012.) Kentucky senator Rand Paul also ended his campaign bid after a poor performance in Iowa.

The next caucus was in Nevada on February 23, 2016, which Donald Trump won. On March 1, Ted Cruz won the Alaska caucus and Marco Rubio won the Minnesota caucus. On March 5, Donald Trump won the Kentucky caucus and Ted Cruz won the Maine and Kansas caucuses. Donald Trump won the Hawaii caucus on March 6 and that in the Northern Mariana Islands on March 15.

In the 2016 election, Sanders's campaign focused heavily on caucus states. Many of the caucus states were states with few electoral votes, such as Hawaii and Alaska, but the hope was that Sanders would be able to overcome Clinton's strength in primary states and allow him to overtake Clinton's pledged delegate lead. Sanders won eleven of the sixteen caucus states. Sanders attempted to take a page out of President Obama's playbook in the 2008 contest against Hillary Clinton, where Obama received 324 pledged delegates from caucus states compared with Clinton's 170 pledged delegates. Some analysts might argue that the story of Obama's success in gaining the nomination is told, in large part, by his victories in these states and his ability to organize large numbers of volunteers, a group crucial to winning in caucus states. (See Table 15.1 in "Measuring Equality: Obama's Attention to Caucus States in the 2008 Presidential Election.") In the end, this approach did not work for Sanders.

Primary Elections

As previously mentioned, a primary election is an election in which voters choose among several candidates who have declared for an office. Primary elections for state and local offices and for U.S. House and Senate nominations are **direct primaries**, in which voters select the individual to represent the party in the general election by voting directly for the candidates on the ballot. By contrast, in a presidential primary election, voters vote for delegates committed to a candidate. These delegates then cast their votes at the political party's national convention to choose the party's presidential candidate.

A **closed primary** is one in which only those affiliated with a particular political party can vote for the party's candidate in the election. The most rigid form of closed primary is one in which a voter must be registered to vote with a political party affiliation in advance of the primary election. (State law determines the date by which people must be registered to vote to participate in a primary election.)

In 2016, nine states used a completely closed primary system: Delaware, Florida, Kentucky, Maryland, Nevada, New Mexico, New York, Oregon, and Pennsylvania.[12] A voter registered as a member of one political party who wants to vote in the primary election of another party must reregister as a member of the other party.[13] Closed primaries are intended to ensure that only voters who are identified as party members will have input into the selection of the party's candidates and to prevent crossover voting, in which voters registered as members of one political party would have input into the selection of a candidate from another party. Closed primaries also help contribute to strong party organization.[14] The deadline for reregistering is usually substantially in advance of the primary, a ruling that makes it more difficult for an individual to change parties. **Political independents** must declare a party affiliation to vote in such primaries.

Direct Primaries Elections in which voters select the individual to represent the party in the general election by voting directly for the candidates on the ballot.

Closed Primary A primary in which only registered members of a particular political party can vote in that party's primary election to choose the party's candidate or delegate.

Political Independents Voters who do not designate a political party affiliation when registering to vote.

Seven states have a closed primary system that is more flexible: Alaska, Connecticut, Idaho, North Carolina, Oklahoma, South Dakota, and Utah.[15] In these states, voters may change their political party affiliation on Election Day or in the weeks close to the election.[16] Under the closed primary system, state law allows political parties the option of choosing whether to allow political independents or voters who are not registered with the party to participate in nomination processes prior to each election cycle.[17]

Other states have a mixed system, where the rules may vary about which voters can participate in which primaries and when and how individuals are able to register to vote in the primary.[18] In 2016, six states used a mixed primary system: California, Oklahoma, Massachusetts, Rhode Island, South Dakota, and West Virginia.[19]

Open Primary A primary election in which a voter does not have to declare a political party affiliation but may participate in the primary election of any party.

An **open primary** is one in which a registered voter can participate in the primary election of any political party without having to be a registered member of that party. In 2016, primary elections in fifteen states were open primaries.[20] In some of these states, voters must request the primary ballot of one particular party at the polls. In other states, voters do not have to declare a party affiliation and they can vote in the primary election of any party. This system permits individuals to choose in which primary they wish to vote when they get to the polls and to request a ballot for that political party's primary.[21]

Six states have partially open primaries where voters can cross party lines. These states are Illinois, Indiana, Iowa, Ohio, Tennessee, and Wyoming. Under the partially open primary system, either voters are required to publicly declare their ballot choice or their ballot selection may be classified as a form of registration with a party.[22]

Open primaries weaken political parties' influence over the nomination process because they permit individuals who are not registered as members of the party to vote in the party's primary.[23] Supporters of the open primary method argue that voters should be able to participate freely in primaries without having to reveal their political preferences or give up their status as political independents, people who are not aligned with either political party.[24]

Plurality Winning of an election by the candidate who receives the most votes (also known as "first past the post").

Majority Winning of an election by the candidate who receives at least 51 percent of the vote.

Runoff Primary A second election held in some states if no candidate in the primary election receives a majority of the votes.

Most primaries use a **plurality** system in which the candidate who receives the most votes is the winner. Nine Southern and border Southern states, however, use a **majority** system in which winning requires receiving more than half of the votes cast. If no candidate receives a majority of the vote in the initial primary election, the top two vote-getters face each other in a **runoff primary**.

The latter system was instituted in the South in the early 1900s when the Democratic Party was the dominant party. The runoff primary was viewed by party officials as a means of ensuring party strength and unity behind one candidate and preventing independent challenges to that candidate.[25] Racial motives were also at work, as many of the Southern states that passed bills imposing a primary and runoff provisions stated explicitly that the intent was to ensure that Whites maintained political control by making it difficult,

measuring equality

Obama's Attention to Caucus States in the 2008 Presidential Election

Caucus votes can be important in presidential primaries, especially in extremely competitive primaries. In the 2008 presidential primaries, then-senator Barack Obama concentrated on caucus states as a strategy to knit together pledged delegates from states with small numbers of electoral votes, at the same time building a strong volunteer network. His campaign's Fifty-State Strategy provided him with numerous routes to get to 270 electoral votes in the general election, and the early attention to the caucus states was integral to this strategy. Table 15.1 shows the importance of the delegates Obama received from caucus states to his overall pledged delegate lead over Hillary Rodham Clinton. In 2012, President Obama did not have a challenger in the presidential primaries, so he did not have to develop a strategy to gain the nomination. But he kept his 2008 network in place in those caucus states that were so important and that network was important to his 2012 campaign strategy. In very competitive presidential primaries, caucus states can mean the difference between victory and defeat. Senator Bernie Sanders tried to follow this strategy in 2016, but he was not as effective as President Obama was in 2008.

TABLE 15.1 **Pledged Delegates from Primaries and Caucuses, 2008 Presidential Election**

Final Results	Pledged Delegates	
	Obama	Clinton
Primaries	1,429	1,463
Caucuses	324	170
American Samoa[a]	1	2
Democrats abroad[a]	4	3
Guam[a]	2	2
Virgin Islands[a]	3	0
Total	1,763	1,640

[a]*"Deemed "territories" by the Democratic National Committee.*

Source: CNN Election Center, http://cnn.com, accessed July 15, 2009.

if not impossible, for Blacks to participate in the primary process.[26] In many Southern jurisdictions, the person who won the primary was the guaranteed winner of the office.

After the Iowa caucuses, the first primary was held in New Hampshire on February 9, 2016. New Hampshire has been the first primary state since 1920. Sanders went on to win the New Hampshire primary. The New Hampshire victory pushed Sanders into becoming a serious contender for the party's nomination.

Although Clinton went on to secure important victories in major states such as California and New York, the reality that it was not a landslide victory across primaries came as a surprise to many pundits.[27] There were unpredictable moments, such as Sanders's victory in the Michigan primary that gave people within the Sanders campaign hope that their victory was viable. The Sanders campaign stated they would continue their campaign until the Democratic National Convention, but Bernie Sanders formally endorsed Hillary Clinton on July 12.[28] The sizeable support that Sanders garnered was unexpected and caused concern among Clinton supporters.

In considering the tumultuous road to victory for Clinton, it is important to keep in mind how racial and ethnic minority voters participated in this process. Although Sanders was relatively successful in gaining delegates, Black and Latino voters were not as swayed by him, as were White millennials and many White progressive voters. According to entrance polls, in Iowa, 58 percent of non-White voters voted for Clinton, and only 34 percent voted for Sanders.[29] According to exit polls taken in Ohio, 71 percent of Black voters supported Clinton, whereas only 28 percent voted for Sanders.[30] Clinton captured a key number of delegates and victories in Florida and Texas, where we see similar patterns by minority voters. In Florida, 81 percent of Black voters and 68 percent of Latino voters supported Clinton. In Texas, 83 percent of Black voters supported Clinton, as did 71 percent of Latino voters.[31] Black voters in the Deep South, or the region that is referred to as the Black Belt (Alabama, Georgia, Louisiana, Mississippi, South Carolina), provided Clinton with a major boost. She won 225 delegates, whereas Sanders only captured 70 delegate votes in those six states. Exit poll data suggest that support from racial and ethnic minority voters assisted tremendously in Clinton's victory over Sanders.

New Hampshire, traditionally considered an important primary, pushed Trump into national headlines as he won the overwhelming number of delegates for the state.[32] By the time of the first Republican primary, twelve candidates were serious contenders for the nomination and actively campaigning. Chris Christie, the governor of New Jersey, had focused his campaign resources into New Hampshire. Christie placed sixth in that race and formally withdrew on February 10. Subsequent to the conclusion of Christie's campaign, Carly Fiorina suspended her campaign that day as well, and Jim Gilmore exited the race following New Hampshire.

As the race continued forward, Trump's increasing share of victories continued, and the remaining candidates left the race, one by one. Jeb Bush withdrew after the South Carolina primary on February 20. One of the key moments for the campaign was Super Tuesday (which occurred on March 1, 2016), known for being the day that the greatest number of states hold their primary elections and caucuses. After Super Tuesday, Ben Carson dropped out. Florida senator Marco Rubio left the race on March 15, after losing his home state. Rubio stated, "America's in the middle of a real political storm, a real tsunami," he said. "And we should have seen this coming."[33] Ted Cruz left May 3, and John Kasich left the race May 4.

On May 26, Donald Trump secured the requisite number of delegates required to attain the Republican nomination of the party. The Republican National Convention was held July 18 to July 21 in Cleveland, Ohio. The Republican platform, with Trump as the designated nominee, has become staunchly more conservative.[34] This includes specific language calling for a wall to be built between Mexico and the United States. The party platform also advocates using religion as a guide for legislation, noting "that man-made law must be consistent with God-given, natural rights."[35]

The number of minority voters in the Republican Party is small. As a result, capturing the trends of Black voters through primary exit polls, for example, is not possible, given the small margin that appear in the sample. Latino voters have a marginally larger presence within the Republican Party. This mattered in Nevada, where Donald Trump claimed he captured the Latino vote.[36] It is important to be mindful of Trump's assertions for several reasons. First, Nevada has a significant Latino population, but a substantial portion are undocumented individuals, who do not participate in the primary process. Second, of Latinos who are citizens and eligible to vote, the vast majority vote as Democrats.[37] Last, the CNN exit poll that Trump utilized to make the claim of getting the majority of the Latino vote is based on a sample of 100 people.[38] Given the small number of individuals captured from very specific precincts, the survey has a large margin of error that is plus or minus 10 percentage points. Given the inconsistency of support from Latinos supporting Trump across states and given this margin of error, it is important to heed caution in accepting the Trump campaign's claims that Republican Latino voters support Trump. Moreover, according to a poll conducted by Latino Decisions of 400 Latino registered voters in Nevada, with a sample that was representative of the state's Latino electorate, the support for Trump looks starkly different than that highlighted by the exit polls.[39] According to this poll, 87 percent of the Latino electorate held unfavorable views of Donald Trump. If we look only at self-identified Republicans, 64 percent of Latino Republicans in the sample held unfavorable views of Donald Trump.[40] In the same sample, 78 percent believed that the Republican either does not care or, more so, may be hostile toward Latinos.[41]

Party Conventions

Party conventions are assemblies held by political parties to nominate candidates, set party rules, and develop a party platform—a statement of the principles and policy positions of the party. Every four years, the Democratic, the Republican, and, in recent years, the Libertarian parties climax the presidential primary season with a convention to nominate their presidential candidate and write the party platform, among other things. These conventions are held in the summer before the November election. Presidential candidates, through either caucus or primary vote, gather pledged delegates who will vote for the candidates at the party's convention.

Both political parties assign each state a specific number of delegates based on population, the number of votes that are cast during the primaries and caucuses, and other factors.[42] In addition to pledged delegates, the Democratic Party has a number of superdelegates who are free to support any candidate, regardless of the popular vote.[43] These superdelegates are Democratic members of Congress, governors, national committee members, and party leaders such as former presidents and vice presidents who are given automatic delegate status.[44]

The Republican Party also has a number of unpledged delegates. These individuals are referred to as unbound delegates, not superdelegates. About 150 delegates were unbound, meaning that they are free to support any candidate.[45] The majority of the Republican unpledged delegates are actually elected, just like the pledged delegates, and are often pledged to a particular candidate.[46] A minority of the unpledged delegates automatically become delegates by virtue of their position as a state party chair or as a national party committee member. By party rule, only the 168 members of the Republican National Committee—a state party chairman and two national committee members in each of the fifty states, five territories, and the District of Columbia—get automatic votes, accounting for about 7 percent of the total convention votes.

In 2016, there were 4,763 delegates to the Democratic National Convention. Of the 718 total superdelegates, 602 expressed support for Hillary Clinton and 47 expressed support for Bernie Sanders.[47] A candidate had to win 2,382 delegates at the convention; Hillary Clinton won 2,807. There were 2,472 delegates to the Republican National Convention. A total of 127 unbound delegates supported Donald Trump and 50 unbound delegates supported Ted Cruz.[48] Trump won a total of 1,542 delegates (1,237 delegates were needed to win the party nomination). There were 4,769 delegates and 347 alternates to the Democratic National Convention and approximately 2,470 delegates and 2,302 alternate delegates from all fifty states to the Republican National Convention in 2016.[49]

Republican Convention. The 2016 Republican National Convention, which the media has described as a "Trump-centered" event, was held in Cleveland, Ohio, from July 18 to July 21.[50] Republican presidential nominee Donald Trump won 1,542 of the 2,472 delegates.[51] A simple majority of 1,237 of the total number is needed to win the presidential nomination. The primary focus of the Republican National Convention was job creation, trade, and economic policy.[52] Convention speakers also offered some remarks on immigration.[53] After a rather unpredictable and tumultuous campaign season, some of the party leadership expressed support for Trump's candidacy, but most leading Republicans—including living Republican presidents and recent Republican presidential nominees—refused to appear at the convention.[54]

Republicans have faced scrutiny over the lack of diversity within the party in general and at the Republican National Convention specifically.[55] The statistics on racial diversity have been particularly troubling during the current election cycle.[56] According to *The Washington Post*, the Republican Party sent fewer Black delegates to the convention in 2016 than it had "at any point in the past century."[57] Less than 1 percent of delegates at the Republican National Convention were African American (only 18 of 2,472).[58] Hispanic delegates made up a slightly higher percentage of delegates than African Americans.[59] According to news reports, there were at least 133 Hispanic delegates at the convention.[60]

One journalist described the convention as the "most flagrant display of GOP racism America has seen in years."[61] Some members of the Republican Party have used racist rhetoric and racist policies to garner support from a conservative White base.[62] Representative Steve King (R-Iowa) caused a firestorm when he defended the lack of diversity, arguing that White people had contributed the most to civilization.[63] Donald Trump has been heavily criticized, including by members of his own party, for the many incendiary, racist, and xenophobic statements he has made since launching his presidential campaign. Nonetheless, a small number of people of color took the convention stage in support of the presidential candidate.[64] Donald Trump and Mike Pence accepted the presidential and vice presidential nominations, respectively, on July 21, 2016.

Democratic Convention. The Democratic National Convention took place in Philadelphia, Pennsylvania, from July 25 to July 28, only a few days after the Republican National Convention. The Democratic conventions in 2008 and 2012 were held in late August and early September, respectively, but the schedule was changed in 2016 to avoid a protracted primary battle and suppress the GOP nominee's momentum following the Republican convention.[65] Hillary Clinton officially accepted the Democratic Party presidential nomination after receiving support from 2,807 of the 4,763 delegates.[66] To win the Democratic nomination, Clinton needed to secure 2,382 delegates and superdelegates.[67] Clinton's nomination was historic because she became the first woman to win the presidential nomination for a major political party.

The Democratic Party had initially struggled to present a unified front during the first couple of days of the convention, following revelations that some party officials were complicit in attempts to undermine Bernie Sanders in his race for the nomination.[68] Tensions subsided after Sanders addressed his supporters and expressed his support for Hillary Clinton. The party platform included raising the minimum wage, supporting public education, implementing a progressive jobs plan, abolishing the death penalty, reviewing trade policy, and working toward Wall Street reform.[69]

In direct contrast to the 2016 Republican National Convention, half of the delegates at the Democratic National Convention were non-White. Twenty-five percent of delegates were Black, 16 percent were Hispanic or Latino, and 9 percent were Asian American or American Indian. According to the Clinton campaign, 1,182 delegates were Black, 747 were Latino, 292 were Asian American, and 147 were American Indian.[70]

On the final day of the Democratic National Convention, Khizr Khan, a Muslim American and Gold Star father, gave a speech about his son, U.S. Army captain Humayan Khan, who had been killed in 2004 during the Iraq War. Khan was accompanied by his wife, Ghazala, who stood silently beside him in support. During the speech, Khizr Khan criticized Republican presidential nominee Donald Trump for his anti-Muslim rhetoric and proposed

Khizr Khan and his wife Ghazala, parents of deceased Muslim U.S. Soldier Humayun S. M. Khan, holds up a booklet of the US Constitution as he delivers remarks asking Republican nominee Donald Trump if he understands the Constitution at the Democratic National Convention on July 28, 2016 in Philadelphia, Pennsylvania.

ban on Muslim immigration. At the end of what has been described as "one of the finest and most damning addresses of the Democratic National Convention," Khizr Khan pulled out a copy of the U.S. Constitution and offered to lend it to Trump.[71]

In the days following Khan's speech, Donald Trump responded to Khan's address in a series of statements, even verbally attacking Ghazala Khan and implying that she was not allowed to speak at the convention because of the Khans' Islamic faith.[72] Many Republican leaders, including senator John McCain (R-Arizona), denounced Trump for his disparaging statements about the Gold Star family.[73] Hillary Clinton and Tim Kaine officially accepted the Democratic Party nominations for president and vice president, respectively, during the 2016 Democratic National Convention on July 26, 2016.

The final vote at the convention is anticlimactic in that the nominee has already secured the necessary number of votes prior to the convention. Everyone already knows who the nominee-elect will be. But the convention serves as a rallying point to energize each party's political base for the fall campaign and to introduce the candidates to the nation as a whole.

Although primaries are the predominant method of selecting candidates for national and statewide office, thirteen states either permit or require conventions for the nomination process. Alabama, Georgia, South Carolina, and Virginia permit political parties to use conventions or primaries to nominate their candidates for national and statewide office.[74] In Virginia in 2013, the Republicans held a convention to nominate their candidates for governor, lieutenant governor, and attorney general. In contrast, Virginia Democrats used a primary election to determine their nominees. State political parties

Democratic presidential and vice-presidential candidates Hillary Clinton and Sen. Tim Kaine, D-Va., take the stage together at a rally in Miami, Saturday, July 23, 2016.

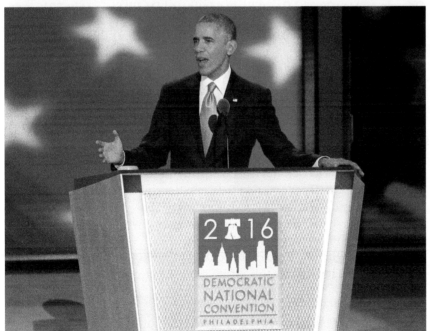

U.S. President Barack Obama delivers remarks at the Democratic National Convention on July 27, 2016 in Philadelphia, Pennsylvania.

decide whether they will nominate candidates in primaries or conventions, but they must follow state election law in carrying out their choice.

Although caucuses and primaries are important tools for established political parties to choose their candidates, they are not advantageous for independents and third-party candidates. These candidates might have to take

Nomination Petitions The number of signatures of registered voters that independent or third-party candidates must collect to qualify for inclusion on a ballot.

out **nomination petitions** and collect a specified number of signatures from registered voters to qualify for inclusion on a ballot. Collecting signatures on nominating petitions is time-consuming and can be difficult if the number of signatures required is sufficiently large that the candidate might have to use volunteers or employ people to circulate petitions. In North Carolina, Michael Munger, a political science professor at Duke University and the Libertarian candidate for governor, had to collect 69,736 signatures of registered voters to gain a position on the 2008 general election ballot for governor. This number represented 2 percent of the total number of people who had voted in the 2004 gubernatorial election. To reach that number of verified signatures, he collected a total of 107,349 and ended up with 73,472 verified signatures—3,736 more than he needed. Nomination petition requirements in some states are aimed at keeping third-party candidates off the ballot. His success in getting on the ballot and in garnering 2.9 percent of the vote in the 2008 general election meant that the 2012 Libertarian candidate for governor did not have to circulate a petition.

In 2016, the former New Mexico governor Gary Johnson was nominated as the Libertarian Party's presidential candidate at its national convention in Orlando on May 29. The Green Party nominated Dr. Jill Stein as its 2016 presidential nominee at its August 6 presidential nominating convention in Houston.

General Elections

General Elections Elections in which the winner is elected to office and takes office after the end of the term of the current officeholder.

General elections are elections in which the winner is elected to office and takes office after the end of the term of the current officeholder. These elections take place on dates specified by state or federal law. In 1845, Congress passed legislation that established the general election date for presidential elections as the first Tuesday after the first Monday in November. As a result, almost all general elections for federal offices—president, House, and Senate—and for most state offices occur on the same November date.

A presidential election is held once every four years. Elections to the House of Representatives are held every two years, with the elections occurring in even-numbered years. Members of the U.S. Senate are elected to six-year terms, with one-third of the Senate up for election every congressional election cycle. Elections to the Senate are held in conjunction with House elections.

Electing the President: How the Electoral College Works

The Electoral College was created by the Founders for several reasons, the most important being to keep the people from having a direct say in the election of the president. The Founders put in place an indirect election process for the presidency that would keep the masses of voters from directly selecting the president. The Founders were suspicious of direct election of the president because they feared that voters could be manipulated and, as a result, that an unsuitable person could be elected president.

To avoid this possibility, the Founders established a system whereby individuals voted for electors, initially chosen by the state legislators and now by the political parties, who would then cast their votes for president at a later date. The Founders believed that, unlike the public, the electors could not be manipulated; they would ensure that only people acceptable to the leaders of the country were elected president. The public's preferences were not to be considered.

Today, presidential electors are chosen by the political parties, and each party has a slate of electors. When individuals go to the polls, they are actually voting for the electors committed to a presidential candidate and not directly for the candidate. Although the Constitution does not prescribe how states are to select their electors, in 1845 Congress passed legislation that electors be appointed on the Tuesday after the first Monday in November of every fourth year (November 8 in 2016), which is the reason elections of the president, and of all national elected officials as a result, occur on the same day in November. In some states, the names of the electors are listed next to the name of the presidential candidate to whom they are committed, but in other states the names are not listed.

In forty-eight states, the presidential candidate who wins the most votes in the state receives all of that state's electoral votes; this is the **winner-take-all** rule. It does not matter if the candidate wins by 500,000 votes or by 537 votes, as George W. Bush did in Florida in 2000. All of the states' electoral votes go to the winner of the state's popular vote. Only two states, Nebraska and Maine, allocate electoral votes via **proportional representation** instead. In each state, two electors are chosen at large by statewide popular vote and the rest are selected by the popular vote in each congressional district.[75] Table 15.2 shows the distribution of electoral votes in presidential elections from 1968 to 2016.

The electors from each state meet on the first Monday after the second Wednesday in December and cast their votes for president.[76] In the 2016 elections, electors met on December 19. In twenty-one states, electors are under no constitutional or statutory requirement to vote for the person to whom they are pledged, but most do so by custom.

There have been some exceptions to this custom. In the 1976 election, a Washington elector pledged to president Gerald Ford voted for Ronald Reagan. In the 1988 election, a West Virginia elector voted for senator Lloyd Bentsen as president and for governor Michael Dukakis as vice president (which was the reverse of their positions on the ticket). In the 2000 presidential election, Al Gore received one less electoral vote than he had won because an elector from Washington, DC, submitted a blank ballot to protest DC's lack of representation in Congress. In 2004, one Minnesota elector voted for the former North Carolina senator John Edwards for both president and vice president. There were no wayward electoral votes in 2008: President-elect Barack Obama and senator John McCain received the electoral votes they had won on election night. In 2012, there were again no renegade electors, with President Obama and Governor Romney receiving the electoral votes they won on election night.

Winner-Take-All An election system in which the candidate who gets the most votes in that district wins the election, even if he or she has not received a majority of the votes and has finished only a few votes ahead of the second-place finisher.

Proportional Representation An election system that uses multimember districts in which seats are awarded by political party roughly in proportion to the results of the election.

TABLE 15.2 Presidential Electoral Votes, 1968–2016

Year	Candidate	Electoral Votes
1968	Richard M. Nixon (R)	301
	Hubert H. Humphrey (D)	191
1972	Richard M. Nixon (R)	520
	George S. McGovern (D)	17
1976	Jimmy Carter (D)	297
	Gerald R. Ford (R)	240
1980	Ronald Reagan (R)	489
	Jimmy Carter (D)	49
1984	Ronald Reagan (R)	525
	Walter F. Mondale (D)	13
1988	George H. W. Bush (R)	426
	Michael S. Dukakis (D)	111
1992	William J. Clinton (D)	370
	George H. W. Bush (R)	168
1996	William J. Clinton (D)	379
	Bob Dole (R)	159
2000	George W. Bush (R)	271
	Albert Gore, (D)	266
2004	George W. Bush (R)	286
	John F. Kerry (D)	251
2008	Barack H. Obama (D)	365
	John W. McCain (R)	173
2012	Barack H. Obama (D)	332
	Mitt Romney (R)	206
2016	Donald J. Trump (R)	306
	Hillary R. Clinton (D)	232

Sources: National Archives, "Electoral Box Scores, 1789–1996," http://www.archives.gov/federal-register /electoral-college/scores.html; "Electoral Box Scores, 2000, 2004, and 2008," http://www.archives.gov /federal-register/electoral-college/scores2.html#2000; 2012 Electoral College Results, http://www.archives .gov/federal-register/electoral-college/2012/election-results.html; 2016 Election Results, http://www.cnn .com/election/results.

Some states, however, require electors to cast their votes according to the popular vote and provide that so-called faithless electors could be fined or disqualified for casting an invalid vote and be replaced by a substitute elector. Despite a law in Washington, DC, along with twenty-six states, that requires electors to vote for the candidate who won the District's electoral vote, in the 2000 presidential election the elector who submitted a blank protest ballot was not penalized in any way. The Supreme Court has found that the Constitution does not make electors free agents in their voting for president and thus that state laws could be passed to require electors to vote for the presidential candidate who won the state's popular vote and for political parties to extract pledges from electors to vote for the party's nominee.[77]

Over the decades, there have been many calls for the abolition of the Electoral College or an overhaul of the method of distributing electoral votes. The outcome of the 2000 presidential election turned on the outcome of the popular vote in Florida, which would determine whether Vice President Gore or Governor George W. Bush would receive the state's 25 electoral votes and thus give one candidate more than 270 electoral votes. The incredible closeness of the vote—less than 1,700 on election night of 6 million votes cast—triggered an automatic recount under Florida law. At the end of the automatic recount and the counting of absentee ballots, Bush led by 537 votes.

After the 2000 presidential contest, in which the Supreme Court ruled in a 5–4 vote that the Florida recount should be halted and George W. Bush declared the winner, the utility of the Electoral College was once again called into question. One proposal, among many, is to eliminate the Electoral College entirely and move to a direct election of the president. If this system had been in place, Al Gore would have been elected president because he received approximately 540,000 more popular votes than George W. Bush did. Another proposal is to keep the Electoral College,

The reverend Jesse Jackson, who ran for president in 1984 and 1988, holds the ballot that Palm Beach voters used to cast their votes during a rally at the Palm Beach elections office, November 9, 2000, in West Palm Beach, Florida. The elections of 2000 and 2004 were marred by charges of intimidation of Black and other racial group voters, coupled with an inordinately high number of invalid ballots in Black precincts in Florida.

but to apportion electoral votes based on the proportion of a state's vote that a candidate receives. A third proposal is to allocate a state's electoral votes based on which candidate wins the popular vote in each congressional district.[78] Nebraska and Maine already allocate their electoral votes this way.

Because each state makes its own determination as to how its electoral votes will be apportioned, these last two proposals mean that each state would have to decide to switch to a proportional allocation system. Despite the controversial 2000 and 2016 elections, the probability that the Electoral College will be eliminated is remote. The all-or-nothing method of apportioning electors gives an advantage to large states with large numbers of electoral votes, and these factors are enduring and powerful. We say more about the Electoral College later, when discussing the winning of the presidential election.

Campaigning for Elections

The election of individuals to public offices in general elections does not "just happen." Candidates put together campaign staffs, hire consultants, use polling, and map strategies for targeting specific groups of voters. Campaigns must also turn their supporters out to the polls for early voting (many states allow voters to vote before the official Election Day), where available, and on

Election Day for those who do not vote early. Candidates must also raise money to pay for everything they will need to win. Thus, to be elected, candidates must be organized.

Developing a Campaign Strategy

After securing the nomination, the major party nominees face each other in the general election. Although political campaigns have been ongoing during the nomination process, at this point the campaigns go into full gear. At the presidential level, candidates develop a strategy that will best secure a majority of electoral votes (270). In essence, presidential selection constitutes fifty-one separate elections (fifty states plus the District of Columbia) to award electoral votes.

Prior to the 2008 presidential elections, presidential candidates typically did not focus their attention on the entire nation, instead concentrating their resources in vote-rich states and tending to avoid those states in which they had little chance of winning. For example, in 1996 Bill Clinton ceded Kansas to Bob Dole, who had represented it in the House and Senate for almost a half-century. Prior to the 2008 presidential election, campaigns used to consider the four states with the most electoral votes the most significant: California (55 votes), New York (31 votes), Texas (34 votes), and Florida (27 votes). In 2008, however, other key states that were highly competitive were considered just as important for their electoral votes: Pennsylvania (21 votes), Illinois (21 votes), Ohio (20 votes), Michigan (17 votes), and New Jersey (15 votes). Together, these nine states constituted 243 of the 270 votes needed to secure a majority of electoral votes in 2008.

In 2008, senator Barack Obama focused not only on Democratic and Democratic-leaning, or Blue, states, but also on Republican, or Red, states. His strategy was to pursue as many combinations as possible to reach 270 electoral votes. At the time, many political analysts thought Obama's strategy was foolhardy and that there was no way he was going to be able to make inroads into such traditionally Republican, or Red, states as North Carolina, Virginia, and Ohio. But Obama's strategy of focusing on a variety of states, described as the fifty-state strategy resulted in his winning nine states that had gone for the Republican candidate in 2004: North Carolina, Virginia, Nevada, Colorado, New Mexico, Florida, Indiana, Iowa, and Ohio.[79] When combined with the traditionally Blue states, Obama won with 365 electoral votes compared to McCain's 173.

In 2012, President Obama pursued much the same strategy, although one state that he won in 2008, Indiana, did not receive a great deal of attention from his campaign. The assumption was that Romney would take Indiana, which he did, but Obama's campaign did spend resources in all of the other states. Once again, his campaign was trying to knit together as many combinations as possible to get to 270 electoral votes. In the end, he carried seven of the nine states that he won in 2008, losing Indiana and North Carolina, giving him 332 electoral votes to Mitt Romney's 206. It was less than his number in 2008, but a substantial victory nonetheless.

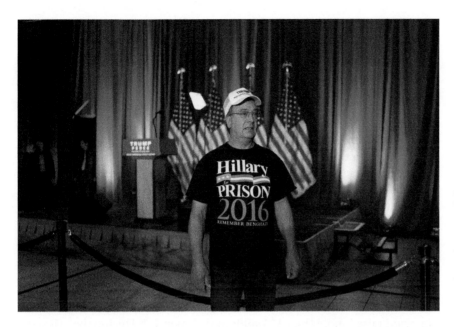

A chant at Trump rallies was to "lock her up" referring to the Democratic presidential nominee Hillary Clinton. An attendee wears a 'Hillary for Prison' shirt at a campaign event for Donald Trump, in Youngstown, Ohio, U.S., on Monday, Aug. 15, 2016.

Clinton's 2016 campaign strategy was different from the approach that she used during her 2008 presidential campaign, when she lost the Democratic nomination to Barack Obama. Although Clinton acknowledged that she is not a "natural campaigner," her primary focus was convincing voters to support her, by appealing to the middle class, and highlighting her electability by emphasizing that she has the skills necessary for governing the country.[80] "Clinton had nearly 100 percent name recognition" among voters, as well as support from many working-class women.[81] The former first lady had an enormous amount of political experience, having served as the secretary of state and senator of New York. Clinton also had a seasoned campaign organization that incorporated much of Obama's machinery from the 2012 election.[82]

The Clinton campaign undertook significant fundraising efforts, and donors raised millions of dollars for the Democratic candidate. Clinton's biggest super PAC supporter, Priorities USA Action, reserved $158 million for an advertising campaign, pumping money into television ads and digital advertising, including on a number of social media platforms.[83]

During the primary season, Clinton's campaign employed a "hyper-local" strategy, identifying a local issue that was of interest to Democratic voters in each state and then championing that issue.[84] To that end, Clinton campaigned against voter identification (ID) laws in Alabama and Missouri, spoke about high concentrations of lead in the water in Jackson, Mississippi, discussed wind energy in Iowa, and focused on the heroin epidemic in New Hampshire.[85]

Clinton focused her presidential bid on several clearly defined issues. Her platform included expanding civil rights for women, racial minorities, and the LGBT community; combating terrorism; instituting a fair tax system;

strengthening Social Security and Medicare; fixing America's infrastructure; comprehensive immigration reform that creates a pathway to full and equal citizenship; making America the world's clean energy superpower; and building an economy that works for all Americans.[86]

Trump's campaign slogan was "Make America Great Again!" His platform included health-care reform, immigration reform (policies centered on deporting all undocumented immigrants and building a wall across the U.S.–Mexican border), restructuring the Department of Veterans Affairs, tax reform, and U.S.–China trade reform.[87] In November 2015, following the Paris terror attacks, Trump advocated a temporary ban on Muslim immigrants, including Syrian refugees, to the United States, as well as expanded surveillance of "certain mosques."[88]

In terms of campaign fundraising, Trump's strategy has been rather unconventional. Initially, Trump stated that his campaign would be fully self-funded and that he would not accept money from donors because "he is rich and didn't need anyone's money."[89] Although Trump's campaign during the primaries was mostly self-funded, by May 2016, donors had raised $5.4 million—significantly less than the amount raised by his Democratic opponent; Clinton's campaign raised more than $25 million that month.[90] During the primaries Trump raised a total of $17 million from individual contributors.[91] After Trump clinched the Republican Party's nomination, he announced that he would write off the $50 million he had lent to the campaign.[92] In early September 2016, the Trump campaign announced that it had raised $90 million during the month of August.[93]

The general election campaigns can be divided into two parts—the "ground war" and the "air war." The **ground war** consists of candidate public appearances, voter registration drives, mobilization of registered voters to get them to the polls on Election Day, fundraising, and public opinion polling, among other efforts. The **air war** consists of advertisements on television, radio, and print. In recent years, presidential campaigns have been waged on the Internet, Twitter, and Facebook as well, with all major candidates hosting campaign websites and having Twitter feeds.

In 2008, Obama effectively used what has come to be called "new media," including text messaging, Facebook and other social networking sites, emails, campaign ads in video games, YouTube, campaign blogs, and user-generated content, among other things.[94] Obama used the Internet and other technologies in 2008 in a manner that echoed John F. Kennedy's groundbreaking use of television as a campaign tool in 1960. Obama's 2008 campaign changed forever how presidential campaigns will be run. His campaign used the same strategy in 2012 and had a much more new-media-savvy campaign operation than did Mitt Romney's.

Presidential and vice presidential candidates also face each other in a series of televised **debates**. Candidates Richard M. Nixon and John F. Kennedy faced off in the first televised presidential debate, but televised debates did not occur again until 1976, when the League of Women Voters, a nonpartisan

Ground War The part of election campaigns conducted using "pavement pounding" methods, including candidate public appearances, voter registration and mobilization, fundraising, and public opinion polling, among others.

Air War The part of election campaigns conducted through broadcast media including radio, television, and the Internet.

Debates Important public face-offs between candidates discussing issues in a variety of formats (including traditional question-and-answer sessions as well as town hall forums) and through a variety of media, most important television and, more recently, the Internet.

group, agreed to sponsor them. In 1987, the Democratic Party and the Republican Party created the Commission on Presidential Debates to administer the debates. The commission consists of a balance of Democrats and Republicans, but no third-party or independent members.

This format disadvantages minor-party candidates. Only once has the commission agreed to allow an independent candidate to participate in the debates: Ross Perot in 1992.[95] John Anderson was allowed by the League of Women Voters, as opposed to the Commission on Presidential Debates, to participate in a debate in 1980, which Jimmy Carter then refused to attend. The two major parties' domination over presidential debates undoubtedly excludes many Americans from the process. In the 2016 presidential election, secretary Hillary Clinton and Donald Trump had three televised debates; the vice presidential candidates, senator Tim Kaine and governor Mike Pence, had one televised debate.

Financing a Campaign

Money is undoubtedly the most important factor in presidential elections. Jesse Unruh, a Democratic politician from California, once said, "Money is the mother's milk of politics."[96] Travel, advertising, support staff, and overhead require a great deal of money. In 1757, George Washington, while seeking a seat in the Virginia House of Burgesses, gave each voter one and a half quarts of rum, wine, or beer.[97] Big business began to play a major role in campaign financing in the election of Ulysses S. Grant and became truly integrated into politics and fundraising with the presidential election of 1896.

William McKinley's campaign manager, "Dollar Mark" Hanna, solicited major business players, such as J. P. Morgan, Standard Oil, and banks, to contribute to McKinley's 1896 campaign, which they did. Hanna raised between $3.5 million and $10 million and established the pattern of major campaign fundraising.[98] McKinley outspent William Jennings Bryant in 1896 and won, a pattern not lost on modern politicians.

As soon as candidates began to solicit funds from big business, legislation was passed to try to keep these funds out of the process or at least limit their influence. As such, a series of campaign finance reform measures was passed during the twentieth century: the Tillman Act of 1907, the Federal Corrupt Practices Act of 1925, the War Labor Disputes Act of 1943, the Taft–Hartley Act of 1947, and the legislation that currently regulates campaign financing, the Federal Election Campaign Act of 1971 (FECA), which was amended in 1974.

In addition to regulating campaign financing, the amended FECA set up the Federal Elections Commission in 1975 to administer and enforce FECA. Congress passed the **Bipartisan Campaign Reform Act (BCRA)** in 2002, also known as the McCain–Feingold Act, which further amended FECA to strengthen the limits, regulations, and reporting of campaign contributions.

BCRA limits individual contributions for 2015–2016 to a candidate for federal office to $2,700 in any given election cycle.[99] This means that individuals can give $2,700 to a candidate during a primary or the same amount to

Bipartisan Campaign Reform Act (BCRA) A campaign finance reform law passed in 2002 that amended the Federal Election Campaign Act of 1971 and strengthened the limits, regulations, and reporting of campaign contributions (also known as the McCain–Feingold Act).

several candidates and then another $2,700 in the general election to one or a similar amount to both. Primary, general, and runoff elections are each considered separate elections. Individuals can contribute up to $33,400[100] to a national party committee per calendar year and a combined limit of $10,000 per calendar year to state, local, or district political parties.[101] Individuals are limited to $5,000 per calendar year in contributions to political action committees (PACs) that support federal candidates.[102] In addition to imposing these individual limits on contributions, the McCain–Feingold Act did the following (among other things):

Soft Money The less regulated money that is raised by a political party to support and maintain the party.

- The act bans **soft money** (unregulated money that that can be used for anything the political parties deem necessary, from pencils to pamphlets to phone banks) and prohibits candidates from using "leadership PACs," which are created to circumvent spending limits in promoting issues.
- The act bans special interests from collecting unlimited and unregulated amounts of money to fund "issue ads," which are designed to push an issue but in reality are used to support or oppose a particular candidate.[103]

Public Funding The financing of election campaigns by the American public through tax allocations as distinct from private fundraising by candidates.

- The act allows candidates who decide to forgo **public funding** for their campaigns to spend without any limits, although contribution limits still apply.[104]
- Under the BCRA, campaign contribution limits can be increased and indexed for inflation every odd-numbered year.[105]

Presidential campaigns in the 1950s through the early 1970s saw the greatest increase in spending, setting the pace for campaigns in the 1980s and 1990s. In 1956, Dwight Eisenhower and his Democratic opponent, Adlai Stevenson, spent a combined $11.6 million in their presidential campaigns. In 1968, Richard Nixon spent around $30 million and Hubert Humphrey laid out around $10 million. The biggest jump in campaign costs came in 1972 when Richard Nixon and George McGovern spent more than $90 million combined.[106]

Campaign costs in the 1980s hovered around $100 million for combined primary spending. But in 1988, the first year with no incumbent running since Richard Nixon in 1968, campaign costs soared to $213 million for the primary alone.[107] In 1988, both the Republicans and the Democrats had numerous candidates vying for their respective nominations.

In the 1996 presidential campaign, Republican candidate Bob Dole spent $34.5 million and incumbent Democratic president Bill Clinton spent $30.4 million.[108] In the 2000 presidential election, both George W. Bush and Al Gore accepted public funding in the general election and each was given $67.6 million to spend. In 2004, both George W. Bush and John F. Kerry accepted public funding and were given $74.6 million each to spend during the general election.

The 2008 presidential election was, until recently, the most expensive on record. Initially, Barack Obama indicated that he would participate in the public financing of the general election, but he changed his mind in June 2008. He then revealed that he thought the public financing system was broken and that if he participated in it, he would not be able to compete effectively against senator John McCain and the Republican Party. Obama therefore decided to forgo public funding, the first time this has happened in a presidential election since public financing was introduced.

Obama was then free to raise and spend as much as he wanted to secure the Democratic nomination during the primary season, as well as during the 2008 general election. It is estimated that Obama raised more than $750 million through traditional fundraising methods and from more than 3 million online donors to his Internet site. McCain accepted public financing and received $83 million in public funds. Obama's financial advantage allowed him to campaign and compete in traditionally Republican states, whereas McCain found it difficult to compete in traditionally Democratic states.

In 2012, Romney enjoyed support from a number of conservative super PACs that either supported his candidacy directly or spent considerable money attacking Obama.[109] The largest pro-Romney super PAC was Restore Our Future, and most of the money it raised came from the financial industry, including private equity executives and hedge fund managers.[110] Restore Our Future raised approximately $157 million during the 2012 campaign, the largest amount raised by any group.[111] The U.S. Supreme Court's 2010 decision in *Citizens United v. Federal Election Commission* ruled that corporations and unions have the same political speech rights as individuals under the First Amendment and are thus able to donate directly to political candidates and PACs.

President Obama initially resisted super PACS, but eventually decided to support their creation on his behalf because of the amounts of money that Romney and his supporters were able to raise. Priorities USA was the main super PAC supporting President Obama, which raised $79 million, significantly less than the super PACs supporting Governor Romney.[112] Despite the support of super PACs, Obama's campaign still focused on individual donors and in the end outraised Romney's campaign, $715 million to $446 million.[113] The super PACs supporting Romney were the source of much of his financial support.

In 2016, Hillary Clinton's super PAC, Priorities USA Action, was a "big-money machine."[114] According to information released by the Federal Election Commission, Priorities USA Action raised more than $100 million between January 1, 2015, and August 22, 2016.[115] A large percentage of the money raised by Priorities USA Action came from twenty individual donors.[116] The group has also collected nearly $1 million through a joint fundraising agreement with EMILY's List.[117] EMILY's List is a PAC that works to help elect pro-choice democratic female candidates to political office. Other pro-Clinton super PACS, namely Blue Answer PAC, Balance of Power PAC, Faith Voters PAC, and America's Teachers, raised a combined total of more than $250,000 during the current election cycle.[118] Priorities USA Action has been devoted to running a multi-million-dollar advertising campaign to boost Hillary Clinton, reserving $158 million for this purpose.[119]

Efforts to fundraise by Donald Trump's supporters fell far short of that of Hillary Clinton's allies, meaning that less money was spent on paid television advertising.[120] During the primaries, Trump criticized major donors and insisted that he did not need the help of super PACs, but by July his campaign announced that it had dropped its opposition to fundraising from super PACs and encouraged donors to provide their financial support.[121] Several competing strategists started collecting money for pro-Trump super PACs in an attempt to try to match Clinton supporters' fundraising efforts.[122] Super PACs supporting Donald Trump raised a combined total of more than $12 million as of August 2016, with Great America PAC bringing in more than half of that amount.[123] Other pro-Trump super PACs included Rebuilding America Now, Make America Great Again PAC, Committee to Restore America's Greatness, Patriots for Trump, and Committee for American Sovereignty. The total cost for both candidates for the 2016 presidential election was approximately $2.6 billion, the most expensive on record.

Running a Campaign

During a campaign, candidates use a number of avenues to get their message across and to gauge how the public is reacting to them and their message. Campaign commercials and public appearances, coupled with polling and media interviews, are some of the most important mechanisms. As mentioned earlier, Obama also used new forms of technology in the campaign to expand his message beyond traditional election approaches.

Candidates invest incredible amounts of money in campaign advertising, which includes not only posters and buttons, but also professional campaign commercials. Purchasing expensive airtime results in the production of thirty-second advertisements that are short on substance and long on symbolism. It is difficult to determine a candidate's stance from these thirty-second features, but they are designed to strike at some value or chord in a targeted group of voters that will pull them toward one candidate and away from another. Moreover, these spots often "shade" the truth or distort the other candidate's position. It is impossible to present anything but short sound bites.

Few candidates can afford to purchase airtime to make a half-hour speech, and many campaign consultants will say that few Americans would listen. Yet in 2008, Obama purchased thirty minutes of airtime on CBS, NBC, Fox, MSNBC, BET, TV One, and Univision on the evening of October 29, 2008, to talk to the American public. Despite the warnings of campaign consultants that no one would listen, Obama drew 33.5 million viewers, more than watched the conclusion of the World Series also airing that evening. Neither Obama nor Romney did this in 2012.

Another aspect of campaign advertising is the use of negative campaign advertisements. Although the American electorate decries it, this type of advertising is extremely effective in putting opponents on the defensive and eroding their support. Most campaigns, whether national or local, have people who are involved in **opposition research**, finding ethical lapses, past

Opposition Research
Campaign activity devoted to undermining the public's confidence in and support of a candidate, a key component of negative campaigning.

problems, or questionable behavior that can be used to undermine the public's confidence in and support for the opposition. Often, campaigns use this "opposition material" in ways that raise ethical concerns, and in some instances candidates will resort to "playing the race card" by tugging at the fragile racial and ethnic threads that are interwoven throughout the fabric of the U.S. political system.

Scholars have identified the 1988 presidential campaign between George H. W. Bush and Michael Dukakis as one in which George Bush played on the racial animus of Whites toward Black Americans to gain an advantage over Dukakis, although racial issues were not at the forefront of the campaign. Bush's campaign determined that Dukakis was vulnerable on the crime issue and that if it played on Whites' fear of being victimized by Blacks, that would bring White votes to Bush. Wanting to avoid a backlash against the official campaign by appealing openly to the racist feelings of Whites, Bush's campaign developed on a two-track system. The official campaign would attack Dukakis's views on crime and his record as governor, while outside groups (taking advantage of a loophole in campaign finance rules) would run an operation that would appeal to the basest instincts of the American public on the subject of race.[124] Thus was born the infamous Willie Horton ad.

Horton was a young Black man convicted of murder and sentenced to life in a Massachusetts prison. He escaped while on furlough and assaulted a White couple in their home, raping the woman. George Bush made Horton a household name by repeatedly mentioning Horton's story and pinning the blame on Michael Dukakis, who was the governor of Massachusetts.[125] Political scientists Donald Kinder and Lynn Sanders later found that the Willie Horton ad had increased the resentment of Whites toward Blacks and moved White voters in Bush's direction.[126]

Bush was not the first presidential candidate to resort to racial appeals. Barry Goldwater's 1964 and Richard Nixon's 1968 campaigns relied implicitly on racial appeals. Ronald Reagan continually used a welfare queen anecdote and other anecdotes on the campaign trail that were code words for race.

Although direct racial appeals were not present in the 2000 election, a racial dynamic was. In 2000, Florida counties with punch-card balloting systems, such as Miami-Dade and Palm Beach, had the highest percentage of uncounted ballots. Palm Beach also had a large number of overvotes, with more than one candidate for president punched; this was, in large part, caused by the format of the ballot, which was a butterfly ballot. Elderly citizens in Palm Beach complained that the ballot layout was so confusing that they found it difficult to find the hole to punch for Al Gore and inadvertently voted for Pat Buchanan instead.[127] The estimate is that more than 19,000 overvotes in Palm Beach County were related to confusion with the ballot that caused people to vote twice in the presidential race.[128]

In 2000, a precinct-by-precinct analysis of Florida counties by the *Washington Post* found that heavily Democratic and African American neighborhoods had lost many more presidential votes than other areas because of outmoded voting machinery and rampant confusion about ballots. In fact, the analysis identified a racial component to Florida's election process: Counties with high proportions of Black voters were more likely to have outmoded voting machinery than were counties with predominately White populations.[129]

As a result of the 2000 debacle, in the presidential election of 2004 massive mobilization efforts occurred, particularly among racial and ethnic communities for the contest between Massachusetts senator John F. Kerry and president George W. Bush. A 2000 Gallup Poll reported that almost 70 percent of Blacks felt "cheated" after the 2000 election, 50 percent felt that Bush had stolen the election, and more than 75 percent said that the U.S. election system is discriminatory.[130] Although non-Whites increased their proportion of all votes, President Bush achieved a decisive reelection victory by increasing his vote margin among White voters, particularly among White women.[131]

Racial appeals were present throughout the 2008 election. For instance, an Inland (California) Republican women's group published an "Obama Bucks" welfare coupon in its October 2008 newsletter. Obama is surrounded by a watermelon, ribs, and a bucket of fried chicken, playing on the worst stereotypes some Americans have of Black Americans. This is but one of many instances of the use of Obama's race as a campaign tactic to push those with negative racial views toward the Republican candidate, senator John McCain, and to degrade Obama at the same time.

In another instance, in Minnesota, racist fliers were mailed to the predominately White constituents in representative Betty McCollum's (D) district. The fliers stated that if Obama were elected, property values would decrease because low-income Blacks would be moving into the neighborhood. The fliers further suggested that criminals, including O. J. Simpson, would be among the new neighbors.

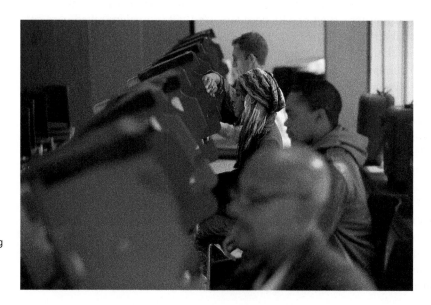

Black voters cast their ballots during early voting at a polling station at Truman College on October 31, 2016 in Chicago, Illinois.

The 2012 race saw more of the same. A bumper sticker began to appear that said "Don't Re-Nig in 2012," with a red line through Obama's campaign symbol. Underneath the phrase were the words "Stop repeat offenders. Don't reelect Obama." There were many versions of this particular sticker and a video of cars with several of them was uploaded to YouTube and went viral. At first, many people thought the stickers were photoedited on the cars, but it soon became apparent that they were real.

During the Republican primaries, Newt Gingrich declared that President Obama was "the food stamp" president. Gingrich said that he was talking about the fact that the number of people on food stamps had increased during President Obama's first term, but most took his comments as alluding to the stereotype that most Blacks are on welfare and rely on government assistance, also harkening back to the "Obama Bucks" welfare coupon from the 2008 election.

At the Republican National Convention, two delegates threw nuts at a Black camerawoman for CNN, saying "This is how we feed the animals." To the convention's credit, the two people were removed from the convention.[132]

Mitt Romney's campaign ran an ad during the general election falsely stating that President Obama had gutted the work requirement in welfare reform. Despite reporters and nonpartisan fact-checker organizations stating that Romney's claim was false, Romney continued to state this as "fact" on the campaign trail. A line in the ad said, "On July 12th, President Obama quietly announced a plan to gut welfare reform by dropping work requirements. Under Obama's plan, you wouldn't have to work and wouldn't have to train for a job. They just send you your welfare check."[133] Again, the allusion was to Blacks not working and a Black president giving them a pass on being responsible. In October 2012, Romney revived this false claim, possibly in the hopes of triggering negative racial attitudes on the part of some White voters.

At a rally for Romney in Lancaster, Ohio, on October 12, a supporter inside the arena was photographed wearing a shirt that said "Put the White back in the White House."[134] When the shirt was called to their attention, the Romney campaign disavowed the supporter. A criticism of Romney is that he never called individuals on these types of actions at the time they happened, only after the fact.

The 2016 Republican primary and presidential general election was rife with race and racism. One of the key undertones to Donald Trump's success in the primaries was his attack of non-Whites. These include explicitly anti-immigrant commentary, policy suggestions meant to profile Muslim Americans, and suggestions of travel bans targeted toward them. As a result of such rhetoric, White nationalists, typically marginalized by the Republican Party, entered the picture and were more vocal in their support of Donald Trump than they had been in past campaigns.[135]

On June 16, 2015, Donald Trump announced his candidacy for the Republican nominee for president.[136] In the one-hour speech, he addressed issues from Chinese oligarchs to ISIS. Most prominent was his discussion on immigration policy and Mexico. Trump stated, "When Mexico sends its people, they're not sending their best—they're not sending you. They're not sending you. They're sending people that have lots of problems and they're bringing those problems with us. They're bringing drugs. They're bringing crime. They're rapists. And some, I assume, are good people."[137] On July 11, Trump held one of his major rallies in Phoenix, Arizona, and incorporated the issue of "illegal immigration" explicitly within this campaign stop.[138] Trump invited Maricopa County sheriff Joe Arpaio, who is notorious for his racial-profiling tactics targeted toward the Latino community. Most notably, Trump suggested building a wall at the U.S.–Mexico border.[139] This idea began a chant in the rally of "Build the Wall!"

On August 25, at a press conference in Iowa, Trump had anchor Jorge Ramos of Univision forcibly removed from the beginning of the press conference when he tried to ask a question.[140] Ramos was escorted from the room by a member of Trump's private security. In the hallway, a middle-age White man, his face flushed with anger, accosted Ramos, jabbing a finger at him. "Get out of my country," he said. "Get out." The man had a Trump sticker on his lapel. Ramos told him that he, too, was a U.S. citizen. Ramos was eventually let back into the room.

Many other instances of racial statements and racial insensitivity occurred during Trump's campaign, including acting as if he did not know who David Duke was, the former grand dragon of the Ku Klux Klan group and neo-Nazi sympathizer who endorsed him. One of the more sensational events that went on for several weeks was Trump's attack in June 2016 on the Mexican American judge Gonzalo Curiel, who was overseeing the fraud case against Trump University in San Diego. Trump began referencing Curiel's Mexican American background and implying that because of it, he could not be fair in his rulings on Trump University because Trump was building a wall and Curiel was a "Mexican."[141]

2016 Independent Congressional candidate Rick Tyler faced a tremendous backlash for a campaign billboard in Tennessee telling voters to "Make America White Again." Tyler took the billboard down 12 hours after it was put up.

Racial appeals were also present in state and local races. Rick Tyler, an independent candidate for Congress from the 3rd Congressional District in Tennessee, put up a billboard along a highway that said "Make America White Again." He said he put it up to make a point that "the 'Leave It to Beaver,' 'Ozzie and Harriet,' 'Mayberry' America of old was vastly superior to what we are experiencing today."[142] David Duke, as a result of Donald Trump's hesitancy to denounce him, decided to run for senator in Louisiana. Duke said that Trump's attacks on Muslims and illegal immigration brought Duke's values and the values of White nationalists into the mainstream of American politics.[143] He also says that Trump's voters are his voters, but an August 2, 2016, poll found that 80 percent of Louisiana voters had an unfavorable opinion of Duke.[144]

Although Clinton did not use race in a pejorative sense in her campaign, she was called out by some, including some members of Black Lives Matters, for comments she made in 1996, when she was first lady and was supportive of her husband's crime bill. In 1994, Congress passed the Violent Crime Control and Law Enforcement Act, a bill that expanded the use of the death penalty, created new three-strikes rules, made it harder for people to get parole, and provided federal funds for states to build more prisons, among other things. Some suggest that the bill increased the incarceration rate for young Black males.[145] Clinton defended her husband's bill in 1996 and made a statement about young Black children that came back to haunt her in the 2016 election: "They are often the kinds of kids that are called 'super-predators, . . .' No conscience, no empathy, we can talk about why they ended up that way, but first we have to bring them to heel."[146] She was heckled at a private fundraiser in February 2016 in Charleston, South Carolina, by a Black Lives Matters protester, Ashley Williams, for her 1996 comments. Williams called Clinton's statement racist and wanted her to apologize for it. Shortly after the event, Clinton said that she regretted having said what she said and disavowed much of the 1994 bill that she says did lead to mass incarceration.[147]

Winning the Election: How Elections Are Decided

Most elections in the United States are decided by a plurality (or first past the post), the candidate who receives the most votes, or a majority, the candidate who receives more than 50 percent of the votes cast in a given election. In a majority system, if no candidate receives 51 percent of the vote, then a runoff election is held between the top two vote-getters.

Most elections for the U.S. House of Representatives and U.S. Senate are decided by a plurality of the votes. In a plurality, or first past the post, electoral system, a candidate can win with any number of votes as long as it is more votes than anyone else receives. Thus, in an election in which there are more than two candidates, an individual can win with only a small proportion of the vote as long as that is the highest percentage received among all of those running.

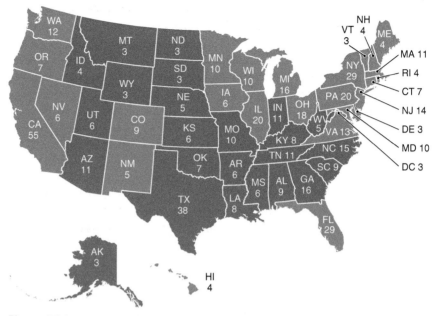

Figure 15.1 2016 Map of Number of Electoral Votes by State

The process by which the United States elects its president is a combination of a plurality system and a majority system, which adds complexity to understanding the process of electing the president. Given the Electoral College system, Americans do not elect the president directly. The votes Americans cast in the presidential election on Election Day are actually votes for a slate of electors who are committed to each presidential candidate. All of the states use a plurality system for determining which slate of electors wins the states' electoral votes. Figure 15.1 shows a map of the Electoral College with the distribution of votes across states.

Voting

The right to vote and the exercise of that right are at the core of the nation's representative form of government. Yet the United States has had a history of denying the vote to certain citizens, experiences lower voter turnout rates than many other countries (especially other Western democracies), and exhibits differences in voter registration and turnout rates based on race, gender, socioeconomic class, and a number of other dimensions.

Factors That Affect Voter Participation

Political scientists have learned that people who follow elections in the newspapers or on television, who have a high level of interest in political campaigns, and who overall are interested in politics and public affairs and follow them closely are more likely to feel that voting is an important thing to do than are those who are not interested in politics and public affairs. Also, people who believed that government is responsive to their needs are more likely to think voting is important and to vote than are people who feel the government is not concerned with them and their needs.[148]

The United States is among the premier democracies in the world, yet the United States has lower voter turnout rates than many countries. An analysis of election turnout by the International Institute for Democracy and Electoral Assistance for all national elections held since 1945 in 172 countries found the United States ranked 139 in average voter turnout (48.3 percent), just ahead of Mexico. Italy was ranked first, with an average voter turnout rate of 92.5 percent. Given the position of the United States as a model democracy that others strive to emulate, why do U.S. citizens vote in such low numbers?

Figure 15.2 shows voter data for the **voting-eligible** (citizen) **population (VEP)** of the United States in presidential elections from 1960 to 2016. (The voter-eligible, or citizen, population is important because only U.S. citizens are eligible to vote.) As Figure 15.2 demonstrates, voter turnout declined continually from 1960 to 1980, jumped up and down a bit between 1984 and 1996, and then steadily increased from 2000 to 2008, although it dipped slightly in 2008. The VEP turnout rate in 2012 was down to 61.8 percent from 63.6 percent in 2008. There turnout rate dropped substantially in 2016 from that of 2012 down to 55.4 percent.

Often, the **voting-age population (VAP)**, which includes both citizens and noncitizens, is used to calculate voter turnout rates. This presents a very

Voting-Eligible Population (VEP) The population of U.S. citizens age eighteen or older.

Voting-Age Population (VAP) The population of both citizens and noncitizens in the United States age eighteen or older.

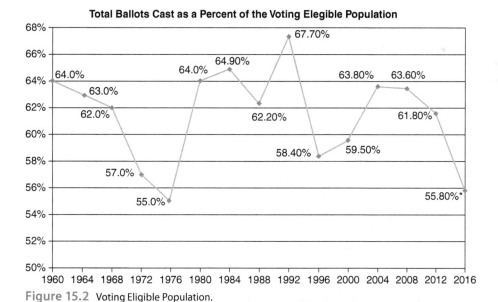

Figure 15.2 Voting Eligible Population.

*Source: Voting-eligible figures 1976–1980 are taken from calculations made by Dr. Michael McDonald, U.S. Election Project, http://www.electproject.org/national-1789-present; Figures for 1980 to 2012 are taken from Table A-6. Reported Voting and Registration for Total and Citizen Voting-age Population by Race and Hispanic Origin: Presidential Elections 1980 to 2012 http://www.census.gov/data/tables/time-series/demo/voting-and-registration/voting-historical-time-series.html; *2016 estimates taken from Dr. McDonald's U. S. Election Project data* different picture from voter turnout rates calculated using VEP. For example, Table 15.3 in "Evaluating Equality: Calculating Voting Turnout Rates" shows that VAP in 2012 was approximately 235.2 million, whereas VEP was 215 million. Using VAP for calculating voter turnout in 2012 yields a 56.5 percent rate, whereas using only VEP produces a higher rate, 61.8 percent. Which is the more accurate number?

These differences are particularly illuminating when we examine voter turnout rates for Whites and Blacks. Using the citizen population only shows that, at least in 2012, the differential between White and Black voter turnout was plus 2.1 percent for Black voter turnout. Additionally, when we look at those Americans who were registered to vote, Black Americans had the highest voter turnout rate, 90.5 percent, of all groups of voters displayed in Table 15.3.

Whether VAP or VEP is used as the basis for calculating voter turnout rates for Latinos and Asians yields quite different results. When VAP is used, Latinos and Asians have extremely low voter turnout rates, 31.8 percent and 31.3 percent, respectively. Yet turnout rates with VEP, although still lower than those of Blacks and Whites, increase approximately 16.2 percentage points for Latinos and 16 percentage points for Asians.

Why Americans Do Not Vote

The reasons for the low voter turnout rate in the United States vary. A survey by the U.S. Census Bureau after the 2012 presidential elections found that of the approximately 153.1 million American citizens who were registered to vote, 8.7 percent, or 20.2 million people, did not vote. The reasons given for not voting included individuals reporting they were too busy to vote or had scheduling conflicts, did not like the candidates and so did not vote, were simply not interested, or just forgot. For others, some lacked transportation, some were ill or disabled, and some were out of town.[149] What are we to make of these reasons, particularly because voting is the least the U.S. government system expects from its citizens?

In a 1992 study of U.S. voting behavior, Ruy Teixeira, a political scientist whose work focuses on political participation and public opinion, concluded that a combination of structural, social, and psychological factors accounts for low voter turnout.[150] The system of voter registration in the United States is complex and varies from state to state. It has been estimated that the labyrinth of laws and administrative procedures that pertains to voting suppresses voter turnout by 9 percent nationally.[151] Individuals must be motivated to register to vote and to work their way through the process. In many countries, voter registration is automatic and done by the state; individuals do not have to seek to be registered on their own.[152]

National Voter Registration Act A law passed in 1993 that provides for voter registration by mail and in departments of motor vehicles (also called the "motor voter" act).

In 1993, Congress passed the **National Voter Registration Act**, which provides for mail registration and for registration at motor vehicle departments and other public offices, such as libraries. This registration process is commonly referred to as motor voter. A 2007 report by the U.S. Election Assistance

evaluating equality

Calculating Voting Turnout Rates

Table 15.3 shows the difference in the calculation of turnout rates using VAP and VEP. The turnout rates are higher when only citizens are taken into account, rather than the total population of those eighteen years of age and older.

TABLE 15.3 **Differences Between Using VAP and VEP for Calculating Voting Turnout Rates**

| 2012 | Population in Thousands | | | | |
	All	White	Black	Latino	Asian
VAP[a]	235,248	155,615	28,709	35,204	12,493
VEP[b]	215,081	152,862	26,915	23,329	8,254
Registered	153,157	112,706	19,680	13,697	4,649
Voted	132,948	98,041	17,813	11,188	3,904

| 2012 | Population in Percentages | | | | |
	All	White	Black	Latino	Asian
Turnout (VAP)	56.5	63.0	62.0	31.8	31.3
Turnout (VEP)	61.8	64.1	66.2	48.0	47.3
Turnout (registered voters)	86.81	86.9	90.5	81.67	83.39
Women (% VEP)	52.10	51.59	55.34	51.29	53.04
Men (% VEP)	47.9	48.41	44.66	48.71	46.96
18–29 (% VEP)	12.8	10.79	16.21	21.10	12.14

Note: Whites include only non-Hispanic Whites. Blacks include only non-Hispanic Blacks. Asians include only non-Hispanic Asians. American Indians and mixed-race groups are not shown.
[a] VAP includes all individuals eighteen years of age and older, regardless of citizenship status in the United States.
[b] VEP includes only U.S. citizens eighteen years of age and older in the United States.
Source: Compiled from Tables 2.1, 2.3, 2.5, and 2.6, Voting and Registration in the Election of 2012, Detailed Tables, http://www.census.gov/hhes/www/socdemo/voting/publications/p20/2012/tables.html, accessed May 10, 2013.

Commission found that making the process of registering to vote easier increased the number of registered voters in 2006 by nearly 12.1 million.[153]

Yet problems have arisen from this legislation. Most notably, voters in the 2000 election who showed up to vote in many jurisdictions around the country found that the motor vehicle departments had never submitted the registration forms to the local registrars' offices. This problem has abated somewhat since 2000, but issues remain in some jurisdictions.

Another barrier is the ability to get to the polls on Election Day. In many countries, Election Day is a holiday or elections are held on the weekend, thereby making it more convenient for people to vote. In the United States, only eleven states have made Election Day a state holiday so that it is easier for people to get to the polls. In eleven other states, state employees are given two hours off to cast their ballots, but in twenty-five states private employers do not give time off on Election Day for their employees to vote.[154] In these states, individuals must vote either before or after work. Only sixteen states open their polls at 6:00 a.m., with most opening at 7:00 a.m., a time at which many Americans are already at or on their way to work. A few states open their polls at 8:00 a.m. Most states close their polls either at 6:00 p.m. or 7:00 p.m., when many people are still commuting home from work. A few states keep their polls open until 8:00 p.m., and New York and Iowa keep their polls open until 9:00 p.m.

In the summer of 2001, a report from the National Commission on Federal Election Reform, formed in the wake of the 2000 election and chaired by former presidents Jimmy Carter and Gerald Ford, recommended, among other things, that Election Day be made a holiday. The reason is not only to provide greater access for people to come to the polls, but also to have more qualified people available to serve as election workers and to allow more schools, which are more accessible for handicapped people, to be used for polling places. The commission also recommended that every state allow provisional voting, that every state adopt a system of statewide voter registration, and that state governments and the federal government take additional steps to ensure the voting rights of all citizens.[155]

Help America Vote Act A law passed in 2002 to reform aspects of the voting process that failed in the 2000 presidential election and to increase voter education and turnout.

In 2002, Congress passed the **Help America Vote Act**, the purpose of which is to reform aspects of the voting process that failed in 2000 and increase voter education and turnout. The act provides money for states to replace outdated voting machines, reforms voter registration procedures, provides better access to voting for the disabled, and offers better training for poll workers. The act also created a new federal registration form to make it easier for new voters to register. In addition, all states now have provisional ballots for voters who believed they are registered to vote but whose names do not appear on the rolls. The provisions of the act were to be phased in, with all provisions being implemented by 2006.[156]

The deadlines were not met. According to a 2008 report by Election Data Services, despite the 2006 deadline on the replacement of lever and punch-card voting machines with whatever new voting machine the local jurisdiction chose, in 2008 approximately 11.3 million registered voters lived in counties that still used lever machines or punch-card ballots.[157] More than $3 billion was sent to the states to upgrade their voting machinery. By the 2012 elections, most of the punch-card and lever machines had been replaced, and "old" technology appeared to be touchscreen voting machines.[158]

Voter ID Laws

As a result of the election and then successful reelection of President Obama and the significance of the votes of racial and ethnic minorities in 2008 and 2012, many Republican-controlled state legislatures passed laws that opponents claimed were aimed at suppressing or making it more difficult for those groups to vote. The push for voter ID laws began in 2003 when Alabama, Colorado, Montana, North Dakota, and South Dakota passed new laws. These laws were the result of provisions in the 2002 Help America Vote Act that required that new registrants provide their driver's license number or the last four digits of their Social Security number with their registration application. In addition, states that allowed individuals to register by mail had to obtain identification from first-time voters. These early laws did not require photo identification to vote and allowed for the use of a number of pieces of identification. For example, in Montana voters could use a driver's license, tribal photo identification, a current utility bill, bank statement, paycheck, government check, or any other document that showed the person's name and current address.[159]

Heading into the 2008 and particularly the 2012 elections, states began to pass stringent photo voter ID laws that were criticized as being aimed at reducing and suppressing the votes of racial and ethnic minorities, who tend to vote Democratic. The argument made by the legislature is that these laws would prevent in-person voter fraud, a problem for which a number of studies have found little to no evidence. (Evidence of in-person voter fraud is virtually nonexistent. An extensive examination of voting found that of 1 billion votes cast between 2000 and 2014, only 31 cases of in-person voting fraud were identified.[160]) These charges were particularly aimed at states controlled by Republican legislatures whose voter ID laws required voters to present state- or federal government–issued photo ID cards. A study by the Brennan Center for Justice identified that 11 percent of voting-eligible Americans—or 21 million citizens—do not have driver's licenses and other nondriver's state-issued IDs.[161] Those without photo IDs are disproportionately seniors (18 percent do not have photo IDs), African Americans (25 percent), the poor (15 percent), and students or people with disabilities.

In 2013, North Carolina's Republican-led legislature had put into place voter ID restrictions by passing legislation that has been described as some of the "most far-reaching" in the United States.[162] On July 29, 2016, the U.S. Court of Appeals for the 4th Circuit struck down North Carolina's voter ID law. The court argued that the law suppressed Black voter turnout because of the way in which it specifically targeted African Americans.[163] The court noted that the law violated the Constitution and the Voting Rights Act and was enacted with "racially discriminatory intent."[164] The North Carolina voter ID law required voters to present state-issued photo identification at the polls and was described as discriminatory for targeting African Americans "with almost surgical precision."[165] In addition to tossing out this requirement, the federal appeals court decision restored voters' ability to register on Election Day and cast early ballots and also allowed individuals who would be eighteen years old on Election Day to register before their eighteenth birthday.[166]

Earlier in July, the 5th Circuit Court of Appeals ruled that a Texas's 2011 photographic voter ID law violated the Voting Rights Act. Commenting on the court's ruling, attorney general Loretta Lynch said, "Texas's highly restrictive voter ID law abridges the right to vote on account of race or color."[167] The law required voters to present only certain government-issued photo IDs when voting and exclude federal or state government IDs and student IDs.[168] Texas was one of nine states that required "strict photo ID," and it only had a few acceptable forms of identification.[169]

In Wisconsin, the U.S. district judge James Patterson ruled that some sections of the state's 2011 voter ID law were unconstitutional because they discriminated against minority voters.[170] Wisconsin's voter ID law required voters to possess specified forms of photo identification to vote. According to the American Civil Liberties Union, the law disproportionately affected Black and Latino voters, who were unlikely to have the types of photo ID required for voting.[171] Judge Patterson's ruling noted that "[Wisconsin's] preoccupation with mostly phantom election fraud leads to real incident of disenfranchisement which undermine rather than enhance confidence in election."[172]

A Kansas voter ID law had also been overturned in May 2016. The law, which had been championed by Republicans,[173] required people to prove American citizenship to register to vote when applying for a driver's license.[174] U.S. district judge Julie Robinson ruled that the state's proof-of-citizenship requirements violated a provision in the National Voter Registration Act, which only requires "minimal information" to determine whether an individual is eligible to vote.[175] Critics of the law had argued that it was implemented in an attempt to "depress voter turnout among groups that lean Democratic, including low-income and minority voters."[176] The rulings in North Carolina, Texas, Wisconsin, and Kansas "suggest a growing judicial suspicion of the wave of voting-restriction legislation" that have been passed by Republicans.[177]

Demographics and Voting

Throughout the book, we have talked about the complexities of the American political system and the inequalities that exist within it. Some of the inequalities were intentional, such as racial and gender inequality, and were implemented through a system of exclusion. Even after the system was changed, institutional and structural barriers were erected to prevent excluded groups from obtaining equality within the system. The effects of the myriad racial and gender inequalities in the United States manifest in differences in voter registration and voter turnout. Voting differences exist on other dimensions as well, such as age, marital status, socioeconomic status, and region of the country.

Race

The data in Table 15.4 show that race plays a role in voter registration and turnout. Although the 2014 mid-term election data are available, voter turnout is lower in mid-term elections than in presidential elections. Therefore, voting data on the 2012 presidential election are used to illustrate demographic voting patterns in the following section. In the 2012 presidential election, non-Hispanic Whites had higher registration and voting rates than did non-Hispanic Asians

TABLE 15.4 **Demographic and Geographic Voting Patterns for Citizen Population in the 2012 National Elections**

	Citizen VEP Population	
	Reported Registered to Vote (%)	Reported Voting (%)
Total citizen VEP[a]	71.2	61.8
Gender		
Male	69.3	59.7
Female	72.9	63.7
Race		
Non-Hispanic White	73.7	64.1
Male	72.2	62.6
Female	75.2	65.6
Non-Hispanic Black	73.1	66.2
Male	69.4	61.4
Female	76.2	70.1
Non-Hispanic Asian	56.3	47.3
Male	54.5	46.0
Female	58.0	48.5
Hispanic	58.7	48.0
Male	56.7	46.0
Female	60.6	49.8
Age		
18–24 years	53.6	41.2
25–44 years	68.7	57.3
45–64 years	75.4	67.9
65–74 years	79.7	73.5
75 years+ and older	79.1	70.0
Marital status		
Married, spouse present	77.1	69.3
Married, spouse absent	61.7	51.6
Widowed	73.4	62.8
Divorced	69.7	58.5
Separated	62.2	49.3
Never married	61.3	50.0
Education level		
Less than 9th grade	49.3	37.1
9th to 12th grade, no diploma	50.6	38.3
High school graduate or GED	63.7	52.6
Some college or associate's degree	74.3	64.2
Bachelor's degree	81.7	75.0
Advanced degree	85.7	81.3
Annual family income		
Less than $10,000	63.2	46.9
$10,000–$14,999	59.5	45.8
$15,000–$19,999	62.8	50.4
$20,000–$29,999	67.7	55.8

(Continued)

TABLE 15.4 *Continued*

	Citizen VEP Population	
	Reported Registered to Vote (%)	Reported Voting (%)
Annual family income (*Continued*)		
$30,000–$39,999	69.2	58.4
$40,000–$49,999	73.8	63.0
$50,000–$74,999	77.4	68.0
$75,000–$99,999	81.7	73.8
$100,000–$149,999	84.9	76.9
$150,000 and over	87.1	80.2
Type of residence		
Owner-occupied units	75.0	66.9
Renter-occupied units	61.3	48.9
Duration of residence		
Less than 1 month	62.2	40.6
1–6 months	66.6	51.5
7–11 months	68.6	53.3
1–2 years	73.3	60.6
3–4 years	77.3	66.4
5 years or longer	84.9	75.9
Region		
Northeast	71.8	62.3
Midwest	74.5	65.0
South	71.1	60.7
West	67.6	60.0

[a] VEP = Voting-eligible population (citizen population eighteen years of age and older).
Source: Compiled from Tables 2.1, 2.3, 2.4, 2.5, 2.6, 3, 5, 7, 8, and 9, Voting and Registration in the Election of 2012 (May 8, 2013), Detailed Tables,
http://www.census.gov/hhes/www/socdemo/voting/publications/p20/2012/tables.html, accessed May 10, 2013.

and Hispanics. Non-Hispanic Whites had slightly higher registration rates, but non-Hispanic Black voter rates were 2.1 percent higher than the voting rate for non-Hispanic Whites. The gap between non-Hispanic White and non-Hispanic Black political participation disappeared in 2012, with Blacks outvoting whites for the first time since the Census Bureau began reporting voting statistics by race. In the 1950s, the difference between Whites and Blacks was significant, but a number of factors—a lowering of de jure and de facto barriers to political participation, mobilization by the Civil Rights Movement, and a dramatic increase in the proportion of Black Americans with higher levels of education and higher status occupations—contributed to a narrowing of the gap.[178] In the 2008 election, the racial gap between non-Hispanic Whites and non-Hispanic Blacks almost disappeared, with only 1.4 percentage points separating the two. Clearly, Barack Obama's candidacy energized Black voters and narrowed the racial gap in voting between Blacks and Whites. The momentum begun in 2008 erased the gap in 2012, with Blacks outvoting Whites.

Yet the gap between non-Hispanic Asians and Whites and Hispanics and Whites remained at 16.8 and 16.1 percent, respectively. The reasons for these continuing lower rates for non-Hispanic Asians and Hispanics can be attributed to a host of factors, among them continued barriers to registration and voting, lower income and education levels, and a higher proportion of younger people not of voting age.

Gender

In 1998, women overall were registered and voted in slightly larger numbers than did men. That year saw the first election in which women outregistered and outvoted men. A number of social changes for women, such as increased participation in the workforce and increased educational attainment (an important contributor to voting), could account for this change. Research in the 1990s found that women were less likely than men to participate in politics.[179]

Yet the 2012 data indicate that increases in women voting occurred among all groups of women: non-Hispanic White, non-Hispanic Black, non-Hispanic Asian, and Hispanic women. Non-Hispanic White, non-Hispanic Black, and Hispanic women were registered and voted in greater numbers than did the men in their respective groups. In fact, Black women had the highest turnout rate, 70.1 percent, of all race and gender categories. Non-Hispanic Asian women registered and voted in higher proportions than non-Hispanic Asian men. The reasons for non-Hispanic White, non-Hispanic Black, non-Hispanic Asian, and Hispanic women voting in larger numbers than their male counterparts vary, but one explanation is that these women experience the American political system both as women and as members of racial groups and that, as political scientists Jane Mansbridge and Katherine Tate describe it, this "doubly bound" situation is a significant contributor to political participation among these women.[180]

Age

Age makes a difference in voter registration and voting. Traditionally, young people age eighteen to twenty-four are registered in lower numbers and the turnout rate is lower, 41.2 percent, as shown in the 2012 data. Voter registration and voting increase with age, with those sixty-five to seventy-four having the highest registration and voter turnout of all of the age categories. Only after age seventy-five do the rates begin to decline, but only slightly.

Research indicates that older Americans are more likely to register and to vote than are younger Americans. Classic voting behavior studies concluded that, by and large, young people do not care much about politics.[181] Yet the 2008 election proved to be an exception to the rule, as voters eighteen to twenty-four were the only age group to show a statistically significant increase in turnout. Moreover, Blacks had the highest turnout rate among this group.[182]

Marital Status

A person's marital status affects voting behavior. People who are married and living with their spouses have significantly higher registration and voting rates than do those who are single. Married persons living with spouses are more settled in a community than are individuals who are divorced or have never married. Data from 2012 indicate that this pattern was present in the recent presidential election—married persons living with their spouses voted in a higher percentage, 69.3 percent, than did all of the other marital categories, particularly those who have never been married.

Socioeconomic Status

Research has found that people who have higher educational and income levels, who own their homes, and who reside in the same place for an extended period of time are more likely to register to vote and to vote than are those who have lower educational and income levels, who rent their homes, and who reside in places for shorter periods of time.[183] The data in Table 15.4 demonstrate that as education increases, registration and voting increase as well. In the 2012 national elections, individuals with less than a ninth-grade education registered to vote (49.3 percent) and voted (37.1 percent) significantly less than did those with advanced degrees (85.7 percent registered and 81.3 percent voted).

The same pattern is present in relation to income. Registration and voting increase progressively as income increases. Only 46.9 percent of those making less than $10,000 voted in the 2012 elections, whereas 80.2 percent of those making more than $150,000 voted.

People who own their homes are more likely to register to vote and to vote than are those who rent. In fact, the difference is substantial—75 percent of homeowners were registered to vote and 66.9 percent voted in the 2012 elections, whereas 61.3 percent of renters were registered to vote and 51.5 percent voted. Those who own their homes might feel that they have a greater stake in what happens politically than do those who rent and most likely move more often. Moving frequently is complicated by variations in voter registration rules from one location to another.

These factors also contribute to racial differences in registration and voting. Census data from 2012 indicate that whereas almost three-fourths (73.6 percent) of non-Hispanic Whites own their homes, only 44.5 percent of non-Hispanic Blacks, 49.1 percent of Hispanics, 56.5 percent of American Indians (2008 data), and 59.5 percent of Asian and Pacific Islanders (2008 data) own their homes.[184] Coupled with home ownership as a contributing factor to registration and voting is length of residence. Those who live in a residence for an extended period of time are more likely to register to vote and to vote than are those who are more transient. Homeowners are more likely to stay in one place than are renters.

Region

The region in which a person lives can influence registration and voting. People in the Midwest have higher levels of voter registration, 74.5 percent, than do those in other parts of the country and a slightly higher percentage of individuals who voted, 65.0 percent. This might be attributed to the fact that in Idaho, Iowa, Minnesota, Wisconsin, and Wyoming, individuals can register to vote on Election Day, and North Dakota no longer has voter registration.

In past elections, Southerners were less likely to vote than were individuals in other regions of the country. Previous lower voter turnout rates in the South have been attributed to lower economic development in the South, along with lower levels of education and income.[185] In 2012, however, voting by Southerners was on par with that of individuals in the West. Given the higher proportion of Black voters in the South and President Obama as the Democratic nominee, Black voter turnout increased during the 2012 election.

In summary, these data from 2012 suggest that older people are more likely to vote than younger people, more highly educated people are more likely to vote than less educated people, people from higher-income families are more likely to vote than people from lower-income families, and people who own homes are more likely to vote than people who rent. The gap between non-Hispanic Whites and Blacks disappeared in 2012, with Whites now lagging behind Blacks, but non-Hispanic Whites are still significantly more likely to vote than non-Hispanic Asians and Hispanics. Women in all racial categories are more likely to vote than are their male counterparts.

The 2016 Presidential Election

The outcome of the 2016 presidential contest was unexpected and counter to virtually every public opinion and tracking poll available, but it was in keeping with the unorthodox and surprise-filled campaign that characterized the election, including the presidential debates. The first debate between the Democratic nominee Hillary Clinton and her Republican counterpart Donald Trump was held on Monday, September 26, 2016, at Hofstra University in Hempstead, New York. Hillary Clinton was clearly substantially more prepared for the debate than was Trump.[186] Clinton dominated most of the exchanges on issues ranging from gender to national security, asserting that Trump did not respect women and warning that he could not be trusted with nuclear codes.[187] Many political commentators agreed that Hillary Clinton scored a decisive victory in the first debate,[188] but some people concluded that Trump won.[189] According to a CNN/ORC poll of voters who watched the debate, 62 percent of voters deemed Hillary Clinton the winner, whereas 27 percent believed Donald Trump prevailed.[190]

Heading into the second debate at Washington University in St. Louis, Missouri, on Sunday, October 9, 2016, Trump's campaign appeared to be coming apart. An audiotape of Trump making vulgar comments about women and bragging about sexually assaulting them had surfaced, causing more than two dozen Republican leaders to disavow their support of the GOP presidential nominee.[191] Although Trump apologized for his grossly inappropriate comments, he brushed his words off as "locker room talk" and denied groping or sexually assaulting women. Hours before the debate, Trump held a press conference with four women who accused Bill Clinton of sexual assault, and during the debate itself, Trump attempted to deflect questions regarding his own assaultive behavior by launching a verbal attack against first Bill and then Hillary Clinton. Trump noted, "If you look at Bill Clinton, far worse. Mine are words, and his was action. His was—what he's done to women, there's never been anybody in the history of politics in this nation that's been so abusive to women . . . Hillary Clinton attacked those same women and attacked them viciously."[192] Although Trump's overall performance in the second debate was a marked improvement from that of the first debate, "Clinton's win in the second debate was decisive."[193] Forty-two percent of voters who watched the debate said Clinton won, including 13 percent of Republicans. Similar to the results of the first debate, only 28 percent of debate watchers believed that Trump won the second debate.

The third and final presidential debate took place at the University of Nevada, Las Vegas, on October 19, 2016, less than three weeks before voters would head to the polls on November 8. As was also the case at the second debate, no handshakes or pleasantries were exchanged before the third debate began.[194] Hillary Clinton presented herself as a well-prepared and experienced politician, and Trump appeared to be a worthy opponent in several ways.[195] Over the course of the debate, both candidates discussed their policy position on a number of important issues, but they also continued to engage in personal attacks and comments on the various scandals that had plagued each other's campaigns.[196] Any gains made by Trump during the first and second debates were reversed when he called Hillary Clinton "a nasty woman" and declined to say whether he would accept the results of the election.[197] Trump later doubled down on his remarks, saying that he would only accept the results if he emerged the winner. Although Trump's comments were shocking, they were not entirely surprising, given that for some time he had been refusing to accept the legitimacy of the election and insisting that the electoral process was "rigged."[198] Overall, the margin tightened following the third debate: 52 percent of debate watchers thought Clinton delivered the better performance, whereas 39 percent believed that Trump won the debate.[199]

Hillary Clinton's primary campaign had largely been overshadowed by the Federal Bureau of Investigation's inquiry into her use of a private email server when she was secretary of state. In the summer, after the conclusion of a full investigation, the FBI announced that it would not recommend filing any criminal charges against Hillary Clinton.[200] The day after the third debate, however, just two weeks before the presidential election, the FBI director James Comey told legislators that the bureau was resuming its investigation[201] as a result of newly discovered email messages found on a laptop seized during a separate criminal investigation of the estranged husband of the Clinton aide Huma Abedin.[202] Comey's letter set off a Republican assault on Clinton, and Trump and his supporters insinuated that the reopening of the investigation indicated that Clinton had, indeed, done something criminal.

On November 6, in a letter addressed to the chairman of the congressional committee, Comey told lawmakers that the FBI upheld their previous findings and stood by their determination that they would not recommend filing charges against Hillary Clinton,[203] issuing the following statement: "Based on our review, we have not changed our conclusions that we expressed in July."[204] Whereas the Clinton campaign welcomed Comey's announcement as a way to finally put to rest concerns about the email scandal, Trump completely rejected it, questioning how it was possible for FBI agents to thoroughly investigate the new emails in such a short period of time.[205] Comey's reopening of the investigation in late October created a firestorm, so his announcement, coming just two days before the November 8 election, was arguably an attempt by the agency to clear "the cloud of suspicion that he had publicly placed" over Clinton's campaign in the last leg of the election.[206] His announcement also renewed skepticism and concern from both Republicans and Democrats about the FBI's handling of the email controversy, however.[207] Although the FBI should remain politically neutral, the organization played a central role in the 2016 presidential election cycle, leading to widespread questions about the agency's integrity.[208]

Clinton appeared to rebound in the polls after the initial dip seen following the release of Comey's October letter. Before the letter's release, early voting had already begun in many states, and by November 8 more than 46 million individuals had already cast their ballots. The projections of which candidate was being helped by early voting were mixed. For example, more than 6 million Florida registered voters voted early but, although Democrats had cast more ballots than Republicans, the number of Democrats was lower than in 2012, which was good news for Trump. The early voting statistics favored Clinton in Nevada, where Latinos turned out in large numbers, and in North Carolina, where Democrats jumped ahead of Republicans. North Carolina was a critical swing state for both Clinton and Trump, as was Nevada for Clinton.

Virtually all of the polls and election models indicated that Clinton was going to win the election and become the first female president of the United States. As the votes began to come in on the evening of November 8, Clinton appeared to be doing well and pulled ahead in several key states, especially Florida. As the night wore on, however, it became clear that although Clinton was leading in the popular vote, the states that had been historically Democratic, her Midwest "blue firewall," were moving in Trump's direction. Three states that had been reliably Democratic in the past—Michigan, Wisconsin, and Pennsylvania—appeared to be leaning toward Trump. Trump ultimately won Wisconsin and its ten electoral votes by about 1 percent of the votes cast, or 27,000 votes.[209] In Pennsylvania, Clinton took Philadelphia and its suburbs by a healthy 635,000 vote margin over Trump, improving on President Obama's margin in the suburban counties in 2012, but falling behind in Philadelphia itself. This was not enough to offset Trump's strength in the rest of the state, however, including three counties that went for Obama in 2012 but flipped to Trump in the 2016 cycle. Trump won Pennsylvania and its twenty electoral votes by 73,224 votes.[210] Trump won Michigan and its sixteen electoral by 11,000 votes, a .28 percent difference over Clinton—47.6 percent to 47.33 percent of the total vote. Macomb County, a traditionally Democratic county, went for Trump, whereas heavily Democratic Detroit and Flint, as well as Wayne County, voted for Clinton.[211]

Trump's messages apparently resonated with White voters in rural areas, who believed they have been left behind by the economic recovery. Seven counties that voted for Obama in North Carolina supported Trump in 2016, primarily because the economic growth experienced by the urban areas has bypassed these counties, many of which have some of the state's highest unemployment rates and lowest incomes. Many of these rural communities have closed factories and most residents have lost their jobs.[212]

Overall, turnout for the 2016 election was the lowest in twenty years (1976), with only 55.8% percent of eligible voters participating. The overall rate in 2012 was 61.8 percent, down from 63.8 percent in 2008. Thus, amid all of the drama and controversy surrounding the 2016 election, fewer voters cast their ballots. Clinton took the majority of the popular vote, 48.1% percent (64,469,963 votes as of November 29, 2016) to Trump's 46.5% percent (62,379,366 votes as of November 29, 2016), but Trump received 306 electoral votes to Clinton's 232.

As Table 15.5 demonstrates, according to the exit polls, Trump took the majority of the White vote (58 percent), whereas Clinton took 88 percent of the Black vote, 65 percent of the Latino vote, 65 percent of the Asian vote, and 56 percent of the vote of those in other categories. Yet, Clinton's margins among these groups was smaller than that of President Obama in 2012, when he received 93 percent of the Black vote, 71 percent of the Latino vote, 73 percent of the Asian vote, and 58 percent of the vote of those in other racial categories.

Clinton needed to carry women in general, and White educated women in particular, in large numbers. She did take the majority of the female vote, 54 percent, but as the exit poll data in Table 15.6 demonstrate, only 43 percent of the White female vote. These percentages are similar to those of Obama in 2012, when he took 55 percent of the female vote, but only 42 percent of the White female vote. Clinton's margin of victory among women came from the

TABLE 15.5 2016 Exit Poll Results by Race

% of Voters	Group	Trump	Clinton	Other/NA
70	White	58%	37%	5%
12	Black	8%	88%	4%
11	Latino	29%	65%	6%
4	Asian	29%	65%	6%
3	Other	37%	56%	7%

TABLE 15.6 2016 Vote by Gender and Race

Total	Trump	Clinton	Other/NA
Vote by Gender and Race			
White men: 34%	63%	31%	6%
White women: 37%	53%	43%	4%
Black men: 5%	13%	80%	7%
Black women: 7%	4%	94%	2%
Latino men: 5%	33%	62%	5%
Latino women: 6%	26%	68%	6%
All others: 6%	32%	61%	7%

votes of Black (94 percent) and Latina women (68 percent). Clinton received 51 percent of the votes of college-educated White women (data not shown), but Trump took 54 percent of college-educated White men, 62 percent of non-college-educated White women, and 72 percent of non-college-educated White men.

We have used the exit poll data for estimates of the voter breakdown, but Edison Research did not poll in all fifty states; only twenty-eight states were included. As a result, there is debate about the accuracy of Trump's support from Latino and Asian American voters as reported in the exit polls. Edison/Mitofsy Election System, which conducts the exit polls for a consortium of news organizations, acknowledges that their sampling frame is not ideal to provide estimates of small, geographically clustered demographic groups.

Latino Decisions, a polling organization that specializes in surveying Latino populations, conducted an election eve national survey of Latinos ($n = 5,600$) and state-level samples in eleven states and interviewed in both English and Spanish. Their data indicate that Clinton received 79 percent of the Latino vote, rather than the 65 percent reported in the exit polls, and Trump received 18 percent rather than 29 percent. According to Latino Decisions, 71 percent of Latino men voted for Clinton compared to 24 percent who voted for Trump, and 86 percent of Latina women voted for Clinton compared to 12 percent for Trump (see Table 15.7). Latinos comprised 7 percent of the electorate in 2000; their proportion increased to 8 percent in 2004, 9 percent in 2008, 10 percent in 2012, and approximately 12 percent in 2016.[213]

Asian American Decisions, a polling group that specializes in surveying Asian Americans, also conducted an election eve national survey of Asian Americans (n = 863), as well as state samples in eight states. Their data indicate that Clinton received 76 percent of the Asian American vote, rather than the 65 percent reported in the exit poll, and Trump received 16 percent, rather than 29 percent. According to Asian American Decisions, 72 percent of Asian

TABLE 15.7 **2016 Latino and Asian American Voters**

Total	Clinton	Trump	Other/NA
	Vote by Race		
Latinos	79%	18%	3%
Latino men	71%	24%	4%
Latina women	86%	12%	2%
Asian Americans	75%	19%	5%
Asian American men	72%	21%	7%
Asian American women	79%	17%	4%

Source: *Latino Decisions, 2016 Latino Election Analysis; Asian American Decisions, The Asian American Vote in 2016.*

American men voted for Clinton compared to 21 percent for Trump, whereas 79 percent of Asian American women voted for Clinton compared to 17 percent for Trump.

There were concerns that the number of Black voters turning out differed from that of 2012 around the country; a comparison of exit polls for both elections suggests this is correct. The Black proportion of the electorate increased from 10 percent in 2000 to 13 percent in 2008; that share was maintained in 2012. In 2016, the Black percentage had declined 1 percentage point, to 12 percent. This 1 percent decline might have made a difference for Democrats, but the assumption is, rather, that Black voters choose not to vote. (Table 15.8 illustrates the changes from 2000 in the racial share of the electorate.) What appears to be lost on commentators is the effect the gutting of Section 5 of the Voting Rights Act has had on Black voters in many states that were formerly covered by Section 5. A November 2016 report by the Leadership Conference Education Fund indicated that formerly covered jurisdictions had 868 fewer polling places than in 2012.[214]

North Carolina dealt with many legal battles addressing voter access during the 2016 election cycle. These lawsuits were filed because of concerns about voter suppression tactics that would primarily affect Black voters in the state. On November 4, 2016, a federal court issued a preliminary injunction barring three North Carolina counties from revoking the voting rights of thousands of residents whose voting eligibility had been challenged by Republican activists and political operatives.[215] The ruling held that voters from the three counties—Beaufort, Cumberland, and Moore—whose voter registrations had been canceled in recent months because of the "individual challenge law" must have their voting privileges reinstated.[216] The National Association for the Advancement of Colored People had filed a lawsuit alleging that the three counties had purged voter rolls through a process that disproportionately targeted Black voters. The judge's ruling was based on the National Voter Registration Act, a federal law that prohibits the cancelation or

TABLE 15.8 National Exit Poll Share of the Electorate: 2000–2016

	Share of Electorate 2000	Share of Electorate 2004	Share of Electorate 2008	Share of Electorate 2012	Share of Electorate 2016
VOTE BY RACE					
White	81%	77%	75%	72%	70%
African-American	10%	11%	13%	13%	12%
Latino	7%	8%	9%	10%	11%
Asian	2%	2%	2%	3%	4%
Other	0%	2%	2%	2%	3%

Source: Nonprofit Vote. 2012. "Nonprofit Voters Increase from 2008." http://www.nonprofitvote.org/. 2016 data taken from the Exit Poll http://www.cnn.com/election/results/exit-polls

blanket removal of voter registrations in the ninety days prior to an election.[217] In the ruling, the judge noted that "electoral integrity is enhanced, not diminished, when all citizens who are eligible to vote are allowed to exercise that right free from interference and burden unnecessarily imposed by others."[218] The North Carolina State Board of Elections revealed that since the 2014 election, officials had removed from voter registration rolls the names of nearly 6,700 voters registered in eight counties.[219] As previously discussed, in August, the Supreme Court issued a decision preventing the state of North Carolina from implementing a strict voting law during the November election. A lower court had previously established that the law was enacted "with almost surgical precision" to specifically target and disenfranchise Black voters.[220]

Several of North Carolina's counties interpreted the 4th Circuit and Supreme Court decisions to require them to open only one early voting site, with their language of at least one site. Guilford County, for example, which includes Greensboro, opened only one early voting site in the first week of early voting, cutting the number of sites from sixteen in 2012 to just one in 2016—a whopping 94 percent cut. As a result, just 12 percent of the 2016 ballots were cast in the first week compared to those cast during the same period in 2012. This was a very successful voter suppression tactic.[221]

There were many other reports of voter suppression tactics around the country. The responsibility for combatting voter suppression tactics falls on the various election boards or civil rights groups. Often, however, there is not enough time remaining for these groups to go to court and get an injunction against those who are attempting to suppress non-White voters. In Arkansas, for example, a Republican election commissioner was accused of voter intimidation after he harassed individuals who were voting early. In a lawsuit filed against the Republican Party of Arkansas and the Jefferson election commissioner Stu Stoffer, Stoffer was accused of yelling at voters, interfering with the voting process, and preventing voters from voting.[222]

our voices

Excerpts from Hillary Clinton's Speech on Donald Trump, the "Alt-Right" Movement, and Mainstreaming Racism*

Everywhere I go people tell me how concerned they are by the divisive rhetoric coming from my opponent in this election. And I understand that concern because it's like nothing we've heard before from a nominee for president of the United States, from one of our two major parties.

From the start, Donald Trump has built his campaign on prejudice and paranoia. He is taking hate groups mainstream and helping a radical fringe take over the Republican Party. His disregard for the values that make our country great is profoundly dangerous.

[Just] this past week, under the guise of outreach to African Americans, Trump has stood up in front of largely White audiences and described Black communities in such insulting and ignorant terms. Poverty, rejection, horrible education, no housing, no homes, no ownership, crime at levels nobody has seen. Right now he said you can walk down the street and get shot. Those are his words.

But when I hear them, I think to myself, how sad. Donald Trump misses so much. He doesn't see the success of Black leaders in every field, the vibrancy of Black-owned businesses, the strength of the Black church . . . He doesn't see the excellence of historically Black colleges and universities or the pride of Black parents watching their children thrive. He apparently didn't see Police Chief Brown of Dallas on television after the murders of five of his officers, conducting himself with such dignity. He certainly doesn't have any solutions to take on the reality of systemic racism and create more equity and opportunity in communities of color, and for every American . . .

Now Trump's lack of knowledge or experience or solutions would be bad enough. But what he's doing here is more sinister. Trump is reinforcing harmful stereotypes and offering a dog whistle to his most hateful supporters. It's a disturbing preview of what kind of president he'd be.

And that's what I want to make clear today. A man with a long history of racial discrimination, who traffics in dark conspiracy theories drawn from the pages of supermarket tabloids and the far dark reaches of the Internet should never run our government our command our military . . .

Maya Angelou, a great American whom I admired very much, she once said, when someone shows you

who they are, believe them the first time. Well throughout his career and this campaign, Donald Trump has shown us exactly who he is, and I think we should believe him. When he was getting his start in business, he was sued by the Justice Department for refusing to rent apartments to Black and Latino tenants. Their applications would be marked with a C, C for colored, and then rejected. Three years later, the Justice Department took Trump back to court because he hadn't changed. And the pattern continued through the decades.

State regulators fined one of Trump's casinos for repeatedly removing Black dealers from the floor. No wonder the turnover rate for his minority employees was way above average. And let's not forget that Trump first gained political prominence leading the charge for the so-called Birthers. He promoted the racist lie that President Obama is not really an American citizen, part of a sustained effort to delegitimize America's first Black president.

And in 2015, Trump launched his own campaign for president with another racist lie. He described Mexican immigrants as rapists and criminals. And he accused the Mexican government of actively sending them across the border. None of that is true . . . I think we all remember when Trump said a distinguished federal judge born in Indiana could not be trusted to do his job because, quote, "he's a Mexican." Think about that . . . Even the Republican Speaker of the House of Representatives, Paul Ryan, described that, and I quote, as the "textbook definition of a racist comment." . . .

But for Trump, that is just par for the course. This is someone who re-tweets White supremacists online, like the user who goes by the name "White Genocide TM." Trump took this fringe bigot with a few dozen followers, and spread his message to 11 million people. His campaign famously posted an anti-Semitic image, a Star of David imposed over a sea of dollar bills that first appeared on White supremacist websites. The Trump campaign has also selected a prominent White national—nationalist leader as a delegate in California, and they only dropped him under pressure.

When asked in a nationally televised interview whether he would disavow the support of David Duke, a former grand wizard of the Ku Klux Klan, Trump wouldn't

our voices *(Continued)*

do it. And only later, again under mounting pressure, did he backtrack. And when Trump was asked about anti-Semitic slurs and death threats coming from his supporters, he refused to condemn them.

Through it all, he has continued pushing discredited conspiracy theories with racist undertones. You remember, he said that thousands of American Muslims in New Jersey cheered the 9/11 attacks. They didn't. He suggested that senator Ted Cruz's father was involved in the Kennedy assassination . . . Just recently, Trump claimed that President Obama founded ISIS. And he has repeated that over and over again . . . You know I've stood by President Obama's side as he made the toughest decisions a commander-in-chief has to make. In times of crisis, our country depends on steady leadership, clear thinking, calm judgment, because one wrong move can mean the difference between life and death. I know we have veterans here and I know we have families, mothers, and spouses, and children of people currently serving. The last thing we need in the situation room is a loose cannon who can't tell the difference—or doesn't care to—between fact and fiction. And who buys so easily into racially tinged rumors.

Someone so detached from reality should never be in charge of making decisions that are as real as they come. And that is yet another reason why Donald Trump is simply temperamentally unfit to be president of the United States . . .

He says that children born to undocumented parents in America are anchor babies and should be deported, millions of them. He'd ban Muslims around the world from entering our country just because of their religion . . . Under Donald Trump, America would distinguish itself as the only country in the world to impose a religious test at the border. Now come to think of it, there actually may be one other place that does that, the so called Islamic State, the territory that ISIS controls. What a cruel irony that someone running for president would equate us with them.

[Trump] hired Stephen Bannon, the head of a right-wing website called Breitbart.com, as [his] campaign's CEO . . . According to the Southern Poverty Law Center, which tracks hate groups, Breitbart embraces ideas on the extremist fringe of the conservative right. This is not conservatism as we have known it. This is not Republicanism as we have known it.

These are racist ideas, race-baiting ideas, anti-Muslim, anti-immigrant, anti-woman, all key tenets making up an emerging racist ideology known as the alt-right. Now,

alt-right is short for alternative-right. The *Wall Street Journal* describes it as a loose but organized movement, mostly online, that rejects mainstream conservatism, promotes nationalism, and views immigration and multiculturalism as threats to White identity.

So the de facto merger between Breitbart and the Trump campaign represents a landmark achievement for this group, a fringe element has effectively taken over the Republican party. And this is part of a broader story—the rising tide of hard-line, right-wing nationalism around the world . . . My friends, this is a moment of reckoning for every Republican dismayed that the party of Lincoln has become the party of Trump. It's a moment of reckoning for all of us who love our country and believe that America is better than this.

Twenty years ago when Bob Dole accepted the Republican nomination, he pointed to the exits in the convention hall, and told any racist in the party to get out. The week after 9/11 George W. Bush went to a mosque and declared for everyone to hear that Muslims love America just as much as I do. In 2008, John McCain told his own supporters that they were wrong about the man he was trying to defeat. Senator McCain made sure they knew Barack Obama, he said, was an American citizen and a decent person. We need that kind of leadership again . . .

How many of you saw any of the Olympics? . . . I was—I was so proud I always get carried away every time the Olympics are on. And you look at the diversity of our athletes. Look at our fabulous Olympic team, representing the United States of America. Ibtihaj Muhammad, an African American Muslim from New Jersey, won the bronze medal in fencing with grace and skill. Would she even have a place in Donald Trump's America? And I'll tell you, when I was growing up, in so many parts of our country, Simone Manuel and Katie Ledecky would not have been allowed to swim in the same public pool. And now together on our swimming team, they're winning Olympic medals as teammates . . .

We want to build an America where everyone has a place; where if you work hard and you do your part, you can get ahead and stay ahead. That's a basic bargain of America. And we cannot get to where we need to be unless we move forward together and stand up against prejudice and paranoia, and prove again that America is great because America is good.

*Excerpted (and edited) version of Hillary Clinton's speech delivered at a campaign rally that was held at Truckee Meadows Community College in Reno, Nevada on August 25, 2016.

American Indians were the last group of Americans to be granted citizenship and obtain the right to vote, which occurred in 1924. But their right to vote was contested by a number of states in the 1960s. American Indians cast their ballots in Maine for the first time in Old Town, Maine, on September 12, 1955. American Indian votes were pivotal to the election of Democratic senators in Montana and North Dakota in 2012.

In Florida, a political advisory committee known as the Florida Citizens for Honest Elections, placed an ad in newspapers across the state offering a $5,000 cash reward for information that could lead to "the arrest and felony conviction of dishonest persons involved in voter fraud."[223] In Texas, a Republican political consultant promoted an "Election Integrity Tip Hotline" offering a $5,000 reward for any fraud-related tips that led to a felony conviction. In response, some Democrats expressed concern that tips about election fraud should go to election officials instead, emphasizing concerns that the hotline was "a systematic and deliberate attempt to suppress votes in the Latino community, specifically targeting the elderly."[224]

American Indians also experienced difficulty in voting in some jurisdictions. The Department of Justice sent election monitors into San Juan County, Utah, which includes a portion of the Navajo Nation. San Juan County has been sued numerous times since 1980 over American Indian voting rights, including brought by the Department of Justice itself. Recently, a federal court ruled in favor of the Navajo Nation in a lawsuit claiming that the county's school districts were drawn in ways that violated the equal-protection clause and that the county had intentionally discriminated against Navajo citizens in setting up commission districts.[225]

San Juan County has a population of 15,000, almost evenly split between Whites and Navajo, yet the county commission has always been majority white. In 2014, the county began to conduct all elections by mail ballot, but many residents of the Navajo Nation do not have street addresses and have to receive their mail at a post office. In some instances, the distance between their home and their post office might be several hundred miles, so getting their mail in a timely fashion is extremely difficult and many of the elderly do not read or write English. If Navajo citizens wanted to vote in person, many had to travel a 400 mile round trip to do so.[226] On Election Day in 2016, there were malfunctioning voting machines and the temporary lack of paper ballots made it difficult for many individuals to vote in San Juan County.

Conclusion

On July 5, 1852, Frederick Douglass, the great abolitionist leader and former slave, gave a speech at an event celebrating the signing of the Declaration of

Independence. Douglass thought it ironic and insulting that he, a former slave now fighting the enslavement of members of his race, was asked to speak at the event. In his famous "The Meaning of July Fourth for the Negro" speech, Douglass saw the Declaration of Independence as a sham because Blacks were enslaved in the land of liberty. Yet Douglass was hopeful that things would change, slavery would be abolished, and the United States would live up to its ideals.

On the evening of November 4, 2008, Barack Obama's election was a manifestation of the nation living up to the ideals Frederick Douglass had felt it capable of more than 150 years earlier. His reelection was an even further ratification of the ideals Douglass thought possible. Although there is still a long way to go on the "long steady march" toward racial equality, the ability of Barack Obama to be elected and then reelected president of the United States in the present electoral system says a lot about the ability of the system to produce outcomes that a majority of the people in the country favor. Moreover, his election highlights the significance of the registration and voting of Blacks, Latinos, Asian Americans, and American Indians. Maybe the country is finally on the path toward "We the People" that Douglass envisioned. With the election of Donald J. Trump as the 45th President of the United States will all of the promise and accomplishments of President Obama be reversed and the gains made by Blacks, Latinos, Asian Americans, American Indians and LGBTQ citizens be reversed? Is the United States entering a second Nadir of the political influence of citizens of color?

REVIEW QUESTIONS

1. What are the purposes of elections?
2. How does the Electoral College work?
3. Why has money become so central to presidential campaigns?
4. How do structural inequalities result in differential voter registration and voter turnout rates?
5. Why was President Obama's reelection campaign for the presidency successful?

KEY TERMS

Air War p. 486

Bipartisan Campaign Reform Act (BCRA) p. 487

Closed Primary p. 471

Debates p. 486

Direct Primaries p. 471

Elections p. 468

General Elections p. 480

Ground War p. 486

Help America Vote Act p. 500

Majority p. 472

National Voter Registration Act p. 498

Nomination Petitions p. 480

Open Primary p. 472

Opposition Research p. 490

Pledged Delegates p. 469

Plurality p. 472

Political Independents p. 471

Proportional Representation p. 481

Public Funding p. 488

Runoff Primary p. 472

Soft Money p. 488

Voting-Age Population (VAP) p. 497

Voting-Eligible Population (VEP) p. 497

Winner-Take-All p. 481

readings

ADDITIONAL READINGS

Paula D. McClain and Joseph Stewart Jr., *"Can We All Get along?": Racial and Ethnic Minorities in American Politics*, 6th ed. (Boulder: Westview Press, 2014).

> This book provides an overview of the history, political attitudes, and behaviors of America's principal racial minority groups.

Tali Mendelberg, *The Race Card: Campaign Strategy, Implicit Messages, and the Norm of Equality* (Princeton, NJ: Princeton University Press, 2001).

> This book studies the use of race as a campaign strategy and its effect on voters.

Ruy A. Teixeira, *The Disappearing American Voter* (Washington, DC: Brookings Institution, 1992).

> This book analyzes the factors that contribute to low voter turnout in the United States.

Sidney Verba, Kay Lehman Schlozman, and Henry E. Brady, *Voice and Equality: Civic Voluntarism in American Politics* (Cambridge, MA: Harvard University Press, 1995).

> This is a landmark study of various aspects of political participation, such as voting and volunteer activities, of the American public.

Ronald W. Walters, *Freedom Is Not Enough: Black Voters, Black Candidates, and American Presidential Politics* (Boulder: Rowman & Littlefield, 2007).

> This is a study of the importance of Black voters to presidential election outcomes.

Michael S. Lewis-Beck, Helmut Northpoth, William G. Jacoby, and Herbert F. Weisberg, *The American Voter Revisited* (Ann Arbor: University of Michigan, 2008).

> This book replicates the approach of the original 1960 *The American Voter* with a focus on the 2000 and 2004 elections.

The Making of Domestic and Foreign Policy: Summing Up American Government in Black and White

Denver police officers arrest a man who sold crack cocaine to an undercover officer, a decoy, during a sting operation. The man took police for a short foot chase, and police officers in the background are looking for money that the suspect ditched. Since the 1980s, prison terms for crack cocaine offenses have been longer than for powder cocaine offenses, a policy that has largely affected African Americans. As a result of political pressure, the policy has been changed by bringing the sentences for the two offenses more into balance.

I n 1994, Edward James Clary, a young Black male, was facing federal district court Judge Clyde Cahill in St. Louis, Missouri, to be sentenced after pleading guilty to possession of 67.76 grams of crack cocaine. Federal drug laws required that Clary be sentenced to a minimum of ten years in prison, even though it would take one hundred times the amount of powder cocaine to receive the same sentence. Edward Clary was not the first person to face such a stringent mandatory minimum sentence, and Judge Cahill was not the first federal judge who would regret imposing such an unjust sentence, especially with the disparity between crack cocaine and powder cocaine sentences. But this case is remarkable because Judge Cahill was one of the first federal judges who disregarded the federal mandatory minimum sentence. Instead of the mandatory ten-year sentence, he gave Clary only four years.

Judge Cahill, who is African American, wrote a lengthy explanation of his departure from the required sentence. The gist of Judge Cahill's opinion was that because African Americans are more likely than Whites to be arrested and prosecuted for crack cocaine, the sentencing disparities between crack and powder cocaine result in racial discrimination in violation of the Fourteenth Amendment equal protection clause. Judge Cahill's densely researched opinion demonstrated that media hype framed crack cocaine as a "Black problem." This media frenzy frightened the public, which then influenced Congress and the president to respond with harsh criminal sentences against crack cocaine users. Judge Cahill's opinion also provided convincing quantitative evidence that most crack cocaine defendants were Black. In short, Judge Cahill attributed the sentencing disparity to unconscious racism among Americans and their political leaders.[1] However, an appeals court reinstated Clary's ten-year prison sentence.[2]

intro

Edward Clary is just one example among thousands of Black males who received disproportionately long prison sentences over the next two decades. A 2010 study demonstrated the overall racial disparities this policy had caused. The average sentence for crack cocaine had been nine years and seven months, whereas the average sentence for powder cocaine had been seven years and three months. Moreover, 79 percent of people sentenced to prison for crack were African American, compared *to only 10 percent of whom were White and 10 percent were Latino. As a result of lobbying from a disparate coalition of civil rights organizations, civil liberties organizations, and even judges, Congress passed the Fair Sentencing Act of 2010, which reduced significantly, but did not erase, the disparity between crack and powder cocaine sentences.3*

This story illustrates the complexities of policymaking in the United States. Policymaking refers to the actions that the government actually takes. There are two kinds of policies in American government: domestic policy and foreign policy. **Domestic policy** *includes the laws, regulations, and programs that directly affect people living in the United States. It includes economic and fiscal concerns, infrastructure, criminal law, health care, housing, education, civil rights, and civil liberties.* **Foreign policy** *is made up of those laws, rules, and programs that affect the relations of the United States with other nations. It includes diplomatic relations, international trade and economics, human rights, global health, national security, and defense.*

Clary's story also demonstrates that policymaking is a dynamic process that occurs across different stages. Media sensationalism and public hysteria over the dangers of crack cocaine convinced public officials to establish the disparate sentences for possession of crack and powder cocaine. Merely enacting a sentencing policy does not ensure that it will be followed, however, and as this story shows, Judge Cahill refused to implement the mandatory minimum sentence for crack cocaine. Implementation is just one of several stages in the policymaking process. In this chapter, we cover all of the stages of policymaking: the agenda-setting stage; the enactment stage, which includes formulation and adoption; and the postformulation stages of implementation and evaluation. (We define these terms as they appear in the chapter.)

In addition to covering the stages of domestic and foreign policymaking, this chapter ties together the preceding chapters of this book. The framework of American government—that is, the Constitution, federalism, civil rights, and civil liberties—provides the context for foreign and domestic policymaking. Moreover, American political institutions—Congress, the presidency, the bureaucracy, and the judiciary—and each aspect of political behavior—public opinion, the media, social movements, interest groups, political parties, and elections—are relevant throughout the policymaking process.

Although domestic and foreign policymaking encompass a wide variety of issues areas, many domestic and foreign policies emphasize minority-group politics. Throughout this book, we have shown how minority-group politics intersects with every aspect of American government. Consequently, this chapter focuses on foreign and domestic policies that affect racial and ethnic minorities.

Domestic Policy Laws, rules, and programs that directly affect people living in the United States.

Foreign Policy Laws, rules, and programs that affect the relationship between the United States and other nations.

Agenda-Setting

Agenda-setting refers to the part of the policymaking process in which certain issues reach a level of public concern that attracts the attention of government officials. The term agenda carries different meanings, and scholars of public policymaking conceive of agenda-setting on several levels. The **agenda universe**

Agenda-Setting The stage in the policymaking process in which certain issues reach a level of public concern that attracts the attention of government officials.

Agenda Universe All possible legitimate issues that could be brought to the attention of the public and possibly of policymakers.

refers to all possible issues that could be brought to the attention of public policymakers. By possible, we mean those ideas that are socially acceptable in American society. For example, even though there are groups that would like to reinstate de jure segregation (e.g., neo-Nazis and the Ku Klux Klan), those goals are not socially acceptable and are therefore not part of the agenda universe.

The next level is the **systemic agenda**, which refers to the issues that policymakers perceive as worthy of their attention and within their authority. Depending on the political and legal climate, issues move from the agenda universe to the systemic agenda. If an issue merits sufficient attention once on the systemic agenda, it proceeds to the **institutional agenda**, where government officials acknowledge that the issue requires their attention. Because government institutions possess finite time and resources, reaching the institutional agenda is an extremely competitive process. In the last stage of the agenda-setting process, the **decision agenda**, a government body resolves to act on an issue.[4]

The key to agenda-setting is to move an issue from the agenda universe to the decision agenda. Many aspects of American politics are important in advancing policies through the agenda-setting process. For example, when political parties include certain issues in their party platforms, those issues are likely to move through the agenda-setting process. The Democratic Party platform in 1948 insisted on ending racial and ethnic discrimination, which engendered a public walkout of Southern Democrats. This dispute between progressives and racists within the Democratic Party certainly highlighted the issue of racial and ethnic discrimination and brought it to the attention of the American public and politicians.

Likewise, the actions of political institutions (Congress, the executive branch, the bureaucracy, and the judiciary) can set the agenda. For example, the failures of the Bush administration (the executive branch) and the Federal Emergency Management Agency (the bureaucracy) during the aftermath of Hurricane Katrina highlighted the issue of African American poverty in New Orleans. Despite the influence of political parties and institutions, it is social movements, individual interest groups, and the media that are most crucial to moving policy items through the agenda-setting process.

Social Movements, Interest Groups, and Agenda-Setting

Social movements and individual interest groups are crucial factors in agenda-setting, especially in minority-group politics. For example, a major goal of the Civil Rights Movement was to set the domestic policy agenda to highlight the discrimination minorities faced and the need to pass meaningful civil rights laws. Members of the Civil Rights Movement staged large-scale protests to highlight the discrimination they endured. Bus boycotts in Southern cities during the 1950s highlighted the injustices of segregation in public transportation. The March on Washington in 1963 demonstrated to many

Systemic Agenda The set of issues that policymakers perceive as worthy of their attention.

Institutional Agenda The set of issues that government officials recognize require their attention.

Decision Agenda The set of issues that a government body formally resolves to address.

Americans who had been unaware of racial discrimination in the South the importance of enacting policies to guarantee civil rights and voting rights to African Americans.

Other racial and ethnic minority groups used protests to set the agenda for civil rights policies. In March 1968, Mexican-American students at Lincoln High School in Los Angeles staged a student strike that lasted for more than a week, and this action sparked attention to the civil rights concerns of Latinos, especially Mexican Americans in the Southwest. The American Indian Movement (AIM) staged more dramatic protests to highlight the injustices that American Indians experienced. In 1972, members of AIM seized the Washington, DC, headquarters of the Bureau of Indian Affairs, and the following year AIM members engaged in an armed standoff with federal agents at Wounded Knee in the Pine Ridge Reservation in South Dakota. Native Hawaiian movements have highlighted income inequality in Hawaii and the ways in which their traditional culture has been hijacked by Americans since Hawaii became a state.[5]

Interest groups can also set the policy agenda without engaging in protests. For example, many racial and ethnic minority interest groups initiate, finance, and manage litigation when the elected branches of government are not receptive to their claims. By sponsoring this litigation campaign, these groups set the agenda in the federal judiciary. The most significant example of an interest group that litigates is the National Association for the Advancement of Colored People Legal Defense and Educational Fund (NAACP-LDF), which has set the U.S. Supreme Court's agenda by bringing cases concerning racial discrimination in housing, voting, and, most notably, education.[6] Groups advocating on behalf of other ethnic and racial minorities also set the agenda for the judiciary by sponsoring cases. These groups include the Mexican American Legal Defense and Educational Fund, the Native American Rights Fund, and the Asian Americans Advancing Justice.[7]

Interest groups also play a key role in agenda-setting for foreign policy. Many interest groups are extremely concerned about foreign policy issues, such as international trade, war, national security, human rights, global health, and relations with particular nations. Racial and ethnic minority interest groups are especially concerned about America's relations with their members' nations of ancestral origin. For example, Amnesty International is a worldwide interest group that promotes human rights throughout the world. Its primary focus is to advocate on behalf of political prisoners throughout the world and against the use of torture. It also supports free expression and opposes the death penalty.[8] Since 2010 the African nation of Uganda passed several laws and took actions that criminalized homosexuality. Amnesty International has highlighted this issue as a fundamental violation of civil rights.[9] Likewise, since 1981 the Cuban American National Foundation is an interest group of Cuban Americans who seek to set the foreign policy agenda to promote democracy in Cuba.[10]

The Media and Agenda-Setting

The media are another significant influence on agenda-setting. Reporters, editors, and publishers control the content of coverage, and the amount of media exposure that an issue receives determines the extent to which it will advance through the agenda-setting process. Stories that are deemed interesting and profitable will receive extensive media coverage, and the policies involved in those stories will feature prominently on the agenda. Stories deemed unimportant will not receive media exposure, and those issues will be unlikely to attract sufficient public and political attention.

The media's coverage of the Civil Rights Movement during the 1960s demonstrates the key role that the media play in agenda-setting for domestic policy. As we discussed in Chapter 11, the media's televised coverage of key civil rights events set the agenda for many Americans who were otherwise uninformed about the hardships Blacks endured in the South. In fact, survey evidence demonstrates that Americans viewed civil rights as a more salient issue after the media covered significant events, such as the Montgomery bus boycott, the desegregation of Central High School in Little Rock, Arkansas, the sit-ins of the early 1960s, and the 1963 March on Washington. In 1965, television and newspaper coverage of the police brutality against civil rights activists at the Edmund Pettus Bridge in Selma, Alabama, especially increased public attention to civil rights issues. Nevertheless, many scholars argue that the media's impact on civil rights is overstated. In fact, the media often set the agenda in a way that reinforces negative stereotypes of African Americans.[11]

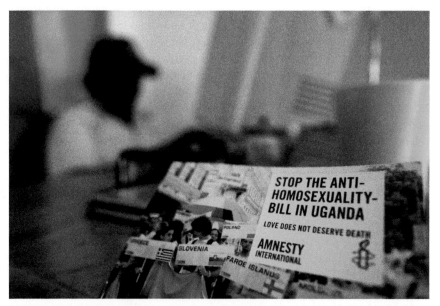

Amnesty International protest against severe anti-LGBT discrimination in Uganda. Amnesty International is an interest group that fights against human rights abuses throughout the world, including the human rights violations taking place in Uganda against LGBT people.

The media are especially important for bringing issues onto the foreign policy agenda, especially concerning human rights violations. By disseminating graphic images of people suffering as a result of famine or genocide (and often both), the media help to make Americans aware of a foreign policy issue about which they otherwise would have remained uninformed. These images often impel the American public to sympathize with the victims and demand that American foreign policy address the problem. For example, during the early 1990s televised coverage of the atrocities that Serbians committed against Bosnian Muslims placed on the agenda the question of whether Americans should economically or militarily intervene on behalf of the Bosnian Muslims.[12]

At the same time as the crisis in the Balkans, genocide and a humanitarian crisis were occurring in the tiny African nation of Rwanda, in which close to 1 million people were slaughtered and refugees overwhelmed neighboring countries. This human rights travesty initially received little media coverage in the United States, particularly in comparison to the Balkan region (which is in Europe). Consequently, it was not on the agenda of the American public. Media critic Tim Graham of MediaWatch notes that a lack of televised coverage of the atrocities in Rwanda ultimately led American policymakers to disregard the issue.[13]

American politicians and the media also influence the agenda in other nations, which in turn affects U.S. foreign policy. "Our Voices: President Obama's 2009 Cairo Speech" provides an excerpt from President Obama's 2009 speech at Cairo University in Egypt. Many people have credited this speech for inspiring the Arab Spring, a series of popular uprisings that overthrew Middle East dictators in 2011. However, detractors, such as conservative scholar Fouad Ajami, refer to that notion as a "myth."[14] Moreover, despite the deposing of these dictators, struggles still exist. For example, although in 2011, Hosni Mubarak was overthrown in Egypt after three decades of rule, and in 2012, Egyptians democratically elected Mohammed Morsi as president, the nation has still been wrought with problems. Morsi is a member of the controversial Muslim Brotherhood, a group that seeks to enact Muslim religious principles into law, and he tried to expand the power of the presidency and eliminate judicial review, which led to more rioting. Then, in early 2013, there was more rioting during the trial of former police officers accused of shooting protestors during the end of Mubarak's regime. These anti-Morsi protests intensified during the spring of 2013, and in July the Egyptian military removed Morsi from power.[15]

Policy Enactment

Once an issue has captured the attention of government leaders, the next stage in the policymaking process involves political actors considering the range of alternatives to best address the issue. This is the stage at which legislators actually make, or enact, the policy, and it entails two distinct steps. The **policy formulation** stage occurs after the government decides to act on a problem

Policy Formulation The stage in the policymaking process in which government actors draft a solution to a problem that they have recognized merits their attention.

our voices

President Obama's 2009 Cairo Speech

American politicians can set the agenda for other nations, which, in turn, affects U.S. foreign policy. For example, President Obama designed his 2009 speech in Cairo, Egypt, to convince the Muslim world that the United States was not an enemy of Islam, even though it would maintain its vigilant fight against terrorism. To substantiate his point, President Obama highlighted his multiethnic background, and his personal experience with Islam, the first U.S. president who could make that claim. He also emphasized the relevance of Islam throughout American history, and he publicly recognized the mistakes of the Iraq War. Finally, in his speech, President Obama stressed the importance of democracy and self-rule for Muslim nations.

There is some indication that the president's focus on democracy set the agenda in foreign nations because there have been popular uprisings in numerous Arab and Islamic nations. In 2011 citizens of Tunisia, Egypt, and Libya, especially youth, overthrew longtime dictators, in what is now called the Arab Spring. Despite the change in repressive regimes, civil unrest still exists in these nations. Moreover, since 2009, there have also been popular uprisings in Iran and Syria, but those governments successfully, albeit brutally, repressed protests. There is considerable debate over whether this speech is responsible for the Arab Spring, but there is no doubt that President Obama's speech and the foreign press coverage of it helped to set the agenda for the pursuit of democratic reform in that region.

Palestinians in Gaza City watch President Obama's Cairo speech. This speech is credited for helping to inspire the Arab Spring, in which popular protests led to the overthrow of longtime Arab dictators, although the progress toward democracy has been uneven and wrought with setbacks.

Remarks by the President on a New Beginning, Cairo University, Cairo, Egypt, June 4, 2009

. . . We meet at a time of great tension between the United States and Muslims around the world—tension rooted in historical forces that go beyond any current policy debate. The relationship between Islam and the West included centuries of coexistence and cooperation, but also conflict and religious wars. . . . Moreover, the sweeping change brought by modernity and globalization led many Muslims to view the West as hostile to the traditions of Islam.

Violent extremists have exploited these tensions in a small but potent minority of Muslims. The attacks of September 11, 2001, and the continued efforts of these extremists to engage in violence against civilians has led some in my country to view Islam as inevitably hostile to not only America and Western countries, but also to human rights.

I've come here to Cairo to seek a new beginning between the United States and Muslims around the world, one based on mutual interest and mutual respect, and one based upon the truth that America and Islam are not exclusive and need not be in competition. . . . That is what I will try to do today—to speak to the truth as best I can, humbled by the task before us, and firm in my belief that the interests we share as human beings are far more powerful than the forces that drive us apart.

. . . Now part of this conviction is rooted in my own experience. I am a Christian, but my father came from a Kenyan family that includes generations of Muslims. As a boy, I spent several years in Indonesia and heard the call of the azaan at the break of dawn and at the fall of dusk. As a young man, I worked in Chicago communities where many found dignity and peace in their Muslim faith.

. . . I also know that Islam has always been part of America's story. . . . And since our founding, American Muslims have enriched the United States. . . . And when the first Muslim American was recently elected to Congress, he took the oath to defend our Constitution using the same Holy Koran that one of our founding fathers—Thomas Jefferson—kept in his personal library.

. . . The fourth issue that I will address is democracy. . . . I know there has been controversy about the promotion of democracy in recent years, and much of this controversy is connected to the war in Iraq. So let me be clear: No system of government can or should be imposed on one nation by any other.

. . . That does not lessen my commitment, however, to governments that reflect the will of the people. Each nation gives life to this principle in its own way, grounded in the traditions of its own people.

America does not presume to know what is best for everyone, just as we would not presume to pick the outcome of a peaceful election. But I do have an unyielding belief that all people yearn for certain things: the ability to speak your mind and have a say in how you are governed, confidence in the rule of law and the equal administration of justice, government that is transparent and does not steal from the people, the freedom to live as you choose. These are not just American ideas; they are human rights. And that is why we will support them everywhere.

Source: Adapted from the White House Office of the Press Secretary, "Remarks by the President on a New Beginning," June 4, 2009, http://www.whitehouse.gov/the_press_office/Remarks-by-the-President-at-Cairo-University-6-04-09, accessed July 29, 2016.

and needs to craft the best solution from the various available alternatives. During the **policy adoption** stage the policy is actually enacted. Government institutions (Congress, the presidency, the bureaucracy, and the courts) play a significant role in policy formulation and adoption, although interest groups, social movements, the media, and political parties are important as well. The policy formulation and adoption stages are especially crucial in foreign and domestic policies that are important to racial and ethnic minorities.

Policy Adoption The stage in the policymaking process in which the policy is actually enacted.

Before proceeding to the discussion of the formulation and adoption stages, we should point out that many issues reach the agenda-setting stage but do not make it to the formulation stage. For example, after Hurricane Katrina struck the Gulf Coast in August 2005, the resulting flooding in New Orleans set the agenda for the need to address the de facto segregation and harsh living conditions of the low-income, largely Black residents of New Orleans. Media coverage of the aftermath of the hurricane revealed to Americans the suffering endured by the residents who lacked the means to evacuate. This focus brought the issue of inner-city poverty and the lack of adequate housing to the forefront of the agenda, and many observers believed that the American government would begin to formulate policies to address this problem.

However, by 2008, the UN Human Rights Council found that poverty and discrimination had still not been addressed, and, in fact, some policies, such as the demolition of public housing, had exacerbated the problems that impoverished and mostly Black Gulf Coast residents faced. Federal and city officials ignored the report.[16]

Policy Formulation

After governments decide to act on a problem, they need to craft the best solution from the various alternatives available to them. This policy formation stage takes place for the most part within political institutions and outside of public view. Members of Congress (and their staff) write bills they plan to introduce formally, presidents and key assistants develop executive orders, independent regulatory commissioners craft rules, and federal judges, with the help of lawyers and law clerks, write opinions.

The extent to which formulated policies favor minorities depends largely, albeit not exclusively, on minority representation in the respective institution. For example, a pressing foreign policy issue concerns the American response to the genocide occurring in the Darfur region of Sudan. People living in the region have been beset with drought and famine, but recently their suffering has been exacerbated by war between Arab Muslim militias backed by the government and non-Arab Africans. More problematic are the numerous reports that government-supported gangs have systematically tortured, raped, and murdered thousands of innocent people.

It has been African-American members of Congress who have taken the lead on formulating American foreign policy to deal with the genocide. The Darfur Genocide Accountability Act of 2005 was introduced into the House of Representatives. The act not only provides for sanctions, such as travel

Sudanese refugees wait to collect water supplies at a water station in Zamzam refugee camp on the outskirts of the Darfur town of el Fasher, Sudan, April 9, 2010, ahead of the April 11 multiparty general elections in Sudan. American foreign policy has sought to end the conflict and famine in Sudan, and although there had been a promise of peace, conditions have deteriorated.

restrictions and economic restrictions, against the government of Sudan, but also authorizes the president to use military force to stop the genocide. This policy was formulated and introduced by the late African-American representative Donald Payne (D-NJ). Four of the other seven members primarily responsible for formulating this policy are also African American.[17] These efforts appeared eventually to pay off when a peace agreement was achieved in 2011, but in 2012 U.S. Ambassador Dane Smith reported that conditions in Darfur had worsened, instead of improving.[18] Moreover, problems with Islamic militants spread to other African nations, most notably Mali. Although in 2013 French military forces defeated Islamic militants in Mali, experts fear that the fighters would hide within the nation and launch a guerilla war.[19]

In the area of domestic policy, Latinos and Asian Americans are concerned about immigration and the rights of undocumented immigrants. For example, in 2015 Representative Luis Gutiérrez (D-IL) introduced a bill that would provide the health care benefits of the Affordable Care Act (aka "Obamacare") for undocumented immigrants.[20] This bill had only six cosponsors—two African Americans (Yvette Clarke (D-NY) and Marc Veasey (D-TX), one Latino (Raúl Grijalva D-AZ), one Asian American (Judy Chu D-CA), and two whites (Zoe Lofgren (D-CA) and Janice Schakowsky (D-IL). Ultimately, the bill died in committee and it will not become law during this legislative session.[21]

Despite the generally closed nature of policy formulation, the public does have input into the process. Political parties, which allow for limited public participation, often try to influence policy formulation by offering in their platforms general outlines of policies the party wants passed. Both party platforms in 2016 outlined foreign and domestic policies that could affect minority-group politics.

On the domestic front, the 2016 Democratic Party platform articulated policies to protect racial and ethnic minorities' voting rights, including keeping early voting, same-day registration, and voting by mail. It also seeks to "rectify" the *Shelby County v. Holder* decision that ended preclearance for regions with a history of voting discrimination (see Chapters 3 and 5). The platform also intends to close the wealth gap between minorities and whites, financially help the people of Puerto Rico, support statehood for Washington, DC, provide more resources for minority serving colleges and universities, and end "systemic racism" (the idea that racism is inexorably mixed into American political, economic, and social institutions). An entire section on indigenous tribes addresses enhancing sovereignty and increasing health care. The Democratic platform also endorses providing a path to citizenship for undocumented immigrants and supports President Obama's policies concerning undocumented immigrants (see Chapter 5). On foreign policy, the Democratic Platform supports more aid for Africa and acceptance of some Muslim refugees from the civil war in Syria.[22] The 2016 Republican Party platform advocates policies that require photo identification to vote and oppose statehood for Washington, DC. It supports statehood for Puerto Rico and sovereignty for indigenous tribes. On the issue of immigration, the Republican platform endorses policies that would cause undocumented immigrants to leave the United States, build a wall along the border of the United States and Mexico, and oppose so-called "sanctuary cities," in which local law enforcement agencies will not report undocumented immigrants in order to ensure that communities cooperate with law enforcement.[23]

The public can also offer direct input into policy formulation. For example, during the early 1980s Congress created the Commission on Wartime Relocation to investigate the internment of Japanese Americans during World War II and suggest policies to redress that severe injustice. The commission was critical in the passage of the Civil Liberties Act of 1988, which apologized to and compensated the victims of internment. Many Japanese-American activists testified before the commission (and even before Congress), and the commission also took essential testimony from the actual victims of the internment. Their testimony helped to shape this important policy in the area of minority-group politics.[24]

Administrative Procedure Act A federal law that requires administrative agencies to publish proposed rules and allow the public to offer comment on them before they go into effect.

Additionally, the **Administrative Procedure Act**, which was first passed in 1946 and has been amended several times since then, requires that any administrative agency seeking to formulate a policy must first promulgate the policy as a proposed rule. Then, for a thirty-day period, the public can comment on the proposed rule. The agency must consider those comments before the rule goes into effect, but it does not need to change the policy in response to public comments or even overwhelming public opposition.[25] Although these opportunities are open to the general public, most people do not avail themselves of this chance to contribute to policy formulation. Instead, well-financed interest groups usually provide comments.

Think Tanks Interest groups that focus on research and scholarly analysis of issues relevant to the people they represent.

Interest groups can also formulate policies, which are then presented to political institutions. **Think tanks** are interest groups that research, analyze, and design policies to address specific issues, and they play a prominent role in policy formulation. Think tanks are composed of intellectuals and scholars, and, although most think tanks are officially nonpartisan, they do harbor ideological biases. In fact, many think tanks focus on formulating polices that are important to racial and ethnic minority groups. For example, the Joint Center for Political and Economic Studies (JCPES) is a think tank that focuses on issues important to all racial and ethnic minorities, with a special emphasis on African Americans. The JCPES publishes reports that make specific policy recommendations to improve the political and economic life of Blacks and other minorities.[26] In 2012, JCPES published a report that found that health outcomes in heavily African-American areas of rural Mississippi were far worse than most other places in the United States. Life expectancy in that region was equal to impoverished nations such as Sri Lanka, Ethiopia, and the Dominican Republic. The report advocated specific policy proposals to improve health, such as providing vouchers to purchase vegetables at farmers markets, increasing transportation to supermarkets that sell healthy foods, and enhancing opportunities for exercise.[27]

Interest groups also formulate policies in the federal judiciary by sponsoring litigation and submitting briefs. Judges read these briefs and often incorporate them into their decisions. In other words, groups sponsoring litigation not only set the agenda, but through their legal arguments and briefs they also help to formulate judicial policies. Even if groups do not participate directly in a case, they can still influence Supreme Court policymaking through *amicus curiae* briefs. These briefs allow parties that are not directly involved in the case to submit a brief to advocate for a particular outcome or suggest a legal policy for the court to formulate. For example, in the crucial 2003 affirmative action cases *Gratz v. Bollinger* and *Grutter v. Bollinger* (see Chapter 5) 107 *amicus curiae* briefs were filed.[28]

Policy Adoption

Merely formulating a policy does not guarantee its existence. The policy has to be approved by the appropriate government institution(s). Legislatures must pass and executives must sign laws for these policies to take effect, or a majority of appellate court judges must agree on a decision for it to take effect. Recall from the preceding definition that policies are actually enacted at the policy adoption stage, and although many policies are formulated, not all are adopted.

Even though most policy adoption takes place within political institutions, the public is still concerned with exactly what a policy will be when it is passed. Members of the public communicate their views through the activities of social movements, interest groups, and the media. Many controversial policies take a long time to be enacted, so members of the public have ample opportunity to mobilize in opposition to a policy or to compel major changes to it.

The policy adoption process often requires political leaders to compromise. For example, during the 1980s, a key foreign policy issue concerned the U.S. response to apartheid in South Africa, which inflicted horrendous suffering on Blacks living there. Many Americans, especially African Americans, wanted to enact sanctions against the White-controlled government of South Africa. These sanctions would have effectively ended American economic ties with South Africa by banning imports or exports between the two nations.

By 1986, there was widespread support for a sanctions bill, and a significant sanctions bill was formulated in the House and Senate. But to secure passage of the bill, members of Congress agreed to change the originally formulated bill by exempting grain sales from sanctions because senators from farm states wanted to keep the grain market open. Another change deleted a provision from the bill that would have required the president to sell U.S. gold reserves to lower the price of gold, a key component of the South African economy.[29] The sanctions bill was passed into law, and Congress overrode President Ronald Reagan's veto. The compromises were essential for the policy to be adopted.

Compromise is even a feature of policy adoption when the U.S. Supreme Court makes policy, which is illustrated in the Court's policy on affirmative action in education. In the 1978 case of *Regents of the University California v. Bakke,* a White applicant to the University of California at Davis Medical School challenged the university's policy of reserving a quota of slots for minority applicants after he was denied admission despite having a higher grades and test scores than minorities who were admitted. Four justices believed that public schools should not be allowed in any way to use race as an admission factor, whereas four other justices were willing to uphold the University of California's quota system.

It was Associate Justice Lewis Powell's compromise opinion that became the Court's policy on affirmative action. Powell ruled that quota systems violate the Fourteenth Amendment equal protection clause—a majority of the Court did want to overrule the use of firm quotas for minority applicants. Justice Powell also allowed the use of racial minority status as a benefit in deciding admissions—a majority of the Court was willing to uphold the general use of affirmative action.[30] In 2003, this compromise policy was upheld in *Grutter v. Bollinger*,[31] which concerned the University of Michigan Law School's admission process.

If the policymaking institution is unable to reach a compromise, the policy will not be adopted. For example, in 2007 a bipartisan group of senators formulated a new policy to overhaul the nation's immigration laws. This policy would have provided more money for the border patrol, funded the building of a wall between the United States and Mexico, and increased enforcement and penalties against employers who knowingly hire illegal immigrants. The bill would also have put in place a process for illegal immigrants to become U.S. citizens and would have established a guest worker system for foreigners to work legally in the United States. This compromise was supported by congressional leaders in both parties and the Bush administration. Two key Latino politicians, Senator Mel Martinez (R-FL) and Secretary of Commerce Carlos Gutierrez, led the fight to adopt this policy.

However, conservatives and labor unions opposed the citizenship and guest worker provisions, and environmentalists and advocates for immigrants opposed the emphasis on border security and the building of a border wall. After a series of parliamentary maneuvers between senators supporting and senators opposing the bill, the opponents in the Senate successfully filibustered the bill. As a result, the policy was not adopted.[32] Although this immigration reform policy was not enacted, the issue still persists. In early 2013 a bipartisan group of U.S. Representatives and Senators formulated a plan that would provide a way for undocumented residents to gain legal status, and at about the same time President Obama proposed a similar policy.[33] Again, the compromise was never reached; therefore the bill never passed.

Moreover, single individuals, such as congressional committee chairs, possess unilateral authority to obstruct the policy adoption process. During the 1950s, members of Congress, such as House Rules Committee chair Howard Smith (D-VA) and Senate Judiciary Committee chair James Eastland (D-MS), prevented the adoption of civil rights bills by not reporting them from their committees.[34]

Through executive orders (see Chapter 7), presidents are able to adopt policies unilaterally without having to compromise with other branches.

Flanked by labor leaders, including AFL-CIO President Richard Trumka, President and Executive Director of Asian American Justice Center Mee Moua, President and CEO of Leadership Conference on Civil and Human Rights Wade Henderson, and Managing Director of United We Dream Cristina Jimenez, President and CEO of National Council of la Raza Janet Murguia speaks to the press after a meeting with U.S. President Barack Obama at the White House, February 5, 2013, in Washington, DC. Obama was meeting with labor leaders to discuss issues including immigration reform, the economy, and deficit reduction. Both Obama and Congress have formulated immigration reform policies, although it is unclear if the policies will be adopted.

An executive order is a directive that the president issues to subordinates, and many of these orders influence public policy, especially in the area of minority politics. For example, during World War II President Franklin Roosevelt issued two executive orders that greatly shaped the fate of racial minorities. Executive Order 8802 forbade racial and ethnic discrimination in the federal government and in defense companies that contracted with the federal government. Executive Order 9066 established the policy of forcibly removing Japanese Americans to internment camps.[35] In July 2012 President Obama issued two executive orders that influenced foreign policy. Executive Order 13619 prevented financial transactions in the United States for any Burmese (a nation in Asia) official who committed human rights abuses. Executive Order 13620 limited exports from the African nation of Somalia because of its human rights abuses.[36]

Although many observers find policy adoption debates to be dry, they can sometimes become heated, especially over controversial issues. There were particularly virulent debates during the process of adopting President Obama's health care reform policy in 2010, especially with many opponents of health care reform focusing on President Obama's race. "Evaluating Equality: Racism and the Public Debate over the Adoption of Health Care Reform Policies" examines this issue in more detail.

evaluating equality

Racial Prejudice and the Public Debate over the Adoption of Health Care Reform Policies

In 2009, President Barack Obama and members of Congress formulated different policies to reform the health care system. These policies contained a variety of proposals, such as reducing health care costs, preventing health insurance companies from denying coverage to people with existing illnesses or canceling coverage to people who get sick, limiting lawsuits against negligent doctors, mandating that every person obtain health insurance, and developing a government-run health insurance option for people to obtain coverage. Given the significance and complexity of this issue, the adoption phase for health care reform has been extremely chaotic.

As members of Congress traveled to their districts during the summer of 2009, the debate over the adoption of a specific set of health care reform policies intensified among the American public. Many members of Congress held "town hall" meetings with their constituents to discuss the issue, and interest groups mobilized both supporters and opponents of these reforms to attend these meetings to express their views. Normally, these town hall meetings are fairly low key, but in summer 2009 these meetings concerning health care reform were extremely boisterous. Initially, opponents of the heath care reforms shouted down members of Congress who supported health care reform, but then supporters of the reforms attended meetings to counter these opponents. Vicious shouting matches and occasional violence ensued.

Vigorous public fights over policy are certainly not new to American

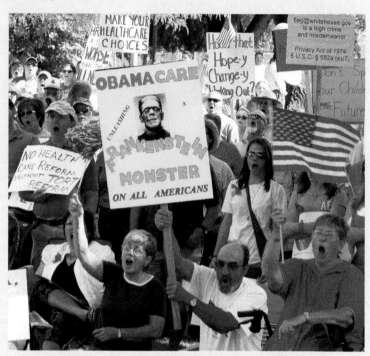

Formulating and adopting major policy changes, such as health insurance reform, can inflame passions among supporters and opponents of the policy. Here, opponents of the Democratic health care reform proposals attend a protest, with signs lambasting health care reform as well as President Obama. Many anti-health-care-reform protestors have referred to President Obama in nasty and racist terms. The health insurance industry, which strongly opposes reform, has provided the financial backing for these protests.

politics, but the specter of racism has emerged in this debate. Because President Obama is Black and is a major proponent of health care reform, much of the opposition to health care has undertones based on racial prejudice.

There have been subtle examples of this prejudice. For example, many protesters at Tea Party and anti-health-care-reform rallies display signs or t-shirts with the words "I Want My Country Back," which suggest that

these people feel they have lost their country because the president is different from them. Likewise, some health care reform opponents claim inaccurately that President Obama is not the legitimate president because he was born in Kenya and not Hawaii, again undermining the legitimacy of a duly elected president who happens to be Black.

An extremely disturbing incident occurred on September 9, 2009, when President Obama formally addressed

Congress to argue for his health care reform proposals. After the president contended that illegal immigrants would not receive benefits under his plan, Representative Joe Wilson (R-SC) shouted, "You lie." Members of Congress are expected to be extremely respectful to the president during a formal address, even if they disagree with his message. Many people interpreted Representative Wilson's outrageously disrespectful interruption to be based on racial prejudice.

There were even blatant examples of racism. Most notably, in July 2009, Dr. David McKalip, a politically active St. Petersburg, Florida, neurosurgeon and head of the Pinellas County Medical Association, disseminated an email opposing health care reform. His email contained an extremely prejudiced and offensive caricature of President Obama dressed as a stereotypical African witch doctor. After public outcry over the photograph, Dr. McKalip apologized and assumed a much lower profile in the debate, but the offensive message was still clear.

The subtle and blatant racial prejudice underlying the health care reform debate became so controversial that former Democratic president Jimmy Carter directly accused the opponents of health care reform of being racists. Other political leaders disagreed. Former Democratic president Bill Clinton argued that the vitriol against the health care reform proposals would be the same if President Obama were White. Members of the Obama administration, including President Obama himself, downplayed the significance of racism in the debate. The intensity of the debate over health care reform abated by 2011, and although it was not central, the issue of health care still emerged during the 2012 election campaign.

- Research newspaper articles and Internet sites that cover the debate over the adoption and implementation of health care reform policies.
- After conducting this research, debate whether racism motivated the opponents of the president's health care reform proposals.
- As you debate this issue, take note of the race and ethnicity of your classmates on each side of the debate.

Postenactment Stages

Despite obstacles in the agenda-setting, policy formulation, and policy adoption stages, the government often will establish policies. The policymaking process does not end there, however. Adopted policies cannot accomplish their goals unless the government and even citizens ensure that the policies are carried out. This stage of the policymaking process is known as **policy implementation**, the process by which government actors and even private citizens execute a policy that has been adopted.

Furthermore, the policymaking process does not cease once a policy is put into effect. After a sufficient time, the government and private citizens need to ensure that the policy has achieved its desired effect. **Policy evaluation** determines the extent to which those goals have been achieved and suggests ways to improve the policy. It is often the case that policy implementation and evaluation intersect with minority-group politics.

Policy Implementation

During the process of policy implementation, government officials must ensure that money is spent and regulations are enforced. The government agencies and officials charged with implementing policies enjoy considerable

Policy Implementation The stage in the policymaking process in which government actors and even private citizens carry out enacted policies.

Policy Evaluation The stage in the policymaking process in which government actors and private citizens determine whether an implemented policy is achieving its intended effect.

discretion; that is, policies are not necessarily implemented according to the intent of those who formulated and adopted them.

Implementation entails the spending of money that has been appropriated or budgeted. Generally, after Congress appropriates money, which is policy adoption, the executive branch and bureaucracy are responsible for laying out the actual expenditures. Occasionally, policy implementation can be affected when money that is targeted to fund policy is not fully spent.

For example, the 2001 No Child Left Behind Act requires testing of schoolchildren as a way to increase their performance. By 2004, school districts throughout the nation had adopted the testing mandates, but according to many estimates, the executive branch underfunded the implementation of this policy by about $9 billion. As a result, many schools had to divert money from other crucial programs to pay for the testing, which greatly affected the more impoverished districts containing a large number of racial and ethnic minorities. Representative Robert Scott (D-VA) estimated that the Richmond, Virginia, school district alone lost about $9 million because this policy was not fully funded.[37] In 2012, President Obama announced that some states were exempted from the strict controls in No Child Left Behind because they had enacted their own reforms designed to improve education outcomes.[38]

Moreover, by spending money, the executive branch can shape how a policy actually affects people. For example, the President's Emergency Plan for AIDS Relief (PEPFAR) is a policy designed to spend billions of dollars to treat and prevent HIV/AIDS in Africa and the Caribbean. When Republican President George W. Bush implemented the program, his administration insisted on emphasizing controversial abstinence-only programs as a way to prevent the spread of the disease. However, in 2010 then Secretary of State Hillary Clinton announced that the Democratic Obama administration would embrace all forms of AIDS prevention, including condoms and sex education, and not solely abstinence.[39]

The executive branch also implements policies by enforcing laws passed by Congress. For example, the Civil Rights Act of 1964 created the Equal Employment Opportunity Commission (EEOC) to enforce civil rights laws, but the chair of the commission, whom the president appoints, possesses discretion in how to enforce these laws. President Ronald Reagan chose the conservative Clarence Thomas, now a U.S. Supreme Court justice, to chair the EEOC. Unlike his predecessors, Thomas did not rely on statistical evidence as proof of discrimination, and by declining to act on discrimination complaints he allowed thousands of cases to lapse.[40] Civil rights laws were enforced less vigorously during the 1980s than they had been previously.

Policy implementation is especially important for the Supreme Court. After the Court adopts a policy—that is, issues a ruling—it relies on others to ensure that the ruling is carried out. Lower court judges often implement the

Supreme Court's rulings. For example, in 1955 the U.S. Supreme Court adopted a policy in its *Brown v. Board of Education of Topeka, Kansas,* known as *Brown II,* decision that required states to desegregate their public schools "with all deliberate speed."[41] The Supreme Court relied on federal district judges to implement this policy.

Although federal district judges are instruments of the national government, they operate entirely within their region and are often subject to local political pressure. When enforcing the "all deliberate speed" mandate, some judges, such as Frank M. Johnson of Alabama, withstood local political pressure from Whites and used their authority to ensure integration in the public schools under their jurisdiction. Other judges, such as T. Whitfield Davidson, who presided over Dallas, Texas, vehemently opposed integration and refused to implement the decision.[42] Consequently, the rate of integration varied throughout the South.

The executive branch is extremely crucial to the implementation of the Supreme Court's policies. After the Supreme Court's *Brown v. Board of Education* opinions, presidents Dwight Eisenhower and John Kennedy used federal military force to ensure that schools were actually integrated. If the president chooses not to enforce a Supreme Court decision, the decision has no effect. For example, in *Worcester v. Georgia,* the Supreme Court in 1832 ruled that a national government treaty with the Cherokee Nation overrode a Georgia law forbidding non-Cherokees from residing on Cherokee land.[43] The decision favored the national government's agreement with the Cherokee Nation over state control, but President Andrew Jackson opposed this decision, and he refused to enforce it.[44]

Local governments often influence policy implementation. For example, after Hurricane Katrina destroyed homes in the Gulf Coast region, FEMA's Individual Assistance Program was adopted to provide temporary trailer housing for displaced people. The policy allows for trailers to be placed on people's property or in existing trailer parks. The policy also requires FEMA to build new trailer parks to accommodate the remaining displaced people. The policy mandates that FEMA search for appropriate places to build the trailer parks and get approval from local governments.

Although local government officials understand that the new trailer parks are necessary to house displaced citizens, these officials generally oppose having the trailer parks built in their jurisdictions because the parks have a reputation for increasing crime and lowering existing property values. As a result, wealthy and powerful local governments are able to influence FEMA's implementation of the Individual Assistance Program in a way that avoids trailer parks in their jurisdiction. In fact, a study found that the more Blacks there were in an area, the greater was the chance that a new trailer park would be built.[45]

Variation in implementation also stems from the formulation and adoption processes. If a policy is formulated in detail, then it is more likely to attract opposition and might not be adopted. To ensure adoption, policy designers therefore often formulate broad policies. Broadly constructed policies invite implementers to insert their own biases into the implementation process. As discussed earlier, the U.S. Supreme Court's *Brown II* decision instituted the vague "all deliberate speed" mandate for school desegregation. Supreme Court justices and law clerks recognized that a detailed ruling would decrease the chances of a unanimous opinion and numerous school districts would ignore it. During the justices' conference, Justice Hugo Black remarked, "The less we say, the better off we are." Thus, the broadly formulated policy allowed Chief Justice Warren to secure a unanimous decision, but as a trade-off the broad decision gave tremendous discretion to federal judges in charge of implementing it.[46] As we have discussed, this discretion led to wide disparities in the speed of integration.

Because sentencing people convicted of a crime is a key element of implementation, variations in implementation can also lead to disparate sentences for the same crime. "Measuring Equality: Racial Disparities in the Punishment of Drug Offenders" explains disparate criminal sentencing in more detail.

Policy Evaluation

The domestic policymaking process does not stop at the implementation stage. Governments, interest groups, and the public need to ensure that the policy has achieved its desired effect, and this stage is known as policy evaluation. Despite the seemingly objective nature of the evaluation task, evaluators enjoy tremendous leeway. Because policymakers are often ambiguous about the objectives of a policy, an evaluator enjoys wide discretion in establishing the goals of a policy. Moreover, the evaluator selects the method to ascertain whether the effects of the policy have met those goals.

The government evaluates policy through the congressional oversight process (see Chapter 6). Inherent in the lawmaking power of Congress is the authority to make sure that laws are enforced according to congressional intentions and to prevent waste, fraud, or abuse in government. Although oversight often features interbranch disputes, it is largely a partisan process. Committee chairs have tremendous discretion in determining whether to conduct oversight investigations. As a result, Congress is less likely to exercise its oversight power in periods of unified government than in periods of divided government. As we discussed in Chapter 6, after the Republicans took control of the House in 2011, they vowed to increase oversight investigations of the Obama administration's perceived inability or unwillingness to enforce immigration laws.

Interest groups, largely through the use of social media, are also engaged in policy evaluation. For example, in 2011 President Obama formulated a policy that sent one hundred U.S. troops to Uganda to track down human rights abuser Joseph Kony, who had sold young girls into sex slavery and forced young boys to be soldiers in his militia. Although this decision garnered some news coverage at the time, Americans soon forgot about the issue and Kony was not apprehended. In 2012, a group called Invisible Children

measuring equality

Racial Disparities in the Punishment of Drug Offenders

Implementation is crucial to policymaking, and policies can be implemented in a way that creates varying results for different racial or ethnic groups. In particular, the implementation of antidrug policies has negatively affected African Americans and Latinos. Here we explore in more detail the extent to which the implementation of drug policies affects Blacks and Latinos. Implementation includes enforcement of antidrug laws and sentencing of drug offenders, and we examine the number of inmates in state prison for drug offenses.

We provide two dimensions of this analysis. We compare sentencing among Whites, Blacks, and Latinos, and we compare drug offense sentences with sentences for other crimes. Specifically, we compare drug crimes to violent crimes (e.g., murder, manslaughter, sexual assault, robbery, and assault), property crimes (e.g., burglary, larceny, fraud, and forgery), public-order crimes (e.g., driving while under the influence, weapons violations, vice, and liquor offenses), and other crimes.

First, we ascertain the percentages of Whites, Blacks, and Latinos incarcerated in state prisons throughout the United States for each offense category. Because some data are missing and because other races are incarcerated (although not reported), these figures do not add up to 100 percent. Therefore, we report the data in Table 16.1 versus a pie chart format. These data suggest that race matters for drug sentences. Whites make up the plurality of state prisoners for property, public order crimes, other crimes; i.e., the less serious offenses. However, for more serious crimes—drug and violent crimes—Blacks comprise the plurality of state prisoners. Latinos are the least represented in all types of crimes.

Second, we provide three pie charts, one for each racial group: Whites (Figure 16.1), Blacks (Figure 16.2), and Latinos (Figure 16.3). For each group, we show the percentage of total inmates by type of crime. Because these figures add up to 100 percent (except for small rounding errors), we use pie charts to report these data.

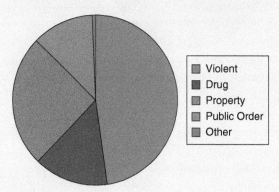

Figure 16.1 Composition of White State Prison Inmates in the United States by Offense Type, 2013.

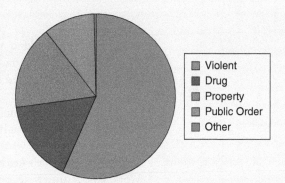

Figure 16.2 Composition of Black State Prison Inmates in the United States by Offense Type, 2013.

TABLE 16.1 Racial and Ethnic Composition of State Prisoners in the United States by Offense Type, 2013

Crime	White %	Black %	Latino %
Drug	32.6	38.4	19.2
Violent	31.8	40.0	23.0
Property	46.0	32.0	14.5
Public order	38.3	34.9	22.8
Other	31.1	19.8	13.2

A solid majority (close to 60 percent) of Blacks and Latinos are imprisoned for violent offenses, but for Whites, this figure is only a plurality, but not a majority—47.8 percent. For White inmates, the next highest category is property crimes (25.1 percent), which is then followed by drug offenses (14.1 percent). For Black and Latino inmates, property crimes and drug offenses are about equal. Unlike White inmates, who are more likely

measuring equality *(Continued)*

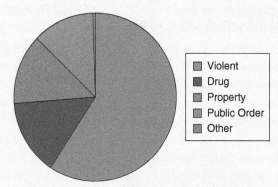

Figure 16.3 Composition of Latino State Prison Inmates in the United States by Offense Type, 2013.

to be serving time for property crimes than for drug crimes, Black and Latino inmates are as likely to be serving prison time for property crimes as they are for drug crimes.

These results show that Whites are incarcerated differently from Blacks and Latinos. There are, however, several ways to interpret these data. First, it is possible

that Blacks and Latinos are more likely than Whites to commit drug crimes. In that case, implementation reflects the crimes being committed. Second, it is possible that drug crimes are being committed at an equal level, but that Blacks and Latinos are more likely than Whites to be arrested. In that case then, when police implement drug laws, they would be discriminating against Blacks and Latinos. Third, it is possible that crimes are committed and arrests are made at the same rate, but Blacks and Latinos receive longer sentences than Whites. In this case, the judges implementing the drug laws would be discriminating against Blacks and Latinos. Which of the three interpretations is most plausible? What role might property ownership play in the incarceration rates for property crimes? How would you go about conducting further research on these topics?

Source: Data adapted from E. Ann Carson, "Appendix Table 4, Estimated Number of Sentenced Prisoners Under State Jurisdiction by Offense, Sex, Race, Hispanic Origin Year, December 31, 2013," *Prisoners in 2015* (Washington, DC: Bureau of Justice Statistics, December 2015), 30, http://www.bjs.gov /content/pub/pdf/p14.pdf, accessed August 1, 2016.

launched a viral video that highlighted Kony's transgressions and raised awareness on how he had not been caught, despite the president's policy. In April of 2013 the United States government announced a $5 million bounty for Kony's capture.[47]

The manner in which governments interpret an evaluation can also be biased. Those who initially supported a policy will interpret an evaluation as indicative of success, whereas those who opposed the policy will interpret the same evaluation less favorably. For example, the Personal Responsibility and Work Opportunity Reconciliation Act of 1996 (welfare reform) gave states more authority to distribute aid to the needy, established time limits for receiving aid, and insisted that aid recipients work or attend a training program. In 1999, the federal government collaborated with the Urban Institute—a think tank that focuses on poverty and race—to evaluate this policy, and it reported that welfare rolls had diminished throughout the nation. President Bill Clinton, who willingly signed the act, hailed this evaluation as evidence that the policy was working.

Opponents of the law interpreted the study quite differently. Georgetown University law professor Peter Edelman, who had resigned from the Clinton administration because he opposed the welfare reform policy, emphasized that the evaluation showed that many of those individuals who left welfare took menial jobs and would once again return to welfare.[48] In fact, a subsequent evaluation of welfare reform within the state of Wisconsin found that compared to Whites, Blacks and Latinos were disproportionately sanctioned for failing to meet the requirements of the welfare reform program.[49]

Conclusion

Policymaking refers to what government actually does, and it entails several stages. This chapter has traced the policymaking process in both domestic and foreign policies. In the initial agenda-setting stage, an issue is brought to the attention of the American public, largely, albeit not exclusively, through the media, social movements, and individual interest groups.

Next is the policy enactment stage, which includes both formulation and adoption. In policy formulation, political actors actually create the policies. Although formulation is generally dominated by political institutions, the public and interest groups can influence policy formulation. Policy adoption occurs when the formulated policy is formally established, and it often requires compromise.

Finally, there are the postenactment stages, which comprise implementation and evaluation. During implementation, the policy is actually carried out. The actors responsible for implementing policies often enjoy tremendous discretion to alter a policy's desired effect or even refuse to carry out certain policies. In policy evaluation, the policy is assessed to determine whether it has achieved its intended goals. Although the evaluation stage is supposed to be objective, the biases of the evaluators can influence this stage of the policy-making process.

Because the policymaking process entails each of the aspects of government that we have covered throughout this book, this chapter also served to tie together the book's previous chapters. Most notably, this chapter reemphasized our focus on minority-group politics. Minority groups rely on the media, interest groups, and social movements to set the agenda on domestic and foreign policies relevant to racial and ethnic minorities. Minority representation in government institutions is crucial for the formulation of policies favorable to racial and ethnic minority groups, and compromise is crucial for those policies being successfully adopted. The discretion that policy implementers enjoy greatly influences how policies actually affect racial and ethnic minorities, and biases inherent in the evaluation process shape how those policies are assessed.

The story of Edward Clary clearly highlights the intersection between policy-making and minority-group politics. The media hype over crack cocaine, which largely framed the issue as a "Black" problem, set the agenda among the public and then among political institutions that tougher policies against crack cocaine were needed. Accordingly, Congress and the president tremendously increased the penalties for crack cocaine, which resulted in a 100:1 differential between crack and powder cocaine sentences. But, during the implementation of the policy, Judge Cahill, an African American, opted not to adhere to the minimum guideline because it negatively affected Black defendants. Although Judge Cahill's departure from the minimum sentence was overturned on appeal, the crack cocaine policy was eventually evaluated and the disparity has been reduced substantially. Undoubtedly, race played a key role throughout the process.

REVIEW QUESTIONS

1. How have various civil rights movements and interest groups set the agenda on domestic and foreign affairs issues important to racial and ethnic minorities?

2. Do policies in general and those important to racial and ethnic minorities in particular necessarily advance from the agenda-setting stage to the formulation stage? Why or why not?

3. How important is compromise in the policy adoption process, especially for foreign and domestic policies relevant to racial and ethnic minorities?

4. How does executive branch and bureaucratic discretion in policy implementation affect racial and ethnic minorities?

5. Do interested parties interpret policy evaluations similarly, especially when concerned with issues affecting the people living near or below the poverty line and racial and ethnic minorities?

KEY TERMS

Administrative Procedures Act p. 530
Agenda-Setting p. 521
Agenda Universe p. 521
Decision Agenda p. 522
Domestic Policy p. 521

Foreign Policy p. 521
Institutional Agenda p. 522
Policy Adoption p. 527
Policy Evaluation p. 535
Policy Formulation p. 525

Policy Implementation p. 535
Systemic Agenda p. 522
Think Tanks p. 530

ADDITIONAL READINGS

Thomas D. Boston, ed., *A Different Vision: Race and Public Policy*, vol. 2 (London: Routledge, 1997).
This second part of a two-volume edited work focuses on public policies addressing income inequality among Blacks.

Fred Grünfeld and Anke Huijboom, *The Failure to Prevent Genocide in Rwanda: The Role of Bystanders* (Leiden, the Netherlands: Koninklijjke Brill, 2007).
This book thoroughly evaluates the failures that led to the genocide committed in Rwanda during the 1990s, one of the worst examples of human rights violations in African history.

Leslie T. Hatamiya, *Righting a Wrong: Japanese Americans and the Passage of the Civil Liberties Act of 1988* (Palo Alto, CA: Stanford University Press, 1993).
This book traces the history of the agenda-setting, formulation, and adoption stages of the legislation that apologized for and compensated the victims of the internment of Japanese Americans during World War II.

C. Michael Henry, ed., *Race, Poverty, and Domestic Policy* (New Haven, CT: Yale University Press, 2004).
This book, a collection of scholarly essays from the Inner City Poverty Conference sponsored by the Institution of Special and Policy Studies at Yale University, covers a wide range of topics, such as racism, measurement of income inequality, crime and law enforcement, education, family concerns, and welfare.

Doris Marie Provine, *Unequal Under Law: Race in the War on Drugs* (Chicago: University of Chicago Press, 2007).
This book examines how the "War on Drugs" stems from and exacerbates racism in the United States.

The Declaration of Independence

When in the course of human events, it becomes necessary for one people to dissolve the political bands which have connected them with another, and to assume, among the powers of the earth, the separate and equal station to which the Laws of Nature and of Nature's God entitle them, a decent respect to the opinions of mankind requires that they should declare the causes which impel them to the separation.

We hold these truths to be self-evident, that all men are created equal, that they are endowed by their Creator with certain unalienable Rights, that among these are life, liberty and the pursuit of happiness. That to secure these rights, governments are instituted among men, deriving their just powers from the consent of the governed; that whenever any form of government becomes destructive of these ends, it is the right of the people to alter or to abolish it, and to institute new Government, laying its foundation on such principles and organizing its powers in such form, as to them shall seem most likely to effect their safety and happiness. Prudence, indeed, will dictate that Governments long established should not be changed for light and transient causes; and, accordingly, all experience hath shown, that mankind are more disposed to suffer, while evils are sufferable, than to right themselves by abolishing the forms to which they are accustomed. But when a long train of abuses and usurpations, pursuing invariably the same object evinces a design to reduce them under absolute despotism, it is their right, it is their duty, to throw off such government, and to provide new guards for their future security. Such has been the patient sufferance of these colonies; and such is now the necessity which constrains them to alter their former systems of government. The history of the present King of Great Britain is a history of repeated injuries and usurpations, all having in direct object the establishment of an absolute tyranny over these States. To prove this, let facts be submitted to a candid world:

- He has refused his assent to laws, the most wholesome and necessary for the public good.
- He has forbidden his governors to pass laws of immediate and pressing importance, unless suspended in their operation till his assent should be obtained; and, when so suspended, he has utterly neglected to attend to them.
- He has refused to pass other laws for the accommodation of large districts of people, unless those people would relinquish the right of representation in the legislature, a right inestimable to them and formidable to tyrants only.

- He has called together legislative bodies at places unusual, uncomfortable, and distant from the depository of their public records, for the sole purpose of fatiguing them into compliance with his measures.
- He has dissolved representative houses repeatedly, for opposing with manly firmness his invasions on the rights of the people.
- He has refused for a long time, after such dissolutions, to cause others to be elected; whereby the legislative powers, incapable of annihilation, have returned to the People at large for their exercise; the State remaining in the mean time exposed to all the dangers of invasion from without, and convulsions within.
- He has endeavored to prevent the population of these States; for that purpose obstructing the laws for naturalization of foreigners; refusing to pass others to encourage their migrations hither, and raising the conditions of new appropriations of lands.
- He has obstructed the administration of justice, by refusing his assent to laws for establishing judiciary powers.
- He has made judges dependent on his will alone, for the tenure of their offices, and the amount and payment of their salaries.
- He has erected a multitude of new offices, and sent hither swarms of officers to harass our people, and eat out their substance.
- He has kept among us, in times of peace, standing armies without the consent of our legislatures.
- He has affected to render the Military independent of, and superior to, the civil power.
- He has combined with others to subject us to a jurisdiction foreign to our constitution and unacknowledged by our laws; giving his assent to their acts of pretended legislation:
- For quartering large bodies of armed troops among us;
- For protecting them, by a mock trial, from punishment for any murders which they should commit on the inhabitants of these States;
- For cutting off our trade with all parts of the world;
- For imposing taxes on us without our Consent;
- For depriving us, in many cases, of the benefits of Trial by Jury;
- For transporting us beyond Seas to be tried for pretended offences;
- For abolishing the free System of English Laws in a neighbouring Province, establishing therein an Arbitrary government, and enlarging its Boundaries so as to render it at once an example and fit instrument for introducing the same absolute rule into these colonies;
- For taking away our charters, abolishing our most valuable laws, and altering fundamentally the forms of our governments;
- For suspending our own legislatures, and declaring themselves invested with power to legislate for us in all cases whatsoever.

- He has abdicated government here, by declaring us out of his protection and waging war against us.
- He has plundered our seas, ravaged our coasts, burnt our towns, and destroyed the lives of our people.
- He is at this time transporting large armies of foreign mercenaries to complete the works of death, desolation and tyranny, already begun with circumstances of cruelty and perfidy scarcely paralleled in the most barbarous ages, and totally unworthy the head of a civilized nation.
- He has constrained our fellow citizens taken captive on the high seas to bear arms against their country, to become the executioners of their friends and brethren, or to fall themselves by their hands.
- He has excited domestic insurrections amongst us, and has endeavored to bring on the inhabitants of our frontiers, the merciless Indian savages, whose known rule of warfare, is an undistinguished destruction of all ages, sexes and conditions.

In every stage of these oppressions we have petitioned for redress in the most humble terms; our repeated petitions have been answered only by repeated injury. A prince whose character is thus marked by every act which may define a tyrant, is unfit to be the ruler of a free people.

Nor have we been wanting in attentions to our British brethren. We have warned them from time to time of attempts by their legislature to extend an unwarrantable jurisdiction over us. We have reminded them of the circumstances of our emigration and settlement here. We have appealed to their native justice and magnanimity, and we have conjured them by the ties of our common kindred to disavow these usurpations, which, would inevitably interrupt our connections and correspondence. They, too, have been deaf to the voice of justice and of consanguinity. We must, therefore, acquiesce in the necessity, which denounces our separation, and hold them, as we hold the rest of mankind, enemies in war, in peace friends.

We, therefore, the representatives of the United States of America, in general Congress, assembled, appealing to the Supreme Judge of the world for the rectitude of our intentions, do, in the name, and by the authority of the good people of these colonies, solemnly publish and declare, that these united colonies are, and of right ought to be free and independent states; that they are absolved from all allegiance to the British Crown, and that all political connection between them and the state of Great Britain, is and ought to be totally dissolved; and that, as free and independent states, they have full power to levy war, conclude peace, contract alliances, establish commerce, and to do all other acts and things which independent states may of right do. And for the support of this declaration, with a firm reliance on the protection of Divine Providence, we mutually pledge to each other our lives, our fortunes and our sacred honor.

The Constitution of the United States of America

We the People of the United States, in Order to form a more perfect Union, establish Justice, insure domestic Tranquility, provide for the common defence, promote the general Welfare, and secure the Blessings of Liberty to ourselves and our Posterity, do ordain and establish this Constitution for the United States of America.

Article I

Section 1

All legislative Powers herein granted shall be vested in a Congress of the United States, which shall consist of a Senate and House of Representatives.

Section 2

The House of Representatives shall be composed of Members chosen every second Year by the People of the several States, and the Electors in each State shall have the Qualifications requisite for Electors of the most numerous Branch of the State Legislature.

No Person shall be a Representative who shall not have attained to the Age of twenty five Years, and been seven Years a Citizen of the United States, and who shall not, when elected, be an Inhabitant of that State in which he shall be chosen.

Representatives [and direct Taxes][1] shall be apportioned among the several States [which may be included within this Union, according to their respective Numbers, which shall be determined by adding to the whole Number of free Persons, including those bound to Service for a Term of Years, and excluding Indians not taxed, three fifths of all other Persons].[2] The actual Enumeration shall be made within three Years after the first Meeting of the Congress of the United States, and within every subsequent Term of ten Years, in such Manner as they shall by Law direct. The Number of Representatives shall not exceed one for every thirty Thousand, but each State shall have at Least one Representative; and until such enumeration shall be made, the State of New Hampshire shall be entitled to choose three, Massachusetts eight, Rhode-Island and Providence Plantations one, Connecticut five, New York six,

[1] Modified by the Sixteenth Amendment.
[2] Negated by the Fourteenth Amendment.

New Jersey four, Pennsylvania eight, Delaware one, Maryland six, Virginia ten, North Carolina five, South Carolina five, and Georgia three.

When vacancies happen in the Representation from any State, the Executive Authority thereof shall issue Writs of Election to fill such Vacancies.

The House of Representatives shall choose their Speaker and other Officers; and shall have the sole Power of Impeachment.

Section 3

The Senate of the United States shall be composed of two Senators from each State, chosen [by the Legislature thereof]³ for six Years; and each Senator shall have one Vote.

Immediately after they shall be assembled in Consequence of the first Election, they shall be divided as equally as may be into three Classes. The Seats of the Senators of the first Class shall be vacated at the Expiration of the second Year, of the second Class at the Expiration of the fourth Year, and of the third Class at the Expiration of the sixth Year, so that one third may be chosen every second Year[; and if Vacancies happen by Resignation, or otherwise, during the Recess of the Legislature of any State, the Executive thereof may make temporary Appointments until the next Meeting of the Legislature, which shall then fill such Vacancies].⁴

No Person shall be a Senator who shall not have attained to the Age of thirty Years, and been nine Years a Citizen of the United States, and who shall not, when elected, be an Inhabitant of that State for which he shall be chosen.

The Vice President of the United States shall be President of the Senate, but shall have no Vote, unless they be equally divided.

The Senate shall choose their other Officers, and also a President pro tempore, in the Absence of the Vice President, or when he shall exercise the Office of President of the United States.

The Senate shall have the sole Power to try all Impeachments. When sitting for that Purpose, they shall be on Oath or Affirmation. When the President of the United States is tried, the Chief Justice shall preside: And no Person shall be convicted without the Concurrence of two thirds of the Members present.

Judgment in Cases of Impeachment shall not extend further than to removal from Office, and disqualification to hold and enjoy any Office of honor, Trust or Profit under the United States: but the Party convicted shall nevertheless be liable and subject to Indictment, Trial, Judgment and Punishment, according to Law.

Section 4

The Times, Places and Manner of holding Elections for Senators and Representatives, shall be prescribed in each State by the Legislature thereof; but the Congress may at any time by Law make or alter such Regulations, except as to the Places of chusing Senators.

³ Changed by the Seventeenth Amendment.
⁴ Modified by the Seventeenth Amendment.

[The Congress shall assemble at least once in every Year, and such Meeting shall be on the first Monday in December, unless they shall by Law appoint a different Day.][5]

Section 5

Each House shall be the Judge of the Elections, Returns and Qualifications of its own Members, and a Majority of each shall constitute a Quorum to do Business; but a smaller Number may adjourn from day to day, and may be authorized to compel the Attendance of absent Members, in such Manner, and under such Penalties as each House may provide.

Each House may determine the Rules of its Proceedings, punish its Members for disorderly Behaviour, and, with the Concurrence of two thirds, expel a Member.

Each House shall keep a Journal of its Proceedings, and from time to time publish the same, excepting such Parts as may in their Judgment require Secrecy; and the Yeas and Nays of the Members of either House on any question shall, at the Desire of one fifth of those Present, be entered on the Journal.

Neither House, during the Session of Congress, shall, without the Consent of the other, adjourn for more than three days, nor to any other Place than that in which the two Houses shall be sitting.

Section 6

The Senators and Representatives shall receive a Compensation for their Services, to be ascertained by Law, and paid out of the Treasury of the United States. They shall in all Cases, except Treason, Felony and Breach of the Peace, be privileged from Arrest during their Attendance at the Session of their respective Houses, and in going to and returning from the same; and for any Speech or Debate in either House, they shall not be questioned in any other Place.

No Senator or Representative shall, during the Time for which he was elected, be appointed to any civil Office under the Authority of the United States, which shall have been created, or the Emoluments whereof shall have been increased during such time; and no Person holding any Office under the United States, shall be a Member of either House during his Continuance in Office.

Section 7

All Bills for raising Revenue shall originate in the House of Representatives; but the Senate may propose or concur with Amendments as on other Bills.

Every Bill which shall have passed the House of Representatives and the Senate, shall, before it become a Law, be presented to the President of the United States: If he approve he shall sign it, but if not he shall return it, with his Objections to that House in which it shall have originated, who shall enter the Objections at large on their Journal, and proceed to reconsider it. If after such Reconsideration two thirds of that House shall agree to pass the Bill, it shall be

---

[5]Changed to January 3 by the Twentieth Amendment.

sent, together with the Objections, to the other House, by which it shall likewise be reconsidered, and if approved by two thirds of that House, it shall become a Law. But in all such Cases the Votes of both Houses shall be determined by yeas and Nays, and the Names of the Persons voting for and against the Bill shall be entered on the Journal of each House respectively. If any Bill shall not be returned by the President within ten Days (Sundays excepted) after it shall have been presented to him, the Same shall be a Law, in like Manner as if he had signed it, unless the Congress by their Adjournment prevent its Return, in which Case it shall not be a Law.

Every Order, Resolution, or Vote to which the Concurrence of the Senate and House of Representatives may be necessary (except on a question of Adjournment) shall be presented to the President of the United States; and before the Same shall take Effect, shall be approved by him, or being disapproved by him, shall be repassed by two thirds of the Senate and House of Representatives, according to the Rules and Limitations prescribed in the Case of a Bill.

Section 8

The Congress shall have Power

To lay and collect Taxes, Duties, Imposts and Excises, to pay the Debts and provide for the common Defence and general Welfare of the United States; but all Duties, Imposts and Excises shall be uniform throughout the United States;

To borrow Money on the credit of the United States;

To regulate Commerce with foreign Nations, and among the several States, and with the Indian Tribes;

To establish an uniform Rule of Naturalization, and uniform Laws on the subject of Bankruptcies throughout the United States;

To coin Money, regulate the Value thereof, and of foreign Coin, and fix the Standard of Weights and Measures;

To provide for the Punishment of counterfeiting the Securities and current Coin of the United States;

To establish Post Offices and post Roads;

To promote the Progress of Science and useful Arts, by securing for limited Times to Authors and Inventors the exclusive Right to their respective Writings and Discoveries;

To constitute Tribunals inferior to the supreme Court;

To define and punish Piracies and Felonies committed on the high Seas, and Offences against the Law of Nations;

To declare War, grant Letters of Marque and Reprisal, and make Rules concerning Captures on Land and Water;

To raise and support Armies, but no Appropriation of Money to that Use shall be for a longer Term than two Years;

To provide and maintain a Navy;

To make Rules for the Government and Regulation of the land and naval Forces;

To provide for calling forth the Militia to execute the Laws of the Union, suppress Insurrections and repel Invasions;

To provide for organizing, arming, and disciplining the Militia, and for governing such Part of them as may be employed in the Service of the United States, reserving to the States respectively, the Appointment of the Officers, and the Authority of training the Militia according to the discipline prescribed by Congress;

To exercise exclusive Legislation in all Cases whatsoever, over such District (not exceeding ten Miles square) as may, by Cession of particular States, and the Acceptance of Congress, become the Seat of the Government of the United States, and to exercise like Authority over all Places purchased by the Consent of the Legislature of the State in which the Same shall be, for the Erection of Forts, Magazines, Arsenals, dock-Yards, and other needful Buildings;—And

To make all Laws which shall be necessary and proper for carrying into Execution the foregoing Powers, and all other Powers vested by this Constitution in the Government of the United States, or in any Department or Officer thereof.

Section 9

The Migration or Importation of such Persons as any of the States now existing shall think proper to admit, shall not be prohibited by the Congress prior to the Year one thousand eight hundred and eight, but a Tax or duty may be imposed on such Importation, not exceeding ten dollars for each Person.

The Privilege of the Writ of Habeas Corpus shall not be suspended, unless when in Cases of Rebellion or Invasion the public Safety may require it.

No Bill of Attainder or ex post facto Law shall be passed.

[No Capitation, or other direct, Tax shall be laid, unless in Proportion to the Census or enumeration herein before directed to be taken.][6]

No Tax or Duty shall be laid on Articles exported from any State.

No Preference shall be given by any Regulation of Commerce or Revenue to the Ports of one State over those of another; nor shall Vessels bound to, or from, one State, be obliged to enter, clear, or pay Duties in another.

No Money shall be drawn from the Treasury, but in Consequence of Appropriations made by Law; and a regular Statement and Account of the Receipts and Expenditures of all public Money shall be published from time to time.

No Title of Nobility shall be granted by the United States: And no Person holding any Office of Profit or Trust under them, shall, without the Consent of the Congress, accept of any present, Emolument, Office, or Title, of any kind whatever, from any King, Prince, or foreign State.

Section 10

No State shall enter into any Treaty, Alliance, or Confederation; grant Letters of Marque and Reprisal; coin Money; emit Bills of Credit; make any Thing but gold and silver Coin a Tender in Payment of Debts; pass any Bill of Attainder, ex post facto Law, or Law impairing the Obligation of Contracts, or grant any Title of Nobility.

[6] Modified by the Sixteenth Amendment.

No State shall, without the Consent of the Congress, lay any Imposts or Duties on Imports or Exports, except what may be absolutely necessary for executing it's inspection Laws: and the net Produce of all Duties and Imposts, laid by any State on Imports or Exports, shall be for the Use of the Treasury of the United States; and all such Laws shall be subject to the Revision and Control of the Congress.

No State shall, without the Consent of Congress, lay any Duty of Tonnage, keep Troops, or Ships of War in time of Peace, enter into any Agreement or Compact with another State, or with a foreign Power, or engage in War, unless actually invaded, or in such imminent Danger as will not admit of delay.

Article II

Section 1

The executive Power shall be vested in a President of the United States of America. He shall hold his Office during the Term of four Years, and, together with the Vice President, chosen for the same Term, be elected, as follows:

Each State shall appoint, in such Manner as the Legislature thereof may direct, a Number of Electors, equal to the whole Number of Senators and Representatives to which the State may be entitled in the Congress: but no Senator or Representative, or Person holding an Office of Trust or Profit under the United States, shall be appointed an Elector.

[The Electors shall meet in their respective States, and vote by Ballot for two Persons, of whom one at least shall not be an Inhabitant of the same State with themselves. And they shall make a List of all the Persons voted for, and of the Number of Votes for each; which List they shall sign and certify, and transmit sealed to the Seat of the Government of the United States, directed to the President of the Senate. The President of the Senate shall, in the Presence of the Senate and House of Representatives, open all the Certificates, and the Votes shall then be counted. The Person having the greatest Number of Votes shall be the President, if such Number be a Majority of the whole Number of Electors appointed; and if there be more than one who have such Majority, and have an equal Number of Votes, then the House of Representatives shall immediately choose by Ballot one of them for President; and if no Person have a Majority, then from the five highest on the List the said House shall in like Manner choose the President. But in choosing the President, the Votes shall be taken by States, the Representation from each State having one Vote; A quorum for this purpose shall consist of a Member or Members from two thirds of the States, and a Majority of all the States shall be necessary to a Choice. In every Case, after the Choice of the President, the Person having the greatest Number of Votes of the Electors shall be the Vice President. But if there should remain two or more who have equal Votes, the Senate shall choose from them by Ballot the Vice President.][7]

---

[7] Changed by the Twelfth and Twentieth Amendments.

The Congress may determine the Time of choosing the Electors, and the Day on which they shall give their Votes; which Day shall be the same throughout the United States.

No Person except a natural born Citizen, or a Citizen of the United States, at the time of the Adoption of this Constitution, shall be eligible to the Office of President; neither shall any Person be eligible to that Office who shall not have attained to the Age of thirty five Years, and been fourteen Years a Resident within the United States.

In Case of the Removal of the President from Office, or of his Death, Resignation, or Inability to discharge the Powers and Duties of the said Office, the Same shall devolve on the Vice President, and the Congress may by Law provide for the Case of Removal, Death, Resignation or Inability, both of the President and Vice President, declaring what Officer shall then act as President, and such Officer shall act accordingly, until the Disability be removed, or a President shall be elected.

The President shall, at stated Times, receive for his Services, a Compensation, which shall neither be increased nor diminished during the Period for which he shall have been elected, and he shall not receive within that Period any other Emolument from the United States, or any of them.

Before he enter on the Execution of his Office, he shall take the following Oath or Affirmation:—"I do solemnly swear (or affirm) that I will faithfully execute the Office of President of the United States, and will to the best of my Ability, preserve, protect and defend the Constitution of the United States."

Section 2

The President shall be Commander in Chief of the Army and Navy of the United States, and of the Militia of the several States, when called into the actual Service of the United States; he may require the Opinion, in writing, of the principal Officer in each of the executive Departments, upon any Subject relating to the Duties of their respective Offices, and he shall have Power to grant Reprieves and Pardons for Offences against the United States, except in Cases of Impeachment.

He shall have Power, by and with the Advice and Consent of the Senate, to make Treaties, provided two thirds of the Senators present concur; and he shall nominate, and by and with the Advice and Consent of the Senate, shall appoint Ambassadors, other public Ministers and Consuls, Judges of the supreme Court, and all other Officers of the United States, whose Appointments are not herein otherwise provided for, and which shall be established by Law: but the Congress may by Law vest the Appointment of such inferior Officers, as they think proper, in the President alone, in the Courts of Law, or in the Heads of Departments.

The President shall have Power to fill up all Vacancies that may happen during the Recess of the Senate, by granting Commissions which shall expire at the End of their next Session.

Section 3

He shall from time to time give to the Congress Information of the State of the Union, and recommend to their Consideration such Measures as he shall judge necessary and expedient; he may, on extraordinary Occasions, convene both Houses, or either of them, and in Case of Disagreement between them, with Respect to the Time of Adjournment, he may adjourn them to such Time as he shall think proper; he shall receive Ambassadors and other public Ministers; he shall take Care that the Laws be faithfully executed, and shall Commission all the Officers of the United States.

Section 4

The President, Vice President and all civil Officers of the United States, shall be removed from Office on Impeachment for, and Conviction of, Treason, Bribery, or other high Crimes and Misdemeanors.

Article III

Section 1

The judicial Power of the United States shall be vested in one supreme Court, and in such inferior Courts as the Congress may from time to time ordain and establish. The Judges, both of the supreme and inferior Courts, shall hold their Offices during good Behaviour, and shall, at stated Times, receive for their Services a Compensation, which shall not be diminished during their Continuance in Office.

Section 2

The judicial Power shall extend to all Cases, in Law and Equity, arising under this Constitution, the Laws of the United States, and Treaties made, or which shall be made, under their Authority;—to all Cases affecting Ambassadors, other public Ministers and Consuls;—to all Cases of admiralty and maritime Jurisdiction;—to Controversies to which the United States shall be a Party;—to Controversies between two or more States;[—between a State and Citizens of another State;—][8]

between Citizens of different States;—between Citizens of the same State claiming Lands under Grants of different States, [and between a State,][9] or the Citizens thereof[, and foreign States, Citizens or Subjects].[10]

In all Cases affecting Ambassadors, other public Ministers and Consuls, and those in which a State shall be Party, the supreme Court shall have original Jurisdiction. In all the other Cases before mentioned, the supreme Court shall have appellate Jurisdiction, both as to Law and Fact, with such Exceptions, and under such Regulations as the Congress shall make.

The Trial of all Crimes, except in Cases of Impeachment, shall be by Jury; and such Trial shall be held in the State where the said Crimes shall have been committed; but when not committed within any State, the Trial shall be at such Place or Places as the Congress may by Law have directed.

[8] Altered by the Twelfth Amendment.
[9] Altered by the Twelfth Amendment.
[10] Altered by the Twelfth Amendment.

Section 3

Treason against the United States, shall consist only in levying War against them, or in adhering to their Enemies, giving them Aid and Comfort. No Person shall be convicted of Treason unless on the Testimony of two Witnesses to the same overt Act, or on Confession in open Court.

The Congress shall have Power to declare the Punishment of Treason, but no Attainder of Treason shall work Corruption of Blood, or Forfeiture except during the Life of the Person attainted.

Article IV

Section 1

Full Faith and Credit shall be given in each State to the public Acts, Records, and judicial Proceedings of every other State. And the Congress may by general Laws prescribe the Manner in which such Acts, Records and Proceedings shall be proved, and the Effect thereof.

Section 2

The Citizens of each State shall be entitled to all Privileges and Immunities of Citizens in the several States.

A Person charged in any State with Treason, Felony, or other Crime, who shall flee from Justice, and be found in another State, shall on Demand of the executive Authority of the State from which he fled, be delivered up, to be removed to the State having Jurisdiction of the Crime.

[No Person held to Service or Labour in one State, under the Laws thereof, escaping into another, shall, in Consequence of any Law or Regulation therein, be discharged from such Service or Labour, but shall be delivered up on Claim of the Party to whom such Service or Labour may be due.][11]

Section 3

New States may be admitted by the Congress into this Union; but no new State shall be formed or erected within the Jurisdiction of any other State; nor any State be formed by the Junction of two or more States, or Parts of States, without the Consent of the Legislatures of the States concerned as well as of the Congress.

The Congress shall have Power to dispose of and make all needful Rules and Regulations respecting the Territory or other Property belonging to the United States; and nothing in this Constitution shall be so construed as to Prejudice any Claims of the United States, or of any particular State.

Section 4

The United States shall guarantee to every State in this Union a Republican Form of Government, and shall protect each of them against Invasion; and on Application of the Legislature, or of the Executive (when the Legislature cannot be convened), against domestic Violence.

[11] Repealed by the Thirteenth Amendment.

Article V

The Congress, whenever two thirds of both Houses shall deem it necessary, shall propose Amendments to this Constitution, or, on the Application of the Legislatures of two thirds of the several States, shall call a Convention for proposing Amendments, which, in either Case, shall be valid to all Intents and Purposes, as Part of this Constitution, when ratified by the Legislatures of three fourths of the several States, or by Conventions in three fourths thereof, as the one or the other Mode of Ratification may be proposed by the Congress; Provided that no Amendment which may be made prior to the Year One thousand eight hundred and eight shall in any Manner affect the first and fourth Clauses in the Ninth Section of the first Article; and that no State, without its Consent, shall be deprived of its equal Suffrage in the Senate.

Article VI

All Debts contracted and Engagements entered into, before the Adoption of this Constitution, shall be as valid against the United States under this Constitution, as under the Confederation.

This Constitution, and the Laws of the United States which shall be made in Pursuance thereof; and all Treaties made, or which shall be made, under the Authority of the United States, shall be the supreme Law of the Land; and the Judges in every State shall be bound thereby, any Thing in the Constitution or Laws of any State to the Contrary notwithstanding.

The Senators and Representatives before mentioned, and the Members of the several State Legislatures, and all executive and judicial Officers, both of the United States and of the several States, shall be bound by Oath or Affirmation, to support this Constitution; but no religious Test shall ever be required as a Qualification to any Office or public Trust under the United States.

Article VII

The Ratification of the Conventions of nine States, shall be sufficient for the Establishment of this Constitution between the States so ratifying the Same.

The Word, "the," being interlined between the seventh and eighth Lines of the first Page, the Word "Thirty" being partly written on an Erazure in the fifteenth Line of the first Page, The Words "is tried" being interlined between the thirty second and thirty third Lines of the first Page and the Word "the" being interlined between the forty third and forty fourth Lines of the second Page.

Attest William Jackson Secretary

Done in Convention by the Unanimous Consent of the States present the Seventeenth Day of September in the Year of our Lord one thousand seven hundred and Eighty seven and of the Independence of the United States of America the Twelfth In witness whereof We have hereunto subscribed our Names,

G°. WASHINGTON
Presidt and deputy from Virginia

Delaware
Geo: Read
Gunning Bedford jun
John Dickinson
Richard Bassett
Jaco: Broom

Maryland
James McHenry
Dan of St Thos. Jenifer
Danl. Carroll

Virginia
John Blair
James Madison Jr.

North Carolina
Wm. Blount
Richd. Dobbs Spaight
Hu Williamson

South Carolina
J. Rutledge
Charles Cotesworth
 Pinckney
Charles Pinckney
Pierce Butler
Georgia
William Few
Abr Baldwin
New Hampshire
John Langdon
Nicholas Gilman

Massachusetts
Nathaniel Gorham
Rufus King

Connecticut
Wm. Saml. Johnson
Roger Sherman

New York
Alexander Hamilton

New Jersey
Wil: Livingston
David Brearley
Wm. Paterson
Jona: Dayton

Pennsylvania
B Franklin
Thomas Mifflin
Robt. Morris
Geo. Clymer
Thos. FitzSimons
Jared Ingersoll
James Wilson
Gouv Morris

[B] Articles

In addition to, and Amendment of the Constitution of the United States of America, proposed by Congress, and ratified by the Legislatures of the several States, pursuant to the fifth Article of the original Constitution.

(The first ten amendments to the U.S. Constitution were ratified December 15, 1791, and form what is known as the "Bill of Rights.")

Amendment I

Congress shall make no law respecting an establishment of religion, or prohibiting the free exercise thereof; or abridging the freedom of speech, or of the press; or the right of the people peaceably to assemble, and to petition the Government for a redress of grievances.

Amendment II

A well regulated Militia, being necessary to the security of a free State, the right of the people to keep and bear Arms, shall not be infringed.

Amendment III

No Soldier shall, in time of peace be quartered in any house, without the consent of the Owner, nor in time of war, but in a manner to be prescribed by law.

Amendment IV

The right of the people to be secure in their persons, houses, papers, and effects, against unreasonable searches and seizures, shall not be violated, and no Warrants shall issue, but upon probable cause, supported by Oath or affirmation, and particularly describing the place to be searched, and the persons or things to be seized.

Amendment V

No person shall be held to answer for a capital, or otherwise infamous crime, unless on a presentment or indictment of a Grand Jury, except in cases arising in the land or naval forces, or in the Militia, when in actual service in time of War or public danger; nor shall any person be subject for the same offence to be twice put in jeopardy of life or limb; nor shall be compelled in any criminal case to be a witness against himself, nor be deprived of life, liberty, or property, without due process of law; nor shall private property be taken for public use, without just compensation.

Amendment VI

In all criminal prosecutions, the accused shall enjoy the right to a speedy and public trial, by an impartial jury of the State and district wherein the crime shall have been committed, which district shall have been previously ascertained by law, and to be informed of the nature and cause of the accusation; to be confronted with the witnesses against him; to have compulsory process for obtaining witnesses in his favor, and to have the Assistance of Counsel for his defence.

Amendment VII

In Suits at common law, where the value in controversy shall exceed twenty dollars, the right of trial by jury shall be preserved, and no fact tried by a jury, shall be otherwise re-examined in any Court of the United States, than according to the rules of the common law.

Amendment VIII

Excessive bail shall not be required, nor excessive fines imposed, nor cruel and unusual punishments inflicted.

Amendment IX

The enumeration in the Constitution, of certain rights, shall not be construed to deny or disparage others retained by the people.

Amendment X

The powers not delegated to the United States by the Constitution, nor prohibited by it to the States, are reserved to the States respectively, or to the people.

Amendment XI

Passed by Congress March 4, 1794. Ratified February 7, 1795.

Note: Article III, Section 2, of the Constitution was modified by Amendment XI.

The Judicial power of the United States shall not be construed to extend to any suit in law or equity, commenced or prosecuted against one of the United States by Citizens of another State, or by Citizens or Subjects of any Foreign State.

Amendment XII

Passed by Congress December 9, 1803. Ratified June 15, 1804.

Note: A portion of Article II, Section 1, of the Constitution was superseded by the Twelfth Amendment.

The Electors shall meet in their respective states and vote by ballot for President and Vice-President, one of whom, at least, shall not be an inhabitant of the same state with themselves; they shall name in their ballots the person voted for as President, and in distinct ballots the person voted for as Vice-President, and they shall make distinct lists of all persons voted for as President, and of all persons voted for as Vice-President, and of the number of votes for each, which lists they shall sign and certify, and transmit sealed to the seat of the government of the United States, directed to the President of the Senate;—the President of the Senate shall, in the presence of the Senate and House of Representatives, open all the certificates and the votes shall then be counted;—The person having the greatest number of votes for President, shall be the President, if such number be a majority of the whole number of Electors appointed; and if no person have such majority, then from the persons having the highest numbers not exceeding three on the list of those voted for as President, the House of Representatives shall choose immediately, by ballot, the President. But in choosing the President, the votes shall be taken by states, the representation from each state having one vote; a quorum for this purpose shall consist of a member or members from two-thirds of the states, and a majority of all the states shall be necessary to a choice. [And if the House of Representatives shall not choose a President whenever the right of choice shall devolve upon them, before the fourth day of March next following, then the Vice-President shall act as President, as in case of the death or other constitutional disability of the President.—][12] The person having the greatest number of votes as Vice-President, shall be the Vice-President, if such number be a majority of the whole number of Electors appointed, and if no person have a

---

[12] Superseded by Section 3 of the Twentieth Amendment.

majority, then from the two highest numbers on the list, the Senate shall choose the Vice-President; a quorum for the purpose shall consist of two-thirds of the whole number of Senators, and a majority of the whole number shall be necessary to a choice. But no person constitutionally ineligible to the office of President shall be eligible to that of Vice-President of the United States.

Amendment XIII

Passed by Congress January 31, 1865. Ratified December 6, 1865.

Note: A portion of Article IV, Section 2, of the Constitution was superseded by the Thirteenth Amendment.

Section 1

Neither slavery nor involuntary servitude, except as a punishment for crime whereof the party shall have been duly convicted, shall exist within the United States, or any place subject to their jurisdiction.

Section 2

Congress shall have power to enforce this article by appropriate legislation.

Amendment XIV

Passed by Congress June 13, 1866. Ratified July 9, 1868.

Note: Article I, Section 2, of the Constitution was modified by Section 2 of the Fourteenth Amendment.

Section 1

All persons born or naturalized in the United States, and subject to the jurisdiction thereof, are citizens of the United States and of the State wherein they reside. No State shall make or enforce any law which shall abridge the privileges or immunities of citizens of the United States; nor shall any State deprive any person of life, liberty, or property, without due process of law; nor deny to any person within its jurisdiction the equal protection of the laws.

Section 2

Representatives shall be apportioned among the several States according to their respective numbers, counting the whole number of persons in each State, excluding Indians not taxed. But when the right to vote at any election for the choice of electors for President and Vice-President of the United States, Representatives in Congress, the Executive and Judicial officers of a State, or the members of the Legislature thereof, is denied to any of the male inhabitants of such State, being twenty-one years of age,[13] and citizens of the United States, or in any way abridged, except for participation in rebellion, or other crime, the basis of representation therein shall be reduced in the proportion which the number of

[13] Changed by Section 1 of the Twenty-Sixth Amendment.

such male citizens shall bear to the whole number of male citizens twenty-one years of age in such State.

Section 3

No person shall be a Senator or Representative in Congress, or elector of President and Vice-President, or hold any office, civil or military, under the United States, or under any State, who, having previously taken an oath, as a member of Congress, or as an officer of the United States, or as a member of any State legislature, or as an executive or judicial officer of any State, to support the Constitution of the United States, shall have engaged in insurrection or rebellion against the same, or given aid or comfort to the enemies thereof. But Congress may by a vote of two-thirds of each House, remove such disability.

Section 4

The validity of the public debt of the United States, authorized by law, including debts incurred for payment of pensions and bounties for services in suppressing insurrection or rebellion, shall not be questioned. But neither the United States nor any State shall assume or pay any debt or obligation incurred in aid of insurrection or rebellion against the United States, or any claim for the loss or emancipation of any slave; but all such debts, obligations and claims shall be held illegal and void.

Section 5

The Congress shall have the power to enforce, by appropriate legislation, the provisions of this article.

*Changed by Section 1 of the Twenty-Sixth Amendment.

Amendment XV

Passed by Congress February 26, 1869. Ratified February 3, 1870.

Section 1

The right of citizens of the United States to vote shall not be denied or abridged by the United States or by any State on account of race, color, or previous condition of servitude.

Section 2

The Congress shall have the power to enforce this article by appropriate legislation.

Amendment XVI

Passed by Congress July 2, 1909. Ratified February 3, 1913.

Note: Article I, Section 9, of the Constitution was modified by Amendment XVI.

The Congress shall have power to lay and collect taxes on incomes, from whatever source derived, without apportionment among the several States, and without regard to any census or enumeration.

Amendment XVII

Passed by Congress May 13, 1912. Ratified April 8, 1913.

Note: Article I, Section 3, of the Constitution was modified by the Seventeenth Amendment.

The Senate of the United States shall be composed of two Senators from each State, elected by the people thereof, for six years; and each Senator shall have one vote. The electors in each State shall have the qualifications requisite for electors of the most numerous branch of the State legislatures.

When vacancies happen in the representation of any State in the Senate, the executive authority of such State shall issue writs of election to fill such vacancies: Provided, That the legislature of any State may empower the executive thereof to make temporary appointments until the people fill the vacancies by election as the legislature may direct.

This amendment shall not be so construed as to affect the election or term of any Senator chosen before it becomes valid as part of the Constitution.

Amendment XVIII

Passed by Congress December 18, 1917. Ratified January 16, 1919. Repealed by Amendment XXI.

Section 1
After one year from the ratification of this article the manufacture, sale, or transportation of intoxicating liquors within, the importation thereof into, or the exportation thereof from the United States and all territory subject to the jurisdiction thereof for beverage purposes is hereby prohibited.

Section 2
The Congress and the several States shall have concurrent power to enforce this article by appropriate legislation.

Section 3
This article shall be inoperative unless it shall have been ratified as an amendment to the Constitution by the legislatures of the several States, as provided in the Constitution, within seven years from the date of the submission hereof to the States by the Congress.

Amendment XIX

Passed by Congress June 4, 1919. Ratified August 18, 1920.

The right of citizens of the United States to vote shall not be denied or abridged by the United States or by any State on account of sex.

Congress shall have power to enforce this article by appropriate legislation.

Amendment XX

Passed by Congress March 2, 1932. Ratified January 23, 1933.

Note: Article I, Section 4, of the Constitution was modified by Section 2 of this amendment. In addition, a portion of the Twelfth Amendment was superseded by Section 3.

Section 1

The terms of the President and the Vice President shall end at noon on the 20th day of January, and the terms of Senators and Representatives at noon on the 3d day of January, of the years in which such terms would have ended if this article had not been ratified; and the terms of their successors shall then begin.

Section 2

The Congress shall assemble at least once in every year, and such meeting shall begin at noon on the 3d day of January, unless they shall by law appoint a different day.

Section 3

If, at the time fixed for the beginning of the term of the President, the President elect shall have died, the Vice President elect shall become President. If a President shall not have been chosen before the time fixed for the beginning of his term, or if the President elect shall have failed to qualify, then the Vice President elect shall act as President until a President shall have qualified; and the Congress may by law provide for the case wherein neither a President elect nor a Vice President shall have qualified, declaring who shall then act as President, or the manner in which one who is to act shall be selected, and such person shall act accordingly until a President or Vice President shall have qualified.

Section 4

The Congress may by law provide for the case of the death of any of the persons from whom the House of Representatives may choose a President whenever the right of choice shall have devolved upon them, and for the case of the death of any of the persons from whom the Senate may choose a Vice President whenever the right of choice shall have devolved upon them.

Section 5

Sections 1 and 2 shall take effect on the 15th day of October following the ratification of this article.

Section 6

This article shall be inoperative unless it shall have been ratified as an amendment to the Constitution by the legislatures of three-fourths of the several States within seven years from the date of its submission.

Amendment XXI

Passed by Congress February 20, 1933. Ratified December 5, 1933.

Section 1

The eighteenth article of amendment to the Constitution of the United States is hereby repealed.

Section 2

The transportation or importation into any State, Territory, or Possession of the United States for delivery or use therein of intoxicating liquors, in violation of the laws thereof, is hereby prohibited.

Section 3

This article shall be inoperative unless it shall have been ratified as an amendment to the Constitution by conventions in the several States, as provided in the Constitution, within seven years from the date of the submission hereof to the States by the Congress.

Amendment XXII

Passed by Congress March 21, 1947. Ratified February 27, 1951.

Section 1

No person shall be elected to the office of the President more than twice, and no person who has held the office of President, or acted as President, for more than two years of a term to which some other person was elected President shall be elected to the office of President more than once. But this Article shall not apply to any person holding the office of President when this Article was proposed by Congress, and shall not prevent any person who may be holding the office of President, or acting as President, during the term within which this Article becomes operative from holding the office of President or acting as President during the remainder of such term.

Section 2

This article shall be inoperative unless it shall have been ratified as an amendment to the Constitution by the legislatures of three-fourths of the several States within seven years from the date of its submission to the States by the Congress.

Amendment XXIII

Passed by Congress June 16, 1960. Ratified March 29, 1961.

Section 1

The District constituting the seat of Government of the United States shall appoint in such manner as Congress may direct:

A number of electors of President and Vice President equal to the whole number of Senators and Representatives in Congress to which the District would be entitled if it were a State, but in no event more than the least populous State; they shall be in addition to those appointed by the States, but they shall be considered, for the purposes of the election of President and Vice President, to be electors appointed by a State; and they shall meet in the District and perform such duties as provided by the twelfth article of amendment.

Section 2

The Congress shall have power to enforce this article by appropriate legislation.

Amendment XXIV

Passed by Congress August 27, 1962. Ratified January 23, 1964.

Section 1

The right of citizens of the United States to vote in any primary or other election for President or Vice President, for electors for President or Vice President, or for Senator or Representative in Congress, shall not be denied or abridged by the United States or any State by reason of failure to pay poll tax or other tax.

Section 2

The Congress shall have power to enforce this article by appropriate legislation.

Amendment XXV

Passed by Congress July 6, 1965. Ratified February 10, 1967.

Note: Article II, Section 1, of the Constitution was affected by the Twenty-Fifth Amendment.

Section 1

In case of the removal of the President from office or of his death or resignation, the Vice President shall become President.

Section 2

Whenever there is a vacancy in the office of the Vice President, the President shall nominate a Vice President who shall take office upon confirmation by a majority vote of both Houses of Congress.

Section 3

Whenever the President transmits to the President pro tempore of the Senate and the Speaker of the House of Representatives his written declaration that he is unable to discharge the powers and duties of his office, and until he transmits to them a written declaration to the contrary, such powers and duties shall be discharged by the Vice President as Acting President.

Section 4

Whenever the Vice President and a majority of either the principal officers of the executive departments or of such other body as Congress may by law provide, transmit to the President pro tempore of the Senate and the Speaker of the House of Representatives their written declaration that the President is unable to discharge the powers and duties of his office, the Vice President shall immediately assume the powers and duties of the office as Acting President.

Thereafter, when the President transmits to the President pro tempore of the Senate and the Speaker of the House of Representatives his written declaration that no inability exists, he shall resume the powers and duties of his office unless the Vice President and a majority of either the principal officers of the executive department or of such other body as Congress may by law provide, transmit within four days to the President pro tempore of the Senate and the Speaker of the House of Representatives their written declaration that the President is unable to discharge the powers and duties of his office. Thereupon Congress shall decide the issue, assembling within forty-eight hours for that purpose if not in session. If the Congress, within twenty-one days after receipt of the latter written declaration, or, if Congress is not in session, within twenty-one days after Congress is required to assemble, determines by two-thirds vote of both Houses that the President is unable to discharge the powers and duties of his office, the Vice President shall continue to discharge the same as Acting President; otherwise, the President shall resume the powers and duties of his office.

Amendment XXVI

Passed by Congress March 23, 1971. Ratified July 1, 1971.

Note: Amendment XIV, Section 2, of the Constitution was modified by Section 1 of the Twenty-Sixth Amendment.

Section 1

The right of citizens of the United States, who are eighteen years of age or older, to vote shall not be denied or abridged by the United States or by any State on account of age.

Section 2

The Congress shall have power to enforce this article by appropriate legislation.

Amendment XXVII

Originally proposed Sept. 25, 1789. Ratified May 7, 1992.

No law, varying the compensation for the services of the Senators and Representatives, shall take effect, until an election of representatives shall have intervened.

Glossary

Abolitionists Nineteenth-century political activists who sought to end slavery.

Administrative Adjudication The quasi-judicial process by which a bureaucratic agency resolves a dispute between the agency and a private citizen.

Administrative Law A type of law pertaining to the rules made by bureaucrats and administrative agencies.

Administrative Procedures Act A federal law that requires administrative agencies to publish proposed rules and allow the pubic to offer comment on them before they go into effect.

Affirmative Action Corrective policies that attempt to help racial and ethnic minorities (as well as women) achieve equality in education and the workforce by providing them with advantages in college admission, hiring, promotion, and the awarding of contracts.

Agenda Setting The stage in the policymaking process in which certain issues reach a level of public concern that attracts the attention of government officials; also the media's power to influence the importance that the public places on issues.

Agenda Universe All possible legitimate issues that could be brought to the attention of the public and possibly of policymakers.

Air War The part of election campaigns conducted through broadcast media including radio, television, and the Internet.

Amicus Curiae (Friend of the Court) Briefs Briefs filed by parties that have an interest in the outcome of a case but are not directly involved in it.

Antifederalists Opponents of the Constitution during the ratification process.

Appellate Jurisdiction The types of cases in which the Supreme Court reviews legal issues decided by a lower court.

Bicameral Legislature A legislature with two bodies, usually referred to as the upper and lower chambers, or, as is most common in the United States, the House and the Senate.

Bill of Attainder A law passed by a legislative body that punishes specific people without convicting them in a court.

Bill of Rights The first ten amendments to the Constitution, which focus primarily on individual liberties and basic rights.

Bipartisan Campaign Reform Act (BCRA) A campaign finance reform law passed in 2002 that amended the Federal Election Campaign Act of 1971 and strengthened the limits, regulations, and reporting of campaign contributions (also known as the McCain–Feingold Act).

Black and Tan Republicans A wing of the Republican Party that supported civil rights for African Americans.

Black Codes Laws passed in Southern states during the immediate aftermath of the Civil War that singled out African Americans for mistreatment and discrimination.

Block Grants Grants-in-aid from the national government that are general, contain minimal regulations, and give state and local governments considerable discretion on how the money should be used.

Blog A website in which the operator states his or her opinion, allows readers to post comments, and provides links to news stories and other blogs.

Bradley Effect The difference between how Black candidates poll and how they perform at the ballot box (also called the Wilder effect).

Brown v. Board of Education A landmark 1954 Supreme Court case that prohibited government-sponsored segregation as a violation of the Fourteenth Amendment equal protection clause.

Bureaucracy A large, complex organization in which employees work within specific levels of rank and authority to carry out the policies of that organization.

Bureaucrats The employees who work in a bureaucracy.

Cabinet The key presidential aides, each of whom heads an executive branch department, as well as others that the president designates.

Cabinet Departments The major divisions within the executive branch, with each performing a specific function.

Casework Favors and other forms of assistance that members of Congress provide to their constituents.

Catalyst An event that energizes and coalesces a social movement.

Catalytic Leadership Social activists who create or recognize opportunities to galvanize people to organized action.

Categorical Grants Grants-in-aid that contain numerous, detailed provisions on how the states and local governments use the money.

Caucus A method for political parties to select their candidates for office whereby party members convene at local meetings.

Caucuses Informal organizations within Congress.

Central Clearance A requirement that all agency budget requests receive approval from the Office of Management and Budget before the president submits them to Congress.

Chief of Staff A key assistant to the president who coordinates executive branch employees and serves as a link between other presidential advisers and the president.

Civic Virtue The subordination of individualism and individual self-interest to the interest of society.

Civil Law A type of law that pertains to a dispute between two parties, at least one of which is a non-governmental private party.

Civil Liberties The constitutional freedoms that Americans enjoy and on which the government may not encroach.

Civil Rights The protections against unequal treatment that the government guarantees to all groups.

Civil Rights Act of 1964 A federal law that prevents private businesses from discriminating in service and personnel policies.

Civil Servants Federal bureaucrats who are not political appointees, but instead are hired according to their education and performance on an examination.

Civil Unions Government policies that provide official legal recognition of same-sex couples without sanctioning marriage.

Classical Liberalism A body of Western European political philosophy that is concerned with the freedom of the individual and the role of government in protecting that freedom.

Classical Republicanism A theory that rule by the people ought to be indirect through representatives.

Clear and Present Danger Test A guideline that requires the government to demonstrate that banned expression poses a definite and immediate threat to peace or national security.

Closed Primary A primary in which only registered members of a particular political party can vote in that party's primary election to choose the party's candidate or delegate.

Cloture Vote A procedure in the Senate to stop a filibuster that requires three-fifths of the senators (sixty) agreeing to end debate.

Collective Good Any benefit that if available to one member of the community cannot be denied to any other, regardless of whether he or she bore any of the costs of providing it.

Commerce Clause A constitutional provision that gives the national government the authority to regulate commerce among the states, foreign nations, and Indian tribes; it has been used to expand the power of the national government.

Comptroller General The head of the Government Accountability Office.

Concurrent Powers Powers shared by the national government and state governments, such as the power to tax and borrow money.

Concurring Opinion An opinion that agrees with the outcome of a Supreme Court case but for reasons different from those expressed in the majority opinion.

Confederation A system in which states or other types of government units organize a weak central government with limited scope and powers while reserving ultimate power for themselves.

Conference committee A committee composed of members of the House and the Senate that reconciles different versions of the same bill.

Congressional Black Caucus An informal organization consisting of African Americans elected to the United States Congress.

Congressional Record The published record of the official proceedings of Congress.

Congressional War Powers The power granted by the Constitution (in Article 1, Section 8) to Congress to decide when the United States goes to war.

Conservative Individual who believes that government should play a limited role in the lives of individuals and that government is not the source of solutions for problems.

Constituency The people who choose a representative to act on their behalf.

Constitution A set of formal written rules and principles governing a state.

Constitutional Democracy A government that derives its authority from a constitution.

Constitutional Law A type of law pertaining to the rules for our government expressed in the Constitution.

Cooperative Federalism A view of federalism in which the national government expands its power and blurs the lines between national and state authority.

County Commissions Representative bodies that make policies that apply to the county.

Coverture A doctrine and system in British common law according to which marriage merged a woman's legal identity with that of her husband.

Criminal Law A type of law that pertains to violations of a code of behavior specified in local, state, and federal statutes.

Dealignment A period in which voters abandon their ties to the political parties, resulting in a balance of power between Republicans and Democrats.

Debates Important public face-offs between candidates discussing issues in a variety of formats (including traditional question-and-answer sessions as well as town hall forums) and through a variety of media, most important television and more recently, the Internet.

Decision Agenda The set of issues that a government body formally resolves to address.

De Facto Segregation Physical separation of groups that is not legally sanctioned or imposed by the government but instead stems from individual preferences and economic forces.

De Jure Segregation Physical separation of groups that results from laws or official government actions.

Democracy A system of government in which political power is exercised by the people.

Democratic Party One of the two major political parties, established by Andrew Jackson in the 1820s to champion the interests of commoners.

Democratic-Republicans An early political party that Thomas Jefferson formed to oppose the nationalist policies of John Adams and Alexander Hamilton.

Descriptive Representation The extent to which the characteristics of a representative correspond with the general characteristics of his or her constituency.

Devolution A view of federalism that advocates partially returning power to state and local governments.

Dillon's Rule A principle of local governance in which municipal governments lack independent authority; they can only draw power from their state governments.

Direct Democracy A democracy in which the people are able to participate directly in decision making.

Direct Primaries Elections in which voters select the individual to represent the party in the general election by voting directly for the candidates on the ballot.

Disenfranchisement A government denying a group the right to vote.

Dissenting Opinion An opinion that disagrees with the winning side of a Supreme Court case and explains why.

Divided Government A period in which the president is of one political party and the majority of one or both houses of Congress is of the other party.

Domestic Policy Laws, rules, and programs that directly affect people living in the United States.

Dred Scott v. Sandford A controversial 1857 Supreme Court decision that ruled Congress lacked power to regulate slavery and Blacks had no civil rights.

Dual Federalism A view of federalism in which the national government is limited to a strict interpretation of the powers granted in the Constitution, while states enjoy broad police power to rule within their own territory.

Due Process Clause A specific provision of the Fourteenth Amendment that requires states to use normal judicial and criminal procedures before denying a citizen life, liberty, or property.

Electioneering Working actively on behalf of a political candidate or political party with activities that might include publicly endorsing a candidate, making a campaign contribution, or making phone calls.

Elections The process by which individuals make political choices by voting.

Electoral College The entity that selects the president and vice president, consisting of 538 electors chosen from the fifty states and the District of Columbia.

Emancipation Proclamation, The An executive order issued by president Abraham Lincoln during the Civil War that freed the slaves in the Confederacy.

Eminent Domain A provision in the Fifth Amendment to the Constitution that requires the government to provide compensation when it takes private property for public use.

Enemy Combatants The status given to individuals captured in battle who do not belong to any national military force.

Enumerated Powers Powers of the federal government specifically stated in the Constitution.

Environmental Racism Intentional or unintentional racial discrimination in the enforcement of environmental laws and regulations and in the targeting of racial minority communities for the siting of pollution-producing industries or hazardous waste sites and other related environmentally hazardous entities.

Equal Protection Clause A specific provision of the Fourteenth Amendment that prevents states from passing laws that treat people differently on account of race or ethnicity.

Equal Rights Amendment A proposed, but unratified, constitutional amendment that would have prevented gender discrimination to the same extent that the Fourteenth Amendment prevents racial and ethnic discrimination.

Establishment Clause A provision in the First Amendment to the U.S. Constitution that prevents the government from endorsing religion.

Ethnicity A socially constructed classification of people based on national origin or culture.

Ex Post Facto Law A criminal sanction that applies retroactively and could result in governments charging people for acts committed before they were outlawed.

Exclusionary Rule A judicially created civil liberties protection that prohibits the use of evidence gathered in violation of the Fourth Amendment.

Executive Agreements Agreements between the president and foreign nations that, because they are not treaties, do not need the approval of the Senate.

Executive Office of the President (EOP) A part of the executive branch that is divided into specific offices and contains key advisers who assist the president in managing the executive branch and developing policies.

Executive Orders Directives that the president issues to subordinates in the executive branch and that have the force of law.

Executive Privilege Presidential authority to keep some of the communications among executive branch personnel private and free from Congress, the courts, and the public.

Extradition Clause A provision in the Constitution stipulating that if a person is charged with a crime in one state and flees to another state, then the second state must transport the accused criminal back to the first state.

Factionalism Divisions that develop within a movement that may weaken it or cause its demise.

Federal Communications Commission (FCC) An independent regulatory commission that licenses and regulates the content of broadcast radio and television.

Federalism The balance of power between the national government on one side and the state and local governments on the other side.

Federalist Papers, The A collection of the eighty-five articles written by James Madison, Alexander Hamilton, and John Jay in support of the ratification of the Constitution.

Federalist Party An early political party led by John Adams and Alexander Hamilton that supported nationalizing the economy.

Federalists Proponents of the Constitution during the ratification process.

Feudalism A system of landholding involving a network of allegiances and obligations.

Fifteenth Amendment An amendment to the Constitution that prevents states from denying the right to vote on the basis of race or ethnicity.

Fighting Words Derisive, insulting, or offensive words that inflict damage on other people and are therefore not protected by the First Amendment.

Filibuster A parliamentary technique in the Senate that allows senators to delay or block votes by talking endlessly.

Foreign Policy Laws, rules, and programs that affect the relationship between the United States and other nations.

Fourteenth Amendment An amendment to the Constitution that prevents states from denying on the basis of race full citizenship to their residents.

Framing The media's ability to shape how viewers interpret political events and issues.

Franking Privilege The ability of members of Congress to send noncampaign material to their constituents free of charge.

Free Exercise Clause A provision in the First Amendment to the U.S. Constitution that prevents the government from prohibiting people from practicing their religion.

Free Rider A person who profits from the activities of others without participating in those activities.

Fugitive Slave Clause A clause in the Constitution stipulating if slaves escaped from a slave state to a free state the free state must return them to their owners in the slave state.

Full Faith and Credit Clause A constitutional provision requiring states to recognize official documents and records from other states.

Gender Social relations between the sexes and attitudes about how the sexes interact and the roles that society assumes they will play.

Gender Gap The difference between men and women on such crucial issues as partisan identification and voting for certain candidates.

General Elections Elections in which the winner is elected to office and takes office after the end of the term of the current officeholder.

Gerrymandering The practice in which a group, usually a political party, uses redistricting to maximize its chances of winning elections.

Government A social institution that controls the behavior of people; the political and administrative hierarchy of an organized state.

Government Accountability Office (GAO) The part of the legislative branch that is responsible for auditing how bureaucratic agencies spend money appropriated by Congress.

Government Corporations Parts of the federal bureaucracy that charge fees for the services that they provide to the American public.

Grandfather Clauses A policy designed to disenfranchise Blacks by exempting Whites, but not Blacks, from literacy tests.

Grants-in-Aid National government expenditures that provide money or property to the states to accomplish a policy goal.

Great Compromise (or Connecticut Compromise) Worked out by a committee at the 1787 Constitutional Convention, a compromise that called for membership in the House of Representatives based on population, with states having equal representation in the Senate.

Ground War The part of election campaigns conducted using "pavement pounding" methods including candidate public appearances, voter registration and mobilization, fundraising, and public opinion polling, among others.

Hard Money The heavily regulated money that is directly raised by political candidates.

Hatch Act A federal law passed in 1939 and amended in 1993 that restricts federal employees' partisan political activities.

Hate Crime Legislation Laws that enhance criminal penalties for crimes committed out of prejudice toward certain groups.

Hate Speech A form of expression that is hostile toward a particular race, ethnicity, gender, religion, nationality, or sexual orientation.

Help America Vote Act A law passed in 2002 to reform aspects of the voting process that failed in the 2000 presidential election and to increase voter education and turnout.

Home Rule A principle of local governance in which local governments can govern themselves independently of the state governments.

House Majority Leader The second most powerful leader in the House of Representatives; the person who assists the Speaker in passing the majority party's legislative priorities.

House Minority Leader The leader of the minority party in the House of Representatives; the person who articulates the legislative priorities of the minority party and opposes the majority party's priorities but exerts minimal control over the outcome of legislation.

Impeachment The process by which the House of Representatives charges a president, vice-president, or federal judge with a high crime or misdemeanor; the Senate can then decide to remove that official from office with a two-thirds vote.

Implementation The day-to-day process by which bureaucrats enforce laws and carry out policies.

Implied Powers Government powers that are inferred from the powers expressly enumerated in the Constitution.

Incorporation The application of the Bill of Rights to state and local governments.

Independent Executive Agencies Parts of the federal bureaucracy with specified functions that are independent from cabinet departments, do not regulate, and do not charge fees for their services.

Independent Regulatory Commissions Government bodies that issue and enforce regulations on specified economic and social interests.

Indirect (or Representative) Democracy A democracy in which people do not participate directly in decision making and instead elect individuals to represent their interests.

Inegalitarianism A tradition of excluding large segments of the American population from participation in the political system despite the language of equality, liberty, and freedom (*see also* Tradition of exclusion).

Inequality The extent to which one group enjoys more political, social, or economic benefits than another group.

Inequality of Opportunity A form of inequality in which laws or official actions deny specific groups social, political, or economic benefits that are available to other groups.

Inequality of Outcome A form of inequality in which social and demographic forces, not official laws or policies, cause one group to enjoy more political, social, or economic benefits than another group.

Institutional Agenda The set of issues that government officials recognize require their attention.

Interest Group Litigation The practice of interest groups arguing cases before the judiciary as a means of influencing public policy.

Interest Groups Organizations whose members act together to influence public policy to promote their common interests (also known as pressure groups).

Interstate Compact Clause A clause in Article I, Section 10 of the Constitution that requires the approval of Congress when states enter into official agreements with one another.

Iron Triangle A conception of bureaucratic policymaking in which policymaking is dominated by congressional committees, interest groups, and bureaucratic agencies.

Issue Networks A conception of policymaking as dynamic and not controlled by any particular set of groups or institutions.

Jim Crow Laws The southern practice of racially segregating all public facilities, such as transportation, schools, libraries, hotels, hospitals, theaters, parks, and cemeteries.

Judicial Activism A conception of judicial review that believes courts should overturn laws or government actions even if there is no clear constitutional directive.

Judicial Restraint A conception of judicial review that believes courts should not overturn laws or government actions unless there is a clear directive in the Constitution.

Judicial Review The power of a court to overturn a law or official government action because it is deemed unconstitutional.

Justiciable The requirement that there must be an actual case or controversy between two parties for the federal judiciary to decide a case.

Latino An ethnic category describing people of Spanish or Portuguese colonial ancestry from the Caribbean, Central America, and South America.

Legislative Veto An act of one or both houses of Congress that overturned an administrative action. The Supreme Court invalidated such acts in 1983.

Libel The publication of written material that damages a person's reputation.

Liberal Individual who believes that government has a role to play in the lives of individuals and that government can provide solutions to policy problems.

Lily White Republicans A wing of the Republican Party that opposed civil rights for African Americans.

Line-Item Veto Governors' power to reject specific expenditures and taxes, while allowing the remainder of a bill to stand.

Literacy Tests A form of disenfranchisement in which potential voters need to demonstrate the ability to read as a condition for registering to vote.

Living Constitution A belief that the Constitution should be interpreted to reflect contemporary times.

Lobbying The process by which an individual, a group, or an organization seeks to influence government policymakers.

Logic of Collective Action The view that the costs of large groups collectively organizing are high and the benefits to individual members are relatively low; thus the appeal to rational members is one of deterrence to organizing collectively.

Logrolling The practice by members of Congress of trading votes or other favors to enhance members' mutual interests.

Lynching The practice of killing people by mob action outside of the formal judicial process. In the United States, lynching was used as an intimidation tactic against Black Americans.

Majority Winning of an election by the candidate who receives at least 51 percent of the vote.

Majority-Minority Districts Legislative districts that contain a population made up of more than 50 percent of a racial or ethnic minority group.

Majority Opinion The opinion reflecting the winning outcome of a Supreme Court case that is signed by at least a plurality of the justices.

Majority Party The political party in the House or the Senate that has more than half of the seats and therefore controls the leadership, rules, and outcome of legislation.

Mandate A president's claim to Congress that his election victory signifies the public's support for his policy preferences.

Mass Media Sources of information, including print, radio, television, and the Internet, that reach a large number of people.

Merit System A system of selecting state judges in which a nonpartisan commission presents the governor with a short list of judicial candidates, out of which the governor selects one name; that judge later appears before the voters in a retention election.

Minor Parties Political parties in a two-party system that are not one of the dominant two political parties.

Minority Party The political party in the House or the Senate that has fewer than half of the seats and therefore does not control the leadership, rules, or outcome of legislation.

Miranda Rights The Supreme Court's requirement that law enforcement must inform criminal suspects of the following: (1) that they have the right to remain silent, (2) that anything they say can be used against them in court, (3) that they have the right to the presence of an attorney, and (4) that if they cannot afford an attorney, then the court will appoint one before the interrogation takes place.

Modern Presidency Since Franklin Roosevelt in 1933, the conception of the presidency, which is characterized by a powerful president who seeks to lead Congress, connects with the American public, and presides over an enormous executive branch.

Monopoly A situation in which one company controls an entire industry.

Mootness An aspect of justiciability that requires that the conflict causing the case must still be germane; it could not have resolved itself on its own.

Municipalities The incorporated districts, usually cities or towns, that comprise the local government.

National Committee The organization responsible for making rules and regulations for a party when the conventions are not in session, raising money for the party, and directing the party's electoral strategy.

National Committee Chair The head of each party's national committee, who is most responsible for directing the party's electoral strategies.

National Government A system of government in which powers are distributed between the central government (federal government) and subunits, such as states.

National Voter Registration Act A law passed in 1993 that provides for voter registration by mail and in departments of motor vehicles (also called the "motor voter" act).

Natural Law Law that comes from nature and is superior to statutory law.

Natural Rights Rights to which every person is entitled, such as life and liberty; rights that are not dependent on government.

Necessary and Proper Clause A clause in Article 1 of the Constitution giving Congress the authority to make whatever laws are necessary and proper to carry out its enumerated responsibilities (sometimes called the elastic clause).

New Deal Coalition The groups that supported president Franklin Roosevelt's policies and as a result made the Democrats the dominant party during the 1930s and 1940s.

New Jersey Plan Drafted by William Paterson of New Jersey at the 1787 Constitutional Convention, a proposal for a system of government that called for the maintenance of a confederation with a unicameral legislature in which all states were represented equally, a multimember executive without the power to veto legislation, and a supreme court.

Nineteenth Amendment An amendment to the Constitution that prevents states from denying women the right to vote because of their sex.

Nomination Petitions The certain number of signatures of registered voters that independent or third-party candidates must collect to qualify for inclusion on a ballot.

Open Primary A primary election in which a voter does not have to declare a political party affiliation but may participate in the primary election of any party.

Opposition Research Campaign activity devoted to undermining the public's confidence in and support of a candidate, a key component of negative campaigning.

Original Intent A belief that the Constitution should be interpreted only according to the intent of its authors.

Original Jurisdiction A defined set of cases that avoids a lower court and goes directly to the Supreme Court.

Parallel Press Newspapers and other forms of media geared toward specific racial and ethnic minority groups.

Partisan Identification The political party an individual most identifies with.

Party Platform A statement a political party produces at its national convention that summarizes the basic policy principles of the party.

Patronage A system of hiring bureaucrats because they supported the winning political candidate, not because they had the skill, training, and experience for their jobs.

Pendleton Act A federal law passed in 1883 that required bureaucrats to be hired and retained according to their demonstrated skill, not their political affiliation.

Penny Press Nineteenth-century newspapers that eschewed coverage of politics and instead focused on human interest stories.

Peremptory Challenges The right of each side in a legal case to discard a set number of potential jurors without needing to express a reason for doing so.

Pledged Delegates Party members elected or chosen on the state and local levels to support a particular candidate at the party's national convention.

Plessy v. Ferguson A controversial 1896 Supreme Court decision that ruled that under the Fourteenth Amendment, states were allowed to segregate by race.

Pluralism A theory of politics that contends that power is group based and that, because there are multiple points of access within American government, each

group possesses an equality of opportunity when competing with other groups for power and resources (also known as interest group theory).

Plurality Winning of an election by the candidate who receives the most votes (also known as "first past the post" [FPTP]).

Pocket Veto A way for the president to overturn a bill passed by Congress when the president does not act on a bill within ten days of passage (excluding Sundays) and Congress adjourns in the meantime.

Police Power A general, unwritten power to regulate health, safety, and morals.

Policy Adoption The stage in the policymaking process in which the policy is actually enacted.

Policy Evaluation The stage in the policymaking process in which government actors and private citizens determine whether an implemented policy is achieving its intended effect.

Policy Formulation The stage in the policymaking process in which government actors draft a solution to a problem that they have recognized merits their attention.

Policy Implementation The stage in the policymaking process in which government actors and even private citizens carry out enacted policies.

Political Culture The attitudes, beliefs, and values that undergird or are at the foundation of a political system.

Political Independents Voters who do not designate a political party affiliation when registering to vote.

Political Party Mass organizations that seek to elect candidates to public office and influence policymaking.

Political Socialization The process through which a person gains political understanding and forms a set of political beliefs.

Politics The conflict, competition, and compromise that occur within a political system.

Poll Taxes Fees that states charged citizens to vote and that disenfranchised the poor and minority citizens.

Pork Barrel Spending Federal money spent on projects that benefit only a specific member's district or state.

Precedent A principle articulated in a previous case that judges use to decide current cases.

Preemption A concept that permits the national government to overturn state and local laws.

Press Conferences Formal question-and-answer sessions that the president or the press secretary holds with the White House press corps.

Press Secretary A member of the president's staff who conducts daily briefings with members of the media.

Primary A method for political parties to select their candidates for office whereby people vote in an election.

Priming The media's ability to influence how the public perceives politicians and candidates.

Prior Restraint A usually impermissible government regulation that prevents the publication of printed material.

Private Law A type of law in which the government is a party to the case.

Privileges and Immunities Clause A provision in Article IV of the Constitution that prevents states from discriminating against citizens of other states.

Probability Sampling A general term for a sample selected in accordance with probability theory, which ensures that every person in the population has an equal chance of being selected for the sample.

Probable Cause A legal requirement that there be more evidence indicating guilt than indicating innocence before a law enforcement officer can act.

Proportional Representation An election system that uses multi-member districts and in which seats are awarded by political party roughly in proportion to the results of the election.

Public Funding The financing of election campaigns by the American public through tax allocations as distinct from private fundraising by candidates.

Public Good A government policy or action that benefits society as a whole rather than a specific individual.

Public Law A type of law that concerns disputes between individuals.

Public Opinion The collective opinions of large segments of the population on an issue, candidate, or public policy on which the public might be much divided and lack a consensus.

Quota Sampling A type of sample in which individuals to be interviewed are selected based on their proportion or quota in the general population being polled.

Race A socially constructed classification of people based on their physical characteristics, especially skin color.

Racial Profiling A law enforcement technique that singles out suspects on the basis of their race or ethnicity.

Realignment Periods when voter allegiances toward the political parties shift for an extended period of time, resulting in one party emerging as dominant.

Reapportionment The process of assigning states a number of representatives to the House of Representatives after each decennial census.

Reconstruction The period from 1865 to 1877 in which former Confederate states were brought back into the Union, often characterized by a military presence in the South and civil rights progress for Blacks.

Redistricting The process by which a state is divided into geographical regions, with each region electing a member of the House of Representatives.

Reparations A concept or tool for providing monetary payments to members of aggrieved groups based on past wrongful actions against them or their ancestors.

Representative A person chosen to make policy decisions on behalf of a defined group of people.

Republican Form of Government A government whose powers are exercised by elected representatives who are directly or indirectly accountable to the people governed.

Republican Party One of the two major political parties, founded in the 1850s by former Whigs who opposed slavery.

Reservations Portions of land set aside for American Indians removed from their ancestral lands by the federal government.

Retention Election A type of judicial election in which voters decide only whether to keep the judge in office; there are no opposition candidates.

Right to Die An extension of the right to privacy that includes an individual's right to refuse life-saving medical treatment but does not include the right to commit suicide.

Rule of Law The predominance of law over discretionary authority.

Rulemaking The process by which bureaucrats issue regulations that have the force of law.

Runoff Primary A second election held in some states if no candidate in the primary election receives a majority of the votes.

Sample A small set of people carefully drawn from a larger population to reflect its overall characteristics.

Sampling Error The degree of expected error in sampling results that comes from estimating the responses of the population from a sample.

School Districts Local government entities that create policies for public schools.

Search Warrant A legal document that allows law enforcement to search someone's person, home, or business.

Sedition Act A 1798 law that criminalized harsh criticism of president John Adams and his policies.

Segregation Physical separation of a dominant group from a subordinate group.

Selective Incorporation The process by which the Supreme Court has gradually incorporated specific liberties deemed absolutely necessary in a free society.

Senate Majority Leader The most powerful position in the Senate; the person who articulates the majority party's legislative priorities and works to pass them.

Senate Majority Whip (also called the assistant majority leader) A majority party leader in the Senate who counts votes, persuades members to vote according to the leadership's wishes, and assists the majority leader in passing the majority party's legislation.

Senate Minority Leader The leader of the minority party of the Senate; the person who articulates the legislative priorities of the minority party and opposes the majority party's priorities but exerts limited control over the outcome of legislation.

Senatorial Courtesy The practice whereby a president consults with senators in his party to find potential lower court vacancies that occur in the senators' states.

Senior Executive Service High-level bureaucrats the president places in different agencies to ensure compliance with his directives.

Separate but Equal Principle A legal principle that allowed states to segregate the races in public facilities, as long as the state provided each race with basic access to the public facility in question.

Separation of Church and State A constitutional principle that prevents the government (federal, state, or local) from interfering with or advancing religion or religious activity.

Separation of Powers The manner in which the Constitution divides power among the three branches of government—the legislature, the executive, and the judiciary.

Sexual Harassment Unwelcome sexual comments or treatment in the workplace or an educational institution.

Shared Grievances Complaints against the political system (national, state, or local) by a group of people who agree generally on the causes of the complaints.

Signing Statements Presidential declarations issued along with legislative bill signings that express reservations about parts of a bill or announce an unwillingness to enforce aspects of the bill.

Sit-ins A form of protest against segregated restaurants in which Black patrons refused to move from Whites-only sections.

Social Construction of Race The construction of a group of people of various phenotypes, skin colors, and physical characteristics for political and social purposes such as enslavement and exclusion.

Social Contract Individuals creating government by entering into a contract with it.

Social Movement A sustained challenge to those in power put forth by individuals, acting in concert with others, who have been excluded from the political process or who consider themselves political outsiders.

Soft Money The less regulated money that is raised by a political party to support and maintain the party.

Solicitor General A high-ranking lawyer in the Justice Department who argues cases before the Supreme Court on behalf of the U.S. government.

Southern Christian Leadership Conference (SCLC) Group designed to be the umbrella organization that would link church-based affiliates throughout the South in the nonviolent struggle for racial justice.

Sovereignty A government policy toward American Indians that allows each tribe to regulate its own people and operate according to its own customs; also complete political power and authority.

Speaker of the House The most powerful position in the House of Representatives; the leader of the majority party; the person who articulates the House's legislative priorities and ensures their passage.

Standing An aspect of justiciability that requires the party bringing the case to show that the policy in question has caused it an injury.

State of the Union Address An annual occasion in which the president speaks before Congress to suggest laws that Congress should pass.

Statutory Law A type of law pertaining to rules made by legislatures, especially Congress.

Student Non-Violent Coordinating Committee (SNCC) Organization of college students dedicated to continuing the campaign for social justice started by the North Carolina A&T students.

Substantive Representation The extent to which representatives advocate policies that benefit their constituents.

Suffrage Movement Large-scale efforts of organizations and activists during the late nineteenth and early twentieth centuries to secure the right to vote for women.

Super PACs Political action committees allowed to raise an unlimited amount of money from any source, including individuals, corporations, labor unions, and interest groups. These committees are then allowed to spend this money in support of or opposition to any political candidate, including people running for president, so long as their activities are not directly coordinated with a campaign.

Superdelegates Delegates to the Democratic National Convention who are not selected by primaries or caucuses but instead are established party leaders.

Supportive Environment An environment receptive to the ideals and demands of a social movement.

Supremacy Clause A clause in Article VI of the Constitution stipulating that the Constitution and national laws are supreme, meaning that when state laws conflict with national laws, national laws take precedence.

Survey Research Administration of questionnaires to a sample of respondents selected from a particular population, useful for making descriptive and explanatory studies of large populations.

Symbolic Representation The extent to which constituents trust and accept their representative and the legislative institution as a whole.

Systemic Agenda The set of issues that policymakers perceive as worthy of their attention.

Tea Party A conservative political movement that advocates for drastically cutting government spending, reducing taxes, and ending most forms of regulations.

Tenth Amendment An amendment to the Constitution that guarantees states powers not given to the national government or forbidden to the states.

Think Tanks Interest groups that focus on research and scholarly analysis of issues relevant to the people they represent.

Thirteenth Amendment An amendment to the Constitution that prohibits slavery throughout the United States.

Three-Fifths Compromise A compromise reached at the Constitutional Convention over how state populations were to be counted for purposes of allocating seats in the House of Representatives; each slave was to be counted as three-fifths of a person for representational purposes.

Tradition of Exclusion A tradition that excludes groups from the political system based on their ascribed traits, such as race, gender, and religion (*see also* Inegalitarianism).

Twelfth Amendment An amendment to the Constitution that requires the president and vice president to be elected on separate ballots.

Two-Party System A government system in which only two political parties compete for elected offices.

Unfunded Mandates Directives the national government issues to state and local governments without compensating them for complying.

Unicameral Form of Government A government system that consists of only one legislative body (rather than two or more).

Unified government A period in which both houses of Congress are controlled by the same party as the president.

Unitary Form of Government A system in which the central government exercises complete control and authority over subunits of government, which means that states or other governmental units do not have autonomous powers.

Veto The president's ability to cancel legislation passed by Congress.

Virginia Plan Drafted by James Madison of Virginia at the 1787 Constitutional Convention, a proposal for a system of government that called for the establishment of a strong central government with three branches: a bicameral legislature, a chief executive chosen by the legislature, and a powerful judiciary.

Voting-Age Population (VAP) The population of both citizens and noncitizens in the United States age eighteen or over.

Voting-Eligible Population (VEP) The population of U.S. citizens age eighteen or over.

Voting Rights Act of 1965 A federal law that significantly curtailed disenfranchisement of racial and ethnic minorities by banning literacy tests and requiring federal supervision of jurisdictions with a history of voting discrimination.

Whigs A political party founded in the 1830s to oppose the politics and policies of president Andrew Jackson.

Whip A legislative leader who assists the party by counting votes and persuading members to vote according to the party leaders' wishes.

Whistleblowers Bureaucrats who publicly expose waste, fraud, or abuse in their agency.

White Citizens Council Formed in 1954 in Mississippi to prevent the implementation of *Brown v. Board of Education*, the White Citizens Council's membership consisted of plantation owners, bankers, doctors, legislators, and others opposed to Black civil rights and determined to maintain segregation.

White House Press Corps Those elite journalists responsible for covering the president and key executive branch officials.

White House Staff The president's personal advisers, who do not need senatorial approval when appointed and provide critical political and policy advice to the president.

White Primary A practice by Southern state Democratic parties in the nineteenth and early twentieth centuries intended to disenfranchise Blacks by preventing them from voting in the crucial Democratic Party primary elections.

Winner-Take-All An election system in which the candidate who gets the most votes in that district wins the election, even if he or she has not received a majority of the votes and has finished only a few votes ahead of the second-place finisher.

Writ of Certiorari A formal legal document filed by the losing party in a lower court case that asks the Supreme Court to hear an appeal.

Yellow Journalism A form of journalism popular during the late eighteenth and early nineteenth centuries that sensationalized stories and distorted facts to sell more papers.

Notes

Chapter 1

1 Justin Wm. Moyer. 2016 "Delaware Apologizes for Slavery and Jim Crow. No reparations forthcoming." *The Washington Post*, February 11. https://www.washingtonpost.com/news/morning-mix/wp/2016/02/11/delaware-apologizes-for-slavery-and-jim-crow-no-reparations-forthcoming/

2 "House Apologizes for Slavery, 'Jim Crow' Injustices," CNNPolitics.com, July 29, 2008, accessed July 29, 2008.

3 Krissah Thompson, "Senate Backs Apology for Slavery," Washingtonpost.com, June 19, 2009, accessed July 14, 2009.

4 Andrew DeMillo, "Gov. Questions Need for Slavery Apology," Washingtonpost.com, June 5, 2007, accessed June 5, 2007.

5 "States Debate Formal Slavery Apologies; Arguments Question Resolutions' Necessity," *Grand Rapids Press* (Michigan), A5, accessed June 3, 2007, Lexis Nexis.

6 "John Hope Franklin: Apologies Aren't Enough," *Independent Weekly*, April 18, 2007, www.indyweek.com, accessed June 5, 2007.

7 "National," *Sun-Sentinel* (Fort Lauderdale, Florida), Broward metro ed., 3A, http://www.sun-sentinel.com, accessed June 3, 2007.

8 General Assembly of North Carolina, Resolution 2007–21 (Senate Joint Resolution 1557), April 12, 2007.

9 Richard Johnson, "Graphic: Mapping a Superpower-Sized Military," *National Post*, October 28, 2011, http://news.nationalpost.com/2011/10/28/graphic-mapping-a-superpower-sized-military/

10 Lisa King, "Olympics 2012: Title IX Made Women Gold Medalists Possible at the 2012 Olympics." *Washington Times*, August 1, 2012, http://communities.washingtontimes.com/neighborhood/london-2012-summer-olympic-games/2012/aug/1/Title-IX-American-women-gold-2012-Olympics/

11 R. Vivian Acosta and Linda Jean Carpenter. "Women in Intercollegiate Sport. A Longitudinal, National Study, Thirty Five Year Update. 1977–2012." Unpublished manuscript. Available for downloading at http://acostacarpenter.org/AcostaCarpenter2012.pdf

12 Association of Public and Land-Grant Universities, "Land Grant Heritage." http://www.aplu.org/page.spx?pid=1565

13 Sarah Thomson, Robin Osborn, David Squires, and Sarah Jane Reed. "International Profiles of Health Care Systems, 2011." New York: The Common Wealth Fund, 2011.

14 Michael Curtis, Jean Blondel, Bernard E. Brown, Joseph Fewsmith, Roger E. Kanet, Donald Kommers, Theodore McNelly, Martin C. Needler, John S. Reshetar, and Stephen Wright, *Introduction to Comparative Government*, 4th ed. (New York: Longman, 1997), 13.

15 Paula D. McClain and Joseph Stewart Jr., *"Can We All Get along?": Racial and Ethnic Minorities in American Politics*, 6th ed. (Boulder, CO: Westview Press, 2014).

16 Quoted in Lee Cameron McDonald, *Western Political Theory: The Modern Age* (New York: Harcourt, Brace and World, 1962), 7.

17 Rogers M. Smith, "Beyond Tocqueville, Myrdal, and Hartz: The Multiple Traditions in America," *American Political Science Review* 87 (September 1993): 549–566; Rogers M. Smith, *Civic Ideals: Conflicting Visions of Citizenship in U.S. History* (New Haven, CT: Yale University Press, 1997), 3.

18 Lee Cameron McDonald, *Western Political Theory: The Modern Age* (New York: Harcourt, Brace and World, Inc., 1962), 243.

19 Stephen Holmes, *The Anatomy of Antiliberalism* (Cambridge, MA: Harvard University Press, 1993), 3–4.

20 M. N. S. Sellers, *American Republicanism: Roman Ideology in the United States Constitution* (New York: New York University Press, 1994), 47.

21 McDonald, 188.

22 Smith, *Civic Ideals*, chap. 1.

23 Joan Hoff Wilson, "The Illusion of Change: Women in the American Revolution" in *The American Revolution: Explorations in the History of American Radicalism*, ed. Alfred F. Young (DeKalb: Northern Illinois University Press, 1976), 386–445.

24 Linda K. Kerber, *Women of the Republic: Intellect and Ideology in Revolutionary America.* (Chapel Hill: University of North Carolina Press, 1980), 23.

25 Jean-Jacques Rousseau, *Emile*, trans. Barbara Foxley (London: J. M. Dent & Sons, 1957), 322.

26 Linda K. Kerber, "The Paradox of Women's Citizenship in the Early Republic: The Case of *Martin v. Massachusetts, 1805*," *American Historical Review* 97 (April 1992): 349–378.

27 Winthrop D. Jordan, *White over Black: American Attitudes toward the Negro, 1550–1812* (Baltimore, MD: Penguin Books, 1968), 20, 23, 56.

28 McClain and Stewart, *"Can We All Get along?"*

29 Smith, *Civic Ideals*.

30 Thomas Jefferson, *Notes on the State of Virginia*, ed. William Peden (Chapel Hill: University of North Carolina Press, [1785] 1982).

31 John Chester Miller, *The Wolf by the Ears: Thomas Jefferson and Slavery* (Charlottesville: University Press of Virginia, 1991).

32 Louisiana and North Carolina used the one-sixteenth criterion (one great-great-grandparent). One eighth (one great-grandparent) was the standard in Florida, Indiana, Maryland, Mississippi, Missouri, Nebraska, North Dakota, South Carolina, and Tennessee. Oregon used a one quarter standard (one grandparent) (McClain and Stewart, *"Can We All Get along,"* 9).

33 Vine Deloria, Jr. and David E. Wilkins, *Tribes, Treaties, and Constitutional Tribulations* (Austin: University of Texas Press, 1999), 6.

34 Ibid., 7.

35 Ibid.

36 Smith, *Civic Ideals*, 61.

37 Ibid., 17.

38 Smith, "Beyond Tocqueville," 563, n.4.

39 Linda K. Kerber, "A Constitutional Right to Be Treated Like American Ladies: Women and the Obligations of Citizenship," in *U.S. History as Women's History*, ed. Linda K. Kerber, Alice Kessler-Harris, and Kathryn Kish Sklar (Chapel Hill: University of North Carolina Press, 1995), 18.

40 McClain and Stewart, *"Can We All Get along?"* 10.

41 Sidney L. Gulick, *American Democracy and Asiatic Citizenship* (New York: Scribner's, 1918), 55–56.

42 Donald L. Robinson, *Slavery in the Structure of American Politics, 1765–1820* (New York: Harcourt Brace Jovanovich, 1971), 86.

43 Ibid., 136.

44 Bruce E. Johansen, *Forgotten Founders: How the American Indian Helped Shape Democracy* (Boston: Harvard Common Press, 1982); Donald A. Grinde Jr., *The Iroquois and the Founding of the American Nation* (San Francisco: Indian Historian Press, 1977).

45 Ibid.

46 Ibid.

47 Ibid.

48 Rogers M. Smith, "Response to Jacqueline Stevens," *American Political Science Review* 89 (December 1995): 990–995.

Chapter 2

1 Tyler Kingkade. 2015. "UMD Frat Brother Allegedly Sent Racist Email, Signed Off With 'F*** Consent.'" *HuffPost College* (March 14) http://www.huffingtonpost.com /2015/03/13/umd-racist-frat-email_n_6863386.html. Accessed May 26, 2016.

2 Dana Hedgepeth and Susan Svrluga. 2015. "After Racist, Sexist Email Surfaces, U-Md. Student Leaves Fraternity." *The Washington Post Online* https://www.washingtonpost .com/local/education/u-of-md-investigates-e-mail-with -vulgar-language-allegedly-from-someone-associated -with-a-fraternity/2015/03/13/567e0baa-c97f-11e4-aa1a -86135599fb0f_story.html. Accessed May 26, 2016.

3 (esilvermandbk@gmail.com). 2015. "UMD investigation finds no policy violation in racist, sexist email." *The Diamondback* http://www.dbknews.com/archives /article_50c3b0d6-d8b9-11e4-bc1d-7bf3c631a532.html Accessed May 26, 2016.

4 Jack P. Greene, *Understanding the American Revolution: Issues and Actors* (Charlottesville: University Press of Virginia, 1995), 80.

5 Ibid., chap. 5.

6 Colin Bonwick, *The American Revolution* (London: Macmillan, 1991), chap. 3.

7 Greene, *Understanding the American Revolution*, chap. 12.

8 Bonwick, *The American Revolution*, chap. 4.

9 Martin Diamond, "The American Idea of Equality: The View from the Founding." *The Review of Politics* 38(3), 313–331.

10 Lester J. Cappon (Ed.), *The Adams-Jefferson Letters: The Complete Correspondence between Thomas Jefferson and Abigail and John Adams* (2 vols., Chapel Hill: University of North Carolina Press for the Institute of Early American History and Culture, Williamsburg, VA, 1959).

11 Merrill Jensen, *The Articles of Confederation: An Interpretation of the Social-Constitutional History of the American Revolution, 1774–1781* (Madison: University of Wisconsin Press, 1940), 126.

12 Ibid., chap. 12.

13 National Archives, "America's Founding Fathers: Delegates to the Constitutional Convention," http:// www.archives.gov/exhibits/charters/constitution_ founding_fathers_overview.html

14 Richard Vetterli and Gary Bryner, *In Search of the Republic: Public Virtue and the Roots of American Government* (Totowa, NJ: Rowman and Littlefield, 1987).

15 U.S. Census Bureau, "Congressional Apportionment: Historical Perspective," http://www.census.gov/population /www/censusdata/apportionment/history.html

16 Morton Borden, ed., *The Antifederalist Papers* (East Lansing: Michigan State University Press, 1965), x.

17 *McCulloch v. Maryland, 4 Wheat. 316* (1819).

18 Morton Keller, "Failed Amendments to the Constitution," *The World and I* (September 1987): 87–93.

Chapter 3

1 Rob O'Dell, Yvonne Wingett Sanchez, and Caitlin McGlade, "Lack of Polling Sites, Not Independents, Caused Maricopa Election Chaos," *Arizona Republic*, March 24, 2016, http://www.azcentral.com/story/news /politics/elections/2016/03/23/maricopa-county

-presidential-primary-election-chaos-arizona/
82174876/, accessed April 13, 2016.

2 United States Census Bureau, "QuickFacts: Maricopa County, Arizona," http://www.census.gov/quickfacts/ table/PST045215/04013, accessed April 13, 2016.

3 Slip Opinion, *Shelby County, AL v. Holder*, No. 12-96, http://www.supremecourt.gov/opinions/12pdf/12 -96_6k47.pdf, accessed April 13, 2016.

4 Michael Kiefer, "Justice Department to Investigate Maricopa County in Election Fiasco," *Arizona Republic*, April 5, 2016, http://www.azcentral.com/story/news /politics/elections/2016/04/04/doj-maricopa-county -helen-purcell-presidential-preference-election/ 82625974/, accessed April 13, 2016.

5 National Conference of State Legislatures, "2016 Legislative Session Calendar," http://www.ncsl.org /documents/ncsl/sess2016_3_22_2016.pdf, accessed April 16, 2016.

6 *Reynolds v. Sims*, 377 U.S. 84 (1964).

7 *Thornburg v. Gingles*, 478 U.S. 30 (1986).

8 For a brief time during the 1990s, the U.S. president had the line-item veto authority, but in *Clinton v. City of New York*, 524 U.S. 417 (1998) the U.S. Supreme Court ruled that the line-item veto violated the Constitution.

9 Christopher Famighetti, Amanda Melillo, and Myrna Pérez, *Election Day Long Lines: Resource Allocation* (New York: Brennan Center for law and Justice at New York University, 2014), https://www.brennancenter.org/sites /default/files/publications/ElectionDayLongLines- ResourceAllocation.pdf; accessed April 16, 2016.

10 Steve Bousquet, "Governor Scott Defends Florida Election, as His Chief Admits 'We Could Have Done Better,'" *Tampa Bay Times*, November 10, 2012, http://www .tampabay.com/news/politics/national/gov-rick-scott -defends-florida-election-as-his-chief-says-we-could -have/1260762, accessed April 16, 2106.

11 Steve Bousquet, "Scott Pushes for More Early Voting Days, Sites," *Tampa Bay Times*, January 18, 2013, 1A.

12 Bill Cotterell, "Florida Non-Citizen Voter Purge Postponed: Elections Official," *Reuters*, March 27, 2014, http://www.reuters.com/article/2014/03/27/us-usa -florida-politics-idUSBREA2Q2DH20140327, accessed April 16, 2016.

13 For examples of research finding the existence of racially polarized voting, see Chandler Davidson and Bernard Grofman, *Quiet Revolution in the South* (Princeton, NJ: Princeton University Press, 1994); Bernard Grofman, Lisa Handley, and Richard Niemi, *Minority Representation and the Quest for Voting Equality* (Cambridge, UK: Cambridge University Press, 1992); and David Lublin, "The Election of African Americans and Latinos to the U.S. House of Representatives, 1972–1994," *American Politics Quarterly* 25 (1997): 286–296. However, a study of a Los Angeles mayoral race demonstrates that issue voting can trump voting based on race and ethnicity. See Marisa A. Abrajano, Jonathan Nagler, and R. Michael Alvarez,

"A Natural Experiment of Race-Based and Issue Voting: The 2001 City of Los Angeles Elections," *Political Research Quarterly* 58 (2005): 203–218.

14 United States Census Bureau, "QuickFacts New Mexico," https://www.census.gov/quickfacts/table/PST045215/35, accessed April 16, 2016.

15 National Center for State Courts, "Judicial Selection in the States," http://www.judicialselection.us/, accessed April 17, 2016. In New Jersey, the state Senate must confirm the nomination. California judges serve a twelve-year term and must run in a retention election to serve another term.

16 Roy Schotland, "Comment: Judicial Independence and Accountability," *Law & Contemporary Problems* 61 (1998): 149–150.

17 For example, see Paul Brace and Brent D. Boyea, "State Public Opinion, the Death Penalty, and the Practice of Electing Judges," *American Journal of Political Science* 52 (2008): 360–372; Melinda Gann Hall, "Electoral Politics and Strategic Voting in State Supreme Courts," *Journal of Politics* 54 (1992): 427–446; Melinda Gann Hall, "Justices as Representatives: Elections and Judicial Politics in the American States," *American Politics Quarterly* 23 (1995): 485–503.

18 For a spirited theoretical and empirical justification of judicial elections see, Chris W. Bonneau and Melinda Gann Hall, *In Defense of Judicial Elections* (New York: Routledge, 2009).

19 *Chisom v. Roemer*, 501 U.S. 380 (1991).

20 Greg Goelzhauser, "Diversifying State Supreme Courts," *Law and Society Review* 45 (2011): 761–781.

21 Barbara Luck Graham, "Do Judicial Selection Systems Matter?: A Study of Black Representation on State Courts," *American Politics Quarterly* 18 (1990): 316–336; Mark S. Hurwitz and Drew Noble Lanier, "Diversity in State and Federal Appellate Courts: Change and Continuity Across 20 Years," *The Justice System Journal* 29 (2008): 47–70.

22 Robert C. Luskin, Christopher N. Bratcher, Christopher G. Jordan, Tracy K. Renner, and Kris S. Seago, "How Minority Judges Fare in Retention Election," *Judicature* 77 (1994): 316–321.

23 United States Census Bureau, "QuickFacts: Washington city, District of Columbia," https://www.census.gov/ quickfacts/table/PST045215/1150000, accessed April 17, 2016.

24 William Cummings, "Pot Now Legal in D.C. Despite Threats from Congress," *USA Today*, February 26, 2015, http://www.usatoday.com/story/news/nation/2015/ 02/25/dc-marijuana-legalization/24033803/, accessed April 17, 2016.

25 For more on the comparison between FEMA's response to Hurricanes Katrina and Sandy see, Valerie Bauerline, "Lessons Learned from the Response to Katrina's Havoc," *Wall Street Journal*, August 28, 2015, http://www .wsj.com/articles/lessons-learned-from-failed-response -to-katrina-1440787007, accessed April 17, 2016.

26 United States Census Bureau, "QuickFacts California," https://www.census.gov/quickfacts/table/PST045215/06; "QuickFacts Wyoming," https://www.census.gov/quickfacts/table/PST045215/56, accessed April 19, 2016.

27 Daniel J. Elazar, "Federal-State Collaboration in the Nineteenth-Century United States," *Political Science Quarterly* 79 (1964): 248–281.

28 *McCulloch v. Maryland*, 17 U.S. 316 (1819).

29 *Gibbons v. Ogden*, 22 U.S. 1 (1824).

30 *Prigg v. Pennsylvania*, 41 U.S. 539 (1842).

31 *Dred Scott v. Sandford*, 60 U.S. 393 (1857).

32 Paula D. McClain and Joseph Stewart, Jr., *"Can We All Get along?": Racial and Ethnic Minorities in American Politics*, 6th ed. (Boulder, CO: Westview Press, 2014), 18.

33 Martin Grodzins, "The American Federal System," in *A Nation of States*, ed., Robert A. Goldwin (Chicago: Rand McNally, 1963).

34 For more on the concept of dual federalism, see Edward S. Corwin, "The Passing of Dual Federalism," *Virginia Law Review* 36 (February 1950): 1–24.

35 *United States v. E.C. Knight Company*, 156 U.S. 1 (1895).

36 *Hammer v. Dagenhart*, 247 U.S. 251 (1918).

37 For more on the Second Land Grant Act HBCUs see, Ralph D. Christy and Lionel Williamson, eds., *A Century of Service: American Land Grant Colleges and Universities, 1890–1990* (New Brunswick, NJ: Transaction Publishers, 1992).

38 *Plessy v. Ferguson*, 133 U.S. 537 (1896).

39 *United States v. Reese*, 92 U.S. 214 (1876).

40 *United States v. Cruikshank*, 92 U.S. 542 (1875).

41 Grodzins, *The American Federal System*.

42 *Palko v. Connecticut*, 302 U.S. 319 (1937).

43 See, for example, *Schechter Poultry Corporation v. United States*, 295 U.S. 495 (1935); *United States v. Butler*, 297 U.S. 1 (1936); and *Carter v. Carter Coal Company*, 298 U.S. 238 (1936).

44 *National Labor Relations Board v. Jones & Laughlin Steel Corp.*, 301 U.S. 1 (1937).

45 *United States v. Darby Lumber Co.*, 312 U.S. 100 (1941).

46 *Wickard v. Filburn*, 317 U.S. 11 (1942).

47 For more on Medicaid see, "Medicaid.gov: Keeping America Healthy," http://www.medicaid.gov/, accessed April 22, 2012.

48 U.S. Department of Health & Human Services, Administration for Children & Families, Office of Head Start, "History of Head Start," http://www.acf.hhs.gov/programs/ohs/about/history-of-head-start, accessed April 22, 2016.

49 *National League of Cities v. Usery*, 426 U.S. 833 (1976).

50 *Garcia v. San Antonio Metropolitan Transit Authority*, 469 U.S. 528 (1985).

51 For more on the controversy over unfunded mandates, see Edward Koch, "The Mandate Millstone," *The Public Interest* 61(Fall 1980): 42–57.

52 *Brown v. Board of Education*, 347 U.S. 483 (1954).

53 *Heart of Atlanta Motel v. United States*, 379 U.S. 241 (1965); *Katzenbach v. McClung*, 379 U.S. 294 (1965).

54 Slip Opinion, *Shelby County, AL v. Holder*, No. 12-96, http://www.supremecourt.gov/opinions/12pdf/12-96_6k47.pdf, accessed April 22, 2106.

55 Thomas E. Mann and Raffaela L. Wakeman, "Voting Rights After *Shelby County v. Holder*," *Brookings: Up Front*, June 28, 2013, https://www.brookings.edu/2013/06/25/voting-rights-after-shelby-county-v-holder/, accessed April 22, 2016.

56 McClain and Stewart 2014, 270–274.

57 *Reed v. Reed*, 404 U.S. 71 (1971).

58 *Roe v. Wade*, 410 U.S. 413 (1973).

59 William J. Clinton, "Address Before a Joint Session of the Congress on the State of the Union," January 23, 1996. Online by Gerhard Peters and John T. Woolley, *The American Presidency Project*, http://www.presidency.ucsb.edu/ws/index.php?pid=53091, accessed April 22, 2016.

60 Department of Housing and Urban Development, Community Development Block Grant Program, http://portal.hud.gov/hudportal/HUD?src=/program_offices/comm_planning/communitydevelopment/programs, accessed April 22, 2016.

61 Department of Health and Human Services, "Temporary Assistance for Needy Families," http://www.acf.hhs.gov/programs/ofa/programs/tanf, accessed April 22, 2016.

62 For example, see LaDonna Pavetti and Liz Schott, "TANF's Inadequate Response to Recession Highlights Weakness of Black Grant Structure," *Center for Budget Priorities*, July 14, 2011, http://www.cbpp.org/cms/?fa=view&id=3534, accessed April 22, 2016.

63 National Association of Black Social Workers Steering Committee, "Welfare Reform," *National Association of Black Social Workers*, October 2002, http://c.ymcdn.com/sites/nabsw.org/resource/resmgr/position_statements_papers/welfare_reform.pdf, accessed April 22, 2016.

64 *South Dakota v. Dole*, 483 U.S. 203 (1987).

65 Phillip Rucker, "Last Republican Governor Agrees to Accept Stimulus Aid," *Washington Post*, April 9, 2009, http://www.washingtonpost.com/wp-dyn/content/article/2009/04/03/AR2009040301776.html, accessed April 22, 2016.

66 *National Federation of Independent Business v. Sebelius*, 132 S.Ct. 2566 (2012).

67 *Gonzalez v. Raich*, 545 U.S. 1 (2005).

68 Brady Dennis, "Obama Administration Will Not Block State Marijuana Laws if Distribution is Regulated," *Washington Post*, August 29, 2013, https://www.washingtonpost.com/national/health-science/obama-administration-will-not-preempt-state-marijuana-laws--for-now/2013/08/29/b725bfd8-10bd-11e3-8cdd-bcdc09410972_story.html, accessed April 22, 2016.

69 Marijuana Policy Project, "2016 Presidential Candidates: Where do they Stand on Marijuana Policy," https://www.mpp.org/2016-presidential-candidates/, accessed April 22, 2016.

70 Timothy J. Conlon and Paul L. Posner, "Inflection Point? Federalism and the Obama Administration," *Publius: Journal of Federalism* 41 (2011): 421–446.

71 *United States v. Lopez*, 514 U.S. 549 (1995), at 567.

72 *United States v. Morrison*, 529 U.S. 528 (2000).

73 *Gonzales v. Raich*, 545 U.S. 1 (2005).

74 *Gregory v. Ashcroft*, 501 U.S. 452 (1991).

75 *Planned Parenthood v. Casey*, 503 U.S. 833 (1992).

76 *Swann v. Charlotte-Mecklenburg Board of Education*, 402 U.S. 1 (1971).

77 *Board of Education of Oklahoma City v. Dowell*, 498 U.S. 237 (1991).

78 *Parents Involved in Community Schools v. Seattle School District, No. 1*, 551 U.S. 707 (2007).

79 *Seminole Tribe of Florida v. Florida*, 517 U.S. 44 (1996).

Chapter 4

1 U.S. Census Bureau, Quick Facts: North Charleston City, South Carolina," https://www.census.gov/quickfacts /table/PST045215/4550875, accessed April 27, 2016.

2 Bruce Smith and Jeffrey Collins, "White Officer Charged in Unarmed Black Man's Death," *U.S. News & World Report*, April 8, 2015, http://www.usnews.com/news/us /articles/2015/04/08/protest-planned-after-white-sc -officer-charged-with-murder, accessed April 27, 2016.

3 Catherine E. Choichet and Chandler Friedman, Walter Scott Case: Michael Slager Released From Jail After Posting Bond," *CNN.com*, January 5, 2015, http://www.cnn .com/2016/01/04/us/south-carolina-michael-slager-bail/, accessed April 27, 2016.

4 Alexander Hamilton. "Federalist Paper No. 84," Library of Congress, https://www.congress.gov/resources/display /content/The+Federalist+Papers#TheFederalistPapers-84, accessed May 2, 2016.

5 For more on the history of the ratification of the Bill of Rights, see Bernard Schwartz, *The Great Rights of Mankind: A History of the American Bill of Rights* (Lanham, MD, Rowman & Littlefield, 1992).

6 *Barron v. Mayor and City Council of Baltimore*, 32 U.S. 243 (1833).

7 *Hurtado v. California*, 110 U.S. 516 (1884). Justice John Marshall Harlan's dissent argued that the Bill of Rights should be incorporated through the due process clause.

8 *Palko v. Connecticut*, 302 U.S. 319 (1937).

9 *Schenck v. United States*, 249 U.S. 47 (1919), 52.

10 For more on Emma Goldman, see the University of California, Berkeley, *Emma Goldman Papers*, http://www .lib.berkeley.edu/goldman/index.html. For Emma Goldman's contribution to freedom of expression, see specifically the section entitled, "Emma Goldman and Free Speech," http://www.lib.berkeley.edu/goldman /MeetEmmaGoldman/emmagoldmanandfreespeech .html, both accessed May 2, 2016.

11 *Brandenburg v. Ohio*, 395 U.S. 444 (1969).

12 *Texas v. Johnson*, 491 U.S. 397 (1989).

13 *Miller v. California*, 413 U.S. 15 (1973).

14 *Chaplinsky v. New Hampshire*, 315 U.S. 568 (1942).

15 *Cohen v. California*, 403 U.S. 15 (1971). California had initially sentenced Cohen to thirty days in jail after he was convicted of disturbing the peace because he wore a jacket displaying the words "Fuck the Draft."

16 *R.A.V. v. City of St. Paul, MN*, 505 U.S. 377 (1992).

17 *Wisconsin v. Mitchell*, 508 U.S. 476 (1993).

18 *Virginia v. Black*, 538 U.S. 123, 343 (2003).

19 *Walker v. Texas Division, Sons of Confederate Veterans*, 135 S.Ct. 2239 (2015).

20 *New York Times v. United States*, 403 U.S. 713 (1971).

21 *Near v. Minnesota*, 283 U.S. 697 (1931).

22 *New York Times v. Sullivan*, 376 U.S. 254 (1964).

23 *Federal Communications Commission v. Pacifica Foundation*, 438 U.S. 726 (1978).

24 See *Reno v. American Civil Liberties Union*, 521 U.S. 844 (1997); *Ashcroft v. American Civil Liberties Union*, 542 U.S. 656 (2004).

25 *Everson v. Board of Education Ewing Township*, 330 U.S. 1 (1947).

26 *Engle v. Vitale*, 370 U.S. 421 (1962); *Abington Township School District v. Schempp*, 374 U.S. 203 (1963); *Lee v. Wiseman*, 505 U.S. 577 (1991); *Santa Fe Independent School District v. Doe*, 530 U.S. 790 (2000). Rebecca Riffkin, "In U.S., Support for Daily Prayer in Schools Dips Slightly," *Gallup*, September 25, 2014, http://www .gallup.com/poll/177401/support-daily-prayer-schools -dips-slightly.aspx, accessed May 2, 2016.

27 *Zelman v. Simmons-Harris*, 536 U.S. 639 (2002).

28 The White House, "About the Office of Faith-based and Neighborhood Partnerships," https://www.whitehouse.gov/ administration/eop/ofbnp/about, accessed May 2, 2016.

29 Michael B. Henderson, Paul E. Peterson, and Martin West, "The 2015 EdNext Poll on School Reform" *Education Next* 16(1) (Winter 2016), http://educationnext .org/2015-ednext-poll-interactive/, accessed May 2, 2016.

30 *Braunfeld v. Brown*, 366 U.S. 599 (1961).

31 *Sherbert v. Verner*, 374 U.S. 398 (1963) and *Wisconsin v. Yoder*, 406 U.S. 205 (1972).

32 *Bob Jones University v. United States*, 461 U.S. 574 (1983).

33 *O'Lone v. Shabazz*, 482 U.S. 342 (1987).

34 *Employment Division, Department of Human Resources of Oregon v. Smith*, 494 U.S. 872 (1990).

35 Santeria is a religion started by African slaves brought to the Caribbean. It combines elements of Catholicism with traditional African and Indian religions, and a major Santeria ritual involves animal sacrifice.

36 *Church of the Lukumi Babalu Aye v. City of Hialeah*, 508 U.S. 520 (1993).

37 *Gonzales v. O Centro Espirita Beneficiente Uniao Do Vegetal*, 126 S.Ct. 1211 (2006).

38 *Equal Employment Opportunity Commission v. Abercrombie & Fitch Stores*, 135 S.Ct. 2028 (2015).

39 *Holt v. Hobbs*, 135 S.Ct. 853 (2015).

40 For more on the exclusionary rule and "good faith" exception see *Massachusetts v. Sheppard*, 468 U.S. 981 (1984) and *United States v. Leon*, 468 U.S. 897 (1984).

41 *Katz v. United States*, 389 U.S. 347 (1967).

42 *American Civil Liberties Union v. National Security Agency*, 438 F. Supp. 2d 754 (2006); *American Civil Liberties Union v. National Security Agency*, 493 F3d. 644 (2007), cert. denied, *American Civil Liberties Union v. National Security Agency*, 552 U.S. 1179 (2008).

43 *American Civil Liberties Union v. Clapper*, 785 F.3d. 787 (2015).

44 Jeremy Diamond, "NSA Surveillance Bill Passes After Weeks-Long Showdown," CNN.com, September 7, 2015, http://www.cnn.com/2015/06/02/politics/senate -usa-freedom-act-vote-patriot-act-nsa/, accessed April 28, 2016.

45 Evan P. Schultz, "Racial Profiling Is Back, but It's Not the Answer to Terrorism," *Fulton County (GA) Daily Report*, October 2, 2001.

46 Peter Siggins, "Racial Profiling in Age of Terrorism," Santa Clara University: Markkula Center for Applied Ethics, March 12, 2002, https://www.scu.edu/ethics /focus-areas/more/resources/racial-profiling-in-an-age -of-terrorism/, accessed May 2, 2016.

47 *Escobedo v. Illinois*, 378 U.S. 478 (1964).

48 *Miranda v. Arizona*, 384 U.S. 436 (1966).

49 *Gideon v. Wainwright*, 372 U.S. 335 (1963).

50 Colorado Commission on Criminal and Juvenile Justice, "Recommendation Presented to the CCCJ: Justice Agencies to Track Racial and Ethnic Diversity of Staff," October 12, 2012, https://cdpsdocs.state.co.us/ccjj /Meetings/2012/2012-10-12_MORRec_FY13-MOR1.pdf, accessed May 3, 2016.

51 See, for example, *Strauder v. West Virginia*, 100 U.S. 303 (1880); *Swain v. Alabama*, 380 U.S. 202 (1965).

52 *Batson v. Kentucky*, 476 U.S. 79 (1986).

53 Jeff Rosen, "Jurymandering," *New Republic* 207(23) (1992): 15–18.

54 Shari Seidman Diamond, Destiny Peery, Francis J. Dolan, and Emily Dolan, "Achieving Diversity on the Jury: Jury Size and the Peremptory Challenge," *Journal of Empirical Legal Studies* 6 (September 2009): 425–449.

55 *Hudson v. McMillan*, 503 U.S. 1 (1992).

56 *Harmelin v. Michigan*, 501 U.S. 957 (1991).

57 The Sentencing Project, State By State Data: U.S. Total," http://www.sentencingproject.org/the-facts#map, accessed April 28, 2016.

58 *Wilkerson v. Utah*, 99 U.S. 130 (1878) upheld execution by firing squad, hanging, or beheading. More recently, in *Glossip v. Gross*, 135 S.Ct. 2726 (2015) the Supreme Court upheld the use of midazolam in lethal injection procedures, despite claims that the drug does not suffi-ciently anesthetize the condemned inmate, which causes intense suffering.

59 Death Penalty Information Center, "States With and Without the Death Penalty," http://www.deathpenaltyinfo .org/states-and-without-death-penalty, accessed April 29, 2016.

60 See, for example, David Baldus, George Woodworth, and Charles Pulaski, *Equal Justice and the Death Penalty:*

A Legal and Empirical Analysis (Boston: Northeastern University Press, 1990).

61 *McCleskey v. Kemp*, 481 U.S. 279 (1987).

62 *Bowers v. Hardwick*, 478 U.S. 176 (1984).

63 *Lawrence v. Texas*, 539 U.S. 558 (2003).

64 *Cruzan v. Director of Missouri Department of Health*, 497 U.S. 261 (1990).

65 *Griswold v. Connecticut*, 381 U.S. 479 (1965).

66 *Roe v. Wade*, 410 U.S. 113 (1973).

67 See *Planned Parenthood of Southeastern Pennsylvania v. Casey*, 505 U.S. 833 (1992).

68 Peter Sullivan, "Democrats Block 20-Week Abortion Ban," *The Hill*, September 22, 2015, http://thehill.com /policy/healthcare/254497-dems-block-20-week -abortion-ban#, accessed May 1, 2016.

69 Guttmacher Institute, "Targeted Regulation of Abortion Providers," https://www.guttmacher.org/state-policy /explore/targeted-regulation-abortion-providers, accessed May 1, 2016.

70 Adam Liptak, "Supreme Court Strikes Down Texas Abortion Restrictions," *New York Times*, June 26, 2016.

71 David Wahlberg, "Mississippi Sets Bar for Restrictions on Abortion," *Atlanta Journal Constitution*, April 11, 2005, 1A.

72 Robert Brown, R. Todd Jewell, and Jeffrey J. Rous, "Provider Availability, Race, and Abortion Demand," *Southern Economic Journal* 67 (2001): 656–671.

73 The Henry J. Kaiser Family Foundation, "Reported Legal Abortions by Race of Woman Who Obtained Abortion by the State of Occurrence: Timeframe 2012," http://kff .org/womens-health-policy/state-indicator/abortions -by-race/, accessed May 1, 2016.

74 John P. Bartowski, Aida I. Ramos-Wada, Chris G. Ellison, and Gabriel A. Acevedo, "Faith, Race-Ethnicity, and Public Policy Preferences: Religious Schemas and Abortion Attitudes Among U.S. Latinos," *Journal for the Scientific Study of Religion* 51 (2012): 343–358.

Chapter 5

1 Tim Rogers, "Citizenship Can Feel Like a Guilty Privi-lege When Your Parents Are Undocumented," Fusion, April 17, 2016, http://fusion.net/story/291636/supreme -court-dapa-decision/, accessed May 20, 2016.

2 Michael D. Shear, "Obama, Daring Congress, Acts to Overhaul Immigration," *New York Times*, November 20, 2014, http://www.nytimes.com/2014/11/21/us/obama -immigration-speech.html, accessed May 21, 2016.

3 Steven Nelson, "Dreamers' Nightmare Deferred by Supreme Court Immigration Split," *U.S. News & World Report*, June 23, 2016, http://www.usnews.com/news /articles/2016-06-23/dreamers-nightmare-deferred-by -supreme-court-immigration-split, accessed August 8, 2016.

4 Jens Manuel Krogstad and Jeffrey S. Passel, "Five Facts About Illegal Immigration in the U.S.," Washington, DC: Pew Hispanic Center, November 19, 2015 http://www

.pewresearch.org/fact-tank/2015/11/19/5-facts-about
-illegal-immigration-in-the-u-s/, accessed May 21, 2016.

5 Paula D. McClain and Joseph Stewart, Jr., *"Can We All
Get along?": Racial and Ethnic Minorities in American Politics*, 6th ed. (Boulder, CO: Westview Press, 2014), 9.

6 Megan Smolenyak, "What Race is Bruno Mars?" *Huffington
Post: HUFFPOST CELEBRITY*, January 12, 2013, http://
www.huffingtonpost.com/megan-smolenyak-smolenyak
/what-race-is-bruno-mars_b_2116984.html, accessed
May 21, 2016.

7 For more on the question of whether Judaism is an ethnicity, see Zvi Gitelman, ed., *Religion or Ethnicity: Jewish
Identities in Evolution* (New Brunswick, NJ: Rutgers University Press, 2009).

8 Albert P. Blaustein and Robert L. Zangrando, *Civil Rights
and the Black American: A Documentary History* (New York:
Clarion, 1970), 42–44.

9 Ibid., 44–47.

10 *Prigg v. Pennsylvania*, 41 U.S. 539 (1842).

11 *Dred Scott v. Sandford*, 60 U.S. 393 (1857).

12 National Archives, "African American Records: The
Freedman's Bureau, 1865–1872," http://www.archives
.gov/research/african-americans/freedmens-bureau/#intro,
accessed May 25, 2016.

13 Rutherford B. Hayes Presidential Center, "Disputed
Election of 1876," http://www.rbhayes.org/hayes
/president/display.asp?id=511&subj=president, accessed
May 22, 2016.

14 Ferris State University Jim Crow Museum of Racist
Memorabilia, "Who Was Jim Crow," http://www.ferris
.edu/jimcrow/who.htm, accessed May 22, 2016.

15 *Plessy v. Ferguson*, 163 U.S. 537 (1896).

16 Donald G. Nieman, *Promises to Keep: African Americans
and the Constitutional Order, 1776 to the Present* (New
York: Oxford University Press, 1991), 115–119.

17 *United States v. Cruikshank*, 92 U.S. 542 (1876).

18 Steven F. Lawson, *Running for Freedom: Civil Rights and
Black Politics in America since 1941*, 2nd ed. (New York:
McGraw-Hill, 1997), 81. African American population
figures come from United States Census, "No. 23:
Population, By Race, By State 1940 to 1960," 31, http://
www2.census.gov/prod2/statcomp/documents/1961-02
.pdf, accessed August 8, 2016

19 Gunnar Myrdal, *An American Dilemma: The Negro
Problem and American Democracy* (New York: Harper &
Brothers, 1944).

20 For more on World War II and its economic impact on
civil rights, see Daniel Kryder, *Divided Arsenal: Race and
the American State During World War II* (New York:
Cambridge University Press, 2000).

21 National Association for the Advancement of Colored
People, "NAACP: 100 Years of History," http://www
.naacp.org/pages/naacp-history, accessed May 22, 2016.

22 *Guinn and Beal v. United States*, 247 U.S. 347 (1915).

23 For a good history of the creation of the NAACP Legal Defense and Education Fund, see Jack Greenberg, *Crusaders in
the Courts: How a Dedicated Band of Lawyers Fought for the
Civil Rights Revolution* (New York: Basic Books, 1994).

24 *Brown v. Board of Education, Topeka, Kansas*, 347 U.S. 483
(1954), 495.

25 Slip Opinion, *Shelby County v. Holder*, No. 12-96, http://
www.supremecourt.gov/opinions/12pdf/12-96_6k47
.pdf, accessed March 19, 2014.

26 Nieman, *Promises to Keep*, 180.

27 *Swann v. Charlotte-Mecklenburg County Board of Education*,
402 U.S. 1 (1971).

28 Gary Orfield and Chungmei Lee, "Racial Transformation
and the Changing Nature of Segregation," Civil Rights
Project, Harvard University, January 2006, 14, http://
civilrightsproject.ucla.edu/research/k-12-education
/integration-and-diversity/racial-transformation-and
-the-changing-nature-of-segregation/orfield-racial
-transformation-2006.pdf, accessed May 24, 2016.

29 *Board of Education v. Dowell*, 498 U.S. 237 (1991).

30 *Parents Involved in Community Schools v. Seattle School
District*, 551 U.S. 701 (2007).

31 Orfield and Lee, "Racial Transformation."

32 United States Government Accountability Office,
"Report to Congressional Requesters: K–12 Education,
Better use of Information Could Help Agencies Identify
Disparities and Address Racial Discrimination," April
2016, http://www.gao.gov/assets/680/676745.pdf,
accessed May 24, 2016.

33 Stephen Carter, *Reflections of an Affirmative Action Baby*
(New York: Basic Books, 1991).

34 *Regents of the University of California v. Bakke*, 438 U.S.
265 (1978).

35 *Grutter v. Bollinger*, 539 U.S. 306 (2003).

36 *Fisher v. University of Texas*, 570 U.S. ___ (2103). See also,
Adam Liptak, "Justices Take Up Race as a Factor in
College Entry," *New York Times*, February 22, 2012, A1.

37 Adam Liptak, "Supreme Court Upholds Affirmative
Action Program at University of Texas," *New York Times*,
June 23, 2016, http://www.nytimes.com/2016/06/24/us
/politics/supreme-court-affirmative-action-university-of-
texas.html?_r=0, accessed August 8, 2016.

38 Robert Barnes, "Judge Blocks ID Law in Pa.," *Washington
Post*, October 3, 2012, A1; Sari Horowitz, "Pennsylvania
Judge Strikes Down Voter ID Law," *Washington Post*,
January 17, 2014, http://www.washingtonpost.com
/world/national-security/pennsylvania-judge-strikes
-down-voter-id-law/2014/01/17/472d620e-7fa2-11e3
-93c1-0e888170b723_story.html, accessed May 25, 2016.

39 Holly Yeager, "Justice Department to Sue North Carolina
Over Voting Law," *Washington Post*, September 30, 2013,
http://www.washingtonpost.com/politics/justice
-department-to-sue-north-carolina-over-voting
-law/2013/09/29/123cbbce-292d-11e3-8ade
-a1f23cda135e_story.html, accessed May 25, 2016.

40 Michael Wines and Alan Blinder, "Federal Appeals
Court Strikes Down North Carolina Voter ID Requirement," July 29, 2016, http://www.nytimes.com/2016

/07/30/us/federal-appeals-court-strikes-down-north
-carolina-voter-id-provision.html?_r=0, accessed
August 9, 2016.

41 Steve Bousquet, "U.S. Justice Department Okays
Florida Early Voting Plan for Five Counties," *Tampa Bay
Times*, September 6, 2012, http://www.tampabay.com
/news/politics/national/us-justice-department-okays
-florida-early-voting-plan-for-five-counties/1249884,
accessed May 25, 2016. Joe Palazzolo, "Judge Blocks
Limits on Early Voting in Ohio," *Wall Street Journal*,
August 31, 2012, http://online.wsj.com/article
/SB10000872396390444772804577623763333125998
.html, accessed September 12, 2012.

42 Lynette Clemetson, "Hispanics Now Largest Minority,
Census Shows," *New York Times*, January 22, 2003,
http://www.nytimes.com/2003/01/22/us/hispanics
-now-largest-minority-census-shows.html, accessed
May 25, 2016.

43 LULAC, "All for One—One for All," http://lulac.org
/about/history/, accessed May 25, 2016.

44 McClain and Stewart, *"Can We All Get along?"* 55–56.

45 United States Department of Justice, "About Language
Minority Voting Rights," https://www.justice.gov/crt
/about-language-minority-voting-rights, accessed
May 25, 2016.

46 McClain and Stewart, *"Can We All Get along?"* 45.

47 Ben Fox and Danica Coto, "Puerto Rico Vote Endorses
Statehood with Asterisk," *Yahoo News*, November 7,
2012, https://www.yahoo.com/news/puerto-rico-vote
-endorses-statehood-asterisk-205404726.html, accessed
May 25, 2016; Jim Malewitz, "Statehood for Puerto Rico?
Romney Supports a 51st State," *Stateline*, August 30,
2012, http://www.pewstates.org/projects/stateline
/headlines/statehood-for-puerto-rico-romney-supports
-a-51st-state-85899414495, accessed May 25, 2016.

48 Laura Litvan and Billy House, "Puerto Rico Debt Crisis
Bill Clears First U.S. House Hurdle," *Bloomberg Politics*,
May 25, 2016, http://www.bloomberg.com/politics/
articles/2016-05-25/puerto-rico-debt-crisis-measure
-nears-u-s-house-committee-vote, accessed May 25, 2016.

49 See for example, Carmen Teresa Whalen and Victor
Vázquez-Hernández, eds., *The Puerto Rican Diaspora:
Historical Perspectives* (Philadelphia: Temple University
Press, 2005).

50 McClain and Stewart, *"Can We All Get along?"* 19–20, 285

51 Brian Bennett, "Program May Halt Deportations for
Many in the U.S. Illegally," *Los Angeles Times*, November
18, 2011, A15.

52 Time Staff, "Here's Donald Trump's Presidential
Announcement Speech," *Time*, June 16, 2015, http://
time.com/3923128/donald-trump-announcement-
speech/, accessed May 25, 2016.

53 Randal C. Archibold, "Arizona Enacts Stringent Law on
Immigration," *New York Times*, April 24, 2010, A1.

54 Marc Lacey and Katherine Q. Seelye, "Recall Election
Claims Arizona Anti-Immigration Champion,"

New York Times, November 10, 2011, http://www.nytimes
.com/2011/11/10/us/politics/russell-pearce-arizonas
-anti-immgration-champion-is-recalled.html, accessed
May 25, 2016.

55 Slip Opinion, *Arizona, et. al. v. United States*, No. 11-182,
http://www.supremecourt.gov/opinions/11pdf/
11-182b5e1.pdf, accessed May 26, 2016.

56 Alex Seitz-Wald, "Rep. Steve King: Immigrants are Like
Dogs," *Salon*, May 22, 2012, http://www.salon.com
/2012/05/22/rep_steve_king_immigrants_like_dogs/,
accessed March 20, 2014.

57 Anti-Defamation League, *Immigrants Targeted: Extremist
Rhetoric Moves into the Mainstream*, 2008, http://archive
.adl.org/civil_rights/anti_immigrant/rhetoric.html#
.V0eQhPkrLIU, accessed May 26, 2016.

58 The National Archives and Records Administration,
"The Chinese Exclusion Act (1882)," http://www
.ourdocuments.gov/document_data/pdf/doc_047.pdf,
accessed May 26, 2016.

59 McClain and Stewart, *"Can We All Get along?"* 21–22.

60 *Korematsu v. United States*, 323 U.S. 214 (1944).

61 McClain and Stewart, *"Can We All Get along?"* 22.

62 Japanese American Citizens League, "History," https://
jacl.org/about/history/, accessed May 26, 2016.

63 Chinese American Citizens Alliance, "History of CACA,"
http://www.cacanational.org/, accessed May 26, 2016.

64 Chinese for Affirmative Action, "Issue Advocacy,"
http://www.caasf.org/v2/what-we-do/issue-advocacy/,
accessed May 26, 2016.

65 The Cherokee Nation, "A Brief History of the Trail of
Tears," http://www.cherokee.org/AboutTheNation
/History/TrailofTears/ABriefHistoryoftheTrailofTears
.aspx, accessed May 26, 2016.

66 McClain and Stewart, *"Can We All get along?"* 17–18.

67 Ibid., 57–58.

68 Kevin Fagan, "Casinos Riches Elude Majority of State's
Indians; Inequities Anger Many Who Lobbied for Expansion," *San Francisco Chronicle*, April 20, 2008, A10.

69 See, for example, *Reed v. Reed*, 404 U.S. 71 (1971);
Geduldig v. Aiello, 417 U.S. 484 (1974).

70 Nancy E. McGlen and Karen O'Connor, *Women's Rights:
The Struggle for Equality in the 19th and 20th Centuries*
(New York: Praeger, 1983), 380.

71 Library of Congress, Congress.Gov, "H.J. Res. 51:
Removing the Deadline for the Ratification of the Equal
Rights Amendment," 114th Congress, https://www
.congress.gov/bill/114th-congress/house-joint
-resolution/51, accessed May 26 November 25, 2016.

72 Equal Employment Opportunity Commission, "The
Equal Pay Act of 1963," https://www.eeoc.gov/laws
/statutes/epa.cfm, accessed May 27, 2016.

73 *Meritor Savings Bank v. Vinson*, 477 U.S. 57 (1986).

74 *Lawrence v. Texas*, 539 U.S. 558 (2003).

75 David S. Cloud and David Zucchino, "Military Gays
Celebrate Freedom," *Los Angeles Times*, September 21,
2011, A1.

76 *Obergefell v. Hodges* (2016), Slip Opinion, http://www
.supremecourt.gov/opinions/14pdf/14-556_3204.pdf,
accessed May 28, 2016.

77 Sandhya Somashekhar, "Judge: Kim Davis May Keep
her Name Off Marriage Licenses," *Washington Post*,
February 10, 2016, https://www.washingtonpost.com
/news/post-nation/wp/2016/02/10/judge-kim-davis
-may-keep-her-name-off-marriage-licenses/, accessed
May 28, 2016.

78 Human Rights Campaign, "Research Overview: Hate
Crimes and Violence Against Lesbian, Gay, Bisexual,
and Transgender People," Washington, DC: Human
Rights Campaign, 2014), 6, http://hrc-assets.s3-website
-us-east-1.amazonaws.com/files/assets/resources/HRC
-Hate-Crimes-Guide-2014.pdf, accessed May 28, 2016.

79 Ibid., 17.

80 Vicki Hyman, "Bruce Springsteen Joins Boycott of N.C. Over
Anti-Transgender Law: Cancels Weekend Show," *N.J.Com*,
April 8, 2106, http://www.nj.com/entertainment/celebrities
/index.ssf/2016/04/bruce_springsteen_cancels_concert
_hb2_north_caroli.html, accessed May 28, 2016.

81 David Montgomery and Alan Blinder, "States Sue
Obama Administration Over Transgender Bathroom
Policy," *New York Times*, May 25, 2016, http://www
.nytimes.com/2016/05/26/us/states-texas-sue-obama
-administration-over-transgender-bathroom-policy
.html, accessed May 28, 2016.

82 The American Association of Retired Persons, *Age Discrimination: What Employers Need to Know,* http://assets
.aarp.org/www.aarp.org_/articles/money/employers
/age_discrimination.pdf, accessed May 28, 2016.

83 Disability Rights Education & Defense Fund, "About
DREDF," http://dredf.org/about-us/, accessed May 28,
2016.

Chapter 6

1 United States Census, "My Congressional District,
114th Congress: Texas, Congressional District 23,"
http://www.census.gov/mycd/, accessed June 4, 2016.

2 Congressman Will Hurd: 23rd District of Texas,
"About: Biography," https://hurd.house.gov/about
/full-biography, accessed June 4, 2016.

3 See for example Representative Hurd's Biography,
https://hurd.house.gov/about/full-biography, accessed
November 16, 2016.

4 Katie Leslie, "Rep. Will Hurd Keeping Distance from
Donald Trump, Pushing Back Against Pete Gallego Attack
Ads," *Dallas Morning News*, May 6, 2016, http://trailblaz-
ersblog.dallasnews.com/2016/05/rep-will-hurd-keeping-
distance-from-donald-trump-pushes-back-against-pete-
gallego-attack-ads.html/, accessed June 4, 2016

5 John T. Bennett, "GOP's Will Hurd Re-Elected in Texas's 23rd District," Roll Call, November 9, 2016,
http://www.rollcall.com/news/politics/gops-will-hurd
-re-electedloses-rematch-in-texas-23rd-district, accessed
November 16, 2016.

6 Technically the representative from Puerto Rico is called
a resident commissioner, but the position enjoys the
same rights and privileges as other nonvoting delegates.

7 U.S. Census Bureau, "QuickFacts: Washington City,
District of Columbia," http://www.census.gov/quickfacts
/table/PST045215/1150000, accessed June 8, 2016.

8 To keep the size of the House an odd number, the proponents of the bill wanted to add a 437th seat after adding
the new seat from Washington, DC. Utah was next in line
to receive another representative after the reapportionment
following the 2000 census; therefore, it would receive the
extra seat. Redistricting the state would be too complicated, so the seat would be at-large. Moreover, because the
DC seat would most likely be filled by a Democrat, proponents of the bill figured that the Utah at-large seat, which
would most likely be filled by a Republican, would not
change the partisan composition of the House.

9 "Bill for D.C. Rep Put on Hold," *Bergen Record* (Bergen
County, NJ), March 11, 2009, A9.

10 Stephan Dinan, "Boehner Takes Reins of the House,"
Washington Times, January 6, 2011, 1.

11 United States House of Representatives, "History, Art,
and Archives: Historical Highlights 1911 Reapportionment," http://history.house.gov/Historical-Highlights
/1901-1950/The-1911-House-reapportionment/, accessed
June 8, 2016.

12 *Wesbery v. Sanders*, 376 U.S. 1 (1964).

13 *Karcher v. Daggett*, 462 U.S. 725 (1983).

14 See *Shaw v. Reno*, 509 U.S. 630 (1993); *Miller v. Johnson*,
512 U.S. 622 (1995); *Bush v. Vera*, 517 U.S. 952 (1996);
and *Shaw v. Hunt*, 517 U.S. 899 (1996).

15 For more on these views of representation, see Hanna
Fenichel Pitkin, *The Concept of Representation* (Berkeley:
University of California Press, 1967).

16 For more on the impact of majority-minority districts,
see Charles Cameron, David Epstein, Sharyn
O'Halloran, "Do Majority-Minority Districts Maximize
Black Representation in Congress?," *American Political
Science Review* 90 (1996) pp. 794–812; Kevin A. Hill,
"Does the Creation of Majority Black Districts Aid
Republicans? An Analysis of the 1992 in Eight Southern
States," *Journal of Politics* 57 (1995) 384–401.

17 For more on majority party control in the House of
Representatives, see Gary W. Cox and Matthew D.
McCubbins, *Legislative Leviathan: Party Government in
the House,* 2nd ed. (New York: Cambridge University
Press, 2007).

18 Ben Pershing, "Clyburn Leadership Role a 'Work in
Progress,'" *Washington Post*, May 10, 2011, A15.

19 Gregory Korte, "Obama Vetoes GOP Attempt to Repeal
Obamacare," *USA Today*, January 6, 2016, http://www
.usatoday.com/story/news/politics/2016/01/08/obama
-vetoes-gop-attempt-repeal-obamacare/78506800/,
accessed June 9, 2016.

20 Congressional Black Caucus, "Voter Protection and
Empowerment Working Group," https://cbc-butterfield

.house.gov/about/cbc-taskforces/voter-protection-and
-empowerment-working-group-0, accessed June 12, 2016.

21 Congressional Black Caucus, "Members," https://cbc
-butterfield.house.gov/members, accessed June 12, 2016.

22 Congressional Hispanic Caucus, "Immigration and Border
Issues," http://congressionalhispaniccaucus-sanchez
.house.gov/issues/immigration, accessed June 12, 2016.

23 Congressional Hispanic Caucus, "Members," http://
congressionalhispaniccaucus-sanchez.house.gov/
members, accessed June 12, 2016.

24 Congressional Asian Pacific American Caucus,
"Members," http://capac-chu.house.gov/members,
accessed June 12, 2016.

25 House of Representatives Committee on Rules,
"About the Committee on Rules—History and
Processes," https://rules.house.gov/about, accessed
June 12, 2016.

26 For more on Representative Howard Smith's tenure as
chair of Rules Committee, see Bruce J. Dierenfield,
*Keeper of the Rules: Congressman Howard W. Smith of
Virginia* (Charlottesville, VA: University Press of
Virginia, 1987).

27 Johanna Neuman, "The Senate Says No to D.C. Voice in
Congress," *Los Angeles Times*, September 19, 2007, A14.

28 Michael Grunwald, "Missouri Senate Race Is Heating Up
Early: Rejection of Judge Puts Ashcroft on Spot,"
Washington Post, October 23, 1999, A6.

29 Kenneth J. Cooper, "Hastings Joins His Accusers,"
Washington Post, January 6, 1993, A10; United States
Census, "My Congressional District," http://www
.census.gov/mycd/, accessed June 12, 2016.

30 Gail Russell Chaddock, "With New Oversight Powers,
House GOP Aims to Put Obama on Defensive," *Christian
Science Monitor*, January 13, 2011.

31 David R. Mayhew, *Congress: The Electoral Connection*
(New Haven, CT: Yale University Press, 1974).

32 Richard Fenno, *Home Style: House Members in Their
Districts* (Boston: Little Brown, 1978).

33 Morris P. Fiorina, *Congress: Keystone of the Washington
Establishment*, 2nd ed. (New Haven, CT: Yale University
Press, 1989).

34 Christian R. Grose, *Congress in Black and White: Race
and Representation in Congress and at Home* (New York:
Cambridge University Press, 2011).

35 United States House of Representatives Committee on
House Administration, "What Is the Frank?" https://
cha.house.gov/franking-commission/what-frank,
accessed June 12, 2016

36 Eric Schmitt, "House Approves Ending Schooling of
Illegal Aliens," *New York Times*, March 21, 1996, D25.

37 Fiorina 1989 also discusses the role that pork barrel
spending plays in members' reelection prospects.

38 Bret Schulte, "A Bridge (Way) Too Far," *U.S. News &
World Report*, July 8, 2005, http://www.usnews.com
/usnews/news/articles/050808/8highway.htm, accessed
January 27, 2013.

39 Japanese American Citizens League, "History," https://
jacl.org/about/history/, accessed August 19, 2016;

40 League of United Latin American Citizens, "Advocacy,"
http://lulac.org/advocacy/, accessed August 19, 2016.

41 Fiorina 1989, 56.

Chapter 7

1 Dinesh D'Souza, "Obama and the End of Racism,"
Townhall, September 1, 2008, http://townhall.com
/columnists/dineshdsouza/2008/09/01/obama_and
_the_end_of_racism, accessed June 22, 2016.

2 Laura Shin, "The Racial Wealth Gap: Why a Typical
White Household Has 16 Times the Wealth of a Black
One," *Forbes*, March 26, 2015, http://www.forbes.com
/sites/laurashin/2015/03/26/the-racial-wealth-gap
-why-a-typical-white-household-has-16-times-the
-wealth-of-a-black-one/#5ec900806c5b, accessed
June 22, 2016.

3 Paula D. McClain and Joseph Stewart, Jr., *Can We All
Get along: Racial and Ethnic Minorities in American
Politics*, 6th *edition* (Boulder, CO: Westview Press, 2014),
153–157.

4 John Woolley and Gerhard Peters, "Election of 2008,"
The American Presidency Project (Santa Barbara CA:
University of California at Santa Barbara, 1999–2016),
http://www.presidency.ucsb.edu/showelection
.php?year=2008, accessed June 22, 2016.

5 John Woolley and Gerhard Peters, "Election of 2012,"
The American Presidency Project (Santa Barbara CA:
University of California at Santa Barbara, 1999–2016),
http://www.presidency.ucsb.edu/showelection
.php?year=2012, accessed June 22, 2016.

6 CNN Politics, "Election Results: Presidential," http://
edition.cnn.com/election/results/president, accessed
November 16, 2016.

7 U.S. Census Bureau, "QuickFacts: Iowa and New
Hampshire," https://www.census.gov/quickfacts/table
/PST045215/33,19,00, accessed June 23, 2016.

8 Specifics on the 1876 election from the Rutherford B.
Hayes Presidential Center, "The Disputed Election of
1876: Frequently Asked Questions about the Disputed
Election of 1876," http://www.rbhayes.org/hayes
/president/display.asp?id=511&subj=president, accessed
June 23, 2016.

9 *Bush v. Gore*, 531 U.S. 98 (2000).

10 John Woolley and Gerhard Peters, "Election of 2000,"
The American Presidency Project (Santa Barbara CA:
University of California at Santa Barbara, 1999–2016),
http://www.presidency.ucsb.edu/showelection.
php?year=2000, accessed June 23, 2016.

11 For more on the Obama campaign's use of high-tech
data mining see, Tim Murphy, "Inside the Obama Campaign's Hard Drive," *Mother Jones*, September/October
2012, http://www.motherjones.com/politics/2012/10
/harper-reed-obama-campaign-microtargeting, accessed
June 23, 2016.

12 *Washington Post*, "Money Raised as of Oct. 19," https://www.washingtonpost.com/graphics/politics/2016-election/campaign-finance/, accessed November 16, 2016.

13 Center for Responsive Politics, "Super PACs," *Open Secrets*, http://www.opensecrets.org/pacs/superpacs.php?cycle=2012, accessed May 9, 2014.

14 Alexander Hamilton, *The Federalist Papers*, No. 70, ed. Michael Genovese (New York: Palgrave Macmillan, 2009), 199.

15 See Russell L. Riley, *The Presidency and the Politics of Racial Inequality: Nation Keeping from 1831 to 1965* (New York: Columbia University Press, 1999).

16 Jerry Markon, "Justice Dept. Steps Up Civil Rights Enforcement," *Washington Post*, June 4, 2010, A16.

17 For more on signing statements, see John T. Woolley, "Presidential Signing Statements: Frequently Asked Questions" *American Presidency Project* (Santa Barbara, CA: University of California at Santa Barbara, 1999–2016), http://www.presidency.ucsb.edu/signingstatements.php#q1, accessed June 24, 2016.

18 Charlie Savage, "Bush Move on Darfur Law Criticized: Critics Say He Undercuts Law on Divestment, President Cites Policy Role," *Boston Globe*, February 9, 2008, A2.

19 The authors counted Obama signing statements reported for each year by Woolley, "Presidential Signing Statement," http://www.presidency.ucsb.edu/signingstatements.php#q1, accessed June 24, 2016.

20 Peter Nicholas, "Obama Signs Defense Bill," *Los Angeles Times*, January 1, 2012, A3.

21 Paula D. McClain and Joseph Stewart, Jr., *"Can We All Get along?": Racial and Ethnic Minorities in American Politics*, 6th ed. (Boulder, CO: Westview Press, 2014), 148.

22 Lyndon Johnson: "Executive Order 11246—Equal Employment Opportunity," September 24, 1965. Gerhard Peters and John T. Woolley, *The American Presidency Project* (Santa Barbara, CA; University of California, Santa Barbara, 1999–2016). http://www.presidency.ucsb.edu/ws/?pid=59153, accessed June 24, 2016.

23 Barack Obama: "Executive Order 13620—Taking Additional Steps to Address the National Emergency with Respect to Somalia," July 20, 2012, Gerhard Peters and John T. Woolley, *The American Presidency Project* (Santa Barbara, CA: University of California at Santa Barbara, 199-2014). http://www.presidency.ucsb.edu/ws/index.php?pid=101397&st=&st1=, accessed June 24, 2016.

24 Adam Liptak and Michael D. Shear, "Supreme Court Tie Blocks Obama Immigration Plan," *New York Times*, June 23, 2016, http://www.nytimes.com/2016/06/24/us/supreme-court-immigration-obama-dapa.html?_r=0, accessed June 24, 2016.

25 Michael Oreskes, "Senate Rejects Tower 53–47," *New York Times*, March 10, 1989, A1.

26 United States Senate, "Senate History: Nominations," http://www.senate.gov/artandhistory/history/common/briefing/Nominations.htm#10, accessed June 24, 2016.

27 *United States v. Curtiss-Wright Export Corp.*, 299 U.S. 304, 319 (1936).

28 Jake Thompson, "ABM Treaty Officially Ends After 30 Years," *Omaha World-Herald*, June 14, 2002, 5A.

29 *United States v. Belmont*, 301 U.S. 324 (1937); *United States v. Pink*, 313 U.S. 203 (1942).

30 David O'Brien, *Constitutional Law and Politics, Vol. 1: Struggles for Power and Governmental Accountability*, 7th ed. (New York: Norton, 2008), 252.

31 *Hamdan v. Rumsfeld*, 548 U.S. 557 (2006); *Boumediene v. Bush*, 553 U.S. 723 (2008).

32 Greg Miller and Julian E. Banes, "The United States Will Not Torture, Obama Says: President Says Terror War Will Be Won on Our Own Terms," *Baltimore Sun*, January 23, 2009, 1A.

33 Micah Zenko, "Obama's Embrace of Drone Strikes Will be a Lasting Legacy," *New York Times*, January 12, 2016, http://www.nytimes.com/roomfordebate/2016/01/12/reflecting-on-obamas-presidency/obamas-embrace-of-drone-strikes-will-be-a-lasting-legacy, accessed June 24, 2016.

34 Congress.gov, "S. 321 – Indian Preference Act: 101st Congress (1989-1990), https://www.congress.gov/bill/101st-congress/senate-bill/321, accessed August 23, 2016.

35 U.S. Senate, "Art & History: The State of the Union Address," http://www.senate.gov/artandhistory/history/common/generic/News_State_of_the_Union.htm, accessed June 25, 2016.

36 Office of the Historian and Office Art & Archives U.S. House of Representatives, "The State of the Union Address," http://history.house.gov/Institution/SOTU/State-of-the-Union/; Clerk U.S. House of Representatives, "Historical Highlights: The First Evening Televised State of the Union Address, January 4, 1965" http://history.house.gov/Historical-Highlights/1951-2000/The-first-televised-evening-State-of-the-Union-Address/, both accessed June 25, 2016.

37 Lyndon B. Johnson, "Annual Message to Congress on the State of the Union," January 4, 1965, Gerhard Peters and John T. Woolley, *The American Presidency Project* (Santa Barbara, CA; University of California at Santa Barbara, 1999–2016). http://www.presidency.ucsb.edu/ws/index.php?pid=26907, accessed June 25, 2016.

38 For more on President Obama's relationship with Congress over immigration, see David A. Graham, "Immigration Advocates Place Their Faith in Obama," *The Atlantic*, June 1, 2015, http://www.theatlantic.com/politics/archive/2015/06/immigration-advocates-place-their-faith-in-obama/394388/, accessed June 25, 2016.

39 Marc Landler, "Obama's Growing Trust in Biden Is Reflected in His Call on Troops," *New York Times*, June 25, 2011, A4.

40 U.S. Senate, "Charles Curtis: A Featured Biography," http://www.senate.gov/artandhistory/history/common/generic/Featured_Bio_Curtis.htm, accessed January 25, 2012.

41 Jennifer Epstein, "FLOTUS a 'Huge Force' in Grassroots Outreach," *POLITICO*, http://www.politico.com/news

/stories/0912/81800.html, accessed June 25, 2016; Christi Parsons, "As First Lady, Obama Takes Time to Learn: Aware of the Perils of a Big Early Agenda, She Sets Out Slowly," *Chicago Tribune*, February 24, 2008, 8.

42 U.S. Department of Interior, "Tribal Nations," https:// www.doi.gov/tribes, accessed June 25, 2016.

43 Robert E. DiClerico, *The American President*, 5th ed. (Upper Saddle River, NJ: Prentice-Hall, 2000), 208.

44 Kathryn Dunn Tenpas, PhD, "A Curious Strategy for the Obama Administration's Final Stretch," *FixGov: Making Government Work* (Washington, DC: Brookings, September 14, 2014), http://www.brookings.edu/blogs /fixgov/posts/2014/09/15-obama-final-stretch-cabinet -meetings-tenpas, accessed June 25, 2016.

45 John O'Sullivan, "Give Powell Credit as Peacemaker, but Brain Behind U.S. War Strategy Clearly Is Rumsfeld," *Chicago Sun-Times*, November 27, 2001, 29.

46 Mark Mazzetti, Helene Cooper, and Peter Baker, "Behind the Hunt for Bin Laden," *New York Times*, May 3, 2011, A1.

47 NBC News Latino, "Labor Sec. Tom Perez: President Has Authority on Immigration Matters," *NBC News*, April 15, 2016, http://www.nbcnews.com/news/latino/labor -sec-tom-perez-president-has-authority-immigration -matters-n556661, accessed June 26, 2016.

48 Secretary Cavazos served in both the Reagan and the first Bush administrations.

49 He spoke these words to the National Association for the Advancement of Colored People during his campaign; see "Clinton Vows Racial Accord," *Chicago Sun-Times*, July 12, 1992, 16.

50 Christi Parsons and Michael A. Memoili, "Obama Cabinet Starts Looking Less Diverse," *Los Angeles Times*, January 10, 2013, AA2.

51 The White House, President Barack Obama, "The National Security Council," https://www.whitehouse .gov/administration/eop/nsc, accessed June 26, 2016.

52 The White House, President Barack Obama, "The Office of Management and Budget," https://www.whitehouse .gov/omb, accessed June 26, 2016.

53 Gromer Jeffers, Jr., "Ron Kirk Back Home in Dallas After Resigning as U.S. Trade Rep," *Dallas Morning News*, accessed June 26, 2016.

54 Richard Neustadt, *Presidential Power and the Modern Presidents: The Politics of Leadership From Roosevelt to Reagan* (New York: Free Press, 1990).

55 Samuel Kernell, *Going Public: New Strategies of Presidential Leadership*, 2nd ed. (Washington, DC: Congressional Quarterly Press, 1993).

56 Ann Devroy, "Bush Vetoes Civil Rights Bill," *Washington Post*, October 23, 1990, A1.

57 Adam Clymer, "Civil Rights Bill Is Passed by House," *New York Times*, November 8, 1991, A15.

58 Jonathan Weisman and Ashley Parker, "Republicans Back Down, Ending Crisis Over Shutdown and Debt Limit," *New York Times*, October 16, 2013, http://www .nytimes.com/2013/10/17/us/congress-budget-debate .html?_r=0, accessed June 25, 2016.

59 For more on the comparison between Presidents Kennedy and Johnson and their abilities to secure civil rights policies, see Mark Stern, *Calculating Visions: Kennedy, Johnson, and Civil Rights* (New Brunswick, NJ: Rutgers University Press, 1992).

60 Kernell, *Going Public*, supra note 48.

61 Gallup Presidential Approval Center, http://www.gallup .com/poll/124922/presidential-approval-center.aspx, accessed June 26, 2016.

62 *United States v. Nixon*, 418 U.S. 683 (1974).

63 *Cheney v. U.S. District Court for the District of Columbia*, 542 U.S. 367 (2004).

64 Ed O'Keefe and Sari Horowitz, "Holder Is Held in Contempt of Congress," *Washington Post*, June 29, 2012, A1.

Chapter 8

1 United States Census Bureau, "QuickFacts: Flint City, Michigan," https://www.census.gov/quickfacts/table /PST045215/2629000, accessed July 1, 2016.

2 Clare Groden, "How Michigan's Bureaucrats Created the Flint Water Crisis," *Fortune*, http://fortune.com /flint-water-crisis/; Merritt Kennedy, "Lead-Laced Water in Flint: A Step-By-Step Look at the Makings of a Crisis," *National Public Radio*, April 20, 2016, http://www.npr .org/sections/thetwo-way/2016/04/20/465545378 /lead-laced-water-in-flint-a-step-by-step-look-at-the -makings-of-a-crisis, both accessed July 1, 2016.

3 United States Department of Justice, Civil Rights Division, "About the Division," https://www.justice.gov /crt/about-division, accessed July 2, 2016.

4 United States Department of Homeland Security Federal Emergency Management Agency, "About the Agency," https://www.fema.gov/about-agency, accessed July 2, 2016.

5 Gerald Shields, "Ex–FEMA Chief Witt Described as 'Real Deal,'" *The Advocate* (Baton Rouge, LA), March 1, 2006, B1; "Short Takes: Quick Witt Helps," *Atlanta Journal and Constitution*, February 12, 1996, 8A.

6 Christopher Cooper and Robert Block, *Disaster: Hurricane Katrina and the Failure of Homeland Security* (New York: Times Books, 2006); Michael Grunwald and Susan B. Glaser, "Brown's Turf War Sapped FEMA's Strength; Director Who Symbolized Incompetence in Katrina Predicted Agency Would Fail," *Washington Post*, December 23, 2005, A1.

7 Arloc Sherman and Isaac Shapiro, "Essential Facts on the Victims of Hurricane Katrina," *Center on Budget and Policy Priorities*, http://www.cbpp.org/research/essential -facts-about-the-victims-of-hurricane- katrina?fa=view&id=658, accessed July 2, 2016.

8 *Humphrey's Executor v. United States*, 295 U.S. 602 (1935).

9 Equal Employment Opportunity Commission, "About EEOC," http://www.eeoc.gov/eeoc/index.cfm, accessed February 13, 2012.

10 "Congressional Study Says Job Bias Cases Are Poorly Handled," *New York Times*, October 12, 1988, A23.

11 Equal Employment Opportunity Commission, "Jenny R. Yang, Chair," https://www.eeoc.gov/eeoc/yang.cfm, accessed July 2, 2016

12 Roy Maurer, "EEOC Targets Emerging Workforce Technology Trends," Society for Human Resource Management, March 16, 2016, https://www.shrm.org/hrdisciplines/staffingmanagement/articles/pages/jenny-yang-eeoc-chair-shrm-conference.aspx, accessed July 2, 2016.

13 CIA, "About CIA," https://www.cia.gov/about-cia/index.html, accessed February 16, 2012.

14 Steven J. Dick, "Why We Explore: The Birth of NASA," http://www.nasa.gov/exploration/whyweexplore/Why_We_29.html, accessed July 2, 2016.

15 U.S. Commission on Civil Rights, "About Us," http://www.usccr.gov/about/index.php, accessed July 2, 2016.

16 Mary Frances Berry.com, "Home," http://www.maryfrancesberry.com/, accessed February 16, 2012.

17 Patty Reinert, "Critics Pounce on Florida: Civil Rights Panel Vows to Keep Tabs on Reform Efforts," *Houston Chronicle*, March 10, 2001, A1.

18 Peter Schmidt, "Civil Rights Commission Pressures Law Schools on Affirmative Action," *Chronicle of Higher Education* 36, no. 2 (September 7, 2007): 36.

19 Bill Briggs, "Civil Rights Commission Urged to Order Audit of Military Sex-Assault Cases," *U.S. News & World Report/NBC News.com*, January 11, 2013, http://usnews.nbcnews.com/_news/2013/01/11/16469177-civil-rights-commission-urged-to-order-audit-of-military-sex-assault-cases?lite, accessed July 2, 2016; U.S. Commission on Civil Rights, "Martin R. Castro, Chair," http://www.usccr.gov/about/bio/Castro.php, accessed July 2, 2016.

20 Ashley Halsey III, "House GOP Set to Ax Transportation Fund," *Washington Post*, July 6, 2011, A2.

21 Office of Personnel Management, "Executive Branch Civilian Employment Since 1940," https://www.opm.gov/policy-data-oversight/data-analysis-documentation/federal-employment-reports/historical-tables/executive-branch-civilian-employment-since-1940/, accessed July 2, 2016.

22 For more on Andrew Jackson and the establishment of the "spoils system," see Leonard D. White, *The Jacksonians: A Study in Administrative History, 1829–1861* (New York: MacMillan, 1954).

23 See Steven P. Erie, *Rainbow's End: Irish Americans and the Dilemmas of Urban Machine Politics, 1840–1985* (Berkeley and Los Angeles: University of California Press, 1988).

24 U.S. Office of Personnel Management, "Our Mission, Role & History," http://www.opm.gov/about-us/our-mission-role-history/, accessed July 2, 2016

25 Richard E. Moffit, "Gutting the Hatch Act: Congresses Plan to Re-Politicize the Civil Service," *Heritage Research Reports*, July 6, 1993, http://www.heritage.org/research/reports/2003/07/gutting-the-hatch-act-congresss-plan-to-repoliticize-the-civil-service, accessed July 2, 2016.

26 *Washington v. Davis*, 426 U.S. 229 (1976).

27 James W. Fesler and Donald F. Kettl, *The Politics of the Administrative Process* (Chatham, NJ: Chatham House, 1996), 152–153.

28 *Johnson v. Transportation Agency, Santa Clara (CA) County*, 480 U.S. 616 (1987).

29 See the Administrative Procedure Act, § 553 Rule Making, https://www.archives.gov/federal-register/laws/administrative-procedure/553.html; Emily S. Bremer, "A Primer on the Informal Rulemaking Process," Administrative Conference of the United States, May 10, 2013, https://www.acus.gov/newsroom/administrative-fix-blog/primer-informal-rulemaking-process; both accessed July 3, 2016.

30 Federal Aviation Administration, "FAA Regulations," https://www.faa.gov/regulations_policies/faa_regulations/, accessed July 3, 2016.

31 U.S. Environmental Protection Agency, "Regulations," https://www.epa.gov/laws-regulations/regulations, accessed July 3, 2016.

32 Government Printing Office, "Federal Housing Finance Agency 12 CFR 1207 RIN 2590-AA28 Minority and Women Inclusion," *Federal Register* 75 (248, Tuesday, December 28, 2010): 81395–81405.

33 Equal Employment Opportunity Commission, "Facts about Mediation," http://www.eeoc.gov/eeoc/mediation/facts.cfm, accessed July 3, 2016.

34 See for example, Theodore J. Lowi, *The End of Liberalism: The Second Republic of the United States*, 2nd ed. (New York: Norton, 1979).

35 Hugh Heclo, "Issue Networks and the Executive Establishment," In Anthony Kind, ed., *The New American Political System* (Washington, DC: The American Enterprise Institute, 1978), 87–124.

36 Todd J. Gillman and Laura Isensee, "Bush Commutes Sentences of Border Control Agents," *Dallas Morning News*, January 20, 2009, 1A; Michelle Middelstadt, "Rift between Border Patrol Agents, Leaders Widening," *Houston Chronicle*, April 26, 2007, A7.

37 National Border Patrol Council, "Overzealous Prosecution Results in Excessive Sentence in Jesus Diaz Case," April 18, 2012, http://www.bpunion.org/index.php/newsroom/press-releases/100-overzealous-prosecution-results-in-excessive-sentence-in-jesus-diaz-case, accessed July 3, 2016.

38 U.S. Office of Personnel Management, "Senior Executive Service," https://www.opm.gov/policy-data-oversight/senior-executive-service/, accessed April 23, 2014.

39 The White House, Office of Management and Budget, "The Mission and Structure of the Office of Management and Budget," https://www.whitehouse.gov/omb/organization_mission/, accessed July 3, 2016.

40 Office of the Inspector General Social Security Administration, "Whistleblower Protection History," https://oig

.ssa.gov/whistleblower-protection/history, accessed July 3, 2016.

41 Marsha Coleman-Adebayo, *No Fear: A Whistleblower's Triumph Over Corruption and Retaliation at the EPA* (Chicago: Chicago Review Press, 2011); Daryl Fears, "Coming Soon: A Tale of Whistleblowing at the EPA," *Washington Post*, July 10, 2006, http://www.washingtonpost.com/wp-dyn /content/article/2006/07/09/AR2006070900741_pf.html, accessed July 3, 2016.

42 Spencer S. Hsu, "FEMA Knew of Toxic Gas in Trailers; Hurricane Victims Reported Illness," *Washington Post*, July 20, 2007, A1.

43 U.S. Government Accountability Office, "About GAO," http://www.gao.gov/about/index.html, accessed July 3, 2016.

44 See for example, Government Accountability Office, *Statement of Comptroller General David Walker: Hurricane Katrina: GAO's Preliminary Observations Regarding Preparedness, Response, and Recovery*, March 8, 2006, http:// www.gao.gov/assets/120/112976.pdf and Government Accountability Office, *Report to Congressional Committees: Hurricane Katrina: Better Plans and Exercises Needed to Guide the Military's Response to Natural Disasters*, May 2006, http://www.gao.gov/new.items/d06643.pdf, both accessed July 3, 2016.

45 *Immigration and Naturalization Service v. Chadha*, 462 U.S. 919 (1983).

46 *U.S. v. Brignoni-Ponce*, 422 U.S. 873 (1975).

47 MALDEF, "Protecting Immigrants' Rights," http:// www.maldef.org/immigration/index.html, accessed April 23, 2014.

Chapter 9

1 California Supreme Court website, "Associate Justice Goodwin Liu," http://www.courts.ca.gov/15450.htm, accessed July 11, 2016.

2 Perry Bacon, Jr., "Appeals Court Nomination Advances," *Washington Post*, May 14, 2010, A14; Charlie Savage, "Appeals Court Nominee Ignites a Partisan Battle," *New York Times*, April 13, 2010, A15.

3 Josh Richman, "GOP Blocks UC Berkeley Law Professor's Vote to Bench," *San Jose Mercury News*, May 19, 2011.

4 U.S. Senate, "Roll Call Votes 108th Congress," http:// www.senate.gov/legislative/LIS/roll_call_lists/roll_call _vote_cfm.cfm?congress=108&session=1&vote=00312, accessed July 11, 2016.

5 Maura Dolan, "Accolades as Justice Confirmed," *Los Angeles Times*, September 1, 2011, AA1.

6 Warren Richey, "How New Senate Filibuster Rules Could Change Balance of Power on Courts," *Christian Science Monitor*, November 21, 2013, http://www.csmonitor .com/USA/Politics/DC-Decoder/2013/1121/How-new -Senate-filibuster-rule-could-change-balance-of-power -on-courts-video, accessed July 11, 2016.

7 Henry J. Abraham, *The Judicial Process: An Introductory Analysis of the Courts of the United States, England, and*

Great Britain, 6th ed. (New York: Oxford University Press, 1993), 7.

8 For more on the Judiciary Act of 1789, see Library of Congress, "Primary Documents in American History: The Judiciary Act of 1789," https://www.loc.gov/rr/ program/bib/ourdocs/judiciary.html, accessed July 11, 2016.

9 United States Courts, "U.S. District Courts—Judicial Business 2015," http://www.uscourts.gov/statistics -reports/us-district-courts-judicial-business-2015, accessed July 11, 2016.

10 *Brown v. Board of Education*, 349 U.S. 294 (1955).

11 For more on the role of federal district court judges in desegregation see J. W. Peltason, *Fifty-Eight Lonely Men: Southern Federal Judges and School Desegregation* (New York: Harcourt, Brace, and World, 1961).

12 United States Courts, "U.S. Courts of Appeals—Judicial Business 2015," http://www.uscourts.gov/statistics -reports/us-courts-appeals-judicial-business-2015, accessed July 11, 2016.

13 For more on the use of judicial review in the states prior to *Marbury v. Madison*, see Michael William Treanor, "Judicial Review Before Marbury," *Stanford Law Review* 58 (2005): 455–562, 497–517.

14 *Marbury v. Madison*, 1 Cranch. 137 (1803).

15 For more on the legal and political issues surrounding *Marbury v. Madison* and John Marshall, see Mark A. Graber, "Establishing Judicial Review: Schooner Peggy and the Early Marshall Court," *Political Research Quarterly* 51 (1998) 221–239; Jack Knight and Lee Epstein, "On the Struggle for Judicial Supremacy," *Law & Society Review* 30 (1996): 87–120; William E. Nelson, *Marbury v. Madison: The Origins and Legacy of Judicial Review* (Lawrence, KS; University of Kansas Press, 2000); James O'Fallon, "*Marbury*," *Stanford Law Review* 44 (1992): 219–260.

16 For more on the different approaches to constitutional interpretation, consult Walter F. Murphy, C. Herman Pritchett, Lee Epstein, and Jack Knight, *Courts, Judges, and Politics: An Introduction to the Judicial Process*, 6th ed. (Boston: McGraw-Hill, 2006), 539–616.

17 *Brown v. Board of Education*, 347 U.S. 483 (1954).

18 Ibid., Footnote 11, 494.

19 *Worcester v. Georgia*, 6 Pet. 515 (1832). For more on Jackson's actions after this decision consult, Matthew L. Sundquist, "*Worcester v. Georgia*: A Breakdown in the Separation of Powers," *American Indian Law Review* 35 (2010–2011): 239–255.

20 *Brown v. Board of Education*, I n15 and II n9.

21 *Dred Scott v. Sandford*, 19 How. 393 (1857).

22 *Wards Cove Packing, Inc. v. Atonio*, 490 U.S. 642 (1989).

23 For a full text of the Civil Rights Act of 1991, see Equal Employment Opportunity Commission, "Civil Rights Act 1991," https://www.eeoc.gov/eeoc/history/35th /thelaw/cra_1991.html, accessed July 11, 2016.

24 *United States v. SCRAP*, 412 U.S. 669 (1973).

25 *Lujan v. Defenders of Wildlife*, 504 U.S. 555 (1992).

26 *DeFunis v. Odegaard*, 416 U.S. 312 (1974).

27 *Plessy v. Ferguson*, 163 U.S. 537 (1896).

28 *Brown* I, 492.

29 *Metro Broadcasting v. Federal Communication Commission*, 497 U.S. 547 (1990).

30 *Adarand Constructors, Inc. v. Peña*, 515 U.S. 200 (1995).

31 David M. O'Brien, *Storm Center: The Supreme Court in American Politics*, 8th ed. (New York: Norton, 2008), 35.

32 The Supreme Court of the United States, "Biographies of Current Justices of the Supreme Court," http://www .supremecourt.gov/about/biographies.aspx, accessed July 11, 2016.

33 Henry J. Abraham, *Justices and Presidents: A Political History of Appointments to the Supreme Court*, 3rd ed. (New York: Oxford University Press, 1992), 255–257.

34 Sheldon Goldman, Elliot Slotnick, Gerard Gryski, Gary Zuk, and Sara Schiavoni, "W. Bush Remaking the Federal Judiciary: Like Father, Like Son?" *Judicature* 86 (2007): 304, 308; Sheldon Goldman, Elliot Slotnick, and Sara Schiavoni, "Writing the Book of Judges: Obama's Appointment Record After His First Six Years," *Journal of Law and Courts* 3 (2015): 331–367; 356, 364.

35 Nina Totenberg, "Supreme Court Justice Souter to Retire," *National Public Radio*, April 30, 2009, http:// www.npr.org/templates/story/story.php?storyId= 103694193, accessed July 16, 2016.

36 "Clement M. Haynesworth Junior: Judge Was Rejected as 1969 Supreme Court Nominee," *Los Angeles Times*, November 23, 1989, http://articles.latimes.com/1989-11 -23/news/mn-3_1_supreme-court, accessed July 11, 2016.

37 "Anita Hill vs. Clarence Thomas: The Back Story," *CBS News*, October 20, 2010, http://www.cbsnews.com/news /anita-hill-vs-clarence-thomas-the-backstory/, accessed July 11, 2016.

38 Andrew Cohen, "The Sad Legacy of Robert Bork," *The Atlantic*, December 12, 2012, http://www.theatlantic .com/politics/archive/2012/12/the-sad-legacy-of-robert -bork/266456/, accessed July 11, 2016.

39 Amita Kelly, "McConnell: Blocking Supreme Court Nomination 'About a Principle, Not a Person,'" *National Public Radio*, March 16, 2016, http://www.npr .org/2016/03/16/470664561/mcconnell-blocking -supreme-court-nomination-about-a-principle-not-a -person, accessed July 11, 2016.

40 Russell Wheeler, "Judicial Nominations and Confirmations: Fact and Fiction," *FixGov: Making Government Work* (Washington, DC: Brookings, December 30, 2013), http://www.brookings.edu/blogs/fixgov/posts/2013/12 /30-staffing-federal-judiciary-2013-no-breakthrough -year, accessed July 11, 2016.

41 Data Adapted from American Bar Association Commission on Women in the Profession, *A Current Glance at Women in the Law, 2014* (Chicago: American Bar Association, July 2014), 5, http://www.americanbar.org/content /dam/aba/marketing/women/current_glance_statistics _july2014.authcheckdam.pdf, accessed July 11, 2016.

42 Jonathan Jew-Lim, "A Brief Overview of President Obama's Asian American Judicial Nominees in 2010," *Asian American Law Journal* 17 (2010): 227–238; Josh Richman, "U.S. Senate Confirms Chen to Federal Bench," *San Jose Mercury News*, May 10, 2011.

43 Luz Lazo, "Area Hispanics Praise Selection of Sotomayor," *Richmond (VA) Times Dispatch*, May 27, 2009, A4.

44 Wes Allison, "The Buzz Florida Politics: Martinez Liking Sotomayor," *St. Petersburg Times*, June 7, 2009, 3B.

45 *Ricci v. DeStefano*, 530 F.3d. 87 (2008); *Ricci v. DeStefano*, 129 S.Ct. 2658 (2009).

46 Wes Allison, "The Ruling That Has Nominee Under Fire," *St. Petersburg Times*, May 31, 2009, 1A.

47 United States Senate, "Supreme Court Nominations, present–1789," http://www.senate.gov/pagelayout /reference/nominations/Nominations.htm, accessed July 11, 2016. Senator Edward Kennedy (D-MA) was still in the Senate then, but he did not vote because he was too ill.

48 United States Supreme Court, "Frequently Asked Questions," http://www.supremecourt.gov/faq.aspx#faqgi9, accessed July 11, 2016.

49 See, Samuel Krislov, "Amicus Curiae: From Friendship to Advocacy," *Yale Law Journal* 72 (1963): 694–721.

50 *Plessy*, Justice Harlan's dissent on 552–564.

51 *Brown* I.

52 See for example, Sean Farhang and Gregory Wawro, "Institutional Dynamics on the U.S. Courts of Appeals: Minority Representation Under Panel Decision Making," *Journal of Law, Economics, & Organization* 20 (2004): 299–330 and Darrell Steffensmeier and Chester L. Britt, "Judges Race and Judicial Decision Making: Do Black Judges Sentence Differently?" *Social Science Quarterly* 82 (2002): 749–764. Steffensmeier and Britt actually unearth some evidence that in certain cases Black judges sentence more harshly than White judges.

53 Sherrilyn A. Ifill, "Racial Diversity on the Bench: Beyond Role Models and Public Confidence," *Washington & Lee Law Review* 57 (2000): 405–495.

54 See for example, Susan Welch, Michael Combs, and John Gruhl, "Do Black Judges Make a Difference?" *American Journal of Political Science* 32 (1988): 126–136.

55 See for example, Susan W. Johnson and Donald R. Songer, "Judge Gender and Voting Behavior of Justices on Two North American Supreme Courts," *Justice System Journal* 30 (2009): 265–279.

56 See for example David W. Allen and Diane E. Wall, "Role Orientations and Women State Supreme Court Justices," *Judicature* 77 (1993): 156–165; Susan W. Johnson, Ronald Stidham, Robert A. Carp, and Kenneth Manning, "The Gender Influence on U.S. District Court Decisions: Updating the Traditional Judge Attribute Model," *Journal of Women, Politics, & Policy* 29 (2008): 497–526.

57 See for example, Christina L. Boyd, Lee Epstein, and Andrew D. Martin, "Untangling the Causal Effects of Sex on Judging," *American Journal of Political Science*

54 (2010): 389–411; John Gruhl, Cassia Spohn, and Susan Welch, "Women as Policy Makers: The case of Trial Judges," *American Journal of Political Science* 25 (1981): 308–322; Jennifer Segal, "Representative Decision Making on the Federal Bench: Clinton's District Court Appointments," *Political Research Quarterly* 53 (2000): 147–150; Donald R. Songer and Kelley Crews-Meyer, "Does Gender Matter? Decision Making in State Supreme Courts," *Social Science Quarterly* 81 (2000): 750–762; and Thomas G. Walker and Deborah J. Barrow, "The Diversification of the Federal Bench: Policy and Process Ramifications," *Journal of Politics* 47 (1985): 596–617.

58 Jeffrey A. Segal and Harold J, Spaeth, *The Supreme Court and the Attitudinal Model Revisited* (New York: Cambridge University Press, 2002).

59 See, for example, Rebecca Salokar, *The Solicitor General: The Politics of Law* (Philadelphia: Temple University Press, 1992); Jeffrey A. Segal and Cheryl D. Reedy, "The Supreme Court and Sex Discrimination: The Role of the Solicitor General," *Western Political Quarterly* 41 (1988): 553–568.

60 O'Brien, *Storm Center*, 139.

61 In housing: *Shelley v. Kraemer*, 344 U.S. 1 (1948). See also, Clement E. Vose, *Caucasians Only: The Supreme Court, the NAACP, and the Restrictive Covenant Cases* (Berkeley: University of California Press, 1959). In voting: *Nixon v. Herndon*, 273 U.S. 536 (1927); *Smith v. Allwright*, 321 U.S. 649 (1944). See also, Steven C. Tauber, The Influence of the NAACP Legal Defense Fund on the U.S. Supreme Court's Minority Voting Rights Law," In Christopher P. Banks and John C. Green, *Superintending Democracy: The Courts and the Political Process* (Akron, OH: University of Akron Press, 2001).

62 *Brown* I. See also Jack Greenberg, *Crusaders in the Courts: How a Dedicated Band of Lawyers Fought for the Civil Rights Revolution* (New York: Basic Books, 1994).

63 NAACP Legal Defense and Education Fund, "Program Areas," http://www.naacpldf.org/program-areas, accessed July 11, 2016.

64 Mexican American Legal Defense Fund, "MALDEF: The Latino Legal Voice for Civil Rights in America," http://www.maldef.org/, accessed July 12, 2016.

65 The Native American Rights Fund, "Our Work," http://www.narf.org/our-work/, accessed July 11, 2016.

66 Asian Americans Advancing Justice "Programs," http://www.advancingequality.org/what-we-do/programs, accessed July 11, 2016.

67 David D. Kirkpatrick, "Seeing Slavery in Liberalism: Janice Rogers Brown," *New York Times*, June 9, 2005, A22.

Chapter 10

1 The Associate Press–NORC Center for Public Affairs Research. "Law Enforcement and Violence: The Divide between Black and White Americans." August 2015. http://www.apnorc.org/projects/Pages/law-enforcement -and-violence-the-divide-between-black-and-white -americans.aspx Accessed June 9, 2016.

2 Quoted in "Propaganda in the Civil War," http://www .civilwarhome.com, accessed July 12, 2009.

3 Phillip S. Paludan. "The Better Angels of Our Nature: Lincoln, Propaganda, and Public Opinion in the North during the Civil War," in *On the Road to Total War: The American Civil War and the German Wars of Unification, 1861–1871*, ed. Stig Förster and Jörg Nagler (New York: Cambridge University Press, 1997), 362–363.

4 Daniel Stevens, "Public Opinion and Public Policy: The Case of Kennedy and Civil Rights," *Presidential Studies Quarterly* 32 (March 2002): 111–136.

5 American RadioWorks, "John F. Kennedy: The Mississippi Crisis," http://americanradioworks .publicradio.org/features/prestapes/a1.html, accessed July 22, 2009.

6 Stevens, "Public Opinion and Public Policy," 123–125.

7 See, for instance, Mark A. Lorell and Charles Kelley, Jr., *Casualties, Public Opinion, and Presidential Policy During the Vietnam War* (Santa Monica, CA: Rand Project Air Force, 1985); William Schneir and Miriam Schneir, "How the Military Cooked the Books: The Uncounted Vietcong," *The Nation* 283 (May 1984): 570–577; James J. Wirtz, "Intelligence to Please? The Order of Battle Controversy During the Vietnam War," *Political Science Quarterly* 106 (Summer 1991): 239–263.

8 Elizabeth Becker, "In the War on Terrorism, a Battle to Shape Public Opinion," *New York Times*, November 11, 2001, A1.

9 Gabriel Almond and Sidney Verba, *The Civic Culture: Political Attitudes and Democracy in Five Nations* (Princeton, NJ: Princeton University Press, 1963).

10 Carroll J. Glynn, Susan Herbst, Garrett J. O'Keefe, Robert Y. Shapiro, and Mark Lindeman, *Public Opinion* (Boulder, CO: Westview Press, 2004), 8.

11 Richard D. Pineda and Stacey K. Sowards, "Flag Waving as Visual Argument: 2006 Immigration Demonstrations and Cultural Citizenship," *Argumentation and Advocacy* (December 22, 2007).

12 http://i.abcnews.com/Technology/story?id=7463348#at, accessed October 29, 2009.

13 Until 2002, the ANES was conducted every presidential and midterm election year. Currently, the ANES is conducted only during presidential election years.

14 Glynn et al., *Public Opinion*, 60.

15 Earl R. Babbie, *The Practice of Social Research*, 3rd ed. (Belmont, CA: Wadsworth, 1983), 145.

16 Ibid., 143.

17 Ibid., 145.

18 Herbert Asher, *Polling and the Public: What Every Citizen Should Know*, 7th ed. (Washington, DC: Congressional Quarterly Press, 2007), 69–76.

19 Jillesa G. "Does Question Order Affect the Type of Survey Response You Receive?" SurveyMonkey Blog.

June 20, 2016. https://www.surveymonkey.com/blog/2016/06/20/aapor/

20 Pew Research Center for the People and the Press, "The Impact of 'Cells-Only' on Public Opinion Polling," January 31, 2008.

21 Steven Shepard, "Gallup Blew Its Presidential Polls, but Why?" *National Journal*, November 18, 2012, http://www.nationaljournal.com/politics/gallup-blew-its-presidential-polls-but-why--20121118. Accessed February 7, 2013.

22 U.S. Census Bureau, "Projections of the Size and Composition of the U. S. Population: 2014-2060." Table 2. March 2015. http://www.census.gov/content/dam/Census/library/publications/2015/demo/p25-1143.pdf. Accessed June 9, 2016.

23 U.S. Census Bureau, "California Quick Facts from the US Census Bureau," http://www.census.gov/quickfacts/table/PST045215/06. Accessed June 9, 2016

24 Paula D. McClain and Joseph Stewart, Jr., *"Can We All Get along?": Racial and Ethnic Minorities in American Politics*, 6th ed. (Boulder, CO: Westview Press, 2014).

25 Ian Ayres, *Pervasive Prejudice? Unconventional Evidence of Race and Gender Discrimination* (Chicago: University of Chicago Press, 2001).

26 Paul R. Abramson, "Political Efficacy and Political Trust Among School Children: Two Explanations," *Journal of Politics* 34 (1972): 1243–1275.

27 Gallup Poll, June 13 to July 10, 2015. http://www.gallup.com/poll/1687/race-relations.aspx

28 Randall Kennedy, *Race, Crime, and the Law* (New York: Pantheon, 1997), chap. 4; Patricia Warren and Donald Tomaskovic-Devey, "Racial Profiling and Searches: Did the Politics of Racial Profiling Change Police Behavior?" *Criminology and Public Policy* 8 (2): 343–369; Seth W. Fallik and Kenneth J. Novak, "The Decision to Search: Is Race or Ethnicity Important?" *Journal of Contemporary Criminal Justice* 28 (2): 146–165; Mary Romero, "Racial Profiling and Immigration Law Enforcement: Rounding Up the Usual Suspects in the Latino Community," *Critical Sociology* 32 (2–3): 447–473; Kenneth J. Novak and Mitchell B. Chamlin, "Racial Threat, Suspicion, and Police Behavior: The Impact of Race and Place in Traffic Enforcement," *Crime and Delinquency* 58 (2): 275–300.

29 Howard Schumann, Charlotte Steeh, Lawrence Bobo, and Maria Krysan, *Racial Attitudes in America: Trends and Interpretations* (Cambridge, MA: Harvard University Press, 1997), chaps. 3, 5; Donald R. Kinder and Lynn M. Sanders, *Divided by Color: Racial Politics and Democratic Ideals* (Chicago: University of Chicago Press, 1996), chap. 6.

30 Rodney E. Hero, *Latinos and the U.S. Political System* (Philadelphia: Temple University Press, 1992); Robert S. Smith and Richard Seltzer, *Race, Class, and Culture* (Albany: State University of New York Press, 1992); Katherine Tate, *From Protest to Politics: The New Black Voters in American Elections* (Cambridge, MA: Harvard University Press and Russell Sage Foundation, 1993).

31 The data sets are the 1984 and 1988 National Black Election Study, the 1993 National Black Politics Study, the 1996 National Black Election Study, the 2004 CBS News/Black Entertainment Television Monthly Poll, and the 2008 Joint Center for Political and Economic Studies National Opinion Poll.

32 Tate, *From Protest to Politics*, 31–32, 38.

33 Hero, *Latinos and the U.S. Political System*, 1992.

34 Rodolfo O. de la Garza, Louis DeSipio, F. Chris Garcia, John Garcia, and Angelo Falcon, *Latino Voices: Mexican, Puerto Rican, and Cuban Perspectives on American Politics* (Boulder, CO: Westview Press, 1992), 90.

35 Lawrence D. Bobo and Devon Johnson, "A Taste for Punishment: Black and White Americans' Views on the Death Penalty and the War on Drugs," *Du Bois Review* 1 (2004): 151–180; Devon Johnson, "Racial Prejudice, Perceived Injustice, and the Black–White Gap in Punitive Attitudes," *Journal of Criminal Justice* 36 (2008): 198–206.

36 Bobo and Johnson, "A Taste for Punishment"; Randall Kennedy, *Race, Crime, and the Law* (New York: Pantheon, 1997), chap. 4.

37 Harold M. Rose and Paula D. McClain, *Race, Place, and Risk: Black Homicide in Urban America* (Albany: State University of New York Press, 1990); Darnell F. Hawkins, ed., *Violent Crime: Assessing Race and Ethnic Differences* (New York: Cambridge University Press, 2003); Randall Kennedy, "Racial Trends in the Administration of Criminal Justice," in *America Becoming: Racial Trends and Their Consequences*, vol. 2, ed. Neil J. Smelser, William Julius Wilson, and Faith Mitchell (Washington, DC: National Academy Press, 2001).

38 United Nations Office of Drug and Crime. "Global Study on Homicide 2013." https://www.unodc.org/documents/gsh/pdfs/2014_GLOBAL_HOMICIDE_BOOK_web.pdf. Accessed June 9, 2016.

39 Kristi Andersen, "Gender and Public Opinion," in *Understanding Public Opinion*, ed. Barbara Norrander and Clyde Wilcox (Washington, DC: Congressional Quarterly Press, 1997).

40 Ibid.

41 Ibid.

42 Karen M. Kaufmann, "The Gender Gap," *PS: Political Science and Politics* 39 (July 2006): 447–453.

43 Ronald B. Rapoport, Walter J. Stone, and Alan I. Abramowitz, "Sex and the Caucus Participant: The Gender Gap and Presidential Nominations," *American Journal of Political Science* 34 (1990): 725–740; Martin Gilens, "Gender and Support for Reagan: A Comprehensive Model of Presidential Approval," *American Journal of Political Science* 32 (1988): 19–49.

44 Kaufmann, "The Gender Gap"; Karen M. Kaufmann and John R. Petrocik, "The Changing Politics of American Men: Understanding the Sources of the Gender Gap," *American Journal of Political Science* 43 (1999): 864–887.

45 Kaufmann and Petrocik, "The Changing Politics of American Men."

46 Center for the American Woman and Politics, *The Gender Gap: Voting Choices in Presidential Elections* (New Brunswick, NJ: Eagleton Institute, Rutgers University, 2005).

47 CNN Election Center 2008, "Presidential National Exit Poll," http://www.cnn.com/ELECTION/2008/results /polls/#val=USP00p1. Accessed February 5, 2009.

48 CNN Election Center 2016. "Presidential National Exit Poll," http://www.cnn.com/election/results/exit-polls

49 Patricia Gurin, "Women's Gender Consciousness," *Public Opinion Quarterly* 49 (1985): 143–163.

50 Gilens, "Gender and Support for Reagan"; Ethel Klein, *Gender Politics* (New York: Cambridge University Press, 1984).

51 Elizabeth Adell Cook and Clyde Wilcox, "Feminism and the Gender Gap: A Second Look," *Journal of Politics* 53 (1989): 1111–1122.

52 Vincent L. Hutchings, *Public Opinion and Democratic Accountability: How Citizens Learn About Politics* (Princeton, NJ: Princeton University Press, 2003), 56–57.

53 Kaufmann and Petrocik, "The Changing Politics of American Men."

54 Kaufmann, "The Gender Gap."

55 Sidney Verba and Norman H. Nie, *Participation in America: Political Democracy and Social Equality* (New York: Harper & Row, 1972), chap. 12.

56 Ibid., chaps. 10, 12.

57 Tasha Philpot, *Race, Republicans, and the Return of the Party of Lincoln* (Ann Arbor: University of Michigan Press, 2007). See also Michael K. Fauntroy, *Republicans and the Black Vote* (Boulder, CO: Lynne Rienner, 2007).

58 Philpot, *Race*, 47–48.

59 Phillip Bump, 2016. "There Are Likely Fewer Black Delegates to the Republican Convention Than at Any Point in at Least a Century." *The Washington Post* (July 19, 2016). https://www.washingtonpost.com/news /the-fix/wp/2016/07/19/there-are-likely-fewer-black -delegates-to-the-republican-convention-than-at-any -point-in-at-least-a-century/?tid=sm_tw_pp, accessed August 13, 2016.

60 Ibid.

61 Hutchinson, Earl Ofari. 2016. "The 2016 GOP Convention: The Whitest of the Whitest Conventions." *The Huffington Post* (July 17, 2016). http://www.huffingtonpost.com /earl-ofari-hutchinson/the-2016-gop-conventionth _b_11028190.html, accessed August 13, 2016.

62 NBC News. 2016. "GOP: At Least 133 Latino Delegates at Republican Convention." http://www.nbcnews.com/ storyline/2016-conventions/gop-least-133-latino -delegates-republican-convention-n614376, accessed August 13, 2016.

63 Frostenson, Sarah. 2016. "Half of the Democratic Delegates Were People of Color. For Republicans, It Was Only 6%." (July 29, 2016). http://www.vox.com/2016 /7/29/12295830/republican-democratic-delegates -diversity-nonwhite, accessed August 13, 2016.

64 Philpot, Ibid.

65 Gallup Poll, April 21, 1937; Gallup Poll, April 1981; Gallup Poll, July 13–14, 1998.

66 "The News Media/Communications," Polling Report. com, Media Studies Center survey conducted by the University of Connecticut, January 11–18, 1999 (*n* = 1,002 adults nationwide).

67 Pew Research Center for the People and the News. "In Changing News Landscape, Even Television Is Vulnerable: Trends in News Consumption, 1991–2012," September 27, 2012, http://www.people-press.org /2012/09/27/in-changing-news-landscape-even -television- is-vulnerable/. Accessed February 7, 2013.

68 Gallup Poll, July 8, 2013. http://www.gallup.com/poll /163412/americans-main-source-news.aspx

69 Rasmussen Reports, "Nearly One-Third of Younger Americans See Colbert, Stewart as Alternatives to Traditional News Outlets," March 25, 2009, http://www .rasmussenreports.com/public_content/lifestyle /entertainment/march_2009/nearly_one_third_of _younger_americans_see_colbert_stewart_as _alternatives_to_traditional_news_outlets. Accessed February 26, 2012.,

70 Center of Political Communication, University of Delaware. "National Survey Shows Public Overwhelmingly Opposes Internet 'Fast Lanes.'" November 10, 2014. https://www.cpc.udel.edu/content-sub-site/Documents /UD-CPC-NatAgenda2014PR_2014NetNeutrality.pdf

71 Public Religion Research Institute and the Brookings Institute. *What Americans Want from Immigration Reform in 2014.* June 10, 2014. http://www.brookings.edu/~/media/research/ files/reports/2014/06/10%20immigration%20reform%20 survey/finalimmigrationsurvey%20%282%29.pdf

72 Pew Research Center: Journalism and Media, "The 2016 Presidential Campaign—A News Event That's Hard to Miss" February 4, 2016. http://www.journalism.org /2016/02/04/the-2016-presidential-campaign-a -news-event-thats-hard-to-miss/ Accessed June 9, 2016.

73 Pew Research Center: Journalism and Media, "Millennials and Political News: Social Media—the Local TV for the Next Generation?" June 1, 2015. http://www .journalism.org/2015/06/01/millennials-political-news/ Accessed June 9, 2016.

74 Alvin Schexnider, "The Politics of Pragmatism: An Analysis of the 1989 Gubernatorial Election in Virginia," *PS: Political Science and Politics* 23 (June 1990): 154–156.

75 Daniel J. Hopkins, "No More Wilder Effect, Never a Whitman Effect: When and Why Polls Mislead about Black and Female Candidates" (unpublished paper, August 4, 2008).

76 Diane Eicher, "The ABCs of Menus: Area Schools Out of Sync with Fed Plan," *Denver Post*, September 26, 1996, E01; Sara Fritz, "As Bush Sinks in Polls, He Tries New Direction," *St. Petersburg Times*, July 2, 2001, 1A.

77 Asher, *Polling and the Public*, chap. 9.

78 Ibid.

79 "Gallup Poll Presidential Approval Ratings: Truman–Bush," facsimile copy sent from the Gallup Organization, May 6, 1999.

80 Michael W. Traugott and Paul J. Lavrakas. *The Voter's Guide to Election Polls*, 2nd ed. (New York: Chatham House, 2000), 79.

81 Don Frederick, "John McCain's Own Polling Gives Him Hope, Aide Says," *Los Angeles Times*, October 27, 2008. http://latimesblogs.latimes.com/washington/2008/10/john-mccains-ow.html. Accessed February 5, 2009.

82 Rosalee A. Clawson and Zoe M. Oxley, *Public Opinion: Democratic Ideals and Democratic Practice* (Washington, DC: Congressional Quarterly Press, 2008), chaps. 10, 11, 12.

Chapter 11

1 White House Correspondence Association, "History of the WHCA," http://www.whca.net/history.htm, accessed July 13, 2016.

2 Cynthia Littleton, "Larry Wilmore's 'Nightly Show' Cancelled at Comedy Central," *Variety*, August 15, 2016, http://variety.com/2016/tv/news/larry-wilmore-nightly-show-canceled-comedy-central-1201837298/, accessed September 9, 2016.

3 Chris Cillizza, "Larry Wilmore's Controversial, Confrontational White House Correspondents' Dinner Speech," *Washington Post*, May 2, 2016, https://www.washingtonpost.com/news/the-fix/wp/2016/05/02/larry-wilmores-controversial-confrontational-white-house-correspondents-dinner-speech/, accessed July 14, 2016.

4 Fresh Air, "Larry Wilmore on 'Breaking Taboos' at the White House Correspondents' Dinner," *National Public Radio*, May 3, 2016, http://www.npr.org/2016/05/03/476598311/larry-wilmore-on-breaking-taboos-at-the-white-house-correspondents-dinner, accessed September 9, 2016.

5 For more on media and framing, see Shanto Iyengar and Donald R. Kinder, *News That Matters: Television and American Opinion* (Chicago: University of Chicago Press, 1987); Dietram A. Scheufele and David Tewksbury, "Framing, Agenda Setting, and Priming: The Evolution of Three Media Effects Models," *Journal of Communication* 57 (2007), 9–20.

6 Andy Greene, "Fox News Attacks Rapper Common Over White House Invite," *Rolling Stone*, May 10, 2011, http://www.rollingstone.com/music/news/fox-news-attacks-rapper-common-over-white-house-invite-20110510, accessed July 16, 2016.

7 Sarah Gray, "Twitter is Exploding After Larry Wilmore's White House Correspondents' Dinner Ending," *Attn:*, May 1, 2016, http://www.attn.com/stories/7930/twitter-response-to-larry-wilmore-using-n-word-at-whcd, accessed July 16, 2016.

8 For more on agenda setting and the media, see Iyengar and Kinder *News that Matters* and Scheufele and Tewksbury 2007.

9 Shelley Streeby, *American Sensations: Class, Empire, and the Production of Popular Culture* (Berkeley: University of California Press, 2002), 38–77.

10 Truman Nelson, ed., "Introduction," In *Documents of Upheaval: Selections from William Lloyd Garrison's* The Liberator, *1831–1835* (New York: Hill and Wang, 1966), ix–xxii.

11 Patrick Washburn, *The African American Newspaper: Voice of Freedom* (Evanston, IL: Northwestern University Press, 2006), 28–36.

12 David Nasaw, *The Chief: The Life of William Randolph Hearst* (Boston: Houghton Mifflin, 2000), 79–80.

13 Stephanie Greco Larson, *Media and Minorities: The Politics of Race in News and Entertainment* (Lanham, MD: Rowman and Littlefield, 2006), 110.

14 Washburn, *The African American Newspaper*, 80–100.

15 Nicolas Kanellos and Helvetia Martell, *Hispanic Periodicals in the United States, Origins to 1960: A Brief History and Comprehensive Bibliography* (Houston, TX: Arte Público Press, 2000), 3–116; Larson, *Media and Minorities*, 125–129.

16 Larson, *Media and Minorities*, 115–116.

17 For more on Roosevelt's fireside chats, see David Michael Ryfe, "Franklin Roosevelt and the Fireside Chats," *Journal of Communication* 49 (1999), 80–103.

18 The Museum of the Moving Image, "1952: Eisenhower vs. Stevenson," In *The Living Room Candidate: Presidential Campaign Commercials 1952–2012*, http://www.livingroomcandidate.org/commercials/1952, accessed July 16, 2016.

19 Larson, *Media and Minorities*, 171–173.

20 Ibid., 145–192.

21 For more on Black Entertainment Television, see http://www.bet.com; and Brett Pulley, *The Billion Dollar BET: Robert Johnson and the Inside Story of Black Entertainment Television* (Hoboken, NJ: Wiley, 2004).

22 For more on Noticiero Univision, see http://www.univision.com/shows/noticiero-univision.

23 Kenneth Olmstead, Mark Jurkowitz, Amy Mitchell, and Joni Edna, "How Americans Get TV News at Home," *Pew Research Journalism Project*, October 11, 2013, http://www.journalism.org/2013/10/11/how-americans-get-tv-news-at-home/, accessed July 16, 2016.

24 For more on CSPAN, see http://www.c-span.org/, accessed July 16, 2016.

25 Fox Business, "Lou Dobbs," http://www.foxbusiness.com/person/d/lou-dobbs.html, accessed July 16, 2016.

26 Heidi Beirich and Mark Potok, "CNN's Lou Dobbs Refuses to Cover Anti-Latino Racism in Anti-Immigration Activist Groups and Citizen Border Patrols," *Southern Poverty Law Center: Intelligence Report*, January 31, 2006 https://www.splcenter.org/fighting-hate/intelligence-report/2006/cnn%E2%80%99s-lou-dobs-refuses-cover-anti-latino-racism-anti-immigration-activist-groups-and-citzen-border-patrols, accessed July 16, 2016.

27 Marisol Bello, "Comics' Restore Rally Not Politics-as-Usual," *USA Today*, November 1, 2010, 3A; see also

Geoffrey Baym, *From Cronkite to Colbert: The Evolution of Broadcast News* (Boulder, CO: Paradigm Publishers, 2009).

28 Mark Dawidziak, "Seriously Funny: Is This Man a Jester or Journalist? Jon Stewart Is Blurring the Lines," *Cleveland Plain Dealer*, April 12, 2009, E1.

29 http://www.youtube.com/user/whitehouse, accessed July 16, 2016.

30 Frank Rich, "2006: The Year of the 'Macaca,'" *New York Times*, November 12, 2006, 4–12.

31 For more on these blogs, see http://www.dailykos.com and http://redstate.com/.

32 http://www.chicagodefender.com.

33 Matthew Mosk, "An Attack That Came Out of the Ether: Scholar Looks at First Link in Email Chain about Obama," *Washington Post*, June 28, 2008, C1; Cristina Silva, "Whoomp! That Is Not Obama in Music Video," *St. Petersburg Times*, June 9, 2010, 1A.

34 See Sahar Khamis and Katherine Vaughn, "Cyber-activism in the Egyptian Revolution: How Civic Engagement and Citizen Journalism Tilted the Balance," *Arab Media & Society* 13 (Summer 2011), http://www.arabmediasociety.com/?article=769, accessed July 17, 2016.

35 Michael Barthel, Elisa Shearer, Jeffery Gottfried, and Amy Mitchell, "News Use on Facebook and Twitter is on the Rise," *Pew Research Center: Journalism & Media*, July 14, 2015, http://www.journalism.org/2015/07/14/news-use-on-facebook-and-twitter-is-on-the-rise/, accessed July 17, 2016.

36 Jeffrey Gottfried, Michael Barthel, Elisa Shearer, and Amy Mitchell, "The 2016 Presidential Campaign: A News Event That's Hard to Miss," *Pew Research Center: Journalism & Media*, February 4, 2016, http://www.journalism.org/2016/02/04/the-2016-presidential-campaign-a-news-event-thats-hard-to-miss/, accessed July 17, 2016.

37 Bijan Stephen, "Get Up, Stand Up: Social Media Helps Black Lives Matter Fight the Power," *Wired*, October 2015, http://www.wired.com/2015/10/how-black-lives-matter-uses-social-media-to-fight-the-power/, accessed July 17, 2016.

38 Kali Holloway, "These are the 10 Most Racist Cities in America According to Twitter," *AlterNet*, March 16, 2016, http://www.alternet.org/media/these-are-10-most-racist-cities-america-according-twitter, accessed July 17, 2016.

39 Jon Greenberg, "Trump's Pants on Fire Tweet that Blacks Killed 81% of White Homicide Victims," *PolitiFact*, November 23, 2015, http://www.politifact.com/truth-o-meter/statements/2015/nov/23/donald-trump/trump-tweet-blacks-white-homicide-victims/, accessed July 17, 2016.

40 Eric Pryne, "Last Edition of the Post-Intelligencer Set for Tuesday," *Seattle Times*, March 16, 2009; Dave Thier, "For New Orleans, a Daily That Is No Longer Daily," *New York Times*, September 30, 2012, http://www.nytimes.com/2012/10/01/us/times-picayune-publishes-last-daily-issue.html?_r=0, accessed July 17, 2016.

41 See http://www.gannett.com/ and http://www.mcclatchy.com/

42 See http://www.iheartmedia.com/Pages/Home.aspx

43 See http://corporate.comcast.com/our-company/businesses/nbcuniversal and http://www.disneyabcpress.com/disneyabctv/

44 Ashley Lutz, "These 6 Corporations Control 90% of the Media in America," *Business Insider*, June 14, 2012, http://www.businessinsider.com/these-6-corporations-control-90-of-the-media-in-america-2012-6, accessed July 17, 2016.

45 Richard Davis, *The Press and American Politics: The New Mediator* (Upper Saddle River, NJ: Prentice Hall, 2001), 115.

46 See Larry J. Sabato, *Feeding Frenzy: Attack Journalism & American Politics* (Lanham, MD: Lanham Publishing, 2000).

47 American Society of Newspaper Editors, "Table-L: Numbers and Percentages of Women by Job Category," *2015 Census*, July 28, 2015, http://asne.org/content.asp?contentid=144, accessed July 17, 2016.

48 For more on priming, see Iyengar and Kinder, 1987 and Scheufele and Tewksbury, 2007.

49 Larson, *Media and Minorities*, 202–228, 237–267.

50 Steve Kornacki, "Media Fascination with Obama Is No Liberal Conspiracy," *New York Observer*, July 23, 2008.

51 Kathryn Q. Seelye, "Wright Dominated News Coverage," *New York Times*, May 6, 2008, http://thecaucus.blogs.nytimes.com/2008/05/06/wright-dominated-news-coverage/, accessed May 1, 2014.

52 See for example, Dr. Milton Wolf, "Liberal Media Cues Up Cain and Friends: All in for Obama While GOP Gets Snookered," *Washington Times*, November 10, 2011, B1.

53 Katy Waldman, "The Problem with Palin's 'Shuck and Jive,'" *Slate.com*, October 25, 2012, http://www.slate.com/blogs/browbeat/2012/10/25/shuck_and_jive_meaning_and_history_of_phrase_palin_used_is_it_racist.html, accessed July 19, 2016.

54 Ben Jacobs, "Rupert Murdoch Implies that Obama is not 'Real Black President' in Tweet Praising Carson," *The Guardian*, October 7, 2015, https://www.theguardian.com/media/2015/oct/08/rupert-murdoch-obama-not-real-black-president-tweet-ben-carson, accessed July 19, 2016.

55 For more on press secretaries, see W. Dale Nelson, *Who Speaks for the President: The White House Press Secretary from Cleveland Through Clinton* (Syracuse, NY: Syracuse University Press, 1998).

56 American Urban Radio Networks, "White House Report With April Ryan," http://www.aurn.com/WHR/, accessed July 19, 2016.

57 NBC News, "About Us: Kristen Welker NBC News White House Correspondent," http://www.nbcnews.com/id/39619632/ns/nbc_nightly_news_with_brian_williams-about_us/t/kristen-welker/#.V47GHOgrKhc, accessed July 19, 2016.

58 *Media Life Magazine*, March 15, 2012, http://www.medialifemagazine.com/myles-miller-becomes

-washington-correspondent-at-the-daily/, accessed July 19, 2016.

59 Larson, *Media and Minorities,* 207.

60 *Near v. Minnesota,* 283 U.S. 697 (1931).

61 *New York Times v. United States,* 403 U.S. 713 (1971).

62 *Cox Broadcasting Company v. Cohn,* 420 U.S. 469 (1975).

63 *Smith v. Daily Mail Publishing Co.,* 443 U.S. 97 (1979); *Globe Newspaper Co. v. Superior Court for the County of Norfolk,* 457 U.S. 596 (1982).

64 *Nebraska Press Association v. Stuart,* 427 U.S. 539 (1976).

65 *Branzburg v. Hayes,* 408 U.S. 665 (1971).

66 *Federal Communications Commission v. Pacifica Foundation,* 438 U.S. 726 (1978).

67 *Denver Area Educational Telecommunications Consortium v. Federal Communications Commission,* 518 U.S. 727 (1996).

Chapter 12

1 Taylor Branch, *Parting the Waters: America in the King Years, 1954–63* (New York: Touchstone, 1988), 19–24; Donald P. Baker, "Shame of a Nation: The Lessons and Legacy of the Prince Edward School Closings," *Washington Post,* March 4, 2001, W08.

2 John Hope Franklin, *From Slavery to Freedom: A History of Negro Americans,* 3rd ed. (New York: Vintage, 1969), 332–343.

3 Sidney Tarrow, *Power in Movement: Social Movements, Collective Action, and Politics* (Cambridge, UK: Cambridge University Press, 1994), 1.

4 Madeleine Adamson and Seth Borgos, *This Mighty Dream: Social Protest Movements in the United States* (Boston: Routledge and Kegan Paul, 1984), 32.

5 Ibid.

6 John D. McCarthy and Mayer N. Zald, "Resource Mobilization and Social Movements: A Partial Theory," *American Journal of Sociology* 82 (May 1977): 1214.

7 Barry D. Adam, *The Rise of a Gay and Lesbian Movement,* rev. ed. (New York: Twayne, 1995), 80.

8 Ibid.

9 Ibid., 85.

10 Ibid., 89.

11 McCarthy and Zald, "Resource Mobilization and Social Movements," 1216.

12 J. Craig Jenkins, "The Transformation of a Constituency into a Movement," in *Social Movements of the Sixties and Seventies,* Jo Freeman, ed. (New York: Longman, 1983), 63.

13 Ibid., 64.

14 Michael Janofsky, "Federal Parks Chief Calls 'Million Man' Count Low," *New York Times,* October 21, 1995, http://www.nytimes.com/1995/10/21/us/federalparks -chief-calls-million-man-count-low.html. Accessed October 23, 2012.

15 Theodore J. Lowi, *The Politics of Disorder* (New York: Basic Books, 1971), 54.

16 Hazel Erskine, "The Polls: Pollution and Its Costs," *Public Opinion Quarterly* 36 (Spring 1972): 120.

17 Gallup Poll, "Environment—Summary Data," http:// www.gallup.com/poll/1615/environment.aspx#1. Accessed October 23, 2012.

18 Charles C. Euchner, *Extraordinary Politics: How Protest and Dissent Are Changing American Democracy* (Boulder, CO: Westview Press, 1996), 212.

19 Ibid., 218.

20 Susan E. Howell and William P. McLean, "Performance and Race in Evaluating Minority Mayors," *Public Opinion Quarterly* 65 (2001): 231–243; Melissa J. Marschall and Anirudh V. S. Ruhil, "Substantive Symbols: The Attitudinal Dimension of Black Political Incorporation in Local Government," *American Journal of Political Science* 51 (2007): 17–33.

21 Betty A. Dobratz and Stephanie L. Shanks-Meile, *White Power, White Pride! The White Separatist Movement in the United States* (New York: Twayne, 1997).

22 Ibid., 150–151.

23 Southern Poverty Law Center, "Active Hate Groups in the U.S. in 2015," https://www.splcenter.org/hate-map. Accessed July 5, 2016.

24 Dobratz and Shanks-Meile, *White Power,* 150–151; Southern Poverty Law Center, "Active Patriot Groups."

25 Southern Poverty Law Center, "Hate Maps," http://www .splcenter.org/get-informed/hate-map, accessed September 11, 2012.

26 Josephine Wolff, "The Secret Agents Who Stake Out the Ugliest Corners of the Internet." *The Atlantic,* July 22, 2015. http://www.theatlantic.com/technology/archive /2015/07/secret-service-online-threat-president/399179/ Accessed July 5, 2016.

27 C. Wendell King, *Social Movements in the United States* (New York: Random House, 1956), 27.

28 *Plessy v. Ferguson,* 163 U.S. 537 (1896).

29 Kwame A. Appiah and Henry Louis Gates, Jr., eds., *Africana: The Encyclopedia of the African and African American Experience* (New York: Basic Civitas Books, 1999), 442.

30 Melissa V. Harris-Lacewell, *Barbershops, Bibles, and BET: Everyday Thought and Black Political Talk* (Princeton, NJ: Princeton University Press, 2004).

31 *Missouri ex rel. Gaines v. Canada,* 305 U.S. 337 (1938).

32 Appiah and Gates, *Africana,* 445.

33 Ralph J. Bunche, *World View of Race* (Washington, DC: The Associates in Negro Folk Education, 1936).

34 Paula D. McClain and Joseph Stewart, Jr., *"Can We All Get along?": Racial and Ethnic Minorities in American Politics,* 5th ed. (Boulder, CO: Westview Press, 2010).

35 Branch, *Parting the Waters,* 193.

36 McClain and Stewart, *"Can We All Get along?"*

37 Appiah and Gates, *Africana,* 447.

38 Ibid., 449; Branch, *Parting the Waters,* 271.

39 Appiah and Gates, *Africana,* 449.

40 Martin Luther King Jr., "Letter from Birmingham Jail," http://www.mlkonline.net/jail.html, accessed July 21, 2009.

41 Paula D. McClain, "Foreword," in *Legacies of the 1964 Civil Rights Act*, ed. Bernard Grofman (Charlottesville: University Press of Virginia, 2000), xii.

42 Appiah and Gates, *Africana*, 451.

43 Ibid.

44 Branch, *Parting the Waters*, 821.

45 Appiah and Gates, *Africana*, 452.

46 Ibid., 445; Marco Giugni, "How Social Movements Matter: Past Research, Present Problems, Future Development," in *How Social Movements Matter*, ed. Marco Giugni, Doug McAdams, and Charles Tilly (Minneapolis: University of Minnesota Press, 1999), xiii.

47 Martin Luther King, Jr., "I Have a Dream" Address at March on Washington, August 28, 1963, http://www.mlkonline.net/dream.html, accessed August 8, 2008.

48 Appiah and Gates, *Africana*, 455.

49 Sara M. Evans, *Born for Liberty: A History of Women in America* (New York: Basic Books, 1971), 54.

50 Ellen Carol DuBois, *Feminism and Suffrage: The Emergence of an Independent Women's Movement in America, 1848–1869* (Ithaca, NY: Cornell University Press, 1978), 22.

51 Frederick Douglass, "The Rights of Women," *North Star*, July 28, 1848, http://www.iath.virginia.edu/utc/abolitn/abwm03dt.html. Accessed August 18, 2008.

52 Legacy 98, "Living the Legacy: The Women's Rights Movement, 1848–1998," http://www.legacy98.org/move-hist.html, accessed August 18, 2008.

53 Ibid.

54 Beverly Guy-Sheftall. *Words of Fire: An Anthology of African American Feminist Thought.* (New York, NY: The New Press, 1995), 1.

55 Nell Irvin Painter. *Sojourner Truth: A Life, A Symbol.* (New York, NY: W. W. Norton & Company, 1996); Guy-Sheftall, 35.

56 Painter, 98.

57 Ibid.

58 Aida Hurtado. "Relating to Privilege: Seduction and Rejection in the Subordination of White Women and Women of Color." *Signs*, 14(4), *Common Grounds and Crossroads: Race, Ethnicity, and Class in Women's Lives* (Summer, 1989): 833–855.

59 Guy-Sheftall, 35.

60 Dubois, 70.

61 Ibid.

62 Ibid., 69.

63 Guy-Sheftall, 35.

64 Evans, *Born for Liberty*, 123–124.

65 Elizabeth Cady Stanton, "Letter to the National Anti-Slavery Standard," December 26, 1865, in *Selected Papers of Elizabeth Cady Stanton and Susan B. Anthony*, ed. Ann D. Gordon (New Brunswick, NJ: Rutgers University Press, 1997), 54–55.

66 Ula Taylor, "The Historical Evolution of Black Feminist Theory and Praxis," *Journal of Black Studies* 29 (1998): 234–253.

67 Evans, *Born for Liberty*, 153.

68 Taylor, "The Historical Evolution of Black Feminist Theory."

69 Legacy 98, "Living the Legacy."

70 Ibid.

71 Evans, *Born for Liberty*, 267.

72 Legacy 98, "Living the Legacy."

73 Evans, *Born for Liberty*, 291.

74 Ibid.

75 Ibid.

76 Legacy 98, "Living the Legacy."

77 Kate Alexander, "Capitol Rally Aims to Reignite Women's Rights Movement," *Houston Chronicle*, April 29, 2012, http://www.chron.com/news/article/Capitol-rally-aims-to-reignite-women-s-rights-3519255.php. Accessed January 15, 2013.

78 Adamson and Borgos, *This Mighty Dream*, 39.

79 Marc Karson, *American Labor Unions and Politics: 1900–1918* (Boston: Beacon Press, 1958).

80 Adamson and Borgos, *This Mighty Dream*, 39.

81 Thomas R. Brooks, *Toil and Trouble: A History of American Labor*, 2nd ed. (New York: Delacorte Press, 1971), 58–59.

82 Melvyn Dubofsky and Foster Rhea Dulles, *Labor in America: A History*, 7th ed. (Arlington Heights, IL: Harland Davidson, 2004).

83 Larry Tye, *Rising from the Rails: Pullman Porters and the Making of the Black Middle Class* (New York: Macmillan, 2005); Beth Tompkins Bates, *Pullman Porters and the Rise of Protest Politics in Black America, 1925–1945* (Chapel Hill: University of North Carolina Press, 2001).

84 Paula J. Giddings, *Ida: A Sword among Among Lions* (New York: Amistad, 2008), 634–641.

85 Harry Bruinius, "Pullman Porters Tell Tales of a Train Ride through History," *Christian Science Monitor*, February 29, 2008, http://www.csmonitor.com/2008/0229/p20s01-ussc.html, accessed July 21, 2009.

86 Ibid.

87 R. W. Hurd, "Contesting the Dinosaur Image: The Labor Movement's Search for a Future," *Labor Studies Journal* 22 (Winter 1998): 5–30.

88 Michael Schiavone, *Unions in Crisis? The Future of Organized Labor in America* (Westport, CT: Praeger, 2008).

89 Steven E. Abraham, "The Impact of the Taft-Hartley Act on the Balance of Power in Industrial Relations,"- *American Business Law Journal* 33 (1996): 341–372.

90 Melvyn Dubofsky, *The State and Labor in Modern America* (Chapel Hill: University of North Carolina Press, 1994), 223.

91 Hurd, "Contesting the Dinosaur Image."

92 Benjamin Kline, *First Along the River: A Brief History of the U.S. Environmental Movement* (San Francisco: Acada Books, 1997); Philip Shabecoff, *A Fierce Green Fire: The American Environmental Movement* (New York: Hill and Wang, 1993).

93 Gregory Dicum, "Justice in Time: Meet Robert Bullard, the Father of Environmental Justice," *Grist: Environmental News and Commentary*, March 14, 2006, http://www.grist.org/news/maindish/2006/03/14/dicum. Accessed July 6, 2009.

94 Robert D. Bullard, *Dumping in Dixie: Race, Class, and Environmental Quality* (Boulder, CO: Westview Press, 2000).

95 Material for this paragraph and the following are taken from Jennifer Rosenberg, "Vietnam War," http://history1900s.about.com/od/vietnamwar/a/vietnamwar.htm; Accessed January 15, 2013. Edmund J. Malesky, "Vietnam War," *International Encyclopedia of the Social Sciences*, 2nd ed., ed. William A. Darity, Jr. (New York: Thompson, 2008), 612–617.

96 Ibid.

97 Malesky, 614.

98 Marvin E. Gettleman, Jane Franklin, and Marilyn Young, *Vietnam and America: A Documented History* (New York: Grove Atlantic, 1995), 296.

99 Ibid., 297.

100 Paul M. Holsinger, *War and American Popular Culture: A Historical Encyclopedia* (Westport, CT: Greenwood, 1998).

101 "The Greatest Is Gone," *Time*, February 27, 1978, http://www.time.com/time/magazine/article/0,9171,919377,00.html, accessed July 6, 2009.

102 David Farber, *Chicago '68* (Chicago: University of Chicago Press, 1994).

103 Ibid., 196.

104 Ibid., 202.

105 Ibid., 204.

106 Gettleman et al., *Vietnam and America*, 299.

107 Jonathan Sutherland, *African Americans at War: An Encyclopedia* (Santa Barbara, CA: ABC-CLIO, 2004), 502.

108 Material for this paragraph and some of the material in the second paragraph are drawn from these sources: *lgbt: Encyclopedia of Lesbian, Gay, Bisexual, and Transgender History in America*, ed. Marc Stein (New York: Charles Scribner's Sons/Thomson Gale, 2003); Raymond Smith, *Gay and Lesbian Americans and Political Participation: A Reference Handbook* [electronic resource] (Santa Barbara, CA: ABC-CLIO, 2002).

109 Ibid.

110 Michael Levy, "Gay Rights Movement," *The History Channel website* (2011), accessed February 1, 2013.

111 Jim Farber, "Before the Stonewall Uprising, there was the "Sip-In," *New York Times*, April 20, 2016. http://www.nytimes.com/2016/04/21/nyregion/before-the-stonewall-riots-there-was-the-sip-in.html?login=email&_r=0 Accessed April 21, 2016.

112 Levy, Ibid.

113 Michael Janofsky, "Man Is Convicted in Killing of Gay Student," *New York Times*, November 4, 1999, http://www.nytimes.com/1999/11/04/us/man-is-convicted-in-killing-of-gay-student.html?ref=aaronjamesmckinney Accessed February 1, 2013.

114 The Leadership Conference, "LLEHCPA 2009-Endorsing Organizations," http://www.civilrights.org/hatecrimes/llehcpa/organizations.html Accessed February 1, 2013.

115 All of the dates for events in this section come from PBS, "Stonewall Uprising: Timeline: Milestones in the American Gay Rights Movement" (2013), http://www.pbs.org/wgbh/americanexperience/features/timeline/stonewall/ Accessed February 1, 2013.

116 Andrew R. Flores, "National Trends in Public Opinion on LGBT Rights in the United States." The Williams Institute, November 2014. http://williamsinstitute.law.ucla.edu/wp-content/uploads/POP-natl-trends-nov-2014.pdf Accessed July 4, 2016.

117 Justine McCarthy, "Record-High 60% of Americans Support Same-Sex Marriage." Gallup Poll, May 19, 2015. http://www.gallup.com/poll/183272/record-high-americans-support-sex-marriage.aspx Accessed July 4, 2016.

118 John Schwartz, "Highlights from the Supreme Court Decision on Same-Sex Marriage." *New York Times*, June 26, 2015. http://www.nytimes.com/interactive/2015/us/2014-term-supreme-court-decision-same-sex-marriage.html Accessed July 4, 2016.

119 NPR, "Court Overturns DOMA, Sidesteps Broad Gay Marriage Ruling," June 26, 2013. http://www.npr.org/sections/thetwo-way/2013/06/26/195857796/supreme-court-strikes-down-defense-of-marriage-act

120 Neal Braverman, "At Least 11 Alabama Counties Refuse to Comply With Marriage Equality," *The Advocate*, January 20, 2016. http://www.advocate.com/marriage-equality/2016/1/20/least-11-alabama-counties-refuse-comply-marriage-equality Accessed July 4, 2016.

121 Dave Phillips, "North Carolina Bans Local Anti-Discrimination Policies," *New York Times*, March 24, 2016. http://www.nytimes.com/2016/03/24/us/north-carolina-to-limit-bathroom-use-by-birth-gender.html Accessed July 4, 2016.

122 Beau Minnick, "HB2 changes don't guarantee NBA All-Star game will stay in Charlotte," WNCN.com July 4, 2016. http://wncn.com/2016/07/04/hb2-changes-dont-guarantee-nba-all-star-game-will-stay-in-charlotte/ Accessed July 4, 2016.

123 Joe Sterling, Eliott C. McLaughlin and Joshua Berlinger, "North Carolina, U.S., square off over transgender rights." CNN.com, May 9, 2016. http://www.cnn.com/2016/05/09/politics/north-carolina-hb2-justice-department-deadline/ Accessed July 4, 2016.

124 Adrian Wojnarowski, "NBA pulls 2017 All-Star Game from Charlotte, focuses on New Orleans." http://sports.yahoo.com/news/nba-pulls-2017-all-star-game-from-charlotte-focuses-on-new-orleans-190148437.html

125 Sterling, McLaughlin and Berlinger.

126 Elon University, "Elon Poll: Cooper Pulls Ahead in N.C. Gubernatorial Race." April 10–16, 2016. http://www.elon.edu/e-web/elonpoll/041916.xhtml Accessed July 4, 2016.

127 Mark Berman, "Mississippi governor signs law allowing businesses to refuse service to gay people," *Washington Post* April 5, 2016. https://www .washingtonpost.com/news/post-nation/wp/2016/04 /05/mississippi-governor-signs-law-allowing-business -to-refuse-service-to-gay-people/?utm_term= .a2fac002eca1 Accessed July 4, 2016.

128 Emma Green, "Why Mississippi's Law on Religious Rights and LGBT Discrimination Got Blocked," *The Atlantic*, July 1, 2016. http://www.theatlantic.com /politics/archive/2016/07/why-mississippis-law-on -religious-rights-and-lgbt-got-blocked/489731/ Accessed July 4, 2016.

129 Carlos Muñoz, Jr., *Youth, Identity, Power: The Chicano Movement*, rev. and expanded ed. (London: Verso Press, 2007).

130 This section is indebted to David E. Wilkins, *American Indian Politics and the American Political System*, 2nd ed. (Lanham, MD: Rowman and Littlefield, 2006).

131 William Wei, *The Asian American Movement* (Philadelphia: Temple University Press, 1993).

132 Lawrence S. Wittner, *The Struggle Against the Bomb: A History of the World Nuclear Disarmament Movement* (Stanford, CA: Stanford University Press, 1993); Lawrence S. Wittner, *Toward Nuclear Abolition: A History of the World Nuclear Disarmament Movement, 1971–Present.* (Stanford, CA: Stanford University Press (2003).

133 "Fundamentalism," in *Dictionary of the Social Sciences*, ed. Craig Calhoun (New York: Oxford University Press, 2002); "Fundamentalism," in *The Oxford Dictionary of the Christian Church*, eds. F. L. Cross and E. A. Livingstone, Oxford University Press Inc., Oxford Reference Online, http://www. oxfordreference.com /views//ENTRY.html?subview=Main&entry=t257 .e2750, accessed November 6, 2009; Robert Withnow, ed., *Encyclopedia of Politics and Religion* (Washington, DC: CQ Press, 2007).

134 Doug McAdam, "The Decline of the Civil Rights Movement," in *Waves of Protest: Social Movements Since the Sixties*, eds. Jo Freeman and Victoria Johnson (Lanham, MD: Rowman and Littlefield, 1999), 325–348.

135 Ronald T. Libby, *Eco-Wars: Political Campaigns and Social Movements*. New York: Columbia University Press, 1998, chap. 5.

136 Euchner, *Extraordinary Politics*, 48.

137 Adamson and Borgos, *This Mighty Dream*, 46.

138 Ibid., 47–48.

139 A. Garza. "A Herstory of the #BlackLivesMatter Movement," *thefeministwire.org* (http://www.thefeministwire. com/2014/10/blacklivesmatter-2/).

140 M. D. Smith. "How Trayvon Martin's Death Launched a New Generation of Black Activism," *The Nation*. 2014 Available at http://www.thenation.com/article/how -trayvon-martins-death-launched-new-generation -black-activism.

141 Ibid.

142 V. Zarya, "Founders of #BlackLivesMatter: Getting credit for your work matters." *Fortune Magazine*. July 19, 2015. Available online at http://fortune.com/2015/07 /19/blacklivesmatter-work-credit/

143 Ibid.

144 Smith, 2014.

145 Ruffin, H. G. 2016. "Black Lives Matter: The Growth of a New Social Justice Movement." Available at http://www.blackpast.org/perspectives/black-lives -matter-growth-new-social-justice-movement

146 Zarya, ibid.

147 Johnson, Kevin. "Black Lives Matter Finds Canadian Voice" *USA Today*. May 11, 2016. http://www.usatoday .com/story/news/world/2016/05/11/black-lives-matter -canada/83827764/

148 Tamari, S., "From Ferguson to Palestine, We See Us." *Huffington Post*. 2015. Available at http://www .huffingtonpost.com/sandra-tamari/from-ferguson -to-palestine_b_8307832.html

149 Henderson, N. "How Black Lives Matter activists are influencing 2016 race." http://www.cnn.com/2015/08 /18/politics/black-lives-matter-2016-presidential-race/

150 "Times Topics: Tea Party Movement," *New York Times*, August 12, 2012, http://topics.nytimes.com/top /reference/timestopics/subjects/t/tea_party_movement /index.html. Accessed February 11, 2013.

151 Jared A. Goldstein. 2011. "The Tea Party Movement and the Perils of Popular Originalism," *Arizona Law Review* 53 (2011): 831.

152 Ibid.

153 CNN Political Unit. 2010. "Time Line: Rise of the Tea Party," http://politicalticker.blogs.cnn.com/2010 /11/02/timeline-rise-of-the-tea-party/, accessed February 11, 2013.

154 Ibid.

155 Amanda Fallin, Rachel Grana, and Stanton A. Glantz, "'To Quarterback Behind the Scenes, Third Party Efforts': The Tobacco Industry and the Tea Party," *Tobacco Control* (2013), doi:10.1136/ tobaccocontrol-2012-050815.

156 "Times Topics, Tea Party Movement," *New York Times*, August 12, 2012.

157 Kate Zernike and Megan Thee-Brenan, "Poll Finds Tea Party Backers Wealthier and More Educated." *New York Times*, April 14, 2010. http://www.nytimes. com/2010/04/15/us/politics/15poll.html

Chapter 13

1 Reuters. 2016. "Donald Trump's Proposed Muslim Ban is Likely Illegal But . . ." *Newsweek* (June 16, 2016). Retrieved from http://www.newsweek.com/donald -trump-muslims-ban-terrorism-radical-islam-guns -orlando-shooting-legal-470470

2 Sethi, Arjun Singh. 2016. "The FBI Needs to Stop Spying on Muslim Americans." *Politico* (March 29, 2016). Re-

trieved from http://www.politico.com/magazine/story/2016/03/muslim-american-surveillance-fbi-spying-213773

3 Council on American-Islamic Relations (CAIR). 2016. "CAIR: Who We Are." Retrieved from http://www.cair.com/about-us/cair-who-we-are.html

4 Blake, Andrew. 2016. "Muslim Group CAIR Sues Over Secret Government Watch Lists." *The Washington Times* (April 6, 2016). Retrieved from http://www.washingtontimes.com/news/2016/apr/6/muslim-group-sues-over-secret-government-watch-lis/

5 Ibid.

6 Ibid.

7 Dennis S. Ippolito and Thomas G. Walker, *Political Parties, Interest Groups, and Public Policy: Group Influence in American Politics* (Englewood Cliffs, NJ: Prentice Hall, 1980), 1.

8 National Association for the Advancement of Colored People, "100: NAACP Centennial Celebration," http://www.naacp.org/about/history/, accessed July 9, 2009.

9 National Urban League, "History of the National Urban League," http://www.nul.org/history.html, accessed July 9, 2009.

10 James Madison, "Federalist No. 10," in *The Federalist Papers*, ed. Clinton Rossiter (New York: Mentor Books, 1961), 78.

11 Ibid., 79.

12 Quoted in H. R. Mahood, *Interest Groups in American National Politics: An Overview* (Upper Saddle River, NJ: Prentice Hall, 2000); see also Arthur F. Bentley, *The Process of Government: A Study of Social Pressures*, 2nd ed. (New Brunswick, NJ: Transaction Press, 1995).

13 Mahood, *Interest Groups*, 12–13; Bentley, *The Process of Government*.

14 David B. Truman, *The Governmental Process: Political Interests and Public Opinion* (New York: Knopf, 1951).

15 Mahood, *Interest Groups*, 15.

16 Robert A. Dahl, *Who Governs?: Democracy and Power in an American City* (New Haven, CT: Yale University Press, 1961).

17 E. E. Schattschneider, *The Semisovereign People: A Realist's View of Democracy in America* (New York: Harcourt Brace, 1975); Mahood, *Interest Groups*, 17.

18 Schattschneider, *The Semisovereign People*, 34.

19 Theodore J. Lowi, *The End of Liberalism* (New York: Norton, 1979).

20 Ibid.

21 Ibid.

22 Kay Lehman Schlozman and John Tierney, *Organized Interests and American Democracy* (New York: Harper and Row, 1986), 123–125.

23 Ibid.

24 Ibid.

25 James Q. Wilson, *Political Organizations* (New York: Basic Books, 1973), chap. 3.

26 American Association for Retired People, http://www.aarp.org/about-aarp/ accessed July 15, 2016.

27 Alexis de Tocqueville, *Democracy in America, Volumes 1 and 2*. Translated by Henry Reeve. The Penn State Electronic Classics Series Publication, 2002, 584, http://seas3.elte.hu/coursematerial/LojkoMiklos/Alexis-de-Tocqueville-Democracy-in-America.pdf

28 Mahood, *Interest Groups*, 28.

29 Norman J. Ornstein and Shirley Elder, *Interest Groups, Lobbying, and Policymaking* (Washington, DC: Congressional Quarterly Press, 1978), 44.

30 Mahood, *Interest Groups*, 29.

31 William B. Browne, *Groups, Interests, and U.S. Public Policy* (Washington, DC: Georgetown University Press, 1998), 33.

32 U.S. Chamber of Commerce, "About Us," http://www.uschamber.com/default, accessed May 12, 2009.

33 Business Roundtable, "About Us," http://www.businessroundtable.org/, accessed May 12, 2009.

34 Browne, *Groups, Interests, and U.S. Public Policy*, 32.

35 Beth Sussman, "Associations Band Together on Derivatives Fight," *National Journal Online*, September 25, 2009, http://undertheinfluence.nationaljournal.com/2009/09/associations-band-together-on.php, accessed October 1, 2009.

36 http://www.bls.gov/opub/ted/2013/ted_20130124.htm, accessed February 14, 2013. Union Affiliation data from Current Population Survey available at: http://www.bls.gov/cps/cpslutabs.htm accessed July 1, 2016.

37 https://www.opensecrets.org/orgs/list.php accessed July 15, 2016.

38 http://www.modernhealthcare.com/article/20130509/NEWS/305099950.

39 American Bar Association, "About Us," http://www.americanbar.org/utility/about_the_aba.html accessed July 15, 2016.

40 Ibid.

41 NAACP. 2016. "NAACP Announces 2016 Convention Theme 'Our Lives Matter, Or Votes Count.'" http://www.naacp.org/press/entry/naacp-announces-2016-convention-theme-our-lives-matter-our-votes-count Accessed on July 25, 2016; Brock, Roslyn M. 2014. "From the Chairman." All in for Justice and Equality: NAACP Annual Report. http://action.naacp.org/page/-/annual%20reports/NAACP2014AnnualReportWEB.pdf accessed on July 25, 2016; NAACP. 2016. "Our Mission." http://www.naacp.org/pages/our-mission. Accessed on July 25, 2016; NAACP Facebook; NAACPConnect Google Plus; NAACP Twitter. Accessed on July 25, 2016.

42 National Council of La Raza (NCLR). 2016. "About Us." http://www.nclr.org/about-us/ Accessed on July 25, 2016.

43 National Organization for Women (NOW). 2016. "How Many Members Does NOW Currently Have?" http://now.org/faq/how-many-members-does-now-currently-have/ accessed on July 25, 2016; National Organization for Women (NOW). 2016. "Who We Are." http://now.org/about/who-we-are/ accessed on July 25, 2016;

44 National League of Cities (NLC). 2016. "About NLC." http://www.nlc.org/about-nlc Accessed on July 25, 2016

45 http://www.afscme.org, accessed July 9, 2009.

46 Mahood, *Interest Groups*, 40.

47 Libertarians believe that individual liberty is paramount.

48 Cato Institute. 2016. http://www.cato.org accessed July 30, 2016.

49 http://www.pfaw.org/about-us/our-mission-and-vision, accessed July 15, 2016.

50 Public Citizen. 2016. "About Us." http://www.citizen.org/Page.aspx?pid=2306 accessed July 26, 2016.

51 Ibid.

52 Public Citizen. 2016. "Public Citizen Applauds Expected Release of Final Silica Rule After Decades of Delay." http://www.citizen.org/pressroom/pressroomredirect.cfm?ID=5842 accessed July 26, 2016; Public Citizen. 2016. "Accomplishments." http://www.citizen.org/Page.aspx?pid=2307 Accessed July 26, 2016.

53 Mahood, *Interest Groups*, 44.

54 MADD. 2016. "Frequently Asked Questions." http://www.madd.org/about-us/faqs/ Accessed July 26, 2016.

55 MADD. 2016. "Mission Statement." http://www.madd.org/about-us/mission/ Accessed July 30, 2016.

56 MADD. 2016. "MADD's Campaign." http://www.madd.org/drunk-driving/campaign/ Accessed July 30, 2016.

57 Christian Coalition of America. 2016. http://www.cc.org/about_us Accessed July 30, 2016.

58 The National Council of Churches of Christ. 2016. "About the National Council of Churches." http://nationalcouncilofchurches.us/about-us/ accessed July 30, 2016.

59 Lester Milbrath, *The Washington Lobbyists* (Chicago: Rand McNally, 1963), 8.

60 National Public Radio, "A Lobbyist by Any Other Name?" January 22, 2006.

61 Ronald J. Hrebenar and Ruth K. Scott, *Interest Group Politics in America* (Englewood Cliffs, NJ: Prentice Hall, 1982), 61–72.

62 Federal Election Commission, "Number of Federal PACS Increases," news release, March 9, 2009.

63 Federal Election Commission (FEC). 2016. "Contribution Limits for 2015–2016 Federal Elections." http://www.fec.gov/info/contriblimitschart1516.pdf

64 Federal Election Commission (FEC). 2016. "PAC Count—1974 to Present." http://www.fec.gov/press/resources/paccount.shtml#search=pac%20count, accessed July 30, 2016.

65 L. Sandy Maisel, "BCRA's Unintended Consequences: The 527s Controversy," *Central Maine Morning Sentinel*, September 17, 2004, A7.

66 Ibid.

67 Warren Richey, "Supreme Court: Campaign Finance Overhaul in 'Hillary' Case?" *Christian Science Monitor Online*, September 8, 2009, www.csmonitor.com, accessed September 10, 2009.

68 Jeffrey M. Berry, *The Interest Group Society*, 3rd ed. (New York: Longman, 1997), 122.

69 Ibid., 123.

70 Ibid., 365.

71 Schlozman and Tierney, *Organized Interests*, 358.

72 *District of Columbia et al. v. Heller*, 554 U.S., 128 S.Ct. 2783, 171 L.Ed. 2d 637 (2008); Ariane de Vogue, "Supreme Court Shoots Down D.C. Gun Ban," ABC News, June 26, 2008, http://abcnews.go.com/TheLaw/SCOTUS/story?id=5037600, accessed July 9, 2009.

73 Dolan, Maura. 2008. "Gun Advocates Armed for Legal Fight." *Los Angeles Times* (June 27, 2008). http://articles.latimes.com/2008/jun/27/nation/na-legal27 Accessed July 30, 2016.

74 Associated Press. 2008. "NRA Sues to Overturn S.F. Gun Ban." http://www.nbcnews.com/id/25419519/ns/us_news-life/t/nra-sues-overturn-sf-gun-ban/#.V50tPmWgDiU Accessed July 30, 2016.

75 Ferraro, Thomas. 2013. "U.S. Senate Extends Gun Ban; Rejects Bid Address 3-D Plastic Firearms." *Reuters*. (December 20, 2013). http://www.reuters.com/article/us-usa-congress-guns-idUSBRE9B900Q20131210 Accessed July 30, 2016.

76 Bradner, Eric, and Gregory Krieg. 2016. "Emotional Obama Calls for 'Sense of Urgency' to Fight Gun Violence." http://www.cnn.com/2016/01/05/politics/obama-executive-action-gun-control/ Accessed July 30, 2016.

77 Newsweek. 2016. "Quora Question: Why the NRA Opposes Gun Control Legislation." (June 25, 2016). http://www.newsweek.com/quora-question-why-nra-opposes-gun-legislation-472955 Accessed July 30, 2016.

78 Stohr, Greg. 2016. "NRA Rejected U.S. Supreme Court on San Francisco Gun Law." *Bloomberg.* http://www.bloomberg.com/news/articles/2015-06-08/nra-rejected-by-u-s-supreme-court-on-san-francisco-gun-law Accessed July 30, 2016.

79 Marcia Coyle, "Amicus Briefs Are Ammo for Supreme Court Gun Case," *National Law Journal* (March 10, 2008), http://www.law.com/jsp/article.jsp?id=1205146037339, accessed July 9, 2009.

80 "Bork's Nomination Pleases Some, Infuriates Others," *The Record* (New Jersey), October 4, 1987, O3.

81 Schlozman and Tierney, *Organized Interests*, 363.

82 Hrebenar and Scott, *Interest Group Politics*, 93.

83 Ibid., 94.

84 We Card, "Frequently Asked Questions," http://www.wecard.org/index.php?option=com_content&task=view&id=16&Itemid=33, accessed November 4, 2009.

85 http://www.wecard.org.

86 Hrebenar and Scott, *Interest Group Politics*, 96.

87 Kate Kaye, "Bailout Drives Search Efforts for Automakers, Advocacy Groups," December 15, 2008, http://www.clickz.com/3632087, accessed November 4, 2009.

88 Lila Guterman, "Scientists Accuse Toxicology Journal of Industry Ties, Urge Disclosure of Conflicts of Interest," *Chronicle of Higher Education*, November 20, 2002, http://chronicle.com/daily/2002/11/2002112003n.htm.

89 Ibid.

90 Kevin Borgardus, "Nonprofits' Spending Was Dominated by Card-Check," The Hill, March 2, 2009, http://thehill .com/business—lobby/nonprofits-spending-was -dominated- by-card-check-2009-03-02.html, accessed July 9, 2009.

91 Hrebenar and Scott, *Interest Group Politics*, 197.

92 Ibid.

93 American Civil Liberties Union (ACLU). 2016. "ACLU Annual Report 2015." https://www.aclu.org/aclu -annual-report-2015, accessed July 30, 2016.

94 Dara Z. Strolovitch, "Do Interest Groups Represent the Disadvantaged? Advocacy at the Intersections of Race, Class, and Gender," *Journal of Politics* 68 (2006): 894–910.

95 Ibid.

Chapter 14

1 "About Donna," donnabrazile.com, http://donnabrazile. com/?page_id=2 , accessed July 25, 2015; "Donna Brazile: Born for Politics," *USA Today: Opinion*, May 23, 2000, http://usatoday30.usatoday.com/news/opinion /e1861.htm, accessed July 25, 2016.

2 Jeff Adelson, "DNC Chair Donna Brazile Casts November Election as Part of Civil Rights Struggle in Speech to Progressive Baptists," *The New Orleans Advocate*, August 10, 2016, http://www.theadvocate.com /new_orleans/news/article_35efe80e-5f4c-11e6-8d52 -bbd58dc0174a.html, accessed September 22, 2016.

3 Michael Grynbaum, "CNN Parts Ways with Donna Brazile, A Hillary Clinton Supporter," New York Times, October 31, 2016, http://www.nytimes.com/2016/11/01 /us/politics/donna-brazile-wikileaks-cnn.html, accessed November 25, 2016.

4 Matthew J. Burbank, Ronald J. Hrebenar, and Robert C. Benedict, *Parties, Interest Groups, and Political Campaigns*, 2nd edition (New York: Oxford University Press, 2008), 6–12; John F. Bibby and Brian F. Schaffner, *Politics, Parties, & Elections in America*, 6th edition (Boston: Thomson Wadsworth, 2008), 21–23.

5 Burbank, Hrebenar, and Benedict, *Parties, Interest Groups, and Political Campaigns*, 12–15; Bibby and Schaffner, *Politics, Parties, & Elections in America*, 23–24

6 See Steven P. Erie, *Rainbow's End: Irish Americans and the Dilemmas of Urban Machine Politics, 1840–1985* (Berkeley and Los Angeles: University of California Press, 1988).

7 Burbank, Hrebenar, and Benedict, *Parties, Interest Groups, and Political Campaigns*, 15–18; Bibby and Schaffner, *Politics, Parties, & Elections in America*, 24–25.

8 Burbank, Hrebenar, and Benedict, *Parties, Interest Groups, and Political Campaigns*, 18–22; Bibby and Schaffner, *Politics, Parties, & Elections in America*, 27–30.

9 For more on the issue of partisan realignments see, Walter Dean Burnham, *Critical Elections and the Mainsprings of American Politics* (New York: Norton, 1970); V. O. Key, Jr., "A Theory of Critical Elections," *Journal of Politics* 17 (1955): 3–18; V. O. Key, Jr., "Secular Realignment and the Party System," *Journal of Politics* 21 (1959): 198–210; Arthur Paulson, *Realignment and Party Revival: Understanding Electoral Politics at the Turn of the Twenty-First Century* (Westport, CT: Praeger, 2000); John Kenneth White and Matthew R. Kerbel, *Party On! Political Parties from Hamilton and Jefferson to Today's Networked Age* (Boulder, CO: Paradigm Press, 2012), 117–123.

10 David R. Mayhew, *Electoral Realignments: A Critique of an American Genre* (New Haven, CT: Yale University Press, 2002).

11 Rutherford B. Hayes Presidential Center, "Disputed Election of 1876," http://www.rbhayes.org/hayes /president/display.asp?id=511&subj=president, accessed July 25, 2016.

12 For more on these terms, see Paula D. McClain and Joseph Stewart, Jr., *"Can We All Get along?" Racial and Ethnic Minorities in American Politics*, 6th edition (Boulder, CO: Westview Press, 2014), 90.

13 Burbank, Hrebenar, and Benedict, *Parties, Interest Groups, and Political Campaigns*, 22–24; Bibby and Schaffner, *Politics, Parties, & Elections in America*, 30–32.

14 John Woolley and Gerhard Peters, "Elections: The Election of 1948," *The American Presidency Project* (Santa Barbara, CA: University of California, Santa Barbara, 1999–2016), http://www.presidency.ucsb.edu /showelection.php?year=1948, accessed July 26, 2016.

15 For more on dealignment, see White and Kerbel, *Party On!*, 123–126.

16 John Woolley and Gerhard Peters, "Elections: The Election of 1968," *The American Presidency Project* (Santa Barbara, CA: University of California, Santa Barbara, 1999–2016), http://www.presidency.ucsb.edu /showelection.php?year=1968, accessed July 26, 2016.

17 See Kevin P. Phillips, *The Emerging Republican Majority* (New Rochelle, NY: Arlington House, 1969).

18 http://www.prohibitionparty.org/

19 http://www.usmjparty.com/

20 John Woolley and Gerhard Peters, "Elections: The Election of 1912," *The American Presidency Project* (Santa Barbara, CA: University of California, Santa Barbara, 1999–2016), http://www.presidency.ucsb.edu /showelection.php?year=1912, accessed July 26, 2016.

21 Ibid., "Elections: The Election of 1948" and "Elections: The Election of 1968," http://www.presidency.ucsb.edu /showelection.php?year=1948; http://www.presidency .ucsb.edu/showelection.php?year=1968, accessed September 22, 2016.

22 Bibby and Schaffner, *Politics, Parties, & Elections in America*, 138–141.

23 David Weigel, "Democrats Vote to Bind Most Superdelegates to State Primary Results," *Washington Post*, July 23, 2016, https://www.washingtonpost.com/news/post -politics/wp/2016/07/23/democrats-vote-to-bind-most -superdelegates-to-state-primary-results/, accessed July 26, 2016.

24 Republican National Convention, *Republican Platform 2016*, https://prod-static-ngop-pbl.s3.amazonaws.com/media/documents/DRAFT_12_FINAL[1]-ben_1468872234.pdf, accessed September 22, 2016.

25 Burbank, Hrebenar, and Benedict, *Parties, Interest Groups, and Political Campaigns*, 47–48.

26 *McConnell v. Federal Election Commission*, 540 U.S. 93 (2004).

27 Burbank, Hrebenar, and Benedict, *Parties, Interest Groups, and Political Campaigns*, 48–49; Louis Jacobsen, "Looking Back at Howard Dean's 50-State Strategy," *Governing*, May 6, 2013, http://www.governing.com/blogs/politics/gov-democrat-howard-deans-fifty-state-strategy.html, accessed July 26, 2016.

28 Steven A. Holmes, *Ron Brown: An Uncommon Life* (New York: Wiley, 2000).

29 Larry Lipman, "Martinez Resigns as Republican Chairman," *Palm Beach Post*, October 20, 2007, 10A.

30 Paul West, "Steele Elected Chair of the RNC: MD's Ex-Lieutenant Governor Becomes the First Black Head of GOP," *Baltimore Sun*, January 31, 2009, 1A.

31 Steve Peoples, "Reince Priebus Re-Elected GOP National Chairman," *Associated Press*, January 25, 2013, http://bigstory.ap.org/article/rnc-chair-priebus-reelected, accessed July 26, 2016.

32 Democratic National Committee, "People," http://www.democrats.org/, accessed July 26, 2016.

33 Democratic National Committee, "Our Leaders," https://www.democrats.org/about/our-leaders, accessed July 26, 2016.

34 Republican National Committee, "National Leadership," https://www.gop.com/leaders/national/, accessed July 26, 2016.

35 Republican National Committee, "GOP Hispanics," https://www.gop.com/groups/gop-hispanics/; "Black Republican Activists," https://www.gop.com/groups/black-republican-activists/; "Asian Pacific Americans," https://www.gop.com/groups/asian-pacific-americans/, all accessed July 26, 2016.

36 Burbank, Hrebenar, and Benedict, *Parties, Interest Groups, and Political Campaigns*, 37–44.

37 Ibid., 19–20, 22

38 *Elrod v. Burns*, 427 U.S. 347 (1976); *Rutan v. Republican Party of Illinois*, 497 U.S. 62 (1990).

39 *Smith v. Allwright*, 321 U.S. 649 (1944).

40 Terry Gildea, "Utah GOP Elects James Evans Party Chairman," Utah Public Radio, KUER, May 16, 2013, http://kuer.org/post/utah-gop-elects-james-evans-party-chairman#stream/0, accessed July 27, 2016.

41 David Catanese, "Colo. Dems Tap Latino Chair, Pozen Plays Hard to Get," *Politico.com*, March 5, 2011, http://www.politico.com/blogs/davidcatanese/0311/Colo_Dems_tap_Latino_chair_Pozen_plays_hard_to_get.html#; Colorado Democrats, "Rick Palacio," http://www.coloradodems.org/people/rick-palacio, both accessed July 27, 2016.

42 Burbank, Hrebenar, and Benedict, *Parties, Interest Groups, and Political Campaigns*, 84–87.

43 Pew Research Center U.S. Policy & Politics, "A Deep Dive into Party Affiliation: Sharp Differences by Race, Gender, Generation, and Education," April 7, 2015, http://www.people-press.org/2015/04/07/a-deep-dive-into-party-affiliation/, accessed July 27, 2016.

44 "President Exit Polls," *New York Times*, http://elections.nytimes.com/2012/results/president/exit-polls, accessed July 27, 2016.

45 Democratic National Committee, "People: Young People and Students," https://www.democrats.org/people/young-people-and-students; Republican National Committee, "Millennials," https://www.gop.com/groups/gop-millennials/, both sites accessed July 27, 2016.

46 Pew Research Center U.S. Policy & Politics, "Party Identification Detailed Tables," April 7, 2015, http://www.people-press.org/2015/04/07/2014-party-identification-detailed-tables/, accessed July 27, 2016.

47 Ibid.

48 Ibid.

49 "President Exit Polls," *New York Times*, http://elections.nytimes.com/2012/results/president/exit-polls, accessed July 27, 2016.

50 For more on racial and ethnic minorities and party identification, consult McClain and Stewart, *"Can We All Get along?"*, 89–100.

51 James G. Muhammad, "Rev. Jesse Jackson: Why Blacks MUST Vote for Kerry," *N'DIGO* (October 28–November 3, 2004): 4.

Chapter 15

1 Carl M. Brauer, "John F. Kennedy," in *The Presidents: A Reference History*, ed. Henry F. Graff, 2nd ed. (New York: Scribner's, 1996).

2 President-Elect Barack Obama's Acceptance Speech, Grant Park, Chicago, IL, November 5, 2008, http://www.huffingtonpost.com/2008/11/04/obama-victory-speech_n_141194.html, accessed July 12, 2009.

3 L. Sandy Maisel and Mark D. Brewer, *Parties and Elections in America: The Electoral Process*, 5th ed. (Boulder: Rowman & Littlefield, 2007), 32.

4 Ibid., 36.

5 William G. Mayer, "An Incremental Approach to Presidential Nomination Reform," *PS: Political Science and Politics* 42 (January 2009): 65–69.

6 The fourteen Democratic caucus states in 2012 were Alaska, Colorado, Hawaii, Idaho, Iowa, Kansas, Maine, Minnesota, Nebraska, Nevada, North Dakota, Utah, Washington, and Wyoming. The thirteen Republican caucus states were Alaska, Colorado, Hawaii, Idaho, Iowa, Kansas, Maine, Minnesota, Missouri, Nevada, North Dakota, Washington, and Wyoming.

7 "Who Is Running for President?" *The New York Times*, http://www.nytimes.com/interactive/2016/us/elections/2016-presidential-candidates.html, accessed July 14, 2016.

8 David Frum, "Run, Warren, Run," *The Atlantic*, January 13, 2015. http://www.theatlantic.com/politics/archive/2015/01/run-warren-run/384490/, accessed July 14, 2016.

9 Patrick Healy, "Little Separates Bernie Sanders and Hillary Clinton in Tight Race in Iowa," *The New York Times*, February 2, 2016, http://www.nytimes.com/2016/02/02/us/bernie-sanders-hillary-clinton-democratic-iowa-caucus.html, accessed July 14, 2016.

10 Marian Tupy, "Bernie Is Not a Socialist and America Is Not Capitalist," *The Atlantic*, March 1, 2016, http://www.theatlantic.com/international/archive/2016/03/bernie-sanders-democratic-socialism/471630/, accessed July 14, 2016.

11 Ibid., "Who Is Running for President?"

12 National Conference of State Legislators, "State Primary Election Types," 2016, http://www.ncsl.org/research/elections-and-campaigns/primary-types.aspx#closed, accessed August 22, 2016.

13 John F. Bibby and Thomas M. Holbrook, "Parties and Elections," in *Politics in the American States*, ed. Virginia Gray, Russell L. Hanson, and Herbert Jacob (Washington, DC: Congressional Quarterly Press, 1999), 88.

14 National Conference of State Legislators, ibid.

15 Ibid.

16 Ibid.

17 Ibid.

18 Ballotpedia, "Hybrid Primary," 2016, https://ballotpedia.org/Hybrid_primary, accessed August 22, 2016.

19 National Conference of State Legislators, 2016.

20 Ibid.

21 Malcolm Jewell and Sarah M. Morehouse, *Political Parties and Elections in American States*, 4th ed. (Washington, DC: Congressional Quarterly Press, 2001), 103.

22 National Conference of State Legislators, 2016.

23 Jewel and Morehouse, *Political Parties and Elections*, 274.

24 Ibid., 106.

25 L. Sandy Maisel and Kara Z. Buckley, *Parties and Elections in America: The Electoral Process*, 4th ed. (Boulder: Rowman & Littlefield, 2004), 218.

26 J. Morgan Kousser, "Origins of the Run-Off Primary," *The Black Scholar* (September–October 1984): 23–26.

27 Carl Bialik, "Why the Polls Missed Bernie Sanders's Michigan Upset," *FiveThirtyEight*, March 9, 2016, http://fivethirtyeight.com/features/why-the-polls-missed-bernie-sanders-michigan-upset/, accessed September 22, 2016.

28 M. J. Lee, Dan Merica, and Jeff Zeleny, "Bernie Sanders Endorses Hillary Clinton," CNN.com. July 12, 2016, http://www.cnn.com/2016/07/11/politics/hillary-clinton-bernie-sanders/, accessed September 22, 2016.

29 "Iowa Entrance Polls," CNN.com, Election Center 2016, February 1, 2016, http://www.cnn.com/election/primaries/polls/ia/Dem, accessed September 22, 2016.

30 "Ohio Exit Polls," CNN.com, Election Center 2016, March 15, 2016, http://www.cnn.com/election/primaries/polls/oh/Dem, accessed September 22, 2016.

31 "Texas Exit Polls," CNN.com, Election Center 2016, March 1, 2016, http://www.cnn.com/election/primaries/polls/TX/Dem, accessed September 22, 2016.

32 "After New Hampshire: Updates, Analysis and Results," *The New York Times*, http://www.nytimes.com/live/new-hampshire-primary-2016-election/, accessed September 22, 2016.

33 "Who Is Running for President?" *The New York Times*, http://www.nytimes.com/interactive/2016/us/elections/2016-presidential-candidates.html, accessed September 22, 2016.

34 Jeremy W. Peters, "Emerging Republican Platform Goes Far to the Right," *The New York Times*, July 12, 2016, http://www.nytimes.com/2016/07/13/us/politics/republican-convention-issues.html, accessed September 22, 2016.

35 Ibid.

36 Janell Ross, "Donald Trump Apparently Won the Latino Vote in Nevada. It Doesn't Mean Latinos Suddenly Love Him," *The Washington Post*, February 24, 2016, https://www.washingtonpost.com/news/the-fix/wp/2016/02/24/donald-trump-apparently-won-the-latino-vote-in-nevada-it-doesnt-mean-latinos-suddenly-love-him/, accessed September 22, 2016.

37 David Damore, "Nevada Latino Voters in the 2016 Election," April 22, 2016, http://www.latinodecisions.com/files/8714/6134/1022/AV_Wave_1_NV_Deck_April_2016.pdf, accessed September 22, 2016.

38 Ross, "Donald Trump Apparently Won the Latino Vote in Nevada. It Doesn't Mean Latinos Suddenly Love Him."

39 Damore, "Nevada Latino Voters in the 2016 Election."

40 Ibid.

41 Ibid.

42 "Who's Winning the Presidential Delegate Count?" Bloomberg Politics, 2016, http://www.bloomberg.com/politics/graphics/2016-delegate-tracker/, accessed August 19, 2016.

43 "2016 Democratic National Convention: Unpledged Delegates—By State," Vox, 2016, https://cdn1.vox-cdn.com/uploads/chorus_asset/file/6622695/Unpledged_Delegate_List_5.27.16.0.pdf, accessed August 19, 2016.

44 "Why Delegates Matter in the Presidential Race," CNN.com, Election Center 2008, http://edition.cnn.com/2008/POLITICS/01/02/delegate.explainer/index.html, accessed July 7, 2009.

45 Marshall Cohen, "Donald Trump Picks Up More Unbound GOP Delegates," May 9, 2016, http://www.cnn.com/2016/05/09/politics/trump-gop-delegates-unbound/, accessed August 19, 2016.

46 Nate Silver, "The G.O.P.'s Fuzzy Delegate Math," *New York Times*, February 25, 2012, http://fivethirtyeight.blogs.nytimes.com/2012/02/25/the-g-o-p-s-fuzzy-delegate-math/, accessed May 26, 2013.

47 CNN Politics. "Election Center," http://www.cnn.com/election/primaries, accessed August 19, 2016.

48 Ibid.

49 DNC Office of Party Affairs and Delegate Selection, "2016 Democratic National Convention: Delegate /Alternate Allocation," 2016, https://ballotpedia.org /wiki/images/c/ce/Appendix_B_-_Allocation_Chart _1.29.16.pdf.pdf, accessed August 19, 2016; Republican National Convention, "About," 2016, http://convention .gop/about, accessed August 19, 2016.

50 Boris Heersink and Sidney M. Milkis, "These 2 Trends Are What Produced Such a Negative Republican National Convention," *The Washington Post*, July 24, 2016, https://www.washingtonpost.com/news/monkey -cage/wp/2016/07/24/these-2-trends-are-what-produced -such-a-negative-republican-national-convention/, accessed August 13, 2016.

51 "Election 2016 Primaries + Caucuses," CNN.com, 2016, http://www.cnn.com/election/primaries, accessed August 13, 2016.

52 Nicholas Confessore, "G.O.P. Convention Day 2 Takeaways: A Party United, At Least for a Night," *The New York Times*, July 19, 2016, http://www.nytimes .com/2016/07/19/us/politics/republican-national -convention.html, accessed August 13, 2016.

53 Melanie Mason, "A More Restrained Tone and an Appeal to Populism: 5 Takeaways from Donald Trump's Accep- tance Speech," *Los Angeles Times*, July 22, 2016, http:// www.latimes.com/nation/politics/trailguide/la-na -republican-convention-2016-trump-speech-updates -htmlstory.html, accessed August 13, 2016.

54 Heersink and Milkis, "These 2 Trends Are What Produced Such a Negative Republican National Convention."

55 Ericka Cruz Guevarra, "Roundup: The Republican National Convention and Race (So Far)," *NPR: North Carolina Public Radio*, 2016, http://www.npr.org/sections /codeswitch/2016/07/21/486604305/roundup-the -republican-national-convention-and-race-so-far, accessed August 13, 2016.

56 Breakdown of delegates by race. Black/African American: 18; Hispanic: approximately 133; Asian American: no estimates available.

57 Phillip Bump, "There Are Likely Fewer Black Delegates to the Republican Convention Than at Any Point in at Least a Century," *The Washington Post*, July 19, 2016, https://www.washingtonpost.com/news/the-fix/wp/2016 /07/19/there-are-likely-fewer-black-delegates-to-the -republican-convention-than-at-any-point-in-at-least-a -century/?tid=sm_tw_pp, accessed August 13, 2016.

58 Ibid.

59 Earl Ofari Hutchinson, "The 2016 GOP Convention: The Whitest of the Whitest Conventions," *The Huffington Post*, July 17, 2016, http://www.huffingtonpost.com/earl-ofari -hutchinson/the-2016-gop-conventionth_b_11028190 .html, accessed August 13, 2016.

60 "GOP: At Least 133 Latino Delegates at Republican Convention," NBC News, 2016, http://www.nbcnews .com/storyline/2016-conventions/gop-least-133-latino -delegates-republican-convention-n614376, accessed August 13, 2016.

61 Zak Cheney Rice, "The RNC Was the Most Flagrant Display of GOP Racism America Has Seen in Years," *Identities.Mic*, July 22, 2016, https://mic.com/articles /149140/the-rnc-was-the-most-flagrant-display-of-gop -racism-america-has-seen-in-years#.uetHD333I, accessed August 13, 2016.

62 Ibid.

63 Bump, "There Are Likely Fewer Black Delegates to the Republican Convention Than at Any Point in at Least a Century."

64 Guevarra, "Roundup: The Republican National Conven- tion and Race (So Far)."

65 Julie Westfall, "2016 Democratic Convention to Be Held Right after GOP Gathering," *Los Angeles Times*, January 23, 2016, http://www.latimes.com/nation/politics /politicsnow/la-pn-dnc-right-after-republican-convention -20150123-story.html, accessed August 13, 2016.

66 "Election 2016 Primaries + Caucuses," CNN.com, 2016, http://www.cnn.com/election/primaries, accessed August 13, 2016.

67 "Factbox: The Race to the U.S. Presidential Nominations: How Delegates Are Selected," Reuters, February 24, 2016, http://www.reuters.com/article/us-usa-election -delegates-factbox-idUSKCN0VY094, accessed August 13, 2016.

68 Patrick Healy and Jonathan Martin, "Democrats Strug- gle for Unity on First Day of Convention," *The New York Times*, July 25, 2016, http://www.nytimes.com/2016 /07/26/us/politics/dnc-speakers-protests-sanders.html, accessed August 13, 2016.

69 Democratic National Convention, "Democratic Platform Drafting Meeting Concludes," https://www .demconvention.com/news/democratic-platform -drafting-meeting-concludes/, accessed August 13, 2016.

70 Sarah Frostenson, "Half of the Democratic Delegates Were People of Color. For Republicans, It Was Only 6%," July 29, 2016, http://www.vox.com/2016/7/29/12295830/ republican-democratic-delegates-diversity-nonwhite, accessed August 13, 2016.

71 Katie Zezima, "Republicans Denounce Trump as Con- frontation with Muslim Parents Escalates," *The Washington Post*, August 1, 2016, https://www.washingtonpost .com/politics/republicans-denounce-trump-as -confrontation-with-muslim-parents-escalates/2016/07/ 31/54397028-5722-11e6-9aee-8075993d73a2_story .html, accessed August 13, 2016.

72 Stephanie McCrummen, "Khizr Khan Responds to the Latest from Trump: 'Typical of a Person Without a Soul,'" *The Washington Post*, July 31, 2016, https://www .washingtonpost.com/politics/khizr-khan-responds -to-the-latest-from-trump-what-he-said-originally--that -defines-him/2016/07/31/450f78dc-56d6-11e6-b7de -dfe509430c39_story.html, accessed August 13, 2016.

73 Katie Zezima, "Republicans Denounce Trump as Confrontation with Muslim Parents Escalates," *The Washington Post*, August 1, 2016, https://www .washingtonpost.com/politics/republicans-denounce -trump-as-confrontation-with-muslim-parents-escalates /2016/07/31/54397028-5722-11e6-9aee-8075993d73a2 _story.html, accessed August 13, 2016.

74 Bibby and Holbrook, "Parties and Elections," 89.

75 Office of the Federal Register, National Archives and Records Administration, "A Procedural Guide to the Electoral College," http://www.nara.gov/fedreg/electcoll /proced.html, accessed July 7, 2009.

76 Ibid.

77 *Ray v. Blair*, 343 U.S. 214 (1952); Office of the Federal Register, National Archives and Records Administration, "Frequently Asked Questions on the Electoral College," http://www.nara.gov/fedreg/electcoll/faq.html, accessed July 10, 2009.

78 Congressional Research Service, "CRS Report to Congress—The Electoral College: Reform Proposals in the 109th Congress," March 12, 2007.

79 Kyle Trygstad, "Obama's 50 State Strategy," *Real Clear Politics*, June 26, 2016, http://www.realclearpolitics.com /articles/2008/06/obamas_50_state_strategy.html, accessed July 9, 2009.

80 Martha T. Moore and Catalina Camia, "Hillary Clinton Launches 2016 Presidential Bid," *USA Today*, 2016, http:// www.usatoday.com/story/news/politics/elections/2015 /04/12/hillary-clinton-president-announcement-2016 /22018067/, accessed September 8, 2016; Liz Kreutz, "How Hillary Clinton's Campaign Has Changed in the New Year," January 8, 2016, http://abcnews.go.com /Politics/hillary-clintons-campaign-changed-year/story ?id=36158940, accessed September 8, 2016; Mark Binelli, "Hillary Clinton vs. Bernie Sanders: The Good Fight," *Rolling Stone*, March 9, 2016, http://www.rollingstone .com/politics/news/hillary-clinton-vs-bernie-sanders -the-good-fight-20160309, accessed September 8, 2016.

81 Amy Chozick, "What Hillary Clinton Would Need to Do to Win." *The New York Times*, April 12, 2015, http:// www.nytimes.com/interactive/2016/us/elections /hillary-clinton.html, accessed September 8, 2016.

82 Katie Glueck, "The Power Players behind Hillary Clinton's Campaign." *Politico*, April 12, 2016, http://www.politico .com/story/2015/04/hillary-clintons-power-players -116874, accessed September 8, 2016.

83 Zeke J. Miller, "Mismatch 2016," *Time Magazine*, 2016, http://time.com/trump-clinton-mismatch, accessed September 8, 2016.

84 James Hohmann, "The Daily 202: Hillary Clinton Is Winning with a Hyper-Local Strategy," *The Washington Post*, March 8, 2016, https://www.washingtonpost.com/ news/powerpost/paloma/daily-202/2016/03/08/daily -202-hillary-clinton-is-winning-with-a-hyper-local -strategy/56de2040981b92a22d7612d7/, accessed September 8, 2016.

85 Hohmann, "The Daily 202: Hillary Clinton Is Winning with a Hyper-Local Strategy."

86 Hillary for America, 2016, https://www.hillaryclinton .com/issues/, accessed September 8, 2016.

87 Donald J. Trump for President, https://www .donaldjtrump.com/POSITIONS, accessed September 9, 2016.; Timm, Jane C, "A Full List of Donald Trump's Rapidly Changing Policy Positions," 2016, http://www .nbcnews.com/politics/2016-election/full-list-donald -trump-s-rapidly-changing-policy-positions-n547801, accessed September 9, 2016.

88 Maggie Haberman, "Donald Trump Calls for Surveillance of 'Certain Mosques' and a Syrian Refugee Database," *The New York Times*, November 21, 2016, http:// www.nytimes.com/2015/11/22/us/politics/donald -trump-syrian-muslims-surveillance.html, accessed September 9, 2016.

89 Adam B. Lerner, "The 10 Best Lines from Donald Trump's Announcement Speech," *Politico*, June 16, 2016, http://www.politico.com/story/2015/06/donald-trump -2016-announcement-10-best-lines-119066, accessed September 9, 2016.

90 Candace Smith, "Trump Campaign Announces $90 Million Fundraising Haul in August," September 8, 2016, http://abcnews.go.com/Politics/trump -campaign-announces-90-million-fundraising-haul -august/story?id=41952316, accessed September 9, 2016.

91 Anu Narayanswamy, Darla Cameron, and Matea Gold, *The Washington Post*, 2016, https://www.washingtonpost .com/graphics/politics/2016-election/campaign-finance/, accessed September 9, 2016.

92 Smith, "Trump Campaign Announces $90 Million Fundraising Haul in August"; Narayanswamy et al., 2016.

93 Smith, "Trump Campaign Announces $90 Million Fundraising Haul in August."

94 Audrey A. Haynes and Brian Pitts, "Making an Impression: New Media in the 2008 Presidential Nomination Campaigns," *PS: Political Science and Politics* 42 (January 2009): 53–58.

95 Shirley Anne Warshaw, *The Keys to Power: Managing the Presidency* (New York: Addison Wesley Longman, 2000), 68–71.

96 John Jay Douglass, "The Mother's Milk of Elections," *World and I* 15 (March 2000): 1.

97 Ibid.

98 Peter Baida, "The Legacy of Dollar Mark Hanna," *Forbes* 142 (October 24, 1988): 3.

99 Amount is indexed for inflation during odd numbered years; Federal Election Commission; "Presidential Election Campaign Fund (Updated May 13, 2016)." http:// www.fec.gov/press/bkgnd/fund.shtml#search=bcra%20 2016, accessed August 26, 2016.

100 Amount is indexed for inflation during odd numbered years.

101 The Center for Responsive Politics, "2016 Campaign Contribution Limits," https://www.opensecrets.org /overview/limits.php, accessed August 26, 2016.

102 Federal Election Commission, "Contribution Limits for 2013–2014," http://www.fec.gov/info /contriblim-itschart1314.pdf, accessed April 14, 2013; Anthony Corrado, "The Changing Environment of Presidential Campaign Finance," in *In Pursuit of the White House: How We Choose Our Presidential Nominees*, ed. William G. Mayer (Chatham, NJ: Chatham House, 1996), 220–253.

103 "Key Provisions of the McCain–Feingold–Cochran Bill (S. 27)," *Public Citizen*, http://citizen.org/congress /reform/mcfinkeyprovisions.htm. Accessed January 12, 2009.

104 Ibid.

105 Federal Election Commission, "Bipartisan Campaign Reform Act of 2002," http://www.fec.gov/pages/bcra /bcra_update.shtml, accessed August 26, 2016.

106 Corrado, "The Changing Environment of Presidential Campaign Finance," 221.

107 Ibid., 227.

108 Stephen J. Wayne, *The Road to the White House 2000: The Politics of Presidential Selection* (New York: Bedford/ St. Martin's Press, 2000).

109 Phil Hirschkorn, "Top Super PAC Donors Giving Multimillions in 2012," CBS News, September 24, 2012, http://www.cbsnews.com/8301-250_162 -57519344/top-super-pac-donors-giving-multimillions -in-2012/, accessed January 7, 2013.

110 Ibid.

111 Center for Responsive Politics (OpenSecrets.org), "Super PACS," February 18, 2013, http://www.opensecrets .org/pacs/superpacs.php, accessed March 11, 2013.

112 Ibid.

113 Center for Responsive Politics (OpenSecrets.org), "2012 Presidential Race," January 14, 2013, http:// www.opensecrets.org/pres12/index.php. Accessed March 11, 2013.

114 Ivona Iacob, "The Top Donors Backing Hillary Clinton's Super PAC," *Forbes*, May 27, 2016, http://www.forbes .com/sites/ivonaiacob/2016/05/27/top-donors-hillary -clinton-superpac/#5ed9d7992740, accessed August 30, 2016.

115 Center for Responsive Politics, "Hillary Clinton: Candidate Summary, 2016 Cycle," 2016, https://www .opensecrets.org/pres16/candidate.php?id=N00000019, accessed August 30, 2016.

116 Iacob, "The Top Donors Backing Hillary Clinton's Super PAC."

117 Schouten, Fredreka, "Hillary Clinton Super PAC Stock- piles $40 Million for Donald Trump Attacks," July 20, 2016, http://www.usatoday.com/story/news/politics /onpolitics/2016/07/20/hillary-clinton-super-pac -stockpiles-40-million-donald-trump-attacks /87347474/, accessed August 30, 2016.

118 Center for Responsive Politics, "Hillary Clinton: Candidate Summary, 2016 Cycle."

119 Fredreka Schouten, "Hillary Clinton Super PAC Stock- piles $40 Million for Donald Trump Attacks."

120 Rebecca Ballhaus, "Hillary Clinton Super Pac Outpaces Donald Trump Groups in July," *The Wall Street Journal*, August 20, 2016, http://www.wsj.com /articles/hillary-clinton-super-pac-outpaces-donald -trump-groups-in-july-1471731438, accessed August 30, 2016.

121 Alex Isenstadt and Kenneth P. Vogel, "Trump Blesses Major Super PAC Effort," *Politico*, July 20, 2016, http:// www.politico.com/story/2016/07/trump-super-pac -donors-225892, accessed, August 30, 2016.

122 Fredreka Schouten, "Hillary Clinton Super PAC Stock- piles $40 Million for Donald Trump Attacks."

123 Center for Responsive Politics, "Donald Trump: Candidate Summary, 2016 Cycle," 2016, https:// www.opensecrets.org/pres16/candidate.php?id= N00023864, accessed August 30, 2016.

124 Tali Mendelberg, *The Race Card: Campaign Strategy, Implicit Messages, and the Norm of Equality* (Princeton, NJ: Princeton University Press, 2001), 3.

125 Ibid.

126 Donald Kinder and Lynn M. Sanders, *Divided by Color: Racial Politics and Democratic Ideals* (Chicago: University of Chicago Press, 1996), chap. 6.

127 Gwyneth K. Shaw, Jim Leusner, and Sean Holton, "Uncounted Ballots May Add Up to 180,000," *Orlando Sentinel*, November 15, 2000.

128 Frances Robles and Geoff Dougherty, "Ballot Errors Rate High in Some Black Precincts," *Miami Herald*, November 15, 2000.

129 John Mintz and Dan Keating, "Fla. Ballot Spoilage Likelier for Blacks," *Washington Post*, December 3, 2000, A1, A28.

130 Paula D. McClain and Joseph Stewart Jr., *"Can We All Get along?": Racial and Ethnic Minorities in American Poli- tics*, 5th ed. (Boulder, CO: Westview Press, 2010), 113.

131 Kinder and Sanders, *Divided by Color*, 42–43.

132 CNN Political Unit, "Two People Removed from RNC Convention after Taunting Black Camera Operator," August 29, 2012, http://politicalticker.blogs.cnn.com /2012/08/29/two-people-removed-from-rnc-after -taunting-black-camera-operator/, accessed January 7, 2013.

133 Ari Shapiro, "Despite Fact Checks, Romney Escalates Welfare Work Requirement Charge," NPR, August 22, 2012, http://www.npr.org/blogs/itsallpolitics/2012/08 /22/159791065/despite-fact-checks-romney-escalates -welfare-work-requirement-charge, accessed January 7, 2013.

134 The Grio, "'Put the White Back in the White House' T-Shirt Spotted at Romney Rally Goes Viral," October 14, 2012, http://thegrio.com/2012/10/14/put-the-white -back-in-the-white-house-t-shirt-spotted-at-romney

-rally-goes-viral/#s:offensive-anti-obama-tshirt, accessed January 7, 2013.

135 Confessore, Nicholas, "For Whites Sensing Decline, Donald Trump Unleashes Words of Resistance," July 13, 2016, http://www.nytimes.com/2016/07/14/us/politics /donald-trump-white-identity.html?_r=0, accessed September 22, 2016.

136 Aaron Rupar and Bryan Dewan, "Timeline: How Trump Took the Low Road to the Top of the Republican Party," March 1, 2016, http://thinkprogress.org /politics/2016/03/01/3755255/donald-trump-super -tuesday-timeline/, accessed September 22, 2016.

137 Alexander Burns, "Choice Words from Donald Trump, Presidential Candidate," June 16, 2016, http://www .nytimes.com/politics/first-draft/2015/06/16/choice -words-from-donald-trump-presidential-candidate /?mtrref=www.nytimes.com, accessed September 22, 2016.

138 "Trump's Bizarre Strategy to Win Back Latino Supporters Is Definitely Not Working," ThinkProgress.com, July 11, 2015, http://thinkprogress.org/immigration /2015/07/11/3679417/donald-trump-joe-arpaio/, accessed September 22, 2016.

139 Curtis Lee, "Arizona Crowd Welcomes Donald Trump's Tough Stance on Immigration," July 11, 2015, http:// www.latimes.com/nation/politics/la-na-trump -arizona-rally-20150710-story.html, accessed September 22, 2016.

140 "Donald Trump vs. Univision's Jorge Ramos," CNN .com, 2016, http://www.cnn.com/videos/politics/2015 /08/26/donald-trump-jorge-ramos-argue-immigration -origwx-bw.cnn/video/playlists/donald-trump -immigration/, accessed September 22, 2016; William Finnegan, "The Man Who Wouldn't Sit Down," The New Yorker, October 5, 2015, http://www.newyorker .com/magazine/2015/10/05/the-man-who-wouldnt-sit -down, accessed September 22, 2016.

141 Nina Totenberg, "Who Is Judge Gonzalo Curiel, the Man Trump Attacked for His Mexican Ancestry?" June 7, 2016, http://www.npr.org/2016/06/07/481140881/who -is-judge-gonzalo-curiel-the-man-trump-attacked-for -his-mexican-ancestry, accessed September 22, 2016.

142 Lindsey Bever, "'Make America White Again': A Politician's Billboard Ignites Uproar," June 23, 2016, https:// www.washingtonpost.com/news/the-fix/wp/2016 /06/23/make-america-white-again-a-politicians -billboard-ignites-uproar/, accessed September 22, 2016.

143 Camila Domonoske, "Former KKK Leader David Duke Says 'Of Course' Trump Voters Are His Voters," NPR, August 5, 2016, http://www.npr.org/sections /thetwo-way/2016/08/05/488802494/former-kkk -leader-david-duke-says-of-course-trump-voters-are -his-voters, accessed September 22, 2016.

144 Eric Garcia, "Poll Shows Louisiana Doesn't Like David Duke," Roll Call, August 2, 2016, http://www.rollcall .com/news/politics/david-dukes-unpopularity-sky -high, accessed September 22, 2016.

145 Michelle Alexander, "Why Hillary Clinton Doesn't Deserve the Black Vote," The Nation, February 29, 2016, https://www.thenation.com/article/hillary-clinton -does-not-deserve-black-peoples-votes/, accessed September 22, 2015.

146 Anne Gearan and Abby Phillip, "Clinton Regrets 1996 Remark on 'Super-predators' After Encounter with Activist," Washington Post, February 2, 2016, https://www .washingtonpost.com/news/post-politics/wp/2016/02 /25/clinton-heckled-by-black-lives-matter-activist/, accessed September 22, 2016.

147 Ibid.

148 Kinder and Sanders, Divided by Color, 42–43.

149 U.S. Census Bureau, "Voting and Registration in the Election of November 2012," Table 10, May 8, 2013, http://www.census.gov/hhes/www/socdemo/voting /publications/p20/2012/tables.html.

150 Ruy A. Teixeira, The Disappearing American Voter (Washington, DC: Brookings Institution, 1992).

151 McClain and Stewart, "Can We All Get along?," 82.

152 Teixeira, The Disappearing American Voter, 13.

153 U.S. Election Assistance Commission, "The Impact of the National Voter Registration Act on the Administration of Elections for Federal Office, 2005–2006," http://www.eac.gov/clearinghouse/docs/the-impact-of -the-national-voter-registration-act-on-federal -elections-2005–2006/attachment_download/file, accessed April 15, 2007.

154 Federal Election Commission, "Frequently Asked Questions about Election Day and Voting Procedures," http://www.fec.gov/pages/faqvdayeprocedures.htm, accessed July 9, 2009.

155 Janelle Carter, "Election-Overhaul Panel Advises National Holiday for Voting," Herald Sun (Durham, NC), July 31, 2001, A1, A7.

156 McClain and Stewart, "Can We All Get along?"

157 Jennifer C. Kerr, "Farewell Lever and Punch-Card Machine." The Seattle Times, November 2, 2012, http:// seattletimes.com/html/politics/2019583491 _apushowamericavotes.html, accessed January 7, 2013.

158 Election Data Services, "Nation Sees Drop in Use of Electronic Voting Equipment for 2008 Election—A First," http://electiondataservices.com/images/File /NR_VoteEquip_Nov-2008wAppendix2.pdf, accessed March 13, 2009.

159 National Conference of State Legislatures, "Voter Identification Requirements," January 14, 2013, http:// www.ncsl.org/legislatures-elections/elections/voter-id .aspx, accessed February 5, 2013.

160 Justin Levitt, "A Comprehensive Investigation of Voter Impersonation Finds 31 Credible Incidents out of One Billion Ballots Cast," Washington Post, August 6, 2014, https://www.washingtonpost.com/news/wonk/ wp/2014/08/06/a-comprehensive-investigation-of -voter-impersonation-finds-31-credible-incidents-out -of-one-billion-ballots-cast/.

161 Wendy Weiser and Diana Kasdan, *Voting Law Changes: Election Update* (New York: Brennan Center for Justice, New York University School of Law, 2012).

162 Robert Barnes and Ann E. Marimow, "Appeals Court Strikes down North Carolina's Voter-ID Law," *The Washington Post*, July 29, 2016, https://www .washingtonpost.com/local/public-safety/appeals -court-strikes-down-north-carolinas-voter-id-law /2016/07/29/810b5844-4f72-11e6-aa14-e0c1087f7583 _story.html, accessed August 1, 2016.

163 Michael Wines and Alan Blinder, "Federal Court Strikes down North Carolina Voter ID Requirement," *The New York Times*, July 29, 2016, http://www.nytimes .com/2016/07/30/us/federal-appeals-court-strikes -down-north-carolina-voter-id-provision.html, accessed August 1, 2016.

164 Jason Hanna, John Newsome, and Ariane de Vogue, "North Carolina Voter ID Law Overturned on Appeal," http://www.cnn.com/2016/07/29/politics/north -carolina-voter-id/, accessed August 1, 2016.

165 Josh Gerstein, "Court Strikes down North Carolina Voter ID Law," *Politico*, July 29, 2016, http://www .politico.com/story/2016/07/court-strikes-down-north -carolina-voter-id-law-226438, accessed August 1, 2016.

166 Robert Barnes and Ann E. Marimow, "Appeals Court Strikes down North Carolina's Voter-ID Law," *The Washington Post*, July 29, 2016, https://www .washingtonpost.com/local/public-safety/appeals -court-strikes-down-north-carolinas-voter-id-law /2016/07/29/810b5844-4f72-11e6-aa14-e0c1087f7583 _story.html, accessed August 1, 2016.

167 Ariane De Vogue, "Appeals Court: Texas Voter ID Law Violates Voting Rights Act," 2016, http://www.cnn .com/2016/07/20/politics/texas-voter-id-law/index .html, accessed August 1, 2016.

168 Ibid.

169 Jim Malewitz, "Texas Voter ID Law Violates Voting Rights Act, Court Rules," *The Texas Tribune*, July 20, 2016, https://www.texastribune.org/2016/07/20/ appeals-court-rules-texas-voter-id/, accessed August 1, 2016.

170 Emily Tamkin, "Parts of Wisconsin Voter ID Law Ruled Unconstitutional," 2016, http://www.slate.com/blogs /the_slatest/2016/07/30/federal_judge_declares_parts _of_wisconsin_s_voter_id_laws_unconstitutional.html, accessed August 1, 2016.

171 American Civil Liberties Union, "*Frank v. Walker*: Fighting Voter Suppression in Wisconsin," 2016, https://www.aclu.org/cases/frank-v-walker-fighting -voter-suppression-wisconsin, accessed August 1, 2016.

172 Michael Wines and Alan Blinder, "Federal Court Strikes down North Carolina Voter ID Requirement," *The New York Times*, July 29, 2016, http://www.nytimes .com/2016/07/30/us/federal-appeals-court-strikes -down-north-carolina-voter-id-provision.html, accessed September 22, 2016.

173 Julie Bosman, "Voter ID Battle Shifts to Kansas," *The New York Times*, October 15, 2016, http://www .nytimes.com/2015/10/16/us/politics/kansas-voter-id -law-sets-off-a-new-battle-over-registration.html, accessed August 1, 2016.

174 Kevin Murphy, "ACLU Asks Federal Court to Block Kansas Voter ID Law," *Reuters* April 4, 2016, http:// www.reuters.com/article/us-kansas-voterid -idUSKCN0XB17F, accessed August 1, 2016.

175 "Judge Slams Kansas Voter ID Law's 'Magnitude of Harm,'" CBS.com, 2016, http://www.cbsnews.com /news/judge-kansas-rejects-citizenship-proof-to-vote/, accessed August 1, 2016.

176 Bosman, "Voter ID Battle Shifts to Kansas."

177 Barnes and Marimow, "Appeals Court Strikes down North Carolina's Voter-ID Law."

178 Sidney Verba, Kay Lehman Schlozman, and Henry E. Brady, *Voice and Equality: Civic Voluntarism in American Politics* (Cambridge, MA: Harvard University Press, 1995), 230.

179 Ibid., 252.

180 Jane Mansbridge and Katherine Tate, "Race Trumps Gender: Black Opinion on the Thomas Nomination," *PS: Political Science and Politics* 25 (1992): 488–492.

181 Bernard R. Berelson, Paul F. Lazarsfeld, and William N. McPhee, *Voting: A Study of Opinion Formation in a Presidential Campaign* (Chicago: University of Chicago Press, 1954), 91.

182 U.S. Census Bureau News, "Voter Turnout Increases by 5 Million in 2008 Presidential Election," July 20, 2009.

183 Verba et al., *Voice and Equality*.

184 U.S. Census Bureau, "Homeownership Rates by Race and Ethnicity of Householder: 1994 to 2008," Table 22, National Low Income Housing Coalition, "Home- ownership Rates Drop for All Races, Especially for Hispanics, February 13, 2013," http://nlihc.org/article /homeownership-rates-drop-all-races-especially -hispanics, accessed May 26. 2013.

185 Carol A. Cassel, "Change in Electoral Participation in the South," *Journal of Politics* 41 (August 1979): 907–917.

186 J.P.P., 2016.

187 Burns and Flegenheimer, 2016.

188 Ariel Edwards-Levy, "Hillary Clinton Won the First Presidential Debate, Polling Finds," *The Huffington Post*, September 28, 2016. http://www.huffingtonpost.com /entry/poll-hillary-clinton-won-first-presidential -debate_us_57ec15c5e4b082aad9b8be8a, accessed October 10, 2016.

189 J.P.P., 2016.

190 Jennifer Agiesta, "Post-Debate Poll: Hillary Clinton Takes Round One," September 27, 2016. http://www .cnn.com/2016/09/27/politics/hillary-clinton-donald -trump-debate-poll/, accessed October 10, 2016.

191 NPR Staff, "Fact Check: Clinton and Trump Debate for the 2nd Time," October 9, 2016. http://www.npr .org/2016/10/09/497056227/fact-check-clinton-and

-trump-debate-for-the-second-time, accessed October 26, 2016.

192 Meghan Keneally, Veronica Stracqualursi, Shushannah Walshe, Meridith McGraw, and Julia Jacobo, "2nd Presidential Debate: 11 Moments That Mattered," ABC News, October 9, 2016. http://abcnews.go.com /Politics/presidential-debate-11-moments-mattered /story?id=42687340, accessed October 26, 2016.

193 Anna Palmer and Jake Sherman, "Poll: Hillary Clinton Won the Second Debate," *Politico*, October 11, 2016. http://www.politico.com/story/2016/10/clinton -trump-debate-poll-229581, accessed October 26, 2016.

194 Allan Rapperport, "Who Won the Debate? Hillary Clinton, the 'Nasty Woman,'" *The New York Times*, October 20, 2016. http://www.nytimes.com/2016/10 /21/us/politics/who-won-the-third-debate.html, accessed October 26, 2016.

195 Ed Rogers, "Trump Won the Third Debate," *The Washington Post*, October 19, 2016. https://www .washingtonpost.com/blogs/post-partisan/wp/2016 /10/19/trump-won-tonights-debate/?utm_term= .b6d005181f14, accessed October 26, 2016.

196 Leigh Ann Caldwell, "5 Major Takeaways from the Third and Final Presidential Debate," NBC News, October 20, 2016. http://www.nbcnews.com /storyline/2016-presidential-debates/5-major -takeaways-third-final-presidential-debate-n669831, accessed October 26, 2016.

197 Eric Bradner, "Trump Always Takes the Bait and Other Debate Takeaways," CNN Politics, October 20, 2016. http://www.cnn.com/2016/10/20/politics/presidential -debate-takeaways/, accessed October 23, 2016.

198 Caldwell, 2016.

199 Jennifer Agiesta, "Hillary Clinton Wins Third Presidential Debate, According to CNN/ORC Poll," CNN Politics, October 20, 2016. http://www.cnn .com/2016/10/19/politics/hillary-clinton-wins-third -presidential-debate-according-to-cnn-orc-poll/index .html, accessed October 26, 2016.

200 Emily Schultheis, "FBI Director to Congress: Still No Charges Recommended after Latest Clinton Emails Reviewed," CBS News, November 6, 2016. http://www .cbsnews.com/news/fbi-director-comey-congress-new -letter-hillary-clinton-emails-still-no-charges/, accessed November 8, 2016.

201 Ellen Nakashima, Sari Horwitz, and Matt Zapotosky, "For FBI, Email Investigation Yields Little but Criticism," *The Washington Post*, November 6, 2016. https:// www.washingtonpost.com/politics/fbi-director-comey -says-agency-wont-recommend-charges-over-clinton -email/2016/11/06/f6276b18-a45e-11e6-ba59 -a7d93165c6d4_story.html, accessed November 8, 2016.

202 Josh Gerstein, "Comey Says FBI Stands by Decision to Not Pursue Case against Clinton," *Politico*, November 6, 2016. http://www.politico.com/story/2016/11/fbi -director-comey-says-agency-stands-by-decision-to

-not-pursue-case-against-clinton-230842, accessed November 8, 2016.

203 Julia Edwards, "FBI Agents, Lawmakers Hammer Comey over Clinton Emails Inquiry," *Reuters*, November 7, 2016. http://www.reuters.com/article /us-usa-justice-comey-idUSKBN1322K6, accessed November 8, 2016.

204 Eric Bradner, Pamela Brown, and Evan Perez, "FBI Clears Clinton—Again," CNN Politics, November 7, 2016. http://www.cnn.com/2016/11/06/politics /comey-tells-congress-fbi-has-not-changed -conclusions/index.html, accessed November 8, 2016.

205 Gerstein, "Comey Says FBI Stands by Decision to Not Pursue Case against Clinton."

206 Matt Apuzzo, Michael S, Schmidt, and Adam Goldman, "Emails Warrant No New Action against Hillary Clinton, FBI Director Says," *The New York Times*, November 6, 2016. http://www.nytimes.com/2016/11 /07/us/politics/hilary-clinton-male-voters-donald -trump.html, accessed November 8, 2016.

207 Nakashima et al., "For FBI, Email Investigation Yields Little but Criticism."

208 Edwards, "FBI Agents, Lawmakers Hammer Comey over Clinton Emails Inquiry."

Chapter 16

1 See *U.S. v. Clary*, 846 F. Supp. 768 (1994); and Doris Marie Provine, *Unequal Under the Law: Race in the War on Drugs* (Chicago: University of Chicago Press, 2007), 1–36.

2 *U.S. v. Clary*, 34 F.3d. 709 (1994); *certiorari* denied, 513 U.S. 1182 (1995).

3 Danielle Kurtzleben, "Data Show Racial Disparity in Crack Sentencing: Obama Signed the Fair Sentencing Act to Make Punishments for Crack and Cocaine More Equal," *U.S. News and World Report*, August 3, 2010, http:// www.usnews.com/news/articles/2010/08/03/data-show -racial-disparity-in-crack-sentencing, accessed October 2, 2016; John Schwartz, "Drug Terms Reduced, Freeing Prisoners," *New York Times*, November 2, 2011, A18.

4 See Thomas A. Birkland, *An Introduction to the Policy Process: Theories, Concepts, and Models of Public Policy Making* (Armonk, NY: Sharpe, 2001), 105–112; Roger W. Cobb and Charles D. Elder, *Participation in American Politics: The Dynamics of Agenda Building* (Boston: Allyn & Bacon, 1972); John W. Kingdon, *Agendas, Alternatives, and Public Policies* (Boston: Little, Brown, 1984).

5 Paula D. McClain and Joseph Stewart, Jr., *"Can We All Get along?": Racial and Ethnic Minorities in American Politics*, 6th ed. (Boulder, CO: Westview Press, 2014), 55–63.

6 In housing: *Shelley v. Kraemer*, 344 U.S. 1 (1948). In voting: *Nixon v. Herndon*, 273 U.S. 536 (1927); *Smith v. Allwright*, 321 U.S. 649 (1944). In education: *Missouri ex. Rel. Gaines v. Canada*, 305 U.S. 337 (1938); *Sweatt v. Painter*, 339 U.S. 692 (1950); *McLaurin v. Oklahoma*, 339 U.S. 637 (1950); *Brown v. Board of Education*,

347 U.S. 483 (1954). For more on the NAACP Legal Defense and Educational Fund's work on discrimination litigation, see Jack Greenberg, *Crusaders in the Courts: How a Dedicated Band of Civil Rights Lawyers Fought for the Civil Rights Revolution* (New York: Basic Books, 1994).

7 See http://www.maldef.org/; http://www.narf.org; and http://www.advancingequality.org/, accessed July 29, 2016.

8 Amnesty International, "Who We Are," https://www.amnesty.org/en/who-we-are/, accessed July 29, 2016.

9 Amnesty International, "Uganda: Discriminatory Legislation Fuels Repression and Abuse," October 16, 2014, https://www.amnesty.org/en/latest/news/2014/10/uganda-discriminatory-legislation-fuels-repression-and-abuse/, accessed July 29, 2016.

10 Cuban American National Foundation, "About Us," http://canf.org/about-us, accessed October 2, 2016.

11 Stephanie Greco Larson, *Media and Minorities: The Politics of Race in News and Entertainment* (Lanham, MD: Rowman and Littlefield, 2006), 145–192.

12 Dusan Djordjevich, "Death Camps and Desert Storm Frame Bosnia Coverage," *Fairness & Accuracy in Reporting*, October 1, 1992, http://fair.org/extra/death-camps-and-desert-storm-frame-bosnia-coverage/, accessed July 29, 2016.

13 Joyce Price, "Why Rwanda Was Ignored: Months of Carnage Passed Before Congress Urged Aid," *Washington Times*, July 31, 1994, A4.

14 Fouad Ajami, "5 Myths About the Arab Spring," *Washington Post*, January 15, 2012, B2.

15 David D. Kirkpatrick, "Army Ousts Egypt's President; Morsi is Taken into Military Custody," *New York Times*, July 3, 2014, http://www.nytimes.com/2013/07/04/world/middleeast/egypt.html?pagewanted=all&_r=0, accessed July 29, 2016.

16 John Moreno Gonzales, "U.N. Finding of Discrimination in Katrina Recovery Mostly Ignored," *Associated Press State and Local Wire*, February 28, 2008.

17 Library of Congress, Congress.Gov, "H.R. 1424: Darfur Genocide Accountability Act, of 2005," https://www.congress.gov/bill/109th-congress/house-bill/1424, accessed July 29, 2016.

18 Radio Dbanga, "Sudan: Ambassador Smith—'Security Situation in Darfur Deteriorated Compared to 2011,'" *allAfrica*, September 19, 2012, http://allafrica.com/stories/201209200049.html, accessed July 29, 2016.

19 Peter Tinti and Adam Nossiter, "Militants Infiltrate Towns in Freed Areas of Mali, Raising Peril of Guerilla War," *New York Times*, February 17, 2013, A8.

20 Representative Luis Gutiérrez, "Rep. Gutiérrez' New Bill Expands Access to Obamacare to Undocumented Immigrants," September 30, 2015, https://gutierrez.house.gov/press-release/rep-guti%C3%A9rrez%E2%80%99-new-bill-expands-access-obamacare-undocumented-immigrants, accessed July 29, 2016.

21 GovTrack.us, "HR 3659: Exchange Inclusion for a Healthy America Act of 2015," https://www.govtrack.us/congress/bills/114/hr3659/details, accessed July 29, 2016.

22 Democratic National Convention, "Democratic Party Platform 2016, July 21, 2106" Gerhard Peters. "Political Party Platforms of Parties Receiving Electoral Votes." *The American Presidency Project*. Ed. John T. Woolley and Gerhard Peters. Santa Barbara, CA: University of California. 1999–2016, http://www.presidency.ucsb.edu/papers_pdf/117717.pdf, accessed August 1, 2016.

23 Republican National Convention, "Republican Platform 2016," Gerhard Peters. "Political Party Platforms of Parties Receiving Electoral Votes." *The American Presidency Project*. Ed. John T. Woolley and Gerhard Peters. Santa Barbara, CA: University of California. 1999–2016, http://www.presidency.ucsb.edu/papers_pdf/117718.pdf, accessed August 1, 2016.

24 For more on the formulation of the policy redressing victims of internment, see Leslie T. Hatamiya, *Righting a Wrong: Japanese Americans and the Passage of the Civil Liberties Act of 1988* (Palo Alto, CA: Stanford University Press, 1994).

25 Administrative Procedure Act, "Rule Making," Title 5, Part 1, Chapter 5, Subchapter II, Section 553, National Archives, http://www.archives.gov/federal-register/laws/administrative-procedure/553.html, accessed August 1, 2016.

26 Joint Center for Political and Economic Studies, "About," http://jointcenter.org/about/about, accessed August 1, 2016.

27 Joint Center for Political and Economic Studies, *Place Matters for Health in the Delta South: Ensuring Opportunities for Good Health for All: A Report on Heath Inequities in Delta South, Mississippi*, November 2012, http://jointcenter.org/docs/40944_SouthDelta[1].pdf, accessed August 1, 2016.

28 David M. O'Brien, *Storm Center: The Supreme Court in American Politics*, 10th ed. (New York: Norton, 2014), 230.

29 Steven V. Roberts, "Senate Votes Bill to Prod Pretoria," *New York Times*, August 16, 1986, 1.

30 *Regents of the University of California v. Bakke*, 438 U.S. 235 (1978); see also O'Brien, *Storm Center*, 298–300.

31 *Grutter v. Bollinger*, 539 U.S. 306 (2003).

32 Jonathan Weisman, "Immigration Bill Dies in Senate: Bipartisan Compromise Fails to Satisfy the Right or the Left," *Washington Post*, June 29, 2007, A1.

33 Alan Gomez, "White House Immigration Plan Offers Plan to Residency," *USA Today*, February 17, 2013, http://www.usatoday.com/story/news/nation/2013/02/16/obama-immigration-bill/1925017/, accessed August 1, 2016.

34 See Mark Stern, *Calculating Visions: Kennedy, Johnson, and Civil Rights* (New Brunswick, NJ: Rutgers University Press, 1992).

35 McClain and Stewart, *"Can We All Get along?"* 148.

36 John T. Woolley and Gerhard Peters, "Executive Orders, J. Q. Adams–Obama" *The American Presidency Project*. Ed. John T. Woolley and Gerhard Peters. Santa Barbara, CA: University of California. 1999–2016, http://www.presidency.ucsb.edu/executive_orders.php?year= 2012&Submit=DISPLAY, accessed October 2, 2016.

37 Jason Wermers, "Education Law Is Faulted: No Child Left Behind Is Called Underfunded, Straining Poorer Schools," *Richmond Times Dispatch*, March 23, 2004, B3.

38 The White House Office of the Press Secretary, "President Obama: Our Children Can't Wait for Congress to Fix No Child Left Behind, Announces Flexibility in Exchange for Reform in Ten States," February 9, 2012, https://www.whitehouse.gov/the-press-office/2012/02/09/president-obama-our-children-can-t-wait-congress-fix-no-child-left-behin, accessed August 1, 2016.

39 Department of State, "Remarks of Hillary Rodham Clinton The Global Health Initiative: The Next Phase of American Leadership in Health Around the World" August 16, 2010, http://www.state.gov/secretary/20092013clinton/rm/2010/08/146002.htm , accessed October 2, 2016; Sheryl Gay Stolberg, "In Global Battle on AIDS, Bush Creates Legacy," *New York Times*, January 5, 2008, A1.

40 Tinsley E. Yarbrough, "Bush and the Courts," in *The Bush Presidency: Triumphs and Adversities*, ed. Dilys M. Hill and Phil Williams (New York: St. Martin's Press, 1994), 97–98.

41 *Brown v. Board of Education of Topeka, KS*, 349 U.S. 294 (1955).

42 McClain and Stewart, *"Can We All Get along?"* 180–181.

43 *Worcester v. Georgia*, 6 Peters 515 (1832).

44 For more on Jackson's actions after this decision consult, Matthew L. Sundquist, *"Worcester v. Georgia*: A Breakdown in the Separation of Powers," *American Indian Law Review* 35 (2010–2011), 239–255.

45 Belinda Creel Davis and Valentina A. Bali, "Examining the Politics of Race, NIMBY, and Local Politics in FEMA Trailer Park Placement," *Social Science Quarterly* 89 (2008): 1175–1194.

46 David M. O'Brien, *Storm Center*, 323.

47 Joseph Kron and David Goodman, "Online, a Distant Conflict Soars to No. 1," *New York Times*, March 9, 2012, A1; Gabrielle Levy, "$5 Million Bounty Offered for Joseph Kony," *UPI.com*, April 3, 2013, http://www.upi.com/blog/2013/04/03/5-million-bounty-offered-for-Joesph-Kony/2981365016264/, accessed August 1, 2016.

48 Jonathan Weisman, "Welfare Rolls Reduced Sharply," *Baltimore Sun*, August 4, 1999, 1A.

49 Steve Schultze, "Minority W-2 Clients Faced More Penalties, Study Says," *Milwaukee Journal Sentinel*, March 29, 2003, 2B.

Credits

Photos

Front matter

p. xxv: Les Todd, Duke University Photography; p. xxv: University of South Florida

Chapter 1

p. 1: AP photo/Steve Ruark; p. 4: Copyright Bettmann/Corbis/AP Images; p. 6: AP Photo/Gerry Broome; p.13: Universal History Archive/Getty Images; p. 14: Copyright Bettmann/Corbis/AP Images; p. 14: Hulton Archive/Getty Images; p. 17: Library of Congress Prints and Photographs Division Washington, D.C. 20540 USA; p. 19: AP Photo/The Daily Progress, Dan Lopez; p. 21: Terra Foundation for American Art, Chicago/Art Re- source, NY; p. 23: North Wind Picture Archives via AP Images

Chapter 2

p. 27: Maryland Technology Enterprise Institute, A. James Clark School of Engineering, University of Maryland; p. 31: North Wind Picture Archives via AP Images; p. 32: Copyright Bettmann/Corbis/AP Images; p. 34: AP Photo; p. 42: North Wind Picture Archives via AP Images; p. 53: JEWEL SAMAD/AFP/Getty Images

Chapter 3

p. 57: AP Photo/Matt York p. 66: Mark Wilson/Getty Images; p. 70: Bill Clark/Roll Call/Getty Images; p. 71: Leigh Vogel/Getty Images for AOL; p. 71: Reuters Pictures; p. 71: Justin Sullivan/Getty Images; p. 81: © Louie Psihoyos/CORBIS; p. 83: Walter Sanders/Time Life Pictures/Getty Images; p. 83: Copyright Bettmann/Corbis/AP Images

Chapter 4

p. 99: Reuters Pictures; p. 105: Copyright Bettmann/Corbis/AP Images; p. 107: AP Photo/Tribune-Star, Michael A. Curlett, File; p. 109: Reuters Pictures/Mario Anzuoni; p. 114: Courtesy John Vachon Collection.; p. 117: © Tribune Media Services, Inc. All Rights Reserved. Reprinted with permission.; p. 117: LALO ALCARAZ ©2002 Dist. by UNIVERSAL UCLICK. Reprinted with permission. All rights reserved.; p. 119: AP Photo/Lou Krasky; p. 127: AP Photo/Manuel Balce Ceneta

Chapter 5

p. 131: Courtesy: © 2016 Fusion Media Network, LLC. Photo by Tim Rogers http://fusion.net/story/291636/supreme-court-dapa-decision/; p. 137: Russell Lee/Library of Congress/Getty Images; p. 138: North Wind Picture Archives via AP Images; p. 144: Don Cravens// Time Life Pictures/Getty Images; p. 146: AFP/Getty Images; p. 157: Andrew Renneisen/Getty Images; p. 159: Library of Congress Prints and Photographs Division Washington, D.C. 20540 USA.; p. 160: Copyright Bettmann/Corbis/AP Images; p. 160: 04-06-06 @ Timothy Swope. Copyright © 2013 iStockphoto LP.; p. 165: © Elaine Thompson/AP/Corbis

Chapter 6

p. 171: AP Photo/Cliff Owen, File; p. 175: WOSU Public Media; p. 176: Douglas Graham/CQ Roll Call; p. 182: Stephen Crowley/ The New York Times; p. 185: Alex Wong/Getty Images; p. 189: Image courtesy of ThinkProgress (http://thinkprogress.org). Used by permission.; p. 190: © The Curators of the University of Missouri, Jan 2015, St. Louis Public Radio, University of Missouri; p. 197: AP Photo/Jae C. Hong

Chapter 7

p. 205: Christopher Gregory/Getty Images; p. 222: AP Photo/Brennan Linsley; p. 225: Alex Wong/Getty Images; p. 226: AP Photo/Paul Sancya; p. 227: Copyright Bettmann/Corbis/AP Images; p. 230: AP Photo/J. Scott Applewhite; p. 232: PETE SOUZA/The New York Times; p. 236: JEWEL SAMAD/AFP/Getty Images

Chapter 8

p. 243: (Jake May/The Flint Journal-MLive.com via AP); p. 249: AP Photo/Eric Gay; p. 251: Photo credit Jim Abbott. Used by permission of Mary Frances Berry.; p. 254: The Granger Collection, New York; p. 256: Sari O'Neal/Shutterstock; p. 263: AP Photo/The Sun, Alfred J. Hernandez; p. 265: © Roger Ressmeyer/CORBIS

Chapter 9

p. 269: AP Photo/Charles Dharapak; p. 280: Library of Congress Prints and Photographs Division Washington, D.C. 20540 USA; p. 281: Reuters Pictures; 284: AP Photo/Susan Walsh; p. 288: AP Photo/Andres Leighton; p. 294: AP Photo

Chapter 10

p. 297: Shutterstock/Rena Schild; p. 301: AP Photo/Jim Bourdier; p. 301: Copyright Bettmann/Corbis/AP Images; p. 304: AP Photo/Alan Diaz; p. 307: AP Photo/Byron Rollins, file; p. 320: Pete Marovich/Getty Images

Chapter 11

p. 331: AP Photo/Susan Walsh; p. 336: Library of Congress Prints and Photographs Division Washington, D.C. 20540 USA; p. 338: AP Photo/Alan Diaz; p. 339: AP Photo/ Bill Hudson; p. 341: Dennis Whitehead/MMImedia; p. 342: Reuters Photos; p. 344: Twitter.com/Donald J. Trump; p. 345: AP Photo/Dave Martin; p. 356: Chris Graythen/Getty Images

Chapter 12

p. 359: Hank Walker/Time & Life Pictures/Getty Images; p. 364: Cathy Murphy/Getty Images; p. 366: REUTERS/Crockett County Sheriff's Department/Handout (UNITED STATES); p. 371: AP Photo/Bill Hudson; p. 373: Library of Congress Prints and Photographs Division Washington, D.C. 20540 USA; p. 374: Randall Studio – National Portrait Gallery, Smithsonian Institution; p. 376: AP Photo; p. 380: Copyright Bettmann/Corbis/AP Images; p. 386: Paul Connell/The Boston Globe via Getty Images; p. 388: Fred W. McDarrah/Getty Images; p. 391: Shutterstock/J. Bicking; p. 398: Win McNamee/Getty Images

Chapter 13

p. 405: AP Photo/Julio Cortez; p. 408: The Granger Collection, New York; p. 418: © Bettmann/CORBIS; p. 419: John Sommers II/ Getty Images; p. 420: AP Photo /Russell Contreras, File; p. 421:© Najlah Feanny/CORBIS SABA; p. 424: Shutterstock/txking

Chapter 14

p. 437: AP Photo/J. Scott Applewhite; p. 442: Library of Congress Prints and Photographs Division Washington, D.C. 20540 USA; p. 446: MPI/Getty Images; p. 450: Buyenlarge/Getty Images; p. 451: AP Photo/Carolyn Kaster; p. 455: Photo by Jerry Baker; p. 457: AP Photo/Pablo Martinez Monsivais

Chapter 15

p. 465: Olivier Douliery/Sipa USA via AP; p. 469: AP Photo/Mark J. Terrill; p. 478: Alex Wong/Getty Images; p. 479: AP Photo/Andrew Harnik; p. 479: Photo by Paul Morigi/WireImage/Getty Images; p. 483: AP Photo/Marta Lavandier; p. 485:Ty Wright/Bloomberg via Getty Images; 492: Joshua Lott/Stringer; p. 494:Rick Tyler for Congress; p. 517: AP Photo

Chapter 16

p. 519: Andy Cross/*The Denver Post* via Getty Images; p. 524: European PressPhoto Agency; p. 526: REUTERS/Suhaib Salem; p. 528: AP Photo/Nasser Nasser; p. 533: Alex Wong/Getty Images; p. 534: AP Photo/Ed Andrieski

Figures

Chapter 1

p. 22: U.S. Census, 1790

Chapter 3

p. 60: U.S. Census Bureau, 2010 Census Redistricting Data (Public Law 94-171) Summary File, Table P1.; p. 61: U.S. Census Bureau, 2010 Census Summary File 1.; p. 61: U.S. Census Bureau, 2010 Census Redistricting Data (Public Law 94-171) Summary File, Table P1.; p. 62: U.S. Census Bureau, 2010 Census Redistricting Data (Public Law 94-171) Summary File, Table P1.; p. 64: Data adapted from National Conference of State Legislatures, "Number of African American Legislators 2009," http://www.ncsl.org/legislatures-elections/legisdata/african-american-legislators-1992-to-2009.aspx and "2009 Latino Legislators," http://www.ncsl.org/legislatures-elections/legisdata/latino-legislators-overview.aspx; United States Census Bureau, "State and County QuickFacts," http:// quickfacts.census .gov/qfd/index.html, websites accessed December 22, 2012

Chapter 4

p. 125: Adapted from Deborah Fins, Criminal Justice Project of the NAA CP Legal Defense Fund, Death Row, USA: Winter 2016, 36–37, http://www.naacpldf.org/files/publications/DRUSA _Winter_2016.pdf, accessed April 30, 2016; U.S. Census Bureau, "State and County Quick Facts," https://www.census.gov/quickfacts/table/PST 045215/00, accessed April 30, 2016.; p. 128: Data adapted from the Pew Forum on Religion and Public Life, Public Opinion on Abortion: Views on Abortion, 1995–2016, April 8, 2016, http://www.pewforum.org/2016/04/08/public-opinion-on-abortion-2/, accessed May 1, 2016

Chapter 5

p. 147: Data compiled from Charles S. Bullock III and Ronald Keith Gaddie, The Triumph of Voting Rights in the South (Norman, OK: University of Oklahoma Press, 2009), pp. 42, 68, 92, 124, 148, 176, 204, 238, 266, 294, 313.; p. 148–149: Data adapted from Gary Orfield, John Kucsera, and Genevieve Sigel-Hawley, E Pluribus. . . Separation: Deepening Double Segregation for More Students (Los Angeles: The UCLA Civil Rights Project, September 2012), Table 11, p. 34; p. 156: Data adapted from Andrew Kohut, p. 164: Adapted from United States Census, "Historical Income Tables: People: Table P-2. Race and Hispanic Origin by Median income and Sex, 1947–2014: All Races," https://www.census.gov/hhes/www/income/data/historical/people/, accessed May 27, 2016. p. 166: Adapted from Gallup, "In Depth: Topics A to Z: Marriage," http://www.gallup.com/poll/117328/marriage.aspx, accessed May 28, 2016

Chapter 6

p. 179: Adapted from Table 5-2 Members of Congress: Female, Black, Hispanic, Marital Status, and Age, 1971–2011. In Vital Statistics on American Politics 2011–2012, edited by Harold W. Stanley, and Richard G. Niemi, 193–194. Washington, DC: CQ Press, 2011. http://library.cqpress.com/ vsap/vsap11_tab5-2, accessed January 26, 2013. Information for 2013–2015 updated by authors.; p. 194: Adapted from Lexis/Nexis, "How a Bill Becomes Law," http://www.lexisnexis.com/help/cu/The_Legislative_Process/How_a_Bill_Becomes_ Law.htm, accessed June 11, 2009.; pp. 198–199: Data adapted from National Hispanic Leadership Agenda, Congressional Scorecard, First and Second Session, 113th Congress. August 2014, pp. 4–5 https://nationalhispanicleadership.org/images/Scorecards/NHLA_2014scorecard_090915_forweb_2.pdf, accessed June 12, 2016

Chapter 7

pp. 213–214: Vote result data from John Woolley and Gerhard Peters, "Election of 2012," The American Presidency Project, http://www.presidency.ucsb.edu/showelection.php?year=2012, accessed January 18, 2013. Population data from U.S. Census, "State and County Quick Facts," http://quickfacts.census.gov/qfd/index.html, accessed January 18, 2013.; pp. 215–216: CNN , "Presidential Results," http://www.cnn.com/election/results/president and United States Census Bureau, "Quick Facts, https://www.census.gov/quickfacts/table/SE X255215/00, both accessed November 13, 2016; p. 217: Adapted from Center for Responsive Politics,

"SuperPACs,"OpenSecrets. http://www.opensecrets.org/pacs/superpacs.php?cycle=2012, accessed May 9, 2014.; p. 220: Adapted from Gerhard Peters and John T. Woolley, "Executive Orders," The American Presidency Project. Ed. John T. Woolley and Gerhard Peters. Santa Barbara, CA. 1999–2016. Available from the World Wide Web: http://www.presidency.ucsb.edu/data/orders.php., accessed June 27, 2016; p. 238: Clinton and Obama data adapted from, Frank Newport, "Blacks and Whites Continue to Differ Sharply on Obama," Gallup Politics, http://www.gallup.com/poll/141725/Blacks-Whites-Continue-Differ-Sharply-Obama.aspx, accessed September 30, 2012. Bush data adapted from Frank Newport, "Bush Job Approval Rating: Little Difference Among Whites, Hispanics; Blacks Very Low in Job Approval," Gallup Politics, http://www.gallup.com/poll/28009/Bush-Job-Approval- Rating-Little-Difference-Among-Whites-Hispanics.aspx, accessed September 30, 2012

Chapter 8

p. 259: Bureaucracy statistics are adapted from Office of Personnel Management, Annual Report to the Congress: Federal Equal Opportunity Recruitment Program, Fiscal Year 2010, 15, 25, 35, 45, http://www.opm.gov/About_OPM/ Reports/FEORP/2010/feorp2010.pdf, accessed February 13, 2012. GS salary data are from "Salary Table 2010-GS," http:// www.opm.gov/oca/10tables/pdf/gs.pdf; and from "Salary Table No. 2010-EX," http://www.opm.gov/oca/10tables/pdf/ ex.pdf, both accessed February 13, 2012. Population data are from U.S. Census, "Quick Facts: USA 2010," http://quickfacts.census.gov/qfd/states/00000.html, accessed February 14, 2012

Chapter 9

p. 287: Data adapted from Sheldon Goldman, Elliot Slotnick, and Sara Schiavoni, "Writing the Book of Judges: Part 1 Obama's Judicial Appointment Record After Six Years," Journal of Law and Courts, vol. 3 (2015): 331–367: 356, 364; Jennifer Segal Diascro and Rorie Spill Solberg, "George W. Bush's Legacy on the Federal Bench: Policy in the Face of Diversity," Judicature 92, 6 (2009): 294–295

Chapter 10

p. 314: Source: Gallup Poll, June 15-July 10, 2015. All rights reserved. The content is used with permission; however, Gallup retains all rights of republication.; p. 320:"Obama and Cruz: Born in the U.S.?" Public Policy Polling, Aug. 28–30; p. 326: Pew Research Center, January 12–27,

2016. http://www.journalism.org/2016/02/04/the-2016-presidential-campaign-a-news-event-thats-hard-to-miss/

Chapter 11

pp. 348–349: Data adapted from Bob Papper, "DRTNA Research: Women and Minorities in Newsrooms," Radio-Television News Directors Association, July 11, 2016, http://www.rtdna.org/article/rtdna_research_women_and_minorities_in_newsrooms, accessed July 20, 2016; United States Census Bureau, "Table 1: Population by Hispanic or Latino Origin and by Race for the United States," Overview of Race and Hispanic Origin: 2000, https://www.census.gov/prod/2001pubs/c2kbr01-1.pdf, Accessed July 20, 2016; United States Census, "Quick Facts: United States," https://www.census.gov/quickfacts/table/PST045215/00, accessed July 20, 2016; p. 350: American Society for Newspaper Editors, "Table A: Minority Employment in Daily Newspapers," Newsroom Diversity Survey: 2015 Census, July 28, 2015, http://asne.org/content.asp?pl=140&sl=129&contentid=129, accessed July 19, 2016

Chapter 12

p. 382: "Union Membership" Bureau of Labor Statistics 1983–2012." Update based on: Bureau of Labor Statistics - "40. Union affiliation of employed wage and salary workers by selected characteristics"; http://www.bls.gov/cps/cpsaat40.pdf.; p. 382: "Median Weekly Wage, Bureau of Labor Statistics 1983–2012." Update based on: Bureau of Labor Statistics – "41. Median weekly earnings of full-time wage and salary workers by union affiliation and selected characteristics," http://www.bls.gov/cps/cpsaat41.pdf/

Chapter 14

p. 451: Data Adapted from David A. Bositis, "Table 8: Black Delegates at the Republican National Conventions,

1912–2012," in Blacks & the 2012 Republican National Convention (Washington, DC: Joint Center for Political and Economic Studies 2012), 17, accessed online at http://www.jointcenter.org/sites/default/files/upload/research/files/Blacks%20and%20the%202012%20Republican%20National%20Convention.pdf; David A. Bositis, "Black Delegates at the Democratic National Conventions, 1932–2012," in Blacks & the 2012 Democratic National Convention (Washington, DC: Joint Center for Political & Economic Studies, 2012), 13, accessed online at http://www.jointcenter.org/sites/default/files/upload/research/files/Blacks%20and%20the%202012%20Democratic%20National%20Convention.pdf, both sites accessed February 9, 2013.; p. 462: Data adapted from Robert Suro et al., Changing Faiths: Latinos and the Transformation of American Religion (Washington, DC: PEW Research Center, 2007), 82–83, http://pewforum.org/newassets/surveys/hispanic/hispanics-religion-07-final-mar08.pdf, accessed June 27, 2009, and October 14, 2009

Chapter 15

p. 497: McDonald, Michael P. 2012. "Total Ballots Cast as a Percent of the Voting Eligible Population" United States Elections Project

Chapter 16

pp. 539–540: Data adapted from Heather C. West, William J. Sobol, and Sarah J. Greenman, "Appendix Table 16a, Estimated Number of Sentenced Prisoners Under State Jurisdic- tion by Offense, Sex, Race, Hispanic Origin Year End 2006," Prisoners 2009 (Washington, DC: Bureau of Justice Statistics, 2010), 29, http:// www.bjs.gov/content/pub/pdf/p09.pdf, accessed March 9, 2012

Index

Note: Page numbers followed by *t* indicate a table. Italicized page numbers indicate a figure

*This book is dedicated
to my dear friend, colleague, and
one of Lightroom's guiding lights,
Winston Hendrickson.
You taught us so much, about so much.
We will miss you, always.
1962–2018*

ACKNOWLEDGMENTS

I start the acknowledgments for every book I've ever written the same way—by thanking my amazing wife, Kalebra. If you knew what an incredible woman she is, you'd totally understand why.

This is going to sound silly, but if we go grocery shopping together, and she sends me off to a different aisle to get milk, when I return with the milk and she sees me coming back down the aisle, she gives me the warmest, most wonderful smile. It's not because she's happy that I found the milk; I get that same smile every time I see her, even if we've only been apart for 60 seconds. It's a smile that says, "There's the man I love."

If you got that smile, dozens of times a day, for 29 years of marriage (in September of this year), you'd feel like the luckiest guy in the world, and believe me—I do. To this day, just seeing her puts a song in my heart and makes it skip a beat. When you go through life like this, it makes you one incredibly happy and grateful guy, and I truly am.

So, thank you, my love. Thanks for your kindness, your hugs, your understanding, your advice, your patience, your generosity, and for being such a caring and compassionate mother and wife. I love you.

Secondly, a big thanks to my son, Jordan. I wrote my first book when my wife was pregnant with him (21+ years ago), and he has literally grown up around my writing, so you can imagine how incredibly proud I was when he completed his first book (a 243 page fantasy novel) last year. It has been a blast watching him grow up into such a wonderful young man, with his mother's tender and loving heart, and compassion way beyond his years. As he heads into his senior year of college, he knows that his dad just could not be prouder, or more excited for him. Throughout his life he has touched so many people, in so many different ways, and even though he's still a young man, he's already inspired so many people, and I just cannot wait to see the amazing adventure, and the love and laughter this life has in store for him. Hey, little buddy—this world needs more "yous!"

Thanks to our wonderful daughter, Kira, for being the answer to our prayers, for being such a blessing to your older brother, for being such a strong little girl, and for proving once again that miracles happen every day. You are a little clone of your mother, and believe me, there is no greater compliment I could give you. It is such a blessing to get to see such a happy, hilarious, clever, creative, and just awesome little force of nature running around the house each day—she just has no idea how happy and proud she makes us. She's what happens when a magical unicorn, a leprechaun, and a fairy princess cosmically collide, and the result gets covered in chocolate sprinkles and cherries. It doesn't get much better than that.

A special thanks to my big brother, Jeff. I have so much to be thankful for in my life, and having you as such a positive role model while I was growing up is one thing I'm particularly thankful for. You're the best brother any guy could ever have, and I've said it a million times before, but one more surely wouldn't hurt—I love you, man!

My heartfelt thanks go to my entire team at KelbyOne. I know everybody thinks their team is really special, but this one time—I'm right. I'm so proud to get to work with you all, and I'm still amazed at what you're able to accomplish day in, day out, and I'm constantly impressed with how much passion and pride you put into everything you do.

A warm word of thanks goes to my in-house Editor, Kim Doty. It's her amazing attitude, passion, poise, and attention to detail that has kept me writing books. When you're writing a book like this, sometimes you can really feel like you're all alone, but she really makes me feel that I'm not alone—that we're a team. It often is her encouraging words or helpful ideas that keep me going when I've hit a wall, and I just can't thank her enough. Kim, you are "the best!"

I'm equally as lucky to have the brilliant Jessica Maldonado doing the design of my books. I just love the way Jessica designs, and all the clever little things she adds throughout. She's not just incredibly talented and a joy to work with, she's a very smart designer and thinks five steps ahead in every layout she builds. We hit the jackpot when we found you!

http://kelbyone.com

Also, a big thanks to our copy editor, Cindy Snyder, whom I feel very blessed to have still working with us on these books. Thank you, Cindy!

Thanks to my friend and business partner, Jean A. Kendra, for her support and friendship all these years. You mean a lot to me, to Kalebra, and to our company.

A big thanks to my dear friend, rocket photographer, professor of Tesla studies, unofficial but still official Disney Cruise guide, landscape photography sojourner, and Amazon Prime aficionado, Mr. Erik Kuna. You are one of the reasons I love coming to work each day. You're always uncovering cool things, thinking outside-the-box, and making sure we always do the right thing for the right reasons. Thanks for your friendship, all your hard work, and your invaluable advice.

Thanks to Jeanne Jilleba, my Executive Assistant, for constantly putting my wheels back on the track. I know even finding where I'm at in the building is a challenge, but you just seem to take it all in stride. I'm very grateful to have your help, talent, and immeasurable patience every day.

Thanks to Kleber Stephenson for making sure all sorts of awesome things happen, doors open, and opportunities appear. I particularly enjoy our business trips together where we laugh too much, eat way too much, and have more fun on a business trip than was previously scheduled.

High-five to the crew at Peachpit Press, and to my editor, Laura Norman, for taking over the helm and guiding my books safely to their birth.

Thanks to Rob Sylvan, Serge Ramelli, Matt Kloskowski, Terry White, and all the friends and educators who have helped and supported me on my Lightroom education journey. Thanks to Manny Steigman for always believing in me, and for his support and friendship all these years. Thanks to Gabe, Rebecca, Steve, Joseph, and all the wonderful folks at B&H Photo. It is the greatest camera store in the world, but it's so much more.

Thanks to these friends who had nothing to do with this book, but so much to do with my life, and I just want to give them the literary version of a hug: Jeff Revell, Ted Waitt, Don Page, Juan Alfonso, Moose Peterson, Brandon Heiss, Eric Eggly, Larry Grace, Rob Foldy, Merideth Duffin, Dave Clayton, Victoria Pavlov, Dave Williams, Larry Becker, Peter Treadway, Roberto Pisconti, Fernando Santos, Mike McCaskey, Marvin Derizen, Mike Kubeisy, Maxx Hammond, Michael Benford, Brad Moore, Nancy Davis, Mike Larson, Joe McNally, Annie Cahill, Rick Sammon, Mimo Meidany, Tayloe Harding, Dave Black, John Couch, Greg Rostami, Matt Lange, Barb Cochran, Jack Reznicki, Frank Doorhof, Karl-Franz, Peter Hurley, Kathy Porupski, and Vanelli .

I owe a debt of thanks to some awesome people at Adobe: Jeff Tranberry, who I nominate as the world's most responsive superhero. Lightroom Product Manager, Sharad Mangalick, for all his help, insights, and advice. Tom Hogarty for answering lots of questions and late-night emails, and for always helping me to see the bigger picture. You guys are the best!

Thanks to my friends at Adobe Systems: Bryan Hughes, Terry White, Stephen Nielson, Bryan Lamkin, Julieanne Kost, and Russell Preston Brown. Gone but not forgotten: Barbara Rice, Rye Livingston, Jim Heiser, John Loiacono, Kevin Connor, Deb Whitman, Addy Roff, Cari Gushiken, Karen Gauthier, and Winston Hendrickson, to whom this book is dedicated.

Thanks to my mentors, whose wisdom and whip-cracking have helped me immeasurably, including John Graden, Jack Lee, Dave Gales, Judy Farmer, and Douglas Poole.

Most importantly, I want to thank God, and His Son Jesus Christ, for leading me to the woman of my dreams, for blessing us with two amazing children, for allowing me to make a living doing something I truly love, for always being there when I need Him, for blessing me with a wonderful, fulfilling, and happy life, and such a warm, loving family to share it with.

OTHER BOOKS BY SCOTT KELBY

Photoshop for Lightroom Users

Professional Portrait Retouching Techniques for Photographers Using Photoshop

The Digital Photography Book, parts 1, 2, 3, 4 & 5

Light It, Shoot It, Retouch It: Learn Step by Step How to Go from Empty Studio to Finished Image

The Adobe Photoshop CC Book for Digital Photographers

The Photoshop Elements Book for Digital Photographers

The iPhone Book

Professional Sports Photography Workflow

Photo Recipes Live: Behind the Scenes: Your Guide to Today's Most Popular Lighting Techniques, parts 1 & 2

It's a Jesus Thing: The Book for Wanna Be-lievers

ABOUT THE AUTHOR

Scott Kelby

Scott is Editor and Publisher of *Lightroom Magazine*; producer of LightroomKillerTips.com, Editor and co-founder of *Photoshop User* magazine; host of *The Grid*, the influential, live, weekly talk show for photographers; and is founder of the annual Scott Kelby's Worldwide Photo Walk.™

He is President and CEO of KelbyOne, an online educational community for learning Lightroom, Photoshop, and photography.

Scott is a photographer, designer, and award-winning author of more than 90 books, including *Light It, Shoot It, Retouch It: Learn Step by Step How to Go from Empty Studio to Finished Image*; *The Adobe Photoshop Book for Digital Photographers*; *Professional Portrait Retouching Techniques for Photographers Using Photoshop*; *How Do I Do That In Lightroom?*; and *The Digital Photography Book* series. The first book in this series, *The Digital Photography Book*, part 1, has become the top-selling book on digital photography in history.

For six years in a row, Scott has been honored with the distinction of being the world's #1 best-selling author of photography techniques books. His books have been translated into dozens of different languages, including Chinese, Russian, Spanish, Korean, Polish, Taiwanese, French, German, Italian, Japanese, Hebrew, Dutch, Swedish, Turkish, and Portuguese, among many others. He is recipient of the prestigious ASP International Award, presented annually by the American Society of Photographers for "…contributions in a special or significant way to the ideals of Professional Photography as an art and a science," and the HIPA Special Award presented for his worldwide contributions to photography education.

Scott is Conference Technical Chair for the annual Photoshop World Conference and a frequent speaker at conferences and trade shows around the world. He is featured in a series of online learning courses at KelbyOne.com and has been training Photoshop users and photographers since 1993.

For more information on Scott, visit him at:

His daily Lightroom blog: **lightroomkillertips.com**

His personal blog: **scottkelby.com**

Twitter: **@scottkelby**

Facebook: **facebook.com/skelby**

Instagram: **@scottkelby**

Google+: **+ScottKelby**

TABLE OF CONTENTS

http://kelbyone.com

CHAPTER 4   **109**

▼ CUSTOMIZING
HOW TO SET THINGS UP YOUR WAY

CHAPTER 5   **127**

▼ EDITING YOUR IMAGES
HOW TO TWEAK YOUR IMAGES LIKE A PRO!

CHAPTER 6   **163**

▼ PAINTING WITH LIGHT
THE ADJUSTMENT BRUSH & OTHER TOOLBOX TOOLS

CHAPTER 7   **189**

▼ SPECIAL EFFECTS
MAKING STUFF LOOK...WELL...SPECIAL!

TABLE OF CONTENTS

CHAPTER 8   231
▼ PROBLEM PHOTOS
DEALING WITH COMMON IMAGE PROBLEMS

CHAPTER 9   271
▼ EXPORTING IMAGES
SAVING JPEGS, TIFFS, AND MORE

CHAPTER 10   295
▼ LR WITH PHOTOSHOP
HOW AND WHEN TO USE PHOTOSHOP

CHAPTER 11   313
▼ PHOTO BOOKS
CREATING BEAUTIFUL BOOKS WITH YOUR IMAGES

http://kelbyone.com

Seven (or So) Things You'll Wish You Had Known Before Reading This Book

I really want to make sure you get the absolute most out of reading this book, and if you take two minutes and read these seven (or so) things now, I promise it will make a big difference in your success with Lightroom Classic, and with this book, in general (plus, it will keep you from sending me an email asking something that everyone who skips this part will wind up doing). By the way, the captures shown here are just so there's not big, blank spaces—they're essentially for looks (hey, we're photographers—how things look, matters).

(1) This book is for Lightroom Classic users (the version of Lightroom that has been around for 11 years now— the one we all know and love). If your Lightroom looks like the one you see here, you're in the right place. If your Lightroom doesn't look like this (you don't see Library, Develop, Map, etc., across the top like you see here), you're using a different version of Lightroom that is based on storing your images in the cloud, and its name is Lightroom CC. While we do take a quick look at it toward the end of the book, this book does not cover this cloud-storage version. You are still welcome to stay and look at the pictures, though.

(2) You can download many of the key photos used here in the book, so you can follow along using many of the same images that I used, at **http://kelbyone .com/books/lrclassic7**. See, this is one of those things I was talking about that you'd miss if you skipped over this and jumped right to Chapter 1. Then you'd send me an angry email about how I didn't tell you where to download the photos. You wouldn't be the first.

(3) If you've read my other books, you know they're usually "jump in anywhere" books, but with Lightroom, I wrote the book in the order you'll probably wind up using the program, so if you're new to Lightroom, I would really recommend you start with Chapter 1 and go through the book in order. But hey—it's your book—if you decide to just hollow out the insides and store your valuables in there, I'll never know. Also, make sure you read the opening to each project, up at the top of the page. Those actually have information you'll want to know, so don't skip over them.

(4) The official name of the software is "Adobe Photoshop Lightroom Classic CC" because it's part of the Photoshop family, and part of Adobe's Creative Cloud offering, but if every time I referred to it throughout the book, I called it "Adobe Photoshop Lightroom Classic CC," you would eventually want to strangle me (or the person sitting nearest you). So, from here on out, I usually just refer to it as "Lightroom" or "Lightroom Classic."

(5) Warning: The intro page at the beginning of each chapter is designed to give you a quick mental break, and honestly, they have little to do with the chapter. In fact, they have little to do with anything, but writing these quirky chapter intros is kind of a tradition of mine (I do this in all my books, and I even released a book of just the best chapter intros from all of my books. I am not making this up). But, if you're one of those really "serious" types, you can skip them, because they'll just get on your nerves. The rest of the book is normal, but that one single page, at the beginning of each chapter, well…it's not normal. Just so ya know.

Continued

(6) At the end of the book is a special bonus chapter, where I share my own start-to-finish workflow. However, don't read it until you've read the entire book first, or you might not know how to do certain things that I'll be telling you to do (that's why I put it at the end of the book).

(7) Where are the chapters on the Web module and the Slideshow module? They're on the web (you'll find them at the address in #7.2). I put them there because Adobe has…well…I think they've kind of abandoned them (not officially mind you, but come on—they haven't really added any new features in the past four versions, so I can't [with a straight face] recommend that you use them at all). Though, I do have one really good use for the Slideshow module, and I put that in the Video chapter. But, just in case, I still posted those chapters on the web, so just think of them as bonus chapters you won't ever read for features you won't ever use.

(7.1) Who's up for some cool, free Lightroom presets? I think you've earned 'em (well, at least you will have by the time you finish this book). Now, if you're a brand-new user and you're not sure what presets are yet, they are basically "one-click wonders" that make your photos look awesome. There's a huge market for presets and people sell presets like these all day long (for bunches of money). But, because I dig you with the passion of a thousand burning suns (or because you bought this book—I'll let you decide which reason fits you best), I'm giving you a whole bunch of them we created here in-house. Anyway, the link to them, and samples of how they look, are found on the downloads page (mentioned below in #7.2). See, I care.

(7.2) I created a couple bonus videos for you. One shows you how to get started by moving all your images onto an external hard drive (which you'll learn about in Chapter 1), and the other shows you how to create a custom border in Photoshop that you can add to your prints (you'll learn how to do this in Chapter 12). You can find these at **http://kelbyone.com/books/lrclassic7**. Okay, now turn the page and let's get to work.

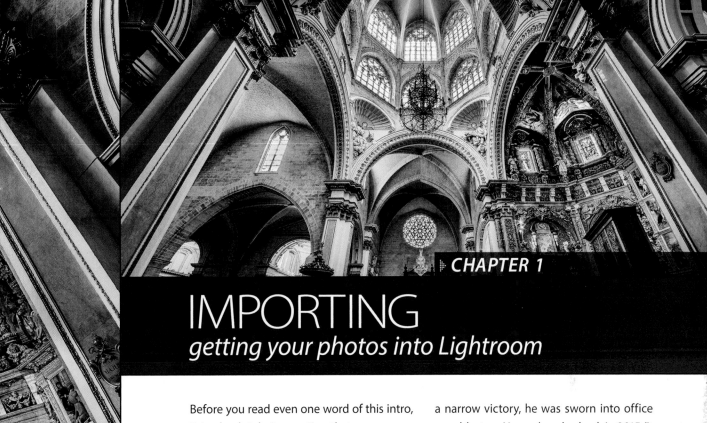

CHAPTER 1

IMPORTING
getting your photos into Lightroom

Before you read even one word of this intro, it is absolutely imperative that you pause for a moment (hit the pause button; it's the one with two vertical lines on it), go back to page xiii, and carefully re-read #5 in "Seven (or So) Things You'll Wish You Had Known Before Reading This Book." The reason this is so important (it's a sad story, really) is that in the previous edition of this book, there was a reader who just kind of skimmed that section (I believe he was from Canterbury, England, quite near the birthplace of Austin D. Powers), so he had no warning for what he was getting into with my chapter intros. Anyway, he assumed the rest of the book was like this, and…well, quite frankly, it drove him mad. Mad, I tell you! He would dress each day in nothing but aluminum foil and he began selling goldfish sandwiches on the street. At some point, it was clear to everyone around him that he would have no choice but to run for political office. After

a narrow victory, he was sworn into office on a blustery November day back in 2015 (it was a Tuesday, if I remember correctly). He stood nobly on the steps of the courthouse, wind rippling through his foil gown, and he swore an oath to bear true allegiance to Her Majesty Queen Histogram, Her Heirs and Successors, according to law. He pledged to import his images into Lightroom in such a manner as to bring great honor and prestige to the sovereign base areas of Loupe View and the Keyword Islands. However, after being in office for just five months, a press conference was hastily called after rumors surfaced of missing image warnings and a corrupt catalog. When asked by *The Guardian* Senior Political Editor Simon Jollybotum if the rumors were true, he looked Simon dead in the eye and said, "Hashtag Fakenews, Hashtag Sad," and shouted at Simon to get off his lawn. You can't make this stuff up, kids.

First: Move All Your Photos onto One External Hard Drive

Before you dive into Lightroom, in fact, before you even launch it, to have a happy Lightroom life, start by setting up an external hard drive to hold all your photos (don't use the one in your computer—it will be full before you know it). This step is more important than it sounds, and it will save you loads of frustration down the road (and that road always gets here sooner than you'd think). The good news is, external hard drives have never been cheaper than they are today (I recently saw a 4-terabyte WD external hard drive for just $88, which is just incredible for that much storage).

Make That Move:

Okay, now that you've got your external hard drive connected to your computer, you are going to *move all* your photos onto that one, single, external hard drive. All of them. So, gather all your photos—from old CDs and DVDs, and other older portable drives—and put them all on this one external hard drive. Also, make sure you move them (don't just copy them—move them) from your computer onto your external hard drive (once you've verified that they're on your external hard drive, you can delete the copies still on your computer—you only want to be working with the images on that external hard drive). Getting these all together in one place takes a little doing (I made a short video that will help if you're stuck on how to do this—it's on the book's companion webpage; see page xv for the link). Besides the sheer peace-of-mind of finally having all your images in one, single, easy-to-back-up place, the good news is people have told me time and time again that doing this turned out to be much easier and faster than they thought it would be. TIP: When you buy your external hard drive, buy one that's way larger than you think you'll need (at least 4 terabytes minimum). Anyway, whichever external storage unit you choose, it will fill up faster than you ever imagined, thanks to today's crazy-high-megapixel cameras that have become standard (and they're only getting larger going forward). But, for now, go gather all your portable hard drives, CDs, and DVDs, and let's bring them all together onto this one external hard drive.

That question mark on a folder in Lightroom's Folders panel just means that when you moved your folders of photos off your computer and onto that external hard drive, Lightroom doesn't know where they are anymore. No biggie—you just have to tell Lightroom where you moved 'em, and it will relink the photos automatically. If you're an advanced Lightroom user, and you're switching to this organization system I'm teaching here in the book, you might be able to get around this whole question mark thing altogether (read on for how to get around it).

What to Do When You See a Question Mark on Your Photos Folder

How to Tell Lightroom Where You Moved Your Folders:

After you've moved your images from your computer over onto that external hard drive, if you look over in the Library module's Folders panel, you'll see a bunch of grayed-out folders with question marks on them. That just means that Lightroom no longer knows where those original images are. The fix? Just tell Lightroom where you moved 'em—Right-click on any folder with a question mark, and from the pop-up menu, choose **Find Missing Folder** (as shown here). This brings up the standard Open dialog, so just navigate your way to your external hard drive, find the missing folder, and click the Choose button. That's it—Lightroom knows where they are now and it's business as usual.

Advanced Lightroom Users:

If you're really comfortable working in the Folders panel, instead of dragging the folders from your computer onto your external hard drive, go ahead and do it from right within the Folders panel itself. When you make the move within this panel, since you're moving them using Lightroom, it knows where you moved them, and you don't have to do any relinking. *Note:* If you plug in a new, empty, external hard drive, Lightroom won't recognize it (the drive won't appear in the Folders panel), so click the + (plus sign) button on the right side of the Folders panel header, navigate to the new external hard drive, and make a new empty folder on the drive. Now that drive will appear in the Folders panel and you can drag-and-drop your folders directly onto that external drive.

You Need a Second Backup Hard Drive

It's good that external hard drives are so cheap, because you're going to need *two* of them. Why two? Because all hard drives eventually crash and die (sometimes on their own, or we knock them over, or lightning strikes, or the dog pulls it off your desk by accident). It's not just hard drives that die—every media storage unit goes bad at some point (CDs, DVDs, portable drives, optical drives, you name it), and you're going to need a backup when yours goes to the place where hard drives go to die (the most prevalent theory is that they go to Cleveland, since that's where promising quarterbacks go to die. Sorry, somebody had to say it).

It Has to Be a Totally Separate Drive:

Your backup has to be a totally independent external hard drive from your main external hard drive—not just a partition or another folder on the same external hard drive. I talk to photographers who use partitions not realizing that, when your hard drive dies, both your main folder of photos and your backup folder on the partition will both die at the same time. The result is the same—all your images are probably lost forever.

Where to Keep Your External Hard Drives:

Not only do you need two separate drives, but, ideally, they would be kept in *two* separate locations. For example, I keep one at home and the other at the office, and about once a month I bring the one from home to the office and sync 'em up, so they have all the stuff I've added in the past month. By keeping them in two separate places, if a fire strikes or there's a break-in, or a flood, or a tornado, I still have a backup drive at a different location. Also, this is the reason why you can't use your computer as a backup (what if it dies in a flood or fire or is stolen?), and you cannot put your backup drive right there on your desk next to your main external hard drive (for the same reasons).

©ADOBESTOCK/DRUMCHEG

Oh, come on, this is overkill!!! Really, three backups? Yup. You've gotta have a cloud backup—ask anybody that experienced the epic floods in Houston or Hurricane Katrina or any of the myriad of natural disasters these past few years where people lost all their photos. We're talking about the visual history of your life here—irreplaceable photos, along with client images, and family photos, and stuff you just can't put a price on. This third leg of protection has never been more important. You don't have to do it, but you'll sure sleep better if you do.

And You Need a Cloud Backup, Too

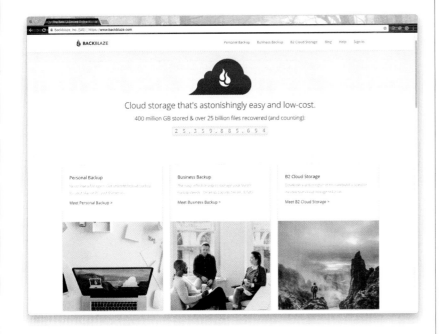

Why You Should Add a Cloud Backup, Too:

If a natural disaster (hurricane, major flood, etc.) hits your area, you could lose both your photo drives, even though they're in different locations. That's why I recommend having a cloud-based backup, as well (ask folks who have survived major hurricanes, but still lost everything). I use Backblaze.com as my cloud backup for one simple reason: it's only $5 per month for (get this) unlimited storage! It works in the background and automatically backs up your external hard drive to the cloud.

Don't Look at the Upload Progress:

The thing about Backblaze (or any cloud-based backup) is that you have to copy your entire photo library up to the cloud—terabytes of images, most likely—and that takes time. How much time? I'd say, for most folks, a month at the quickest, but probably six weeks to two months for serious photographers, and perhaps longer for working pros. The upload speed for most Internet connections is a fraction of the download speed, so I recommend that you don't even look at the upload progress for at least a month, or you'll be like "It's only 6%! Arg#%$&!" Save yourself the aggravation—tell it to back up your external hard drive, and then just go about your life. In six weeks from now, you can have your photo library fully backed up in the cloud…or not—the time is going to pass either way.

Get Your Photos Organized FIRST, Before You Launch Lightroom

I talk to photographers almost every day who are somewhat or totally confused about where their photos are located. They're frustrated and feel disorganized and all that has nothing to do with Lightroom. However, if you get organized first (I'm about to share a really simple way to do this), before you start using Lightroom, it will make your Lightroom life sooooooo much easier. Plus, not only will you know exactly where your photos are, you'll be able to tell someone else their exact location, even when you're not in front of your computer.

Step One:

Go to your external hard drive (see page 2) and, on that drive, create a single new folder. This is your main photo library folder and creating this one folder, and putting all your images (old ones you've taken in years past and new ones you're about to take) inside this one folder is the key to staying fully organized before you ever even get to the Lightroom part of this. By the way, I name this one all-important folder "Lightroom Photos," but you can name yours anything you like. Whatever you name it, just know this is the new home for your entire photographic library. Also know that when you need to back up your entire library, you only have to back up this one folder. Pretty sweet already, right?

Step Two:

Inside that folder, you're going to create more folders and name them with topics of things you shoot. For example, I have nine separate folders: Architecture, Automotive, Aviation, Family, Landscapes, Misc, People, Sports, and Travel—all separate folders within my Lightroom Photos folder. Now, since I shoot a lot of different sports, inside my Sports folder, I have created separate folders for football, baseball, motorsports, basketball, hockey, and other sports. You don't have to do that last part; I just do it because, again, I shoot a lot of different sports and that makes it easier to find stuff when I'm not in Lightroom.

Step Three:

Now, you probably have lots of folders full of photos on your computer already. Your job (this is easier than it sounds) is to drag those folders from your computer onto your external hard drive, directly into the topic folder that matches what they are. So, if you have a folder with photos from your trip to Hawaii, drag that folder into your Lightroom Photos folder, and into the Travel folder. By the way, if your folder of Hawaii vacation images isn't named something really easy, like "Maui Trip," now would be the time to rename it. The simpler and more descriptive your folder names, the better. Let's continue: If you shot your daughter's softball champion-ship game, drag that folder into your Light-room Photos folder, and into the Sports folder. Now, you might decide, since the photos are of your daughter, to instead put them in your Family folder. No prob-lem, that's your choice, but if you choose your Family folder, then from now on, all your kid's sports should go in that Family folder—not some in Sports and some in Family. Consistency is key.

Step Four:

So, how long will it take to move all these images from your hard drive into the right folders? Not as long as you'd think. A few hours tops in most cases. What does this accomplish? Well, for starters, you'll know exactly where every photo you've taken is, without even being in front of your computer. For example, if I asked you, "Where are your photos from your trip to Italy?" You would already know they were in your Lightroom Photos folder, in your Travel folder, in a folder called "Italy." If you went to Italy more than once, maybe you'd see three fold-ers there—Italy Winter 2015, Italy Spring 2016, and Italy Christmas 2017—and I'd be totally jealous that you got to go to Italy three times, so I probably wouldn't ask you this question in the first place. But, if I did, at least you'd know the answer. But there's more.

Continued

Step Five:

There's a trap you might be tempted to fall into that I want to save you from, and that trap is organizing folders by date. It's a trap because it really relies on you remembering when you did…well…everything. Besides, Lightroom is already keeping track of the exact time and date (even the day of the week) that every single photo in your library was taken (it does this by looking at the camera info embedded by your camera when you took the shot). So, if you ever have the urge to see your photos organized by date, press the \ **[backslash] key** to bring up the Library Filter bar across the top of Lightroom's Grid view, then click on Metadata, and in the first column, choose **Date** from the pop-up menu. Now, click on any year, then on a month, to see just the photos taken on an exact date. It's already doing the date stuff for you, so you don't have to.

Step Six:

Now, if you shoot a lot of landscape photos, and I asked, "Where are your shots from Yosemite?" You'd say, "On my external hard drive, in my Lightroom Photos folder, inside my Landscapes folder." End of story. That's where they are, and your computer can put them in alphabetical order, making them even easier to find. How easy is that? As long as you use simple, descriptive names for all your shoot folders, like "Acadia National Park" or "Rome" or "Family Reunion 2016," you're in a happy place. Yes, it can be that easy. Just spend a little time now (again, probably not more than a few hours) dragging all your images into their proper topic folders, and you'll reap the glorious benefits forever (they're not actually glorious, but it's such an awesome adjective, and one I don't get to use often, so I exercised some artistic writer's license there).

Step Seven:

What if you're importing new images from your camera's memory card? You do the same thing: you'll copy them from the card directly into the right topic folder, and then inside that topic folder, you'd create a new folder for these images with a simple name describing the shoot. So, let's say you took photos at a KISS and Def Leppard concert (awesome show, by the way). They would go onto your external hard drive, inside your Lightroom Photos folder, inside your Concerts folder, and inside your Kiss_Def Leppard folder. (*Note:* If you're an event photographer, you might need a topic folder called "Events," with a bunch of other subfolders inside, like Concerts, Celebrities, Award Shows, and Political Events, to stay organized.)

Step Eight:

Another example: if you're a wedding photographer, you'd have a Weddings folder, and inside that you'd see other folders with simple names like Johnson _Anderson Wedding and Smith_Robins Wedding and so on. That way, if Mrs. Garcia calls and says, "I need another print from our wedding," you'd know exactly where their photos are: inside your Lightroom Photos folder, inside Weddings, inside the Garcia_Jones Wedding folder! Couldn't be easier (well, it actually can be easier, in Lightroom, but that comes later because you do all this organizing before you ever even launch Lightroom). This simple organization of your photo library is the secret. Now, while we're passing on secrets, here's the secret to a happy marriage. It's simple, but it works. The secret is… (wait for it, wait for it…) separate bathrooms. There. I said it. Two secrets, both in one book. Whodathunkit?

Importing Photos Already On Your Hard Drive

One of the most important concepts to understand about Lightroom is this: while Adobe calls this process "Importing," it doesn't actually move or copy images *into* Lightroom. Your images never move—they're still right on your external hard drive. Lightroom is just "managing" them now. It's like you told Lightroom, "See those images on my external drive? Manage those for me." Of course, they would be impossible to manage if you couldn't see them, so Lightroom creates thumbnail previews of the images and that's what you're seeing in Lightroom. Your actual images never actually move or get copied "into" Lightroom.

Step One:

First, make sure you read that intro above—it's the most important thing to understand—before you start to import your photos. Luckily, importing images into Lightroom is about the easiest thing in the world. Go to your external hard drive and simply drag-and-drop the folder of images you want to import directly onto Lightroom's icon (in your Dock on a Mac, or on your desktop on a PC). This brings up Lightroom's Import window (seen here). It assumes you want all the images imported, that's why there's a checkbox next to every one. If there's a photo you don't want imported, click on its checkbox to uncheck it, and it won't get imported. To see any image larger, double-click on it. To return to the regular thumbnail grid view, double-click again or press the letter **G** on your keyboard. If you want to see all these thumbnails larger, drag the Thumbnails slider (at the bottom) to the right.

Step Two:

All you have to do at this point is simply make sure Add is selected at the top of the window, then click the Import button at the bottom right (yes, for now, ignore all the buttons and knobs and stuff), and your images will appear in Lightroom. Pretty simple. There are a few options you can tweak (we'll get to those shortly), but that's really all there is to doing a simple import and having Lightroom manage those images for you.

Lightroom builds image previews in different sizes: thumbnail, standard screen size, and 100% (called 1:1 in Lightroom speak). The larger the preview size, the longer it takes Lightroom to render it when you first import. Luckily, you can choose how fast these are displayed based on your personal level of patience. I have the patience of a hamster, so I want it to show me my thumbnails *now* (but, there's a price to pay for this speed)! You'll need to find which preview method suits your personality.

Choosing How Fast Your Photos Appear

Choose from one of these:

At the top right of the Import window, in the File Handling panel, from the Build Previews pop-up menu, you get four choices for how fast your image previews (your thumbnails and sizes larger than just thumbnails) will appear when you zoom in on a photo in Lightroom. We'll go from the fastest to slowest:

(1) Minimal (for Very Fast Thumbnails)

If you shoot in RAW and choose this, Lightroom grabs the smallest JPEG preview it can from the one the camera manufacturer includes within the RAW image (the same JPEG preview you see on the back of your camera when you shoot in RAW). It uses that as your thumbnail and it appears super-fast! (*Note:* This is the option I always choose.) These super-fast Minimal previews are not the most color-accurate, so you're definitely trading color accuracy for speed. If you have to zoom in on a photo, that's pretty quick, too, as long as the camera manufacturer included a decent-sized preview with their RAW image. If they didn't, Lightroom will create those larger previews (you just have to wait a few seconds longer for them to appear). *Note:* If you shoot in JPEG, your thumbnails will appear quickly anyway—zooming in is quick too, and the color will be fairly accurate. Score two-points for JPEG!

TIP: Rendering Larger Previews

If you want larger, higher-quality previews for any embedded previews, just click on the little, black, double-arrow icon in the top left of the thumbnail in Grid view.

Continued

(2) Embedded & Sidecar

Choose Embedded & Sidecar to get the largest previews created by your camera. It puts thumbnails in Lightroom fairly quickly, and if you double-click to zoom in, you'll wait while it builds the larger preview before you can see it (you'll see a message onscreen that says "Loading"). If you zoom in even closer, you'll have to wait a few moments more (the message will read "Loading" again). That's because it doesn't create these larger, higher-quality previews until you try to zoom in.

(3) Standard

Choosing the Standard preview means you're willing a wait a bit, until all the standard-sized previews are rendered, so when you double-click on images later, you won't get any of those "Loading" messages. Standard previews are what you see when you double-click on a thumbnail, or you take the image over to the Develop module. You'll still see the thumbnails appear, but wait until you see the progress bar up in the top-left corner show that all the previews are rendered before you start looking at your images at that larger size. However, if you zoom in even closer, to a 1:1 view probably, you'll have to wait a few seconds more while that 1:1 preview renders.

(4) 1:1 (Full 100% Size)

You choose this size if you never want to see a "Loading" message ever—you want crisp, super-large previews available anytime, and you're a very patient person. Rendering these full-sized previews is notoriously slow. It's a "sloth covered in molasses" type of slow. It's "click the Import button, maybe make a sandwich, and then mow the lawn" type of slow before it renders all the previews. But, when it's finally done, you're in the express lane—the "Loading" messages are behind you now and it's full speed ahead.

This easy method is designed for people who are new to Lightroom and might be concerned about where it's putting your images during the import process. (*Note:* If you've been using Lightroom for a while now, you can skip this and jump to page 15.) While this simple method doesn't make use of all the importing options, you'll still sleep better at night because you'll know exactly where the images you imported are stored.

Importing from Your Camera (Easy Method)

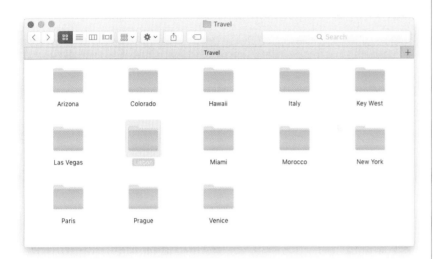

Step One:
Don't launch Lightroom (well, not yet anyway). Instead, just plug your card reader with your memory card into your computer, select all the photos on your card, and drag-and-drop them into the folder where you want to store them on your external hard drive. For example, if they're travel photos (like these photos from Lisbon), you'd drag them onto your external hard drive, into a folder named Travel, and inside your Travel folder, you'd make a new folder named, "Lisbon." That's where you drag them—into that new Lisbon folder. Now, is there any question where your photos are? Of course not—they're on your external hard drive, in your Travel folder, in a folder named Lisbon. This location, where they're at right now, will not change once you import them into Lightroom (your images don't move or get copied inside of Lightroom—they stay right there on your external drive).

Step Two:
Now, take that Lisbon folder and drag-and-drop it onto Lightroom's icon (in your Dock on a Mac, or on your desktop on a PC). This brings up Lightroom's Import window (seen here). From the Build Previews pop-up menu (at the top right of the window, in the File Handling panel), choose how long you want to wait for your previews to build (we just looked at this on page 11). I chose Embedded & Sidecar, here, but there are a couple of other options you might consider.

Continued

Step Three:

There are other options in the Import window, but we haven't covered them yet (we will later on), so explaining them at this point wouldn't do a lot of good, but there's one option we can cover now—Don't Import Suspected Duplicates. When this option is turned on, if it sees a file already in the folder with the same exact filename, it skips it. This helps when you're downloading from the same memory card over a couple of days (like when you're on vacation), so you don't wind up with a bunch of duplicates of the same photo. Again, the other options we'll cover later (in the advanced import workflow, on the next page, but don't read that until you're really comfortable about where your photos are being imported and stored).

Step Four:

Now, just make sure Add is selected at the top of the window, then click the Import button at the bottom right and your images will appear in Lightroom, and you can start scrolling through the previews, double-clicking to see them larger, and even zooming in to 100% to check for sharpness. At this point, you can start the process of finding the best images from your shoot (and I'll take you through my process in the next chapter).

If you've been using Lightroom for a while now, and you're totally comfortable with where your photos are stored—you know exactly where they are and have zero amount of stress over where your images reside—then this is for you. When you're done with this section, you'll be importing images like a SpaceX re-entry booster lead engineer, and you'll be clicking so many features and options that even Adobe doesn't know what they do. In short, buckle up—let's light this candle!

Importing from Your Camera (Advanced Users)

Step One:
If you have Lightroom open, and connect your camera or memory card reader to your computer, the Import window you see here appears over your Lightroom window. The top section of this Import window is important because it shows you what's about to happen. From left to right: (1) it shows where the photos are coming from (in this case, your camera's memory card); (2) what's going to happen to these images (in this case, they're getting copied); and (3) where they're going to (in this case, onto your external hard drive, into your Weddings folder).

Step Two:
If your memory card is connected to your computer, Lightroom assumes you want to import photos from that card, and you'll see it listed next to "From" in the top-left corner of the window (circled here). If you want to import from a different card (you could have two card readers connected to your computer), click on the From button, and the pop-up menu you see here will appear. This is where you can choose your other card reader, or you can choose to import photos from somewhere else, like your desktop, or Pictures folder, or any recent folders you've imported from.

Continued

Step Three:

There is a Thumbnails size slider below the bottom-right corner of the center Preview area that controls the size of the thumbnail previews, so if you want to see them larger, just drag that slider to the right. If you want to see any photo you're about to import at a large, full-screen size, just double-click on it to zoom in, or click on it, and then press the letter **E**. Double-click to zoom back out, or press the letter **G**.

TIP: Shortcuts for Thumbnail Size

To see the thumbnails larger in the Import window, press the **+ (plus sign) key** on your keyboard or press the **– (minus sign) key** to make them smaller again.

Step Four:

As I mentioned earlier, by default, all the photos have a checkmark at the top left of their grid cell (meaning they are all marked to be imported). If you see one or more photos you don't want imported, just turn off their checkboxes. Now, what if you have 300+ photos on your memory card, but you only want a handful of them imported? You'd click the Uncheck All button at the bottom of the window to uncheck every photo, then Command-click (PC: Ctrl-click) on just the photos you want to import, and then turn on the checkbox for any of these selected photos, and all the selected photos become checked and will be imported.

TIP: Selecting Multiple Photos

If the photos you want are contiguous, then click on the first photo, press-and-hold the Shift key, scroll down to the last photo, and click on it to select all the photos in between at once.

Step Five:

There are some other options at the top center of the Import window: again, Copy copies the files "as is" from your memory card (if they're RAW photos or JPEGs, they stay that way); Copy as DNG converts your RAW photos to Adobe's DNG format as they're being imported (see page 24 for more on DNG). I just leave mine set at Copy all the time. Neither choice moves your originals off the memory card (you'll notice Move is grayed out), it only copies them, so you'll still have the original images on your memory card. Below those are some view options: (1) All Photos (the default) displays all the photos on your memory card. (2) If you click on New Photos, it only shows the new photos on the card that you haven't imported yet, and it hides the rest from view.

Step Six:

On the right side of the window there are more options (but, if you're reading this advanced import process, you probably already know what these do): In the File Handling panel is the option to create smart previews (I only turn this on if I'm working on my laptop and I know I won't have the high-res original images with me, but I still need to edit them in the Develop module). There's an option to copy the images you're importing to a second external drive, but these second-drive backup photos don't get any of the edits you make in Lightroom—it's just a straight copy off the memory card. The last option in this panel is to import directly into an existing collection (or create a new collection from scratch and import into that). There's also the Apply During Import panel, where you can apply a Develop module preset to your images as they're imported, along with your copyright info (from the Metadata pop-up menu), and you can type in keywords (search terms) in the Keywords field, if you like.

Continued

Step Seven:

Below the File Handling panel is the File Renaming panel, where you can have your photos renamed automatically as they're imported. I always use this to give my files a very descriptive name (in this case, something like Williams Wedding makes more sense to me than _K1_8115 .CR2, especially if one day I have to search for them). If you turn on the Rename Files checkbox, there's a Template pop-up menu where you have serveral different choices. I choose **Custom Name - Sequence**, so it adds my custom name "Williams Wedding" followed by a numeric sequence (so, they become Williams Wedding-1.CR2, Williams Wedding-2.CR2, and so on). Just by looking at the pop-up menu, you can see how it will rename your files, so choose whichever one you like best, or create your own by choosing **Edit** at the bottom of the menu (I take you through that whole process in Chapter 3).

Step Eight:

Finally, if you click-and-hold on "To" at the top right, a pop-up menu appears (shown here) that lets you choose where you want the images you're importing stored. In our case, you'd want them stored on your external hard drive, so chose **Other Destination** from this pop-up menu and choose the category folder where you want these images stored (like Travel or Portrait or Family, or in this case, Weddings). In the Destination panel, I also turn on the Into Subfolder checkbox, name the subfolder with a descriptive name, like "Williams_Arnone Wedding," and choose Into One Folder from the Organize pop-up menu. So, at this point, you know three things: (1) the photos are coming from your memory card; (2) they're being copied from that card; and (3) those copies are going onto your external hard drive, into your Weddings folder, into a new folder inside it named "Williams_Arnone Wedding."

If you work on a laptop, you probably (hopefully) have stored your images on an external hard drive, but if you disconnect that drive, you can't change things like Exposure, or White Balance, and so on, because you don't have access to the original high-res files (which are on that external hard drive you disconnected). All you have now are thumbnails, which are handy for sorting and stuff, but you can't do any Develop module editing. Well, creating smart previews changes all that.

Using Lightroom with a Laptop? You'll Love Smart Previews

Step One:
To be able to still edit your images when they're "offline" (the external hard drive with your images is not currently attached to your laptop), you need to turn this feature on in the Import window. Just turn on the Build Smart Previews checkbox in the top-right corner (in the File Handling panel; it's shown circled here in red). This tells Lightroom to make a special larger preview that allows you to make edits in the Develop module, and later, when you reconnect your laptop to your external hard drive, it applies those same edits to your high-resolution images. It's a beautiful thing.

Step Two:
Once your images are imported, click on one of them, then look right underneath the histogram at the top right and you'll see "Original + Smart Preview," which lets you know that you're seeing the real original image (since the hard drive with the real original file is connected—look over in the left side Panels area here, in the Folders panel, and you'll see "External Hard Drive" listed as one of my mounted drives), but that the image also has a smart preview.

TIP: Smart Previews After Importing
If you forgot to turn on the Build Smart Previews checkbox on import, no sweat. In Grid view, just select the photos you want to have smart previews, then go under the Library menu, under Previews, and choose **Build Smart Previews**.

Save Time Importing Using Import Presets (and a Compact View)

If you find yourself using the same settings when importing images, you're probably wondering, "Why do I have to enter this same info every time I import?" Luckily, you don't. You can just enter it once, and then turn those settings into an Import preset that remembers all that stuff. Then, you can choose the preset, add a few keywords, maybe choose a different name for the subfolder they're being saved into, and you're all set. In fact, once you create a few presets, you can skip the full-sized Import window altogether and save time by using a compact version instead. Here's how:

Step One:

Here, we'll assume you're importing images from a memory card, and you're going to copy them onto your external hard drive, into your Lightroom Photos main folder, then into your Portraits folder. You want your copyright info added as they're imported (see Chapter 3), and we'll choose Embedded & Sidecar so the thumbnails and previews show up fast. Now, go to the very bottom center of the Import window, and click-and-hold where it says "None." From the pop-up menu that appears, choose **Save Current Settings as New Preset** (as shown here) and give it a descriptive name.

Step Two:

Click the Show Fewer Options button (the up-facing arrow) in the bottom-left corner of the Import window, and it switches to a compact view (as seen here). So, from now on, all you have to do is choose your preset from the pop-up menu at the bottom (as shown here, where I'm choosing my From Memory Card preset), and then enter just the few bits of info that do change when you import a new set of photos, like the descriptive name of the subfolder you want to save these photos inside. So, how does this save you time? Well, now you only have to choose a folder, then type in your subfolder's name, and click the Import button. That's fast and easy! *Note:* You can return to the full-size Import window anytime by clicking the Show More Options button (the down-facing arrow) in the bottom-left corner.

I put the import preferences toward the end of the Importing chapter because I figured that, by now, you've imported some photos and you know enough about the importing process to know what you wish was different. That's what preferences are all about (and Lightroom has preference controls because it gives you lots of control over the way you want to work).

Choosing Your Preferences for Importing Photos

Step One:
The preferences for importing photos are found in a couple different places. First, to get to the Preferences dialog, go under the Lightroom menu on a Mac or the Edit menu on a PC, and choose **Preferences** (as shown here).

Step Two:
When the Preferences dialog appears, first click on the General tab up top (shown highlighted here). Under Import Options in the middle, the first preference lets you tell Lightroom how to react when you connect a memory card from your camera to your computer. By default, it opens the Import window. However, if you'd prefer it didn't automatically open that window each time you plug in a camera or card reader, just turn off its checkbox (as shown here). The second preference here was added back in Lightroom 5. In all previous versions, if you used the keyboard shortcut to start importing photos while in another module, Lightroom left whatever you were working on and jumped over to the Library module to show you the images as they were importing (basically, it assumed you wanted to stop working on whatever you were doing, and start working on these currently importing images). Now, you can choose to stay in the folder or collection you are in and just have those images import in the background by turning off the Select the "Current/Previous Import" Collection During Import checkbox.

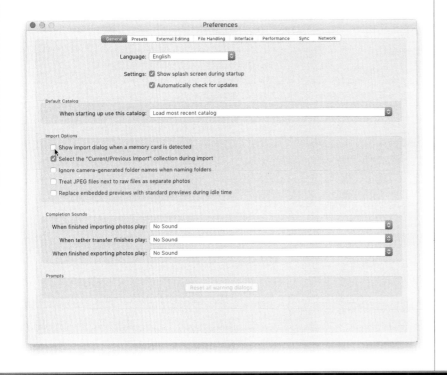

Continued

Step Three:

If you choose to use the Embedded & Sidecar previews when you import photos (see page 11), there's an option you can turn on if you want to have Lightrotom build the larger previews when it's not doing anything else important. Just turn on the Replace Embedded Previews with Standard Previews During Idle Time checkbox and it will create those larger, more color-accurate previews in the background for you.

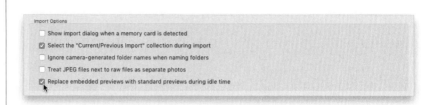

Step Four:

There are two other importing preference settings I'd like to mention that are also found on the General tab. In the Completion Sounds section, you not only get to choose whether or not Lightroom plays an audible sound when it's done importing your photos, you also get to choose which sound (from the pop-up menu of system alert sounds already in your computer, as seen here).

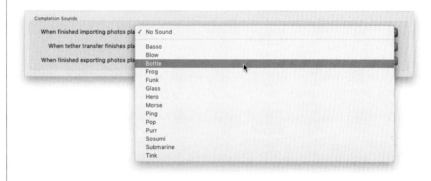

Step Five:

While you're right there, directly below the menu for choosing an "importing's done" sound are two other pop-up menus for choosing a sound for when your tether transfer finishes and for when your exporting is done. I know, the second one isn't an importing preference, but since we're right there, I thought…what the heck. I'll talk more about some of the other preferences later in the book, but since this chapter is on importing, I thought I'd better tackle these here.

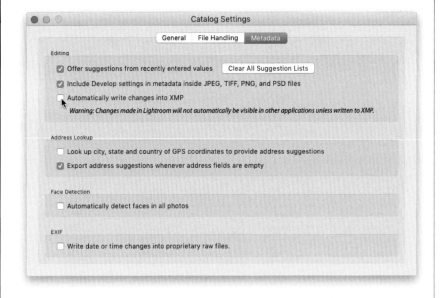

Step Six:

Now, close the Preferences dialog, and then go back under the Lightroom menu on a Mac or the Edit menu on a PC, and this time choose **Catalog Settings**. In the Catalog Settings dialog (shown here), click on the Metadata tab. Here you can determine whether you want to take the metadata you add to your RAW photos (copyright, keywords, etc.) and have it written to a totally separate file, so then for each photo you'll have two files—one that contains the photo itself and a separate file (called an XMP sidecar) that contains that photo's metadata. You do this by turning on the Automatically Write Changes into XMP checkbox, but why would you ever want to do this? Well, normally Lightroom keeps track of all this metadata you add in its database file—it doesn't actually embed the info until your photo leaves Lightroom (by exporting a copy over to Photoshop, or exporting the file as a JPEG, TIFF, or PSD—all of which support having this metadata embedded right into the photo itself). However, some programs can't read embedded metadata, so they need a separate XMP sidecar file.

Step Seven:

Now that I've shown you that Automatically Write Changes into XMP checkbox, I don't actually recommend you turn it on, because writing all those XMP sidecars takes time, which slows Lightroom down. Instead, if you want to send a file to a friend or client and you want the metadata written to an XMP sidecar file, first go to the Library module and click on an image to select it, then press **Command-S (PC: Ctrl-S)**, which is the shortcut for **Save Metadata to File** (which is found under the Metadata menu). This writes any existing metadata to a separate XMP file (so you'll need to send both the photo and the XMP sidecar together).

Converting RAW Photos to the Adobe DNG Format

You have the option of converting your RAW images from your camera manufacturer's proprietary RAW format to Adobe's open format DNG (Digital Negative) format. DNG was created by Adobe out of concern that one day, one or more manufacturers might abandon their proprietary RAW format, leaving photographers shooting RAW out in the cold. Unfortunately, none of the big three camera manufacturers embraced this DNG format, and even I stopped converting my images a few years ago. However, if you want to convert to DNG, here's how:

Two DNG Advantages:

There are two advantages of the DNG format: (1) DNG files maintain the RAW properties, but are about 20% smaller in file size, and (2) if you need to share an original RAW image file with someone, and you want that file to include any changes you made to it in Lightroom (including keywords, copyright, meta-data, etc.), you don't have to generate a separate XMP sidecar file (a separate text file that stores all that info). With DNG, all that data is backed right into the file itself, so there is no need for a second file. There are disadvantages to DNG, as well, including importing taking longer because your RAW files have to be converted to DNG first. Also, DNGs aren't supported by many other photo applications. Just so you know.

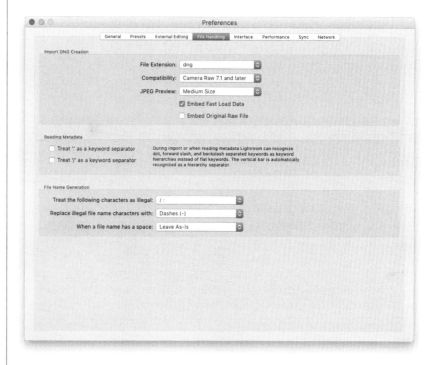

Setting Your DNG Preferences:

If you want to convert your RAW files to DNG format as they're imported, first press **Command-, (PC: Ctrl-,)** to bring up Lightroom's Preferences dialog, then click on the File Handling tab (as seen above). In the Import DNG Creation section at the top, you can choose the three-letter File Extension, how backward compatible with older versions of Adobe Camera Raw you want to make them, and the size of the preview that gets embedded in DNG images. Although you can embed the original proprietary RAW file, it adds to the file size, and pretty much kills advantage #1 above. By the way, you choose Copy as DNG at the top center of the Import window (as shown here).

Now that your images have been imported, there are some tips about working with Lightroom's interface you're going to want to know about right up front that will make working in it much easier.

Four Things You'll Want to Know Now About Getting Around Lightroom

Step One:
There are seven modules in Lightroom, and each does a different thing. When your imported photos appear in Lightroom, they always appear in the center of the Library module, which is where we do all our sorting and organizing. The Develop module is where you do your photo editing (changing the exposure, white balance, tweaking colors, etc.), and it's pretty obvious what the other five do (I'll spare you). You move from module to module by clicking on the module's name up in the taskbar across the top, or you can use the shortcuts **Command-Option-1** for Library, **Command-Option-2** for Develop, and so on (on a PC, it would be **Ctrl-Alt-1, Ctrl-Alt-2**, and so on).

Step Two:
There are five areas in the Lightroom interface overall: that taskbar along the top, the left and right side Panels areas, a Filmstrip across the bottom, and your photos always appear in the center Preview area. You can hide any panel (which makes the Preview area, where your photos are displayed, larger) by clicking on the little gray triangle in the center edge of the panel. For example, go ahead and click on the little gray triangle at the top center of the interface, and you'll see it hides the taskbar. Click it again; it comes back.

Continued

Step Three:

The #1 interface complaint I hear from Lightroom users is how they hate the Auto Hide & Show feature (which is on by default). The idea behind it sounds great: if you've hidden a panel and need it again to make an adjustment, you move your cursor over where the panel used to be, and it pops out. When you're done, you move your cursor away, and it automatically tucks back out of sight. Sounds great, right? The problem is one of those panels pops out anytime you move your cursor to the far right, left, top, or bottom of your screen. It really drives people nuts (I'm on that list), and I've had people literally offer me money to show them how to turn that "feature" off. To turn off Auto Hide & Show, Right-click on the little gray triangle next to any panel and choose **Manual** from the pop-up menu (as shown here). This works on a per-panel basis, so you'll have to do it to each of the four panels.

Step Four:

I use Manual mode, so I can just open and close panels as I need them. You can also use the keyboard shortcuts: **F5** closes/opens the top taskbar, **F6** hides the Filmstrip, **F7** hides the left side Panels area, and **F8** hides the right side (on a newer Mac keyboard or a laptop, you may have to press the Fn key with these). You can hide both side Panels areas by pressing the **Tab key**, but the one shortcut I probably use the most is **Shift-Tab**, because it hides all the panels at once and leaves just your photos visible (as shown here). Also, each module's panels kind of follow the same basic idea: the left side Panels area is used primarily for presets and templates and giving you access to your collections; the right side Panels area has all the adjustments.

Before we get to organizing our photos (which we cover in the next chapter), lets take a minute to learn the ins and outs of how Lightroom lets you view your imported photos.

Viewing Your Imported Photos

Step One:
When your imported photos appear in Lightroom, they are displayed as small thumbnails in the center Preview area (as seen here). You can change the size of these thumbnails using the Thumbnails slider that appears on the right side of the toolbar (the dark gray horizontal bar that appears directly below the center Preview area). Drag it to the right, and they get bigger; drag it to the left, and they get smaller (the slider is circled here). You can also press **Command-+ (PC: Ctrl-+)** to zoom in, or **Command-– (PC: Ctrl-–)** to zoom out.

Step Two:
To see any thumbnail at a larger size, just double-click on it, press the letter **E** on your keyboard, or press the **Spacebar**. This larger size is called Loupe view (as if you were looking at the photo through a loupe), and by default it zooms in so you can see your entire photo in the Preview area surrounded by a light gray background. This is called Fit in Window view. If you don't like seeing that gray background, go up to the Navigator panel in the top left, click on Fill, and now when you double-click on a thumbnail, it will zoom in to fill the whole Preview area (no gray background). Choosing 1:1 will zoom your photo in to a 100% actual size view when it's double-clicked, but it's kind of awkward to go from a tiny thumbnail to a huge, tight, zoomed-in image like that.

Continued

Step Three:

I leave my Navigator panel setting at Fit, so when I double-click I can see the entire photo fitting in the center Preview area, but if you want to get in closer to check sharpness, you'll notice that when you're in Loupe view, your cursor has changed into a magnifying glass. If you click it once on your photo, it jumps to a 1:1 view of the area where you clicked. To zoom back out, just click it again. To return to the thumbnail view (called Grid view), just press the letter **G** on your keyboard. This letter "G" is one of the most important keyboard shortcuts to memorize. This is particularly handy, because when you're in any other module, pressing G brings you right back here to the Library module and your thumbnail grid, which is kind of "home base" for Lightroom Classic.

Step Four:

The area that surrounds your thumbnail is called a cell, and each cell displays information about the photo, from the filename, to the file format, dimensions, etc.—you get to customize how much or how little it displays, as you'll see in Chapter 4. But in the meantime, here's another keyboard shortcut you'll want to know about: press the letter **J**. Each time you press it, it toggles you through the three different cell views, each of which displays different groups of info—an expanded cell with lots of info, a compact cell with just a little info, and one that hides all that distracting stuff altogether (great for when you're showing thumbnails to clients). Also, you can hide (or show) the toolbar by pressing **T**. If you press-and-hold T, it only hides it temporarily—only for as long as you have the T key held down.

The default cell view is called Expanded and gives you the most info

Press J to switch to Compact view, which shrinks the size of the cell, hides all the info, and just shows the photos

Press J one more time and it adds back some info and numbers to each cell

There are two really large views that you'll probably use fairly often: One hides most of the panels and tools and stuff, and gives you a large clutter-free view. The other takes over your screen and hides everything but the photo. You'll find the one you like best, but give them both a try and see which one is for you.

The Two Flavors of Full-Screen View

Step One:
Press **Shift-Tab** to hide all the panels (left, right, top, and bottom), but Lightroom's menus and its title bar will still be visible along the top. If you keep the gray toolbar along the bottom of the Preview area visible, you'll also still see it in this Shift-Tab view. To toggle the toolbar on/off, press the letter **T**. If you are in Grid view and keep the Library Filter bar along the top of the screen visible, you'll still see that, too. To toggle it on/off, press the **\ (backslash) key**. (*Note:* If you have your Navigator panel [on the top of the left side Panels area] set to Fit, your entire image will fit onscreen, and you'll see a gray background around it [as seen here]. If you chose Fill instead, it will zoom in to fill the screen.) Lastly, pressing Shift-Tab will be bring everything back. Seems like a lot of decisions for just a larger view, right?

Step Two:
If you want a simple full-screen view, just press the letter **F** on your keyboard. To return to regular view, press F again. That's a whole lot easier.

CHAPTER 2

GETTING ORGANIZED
my system for a happy Lightroom life

There are lots of ways to organize your images in Lightroom, and that's actually part of the problem—there are so many different schemes and methods that you'll hardly run into anyone who does it the same way as anyone else. The worst part is that many are so overly complex and confusing that some folks actually need to keep a spreadsheet printout next to their computer just so they can keep track of everything. That's crazy, and it's also precisely why a few years ago I set out to introduce a new organizational system that would be easy, efficient, and one anyone could employ. Now users would not only be able to quickly and easily find their images in Lightroom, they'd also be triple backed up in case of disaster. I call my system the "SLIM" system, which stands for the "Simplified Lightroom Image Management" system and you're going to learn that

very system in this chapter. This replaces a few earlier systems that I used that didn't pan out. The first was my "Catalog Hierarchy Unified Backup By Year" system or "CHUBBY" system for short. It was okay for a while, but many users complained that while they were CHUBBY, they had trouble with dates. Little by little, this system kept growing and growing until it reached some pretty large proportions. That's when I realized that this system could no longer fit comfortably into most situations. It had evolved into an even larger system, one that I would eventually call my "Filter And Tag" system. However, after taking my laptop with me on a cruise, I realized that my "FAT" system no longer fit— it had bloated into what I now call the "Pro Organizational Responsive Keyword Yield" system, which essentially just sits on your couch and eats chips.

Four Important Things to Know First!

In this chapter, you're going to learn an organizational system—the same one I use for organizing my own images. I call it the "SLIM" system, which stands for the "Simplified Lightroom Image Management" system. First, the good news: you've already tackled a good chunk of it, because all that organizing you did in Chapter 1 when you moved all your photos onto one external hard drive and sorted them into the topics that you shoot, that's a core part of the SLIM system because we mimic that in Lightroom. But, there are a few more things you'll need to know up front (well, four, to be exact).

#1: Stay Away from the Folders Panel

When I meet somebody with a sad story about losing some (or all) of their photos forever, it was because they were messing around in Lightroom's Folders panel. That's why I don't recommend working in the Folders panel at all. It's too risky—make a mistake there and it's forever. Here's a car analogy: we can drive around, get to where we want, and be happy just driving, but if we open the hood and start messing around with the engine, and we don't really know what we're doing, we can mess up our car, right? Treat the Folders panel the same way—you can live a happy life without opening Lightroom's "hood" and messing around with stuff. Now, the Folders panel (like your car's engine) is essential for Lightroom to operate, but let's consider it an "under-the-hood" part of Lightroom and just stay out of there.

#2: Lightroom Was Designed for You to Use Collections Instead

That's why the Collections panel is available in all seven modules, but the Folders panel is only in the Library module. Collections are safe. They're forgiving. They protect you from messing up. Plus, you can put the same photo in multiple collections (you can have a photo of your dog in your Dogs collection, and in your Family collection, and Pets collection, and all is still right with the world)—with folders, you can't. If you've already been working in folders, don't sweat it. To make any folder a collection, just Right-click on it and choose **Create Collection**. Can it really be that easy? Yup.

#3: Think of Collections as Photo Albums

Think back to the film days—we'd get our film developed, then we'd take our favorite prints and organize them in a photo album, right? Well, we do the same thing in Lightroom, but instead of calling them "photo albums," we call them "collections." We can drag-and-drop our favorite images into them, and arrange them in any order, and even have the same image appear in multiple collections. In short: collections are awesome!

#4: You Organize Your Collections Inside Collection Sets

If you've got a bunch of related collections, like collections from your trips to Italy and San Francisco, and Hawaii, and your trip to Paris, you can organize all those inside a collection set (and you'd probably name that set "Travel"). That way, all your travel collections are together (like the folders on your hard drive). If you look at a collection set's icon, it looks like that box you buy at Office Depot or Staples to put file folders inside of, and that's essentially what is it— a collection you can put other collections inside. You can even put other collection sets inside of it. For example, if you create a "Sports" collection set, you can put another collection set inside it called "Football," and then all the football games you shot can go inside that. If you shoot high school and college football, you can have a collection set for each of these—one with all your high school games ("Predators vs. Blazers," "Sabercats vs. Huskies"), then your college games in a separate collection set ("Buckeyes vs. Seminoles," "Vols vs. Crimson Tide"). Working with collections and collection sets also opens up a whole new world of features that you can only access if you work in collections. For example, if you want to work with Lightroom on your phone or tablet (see Chapter 14 for more on this), you have to use collections (you can't do this with folders). The future of Lightroom is a collections-based workflow, so no sense in fighting it, let's do it right from the start.

Want a Happy Lightroom Life? Use Just One Catalog

You may think it might be too late for you—you might already have a dozen different catalogs—but don't worry, it's not too late (we're about to learn how to fix that). If you want a happy, organized Lightroom life (and avoid a mountain of time-wasting frustration), go with just one single catalog for everything. So, how many images can you have in a single catalog and still work at full speed? We don't know the limit—Adobe has users with over 6 million images, and they're still rocking right along, so stick with one catalog and life will be good.

Step One:
If you're new to Lightroom, this is the easiest thing in the world. When you open Lightroom, what you see onscreen with your photos, that's your catalog. Just don't create a new one. That is your catalog, and that's what you're working with. But, what if you have three, five, or 15 different catalogs? You have two choices: (1) Combine all your catalogs into just one single existing catalog (ahhh, that's a beautiful place to be). Don't worry, it keeps everything intact—all your sorting, metadata, edits, and so on—that's why there's nothing hard about doing this. Start by opening whichever catalog is your favorite (or is the most complete, or the one you like the best etc.), and that will be the catalog you build upon. So, make that decision now.

Step Two:
Now, find your other catalogs and import them all (yes, all of them) into this one catalog. To do that, go under the File menu, choose **Import from Another Catalog**, then go to wherever you store your Lightroom catalogs on your computer (I'm guessing it's in a folder named "Lightroom" inside either your computer's Pictures folder or My Pictures folder). Once you find one of those catalogs, click Choose to start the process.

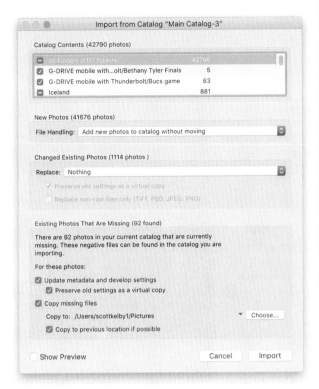

Step Three:

When you hit that Choose button, it's going to bring up the Import from Catalog dialog you see here. In the center is a list of all the collections in this other catalog and how many photos are in each. The only reason I would turn off one of these (and not have it import) is if I knew I already had a collection with the same name and photos as one in the catalog I currently have open. Also, leave the File Handling pop-up menu set to **Add New Photos to Catalog without Moving**. Otherwise, I just hit the Import button at the bottom right, and I go make a cup of coffee (it's a Keurig machine, so it's pretty quick), and then all those collections are added to my currently open catalog. Once I confirm they're there, I do two things: (1) I sort all the images into their proper collection sets by topic, and (2) I throw away the old catalog (there's no reason to keep it now—I've combined that catalog into this one). Now do that for all your other catalogs (this will take much less time than you think), and when you're done, all your photos are finally in just one catalog. Ahhhh, life is good.

Step Four:

The other option (2) is if you have multiple catalogs, but you really don't like any particular one, so you don't have one you want to start with. In that case, just create a brand new, clean, empty catalog and import all your other catalogs into it. Go under the File menu and choose **New Catalog**. This creates a new catalog with nuthin' in it, ready for you to start importing all your other catalogs using the method I just showed. The result is the same: one single catalog with all your photos in it, and you are on your way to a happy Lightroom life.

Where to Store Your Catalog

While we do want to store our images on an external hard drive, to get the best performance from Lightroom, you'll want to store your Lightroom catalog directly on your computer.

Step One:

If you've been using Lightroom for a while (or you just recently started), and you've stored your catalog on an external hard drive, it's easy to copy it back onto your computer (where you'll get the best performance), but you need to do this right, so everything works like it should. Before simply drag your catalog over to your computer, I recommend first creating a new folder on your external hard drive, naming it "Catalog Backup," and then dragging your existing catalog into that folder, along with the files named "Previews." That does two things: (1) It creates a backup we can use in the unlikely case that something goes wrong during this process (it won't, but just in case). And, (2) since you're changing the location of the catalog, if you were to launch Lightroom, it won't launch this backup catalog on your external hard drive by mistake.

Step Two:

Now go into that Catalog Backup folder and click-and-drag these files: (1) the one with the extension .lrcat (that's your actual catalog file); (2) the one with the extension .lrdata (those are your thumbnail previews); and (3) if you've created any smart previews, you'll see a third file with the .lrdata extension, but it will have "Smart Previews" in its filename. All three of those go onto your computer (put them inside your Pictures or My Pictures folder), inside a folder named "Lightroom" (you may already have one named that). Once that's done, double-click that .lrcat file you just copied onto your computer, and from now on, you'll be working from that catalog.

Okay, we've got to get off using folders—they're just too dangerous (and if you read that and you're like, "What?!" it just means you didn't read the "Four Important Things…" at the beginning of this chapter, so go back and read those now. Anyway, we're getting off folders before something bad happens, so here's how to make a collection from a folder. Now, just so ya know, we're not deleting any folders, we're just going to use collections instead. Those folders are sacred because our actual photos are inside, so we're just going to leave them alone once we make our collections.

How to Make a Collection from a Folder

Step One:
This used to be more complicated, but thankfully Adobe made the process of creating a collection from a folder amazingly simple. Just go to the Folders panel, Right-click on the folder you want to also have as a collection, and from the pop-up menu that appears, choose **Create Collection**. Boom. Done. Drops the mic. That's really all there is to it. Go and look in the Collections panel and you'll see your new collection (they appear in alphabetical order).

Step Two:
If you have a folder with other folders inside of it, then you only change one thing: when you Right-click on the folder (the one with other folders inside it), choose **Create Collection Set**, instead. That creates a collection set and keeps all those nested folders inside intact, but now you've created collections from them. Everything's the same, but now you're working in collections, and it's a happy place, with puppies and rainbows, and where small animals will come up and eat from your hand. You're on your way to a happier, healthier Lightroom life using collections.

WARNING: I know I've said this before (like up in the introduction on this page), but now that you've made collections from your folders, *do not delete any folders*. They contain your actual image files. Just ignore them. Leave them alone. Don't mess with them, etc. You're a collections person now, so just ignore that old way of working.

Organizing Photos Already On Your Hard Drive

I'm going to take you through my simple system for organizing the images already on your external hard drive (I say "external hard drive" because I'm hoping you've already moved them all onto an external hard drive, but if for some reason you haven't done that yet, you can of course still use this exact system, so don't let that hold you back).

Step One:

Okay, I'm counting on you having already read the first part of this chapter, so we can dive right in. Here's what we're going to do: Remember those topic folders you created on your external hard drive back in Chapter 1? The ones you created to organize your images before you even launched Lightroom? Well, we're going to mimic that same setup here in Lightroom using collection sets and collections. So, start by going to the Collections panel, clicking on the + (plus sign) button on the right side of the panel header, and choosing **Create Collection Set**. Give it the name of one of those folders on your external hard drive.

Step Two:

Once you create that first collection set, you're then going to drag your existing collections that fit into that topic inside this collection set. Let's say the first collection set you created is called "Sports," and you have collections from all the different sports you shoot. You simply drag-and-drop them right on this collection set and they move inside of it. If you have a lot of a particular topic, let's say you shoot a lot of car racing, you might need to create a Racing collection set inside that Sports collection set, and then drag your racing shoots inside that collection set. Inside my own Sports collection set, I have collection sets for Football, Baseball, Tennis, Motorports, Misc Sports, Hockey, and Basketball. However, inside my Football collection set, I have a collection set for College and another for NFL, and inside NFL I have two more: one to keep all my Bucs games together and one for all my Falcons games.

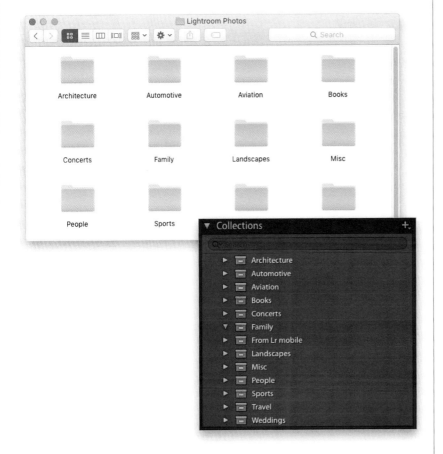

Step Three:

Now you're going to create a collection set for every topic folder you have on your external hard drive. Then, you're going to drag-and-drop any collections you've created from folders, or already had in your Collections panel, or whatever, and put them into their corresponding topics (here, I'm dragging my Oregon Landscapes collection into my Landscapes collection set). So, shots from a high school football game go in Sports; shots from your son's graduation get dragged into the Family collection set. That one time you shot close-up photos of flowers, goes in the Misc collection set (unless you start shooting flowers a lot, then you'd create a topic called Flowers at some point). Now, what if you have shots from your kid's football game, and you're not sure whether to put them in Sports or Family? Why not create a collection in both? That's the great thing about collections—your images can be in more than one location (whereas they can't if you're still using folders).

TIP: Deleting Collections

If you want to delete a collection or collection set, just Right-click on it, and from the pop-up menu, choose **Delete**. It'll remind you that the photos in that collection will still remain in your catalog (which is a good thing).

Step Four:

Here, at the top, is what it should look like on your external hard drive (you're seeing my topics—of course yours will reflect the topics you shoot), and here's what your Lightroom Collections panel should look like after you're done mimicking that structure with collection sets. If you click on a little "flippy" triangle, it expands the set and shows you all the collections inside.

Why You Need to Use Pick Flags Instead of Star Ratings

If I'm teaching a workshop and I see one of my students stuck, it's almost a lock that it's one of two things they're stuck on, and one of them is the massive time-suck that is the 1–5 star rating system. They'll ask me, "What do you think? Is this a 2-star or a 3-star?" Who cares? You're just wasting your time! Either it's one of your best shots or it's one of those out-of-focus, probably-should-just-delete shots (you should ignore the rest altogether). That's why Pick flags make so much sense. It's either a good shot or not. Here's how we use them as the core of our organizational system:

Step One:
When you boil it down, we're looking for the best photos from our shoot, and we also want to get rid of the photos where the subject is out of focus, you pressed the shutter by accident, the flash didn't fire, etc. There's no sense in storing photos that you'll never use, right? Pick flags make marking your "keepers" (shots that are in the running), and the really bad shots you need to delete, super-quick and easy. First, you'll want to see images at a large size, so double-click on a photo, and then either press **Shift-Tab** to hide all the panels, or press **F** on your keyboard to go full screen. Now, take a quick look at the photo (good photos stand out even at a quick glance), and if it's a good shot, press the letter **P** to mark it as a Pick. If you hid the panels, you'll see "Flag as Pick" appear near the bottom of the image (as seen here). If you're in full screen, you'll just see a small white flag appear onscreen.

Step Two:
That's that the plan—if you see a good shot, you press P; if it's not good, you don't do anything, you just move on by pressing the **Right Arrow key** on your keyboard. If you see a really bad shot (out of focus, like the shot here, the subject's eyes are closed, etc.), press the letter **X** to mark it as a Reject. If you mark an image as a Pick or Reject, and you change your mind, just press **U** to unflag that image.

TIP: Using Auto Advance for Picks
If you turn on **Auto Advance**, under the Photos menu, when you mark a Pick, it automatically moves to the next image.

Step Three:

When we get into the system (starting on the next page), we'll get into what to do with those Picks, but at this point, you can just deal with those Rejects (you can really deal with them at any time, but the sooner you get them out of your life, the less time they'll appear onscreen just taking up space, so I like to deal with them early in the process). To get rid of all your Rejects at once, go under the Photo menu up top, and all the way at the bottom of the menu, choose **Delete Rejected Photos** (as shown here). When you're in Grid view, this displays all the photos you're about to delete (I guess to give you one last chance to change your mind). A dialog will appear asking if you just want these out of Lightroom or deleted from your disk. I always choose Delete from Disk because if I marked them as Rejects, they truly are rejects, and I want them out of my life.

Step Four:

So, do we ever use star ratings? Yes. But only one: the 5-star rating (here, I pressed the number **5** on my keyboard to assign a 5-star rating to this photo). We'll talk about why (and how it comes in handy having this second style of rating), but we don't use the 1-, 2-, 3-, or 4-star, just the 5-star). If you're an "anti-starite" and don't want to use stars, you could go with color labels instead, but the downside of these is that they don't transfer to Lightroom CC on mobile devices, so I skip them in my rating process. However, here's where I do use color labels: If I do a shoot with a professional model, and I have a makeup artist, fashion stylist, and hair stylist onset, I let them use color labels to mark their favorites. That way, I can quickly find their favorites, and I can email or text them finals for their portfolios or social media.

Organizing Photos You're Importing from Your Camera

Here, we're going to look at how to organize your images from a shoot you just imported, and I'm going to show you the same method I use for organizing my shoots. It's pretty straightforward, but like any part of this system, the key is consistency.

Step One:

In reality, of course, Step One is to import your photos from your camera's memory card, so we're going to pick this up from the point where you literally just imported your photos. When you import your photos, they appear in Grid view, waiting for you to sort, edit, etc., but before you do anything, go to the Collections panel, click the + (plus sign) button on the right of the panel header, and from the pop-up menu, choose **Create Collection Set**, and then give that new set a very descriptive name. In our example here, these are shots from Lisbon, so I'm naming the collection set (wait for it…wait for it…) "Lisbon." I have a collection set called "Travel" with all my travel photos inside, so in the Create Collection Set dialog, I'd turn on the Inside a Collection Set checkbox, choose **Travel** from the pop-up menu, then click Create.

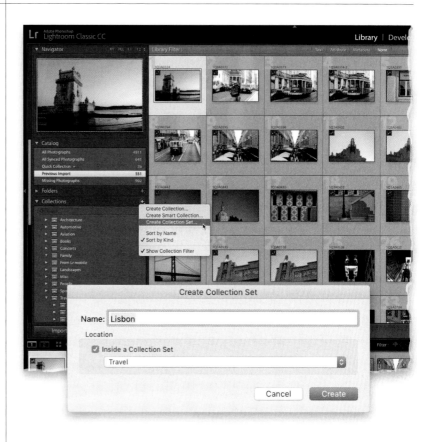

Step Two:

At this point, you have an empty collection set named Lisbon (inside your main Travel collection set), so go under the Edit menu and choose **Select All** (or press **Command-A [PC: Ctrl-A]**) to select all those photos from Lisbon you just imported. Go back to the Collections panel, click the + sign button again, but this time choose **Create Collection** from the pop-up menu. When the Create Collection dialog appears, name this new collection "Full Shoot" (that way, any time you want to see all the images from your Lisbon shoot, you'll just click on this Full Shoot collection).

Step Three:

In the Location section, turn on the Inside a Collection Set checkbox, and from the pop-up menu below, choose Lisbon (all the collection sets you've created will appear in this menu). Below that, in the Options section, the Include Selected Photos checkbox should already be turned on, but if for some reason it's not, turn it on (otherwise, it will ignore the photos you just selected to be in this new collection). Now you can click Create, and it puts this new "Full Shoot" collection inside of your Lisbon collection set. Okay, so far, so good. Now it gets more fun (not harder, it actually does get more fun at this point).

Step Four:

This is where I begin the process of finding my best images from the shoot using the Pick flag method I showed back on page 40. I double-click on the first image to see it larger onscreen (this puts it in what Lightroom calls "Loupe view"), then I get all the panels out of the way by pressing **Shift-Tab**, and then I start going through my images. If I see an image I like, I press **P** on my keyboard. If I don't like the photo, I don't do anything—I just hit the **Right Arrow key** on my keyboard and move on. If I see a photo that's so messed up it needs to be deleted, I press **X**. If I mess up doing either, I press **U** to unflag it. I do this pretty quickly, because I'll have an opportunity to be really choosy in the next stage, but for now, when the image appears onscreen, I make a quick decision—it's a Pick or I move on. You'll be amazed at how quickly you'll move through an entire shoot using this method. Okay, we're not done yet, but we're well on our way.

Continued

Step Five:

Once you've got your Picks and Rejects flagged, let's get rid of the Rejects. Switch back to Grid view **(G)**, and in the Catalog panel (press Shift-Tab again to make it visible), click on Previous Import. Then, go under the Photo menu and choose **Delete Rejected Photos**. This displays just the photos you've marked as Rejects, and a dialog appears asking if you want to remove them from Lightroom. Go ahead and click on the Delete from Disk button to remove them from your hard drive.

Step Six:

Now to see just your Picks (and hide the rest), click back on your Full Shoot collection in your Lisbon collection set, and make sure the Filmstrip along the bottom is visible. Near the top right of the Filmstrip, you'll see the word "Filter," and to the right of it are three grayed-out flags. To see just your Picks, click twice on the first flag (the white one), and it will display just your Picks. By the way, you only have to click twice like that the first time you use it, and just in case you were curious, clicking the center flag would display just the images you didn't flag.

TIP: Use the Other Picks Filter

You can also choose to see just your Picks, Rejects, or your unflagged photos from the Library Filter bar that appears across the top of the center preview area (if you don't see it, just press the **\ [backslash] key** on your keyboard). Just click on Attribute and a bar pops down. Click on the white Pick flag, and now just your Picks are visible.

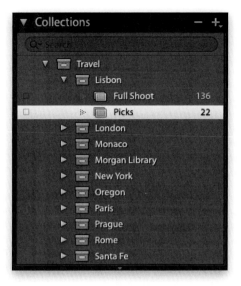

Step Seven:

Now that only your Picks are visible, press **Command-A (PC: Ctrl-A)** to select all the currently visible photos (your Picks), and then let's put them into a collection. Press **Command-N (PC: Ctrl-N)**—that's the keyboard shortcut to create a new collection (well, to bring up the Create Collection dialog anyway), and this is a good one to know because you're going to create a *lot* of new collections. When the Create Collection dialog appears, name this collection "Picks" and, of course, you are going to choose to put this in that same Lisbon collection set, because these are the Picks from that shoot, so choose Lisbon from the Inside a Collection Set pop-up menu (if it's not already selected for you), leave the Include Selected Photos checkbox turned on (we always leave that on), and click Create. So, where are we now in this process? Inside our Travel collection set, we have a collection set named Lisbon, and inside of that we have a regular collection called "Full Shoot" and one called "Picks." We're almost there.

Step Eight:

Within our Picks collection, there are some shots that really stand out—the best of the best, the ones you actually will want to email to the client, or print, or add to your portfolio. So, we need to refine our sorting process a little more to find our best shots from this group of keepers—our "Selects." We're already done with our Pick flags since all our Picks are already in their own collection. So, we could just select all the photos in our Picks collection and press the letter U to unflag them all (as seen here), and then we could use the Pick flags all over again to narrow our Picks down to the best-of-the-best (our Selects). But what if, instead, we use that 5-star rating we've been saving for just such an occasion? Doing this will come in really handy later (when we get into smart collections) and those Pick flags won't help us then (more on this later).

Continued

Step Nine:

So, we're going with just using the 5-star rating for separating our very best shots from the Picks—our "good shots" (you'll be glad later that you did it this way). Okay, now we're looking for our best-of-the-best shots from our shoot (again, I call these our "Selects"). Getting to these Selects is when we really take our time. We get much pickier (no pun intended) about which photos make the cut, and we don't zoom through the images (and we don't have to, because we're starting with our Picks and it should be a much smaller number of images than our full shoot). In your Picks collection, double-click on the first photo (the first thumbnail in the top-left corner) to make it larger (take it into Loupe view), press **Shift-Tab** (or go full screen), and let's start finding our 5-star images.

Step 10:

Start going through your images, and when you see a shot that's really good (one that you might fully edit, share online, send to the client, etc.), just press the number **5** on your keyboard, and you'll see "Set Rating to 5" appear onscreen (if you're in full-screen mode, you'll see five stars appear across the bottom of the screen. Not the words "5 stars," you'll actually see five stars).

Step 11:
Once you've carefully made your choices on which Picks should be your 5-star images, it's time to put them in our third and final collection. But first, we have to see only those 5-star images. So, go to the Filmstrip again, and to the right of the Pick flags, you'll see five grayed-out stars. Click-and-drag your cursor from left to right to highlight all five stars (as shown here), and it filters out everything else, leaving your 5-star-rated images visible. You probably know what to do from here: select all and press Command-N (PC: Ctrl-N) to create a new collection, name it "Selects," and save it inside the Lisbon collection set.

Step 12:
Now, if you look in your Lisbon collection set, you'll see three individual collections: (1) Full Shoot, (2) Picks, and (3) Selects. From here on out, you'll probably just work with your Selects collection, and that's okay—those are your best images from the Lisbon shoot. If you need extra images (maybe for a photo book or slide show), you'd look in your Picks, because those are still at least "good shots." Okay, now that you know the routine, what would a portrait shoot's collection set look like? It would be in my Portraits collection set, named with my subject's name (like "Allison's Headshots"), and inside that collection set, you'd find three collections: Full Shoot, Picks, and Selects. What if it was a landscape shoot from Yosemite? Then, it would be in my Landscapes collection set, inside a collection set named "Yosemite," and inside that Yosemite collection set would be three collections: Full Shoot, Picks, and Selects. It doesn't matter what the topic is, each shoot breaks down the same way—Full Shoot, Picks, and Selects. Keep it consistent like this and the process gets really quick (and you'll be able to find anything really quickly).

Two Tools to Help You Find Your Best Shots: Survey and Compare View

Sometimes it's tough getting down to just a few shots that are your best of the best—especially if the shots look very much alike (like from a portrait shoot). But, there are two tools built into Lightroom that can help make the process easier: they are Survey view and Compare view.

Step One:

I use Survey view when I have a number of shots that are similar (like a number of shots of the same basic pose) and I'm trying to find the best ones from that group. You enter Survey view (seen here) by selecting the similar photos (click on one, then press-and-hold the Command [PC: Ctrl] key and click on the others— I selected a group of six images here), and then pressing the letter **N** on your keyboard. While it's hard picking which images from a similar set of shots are the best ones, it's much easier picking which ones from a set you like the least. That's what Survey view is all about—the process of elimination. See which image you like the least, then move your cursor over it and an "X" appears in the bottom-right corner (as shown here).

Step Two:

Click on that X to remove that image from screen. It doesn't delete it, and it doesn't remove it from the collection or anything like that, it literally just removes it from the screen for now (as seen here, where there are now just five images left onscreen). Then, do the same for the next image you like least, and the next, and so on, clicking on that X in the bottom-right corner of any image you don't like, and it's removed from the screen.

Step Three:

Here, I'm down to just three images. If you like all three, you could mark them all as 5-star images, or continue on, and when there's only one left, that's the shot that made it through (in this case) all six rounds of elimination. Press the number **5** on your keyboard to mark it as a 5-star image for your Selects collection. Another method for narrowing things down is using Compare view. Instead of putting a bunch of images onscreen at once, it's more like a head-to-head battle between two images at a time. Press **Shift-Tab** to hide all the panels, then start by selecting the group of images you want to narrow down, and press the letter **C** to enter Compare view. This puts one image on the left, called the "Select," and one on the right, called the "Candidate" (as seen below).

Step Four:

At the end, whichever image winds up as the Select is your favorite, but for now (when you first start), you need to decide which of these two you like better. If you like the image on the left (the Select) better than the one on the right (the Candidate), press the **Right Arrow key** on your keyboard. The Select image stays the same, but a new Candidate image appears to challenge your current Select. Or, if you like the Candidate better than the Select, click the Swap button (circled here) down in the toolbar, and it moves over to the left to become the Select and a new photo appears as the Candidate. (*Note:* If you don't see the toolbar, press **T**.) That's pretty much it. If you selected seven images to start, when you get to the last image to be compared, it stops there (no more images will appear as the Candidate). It's now down to these last two. If you still think the Select looks best, well, that's your favorite (it beat all the other contenders). If you like that Candidate best, hit the Swap button, then click the Done button in the toolbar to go to Loupe view, where you can then press 5 on your keyboard to mark the winning image as your Select. That's it.

Smart Collections: Your Organizational Assistant

Wouldn't it be awesome to have an assistant that you could assign Lightroom housekeeping tasks to, like "Gather all my 5-star photos from the last 60 days, but only ones that were taken with my 5D Mark IV, and only ones that I shot horizontally, and that have GPS data, and put them in a collection for me automatically"? That's what smart collections do—they gather photos based on a range of criteria you choose, and put them in a collection for you automatically. Like an assistant. Or a magical photo butler. Let's go with that second one.

Step One:

To understand the power of smart collections, let's build one that creates a collection of all your best shots from the last year, and all in horizontal format, so you can create a calendar with your favorite shots as a gift for friends and family (ya know, in lieu of a really good gift ;-). In the Collections panel, click on the + (plus sign) button on the right side of the panel header, and choose **Create Smart Collection** from the pop-up menu. This brings up the Create Smart Collection dialog. In the Name field at the top, name your smart collection (maybe something like, "Best of 2017 for Calendar"), and from the Match pop-up menu, choose **All**, so any criteria we add will be included in our smart collection.

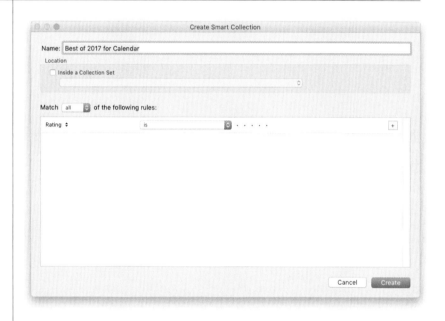

Step Two:

Then, from the pop-up menu beneath that, to the right of "Rating" (that's the default for the first pop-up menu), make sure it's set to **Is**, and you'll see five black dots to the right. Click on the fifth dot and it changes to five stars. If you clicked the Create button at this point, it would create a new collection with every 5-star image in your entire catalog, but let's add another line of criteria, so we get just the 5-stars from 2017. To create another line of criteria, click on the little + (plus sign) button on the far right of those stars. From the first pop-up menu, under Date, choose **Capture Date**, then from the menu to the right of that, choose **Is in the Range**, and then in the text fields that appear, enter "2017-01-01" to "2017-12-31."

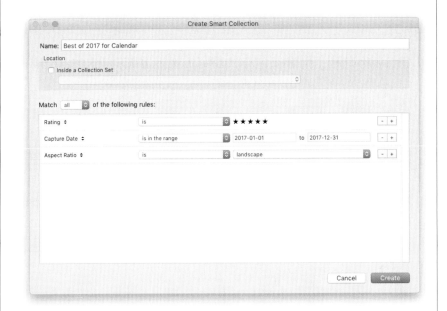

Step Three:
At this point, if you clicked the Create button, you'd have a collection of all your 5-star images from 2017. Pretty handy, but for our calendar, we need all the images to be wide (not tall), so let's add another line of criteria. Click the + button on the far right of the last line of criteria, and from the first pop-up menu, under Size, choose **Aspect Ratio**. From the next menu, choose **Is**, and then from the menu to the right of that, choose **Landscape**. Now, if you click Create, you'd get all your 5-star images from 2017 that are wide, and if you were to import a photo today that matches those criteria, it would be added to that smart collection automatically.

ADVANCED TIP:
Adding Sub-Criteria
If you're looking for even smarter smart collections, press-and-hold the Option (PC: Alt) key and the + button next to a line of criteria changes to the # (number sign) button. Click it, and it adds a sub-criteria line with more advanced options for creating smart collections.

Step Four:
So, when you hit the Create button, it compiles all the photos that match that criteria, puts them in a collection, and adds it to your Collections panel. You'll be able to instantly see which collections are smart collections because they have a little "gear" icon in the bottom-right corner of their collection icon. A couple of things to note: If you decide you want to change, add, or delete any criteria from this smart collection, just double-click on it and it opens the Edit Smart Collection dialog, where you can add (hit the + button) or take away (hit the – button) criteria. Also, smart collections don't have to have this level of depth—they can be "one liners" that compile any photos that don't have your copyright data added, or have a particular keyword (or are missing keywords altogether), or don't have GPS data (you can add missing GPS data—see page 66), so don't think they always have to be these in-depth multi-criteria searches.

Reducing Clutter Inside Your Collections by Using Stacks

One way to simply "de-clutter" any collection is to use Lightroom's Stacking feature, where you use one thumbnail to represent a bunch of photos that pretty much look alike. A great use for this would be when you shoot a pano with a bunch of frames (that look just slightly different) or an HDR, where you took seven frames, but just need one frame to represent all seven (since it's the exact same scene, just brighter or darker). You can do this manually, but you'll love the automatic method even more.

Step One:
Here, we've imported images from a model shoot, and you can see what I was talking about above, where there are several shots that include the same pose (I made the thumbnails really, really small and there are still parts of the shoot that aren't visible). To cut through the clutter of seeing all these similar images, we're going to group similar poses into a stack with just one thumbnail showing (the rest of the photos are grouped behind that photo), but with the number of photos behind it visible right on the thumbnail. Start by clicking on the first photo of a similar pose (as seen highlighted here), then press-and-hold the Shift key and click on the last photo that has the same pose (as shown here) to select them all (you can also select photos in the Filmstrip, if you prefer).

Step Two:
Now press **Command-G (PC: Ctrl-G)** to put all your selected photos into a stack (this keyboard shortcut is easy to remember, if you think of G for Group). If you look in the grid now, you can see there's just one thumbnail visible with that pose. It didn't delete or remove those other photos—they are stacked behind that one thumbnail (in a computery, technical, you'll-just-have-to-trust-that's-what's-happening kind of way). If you look in the top-left corner of that thumbnail, you'll see the number 28 in a small white box. That's letting you know there are 27 similar images stacked behind this one thumbnail.

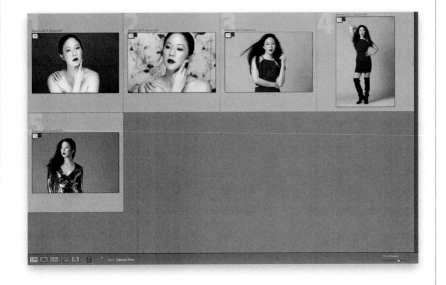

Step Three:

Here, I selected each set of images of the same pose, pressed Command-G (PC: Ctrl-G) to stack them, and now I'm down to just these five thumbnails, which represent all the images you saw in Step One. Talk about cutting the clutter! The view you're seeing here is called the Collapsed view. To see all the photos in a stack, click on it and press the letter **S** on your keyboard, or you can click on that little number in the top-left corner of each stack's thumbnail, or click on one of the two little thin bars that appear on either side of the thumbnail. (To collapse the images back into the stack, just do any of these again.) To add a photo to an existing stack, just drag-and-drop it right onto the existing collapsed stack. To stop stacking, Right-click on a stack's thumbnail, and from the pop-up menu, under Stacking, choose **Unstack**.

TIP: Pick Your Stack Cover Photo

The first photo you selected when creating a stack becomes the cover thumbnail. To choose a different photo in your stack to be the cover thumbnail, expand the stack, hover over the photo you want, then click on its stack number in the top-left corner. That moves it to the front, and it becomes the new cover image.

Step Four:

Manually stacking takes time, which is why I love having Lightroom do it for me automatically, based on the time photos were taken. Go under the Photo menu, under Stacking, and choose **Auto-Stack by Capture Time** (as shown here). This brings up a dialog with a slider, and it shows how many stacks it would create automatically based on whether you want it to stack images with less time between them (drag left) or more time (drag the slider right). When you click Stack, it looks like nothing happened—that's because the stacks are expanded. To see the tidied up look, go back under the Stacking menu and choose **Collapse All Stacks**.

Adding Keywords (Search Terms)

There are a number of pros, including journalists, commercial photographers, and folks who sell their images as stock, who have to add keywords (search terms) as part of their job. For the rest of us, it just takes a lot of time, and it may even be a big waste of time if you're pretty organized, in which case, finding the images you're looking for is quick and easy even without keywords (I don't usually use keywords myself). If you're not organized, keywords are your only hope, and for those folks (and people who just like keywording), here's how to add them:

Step One:

I just want to mention up front that I'm going to start with the keywording basics, as most folks won't need the level of keywording I get into after just a couple of pages. But, if you're a commercial photographer, or if you work with a stock photo agency, keywording all your images is pretty much what you have to do. Luckily, Lightroom makes the process fairly painless. There are a few ways to add specific keywords, and there are different reasons why you might choose one way over another. We'll start with the Keywording panel in the right side Panels area. When you click on a photo, it will list any keywords already assigned to that photo near the top of the Keywording panel (as shown here). By the way, we don't really use the word "assigned," we say a photo's been "tagged" with a keyword, as in, "It's tagged with the keyword NFL."

Step Two:

I tagged all the photos here with some kinda generic keywords when I imported them, like Alabama, Clemson, and Raymond James Stadium. To add another keyword, you'll see a text field below the keyword field where it literally reads, "Click here to add keywords." Just click in that field, and type in the keyword you want to add (if you want to add more than one keyword, just put a comma between them), then press the **Return (PC: Enter) key**. So, for the selected photo in Step One, I added the keyword "End Zone." Easy enough.

Step Three:
If you want to apply the same keyword(s) to a bunch of photos at once, like 71 photos taken during the celebration, you'd select those 71 photos first (click on the first one, press-and-hold the Shift key, then scroll down to the last one, and click on it to select all the photos in between), then in the Keywording panel, add your keyword(s) in the Keyword Tags text field. For example, here I typed "Celebration" and it added that keyword to all 71 selected photos. So, the Keywording panel would be my first choice if I needed to tag a number of photos from a shoot with the same keywords.

TIP: Choosing Keywords
Here's how I'd choose my keywords: I'd ask myself, "If, months from now, I was trying to find these same photos, what words would I most likely type in the Search field?" Then, I'd use those words. It works better than you'd think.

Step Four:
Say you wanted to add some specific keywords to just certain photos, like adding the name of a particular player to shots of just him. You'd Command-click (PC: Ctrl-click) on the photos of him to select them, then use the Keywording panel to add this keyword, and it would add it to just those photos.

TIP: Create Keyword Sets
If you use the same keywords often, you can save them as a Keyword Set, so they're just one click away. To create a set, just type the keywords in the Keyword Tags text field, then click on the Keyword Set pop-up menu near the bottom of the panel. Choose **Save Current Settings as New Preset** and they're added to the list, along with built-in sets like Wedding, Portrait, etc.

Continued

Step Five:

The next panel down, Keyword List, lists all the keywords you've created or that were already embedded into the photos you've imported. The number to the right of each keyword tells you how many photos are tagged with that keyword. If you hover your cursor over a keyword in the list, a white arrow appears on the far right. Click on it and it displays just the photos with that keyword (in the example shown here, I clicked on the arrow for Deshaun Watson, and it brought up the only two photos in my entire catalog tagged with that keyword).

TIP: Drag-and-Drop and Delete Keywords

You can drag-and-drop keywords in the Keyword List panel right onto photos to tag them and vice-versa—you can drag-and-drop photos right onto keywords. To remove a keyword from a photo, in the Keywording panel, just delete it from the Keyword Tags field. To delete a keyword entirely (from all photos and the Keyword List panel itself), scroll down to the Keyword List panel, click on the keyword, then click the – (minus sign) button on the left side of the panel header.

Step Six:

It doesn't take long for your list of keywords to get really long. So, to keep things organized, you can create a keyword that has sub-keywords (like College Football as the main keyword, then inside that is Alabama, Clemson, and so on). Besides having a shorter keyword list, it also gives you more sorting power. For example, if you click on College Football (the top-level keyword) in the Keyword List panel, it will show you every image in your catalog tagged with Alabama, Clemson, etc. But, if you click on Alabama, it will show you only the photos tagged with Alabama. This is a huge time-saver, and I'll show you how to set this up in the next step.

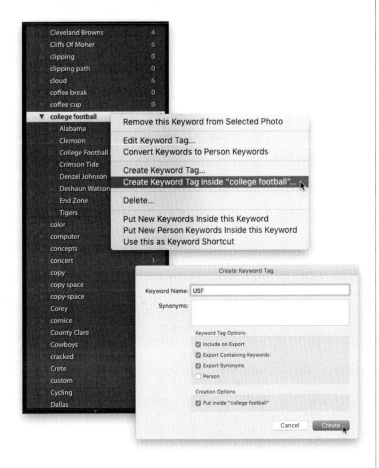

Step Seven:

To make a keyword into a top-level one, just drag-and-drop other keywords directly onto it. That's all you have to do. If you haven't added the keywords you want as sub-keywords yet, do this instead: Right-click on the keyword you want as a top-level keyword, then from the pop-up menu, choose **Create Keyword Tag Inside** (as shown here) to bring up a dialog where you can create your new sub-keyword. Click the Create button, and this new keyword will appear under your main keyword. To hide the sub-keywords, click the triangle to the left of your main keyword.

TIP: "Painting" On Keywords

Another way to add keywords is to paint them on using the Painter tool. Click on the Painter tool down in the toolbar, then from the pop-up menu to its right, choose **Keywords** and a text field will appear to its right. Type in your keyword(s) that relates to particular photos, then click-and-drag that paint can over just those photos you want to have that keyword(s). You'll see a confirmation appear onscreen as they're tagged.

Step Eight:

Besides working in the Keywording and Keyword List panels, once you've tagged your images with keywords, you can then use the Library Filter to search for images by their keyword. For example, if you're looking for shots of a particular player, you can just press **Command-F (PC: Ctrl-F)** and the Text Search field will appear in the top right, above your thumbnail grid. Type in the name of the player, and just the shots of him you tagged with his name will instantly appear in the grid below. Keywords really are just that—search terms. Some you add are generic (like NCAA football), but you can add more specific ones (like Deshaun Watson), as well.

Face Tagging to Find People Fast

Lightroom uses facial recognition software to help you find, and then tag, people easily. When it works, it's pretty helpful, but well…it's still "a work in progress," shall we say? If you're ever depressed and need a good laugh, turn on face tagging and watch it bring up things like a potato, as it asks, "Is this Larry?" Then, a bar of soap, "Is this Larry?" and then plate of scrambled eggs, "Is this Larry?" Sometimes it actually brings up Larry. Okay, it's not quite that bad, but it's not quite that good either. It may be worth using for tagging family members with their names (to use with keywords for searching).

Step One:

First, a heads-up: While we might refer to Lightroom's face tagging as "automatic," it's going to feel more semi-automatic because you do a lot of the initial work yourself. At first, it only recognizes that there's a face in the photo—it doesn't know who it is. That part is up to you, as you have to tell it who it is, so that it can go about its business of mis-assigning that face to the wrong person. So, if you have a decent-sized catalog, and you want your entire catalog set up with face tagging, you might need to set aside a morning to initially set this up. Okay, now that you know that, to start face tagging, go to the Library module and click on the People icon in the toolbar (shown circled here; or choose **People** from the View menu, or just press the letter **O** to jump there fast).

Step Two:

The first time you launch this, you get a screen that lets you know that it takes a while for Lightroom to go through your catalog and search each image for faces (luckily, it does this in the background, so it doesn't stop you from working). But, it does give you a choice: start now and do your entire catalog in the background, or just do it when you actually click the People icon. Choose whichever option you want, and it starts searching for faces. (By the way, as I'm writing this, Lightroom just displayed a lamp post, an archway, and a group of flags for faces. I am not making this up.)

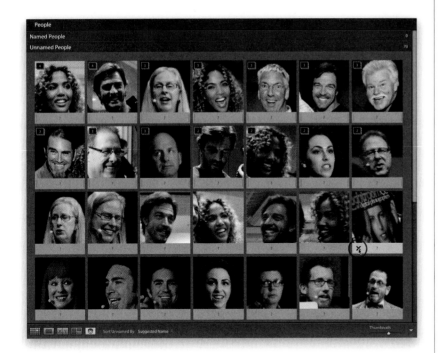

Step Three:

As it finds what it thinks are faces, they'll be displayed in the Unnamed People section with a "?" below each thumbnail showing that it doesn't know whose face that is (which makes sense—you haven't told Lightroom who's who yet). It found some blurry faces of people in the background in some of the photos, which I don't need tagged, along with the face of the cover model on my last Lightroom book, so I would just delete those from People view. To remove faces you don't want tagged, move your cursor over a thumbnail and click the "X" icon that appears in the bottom-left corner of the thumbnail (as seen here in the last thumbnail in the third row). *Note:* It doesn't remove these photos from Lightroom, just from this People view.

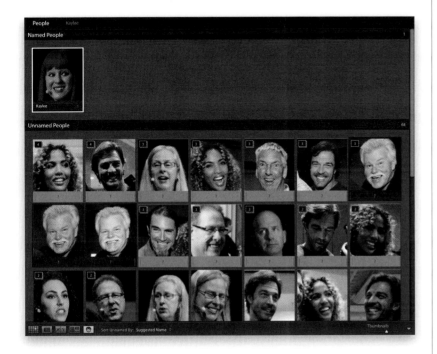

Step Four:

To tag any one of those photos with a name (you're actually tagging them with a special type of keyword used for searching), just click your cursor on the little question mark below the photo, and a text field appears. Type in their name and press the **Return (PC: Enter) key** on your keyboard. Once you tag a face with a name, it moves up top to the Named People section (seen here). If you see faces in the Unnamed People section that match someone in the Named People section up top, you can just drag-and-drop them right on their thumbnail in Named People.

Continued

Step Five:

If it recognize faces that it thinks are the same person, it groups them together in a stack to help keep things tidy. Take a look at the last thumbnail in the top row here—it found three similar faces and it grouped them together (there's a "3" in the top left of the thumbnail). To see the faces in a stack, click on its thumbnail, then press **S** on your keyboard and the stack expands (as seen here for that stack). To collapse it, press S again. To just take a quick peek inside a stack, press-and-hold the S key to see inside, then when you release that key, it collapses back again. If this stack appears in Unnamed People, click your cursor on the question mark below the thumbnail, so you can click and type in that person's name (that's Moose Peterson in those photos, so I tagged the first one "Moose"). After a few minutes, it will start "catching on" and a you'll start to see names followed by a question mark, like this: "Julieanne?" If it is her, click the checkmark button (as shown here at the bottom) and it moves that to her thumbnail up in Named People. If it's not, click the "No!" symbol. Also, once you tag someone, give Lightroom a minute or two to find and tag other similar faces. It learns as it goes.

Step Six:

At this point, we're at the stage where it has found all the faces it can find, and grouped the ones it thinks are the same person, and you're still left with a whole bunch of Unnamed People. So, it's now up to you to name them or drag-and-drop unnamed faces onto the proper thumbnails up in the Named People section. You'll see a green + (plus sign) appear when you're over the named thumbnail, letting you know that you're adding this face to that tag. This could be a quick process, or a long one, depending on which option you chose in Step Two (the full catalog or just the collection you're in). Either way, it's on you at this point to do the rest of the work.

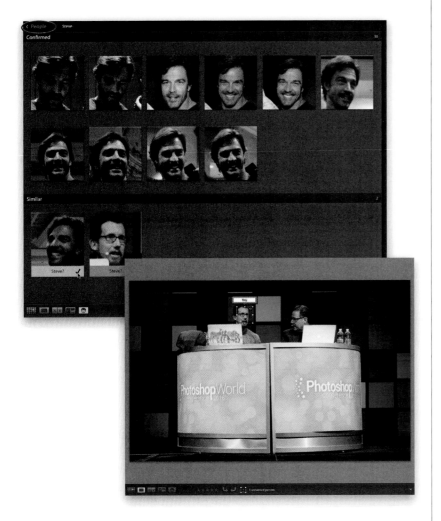

Step Seven:

If you double-click on a tagged photo in the Named People section, it takes you to the Confirmed section, which shows you which photos are confirmed to be that person. In the Similar section below, it shows you other photos it thinks may be that person (if you move your cursor over a thumbnail, a question mark appears after the person's name, as seen here. Expect this to happen pretty frequently). To confirm it's Steve, click on the checkmark, and that image moves up to the Confirmed section. Lightroom now uses that information to present other images, "How about these? These look similar, right?" Um. No. That's Trey in the Similar section. That's okay, because you can just return to People view by clicking on the word "People" in the top-left corner (shown circled here in red) and keep tagging other images. What happens if you double-click on an untagged photo? It opens the photo in a large Loupe-view-sized window and displays a rectangle around the region it thinks is a face. Click on the question mark and type in who that is. Also, you can create a new region over a face it missed, by simply clicking-and-dragging over a face. To remove an errant "face region," click on its little "X."

Step Eight:

Once you've got these people keywords applied, they work like regular keywords to help you find tagged images fast. Just go to the Keyword List panel (in this case, we're looking for images I tagged with "Moose"), and when you move your cursor over the Moose keyword, an arrow appears to its right. Click on that, and it now displays just those images that are tagged with "Moose." You can also search using the standard old **Command-F (PC: Ctrl-F)** text search by typing in the name of the person you're trying to find and they'll come right up.

Renaming Your Photos

If you didn't rename your photos when you imported them from your camera's memory card, it's really important (for searching purposes, if nothing else) that you rename them now with descriptive names (we name collections, sets, photos—everything—with descriptive names). If all you have are the numeric names assigned by your camera, like "_DSC0035.jpg," your chances of finding your images using a text search are pretty dim. Here's how to rename your photos to something that makes sense (and makes searching easy):

Step One:

Press **Command-A (PC: Ctrl-A)** to select all of the photos in your current collection, then go under the Library menu and choose **Rename Photos**, or press **F2** on your keyboard to bring up the Rename Photos dialog (shown here). From the File Naming pop-up menu, choose whichever preset you want to use. I always use the Custom Name - Sequence preset, which lets you type in a custom name, and then it starts automatically numbering each image, starting with whatever number you like (I generally choose to start with the number 1). That's all there is to it.

Step Two:

Now just click OK, and all the photos are renamed in an instant. This whole process takes just seconds, but makes a big difference when you're searching for photos—not only here in Lightroom, but especially outside of Lightroom in folders, in emails, etc., plus it's easier for clients to find photos you've sent them for approval.

To make finding our photos easier, we gave them descriptive names (either when we imported them, or when we renamed them afterward), and because we did that simple step, searching for our images by name is a breeze (of course, we can search by more than the name—we can search by everything from your camera's make and model, to the lens you used, and more).

Finding Photos Using a Simple Search

Step One:
Before you start searching, first you need to tell Lightroom where you want it to search. If you want to search just within a particular collection, go to the Collections panel and click on that collection. If you want to search your entire photo catalog, then look down on the top-left side of the Filmstrip and you'll see the path to the current location of the photos you're viewing. Click-and-hold on that path and, from the pop-up menu that appears, choose **All Photographs** (some other choices here are to search the photos in your Quick Collection, your last import of photos, or any of your recent folders or collections).

Step Two:
Now that you've chosen where to search, the easiest way to start a search is to use a familiar keyboard shortcut: **Command-F (PC: Ctrl-F)**. This brings up the Library Filter bar across the top of the Library module's Grid view. Chances are you're going to search by text, so just type in the word(s) you're searching for in the search field, and by default it searches for that word everywhere it can—in the photo names, in any keywords, captions, embedded EXIF data, you name it. If it finds a match, those photos are displayed (here, I searched for "Bucs vs Raiders"). You can narrow your search using the two pop-up menus to the left of the search field. For example, to limit your search to just captions, or just keywords, choose those from the first pop-up menu.

Continued

Step Three:

Another way to search is by attribute, so click on the word Attribute in the Library Filter and those options appear. Earlier in this chapter, we used the Attribute options to narrow things down to where just our Picks were showing (you clicked on the white Pick flag), so you're already kind of familiar with this, but I do want to mention a few other things: As for the star ratings, if you click on the fourth star, it filters things so you just see any photos that are rated four stars or higher (so you'd see both your 4-star and 5-star images, but of course I'm hoping you're following the system and not using any 4-star ratings at all). If you want to see your 4-star rated images only, then click-and-hold on the ≥ (greater than or equal to) sign that appears to the immediate right of the word Rating, and from the pop-up menu that appears, choose **Rating Is Equal to**, as shown here. You can also now use the Library Filter to see photos based on whether they've been edited yet using the Edits icons to the left of the star ratings.

Step Four:

Besides searching by text and attributes, you can also find the photos you're looking for by their embedded metadata (so you could search for shots based on which kind of lens you used, or what your ISO was set to, or what your f-stop was, or a dozen other settings). Just click on Metadata in the Library Filter, and a series of columns will pop down where you can search by date, camera make and model, lenses, or labels (as shown here). However, I have to tell you, if the only hope you have of finding a photo is trying to remember which lens you used the day you took the shot, you've done a really lame job of naming your files with descriptive names. This should truly be your "search of last resort."

Your camera doesn't need GPS to do this—in fact, you'll learn two easy ways to use this feature without even having GPS. But, if your camera does have built-in GPS, Lightroom places your images on a world map for you, automatically, behind the scenes without you even asking. Pretty amazing stuff! Next thing you know, they'll put a man on the moon and people will be driving around in electric cars.

Lightroom is Automatically Organizing Your Images on a Map

Step One:
If you've imported any photos that were taken with a camera that has built-in (or add-on) GPS, click on one of those photos, then in the Library module, go to the Metadata panel in the right side Panels area. Near the bottom of the EXIF section, you'll see a metadata field labeled GPS with the exact coordinates of where that shot was taken (shown circled here in red). Click on the little arrow that appears to the far right of the GPS field.

Step Two:
When you click on that little arrow, Lightroom takes you over to the Map module and displays a full-color satellite image with a pin at the exact location you were standing when you took the shot. How cool is that?! It's not just this one shot that's organized on the map—Lightroom automatically adds all your GPS-tagged shots to the map for you, so now you can find images by their location on the map, instead of just by name or keyword. To see all the photos represented by that little pin, hover your cursor over it and a preview window pops up that shows you a thumbnail of the first image. (By the way, if you double-click on the pin, the preview window pops up and stays.) To see more photos, just click the left and right arrows on the sides of the preview window (or you can use the **Left/Right Arrow keys** on your keyboard).

Map Organizing Even If Your Camera Doesn't Have GPS

There are two ways to add your photos to the global map, at the right location, without having GPS built-in to your camera. The first method gets your photos very close to the right location, and the second uses a clever trick to get your photos to the exact GPS location.

Step One:

The first method is to simply search the map and find the location where you took the shot (either with a simple city/country search for a general location, or by searching for an exact place or monument, like the Eiffel Tower in Paris or Rockefeller Center in New York City). You do this in the top-right corner of the Map module—in that Search field, type in the location you're looking for and a pin appears marking that location (here, I searched for Venice, Italy). *Note:* Lightroom's Map module uses a special version of Google Maps, so you'll have to be connected to the Internet for this GPS/map feature to work.

Step Two:

Now, in the Filmstrip along the bottom, select the images you took at that location, and then drag-and-drop them directly onto that pin on the map. Not only does it add those photos to the map, it also embeds that exact GPS data directly into the images (as seen here, circled in red). There's another method that's a bit more accurate, but you'll have to do a little trick to get the exact GPS coordinates without having GPS in your camera.

Step Three:
The second method starts while you're still at the location shooting. Before you leave, take one photo with your phone's camera. Your cell phone has built-in GPS, so that one shot will have the GPS coordinates embedded in it (if you have this feature turned on). Once you import the photos from your camera into Lightroom, import that one shot from your cell phone, too, because we're going to use its location on the map to add our non-GPS images to the map, as well.

TIP: Saving Your Favorite Locations
You can name any pin as a favorite location, so you can get back to it on the map without searching. First, click on a pin, then go to the Saved Locations panel (in the left side Panels area) and click the + (plus sign) button on the right side of the panel header. Give this location a name, then use the Radius slider to determine how far out you want other nearby photos tagged with that same location. As you drag the slider, it visually shows the radius as a white circle on the map, so you can see the area being covered. Turning on the Private checkbox tells Lightroom to strip out your GPS data if you save these files outside of Lightroom. Click Create, and this location is added to your Saved Locations panel.

Step Four:
Drag that cell phone photo into the same collection as your camera shots. Click on it, then go to the Metadata panel, down to GPS data, and click the little arrow to the right. This takes you to the Map module with a pin at the exact location where you took that cell phone photo. Now, go to the Filmstrip, select all the images you took with your regular camera at that location, and drag-and-drop them directly onto that pin where you took that cell phone photo. Not only does it add those camera images to the map, it's also embeds the GPS data directly into all the images.

Making Collections from Locations on the Map

Since now we know that behind-the-scenes Lightroom is automatically adding any of our images that have embedded GPS data to a map of the world, we can use that to make collections from any location. For example, if you see it added a bunch of shots you took in Paris to a tag over Paris in the Map module, you can instantly turn that tag into a collection, and then all those shots from Paris are instantly in a collection. It's almost too easy because Lightroom is pretty much doing all the work for you.

Step One:

Go to the Map module (I chose to view the map in a satellite view, here—you choose these different views from the Map Style pop-up menu in the left side of the tool-bar). Here, you can see a pin representing 70 photos I took in Marrakesh, Morocco. Lightroom automatically added these images to the map for me because I had the GPS feature turned on in my DSLR. To put those 70 photos from Marrakesh into a collection, start by Right-clicking on the pin, and from the pop-up menu that appears, choose **Create Collection** (as shown here).

Step Two:

This brings up the Create Collection dialog (seen here) where you can name your new collection (I gave mine a rather obvious name), and of course, all the standard options for creating a new collection are here, including the option to add this new collection to an existing collection set (ya know, putting it under my Travel collection set sounds like a pretty good choice). Click the Create button, and your new collection is created and added to the Collections panel, with just those images from Marrakesh, and Lightroom did all the gathering of those images for you automatically. Not too shabby.

If you work for any amount of time in Lightroom, at some point, you're going to take an image to the Develop module and see the warning "The file could not be found." If you go back to Grid view, you'll see a little exclamation point icon in the top right of the thumbnail, which is telling you that Lightroom can't find the original photo. All this means is that you moved the photo and Lightroom doesn't know where you moved it to, and all you have to do to fix this problem is simply tell Lightroom where you moved it.

Dealing with "The File Could Not Be Found" Message

"Morocco 6.jpg" could not be used because the original file could not be found. Would you like to locate it?

Previous location: /Volumes/External Hard Drive/Lightroom Photos/Travel/Lisbon/Finals/Morocco 6.jpg

Cancel   Locate

Step One:

In the thumbnails shown here, you can see one of them has a little exclamation point icon, letting you know Lightroom can't find the original high-resolution photo (so it only has this low-res thumbnail). If you took this photo over to the Develop module, you'd see the dreaded "The file could not be found" warning appear near the top of the image. This usually means that either (a) you moved the photo to another location, so Lightroom has lost track of it (nothing wrong with that—you should be able to move your photos wherever you want, right?), or (b) the original photo is stored on an external hard drive and that drive isn't connected to your computer right now, so Lightroom can't find it. Either way, it's a pretty easy fix, but first let's figure out which of those two scenarios it is.

Step Two:

To find out where the missing photo was last seen, click on that little exclamation point icon and a dialog will pop up telling you it can't find the original file (which you already knew), but more importantly, under the scary warning it shows you its previous location (so you'll instantly be able to see if it was indeed on a removable hard drive, flash drive, etc., or if you moved the file from where Lightroom last saw it).

Continued

Step Three:

Click on the Locate button, and when the Locate dialog appears (shown here), navigate your way to where that photo is now located. (I know you're thinking to yourself, "Hey, I didn't move that file!" but come on—files just don't get up and walk around your hard drive. You moved it—you just probably forgot you moved it, which is what makes this process so tricky.) Once you find it, click on it, then click the Select button, and it relinks the photo. If you moved an entire folder, then make sure you leave the Find Nearby Missing Photos checkbox turned on, so that when you find any one of your missing photos, it will automatically relink all the missing photos in that entire folder at once, and you can then edit your photos in the Develop module once again.

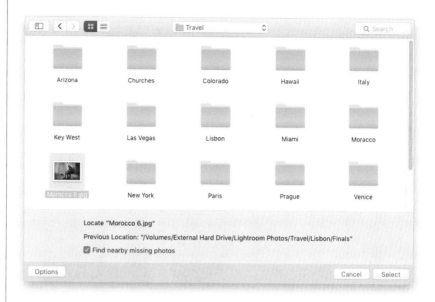

TIP: Keeping Everything Linked

If you want to make sure that all your photos are linked to the actual files (so you never see the dreaded exclamation point icon), go to the Library module, and under the Library menu up top, choose **Find All Missing Photos**. This will bring up any photos that have a broken link in Grid view, so you can relink them using the technique we just learned here.

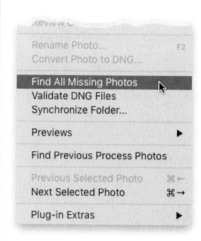

NOTE: If You Work in Folders

If you use folders instead of collections (don't get me started), and the folder is grayed out with a question mark in the right corner of the folder icon, it's the same scenario: you either moved that folder of images, or the drive it's on is disconnected. Right-click on that folder in the Folders panel and choose **Find Missing Folder**. Then, navigate to its new location, choose it, and now Lightroom knows where this missing folder is located. If you can't find this folder anywhere, it's possible that you accidentally deleted it, or its contents (which is a big reason you shouldn't be working in folders in the first place), in which case, here's hoping you have a backup of it someplace.

I mentioned earlier that you don't need to organize your photos by date, because Lightroom is actually already doing this for you automatically behind-the-scenes, using the exact time, day, month, and year embedded in the image file by your camera. Here's how to see your entire library organized by date:

Lightroom Is Automatically Organizing Your Photos by Date Behind the Scenes

Step One:
In the Library module, along the top of the Preview area is the Library Filter (if you don't see it, press the **\ [backslash] key** on your keyboard to bring it up). This searches based on where you're currently working in Lightroom (so if you're currently in a collection, it shows the details of what's in that collection), so go to the Catalog panel (near the top of the left side Panels area) and click on All Photographs, so we're looking at our entire catalog of images and not just one collection. There are four tabs across the top. Click on the Metadata tab, and it brings up four data columns: The first one on the left is your catalog sorted by Date, starting with the earliest year you have photos for in Lightroom.

Step Two:
To see the images taken in a particular year, click the right-facing arrow to the left of the year (in this case, I'm clicking on 2016), and it shows you each month in that year that I took a photo, and how many photos were taken in that particular month. Click on the arrow to the left of a month, and it displays all the days of that month represented by photos, along with the day of the week they were taken (helpful if you know the photos you're looking for were taken on a weekend) and the number of photos taken on that day. Click on one of those days, and the photos taken on that date are displayed in the grid below.

Continued

Step Three:

Did you notice that the other three columns to the right dynamically update to show you even deeper data on those photos? For example, I clicked on Monday, May 16, 2016, and in the second and third columns, it shows me which camera(s) I used to take the photos on that day, and it breaks down which lenses I used for each as well, so I can filter things down by camera make and model, or by lens used on that particular date. This is handy if you know you used a particular lens in the shot you're searching for (maybe you remember it was a fisheye shot, or maybe taken with a tilt-shift or a macro lens).

TIP: Searching by
Multiple Criteria

If you Command-click (PC: Ctrl-click) on more than one of the three search options in the Library Filter, they're additive. So, you could Command-click on Text, then Attribute, then Metadata, and they just pop down one after another. Now you can search for a photo with a specific keyword, that's marked as a Pick, with a Red label, that was taken at ISO 100, with a Canon EOS 5D Mark IV, using a 24–70mm lens, and is in Landscape (wide) orientation (and the results appear below it). You can even save these criteria as a search preset from the pop-up menu on the far right.

Step Four:

The last column is set to Label, by default, and shows you if any color labels were assigned to these photos, but if you click-and-hold directly on the column header "Label," you can choose from a long list of search attributes that might be more helpful to you (especially if you don't use color labels). You can change any of these four headers to search by whichever criteria you'd like.

Backing Up Your Catalog (This Is VERY Important)

All the sorting into collections, all the Develop module edits, all the copyright info, keywords, and stuff you do to your photos in Lightroom is stored in your Lightroom catalog file. As you might imagine, this is one incredibly important file, and if for some reason or another, one day you open up your catalog and get a warning that it has become corrupted, if you don't have a backup, you will be starting over from scratch. The good news is Lightroom will back up your catalog for you, and even ask you to do it, but you have to tell it to. Here's how:

Step One:

When you quit Lightroom, you'll notice that from time to time it will bring up the Back Up Catalog dialog, giving you the opportunity to make a backup of your all-important catalog (it has all your edits, sorting, metadata, Pick flags, etc., stored in its database). At the top, it even has a pop-up menu where you can choose how often to bring up this dialog, giving you the opportunity to back up from once a day to once a month (I would choose how often to back up based on how many days of work you're willing to lose if your catalog did become corrupt, and you had to use a backup catalog). By default, it stores this backup in a folder called (wait for it…wait for it…) "Back-ups" inside the Lightroom folder where your regular catalog is stored on your computer. *Note:* Even though you store your photos on an external hard drive, for the best performance, you should store your catalog right on your computer (we covered this back on page 36).

Step Two:

If you want, you can change the location where your backup catalog is stored (maybe to your external drive or to a cloud backup, in case your computer was to get stolen, so you'd still have a working backup). I leave the two Also checkboxes turned on just for good housekeeping.

Step Three:
So, what do you do if "the unthinkable" happens: you launch Lightroom one day, and you get a warning dialog letting you know that your catalog is "...corrupt and cannot be used or backed up until it is repaired"? Well, first you'd click the Repair Catalog button, and say a few prayers, and with any luck at all it will fix whatever was wrong with your catalog, and you're back up and running. But, what if, for whatever reason, you get the dialog seen here at bottom and it can't repair your catalog? Well, we go to Plan B.

TIP: Why You Might Not Need to Back Up At All
If you have an automated backup for your entire computer (I use Apple's Time Capsule for daily complete backups), then you may not need this Lightroom backup catalog because you already have a backup catalog on your backup computer hard drive.

Step Four:
Plan B is to restore your latest backup copy of your catalog. Here's how: In the "I can't repair your catalog" second warning dialog, click the Choose a Different Catalog button, and when the catalog chooser dialog appears (I have no idea if that's its proper name, by the way), click on Create New Catalog. You're doing this just so you can access Lightroom's menus (without a catalog open, you can't get to those menus), so name it "Trash Me," or whatever (it's just temporary). Once it opens this empty catalog, go under Lightroom's File menu and choose **Open Catalog**. In the dialog, navigate to your Backups folder (wherever you chose to save it in Step Two), and you'll see all your backups listed in folders by date and 24-hour time. Open the folder for the most recent backup, double-click on the .lrcat file (that's your backup), click the Open button, and you're back in business.

CHAPTER 3

ADVANCED STUFF
that next level of importing & organizing

Editions of this book have been around for 11+ years, but this is the first one to have a separate advanced importing and organization chapter. I think by doing this I have created an entirely new genre of Lightroom braggadocio. Just imagine how reading this chapter could play out for you. You're out one night attending a gala Lightroom charity ball, and you're making your entrance on the red carpet (point of order: at Lightroom events like this, technically, it is always a neutral gray carpet, but for the TV viewers watching at home, E! and ABC still refer to it as a "red carpet"). Of course, the TV hosts wave you over to ask the usual questions: "Who designed that gorgeous outfit?" "Where's that stunning necklace from?" And, "How much is too much Clarity on a typical landscape image?" The usual stuff. You answer their questions with a casual grace and elegance, as a passing waiter hands you a glass of champagne. It's at that moment—when all eyes are upon you, as you're looking radiant in your Schiaparelli haute couture gown and Sergio Rossi shoes—that you breezily turn to the hosts and say, "Tonight's really not about me…I'm just happy to be supporting the great work of the charity, helping raise money for these wonderful kids, and of course, staying focused on my advanced importing and organizational work in Lightroom." Trust me, at that moment, it will be as if all the oxygen has been sucked out of the room. Children will start crying, guests will be fainting, entire plates of ginger-soy-glazed mahi mahi will crash to the ground. It's because, single-handedly, you just created a major seismic shift in the Lightroom upper echelon, and there won't be a person in that room who doesn't realize what they just witnessed. It will be just as the Oracle had prophesied: you are "The Advanced One."

Shooting Tethered (Go Straight from Your Camera, Right Into Lightroom)

One of my favorite features in Lightroom is the built-in ability to shoot tethered (shooting directly from your camera into Lightroom), without using third-party software, which is what we used to do. The advantages are: (1) you can see your images much bigger on your computer's screen than on that tiny LCD on the back of the camera, so you'll make better images; and (2) you don't have to import after the shoot—the images are already there. Warning: Once you try this, you'll never want to shoot any other way.

Step One:
The first step is to connect your camera to your computer using that little USB cable that came with your camera. (Don't worry, it's probably still in the box your camera came in, along with your manual and some other weird cables that come with digital cameras. So, go look there for it.) Go ahead and connect your camera now. In the studio, and on location, I use the tethered setup you see here (which I learned about from world-famous photographer Joe McNally). The bar is the Tether Tools Rock Solid 4-Head Tripod Cross Bar, with the TetherTable Aero attached, along with the Aero Secure-Strap and TetherPro USB cable.

Step Two:
Now go under Lightroom's File menu, under Tethered Capture, and choose **Start Tethered Capture**. This brings up the dialog you see here, where you enter pretty much the same info as you would in the Import window (you type in the name of your shoot at the top in the Session Name field, and you choose whether you want the images to have a custom name or not. You also choose where on your hard drive you want these images saved, and if you want any metadata or keywords added—just like usual). However, there is one important feature here that's different—the Segment Photos By Shots checkbox (shown circled in red here)—which can be incredibly handy when you're shooting tethered (as you'll see).

Step Three:

The Segment Photos By Shots feature lets you organize your tethered shots as you go. So, let's say you're doing a location shoot, and you're shooting in two different locations there: one by a window, and the other outside. You can separate each of these locations into its own folder by clicking the Shot Name (this will make more sense in a moment). Try it out by turning on the Segment Photos By Shots checkbox and clicking OK. When you do this, a naming dialog appears (shown here), where you can type in a descriptive name for your first shoot.

Step Four:

When you click OK, the Tethered Capture window appears (seen here). If Lightroom sees your camera, its model name will appear on the left (if you have more than one camera connected, you can choose which one to use by clicking on the camera's name and choosing from the pop-up menu). If Lightroom doesn't see your camera, it'll read "No Camera Detected," in which case you need to make sure your USB cable is connected correctly, and that Lightroom supports your camera's make and model. To the right of the camera's model, you'll see its current settings, including shutter speed, f-stop, and ISO. To the right of that, you can apply a Develop module preset (see Chapter 7 for more on those, but for now, leave it set at None).

TIP: Hiding or Shrinking the Tethered Capture Window

Press **Command-T (PC: Ctrl-T)** to show/hide it. If you want to keep it onscreen, but you want it smaller (so you can tuck it to the side of your screen), press-and-hold the Option (PC: Alt) key and the little X in the top right that you'd click on to close the window changes into a – (minus sign). Click on that and the window shrinks down to just the shutter button. To bring it back full size, Option-click (PC: Alt-click) in the top right again.

Continued

Step Five:

The round button on the right side of the Tethered Capture window is actually a shutter button, and if you click on it, it'll take a photo just as if you were pressing the shutter button on the camera itself (pretty slick). When you take a shot now, in just a few moments, the image will appear in Lightroom. The image doesn't appear quite as fast in Lightroom as it does on the back of the camera, because you're trans- ferring the entire file from the camera to the computer over that USB cable (or wire- less transmitter, if you have one connected to your camera), so it takes a second or two. Also, if you shoot in JPEG mode, the file sizes are much smaller, so your images appear in Lightroom much faster than RAW images. Here's a set of images taken during a tethered shoot. The problem is if you view them in the Library module's Grid view like this, they're not much bigger than the LCD on the back of your camera. *Note:* Canon and Nikon react to tethering differently. For example, if you shoot Canon, and you have a memory card in the camera while shooting tethered, it writes the images to your hard drive and the memory card, but Nikons write only to your hard drive.

Step Six:

Of course, the big advantage of shooting tethered is seeing your images really large (you can check the lighting, focus, and overall result much easier at these larger sizes, and clients love it when you shoot tethered when they're in the studio, because they can see how it's going without looking over your shoulder and squinting to see a tiny screen). So, double- click on any of the images to jump up to Loupe view (as shown here), where you get a much bigger view as your images appear in Lightroom. (*Note:* If you do want to shoot in Grid view, and just make your thumbnails really big, then you'll probably want to go to the toolbar and, to the left of Sort Order, click on the A–Z button, so your most recent shot always appears at the top of the grid.

Step Seven:
Now let's put that Segment Photos By Shots feature to use. Let's say you finish this round of shots with your subject near the window and now you're going to shoot outside. Just click directly on the words "By Window" in the Tethered Capture window (or press **Command-Shift-T [PC: Ctrl-Shift-T]**) and the Shot Name dialog appears. Give this new set of shots a name (I named mine "Outside"), and then go back to shooting. Now these images will appear in their own separate folder, but all within my main Location Shoot folder.

TIP: Shortcut for Triggering Tethered Capture
You can trigger a tethered capture by pressing **F12** on your keyboard.

Step Eight:
When I'm shooting tethered, rather than looking at the Library module's Loupe view, I switch to the Develop module, so if I need to make a quick tweak to anything, I'm already in the right place. Also, when shooting tethered, my goal is to make the image as big as possible onscreen, so I hide Lightroom's panels by pressing **Shift-Tab**, which enlarges the size of your image to take up nearly the whole screen. Then lastly, I press the letter **L** twice to enter Lights Out mode (see page 92 for more on this), so all I see is the full-screen-sized image centered on a black background, with no distractions (as shown here). If I want to adjust something, I press L twice, then Shift-Tab to get the panels back.

Using Image Overlay to See If Your Images Fit Your Layout

This is one of those features that once you try it, you fall in love with it, because it gives you the opportunity to make sure an image you're shooting for a specific project (like a magazine cover, brochure cover, inside layout, wedding book, etc.) looks and fits the way you want it to, because you get to see the artwork as an overlay in front of your image as you're shooting tethered. This is a big time and frustration saver, and it's simple to use (you just need a little tweaking in Photoshop to set up your artwork).

Step One:

You'll need to start in Photoshop by opening the layered version of the cover (or other artwork) you want to use as an overlay in Lightroom. The reason is this: you need to make the background for the entire file transparent, leaving just the type and graphics visible. In the cover mock-up we have here, the cover has a solid gray background (of course, once you drag an image in there inside of Photoshop, it would simply cover that gray background). We need to prep this file for use in Lightroom, which means: (a) we need to keep all our layers intact, and (b) we need to get rid of that solid gray background.

Step Two:

Luckily, prepping this for Lightroom couldn't be simpler: (1) Go to the Background layer (the solid gray layer in this case), and delete that layer by dragging it onto the Trash icon at the bottom of the Layers panel (as shown here). Now, (2) all you have to do is go under the File menu, choose Save As, and when the Save As dialog appears, from the Format pop-up menu (where you choose the file type to save it in), choose **PNG**. This format lets you keep the layers intact and, since you deleted the solid gray background layer, it makes the background transparent (as seen here). By the way, in the Save As dialog, it will tell you that it has to save a copy to save in PNG format, and that's fine by us, so don't sweat it.

Step Three:
That's all you have to do in Photoshop, so head back over to Lightroom and go to the Library module. Now, go under the View menu, under Loupe Overlay, and select **Choose Layout Image** (as shown here). Then, find that layered PNG file you just created in Photoshop and choose it.

Step Four:
Once you select your layout overlay image, your cover appears over whichever image you currently have onscreen (as shown here). To hide the cover, go under the same Loupe Overlay menu, and you'll see that Layout Image has a checkmark by it, letting you know it's visible. Just choose Layout Image to hide it from view. To see it again, choose it again. Or press **Command-Option-O (PC: Ctrl-Alt-O)** to show/hide it. Remember, if you hadn't deleted the Background layer, what you'd be seeing here is a bunch of text over a gray background (and your image would be hidden). That's why it's so important to delete that Background layer and save in PNG format. Okay, let's roll on, because there are a few more features here you'll want to know about.

Continued

Step Five:

Now that your layout image overlay is in place, you can use the Left/Right Arrow keys on your keyboard to try different images on your cover (or whatever file you used). Here's what it would look like with a different shot.

Step Six:

When you look at the image in the previous step, did you notice that the word Photographer goes over part of her head? Luckily, you can reposition the cover to see what it would look like if you moved her over to the left a bit. Just press-and-hold the Command (PC: Ctrl) key and your cursor changes into the grabber hand (shown circled here in red). Now, just click-and-drag on the cover and it moves left/right and up/down. What's kind of weird at first is that it doesn't move your image inside the cover. It actually moves the cover. It takes a little getting used to at first, but then it becomes second nature.

Step Seven:
You can control the Opacity level of your overlay image, as well (I switched to a different image here). When you press-and-hold the Command (PC: Ctrl) key, two little controls appear near the bottom of the overlay image. On the left is Opacity, and you just click-and-drag to the left directly on the word "Opacity" to lower the setting (as seen here, where I've lowered our cover overlay to 45%). To raise the opacity back up, drag back to the right.

Step Eight:
The other control, which I actually think is more useful, is the Matte control. You see, in the previous step, how the area surrounding the cover is solid black? Well, if you lower the Matte amount, it lets you see through that black background, so you can see the rest of your image that doesn't appear inside the overlay area. Take a look at the image here. See how you can see the background outside on the left, top, and bottom of the cover? Now I know that this image has room for me to rearrange her position on the cover if I need to. Pretty handy, and it works the same as the Opacity control—press-and-hold the Command (PC: Ctrl) key and click-and-drag right on the word "Matte."

Creating Your Own Custom File Naming Templates

Staying organized is critical when you have thousands of photos, and because digital cameras generate the same set of names over and over, it's really important that you rename your photos with a unique name right during import. A popular strategy is to include the date of the shoot as part of the new name. Unfortunately, only one of Lightroom's import naming presets includes the date, and it makes you keep the camera's original filename along with it. Luckily, you can create your own custom file naming template just the way you want it. Here's how:

Step One:

Start in the Library module, and click on the Import button on the bottom-left side of the window (or use the keyboard shortcut **Command-Shift-I [PC: Ctrl-Shift-I]**). When the Import window appears, click on Copy at the top center and the File Renaming panel will appear on the right side. In that panel, turn on the Rename Files checkbox, then click on the Template pop-up menu and choose **Edit** (as shown here) to bring up the Filename Template Editor (shown below in Step Two).

Step Two:

At the top of the dialog, there is a pop-up menu where you can choose any of the built-in naming presets as a starting place. For example, if you choose Custom Name – Sequence, the field below shows two blue tokens (that's what Adobe calls them; on a PC, the info appears within braces) that make up that preset: The first represents the text (to type in your own custom text, double-click on that blue Custom Text token and it highlights, so you can type in whatever name you like). The second blue token represents the auto numbering. To remove either token, click on it, then press the Delete (PC: Backspace) key on your keyboard. If you want to just start from scratch (as I'm going to do), delete both tokens, choose the options you want from the pop-up menus below, and it automatically inserts the tokens for you (there's no need to click Insert if you choose from a menu).

Filename Template Editor

Preset: Custom Name - Sequence (edited)

Example: untitled.RAW

Custom Text

Image Name

Filename — Insert

Numbering

Import # (1) — Insert

Image # (1) — Insert

Sequence # (001) — Insert

Additional

Date (YYYY) — Insert

Dimensions — Insert

Custom

Shoot Name — Insert

Custom Text — Insert

Cancel | Done

Step Three:

Let's go ahead and make one from scratch (this is only an example—you can create a custom template later that fits your needs). We'll start by adding a Custom Text token (later, when we're actually doing an import, we'll customize this name to fit the images we're importing), so near the bottom of the dialog, click the Insert button to the right of Custom Text to add a Custom Text token (as seen here). By the way, if you look right above where the tokens appear, where it says "Example," it shows you a preview of the filename you're creating. At this point, our name is just "untitled.RAW" (it will show whatever the actual file extension is, so if it's a JPG or CR2 or NEF, that's what it will show for the extension).

Filename Template Editor

Preset: Custom Name - Sequence (edited)

Example: untitled_Jun.RAW

Custom Text _ Date (Mon) ⌄

Image Name

Filename — Insert

Numbering

Import # (1) — Insert

Date (Month DD, YYYY)
Date (YYYYMMDD) — Insert
Date (YYMMDD) — Insert
Date (YYYY)
Date (YY)
Date (Month)
✓ Date (Mon) — Insert
Date (MM)
Date (DD) — Insert
Julian Day of the Year
Hour
Minute — Insert
Second
Custom Text — Insert

Cancel | Done

Step Four:

Now, let's add the month it was taken (dates are drawn automatically from the metadata embedded into your photo by your camera when the shot was taken), but if you just add the month, it doesn't put a space between the letters, so the month's name will butt right up against our custom name. Luckily, we can add a hyphen or underscore to create some visual separation. So, press-and-hold the Shift key, then press the hyphen (dash) key, and it adds an underscore after the custom name. Now, we'll have some visual separation when we add the month after it. Go down to the Additional section, and from the Date pop-up menu, choose **Date (Mon)**, as shown here. This gives you the month's three-letter abbreviation, rather than the full month (the letters in the parentheses show you how the date will be formatted. For example, choosing Date [MM] would show the two-digit month, like "06," instead of showing "Jun").

Continued

Step Five:

Now let's add the year (by the way, Lightroom is keeping track of all your images by date automatically—you can access this sorting by going to the Library Filter bar, clicking on the Metadata tab at the top, and choosing Date in the first column [see page 71]—so I don't actually add the date to my filenames. This is just to help you learn how to use the Filename Template Editor). You could add another underscore between the month and year, but to visually change things up, let's add a dash. Now let's choose the year. In this case, I went with the four-digit year option (as shown here), and it adds it after our dash. Take a look at our name example now, it's "untitled_Jun-2018.RAW."

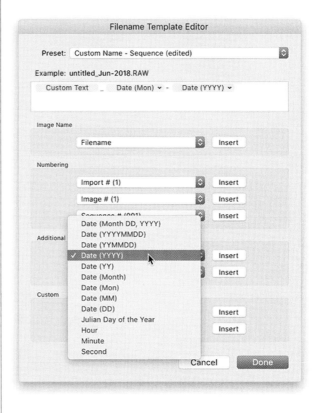

Step Six:

Lastly, you're going to have Lightroom automatically number these photos sequentially. To do that, go to the Numbering section and choose your numbering sequence from the third pop-up menu down. Here, I added a dash and then chose the Sequence # (001) token, which adds three-digit auto-numbering to the end of your filename. So, now my files will be named "untitled_Jun-2018-001.RAW," "-002.RAW," and so on (you can see this in the Example).

Step Seven:

Once the little naming example looks right to you, go under the Preset pop-up menu up top, choose **Save Current Settings as New Preset** (as shown here), and a dialog will appear where you can name your preset. Type in a descriptive name (so you'll know what it will do the next time you want to apply it—I chose "Name, Mon, Year, Seq"), click Create, and then click Done in the Filename Template Editor. Now, next time you're importing some images in the Import window and you click on the File Renaming panel's Template pop-up menu, you'll see your custom naming template as one of the preset choices (as seen selected in the next step).

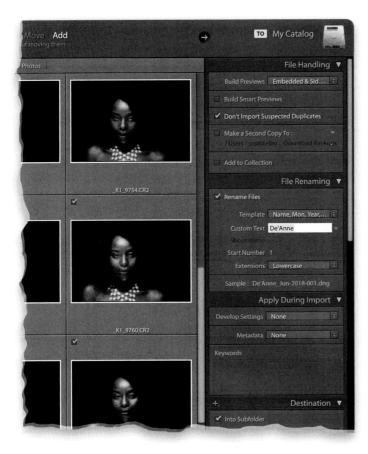

Step Eight:

So, how does this work for other shoots? Smooth as glass. Here's why: After you choose this new naming template from the Template pop-up menu, click below it in the Custom Text field (this is where that Custom Text token we added earlier comes into play) and type in the descriptive part of the filename (in this case, I typed in "De'Anne"2—don't include spaces between words). That custom text will appear before an underscore, giving you a visual separator so everything doesn't run together (see, it all makes sense now). Once you type it in, if you look at the Sample at the bottom of the File Renaming panel, you'll see a preview of how the photos will be renamed. Once you've chosen all your Apply During Import and Destination panel settings, you can click the Import button.

Creating Your Own Custom Metadata (Copyright) Templates

I mentioned earlier in the book that you'll want to set up your own custom metadata template, so you can easily and automatically embed your own copyright and contact information right into your photos as they're imported into Lightroom. Well, here's how to do just that. Keep in mind that you can create more than one template, so if you create one with your full contact info (including your phone number), you might want to create one with just basic info, or one for when you're exporting images to be sent to a stock photo agency, etc.

Step One:
You can create a metadata template from right within the Import window, so press **Command-Shift-I (PC: Ctrl-Shift-I)** to bring it up. Once the Import window appears, go to the Apply During Import panel, and from the Metadata pop-up menu, choose **New** (as shown here).

Step Two:
A blank New Metadata Preset dialog will appear. First, click the Check None button at the bottom of the dialog, as shown here (so no blank fields will appear when you view this metadata in Lightroom—only fields with data will be displayed).

New Metadata Preset

Preset Name: Scott Copyright (Full)

Preset: Custom

▼ ☐ IPTC Content

Headline

IPTC Subject Code

Description Writer

Category

Other Categories

▼ ☑ IPTC Copyright

Copyright © 2018 Scott Kelby

Copyright Status Copyrighted

Rights Usage Terms All rights reserved. No reproduction of any kind without

Copyright Info URL http://scottkelby.com/usage

▼ ☐ IPTC Creator

Creator Scott Kelby

Creator Address 118 Douglas Road E.

Creator City Oldsmar

Creator State / Province FL

Creator Postal Code 34677

Creator Country USA

Creator Phone 813-433-5000

Creator E-Mail skelby@photoshopuser.com

Creator Website http://scottkelby.com

Check All   Check None   Check Filled   Cancel   Create

Edit Metadata Presets

Prese ✓ Scott Copyright (Full)
Scott's Copyright

Save Current Settings as New Preset...
Restore Default Presets
Delete preset "Scott Copyright (Full)"...
Rename preset "Scott Copyright (Full)"...

Caption

▼ ☐ Camera Info

User Comment

GPS

Altitude

Direction

▼ ☐ IPTC Content

Headline

IPTC Subject Code

Description Writer

Category

Other Categories

▼ ☑ IPTC Copyright

Copyright © 2018 Scott Kelby

Copyright Status Copyrighted

Rights Usage Terms All rights reserved. No reproduction of any kind without

Copyright Info URL http://scottkelby.com/usage

Check All   Check None   Check Filled   Done

Step Three:

In the IPTC Copyright section, type in your copyright information (as seen here). Next, go to the IPTC Creator section and enter your contact info (after all, if someone goes by your website and downloads some of your images, you might want them to be able to contact you to arrange to license your photos). Now, you may feel that the Copyright Info URL (web address) that you added in the previous section is enough contact info, and if that's the case, you can skip filling out the IPTC Creator info (after all, this metadata preset is to help make potential clients aware that your work is copyrighted, and tell them how to get in contact with you). Once all the metadata info you want embedded in your photos is complete, go up to the top of the dialog, give your preset a name—I chose "Scott Copyright (Full)"—and then click the Create button.

Step Four:

As easy as it is to create a metadata template, deleting one isn't much harder. Go back to the Apply During Import panel and, from the Metadata pop-up menu, choose **Edit Presets**. That brings up the Edit Metadata Presets dialog (which looks just like the New Metadata Preset dialog). From the Preset pop-up menu at the top, choose the preset you want to delete. Once all the metadata appears in the dialog, go back to that Preset pop-up menu, and now choose **Delete Preset [Name of Preset]**. A warning dialog will pop up, asking if you're sure you want to delete this preset. Click Delete, and it is gone forever.

Using Lights Dim, Lights Out, and Other Viewing Modes

One of the things I love best about Lightroom is how it gets out of your way and lets your photos be the focus. That's why I love the Shift-Tab shortcut that hides all the panels. But if you want to really take things to the next level, after you hide those panels, you can dim everything around your photo, or literally "turn the lights out," so everything is blacked out but your photos. Here's how:

Step One:
Press the letter **L** on your keyboard to enter Lights Dim mode, in which everything but your photo(s) in the center Preview area is dimmed (kind of like you turned down a lighting dimmer). Perhaps the coolest thing about this dimmed mode is the fact that the Panels areas, taskbar, and Filmstrip all still work—you can still make adjustments, change photos, etc., just like when the "lights" are all on.

Step Two:
The next viewing mode is Lights Out (you get Lights Out by pressing **L** a second time), and this one really makes your photo(s) the star of the show because everything else is totally blacked out, so there's nothing (and I mean nothing) but your photo(s) onscreen (to return to regular Lights On mode, just press L again). To get your image as big onscreen as possible, right before you enter Lights Out mode, press **Shift-Tab** to hide all the panels on the sides, top, and bottom—that way you get the big image view you see here. Without the Shift-Tab, you'd have the smaller size image you see in Step One, with lots and lots of empty black space around it.

TIP: Controlling Lights Out Mode

You have more control over Lightroom's Lights Out mode than you might think: just go to Lightroom's preferences (under the Lightroom menu on a Mac or the Edit menu on a PC), click on the Interface tab, and you'll find pop-up menus that control both the Dim Level and the Screen Color when you're in full Lights Out mode.

Step Three:

If you want to view your grid of photos without distractions, first press Shift-Tab to hide all the panels. Then press **Command-Shift-F (PC: Ctrl-Shift-F)** on your keyboard. That makes the window fill your screen and hides the window's title bar and the menu bar at the top of your screen. If you really want the maximum effect, press **T** to hide the toolbar, and if you have the Library Filter bar showing across the top, you can hide it, too, by pressing the **\ (backslash) key** to get the view you see here at the top, which is just your photos on a solid, top-to-bottom gray background. If you want a black background behind your images with even the file names hidden, press L twice to see your grid in Lights Out mode (seen here at the bottom). Press L once to return to Lights On view, and then press **Shift-F** to return to your normal view.

Using Guides and Grid Overlays

Just like in Photoshop, Lightroom has its own moveable, non-printing guides (only these may be better than Photoshop's). But, beyond these guides, you also have the ability to put a resizable, non-printing grid over your image, as well (helpful for lining things up or for straightening a part of your image), but it's not just a static grid, and it's not just resizable. We'll start with the guides.

Step One:
To make the guides visible, go under the View menu, under Loupe Overlay, and choose **Guides**. A white horizontal guide and white vertical guide will appear centered on your screen. To move them in tandem, press-and-hold the Command (PC: Ctrl) key, then move your cursor directly on the black circle in the middle where they intersect. Your cursor changes from the zoom tool (magnifying glass) to the hand tool (as shown here), and you can then drag the two guide lines wherever you'd like. To move either guide individually, move your cursor away from the center, hover it right over either guide, and now you can drag that individual guide where you want it. To clear the guides, press **Command-Option-O (PC: Ctrl-Alt-O)**.

Step Two:
You also have a grid that pretty much works the same way. Go under the View menu, under Loupe Overlay, and choose **Grid**. This puts a non-printing grid over your image, which you can use for alignment (or anything else you want). If you press-and-hold the Command (PC: Ctrl) key, a control bar appears at the top of the screen. Click directly on the word "Opacity" to change how visible the grid is (here, I cranked it up to 100%, so the lines are solid). Click directly on the word "Size," to change the size of the grid blocks themselves—drag left to make the grid smaller or right to make it larger. To clear the grid, press **Command-Option-O (PC: Ctrl-Alt-O)**. *Note:* You can have more than one overlay, so you can have both the guides and grid visible at the same time.

Let's say you're having a business lunch with a potential client, and you learn that the client is a car buff. You have some collections of car shots you've taken, but you want to quickly put something together to show him some of your work. You won't need this after this meeting—you just want to go through your collections, find some favorites, and put them in a temporary collection to show him in a quick slide show. Well, that's a job for Quick Collections.

When to Use a Quick Collection Instead

Step One:
There are a lot of reasons why you might want a temporary collection, but most of the time, I use Quick Collections when I need to gather images from a number of different collections into one collection, just temporarily. We'll use the example I laid out in the intro above, and we'll look though our automotive collections and choose some of our individual favorites from each to be in our quick, simple slide show. So, start by looking in one of your automotive collections, and when you see a shot you might want to include, just press the letter **B** and that image gets added to your Quick Collection (you get a message right onscreen letting you know it has been added, as seen here).

Step Two:
Now go to another automotive collection and do the same thing—each time you see an image you want in your Quick Collection, press B and it's added. Using this method, in no time at all, I can whip through 10 or 15 "Select" collections and mark the ones I want in my Quick Collection as I go. (You can also add photos to your Quick Collection by clicking on the little circle that appears in the top-right corner of each thumbnail in Grid view when you move your cursor over the thumbnail—it'll turn gray with a thick black line around it when you click on it. *Note:* You can hide that gray dot by pressing **Command-J [PC: Ctrl-J]**, clicking on the Grid View tab up top, then turning off the checkbox for Quick Collection Markers, as shown on the bottom here.)

Continued

Step Three:

To see the photos you put in a Quick Collection, go to the Catalog panel (in the left side Panels area), click on Quick Collection (as shown here), and now just those photos are visible. To remove a photo from your Quick Collection, just click on it and press the **Delete (PC: Backspace) key** on your keyboard (it doesn't delete the original, it just removes it from this temporary Quick Collection). You can also click on any photo, press B again, and it will remove the image from your Quick Collection.

TIP: If You Want to Save This Quick Collection

If you decide you want your Quick Collection to be saved as a regular collection, just go to the Catalog panel, Right-click on Quick Collection, choose **Save Quick Collection** from the pop-up menu, and a dialog appears where you can give your new collection a name.

Step Four:

Now that your photos from all those different collections are in a Quick Collection, you can see these images as a slide show at any time by pressing **Command-Return (PC: Ctrl-Enter)**. This kicks in Lightroom's Impromptu Slideshow feature, which plays a full-screen slide show (as seen here) of the photos in your Quick Collection, using the Default preset in Lightroom's Slideshow module. To stop the slide show, just press the Esc key. So, when you're done, do you have to delete this Quick Collection? That's up to you. As I mentioned in the tip above, you can save it and make it a real collection (with its own name and all that) or you can clear all the photos out of that Quick Collection by Right-clicking on it (in the Catalog panel) and choosing **Clear Quick Collection**. Now you can use it for something else.

We just talked about Quick Collections and how you can temporarily toss things in there for an impromptu slide show, or until you figure out if you actually want to create a collection of those images, but something you might find more useful is to replace the Quick Collection with a target collection. You use the same keyboard shortcut, but instead of sending things to the Quick Collection, now they go to an existing collection. So, why would you want to do that? Read these two pages and you'll totally see why these are so handy (you are soooo going to dig this!).

Using Target Collections (and Why They're So Handy)

Step One:

Let's say, during your travels abroad, you wind up shooting a lot of cathedrals (if you take any guided tours when you're overseas, trust me, your tour operator will be taking you to every cathedral they can find). Well, wouldn't it be handy to have one collection of all your favorite cathedral images, so they're all just one click away? If that sounds handy to you (it sure does to me), then create a new collection and name it "Cathedrals." Once it appears in the Collections panel, Right-click on it and choose **Set as Target Collection**. This adds a + (plus sign) to the end of the collection's name, so you know at a glance it's your target collection (as seen here). *Note:* You can't make a smart collection into your target collection. Just so ya know.

Step Two:

Now that you've created your target collection, adding images to it is easy— when you see a cathedral image you like, no matter which collection it's in, press **B** on your keyboard (the same shortcut you used for Quick Collection), and that image is added to your Cathedrals target collection. For example, here we're look- ing at a shot of the ceiling in St. Stephen's Cathedral in Passau, Germany. It's in my Danube River collection, and I want it added to my Cathedrals target collec- tion, so I clicked on it and pressed B. I get a confirmation onscreen that reads, "Add to Target Collection 'Cathedrals,'" so I know it was added. It doesn't remove it from my Danube River collection, it just adds it to the Cathedrals target collection, as well.

Continued

Step Three:

Now, if I click on that Cathedrals target collection, I see that St. Stephen's Cathedral image, plus cathedral images from other collections, as well, because now all my cathedral finals are in one place (I told you this was pretty handy, right?).

Step Four:

If you wind up creating these target collections fairly often, here's a time-saver: anytime you create a new collection, there's a checkbox in the Create Collection dialog that will make your new collection the target collection—just turn on the Set as Target Collection checkbox and this new collection is your new target collection. By the way, you can only have one target collection at a time, so when you choose a different collection to become the target collection, it removes the target from the previously selected collection (the collection is still there—it doesn't delete it. But, pressing B doesn't send images to that collection anymore— it sends them to the new collection you just designated as the target collection). Also, just keep in mind that if you want to go back to creating a Quick Collection (using the B keyboard shortcut), you'll need to turn off your target collection, by just Right-clicking on it and choosing **Set as Target Collection**.

Your digital camera automatically embeds all kinds of info right into the photo itself, including everything from the make and model of the camera it was taken with, to the type of lens you used, and even whether your flash fired or not. Lightroom can search for photos based on this embedded information, called EXIF data. Beyond that, you can embed your own info into the file, like your copyright info, or photo captions for uploading to news services.

Adding Copyright Info, Captions, and Other Metadata

Step One:
You can see the info embedded in a photo (called metadata) by going to the Metadata panel in the right side Panels area in the Library module. By default, it shows you some of the different kinds of data embedded in your photo, so you see a little bit of the stuff your camera embedded (called EXIF data—stuff like the make and model of camera you took the photo with, which kind of lens you used, etc.), and you see the photo's dimensions, any ratings or labels you've added in Lightroom, and so on, but again, this is just a small portion of what's there. To see all of just what your camera embedded into your photo, choose **EXIF** from the pop-up menu in the left side of the panel header (as shown here), or to see all the metadata fields (including where to add captions and your copyright info), choose **EXIF and IPTC**.

TIP: Get More Info or Search
While in Grid view, if you see an arrow to the right of any metadata field, that's a link to either more information or an instant search. For example, scroll down to the EXIF metadata (the info embedded by your camera). Now, hover your cursor over the arrow that appears to the right of ISO Speed Rating for a few seconds and a little message will appear telling you what that arrow does (in this case, clicking that arrow would show you all the photos in your catalog taken at 400 ISO).

Continued

Step Two:

Although you can't change the EXIF data embedded by your camera, there are fields where you can add your own info. For example, if you need to add captions (maybe you're going to be uploading photos to a wire service), just go to the Caption field in the IPTC metadata, click your cursor inside the field, and start typing (as shown here). When you're done, just press the **Return (PC: Enter) key**. You can also add a star rating or label here in the Metadata panel, as well (though I usually don't do that here).

Note: This metadata you're adding is stored in Lightroom's database, and when you export your photos from Lightroom as either JPEGs, PSDs, or TIFFs, this metadata (along with all your color correction and image editing) gets embedded into the file itself at that moment. However, it's different when working with RAW photos (as you'll see in a moment).

Step Three:

If you created a Copyright Metadata preset (see page 90), but didn't apply it when you imported these photos, you can apply that now from the Preset menu at the top of the Metadata panel. Or if you didn't create a copyright preset at all, you can add your copyright info manually. Scroll down to the bottom of the Metadata panel to the Copyright section, and just type in your copyright info (and make sure you choose **Copyrighted** from the Copyright Status pop-up menu). By the way, you can do this for more than one photo at a time. First, Command-click (PC: Ctrl-click) to select all the photos you want to add this copyright info to, then when you add the information in the Metadata panel, it's instantly added to every selected photo.

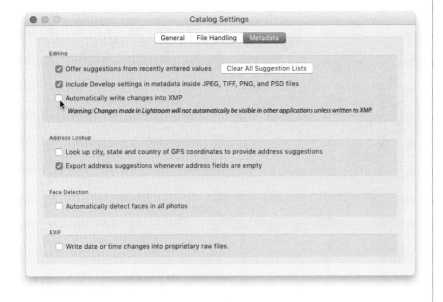

Step Four:

If you want to give someone your original RAW file (maybe a client or co-worker) or if you want to use your original RAW file in another application that processes RAW images, the metadata you've added in Lightroom (including copyright info, keywords, and even color correction edits to your photo) won't be visible because you can't embed info directly into a RAW file. To get around that, all this information gets written into a separate file called an XMP sidecar file. These XMP sidecar files aren't created automatically—you create them by pressing **Command-S (PC: Ctrl-S)** before you give someone your RAW file. After you press this, if you look in the photo's folder on your computer, you'll see your RAW file, then next to it an XMP sidecar file with the same name, but with the .xmp file extension (the two files are circled here in red). These two files need to stay together, so if you move it, or give the RAW file to a co-worker or client, be sure to grab both files.

Step Five:

Now, if you converted your RAW file into a DNG file when you imported it, then when you press Command-S (PC: Ctrl-S), it does embed the info into the single DNG file (a big advantage of DNG—see Chapter 1), so there will be no separate XMP file. There actually is a Lightroom catalog preference (choose **Catalog Settings** from the Lightroom menu on a Mac, or the Edit menu on a PC, then click on the Metadata tab, shown here) that automatically writes every change you make to a RAW file to the XMP sidecar, but the downside is a speed issue. Each time you make a change to a RAW file, Lightroom has to write that change into XMP, which slows things down a bit, so I leave the Automatically Write Changes into XMP checkbox turned off.

From Laptop to Desktop: Syncing Catalogs on Two Computers

If you're running Lightroom on a laptop during your location shoots, you might want to take all the edits, keywords, metadata, and of course the photos themselves, and add them to the Lightroom catalog on your studio computer. It's easier than it sounds: basically, you choose which collection to export from your laptop, then you take the folder it creates over to your studio computer and import it—Lightroom does all the hard work for you, you just have to make a few choices about how Lightroom handles the process.

Step One:

Okay, we're on location (or on the road), and we've imported our images, organized them in a collection set, and tweaked some of them—we pretty much did everything we need to do to these images on our laptop.

Step Two:

Once you get back home, on your laptop, go to the Collections panel and Right-click on the collection set you created—the one you want to merge with your desktop computer in your studio. (*Note:* If you work in folders, instead of collections, the only difference would be you'd go to the Folders panel and Right-click on the folder from that shoot instead.) From the pop-up menu that appears, choose **Export this Collection Set as a Catalog** (as shown here).

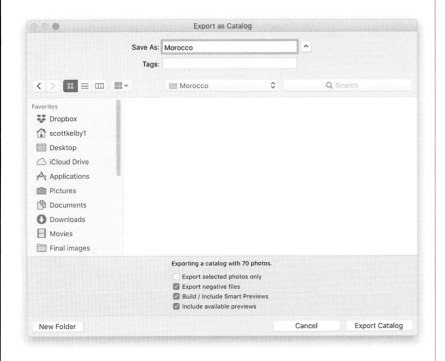

Step Three:

When you choose this, it brings up the Export as Catalog dialog (shown here). First, let's choose where to save this exported catalog. Since you'll need to get these images from your laptop to your desktop computer, I recommend using either a small portable hard drive or a USB flash drive with enough free space to hold your exported catalog, previews, and your original images (you can get a SanDisk 16GB USB flash drive for $6. That's cheaper than an appetizer at Chili's). So, give your exported collection a name, choose that portable drive to save it onto, then turn on the Export Negative Files checkbox (near the bottom of the dialog), so that it not only saves your edits, but it saves your images to that portable drive, too. Make sure to turn on the Include Available Previews checkbox, as well (so you don't have to wait for them to render when you import them later). You can also choose to include smart previews if you'd like.

Step Four:

When you click the Export Catalog button, it exports your collection (it usually doesn't take very long, but of course the more photos in your collection or folder, the longer it will take), and when it's done exporting, you'll see a new folder on your portable drive (or USB flash drive). If you look inside that folder, you'll see three or four files (depending on whether you chose to export smart previews or not). You'll see (1) a folder with the actual photos; (2) a file that includes the previews; (3) a file that includes any smart previews, if you chose to export those; and (4) the catalog file itself (it has the file extension LRCAT (as seen here).

Continued

Step Five:

Now, on your desktop computer, go under Lightroom's File menu and choose **Import from Another Catalog.** Navigate to that folder you created on your portable drive, then inside that folder, click on the file that ends with the file extension LRCAT (that's the catalog file you're importing), and then click the Choose button. That brings up the Import from Catalog dialog (seen here). If you want to see thumbnails of the images you're about to import, turn on the Show Preview checkbox in the bottom-left corner, and the thumbnails will appear on the right side of the dialog (seen here). If, for some reason, you don't want one or more of these photos imported, uncheck the checkbox in the top-left corner of its thumbnail.

Step Six:

So far we're just importing your previews and the edits you made on your laptop, but we haven't moved the photos from that folder on your portable or USB flash drive over to your desktop computer's storage device (which I'm hoping is an external hard drive—see Chapter 1). To make sure your original images get moved over as well, go to the New Photos section on the left and, from the File Handling pop-up menu, choose **Copy New Photos to a New Location and Import** (as shown here). When you choose this, a button appears right below asking you to choose where you want these images copied to. In our case, they would go onto your desktop computer's external hard drive, inside your main folder, inside your Travel folder. So, navigate there and click the Choose button. Now, click Import, and your exported collection will be added to your desktop computer's catalog, with all your edits, previews, metadata, etc., all intact, and copies of your original images will be copied onto your external hard drive.

It's pretty unlikely that you'll have a major problem with your Lightroom catalog (after all these years of using Lightroom, it has only happened to me once), and if it does happen, chances are Lightroom can repair itself (which is pretty handy). However, the chances of your hard drive crashing, or your computer dying, or getting stolen (with the only copy of your catalog on it) are much higher. Here's how to deal with both of these potential disasters in advance, and what to do if the big potty hits the air circulation device:

Dealing with Disasters (Troubleshooting)

Step One:
If you launch Lightroom and you get a warning dialog like you see here (at top), then go ahead and give Lightroom a chance to fix itself by clicking the Repair Catalog button. Chances are pretty likely it'll fix the catalog and then you're all set. However, if Lightroom can't fix the catalog, you'll see the bottom warning dialog instead, letting you know that your catalog is so corrupt it can't fix it. If that's the case, it's time to go get your backup copy of your catalog (ya know, the one we talked about back in Chapter 2).

Step Two:
Now, as long as you've backed up your catalog, you can restore that backup catalog, and you're back in business (just understand that if the last time you backed up your catalog was three weeks ago, everything you've done in Lightroom since then will be gone. That's why it's so important to back up your catalog fairly often, and if you're doing client work, you should back up daily). Luckily, restoring from a backup catalog is easy. First, go to your backup hard drive (remember, your backup catalog should be saved to a separate hard drive. That way, if your computer crashes, your backup doesn't crash along with it), and locate the folder where you save your Lightroom catalog backups (they're saved in folders by date, as seen here, so double-click on the folder with the most current date), and inside you'll see your backup catalog.

Continued

Step Three:
Next, find the corrupt Lightroom catalog on your computer (on my computer, it's in my Lightroom folder that's in my Pictures folder), and delete that file (drag it into the Trash on a Mac, or into the Recycle Bin on a PC). Now, drag-and-drop your backup catalog file into the folder on your computer where your corrupt file used to be (before you deleted it).

TIP: Finding Your Catalog
If you don't remember where you chose to store your Lightroom catalogs—don't worry—Lightroom can tell you. Go under the Lightroom (PC: Edit) menu and choose **Catalog Settings**. Click on the General tab, then under Location it will show the path to your catalog. Click on the Show button, and it will take you there.

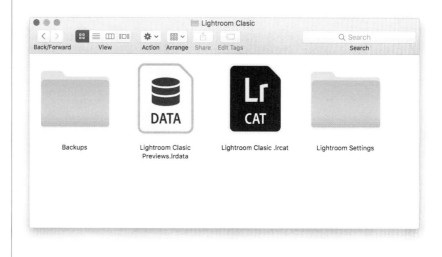

Step Four:
The final step is simply to open this new catalog in Lightroom by going under the File menu and choosing **Open Catalog**. Now, go to where you placed that backup copy of your catalog (on your computer), find that backup file, click on it, then click OK, and everything is back the way it was (again, provided you backed up your catalog recently. If not, it's back to what your catalog looked like the last time you backed it up). By the way, it even remembers where your photos are stored (but if it doesn't, go back to Chapter 2 where we looked at how to relink them).

TIP: If Your Computer Crashed...
If, instead of a corrupt catalog, your computer crashed (or your hard drive died, or your laptop got stolen, etc.), then it's pretty much the same process—you just don't have to find and delete the old catalog first, because it's already gone. So, you'll start by just dragging your backup copy of the catalog into your new, empty Lightroom folder (which is created the first time you launch Lightroom on your new computer, or new hard drive, etc.).

Step Five:

If you think your catalog's okay, but Lightroom has locked up or is just acting wonky, a lot of the time, simply quitting Lightroom and restarting will do the trick (I know, it sounds really simple, and kind of "Duh!" but this fixes more problems than you can imagine). If that didn't work, and Lightroom is still acting funky, it's possible your preferences have become corrupt and need to be replaced (hey, it happens). To do that, quit Lightroom, then press-and-hold **Option-Shift (PC: Alt-Shift)**, and relaunch Lightroom. Keep holding those keys down until the dialog appears asking if you want to reset your preferences. If you click on Reset Preferences, it builds a new, factory-fresh set of preferences, and chances are all your problems will be gone.

Step Six:

Next, if you have installed Lightroom plug-ins, it's possible one of them has gotten messed up or is outdated, so check the plug-in manufacturers' sites for updates. If your plug-ins are all up to date, then go under the File menu and choose **Plug-in Manager**. In the dialog, click on a plug-in, then to the right, click the Disable button, and see if the problem is still there. Turn each off, using the process of elimination, until you find the one that's messing things up. If you wind up disabling them all, and the problem is still there, then it's time to do a reinstall, either from the original install files (if you have Lightroom 6) or from the Adobe Creative Cloud app (if you use Lightroom Classic CC). Start by uninstalling Lightroom from your computer (it won't delete your catalogs), and then do your install. One of those will most surely fix your problem. If none of those worked, it may be time to call Adobe, 'cause something's crazy messed up (but at least you'll have already done the first round of things Adobe will tell you to try, and you'll be that much closer to a solution).

CHAPTER 4

CUSTOMIZING
how to set things up your way

This chapter about is about personalizing your Lightroom experience, so it works best for you. But, before you read this chapter, you really should be a bit more advanced in your Lightroom learning. The problem is that there's no one really there to police this, to stop you from reading a chapter you're not really emotionally prepared to handle. This is the type of stuff we tell our 12-year-old daughter that falls under the broad and all-encompassing header of "It's inappropriate." This officially replaces the previous phrase adored and used liberally by parents all over the world, which was, "Because I said so." When you think about it, that was a really lame response (at least it was when I heard it from my parents) because there was a reason, but they didn't want to tell you what it was. Of course, the real reason could have ranged from they just didn't feel like dealing with it, to they were lazy,

mean, or all of the above, but not giving us some reasonable explanation was certainly frustrating. That's why we, as parents (and Lightroom book authors), love the phrase, "It's inappropriate," because it infers there is a reason, but if we explained the reason, our explanation would have to be deemed inappropriate, too. So, our kids just assume it's something naughty, and go about their day knowing their parents love and care deeply about them experiencing anything that could be inappropriate for their age group (or Lightroom experience level). So, just know, dear reader, that I love you and I'm concerned about you being exposed to naughty Lightroom features. You can take a peek at this chapter, but if you see anything that you don't understand, or after seeing it you're uncomfortable and need to talk, just know that's something you should go ask your mother.

Choosing What You See in Loupe View

When you're in Loupe view (the zoomed-in view of your photo), besides just displaying your photo really big, you can display as little (or as much) information about your photo as you'd like as text overlays, which appear in the top-left corner of the Preview area. You'll be spending a lot of time working in Loupe view, so let's set up a custom Loupe view that works for you.

Step One:
In the Library module's Grid view, click on a thumbnail and press **E** on your keyboard to jump to the Loupe view (in the example shown here, I hid everything but the right side Panels area, so the photo would show up larger in Loupe view).

Step Two:
Press **Command-J (PC: Ctrl-J)** to bring up the Library View Options dialog and then click on the Loupe View tab. At the top of the dialog, turn on the Show Info Overlay checkbox. The pop-up menu to the right lets you choose from two different info overlays: Info 1 overlays the filename of your photo (in larger letters) in the upper-left corner of the Preview area (as seen here). Below the filename, in smaller type, is the photo's capture date and time, and its cropped dimensions. Info 2 also displays the filename, but underneath, it displays the exposure, ISO, and lens settings.

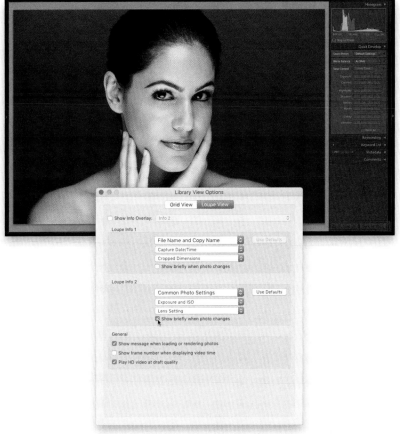

Step Three:

Luckily, you can choose which info is displayed for both info overlays using the pop-up menus in this dialog. So, for example, instead of having the filename show up in huge letters, for Loupe Info 2, you could choose something like **Common Photo Settings** from the first pop-up menu (as shown here). By choosing this, instead of getting the filename in huge letters, you'd get the same info that's displayed under the histogram (like the shutter speed, f-stop, ISO, and lens setting) found in the top panel in the right side Panels area. You can customize both info overlays separately by simply making choices from these pop-up menus. (*Remember:* The top pop-up menu in each section is the one that will appear in really large letters.)

Step Four:

Any time you want to start over, just click the Use Defaults button to the right and the default Loupe Info settings will appear. Personally, I find this text appearing over my photos really, really distracting most of the time. The key part of that is "most of the time." The other times, it's handy. So, if you think this might be handy, too, here's what I recommend: (a) Turn off the Show Info Overlay checkbox and turn on the Show Briefly When Photo Changes checkbox below the Loupe Info pop-up menus, which makes the overlay temporary—when you first open a photo in Loupe view, it appears on the photo for around four seconds and then hides itself. Or, you can do what I do: (b) leave those off, and when you want to see that overlay info, press the letter **I** to toggle through Info 1, Info 2, and Show Info Overlay off. At the bottom of the dialog, there's also a checkbox that lets you turn off those little messages that appear onscreen, like "Loading" or "Assigned Keyword," etc., along with some video option checkboxes.

Choosing What You See in Grid View

Those little cells that surround your thumbnails in Grid view can either be a wealth of information or really distracting (depending on how you feel about text and symbols surrounding your photos), but luckily you get to totally customize not only how much info is visible, but in some cases, exactly which type of info is displayed (of course, you learned in Chapter 1 that you can toggle the cell info on/off by pressing the letter **J** on your keyboard). At least now when that info is visible, it'll be just the info you care about.

Step One:

Press **G** to jump to the Library module's Grid view, then press **Command-J (PC: Ctrl-J)** to bring up the Library View Options dialog (shown here), and click on the Grid View tab at the top (seen highlighted here). At the top of the dialog, there's a pop-up menu where you can choose the options for what's visible in either the Expanded Cells view or the Compact Cells view. The difference between the two is that you can see more info in the Expanded Cells view.

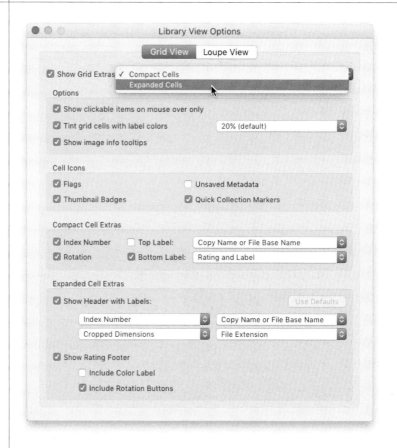

Step Two:

We'll start at the top, in the Options section. If you add a Pick flag and left/right rotation arrows to your cell, and turn on the Show Clickable Items on Mouse Over Only checkbox, it means they'll stay hidden until you move your mouse over a cell, then they appear so you can click on them. If you leave it unchecked, you'll see them all the time. The Tint Grid Cells with Label Colors checkbox only kicks in if you've applied a color label to a photo. If you have, turning this on tints the gray area around the photo's thumbnail the same color as the label, and you can set how dark the tint is with the pop-up menu. With the Show Image Info Tooltips checkbox turned on, when you hover your cursor over an icon within a cell (like a Pick flag or a badge), it'll show you a description of that item. Hover your cursor over an image thumbnail, and it'll give you a quick look at its EXIF data.

The thumbnail badges show you (from L to R) that a keyword has been applied, the photo has GPS info, it has been added to a collection, it has been cropped, and it has been edited

The black circle in the upper-right corner is actually a button—click on it to add this photo to your Quick Collection

Step Three:

The next section down, Cell Icons, has two options for things that appear right over your photo's thumbnail image, and two that appear just in the cell. Thumbnail badges appear in the bottom-right corner of a thumbnail to let you see if: (a) the photo has had keywords added, (b) the photo has GPS info, (c) the photo has been added to a collection, (d) the photo has been cropped, or (e) the photo has been edited in Lightroom (color correction, sharpening, etc.). These tiny badges are actually clickable shortcuts. For example, if you wanted to add a keyword, you could click the Keyword badge (whose icon looks like a tag), and it opens the Keywording panel and highlights the keyword field, so you can just type in a new keyword. The other option on the thumbnail, Quick Collection Markers, adds a black circle (that's actually a button) to the top-right corner of your photo when you mouse over the cell. Click on it to add the photo to (or remove it from) your Quick Collection (it becomes a gray dot).

Step Four:

The other two options don't put anything over the thumbnails—they add icons in the cell area itself. When you turn on the Flags checkbox, it adds a Pick flag to the top-left side of the cell, and you can then click on this flag to mark this photo as a Pick (shown here on the left). The last checkbox in this section, Unsaved Metadata, adds a little icon in the top-right corner of the cell (shown here on the right), but only if the photo's metadata has been updated in Lightroom (since the last time the photo was saved) and these changes haven't been saved to the file itself yet (this sometimes happens if you import a photo, like a JPEG, which already has keywords, ratings, etc., applied to it, and then in Lightroom you added keywords, or changed the rating). If you see this icon, you can click on it to bring up a dialog that asks if you want to save the changes to the file (as shown here).

Click the flag icon to mark it as a Pick

Click the Unsaved Metadata icon to save the changes

The metadata for this photo has been changed in Lightroom. Save the changes to disk?

☐ Don't show again   Cancel   Save

Continued

Step Five:

We're going to jump down to the bottom of the dialog to the Expanded Cell Extras section, where you choose which info gets displayed in the area at the top of each cell in Expanded Cells view. By default, it displays four different bits of info (as shown here): It's going to show the index number (which is the number of the cell, so if you imported 63 photos, the first photo's index number is 1, followed by 2, 3, 4, and so on, until you reach 63) in the top left, then below that will be the pixel dimensions of your photo (if the photo's cropped, it shows the final cropped size). Then in the top right, it shows the file's name, and below that, it shows the file's type (JPEG, RAW, TIFF, etc.). To change any one of these info labels, just click on the label pop-up menu you want to change and a long list of info to choose from appears (as seen in the next step). By the way, you don't have to display all four labels of info, just choose None from the pop-up menu for any of the four you don't want visible.

Step Six:

Although you can use the pop-up menus here in the Library View Options dialog to choose which type of information gets displayed, check this out: you can actually do the same thing from right within the cell itself. Just click on any one of those existing info labels, right in the cell itself, and the same exact pop-up menu that appears in the dialog appears here. Just choose the label you want from the list (I chose ISO Speed Rating here), and from then on it will be displayed in that spot (as shown here on the right, where you can see this shot was taken at an ISO of 200).

Step Seven:

At the bottom of the Expanded Cell Extras section is a checkbox, which is on by default. This option adds an area to the bottom of the cell called the Rating Footer, which shows the photo's star rating, and if you keep both checkboxes beneath Show Rating Footer turned on, it will also display the color label and the rotation buttons (which are clickable and will appear when you move your cursor over a cell).

Step Eight:

The middle section we skipped over is the Compact Cell Extras section. The reason I skipped over these options is that they work pretty much like the Expanded Cell Extras, but with the Compact Cell Extras, you have only two fields you can customize (rather than four, like in the Expanded Cell Extras): the filename (which appears on the top left of the thumbnail), and the rating (which appears beneath the bottom left of the thumbnail). To change the info displayed there, click on the label pop-up menus and make your choices. The other two checkboxes on the left hide/show the index number (in this case, it's that huge gray number that appears along the top-left side of the cell) and the rotation arrows at the bottom of the cell (which you'll see when you move your cursor over the cell, as shown here). One last thing: you can turn all these extras off permanently by turning off the Show Grid Extras checkbox at the top of the dialog.

Make Working with Panels Faster & Easier

Lightroom has an awful lot of panels, and you can waste a lot of time scrolling up and down in these panels just searching for what you want (especially if you have to scroll past ones you never use). This is why, in my live Lightroom seminars, I recommend: (a) hiding panels you find you don't use and (b) turning on Solo mode, so when you click on a panel, it displays only that one panel and tucks the rest out of the way. Here's how to use these somewhat hidden features:

Step One:

Start by going to any side panel, then Right-click on the panel header and a pop-up menu will appear with a list of all the panels on that side. Each panel with a checkmark beside it is visible, so if you want to hide a panel from view, just choose it from this list and it unchecks. For example, here in the Develop module's right side Panels area, I've hidden the Calibration panel. Next, as I mentioned in the intro above, I always recommend turning on Solo mode (you choose it from this same menu, as seen here).

Step Two:

Take a look at the two sets of side panels shown here. The one on the left shows how the Develop module's panels look normally. I'm trying to make an adjustment in the Split Toning panel, but I have all those other panels open around it (which is distracting), and I have to scroll down past them just to get to the panel I want. However, look at the same set of panels on the right when Solo mode is turned on—all the other panels are collapsed out of the way, so I can just focus on the Split Toning panel. To work in a different panel, I just click on its name, and the Split Toning panel tucks itself away automatically.

The Develop module's right side Panels area with Solo mode turned off

The Develop module's right side Panels area with Solo mode turned on

Lightroom supports using two monitors, so you can work on your photo on one screen and also see a huge, full-screen version of your photo on another. But Adobe went beyond that in this Dual Display feature and there are some very cool things you can do with it, once it's set up (and here's how to set it up).

Using Two Monitors with Lightroom

Step One:
The Dual Display controls are found in the top-left corner of the Filmstrip (shown circled in red here), where you can see two buttons: one marked "1" for your main display and one marked "2" for the second display. If you don't have a second monitor connected and you click the Second Window button, it just brings up what would be seen in the second display as a separate floating window (as seen here).

Step Two:
If you do have a second monitor connected to your computer, when you click on the Second Window button, the separate floating window appears in Full Screen mode, set to Loupe view, on the second display (as seen here). This is the default setup, which lets you see Lightroom's interface and controls on one display and then the larger zoomed-in view on the second display.

Continued

Step Three:

You have complete control over what goes on the second display using the Secondary Window pop-up menu, shown here (just click-and-hold on the Second Window button and it appears). For example, you could have Survey view showing on the second display, and then you could be zoomed in tight, looking at one of those survey images in Loupe view on your main display (as shown at bottom). By the way, just add the **Shift key** and the Survey view, Compare view, Grid view, and Loupe view shortcuts are all the same (so, **Shift-N** puts your second display into Survey view, etc.).

Step Four:

Besides just seeing things larger with the Loupe view, there are some other pretty cool Second Window options. For example, click on the Second Window button and choose **Loupe – Live** from the Secondary Window pop-up menu, then just hover your cursor over the thumbnails in the Grid view (or Filmstrip) on your main display, and watch how the second display shows an instant Loupe view of any photo you pass over (here, you can see on my main display the third photo is selected, but the image you see on my second display is the one my cursor is hovering over—the fourth image).

Step Five:

Another Second Window Loupe view option is called **Loupe – Locked** and when you choose this from the Secondary Window pop-up menu, it locks whatever image is currently shown in Loupe view on the second display, so you can look at and edit other images on the main display (to return to where you left off, just turn Loupe – Locked off).

Here's the second display default view, with the navigation bars at the top and bottom visible

Step Six:

The navigation bars at the top and bottom of your image area will be visible on the second display. If you want those hidden, click on the little gray arrows at the top and bottom of the screen to tuck them out of sight and give you just the image onscreen. You can also Right-click on either arrow to bring up the hide and show options for these bars.

Here's the second display with the navigation bars hidden, which gives a larger view

Continued

TIP: Show Second Monitor Preview

There's a feature found under the Second-ary Window pop-up menu called Show Second Monitor Preview, where a small floating Second Monitor window appears on your main display, showing you what's being seen on the second display. This is pretty handy for presentations, where the second display is actually a projector, and your work is being projected on a screen behind you (so you can face the audience), or in instances where you're showing a client some work on a second screen and the screen is facing away from you (that way, they don't see all the controls, and panels, and other things that might distract them).

Just like you can choose what photo information is displayed in the Grid and Loupe views, you can also choose what info gets displayed in the Filmstrip, as well. Because the Filmstrip is pretty short in height, I think it's even more important to control what goes on here, or it starts to look like a cluttered mess. Although I'm going to show you how to turn on/off each line of info, my recommendation is to keep all the Filmstrip info turned off to help avoid "info overload" and visual clutter in an already busy interface. But, just in case, here's how to choose what's displayed down there:

Choosing What the Filmstrip Displays

Step One:

Right-click on any thumbnail in the Filmstrip and a pop-up menu appears (seen here). At the bottom of it are the View Options for the Filmstrip. There are four options: Show Ratings and Picks adds tiny flags and star ratings to your Filmstrip cells. If you choose Show Badges, it adds mini-versions of the same thumbnail badges you see in Grid view (which show if the photo is in a collection, whether keywords have been applied, whether it has been cropped, or if it has been adjusted in Lightroom). Show Stack Counts adds a stack icon with the number of images inside the stack. The last choice, Show Image Info Tooltips, kicks in when you hover your cursor over an image in the Filmstrip—a little window pops up showing you the info you have chosen in the View Options dialog for your Info Overlay 1. If you get tired of accidentally clicking on badges that launch stuff when you're navigating around the Filmstrip, you can leave the badges visible but turn off their "click-ability" (if that's even a word) by choosing **Ignore Clicks on Badges** here, too.

Step Two:

Here's what the Filmstrip looks like when these options are turned off (top) and with all of them turned on (bottom). You can see Pick flags, star ratings, and thumbnail badges (with unsaved metadata warnings). I hovered my cursor over one of the thumbnails, so you can see the little pop-up window appear giving me info about the photo. The choice is yours—clean or cluttered.

Adding Your Studio's Name or Logo for a Custom Look

The first time I saw Lightroom, one of the features that really struck me as different was the ability to replace the Lightroom logo (that appears in the upper-left corner of the interface) with either the name of your studio or your studio's logo. I have to say, when you're doing client presentations, it does add a nice custom look to the program (as if Adobe designed Lightroom just for you), but beyond that, the ability to create an Identity Plate goes farther than just giving Lightroom a custom look (but we'll start here, with the custom look).

Step One:
First, just so we have a frame of reference, here's a zoomed-in view of the top-left corner of Lightroom's interface, so you can clearly see the logo we're going to replace starting in Step Two. Now, you can either replace Lightroom's logo using text (and you can even have the text of the modules in the taskbar on the top right match) or you can replace the logo with a graphic of your logo (we'll look at how to do both).

Step Two:
Go under the Lightroom menu (the Edit menu on a PC) and choose **Identity Plate Setup** to bring up the Identity Plate Editor (shown here). By default, the first Identity Plate pop-up menu at the top is set to Lightroom Classic CC (or Adobe ID), so you'll need to change it to **Personalized**. To have your name replace the Lightroom logo seen above, type it in the large black text field on the left side of the dialog. If you don't want your name as your Identity Plate, just type in whatever you'd like (the name of your company, studio, etc.), then while the type is still highlighted, choose a font, font style (bold, italic, condensed, etc.), and font size from the pop-up menus (directly below the text field).

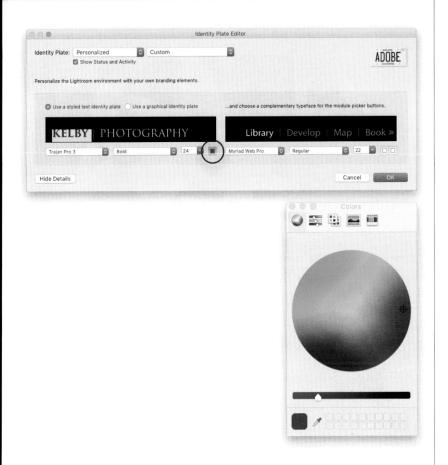

Step Three:

If you want to change only part of your text (for example, if you wanted to change the font of one of the words, the font size, or color of a word), just highlight the word you want to adjust before making the change. To change the color, click on the little square color swatch to the right of the Font Size pop-up menu (it's shown circled here). This brings up the Colors panel (you're seeing the Macintosh Colors panel here; the Windows Color panel will look somewhat different, but don't let that freak you out. Aw, what the heck—go ahead and freak out!). Just choose the color you want your selected text to be, then close the Colors panel.

Step Four:

If you like the way your custom Identity Plate looks, you definitely should save it, because creating an Identity Plate does more than just replace the current Lightroom logo—you can add your new custom Identity Plate text (or logo) to any slide show, web gallery, or final print by choosing it from the Identity Plate pop-up menu in all three modules (see, you were dismissing it when you thought it was just a taskbar, feel good feature). To save your custom Identity Plate, from the second pop-up menu, choose **Save As** (as shown here). Give your Identity Plate a descriptive name, click OK, and now it's saved. From here on out, it will appear in that pop-up menu, where you can get that same custom text, font, and color with just one click.

Continued

Step Five:

Once you click the OK button, your new Identity Plate text replaces the Lightroom logo that was in the upper-left corner (as shown here).

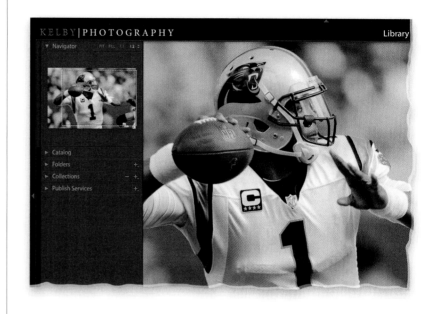

Step Six:

If you want to use a graphic (like your company's logo) instead, just go to the Identity Plate Editor again, but this time, click on the radio button for Use a Graphical Identity Plate (as shown here), instead of Use a Styled Text Identity Plate. Next, click on the Locate File button (found above the Hide/Show Details button near the lower-left corner) and find your logo file. You can put your logo on a black background so it blends in with the Lightroom background, or you can make your background transparent in Photoshop, and save the file in PNG format (which keeps the transparency intact). Now click the Choose button to make that graphic your Identity Plate.

Note: To keep the top and bottom of your graphic from clipping off, make sure your graphic isn't taller than 57 pixels.

Step Seven:
When you click OK, the Lightroom logo (or your custom text—whichever was up there last) is replaced by the new graphic file of your logo (as shown here). If you like your new graphical logo file in Lightroom, don't forget to save this custom Identity Plate by choosing Save As from the second pop-up menu at the top of the dialog.

Step Eight:
If you decide, at some point, that you'd like the original Lightroom logo back instead, just go back to the Identity Plate Editor and change the first Identity Plate pop-up menu to **Lightroom Classic CC** (as shown here). Remember, we'll do more with one of your new Identity Plates later in the book when we cover the modules that can use it.

CHAPTER 5

EDITING YOUR IMAGES
how to tweak your images like a pro!

If you're one of those lucky people for whom Lightroom was your first experience with editing digital images, you have no idea how lucky you are. Today, it's an incredibly mature, robust, fairly awesome program, but before Lightroom came along, it was a dark, dark time. Back then, we used Camera Raw (which was actually quite good), but it was part of a program called Adobe Bridge (which was actually quite bad). Well…now, I take that back. I don't want to say anything disparaging about Adobe Bridge, but if I did say something, it would be simply that it's absolute crap. Now, since a copy of all instructional books are included in the US government's National Archives within the Library of Congress, I think it's important that when talking about "The Bridge," for history's sake, we're accurate in our description, so tossing around a borderline word like "crap" is probably not going to sit well with the librarians there.

This is one of those cases where it will be vitally important (for official purposes) for you to "fill in the blanks" with more precise and articulate phrases than I was able to muster here. I will give you a descriptive phrase, and you will replace the last word of that phrase with a word that more accurately describes Bridge. Shall we begin? Let's. "Adobe Bridge is a steaming pile of 'carrots.'" Be thoughtful with your response—this is for posterior. Darn autocorrect! That was supposed to read, "this is for posterity." Let's try another: "Adobe Bridge is an absolute piece of 'steel.'" Time to pick your anus. Sorry, stupid autocorrect again. That was supposed to read: "Time to pick your answer." Okay, last one: "Adobe Bridge is a total pain in the 'ear.'" There are a number of prostate answers here. Rats! That was supposed to be "possible answers." Okay, that's it. I'm turning my autocorrect orifice! I mean, off! Ugh.

My Lightroom Editing Cheat Sheet

Here's a quick look at the sliders in the Basic panel (this isn't "official"—it's just how I think of them). By the way, although Adobe named this the "Basic" panel, I think it may be the most misnamed feature in all of Lightroom. It should have been called the "Essentials" panel, since this is precisely where you'll spend most of your time editing images. Also, something handy to know: dragging any of the sliders to the right brightens or increases its effect; dragging to the left darkens or decreases its effect.

Apply a RAW Profile:

From the Profile pop-up menu, you can choose the overall "look" you want to apply to your RAW photo. Do you want a flat, untouched starting point, or something a bit more colorful and contrasty?

Automatic Toning:

If you're not sure where to start, try clicking the much improved Auto button, which automatically tries to balance out the tones in an image for you. It's low risk—if you don't like the results, just press **Command-Z (PC: Ctrl-Z)** to Undo the Auto adjustment.

Brightening or Darkening:

I use these three sliders together: First, I set the white and black points to expand the image's tonal range (see page 144 for how Lightroom can do this for you automatically), and after that, if the image looks a little too bright or a little too dark, I tweak the overall brightness by dragging the Exposure slider to the left to darken or to the right to brighten.

Fixing Problems:

If there are exposure problems (often caused by the limitations of our camera's sensors), one or both of these sliders will usually provide the fix. I use the Highlights slider when the brightest areas of my photo are too bright (or the sky is way too bright), and the Shadows slider opens up dark areas in your photo and makes things "hidden in the shadows" suddenly appear—great for fixing backlit subjects (see page 151).

Fixing Flat-Looking Photos:

If your photo looks flat and drab, drag the Contrast slider to the right—it makes the brightest parts brighter, the darkest parts darker, and makes your colors punchier.

Enhancing Detail:

Technically, the Clarity slider controls midtone contrast, but what it really does when you drag it to the right is it brings out texture and detail in your photo. It also tends to make your photo a little darker if you apply a lot of it, so you might have to drag the Exposure slider a tad to the right after increasing the amount of Clarity.

Reducing Fog or Haze:

The Dehaze slider works miracles in reducing or even eliminating fog and haze—just drag it to the right. It's actually another form of contrast, so you can use it on non-hazy images to add heavy contrast. If you drag it to the left, it adds a hazy effect.

Getting Your Color Right:

These two White Balance sliders help you either correct the white balance in your image (i.e., you'd drag the Temp slider to the right to reduce a blue color cast, or to the left to remove a yellow color cast by adding in some blue), or you'll use these to get creative, like making a slightly yellow sunset a glorious orange, or a drab sky a gorgeous blue.

Making Your Colors More Colorful:

I drag the Vibrance slider to the right when my image needs a color boost (see page 153). You'll notice I didn't mention the Saturation slider. That's because I stopped using it years ago when Vibrance was introduced. Now, I only use the Saturation slider (dragging it to the left) if I want to wash out or remove color altogether. I never drag it to the right. Yeech!

If You Shoot in RAW, You Need to Start Here

In the spring of 2018, Adobe changed the way we process our RAW images (for the better), but it's important to understand what they did (and why they did it), so you can add it to your RAW editing workflow. On these first two pages, I'm going to explain something that will help you really understand why Lightroom does things a certain way, but to do that we have to start in your camera. If you're shooting in JPEG, you can skip these five pages altogether, and instead, your workflow starts on page 135 (shooting in JPEG is not a bad thing, but what I'm teaching here doesn't apply to JPEG images, so I don't want to waste your time or create confusion).

Step One:
Note: Again, this only applies to you, if you shoot in RAW. If you shoot in JPEG, skip these five pages.

When you shoot in JPEG, your camera automatically applies all sorts of processing adjustments to your JPEG images in-camera—like contrast, vibrance, sharpening noise reduction, and so on—to make your JPEG image look really good straight out of the camera. That's why JPEG images look so much better out of the camera than RAW images—RAW images don't have any of that stuff applied to them.

Step Two:
Besides JPEGs looking better by default, most cameras allow you to further tweak JPEGs by applying camera profiles right in your camera to make even better looking JPEGs. These profiles are named by the subject you're shooting, so for example, if you're shooting a landscape, you'd apply the Landscape camera profile to get more saturated colors, more sharpness, and more contrast. You can take it a step further by choosing Vivid, and now your image looks even more colorful. If you're shooting portraits, you can choose the Portrait camera profile and it provides flatter, less contrasty looks and tones that should be more pleasing for skin tones.

Step Three:

When you switch your camera to shoot in RAW mode, you're telling your camera, "Turn off the sharpening, the contrast, the vibrance, the noise reduction—turn off all that stuff that's added to make the image look great, and just give me the untouched RAW image, straight out of the camera, so I can add my own sharpening, contrast, and so on, in Lightroom (or Photoshop, or whatever)." This "turn all that in-camera stuff off" for RAW photos also applies to those camera profiles you just learned about. If you applied a Landscape or Portrait camera profile to your RAW photo, since it's RAW, Lightroom just ignores it (in short, they really only work for JPEG images). The good news is, you can apply these same types of camera profiles in Lightroom to RAW images. But, the news gets even better (well, not yet, in the step after the next step).

Step Four:

When your RAW image opens in Lightroom, for the sake of speed, it first displays the JPEG version of your photo (it's a small JPEG file embedded right into your RAW photo. That's what you see on the back of your camera—that JPEG preview. So, even through you're shooting in RAW, it still shows you the more colorful, more contrasty, sharper JPEG on the back of your camera. Good to know). So, that JPEG preview appears onscreen first, while Lightroom processes the actual RAW photo in the background (it displays a message onscreen that says "Loading," as seen here). Now, it used to process that RAW image using a profile Adobe engineers created 11+ years ago, which they felt provided the most accurate interpretation of what your camera captured. This profile (it was found in the Camera Calibration panel, as seen here) was called "Adobe Standard." I used to joke it should have been named "Adobe Dull" because the result was so flat looking, but it was very accurate as to what the camera captured.

Continued

Step Five:

So, for 11+ years, I've been telling photographers that they could have a better starting place than Adobe Standard by applying one of Adobe's camera profiles hidden down in the Camera Calibration panel (well, they were there in the previous versions of Lightroom anyway). They could choose Camera Landscape or Camera Vivid (depending on their camera), and their RAW image would then look more like the JPEG preview—with more contrast, more color, and a more JPEG-looking starting place for processing their RAW images. Well, in the spring of 2018, Adobe released a replacement for Adobe Standard, called "Adobe Color" (which is the new default RAW image look for Lightroom). This is such a better starting place, as Adobe Color gives your RAW image a more pleasing overall color with added warmth, contrast, and vibrance. Plus, Adobe moved the Profile options to the top of the Basic panel (as seen here). You don't have to do anything to use the Adobe Color profile— it's added by default. But, the even better news is, you now have more choices— more potential starting places that you might want to consider.

Step Six:

For example, from the Profile pop-up menu, choose the Adobe Landscape profile and it will look better for most landscape images (I think it looks even better than the in-camera profiles), and some images will look even better with Adobe Vivid applied. You won't know until you try 'em out. While Adobe added the Adobe RAW profiles as Favorites in the Profile pop-up menu, you can find others by choosing **Browse** (as shown here). You can also click the little icon with four squares just to the right of the Profile pop-up menu—either one will bring up the Profile Browser (seen in the next step).

Step Seven:

In the Profile Browser, under Adobe Raw, you'll find the new RAW profiles. The thumbnails here give you a preview of how your image would look if you chose one of those profiles. Even better, if you hover your cursor over one of them, you get a full-size preview of how that profile would look on your image. Incredibly helpful. Here, I chose the Adobe Vivid profile, and look at how much better the After image on the right looks already (you can see a split-screen before and after like this by pressing the letter **Y** anytime you're in the Develop module. More about these on page 141). It made my starting place that much better!

Step Eight:

Besides Adobe's new and improved RAW camera profiles, you still have access to the camera profile choices from earlier versions of Lightroom. These are found under Camera Matching, and they're named Camera Matching because these are same profiles you could have applied in your camera if you were shooting in JPEG mode (the list will look somewhat different depending on your camera make). These old camera profiles are there in case you wanted to work on a RAW image you previously edited in an older version of Lightroom where you had applied one of those older profiles without it being automatically changed to a new profile. That being said, I wouldn't recommend applying these old Camera Matching profiles to new photos you've just imported into Lightroom—they're not nearly as good as the new ones—but if you have bad taste in editing, at least you know they're there.

Continued

Step Nine:

If you want, you can change the thumbnail options in the Profile Browser. The standard view is called "Grid," which is what you see here at the far left. For larger thumbnails, choose **Large** from the pop-up menu near the top right (as shown here, in the center) to get large, single-column, full-width thumbnails, or choose **List** (as shown, far right) to see just a text-only list. To see even larger thumbnails, you can make the entire right side Panels area wider by clicking-and-dragging the left edge of the Panels area out to the left (you'll hit a point where it stops and you can't drag any farther, but you can make these panels quite a bit wider than their default settings).

The default: Grid   Large size   List view (text only)

Step 10:

To save a profile as a Favorite (so it appears in the Profile pop-up menu—no more scrolling through panels, digging for profiles), move your cursor over the profile thumbnail you want to save and click the star icon that appears in the upper-right corner (as shown here, left). Now that profile will appear in the Profile pop-up menu (as seen here, at right) when the Profile Browser is hidden, and also under Favorites when it's open (just click on a star icon, again, to remove a Favorite). There is a Monochrome choice in both the Adobe Raw and Camera Matching profile sets, and we'll cover those when we look at converting to black and white in Chapter 7. Lastly, you'll notice that below the Camera Matching profiles there are even more profiles. Those are actually creative effects you can apply to get certain "looks" (kind of like presets, but better). More on these also in Chapter 7—they're pretty awesome (and you can also add these to your Favorites if you find you use some of them often).

I start editing my photos by setting the white balance first. I do this for two reasons: (1) Changing the white balance affects the overall exposure of your image big time (take a look at the histogram while you drag the Temp slider back and fourth a few times, and you'll see what a huge effect white balance has on your exposure). And, (2) I find it hard to make reasonable decisions about my exposure if the color is so off it's distracting. I find that when the color looks right, my exposure decisions are better. But hey, that's just me. Or is it?

Setting the White Balance

Step One:
The White Balance controls are found near the top of the Develop module's Basic panel. Your photo reflects whichever white balance you had selected in your camera, so that's why the WB pop-up menu is set to "As Shot"—you're seeing the white balance "as it was shot," which in this case, is way too blue (I had been shooting under fluorescent lights earlier, then wound up shooting in this natural light setting and forgot to change my white balance to match the lighting conditions). There are three ways to set the white balance in Lightroom, and I'm going to show all three, but I use the third way most of the time because it's just so fast and easy. Still, it's important to know all three methods because you might prefer one of the other methods for certain types of photos.

Step Two:
First, you can try the built-in White Balance presets. If you shot in RAW, click-and-hold on As Shot and a pop-up menu of White Balance presets appears. Here, you can choose the same white balance presets (seen here on the left) you could have chosen in your camera. If you shot in JPEG mode, you only get one preset, Auto (seen here on the right), because your white balance choice was already embedded in the file by your camera. You can still change the white balance for JPEG images, but you'll have to use the next two methods instead. *Note:* If your list looks different than mine here on the left, it's because you're using a different make/model of camera. The WB pop-up menu is based on which camera brand you shot with.

Continued

WB presets if you shot in RAW

WB presets if you shot in JPEG

Step Three:

In our photo in Step One, the overall tone is really blue, so it definitely needs a white balance adjustment. (*Note:* If you want to follow along using this same image, you're welcome to download it from the book's companion webpage, mentioned in the book's introduction.) I usually start by choosing Auto from the White Balance pop-up menu to see how that looks (as you can see here, it's much better all around. In person, her skin has a warmer tone, but the Auto preset is actually a little too warm [yellow]). Go ahead and try out the next three presets, but spoiler alert: Daylight will be a bit warmer, with Cloudy and Shade being progressively even warmer. So, I'd choose Cloudy or Shade (just so you can see how much warmer that will make her skin tone, as well as the whole photo for that matter). You can skip Tungsten and Fluorescent—they're going to be way crazy blue (in fact, it was Fluorescent that we accidentally had our white balance set to from the beginning). By the way, the last preset isn't really a preset at all—Custom just means you're going to set the white balance manually instead of using a preset.

Step Four:

If you go through the WB presets and one looks right to you (or if you shot in JPEG, so your only choice was Auto, and it didn't look right), then we move on to Method #2, which is to choose the WB preset that is the closest to being right (in this case, for me, it was Auto), then drag the Temp and Tint sliders (found right below the pop-up menu) to tweak the color more to your liking. Take a look at those two sliders. Without me even explaining how they work, if I wanted more blue in this photo, which way would I drag the Temp slider? Right—those color bars behind the sliders are a huge help. In this case, I think her skin is too yellow, so I dragged the Temp slider away from the yellow side and more toward blue, looking at the image while I dragged. I didn't have to drag it very far and now it looks pretty good overall.

Step Five:

Method #3 is my favorite way to set white balance and is the one I use most of the time. Instead of using a preset or the sliders, I use the White Balance Selector tool (it's that huge eyedropper on the top-left side of the white balance section, or you can just press **W** on your keyboard to get it). It couldn't be easier to use—you simply take the tool and click on an area in your image that should be a light-to-medium gray. Not white (that's for setting the white balance for video cameras)—gray! If there's no gray in the photo, look for an area that's kind of a neutral color, like a tan, ivory, taupe, or beige. Boom. Done. Now, the nice thing about this tool is this: if you don't like how the white balance looks where you clicked, just click somewhere else until it looks good to you. So, let's give it a try—go back to the WB preset pop-up menu, choose As Shot, so it looks blue again, then get the White Balance Selector tool and click it on an area that is supposed to be either gray or neutral (the floor or the lighter areas of that background should do).

Step Six:

What happens if you click in the wrong spot? Trust me, you'll know (see how the whole image turned green here?). If that happens (and it will), don't sweat it—just click somewhere else, including trying a place you wouldn't think would give you an accurate white balance. Now, you see that grid that follows your eyedropper around? We simply call that the "useless annoying grid." Theoretically, it's supposed to help you find a neutral color by showing you the pixels under the location of your cursor, along with the RGB values, and if you to get all three of those numbers to match up (it happened once, in a sci-fi movie), that would be a truly neutral color. I only recommend using this grid to people I don't really like. It kind of evens the score. Anyway, to turn it off, turn off the Show Loupe checkbox (shown circled here in red) down in the toolbar.

Continued

Step Seven:

This is more of a tip than a step, but it's super-helpful. When you're using the White Balance Selector tool, look over at the Navigator panel at the top of the left side Panels area. As you hover the White Balance Selector tool over different parts of your photo, it gives you a live preview of what the white balance would look like if you clicked there (as shown here, where I'm hovering over her leg and the preview shows a very yellowish white balance. If I clicked on that spot, that's what I would get). This can save you lots of clicks and lots of time when trying to find a white balance that looks good to you—move your cursor around the image, and when the preview looks good, just click. When you're done, click the Done button down in the toolbar, or click the tool back where you got it from over in the Basic panel.

TIP: Dismiss the White Balance Selector Tool

In the toolbar, there's an Auto Dismiss checkbox. With this turned on, after you click the White Balance Selector tool once, it automatically returns to its home in the Basic panel.

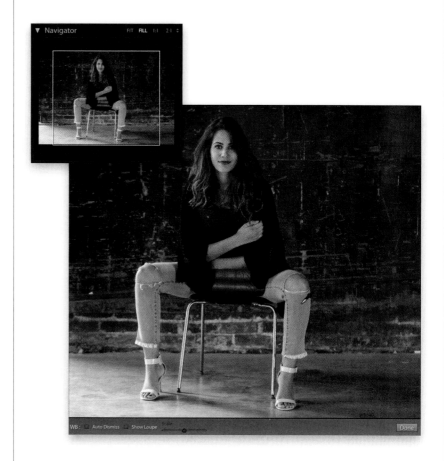

Step Eight:

Here's a before/after using the White Balance Selector tool method.

TIP: For Creative White Balance, Use the Temp/Tint Sliders

Here we learned how to get an accurate white balance because our subject is a person and we want their skin tone to look normal. However, there are times, like when we're doing landscape photos, when we might want to get creative and choose a white balance that makes the image look awesome, rather than accurate. In those cases, I drag the Temp and Tint sliders until I see something I like.

The fact that you can shoot tethered directly from your camera, straight into Lightroom, is one of my favorite features in Lightroom, but when I learned the trick of having the correct white balance applied automatically, as the images first come into Lightroom, it just put me over the top. So much so that I was able to include a free, perforated, tear-out 18% gray card in the back of this book, so you can do the exact same thing (without having to go out and buy a gray card. A big thanks to my publisher, Peachpit Press, for letting me include this). You are going to love it!

Setting Your White Balance Live While Shooting Tethered

Step One:

Start by connecting your camera to your computer (or laptop) using a USB cable, then go under Lightroom's File menu, under Tethered Capture, and choose **Start Tethered Capture** (as shown here). This brings up the Tethered Capture Settings dialog, where you choose your preferences for how the images will be handled as they're imported into Lightroom (see Chapter 3 for more details on this dialog and what to put in where).

Step Two:

Once you get your lighting set up the way you want it (or if you're shooting in natural light), place your subject into position, then go to the back of this book, and tear out the perforated 18% gray card. Hand the gray card to your subject and ask them to hold it while you take a test shot (if you're shooting a product instead, just lean the gray card on the product, or somewhere right near it in the same light). Now, take your test shot with the gray card clearly visible in the shot (as shown here).

Continued

Step Three:

When the photo with the gray card appears in Lightroom, get the White Balance Selector tool **(W)** from the top of the Develop module's Basic panel, and click it once on the gray card in the photo (as shown here). That's it—your white balance is now properly set for this photo. Now, we're going to take that white balance setting and use it to automatically fix the rest of the photos as they're imported.

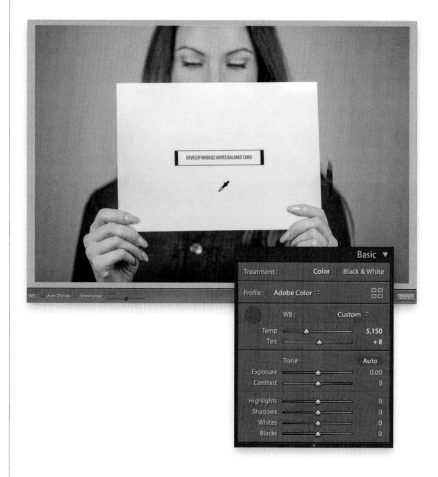

Step Four:

Go to the Tethered Capture window (press **Command-T [PC: Ctrl-T]** if it's no longer visible) and on the right side, from the Develop Settings pop-up menu, choose **Same as Previous**. That's it—now you can take the gray card out of the scene (or get it back from your subject, who's probably tired of holding it by now), and you can go back to shooting. As the next photos you shoot come into Lightroom, they will have that custom white balance you set in the first image applied to the rest of them automatically. So, now, not only will you see the proper white balance for the rest of the shoot, that's just another thing you don't have to mess with in post-production afterward. Again, a big thanks to my publisher, Peachpit Press, for allowing me to include this gray card in the book for you.

In the white balance project, I showed a before and after, but I didn't get a chance to show you how I did that. I love the way Lightroom handles the whole before and after process because it gives you a lot of flexibility to see these the way you want to see them. Here's how:

Seeing a Before and After

Step One:
If you're working in the Develop module and want to see your image before you started tweaking it (the "before" image), just press the **\ (backslash) key** on your keyboard. You'll see the word "Before" appear in the upper-right corner of your image (as seen here). This is probably the Before view I use the most in my own workflow. To return to your After image, press the \ key again (it doesn't say "After;" the Before just goes away).

Step Two:
To see a side-by-side Before and After view, with the before on the left and the after on the right (as seen here), press the letter **Y** on your keyboard. Press Y again to return to the normal view. There are some other before/after options, but to access those, you'll need to make sure the toolbar beneath the Preview area is visible (as seen here). If it's not, press the letter **T**.

Step Three:
If you prefer a different before/after layout, like a split-screen view, where your image is split down the center with the left half in the Before view and the right half in the After, click the Before and After Views button (circled here in red) once in the toolbar. Click it again for a top/bottom split-screen before and after. The three buttons to the right of Before & After do this: the first one copies the Before image's settings to the After image, the second one copies the After's settings to the Before, and the third just swaps the Before/After settings. To return to normal view, press the letter **D** on your keyboard.

Want to Copy a Particular Look? Reference View Can Help

If you have an image you've processed in Lightroom (maybe last year or even five years ago), and you want to match that look on a current photo you're editing, Reference view lets you put them side by side, so you can see the original (the reference photo) while you edit your current photo to match it. This also works great for nailing the look of an image you saw online—download it, use it as your reference image, and work on matching that same look.

Step One:
In this case, I want my Reference photo to be a shot of Venice's Grand Canal near sunset, and I want to apply its look to a shot I took earlier of that same cathedral across the canal. I want them both to have the same look, but I can't just copy-and-paste the settings because my Grand Canal photo is a flattened JPEG I edited in Photoshop. But, I'm able to put it up as my Reference photo, while I tweak the other image on the right, and I can see my edits live on the Active image as I'm tweaking. To enter this view, in the Develop module's toolbar, click the Reference view button (the second button from the left, shown circled here in red, or press **Shift-R**). Your Reference photo will be displayed on the left (you'll see the word "Reference" at the top right), and the photo you're actively editing will be displayed on the right as the "Active" image.

Step Two:
Now you can make your edits right alongside the Reference photo. Here, I made the Active image much warmer, dragging the Temp and Tint sliders way over to the right. I pulled the Exposure back to –0.75, and the Highlights back to –100, and brought up the Contrast a bit, as well. I didn't "nail" it, but I got in the ballpark, thanks to having the Reference photo right there. (*Note:* In this case, I'm using one of my own photos, but I've also used this Reference view feature to help figure out the look applied to a photo I downloaded from the web).

Adobe finally made this feature pretty awesome. We used to joke the old Auto Tone feature was simply the "overexpose by two stops" button. It was fairly useless, but now Adobe went and put some serious math and muscle behind the Auto Tone button (it uses Sensei, Adobe's artificial intelligence and machine learning platform, previously known as Skynet), and now it's actually pretty darn good (and at the very least, a decent starting place).

Auto Tone (It's Finally Actually Really Kinda Pretty Good)

Step One:

Auto Tone is a one-click fix (or at least, a good starting place) and the worse your photo looks at the start, the better job it seems to do. It uses this new AI and machine learning, called "Adobe Sensei," and by golly, it ain't bad! Here's an under-exposed, dull, flat-looking original RAW image. Click the Auto button once (it's in the Basic panel, in the Tone section, just to the right of the word "Tone"), and Lightroom quickly analyzes the image and applies what it thinks is the proper correction for this photo. It only moves the sliders it thinks are needed to make the image look decent (the obvious ones, like Exposure, Contrast, Shadows, and the other stuff in the Tone section of the Basic panel, but it'll also adjust Vibrance and Saturation. At this point, though, it does not adjust the Clarity amount).

Step Two:

Just one click and look at how much better the image looks. Compare the slider settings now versus the previous step. Also, I find that if you apply Auto Tone and it looks a little funky, it's because sometimes it applies too much of the Shadows slider and lowers the Contrast too much. So, just lower the Shadows amount a bit, and increase the Contrast amount a bit, and then see how that looks (but, again, only do this if the Auto Tone results look funky). By the way, if you don't like the results from the Auto Tone button, no harm done, just press **Command-Z (PC: Ctrl-Z)** to undo the auto toning.

Expanding Your Tonal Range by Setting Your White and Black Points

Back in the days before Lightroom, when we just used Photoshop for toning our images, we started the process in Levels by dragging the whites over as bright as we could get them without clipping the highlights. Then, we'd drag the blacks over as dark as we could get them, without them turning solid black. It was called "setting our white and black points," and doing this actually expanded the tonal range of our photos. Now, not only can we do this same thing in Lightroom, we can have Lightroom do it for us automatically (you just have to know the secret handshake).

Step One:

Here's the original image and you can see it looks pretty flat. I use the technique you're about to learn (which expands the image's tonal range) on pretty much every image, but this is another technique where the worse the original looks, the more dramatic the results. There are two ways to do it: Lightroom can do this for you by expanding the amount of whites in the image as bright as they can get without damaging your highlights, and increasing the amount of blacks, so the dark areas are nearly solid black, but it stops short so you still have some detail. Yup, it'll do all that automatically. Or, you can do it yourself (I never do it the manual way—I always let Lightroom set it for me).

Step Two:

Here's how to have Lightroom automatically set your white and black points, expanding your tonal range, near the start of your editing process (it's so simple): Just press-and-hold the Shift key, then double-click directly on the word "Whites," or on its slider knob in the Basic panel. That sets your white point. Now, Shift-double-click on the word "Blacks" (as shown here in the inset), or on its slider knob, and it automatically sets your black point. That's it. It's that easy, and that's how I do it in my own workflow (but I add one extra thing, which you'll learn after the next page). By the way, if you Shift-double-click on either one and it barely moves or doesn't move at all, that means your original capture already pretty much has its tonal range expanded.

Step Three:

If, instead, you want to do this process manually, you'll want to make sure you don't "clip" any of your highlights (making them so bright you lose data in the brightest areas of your image, or so dark that parts of the image turn solid black and thus have no detail). Luckily, Lightroom can warn you using an onscreen clipping warning. Here's how: Press-and-hold the Option (PC: Alt) key before you drag the Whites slider. This turns the screen solid black (as seen here, at top). As you drag to the right, any areas that start to clip will become visible. If you see red, blue, or yellow, it means you're clipping in just that individual channel (not as big a worry). However, if you see solid white areas, you're clipping in all three channels, and you've gone too far. So, pull it back to the left until those white areas go away. Now, do the same thing with the Blacks slider: press-and-hold the Option key as you drag to the left, and stop when you see black areas appear, then pull back to the right (as seen here, below, where I backed off, so I'm only really clipping in the blues. I can live with that little bit of clipping).

Step Four:

Here's a before and after where I used the automatic "Shift-double-click the Whites/Shift-double-click the Blacks" method to expand the image's tonal range. There's still work to be done (including what I do on the next page in conjunction with this), which will give me my overall exposure. So, what you're seeing here is not the final product—that's just a double-click on two different words. Not bad for a couple of double-clicks, though.

Controlling Overall Brightness (Exposure)

The Exposure slider controls the overall brightness of your image. If you look at the histogram (at the top of the right side Panels area) as you drag the Exposure slider (or heck, just hover your cursor over the Exposure slider itself, then glance up at the histogram), you'll see a light-gray shaded area that covers the center 1/3 (if not more) of the entire histogram. It controls the midtones, but really more than that because it also controls the lower highlights and upper shadows, too, all by itself. If you drag it all the way to the left, it will turn your image almost solid black—to the right, almost solid white.

Step One:

Here's our image, and you can see it's way overexposed (there are no lights here, except for those inside the elevator car and the natural light coming in from above—it looks dark and futuristic inside this "cone," in the City of Arts and Sciences complex in Valencia, Spain). To lower the overall brightness of an image, I reach for the Exposure slider in the Basic panel. This is one powerful slider, and as I mentioned above, it covers a wide range of midtones, lower highlights, and upper shadow areas. So, when I need something a little brighter or darker overall, this is the slider I reach for.

TIP: Get a Larger Working Space

Since the controls we're going to use for editing our image are in the right side Panels area, let's close the left side Panels area, so our image appears much larger onscreen. Just press **F7** on your keyboard, or click on the little, gray, left-facing triangle on the far-left center edge to collapse it and tuck it out of sight.

Step Two:

To darken the overall brightness of the image, drag the Exposure slider to the left until the exposure looks good to you. Here, I dragged it to the left quite a bit (down to –1.35, so it was nearly a stop-and-a-half overexposed). While I do grab this slider to make the overall image brighter or darker, I think you get better results if you use it in conjunction with setting the white and black points (see the next page).

In my own daily workflow, I combine setting the Whites slider, the Blacks slider, and the Exposure slider to give me my overall exposure, and I think the results are far better. I start by setting the white and black points (well, I let Lightroom do this for me automatically; see page 144) to expand my tonal range, and then if the image still looks too dark or too bright, I only have to tweak the Exposure amount a little bit, dragging it left (if I think the overall image is still too bright) or right to brighten it.

My Power Trio: Combining Whites + Blacks + Exposure

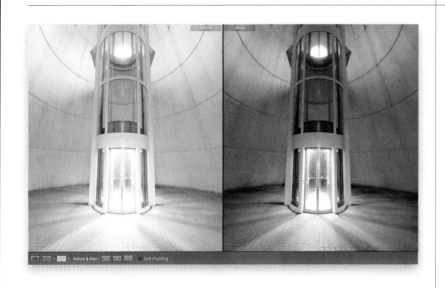

Step One:

I'm using the same image we used on the previous page, and I did the same thing here that I did there—I saw the image was overexposed (too bright), so I dragged the Exposure slider to the left until the exposure looked right to me (as seen here in the After photo). So, now the baseline exposure is correct, but we can make this image look better (and this is what I do in my own workflow) if instead of grabbing the Exposure slider first, we use it after we have Lightroom set the Whites and Blacks sliders for us (again, see page 144). That way, those sliders expand the tonal range first, then we can make the final adjustment with the Exposure slider, tweaking it to be darker or lighter with just a small move. I think the result looks much better overall doing it this way.

Step Two:

Here, I used my "Power Trio" technique by first Shift-double-clicking on Whites, and then Shift-double-clicking on Blacks. Then, I took a look at how the overall brightness of the image looked. I felt it needed to be a bit darker overall, so I dragged the Exposure slider to the left. The difference will look more subtle here in a printed version of a screen capture, but when you try it yourself (try it on one of your images, or download this same one), you'll see quite a difference. (By the way, the name "Power Trio" is actually used to describe rock bands that only have drums, bass, and one guitar [no second rhythm guitar or keyboards]. Think bands like ZZ Top, Rush, or Motörhead.)

Adding Contrast (Important Stuff!)

I host a live weekly photography show called *The Grid* (it's now in its seventh year), and once a month, we invite our viewers to submit images for a blind photo critique (we don't mention the photographer's name on the air, so we can give honest critiques without embarrassing anyone). So, what's the #1 most common post-processing issue we see? Flat-looking photos. That's a shame because it's fixed so easily, and with just one slider.

Step One:

Here's our flat, lifeless image. Before we actually apply any contrast (which makes the brightest parts of the image brighter and the darkest parts darker), here's why contrast is so important: when you add contrast it (a) makes the colors more vibrant, (b) expands the tonal range, and (c) makes the image appear sharper and crisper. That's a lot for just one slider, but that's how powerful it is (in my opinion, perhaps the most underrated slider in Lightroom). Now, for those of you coming from a much earlier version of Lightroom, the Contrast slider used to have so little effect that we really didn't use it at all—we had to use the Tone Curve to create a decent amount of contrast. But, Adobe fixed the math behind it back in Lightroom 4, and now it's awesome.

Step Two:

Here, all I did was drag the Contrast slider to the right, and look at the difference. It now has all the things I mentioned above: the colors are more vibrant, the tonal range is greater, and the whole image looks sharper and snappier. This is such an important tweak, especially if you shoot in RAW mode, which turns off any contrast settings in your camera (the ones that are applied when you shoot in JPEG mode), so your RAW images look less contrasty right out of the camera. Adding that missing contrast back in is pretty important, and it's just one slider. By the way, I never drag it to the left to reduce contrast—I only drag it to the right to increase it.

One of the things we worry about most while shooting is making sure that we don't clip off important highlight detail. It's why most cameras have a built-in highlight warning feature, because if the brightest highlights get too bright, they literally clip off, leaving no pixels, no detail, no nuthin'. If you were to print the image, there wouldn't even be any ink on those areas. If you didn't catch the problem in-camera, no worries, we can usually recover those clipped highlights right in Lightroom.

Dealing With Highlight Problems (Clipping)

Step One:
Here's a shot of one of the spiral staircases in the wonderful Tate Britain museum in London. Not only is the staircase fairly white, but I overexposed the image a bit when I shot it. That doesn't necessarily mean we have clipping (see the intro above for what clipping means), but Lightroom will warn us if we do. Take a look at the triangle up in the top-right corner of the histogram (seen here). That triangle is normally gray, which means everything's okay—no clipping. If you see a color inside that triangle (red, yellow, or blue), that mean the highlights are clipping in just that color channel, which isn't the end of the world. However, if you see that triangle filled with white, then it's clipping the highlights in all your channels, and you'll need to deal with it if it's an area where there's supposed to be detail.

Step Two:
Okay, now we know we have a highlight clipping problem somewhere in our image, but exactly where? To find out, go up to that white triangle and click directly on it (or press the letter **J** on your keyboard). Now, any areas that are clipping in the highlights will appear in bright red (as seen here, where big parts of the stairs and railings are clipping badly). Those areas will have *no* detail whatsoever (no pixels, no nuthin') if we don't do something about it.

Continued

Step Three:

Technically, you could just drag the Exposure slider over to the left until all those red clipped warning areas go away (as shown here), but that will affect the overall exposure of the image, making the entire image underexposed (and this case, a bit dingy, too). It's like you fixed one problem, but then created another. That's why the Highlights slider is so awesome—it lets you leave the exposure right where it is and it addresses those super-bright clipped areas itself because it just affects the highlights and not the entire exposure.

Step Four:

Let's put the Highlights slider to work. Just drag it to the left until you see the red onscreen clipping warning go away (as shown here). The warning is still turned on, but dragging the Highlights slider to the left fixed the clipping problem and brought back the missing detail, so now there are no areas that are clipping.

TIP: This Rocks for Landscapes

The next time you have a blah sky in a landscape or travel shot, drag the Highlights slider all the way to the left to –100. It usually does wonders with skies and clouds, bringing back lots of detail and definition. I use this trick fairly often.

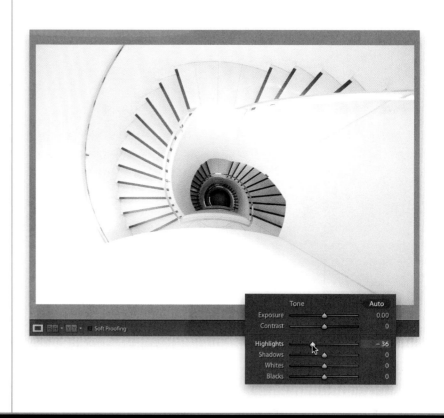

Why do we take so many backlit photos? It's because our eyes are so darn amazing and adjust for such huge differences in tonal range automatically. So, our subject could be standing there totally backlit, but our eyes automatically adjust for it and they look fine to us. The problem is: even the best camera sensors today don't have nearly the range of our eyes, so even though, when we look through our viewfinder, it looks fine to us, when we press the shutter button, the sensor can't handle that much range and we wind up with a backlit photo. Luckily for us, help is just one slider away.

Fixing Backlit Photos and Opening Up Dark Areas

Step One:
Here's the original image and you can see the subject is backlit. While our eyes do an amazing job of adjusting for scenes like this with such a wide range of tones, as soon as we press the shutter button and take the shot, we wind up with a backlit image where our subject is in the shadows (like you see here). As good as today's cameras are (and they are the most amazing they've ever been), they still can't compete with the incredible tonal range of what our eyes can see. So, don't feel bad if you create some backlit shots like this, especially since you're about to learn how easy it is to fix them.

Step Two:
Go to the Shadows slider, drag it to the right, and as you do, just the shadow areas of your photo are affected. As you can see here, the Shadows slider does an amazing job of opening up those shadows and bringing out detail in the image that was just hidden in the shadows. *Note:* Sometimes, if you really have to drag this slider way over to the right, the image can start to look a little flat. If that happens, just increase the Contrast amount (dragging to the right), until the contrast comes back into the photo. You won't have to do this very often, but at least when it happens, you'll know to add that contrast right back in to balance things out.

Clarity: Lightroom's Detail Enhancer

If you're looking for the nerdy technical explanation, the Clarity slider adjusts the amount of midtone contrast, but since that's of little help (well, I guess it is to nerds), then here's how I look at it: I drag this slider to the right when I want to enhance any texture or detail in my image. When you apply a lot of Clarity, it almost looks like you've sharpened the image (but, be careful, you can over-apply Clarity—if you start to see halos around objects in your image or your clouds have drop shadows, that's a warning sign you've gone too far).

Step One:
Which kinds of shots work best with Clarity? Usually anything with wood (from churches to old country barns), landscape shots (because they generally have so much detail), cityscapes (buildings love clarity, so does anything glass or metal), or basically anything with lots of intricate detail (even an old man's craggy face looks great with some Clarity). Here's our original image and there's lots of detail we can enhance—everything from the wood grain in the pews to the ornate adornments throughout the tiny chapel. *Note:* I don't add Clarity to photos where you wouldn't want to accentuate detail or texture (like a portrait of a woman, or a mother and baby, or just a newborn).

Step Two:
To add more punch and bring out the texture and detail in our image here, drag the Clarity slider quite a bit to the right. Here, I dragged it to +74, so you can really see the effect. Look at the added detail in the wood and the altar. If you start seeing a black glow appear on the edges of objects, you know you've dragged too far. If that happens, just back it off a bit until the glow goes away.

Note: The Clarity slider does have one side effect—it can affect the brightness of the photo; sometimes making it look darker, and other times making parts look too bright. That's easily fixed with the Exposure slider, but I just wanted you to keep an eye out in case that happens.

Photos that have rich, vibrant colors definitely have their appeal (that's why professional landscape photographers back in the film days got hooked on Fuji Velvia film and its trademark saturated color). Lightroom has a Saturation slider for increasing your photo's color saturation, but the problem is it increases all the colors in your photo equally, and…well…let's just say it's not awesome (and that's being kind). That's why I love Lightroom's Vibrance slider (a great name for it would have been "Smart Saturation"). It lets you boost colors without trashing your photo, and it does it in a very smart way.

Making Your Colors More Vibrant

Step One:
In the Presence section (at the bottom of the Basic panel) are two controls that affect the color saturation—one is brilliant; one is…well…crappy. There, I said it. It's crappy. I only use the Saturation slider to reduce color (desaturating), never to boost it because the results are pretty awful (it's a very coarse adjustment where every color in your image gets saturated at the same intensity). This is why I use Vibrance instead—it boosts the vibrance of any dull colors in the image quite a bit. If there are already saturated colors in the image, it tries not to boost them very much at all. Lastly, if your photo has people in it, it uses a special mathematical algorithm to avoid affecting flesh tones, so your people don't look sunburned or weird.

Step Two:
Here's a perfect example. Take a look at our tennis player back in Step One. She's wearing a vibrant red visor and red tennis outfit, but the blue service court areas and the green back court behind the baseline are kind of washed out in the direct sun. If I drag the Vibrance slider over to +67 (like I did here), you can see how much it affected the dull blue and green areas—they're now nice and vibrant. But look at her hat and outfit—they've only been boosted a little because they were already pretty vibrant. Most importantly, compare her skin tone in both image—it's only boosted the tiniest amount because Vibrance protects skin tones wonderfully. It truly is "smart saturation."

Removing Haze

Lightroom's Dehaze feature is so awesome it has its own fan base because it does that good of a job at removing haze, fog, etc. (Bonus tip: If you drag the slider to the left, it actually adds fog or haze, so there's that.) It's actually just another form of contrast, but it's a form that loves to cut through haze, so I'm all for it. Here's how it works:

Step One:
Here's our original image, taken in the canals of Phoenix, Arizona (just wanted to see if you're paying attention). It was a foggy morning, but I kept shooting because I knew Dehaze would bail me out.

Step Two:
In the Presence section of the Basic panel, you'll now find the Dehaze slider (it used to be in the Effects panel, which seemed like a weird place for this slider to live—it needed be here in the Basic panel, along with Clarity, Vibrance, and Saturation, so this was a good move). Anyway, drag the Dehaze slider over to the right and the haze literally just goes away (as shown here).

Step Three:

I don't know if you noticed in that last step, but when I dragged that Dehaze slider way over to the right, while it did get rid of the haze, it also made the image a bit darker. That's because Dehaze is a form of contrast, so the darker areas in the image got quite a bit darker. This is why you often have to increase the Exposure slider a bit, and maybe the Shadows slider quite a bit, too (which is what I did here), after applying a heavy dose of Dehaze. Just something to keep in mind. Also, if you have even the slightest amount of vignetting (darkening in the corners) from your lens, cranking Dehaze up will exaggerate it quite a bit, so get rid of any vignetting problems first (we'll look at how to do this in Chapter 9).

Step Four:

Here's a before/after of our image, and you can see what a huge difference it made (but, again, I did increase the Exposure and Shadows amounts afterward, so the image didn't look too dark). Another thing to keep an eye out for when using a high Dehaze setting is that it can introduce a bluish tint into your image. If that happens, you might have to back off the Vibrance slider a bit (to a negative number) to counteract that.

Before

After

Continued

Step Five:

Let's take a look at another image for something else you might run into and a great fix for it. In this case, I tweaked the image (doing the standard stuff: Exposure, Contrast, Clarity, etc.), and I added a decent amount of Dehaze. It actually worked pretty well to get rid of most of the haze in the foreground and middle ground, but the area where the bridge is and behind that is still kind of hazy. If I crank up the Dehaze slider much more, everything will turn blue, and the corners will darken, and it'll start going from bad to worse. That's why it's so awesome to be able to apply Dehaze with the Adjustment Brush. By doing it this way, I can paint over those areas in the back that need an extra amount of Dehaze, without affecting the sky or making everything turn blue.

Step Six:

Click on the Adjustment Brush **(K)** in the toolbar at the top of the right side Panels area, and increase the Dehaze amount by quite a bit (remember, with this brush, you pick an amount, paint, and then go back and choose the right amount. So, don't worry if the amount you choose at this point is the right amount because you'll tweak it after you paint). You can also increase either the Exposure or Shadows, or both (that's what I did here), since Dehaze tends to darken the areas you paint over. Next, take the brush and paint over the bridge, and the surrounding buildings, and they're now nice and crisp. You'd never guess the original image was the one you see on the left on the next page (that was before I made the Exposure, Contrast, etc., tweaks and increased the Dehaze setting). By the way, after I applied Dehaze the first time, I had to lower the Vibrance amount a little to keep the image from looking too blue. I also dragged the white balance Temp slider a little toward yellow to help offset the blue.

Before   After

Automatically Matching Exposures

If you've run into a situation where you have some images where the exposure or overall tone is off, Lightroom can usually fix it for you, pretty much automatically. This is great if you're shooting landscapes and the exposure changes on you as the light changes, or if you're shooting a portrait and your exposure changes as you're taking the shots, or about any time where you want a consistent tone and exposure across a set of images.

Step One:

Take a look at this set of images, taken with natural light. The first one is too bright, the second one's too dark, the third looks about right (well, to me anyway), the fourth and fifth look underexposed, etc. So the exposure for these images is kind of all over the place. One brighter, three darker, and one looks okay. Click on the image that has overall exposure you want (to make it the "most selected" image), then press-and-hold the Command (PC: Ctrl) key and click on the other images to select them, as well. Now, press **D** to jump to the Develop module.

Step Two:

Go under the Settings menu and choose **Match Total Exposures** (as shown here). That's it. There are no settings. There's no dialog. No window. It just does its thing. Press **G** to jump back to the Grid view and compare these images to the ones in Step One, and you can see that they all have a consistent exposure now. This works pretty darn well in most cases, which makes it pretty darn handy.

Now that you've learned all that, I wanted to share the order in which I use all those Basic panel sliders (and yes, I pretty much do the same thing every time, in the same order). While there are still things yet to learn, including local adjustments and special effects and lots of other fun stuff, this is the fundamental image editing I do, and it's often the only editing I do to my image (it just depends on the image). Almost everything else I apply to an image (special effects, or looks) will happen after I'm done with this phase here. I hope you find this helpful.

Putting It All Together (Here's the Order I Use for My Own Editing)

1) I choose my RAW Profile
Adobe Color is pretty good, but if I decide I want more pop, I usually go with Landscape or Vivid as my starting place.

2) I set my white balance
If your color isn't right…it's wrong. I use the White Balance Selector tool most of the time.

3) I have Lightroom automatically set my white and black points
I expand my overall tonal range by Shift-double-clicking on the word "Whites," then on the word "Blacks."

4) I tweak the overall brightness
After setting the white and black points, if I feel the image is too dark or too bright, I drag the Exposure slider a bit, until it looks right.

5) I add contrast and clarity
I always add contrast. As for clarity, I only use it if I want to enhance detail.

6) If I have highlight clipping or detail lost in shadows, I fix it now
This is when I would fix any clipping problems or open up the shadows (dragging the Shadows slider to the right) to reveal hidden detail. This is also when I would use Dehaze if there was a haze or fog issue.

7) Boost colors
Between setting my whites and blacks, and adding contrast, my color is usually pretty vibrant, but if for some reason I think it needs more, I increase the Vibrance amount.

Using the Library Module's Quick Develop Panel

There's a version of the Develop module's Basic panel right within the Library module, called the Quick Develop panel. The idea is that you can make some quick, simple edits right there in the Library module, without having to jump over to the Develop module. The problem is, the Quick Develop panel stinks. Okay, it doesn't necessarily stink, it's just hard to use because there are no sliders—there are buttons you click instead that move in set increments (which makes it frustrating to get just the right amount)—but for a quick edit, it's okay (you can see I'm biting my tongue here, right?).

Step One:
The Quick Develop panel (shown here) is found in the Library module, under the Histogram panel, at the top of the right side Panels area. Although it doesn't have the White Balance Selector tool, it has pretty much the same controls as the Develop module's Basic panel (like Highlights, Shadows, Clarity, etc.; if you don't see all the controls, click on the triangle to the right of the Auto Tone button). Also, if you press-and-hold the Option (PC: Alt) key, the Clarity and Vibrance controls change into the Sharpening and Saturation controls (as seen on the right. *Note:* The Dehaze slider from Develop didn't make it over to Quick Develop yet—hopefully, one day soon). If you click a single-arrow button, it moves that control a little. If you click a double-arrow button, it moves it a lot. For example, if you click the single-right-arrow for Exposure, it increases the Exposure amount by 1/3 of a stop. Click the double-right-arrow and it increases it by a full stop.

Step Two:
One way I use Quick Develop is to quickly see if an image (or a set of images) is worth working on, but without actually doing a full edit in the Develop module. For example, these sunrise images all looked a bit too yellow to me, so to quickly see how they would look with some blue added, I selected them, went to Temperature, and clicked once on the single-left-arrow to move it toward blue. For a bigger jump toward blue, I could have clicked on the double-left-arrow to move it more.

Top-left image: original Contrast

Top-right image: original Contrast

Quick Develop +30 Contrast = +45

Quick Develop +30 Contrast = +57

Step Three:

Another way I use Quick Develop is for comparing changes I'm making to one image to other similar images. For example, here I deselected all the images except for the top-left one. Then, I clicked on the double-right-arrow next to Temperature to make this one image much more yellow (as seen here), which contrasts the other images that I added blue into earlier, and I can see how doing this change compares to the rest.

TIP: Finer Increments in Quick Develop

You can adjust in smaller increments when clicking a single-arrow button. For example, if you Shift-click on the Exposure single-right-arrow, it moves up 1/6 of a stop, instead of a 1/3 of a stop (so, instead of moving +33, it moves just +17 for each Shift-click).

Step Four:

Yet another way to take advantage of Quick Develop is to use it for relative changes. Let's say I had adjusted these images in the Develop module. They look good, but I think they could use more contrast. I had already increased the Contrast to +15 for the first image, the second to +27, the third to +12, and the fourth to +20. If I changed the first one to +30, then used either Sync or Auto Sync, all four images would change their Contrast to +30. Well, that's not what I wanted. I wanted them all to keep the amount of contrast I had originally chosen for each, but add that +30 on top (making the first image's Contrast setting now +45, the second's +57, and so on). I want a relative change added to their current Contrast settings, not absolute where they all change to the same number. Quick Develop lets me do that. I selected the images (in this case, just the top two) and clicked the Contrast double-right-arrow to increase it by +20, then I clicked the single-right-arrow twice to add +10, for a total of +30. This didn't change both images to +30; it added +30 to their current Contrast amounts (as seen here)

Photo by Scott Kelby ⋮ Exposure: 1/125 sec ⋮ Focal Length: 90mm ⋮ Aperture Value: ƒ/8

CHAPTER 6

PAINTING WITH LIGHT
the adjustment brush & other toolbox tools

This chapter is about working with Lightroom's Adjustment Brush and other tools, but you know and I know, what we all really want to talk about is drones, which is great if you do drone photography because then this chapter could be about painting with light on your fabulous drone images. But, I'm just using drones here as an analogy to explain a wider concept, so let's not get hung up on the whole drone thing. Hey, did I mention I got the DJI Mavic Air drone? It's pretty slick, and when you fold in the propellers, it's literally the size of a Coca-Cola can. Anyway, the reason I'm bringing up drones is this: every place has its own drone laws, and they vary from country to country. For example, I went to a country in the Middle East with my buddy Dave, but at Customs in their airport, we learned that drones are forbidden in that country, and they confiscated Dave's Mavic Pro. Luckily, he was able to retrieve it upon leaving the country, after he paid a "storage fee." That's where

this book differs, in that I let you move freely from chapter to chapter without a fee, unlike the Federal Aviation Administration (FAA) here in the US, which currently requires you to register your drone with them and pay a $5 registration fee. So, this got me to thinking: perhaps, before you read this chapter, you should submit a small registration fee, like I dunno, maybe $3? That way, I could officially register you to read a chapter like this, which contains information that is worth considerably more than $3. Now, I know what you're thinking: "But Scott, I bought and paid for this book." Well, I bought and paid for my drone, yet I still had to pay a fee to fly it. You see, just buying a book (or a drone) establishes ownership, but that does not constitute usage and thus, according to several made-up laws, a registration fee should be levied, and that's the story of how I became a junior senator representing Florida's 14th Congressional District. #sendyourfeetome

Adjusting Individual Areas (Dodging & Burning)

Everything we've done so far affects the entire image—if you drag the Exposure slider, it changes the brightness for the entire image (it's a "global adjustment"). But, what if you want to adjust one particular area of your image (a "local" adjustment)? Then, our primary tool is the Adjustment Brush, which lets you "paint with light" just where you want it. In the darkroom days, this was called "dodging and burning," which simply means brightening (dodging) some areas and darkening (burning) others. This is way bigger than it sounds (and you can do more with this brush than just brightening and darkening).

Step One:

Here's the original image, taken in Marrakesh, Morocco. The top center and the light are too bright and the side rooms and the center fountain are too dark. This is where the Adjustment Brush, which lets you "paint with light," totally rocks. I usually get the basic overall exposure decent, and then I use the brush on areas that are too bright or too dark. To help you understand how it works: it's a quick, three-step process where (1) you drag a slider to a random amount (brighter or darker), (2) you paint over the area you want to adjust, and (3) you go back to that slider and dial in the right amount of adjustment. It sounds weird (you're kind of flying blind at first, right?), but it works.

Step Two:

Click on the Adjustment Brush (in the toolbox above the Basic panel or press the letter **K**) to bring up its sliders (it's pretty much the same sliders, in the same order, as the Basic panel). First, reset all the sliders to zero by double-clicking directly on the word "Effect" (circled here), then let's work on brightening the left side of the image. The goal is to balance the light in the image, so drag the Exposure slider to the right a bit (the amount doesn't matter right now because you'll choose the right amount after you paint), then paint over that room and the tile in the archway, but not the top of the arch. When you're done, drag the Exposure slider to where it looks good to you (here, I set it to 1.49). Compare this area on the left here, with the original in Step One.

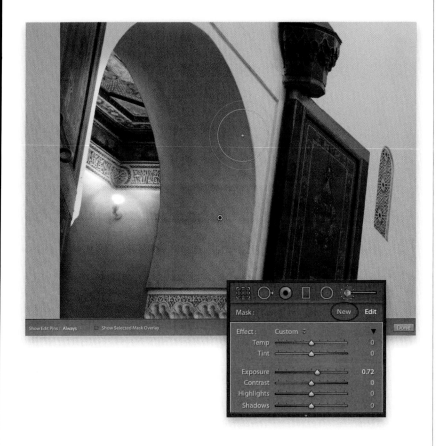

Step Three:

Now let's brighten the archway above the tile on the left. I want to balance the light here, so it's more like the archway on the right side of the image (there's that balancing thing I was talking about. I zoomed in tight here, so you can see the area we're working on more clearly). If I paint with the brush as is (it's set to 1.49), it will be way too bright. To paint in a new area, and be able to use a new, lower exposure setting, we need to tell Lightroom we want to paint someplace new, so click on New (shown circled here) at the top of the panel. Now, we can lower the Exposure amount (I lowered it to 0.72), paint over the top of the archway, and then adjust the Exposure amount without affecting the area where we just painted. You'll also notice that there's now a circle with a black dot on that arch. That's called an "Edit Pin," and it represents the area we just painted over. You'll see a white Edit Pin where we started when we first painted over the room. So, now, your image has two Edit Pins. If you wanted to go back and adjust what you did to the room on the left, you'd click on that white Edit Pin (it would turn into a black dot like this one, letting you know that pin is now active), and it remembers the original Exposure setting.

TIP: Changing Brush Size

Press the **Left Bracket key** to make the brush smaller or the **Right Bracket key** to make it larger.

Step Four:

If you want to see the area a particular pin affects, just hover your cursor over the pin and that area appears in a red tint (as seen here, where I hovered over the pin for the room on the left).

TIP: Leaving This Red Tint On

If you want this red tint (known as the mask overlay) left on, you can either turn on the Show Selected Mask Overlay checkbox in the toolbar beneath the Preview area, or press the letter **O**.

Continued

Step Five:

If you're wondering how I brightened that arch without "going outside the lines" and spilling my brightening onto the wall, I used an awesome feature called Auto Mask. When you turn Auto Mask on (near the bottom of the panel), it senses where the edges of things are and keeps you from accidentally painting over onto other areas. The trick is knowing how it works: You see that little + (plus sign) in the center of the brush (circled here)? That determines what gets affected as you paint, so any area that + travels over gets painted. It's okay if the outside edge of brush strays outside the area (as mine does here), as long as that + in the center doesn't stray over the edge. Keep that + inside the arch and you won't paint over the wall.

TIP: Making Your Brush Faster

Leaving the Auto Mask feature on slows the brush down quite a bit because it's doing math as you paint with it, so I only turn it on when I get near the edge of something I don't want to spill over (press the letter **A** to toggle it on/off).

Step Six:

Now let's work on darkening that center ceiling area with the windows. Click on New (since we're going to be working on a new area), double-click on Effect to reset all the sliders to zero, then drag the Exposure slider way over to the left, so it darkens when we paint, and then paint over the entire center ceiling area. When you're done painting, adjust the Exposure amount (I set mine to –0.67). Now, you're going to unlock more of the brush's power—you can use more than just one slider at a time. The windows in that area could use their highlights pulled back, and the whole area needs more contrast, so drag the Highlights slider to the left, crank up the Contrast, and for even more contrast, crank up the Whites and drag the Blacks to the left (as seen here). Now that ceiling's looking pretty good.

Step Seven:

We've been painting with light (exposure) and contrast, now let's paint with color. Yes, you can paint white balance, so let's warm up both of those side rooms, the hallway right in the center of the image (don't forget to turn on Auto Mask, so you don't spill over and paint on the fountain in the middle), and even the ceiling up top. You do that by clicking on New, double-clicking on Effect to reset the sliders to zero, and then dragging the white balance Temp slider way over to the right, toward yellow. Now, start painting (as shown here, where I'm painting over that hallway wall in the center, with Auto Mask on when I got near that fountain). Click New again, add a bunch of contrast and some clarity, bump up the exposure, and then let's paint over the doors themselves to bring out their detail and dimension.

Step Eight:

The fountain in the center still looks pretty dark, so let's brighten it up. You know the routine by now: click on New, double-click on Effect, increase Exposure, paint, and then adjust the slider to the proper amount. I turned on Auto Mask as I painted, but it isn't 100% all the time—sometimes, depending on the tone and definition of an edge, you still wind up spilling over (which I did on the top left of the fountain here). So, I pressed-and-held the **Option (PC: Alt) key**, to temporarily switch to the Erase brush, and I painted over the spill to erase it (note how the plus sign changes into a minus sign when you switch to the Erase brush).

TIP: How to Delete an Edit Pin

If you want to remove a pin from an area, just click on it and hit Delete (PC: Backspace).

Continued

Step Nine:

That floor is looking kind of dingy and could use just a bit of brightening. You know what to do. Ahhh, that looks better. Now, click on the Edit Pin for the doors you painted over (if you're not sure which pin that is, hover briefly over each pin and the area it affects will appear in red. Once you find the pin for the doors, click on it), and those settings automatically reappear in the panel. Let's use those same settings to paint over the tile pattern above the center doorway to bring out its detail (as shown here).

TIP: Seeing If You Missed a Spot

Click on an Edit Pin, then press the letter **O** on your keyboard to turn on the red mask over that area. If you missed a spot, that area won't appear in red, so just paint over it and it should turn red. When it's all red, you know you haven't missed any spots.

Step 10:

This last step is optional, but since a lot of photographers are adding "light hits" (not an official name; it's just what I call it), I thought I would include this. Doing this adds a large "hit" of light over highlight areas, and even areas where there aren't natural highlights, to make it look like little swatches of light are somehow falling down into your image (maybe through the windows?). Click on New and reset your sliders. Then, set your Exposure amount to 1.00, make your brush size really large, and make sure Auto Mask is turned off, then simply click the brush once in highlight areas (or wherever you want a hit of light to appear—I hovered my cursor over the pin, here, so you can see all the places I clicked with that huge brush). It's definitely a special effect, but it can be a nice finishing effect if done right.

Step 11:

Here, you can see the light hits without the red mask overlay (compare it to the image shown in Step Nine). Before we wrap up our project, two quick things: (1) You have some handy Brush options (along with the Erase brush) in the bottom section of the Adjustment Brush panel. You can choose the Brush Size (using a slider), the amount of Feather (how soft the edges are—I usually keep mine set at 50), and the Flow (whether it paints a solid stroke at 100% opacity or whether you want it to build up as you paint; I leave mine at 100). (2) You actually have two brushes to choose from: "A" (your regular brush) and "B," an alternate brush, and you can choose the settings for each. I usually give my "A" brush (my main brush) a soft edge (with a high Feather amount) and give my "B" brush a hard edge (by lowering the Feather amount to 0, as seen here). So, if I run into a situation where I'm painting along a wall, or other area where a soft edge looks weird, I can toggle over to my "B" brush using the **\ (backslash) key** on my keyboard.

TIP: Moving an Edit Pin

To move a pin, just click-and-drag it where you want it.

Five More Things You Should Know About Lightroom's Adjustment Brush

There are a few other things you need to know that will help you get more comfortable with the Adjustment Brush, and once you learn these (along with the rest of the stuff in this chapter), you'll find yourself making fewer trips over to Photoshop, because you can do so much right here in Lightroom.

#1: You have a choice of how Lightroom displays the Edit Pins, and you make that choice from the Show Edit Pins pop-up menu down in the toolbar beneath the Preview area (as shown here). Choosing Auto means when you move your cursor outside the image area, the pins are hidden. Always means they're always visible, and Never means you never see them. Selected means you only see the currently active pin.

#2: To see your image without the edits you've made with the Adjustment Brush, click the little switch at the bottom left of the panel (circled below in red).

#3: If you press the letter **O**, the red mask overlay stays onscreen, so you can easily see, and fix, areas you've missed.

#4: If you click on the little down-facing triangle to the far right of the Effect pop-up menu, it hides the Effect sliders, and instead gives you an Amount slider (as shown here) that provides a single, overall control over all the changes you make to the currently active Edit Pin.

#5: Below the Auto Mask checkbox is the Density slider, which kind of simulates the way Photoshop's Airbrush feature works, but honestly, the effect is so subtle when painting on a mask, that I don't ever change it from its default setting of 100.

Fixing problems that only appear in certain parts of your image is where the Adjustment Brush comes up big, because you can paint away the problems in these areas. Things like white balance problems when, for example, part of your image is in daylight and part is in the shade. Or painting away noise that just appears in the shadow areas, leaving the rest of the photo untouched (and saving it from the blurring that comes with noise reduction). Incredibly handy.

Selectively Fixing White Balance, Dark Shadows, and Noise Issues

Step One:
Let's start with painting white balance. Take a look at the image here, where the subject is lit, but the background is in the shade. Because I shot this in Auto White Balance on my camera, the background has a fairly strong blue tint to it (pretty typical when part of your image winds up in shade. I face this a lot shooting sports, when part of the field is in shade in late afternoon games and part is in daylight). This is where the ability to paint white balance in just certain areas is incredibly helpful, so press the letter **K** to get the Adjustment Brush.

Step Two:
Double-click directly on the word "Effect" to reset all the sliders to zero. Then, drag the Temp slider over to the right a bit (toward yellow) and start painting over the background. As you do, the yellow white balance you're painting neutralizes the blue in the background (as seen here). Because you have to guess your starting point, the original amount of Temp I used (31) wasn't enough, so I increased the Temp amount to 73 and that looked better. Painting with white balance like this is a huge help. Next, let's paint away noise the same way.

Continued

Step Three:

Here we have an image that is severely backlit from the window. If you look at the before image on the left, you can't even see any detail around the window—it's all just a silhouette. However, when you crank up the Shadows slider and the Exposure slider enough to where the image is properly exposed (I also lowered the Highlights slider a lot to bring some detail back in the area outside the window), you see all the noise big time. Noise usually hides in the shadows, and sometimes when you drastically open up those shadow areas (like we did here), any noise that was in the image is now magnified. So, the window looks great, but the window pane, the shutters, and the area below the window are full of red, green, and blue noise dots that we need to deal with.

Step Four:

So, why don't we just use Lightroom's regular Noise Reduction controls in the Detail panel? It's because that affects the entire image equally—when it reduces noise, it also softens the entire image. Here, by using the Adjustment Brush, we can reduce the noise only in the areas I mentioned and leave the rest of the photo (the brighter areas that don't show much noise) sharp and untouched. By doing it this way, we only make those areas a little soft and not the entire image. To do this, get the Adjustment Brush, and then double-click on the word "Effect" to reset all the sliders to zero. Now, drag the Noise slider all the way to the right, and then paint over those areas to reduce the noise there. How far are you supposed to drag that Noise slider? The idea is to find that sweet spot where it's not too noisy and it's not too blurry. Also, don't forget, all the other sliders here still work, so you could darken just those areas a little, while you're applying noise reduction, which would help to hide the noise, too. Here, I also increased the Sharpness slider to 26.

When it comes to detailed retouching, I generally jump over to Adobe Photoshop, but if you just need to do a quick retouch, it's amazing how many things you can do right here in Lightroom using the Adjustment Brush and the Spot Removal tool, with its healing power. Here's a quick retouch using just those two tools:

Retouching Portraits

Step One:
Here are the things we're going to retouch in this image: (1) remove any major blemishes and wrinkles, (2) soften her skin, (3) brighten the whites of her eyes, (4) add contrast to her eyes and sharpen them, and (5) add some highlights to her hair. Although we're seeing the full image here, for retouching, it's best to zoom in quite a bit. So, go ahead and zoom in nice and tight to start the next step. By the way, I thought her skin looked a little too bright in the original image, so here I reduced the Highlights to –15 (just so you know).

Step Two:
Here, I've zoomed in to a 1:2 view, so we can really see what we're doing (just select this zoom ratio from the pop-up menu at the top right of the Navigator panel, at the top of the left side Panels area). Click on the Spot Removal tool (in the toolbox near the top of the right side Panels area, or just press the letter **Q**). This tool works with just a single click, but you don't want to retouch any more than is necessary, so make the brush Size of the tool a little bit larger than the blemish you're going to remove. Move your brush cursor over the blemish and then just click once. A second circle will appear, showing you where it sampled a clean skin texture. Of course, it's not always 100% right, and if for some reason it chose a bad area of skin to sample from, just click on that second circle, drag it to a clean patch, and it will update your blemish removal. Go ahead and remove any blemishes now using this tool (as shown here).

Continued

Step Three:

Now, let's remove some wrinkles under her eyes. Zoom in tighter (this is a 1:1 view), then take the same Spot Removal tool we've been using (make sure it's set to Heal) and paint a stroke over the wrinkles under her eye on the right (as shown here). The area you've painted over turns white (as seen here), so you can see the area you're affecting.

Step Four:

Lightroom analyzes the area and picks a spot somewhere else in the image to use to repair those wrinkles. It usually picks something nearby, but in this case it chose an area across the bridge of her nose, which, of course, created a bad retouch. Luckily, if you don't like where Lightroom chose to sample from, you can simply have it sample somewhere else by clicking on that second outline (the thinner one of the two) and dragging it somewhere on her face where you think the texture and tone will match better (here, I moved it right up under the original area where the wrinkles were, as shown in the overlay). Also, don't forget to remove the wrinkles beneath the other eye (it's easier to forget than you'd think). *Note:* If our subject is at an age where fully removing the wrinkles is unrealistic, we need to "reduce" the wrinkles instead, so we would decrease the Opacity amount to lower the strength of the removal, bringing back some of the original wrinkles.

Step Five:

Now that the blemishes and wrinkles are removed (I also removed some stray hairs), let's do some skin softening. Switch to the Adjustment Brush (also in the toolbox near the top of the right side Panels area, or just press the letter **K**), then choose **Soften Skin** from the Effect pop-up menu. Now, paint over her face, but be careful to avoid any areas that you don't want softened, like her eyelashes, eyebrows, lips, nostrils, hair, the edges of her face, and so on. This softens the skin by giving you a negative Clarity setting (it's set at –100). Here, I've only painted over the right side of her face, so you can see the difference. This is quite a lot of softening, so once you're done, back off the Clarity amount so you can still see skin detail (I raised my amount to –55).

Step Six:

Next, let's work on her eyes, and we'll start by making the whites brighter. First, click the New button in the top right of the panel, then double-click on the word "Effect" to reset all the sliders to zero. Now, drag the Exposure slider to the right a little bit (here, I dragged it over to 0.50) and paint over the whites of her eyes. If you accidentally paint outside the whites, just press-and-hold the **Option (PC: Alt) key** to switch to the Erase brush and erase away any spillover. Do the same for the other eye and, when you're done, adjust the Exposure slider, as needed, to where the whitening looks natural. Next, let's brighten her irises. Click the New button, and increase the Exposure amount to 1.36 and paint over both irises. Then, to add some contrast, increase the Contrast slider to 33. Lastly, to make those eyes really nice and sharp, increase the Sharpness slider to 22, so the irises get brighter, more contrasty, and sharper, all at the same time.

Continued

Step Seven:

Now, click the New button once again, and let's brighten the highlights in her hair. Start by resetting your sliders to zero, then drag the Exposure slider to the right a little bit (I dragged mine to 0.35), and then paint over the highlight areas to bring them out. Lastly, one of the retouches I get asked the most to do by subjects is to slim them up a bit. I don't think our subject here needs it at all, but if you're asked, here's how it's done: Go to the Transform panel (in the right side Panels area), and in the Transform section, drag the Aspect slider to the right (as seen here at the bottom). As you do, it compresses (narrows) the photo, giving you an instant slimming effect. The farther to the right you drag, the more your subject gets slimmed (here, I dragged to +25). A before/after is shown below.

TIP: Keep from Seeing Too Many Pins

To see just the currently selected Edit Pin, choose **Selected** from the Show Edit Pins pop-up menu in the Preview area toolbar.

The After photo has clearer and smoother skin (plus the highlights have been reduced a little bit); the eyes are brighter, have more contrast, and are sharper; we've enhanced the highlights in her hair; and we've slimmed her face a bit

The Graduated Filter (which is actually a tool) lets you recreate the look of a traditional neutral density gradient filter (these are glass or plastic filters that are dark on the top and then graduate down to fully transparent). They are popular with landscape photographers because you're either going to get a perfectly exposed foreground or a perfectly exposed sky, but not both. However, the Lightroom version actually has some big advantages over using a real neutral density gradient filter.

Richer Skies Using the Graduated Filter

Step One:

Start by clicking on the Graduated Filter tool in the toolbox (it's the second icon to the left of the Adjustment Brush, or press **M**), near the top of the right side Panels area. When you click on it, a set of options pops down that are similar to the effects options of the Adjustment Brush (shown here). Here, we're going to replicate the look of a traditional neutral density gradient filter and darken the sky. Start by choosing **Exposure** from the Effect pop-up menu and then drag the Exposure slider to the left to –1.65 (as shown here). Just like with the Adjustment Brush, at this point, we're just kind of guessing how dark we're going to want our gradient, but we can darken or lighten it later.

Step Two:

Press-and-hold the Shift key (to keep your gradient straight as you drag), click on the top center of your image, and drag straight down until you reach around the middle of the photo (the horizon line). You can see the darkening effect it has on the sky, and the photo already looks more balanced. You might need to stop dragging the gradient before it reaches the horizon line, if it starts to darken your properly exposed foreground, but here, I was able to drag quite a bit lower than the horizon line (it just depends on the photo). In this case, just lowering the exposure didn't do all that much for our sky (as seen here), and this is one area where Lightroom's feature is better than the real filter—we can do more than just darken the exposure.

Continued

Step Three:

Since lowering the Exposure amount didn't make my sky look great (though, honestly, that's usually enough), the next thing I do is add some blue by simply dragging the Temp slider to the left toward blue. What a huge difference that makes! You can also add in some contrast and bring out the clouds by increasing the Whites. That's stuff you could never do with the real filter. Also, here, you can see that I pulled the gradient down so far that it started to darken the mountain just a bit (the Edit Pin shows where the center of your gradient is—you can drag it up/down to reposition). On the next page, I'll show you how to deal with situations like that (and, in the next technique, I'll show you an even better trick), but before we get to all that, just a couple of quick things: (1) To delete your gradient, click on the Edit Pin and press the Delete (PC: Backspace) key. (2) If you don't press-and-hold the Shift key while you drag out your gradient, you can rotate it as you drag (in case you need to).

Step Four:

You're going to run into times where the Graduated Filter covers part of the image you don't want affected, like in this case, where we do want to darken and saturate the sky and graduate down to transparent, but it also darkens and saturates Lisbon's Belem Tower at the same time, which we don't want. Luckily, you can edit that gradient and basically erase the filter just over that tower area. While the Graduated Filter pin is selected, in the Mask section right below the toolbox, click on Brush, as shown here.

Step Five:

Now, scroll down to the bottom of the panel, just below the sliders, click on Erase, and start painting over the tower, and as you do, it removes the darkening and saturation from the areas you're painting over (as seen here). All the same rules apply as you're painting with this brush that apply to the regular Adjustment Brush (you can press the letter **O** to see the mask as you paint, you can change the amount of feathering on the brush, etc.). Also, you can use this brush to add to a mask, instead of just removing like we did here—don't click on Erase, and then you're adding to the mask. Now, if you want an even easier way to do this, instead of using a brush, check out the next technique.

Making Tricky Adjustments Easily Using Color and Luminance Masking

You just learned the technique for adding a gradient to the sky to darken it and make it richer and bluer, and you also learned the somewhat painstaking way to paint away areas from that mask that you didn't want darkened or made bluer. While you were carefully painting, you might have wondered, "There has got to be a better way, right?" Ah yes, my friend, there is, but it's better than that because there are actually two ways—using a Color or a Luminance Range Mask—and I have to say they are pretty darn awesome.

Step One:
Here's the original image (the tower of the Koutoubia Mosque in Marrakesh, Morocco), and you can see the sky is just screaming for us to use the Graduated Filter tool **(M)** to make it darker and richer, and then have it fade to transparent (see the previous technique if you're not sure what I'm talking about).

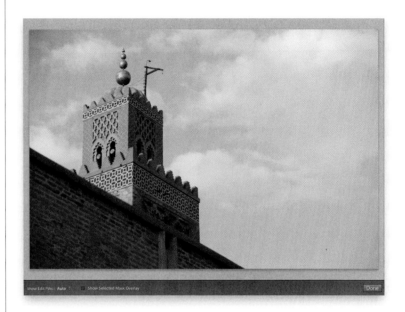

Step Two:
Here, I've applied the Graduated Filter, dragging it from the top down to the bottom, and sure enough it gave us a nice, rich, blue sky as it graduates down to transparent. To get that look, of course, I lowered the Exposure slider quite a bit, but I also dragged the Temp slider a little over toward the blue side to add a lot more blue to the sky, I adjusted the Whites and Blacks, and I cranked up the Contrast and Saturation quite a bit, as well. Now comes the problem: while it did an awesome job on the sky, it also darkened the tower on both sides, as well as the clouds in the sky. As I mentioned in the intro above, we could reach for the Brush tool and carefully paint over these areas, but it's gonna be tricky. Luckily, we have something way faster and better we can use instead.

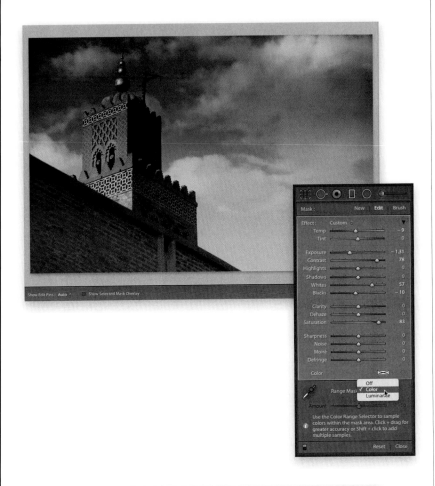

Step Three:
While you still have the Graduated Filter active, scroll all the way to the bottom of its panel and you'll see "Range Mask: Off." There are two different types of Range Masks: Color (which lets us choose which color we want to apply the Graduated filter to) and Luminance (which lets us remove the effect of the Graduated Filter from the darker parts of the image, or the lighter parts, by just dragging a slider). Here, we're going to start by using the Color Range Mask, so click directly on the word "Off," and then choose **Color** from the pop-up menu (as shown here).

Step Four:
Once you choose Color, the Color Range Selector tool (the eyedropper) appears with an Amount slider below it (as seen in the step above). The way this works is really amazingly simple: take the eyedropper and simply click it on the color you want the Graduated Filter applied to (in this case, it's that blue color, so click once in a blue area of the sky), and it instantly masks the tower away (as seen here). If clicking once didn't do the trick (you have lots of different shades of blue in your image), you can add more eyedroppers in different areas of the image by pressing-and-holding the Shift key, clicking once in those areas, and it adds them to what is included in that Graduated Filter adjustment. You can add up to four eyedroppers (as I've done here).

TIP: Click-and-Drag Over Colors
Maybe even more helpful, you can take the eyedropper and click-and-drag out a rectangle over an area to automatically include all the colors in that area.

Continued

Step Five:

If you want to see the mask that's created by the Color Range Mask, press-and-hold the Option (PC: Alt) key, then click on the Amount slider and you'll see a preview of it (as shown here). By the way, dragging the Amount slider to the left includes more areas of colors to be masked away (the dark areas) and dragging to the right masks away fewer colors (press-and-hold the Option key, then drag it back and forth, and you'll instantly see what it does). If you look at the image here at the bottom, you'll see I included a Before/After of the mask, so you can really see what's happening. In the Before image, you can see the mask it applied as a simple gradient—the white areas are affected by all those sliders you moved, and as it moves down to gray, those areas get less of the effect. When it gets down to solid black at the bottom of the image, those black areas are masked out and don't get the effect at all. So, white areas get the full effect, gray partial, and black none. Now look at the mask preview on the After image—the areas in solid black are not affected by the gradient (so the tower doesn't get that darkening or blue over it), and the gray areas, like the clouds, are only partially affected. The white areas (where the blue in the sky is) are the only areas really getting the full effect. Pretty amazing, right?!

How the mask normally looks when the Graduated Filter is applied evenly across the image

After one click on the blue sky, it masks out non-blue areas, like the tower and clouds

Step Six:

Here's a before/after from the point where we added the gradient. The Before image on the left shows how it looks right after you drag the Gradient Filter from top to bottom. The After image on the right is after clicking the eyedropper on the blue part of the sky, which masked out the tower and clouds for a much more realistic look.

How it looks right after you drag the Graduated Filter

How it looks after you add the Color Range Mask by clicking in the blue sky. The tower and the clouds are masked out from the effect

Step Seven:

Two things: (1) The Range Mask isn't just available with the Graduated Filter; it's also available with the Adjustment Brush and the Radial Filter, as well. (2) We haven't used the Luminance Range Mask yet, so let's do that, but we'll use the Adjustment Brush this time, just because we can. We're going to use a different photo (this one from Lisbon). The sky is really washed out, and painting a darker sky between those palm fronds to darken the sky would be really, really tricky and take a ton of time. We'll start by getting the Adjustment Brush **(K)**, darkening the Exposure, and dragging the Temp slider way over toward blue (I took it to –36 here), then just painting over the whole sky—paint right over the palm tree, and if you spill onto the building on the right and skyline below, don't sweat it. No Auto Mask necessary—just paint right over it all.

Step Eight:

Now, go to the bottom of the Adjustment Brush's panel and choose **Luminance** from the Range Mask pop-up menu. This masks away areas based on their darkness or brightness, rather than color. There are two "nubs" on the Range slider: Drag the left one to the right and the darker parts of the image—the palm and the buildings—get masked out of your brush strokes over the sky. To see the mask it created, press-and-hold the Option (PC: Alt) key, click on the Range slider, and it shows the mask (as seen here). Dragging the right nub to the left would subtract any lighter areas from the mask, but in this case, we don't really have any. The Smoothness slider controls how smooth the transition is between the areas that are masked and the effect. Dragging to the right makes the transition smooth; dragging to the left makes it more abrupt and harsh. I added a final before/after on the next page, so you can see how well it masked away that palm and how natural the sky looks behind it.

Continued

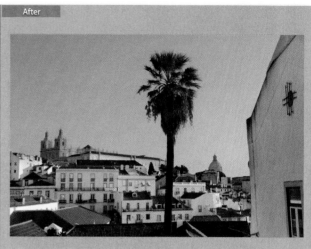

Before painting over the sky

*After painting with the Adjustment Brush
and adding a Luminance Mask*

This feature was designed so you could create an edge-darkening vignette without your subject being right in the center—if you use the Post-Crop Vignetting effect in the Effects panel, it darkens the outside edges all the way around your image equally. That's all well and good, but that's not what I use this filter for. I use this filter to create a soft spotlight effect right where I want it in 10 seconds flat, and it's awesome!

Spotlight Effects (and Off-Center Vignettes) Using the Radial Filter

Step One:

The viewer's eye is drawn to the brightest part of the image first, but unfortunately, in this shot, the lighting is fairly even because of the overcast skies, so our subject blends in to her surroundings more than we'd like. We're going to use the Radial Filter tool to re-light the scene and focus the viewer's attention on our subject by adding a subtle spotlight effect. So, click on the Radial Filter tool in the toolbox near the top of the right side Panels area (it's shown circled here in red; or press **Shift-M**). This tool creates an oval or a circle, and you get to decide what happens inside or outside this shape. To get the spotlight effect, I do two things: (1) I lower the Exposure slider quite a bit (in this case to –1.34), and (2) I make sure the Invert checkbox (near the bottom of the panel) is turned off, so the darkening happens outside the oval.

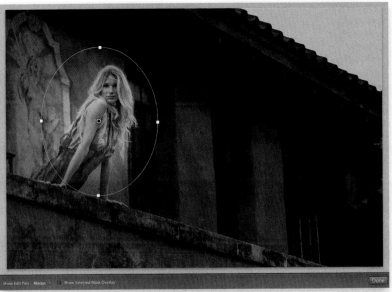

Step Two:

Click-and-drag out the tool over the area where you want the spotlight, and of course, in this case, I would want it over our subject. If, after you drag it out, it's not in the exact spot you want it, just click inside the oval and drag it wherever you want. *Note:* If you need to create a perfect circle using the Radial Filter tool, press-and-hold the Shift key and it constrains the shape to a circle. Also, if you press-and-hold the Command (PC: Ctrl) key and double-click anywhere in your image, it creates an oval as large as it possibly can (you'd use this when you want to create one that affects nearly the entire image, maybe for an overall vignette effect).

Continued

Step Three:

Now that our spotlight is in place, there are lots of things we can do to edit it. For example, if you want to stretch the pool of light out a bit (so it covers all of her), just grab one of the four points around the oval and drag outward. To rotate the spotlight (like I did here), just move your cursor outside the oval and it will change into a two-headed arrow. You can then click-and-drag in the direction you want to rotate your oval. By the way, the transition between the brighter area and the darker area is nice and smooth because the edges of the oval have been feathered (softened) to create that smooth transition (the Feather amount is set to 50, by default. If you want a harder or more abrupt transition, just lower the amount using the Feather slider at the bottom of the panel. Here, I ended up increasing it to 100).

TIP: Removing Ovals

If you want to remove an oval you've created, click on it and then just hit the Delete (PC: Backspace) key.

Step Four:

Let's say you'd like to add another spotlight, a really small one, right over her face. First, to add another spotlight with the same settings, Right-click anywhere inside your oval and choose **Duplicate** (as shown here). That puts another oval right on top of your current one, so the image now looks really dark outside that oval, but you're going to change two things: (1) You're going to make the duplicate really small (slightly larger than her face), and then you're going to click on that center pin and drag it up over her face. It still doesn't look right (well, it does if you're going for a Hollywood Noir effect), because now just her face is lit, and everything else is really dark. So, (2) go to the bottom of the panel, and turn on the Invert checkbox (as seen here; her face will turn really dark), and then drag the Exposure slider over to the right to brighten rather than darken (I took it to 0.42). Now everything looks right.

Step Five:

You can add yet another little spotlight oval using this trick: Let's say we want another one that's inverted (the center of the oval gets affected), so we can put just a little light on that bas-relief piece behind her and to the left. Press-and-hold **Command-Option (PC: Ctrl-Alt)**, and click-and-drag the center of the second small oval on her face and a third oval appears (it's a duplicate of your second one). Drag it to the left, position it over the illustration, shape it so it fits nicely over the bas-relief, and raise the Exposure amount, but not so much that it competes brightness-wise with our subject. Here, I raised it to 0.76. A before/after is shown below. By the way, all these settings I'm using here, I'm choosing by just eyeing it—every photo is different. It's a judgement call, but don't worry, since you made the decision to buy this book, I have great faith in your judgement. :)

TIP: Swapping to the
Inside/Outside

Pressing the **' (apostrophe) key** turns the Invert Mask checkbox on/off, swapping the effect to the inside/outside.

CHAPTER 7

SPECIAL EFFECTS
making stuff look…well…special!

Here's a little known fact: did you know that the Academy of Motion Picture Arts and Sciences (the folks who give out the annual Academy Awards) originally created the Special Effects Oscar category as a way to honor the work done by photographers using Lightroom's Effects panel? Okay, well that's not 100% true. Actually, it's not even 1% true, but if you ever looked in Lightroom's Effects panel and saw that not only are there just two effects in there (Grain and Post-Crop Vignetting), you'd have to ask yourself, are those even effects? Really, is the bar so low for what's allowed into that panel that the simple act of adding noise to your photo is worthy of 50% of an entire panel? I would expect to see some kick butt stuff in that panel, so I figure that Adobe's Lightroom engineers, brilliant as they are, just weren't particularly awesome at putting features in the right spots. I thought it was

one of those left brain/right brain things, but a friend at Adobe, who works closely with the Lightroom team, revealed to me how it's really decided: it's the work of paid lobbyists. I know, it's hard to imagine, but it's a well-known fact out in San Jose, where Adobe is based. Here's how it works: when Lightroom's engineers come into work in the morning, in the lobby of Adobe HQ are small groups of people yelling out where they think certain features should be placed, and they hold up free samples of everything from cans of Monster Energy drink to *Star Wars* action figures (apparently, it was a Boba Fett action figure that shot little missiles and an off-color 12" wampa that got an engineer to move Dehaze to the Basic panel). If I was there with an original Jawa figure with fabric cape, I'll bet I could get the Exposure slider moved to the Split Toning panel. Just sayin'.

Applying Filter-Like "Looks" Using Creative Profiles

Back in Chapter 5, we looked at applying camera profiles to your RAW images. Well, buried in the menu where Adobe put those RAW profiles they also included a bunch of creative profiles for applying more special-effect-style "looks," but using these isn't just limited to RAW photos—you can add them to JPEGs, TIFFs, whatever. These creative profiles have a huge advantage over presets, because presets just move your Develop module sliders to a "pre-set" location (like somebody stepped in and processed the photo for you). However, the profiles don't mess with your sliders—they're their own separate thing, more like special effect filters, so you can still edit your image any way you want after you apply a profile.

Step One:

Here's our original image (remember, the creative profiles don't need a RAW image, you can use them on JPEGs, TIFFs, and PSDs, as well). In the Develop module, at the top of the Basic panel, choose **Browse** from the Profile menu (as shown here), or click the icon with the four little boxes to the right of it. This brings up the Profile Browser with rows of thumbnails (seen in Step Two). There are four sets of creative profiles (behind the scenes, these looks are based on Color Lookup Tables; just throwin' that in for you techie folks). They are: (1) Artistic, (2) B&W (which I cover in this chapter on page 232), (3) Modern, and (4) Vintage.

Step Two:

Two important things to know about the Profile Browser: (1) each thumbnail displays your image with its look applied to it, so you're getting a mini-preview just by looking at the thumbnails, but even better (2) you can audition these looks right on your full-size image by simply hovering your cursor over a thumbnail. So, you can really see whether this is a look you like before committing to it (of course, nothing in Lightroom is really very committed because if you did click on a particular profile and decided you didn't like it after all, you'd just press **Command-Z [Ctrl-Z]** to undo it). Here, I applied the Artistic 08 creative profile.

Step Three:
Let's take this a step further. Scroll down to the Modern profiles, and click on one you like (here, I chose Modern 05, which has kind of a nice desaturated-type look). I actually really like this profile (it's one of my personal favorites out of the whole bunch). You can also see one of the B&W thumbnails at the top of the browser, here (this list of thumbnails scrolls up/down, but the controls at the top, including the all-important Close button, which you click after you're done applying your profile, stay static). By the way, you can add any one or more of these creative profiles to the Favorites section at the top by moving your cursor over a thumbnail, and then clicking on the star icon in the top-right corner.

Step Four:
I like the profile I applied in Step Three, but I wish it wasn't quite so desaturated. Luckily, there's an Amount slider for these creative profiles (unlike with presets) at the top of the Profile Browser, so I can drag this slider to the left, which backs off the intensity, and I can dial in just the right amount (here, I dragged it down to 59; compare it with the full amount in Step Three). This works for any creative profile (there isn't an Amount slider for the RAW profiles), and not only can you back off the amount, if you want a more intense effect, then you can drag the slider to the right.

Virtual Copies— The "No Risk" Way to Experiment

Let's say you added a vignette to a bridal shot. Well, what if you wanted to see a version in black and white, and a version with a color tint, and a really contrasty version, and then maybe a version that was cropped differently? Well, what might keep you from doing that is having to duplicate a high-resolution file each time you wanted to try a different look, because it would eat up hard drive space and RAM like nobody's business. But luckily, you can create virtual copies, which don't take up space and allow you to try different looks without the overhead.

Step One:

You create a virtual copy by just Right-clicking on the original photo and then choosing **Create Virtual Copy** from the pop-up menu (as shown here), or using the keyboard shortcut **Command-'** (apostrophe; **PC: Ctrl-'**). These virtual copies look and act the same as your original photo, and you can edit them just as you would your original, but here's the difference: it's not a real file, it's just a set of instructions, so it doesn't add any real file size. That way, you can have as many of these virtual copies as you want, and experiment to your heart's content without filling up your hard disk.

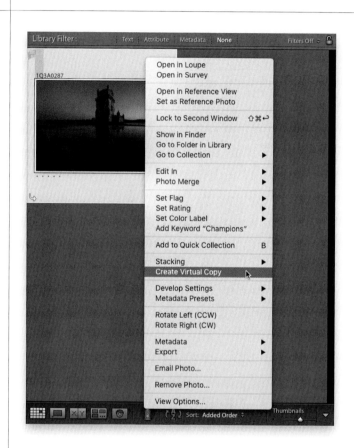

Step Two:

When you create a virtual copy, you'll know which version is the copy because the virtual copies have a curled page icon in the lower-left corner of the image thumbnail (circled in red here) in both Grid view and in the Filmstrip. So now, go ahead and tweak this virtual copy in the Develop module any way you want (here, I increased the Exposure, Contrast, Shadows, Clarity, and Vibrance), and when you return to Grid view, you'll see the original and the edited virtual copy (as seen here).

Step Three:

Now you can experiment away with multiple virtual copies of your original photo, at no risk to that original or your hard drive space. So, click on your first virtual copy, then press Command-' (PC: Ctrl-') to make another virtual copy (that's right—you can make virtual copies of your virtual copy), and then head over to the Develop module, and make some adjustments (here, I made changes to the White Balance, adding more blue and magenta to get this look. I also increased the Exposure, Contrast, Shadows, Clarity, and Vibrance). Now, make some more copies to experiment with (I made a few more copies and tried a few other looks). *Note:* When you make a copy, you can hit the Reset button at the bottom of the right side Panels area to return the virtual copy to its original unedited look. Also, you don't have to jump back to Grid view each time to make a virtual copy—that keyboard shortcut works in the Develop module, too.

Step Four:

Now, if you want to compare all your experimental versions side by side, go back to Grid view, select your original photo and all the virtual copies, then press the letter **N** on your keyboard to enter Survey view (as shown here). If there's a version you really like, of course you can just leave it alone, and then delete the other virtual copies you don't like. (*Note:* To delete a virtual copy, click on it and press the Delete [PC: Backspace] key, and then click Remove in the dialog that appears.) If you choose to take this virtual copy over to Photoshop or export it as a JPEG or TIFF, at that point, Lightroom creates a real copy using the settings you applied to the virtual copy.

Changing Individual Colors

Anytime you have just one color you want to adjust in an image (for example, let's say you want all the reds to be redder, or the blue in the sky to be bluer, or you want to change a color altogether), one place to do that would be in the HSL panel (HSL stands for Hue, Saturation, Luminance). This panel is incredible handy (I use it fairly often) and luckily, because it has a TAT (Targeted Adjustment tool), using it is really easy. Here's how this works:

Step One:

When you want to adjust an area of color, scroll down to the HSL panel in the right side Panels area (by the way, those words in the panel header, HSL/Color, are not just names, they're buttons, and if you click on either of them, the controls for that panel will appear). Go ahead and click on HSL (since this is where we'll be working first), and four buttons appear in the panel: Hue, Saturation, Luminance, and All. The Hue panel lets you change an existing color to a different color by using the sliders. Just so you can see what it does, click-and-drag the Red slider all the way to the left and the Orange slider to –71, and you'll see it changes the red roof to magenta.

Step Two:

If you dragged the Red slider all the way to the right, and left the Orange slider at –71, it would change the color of the red roof to more of an orangeish color. This is a perfect task for the Hue sliders of the HSL panel. Now, what if you wanted to make the orange color more orange, but you've pushed the sliders just about as far as they can go? Well, you'd start by clicking on the word "Saturation" at the top of the panel.

Step Three:

Now, these eight sliders control just the saturation of colors in your image. Drag the Orange slider way over to the right, and the Red not quite as far, and the orange in the roof becomes more vibrant (as seen here). If you know exactly which color you want to affect, you can just drag the sliders. But if you're not sure exactly which colors make up the area you want to adjust, then you can use the TAT (the Targeted Adjustment tool in the top-left corner of the panel). So, if you had a blue sky and wanted to make it more vibrant, you'd click on the TAT, then click it on the sky, and drag it upward to make it bluer (downward to make it less blue). And it wouldn't just move the Blue slider, but would increase the Aqua Saturation amount, as well. You probably wouldn't have realized that there was any aqua in that blue sky, and this is exactly why this tool is so handy here. In fact, I rarely use the HSL panel without using the TAT!

Step Four:

To change the brightness of the colors, click on Luminance at the top of the panel. To brighten the orange color of the roof, take the TAT and click-and-drag straight upward on it, and its color gets brighter (the Luminance for both Red and Orange increased). Two last things: Clicking the All button (at the top of the panel) puts all three panels in one scrolling list and the Color panel breaks them all into sets of three for each color—a layout more like Photoshop's Hue/Saturation. But, regardless of which layout you choose, they all work the same way. A before/after is shown here, after we changed and brightened the color of the roof.

How to Add Vignette Effects

An edge vignette effect (where you darken all the edges around your image to focus the attention on the center of the photo) is one of those effects you either love or that drives you crazy (I, for one, love 'em). Here we're going to look at how to apply a simple vignette, one where you crop the photo and the vignette still appears (called a "post-crop" vignette), and how to use the other vignetting options.

Step One:
To add an edge vignette effect, go to the right side Panels area and scroll down to the Lens Corrections panel (the reason it's in the Lens Corrections panel is this: some particular lenses darken the corners of your photo, even when you don't want them to. In that case, it's a problem, and you'd go to the Lens Corrections panel to fix a lens problem, right? There, you would brighten the corners using the controls in this panel. So, basically, a little edge darkening is bad, but if you add a lot intentionally, then it's cool. Hey, I don't make the rules—I just pass them on). Here's the original image without any vignetting (by the way, we'll talk about how to get rid of "bad vignetting" in Chapter 8—the chapter on how to fix problems).

Step Two:
We'll start with regular full-image vignetting, so click on Manual at the top of the panel, then drag the Vignetting Amount slider all the way to the left. This slider controls how dark the edges of your photo are going to get (the further to the left you drag, the darker they get). The Midpoint slider controls how far in the dark edges get to the center of your photo. So, try dragging it over quite a bit, too (as I have here), and it kind of creates a nice, soft spotlight effect, where the edges are dark, your subject looks nicely lit, and your eye is drawn right where you want it to look.

Step Three:
Now, this works just fine, until you wind up having to crop the photo, because cropping will crop away the edge vignette. To get around that problem, Adobe added a control called "Post-Crop Vignetting," which lets you add vignetting effects after you've cropped. I'm cropping that same photo in tight here, and now most of the edge vignetting I added earlier will be cropped away. So, scroll down to the Effects panel, and at the top, you'll see Post-Crop Vignetting. Before we try that, reset your Vignetting Amount slider (in the Lens Corrections panel) to 0 (zero), so we don't add the post-crop vignetting on top of the little bit of original vignetting still in our photo.

Step Four:
Before we get to the sliders, let's talk about the Style pop-up menu. You have three choices: (1) Highlight Priority, (2) Color Priority, and (3) Paint Overlay (though the only one that really looks good is Highlight Priority, so it's the only one I ever use). Highlight Priority is more like what you get with the regular vignette. The edges get darker, but the color may shift a bit, and I'm totally okay with the edges looking more saturated. This choice gets its name from the fact that it tries to keep as much of the highlights intact, so if you have some bright areas around the edges, it'll try to make sure they stay bright. I made the edges pretty darn dark here—darker than I would make mine, but I wanted you to really see the effect on the cropped image (just for example purposes). The Color Priority style is more concerned with keeping your color accurate around the edges, so the edges do get a bit darker, but the colors don't get more saturated, and it's not as dark (or nice) as the Highlight Priority style. Finally, Paint Overlay gives you the look we had back in Lightroom 2 for post-crop vignetting, which just painted the edges dark gray (yeech!).

Continued

Step Five:
The next two sliders were added to give you more control to make your vignettes look more realistic. For example, the Roundness setting controls how round the vignette is. Just so you know exactly what this does, try this: leave the Roundness set at 0, but then drag the Feather amount (which we'll talk about in a moment) all the way to the left. You see how it creates a very defined oval shape? Of course, you wouldn't really use this look (well, I hope not), but it does help in understanding exactly what this slider does. Well, the Roundness setting controls how round that oval gets (drag the slider back and forth a couple of times and you'll instantly get it). Okay, reset it to zero (and stop playing with that slider). ;-)

Step Six:
The Feather slider controls the amount of softness of the oval's edge, so dragging this slider to the right makes the vignette softer and more natural looking. Here, I clicked-and-dragged the Feather amount to 57, and you can see how it softened the edges of the hard oval you saw in the previous step. So, in short, the farther you drag, the softer the edges of the oval get. The bottom slider, Highlights, helps you to maintain highlights in the edge areas you're darkening with your vignette. The farther to the right you drag it, the more the highlights are protected. The Highlights slider is only available if your Style is set to either Highlight Priority or Color Priority (but you're not going to set it to Color Priority, because it looks kind of yucky, right?). So there ya have it—how to add an edge vignette to focus the viewer's attention on the center of your image by darkening the edges all the way around.

There's a Photoshop effect that started making the rounds a couple years ago, and now it's one of the hottest and most requested looks out there—you see it everywhere from big magazine covers to websites to celebrity portraits to album covers. Anyway, you can get pretty darn close to that look right within Lightroom itself. Now, before I show you the effect, I have to tell you, this is one of those effects that you'll either absolutely love (and you'll wind up over-using it), or you'll hate it with a passion that knows no bounds. There's no in-between.

Getting That Trendy High-Contrast Look

Step One:
Before we apply this effect, I have a disclaimer: this effect doesn't look good on every photo. It looks best on photos that have lots of detail and texture, so it looks great on city shots, landscapes, industrial shots, and even people (especially guys)—anything you want to be gritty and texture-y (if that's even a word). So, you're usually not going to apply this effect to anything you want to look soft and/or glamorous. Here's a shot with lots of detail and that has lots of texture. It's just screaming for this type of treatment.

Step Two:
You're going to really crank up four sliders in the Develop module's Basic panel: (1) drag the Contrast slider all the way over to +100, (2) drag the Highlights slider all the way to –100, (3) drag the Shadows slider all the way to +100 (that opens up the shadows), and (4) drag the Clarity slider all the way to the right to +100. Now, the whole image has that high-contrast look already, but we're not done yet.

Continued

Step Three:

At this point, depending on the photo you applied this effect to, you might have to drag the Exposure slider to the right a bit if the entire image is too dark (that can happen when you set the Contrast at +100). Or, if the photo looks washed out a bit (from cranking the Shadows slider to +100), then you might need to drag the Blacks slider to the left to bring back the color saturation and overall balance. Here, I ended up decreasing the Exposure to −0.20 and the Blacks to −23. Outside of those potential tweaks, the next step is to desaturate the photo a little bit by dragging the Vibrance slider to the left (here, I dragged it over to −25). This desaturation is a trademark of this "look," which kind of gives the feel of an HDR image without combining multiple exposures.

Step Four:

The final step is to add an edge vignette to darken the edges of your photo, and put the focus on your subject. So, go to the Lens Corrections panel (in the right side Panels area), click on Manual at the top, and drag the Vignetting Amount slider to the left (making the edges really dark). Then drag the Midpoint slider pretty far to the left, as well (the Midpoint slider controls how far the darkened edges extend in toward the middle of your photo. The farther you drag this slider to the left, the farther in they go). This made the whole photo look a little too dark, so I had to go back to the Basic panel and increase the Exposure amount a little bit (to +0.10) to bring back the original brightness before the vignette. I included a few befores and afters on the next page just to give you an idea of how it affects different images. Hey, don't forget to save this as a preset (see page 208), so you don't have to do this manually every time you want to apply this look.

Creating Black-and-White Images

There are two methods for converting your images from color to black and white, and I'll start with the method that has been in Lightroom from the start. But, the newer method (definitely my preferred method) gives you more choices, live previews, and, I think, a far better result. Plus, once you've made the conversion, you can use the same techniques you learned in Chapters 5 and 6 to really fine-tune your conversion.

Step One:

Here's our original color image (taken in Banff, Canada), and I thought it would make a good candidate for converting to black and white (not every color image makes a good black-and-white, no matter how good the conversion technique). Before we do the conversion, take a look in the right side Panels area, and you'll see a panel called "HSL/Color." Keep an eye on that panel. Now, at the very top of the Basic panel, in the Treatment section, click on Black & White (as shown here).

Step Two:

Now look at the HSL/Color panel, again. It's no longer visible—it has been replaced by the B&W panel (seen in the inset here), and Lightroom has applied its Adobe Monochrome profile. If you click on the Auto button at the bottom of the panel, it applies an Auto mix (as seen here). Since "it's less than awesome," I don't use it, but instead do it manually. Each of the sliders in this panel affects the underlying tones represented by that color slider. For example, drag the Blues slider back and forth and you'll see how it affects the sky. What these sliders do is brighten or darken parts of your image, and if you just drag each one back and forth a few times, you'll get what they do and how each affects your black-and-white image.

Step Three:

That's what I did here—I double-clicked on Black & White Mix at the top of the panel to remove the Auto mix, then I dragged each slider back and forth a few times to see how each affects the image. The Red slider and the Magenta slider didn't affect this particular image at all, but most of the other sliders did, so I dragged each one, evaluated how it looked to me, and if I liked what a particular slider did, I left it there. This alone won't make a great black-and-white, but it's good to know this is here if you want to tweak a partic-ular part of your image later. What I'm saying here is that I wouldn't use this feature at this stage of the game, but later (when we do our conversion using the better method) we can come back here if we need some part of the photo to be brighter, and we can't think of an easier or faster way to do it.

Step Four:

Okay, hit the Reset button at the bottom of the right side Panels area and let's try the other method. Go to the top of the Basic panel, and from the Profile pop-up menu, choose **Browse** (as shown here). We're going to use a profile to convert to black and white, and we're going to have a lot of choices as to how this conversion happens, and how the final image winds up looking.

Continued

Step Five:

When you choose Browse, it brings up the Profile Browser you see here. Scroll down to the B&W profiles. The awesome thing about these B&W profiles is that they're not presets—they don't move any sliders—so when find one you like and apply it, you can still tweak the resulting image to your heart's content. It shows you a preview of what each B&W profile looks like right on the thumbnail themselves. To find which one looks best to you, just hover your cursor over each thumbnail and you'll get a live preview right on your image. Here, I moved my cursor over each of the thumbnails to find out which one looked best on this particular image, and, for me, it was B&W 07. So, that's what you're seeing here. Just one click.

TIP: Would This Make a Good B&W Image?

If you're looking through your images and wonder if a particular one would make a good black-and-white, just press the letter **V** on your keyboard and it makes the image black and white, and you'll see whether there's potential there or not. If it doesn't look good, press V again to return to the full-color image.

Step Six:

One of the best things about these profiles (besides the fact that they don't move any sliders when you use them) is that you can control their amounts—if you apply one and the effect is too intense, you can use the Amount slider at the top of the panel to back off the intensity. Or, if you like what you see, you can intensify the profile's effect, so that's what I did here, where I increased the Amount by dragging the slider to the right to 152.

Step Seven:

Since the B&W profiles don't move any sliders, you're free to use them to tweak your image. That's what I did here, adding a little more Contrast, backing off the Highlights a bit, and opening up the Shadows and the Whites. After all that, I still felt the top side of the mountain was a bit dark, so I switched to the Adjustment Brush **(K)**, increased the Exposure amount to 0.71, and painted over just that area to brighten it. Or, rather than using the Adjustment Brush, you could go to the B&W panel and tweak individual color sliders (like we did in Step Three). Lastly, I went to the Detail panel and sharpened the living daylights out of it (which I always do with black-and-white images) by setting the Amount to 90 and the Radius to 1.1.

TIP: Add Some Noise!

If you want a more film-like look, go to the Effects panel, under Grain, and increase the Amount to add a film-grain look. The further you drag this slider to the right, the grainier it gets.

The auto conversion to black and white

After applying a B&W profile, then cranking up the amount, and making Basic panel, Adjustment Brush, and Detail panel tweaks

Making Great Duotones

This is such a simple technique, but it's so effective. I learned this trick years ago from my buddy and Adobe Worldwide Evangelist, Terry White, who learned it from another photographer who works for Adobe, and now I'm passing it on to you. Of all the methods I've used to create duotones over the years, this is definitely the easiest, but crazy enough, it's also the best.

Step One:

Although the actual duotone is created in the Split Toning panel (in the right side Panels area), you should convert the photo to black and white first. (I say "should" because you can apply a duotone effect on top of your color photo, but…well… yeech!) So, go to the Profile Browser, by clicking on the icon with the four squares in the top right of the Basic panel, and scroll down to the B&W profiles—see page 202 for more on these, but for now, just find one that looks good to you as a starting point (I chose B&W 01 here), and then click the Close button in the top right of the browser.

Step Two:

The trick to creating duotones is actually incredibly simple: you only add the color tint in the shadows, and you leave the high-lights untouched. So, go to the Split Toning panel, in the right side Panels area, and start by dragging the Shadows Saturation slider to around 25, so you can see some of the tint color (as soon as you start dragging the Saturation slider, the tint appears, but, by default, the hue is a reddish color). Now, drag the Shadows Hue slider over to 35 to get more of a traditional duotone look (I usually pick a hue from 32 to 41, some-where in there. While you're there, lower the Shadows Saturation to 20, as shown here). That's it.

TIP: Reset Your Settings

If you want to start over, press-and-hold the Option (PC: Alt) key, and the word "Shadows" in the Split Toning panel chang-es to "Reset Shadows." Click on it to reset the settings to their defaults.

This matte finish look has become really popular in the last couple of years and luckily, it's pretty easy to pull off. It's just a simple Curves move (and even if you've never used Curves before, you'll be able to do this).

Creating a Matte Look

Step One:

In the Develop module, go down to the Tone Curve panel (if your Tone Curve doesn't look like this one, and instead has sliders under it, click on the little curve icon in the bottom-right corner of the panel to switch to the curve you see here). You're going to add two control points to the diagonal line by just clicking right on that line. So, add one about 1/4 of the way up from the bottom-left corner (you can see the point I added here) and one 1/4 of the way down from the top-right corner (where my cursor is in the image shown here). If you mess up and add a point you didn't mean to, Right-click on it and choose **Delete Control Point**. Adding those two control points locks down most of the curve, so we can adjust the deep shadows and highlights without messing with the rest of the tones of the image. That's the hard part, the rest is easy.

Step Two:

Now, go to the very bottom-left corner, click on that control point, and drag straight up, right along the left edge. Then, do the same thing with the control point up in the very top-right corner, except drag it down a bit along the right edge (as shown here). That's it—you've got the matte look, and now you can rule Instagram like a boss!

Using One-Click Presets (and Making Your Own!)

Lightroom comes with a number of built-in Develop module presets that you can apply to any photo with just one click. These are found in the Presets panel over in the left side Panels area, where you'll find 15 different collections of presets: 14 built-in collections put there by Adobe and a User Presets collection (that one's empty for now, because this is where you store the ones you create on your own). These are huge time savers, so take just minute or two and learn how to put them to use (and how to create your own).

Step One:

We'll start by looking at how to use the built-in presets, then we'll create one of our own, and apply it in two different places. First, let's look at the built-in presets by going to the Presets panel (found in the left side Panels area). There are 14 built-in Lightroom collections (and a User Presets collection, where you can save and store your own presets. If you imported any presets, as I have, you'll also have an Imported Presets collection). When you look inside each collection, you'll see that Adobe named these built-in presets by starting each name with the type of preset it is (for example, within the Classic - Effects presets, you'll find Grain. That's the type of preset, then it says, "Light," "Medium," or "Heavy").

TIP: Renaming Presets

To rename any preset you created (a user preset), just Right-click on the preset and choose **Rename** from the pop-up menu.

Step Two:

You can see a preview of how any of these presets will look, even before you apply them, by simply hovering your cursor over the presets in the Presets panel. A preview will appear above the Presets panel in the Navigator panel (as shown here, where I'm hovering over a Classic - Color preset called Cross Process 3, and you can see a preview of how that color effect would look applied to my photo, up in the Navigator panel, at the top of the left side Panels area).

Step Three:
To actually apply one of these presets, all you have to do is click on it. In the example shown here, I went to the Classic - B&W Filter presets and clicked on the Green Filter preset to create this black-and-white conversion. I could be done right there with one click, but the nice thing is if you want to tweak things after the preset has been applied, you can just grab the sliders in the Basic panel and go to town!

Step Four:
For example, here I increased the Contrast to +44, and I lowered the Highlights a bit more than the preset had (to –98), so I could darken the background a bit. I opened up the Shadows a bit to +10, so you could see more detail in the dark parts of her hair, and I backed off the Clarity amount to +16 to keep the image from looking so "crunchy." Also, once you've applied a preset, you can apply more presets and those changes are added right on top of your current settings, as long as the new preset you chose doesn't use the same settings as the one you just applied. So, if you applied a preset that set the Exposure, White Balance, and Highlights, but didn't use vignetting, if you then chose a preset that just uses vignetting, it adds this on top of your current preset. Otherwise, if the new preset uses Exposure, White Balance, or Highlights, it just moves those sliders to new settings, so it might cancel the look of the original preset. For example, after I applied the Green Filter preset, and tweaked the settings I mentioned above, I went to the Classic - Effects presets collection and applied the preset called "Vignette 1" (as shown here) to add a dark edge effect. The Green Filter didn't have a vignette, so it added it on top.

Continued

Step Five:

Now, of course you can use any built-in preset as a starting place to build your own preset, but here's how build your own custom preset from scratch: Click the Reset button at the bottom of the right side Panels area to reset our photo to how it looked when we started. Now we'll create a look that's kind of like the popular Instagram filter, Clarendon. Choose the Adobe Portrait profile from the Profile pop-up menu, then increase the Exposure amount to +0.62 to brighten things up, bring the Highlights down to –37, and the Shadows up to +11 to open the dark areas a bit. Set the Whites way up to +69, the Blacks to –58, and Vibrance to +7 to add a little more punch to the color. That's it for the Basic panel tweaks.

Step Six:

Now, go the Split Toning panel. In the Highlights section, set the Hue to 59 (for an amber tone) and Saturation to 11, so there's not too much of it. In the Shadows section, set the Hue to 177 (kind of a greenish shade) and the Saturation to 10. The Balance slider in the middle lets you choose the balance between the Highlights Hue and the Shadows Hue. Drag the Balance to –83, so the image is learning toward the greens in the shadows. Okay, we have our Instagram Clarendon-like look. Now, let's save it as a preset so we can apply this same look to other photos in just one click.

Step Seven:
In the Presets panel, click on the + (plus sign) button on the right side of the panel header and choose **Create Preset** to bring up the New Develop Preset dialog (shown here). Give your new preset a name (I named mine "Insta-Clarendon Look"), click the Check None button at the bottom of the dialog (to turn off all the checkboxes), then turn on the checkboxes beside all the settings you edited (as seen here). Now, click the Create button to save all the edits you just made as your own custom preset, which will appear under the User Presets collection in the Presets panel.

Note: To delete a user preset, just click on the preset, then click on the – (minus sign) button, which will appear to the left of the + button on the right side of the Presets panel header.

Step Eight:
Now click on a different photo in the Filmstrip, then hover your cursor over your new preset. Look up at the Navigator panel, and you'll see a preview of the preset (as seen here). Seeing these instant live previews is a huge time saver, because you'll know in a split second whether your photo will look good with the preset applied or not, before you actually apply it. Click on it to apply it.

TIP: Updating a User Preset
If you tweak a user preset and want to update it with the new settings, Right-click on your preset and choose **Update with Current Settings** from the pop-up menu.

Continued

Step Nine:

If you're going to apply a particular preset (either a built-in one or one you created) to a bunch of images you're importing, you can actually have that preset applied to your images as they're imported, so when they appear, they already have your preset applied. You do this right within the Import window. Just go to the Apply During Import panel (seen here), where you'd choose which preset you want from the Develop Settings pop-up menu (as shown here, where I chose that Insta-Clarendon Look preset we just created), and now that preset is automatically applied to each photo as it's imported. There's one more place you can apply these Develop presets, and that's in the Saved Preset pop-up menu, at the top of the Quick Develop panel, in the Library module (see more about the Quick Develop panel in Chapter 5).

TIP: Importing Presets

There are lots of places online where you can download free Develop module presets (like from this book's companion website and my LightroomKillerTips .com site). Once they're downloaded, go to the Presets panel, click the on + (plus sign) button on the right side of the panel header, choose **Import Preset(s)**, and navigate your way to the preset(s) you just downloaded. You can also just Right-click directly on User Presets, and choose **Import** from the pop-up menu (as seen here). Locate the preset(s) you downloaded and click the Import button, and it will now appear in your User Presets.

Sun flare effects are really popular right now, and thankfully, they're pretty darn easy to do. Plus, there are two ways you can pull this off. I'll go with my favorite method first, and I'm adding the second method as a tip, since it uses the same settings—just a different tool.

Sun Flare Effect

Step One:
Here's our original image, and if you look at her hair and the backlighting from the sun, you can already see which side you're going to need to put your sun flare on.

Step Two:
Get the Radial Filter tool in the toolbox near the top of the right side Panels area (it's shown circled here; or press **Shift-M**), but before you click-and-drag it out, drag the Temp slider way over to the yellow side (here, I dragged it over to 78). Now, crank up the Exposure (it is the sun, ya know, and in this case, I dragged it over to the right to 1.51, so basically adding a stop-and-a-half exposure). Then, click-and-drag it out over her shoulder on the left (as seen here). Notice the position of the oval here—I'm intentionally letting it spill a little over onto the side of her face.

Continued

Step Three:

Next, we're going to add some negative Clarity to soften our sunbeam, so drag the Clarity slider way over to the left (here, I dragged it over to –78). It's a little dark, so let's also increase the Exposure to brighten it up (I increased it to 2.93). To better position the flare, click on the little black edit pin and drag it up and to the left a bit (as shown here).

Step Four:

To make the effect look more realistic, you're going to need to somewhat match up the color of the rest of the image with the very warm color you just added with this sun flare. So, go to the Basic panel and drag the Temp slider over to the right a bit, so the sun flare blends in. To finish things off, back off the Contrast a bit (one of the rare times I add negative contrast, but in this case, with the sun bursting in, it helps "sell" the look by lowering the contrast of the rest of the image). A before and after is shown below.

TIP: Optional Second Method

Another way to get a similar effect is to use the Adjustment Brush **(K)** with a really large brush size. Same settings as with the Radial Filter tool—just one or two clicks in the same spot with the brush, and you're there.

The hot look in fashion right now is to add a cross-process effect, and there are a couple of different ways to do this. We'll start with the easy version, and at least uncork the advanced version, which uses Curves.

Cross-Processing Fashion Look

Step One:
These cross-processing effects are usually applied to color images using the Split Toning panel, like we use when creating a duotone look (see page 206), but unlike the duotone, you're going to choose one hue for the highlights and a different hue for the shadows here.

TIP: See a Tint Color Preview
To make it easier to see which color tint you're choosing, press-and-hold the Option (PC: Alt) key, drag the Hue slider, and it will give you a temporary preview of your color tint as if you bumped up the Saturation amount to 100%.

Step Two:
Here, I set the Highlights Hue to 57 and the Shadows Hue to 232. I then set the Shadows Saturation slider to 56 and the Highlights Saturation slider to 51 (a little bit higher than usual, just to add more color). That's all there is to it (I told you this was easy). By the way, the Balance slider (found between the Highlights and Shadows sections) lets you balance the color mix—dragging to the right tips the balance toward the Highlights color and dragging left tips the balance more toward the color in the shadows. You can also choose colors from the color swatches to the right of the words Highlights and Shadows—clicking on either swatch brings up a color picker, and along the top are some common split-tone highlight colors. To close the color picker, click on the X in the upper-left.

Continued

Step Three:

The other method for creating cross-processing looks is to tweak the individual Red, Green, and Blue color channels using the Tone Curve panel (found in the right side Panels area). To pick an individual channel to edit, click on the Channel pop-up menu and choose the channel you want to edit (in our example, the Red channel). Our original image is shown here, and to apply this particular cross-processing effect (you can use this curve to create any color combination you want), you can leave the Red channel alone. Choose Green from the channel pop-up menu (shown bottom middle) and add a point to the curve by clicking once 1/4 of the way up from the bottom of the diagonal line, and then drag it diagonally up to increase the amount of green in the shadows. Add another point 1/4 of the way down from the top and pull it down just a tiny bit. Now, go to the Blue channel and drag the bottom-left corner point straight upward along the left edge a little bit (as shown) to add some blue into the lower midtones. Then, drag the top-right corner point down along the right side (as shown here) to add some blue. Add a point 1/4 of the way down from the top of the curve, and then drag it down just a little, which adds some yellows to the highlights. Finally, add another point 1/4 of the way from the bottom and drag that one up a bit.

Step Four:

Now you have blues, greens, and yellows. If you think the image looks too contrasty or doesn't have enough contrast, go to the Basic panel and adjust the Contrast slider until it looks right to you.

Lightroom's panoramic feature (which stitches multiple frames into one very wide, or very tall, shot) is one of the best out there, and one of the coolest things about it (besides how fast it is, and the great options it has) is that the final panoramic image it creates is still a RAW image. What?!! I know. Crazy, right, but that's how it works (well, that's how it works if you started with RAW images anyway).

Creating Panoramas

Step One:
Start by selecting the images you want combined into a panorama (or pano, for short) in the Library module. Then, go under the Photo menu, under Photo Merge, and choose **Panorama** (as seen here) or just press **Control-M (PC: Ctrl-M)**.

TIP: Overlap 20% or So In-Camera
For Lightroom to successfully stitch together your shots into one single image, when you're taking your pano photos, be sure to overlap each frame by at least 20%. It helps Lightroom determine which frames go together and keeps you from having gaps. Well, it really wouldn't have gaps, it just wouldn't successfully stitch it together—you'd get a warning.

Step Two:
This brings up the Panorama Merge Preview dialog (shown here). It has three Projection choices for creating your pano, but it automatically chooses which one it thinks is best. Personally, I only use Spherical, and according to Adobe, it works best for wide panos. If you shoot architectural panos, where you'd want to keep the lines that are supposed to be straight, straight, Adobe recommends the Perspective projection. Lastly, the Cylindrical projection is a cross between the two, as it's supposed to work better for panos that are really wide, but still need straight vertical lines. All that being said, I still just use Spherical all the time.

Continued

Step Three:

Take a look back at that preview in Step Two. See all that white space around it that needs to be cropped off? Well, you could always crop that away later in Lightroom, but you have two solid options here in this dialog: The first is to have it automatically crop away any of the white gaps around the edges of your image. Just turn on the Auto Crop checkbox (as shown here), and it crops the image tight so none of those white areas are visible. The downside of Auto Crop is cropping this tight makes your pano less tall and less wide. Depending on the photo, that might not be a problem, but it might crop off the tops of mountains or the tops of buildings, etc. The good news is: if you turn it on and you don't like what you see in the preview, you can just toggle it right back off. But, there is a better option.

TIP: This Pano Dialog Is Resizable

You can resize it to whatever size and dimensions you like by just clicking-and-dragging its edges. Since panos are usually wide images, I drag mine out as wide as it can fit onscreen.

Step Four:

Now, behold the wonder that is Boundary Warp. This is my "go-to" option for panos (I use it every time) and simply dragging the slider all the way to the right does as close to magic as you're going to see in Lightroom—it just moves the pano around somehow to fill in those open gaps and yet, when it's done, it doesn't look funky, it looks fantastic! I'm not sure why it's a slider and not a checkbox because I do a lot of panos, and I've never not wanted it at 100% (drag it back to 90% or 80% and you'll see what I mean). Either way, it's pretty darn awesome and I use it on every pano I stitch (I have some comparisons for you on the next page).

Note that the resulting pano file is a DNG image

Step Five:

Just for visual comparison purposes, take a look at the three images here. The top image is the original pano as-is; the middle shot is with the Auto Crop checkbox turned on and the white gaps around the edges trimmed away; and the bottom image is the same pano, but with the Boundary Warp slider dragged all the way over to 100%. There is no answer that is wrong here—you can choose whichever one you want, including making no choice at all and cropping it later in Lightroom or taking it over to Photoshop to use Content-Aware Fill to fill in those gaps. Totally your call.

TIP: If It Can't Find a Lens Profile

If you see a warning icon and it says Lightroom is "Unable to match a lens profile automatically," it'll still make the pano—the results just won't be quite as good. To fix this, click the Cancel button, make sure your pano photos are still selected, then go to the Lens Corrections panel (in the Develop module's right side Panels area) and turn on the Enable Profile Corrections checkbox in the Profile tab. Next, choose your lens make/model from the pop-up menus, then go back and try your pano again, and all should be good.

Step Six:

Now, click the Merge button and it will render the final high-res version of your pano (it renders in the background, but you'll see a progress bar in the upper-left corner of Lightroom). When it's finished, your final stitched pano appears as a DNG file in the same collection as the images you used to create the pano (provided, of course, that the images were in a collection when you started. If not, it'll appear in the same folder, but usually at the bottom of the folder), and you can tweak this pano like you would any other image.

Adding Beams of Light

This effect makes use of the fact that Lightroom has two brushes, and you can make each of the brushes a different size and switch between the two. We use that to create a transition between a small brush and a large brush, and the feathering keeps the transitions smooth. Super-easy to do, and on the right image, it's really effective.

Step One:
Here's the original RAW image we want to add light beams to. If you're thinking, "Scott…that's a pretty lame photo," well, I would have to agree, but it does have one thing going for it: the sun is peeking through the trees. But, I'm with you on the lameness of this shot, which is why in the next step we're at least going to try to take it from lame to not quite as lame.

Step Two:
The first thing we need to do is to warm up the image (color-wise), so in the Basic panel, drag the Temp slider way over to yellow. That's a start. Now let's make it a little bit brighter (maybe 1/4 of a stop or so) by increasing the Exposure to +0.25 and the Contrast to +56. Then, drag the Highlights back quite a bit, so the sun isn't so bright (it's going to get brighter when you add the beams)—I took it over to –60. Now, the woods still look pretty dark, so drag the Shadows slider all the way over to +100. I also dragged the Whites all the way down to –100 because it's really bright where the sun is coming through. Finally, crank up the Clarity to +24 to bring out the detail, and then crank up the Vibrance to +27 to bring out more color, and well…it's still not an awesome photo, but it does look better.

Step Three:

Now, to create our beams, get the Adjustment Brush **(K)** from the toolbox near the top of the right side Panels area, then drag the Temp slider over to 77 (so it paints a very yellow stroke) and crank up the Exposure to around 2.00. At the bottom of the panel, we have two brushes we can use marked "A" and "B." Click on the A brush, set the Feather amount to 100 (to make the edges of your brush soft), and then set the Flow amount to 100 (so we get a consistent amount of the effect we're going to apply). Now, set your Brush size really small at 0.1 (yes, that is one tiny brush), then take that brush and click once right on the sun. It's so small, you won't actually see anything, but you should see a little black edit pin appear in the spot where you clicked (as shown circled here in red).

Step Four:

Now click on the B brush and, again, make sure the Feather and Flow are set at 100, but set this brush at a much larger size (here, I set it to 18.0). Remember, you've already clicked once, right on the sun, right? Now that you have the B brush, move to the bottom of the image, press-and-hold the Shift key (holding the Shift key makes it draw a straight line between where you first clicked on the sun and where you'll click at the bottom of the image), and click once with that larger brush. It will draw a straight line between the two spots, starting at that small size and growing until it reaches the size of the larger brush click at the bottom of the screen. That's how you create a beam, but there's something we can do (on the next page) to make the process of adding more beams a little quicker.

Continued

Step Five:

We're going to continue the process of adding more beams, but to speed things up, instead of going to the bottom of the Adjustment Brush panel every time we need to switch brushes, we're going to use a keyboard shortcut to make the process much faster and easier. Here's what you do: With the A brush selected, click once on the sun, then press the **/ (forward slash) key** to switch to the B brush, press-and-hold the Shift key and click at the bottom of the screen, but to the right or left of your original beam. Each time you press the forward slash key, it toggles between the A and B brushes. So, hit the forward slash key to toggle to the A brush, click once on the sun, press it again to switch to B, press-and-hold the Shift key, and click again somewhere else along the bottom, hit forward slash to return to A, and do it all again, with your beam ending somewhere else, until your image looks like the one you see here.

Step Six:

All of these beams of light you have added are represented by the same edit pin you created the first time you clicked the brush on the sun. This is really handy because you'll probably need to lower the intensity of those beams, so they blend in better with the rest of the image and look more realistic. To do that, simply go to the Exposure slider (you're still in the Adjustment Brush panel, by the way), and back it off some. You were painting at 2.00 (plus 2 stops), so drag it back to the left a bit until it looks like they blend in better (in our case, I lowered the Exposure to 1.04, so I dropped the brightness of my beams by nearly a full stop).

Step Seven:

This is an optional step, but depending on the image, this can add a nice bit of realism, as we add a little haze or fog around our beams. Here's how: First, click on the New button near the top-right corner of the panel, then double-click on the word "Effect" to reset all your Adjustment Brush sliders to zero. Go down to the Dehaze slider and drag it just a little bit to the left (here, I dragged it to –5), and then take a large brush and paint over the area where the beams are, and it adds a foggy haze around the beams (as seen here). Again, it's a totally optional step, but I wanted to give you the option.

TIP: Creating Softer Beams

If you think your beams need to be a little bit softer, drag the Adjustment Brush's Clarity slider over to the left a bit, and you'll see the beams soften.

Step Eight:

Here are a few more examples using the exact same technique, but with the color of the beam varied (which you do by changing the white balance). In the slot canyon shot at the top left, I moved the white balance Temp slider more toward blue to create a whiter beam, but without turning white. In the shot at the Valley of Fire on the top right, I lowered the Temp slider (dragging it to the left), so the beams weren't so yellow, and I lowered the Exposure amount quite a bit. In the concert shot, I made the A brush a lot bigger (I set A to 20 and B to 35), and I changed the white balance of the beam.

Creating
HDR Images

Lightroom lets you take a series of shots that were bracketed in-camera and combine them into a single 32-bit HDR image. But, don't worry—it doesn't create that "Harry Potter on acid" style of HDR. In fact, the merged HDR will look a lot like the normal exposure, but the tonal range is expanded to the extent that you can now do things like opening up the shadows big time without getting a ton of noise. Plus, the final HDR image is a DNG image, so you can edit it like any other RAW image (but with more headroom and tonal depth).

Step One:
Select your bracketed shots in the Library module. Here, I have three bracketed shots (the regular exposure, one shot that is two stops *underexposed*, and one shot that is two stops *overexposed*), but according to Adobe's own engineers, Lightroom doesn't need more than just two frames to do its thing—the one that's two stops under and the one that's two stops over. So, here I selected just those two shots. Now, go under the Photo menu, under Photo Merge, and choose **HDR** (as shown here; or just press **Control-H [PC: Ctrl-H]**).

Step Two:
This brings up the HDR Merge Preview dialog (seen here), and in a few moments, a preview of your HDR image will appear. (*Note:* This dialog is resizable—just click-and-drag the edges to resize it.) Near the top right, the Auto Settings checkbox is on by default (it's the same as Auto Tone from the Basic panel, which I don't generally use on my regular images, but with HDR images, it actually works surprisingly well, so I leave it on). Depending on the image, it can have more detail or it might look brighter in the shadow areas, but it won't look a whole lot different (with Lightroom's brand of HDR, you don't really see the benefits until you "tone" the image in the Develop module).

TIP: Faster HDR Processing
To skip this dialog and have it create your HDR in the background (using whatever settings you used on your last HDR image), just press-and-hold the Shift key as you choose HDR from the Photo menu.

Step Three:

We'll skip the Auto Align checkbox for now because we'll talk about that on the next page. So, for now, just click the Merge button, and it will create your single HDR image, which will appear right next to your individual frames in your collection, as seen here (if you're working in folders, you might have to scroll to the bottom of the folder to find this HDR.dng image). By the way, by just looking at the thumbnails, you can see how your HDR image takes the best from those two images to create an image with more depth.

Step Four:

Now you can tweak your HDR image just like you would any other regular RAW image (yes, the resulting HDR image Lightroom creates is a RAW image). Here, Auto Tone has already been applied (so don't be surprised if you see that some of the sliders have already been moved), but I increased the Contrast and Clarity (as shown here), and I actually decreased the Vibrance a bit because I thought the overall color was a bit too punchy—I wanted more of a gold color than yellow. Anyway, the point is you can tweak it like you would any other image, however, on the next page you'll learn one of the big advantages of creating an HDR image.

Continued

Step Five:

Lightroom's big HDR secret is that with the added tonal range that comes with merging your images to HDR, you can really open up the shadow areas and bring out detail, without getting a bunch of noise. For example, take a look at the normal single-frame image here on the left. When you open up those shadows, you get a ton of noise—it's raining noise in that single image. Now, look at the HDR image on the right, where I opened up the shadows big time. Where's the noise? Exactly! That's one of the big secrets and one of the best reasons to create HDR images like this. The added tonal range rocks!

Step Six:

We're switching images here to discuss the Auto Align checkbox in the HDR Merge Preview dialog. What this helps with (mostly) are shots you hand-held while bracketing—if the alignment is off a little (or a lot), it'll fix that automatically. For example, take a look at the hand-held, bracketed shot of this camel on the left (I know, I know, it only has one hump, so technically it's not a camel, it's a dromedary). You can see it almost has an outline of a second "camel-like animal" along the edges. That's because I hand-held it. Turn on the Auto Align checkbox and now look at the image on the right. It automatically aligns the images for you, and it usually does a pretty amazing job. Of course, if you shot your HDR on a tripod, it doesn't need to align anything, so you can skip the Auto Align checkbox, and it'll process faster. The Deghost Amount feature is different than the Auto Align feature in that Auto Align helps align things if you moved your camera a little when you took the photos. Deghost helps if something was actually moving in your shot (like someone walking in your frame, who now appears like a fully- or semi-transparent ghost, but it doesn't look cool, it looks like a mistake).

Step Seven:

By default, Deghost Amount is turned off (only turn it on if you have visible ghosting). To turn it on, click either Low (for mild deghosting), Medium (for more), or High (if there's a lot of ghosting in the image), and it does a pretty amazing job of basically pulling a non-moving area from one of the bracketed exposures and seamlessly displaying it, rather than the ghosted movement. I always start with the Low amount and only move up to Medium or High if the ghosting is still visible. If you want to see the areas that are being deghosted in your image, you can turn on the Show Deghost Overlay checkbox, and after a few seconds (it has to rebuild a new preview), the areas that are being deghosted will appear in red (as seen here, where I chose Medium).

Step Eight:

Jumping back to our original HDR, I thought I would show you the normal, single image (the one shown here at the top. Note how dark the pews are, and you saw what happens if I increase the shadows in those pews), and the HDR image (shown below). No noise, but a great range of tones.

TIP: Seeing the Expanded Range for Yourself

If you really want to see how much your range has been expanded with an HDR image, go to the Exposure slider and drag it all the way to the right. Notice it didn't stop at +5.00? Now, it goes to +10.00 and –10.00 (if you drag it to the left) stops. You can go from absolutely solid black to absolutely solid white.

Making Streets Look Wet

This is a trick I've been using for a while to make streets look wet in my travel photos, and what I love about it is that it's so simple (you just use two sliders) and yet it's amazingly effective (especially on cobblestone streets, where it looks especially good, but also on just regular ol' asphalt streets, too).

Step One:

In the Develop module, go ahead and make any regular tweaks to the image in the Basic panel (I Shift-double-clicked on the Whites slider and the Blacks slider to have Lightroom automatically set the white and black points. I also decreased the Shadows a bit to bring out detail in the bridge). None of these adjustments have anything to do with the effect you're about to learn, but I thought you might at least want to know what the basic edits I applied to prep the photo were.

Step Two:

Click on the Adjustment Brush tool **(K)** up in the toolbox and then double-click on the word "Effect" to zero out all the sliders. You've got just two sliders to adjust here: (1) Drag the Contrast slider to 100, then drag the Clarity slider to 100, as well. That's it—that's the recipe. Now, paint over the surface you want to appear wet (here, I'm painting over the street in the foreground). As you paint, the area looks wet and appears to add reflections like an actual wet street.

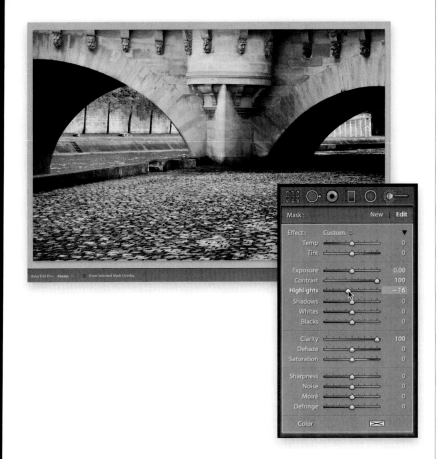

Step Three:

If you paint over the street and it doesn't look "wet" enough, click the New button at the top-left corner of the Adjustment Brush panel and start painting over the same area, but start in a different part of the street (that way, you're stacking this second pass of the look over the first coat of "wet"). By the way, if for any reason the street looks too bright from applying that much Clarity, just lower either the Exposure slider or Highlights slider a little bit for each pin, so it looks to have about the same brightness overall (here, I lowered the Highlights slider to –16. I tried lowering Exposure, as well, but lowering just the Highlights looked better to me).

Step Four:

This technique looks particularly great on cobblestone streets, but it also works for most regular paved streets. I did a before/after here, so you can see an example. Okay, that's it. Instant wet streets.

CHAPTER 8

PROBLEM PHOTOS
dealing with common image problems

Problem photos. We all wind up dealing with them, and while we create some of these issues ourselves, a lot of them are created by our cameras, and we're left to pick up the pieces. Well, I have some advice for you that, if you follow to the letter, not only will help you deal with these types of issues, but will change the way you, and your friends, think about them. Now, you have to have an open mind because this requires a little out-of-the box thinking. So, don't just jump to conclusions before you hear the whole thing because you'll just dismiss it and we'll all lose. Here's the thing: to deal with these types of issues, you're going to have to become an image psychiatrist. Stop snickering, this is important stuff. You're going to need to really analyze each image, and really talk it through, to get to the root of these problems. The first and most important step, before you start any of this is to look and find a very small couch online—one just big enough for a memory card. (You can find these on eBay, Esty, or even Amazon sometimes, but they come from Japan, so while the shipping will only be slightly more, the wait time can often be 4 to 6 weeks.) Now, I know your first thought is, "Oh, this should be easy. I'll just pick up the Barbie Pink Passport 3-Story Townhouse from Amazon." Trust me, it doesn't work (I've tried it. The seats are made of plastic and the card just slides off onto the floor, and then nobody's talking to anybody). You need, at the very least, the KidKraft Shimmer Mansion Dollhouse because they use real wood (not this plastic rubbish Mattel tries to pass off as a couch). Once you get your couch and memory card set up, the first question you should ask is, "Tell me about your sensor."

Fixing Backlit Photos

I think the reason we take so many backlit photos is that our eyes capture such an incredible tonal range, instantly adjusting for things like backlighting, so when we're standing there, our subject doesn't look dark at all. However, our camera's sensor captures only a fraction of the tonal range of what our eyes see. Luckily, as we learned in Chapter 5, Lightroom's Shadows slider was born to fix situations just like this, but there is an extra step you need to know to make it look right.

Step One:

Here's our backlit subject (you can see the sun is behind her on the left, here). While I was standing there, even though she was backlit, to my eyes she looked properly exposed. When I held my DSLR up and looked through the viewfinder, it looked the same, but then this is what my camera's sensor came up with—my subject is nearly a silhouette. This we can deal with.

TIP: Watch Out for Noise

If an image has noise in it, it's usually in the shadow areas, so if you do open the shadows a lot, any noise gets amplified. Keep an eye out for it as you drag that Shadows slider. If things get really noisy in those shadow areas, you might need to get the Adjustment Brush **(K)**, drag the Noise slider to the right, and paint over just that shadow area to keep that noise in check.

Step Two:

In the Develop module, go to the Basic panel and drag the Shadows slider over to the right until your subject's face starts to look balanced with the rest of the light in the image (I dragged it to +80). Don't make it too bright or it'll start to look unnatural. Another thing to look out for, and it's happening in this case, is if you have to drag that Shadows slider pretty far to the right, the photo can start looking washed out (like this one does here). But, we'll fix that with just one simple move.

Step Three:
One way to get rid of that washed-out look is to drag the Contrast slider over to the right a bit (I dragged it to +46, here) until that washed-out look is gone. If you don't like how that looks (it usually does the trick, but depending on the image, hey, ya never know), then set Contrast back to zero and simply push a little bit of blacks into the image by dragging the Blacks slider to the left just a little bit. One of those two methods should do the trick to keep the image from looking washed out after opening up those shadow areas.

Step Four:
Here, I used Lightroom's Before/After view (press **Y**) to show what a big difference this technique (dragging the Shadows slider, then bringing back the contrast) can make.

Reducing Noise

If you wind up shooting at a high ISO or in very low light, chances are your image is going to have some noise—either luminance noise (a visible graininess throughout the photo, particularly in shadow areas) or color noise (those annoying red, green, and blue spots). Lightroom can handle them both, but an added advantage is that it can apply this noise reduction while the image is still in its 16-bit RAW state (most commercial plug-ins can only work once the image has been converted to a regular 8-bit image).

Step One:

To reduce the noise in a "noisy" image like this (it was shot at 800 ISO, but it was way underexposed, so I had to open up the shadows a ton and that's where noise lives), go to the Develop module's Detail panel, to the Noise Reduction section. You see that little warning icon in the top-left corner of the panel? That's letting you know that to really see the changes you make to the image using any of the sliders in this panel, you need to zoom in to at least the full size (1:1) view. If you look at the image in Step Two, I zoomed in even tighter (to 3:1), and now you can really see the noise that's in the tile on the floor, and on the wall.

Step Two:

I usually start by reducing the color noise, simply because it's so distracting (if you shoot in RAW, it automatically applies some color noise reduction). So, start by dragging the Color slider to 0, and then slowly drag it to the right. As soon as the color in the specks goes away, stop, because once it's gone, it doesn't get "more gone" (it just gets blurrier). Here, I stopped at 24. If you feel you lost detail in the process, drag the Detail slider to the right to help it protect color details in edge areas. If you keep this setting really low, you avoid adding colors speckles, but you might get some color bleeding (like they're glowing a bit). Dragging the Smoothness slider to the right softens the color speckles, but I don't mess with this slider because I haven't seen an instance where it didn't make the image look blurry and worse.

Step Three:

Once the color noise has been dealt with, your image now just looks grainy, which is a different kind of noise (luminance noise). So, drag the Luminance slider to the right until the noise is greatly reduced (here, I dragged it over to 38). I gotta tell you, this baby works wonders all by itself, but you have additional control with the other two sliders beneath it. The "catch" is this: your image can look clean, or it can have lots of sharp detail, but it's kinda tricky to have both. The Detail slider (in Adobe speak, the "luminance noise threshold") really helps with seriously blurry images. So, if you think your image looks a little blurry now, drag the Detail slider to the right—just know this may make your image a little more noisy. If, instead, you want a cleaner-looking image, drag the Detail slider to the left—just know that you'll now be sacrificing a little detail to get that smooth, clean look (there's always a trade-off, right?). If you feel you've lost contrast in this process, drag the Contrast slider to the right, but know that it might create some blotchy-looking areas. Again, it's a trade-off and ultimately, you'll decide if using it helps or hurts your particular image.

Before *After*

Continued

Step Four:

Another method for removing noise when you have it in just a particular area, like in the sky or one dark area you opened up, is to "paint" noise reduction using the Adjustment Brush **(K)**. In the Adjustment Brush's panel, you'll see "Noise." Drag this slider to the right a bit, then paint over an area in an image, and it helps to reduce noise where you painted. It's not awesome (as you might expect), and it tends to make those areas blurry to hide the noise, but on some particular images, it works great and only blurs the areas where you paint and not the entire image, like normal Noise Reduction in the Detail panel tends to do. Remember, you can apply the Detail panel's Noise Reduction first, then paint noise reduction over just really bad areas.

Lightroom keeps track of every edit you make to your photo and it displays them as a running list, in the order they were applied, in the Develop module's History panel. So if you want to go back and undo any step, and return your photo to how it looked at any stage during your editing session, you can do that with just one click. Now, unfortunately, you can't just pull out one single step and leave the rest, but you can jump back in time to undo any mistake, and then pick up from that point with new changes. Here's how it's done:

Undoing Anything (or Everything!)

Step One:
Before we look at the History panel, I just wanted to mention that you can undo anything by pressing **Command-Z (PC: Ctrl-Z)**. Each time you press it, it undoes another step, so you can keep pressing it and pressing it until you get back to the very first edit you ever made to the photo in Lightroom, so it's possible you won't need the History panel at all (just so you know). If you want to see a list of all your edits to a particular photo, click on the photo, then go to the History panel in the left side Panels area (shown here). The most recent changes appear at the top. (*Note:* A separate history list is kept for each individual photo.)

Step Two:
If you hover your cursor over one of the history states, the small Navigator panel preview (which appears at the top of the left side Panels area) shows what your photo looked like at that point in history. Here, I'm hovering my cursor over the point a few steps back where I had converted this photo to black and white, but since then I changed my mind and switched back to color.

Continued

Step Three:

If you actually want to jump back to what your photo looked like at a particular stage, then instead of hovering over the state, you'd click once on it and your photo reverts to that state (as shown here). By the way, if you use the keyboard short-cut for your undos (instead of using the History panel), the edit you're undoing is displayed in very large letters over your photo. This is handy because you can see what you're undoing, without having to keep the History panel open all the time.

TIP: Undos Last Forever

Photoshop's History panel only lets you have 20 undos, and if you close the file, they go away. However, in Lightroom, every single change you make to your photo inside Lightroom is tracked and when you change images, or close Light-room, your unlimited undos are saved. So even if you come back to that photo a year later, you'll always be able to undo what you did.

Step Four:

If you come to a point where you really like what you see and you want the option of quickly jumping back to that point, go to the Snapshots panel (right above the History panel) and click on the + (plus sign) button on the right side of the panel header. The New Snapshot dialog appears (seen here, on right) where you can give it a name that makes sense to you (I named mine "Duotone with Vignette," so I'd know that if I clicked on that snapshot, that's what I'd get—a duotone with a vignette). Click Create and that moment in time is saved to the Snapshots panel (as seen here). By the way, you don't have to actu-ally click on a previous step in the History panel to save it as a snapshot. Instead, you can just Right-click on any step and choose **Create Snapshot** from the pop-up menu. Pretty handy.

When I first used the cropping feature in Lightroom, I thought it was weird and awkward—probably because I was so used to the Crop tool in older versions of Photoshop—but once I got used to it, I realized that it's probably the best cropping feature I've ever seen. This might throw you for a loop at first, but if you try it with an open mind, I think you'll wind up falling in love with it. If you try it and don't like it, make sure you read Step Six for how to crop more like you used to in Photoshop (but don't forget that whole "open mind" thing).

Cropping Photos

Step One:
Here's the original photo. The action happened down field a bit, and even though I was shooting a 400mm lens, the action is still pretty far away. So, we need to crop in tight because the shot isn't about all the empty space—the shot is about the receiver catching the ball. Go to the Develop module and click on the Crop Overlay tool (circled here in red) in the toolbox above the Basic panel, and the Crop & Straighten options will pop down below it. This puts a "rule of thirds" grid overlay on your image (to help with cropping composition), and you'll see four cropping corner handles. To lock your aspect ratio (so your crop is constrained to your photo's original proportion), or unlock it if you want a non-constrained freeform crop, click on the lock icon near the top right of the panel (as shown here).

Step Two:
To crop the photo, grab a corner handle and drag inward to resize your Crop Overlay border. Here, I grabbed the bottom-right corner handle and dragged diagonally inward. But, it's still not tight enough.

Continued

Step Three:

Now let's crop in tight on the action (you did download this photo, right? The URL for the downloads is in the book's intro-duction). Just grab the top-left corner and drag it diagonally inward for a nice, tight crop (as seen here). If you need to reposi-tion the photo inside the cropping border, just click-and-hold inside the Crop Overlay border. Your cursor will change into the "grabber hand" (shown here), and now you can drag it where you want it.

TIP: Hiding the Grid

If you want to hide the rule-of-thirds grid that appears over your Crop Overlay border, press **Command-Shift-H (PC: Ctrl-Shift-H)**. Or, you can have it only appear when you're actually moving the crop border itself, by choosing **Auto** from the Tool Overlay pop-up menu in the tool-bar beneath the Preview area. Also, there's not just a rule of thirds grid, there are other grids—just press the letter **O** to toggle through the different ones.

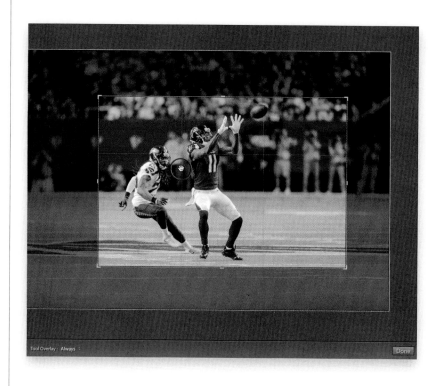

Step Four:

When the crop looks good to you, press the letter **R** on your keyboard to lock it in, remove the Crop Overlay border, and show the final cropped version of the photo (as seen here). But there are two other choices for cropping we haven't looked at yet.

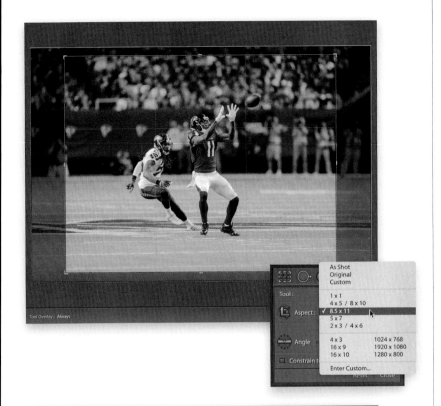

Step Five:

If you know you want a particular size ratio for your image, you can do that from the Aspect pop-up menu in the Crop & Straighten options. Go ahead and click the Reset button, below the right side Panels area, so we return to our original image, and then click on the Crop Overlay tool, again. Click on the Aspect pop-up menu at the top-right side of the Crop & Straighten options, and a list of preset sizes appears (seen here). Choose **8.5x11** from the pop-up menu, and you'll see the left and right sides of the Crop Overlay border move in to show the ratio of what an 8.5x11" crop would be. Now you can resize the cropping rectangle and be sure that it will maintain that 8.5x11 aspect ratio.

Step Six:

The other, more "Photoshop-like," way to crop is to click on the Crop Overlay tool, then click on the Crop Frame tool (shown circled here in red) to release it from its home near the top left of the Crop & Straighten options. Now you can just click-and-drag out a cropping border in the size and position you'd like it. Don't let it freak you out that the original cropping border stays in place while you're dragging out your new crop, as seen here—that's just the way it works. Once you've dragged out your cropping border, it works just like before (grab the corner handles to resize, and reposition it by clicking inside the cropping border and dragging. When you're done, press R to lock in your changes). So, which way is the right way to crop? The one you're most comfortable with.

TIP: Canceling Your Crop

If, at any time, you want to cancel your cropping, just click on the Reset button at the bottom-right side of the Crop & Straighten options panel.

Lights Out
Cropping Rocks!

When you crop a photo using the Crop Overlay tool in the Develop module, the area that will get cropped away is automatically dimmed to give you a better idea of how your photo is going to look when you apply the final crop. That's not bad, but if you want the ultimate cropping experience, where you really see what your cropped photo is going to look like, then do your cropping in Lights Out mode. You'll never want to crop any other way.

Step One:
To really appreciate this technique, first take a look at what things look like when we normally crop an image—lots of panels and distractions, and the area we're actually cropping away appears dimmed (but it still appears). Now let's try Lights Out cropping: First, click on the Crop Overlay tool to enter cropping mode. Now press **Shift-Tab** to hide all your panels.

Step Two:
Press the letter **L** twice to enter Lights Out mode, where every distraction is hidden, and your photo is centered on a black background, but your cropping border is still in place. Now, try grabbing a corner handle and dragging inward, then clicking-and-dragging outside your cropping border to rotate it, and watch the difference—you see what your cropped image looks like live as you're dragging the cropping border. It's the ultimate way to crop (it's hard to tell from the static graphic here, so you'll have to try this one for yourself—you'll never go "dim" again!).

If you've got a crooked photo, Lightroom's got four great ways to straighten it. One of them is pretty precise, two are automatic, and with the last you're pretty much just "eyeing it," but with some photos that's the best you can do.

Straightening Crooked Photos

Step One:
Here's a shot with a pretty bad tilted horizon line (probably something to do with all the wine in Venice. Just a theory). The first method is to get the Crop Overlay tool **(R)**, found in the toolbox, right under the histogram in the Develop module's right side Panels area. Click on the Angle tool, found in the Crop & Straighten options (it looks like a level), then click-and-drag it left to right along something that's supposed to be level in the image (as shown here, where I've dragged it from left to right along the banks of the canal—see the red arrow for direction). This works really well (you can even drag it vertically, so I could have dragged it down the tower). However, there is one catch: you have to have something in the photo that's supposed to be level—like a horizon, or a wall, or a window frame, etc.

Step Two:
The second method is often my first choice because it's just one click and it's totally automated. Above the Angle slider is an Auto button—an auto straighten button (hit the Reset button, at the bottom of the panel, to make the image crooked again). Click it and it attempts to straighten the photo automatically, and if it has a pretty clear visible horizon line, or other obvious straight areas, it does a really nice job. Notice that it doesn't complete the process—it just rotates the cropping border to the precise amount it would take to crop the image. If it looks good to you, click the Done button below the bottom-right corner of the Preview area.

Continued

Step Three:

The third method is kind of like the second method. Really, it's exactly like method #2 in that it's a one-click button to level your image. Go to the Transform panel (in the right side Panels area), and in the Upright section at the top, click the Level button (as shown here), and it auto straightens the photo. Truth be told, the Auto button in the Crop Overlay tool's panel is just a shortcut for the Upright Level feature. Still, I thought you should know about it, just in case you're working in the Transform panel, so you don't leave it and go to the Crop Overlay tool's panel just to straighten your image.

Step Four:

Hit the Reset button (at the bottom of the right side Panels area) to reset the image to where it's crooked again, and we'll try the fourth method, better known as "eyeing it." Now, you could get the Crop Overlay tool, again, and when you move your cursor outside the cropping border (onto the gray background), it changes into a two-headed arrow. Just click-and-drag up/down to rotate your image until it looks straight. However, I prefer to go to the Transform panel, where you'll find a Rotate slider. In this case, drag that slider to the left and it rotates the image counterclockwise. Just stop dragging when it looks straight (as I did here). While this creates those white triangle-shaped gaps around your image, you can have Lightroom automatically crop those away by turning on the Constrain Crop checkbox (as shown here), which will crop away those gaps for you.

This tool is actually pretty well named—it's great for removing spots or the occasional power line or distracting soda bottle in the background on the beach. However, don't confuse it with Photoshop's awesome Healing Brush. I've used the Healing Brush. The Healing Brush was a friend of mine. Spot Removal tool: you are no Healing Brush (but, it's all we've got, so let's at least learn how to use it).

Removing Stuff with the Spot Removal Tool

Step One:

Here's the image we want to retouch, which was taken inside a museum exhibit of beautiful, exotic old cars. Since it's indoors, you can see all the lights in the ceiling reflected on the car, so our goal is to remove at least the most obvious white spots. Click on the Spot Removal tool (shown circled here in red) in the toolbox near the top of the right side Panels area, or just press **Q**, and make the brush a little bigger than the spot you want to remove (you can change brush size by using the **Left and Right Bracket keys** on your keyboard—they're just to the right of the letter P).

Step Two:

Zoom in, so you can see the white spots better, and then just click once over one of those spots and it's gone (as seen here, where I clicked once on a spot on the left side). When you do this, you'll see two outlined areas: (1) the one with the slightly thicker outline is showing the area where you clicked, and (2) the other one (the thinner one) is showing you the area that the Spot Removal tool sampled to make that repair. (*Note:* If you make a mistake, just hit the Delete [PC: Backspace] key to remove your repair). Usually, this sample area is pretty close to the area you're trying to fix, but sometimes (for reasons I can't begin to understand) it decides to sample somewhere totally weird (like in the middle of one of the windows). When that happens (notice I didn't say "if"), there are two things we can do about it.

Continued

Step Three:

The first method is to press the **/ (Forward Slash) key** on your keyboard (named after the lead guitarist for Guns N' Roses). Each you time you press it, Lightroom picks a different area to sample from, and usually its second or third choice is a pretty decent one. That's the automatic way—letting Lightroom choose the new sample spot for you. The second method is the manual way: just click inside the sample circle and drag it to a different area yourself (as seen here, where I dragged it down and over to the right). Notice the little line with an arrow pointing to where you clicked to do your repair. Once you drag the sample circle over to a new area, let go of your mouse button and it does the repair. *Note:* If parts of the repair look see-through, go to the Spot Removal panel (near the top of the right side Panels area) and drag the Feather amount to the left (making the edges of the brush harder). Sometimes that will do the trick. So, those are your choices for fixing a bad repair: press the Forward Slash key or drag the second circle to a better location.

Step Four:

If you want to speed up the process and paint over either a line, or in our case, more than just one reflection spot, you can "paint" a stroke with the Spot Removal tool—just click-and-drag it right over the spots you want to remove. As you paint, the area you're painting over turns white (as shown here), but that's just so you can see where you painted. When you release your mouse button, after just a second or two, it chooses a sample area and removes your spot(s). Once again, it shows an outlined area where it sampled from and if your repair doesn't look good, use the two techniques you just learned in Step Three to find a better area to sample from for a more realistic repair.

Step Five:
So, that's the process (and yes, it can take awhile, like an old person at a 50-item salad bar, who feels they need a tiny bit of all 50 items. But I digress). You navigate around your image, clicking once on small spots with a brush a little larger than the spot you want to remove, and for larger spots or for groups of spots, you'll paint a stroke by clicking-and-dragging the tool over the area you want to repair. Before long, your image will have circles and strokes all over it, because while the tool is active, you can switch to any previous removal you did by just clicking on an edit pin, and then you can drag a circle, or delete it, and try again.

Step Six:
Here's a before/after, with most of the spots removed (I didn't get every single one because…well…it's kind of a pain in the butt, and I have this book to write, and well…I got most of the big stuff anyway).

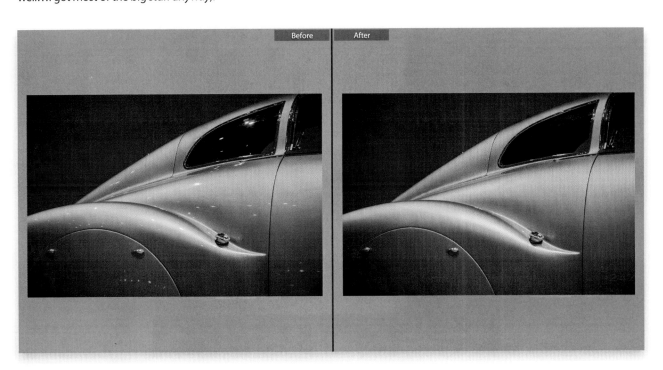

Finding Spots and Specks the Easy Way

There is nothing worse than printing a nice big image, and then seeing all sorts of sensor dust, spots, and specks in your image. If you shoot landscapes or travel shots, it is so hard to see these spots in a blue or grayish sky, and if you shoot in a studio on seamless paper, it's just as bad (maybe worse). I guess I should say, it used to be bad—now it's absolutely a breeze thanks to a feature added back in Lightroom 5 that makes every little spot and speck really stand out so you can remove them fast!

Step One:
Here's an image from Lake Tahoe, Nevada, and you can see a few spots and specks in the sky pretty clearly—I see around eight dust or sensor spots. But it's the spots that you can't see clearly at this size, or against this flat sky, that "Getcha!" Of course, you eventually do see them—like after you've printed the image on expensive paper, or when a client asks, "Are these spots supposed to be there?"

Step Two:
To find any spots, specks, dust, or junk in your image, click on the Spot Removal tool (**Q**; it's shown here circled in red) in the toolbox near the top of the right side Panels area. Down in the toolbar, directly below the main Preview area, is a Visualize Spots checkbox (also circled here). Turn this checkbox on and you get an inverted view of your image, where you can instantly see some more spots now.

Step Three:

I zoomed in a bit here, so you can see the spots better, but another reason why they stand out so amazingly is because I increased the Visualize Spots threshold level (drag the Visualize Spots slider to the right, and now if there are any spots, specks, dust, etc., still hiding, you'll see them in an instant). I drag this slider to the right until I find that point where the spots stand out, but without the threshold overwhelming everything by bringing out what, if you drag too far, looks like snow or noise.

TIP: Click-and-Drag a Brush Size

When using the Spot Removal tool, you can press-and-hold Command-Option (PC: Ctrl-Alt) and click-and-drag out a selection around your spot (start by clicking just to the upper left of the spot, then drag across the spot at a 45° angle). As you do, it lays down a starting point and then your circle drags right over the spot.

Step Four:

Now that the spots are so easily visible, you can take the Spot Removal tool and just click it once, right over each spot, to remove them (as shown here). Use the Size slider or the **Left and Right Bracket keys** to make the tool a little larger than the spot you want to remove. When you're done, turn the Visualize Spots checkbox off and make sure the Spot Removal tool sampled from matching areas. If you see a spot where it didn't, just click on that circle to make it active, then click inside the sampling circle and drag it to a matching area.

Continued

Step Five:

Often, it's dust on your camera's sensor that creates these annoying spots and they'll be in the exact same position in every shot from that shoot. If that's the case, then once you've removed all the spots, make sure the photo you fixed is still selected in the Filmstrip, and select all the similar photos from that shoot, then click the Sync button at the bottom of the right side Panels area. This brings up the Synchronize Settings dialog, shown here. First, click the Check None button, so everything it would sync from your photo is unchecked. Then, turn on the checkboxes for Process Version and Spot Removal (shown here), and click the Synchronize button.

Step Six:

Now, it applies that same spot removal you did to the first photo to all these other selected photos—all at once (as you can see it did here). To see these fixes applied, click on the Spot Removal tool again. I also recommend you take a quick look at the fixed photos, because depending on the subject of your other shots, the fixes could look more obvious than on the photo you just fixed. If you see a photo with a spot repair problem, just click on that particular circle, hit the **Delete (PC: Backspace) key** on your keyboard to remove it, then use the Spot Removal tool to redo that one spot repair manually.

TIP: When to Use Clone

There are two choices for how this tool fixes your spots—Clone or Heal. The only reason to ever switch it to Clone is if the spot you're trying to remove is on or near the edge of an object in your image, or near the edge of the image itself. In these cases, Heal often smudges the image.

If you wind up with red eye in your photos (point-and-shoots are notorious red-eye generators thanks to the flash being mounted so close to the lens), Lightroom can easily get rid of it. This is really handy because it saves you from having to jump over to Photoshop just to remove red eye from a photo of your neighbor's six-year-old crawling through a giant hamster tube at Chuck E. Cheese. Here's how it works:

Removing Red Eye

ROBIN BURGOS

Step One:
Go to the Develop module and click on the Red Eye Correction tool, found in the toolbox right under the Histogram panel (its icon looks like an eye, and it's circled here in red). Click the tool in the center of one of the red eyes and drag down, and when you release the mouse button, it removes the red eye. If it doesn't fully remove all the red, you can expand how far out it removes it by going to the Red Eye Correction tool's options (they appear in the panel once you've released the mouse button), and dragging the Pupil Size slider to the right (as shown here) or clicking-and-dragging the edge of the circle itself (it allows you to reshape it, as well). If you need to move the correction, click-and-drag inside the circle.

Step Two:
Now do the same thing to the other eye (the first eye you did stays selected, but it's "less selected" than your new eye selection—if that makes any sense). As soon as you click, this eye is fixed, too. If the repair makes it look too gray, you can make the eye look darker by dragging the Darken slider to the left (as shown here). The nice thing is that these sliders (Pupil Size and Darken) are live, so as you drag, you see the results right there onscreen—you don't have to drag a slider and then reapply the tool to see how it looks. If you make a mistake and want to start over, just click the Reset button at the bottom right of the tool's options.

Automatically Fixing Lens Distortion Problems

Ever shoot some buildings downtown and they look like they're leaning back? Or maybe the top of a building looks wider than the bottom, or a doorway or just a whole image seems like it's "bulging" out. All these types of lens distortion problems are really pretty common (especially if you use wide-angle lenses), but luckily for us, fixing them is usually just a one- or two- (maybe three-, seldom four-, rarely five-, but I once did six-) click fix.

Step One:

Open an image that has a lens distortion problem. This one has a bunch—from the building bulging outward to it being squashed on its right side. We can fix some of these problems with one click by going to the Lens Corrections panel and turning on the Enable Profile Corrections checkbox (which we'll do in the next step). Doing this searches Lightroom's built-in database of lens fixes and applies the matching one to remove the outward bowing, along with any edge vignetting (darkening) in the corners. If it can't find a lens profile, you'll have to help it out by choosing your lens make and model from the Lens Profile pop-up menus, and then it does the rest. What if you don't see your exact lens there? Just pick a close match.

Step Two:

So, in the Develop module, go to the Lens Corrections panel, in the right side Panels area, turn on that Enable Profile Corrections checkbox, and it applies the lens profile (if it can find one). Although the building is still squashed on its right side, the bulging is now gone (look at how the columns are straight now and no longer curved). Even if this didn't fix anything, it's important to turn this checkbox on because it helps the next corrections work better. Also, there are two Amount sliders in this panel for fine-tuning the profile corrections, and while they're kind of subtle, they can definitely make a difference—drag them back and forth once or twice and you'll get a feel for how they affect your image.

Step Three:

This step is a big one, and your results with it will be improved because you turned on that lens profile in Step Two. There's a correction feature called "Upright," and what it does is helps make buildings that are learning back look more "upright" (it's fairly well-named). You'll find this Upright feature near the top of the Transform panel (in the right side Panels area). In this panel, you'll see six different buttons, but 99.9% of the time I just click the Auto button (as shown here) because it gives the most natural and most balanced correction (some of the others over-correct, and while they'll get things like the vertical lines in buildings perfectly straight, they often do so at the expense of the overall image—it's that whole "the cure is worse than the illness" thing). So, click the Auto button, and as you'll see, it does a fairly good job of balancing the image (its right side is no longer squashed, but it's still pinched just a little bit to that side).

Step Four:

If we click on the Full button, in this particular case, it does a pretty darn good job of straightening out that far-right end—it's no longer pinched. But, to do that, it definitely leaves white gaps at the bottom and top left side. There is a Constrain Crop checkbox at the bottom of this panel and turning that on will automatically crop the image tight, so those white areas will be completely cropped away. In this case, it will leave your image looking more like a long, thin pano, so you might want to consider a "Plan B" (which would make a great name for a gourmet burger joint in Hartford, Connecticut, but of course, I'm just speculating. Try their mini-cheeseburgers. They're insane!).

Continued

Step Five:

Plan B is to get the Crop Overlay tool **(R)** and crop away parts of the white areas, but not all of it, as seen here (the darker areas outside the cropping border will be cropped away). In the next step, we might be able to lessen the amount we have to crop away, but for now, go ahead and crop the image like you see here. By the way, there are two other Upright buttons we haven't discussed yet (we'll look at Guided in the next technique): Vertical straightens the vertical lines in your photo, but it often leaves gaps that are much worse than what you see here. It's very legalistic, as it only considers that one aspect of your photo—not how the final overall image looks. So, this is probably the Upright button I use the least. If you click the Level button, it usually does a great job with the simple act of straightening a crooked photo. So, if that's all your image needs, then click on Level. But, we must move on, because we're still trying to limit our white triangles in the left corners.

Step Six:

The building is still a bit "wonky" and not perfectly flat (now the left side looks a little squashed). You can fix this by going down to the Transform sliders and dragging the Horizontal slider a tiny bit to the left, until the building really looks flat (as shown here). Once you do that, look how little the white triangles in the corners are now. The Horizontal slider controls the side-to-side angle of the image (drag it back and fourth once or twice, and you'll see exactly what it does). The Vertical slider is for manually fixing buildings that are leaning backward (drag it back and forth once or twice and you'll see what I mean). If you use either of these sliders, and the image looks too thin or two wide when you're done, you can bring it back to a normal width by dragging the Aspect slider.

Step Seven:

To finish filling in those white corners, drag the Scale slider to the right until the image grows in size to fill them. You don't want to scale it up too much or you'll start to see pixelization (a loss of quality) and softnesss, so just move this slider a little if you can.

Step Eight:

Here's a before/after view with Lightroom doing most of the work. We (a) turned on the lens profile; (b) clicked the Upright Full button (which is pretty rare, as it's normally the Auto button—go figure); (c) dragged the Horizontal slider to make the building flatter; and lastly, (d) we used the Scale slider to zoom in on the image a bit to cover those white corners. That's not that much to fix a mess like we started with.

Fixing Lens Problems Yourself Using Guided Upright

If I have a shot where buildings or walls are leaning back, and using the automated Upright feature doesn't get the job done, this is my next stop: the "do-it-yourself" version of Upright, called "Guided Upright." You drag out lines along walls or areas that should be straight, and it takes over from there. You can draw up to four lines and reposition them once they're in place, and the image will update live.

Step One:
Here's an image with a serious case of "lean back," courtesy of a super-wide-angle lens and bad camera technique (shhh, don't mention that last part too loud). If the Auto Upright method we looked at in the previous technique didn't do the job for you, then it's time to help Lightroom out by using Guided Upright, where you tell it what's supposed to be straight and it straightens it out for you. Go to the Transform panel (in the right side Panels area) and click on the Guided button (as seen here). When you move your cursor out over the image, it changes into a crosshair. Now, click-and-drag that along an object in your image that's supposed to be vertically straight (like I did here with the column on the far right). At this point, with just one guide, the image looks the same, but that's about to change. By the way, you can reposition your guide by clicking-and-dragging it (as shown here).

Step Two:
Drag another guide out along something else in the image that's supposed to be straight. Here, I placed another guide along the edge of the column on the far left, and those walls now become straight. You'll see white triangle-shaped gaps in the bottom corners (we'll deal with them later), but for now, just take a moment to enjoy how straight those walls are. Ahhh-hhh…those are some straight walls. But, look at the ceiling and the roof. There's still a little work to do, but luckily, we still have two horizontal guides left to help us with those.

Step Three:

Now, you can click-and-drag out a horizontal guide along either the ceiling or the floor. In this case, I tried adding one along the ceiling, right above the columns, and one along the floor below the columns (as seen here). When you add that third guide, it adjusts the image as soon as you add it—same with the fourth guide. This is great because you can see if it looks good, and if it doesn't, you can press **Command-Z (PC: Ctrl-Z)** to Undo adding that guide, try a new location, and it will update live as you add it. Here, you can see all four guides in place, and the image looks pretty straight overall.

Step Four:

We still have to deal with those white triangle gaps in the corners, but we have two choices: (1) Of course, we could jump over to Photoshop (see Chapter 10 for more on doing this) and use the Magic Wand tool (**Shift-W**; while pressing-and-holding the Shift key the whole time) to select both of those areas. Then, go under the Select menu, under Modify, and choose **Expand** to expand those selected areas by 4 pixels (and click OK). Go under the Edit menu, choose Fill, and for Contents, choose **Content-Aware Fill**, and let it take a crack at filling in the gaps (it works fairly well in this case). Or, (2) we could crop them away using Lightroom's Crop Overlay tool **(R)**, which is what I did here. Be sure to unlock the Lock icon (in the top right of the Crop & Straighten options), so you can drag in the sides until those white gaps will be cropped off, and then hit **Return (PC: Enter)** to lock in the final crop. A before/after is on the next page, and you can see the difference this made.

Continued

Vignetting is a lens problem that causes the corners of your photo to appear darker than the rest of the photo. This problem is usually more pronounced when you're using a wide-angle lens, but can also be caused by a whole host of other lens issues. Now, this darkening in the corners is not to be confused with adding a post-crop edge vignette effect all the way around your image (not just the corners), which is something we sometimes intentionally add to focus attention away from the edges (I covered adding edge vignette effects in Chapter 7).

Fixing Edge Vignetting

Step One:
In the photo shown here, you can see how the corner areas look darkened and shadowed. This is the bad vignetting that I mentioned above, and is considered a lens problem because it's caused by the lens you were using when you took the shot. Vignetting like this can happen in expensive lenses and cheaper lenses (it's just often more pronounced in chapter lenses).

Step Two:
Our first line of defense is to go to the Lens Corrections panel in the Develop module's right side Panels area, click on Profile at the top of the panel, and then turn on the Enable Profile Corrections checkbox (as shown here). This applies a fix from Lightroom's built-in database of lens corrections, and it tries to automatically remove the edge vignetting, based on the make and model of the lens you used (it learns all this from the EXIF data embedded in your image). You can see here it did a decent job. It didn't get it all, but it seems to have gotten most of it (but, we'll tweak these results in a moment). If, for some reason, it wasn't able to find a profile for your lens (the pop-up menus in the Lens Profile section are set to none or appear blank), just choose your lens make/model from the pop-up menus.

Continued

Step Three:

Once you apply this Lens Profile correction, if enough of the vignetting didn't go away, you can fine-tune the results in the Amount section (at the bottom of the panel), using the Vignetting slider. Here, I had to drag it all the way over to 200 until nearly all of the vignetting was gone. There's still a tiny bit, and if that bugs you like it does me, it might be time to pull out "the big guns" and do this manually.

Step Four:

Click on Manual at the top of the panel, and you'll see a Vignetting section at the bottom. There are two sliders here: the first slider controls the amount of brightening in the edge areas, and the second slider lets you adjust how far in toward the center of your photo the corners will be brightened. In this photo, the edge vignetting is pretty much contained in the corners and doesn't spread too far into the center of the photo. So, start by slowly clicking-and-dragging the Amount slider to the right, and as you do, keep an eye on the corners of your image. As you drag, the corners get brighter, and your job is to stop when the brightness of the corners matches the rest of the photo (as seen here). In this case, the leftover vignetting is really right up in the corners, but my brightening with the Amount slider is starting to brighten farther into the image than just the corners. So, to keep the brightening to just the ends of the corners, drag the Midpoint slider over to the right until your brightening is just affecting what's up in the very tips of the corners (as I did here). The before/after on the next page shows just how much edge vignetting there really was and how much better it looks after you deal with it.

Sharpening Your Photos

What you see in Lightroom's Detail panel (where Adobe hides the Sharpening controls) depends on which file format you shoot with in your camera. If you shoot in JPEG, your camera applies sharpening in-camera already, so when you come to the Detail panel, your Sharpening Amount will be set to zero. However, if you shoot RAW, the sharpening in your camera is turned off, and by default, Lightroom applies a small amount of capture sharpening. But, it's barely enough sharpening to be noticeable, so it's important to add our own.

Step One:

To sharpen your image, go to the Detail panel in the Develop module, and you'll see four Sharpening sliders. If you shot in RAW, you'll see that a default Sharpening Amount of 25 has already been applied, since your camera turns off internal sharpening when you shoot in RAW. There's a name for sharpening applied with an amount of 25: it's called "barely perceptible to the human eye" (weird thing: dogs can see a slight difference). Anyway, it's at least a starting point. If you shot in JPEG, sharpening was already applied in-camera, so by default, Lightroom sets the Amount at zero (as seen in the bottom inset here) and no sharpening is applied.

Step Two:

At the top of the panel, there's a little preview area that zooms in tight on one small area of the image (if you don't see this preview window, click on the black left-facing triangle to the right of Sharpening at the top of the panel). If you move your cursor over the preview, it changes to the grabber hand, so you can click-and-drag to move around. You can also click the little icon in the upper-left corner of the panel (shown circled here), then move your cursor out over your image, and that area will now appear zoomed, in the preview window (to keep the preview on that area, just click on the area in the main image). To turn this off, click that icon again. If you want to zoom in even tighter, you can Right-click inside the preview window, and choose a 2:1 view from the pop-up menu (shown here).

Step Three:
Just for the record, I bailed on using that tiny preview window years ago—it's just about useless—so, I hide it from view by clicking on the down-facing triangle doohickey to its right. Just so ya know, if you do hide that preview window, you'll see a warning symbol in the top left (shown circled here in red) letting you know that to really see the results of your sharpening, you need to at least be at a 100% full-size view. Luckily, that warning sign is more than a warning—if you click directly on it, it will zoom your image to a 1:1 full-size view for you (as seen here).

Step Four:
The Amount slider does just what you'd expect—it controls the amount of sharpening applied to your photo. Here, I increased it to 130, which is more than I'd normally apply (I'm usually in the 50 to 70 range), but I wanted you to really see the difference here. The Radius slider determines how many pixels out from the edge the sharpening will affect, and I generally leave this set at 1.0, but if I really need some mega-sharpening, I'll bump it up to 1.1 or 1.2. You have to be careful bumping this up because you can start to get a white line or hard-edged halo around the edges of objects, so I usually crank the Amount rather than increase the Radius. Also, I never change the Detail slider. It's designed to keep you from having those halos, and if you increase its amount, it removes your halo protection and gives you crunchier, more haloey (if that's even a word) sharpening, so I leave it as-is.

Continued

Step Five:

The last sharpening slider, Masking, is to me the most amazing one of all, because what it lets you do is control exactly where the sharpening is applied. For example, some of the toughest things to sharpen are things that are supposed to be soft, like a child's skin, or a woman's skin in a portrait, because sharpening accentuates texture, which is exactly what you don't want. But, at the same time, you need detail areas to be sharp—like their eyes, hair, eyebrows, lips, clothes, etc. Well, this Masking slider lets you do just that—it kind of masks away the skin areas, so it's mostly the detail areas that get sharpened. To show how this works, we're going to switch to a portrait.

TIP: Toggling Off the Sharpening

If you want to temporarily toggle off the changes you've made in the Detail panel, just click on the little switch on the far left of the Detail panel's header.

Step Six:

First, press-and-hold the Option (PC: Alt) key and then click-and-hold on the Masking slider, and your image will turn solid white (as shown here). What this solid white image is telling you is that the sharpening is being applied evenly to every part of the image, so basically, everything's getting sharpened.

Step Seven:

As you click-and-drag the Masking slider to the right, parts of your photo will start to turn black, and those black areas are now not getting sharpened, which is our goal. At first, you'll see little speckles of black, but the farther you drag that slider, the more non-edge areas will become black—as seen here, where I've dragged the Masking slider over to 70, which pretty much has the skin areas in all black (so they're not being sharpened), but the detail edge areas, like the eyes, lips, hair, nostrils, and outline, are being fully sharpened (which are the areas still appearing in white). So, in reality, those soft skin areas are being automatically masked away for you, which is really pretty darn slick if you ask me.

Step Eight:

When you release the Option (PC: Alt) key, you see the effects of the sharpening, and here you can see the detail areas are nice and crisp, but it's as if her skin was never sharpened (in fact, I was able to crank up the Amount after the masking). Now, just a reminder: I only use this Masking slider when the subject is supposed to be of a softer nature, where we don't want to exaggerate texture.

TIP: Sharpening a Smart Preview

If you apply sharpening (or noise reduction) to a low-res smart preview of an image, the amount you apply might look just right. But, when you reconnect your hard drive, and it links to the original high-res file, that amount of sharpening (or noise reduction) will actually have much less of an effect. So, you might want to leave the sharpening (and noise reduction) for when you're working on the original file.

Fixing Chromatic Aberrations (a.k.a. That Annoying Color Fringe)

Have you ever seen an image that has either a purple or green color halo or fringe around the edges of things in the image? If you haven't, you're probably just not looking because these color fringes (called "chromatic aberrations") show up fairly often (it's a lens problem), and you can actually exacerbate them (how's that for a $10 word) by applying a lot of contrast or clarity. But, I wouldn't stop applying either one because Lightroom has a very effective way to fix this.

Step One:

Here's the original image, and at the Fit in Window size, you can't tell there's any chromatic aberrations at all, but when you zoom in, you'll find them instantly. They were easily visible at a 1:1 full-size view, but in the next step, I zoomed in even tighter (to an 8:1 view) on the building on the left, so you can really see what's going on.

Step Two:

You can see here that it almost looks like someone traced the left edge of the black space between the windows with a thin yellow/greenish marker, the right edge with a pale purple marker, and along the diagonal part of the reflection on the window with a blue marker.

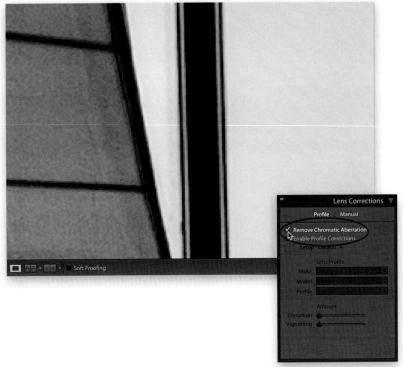

Step Three:

Let's get rid of these by first going to the Develop module's Lens Corrections panel, clicking on Profile at the top, and then turning on the Remove Chromatic Aberration checkbox (as shown here). A lot of the time, just turning on this checkbox is enough to fix the problem (it sure was with this image—take a look here, and in the before/after below, and you'll see the yellow/greenish, purple, and blue edge fringe is all gone). Just one checkbox. How easy is that? Now, what do you do if that doesn't work? Well, you go on to Step Four, that's what ya do.

Step Four:

Click on Manual at the top of the panel (just to the right of Profile), and in the Defringe section, drag the purple Amount slider to the right a little to remove the purple fringe manually—just drag it until the purple line goes away. If it reduces it, but doesn't fully get rid of it, you might have to help it choose the right hue to neutralize it by dragging the Purple Hue sliders around a bit. Do the same thing with the Green Hue and the green Amount sliders until the green fringe is gone. Now, if you're not sure which slider to drag (or moving the sliders doesn't seem to do much), then let Lightroom set them for you. Just click on the Fringe Color Selector tool (the eyedropper in the top left of the Defringe section, shown circled here in red), zoom in really tight, and click it once directly on the color that is fringing. Now, the sliders will move automatically right where they need to, to remove that color fringe.

Basic Camera Calibration in Lightroom

Some cameras seem to put their own color signature on your photos, and if yours is one of those, you might notice that all your photos seem a little red, or have a slight green tint in the shadows, etc. Even if your camera produces accurate color, you still might want to tweak how Lightroom interprets the color of your RAW images. The process for doing a full, accurate camera calibration is kinda complex and well beyond the scope of this book, but I did want to show you what the Calibration panel is used for, and give you a resource to take things to the next level.

Step One:

Before we start, I don't want you to think that camera calibration is something everybody must do. In fact, I imagine most people will never even try a basic calibration, because they don't notice a big enough consistent color problem to worry about it (and that's a good thing. However, in every crowd there's always one, right?). So, here's a quick project on the very basics of how the Calibration panel works: Open a photo, then go to the Develop module's Calibration panel, found at the very bottom of the right side Panels area, (see, if Adobe thought you'd use this a lot, it would be near the top, right?).

Step Two:

The topmost slider is for adjusting any tint that your camera might be adding to the shadow areas of your photos. If it did add a tint, it's normally green or magenta—look at the color bar that appears inside the Tint slider itself. By looking at the color bar, you'll know which way to drag (for example, here I'm dragging the Tint slider away from magenta, toward green, to reduce any reddish color cast in the shadow areas, but the change in this particular photo is so subtle I didn't even see a change).

Step Three:

If your color problems don't seem to be in the shadows, then you'll use the Red, Green, and Blue Primary sliders to adjust the Hue and Saturation (the sliders that appear below each color). Let's say your camera produces photos that have a bit of a red cast to them. You'd drag the Red Primary Hue slider away from red, and if you needed to reduce the overall saturation of red in your photo, you'd drag the Red Primary Saturation slider to the left until the color looked neutral (by neutral, I mean the grays should look really gray, not reddish gray).

Step Four:

Once you get the color dialed in the way you want, you've tested this new color calibration on a few different images from that same camera, and you feel you've neutralized the color bias from your camera with the current Calibration sliders, then you can save a whole lot of time by designating these settings as the new default settings for that particular camera. That way, it will automatically recognize images from that camera and apply your new calibration settings for you. How cool is that? Here's how to set that up: First, make sure you haven't adjusted any settings but those in the Calibration panel (or they'll be baked into your new default settings for that camera). Then, go under the Develop menu and choose **Set Default Settings** (as shown here, above). This brings up the dialog you see here asking if you want to update your default settings for images from this particular camera (it notes the make, model, and possibly the file format, right in the dialog). If you do, click Update to Current Settings (and, obviously, this is also where you go to return to Adobe's default settings, if you ever change your mind and want to go back). That's all there is to it.

CHAPTER 9

EXPORTING
saving JPEGs, TIFFs, and more

"Do we really need an entire chapter on exporting our JPEGs?" Well, I can't say that you personally need a whole chapter, but I know for certain that my publisher does, because in their words, "We prepaid for these pages." You see (prepare yourself, as I reveal some serious book publishing industry secrets that you neither want to know or will ever have any use for as long as we both shall live, so help me God)…. Anyway, because paper costs are so ridiculous these days (it's not like this stuff grows on trees), when they sign a book author to a deal, the publisher is exposing themselves to the risk of paper costs rising significantly between the time they sign the author and the time the book is actually published—often a year or more. So, to protect themselves from these rising costs, they invite new authors to their offices (in my case, in San Francisco). After a light snack and some coffee, they took me to Neiman Marcus in Union Square. It's a very high-end store, and we were just looking around, but then they started pushing me to shoplift some small items. Of course, I resisted, but they kept pushing. They said, "It's okay, everybody out here does it." So, at first, I just took a belt, and then a small bottle of cologne, but they kept telling me that if I wanted to be a successful author, I needed to be bolder. They were putting a lot of pressure on me, and next thing you know, I'm shoving a Maurizio Braschi sable coat under my shirt and I'm sprinting for the door like Usain Bolt. Anyway, apparently my publisher videotaped the whole thing, and they told me that if the price of paper rises before I'm done with the book, they're turning the video over to the police. Well, luckily for me, the paper costs somehow dropped by 1.4% by pub date; I filled the pages in this Exporting chapter with random Springsteen lyrics I copied from the web, and I made enough selling that coat on eBay to pay for a bus ticket home. Overall, it was a petty good trip. Did I mention I got a new belt? And, that I'm (of course) totally making this up?

Saving Your Photos as JPEGs

Since there is no Save command for Lightroom (like there is in Photoshop), one of the questions I get asked most is, "How do you save a photo as a JPEG?" Well, in Lightroom, you don't save it as a JPEG, you export it as a JPEG (or a TIFF, or a DNG, or a Photoshop PSD). It's a simple process, and Lightroom has added some automation features that can kick in once your photo is exported.

Step One:

You start by selecting which photo(s) you want to export as a JPEG (or a TIFF, PSD, or DNG). You can do this in either the Library module's Grid view or down in the Film-strip in any other module by Command-clicking (PC: Ctrl-clicking) on all the photos you want to export (as shown here).

Step Two:

If you're in the Library module, click on the Export button at the bottom of the left side Panels area (circled here in red). If you're in a different module and using the Filmstrip to select your photos for export, then use the keyboard shortcut **Command-Shift-E (PC: Ctrl-Shift-E)**. Whichever method you choose, it brings up the Export dialog (shown in the next step).

Step Three:

Along the left side of the Export dialog, Adobe put some Export presets, which are basically designed to keep you from having to fill out this entire dialog every time from scratch. It comes with a few presets from Adobe, but the real power of this is when you create your own (those will appear under the User Presets header). The built-in Lightroom Presets are at least a good starting place to build your own, so for now, click on Burn Full-Sized JPEGs and it fills in some typical settings someone might use to export their photos as JPEGs and burn them to a disc. However, we'll customize these settings so our files are exported where and how we want them, then we'll save our custom settings as a preset, so we don't have to go through all this every time. If, instead of burning these images to disc, you just want to save these JPEGs in a folder on your hard drive, go to the top of the dialog, and from the Export To pop-up menu, choose **Hard Drive**, as shown here.

Choose where to save your exported images from the Export To pop-up menu

Step Four:

Let's start at the top of the dialog: First, you need to tell Lightroom where to save these files in the Export Location section. If you click on the Export To pop-up menu (as shown here, at top), it brings up a list of likely places you might choose to save your files. The third choice (Choose Folder Later) is great if you're making presets, because it lets you choose the folder as you go. If you want to choose a folder that's not in this list, choose Specific Folder, then click the Choose button to navigate to the folder you want. You also have the option of saving them into a separate subfolder, like I did here, at the bottom. So, now my images will appear in a folder named "Trinity Church" on my desktop. If these are RAW files and you want the exported JPEGs added into Lightroom, turn on the Add to This Catalog checkbox.

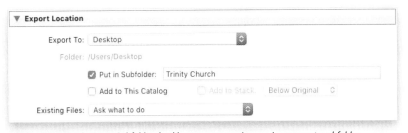

Turn on the Put in Subfolder checkbox to save your images in a separate subfolder

Continued

Step Five:

The next section down, File Naming, is like the file naming feature you learned about back in the Importing chapter. If you don't want to rename the files you're exporting, but want to keep their current names, leave the Rename To checkbox turned off, or turn it on and choose File-name from the pop-up menu. If you do want to rename the files, choose one of the built-in templates, or if you created a custom file naming template (we learned this back in Chapter 3), it will appear in this list, too. In our example, I chose Custom Name – Sequence (which automatically adds a sequential number, starting at 1, to the end of my custom name). Then, I simply named these shots "Trinity Church," so the photos will wind up being named Trinity Church-1, Trinity Church-2, and so on. There's also a pop-up menu for choosing whether the file extension appears in all uppercase (.JPG) or lowercase (.jpg).

Step Six:

Let's say you're exporting an entire collection of images, and inside that collection are some video clips that were shot with your DSLR. If you want them included in your export, in the Video section, turn on the Include Video Files checkbox (shown here). Below that checkbox, you'll choose the video format (H.264 is really compressed, and is for playing on a mobile device; DPX is usually for visual effects). Next, choose your video quality: Max will keep the quality as close to your original video as possible, and High is still good, but may be slower. Choose Medium if you're going to post it to the web, or if you're planning to view it on a high-end tablet. Choose Low for viewing on all other mobile devices. You can see the differences between your format and quality choices by watching the Target size and speed listed to the right of the Quality pop-up menu. Of course, if you don't have any videos chosen when you export, this section will be grayed out.

You can skip the Image Sizing section altogether, unless you need to make the image you're saving smaller than its original size

Step Seven:

Under File Settings, you choose which file format to save your photos in from the Image Format pop-up menu (since we chose the Burn Full-Sized JPEGs preset, JPEG is already chosen here, but you could choose TIFF, PSD, DNG, or if you have RAW files, you could choose Original to export the original RAW photo). Since we're saving as a JPEG, there's a Quality slider (the higher the quality, the larger the file size), and I generally choose a Quality setting of 80, which I think gives a good balance between quality and file size. If I'm sending these files to someone without Photoshop, I choose sRGB as my color space. If you chose a PSD, TIFF, or DNG format, their options will appear (you get to choose things like the color space, bit depth, and compression settings).

Step Eight:

By default, Lightroom assumes that you want to export your photos at their full size. If you want to make them smaller, in the Image Sizing section, turn on the Resize to Fit checkbox, then type in the Width, Height, and Resolution you want. Or you can choose to resize by pixel dimensions, the long edge of your image, the short edge of your image, the number of megapixels in your image, or a percentage from the top pop-up menu.

Continued

Step Nine:

Also, if these images are for printing in another application, or will be posted on the web, you can add sharpening by turning on the Sharpen For checkbox in the Output Sharpening section. This applies the right amount of sharpening based on whether they're going to be seen only onscreen (in which case, you'll choose Screen) or printed (in which case, you'll choose the type of paper they'll be printed on—glossy or matte). For inkjet printing, I usually choose High for the Amount, which onscreen looks like it's too much sharpening, but on paper looks just right (for the web, I choose Standard).

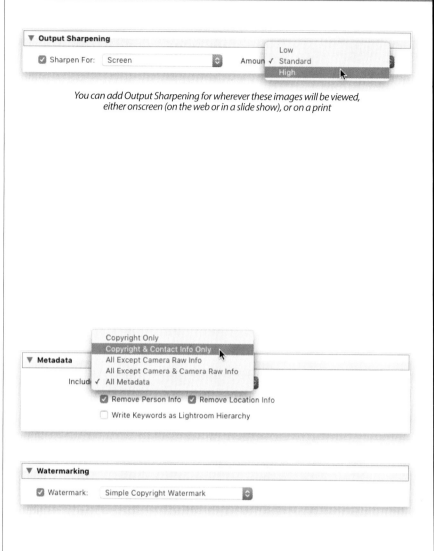

You can add Output Sharpening for wherever these images will be viewed, either onscreen (on the web or in a slide show), or on a print

Step 10:

In the Metadata section, you start by choosing what metadata you want to be exported with your images: everything, everything but your Camera Raw data, everything but your camera and Camera Raw data (this hides all your exposure settings, your camera's serial numbers, and other stuff your clients probably don't need to know), just your copyright and contact info (if you're including your copyright, you probably want to include a way for people to contact you if they want to use your photo), or just your copyright. If you choose All Metadata, All Except Camera Raw Info, or All Except Camera & Camera Raw Info, you can still have Lightroom remove any Person keywords by turning on the Remove Person Info checkbox or any GPS data by turning on the Remove Location Info checkbox.

The next section down lets you add a visible watermark to the images you're exporting (watermarking is covered in detail in the next project), and to add your watermark to each image you're exporting, turn on the Watermark checkbox, then choose a simple copyright or your saved watermark from the pop-up menu.

Step 11:

The final section, Post-Processing, is where you decide what happens after the files are exported from Lightroom. If you choose Do Nothing (from the After Export pop-up menu), they just get saved into that folder you chose back in the beginning. If you choose Open in Adobe Photoshop, they'll automatically be opened in Photoshop after they're exported. You can also choose to open them in another application or in a Lightroom plug-in. Go to Export Actions Folder Now opens the folder where Lightroom stores your export actions. So, if you want to run a batch action from Photoshop, you could create a droplet and place it in this folder. That droplet would then show up in the After Export pop-up menu, and choosing it would open Photoshop and run your batch action on all the photos you were exporting from Lightroom. (*Note:* I show you how to create a batch action in Chapter 11.)

Step 12:

Now that you've customized things the way you want, let's save these settings as your own custom preset. That way, the next time you want to export a JPEG, you don't have to go through these steps again. Now, there are some changes I would suggest that will make your preset more effective. For example, if you saved this as a preset right now, when you use it to export other photos as JPEGs, they'll be saved in that same Trinity Church folder. Instead, this is where it's a good idea to select **Choose Folder Later** (in the Export Location section, as shown here), like we discussed back in Step Four.

Continued

Step 13:

If you know you always want your exported JPEGs saved in a specific folder, then in the Export Location section, click the Choose button, and choose that folder. Now, what happens if you go to export a photo as a JPEG into that folder, and there's already a photo with the same name in it (maybe from a previous export)? Should Lightroom just automatically overwrite this existing file with the new one you're exporting now, or do you want to give this new file a different name, so it doesn't delete the file already in that folder? You get to choose how Lightroom handles this problem using the Existing Files pop-up menu (shown here). I pick **Choose a New Name for the Exported File** (as shown here). That way, I don't accidentally overwrite a file I meant to keep. By the way, when you choose Skip, if it sees a file already in that folder with the same name, it doesn't export the JPEG image—instead, it just skips it.

TIP: Rename Files When Using a Preset

Before you export your photos, make sure you give your files a new custom name, or the shots from your football game will be named Trinity Church-1.jpg, Trinity Church-2.jpg, and so on.

Step 14:

Now you can save your custom settings as a preset: click the Add button at the bottom-left corner of the dialog (shown circled here in red), and then give your new preset a name (in this case, I used Hi-Res JPEGs/Save to Hard Drive. That name lets me know exactly what I'm exporting and where they're going).

Step 15:

Once you click the Create button, your preset is added to the Preset section (on the left side of the dialog, under User Presets), and from now on you're just one click away from exporting JPEGs your way. If you decide you want to make a change to your preset (as I did in this case, where I changed the Color Space to ProPhoto RGB, and I turned the Watermark checkbox off), you can update it with your current settings by Right-clicking on your preset, and from the pop-up menu that appears, choosing **Update with Current Settings** (as shown here).

While you're here, you might want to create a second custom preset—one for exporting JPEGs for use in online web galleries. To do that, you might lower the Image Sizing Resolution setting to 72 ppi, set your sharpening to Screen, set Amount to Standard, set the Metadata to Copyright & Contact Info Only, and you might want to turn the Watermark checkbox back on to help prevent misuse of your images. Then, you'd click the Add button to create a new preset named something like Export JPEG for Web.

Step 16:

Now that you've created your own presets, you can save time and skip the whole Export dialog thing altogether by just selecting the photos you want to export, then going under Lightroom's File menu, under **Export with Preset**, and choosing the export preset you want (in this example, I'm choosing the Export JPEG for Web preset). When you choose it this way, it just goes and exports the photos with no further input from you. Sweet!

Adding a Watermark to Your Images

If your images are going on the web, there's not much to keep folks from taking your images and using them in their own projects (sadly, it happens every day). One way to help limit unauthorized use of your images is to put a visible watermark on them. That way, if someone rips them off, it'll be pretty obvious to everyone that they've stolen someone else's work. Also, beyond protecting your images, many photographers are using a visible watermark as branding and marketing for their studio. Here's how to set yours up:

Step One:

To create your watermark, press **Command-Shift-E (PC: Ctrl-Shift-E)** to bring up the Export dialog, then scroll down to the Watermarking section, turn on the Watermark checkbox, and choose **Edit Watermarks** from the pop-up menu (as shown here). *Note:* I'm covering watermarking here in the Export chapter, because you can add your watermark when you're exporting your images as JPEGs, TIFFs, etc., but you can also add these watermarks when you print an image (in the Print module), or put it in a web gallery (in the Web module).

Step Two:

This brings up the Watermark Editor (seen here), and this is where you either (a) create a simple text watermark, or (b) import a graphic to use as your watermark (maybe your studio's logo, or some custom watermark layout you've created in Photoshop). You choose either Text or Graphic up in the top-right corner (shown circled here in red). By default, it displays the name from your user profile on your computer, so that's why it shows my copyright down in the text field at the bottom of the dialog. The text is also positioned right up against the bottom and left borders of your image, but luckily you can have it offset from the corners (I'll show you how in Step Four). We'll start by customizing our text.

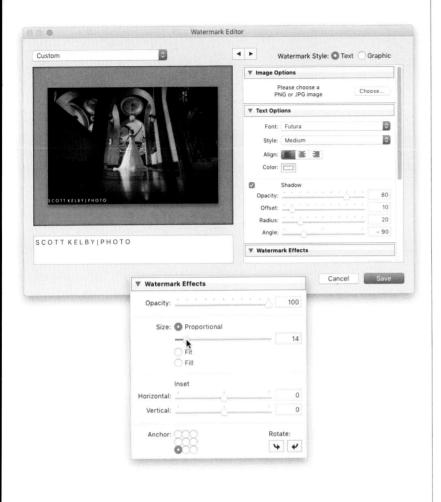

Step Three:

Type in the name of your studio in the text field at the bottom left, then choose your font in the Text Options section on the right side of the dialog. In this case, I chose Futura Medium. (By the way, the little line that separates SCOTT KELBY from PHOTO is called a "pipe," and you create one by pressing Shift-Backslash.) Also, to put some space between the letters, I pressed the Spacebar after each one. You also can choose the text alignment (left justified, centered, or right justified) here, and you can click on the Color swatch to choose a font color. To change the size of your type, scroll down to the Watermark Effects section, where you'll find a Size slider (seen here) and radio buttons to Fit your watermark to the full width of your image, or Fill it at full size. You can also move your cursor over the type on the image preview and corner handles appear—click-and-drag outward to scale the text up, and inward to shrink it down.

Step Four:

You get to choose the position of your watermark in the Watermark Effects section. At the bottom of the section, you'll see an Anchor grid, which shows where you can position your watermark. To move it to the bottom-right corner, click the bottom-right anchor point (as shown here). To move it to the center of your image, click the center anchor point, and so on. To the right of that are two Rotate buttons if you want to switch to a vertical watermark. Also, back in Step Two, I mentioned there's a way to offset your text from the sides of your image—just drag the Horizontal and Vertical Inset sliders (right above the Anchor grid). When you move them, little positioning guides will appear in the preview window, so you can easily see where your text will be positioned. Lastly, the Opacity slider at the top of the section controls how see-through your watermark will be.

Continued

Step Five:

If your watermark is going over a lighter background, you can add a drop shadow using the Shadow controls in the Text Options section. The Opacity slider controls how dark the shadow will be. The Offset is how far from the text your shadow will appear (the farther you drag to the right, the farther away the shadow will be). The Radius is Adobe's secret code name for softness, so the higher you set the Radius, the softer your shadow will become. The Angle slider is for choosing where the shadow appears, so the default setting of –90 puts the shadow down and to the right. A setting of 145 puts it up and to the left, and so on. Just drag it, and you'll instantly see how it affects the position of your shadow. The best way to see if the shadow really looks better or not is to toggle the Shadow checkbox on/off a couple of times.

Step Six:

Now let's work with a graphic watermark, like your studio's logo. The Watermark Editor supports graphic images in either JPEG or PNG format, so make sure your logo is in one of those two formats. Scroll back up to the Image Options section, and where it says Please Choose a PNG or JPEG Image, click the Choose button, find your logo graphic, then click Choose, and your graphic appears (unfortunately, the white background behind the logo is visible, but we'll deal with that in the next step). It pretty much uses the same controls as when using text—go to the Watermark Effects section and drag the Opacity slider to the left to make your graphic see-through, and use the Size slider to change the size of your logo. The Inset sliders let you move your logo off the edges, and the Anchor grid lets you position the graphic in different locations on your image. The Text Options and Shadow controls are grayed out, since you're working with a graphic.

In Photoshop, this logo has a white Background layer, so a white background will appear behind your logo when you bring it into Lightroom's Watermark Editor

Drag the Background layer onto the Trash icon, then save the file in PNG format, and the logo now has a transparent background

Step Seven:

To make that white background transparent, you have to open the layered file of your logo in Adobe Photoshop and do two things: (1) Delete the Background layer by dragging it onto the Trash icon at the bottom of the Layers panel, leaving just your graphics (and text) on their own transparent layers. Then, (2) save the Photoshop document in PNG format. This saves a separate file, and the file appears flattened, but the background behind your logo will be transparent (as shown here at the bottom).

Step Eight:

Now choose this new PNG logo file (in the Image Options section of the Watermark Editor), and when you import it, it appears over your image without the white background (as seen here, where I used a white logo instead). You can now resize, reposition, and change the opacity of your logo graphic in the Watermark Effects section. Once you get it set up the way you want it, you should save it as a watermark preset (so you can use it again, and you can apply it from the Print and Web modules). You do that by clicking the Save button in the bottom right or choosing **Save Current Settings as New Preset** from the pop-up menu in the top-left corner of the dialog. Now your watermark is always just one click away.

Emailing Photos from Lightroom

Back in Lightroom 3 (and earlier versions), if you wanted to email images from Lightroom, it was…well…it was a workaround. You had to jump through a lot of hoops (creating aliases/shortcuts to your email program, and placing those inside one of Lightroom's folders, and on and on). It kinda worked, but it was kinda clunky. Luckily, now, it's built right in, and it couldn't be easier.

Step One:
In Grid view, Command-click (PC: Ctrl-click) on the images you want to email. Now, go under the File menu and choose **Email Photos** (as shown here) to bring up Lightroom's email dialog (shown in the next step).

Step Two:
Here's where you enter the email address of the person you want to email the images to and type in the subject line of your email, and it chooses your default email application (but you can choose a different email application if you like from the From pop-up menu). You'll also see the thumbnails of the images you just selected in Lightroom's Grid view.

TIP: What If Your Email App Isn't Listed?
Then, from the From pop-up menu, choose **Go to Email Account Manager**. There, click the Add button (in the bottom left) and when the New Account dialog appears, choose your email provider from the Service Provider pop-up menu (you'll see AOL, Gmail, Hotmail, etc.). If yours isn't listed there, then choose Other, and you'll have to add the server settings yourself. Now, add your email address and password in the Credential Settings section (it will verify that it's correct), and your email server will be added to your From pop-up menu.

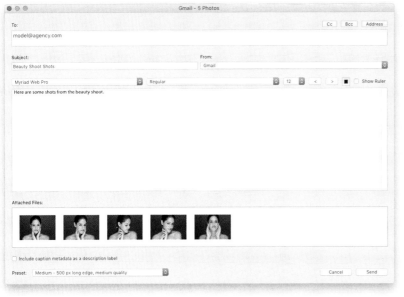

Step Three:

You also get to choose the physical size of the images you're emailing (after all, if you attach enough of them at their full size, chances are your email will bounce back for being too large). There are four built-in size presets you can choose from the pop-up menu in the bottom-left corner of the dialog (as shown here), where you choose both the size and quality. If you've created any presets for emailing, those will appear here, too, or to create one now, choose Create New Preset at the bottom of the menu, and it brings up the standard Export dialog. Enter the settings you want, save it as a preset (click the + [plus sign] button in the bottom-left corner of the Export dialog), and now that preset will appear in your email Preset pop-up menu.

Step Four:

If you're using an email app, when you click the Send button, it launches your email program, fills in all the info you entered in the Lightroom email dialog (address, subject, and so on), and then it attaches your images at the size and quality you selected, so type your message and hit the Send button in your email program, and off it goes. If you're using webmail, once you choose it in the From pop-up menu, the dialog changes to include a message area (seen here at the bottom). Type your message and click the Send button.

TIP: Using the Two Email Presets

Adobe included two email presets in Lightroom's Export dialog: one that brings up the regular email dialog you just learned about (called "For Email"), and the other simply saves your images to your hard drive for you to email later (manually). To save the images for emailing later, go under the File menu, under Export with Preset, and choose **For Email (Hard Drive)**. You'll choose which folder you want to save your images into, and then it just saves them as JPEGs at a small size (640x640 pixels at a quality setting of 50).

Exporting Your Original RAW Photo

So far, everything we've done in this chapter is based on us tweaking our photo in Lightroom and then exporting it as a JPEG, TIFF, etc. But what if you want to export the original RAW photo? Here's how it's done, and you'll have the option to include the keywords and metadata you added in Lightroom—or not.

Step One:

First, click on the RAW photo you want to export from Lightroom. When you export an original RAW photo, the changes you applied to it in Lightroom (including keywords, metadata, and even changes you made in the Develop module) are saved to a separate file called an XMP side-car file, since you can't embed metadata directly into the RAW file itself (we talked about this in Chapter 3), so you need to treat the RAW file and its XMP sidecar file as a team. Now press **Command-Shift-E (PC: Ctrl-Shift-E)** to bring up the Export dialog (shown here). Click on Burn Full-Sized JPEGs just to get some basic settings. From the Export To pop-up menu up top, choose **Hard Drive**, then, in the Export Location section, choose where you want this original RAW file saved to (I chose my desktop). In the File Settings section, from the Image Format pop-up menu, choose **Original** (shown circled here in red). When you choose to export the original RAW file, most of your other choices are grayed out.

TIP: Saving Your RAW Photo as a DNG

From the Image Format pop-up menu, choose **DNG** to bring up the DNG options. Embed Fast Load Data affects how fast the preview appears in the Develop module (it adds a little size to your file). Use Lossy Compression does to RAW images what JPEG compression does to other images—it tosses some info to give you files that are around 75% smaller in size (good for archiving the images the client didn't pick, but you don't want to delete).

Step Two:
Now click Export, and since there's no processing to be done, in just a few seconds your file appears on your desktop (or wherever you chose to save it)—you'll see your file and its XMP sidecar (with the same exact name, but XMP as its file extension) in a folder (as seen here, on my desktop). As long as these two stay together, other programs that support XMP sidecar files (like Adobe Bridge and Adobe Camera Raw, for example) will use that metadata, so your photo will have all the changes you applied to it. If you send this file to someone (or burn it to disc), make sure you include both files. If you decide you want the file to not include your edits, just don't include the XMP file with it.

Here's the image with contrast, highlights, shadows, clarity, and white balance adjustments, and a split toning effect added, when you include the XMP sidecar file

Here's the original image, without contrast, highlights, shadows, clarity, and white balance adjustments, and no split toning effect added, when you don't include the XMP sidecar file

Step Three:
If you export the original RAW file and send it to someone with Photoshop, when they double-click on it, it will open in Camera Raw, and if you provided the XMP file, they'll see all the edits you made in Lightroom, as seen in the top image shown here, where the contrast, highlights, shadows, clarity, and white balance were adjusted, and a split toning effect was added. The bottom image shown here is what they'll see in Camera Raw when you don't include the XMP file—it's the untouched original file with none of the changes I made in Lightroom.

Publish Your Images with Just Two Clicks

If you upload your images pretty regularly to sites like Flickr or Facebook, or maybe you just save them to other hard drives, or even to your iPhone, there's a drag-and-drop way to automate the process. Beyond that, it also helps you keep track of your published images, so the most recent versions of them are the ones that are published. This feature is called Publish Services, and if you take just a few minutes to set this up now, it'll save you a load of time whenever you want to post images online, or save images to your hard drive or external hard drive.

Step One:

The Publish Services panel is in the Library module's left side Panels area. By default, it has four templates you can set up: (1) your hard drive, (2) Adobe Stock, (3) Facebook, and (4) Flickr. Set these up by clicking on the Set Up button on the right side of each. Here, we'll start with the Flickr process, which is the most complicated, and at the end, we'll take a quick look at setting up your hard drive. The Adobe Stock and Facebook processes are pretty similar to Flickr's—click the Set Up button, authorize your account, and you're pretty much good to go. So, click on Set Up next to Flickr.

Step Two:

The main section of the Lightroom Publishing Manager dialog looks like the Export dialog, with two exceptions: (1) near the top, there are Publish Service, and Flickr Account and Title sections, and (2) at the bottom are Flickr's Privacy and Safety options. Start up top by clicking the Authorize button, and a dialog appears (shown on the bottom left) asking you to click another Authorize button to jump over to the Flickr website, so you can log in and give Flickr permission to work with Lightroom, so go ahead and click Authorize. Now the dialog changes to tell you that once you're done at Flickr.com, you need to come back to Lightroom to finish setting everything up (shown on the bottom right).

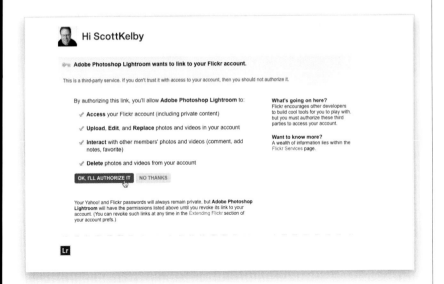

Step Three:

Once you log into your Yahoo account and get to Flickr (if you don't already have a Flickr account, and want to use this feature, go ahead and at least sign up for their free account through Yahoo), you'll find a page with something similar to what you see here, asking you to authorize Flickr to talk back and forth to Lightroom. Once you do, you'll get a confirmation page. Now, back to the Lightroom part.

Step Four:

Once you're done on the Flickr approval page, go back to Lightroom, and click Done in that dialog we saw in Step Two. Now all you have to do is set up the export options like usual (choosing your file format, whether you want sharpening added, watermarking added, etc.), but when you get to the bottom, you'll see options for Flickr's Privacy and Safety control (shown here at the bottom) for the images you're going to upload, so make your choices there now, then click the Save button to save this setup as your Flickr Publish Service.

TIP: Download More Plug-Ins from Adobe

You can add more Publish Services and Export plug-ins by clicking on the Find More Services Online button at the bottom of the Publish Services panel to take you to the Adobe Add-Ons website. Once downloaded and installed, a new Publish Service will show up below your others. To install an Export plug-in, in the Lightroom Plug-In Manager, click Add below the list on the left, locate your downloaded plug-in, and click the Add Plug-In button. You can access it in the Export To pop-up menu at the top of the Export dialog.

Continued

Step Five:

Now select the photos that you'd like to publish to Flickr, and drag-and-drop them onto the Flickr Photostream in the Publish Services panel (you'll see Photostream appear right underneath Flickr, as seen here). Once you've dragged them into this collection (yup, it's a collection), click directly on Photostream and you'll see that the images you just dragged there are waiting to be published (they're not actually published to Flickr until you click the Publish button at the bottom of the left side Panels area or the top right of the center Preview area). What's nice about this is it lets you gather up as many photos, from as many different collections as you'd like, and then publish them all at once with just one click. But for our example here, we'll assume that you just want to publish these five images.

Step Six:

Click the Publish button now, and a split-screen appears in the Preview area, with the five New Photos to Publish appearing in the section on top first. One by one, they'll move down to the Published Photos section below (here, three of the five images have been published). Once all your photos have been published, the New Photos to Publish section disappears, because there are no photos waiting to be published. (By the way, while your photos are being published, a small status bar will appear in the top-left corner of Lightroom to let you know how things are moving along.)

Step Seven:

Switch to your web browser, go to your Flickr Photostream page, and you'll see your images have now been published there (as seen here). Now, you can take things a step further, because the comments that people post online about your published photos can be synced back to Lightroom, so you can read them right there in the Comments panel (in the right side Panels area). For example, on the Flickr website itself, I clicked on the second image and added a comment in the field below it. I wrote: "The watermark needs to be moved to the bottom."

Step Eight:

To see the comments in Lightroom, go to the Publish Services panel, click on your Flickr Photostream, and it displays your published photos. Then, Right-click on your Photostream and choose **Publish Now** from the pop-up menu, and it goes and checks your Flickr account to see if any comments have been added, and downloads them into Lightroom. Now, click on a photo, and then look in the Comments panel (at the bottom of the right side Panels area), and any comments that were added to that image in Flickr will appear there. Also, it displays how many people have tagged that published photo as one of their favorites on Flickr.

Continued

Step Nine:

Okay, so far so good, but what if you make a change to one of those published photos in Lightroom? Here's what to do (and here's where this Publish Services thing works so well): First, click on the Flickr Photostream to display the photos you've already published to Flickr, then click on the photo you want to edit, and press **D** to jump over to the Develop module. In this case, I just made some adjustments in the Basic panel. Now that our edits are done, it's time to get this edited version of the photo back up to our Flickr photostream.

Step 10:

Go back to the Library module, to the Publish Services panel, and click on your Photostream, and you'll see a split screen again, but this time it's showing your edited photo up top waiting to be republished. Click the Publish button and it updates the image on Flickr, so your most recent changes are reflected there. Of course, once you do this, the Modified Photos to Re-Publish section goes away, because now all your photos are republished. Okay, so that's the Flickr Publish Services, and now that you've learned how that works, setting up your hard drive for drag-and-drop publishing is a cinch, so we'll do that next.

Step 11:

Start by clicking on the Set Up button next to Hard Drive in the Publish Services panel. We'll configure this one so it saves any files we drag onto it as high-resolution JPEGs to your hard drive (so think of this as a drag-and-drop shortcut to make JPEGs, rather than having to go through the whole Export dialog). Give this publish service a name now—call this one "Save as JPEG"—then fill out the rest just like you would for exporting a high-res JPEG to your hard disk (like we did back on page 272). When you click Save, it replaces Set Up with the name of your service (in this case, now it reads: "Hard Drive: Save as JPEG," so you know at a glance that it's going to save images you drag-and-drop on it to your hard drive as JPEGs). You can add as many of these as you'd like by Right-clicking next to Hard Drive and choosing **Create Another Publish Service via "Hard Drive."** That way, you can have some that export your images as originals, or some for emailing, or…well…you get the idea (look at the Publish Services panel here where I created a few extra setups, just so you can see what they'd look like).

Step 12:

Now that you've got at least one configured, let's put it to work. In the Library module, go ahead and select four RAW files you want saved as JPEGs (they don't have to be RAW files—they can already be JPEGs that you just want exported from Lightroom), and drag-and-drop those selected photos onto your Hard Drive: Save as JPEG publish service. From here, it's pretty much the same as you just learned with Flickr—the images appear in a New Photos to Publish section until you click the Publish button, then it writes them as JPEGs into whichever folder you chose when you set this publish service up.

CHAPTER 10

LR WITH PHOTOSHOP
how and when to use Photoshop

It's important to know that, even as powerful as Lightroom Classic is today, there are times when you're going to need to jump over to Photoshop to accomplish what you need to do. However, a little historical perspective will help you better understand when and why you need to make this jump: You see, Lightroom 1.0 came out 11+ years ago, which is actually longer than it sounds when you realize that Lightroom was around before even the iPhone. If you were using Lightroom back then and your cell phone rang, it was some weird Motorola or Nokia flip phone, with an awful little monochrome screen that looked like it was from a 1960s Soviet Soyuz mission. There were no apps on your phone, no games, heck, there was no Twitter (if you mentioned "Twitter" to someone, they assumed you were referring to the sound a bird makes). So, if you wound up in a doctor's office, or the DMV, or any type of waiting room, you didn't just pick up your phone and start watching videos or posting on social media. Nope, you just sat there, staring at the wall, sobbing, as you quietly prayed for the sweet angel of death to come and mercifully end your excruciating boredom. Sorry, I got off track. Where was I? Oh, yeah, using Photoshop. Well, back then, Lightroom had very few features and a lot of the sliders weren't actually attached to anything. Adobe, of course, knew all this and held a secret meeting in the vast catacombs beneath their San Jose headquarters, attended by leaders of the World Bank and the Ordo Templi Orientis, where it was decided to make Lightroom work with Photoshop so seamlessly that users wouldn't notice important stuff was missing. Well, the plan worked and, in fact, they'd still be getting away with it to this very day if it weren't for those meddling kids! Well, them and the Illuminati.

Choosing How Your Files Are Sent to Photoshop

When you take a photo from Lightroom over to Photoshop for editing, by default, Lightroom makes a copy of the file (in TIFF format), embeds it with the ProPhoto RGB color profile, sets the bit depth to 16 bits, and sets the resolution to 240 ppi. But if you want something different, you can choose how you'd like your files sent over to Photoshop—you can choose to send them as PSDs (that's how I send mine) or TIFFs, and you can choose their bit depth (8 or 16 bits) and which color profile you want embedded when your image leaves Lightroom.

Step One:

Press **Command-, (comma; PC: Ctrl-,)** to bring up Lightroom's preferences, and click on the External Editing tab up top (seen here). If you have Photoshop on your computer, it chooses it as your External Editor, so in the top section, choose the file format you want for photos that get sent to Photoshop (I set mine to PSD, because the files are much smaller than TIFFs), then from the Color Space pop-up menu, choose your file's color space (Adobe recommends ProPhoto RGB. If you keep it at that, I'd change Photoshop's color space to ProPhoto RGB, as well—whatever you choose, just use the same color space in Photoshop). Adobe also recommends choosing a 16-bit depth for the best results (although, I personally use an 8-bit depth most of the time). You also get to choose the resolution (I leave mine set at the default of 240 ppi). If you want to use a second program to edit your photos, you can choose that in the Additional External Editor section.

Step Two:

Next, there's a Stack With Original checkbox. I recommend leaving this on, because it puts the edited copy of your image right beside your original file (more on this in the next project), so it's easy to find when you return to Lightroom. Lastly, you can choose the name applied to photos sent over to Photoshop. You choose this from the Edit Externally File Naming section at the bottom of the dialog, and you have pretty much the same naming choices as you do in the regular Import window.

While Lightroom is great for so many everyday editing things, it doesn't do heavy special effects or major photo retouching; there are no layers, no filters, and its type controls are very limited, and it doesn't do many of the bazillion (yes, bazillion) things that Photoshop does. So, there will be times during your workflow where you'll need to jump over to Photoshop to do some "Photoshop stuff" and then jump back to Lightroom for printing or presenting. Luckily, these two applications were designed to work together from the start.

How to Jump Over to Photoshop, and How to Jump Back

20-Second Tutorial:

To take the image you're working on over to Photoshop, go under the Photo menu, under Edit In, and choose **Edit in Adobe Photoshop** (as shown here), or just press **Command-E (PC: Ctrl-E)**, and Lightroom sends a copy of your image over to Photoshop. Do anything you want to it in Photoshop and then simply save the image, close the window, and it comes right back to Lightroom. However, if you want to follow along with the project here, I'll take you through the process (plus, you'll get to learn a few Photoshop things along the way). Here's our original image in Lightroom.

Step One:

Now, press Command-E (PC: Ctrl-E) to open the image in Photoshop. If you took the shot in RAW, it just "loans" Photoshop a copy of the image and opens it. However, if you shot in JPEG or TIFF mode, this brings up the Edit Photo with Adobe Photoshop dialog, where you choose (1) to have a copy of your original photo sent to Photoshop, with all the changes and edits you made in Lightroom applied to it, (2) to have Lightroom make a copy of your original untouched photo and send that to Photoshop, or (3) to edit your original JPEG or TIFF in Photoshop without any of the changes you've made thus far in Lightroom. Since we're working with a JPEG here, we'll choose the first option, and work on a copy that has our Lightroom adjustments.

Continued

Step Two:

Here's a copy of our image open in Photoshop CC. We're going to create a blend of two images, kind of a multiple exposure effect with one image blending into the shape of the other (it's a pretty popular effect right now seen in web ads, site banners, etc.). Start by getting the Quick Selection tool from the Toolbar (**W**; it's shown circled here in red). Now, you can either have Photoshop select your subject for you by clicking on the Select Subject button up in the Options Bar (also circled here; this feature works amazingly well), or you can paint over her yourself. Either way will put a selection border around your subject (as seen here). If you decide to paint the selection, you might have to zoom in tight, by pressing **Command-+ (plus sign; PC: Ctrl-+)**, and shrink the size of the brush down (press the **Left Bracket key** on your keyboard to make the brush smaller, or the **Right Bracket key** to make it larger) to help paint in every little area. This tool does a great job in making selections, so it shouldn't take long at all. By the way, to zoom back out, double-click the Hand tool near the bottom of the Toolbar.

Step Three:

Once she's fully selected, press **Command-J (PC: Ctrl-J)** to put a copy of just the subject up on her own separate layer above the Background layer. In the image you see here, I went to the Layers panel and hid the Background layer (the one with the solid white background around her) by clicking on the eye icon to the left of the layer's thumbnail. I did that so you could see that this new layer is just her without the white background. The gray/white checkerboard you now see behind her represents the transparent areas of this layer, so you can see it's just her, on her own separate layer. Having her on her own separate layer like this, without a background behind her, is a key part of this technique.

Step Four:

Now let's open the image we're going to blend with her—it's a shot of the New York City skyline taken from the Top of the Rock observation deck. In Lightroom, click on the image, then press Command-E (PC: Ctrl-E) to open this image in Photoshop, as well. See that tab near the top of the window (the one that says "nyc skyline .jpg")? If you have this Photoshop preference turned on, you can click on these tabs to switch from one image document to another. With this skyline image now open, press **Command-A (PC: Ctrl-A)** to put a selection around the entire image, and then we'll do a simple copy/paste onto our headshot photo document. So, press **Command-C (PC: Ctrl-C)** to copy it, click the BeautyHeadshot1.jpg tab to switch to that image, then press **Command-V (PC: Ctrl-V)** to paste this image on top of your headshot image. It will appear on its own separate layer, so now you'll have three layers: (1) Background is your original image; (2) Layer 1 is that selection of just her on a transparent background; and (3) Layer 2, at the top, is the skyline image.

Step Five:

We need to put a selection back around our subject, and there's a keyboard shortcut that will do that: press-and-hold the Command (PC: Ctrl) key, then click once directly on the image thumbnail for Layer 1 in the Layers panel. When you do this, it puts a selection around your subject (the same selection you made earlier). Now, with that selection in place, make sure the top layer is still active (Layer 2—the skyline shot), then go down to the bottom of the Layers panel and click on the Add Layer Mask icon (it's the third icon from the left, circled here in red). When you do that, it masks the skyline photo into the shape of your subject (as seen here), and the selection automatically deselects itself (so don't be concerned that you don't see it in place any more).

Continued

Step Six:

To blend the skyline in with your subject on the layer below it, you're going to change the layer blend mode of this skyline layer. Layer blend modes determine how the layer you're currently on interacts with the layers below it. When it's set to its default setting—Normal—it doesn't interact, it just covers whatever's on the layer below, so if you change the blend mode, it'll blend. There are 27 different blend modes, and depending on the image, they always look different. So, what I do is press **Shift-+ (plus sign)** again and again, and it toggles through all the different blend modes. Your job? Simply stop at the one that looks good to you. In this case, I used the **Overlay** blend mode, but others I liked were Soft Light, Hard Light, Pin Light, and Subtract (choose whichever one you like best).

Step Seven:

Now we're going to bring back some of our original image, but we still need that lower layer (so the city layer has something to mix with). What we'll do is make a copy of the layer of her with the transparent background, and drag that copy layer to the top of the layer stack. So, in the Layers panel, click on Layer 1 (her with the transparent background), then press Command-J (PC: Ctrl-J), which makes a duplicate of the layer, but this duplicate appears below the skyline, so you can't see that you've done anything. Just click on that layer and drag it up to the top of the layer stack, and at this point, it will look like when we started (as seen here).

Your copy layer is hidden behind a black layer mask

Choose a large, soft-edged brush from the Brush Picker up in the Options Bar, then drag the brush Size slider to 1800 px

Lower the Opacity to 50% up in the Options Bar

Step Eight:

Now you're going to hide this copy layer on top behind a black layer mask, so we can reveal just the parts we want. Press-and-hold the Option (PC: Alt) key and click on the Add Layer Mask icon (the same one you clicked on earlier, at the bottom of the Layers panel). This hides your copy layer behind a black layer mask, so you can't see it at all. It's still there—it's just hidden. Now, go to the Toolbar and get the Brush tool (or just press the letter **B**), then go up to the Brush Picker in the Options Bar, choose a large, soft-edged brush (as shown on the right), and drag the brush Size slider to 1800 pixels. Now, lower the Opacity of the brush to 50% (you also do this up in the Options Bar).

Step Nine:

Look at the bottom of the Toolbar and make sure your Foreground color is set to white (if it's not, press the letter **X** on your keyboard until the white color swatch appears in the front). Then, take the brush and paint over the parts of the image where you want to reveal the original (as I did here where I painted over the left side of her face), and because you're using a soft-edged brush, it blends smoothly. There's still some skyline coming through her face here, but if you want less skyline and more of her face visible, paint over that part of her face again (since you're painting with your brush at 50% Opacity, it builds up as you paint over the same area).

Continued

Step 10:

We're done tweaking the image here in Photoshop, so at this point, you can choose to flatten the image (by choosing **Flatten Image** from the Layers panel's flyout menu), which removes all the layers and leaves you with a single-layer image, like we normally have in Lightroom, or you can keep all the layers intact and send them over to Lightroom (more on this choice on the next page). But, no matter which you choose to do (flattening the image or not), what you do next is the same: just press **Command-S (PC: Ctrl-S)** to Save the changes, then press **Command-W (PC: Ctrl-W)** to Close the image window. Save and close. That's it. Now when you go back to Lightroom, and look in your headshot image collection, you'll find your edited image right beside your original image (as shown here). If you're using folders instead of collections, you'll find this edited image at the end of the images in the folder.

Step 11:

Now that the image is back in Lightroom, you can treat it like any other image, so let's convert it to black and white, and then finish things off by adding a little film grain (I often add grain to black-and-white photos to give them more of a traditional B&W film look). Of course, you can use any of the sliders or profiles in the Develop module, but for now let's just go to the Presets panel in the left side Panels area, and under the B&W presets, click on B&W High Contrast. Then, in that same panel, go down to the Grain presets and choose Medium to apply the film grain effect. So, to recap: press **Command-E (PC: Ctrl-E)** to take your selected image over to Photoshop, do all the tweaking you want there, and when you're done, simply save and close and your edited image appears in Lightroom. Be sure to read the next technique, though, because it's something you'll want to know about saving a layered file back to Lightroom.

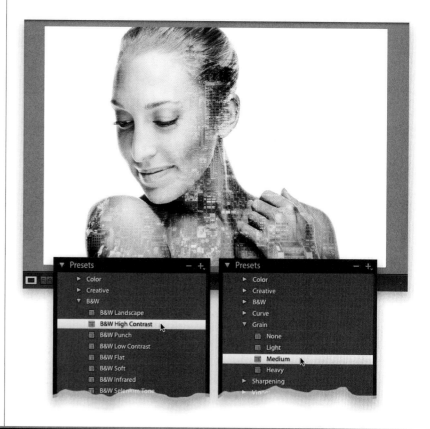

If you take an image over to Photoshop, and you add a bunch of layers, and then you just "save and close," like I've been saying, what happens to those layers? They actually stay intact, even though, in Lightroom, you only see the single image (as if you had flattened the image). The trick is how to reopen the layered image in Photoshop and still have the layers intact.

Keeping Your Photoshop Layers Intact

Step One:
If you have an image with multiple layers (like we did in the previous project), and you save and close the document without flattening it, in Lightroom, you'll just see a flattened version of the image, but the layers are actually still there (you just can't see them because Lightroom doesn't have a layers feature). If you want to see the layers, or work with them, you have to go back to Photoshop. *However*, to do that, when you click on the layered image in Lightroom and press **Command-E (PC: Ctrl-E)** to open it in Photoshop, when the dialog appears asking you if you want to edit a copy with your Lightroom changes, you must choose Edit Original (as seen here).

Step Two:
When you choose Edit Original (and by the way, this is the *only* time we ever choose Edit Original in the Edit Photo with Adobe Photoshop dialog), when the image opens in Photoshop, all the layers are back. If you don't choose Edit Original in that dialog, it sends Photoshop a flattened version of the image. So, if you open a file you know has layers, but you don't see them in Photoshop, you know you chose the wrong option in that dialog.

Adding Photoshop Automation to Your Lightroom Workflow

If there's a "finishing move" you like to do in Photoshop (after you're done tweaking the image in Lightroom), you can add some automation to the process, so once your photos are exported, Photoshop launches, applies your move, and then resaves the file. It's based on you creating an action in Photoshop (an action is a recording of something you've done in Photoshop, and once you've recorded it, Photoshop can repeat that process as many times as you'd like, really, really, fast). Here's how to create an action, and then hook that directly into Lightroom:

Step One:
We start this process in Photoshop, so go ahead and press **Command-E (PC: Ctrl-E)** to open an image in Photoshop (don't forget, you can follow along with the same photo I'm using here, if you like, by downloading it from the site I gave you back in the book's introduction). What we're going to do here is create a Photoshop action that adds a nice, simple matte border around the image, then a simple black frame around the outside, and then it puts your nameplate under the image (it looks better than it sounds). Once we create this action, you'll be able apply a frame with a matte around your image automatically when you export your final image as a JPEG (or TIFF or whatever) from Lightroom.

Step Two:
To create an action, go under the Window menu and choose **Actions** to make the Actions panel visible. Click on the Create New Action icon at the bottom of the panel (it looks just like the Create a New Layer icon in the Layers panel and is circled here), which brings up the New Action dialog (shown here). Go ahead and give your action a name (I named mine "Add Frame") and click the Record button (notice the button doesn't say OK or Save, it says Record, because it's now recording your steps).

Step Three:

We're going to need to get this photo off the Background layer and put it on its own separate layer. To do that, press **Command-A (PC: Ctrl-A)** to put a selection around the entire image (as seen here), then press **Command-Shift-J (PC: Ctrl-Shift-J)** to "cut" the image off the Background layer and put it on its own layer (as seen in the Layers panel here—you can see the image is now on Layer 1 and the Background layer is empty).

Step Four:

Now we're going to add some white space around the image by going under the Image menu and choosing **Canvas Size** (or you can use the shortcut **Command-Option-C [PC: Ctrl-Alt-C]**). When the Canvas Size dialog appears, at the bottom, choose **White** from the Canvas Extension Color pop-up menu, then turn on the Relative checkbox in the middle (that lets us specify how much space we want to add, without having to do any math, by adding it to the current dimensions). For the Width, add 4 inches, and for the Height, add 6 inches, so we'll add more space below the image than on the sides. Click OK to add this space. Now press **V** to switch to the Move tool, and click-and-drag your image up a bit on the canvas (press-and-hold the Shift key to keep it centered), so it's about an inch or so higher than center (as shown here). That leaves us room to add our nameplate in just a minute.

Continued

Step Five:

We need to get the selection back around our image, so go to the Layers panel, press-and-hold the Command (PC: Ctrl) key, and click directly on the layer thumbnail for Layer 1 (your Paris image, in this case), which puts a section around the image. You're going to make that selection around 1/2" larger all the way around your image (this is what we're going to use to create our matte), so go under the Select menu and choose **Transform Selection** to switch your selection into a transformation border. Now, click-and-drag the center handles on each side out about 1/2" from the image (as shown here). It should be about equal distance on all sides (you could technically measure out the sides by making the Rulers visible by pressing **Command-R [PC: Ctrl-R]**, but I honestly just "eye" it). When it looks like what you see here, press **Return (PC: Enter)** to lock in the selection's resizing.

Step Six:

We're going to fill this selected area with white, but we need this matte to appear below our image (not covering it), so click on the Create a New Layer icon at the bottom of the Layers panel (it's the second icon from the right). When this new blank layer appears in the Layers panel, click-and-drag it below your Paris image layer. Your selection will still be in place, so press **D**, then **X**, to set your Foreground color to white, then press **Option-Delete (PC: Alt-Backspace)** to fill your matte selection with white. Deselect by pressing **Command-D (PC: Ctrl-D)**. To create the matte effect, at the bottom of the Layers panel, click on the Add a Layer Style (fx) icon, and choose **Inner Glow** to bring up the Inner Glow options in the Layer Style dialog (seen here). Set your Blend Mode to **Normal**, your Opacity to 26%, and then click on the color swatch and choose black as your glow color. Next, set your Size to 19 pixels, click OK, and it adds a thin shadow inside your white box, which looks like a cut matte.

Step Seven:

Now that our matte is done, we're going to add a thin, black frame border around the outside of the image area. In the Layers panel, click on the Background layer and press Command-A (PC: Ctrl-A) to put a selection around the entire Background layer (as seen here). We'll need to add another blank layer, so click on the Create a New Layer icon at the bottom of the Layers panel to add this new layer directly above the Background layer (as seen here in the Layers panel).

Step Eight:

To add a stroke around the outside of the image, go under the Edit menu and choose **Stroke** to bring up the Stroke dialog (seen here). We want the stroke to appear inside that selected area, so choose Inside for Location, enter 100px for the Width (it's a high-res image, so it won't be nearly as thick as it sounds), then make sure your Color is set to black, and click OK, and it adds a thin black frame to the outside of your image (as seen here). Press Commad-D (PC: Ctrl-D) to Deselect.

Continued

Step Nine:

Now let's add that nameplate below our image. Get the Horizontal Type tool **(T)**, click below your image, and type in your name or the name of your studio. In our example here, I typed in my name, and then I added a "pipe" (a vertical separator line) by pressing **Shift-Backslash**, then "Photography." I typed this nameplate in all caps using the font Gil Sans Light at 24 points. It still needs to be centered, and we need to lower the opacity a bit, so it's gray instead of black and doesn't compete with the image, but that's what Step 10 is for.

Step 10:

To center your text under the image, click on the Move tool in the Toolbar, then in the Layers panel, Command-click (PC: Ctrl-click) on the Background layer, so both the text layer and Background layer are selected. Now, to center your text, go up to the Options Bar and click the Align Horizontal Centers button (shown circled here in red). Then, click on the Type layer in the Layers panel, and in the top-right corner of the panel, lower the Opacity of this layer to 50%, which gives it a gray color, rather than black, and helps it to recede. Now, let's save and close the file by pressing **Command-S (PC: Ctrl-S)**, and then **Command-W (PC: Ctrl-W)**.

Step 11:

You may have forgotten by now, but we've been recording this process the whole time (remember that action we created a while back? Well, it has been recording our steps all along). So, go back to the Actions panel and click on the Stop icon at the bottom of the panel (as shown here). What you've recorded is an action that will apply the effect, then save the file, and then close that file. Now, I generally like to test my action at this point to make sure I recorded it correctly, so head back to Lightroom, click on a different photo, press Command-E (PC: Ctrl-E) to bring that photo over to Photoshop, then in the Actions panel, click on the Add Frame action and click the Play icon at the bottom of the panel. It should apply the effect very, very quickly, then it will save and close the document and send it back to Lightroom. If it looks good, we can move on to the final step.

Step 12:

We're now going to turn that action into what's called a "droplet," and we can use this droplet inside of Lightroom. When you drop an image onto a droplet, it automatically launches Photoshop, opens that photo, and runs the action you turned into a droplet (in our case, it would automatically run the frame action). Then it saves and closes the photo automatically, because you recorded those two steps as part of the action. Pretty sweet. So, to make a droplet, go under Photoshop's File menu, under Automate, and choose **Create Droplet** (as shown here).

Continued

Step 13:

This brings up the Create Droplet dialog (shown here). At the top left of the dialog, click the Choose button, choose your desktop as the destination for saving your droplet, and then name your droplet "Add Frame." Now, in the Play section of this dialog, make sure to choose **Add Frame** (that's what we named our action earlier) from the Action pop-up menu (as seen here). That's it—you can ignore the rest of the dialog, and just click OK in the top-right corner. If you look on your computer's desktop, you'll see an icon that is a large arrow, and the arrow is aiming at the name of the droplet (as seen here at the bottom).

Add Frame

Step 14:

Now that we've built our Add Frame droplet in Photoshop, we're going to add that droplet to our Lightroom workflow using a feature called "Export Actions," which are things that happen after you export an image. To become an Export Action, you have to place this droplet in the folder where Lightroom stores its Export Actions. Luckily, Lightroom can bring this folder right to you. Go back to Lightroom, and under the File menu, choose **Export**. When the Export dialog appears, go down to the Post-Processing section, and from the After Export pop-up menu, choose **Go to Export Actions Folder Now** (as shown here). This brings up the folder on your computer where Lightroom stores Export Actions (shown at the top). All you have to do is drag that droplet you saved earlier on your desktop into this folder, and then simply close the folder—it's now an Export Action in Lightroom.

Step 15:
Okay, let's put it to work: In Lightroom's Grid view, select the photo (or photos) you want to have that effect applied to, then press **Command-Shift-E (PC: Ctrl-Shift-E)** to bring back the Export dialog. In the Preset section on the left, click on the right-facing triangle to the left of User Presets, and then click on the Export JPEG for Web preset we created in Chapter 9 (if you didn't create that one, go ahead and do it now). In the Export Location section, click on the Choose button and select the destination folder for your saved JPEG(s) (if you want to change it). Then, in the File Naming section, you can give your photo(s) a new name (if you'd like). Now, in the Post-Processing section at the bottom, from the After Export pop-up menu, you'll see **Add Frame** (your droplet) has been added as a choice, so choose it (as shown here).

Step 16:
When you click Export, your photo(s) will be saved as a JPEG, then Photoshop will automatically launch, open your photo(s), apply your Add Frame action, then save and close the photo(s). Pretty slick stuff! Here's that image we just selected in Lightroom after having Photoshop run the Add Frame action when we exported it. I love it when a plan comes together.

CHAPTER 11

PHOTO BOOKS
creating beautiful books with your images

It's pretty amazing that today, using Lightroom's Book module, anyone can make a beautiful, hardcover coffee table book, complete with a fancy glossy dust jacket like you see at the bookstore. You don't need the permission of a publisher, or the approval of a bunch of snooty editors. That's right—you are in total control and can have a glorious coffee table book of your own sitting on your coffee table in about four days, and at the same time, have it available for sale in Blurb's online bookstore. So, when other photographers see your coffee table book, and coyly ask, "So, do you sell these? Can people buy them?" Of course, they stand there smirking as they're expecting you to say, "Well, not really," but instead you'll chuckle and say, "Why of course they're for sale," as you casually whip out a card and hand them the pre-printed web address where they can buy your book, as you coyly remark, "They're quite expensive, but I can get you a discount code if you need one." Then, you just pause, not saying anything, just smiling and letting it hang there in the air for a moment, marinating slowly, as their smirk vanishes and is replaced with a look of shame and jealousy, as though a crashing wave of disgrace has washed over them, leaving the unmistakable stench of a loser so strong not even Irish Spring body wash can remove it. Yes, this is the moment you've been waiting for—a chance to even the score with that aloof ex-vice president of your local camera club—and it would all be so perfect if it were not for the fact that nobody will actually see your coffee table book, let alone your coffee table, because people no longer visit people's homes because they're all at home on Facebook, viewing your images 3" wide on the non-color calibrated screen of a factory reconditioned Samsung Galaxy Tab S2 tablet. Sigh. This sounded so much better in my head.

Before You Make Your First Book

Here are just a couple of quick things you'll want to know before you actually build your first book, including what kind of books, sizes, and covers are available through Adobe's partner in book building, Blurb (www.blurb.com):

Step One:

When you jump over to the Book module (up in the taskbar, or just press **Command-Option-4 [PC: Ctrl-Alt-4]**), a Book menu appears up top, and if you go under that menu, at the bottom of it, you'll find **Book Preferences**. Go ahead and choose that before we get rollin' here. Okay, let's start at the top: Just like in the Print, Slideshow, or Web modules, in the Book module, you get to choose whether the default setting for your frames is Zoom to Fill or Zoom to Fit (I leave it set at Zoom to Fill, simply because it usually looks better, but you can choose whichever you like best).

Step Two:

When we build our book project together (after these two pages), you'll have the option of having Lightroom automatically fill all the pages of your book with the photos you've chosen to be in the book (so you don't have to drag-and-drop them into the book one by one). With this preference turned on, as soon as you go to the Book module, it flows your Filmstrip photos into the photo frames on each page and—boom—you've got a book (of course, you can rearrange any pages or swap out photos after the fact, but it's a good starting place).

Step Three:

In the final section, there's a preference to help you visually see where you can add text. Some of the layouts have areas where you can put text, and it's easy to see in the thumbnail, but once you apply it to your actual page, unless there's some text already in place (Filler Text), then you wouldn't know there was a text box there at all. So, choosing Filler Text acts as a reminder (but don't worry—it's just for looks. It doesn't actually print until you erase it and start typing your own text, so you don't have to worry about it showing up in your final book—just like you don't have to worry about guides printing in your final book). Besides Filler Text, if you actually added captions or titles (in the Metadata panel fields in the Library module), you can choose to have Lightroom pull that text instead (which will definitely save you some time). Lastly, Constrain Captions to Text Safe Area just means it will keep your captions from extending into areas where it might get cut off, or extend into the page gutter between pages.

Step Four:

Before you turn the page and we start building a book together, I thought I'd show you the different sizes and types of books you can order directly from Lightroom through Blurb (an online photo book lab that's very popular with photographers, and Adobe's printing partner for Lightroom):

There are five different sizes: Small Square 7x7", Standard Portrait (tall) 8x10", Standard Landscape (wide) 10x8", Large Landscape 13x11", and Large Square 12x12". There are three different cover choices for each: a Softcover, a Hardcover Image Wrap (shown here, on the left and right), and a Hardcover Dust Jacket (you get to choose the inside flap covers and text if you want it, too!). Okay, let's build our book.

Making Your First Book In Just 10 Minutes

This is kind of my quick start guide on how to build a photo book from scratch. It'll take you more time to pick which photos you think you might want in the book than it will to actually make the book (10 minutes, tops). The rest of the chapter will dig in to individual topics, like adding captions, creating custom layouts, etc., but for now, let's just build a book the fast and easy way. When you see how quick (and fun) this is, you'll be making books from here on out.

Step One:

The first step is pretty simple: make a new collection with the finished photos you think you might want to put in your book. It's okay if there are photos in there that don't wind up in the book, and they don't have to be in order at this point—you just need to start somewhere. So, I always start by creating this collection of final images for my book (here, I created a "Morocco for Photo Book" collection inside my Morocco collection set).

Step Two:

Go to the Book module, and thanks to those Preference settings you selected (on the previous two pages), when you jump to the Book module it automatically takes the images in this collection and puts them on the pages of your book, in the order they appear in the collection. Don't sweat it—we can change the order anytime. In fact, we'll be doing that shortly, but this gives you a starting place. Since you won't be doing anything else in the left side Panels area, close it, so you have more room to work with your pages. Now, the default layout puts one photo on the right page and leaves the left blank, but if you want to put one photo on each page (like I have here), then go down to the Auto Layout panel in the right side Panels area, click on the Clear Layout button, then choose **One Photo Per Page** from the Preset menu. Click the Auto Layout button, and it will automatically fill both pages now.

Step Three:

Before you do anything else, you'll need to go up to the Book Settings panel and choose the book's Size (if you change this later, it kind of messes up your layouts). If this is your first book, I recommend going with a 10×8" (or 8×10"), just to keep the cost down. Once you have this process down, then you might want to splurge on a coffee-table-sized book, like the Large Landscape or Large Square. Most of the books I build are the 10×8" Standard Landscape—they cost less and research has shown that people prefer viewing printed photo books at this "magazine" size. Next, choose your Cover style. The vast majority of books I print are softcover—they're perfect bound, so they have a nice look, and they're the least expensive. If you go with either Hardcover Image Wrap (your image wraps around the front and back hardcover) or Hardcover Dust Jacket (a separately printed glossy wrap goes over your hardcover image wrap), they'll cost more. Lastly, choose your Paper Type. I generally go with Standard or Premium Lustre for everyday books (and for gifts). I only upgrade to their ProLine Pearl Photo (which is really nice paper) when I am doing a large, hardcover coffee-table-sized book (because of the extra cost).

Step Four:

Now, before you start customizing the order and layout of your pages, you'll need to know how to get to the different views for your book. There are three, and you choose them by clicking on the little buttons on the left side of the toolbar, right below the Preview area. For example, click on the second button (shown circled here in red) to zoom in to this two-page spread view (or press **Command-R [PC: Ctrl-R]**; you'll use this view a lot). Click on the first button to see your entire book layout (or press **Command-E [PC: Ctrl-E]**). The third button is a single-page view, but you'll really only use that for spell-checking and proofing your text.

Continued

Step Five:

Okay, the boring stuff is out of the way, so now comes the fun part: laying out your book. Like I mentioned in Step Two, Lightroom will automatically fill the pages of your book with your images, but the order and layout of each individual page is totally up to you from this point on. In our spread, here, both pages have images filling the pages, but if you want to change one of the pages to a different layout, click on the page you want to edit (a yellow border will appear around it letting you know it's selected), then click the little down-facing arrow in the bottom-right corner, and a pop-up menu of pre-designed book page layouts appears (as seen here). Here, I clicked on 1 Photo layouts, and in the scrolling list of thumbnails at the bottom, I clicked on the thumbnail that puts a white border around the image, and it immediately applied it to that page (also seen here). That's all there is to it—if you see a thumbnail layout that looks good to you, click on it.

Step Six:

The default layout that Lightroom gives you puts one photo on each page, but if you want to put multiple photos on a page, you can choose from loads of templates with two, three, or four photos, or from templates with pre-designed multi-photo layouts. In this case, I clicked on 2 Photos (as seen here) to see the thumbnail list of two-photo layouts. I then clicked on a layout with two tall, side-by-side images and that thumbnail was applied. Of course, you have to choose another photo to add to this two-photo layout, so for now it just displays a tall, empty, gray box (these are called photo "cells"). *Note:* If a layout is designed with text blocks, you'll see lines that represent where the text block will appear (but, you don't have to add text if you don't want, even if the thumbnail has an area to add text).

Step Seven:

From this point on, it's a "drag-and-drop" world, which makes the rest of this process really easy. To add another photo to this two-photo layout, just make the Filmstrip visible along the bottom, click on a thumbnail, and drag-and-drop it right into that second tall, gray box, and that image now appears in that cell (as seen here). If you wanted to swap the left and right photos, again, it's just a drag-and-drop—click on the left photo and drag it over to the right photo cell, let go, and they swap. *Note:* Take a look back at the tall image on the left in Step Six. Notice how it's kind of off-center in the frame? You can reposition your image within any photo cell by simply clicking-and-dragging it left or right (as I did here where I centered the image). Also, when you click on an image, a Zoom slider appears above it, so you can zoom in/out (if you zoom in too tight, you may not have enough resolution to print the image, and if that happens, you'll see a warning in the upper-right of the photo).

TIP: Adding More Pages

You can always add more pages to your photo book by going to the Page panel (in the right side Panels area) and clicking the Add Page button.

Step Eight:

Now, it's not just dragging-and-dropping within the same page. Like I said, it's a drag-and-drop world at this point. Click-and-drag the image on the left page over onto the tall right photo cell, and the two swap (notice the image that was on the far left is now over on the right page, on the right side—they've swapped).

TIP: Removing a Photo

To remove a photo from a cell, click on it and hit the **Delete (PC: Backspace) key**. It doesn't delete it from your collection, so you can still find it down in your Filmstrip and drop it onto another a page.

Continued

Step Nine:

One of my favorite layouts is a two-page spread, and I include a decent amount of them in every book I create for two reasons: (1) they have a big impact in the book, stretching across both pages like that; and (2) it seems like almost any photo looks great as a two-page spread.

Note: By default, every spread has two pages, right? Well, when you choose one photo to stretch across two pages, that extra photo doesn't just disappear—a new page is created. If you apply a two-page spread to an image on a right page, it adds a new blank page where it used to be, and a new two-page spread is created with your image. You'll have to choose a new image to fill the blank page. If you apply a two-page spread to an image on a left page, it adds a new page to make the two-page spread, and then it takes the page on the right and it moves it to the next page in your book, so now the rest of your layouts are off by one page. Your choices now are: (a) click on the page after your two-page spread, add another page, and drop in another photo, or (b) delete the page that used to be your right page, and that fixes the problem. Your call.

Step 10:

Besides dragging-and-dropping images, you can also drag-and-drop individual pages. Just click on a page to select it, then drag-and-drop it where you want it—even if it breaks up a spread (as I'm doing here, where I dragged the left page in the bottom-left corner and split the two pages in the row above it. The thin yellow line shows where this page will appear when you release the mouse button). You can swap left and right pages the same way. Lastly, if you want to move a full spread, click on the left page to select it, then Command-click (PC: Ctrl-click) on the right page to select them both (as seen here, at the bottom) and drag them where you want them to appear in your book.

Step 11:

Once you have your layouts all in place, your front and back covers designed (see page 339), and the pages in the order you want them (and you've checked any text for typos—there's nothing more embarrassing than receiving your printed book and finding a horrendous typo. I know a guy this happened to and he was crushed. Okay, it was me. I was crushed. Learn from my mistake. See what I did there?). Anyway, once everything looks good to you, click the Send Book to Blurb button at the bottom of the right side Panels area (shown circled here in red). You don't have to worry about resolution issues (outside of what I mentioned in Step Seven), or color space issues, or any of that stuff—Lightroom takes care of all of that, packs it up, and gets it ready for upload to Blurb.

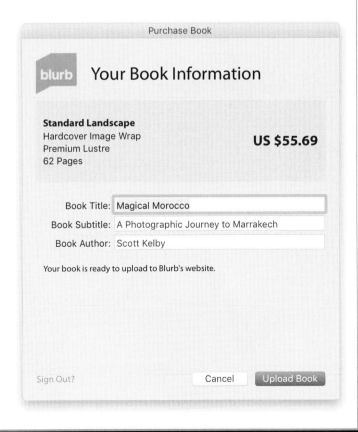

Step 12:

When you click that Send Book to Blurb button, it brings up the Purchase Book dialog you see here. Near the top it shows the specs of your book (including style, paper, number of pages, and price). Below that are fields for the book's title, subtitle, and author (this is helpful since you'll have the opportunity to sell this book publicly on Blurb's website, should you decide to make it available for purchase). If you don't have a Blurb account, you'll be asked to create one (they need your payment info, where to ship the book, etc.), so you'll do that next, and once you're finished, Lightroom compiles everything, uploads it (it doesn't take as long as you'd think), and then in a few days, your book arrives, followed by a reasonable amount of oohing and aahing. That's the process—it's surprisingly straightforward. If you want to dig in more to some of the details, well…that's what the rest of this chapter is all about.

Using Auto Layout to Automate Your Layout Process

In my quick start project, when we switched to the Book module, Lightroom took the images in our collection and arranged them on pages for us, right? That feature is called Auto Layout, but the default layouts are pretty simplistic—one photo, edge-to-edge, on every page, or every right page. Snooze. That's what you'd expect to get doing a photo book at Walgreens. Luckily, we can create and save our own auto layouts, to our specs, which makes a much more interesting-looking book in just one click.

Step One:

If you already have a layout in place, let's go ahead and start from scratch, so we can use the Auto Layout feature. In the Book module, go to the Auto Layout panel, near the top of the right side Panels area, and click the Clear Layout button (as shown here, at the top). There are a set of default presets, and if you click-and-hold on the Preset pop-up menu, you'll see 'em. But, we already know they're pretty lame, so instead, choose **Edit Auto Layout Preset** (as shown here), so we can create our own presets using our own settings.

Step Two:

When you choose that, the Auto Layout Preset Editor appears (seen here). It's split into two parts: the Left Pages and the Right Pages. On the left side, the pop-up menu is set to Same as Right Side or Blank (depending on which preset was originally chosen in the pop-up menu), so whatever you choose for your right side pages (on the right side of the dialog), the same will happen for the left side pages, or they will just be blank. Instead, choose **Fixed Layout** from that pop-up menu. That way, we can choose what appears on our left and right pages separately.

Step Three:

Let's set up a preset to make the left page images square and the right page images full page. Here's what you do: In the Left Pages section, after choosing Fixed Layout from the pop-up menu at the top, choose **1 Photo** from the pop-up menu below that. Now, scroll down to the square image page layout and click on it (as shown here), then just leave the right side at Fixed Layout, with one, full-page photo.

TIP: Hide Info Overlay

By default, info about your book appears in the top left of the Preview area (size, page count, and price). If you'd rather not see this information (it's pretty distracting), then just go under the View menu and choose **Show Info Overlay** (or press the **I** key) to turn it off.

Zoom Photos To: Fit

Zoom Photos To: Fill

Step Four:

There's another option you need to know about with these custom layout presets: you get to choose how your image appears, once you click-and-drag it into place, using the Zoom Photos To pop-up menus below the layout thumbnails. If you choose Fit, it scales your image down to fit inside the frame. So, if you choose Fit with a square layout like we chose, the image will fit fully inside the square (like the image shown here on the top left), but because it fits fully inside that square cell, your photo won't actually appear square. For that to happen, you'd have to choose Fill (like you see here, on the top right, and what I have selected in the previous step). Luckily, you can always change this after the fact, on a per-page basis, by Right-clicking on a photo and choosing **Zoom Photo To Fill Cell** from the pop-up menu to turn it on or off (as shown here at the bottom).

*Right-click on a page to apply
Zoom Photo To Fill Cell anytime*

Continued

Step Five:

Some other options you can choose from are, for example, if you know you're going to want to add some text to your pages, turn on the Add Photo Text checkbox, and your pages will be ready for you to add text by just clicking in the text field on a page and typing. You can also choose a Text Style preset for things like captions and stuff. Of course, you could just choose a layout that has a text area already built-in, but this is at least another option if you want to use a layout that doesn't already have text. For now, though, let's choose a more interesting left page than just that large square, so from the second pop-up menu, choose **2 Photos**, then scroll down and click on the two horizontal images layout seen here, then choose **Fill** from the Zoom Photos To pop-up menu.

Step Six:

Okay, now lets save this layout (two horizontal photos on the left page and one full-bleed photo on the right) by choosing **Save Current Settings as New Preset** from the Preset pop-up menu up top. This will bring up the New Preset dialog (seen below). I name my presets with a descriptive name, calling out what I chose on the left page and the right page (as seen). Now, click the Create button, then Done, and let's give it a try.

Step Seven:

Go back to the Auto Layout panel, click the Clear Layout button (if you already have a layout in place), and then from the Preset pop-up menu, choose the preset you just created (as shown in the inset below on the left). Now, click the Auto Layout button (shown in the inset below on the right) and it fills those blank pages with the images in your collection, using the preset you created (as seen here). Of course, this is just our starting place—now you can edit any page you'd like by clicking on it, then clicking the black arrow in the bottom-right corner and choosing a different layout. *Note:* Have you noticed that it takes your first photo and makes it the front cover, but then it also puts that same image as the first page (as seen here)? That really gets on my nerves. Not much you can do, except replace it with a different photo, which is what I do, but it still kinda frosts my Wheaties that we have to do that.

Step Eight:

I think the real power of Auto Layout is shown when you've created your own custom pages (see page 326) because you can then create auto layouts with pages you've designed, rather than the ones that come with Lightroom. When you make your presets, you can choose **Custom Pages** from the second pop-up menu (under Fixed Layout), and you'll see thumbnails for all the custom pages you've created, and you can choose any one you'd like. Here, I chose the same small, square, custom page for both the left and right and saved it as a preset. Then, I went to the Auto Layout panel, clicked the Clear Layout button to remove that previous layout we applied in Step Seven, and then I chose this L: Sm square – R: Sm square fine art-looking preset. I think this is the real power. Once you make custom pages, it takes things up a notch.

Making Your Own Custom Pages

As far as book page designs go, we have the pre-designed pages that come with Lightroom, and we can mark the ones we use the most as favorites, so we can get to them easily without digging through tons of thumbnails. But, beyond that, we can also create our own custom pages—pages with our own specs (well, within certain limits)—and have them easily available when we want 'em.

Step One:

To make this easy, start by double-clicking on a book page, then clicking on the little down-facing arrow in the bottom-right corner of the page, and then choosing the 1 Photo full bleed layout (as shown here). This will be what we edit to create our custom page. *Note:* We can only create custom single-photo pages. Sadly, we can't do this with two-, three-, or four-image pages.

Step Two:

Move your cursor down to the bottom-right corner of the page, and you'll see it turns into a black bar with a two-headed arrow. Click-and-drag diagonally inward on that corner, and the image will scale proportionally (as shown here). If all you're looking for is a smaller-sized image, like what you see here, or even smaller (remember, it scales proportionally), just keep dragging until the size looks good to you, and then you can save that as a custom page. However, I imagine you want to do a bit more than that (and if you do, keep reading).

Step Three:

To create pages that aren't proportional, go to the Cell panel in the right side Panels area, and you'll find four Padding sliders that control the amount of white space around your image (they control the size of the cell your image resides within). By default, all four sliders are linked together, so if you drag one of them, they all move, which is why things are always proportional. To unlink these sliders, so you can move them independent of each other, turn off the Link All checkbox (as seen here). Now, you can drag each slider independently (if you want things to be really precise), but now that they're unlinked, I just click on the sides, top, or bottom of the image and drag. Here, I'm dragging upward from the bottom, and only the bottom is moving, so it creates a panorama layout, and any photo I drop onto this page now will instantly look like a pano. I use this one a lot in my books.

Step Four:

Okay, now that you've got the idea, let's make a small, square custom page, like the one I have here (there's not one nearly this small, or this square in the built-in presets, except for one that has a torn edge border, which I'm not a fan of, but hey, that's just me). Here, I clicked-and-dragged the four sides inward until it made a square, and when I got pretty close to getting it looking perfectly square, that's when I look to the Cell panel to see if my numbers, especially the Left and Right padding, are equal. If not, I just drag their sliders or highlight a field and type in what I think is the right number. When you've got a page looking like you'd like it, Right-click anywhere on the page, and from the pop-up menu that appears, choose **Save as Custom Page** (as shown here). Now this layout can be applied to any page by choosing it from the Modify Page pop-up menu, under Custom Pages (you can see the two custom pages we just created here).

Adding Text and Captions to Your Photo Book

If you've been using Lightroom for a while, you know the text capabilities have been really limited. But, when it came to books, Adobe added their full-featured type engine right into the Book module, so you have a surprising amount of control over how your type looks and where you can put it. Now, if we can only get them to put a copy of the Book module's type feature over into the Slideshow and Print modules (don't get me started).

Step One:
There are two ways to add text to your photo book: (1) Choose a page layout that has a text area already in place, so all you have to do is click in the text box and start typing. Or, (2) you can add a text caption to any page by going to the Text panel (in the right side Panels area) and turning on the Photo Text check-box (as shown here). Now you'll see a yellow horizontal text box appear across the bottom of your image. To add your caption, just click and start typing.

Step Two:
The Align With Photo checkbox keeps your caption aligned with your photo when you add padding to the photo's cell. So, as you shrink your photo within the cell, your caption will shrink within its cell, too. You can tweak exactly how far away your caption is from your photo using the Offset slider—the farther you drag it to the right, the farther away the text moves from your image (as shown here). Note: If you want to have Lightroom select a text box for you, go under the Edit menu and choose **Select All Text Cells** (this is handy if you have a page with three photos and three captions, and you want to turn all the captions off—just choose Select All Text Cells and then turn the Photo Text checkbox off to hide them from view).

Step Three:

You also have the choice to move your caption above your photo, or to put your caption right over the photo itself (as seen here) using the three buttons below the Offset slider: Above, Over, and Below. Click the Over button and your text box now appears right over the photo, and the Offset slider controls how high your caption appears over it (as you slide it back and forth, you'll see your caption move up and down the photo). *Note:* If you choose to add a caption to a full-page photo layout, the only option you'll have for placement is Over, since there's no white space above or below the photo to fit a caption.

Step Four:

By default, your text is aligned with the left side of your photo, but if you go to the bottom of the next panel down, the Type panel, you'll see alignment buttons—you can choose Align Left, Align Center (as shown here), or Align Right (the fourth choice is Justification, which only comes into play if you're using columns of text). *Note:* If your Type panel doesn't look like this one (you see a lot fewer sliders), then you just need to click on the little black left-facing triangle to the far right of the word "Character" and this expands the panel down to show more options.

Continued

Step Five:

While we're in the Type panel, let's go ahead and highlight our text so we can change the color to white (easier to read over this particular photo) by clicking on the black Character color swatch, and when the Character color picker appears, clicking on the white swatch. Now, click on the Align Left button at the bottom of the Type panel. Look how close the text is to the left edge (it's right on it). If you want to offset that text (scoot it out a little from the edge), there isn't a slider for that. Instead, click off the photo (in that white area around it), then hover your cursor over the left end of the text box and it will change to a two-headed arrow. Now you can click-and-drag your text over to the right a bit (as shown here). *Note:* I have to warn you that getting this two-headed arrow cursor to actually appear may take a few tries. It's, shall we say, "finicky." You can also use it to drag the text box up/down by moving it over the top/bottom of the text box. Again, finicky though.

Step Six:

All the other standard controls that you'd expect for working with type are here (like Size, Opacity, and Leading [the space between two lines of text]), but there are also some more advanced type controls that I didn't expect (like Tracking [the space between all the letters in a word], Kerning [the space between two individual letters], and Baseline [shifting a letter or number above or below the line the text sits on—helpful for writing things like H_2O]). And, of course, you can choose your Font and Style (bold, italic, and so on) from the menus near the top. But, at the top is a very handy thing—Text Style presets, which are already set up using popular fonts and styles. So, if you're working on a travel book and choose Caption – Serif, you get a font style that's appropriate for travel photo books. A nice time saver.

Step Seven:

While we're talking presets: if you tweak your text and like it, you can save the settings as a preset (choose **Save Current Settings as New Preset** from the Text Style Preset pop-up menu). That way, the next time you don't have to start from scratch. If you'd like to add another line of text (besides your caption), go back to the Text panel and turn on Page Text (as shown here). This adds another line of text, lower down the page (you can control how far below the photo it appears using the Offset slider, just like the Photo Text). Of course, you can use the Type panel to choose your font, alignment, and all that stuff just like usual, but remember to highlight your text first.

Step Eight:

If you'd like a more visual approach to your type tweaks (rather than dragging sliders or choosing numbers), then click on the Targeted Adjustment tool (TAT, for short—it's circled in red here). Now you can click-and-drag on your highlighted text to change the Size or Leading. Just move your cursor directly over your text, and click-and-drag up/down to control the space between two lines of text (Leading) or drag left/right to control the Size of your type (that's what I'm doing here). Honestly, I don't find myself using the TAT for Type tasks—it seems easier and faster to just move the sliders, but hey, that's just me. So, that's the scoop on adding captions and text to your photo book. *Note:* If you chose a layout where you can add a lot of text, you can split that text into multiple columns using the Columns slider at the bottom of the Type panel. The Gutter slider controls the amount of space between your columns—dragging to the right increases the amount of space between them.

Adding and Customizing Page Numbers

Another nice Book module feature in Lightroom is automatic page numbering. You have the ability to control the position, the formatting (font, size, etc.), and even which page the numbering starts on (along with how to hide the page numbers on blank pages if you want).

Step One:

To turn on page numbering, go to the Page panel and turn on the Page Numbers checkbox (shown circled here in red). By default, it places page numbers in the bottom-left corner of left pages and the bottom-right of right pages.

Step Two:

You can choose where you'd like them to appear using the pop-up menu to the right of the Page Numbers checkbox. The Top and Bottom options center the page number at the top or bottom of the page (respectively; as shown here, where I moved them to the bottom center). Choosing Side places the page number at the outside center of the page and, obviously, choosing Top Corner will move it to the top corner of the page.

Step Three:
Once your numbers are visible, you can format them (choosing a custom font, size, etc.) by highlighting any page number, then going to the Type panel and choosing how you want them to appear (here, I changed the font to Minion Pro and I lowered the Size to 12 pt).

Step Four:
Besides just customizing their look, you can also choose which page the numbering starts on. For example, if the first page of your photo book is blank (so the images or opening story start on a right page), you can have that right page become page 1 by Right-clicking directly on the page number itself on the right page and, from the pop-up menu that appears, choosing **Start Page Number** (as shown here). Lastly, if you have a blank page(s) in your book (maybe all the left pages), and you don't want it to have a printed page number, just Right-click on the number on the blank page, and from the pop-up menu that appear, choose **Hide Page Number**.

Four Things You'll Want to Know About Layout Templates

There are a few things about making books in Lightroom that aren't really obvious, so I thought I'd put them all together here so you don't have to go digging for them. It's all easy stuff, but since Adobe likes to sneak some features in "under the radar," or give them names that only Stephen Hawking could figure out, I thought this might keep you from reaching for a pistol. Ya know, metaphorically speaking. ;-)

#1: The Advantage of Match Long Edges (and How to Do It Manually)

If you create an Auto Layout preset (see page 322) and choose Zoom Photos to Fit, there's a checkbox for Match Long Edges. With that turned off, if you put a wide photo and a tall photo on the same page, the tall photo will be much larger than the wide photo (as shown here, left). If you turn on Match Long Edges, then it balances the size, even though the two photos have different orientations (as shown here, right). If you didn't use Auto Layout, and you still want that balanced look, just hover your cursor over the corner of the tall image and it changes into a two-headed arrow. Click-and-drag inward to visually shrink the photo until it balances the size.

Match Long Edges off looks way out of balance

Match Long Edges on sizes it down to look more balanced

#2: Saving Your Favorite Layouts

If you see a layout you like and want to use again (without having to remember where to find it), you can save it to your Favorites at the top of the Modify Page pop-up menu by hovering your cursor over it, then clicking on the little circle that looks like a Quick Collection marker (as shown here). If you change your mind, go to your Favorites, and click on the now-gray circle to turn it off. Also, once you've set up some favorites, if you create an Auto Layout preset, one of the page choices in the Editor will be Random From Favorites—it pulls the layout from ones you like. You even get to choose how many photos per page it includes (that way, if you only want 1- or 2-photo favorites, it'll only use those). Cool!

#3: Sorting Pages

You sort pages in Multi-Page View by clicking on the page you want to move to select it, then you click directly on the yellow bar at the bottom where the page number is (as shown here, where I've clicked on page 17), and then you just drag-and-drop that page where you want it in your book. If you want to move a two-page spread, click on the first page to select it, Shift-click on the second page to select it, and then click on either page number area to drag-and-drop the spread to a new location. You can even move groups of pages at once (like pages 10 through 15) by Shift-clicking on those pages to select them, then clicking on any one of the selected pages' yellow bar at the bottom, and dragging them where you want them. By the way, you can swap photos from page to page when you're in the Multi-Page View by just clicking-and-dragging them.

#4: The Front & Back Covers Change If You Choose Dust Jacket

If you choose the Hardcover Dust Jacket cover option for your book, you get to add two extra images on the flaps that fold inside the covers to keep your dust jacket in place (as seen here). You'll only see these side flaps appear if you choose the dust jacket option.

#5: I Know, I Said There Were Only Four, But...

There's one more page you might want to consider in your book: Blurb's logo page, which is the last page in the book. If you let them put their logo at the bottom of the last page, they give you a discount on the price of your book. How much? Well, on this book, the regular price was $46.16 without the logo page. If you turn on the option to allow a logo page (in the Book Settings panel), then the price comes down to $38.99 (that's almost a 20% discount for giving them a logo on a page that was going to be blank anyway. Definitely worth considering).

Customizing Your Backgrounds

By default, all your book pages have white backgrounds, but it doesn't have to be that way. Here are four different ways to colorize or customize your page backgrounds:

Step One:

If you want to change the background color of your page, go to the Background panel and turn on the Background Color checkbox. Choose a new color by clicking on the color swatch to bring up the Background Color picker, and click on any of the preset color swatches at the top, or choose any shade from the gradient bar below. To access all colors, click-and-drag the little horizontal bar on the gradient bar on the far right upward to start revealing the colors.

Step Two:

Besides just a solid color for your background, you can also choose from a collection of built-in background graphics, including one for travel with things like maps and page borders, and one for weddings with elegant little page ornaments. To get to these, turn on the Graphic checkbox, then to the right of the square background graphic well in the center of the panel, click the little black button to bring up the Add Background Graphic menu, with a thumbnail list of built-in backgrounds (as seen here). Just click on a category at the top, then scroll down to the graphic you want to use, click on it, and it appears behind your photo (as seen here). You can control how light/dark the graphic is using the Opacity slider and change its color by clicking on the color swatch (more on this in the next step).

Step Three:

If you want a pattern, rather than a graphic, you can add vertical lines, and better yet, you can choose their color. First, go to the Travel category and choose the lines background from the pop-up menu. Set its Opacity (lightness or darkness), then click on the color swatch to the right of the Graphic checkbox to bring up the Graphic color picker (seen here) and choose any color you'd like for your line pattern (I chose an orange color here, and lowered the Opacity to 32% to make it fade into the background a bit more).

Step Four:

There is one more Background panel option, but before we get to that, look up at the top of the Background panel and you'll find the Apply Background Globally checkbox. Turning this on will repeat your current background throughout the entire book (if that's what you want), and it saves you the time of adding the background manually to every single page (I leave this off, so I can customize my page backgrounds individually). Okay, now on to the last option: using a photo as a background (very popular in wedding albums). In the Filmstrip, find the photo you want to use as a background, drag-and-drop it onto the square background graphic well in the center of the Background panel (as shown here), and that photo becomes your page background. I usually like this background photo to be very light behind my main photo (so it doesn't compete with it), so I lower the Opacity quite a bit—usually to between 10% and 20%. By the way, to remove your background image altogether, Right-click on the background graphic well and choose **Remove Photo**.

Helping with Layouts and Printing Outside of Blurb

Here are a few more things you'll probably want to know about (well, you actually might not need these at all, but if you do, and you go looking for them, at least they're here, right?):

Page Guides:

If you'd like some visual guides to help you align things, Lightroom's got you covered. You turn on/off these non-printing guides in the Guides panel in the right side Panels area. There are four types of guides: (1) Page Bleed, lets you see the small area on the very outside edge of your page that will be cropped off if you choose to have a photo fill the page. It only crops off around 1/8", so you won't even notice it. (2) The Text Safe Area guide shows the area where you can add text without it getting lost in the gutter between spreads or being too close to the outside edges. (3) The Photo Cells guide is the one that appears when you click on a photo anyway, so I leave that off for sure, and lastly, (4) the Filler Text guide puts dummy text in place for layouts that have text (so you'll see where you can add type).

Saving Your Book as a PDF or JPEG:

You don't have to send your book to Blurb for printing—you can save it as a PDF or JPEG and have it printed wherever you'd like. You choose this in the Book Settings panel at the top of the right side Panels area. From the Book pop-up menu, choose either to print to Blurb, or make a PDF or JPEG (it creates an individual JPEG of each page). If you choose PDF or JPEG, you'll then get to choose the quality of the photos (I set this to 80), the color profile (many photo labs recommend sRGB), the resolution (I set mine to 240 ppi), the sharpening strength, and the type of paper (I use High and Glossy).

If you want to create your cover text here in Lightroom's Book module, you're in luck, because it's more powerful and flexible than you might think. You can create multiple lines on the cover, different text blocks with different typefaces, and you can even add text to the spine for hardcover wrap layouts.

Creating Cover Text

Step One:
Click on the Front Cover page to make it active, and you'll see "Add Photo Text" appear over the bottom center of the image. Click on that and a text block appears at the bottom of your image. Any text you enter in this text block will appear over your image. By the way, if for any reason you don't see the Add Photo Text button, go to the Text panel (in the right side Panels area) and turn on the Photo Text checkbox (as seen circled here) and it will appear. In our case, I typed in "Magical Morocco," but it's hard to see because the default type is small and black (don't worry, we'll change that in a few moments).

Step Two:
Like I mentioned, by default your text block appears near the bottom of the image, but you can choose how high on the page this text block appears using the Offset slider in the Photo Text section of the Text panel (as shown here). The farther you drag the Offset slider, the farther up that text block moves (as seen here, where I moved it to the top).

Continued

Step Three:

Once you have your text block positioned where you want it, you can control everything from the color of the text to the size, leading (space between two or more lines of type), tracking (the space between all the letters in your text), and even the justification (left, center, right, justified) in the Type panel. This is a pretty darn surprisingly powerful panel, with lots of nice options to make your type look great. We'll start by changing our font and font size. So, click-and-drag over your text to select it, then in the Type panel, choose a font from the first pop-up menu and adjust the Size (I choose P22 Cezanne Pro at 54 points). If you need to change the color of the type, just click on the Character color swatch to bring up the Character color picker and choose a new color there (I changed it to white here).

Step Four:

Now, all we have to do is adjust the placement, as needed. Here, I clicked on the Align Center button at the bottom of the panel to move the type in the middle, and then I clicked on the top of the text box and dragged it down a bit.

TIP: Getting a Second Text Block

If you go back to the Text panel and turn on the Page Text checkbox, you can add a second block of text that you can position and style any way you'd like.

Step Five:

If you want a second line of type in the same text block, just put your cursor after the last letter and hit the Return (PC: Enter) key on your keyboard. The nice thing is this second line can be edited completely separately from the first line, so you can type in your text, select it, then choose a different font (I chose Minion Pro), change the size (I made it 18 points), and you can control the space between the letters using the Tracking slider. I also used the Leading slider to add more space between them (here, I increased it to 50.3). Finally, I clicked on the top of the text box and dragged it down a bit.

Step Six:

If you're printing a hardcover image wrap book, you also have the option of adding type to the spine. Just move your cursor over the spine (between the front and back cover) and a vertical text block will appear. Click inside it and start typing to add your text sideways down the spine (as seen here). You can edit the font, color, position, etc., just like you would any other text block.

TIP: Choosing a Color for the Spine

Go to the Background panel, turn on the Background Color checkbox, then click on its color swatch and choose a new color. Even better tip: when the Background Color picker appears, click-and-hold your mouse button down anywhere in the picker and, while still holding down the mouse, move the Eyedropper tool out over your cover photo and steal a color.

Custom Template Workaround

If you want a layout for your photo book that is more ambitious than the simple custom page layouts you just learned about, then you can do a pretty slick little workaround (which I learned from Adobe's own Lightroom Evangelist, Julieanne Kost), which is to go to the Print module, design any custom page layout you want (at the same size as your book) with the photos you want, save it as a JPEG file, and import that finished layout into Lightroom as if it was just one photo. It's not actually a template, but it looks like you used one.

Step One:

First, jump over to Lightroom's Print module, and click on the Page Setup button in the lower-left corner. When the Page Setup (PC: Print Setup) dialog appears, from the Paper Size pop-up menu, choose **Manage Custom Sizes** to bring up the dialog you see here (on a PC, click the Properties button, then in the Paper Options section, click the Custom button). You're going to create a new preset size (so you don't have to go through this again). Click the + (plus sign) button (shown circled here in red), and enter 7 in for both Width and Height (PC: Length), for Blurb's Small Square 7x7" book. On a Mac, you'll need to set all your margins (left, top, right, bottom) to 0 in, then click OK twice. Now this template is one click away in the future. While you're here, though, you might want to create presets for all the Blurb sizes (like 10x8", 8x10", 13x10", and 13x13").

Step Two:

Now design any layout you'd like in the Print module. For this layout, I used one of the built-in presets that comes with Lightroom called 4 Wide (found in the Template Browser panel in the left side Panels area). Once the template appeared, I selected the four photos I wanted in this layout, then I turned the Identity Plate checkbox off in the Page panel in the right side Panels area. I only changed two small settings in the Layout panel, so it all fits nicely in the 7x7 square we're using. I set the bottom and top margins to 0.44 in and left the sides at 0.50 in, which gives you the layout you see here (there isn't a layout exactly like this in the Book module's templates).

Step Three:

Although I used a built-in print template here, you can use the Print module's Custom Package feature (found up in the Layout Style panel at the top of the right side Panels area) to start with a blank page and create any type of layout you want (see Chapter 12 for more on this). Okay, once you've got your page set up the way you want it to look here in the Print module, scroll down to the Print Job panel and, where it says Print To, go ahead and choose **JPEG File** (as shown here). Set your Print Sharpening and Media Type to whichever settings you use (again, see Chapter 12 for more on this), then turn on the checkbox for Custom File Dimensions (so it uses the 7x7" custom size you created). Click the Print to File button to save this single 7x7" page as a JPEG file.

Step Four:

Now go to the Library module, and press **Command-Shift-I (PC: Ctrl-Shift-I)** to bring up the Import window. Find that JPEG file you just created and import it into Lightroom. Once it comes in, drag it into the collection you created for your photo book, then jump back to the Book module. Go to the page in your book where you want this 4 Wide image to appear. Right-click on the image on that page and choose **Remove Photo**, so it's just an empty page. From the Modify Page pop-up menu, choose a layout where the photo will fill the entire page, then simply find your 4 Wide image in the Filmstrip and drag it onto this empty page to get the layout you see here. The downside is that it's not a template—it's a fixed page (a flattened JPEG like any other photo). The upside is that you've got a page in your book where you created the layout from scratch exactly the way you wanted it.

CHAPTER 12

PRINTING
unlocking the power of the print

Okay, I'm giving you fair warning. I'm gonna go on a bit of a rant here, because I feel so strongly about making prints. The print is when a photograph is born. What you see on your computer screen isn't real. It's pixels and 1s and 0s trapped behind a thin sheet of glass. You can't touch it, or taste it, or feel it—it's digital. A print is real. But, let's put aside the whole "real" part for now and think about this as saving your images for future generations. Got your photos all backed up on a hard drive? Good! That'll last at least three years, maybe four or five, if you're lucky. If you accidentally knock one over while it's running, or it falls off your desk, it's a goner. It's not just hard drives. You can back up your photos on CDs, DVDs, optical drives—you name it. They all have a short shelf life and it's not "if" they'll die, it's when. But, you know what lasts at least 100 years? Prints. Say what you want about that

old shoebox of prints our parents left us; it worked. The fact they made prints and stuck them in a shoe box is the reason why we have any visual history of our early lives at all. Prints live on after we're gone. So, how can you ensure your prints last even longer? It's easy: make a set of prints of your portfolio images, then book a flight to Spitsbergen, a small Norwegian island in the Arctic Svalbard archipelago. Ask for directions to the Svalbard Global Seed Vault, and when you get there, ask for Earl (tell him I sent you) and let him know you want to store your prints there. Your prints will be pretty secure there thanks to the frigid arctic air, six super-thick steel security doors, and the perennially cranky polar bears that roam nearby looking for a handout. Also, it wouldn't hurt if you took Earl a Bacon Swiss Crispy Chicken Fillet Sandwich from Carl's Jr. and a medium Diet Dr. Pepper. He really likes that.

Printing Individual Photos

If you really like everything else in Lightroom, it's the Print module where you'll fall deeply in love. It's really brilliantly designed (I've never worked with any program that had a better, easier, and more functional printing feature than this). The built-in templates make the printing process not only easy, but also fun (plus, they make a great starting point for customizing and saving your own templates).

Step One:

Before you do anything in the Print module, click on the Page Setup button at the bottom left, and choose your paper size (so you won't have to resize your layout once it's all in place). Now, start in the Template Browser (in the left side Panels area) by clicking on the Fine Art Mat template. The layout you see here should appear, displaying the first photo in your current collection (unless you have a photo selected—then it shows that one). There's a Collections panel here, too, so if you want to change collections, you can do so in the left side Panels area. A few lines of info may appear over the top-left corner of your photo. It doesn't actually print on the photo itself, but if you find it distracting, you can turn this off by pressing the letter **I**, or going under the View menu and choosing **Show Info Overlay**.

Step Two:

If you want to print more than one photo using this same template, go down to the Filmstrip and Command-click (PC: Ctrl-click) on the photos you want to print, and it instantly adds as many pages as you need (here, you see just one image, but if you look down in the toolbar, you can see that this is print 1 of 19). There are three layout styles (in the Layout Style panel at the top right), and this first one is called Single Image/Contact Sheet. This works by putting each photo in a cell you can resize. To see this photo's cell, go to the Guides panel and turn on the Show Guides checkbox. Now you can see the page margins (in light gray), and your image cell (outlined in black, as seen here).

Step Three:

If you look back at the layout in Step Two, did you notice that the image fit the cell side-to-side, but there was a gap on the top and bottom? That's because, by default, it tries to fit your image in that cell so the entire image is visible. If you want to fill the cell with your photo, go to the Image Settings panel and turn on the Zoom to Fill checkbox (as shown here), and now your image fills it up (as seen here). Now, of course, this crops the image a bit, too (well, at least with this layout it did). This Zoom to Fill feature was designed to help you make contact sheets, but as we go through this chapter, I bet you'll totally start to love this little checkbox, because with it you can create some really slick layouts—ones your clients will love. So, even though it does crop the photo a bit, don't dismiss this puppy yet—it's going to get really useful very soon.

Step Four:

Now, let's work on the whole cell concept, because if you "get" this, the rest is easy. First, because your image is inside a cell and you have the Zoom to Fill checkbox turned on, if you change the size of your cell, the size of your photo doesn't change. So, if you make the cell smaller, it crops off part of your image, which is really handy when you're making layouts. To see what I mean, go to the Layout panel, and at the bottom of the panel are the Cell Size sliders. Drag the Height slider to the left (down to 4.41 in), and look at how it starts to shrink the entire image size down right away, until it reaches its original unzoomed width, then the top and bottom of the cell move inward without changing the width further. This kind of gives you a "letter box" view of your image (HD movie buffs will totally get that analogy).

Continued

Step Five:

Now drag the Height slider back to the right, kind of where it was before, then drag the Width slider to the left to shrink the width. This particular photo is wide (in landscape orientation), so while moving the top and bottom of the cell shrank the image, and then the cell, dragging the Width slider like we are here, just shrinks the cell inward (this will all make sense in a minute). See how the left and right sides of your cell have moved in, creating the tall, thin cell you see here? This tall, thin layout is actually kind of cool on some level (well, it's one you don't see every day, right?), but the problem is that the center of the fireplace is on the left side of the frame. We can fix that.

TIP: Print Module Shortcut

When you want to jump over to the Print module, you can use the same keyboard shortcut you do in almost any program that lets you print: it's the standard old **Command-P (PC: Ctrl-P)**.

Step Six:

One of my favorite things about using these cell layouts is that you can reposition your image inside the cell. Just move your cursor over the cell, and your cursor turns into the Hand tool. Now, just click-and-drag the image inside the cell to the position you want it. In this case, I just slid the photo over to the right a bit until the middle of the fireplace was in the center.

Step Seven:

At the bottom of the Cell Size section is a checkbox called "Keep Square." Go ahead and turn on this checkbox, which sets your Height and Width to the exact same size, and now they move together as one unit (since it's perfectly square). Let's try a different way of resizing the cell: click-and-drag the cell borders themselves, right on the layout in the Preview area. You see those vertical and horizontal lines extending across and up/down the page showing the boundaries of your cell? You can click-and-drag directly on them, so go ahead and give it a try. Here, I'm clicking on the top horizontal guide (shown circled here in red), and dragging outward to enlarge my square cell (and the photo inside it). So, by now you've probably realized that the cell is like a window into your photo.

TIP: Rotating Images

If you have a tall photo in a wide cell (or on a wide page), you can make your photo fill as much of that page as possible by going to the Image Settings panel, and turning on the Rotate to Fit checkbox.

Step Eight:

Let's finish this one off with one of my favorite printing features in Lightroom: the ability to change the color of your page background. To do this, just go to the Page panel, turn on the Page Background Color checkbox, and click the color swatch to the right of it to bring up the Page Background Color picker (seen here). In this case, I'm choosing black, but you can choose any color you'd like (dark gray, blue, red—you name it), then close the color picker. Also, you can put a stroke around your image cell by going up to the Image Settings panel, turning on the checkbox for Stroke Border, then choosing a color (just click on the color swatch), and choosing how thick you want your stroke using the Width slider.

Creating Multi-Photo Contact Sheets

The reason you jumped through all those hoops just to print one photo was because the whole Single Image/Contact Sheet was really designed for you to have quick access to multi-photo layouts and contact sheets, which is where this all gets really fun. We're picking up here, with another set of photos, to show you how easy it is to create really interesting multi-photo layouts that clients just love!

Step One:

Start by clicking on any of the multi-photo templates that come with Lightroom (if you hover your cursor over any of the templates in the Template Browser, a preview of the layout will appear in the Preview panel at the top of the left side Panels area). For example, click on the 2x2 Cells template, and it puts your selected photos in two columns and two rows (as shown here). Here, I selected six photos, and if you look down at the right end of the toolbar, you'll see Lightroom will make two prints, although only one will have four photos—the second print will just have those two leftover photos. The layout you see here doesn't look that good, because they're all horizontal photos in vertical cells, but we can fix that. It would look worse if there were tall photos mixed in.

Step Two:

Of course, just printing all your wide photos on a page with wide cells, and then creating a second template with tall cells, would fix that, but an easier way is to go to the Image Settings panel and turn on the Zoom to Fill checkbox (as shown here). This zooms all the images up to fill the cells, so the wide photos zoom in, and how they fill the cells looks uniform (as seen here). Plus, you can reposition the images in their cells by clicking-and-dragging them. However, turning on Zoom to Fill usually crops a tiny bit off of tall shots, and quite a bit off the wide shots, changing the whole look of the photos (luckily, there is a way around this, too).

Step Three:
What you need is a way to print tall images and wide images together at nearly full size, without much cropping. The trick is to turn on the Rotate to Fit checkbox (as shown here), which rotates the wide photos so they best fill the tall cells (as seen here, where the wide photos are now turned sideways to fit in the cells as large as possible). When you turn on Rotate to Fit, it applies that to all your pages, so if you have other wide photos on other pages, it will rotate them, as well.

Step Four:
If you want to print the same photo, at the same exact size, multiple times on the same page, then you can go to the Image Settings panel and turn on the checkbox for Repeat One Photo per Page, as shown here. If you want to print the same photo multiple times on the same page, but you want them to be different sizes (like one 5x7" and four wallet-size photos), then turn to page 364 for details on how to set that up.

Continued

Step Five:

If you click on a different multi-photo layout, like the 4x5 Contact Sheet (as shown here), your photos instantly adjust to the new layout. One nice feature of this template is that the names of your images appear directly below each image. If you want to turn this feature off, go to the Page panel and, near the bottom of the panel, turn off the Photo Info checkbox. By the way, when you have this checkbox turned on, you can choose other text to appear under your images from the pop-up menu to the right of the words Photo Info. Here, I turned on the Zoom to Fill checkbox, but of course, that's totally optional—if you don't want your images cropped, then you should leave Zoom to Fill turned off.

Step Six:

So far, we've been using Lightroom's built-in templates, but half the fun of this process is building your own, and it's surprisingly easy, as long as you don't mind having all your cells being the same exact size, which is the limitation of using the Single Image/Contact Sheet type of layout. You can't have one photo that's square, and two that are rectangular. They're either all square or all rectangular, but don't worry, we'll tackle how to create multiple photos at any size you want a little later. For now, we'll use this contact sheet power to create some cool layouts. Start by selecting some photos (eight or nine should be fine), then click on the template called "Maximize Size" (shown here; it's a decent starting place for building your own templates). Since we're going to be adding photos, I turned off the Rotate to Fit checkbox (it's on by default in this template) in the Image Settings panel.

Step Seven:

You create custom multi-photo layouts in the Layout panel. There's a Page Grid section, which is where you pick how many rows and columns you want in your layout, so start by dragging the Rows slider over to 3, while leaving the Columns set at 1, so you get three photos each in their own row (like you see here). You'll notice that the three photos are stacked one on top of another with no space between them. *(Note:* The black lines you see around the cells are just guides, so you can easily see where the cell borders are. You can get rid of these in the Guides panel by turning off the Image Cells checkbox.)

Step Eight:

To create some vertical space between your photos, go to the Cell Spacing section and click-and-drag the Vertical slider to the right (as shown here, where I dragged it over to 0.68 in to put a little more than a half-inch of space between the photos). Now let's take things up a notch.

Continued

Step Nine:

Now go to the Page Grid sliders and increase the Columns to 3, so you have this layout of three columns wide by three rows deep. Of course, since the default setting is to not have any space between photos, the columns of photos don't have any space between them horizontally.

Step 10:

You add space between the photos in columns by going to the Cell Spacing section, and clicking-and-dragging the Horizontal slider to the right (as shown here). Now that you've got space between your columns, take a look at the page margins. There's lots of space at the top and bottom, and just a little bit of space on the sides of the page.

Step 11:

Although you can drag the Margins sliders to adjust the page margins (right there in the Layout panel), you can also just click directly on the margins themselves and drag them (as shown here). Here, I clicked-and-dragged the top, bottom, and side margins in to where they were about a half-inch from the edge of the page. While we're here, let's go back up to the Image Settings panel and turn on the Zoom to Fill checkbox to fill the cells with the images, as seen here (don't forget, you can reposition your images inside those cells by just clicking-and-dragging them).

Step 12:

If you want to see the full image (not zoomed in tight), but still have them fill the cells, you could turn on the Rotate to Fit checkbox right there in the Image Settings panel, as well. Now all the photos are turned on their sides, so they fit the full width of each cell as large as possible (as seen here).

Continued

Step 13:

Let's wrap this section up with a few examples of cool layouts you can create using these Contact Sheet style layouts (all based on a borderless 8.5x11" page size, which you can choose by clicking the Page Setup button at the bottom of the left side Panels area). Start by turning on the Zoom to Fill checkbox in the Image Settings panel. Then, go to the Layout panel, under Page Grid, and change the number of Rows to 1 and the number of Columns to 3. Drag the Left, Right, and Top Margins sliders to around 0.75 in, and the Bottom Margins slider to around 2.75 (to leave lots of room for your Identity Plate). Jump down to Cell Spacing and set Horizontal to 0.13. Under Cell Size, for the Height, drag it to around 7.50 in, and set the Width at only around 2.24 in, which gives you very tall, narrow cells (as shown here). Now, select three photos and turn on the Identity Plate feature (in the Page panel), make it larger, and click-and-drag it so it's centered below your images, giving you the look you see here (I also turned off the Show Guides checkbox). *Note:* If you like this layout, you can save it as a custom preset (see page 369).

Step 14:

Now let's create four panorama layouts in one photo (you don't need to use real panos—this creates fake panos instantly from any photo you select). Start by turning on the Zoom to Fill checkbox and setting your Rows to 4 and Columns to 1. Then set your Left and Right Margins to 0.50 in, and set the Top to around 0.75 in or 0.80 in. Set your Bottom margin to 1.50 in. Turn off the Identity Plate checkbox in the Page panel, then increase your Cell Size Width to 7.30 in, and your Cell Size Height to 1.81 in to give you thin, wide cells. Now, set the space between your fake panos using the Vertical slider (set it to around 0.50) to give you the layout you see here. I went and clicked on four travel photos, and got this instant pano layout here.

Step 15:

How about a poster, on black, with 36 wide images? Easy. Start by creating a collection made up of only wide images. Then go to the Image Settings panel and turn on the Zoom to Fill checkbox. Go to the Layout panel and set a 1-inch margin all the way around the page, using the Margins sliders. Now, set your Page Grid to 9 Rows and 4 Columns, and set your Horizontal and Vertical Cell Spacing at 0.14 in. Lastly, in the Page panel, turn on the Page Background Color check-box, then click on the color swatch to the right of it, and choose black for your background color. If you have a white border, click on the Page Setup button and choose borderless printing.

Step 16:

Okay, this one's kinda wild—one photo split into five separate thin vertical cells. Here's how it's done: You start by clicking the Page Setup button (at the bottom left), and set your page to be Landscape orientation. Then Right-click on a photo in the Filmstrip and choose **Create Virtual Copy**. You need to do this three more times, so you have a total of five copies of your photo. Now, in the Image Settings panel, turn on Zoom to Fill, then in the Layout panel, set your Margins to 0.50 in all the way around the page. For your Page Grid, choose 1 Rows and 5 Columns. Add a little Horizontal Cell Spacing— around 0.25 in. Then, drag the Cell Size Height slider to around 7.50 in and the Width to around 1.80 in. Select all five photos in the Filmstrip, then you'll click-and-drag each of the five images around inside their cells—dragging left and right—until they appear to be one single image (like you see here).

Creating Custom Layouts Any Way You Want Them

In Lightroom, Adobe also gives you the option to break away from the structured cell layouts of earlier versions to create your own custom cell layouts in any size, shape, and placement, using a Print layout style called "Custom Package." Here's where you can create photos in any size and any layout you want, without being tied into a grid.

Step One:

Start in the Layout Style panel by clicking on Custom Package (we want to start from scratch, so if you see any cells already in place, go to the Cells panel and click the Clear Layout button). There are two ways to get photos onto your page: The first is to go down to the Filmstrip and simply to drag-and-drop images right onto your page (as seen here). The image appears inside its own fully resizable cell, so you can just drag one of the corner handles to resize the image (this image came in pretty small, so I resized it to nearly fill the bottom of the page). It will resize proportionally by default, but if you turn off the Lock to Photo Aspect Ratio checkbox (at the bottom of the Cells panel), then it acts like a regular cell with Zoom to Fill turned on, in that you can crop the photo using the cell. More on that in a minute.

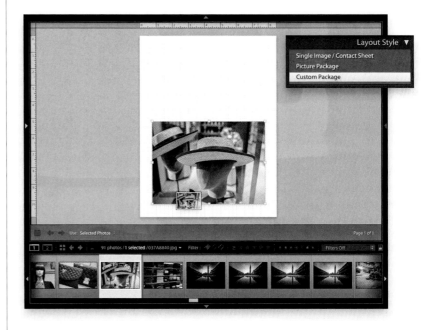

Step Two:

Go ahead and hit the Clear Layout button, so you can try the other way to get your images into your layout, which is to create the cells first, arrange them where you want, then drag-and-drop your images into those cells. You do this by going to the Cells panel, and in the Add to Package section, just click on the size you want. For example, if you wanted to add a 3x7" cell, you'd just click on the 3x7 button (as shown here) and it creates an empty cell that size on the page. Now you can just click inside the cell and drag it anywhere you'd like on the page. Once it's where you like it, you can drag-and-drop a photo into that cell from the Filmstrip.

Step Three:

Let's create a layout using these cell buttons, so hit the Clear Layout button to start from scratch again. Click the 3x7 button to add a long, thin cell to your layout, but then click the Rotate Cell button to make this a tall, thin cell. This cell is actually pretty large on the page, but you can resize it by first making sure the Lock to Photo Aspect Ratio checkbox is turned off, then by grabbing any of the handles, or using the Adjust Selected Cell sliders to choose any size you'd like (here, shrink your Height to around 5.59 in and Width to around 2.21 in). Now, we need to make two more cells just like this one. The quickest way to do that is to press-and-hold the **Option (PC: Alt) key**, then click inside the cell and drag to the right to make a copy. Do this twice until you have three cells and arrange them side by side, as seen here (as you drag a cell, you'll feel it snap to an invisible alignment grid that's there to help you line things up. If you don't feel the snap or see the grid, go to the Rulers, Grid & Guides panel, turn on the checkboxes for Show Guides and Page Grid, and make sure Grid is selected from the Grid Snap pop-up menu).

Step Four:

Next, let's add a larger photo to the bottom of our layout. Click the 4x6 button and it adds a larger cell to the layout, but it's taller and not quite as wide as our three thin cells above. So, set the Height to 3.96 in and the Width to 7.62 in (as seen here). The layout's done, but before you start dragging-and-dropping images, there are two things you need to change first: (1) Because the cells at the top are tall and thin, the checkbox for Lock to Photo Aspect Ratio must be off (we already did this). Otherwise, when you drag-and-drop photos into those thin cells, they will just expand to the full size of the photo. (2) You'll also need to make sure the Rotate to Fit checkbox at the top of the Image Settings panel is turned off, so wide images won't rotate to fit the cell.

Continued

Step Five:

Now you're ready to start dragging-and-dropping photos into your layout. If you drag one that doesn't look good in your layout, just drag another right over it. You can reposition your photo inside a smaller cell by pressing-and-holding the Command (PC: Ctrl) key, then just dragging the image left/right (or up/down), so just the part you want is showing. (*Note:* I turned off the Show Guides checkbox in the Rulers, Grid & Guides panel, here.) Don't forget to save any of these that you like as a custom preset (see page 369 for more).

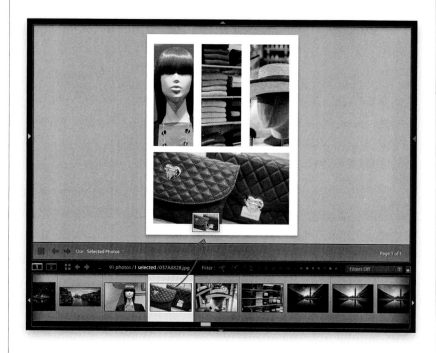

Step Six:

You can stack images so they overlap, almost like they're Photoshop layers. Let's start from scratch again, but first click the Page Setup button (at the bottom left), and turn your page orientation to Landscape. Now go back to the Cells panel, click the Clear Layout button, then click the 8x10 button, resize it, and position it so it takes up most of the page (as shown here). Now, click the 2x2.5 button three times, make each cell a little wider (like the ones seen here), and position them so they overlap the main photo, as shown. Drag-and-drop photos on each cell. You can move the photos in front or behind each other by Right-clicking on the photo, and from the pop-up menu, choosing to send the photo back/forward one level or all the way to the bottom/top of the stack. To add a white photo border around your images (like I did here), in the Image Settings panel, turn on the Photo Border checkbox (turn on the guides to see this better, if you turned them off).

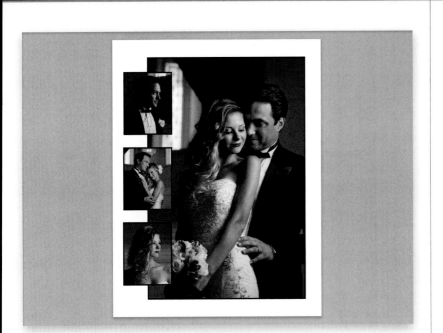

Step Seven:

Want a different look really quick? Try switching your page orientation back to Portrait (tall) and see how that looks. For example, I thought it might make a good wedding book layout, and when I rotated the page, this is pretty much the layout I got without really doing much. Well, I did click-and-drag the side of the main photo to make it a little wider, then I turned off the Photo Border checkbox, turned on the Inner Stroke Border checkbox (also in the Image Settings panel), and added a 2-pt black stroke.

Step Eight:

Here's an alternate look to the page you just created, and it only took about 60 seconds to get from the layout in Step Seven to what you see here. I just changed the Inner Stroke Border to white, and I dragged all of the small images over to the right, so they appear over the main image (instead of peeking in from the side). I also dragged out the sides, top, and bottom of the main image to make it fill the page better. (*Note:* If you saved this layout as a custom preset, you can update it with the changes you made to it by Right-clicking on it in the Template Browser and choosing Update with Current Settings. Again, see page 369 for more on saving custom layouts.)

Adding Text to Your Print Layouts

If you want to add text to your print layouts, it's pretty easy, as well, and like the Web and Slideshow modules, you can have Lightroom automatically pull metadata info from your photos and have it appear on the photo print, or you can add your own custom text (and/or Identity Plate) just as easily. Here's what you can add, and how you can add it:

Step One:
Select a photo, then choose the Fine Art Mat template in the Template Browser and turn on the Zoom to Fill checkbox. The easiest way to add text is to go to the Page panel and turn on the Identity Plate checkbox (see Chapter 4 for how to set it up). Once it's there, you can click-and-drag it right where you want it (in this case, drag it down and position it in the center of the space below the photo, as seen here). Here's the trick I used to get two lines of text, centered, below my photo: I went to my Mac's TextEdit application (any regular text editing application should work), typed and formatted my text there, and copied it into memory. Then, I went to Lightroom's Identity Plate Editor and pasted my copied text (the ol' copy-and-paste routine), and it kept the formatting.

Step Two:
Besides adding your Identity Plate, Lightroom can also pull text from your metadata (things like exposure settings, camera make and model, filename, or caption info you added in the Library module's Metadata panel). In the Page panel, turn on the Photo Info checkbox and choose which type of info you want displayed at the bottom of your cell from the pop-up menu on the right. Here, I chose **Custom Text,** and in the text field that appeared, I typed in the location where the shot was taken (El Centro, California), and you can see it appears directly below my image. You can also change the size of your text from the Font Size pop-up menu right below it.

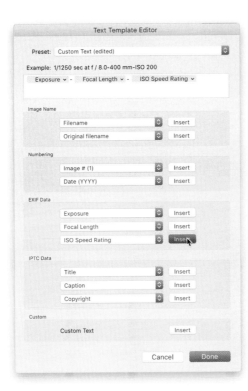

Step Three:

You can also create your own custom list of data that Lightroom will pull from a photo's existing metadata and/or camera data and print under that photo. To do that, in the Page panel, from the Photo Info pop-up menu, choose **Edit** (at the bottom of the menu) to bring up the Text Template Editor (seen here). This is where you choose what info is pulled from the image's metadata, and in this case, I went to the third section down, EXIF Data, where I chose to add text showing the exposure, lens focal length, and ISO by choosing them from the pop-up menus, then clicking the Insert button beside each of these fields. I also typed a dash (on my keyboard), in the text field up top, between each click of the Insert button, so it didn't all run together (it needs that visual separator if you ask me). Now, I can't imagine why anyone would want that type of information printed beneath a photo. But you know, and I know, there's somebody out there right now reading this and thinking, "All right! Now I can put the EXIF camera data right on the print!" The world needs these people.

Step Four:

If you're printing pages for a photo book, you can have Lightroom automatically number those pages. In the Page panel, turn on the Page Options checkbox, then turn on the checkbox for Page Numbers. Lastly, if you're doing a series of test prints, you can have your print settings (including your level of sharpening, your color management profile, and your selected printer) appear near the bottom of the print (as seen here) by turning on the Page Info checkbox.

Printing Multiple Photos on One Page

You saw earlier in this chapter how to print the same photo, at the same exact size, multiple times on the same print. But what if you want to print the same photo at different sizes (like a 5x7" and four wallet sizes)? That's when you want to use Lightroom's Picture Package feature.

Step One:
Start by clicking on the photo you want to have appear multiple times, in multiple sizes, on the same page. Go to the Template Browser in the left side Panels area and click on the built-in template named (1) 4x6, (6) 2x3, which gives you the layout you see here. If you look over in the Layout Style panel at the top of the right side Panels area, you'll see that the selected style is Picture Package (as seen here). *Note:* Here, I made sure the Show Guides checkbox was turned on (in the Rulers, Grid & Guides panel), along with the Image Cells checkbox, so you can see how the cells fit on the page.

Step Two:
By default, this template puts a white border outside each photo. If you don't want the white border, go to the Image Settings panel and turn off the Photo Border checkbox (as seen here), and now the images will be snug up against each other.

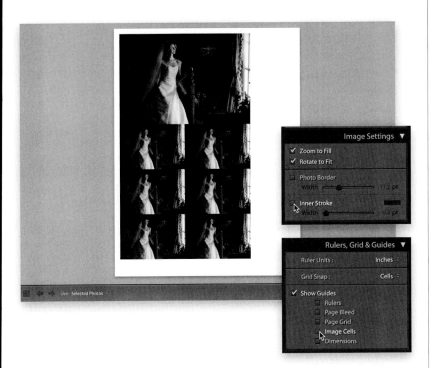

Step Three:

Another option it has on by default is that it puts a black stroke around each image (you can control the size of this stroke, using the Width slider right below the Inner Stroke checkbox). To remove this stroke, turn off the Inner Stroke checkbox (as shown here. You'll still see a thin stroke that separates the images, but don't worry, that doesn't print—that's just the Image Cells guide you're seeing. You can go ahead and turn it off now in the Rulers, Grid & Guides panel, as I have here). Now your images are back to their original cropping, they're right up against each other (there's no extra white border), and you've removed the black stroke around the photos (by the way, if you like this layout, don't forget to save it as your own custom template by clicking on the + [plus sign] button on the right side of the Template Browser header).

Step Four:

Adding more photos is easy—just go to the Cells panel (in the right side Panels area), and you'll see a number of pill-shaped buttons marked with different sizes. Just click on any one of those to add a photo that size to your layout (I clicked on the 2x2.5 button, and it added the new cell you see selected here). So, that's the routine: you click on those buttons to add more photos to your Picture Package layout. To delete a cell, just click on it, then press the **Delete (PC: Backspace) key** on your keyboard.

Continued

Step Five:

If you want to create your own custom Picture Package layout from scratch, go to the Cells panels and click on the Clear Layout button (as shown here), which removes all the cells, so you can start from scratch.

Step Six:

Now you can just start clicking on sizes, and Lightroom will place them on the page each time you click one of those Add to Package buttons (as seen here). As you can see, it doesn't always place the photos in the optimum location for the page dimensions, but Lightroom can actually fix that for you.

Step Seven:
If you click on the Auto Layout button, at the bottom of the Add to Package section (as shown here), it tries to automatically arrange the photos so they fit more logically, and gives you extra space to add more photos. Okay, click the Clear Layout button and let's start from scratch again, so I can show you another handy feature.

TIP: Dragging-and-Copying
If you want to duplicate a cell, just press-and-hold the **Option (PC: Alt) key**, click-and-drag yourself a copy, and position it anywhere you'd like. If one of your photos overlaps another photo, you'll get a little warning icon up in the top-right corner of your page.

Step Eight:
If you add so many cells that they can't fit on one page, Lightroom automatically adds new pages to accommodate your extra cells. For example, start by adding an 8x10, then add a 5x7 (which can't fit on the same letter-sized page), and it automatically creates a new page for you with the 5x7. Now add another 5x7 (so you have two-up), then eight wallet-sized 2.5x3.5s (which won't fit on the same page), and it will add yet another page. Add a couple of 4x6s, and it adds another page. Pretty smart, eh? Also, if you decide you want to add another blank page yourself (this lets you drag an image from one page and drop it on this empty page anywhere you want it), just click on the New Page button (as shown here).

Continued

Step Nine:

If you want to delete a page, just hover your cursor over the page you want to delete, and a little X appears over the top-left corner (as seen here, on the third page). Click on that X and the page is deleted (I already deleted the last two pages we created in the last step, here).

TIP: Zooming In on One Page

Once you have multiple pages like this and you want to work on just one of these pages, you can zoom right in on the page by clicking on it, then clicking on Zoom Page on the right side of the Preview panel header (at the top of the left side Panels area).

Step 10:

You can also manually adjust the size of each cell (which is a handy way to crop your photos on the fly, if you have Zoom to Fill turned on). For example, go ahead and delete the bottom 5x7 image on the second page. Now, click on the top image (to bring up the adjustment handles around the cell), then click-and-drag the bottom handle upward to make the cell thinner (as seen here). You can get the same effect by clicking-and-dragging the Adjust Selected Cell sliders, at the bottom of the Cells panel (there are sliders for both Height and Width), and you can also press-and-hold the Command (PC: Ctrl) key and click-and-drag on the photo to move it within the cell.

If you've come up with a layout you really like and want to be able to apply it at any time with just one click, you need to save it as a template. But beyond just saving your layout, print templates have extra power, because they can remember everything from your paper size to your printer name, color management settings, the kind of sharpening you want applied—the whole nine yards!

Saving Your Custom Layouts as Templates

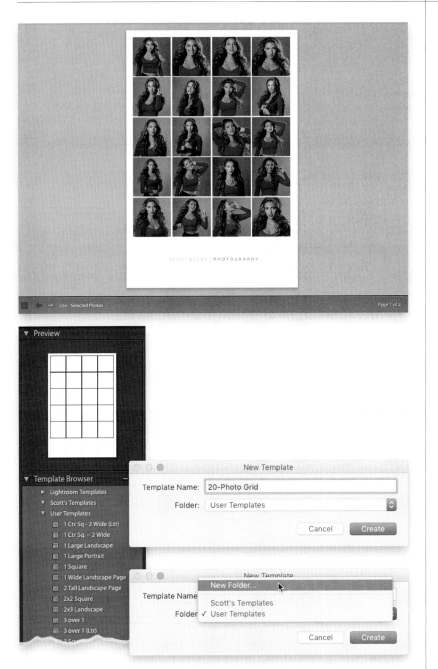

Step One:
Go ahead and set up a page with a layout you like, so you can save it as a print template. The page layout here is based on a 13x19" page (you choose your page size by clicking the Page Setup button at the bottom of the left side Panels area). The layout uses a Page Grid of 5 Rows and 4 Columns. The cell sizes are square (around 3 inches each), and the page has a 1/2" margin on the left, right, and top, with a 3.69" margin at the bottom. I turned on the Stroke Border checkbox and changed the color to white, and turned on my Identity Plate. Also, make sure the Zoom to Fill checkbox (in the Image Settings panel) is turned on.

Step Two:
Once it's set up the way you like it, go to the Template Browser and click the plus sign (+) button on the right side of the header to bring up the New Template dialog (shown here). By default, it wants to save any templates you create into a folder called User Templates (you can have as many folders of print templates as you like to help you organize them. For example, you could have one set for letter-sized, one set for 13x19", one set for layouts that work with portraits, etc.). To create a new template folder, click on the Folder pop-up menu (shown here at bottom), and choose **New Folder**. Give your template a name, click Create, and now this template will appear in the folder you chose. When you hover your cursor over the template, a preview of the template will appear up in the Preview panel at the top of the left side Panels area.

Having Lightroom Remember Your Printing Layouts

Once you've gone through the trouble of creating a cool print layout, with the photos right where you want them on the page, you don't want to lose all that when you change collections, right? Right! Luckily, you can create a saved print, which keeps everything intact—from page size, to the exact layout, to which photos in your collection wound up on the page (and which ones didn't) and in which order. Here's how ya do it:

Step One:

Once you make a print, and you're happy with the final layout (and all your output settings and such, which we'll get into in a bit), click on the Create Saved Print button (shown circled here) that appears above the top-right corner of the center Preview area. This brings up the Create Print dialog (shown here). Here, you'll be saving a print collection. The key thing here, though, is to make sure the Include Only Used Photos checkbox is turned on. That way, when you save this new print collection, only the photos that are actually in this print are saved in it. Also, in the dialog, you'll have the option of including this new print collection inside an existing collection—just turn on the Inside checkbox and then choose the collection or collection set you want it to appear within.

Step Two:

Now click the Create button, and a new print collection is added to the Collections panel (you'll know at a glance that it's a print collection because it will have a printer icon right before the collection's name).That's it! When you click on that print collection and select all the photos in it, you'll see the layout, just the way you designed it, with the images already in order ready to go, including all your output settings (like which printer you printed to, your sharpening and resolution settings—the works!), even if it's a year from now. *Note:* If all your images don't appear in the layout, just go to the Filmstrip and select them all—now they'll appear in your layout.

For all the wonderful things Lightroom's Print module does, one feature it doesn't have is one that lets you backscreen a photo (a staple in most wedding albums). So, I came up with a workaround, where we can use a backscreened image as our page background, and then put another non-backscreened image in front of it on the same page. It's easy, but not really obvious.

Creating Backscreened Prints

Step One:
Choose the photo you want to use as your backscreened image, then create a virtual copy of it by pressing **Command-'** (apostrophe; **PC: Ctrl-'**). We'll use this virtual copy to make our backscreened image, so our original stays intact. Once you've created your virtual copy, go to the Develop module's Tone Curve panel. Make sure the Point Curve is visible (if yours has more sliders below it, and doesn't look like the one you see here, just click on the little Point Curve icon at the bottom-right corner of the panel).

Step Two:
To create the backscreened look, click-and-drag the bottom-left corner point straight up along the left edge until it's about 3/4 or so of the way up to the top (as seen here).

Continued

Step Three:

This is an optional step, but you see this often enough that you might want to consider converting the image you just backscreened to black and white. The advantage is it creates more contrast with the image you're going to put on top of it. To make it a black-and-white image, just go to the top of the Basic panel and click on Black & White (as shown here). That's it—it's black and white. (*Note:* Because the image is backscreened, we can get away with this one-click black-and-white conversion. Otherwise, we'd use the technique for creating high-contrast black-and-whites found in Chapter 7). Now, switch to the Print module, click on the Page Setup button, and choose a borderless 8.5x11" landscape page.

Step Four:

Then, click on Custom Package in the Layout Style panel at the top of the right side Panels area and scroll down to the Cells panel. Click the Clear Layout button, then make sure the Lock to Photo Aspect Ratio checkbox is turned off (turning this off allows you to drag a photo out larger than the page size if necessary). Now, click on your backscreened image, and drag it onto the page. To make your backscreened image fill the page, click-and-drag the image up to the top-left corner of the page, then grab the bottom-right corner point and just drag it out until it fills the entire page, edge to edge (as shown here). If your image won't stretch large enough to extend off the page, that's because you didn't turn off the Lock to Photo Aspect Ratio checkbox at the beginning of this step.

Step Five:

Getting another image to sit on top of this backscreened image is actually easy, but you kind of have to know a trick. The problem is if you add a new cell (like, for example, a 2.5 x 3.5 cell) it doesn't appear on the same page as your backscreened image. Instead, it creates a new page and adds the cell there. So, what you'll need to do is just click-and-drag your full-color photo into that new cell on the extra page (as seen here). Then, click-and-drag the cell onto the first page, and it appears over your backscreened image (as seen in the next step).

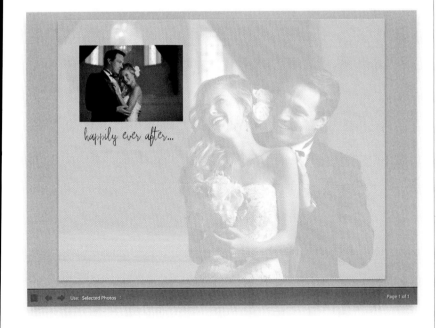

Step Six:

You can now position the image wherever you'd like (you'll see that now-blank additional page is still there, but to get rid of it, just click on the round X button in the top-left corner and it's gone). Here's the final page with the backscreened image and the second image on top of it. I also added a line of text (using the Identity Plate in the Page panel), using the handwritten font, Rough Beauty Script by Pedro Teixeira (from MyFonts.com—I got it on sale for $7).

The Final Print & Color Management Settings

Once you've got your page set up with the printing layout you want, you just need to make a few choices in the Print Job panel, so your photos look their best when printed. Here are which buttons to click, when, and why:

Step One:

Get your page layout the way you want it to look. In the capture shown here, I clicked on Page Setup at the bottom of the left side Panels area, chose a 17x22" page size, set my page to a wide (landscape) orientation, and then I went to the Template Browser and clicked on the Maximize Size template. I set my Left, Right, and Top Margins sliders to 2.00 in, and my Bottom Margins slider to 5.00 in. I also turned on the Zoom to Fill checkbox. Lastly, I added my Identity Plate below the photo, and I lowered the opacity to make it appear gray. Once that's done, it's time to choose our printing options in the Print Job panel, at the bottom of the right side Panels area.

Step Two:

You have the choice of sending your image to your printer, or just creating a high-resolution JPEG file of your photo layout (that way, you could send this finished page to a photo lab for printing, or email it to a client as a high-res proof, or use the layout on a website, or…whatever). You choose whether it's going to output the image to a printer or save it as a JPEG from the Print To pop-up menu, at the top right of the Print Job panel (as seen here). If you want to choose the Print to JPEG File route, go to the next tutorial in this chapter for details on how to use the JPEG settings and export the file.

Step Three:
Since we've already started at the top, we'll just kind of work our way down. The next setting down in the panel is a checkbox for Draft Mode Printing, and when you turn this on, you're swapping quality for speed. That's because rather than rendering the full-resolution image, it just prints the low-res JPEG preview image that's embedded in the file, so the print comes out of your printer faster than a greased pig. It works beautifully—the small images look crisp and clear. However, I would only recommend using this if you're printing multi-photo contact sheets. Notice, though, that when you turn Draft Mode Printing on, all the other options are grayed out. So, for contact sheets, turn it on. Otherwise, leave this off.

Step Four:
Make sure the Draft Mode Printing checkbox is turned off, and now it's time to choose the resolution of your image. For me, this is really simple—I print all my images at the file's native resolution, which means I turn the Print Resolution checkbox off. (*Note:* You'll still see 240 ppi grayed-out in the resolution field to the right when you turn this off.) I would only turn this checkbox on if I need to choose a different resolution (perhaps to up-sample my image size), but I can't even remember the last time I did that. If you search this topic online, you'll find a bunch of outdated posts from 2012, with people arguing back and forth about which setting is right, and they range from 180 to 720 (literally). Again, I don't type in a resolution; I turn off the checkbox and use my image's native resolution, whether I'm printing to my in-house Canon printers or sending my images out for printing at a photo lab. (I also, generally, don't use super-high megapixel cameras. By the way, most of my prints come from an 18-megapixel camera, which by today's standards is low, seeing as $350 entry-level DSLRs are now around 24-megapixel).

Continued

Step Five:

Next is the pop-up menu for Print Sharpening. When you tell Lightroom which type of paper you're printing on and which level of sharpening you'd like, it looks at those, along with the resolution you're printing at, and it applies the right amount of sharpening to give you the best results on that paper media at that resolution (sweet!). So, start by turning on the Print Sharpening checkbox (I always turn this on for every print, and every JPEG file I save), then choose either Glossy or Matte from the Media Type pop-up menu (based on whichever one you're printing to). Now choose the amount of sharpening you want from the Print Sharpening pop-up menu (I generally use High for everything these days. The Low setting seems so subtle that I can't tell it did any sharpening at all, and Medium seems kind of "meh" to me. But, after you do a test, if you think High is too high, then Medium is your next stop). That's all there is to it—Lightroom does all the math for you.

Step Six:

The next checkbox down reveals another feature: 16 Bit Output, which theoretically, gives you an expanded dynamic range on printers that support 16-bit printing. However, as it always is when it comes to printing, there is considerable debate on whether turning this 16 Bit Output checkbox on actually makes a visual difference in your prints—some folks claim you cannot see any difference with the naked eye whatsoever, and others argue it makes a difference. The important thing is: people are arguing about stuff online, and that's what keeps the Illuminati running the show (and it's why we can't have nice things). So, what do I do in regards to the 16 Bit Output? I leave it turned on. It might help, and "it couldn't hurt." (Plus, it gives me something to argue about online.)

Step Seven:

Now it's time to set the Color Management options, so what you see onscreen and what comes out of the printer both match. (By the way, if you have any hope of this happening, you've first got to use a hardware monitor calibrator to calibrate your monitor. Without a calibrated monitor, all bets are off. More on this in a bit.) There are only two things you have to set here: (1) you have to choose your printer profile, and (2) you have to choose your rendering intent. For Profile, the default setting is Managed by Printer (as shown here), which means your printer is going to color manage your print job for you. This choice used to be out of the question, but today's printers have come so far that you'll actually now get decent results leaving it set to Managed by Printer (but if you want "better than decent," read on).

Step Eight:

You'll get better looking prints by assigning a custom printer/paper profile. To get these, go to the website of the company that manufactures the paper you're going to be printing on and download their free ICC color profiles for your printer. So, if I was printing to my Canon imagePROGRAF PRO-1000, on Hahnemühle Photo Rag® Ultra Smooth paper, I'd go to Hahnemühle's website, click on ICC Profile, then click on Download Center, and I'd find the profile that matches my Canon printer (as shown here, where I chose my brand and model from their pop-up menus near the top of the page). Then, I'd download and install the free color profile for my printer. On a Mac, the unzipped profile file should be placed in your Library/ColorSync/Profiles folder. To get to that folder (it's hidden), press-and-hold the Option key, then go under the Go menu, and choose **Library**. There, you'll find the ColorSync folder, and within that, you'll find the Profiles folder. Just drag-and-drop it in there. In Windows, just Right-click on the unzipped file and choose Install Profile.

Continued

Step Nine:

Once your color profile is installed, click-and-hold on the Profile pop-up menu (right where it says Managed by Printer), and choose **Other**. This brings up a dialog (shown here) listing all the color profiles installed on your computer. Scroll through the list and find the paper profiles for your printer, then find the profile(s) for the paper(s) you normally print on (in my case, I'm looking for that Hahnemühle Photo Rag® Ultra Smooth paper for the Canon imagePROGRAF PRO-1000), and then turn on the checkbox beside that paper (as seen here). Once you've found your profile(s), click OK to add it to your pop-up menu.

Step 10:

Return to that Profile pop-up menu in the Print Job panel, and you'll see the color profile for your printer is now available as one of the choices in this menu (as seen here). Choose your color profile from this pop-up menu, if it's not already chosen. In my case, I would choose the Hahnemühle paper profile for my Canon PRO-1000 printer, but in the pop-up menu seen here, they use the cryptic code-name "HFA_CanPro1000_MK_PRUltraSmooth." (They do that to throw off the North Koreans.) Okay, now you've set up Lightroom so it knows exactly how to handle the color for your particular printer, using this particular brand and style of paper. This step is really key to getting the quality prints we're looking for.

Step 11:

Next to Intent, you have two choices: (a) Perceptual, or (b) Relative. Theoretically, choosing Perceptual may give you a more pleasing print because it tries to maintain color relationships, but it's not necessarily accurate as to what you see tonally onscreen. Choosing Relative may provide a more accurate interpretation of the tone of the photo, but you may not like the final color as much. So, which one is right for you? The one that looks best on your own printer for the particular image you're printing. Relative is probably the most popular choice all around, and since you have to pick one, I'd go with that (chances are it will look the best, but to really find out which ones looks best to you, you have to do a couple of test prints and see for yourself). Try one print with Perceptual and the same image with Relative—when the prints come out, you'll know right away which one looks best to you (but know that this is somewhat image dependant). We'll cover the last option, Print Adjustment, after you make your first print.

Step 12:

Now it's time to click the Printer button at the bottom of the right side Panels area. This will bring up the Print dialog (shown here. If you're using a Mac, and you see a small dialog with just two pop-up menus, rather than the larger one you see here, click the Show Details button to expand the dialog to its full size, more like the one shown here).

Continued

Step 13:

Click-and-hold on the Print dialog's main section pop-up menu, and choose **Color Matching** (as shown here). By the way, the part of this dialog that controls printer color management, and your pop-up menu choices, may be different depending on your printer, so if it doesn't look exactly like this, don't freak out. On a PC, click on the Properties button next to the printer Name pop-up menu to locate it instead.

Step 14:

When the Color Matching options appear, you'll see your printer's color management may be turned off already, since you're having Lightroom manage your color (you don't want the printer also trying to manage your color, because when the two color management systems both start trying to manage your color, nobody wins). So, if it's not already set that way, be sure to turn it off. On a PC (this may be different, depending on your printer), on the Main tab, under Color/Intensity, click the Manual radio button, then click the Set button on the Matching tab, under color correction, choose **None**, then click OK. Here, mine was automatically turned off, and grayed out so I couldn't change it.

Step 15:

Now, choose Quality & Media from the pop-up menu (or go to Media Type on a PC) in the Print dialog (again, your pop-up menus may be different, and on a PC, these will be in the Properties dialog for your printer), and for Media Type, choose the paper you'll be printing to from the pop-up menu. (as seen here, I chose Highest Density Fine Art Paper). If your printer supports 16-bit output, turn it on.

CANON U.S.A., INC.: SCOTT KELBY

Step 16:

In that same Quality & Media section, select **High** from the Print Quality pop-up menu. Again, this is for printing to a Canon printer using Hahnemühle paper. If you don't have a Canon printer, choose the one that most closely matches the paper you are printing to. On a PC, for Print Quality, choose High from the pop-up menu. Now sit back and watch your glorious print(s) roll gently out of your printer. So far, so good.

Continued

Step 17:

Once your print comes out of the printer, now it's time to take a good look at the print to see if what we're holding in our hands actually matches what we saw onscreen. If you use a hardware-based monitor calibrator, and you followed all the instructions up to this point on downloading printer profiles and all that stuff, the color of your image should be pretty spot on. If your color is way off, my first guess would be you didn't use a hardware-based calibrator (the X-Rite ColorMunki and the Datacolor Spyder5 [shown here] are both pretty popular) and using one is seriously a no-brainer. You put it on your monitor, launch the software, choose "easy-you-do-it-all-automatically-for-me" mode (not it's actual name), and in about four minutes your monitor is calibrated. This is such a critical step in getting your color right that without hardware calibration of some sort, you really have little hope of the colors on your monitor and your print actually matching.

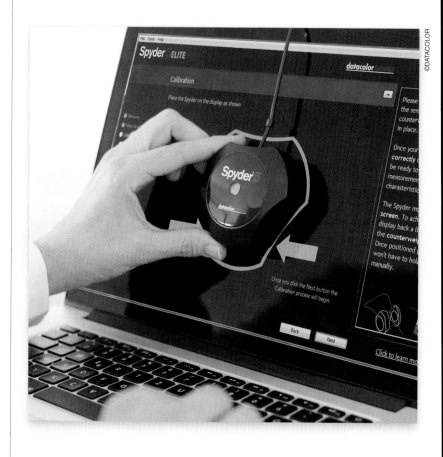

Step 18:

If you've used a hardware calibrator, and followed the instructions in this section of the book, your color should be pretty much spot on, but there's another printing problem you're likely to run up against. Your color probably matches pretty darn well, but my guess is that the print you're holding in your hand right now is quite a bit darker than what you see on your screen. That's mostly because, up to this point, you've been seeing your image on a very bright, backlit monitor, but now your image isn't backlit—it's flat on a printed page (imagine how a backlit sign looks when you turn off the back lighting. Well, that's what you're holding). Luckily, Adobe addressed this problem with the Print Adjustment option at the bottom of the Print Job panel (shown here).

Step 19:

The thing that's so awesome about Print Adjustment is that it doesn't mess with the brightness or contrast of your actual image—your image doesn't change at all, just the print. It literally only affects the brightness of the print, while leaving the image at the same brightness as you had it onscreen. That is incredibly helpful. So, how do you know how much to increase the brightness of the print so it matches your screen? You do a test print. In fact, you kind of have to do a test print, since the changes you make with the Brightness and Contrast sliders aren't seen onscreen (they're only applied as the image is printed). Your test prints don't have to be output on big, expensive, 16x20" sheets of paper—they can be small 4x6" prints.

Step 20:

Once you've made a few test prints at different brightness amounts, compare their brightness to what you see on your screen, and you'll know which ones look right (this is one of those cases where you should add a caption with your brightness setting appearing below the image, like Brightness +10, then Brightness +15, and then a third with Brightness +20. You add these captions in the Photo Info section of the Page panel; we looked at this feature on page 362). Once you see which setting nailed the brightness, that is your Print Adjustment Brightness setting from here on out. I haven't had to increase the Contrast to match my monitor, but if you see a loss of contrast, once you have the Brightness amount nailed down, do test prints to find out the Contrast amount, and you'll be set. *Note:* Different paper types (matte, glossy, fiber, fine art, etc.) display brightness differently, so you may need to do another test for brightness if you change papers and the brightness no longer matches.

Saving Your Layout as a JPEG (for Photo Lab Printing)

You can save any of these print layouts as JPEG files, so you can send them to a photo lab, or have someone else output your files, or email them to your client, or one of the dozen different things you want JPEGs of your layouts for. Here's how it's done:

Step One:
Once your layout is all set, go to the Print Job panel (in the right side Panels area), and from the Print To pop-up menu (at the top right of the panel), choose **JPEG File** (as shown here).

Step Two:
When you choose to print to a JPEG, a new set of features appears. First, ignore the Draft Mode Printing checkbox (it's just for when you're actually printing contact sheets full of small thumbnails). For File Resolution, the default is 300 ppi (and I don't change it), but if for some reason you want to change it, click directly on "300" to highlight the field, and then you can type in a new resolution. Again, I don't change the resolution setting, but just in case you want to, at least you know how.

Step Three:

Next is the pop-up menu for Print Sharpening. What you do here is tell Lightroom which type of paper you'll be printing on (Matte or Glossy), and which level of sharpening you'd like applied (Low, Standard, or High). Lightroom looks at your choices (including resolution) and comes up with the optimum amount and type of sharpening to match your choices. So, start there (I apply this print sharpening to every photo I print or save as a JPEG). If you don't want this output sharpening applied to your exported JPEG, just turn off the Print Sharpening checkbox.

Step Four:

You've got a couple more choices to make before we're done. Next, is JPEG Quality, I usually use 80, because I think it gives a good balance between quality and compression of the file size, but you can choose anything you want, up to 100.

Continued

Step Five:

Below that are the Custom File Dimensions. If you leave the checkbox turned off, it will just use whatever page size you had chosen in the Page Setup dialog. If you want to change the size of your JPEG, turn on the Custom File Dimensions checkbox, then move your cursor over the size fields and use the scrubby slider to change sizes (as shown here, where I changed it to 8.50x11". Depending on the layout, you may have to adjust your margins and cell sizes if you do this).

Step Six:

Lastly, you set your Color Management Profile (many labs require that you use sRGB as your profile, so ask your lab). If you want a custom color profile, go back to the last project for info on how to find those, and you can find info on the rendering Intent setting there, too. Now just click the Print to File button at the bottom of the right side Panels area to save your file.

I wish Lightroom had the built-in ability to add custom borders, edges, and frames around your photos, but unfortunately it just doesn't. However, you can do a little workaround that lets you use your Identity Plate, and a special option in the Identity Plate section, to get the same effect right within Lightroom itself. Here's how it's done:

Adding Custom Borders to Your Prints

Step One:

You can buy royalty-free stock edges, frames, and borders from AdobeStock .com (or any stock photo agency for that matter). But, here, I created our border (in this case, a frame with a matte) from scratch in Photoshop. I've made a short video (it's on the book's downloads page) to teach you exactly how I made it (you'll be stunned at how easy it is). Keep in mind, our border file can't have a solid white background, or it will cover our photo when we bring it into Lightroom. Instead, the background has to be transparent. So, once you build your frame, go to the Layers panel and drag the Background layer into the Trash (at the bottom of the panel; the checkerboard area is transparent). Now, save the file as a PNG, so Lightroom will honor that transparency when you use this frame image.

Step Two:

All right, that's all the prep work in Photoshop—back to Lightroom. Click on the photo you want to have an edge frame, then go to the Print module. In the Page panel, turn on the Identity Plate checkbox. Then, in the Identity Plate pop-up menu, choose **Edit** to bring up the Identity Plate Editor seen here. Click on the Use a Graphical Identity Plate radio button (because we're going to import a graphic, rather than using text), then click on the Locate File button, locate your saved PNG frame file, and click Choose to load it into your Identity Plate Editor (you may not be able to see the edge frame graphic in the small preview window, as shown here).

Continued

Step Three:

When you click OK, your edge frame will appear, hovering over your print (almost like it's on its own layer). The size and position won't be right, so that's the first thing you'll want to fix (which we'll do in the next step, but while we're here, notice how the center of our frame is transparent—you can see right through it to the photo below it. That's why we had to save this file without the Background layer, and as a PNG—to keep that transparency intact).

Step Four:

To resize your border, you can either click-and-drag a corner point outward (as shown here), or use the Scale slider in the Page panel. Once the size looks about right, you can reposition the frame edge by simply clicking-and-dragging inside its borders. You may need to resize your image, as well, using the Margins sliders in the Layout panel.

Step Five:

When it's right where you want it, just click your cursor outside the border and it will deselect. The final photo with the edge frame border is shown here. Now, if you decide you want to keep this border and use it in the future, go back to the Identity Plate Editor and from the Custom pop-up menu at the bottom-left corner of the dialog, choose **Save As** to save this frame border as an Identity Plate you can use anytime to add a quick border effect.

TIP: Frames for Multiple Photos

If you have more than one photo on the page, you can have that Identity Plate frame added to all the photos on the page automatically by going to the Page panel and turning on the Render on Every Image checkbox.

Step Six:

We created a horizontal frame, but how do you add this frame edge to a vertical photo, like the one shown here? If you change your page setup to Portrait (by clicking on the Page Setup button at the bottom of the left side Panels area), the Identity Plate will rotate automatically. If you are printing a vertical photo in a Landscape setup, you can rotate the Identity Plate by clicking on the degree field that appears to the right of the Identity Plate checkbox in the Page panel and choosing the rotation angle (as shown here). You'll probably have to resize and reposition the frame (as I did here) to make it fit just right, but now your single frame edge is doing double duty.

CHAPTER 13

VIDEO
working with video shot with your camera

When you think of Lightroom, you don't think of video, right? What's the first thing you think of? That's right—light. In a room. Which is why the original working title for Lightroom (11+ years ago when it was still in Beta) was actually "table lamp," and it was nearly released as TableLamp 1.0, until someone in marketing at Adobe brought up the fact that just because there's light in a room doesn't mean the light has to come from a lamp on a table. It could come from a hanging lamp, or one of those lamps attached to the underside of a ceiling fan, or just a light fixture in the center of the ceiling, and well…the whole idea just fell apart. For a brief time (I think it was Beta 6, Build 1.3), they considered naming it "Light that hangs from the bottom of a ceiling fan," which internally went by the simple acronym "LTHFTBOACF." That was hard to pronounce, but in print, if you squinted, it looked kinda like "LIFEBOAT," but the "BOA" part is also a real name (well, a nickname for a boa constrictor), so some folks on the engineering team referred to it internally as LIFESNAKE, although some preferrred the more casual SnakeBoat 1.0, with the upper/lower case treatment with InterCaps. Then, an astute quality control expert at Adobe's Seattle office (yes, Adobe also has an office in Seattle, acquired with their purchase of Aldus in August 1994) noticed that the first three letters, "LTH," are, not coincidentally, the Airport Code for Lathrop Wells Airport in Nevada (I am not making this up). So, the Seattle office felt this was a sign, and if it hadn't been for a dyslexic typographer in Adobe's package design department, we'd all be using LathropSnakeLampBoat Classic to this very day. True story.

Trimming Your Video Clips

I think you'll be surprised at all the things you can do with video in Lightroom, and if you don't mind a few simple workarounds, you can pretty much even make your movies (complete with titles, transitions, music, and audio) and save them in HD format. But, before we get to all that (don't worry, it's all amazingly easy), let's start with the thing we usually need to do first—trimming our video clips.

Step One:

You import a video into Lightroom just like you would a photo, but you'll know it's a video because you'll see a video camera icon in the lower-left corner of its thumbnail when it appears in the Import window (Lightroom supports most major DSLR video formats). Once it's in Lightroom, you can put it in a collection, add flags, metadata, and so on, and you'll see the length of the video displayed in the bottom-left corner of its thumbnail (as seen here, where the length of the selected video clip is 11 seconds). You can see a preview of what's on a video clip by moving your cursor over the thumbnail itself and dragging either left or right to quickly "scrub" through the video.

JUAN ALFONSO

Step Two:

If you want to watch your entire video clip, double-click on it and it opens in Loupe view (as seen here). To play the video, you can click the Play button (duh) in the control bar under the video, or just press the **Spacebar** on your keyboard to start/stop it. You can also scrub through the video (kind of like manually fast-forwarding or rewinding) by just dragging the playhead in the control bar. When you play the video, it plays both the video and audio, but there's no volume control for the audio within Lightroom itself, so you'll have to control the audio volume using your computer's volume control.

Step Three:

If your video needs to be trimmed down to size (maybe you need to cut off the end a bit, or crop the video so it starts after a few seconds or so), click on the little gear icon on the far-right side of the control bar and the trim controls pop up (seen here). There are two ways to trim: Just click on an end marker handle on either side of the video clip (they look like two little vertical bars) and drag inward to trim your clip (as shown here). The other way to trim is to set Trim Start and Trim End points (which basically means "start here" and "end here") by hitting the Spacebar to let the video play, then when you reach the point you want your video to actually start, press **Shift-I** to set the Trim Start point. When you reach the point where you want the rest trimmed away, press **Shift-O** to set your Trim End point.

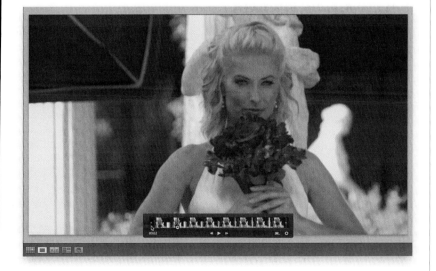

Step Four:

When you trim your clips, it doesn't permanently trim your video—it's non-destructive, so the original is always protected. The trimming is applied to a copy when you export the file (more on exporting later), so while that exported video will be trimmed (and what you see in Lightroom will be trimmed, as well), you can always come back to the original video clip anytime and pull those trim handles right back out (as shown here).

Choosing the Thumbnail for Your Video Clip

Have you ever seen a video (maybe on a blog or on Facebook), and the thumbnail for that video shows them frozen in mid-sentence with their mouth gaping open? Not the most flattering look, right? That's because the thumbnail is chosen randomly from a frame a few seconds into the video clip. Luckily, in Lightroom, you actually get to choose which individual frame becomes the thumbnail you see when your video clip is in Grid view or down in the Filmstrip.

Step One:
Being able to choose your video thumbnail (called a "poster frame" in video speak) is helpful if you have four or five similar-looking clips—you can choose thumbnails that show which video has which important part in it (but, you don't just see it here in Lightroom, that thumbnail goes with it when you export it outside of Lightroom, too). To choose your custom thumbnail, first double-click on your video to see it in Loupe view (as seen here), then play the video until you find the part you'd like as your thumbnail, and then stop (hit the **Spacebar** on your keyboard).

Step Two:
Now go down to the control bar, click-and-hold on the little rectangle icon to the left of the Trim Video button, choose **Set Poster Frame** (as shown here), and now your video clip will have that current image as your thumbnail.

It's called "grabbing a still," where you can take any single frame from your video and make it its own separate JPEG image (this will come in really handy a little later in this chapter, so let's go ahead and learn it now).

Pulling a Photo from Your Video Clip

Step One:
To pull a single frame out of your video and make a still image from it is pretty much the same technique as setting your thumbnail (from the previous page), with just one small exception. You start by playing your video in Loupe view (double-click on the video thumbnail to enter Loupe view), and then stop the video when you see the frame you want to pull out as a still.

Step Two:
Now go down to the control bar, click-and-hold on the little rectangle icon to the left of the Trim Video button, but this time choose **Capture Frame**. This creates a second file (a JPEG image file just like any other photo) and puts it to the left of your selected video clip in the Filmstrip (as seen here). By the way, if you haven't added this video to a collection yet, instead, the JPEG image gets stacked with your video clip and you'll see a "2" in the upper-left corner of your thumbnail (that's letting you know you have two images in your stack. To expand the stack and see both the video and the still, click on the stack and press the letter **S** on your keyboard). Again, you only have to do this if your video wasn't already in a collection.

Editing Your Video Clip (the Easy, but More Limited, Way)

If you take a video clip over to Lightroom's Develop module, it will bring up an alert letting you know "Video is not supported in Develop," but there's another way to do simple edits to your entire video clip at once—stuff like converting it to black and white, making it brighter/darker, adding more contrast, and a handful of other simple things like that—all without going to the Develop module.

Step One:

To do this simple style of editing, you'll need to stay in the Library module, so double-click on the thumbnail you want to edit, so you see it much larger in Loupe view. Now head over to the Quick Develop panel near the top of the right side Panels area. Quick Develop is a simplified version of the Develop module's Basic panel, but instead of using sliders, it uses one-click buttons to make your adjustments. The weird thing is, you can use Quick Develop to edit your video clip.

Step Two:

For example, if you want to make your entire clip black and white, in the Quick Develop panel's Saved Preset section, choose **Black & White** from the Treatment pop-up menu (as shown here). That's it—your entire clip is now black and white. If you want to make it brighter, click the Exposure single-right-arrow button once to increase the brightness 1/3 of a stop, or click the Exposure double-right-arrow button once to increase it a full stop. Some of the adjustments here will be grayed out, so you can't do everything you normally could to a photo in Quick Develop, but you can sure do a lot, like add Contrast, or adjust the White Balance Temperature or Tint, or adjust the Whites and Blacks, as well as the Vibrance amount. If you mess up, you can always Undo any button clicks **(Command-Z [PC: Ctrl-Z])**, or you can click the Reset All button at the bottom of the Quick Develop panel to reset your video clip to how it looked when it was first opened.

While it is true that when you take a video clip over to the Develop module it says "Video is not supported in Develop," that's not actually true. It's more like "Video is not supported in Develop unless you bring a friend (a still photo) along, and then you can edit in the Develop module using a lot more goodies (everything from Curves to Split Toning and more)!" Kinda weird that you can do this workaround, but it's also kinda cool that you can.

Serious Video Clip Editing (Using Lots of Goodies!)

Step One:

You'll start this video-editing-in-the-Develop-module workaround by pulling a still photo from your video, so double-click on your clip to enter Loupe view, then play the video and find a frame you want to pull out as a still. Now, go down to the control bar, click-and-hold on the little rectangle icon, and choose **Capture Frame**. This creates a JPEG file and puts it to the left of your selected video clip in the Filmstrip (if your video is in a collection). Click on the JPEG file first, then press-and-hold the Command (PC: Ctrl) key and click on the video clip (so they're both selected, as shown here, but the JPEG will look brighter because it's the "most selected" of the two thumbnails).

Step Two:

Now press **D** on your keyboard to jump over to the Develop module, and your JPEG image will appear onscreen (since it's selected—and besides, it can't display the video clip). At the bottom of the right side Panels area, make sure you see "Auto Sync" (as shown here. If not, flip on the little switch to the left of Sync to turn it on). What Auto Sync does is this: whatever you do to this selected photo, it also does to the other selected photo (but in this case, the second photo isn't a photo, it's a video, but for some unknown reason, this still works). Now, whatever effects or changes you apply to that JPEG photo, those same changes are applied to your video clip. Freaky, I know. Let's give it a try!

Continued

Step Three:

Let's start by going to the Basic panel and clicking on Black & White in the top right. While we're here, let's increase the Contrast amount to +30. Now, scroll down to the Split Toning panel, and let's apply a duotone effect by dragging the Shadows Saturation slider to around 24 and the Shadows Hue slider to 40 for a brownish tint. Okay, now let's go to the Tone Curve panel, click once right in the center of the curve (the diagonal line), and drag it a little toward the bottom right (as seen here) to bring down the midtones a bit.

TIP: Using Presets in Quick Develop

If you create a cool look in the Develop module and want to use that exact look later on another video clip, save it as a preset (see Chapter 7). That way you can apply it right in the Library module, from the Saved Preset pop-up menu at the top of the Quick Develop panel.

Step Four:

Next, go to the Detail panel, and in the Sharpening section, increase the Amount to 50, then go down to the Effects panel, to the Post-Crop Vignetting section, and drag the Amount slider to the left to –11, so it adds a subtle amount of darkening all around the edges. Now, did you notice that while we were jumping from panel to panel and making edits like we always do, down in the Filmstrip, the video clip's thumbnail is updating, too? It's getting all these same adjustments and effects applied as if it were another still image. How cool is that? *Note:* There are some things in the Develop module that won't affect your video (even though they're not grayed out and it seems like they would). Stuff like profiles, or Clarity, Highlights, and Shadows, or anything in the Lens Corrections panel, and you can't use the Adjustment Brushes either.

Can you really make a wedding video, or a behind-the-scenes video, or an interview or promo right here in Lightroom, with background music, mixing video clips with stills that are animated with movement and smooth transitions, and opening and closing titles, and the save the whole thing in HD format, all without breaking a sweat? Believe it or not, you can (and it's way easier than you'd think).

Let's Make a Short Movie (and Even Save It in HD Quality)!

Step One:

The first step is to simply put all your video clips (trim them first, so this doesn't hold you up later; see page 392) and your final photos (already sharpened, edited, etc.) into a collection. Once they're all in that collection, put them in the order you want them to appear in your video (I try to use a few photos, then a video clip, then a few more stills, then a video clip, etc., just so there's not too much of one format). What's nice is, we're going to add movement to our stills—a Ken Burns–like pan and zoom—so they blend nicely with the moving video clips. So, get them in the basic order you want them (it's a collection, so you'll be able to reorder them later if you need to) by simply dragging-and-dropping them.

Step Two:

Once your images are in order, head up to the taskbar and click on Slideshow to take this collection over to the Slideshow module (that's what we're using to make our movie. Don't worry—it's better than it sounds). In the Template Browser panel near the top of the left side Panels area, click on Widescreen for your template (it's a clean, simple template), but then go over to the Options panel in the top of the right side Panels area and turn on the Zoom to Fill Frame checkbox (as seen here), so you don't have thick black bars at the top and bottom of your slide show…errr… movie. *Note:* You'll find a bonus chapter on using the Slideshow module on the book's companion webpage, mentioned in the book's introduction.

Continued

Step Three:

Now head down to the Titles panel and turn on the Intro Screen checkbox. If you want to change the color of your intro screen's background, click the little color swatch to the right of "Intro Screen" to bring up a color picker where you can choose your new background color (I'll stick with black here). After just a few seconds, your intro screen will disappear. I have no idea why (it seems kinda crazy to me, but it has always been that way). To see it again, click-and-hold on the little Scale slider nub in the Titles panel and it will stay onscreen until you let go. By default, it will show your name (or whatever you have in your Identity Plate), but you can change that (unless it's a promo video, of course).

Step Four:

Let's go ahead and change the name of the text for our title screen (unless, of course, this is a behind-the-scenes video and you want your name there, but we'll assume it isn't for now). In the bottom-right corner of the Add Identity Plate preview window, click the arrow, and from the pop-up menu that appears, choose **Edit** (as shown here). This brings up the Identity Plate Editor, where you can type in your title text, choose your font, size, etc., or you can import a graphic if you want (more on using Identity Plates back in Chapter 4). Once your text is formatted for the opening title, go ahead and do a closing title (right below it), as well, if you like. By the way, you can change the size of your text after the fact, using the Scale slider, and you can also change the text color you chose by turning on the Override Color checkbox and clicking on the color swatch to its right.

Step Five:

Now, let's choose our background music track. Lightroom is a little fussy when it comes to music formats—it likes them in either the AAC (M4A) or MP3 audio format. If you use iTunes for your music (on a Mac or Windows), it can create an AAC music file for you: click on the song in iTunes, then go under File menu, under Convert, and choose **Create AAC Version**. This makes a duplicate of your song in the AAC format, and that's the version you can use in Lightroom. If you don't use iTunes, you'll need to convert the song file to an MP3, and luckily, you can find free utilities online to convert your music track, so do that first, or Lightroom won't let you import the track. Once it's converted, go to the Music panel, click the + (plus sign) icon, choose your music track, and now the track's name will appear at the bottom of the Music panel, along with the length of the track.

Step Six:

Your last stop is the Playback panel (yes, you're already almost done with your video). If you want your slide show to fit the exact length of the song you picked, click the Fit to Music button, and it will do all the math for you (how long each slide will stay onscreen and how long the dissolves between them will need to be, so when the song ends, your last photo or video ends right on time). The Audio Balance slider lets you choose to hear all, some, or none of the audio that your camera picked up (it can be kinda weird when you're mixing still and video and you hear audio just here and there, so I set it all the way over to Music, but it's your call). Next, I turn on the Pan and Zoom checkbox—this puts your stills in motion (à la the Ken Burns effect)—and the slider lets you choose more subtle movement or a lot of movement. The other checkboxes are kind of obvious, and there's a Quality pop-up menu, as well. Pretty simple choices here.

Continued

Step Seven:

At this point, we're ready to look at our movie, so hit the Preview button at the bottom of the right side Panels area and it will play a preview of your video in the Preview area. If you want to see the full-screen version, hit the Play button (to the right of the Preview button). So why would you ever hit Preview instead of Play? It's often smoother and ready to play faster than the full-screen production, so I use Preview just for the sake of time and smoother playbacks, while I'm still in the editing/tweaking phase.

Step Eight:

When you're happy with how everything sounds and looks, hit Play to render the full-size, full-screen version. If it all looks good, it's time to export a copy in which-ever format you need. So, click the Export Video button at the bottom of the left side Panels area and it brings up the Export Slideshow to Video dialog. At the bottom, there's a Video Preset pop-up menu where you choose which size/quality to export. For the highest quality (which also means the largest file size), choose **1080p (16:9)** (that's HD quality and size). If you choose each of the four sizes, a description appears right there next to it, so you know which preset is for what. Choose the one that fits how you're going to share your video and it does the rest. After a few short minutes of rendering, your video is ready to share. That's really all there is to it (and you didn't even have to leave Lightroom).

TIP: Posting Directly to Facebook

You can post your video directly to Face-book using Publish Services (see Chapter 9 for more on how to use them, but I thought you'd want to know you can post your video directly from Lightroom).

Step Nine:

Another way to export your video clips is to use the standard Export button when you're in the Library module (see Chapter 9 to learn all about exporting). When the Export dialog appears, if you scroll down a bit, you'll see an area dedicated to exporting video (seen here). Since you clicked on your video clip to export it, the Include Video Files checkbox should already be turned on, so all you have to do is make two simple choices: (1) Which video format do you want to save your clip in? I use H.264, as it's a widely supported format and makes the file size smaller without losing much (if any) visible quality (kind of like JPEG does for image files). But, of course, how much it's compressed is based on (2) the Quality setting you choose. If you're going to be sharing this somewhere on the web (YouTube, Animoto, etc.), then you'll probably want to consider a lower quality than Max (the physical size and fps will appear to the right when you choose a Quality size from the pop-up menu, so you know what each delivers). However, if you're taking this video over to a dedicated video editing application, that's when you'd want to choose Max quality.

TIP: Video Preferences

There are only two video preferences and they're found in the Library View Options (press **Command-J [PC: Ctrl-J]**), on the Loupe View tab. In the General section, at the bottom, Show Frame Number When Displaying Video Time does just what it says—it adds the frame number beside the time (yawn). The option beneath that, Play HD Video at Draft Quality, is there to make sure the playback of your HD video is smooth if you don't have a super-fast computer—the lower-resolution draft-quality video takes less power to display the video in real time than the full HD version does.

CHAPTER 14

GOING MOBILE
using Lightroom on your phone/tablet & more

This chapter used to be called "Lightroom Mobile" because the app itself used to be called Lightroom Mobile, but Adobe renamed the app "Lightroom CC," probably because they realized that it was too descriptive, too obvious, and made too much sense. Actually, the full name of the app is not Lightroom CC, it's "Adobe Photoshop Lightroom CC," which is what you see on the splash screen that appears for a moment when you first launch the app. But, if you click on the LR icon in the top-left corner, it takes you to the developer credits page, and only there do you see the full and complete name for "the app previously known as Lightroom Mobile," which is (and this is its legal name, and I only know this because a Lightroom rumors site pointed this out and it was listed on a trademark registration page made public by the Freedom of Information Act) "Adobe Photoshop Tito Jermaine Jonathan Livingston Seagull Gordon Lightfoot Keanu Cher Longoria Bailey Hutchinson The Rock Sergio Mendes Marlon Lightroom CC, Sr., III, Esq." It's right there on the registration papers; you can look for yourself. That's a little long if you ask me, and if it were me, personally, I'd drop Gordon, The Rock, and Mendes, making it the shorter, and easier to remember, "Adobe Photoshop Tito Jermaine Jonathan Livingston Seagull Lightfoot Keanu Cher Longoria Bailey Hutchinson Sergio Marlon Lightroom CC, Sr., III, Esq." Apparently, also in that same trademark registration, Adobe is planning on adding a couple additional sliders to Lightroom CC, and the names of these two new sliders would be "Ointment" and "Curd." I can't imagine what those new sliders would actually do, but I know this: I'm not using them during dinner.

Four Really Cool Things About Lightroom CC on Your Mobile Device

You can extend Lightroom's power to your smartphone and tablet using Lightroom mobile (now officially called "Lightroom CC," but we'll call it Lightroom mobile here, for clarity's sake), giving you the option to edit your images pretty much anywhere. Here are four really cool things about the whole "mobile" part of your Lightroom experience:

#1: It Has a Killer Camera App!

Lightoom mobile has its own built-in camera and it's pretty darn awesome. It has a Pro mode where you can manually choose your f-stop, shutter speed, ISO, and white balance, and it even has effect presets you can apply before you take an image. If your camera supports it (like recent iPhones or Samsung phones), you can shoot in RAW. It has a great HDR feature (using the same math from Lightroom Classic on your desktop), and the high-res RAW photos you take with the camera are automatically synced back to your computer. Plus, it has a built-in leveling feature, highlight clipping warnings, and the easiest-to-use Exposure Compensation feature ever (see page 434 for more on using the camera).

#2: You Can Sync Collections from Your Computer

When you first turn on Sync, nothing happens—all your images don't try to stuff their way onto your phone (who has that much free space on their phone, right?). You'll choose which collection(s) in Lightroom Classic (on your desktop) you want synced over to your mobile devices (if any). You turn on a checkbox and it goes over—easy as that. Once it's there, you can do most of the same stuff you do on your desktop, but now on your mobile device—everything from editing your photos to ranking, sorting, and sharing them. By the way, it doesn't sync the full high-res images over, instead it sends smart previews, which look and act like the high-res originals, but only take up around 1 megabyte of space on your mobile device.

#3: You Already Know How to Use It

That's right. It's based off the features in Lightroom Classic, so when you open it and go to edit your images, you'll see all the same familiar sliders you're already used to working with—Exposure, Contrast, Shadows, Highlights, Whites, Blacks, Clarity, Dehaze, and White Balance Temp and Tint. It's the same stuff, using the same math, so really it's just about learning some of the simple interface stuff, and you're off and running. Best of all, the current version of Lightroom mobile's interface is the most like Lightroom Classic on your desktop, so you'll have no trouble getting up to speed fast (well, especially after this chapter).

#4: Your Changes Go Everywhere

When you make an edit on your mobile device or on your computer, that change is automatically updated everywhere. It all stays in sync, so it doesn't really matter where you edit your images—on your phone, tablet, or on your computer—all your changes are reflected everywhere, and it's all handled for you automatically. So, it's pretty much Lightroom wherever you are. Beyond that, your synced images aren't just on your phone, tablet, and desktop, they are also on the web, ready for you to share. Don't worry—it's all password protected, so only you can access them. But, if you want, you can share any collection with friends, family, or the public—all they need is a web browser to see them.

Setting Up Lightroom on Your Mobile Device

This is really easy, but kind of "pain-in-the-butt," stuff because you might have to log into your Adobe account in a couple different places. But, what's nice is, once you've done it, you're done, and it really doesn't get in the way again. Here's how to get up and running quickly:

Step One:

You start in regular ol' Lightroom on your desktop (Lightroom Classic): just click where the Lightroom logo lives (up in the top-left corner of the interface) and a menu will pop down asking if you want to Sync with Lightroom CC. Click on Start. If you're not already, you'll need to sign in with your Adobe ID and password. Simple enough.

TIP Three Ways to Get Images into Lightroom Mobile

(1) You can sync collections from Lightroom Classic on your desktop or laptop computer; (2) you can import photos already on your mobile device from your camera roll; or, (3) you can use Lightroom's built-in camera to take photos and, of course, they go straight into Lightroom on your mobile device.

Step Two:

Now, go to the App Store (on your iPhone or iPad), or Google Play (on your Android phone or tablet), and download the Lightroom CC app (it's free). Once you download it, launch the app and sign in with your Adobe ID and password (this is how it knows Lightroom Classic on your computer and Lightroom on your mobile device are linked to each other). At this point, you won't see any photos in Lightroom mobile (errr, I meant "CC") because you haven't chosen any collections from Lightroom Classic on your desktop to sync over to your mobile device yet (but there will be in a page or two). For now, I just wanted you to get up and running.

You'll notice I said "Collections"—that's a key point because you can't sync folders in Lightroom Classic over to Lightroom mobile; it only syncs collections. So, if you don't have the images you want in Lightroom mobile in a collection, now would be an ideal time to do that (see page 37 for more on how to make a collection out of a folder).

How to Sync Collections over to Lightroom CC (Mobile)

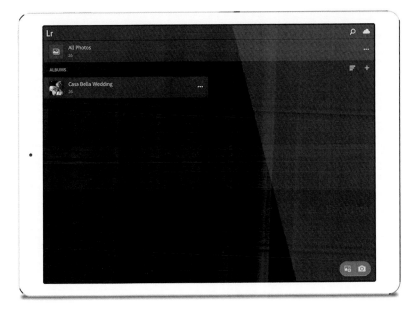

Step One:

Once you turn syncing on in Lightroom Classic on your desktop (we'll just call it "Lightroom desktop" from here on out), you'll see a new little checkbox appear to the far left of each collection's name. To sync one of your collections over to Lightroom mobile, just click on that checkbox, and a little sync icon will appear (as seen here).

Note: Like I mentioned, Lightroom mobile only works with collections from Lightroom desktop, not folders. So, if you have a folder in Lightroom desktop you want synced, you have to make it a collection first by Right-clicking on it in the Folders panel and choosing **Create Collection** from the pop-up menu. You can now sync that collection.

Step Two:

Now, head over to your mobile app (doesn't matter on which device—it syncs to any mobile device you have Lightroom mobile installed on), and you'll see that collection appear in Albums view (as seen here). That's really all there is to it. If you decide you don't want a particular collection synced to Lightroom mobile any longer, just go back to Lightroom desktop and click on that little sync icon to the left of your collection's name, and it no longer syncs.

Note: Adobe no longer calls them "collections" once they hit Lightoom mobile. They now call them "albums," so from here on out, that's what we're callin' 'em, too! Albums.

Working with Your Albums

Here's how to get around the main screen (kind of your Library module in the mobile version), and how to use a new type of Grid view that I wish Adobe would add to the desktop version. *Note:* As luck would have it, the Android version of Lightroom CC for your mobile device was developed quite a bit after the iPhone/iPad version, so it has always lagged behind on features. It's nearly caught up now, and much of it is exactly the same, but don't let it throw you that on an Android device, here and there, things are sometimes just different enough to drive us both mad.

Step One:
When you launch Lightroom CC (just a reminder, that's what the Lightroom mobile app is now called) on your mobile device, you're in Albums view. In this view, small thumbnails for all your collections appear in a tall vertical column, or if you're using a tablet, they appear in two side-by-side columns (as seen here).

TIP: Automatically Add Photos
You can automatically have any photos added to your mobile device's camera roll added to an album by tapping on the three dots to the right of an album's name and tapping **Enable Auto Add**.

Step Two:
To see the images inside any album (collection), just tap on a thumbnail and it shows you the images in the standard Grid view (as seen here). You can change the size of the thumbnails in Grid view by pinching out/in to zoom in/out. I will tell you, though, that this "pinch to zoom to resize thumbnails" is a bit finicky, so you might have to try it a couple of times before they actually change size (not sure why it's so finicky, but that's been my experience on multiple mobile devices, so I guess that's just how it is).

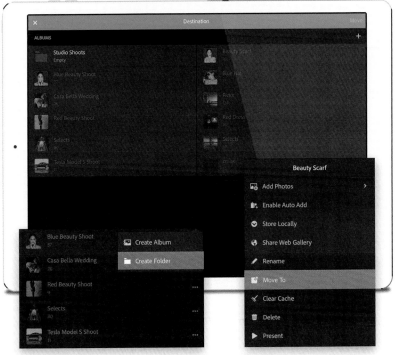

Step Three:

There are actually two different Grid views: the standard Flat view (seen in Step Two), and a Segmented view (seen here), which separates your photos by date or time. To enter Segmented view, tap the three dots in the top right, then in the pop-up menu, tap Grid View, and then tap **Segmented** to give you the date-based layout you see here (tap the three-dots again to hide the pop-up menu). You can set it to segment your photos by year, month, day, or the hour the images were taken by tapping-and-holding on the date displayed near the top left, and a list of choices will appear (as seen here in the inset).

TIP: Reordering Your Thumbnails

If you want to change the order of your photos, in Flat Grid view, tap the three dots in the top right, tap on Sort By, then tap Custom, and then tap directly on the little pencil icon to the right, which takes you to the Reorder screen, where you can tap-and-drag your photos into the order you want them (seems like an awful lot of work to do this, but that's how it is. Whew).

Step Four:

Lightroom mobile doesn't support collection sets created in Lightroom desktop, but you can create a mobile version of a collection set that acts exactly like a collection set, just with a different name—here in Lightroom mobile, it's called a "'folder." You can move albums right into these folders, just like you do with collection sets on your desktop. To create a folder, in Albums view, tap the + (plus sign) icon near the top right, and in the pop-up menu that appears, tap **Create Folder.** Now, just tap on the three dots to the right of an album's name, tap **Move To**, then tap on the new folder in the Destination screen, and then tap Move in the top right. So, if you have a collection set in Lightroom desktop that you want in mobile, start by creating a folder in mobile, and then when those albums are synced over, move them into that folder.

Continued

Step Five:

There is a bunch of hidden information you can display on the thumbnails in Grid view—just tap with two fingers on the screen and it will cycle through the various displays. For example, by default, you see a small badge with the file type (RAW, JPEG, etc.) in the top right of the thumbnail. Tap with two fingers, and it will display any flags or star ratings you assigned to the photos in this album. Two-finger tap again, and it displays the capture date and time, pixel dimensions, and file-name of each image. Two-finger tap again, and it displays the f-stop, ISO, and shutter speed for each image (as seen here). Two-finger tap again, and it shows any "likes" or comments for these images (more on this part later), and one more two-finger tap hides all the data and just shows you the thumbnails (that's the view I stick with—I just want photos, not a bunch of data, but hey, that's just me).

Step Six:

If you want to add a photo to your existing album, go to the bottom-right corner of the screen and tap either the Add Photos icon to add an image from your camera roll (or from all the photos you have synced in Lightroom mobile), or tap the camera icon to take a photo using Lightroom mobile's built-in camera (the photo you take will be added to the currently visible album).

Step Seven:

To see an image larger, just tap on it and it zooms to the Loupe view size you see here. To hide any extra onscreen info and the toolbars, and just see your image presented full screen, tap once on your image and it all quickly hides away. To return to regular Loupe view, just tap the screen once again. To see a filmstrip of the rest of the images in your album across the bottom of the screen:

iPad: Tap the Filmstrip icon in the bottom right of the screen.

Android Tablet: Tap the star icon near the bottom right of the screen.

iPhone/Android Phone: Tap on the Panels pop-up menu in the top left, then tap on Rate & Review.

TIP: Seeing Your Photo's Metadata

To see everything from copyright info to title, caption, and file info, on a phone, tap on the Panels pop-up menu in the top left, then tap **Info**. On an iPad/Android tablet, tap the round "i" icon in the bottom right.

Step Eight:

If you want to copy or move images from one album to another, or even remove images from an album or delete them altogether, in Grid view, tap the three dots in the top right, then tap on what you want to do in the pop-up menu, and then tap on the image(s) you want to do it to (select multiple images by just tapping on them). For example, if you've chosen to move images, tap on them, then tap the arrow in the top right to see a list of albums. Now, just tap the box beside the album where you want to move them to, and then tap **Move** in the top right. To cancel the move (or copy), tap the "X" in the top left. The other functions (Remove from Album and Delete) work similarly. *Note:* Remove from Album removes the image(s) here, and back in the collection in Lightroom desktop, but it does not delete the original file—that's still in the original folder on your computer.

Adding Pick Flags and Ratings to Photos

Adding Pick flags and star ratings is definitely more fun here in Lightroom mobile than it is in Lightroom desktop. Plus, it's nice to just sit back after a shoot, get comfy on the couch, pour a glass of Silver Oak (er, I mean VitaminWater, or tea…yeah…tea), and just swipe through your images, tagging your favorites.

Step One:

You add Pick flags and star ratings in the Rate & Review panel. To get there, you start by tapping once on a photo to enter Loupe view, then:

iPad/Android Tablet: Tap the star icon (circled here in red) near the bottom right of the screen.

iPhone/Android Phone: Tap the Panels pop-up menu in the top left (to the right of the back arrow icon), and then tap on **Rate & Review**.

This adds a row of stars and a flag (or two on an iPad/Android tablet, as seen here below the Filmstrip) that you can tap to add a star rating or Pick flag (or Reject flag), but there's actually a faster way—it's called "Speed Rating."

Step Two:

To flag an image as a Pick, just swipe up/down on the *right* side of the screen and a pop-up display will appear in the center, where you can choose which flag (Pick, Unflagged, or Reject) you want (as seen here). To add a star rating, just swipe up/down on the *left* side of the screen and a pop-up display will appear in the center with 5 stars (as seen here in the inset). Just stop on the star you want. Now, swipe to the right to bring up the next image and do it all again. It's a really quick way to go through a shoot.

Step Three:

To see just your Picks (or just your star-rated images), tap the back arrow icon (in the top left) to return to Grid view, and then tap the little funnel-like icon in the top right to bring up a filtering pop-up menu. You'll see Unflagged (and the number of images you didn't flag listed to the right of it), Picked (and how many images you flagged as Picks), and Rejected (and how many rejects you have, which I'm hoping is not many because if it's a lot, we might need to have an entirely different discussion, but I digress). Tap on any one of those and just your Picks, Unflagged images, or Rejects are displayed. At the bottom of the menu are your star ratings, where you can just tap on the star rating for the images you want to see (hopefully, you're tapping the fifth star because there are so many awesome shots with that rating). To turn all these filters off, just tap **No Filter** (or **Show All**) at the top of the menu, and now all your images in that album are visible again.

Step Four:

If you want to put your Picks, or maybe your 5-star images, into their own separate album, first turn on the Picked (or star rating) filter, then tap the three dots in the top right, choose **Copy To** in the pop-up menu, then tap on all your Picks (or 5-stars) to select them (on an Android device, you'll select them first, then tap Copy to Album). Now, tap the right arrow icon in the top right to choose their destination. This will bring up the Destination screen with all of your albums, but you'll want to tap the + (plus sign) icon in the top right and then tap **Create Album** in the pop-up menu. Name your new album, tap OK, then tap Copy in the top right to copy your Picks into this new album. When you tap the back arrow icon in the top left, it returns you to Albums view, and you'll see your new Picks album listed there alphabetically.

Editing Your Images on Mobile

Good news: you already know this stuff—it's the same sliders that do the same things, using the same math. The interface is slightly different if you turn the screen sideways (it's more like Lightroom desktop, with your panels and sliders on the right side), than if you use it tall (it's a more mobile-like interface, with the sliders along the bottom), but either way, you're already most of the way there, bunky.

Step One:

To edit an image, first tap on the image to enter Loupe view, and then:

iPad/Android Tablet: Tap the Edit icon near the top right of the screen (shown circled here in red) and the Edits panel pops-out on the right.

iPhone/Android Phone: Tap the Panels pop-up menu in the top left (to the right of the back arrow icon), then tap on **Edit** and a row of icons appears across the bottom of the screen. If you turn your phone sideways, the icons move to the right side of the screen, and it's more like Lightroom desktop.

Step Two:

The color and creative profiles (see Chapters 5 and 7) are all here in Lightroom mobile. Tap the Browse button (its icon looks like three photos stacked on one another), and the Profiles browser pops out. As in Lightroom desktop, these thumbnails give you a preview of your image with each look applied. There is no live preview for your image, though—tap to see one applied. If you don't like the look, tap on a different profile. If you don't like any of them, tap the curved left-facing arrow at the top right of the screen or the little X at the top right of the browser (the checkmark at the bottom is the "done" button). To change to a different set of profiles, tap on a different set or tap the menu at the top of the browser where you can choose the same ones from Lightroom desktop. An Amount slider appears below your image for those profiles that allow you to adjust the amount of the effect.

Step Three:
In the Edits panel, Adobe rearranged the sliders in each section, so they make more sense together. Each section (or icon, if you're using a phone) you tap on brings up another set of sliders. For example, tap on Light (or the icon that looks like the sun) and all the sliders that have to do with light (Exposure, Contrast, Highlights, Shadows, Whites, and Blacks) appear (as seen here). At the top of this section is a button for Curves. Just tap along the diagonal line to add a point to the Curve, then drag up to brighten, or down to darken the tones in that area. To remove a point from the Curve, double-tap on it.

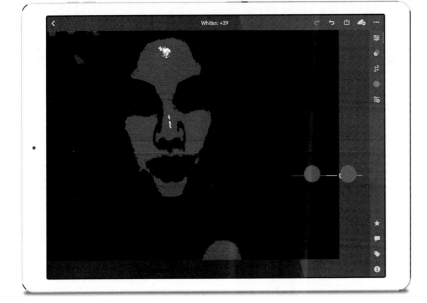

Step Four:
One of my favorite features from Lightroom desktop is here in mobile—it's just kind of hidden—and that's the ability to get a clipping warning if you're blowing out your highlights. You can see this warning onscreen when adjusting the Exposure, Shadows, Highlights, Whites, and Blacks by just pressing two fingers anywhere on the slider you're adjusting. The image will turn black and only display any areas that are clipping the highlights. Here, cranking up the Whites too much clipped her skin in just the Red channel, but clipped all three channels on her forehead, which is some pretty serious damage, and now I know to back down the Whites (or lower the Highlights) to avoid this clipping.

Continued

Step Five:

The vastly improved Auto tone button made its way over to mobile, as well (it's at the top right of the Edits panel. On a phone, its icon looks like a photo with little sparkles on the top right). Just one tap on it and it either looks good or you'll tap the Undo button up top to undo it (like, in this case, where it looks bad—well for beauty-style post-processing anyway).

TIP: There's an Undo button

If you make a mistake, tap the curved left-facing arrow in the top right of the screen to undo your last step. Luckily, you can tap it again and again to keep undoing your last steps.

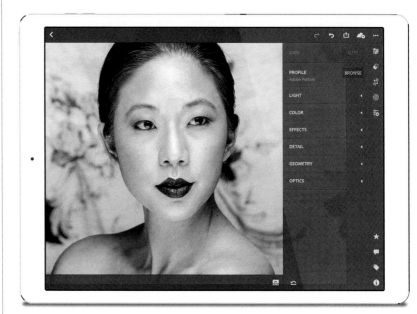

Step Six:

To change your white balance, tap on Color (its icon looks like a thermometer) and the Temp, Tint, Vibrance, and Saturation sliders appear. Near the top center of this section is a pop-up menu of White Balance presets (it's a longer list if you shot in RAW; quite short if you shot in JPEG). The White Balance Selector tool that you know and love (see page 137) is also here (to the right of the WB pop-up menu)—tap on it and it brings up a loupe that you can drag over your image. The preview is live, so as you move it over your image, you'll see how it affects the color as you drag-and-release. When you find an area where the white balance looks good, tap the checkmark on the loupe and it returns to base. To cancel, just tap the eyedropper icon again.

Step Seven:

While we're still in the Color section, there's a B&W button here to convert your image to black and white, but I would avoid this button because it creates a very flat black-and-white. Instead, use the B&W profiles in the Profile browser (seen in Step Two). To the right of the B&W button is an HSL Color Mix button that brings up the HSL sliders to adjust individual colors in your images. (*Note:* The Targeted Adjustment Tool, or "TAT" as it's known, is here, too, once you tap the HSL Color Mix button. It's at the top of the Color Mix section—tap on it to activate it, then tap-and-drag up/down over the area of color in your image you want to adjust.)

TIP: Resetting and Starting Over

If you really mess up and want to reset and start over from scratch, just tap the Reset icon (the downward-facing arrow with a line beneath it) beneath the panels. A pop-up menu will appear asking how much you want to reset: tap Adjustments for just the adjustments you've made; tapping All reverts you back to the original image; To Import takes it back to how it looked when you first opened the image in Lightroom mobile (so it undoes what you did here in mobile, but not stuff you did to it in Lightroom desktop); and To Open will reset it back to when you last opened it.

Step Eight:

The Effects section has sliders like Clarity, Dehaze, and Vignette Amount, and they work the same way they do in Lightroom desktop. There's also a button here for adding color Split Tone effects (hey, shouldn't that be in the Color section? [Insert sound effect of crickets here]). Tapping Detail (the triangle icon) will bring up the same Sharpening sliders you're used to using in Lightroom desktop (as seen here), along with the Noise Reduction sliders. Nothing much to see here, folks. Move along.

Continued

Step Nine:

Besides all the sliders, three of the awesome adjustment brushes and filters made it over to mobile (the Adjustment Brush, the Graduated Filter, and the Radial Filter), and applying them with your finger is actually pretty great. Tap the round Selective Edits icon (the one with the dotted circle around it, shown circled here in red) and a big + (plus sign) icon appears in the top-left corner of the screen. Tap on it and the three adjustment tools appear. Tap on the one you want (we'll tap on the Adjustment Brush here), and a menu pops out from the left center for brush size, feather (softness), and flow. Tap on one, and then drag up/down to change the setting.

TIP: Seeing a Before/After

To see what your image looked like before you started adjusting it, just tap-and-hold on it (you'll see "Before" appear above the image).

Step 10:

Once you tap one of these tools on your image, you'll then need to "Set Adjustments for Your Selection," so tap the adjustment for what you want to do (Light, or Color, or Effects, and so on), then start painting with your finger to adjust that area (if you're using the Graduated Filter, you can tap-and-drag down with your finger, or if you're using the Radial Filter, you can just tap-and-drag outward to create your pool of light). A pin will appear where you first tapped, and if you tap-and-hold on that pin, a menu will appear with options, like for showing the mask as you paint, duplicating the brush edits, or removing the brush edit altogether. When you're done with your adjustments, tap the Done button (or the checkmark icon, if you're using a phone) to apply your edits, or tap Cancel (or the small "X") to cancel your selective edits.

Step 11:

Tapping the Presets icon (the two over-lapping circles) gives you access to a ton of Develop module presets, and each one has a tiny preview beside it. These presets are literally just one-tap effects—tap one and it applies a look. If you like the look, tap the Done button (or checkmark icon)—boom—done! There are seven sections of presets—Color, Creative, B&W, Curve, Grain, Sharpening, and Vignetting—and all you have to do is tap on any one, then tap the Done button to apply it. Of course, once we apply a preset, we can still make adjustments with our sliders (Exposure, Contrast, etc.). *Note:* Currently, you cannot import custom presets you bought or created in Lightroom desktop into Light-room mobile. Don't shoot the messenger.

Step 12:

In some cases you can "stack" presets—having one add its effect on top of anoth-er—and a great place to see this in action is when you use presets that add things like vignette looks (darkening the outside edges of your image) or noise (grain), or apply Curve adjustments. The reason these add on is that most of them don't use the Split Tone sliders or the Color Mix sliders or any other options that might get changed by applying another preset. For example, if you apply a B&W preset, then apply a Color preset, the color overrides the black and white and changes the image back to color. But, adding noise (grain) or a vignette adds on to the look you applied with the first preset because it doesn't use any of the same sliders. Here, I started by applying the B&W preset, B&W Soft. Then, in the overlay, I tapped on the Grain presets and added Medium to enhance the grainy film look.

Continued

Step 13:

One of the most powerful time savers from Lightroom desktop is here, too: the Apply Previous button. It takes the adjustments you made to the previous image and applies them to the current image with one tap (super handy and fast!). To use it, tweak a photo the way you like it, then bring up the Filmstrip, swipe to the image you want to apply this look to, and tap on it. Now, in the Edit panel, tap on the Previous icon (it looks like three sliders with a right-facing arrow) and a pop-up menu appears (seen here), asking if you want just the basic tonal edits you applied, or everything you did to the previous photo, including cropping, rotating, etc. Make your choice and the edits are applied immediately.

Step 14:

There's one more way to get edits from one image applied to another (or a bunch of other images): you can literally copy-and-paste the edits you've made. Once you've applied the edits you want to copy, tap the three dots in the top right and, from the pop-up menu that appears, choose **Copy Settings**. Turn on/off the settings you want to copy in the Copy Settings dialog, and tap OK. Now find an image where you want to apply those same settings, tap the three dots again and, from the pop-up menu, choose **Paste Settings**. That's all there is to it. You can paste those settings to as many images as you'd like.

Step 15:

If you have an image with lens issues, you can apply a lens correction profile by tapping on Optics (the lens icon) and then turning on Enable Lens Corrections. It will choose a built-in lens profile for your particular lens make and model (if one is available, of course). If it doesn't find one, well…you're out of luck. Well, I guess not entirely—you could go on to the next step.

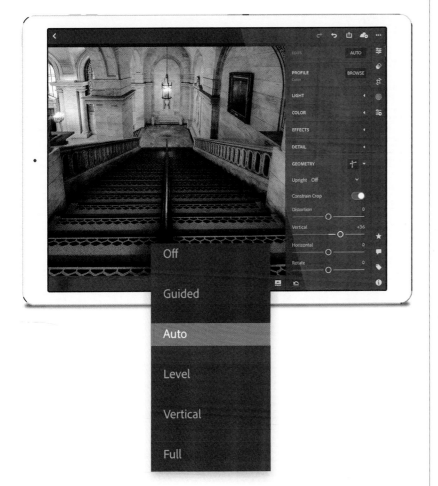

Step 16:

Tap on Geometry (its icon looks like… well…geometry), and you'll find the Upright features, which are automated one-tap fixes for common lens problems (like buildings leaning back, or not being horizontally centered in your image). Upright will even fix a crooked image for you. You'll see the manual sliders in this panel (Distortion, Vertical, Horizontal, Rotate, and Aspect, just like in Lightroom desktop), but at the top, to the right of Upright, you'll see "Off." Tap this to bring up the Upright menu (Auto, Level, Vertical, etc. See page 252 for more on the Upright features). Also in this menu is Guided, which lets you tap-and-draw out lines along parts of your image that are supposed to be straight (for more on Guided Upright see page 256). This feature works really well on mobile devices—it feels more natural than on your desktop. You can draw out up to four lines. If you don't like the results, just tap the trash icon. If you're happy with the results, tap the Done button. Easy as that. There's also a Constrain Crop button near the top of the panel that auto crops away white gaps that may be created when applying either Upright or Guided Upright (I usually leave this turned on. It's a big timesaver most of the time).

Cropping & Rotating

If there's one thing that really translated well on a mobile device, it's cropping and I gotta tell you, I'm not sure if I don't like this better here, than in Lightroom desktop. It really feels quick and intuitive, and you can pretty much do all of the same stuff you do on your computer. But, somehow, it seems smoother and easier here. In short, you'll dig it.

Step One:

If you need to crop your image, just tap on the Crop tool icon. You'll know it's active because it puts a cropping border around your entire image (as seen here), and the Crop and Rotate panel pops out (or if you're using your phone, a row of icons appears along the bottom, or the side, depending on if you have your phone tall or turned sideways). Here, you'll find all the different cropping options from Lightroom desktop.

Step Two:

To apply any of the preset cropping ratios (1x1 Square, 4x3, 16x9, and so on), just tap on the Aspect pop-up menu (or on the icon with the stacked rectangles, if you're using your phone), then tap any preset and your image is cropped to that ratio. Here, I tapped on **16x9** and the cropping border updated to the new ratio. The areas that will be cropped away are still visible, but they're shown in dark gray (you can see here a horizontal strip would be cropped off along the top and bottom if I were to go with this cropping ratio). Now that you've applied a crop, you can reposition your image within that cropping border by just tapping-and-dragging the image right where you want it.

TIP: Resetting the Crop

To return to the original uncropped image, just double-tap anywhere within the cropping border.

Step Three:
Besides just cropping ratios, there's a Locked icon, which gives you a free aspect option. This means you're not constrained to any preset ratio, so once you tap on it to unlock it, you can tap on any corner or side of the cropping border and drag just that part right where you want, without affecting the other three sides (it's like clicking on the Unlock icon for the Crop Overlay tool in Lightroom desktop). Here, I tapped on it to unlock it, and then just tapped-and-dragged each side of the cropping border right where I wanted them. In the Rotate & Flip Image section, if you tap the Flip H icon (the one with the two horizontal triangles), it flips your image horizontally (like I did here—her arm is now on the right side of the image), and of course, tapping the Flip V icon (the one with the two vertical triangles) flips your image upside down.

TIP: Changing the Crop Overlay
When you choose the Crop tool, you can have it temporarily display a Rule of Thirds overlay grid by just two-finger tapping within the cropping border.

Step Four:
If you want to rotate your image within the cropping border, just tap-and-hold outside the cropping border and drag up/down and the image will rotate within the cropping border (so you're rotating the image, not the border). Here, I tapped-and-dragged outside the border and rotated her a little to the left.

TIP: Flipping the Crop to Tall
By default, a crop is applied wide (landscape), but if you want to flip it to the same ratio, but tall (portrait), tap the icon with the rectangle and upward- (or downward-) facing arrow in the Aspect section (or in the top-left corner), and it flips to a tall crop.

Sharing Your Lightroom Albums on the Web

When you sync albums (collections) from Lightroom desktop, of course they are synced to your phone and/or your tablet, but those same albums also appear on a special, private website (that only you have access to). The advantage of having "Lightroom Web" is that you can use it to share your albums with any individual (or the public on social media, if you choose), and it has lots of interesting options and features wrapped around it.

Step One:

While this is an extension of Lightroom mobile (because it's based on syncing one or more albums [collections] from your desktop), you actually don't access this feature through mobile—you access it from a web browser on your desktop (well, I guess you could technically launch a browser on your phone or tablet and see it there, but you already have access to those albums on your mobile device). To see your synced albums, in Lightroom desktop, go under the Help menu and choose **View Your Synced Collection on the Web** (as shown here). If you don't see that option under the Help menu, just go to http://lightroom .adobe.com.

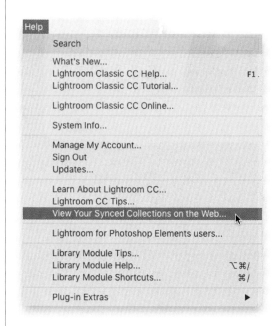

Step Two:

That launches your web browser and takes you to Lightroom Web (your images are password protected, so you might need to sign in with your Adobe ID and password). Here, you'll see all your synced albums right on the web. So, what's the advantage of having them here? Sharing! It makes sharing your albums with anyone really easy. For example, let's say you shot a high school football game and you wanted to share the images with the other parents. You could share that album individually (by emailing or texting the parents), or publicly (by sharing the album directly to Facebook, Twitter, or Google+).

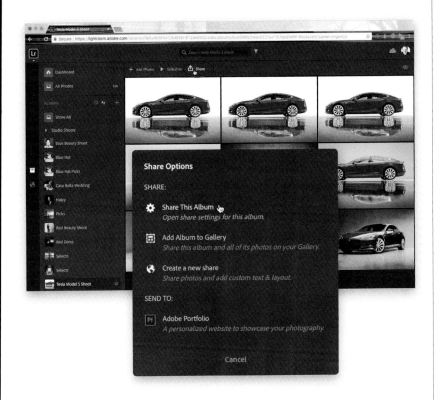

Step Three:

To share any album, click on it and then click on Share near the top of the page (as shown here). This brings up a window asking if you want to Share This Album or Create a New Share (which is a page where you add text and tell a story with your photos). For now, just choose Share This Album. That brings up another window, letting you know it's private, blah, blah, blah, so just click the Share This Album button.

Step Four:

This brings up the Album Settings window. There are four tabs here, but by default, the Share tab will be visible because that's the one you'll use the most. In this tab, it shows you the web address where this album is posted. Click on the clipboard icon to the right of that web address to copy it into memory, so you can email or text this address to a friend or client. If you want to share it publicly, click the Facebook, Twitter, or Google+ icon. Below that are some options for this posted album: you can allow downloads (if you shot that football game, this would allow other parents to download low-resolution photos of their kids); turning on Show Meta-data would include your f-stop, shutter speed, camera info, etc., for each image; and turning on Show Location would share any embedded GPS added by your camera. If you only want to show the Picks, unflagged images, or Rejects in this album, click on the flag option (I'm interested in finding the photographer who wants to share their Rejects. They'd make a great Oprah guest).

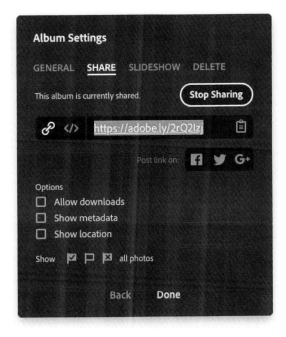

Continued

Step Five:

When someone types that web address into their browser, they'll see what you see here on the right. They can click on any image to see it larger, they can scroll through the images using the arrow keys on their keyboard, and they can hit the Play icon in the top-right corner to see a slide show, complete with transitions (you can choose your slide show options in the Slideshow tab in that Album Settings window seen back in Step Four). When they're viewing a larger image (as seen in the next step), they can see any metadata or GPS info by clicking on the little "i" icon on the right side of the page, and a panel will slide out with those details. That's pretty much all they can do—they can view your images in any web browser, but that might be enough.

Step Six:

If you want the person/client you shared this album with to be able to choose their favorite images or even leave comments to you about a particular shot, then they'll need an Adobe user account (with a user ID and password). Luckily, they are free, so they could just sign up for one. But, what I do is create an account for my clients (just one generic account—like access@KelbyPhoto.com—with a simple password—like "client"). This isn't banking info, so simpler is better, and they'll only see the shoot I'm sharing at that web address, so they can all use the same user ID and password. Now they can log in, and if they see an image they like, they can click the heart icon, and if they want to leave a comment, they can click the comment icon (both in the bottom left), and their comments will appear right within Lightroom desktop.

Step Seven:

When the person you shared your album with marks a photo as a favorite or leaves you a comment, Lightroom lets you know by adding a yellow comment icon to your collection in Lightroom desktop (you'll also see it as a thumbnail badge, like the one shown circled here). To see their written comments (or even respond back), go to the Comments panel at the bottom of the Library module's right side Panels area (as seen here).

TIP: Editing Images in Web

If you want to make edits to your images while you're in Lightroom Web, no problem—the Basic panel adjustments are available right online. Just click on a photo to select it, then tap on the Edit This Photo button in the top-left corner, and the Edit sliders pop-out from the right side.

Step Eight:

If, instead of just sharing an album, you want to use that Create a New Share feature (so you can add text and do some storytelling, like sharing your vacation photo story with friends and family), then back in the Share Options window, click on Create a New Share, give your story a title, and choose a cover photo. Luckily, Adobe has done a great job of putting buttons where you can add text, so you'll have no trouble with that part, but one thing that is kind of hidden is how to create a divider between photos, so you can separate them and add more text. You have to hold your cursor between two images and a break appears, like the images are opening a door to a little + (plus sign; as shown here). Click on it, and it creates a separation at that point, and a new text block button appears, so you can add text. When you're done formatting your story, the share link is already visible in the top-left corner of the page, ready for you to text, email, or post to social media.

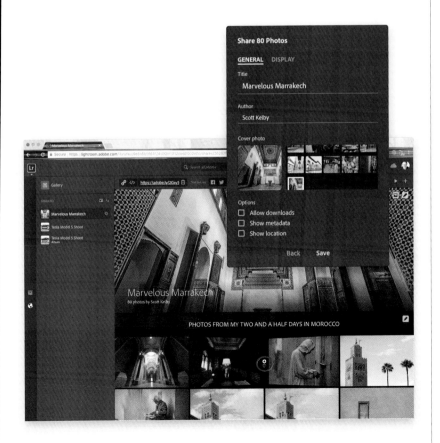

Sharing a Live Shoot to a Phone, Tablet, or the Web

I think this is one of the coolest features of Lightroom mobile, and it really impresses clients because the technology here is really pretty cool. We're going to set things up so that, during a live shoot, we can hand our client our tablet and not only can they see the images coming in live as we shoot, they can make their own Picks, comments, and even share the link with someone at a different location, so they can be part of the shoot, and the approval process, too!

Step One:

You're going to need to shoot tethered, so when you take a shot with your camera, it goes directly into Lightroom desktop (well, in this case, it's going to my laptop, but you know what I mean. See Chapter 3 for how to set up to shoot tethered). Here's a behind-the-scenes shot from a fashion shoot, and as I shoot the images, they come straight into Lightroom Classic on my laptop. I want to be able to hand my client my iPad (or Android tablet) and let them see the images from the shoot on that iPad as I take them, but I also want control over which images my client sees (more on why in a moment).

Step Two:

First, create a new collection in Lightroom desktop/laptop, and when the Create Collection dialog appears, give it a name (I named mine "Red Dress Shoot"), then turn on the Set as Target Collection checkbox (a very important checkbox for this all to work). Also, turn on the Sync with Lightroom CC checkbox (also very important). What that "target collection" stuff means is this: any time I see a photo from this live shoot that I want my client to see on the iPad they're holding, I press the letter **B** on my keyboard. That takes the photo and adds it to that collection (my target collection). I only want my client to see my best shots—not the ones where my subject's eyes are closed, or the flash didn't fire, or my timing was off—so I only tap the B key when I see a good shot.

Create Collection

Name: Red Dress Shoot

Location

☑ Inside a Collection Set

    Fashion

Options

☑ Set as target collection

☑ Sync with Lightroom CC

Cancel   Create

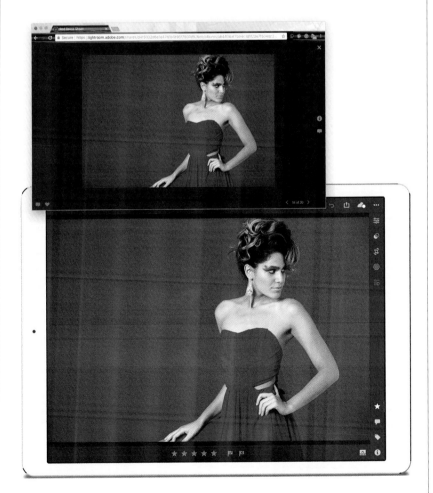

Step Three:

Now that everything's set up and ready to go, I launch Lightroom CC (mobile) on my iPad and there's my newly synced collection (well, it's an "album" in Lightroom mobile on my iPad). I tap on that album and hand it to my client, or art director (or friend, assistant, guest, etc.), who is there on the set, well behind the position where I'm shooting from (most photographers don't like someone looking over their shoulder when they're trying to shoot).

Step Four:

Now I start the shoot, and when I see a shot a like (one I want the client to see), I simply reach over and tap the letter B on my laptop. That image now goes to that targeted collection on my laptop, is synced to the iPad my client is holding, and right there in Lightroom mobile they see the shot. I let my client (friend, family member, etc.) know that if they like the shot, they can tap the Pick flag at the bottom of the screen. Now, if for any reason, you're uncomfortable with handing your client your iPad/tablet, or if you don't have one yet, then instead you'll use Lightroom Web (see page 426), share that synced album, and just text them the album's web address (the one you targeted), and it will work pretty much the same way, but they'll see the images in their web browser, rather than on your iPad. Also, they will use the heart icon to mark their favorites, instead of a Pick flag. They can also leave comments, if they have (or you give them) an Adobe user ID and password (mentioned on page 428). The cool thing about doing it this way is that they can now share that web address with other people (maybe folks back in their office), so they can watch the shoot live, too, right from their web browser. How cool is that?!

Lightroom Mobile's Advanced Search

As a country, as a world, we can't agree on many things these days, but one thing we all can agree on, regardless of our background, is that having to do keywording stinks (and, of course, I wanted to use a stronger term, but you get the gist). Anyway, Adobe knows you hate keywording and that's why you'll love their keywording-free, magical-unicorn-style search feature, which lets you search by describing what you're looking for, like "cars," "guitars," "pizza," or "the kids," and so on. It's another feature powered by Adobe Sensei, and the weird thing is, for the most part, it works pretty darn well.

Step One:
In Albums view, tap on the magnifying glass icon (shown circled here) up in the top-right corner to bring up the Sensei-powered search field. You'll type in a description of what you're looking for and it will use its artificial intelligence to visually search for images that contain that object (no keywording necessary).

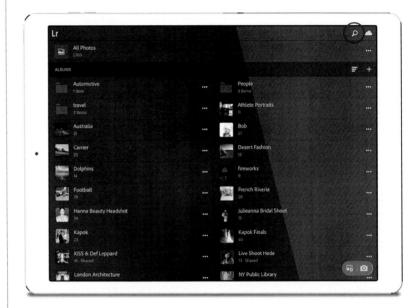

TIP: Safe In-Person Sharing
If you want to hand someone your mobile device, so they can see your images, but without accidentally adding or changing anything (Pick flags, star ratings, edit sliders, etc.), before you hand them your device, turn on Present mode—it disables all that stuff, so you don't have to worry about them accidentally changing anything. Tap the three dots (…) in the top-right corner, then tap on **Present** in the pop-up menu. When they hand your mobile device back to you, just tap the X in the upper-left corner to exit Present mode.

Step Two:
In this case, I wanted to find all my football images, so I typed "football" in the search field, then tapped the Search button on the keyboard. In literally just a second or two it displayed all my images that visually matched that search term, as seen here where it found a bunch of football photos, all from different albums.

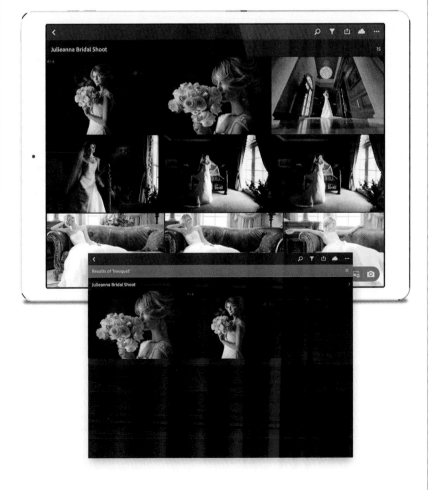

Step Three:

Once your results appear (and they will appear almost immediately), you have a few sorting options. Tap the three dots in the top-right corner and in the menu that pops-up, you'll see that, by default, it sorts by relevancy. Tap on Sort by Relevancy to bring up the other Sort options. If you choose to sort by Capture Date (as I did here), it puts your most-recent images at the top. To reverse the order (and see the oldest shots appearing first), tap the icon to the right of Capture Date (the three lines with the down-facing arrow).

TIP: Save RAW Photos Taken with Lightroom Mobile's Camera App to Your Camera Roll

By default, RAW photos taken with Lightroom mobile's built-in camera app go directly into Lightroom mobile, not into your cell phone's Camera Roll (or Gallery). But, if you want to save one of those RAW images to your Camera Roll (apparently, a lot of folks want to do this), here's how: Tap on the image you want to save to your Camera Roll, then tap on the Share icon up top. In the pop-up menu, tap on Export Original, then tap on **Camera Roll** (or **Gallery**) and the RAW image will be saved to your Camera Roll. Easy as that.

Step Four:

When you start a search from Album view (where all your collections...er... I mean "albums" appear), by default, the Sensei find feature searches through all the images you have in Lightroom mobile. However, if you just wanted to search within a particular album, first tap on that album to display its contents (as I did here), then tap on the magnifying glass icon up top. Now, type in your search term (in this case, I typed in "bouquet") and the results that appear (shown in the inset) display the only two shots in this album where you can see a bouquet.

The Built-In Camera (It's Pretty Sweet!)

I mentioned at the beginning of this chapter that Lightroom mobile has a pretty killer built-in camera feature, and once you start using it, you won't be able to go back to the regular camera app that comes with your phone. Here's how to unlock all those features that take it over-the-top when it comes to usability and results.

Step One:

If you're in Albums view, or if you're in an album, you'll see a blue pill-shaped button in the bottom-right corner of the screen. Tap the camera icon on the right side of that button to bring up Lightroom mobile's camera. If you click on the camera button when you're in an album, the images you shoot with the camera will appear in that album. Otherwise, they will appear in All Photos at the top of Album view.

Step Two:

When the camera appears, it's in Automatic mode, by default, which works like the camera app on your phone (boooo!)—it makes all the exposure decisions for you; you just point-and-shoot (snore). However, if you want full control over the white balance, ISO, shutter speed, and aperture, individually, like you would on a DSLR or mirrorless camera, tap on **Auto** just below the shutter button and a menu will pop-up with different choices, including High Dynamic Range (more on this in a moment), but for now just choose Professional mode (as shown here).

Step Three:

All the Pro adjustment icons will now appear to the left of the shutter button (as seen here). Tap on any one of them and a slider will appear (or icons if you choose White Balance). Also, by default, your camera will be shooting in JPEG format, but if your camera can shoot in RAW format (like the iPhone 6 and up, and many high-end Android phones), just tap on JPG on the left side of the screen and the File Format options will appear (as shown here). Just tap on the button to toggle over to shoot in DNG (Adobe's RAW image format).

Step Four:

When it comes to focusing, it works pretty much like every other camera—you tap-and-hold on the thing you want in-focus and a square focus area box appears. If you want to adjust the exposure (using Exposure Compensation), you can do that easily by tapping-and-dragging left (to darken the exposure) or to the right to brighten it (as seen here). It's quick and easy, and it shows you (in stops) how much Exposure Compensation has been applied by your swiping.

Continued

Step Five:

The three icons above (or to the right of, if you're holding your phone vertically) the shutter button give you (from top to bottom/right to left): live shooting effects (more on this in a moment); an Exposure Lock feature (just tap on the lock icon to lock your exposure, as you recompose your image); and a way to toggle between wide angle and telephoto (if you have a phone that has this two-lens feature built-in, like on an iPhone with two lenses). The live shooting effects feature is cooler than it sounds, because it lets you see and apply a preset effect before you even take the shot. So, you can see, before you even tap the shutter button, if a particular image would look good as a black and white, or with a contrast effect, or creative look applied. When you tap on this option (its icon [circled here] looks like two circles overlapping), a row of live effects appear at the bottom of your image preview area. Tap on one to apply it to your image before you shoot. *Note:* These are non-destructive, so if after you take the shot you change your mind, you can reset the image to the normal look without an effect.

Step Six:

If you tap the three dots in the top left (or top right) of the screen, additional options pop out from the side (or down from the top): Tap on the gear icon for some capture setting preferences for the camera app. The triangle icon turns on/off the Highlight Clipping warning (clipped highlight areas appear with a moving zebra pattern over them). Tap on the grid icon for Grid & Level overlay options (seen here) or to turn on auto level (with haptic feedback on newer iPhones). There's also a self-timer icon, and the last icon lets you choose the aspect ratio of images taken with the camera.

Step Seven:

At the bottom left (or at the top left) is an icon for turning on/off your built-in flash. Just tap on it and the menu you see here pops up. You can choose Auto mode (it senses low-light situations and turns itself on automatically), On (the flash always stays on regardless of the lighting situation), or Off. For the sake of your photography's quality, the right answer is always "Off." (Yes, really.) If you want to take a selfie, there's a camera icon with a circular arrow in the top-left (or top-right) corner and tapping that switches you to the back camera, so you can take your selfie.

Step Eight:

One of my personal favorite features is the built-in HDR mode, which uses the same technology as Lightroom Classic, so you can capture a wider tonal range in situations where you need it. Take, for example, this image I took inside a restaurant. With my Lightroom mobile camera set to Pro mode (seen at the top here), the detail in the textured/glazed glass is gone, and the highlights are blown out so much you can't even make out anything outside the windows. When I switch it to shoot in HDR mode instead, look at the difference (seen here below)—you can see the patio outside, and the texture/glaze in the glass. Even look at the lamp on the table—the detail is back there, too, and the shadow areas are brighter where the champagne bottles are on the far right. It captured a much wider range of tones by combining multiple exposures into one image automatically.

The Desktop Version of Lightroom Mobile Is Lightroom CC

Okay, now that you've learned how to use Lightroom mobile, I wanted to give you a quick look at the desktop version of the mobile app, called "Lightroom CC," which has the same limited number of features, it uses nearly the same layout (no modules—everything's in one place), and even uses albums and folders, just like Lightroom mobile. Lightroom CC on the desktop is the cloud-storage-based version of Lightroom that I mentioned back in the book's introduction (on page xii). Here are the basics:

Step One:
Importing in Lightroom CC on the desktop is the one area that's somewhat different than Lightroom mobile. This is about as simple as it gets because there are hardly any decisions to make here. You don't have to choose where to store your images—they're going to Adobe's cloud storage (there really are barely any options here, well at least compared to Lightroom Classic's Import window). In fact, the only two things you can do here are either uncheck any photos you don't want imported or choose which existing album to add your images into (at the top center, click on Add to Album). You can choose to put them into a new album (as shown here) and that just brings up a naming dialog. That's pretty much it.

Step Two:
This window should look familiar, because it's pretty much the same as Lightroom mobile's main screen, with your folders and albums on the left side, and if you click on an album it shows you the images inside it, just like mobile. At the bottom center are your Pick flags and star ratings. Below the bottom left of your thumbnails, you can choose your different views and sorting options. There's also a Search bar at the top that uses the same Sensei searching that mobile uses.

Step Three:

Just like on mobile, the tools are along the right side—click on one of those icons (here, I clicked on the Edit icon) and your panels pop out. These are the same ones that are in mobile, in the same order, in the same groupings, and they do exactly the same thing (as you can guess). It's literally the same stuff (and it works exactly like the sliders and controls that you learned about in this chapter and in the Develop chapter, starting on page 127). The difference is you tap on the screen in mobile, and you click with a mouse in Lightroom CC on your desktop. Take a look at the iPad version in the inset shown here. It's the same app, with some minor user-interface changes to accommodate a mobile touch screen.

TIP: Don't Use Classic and CC

Adobe recommends using either Lightroom Classic or Lightroom CC—not both at the same time. One reason is if you use Lightroom CC, and then use the mobile app with it, those changes won't sync back to Lightroom Classic, only to Lightrom CC, and confusion will reign as things are out of sync. So, just stick with Classic, and then Lightroom mobile will keep your collections in sync with no issues.

Step Four:

In case you were wondering, yes the Adobe color, camera, B&W, and creative profiles are all here, as well (they're in everything now—in Classic, CC, and mobile). Here, I clicked on one of the B&W profiles to convert my color image to black and white. There are no other modules to choose in Lightroom CC (no Map module, no Print module—in fact, there's just no printing at all—no Slideshow, no Web, no Book module, among lots of other things). Over time, it will get more features, but at this point, it's just what's in the mobile app (with a limited feature set), in a desktop version.

CHAPTER 15

MY WORKFLOW
here's my typical start-to-finish project

For the past few editions of this book, I've been wrapping up the book with a special bonus chapter where I share my own Lightroom workflow. It's a typical start-to-finish project, where I show everything I would do to a particular image so you can see how I deal with different parts of the process. Now, I have to be honest with you, I had fully written this chapter, but then I did the image again, and had to rewrite the whole thing, and each time I reprocessed that image, I wound up having to rewrite the entire chapter. Here's why: I'm old and forget everything. Physically, I'm just in my 50s (and you know what they say, 50s are the new teens), but mentally I'm in my late 90s to early 100s, and I not only can't remember which order to do things in Lightroom, I can't remember where I put my laptop. I was using it yesterday, so I know it's here somewhere. Anyway, instead of fruitlessly rewriting this

chapter on a laptop whose location I can't quite pinpoint in my own home, I thought I would instead make some simple drawings on bar napkins, and that would give you a general idea of what I do in Lightroom. However, I did encounter two minor issues when I started this "napkin notation" process. The first was: without having Lightroom open in front of me, I can't always remember the official names of stuff, so in many cases, I had to describe steps very casually, like "Click that thing up in the right corner by the other thing," or "Go under the menu up top and chose the one that changes the look," or even just "Move the slider that makes the photo look better." I'm pretty sure with the hand-drawn illustrations alongside, it will all make sense. The second problem is that the pen I need to make the drawings and hand-written notes is in my laptop bag. This getting older thing is a blast.

It Starts with the Shoot

What you're about to learn is my typical day-in, day-out, workflow, and it doesn't matter if I'm doing a landscape shoot, portrait shoot, or a sports shoot, I pretty much use Lightroom the same way, in the same order, every time. For this particular example, I'm doing a landscape shoot, so it actually starts with me on location, in this case, in northern Italy's Dolomites mountains. According to my GPS, it says this was taken in "Livinallongo del Col di Lana."

The Location:

My brother Jeff and I drove past this spot on our way to a dawn shoot, and on our way back, we pulled off the road (that's the road at the top of the embankment on the left) and wandered down to this still-water, small lake. The sun wasn't very high in the sky yet, still mostly behind some of the mountains, and the light was still pretty nice. Because of the relatively low-light (it was darker than the behind-the-scenes shot here shows), I used a tripod, and to get a lower perspective, I splayed the legs of the tripod out wide (as seen here). The tripod itself is the Albert model from UK-based tripod designers 3 Legged Thing.

The Camera Info/Settings:

I took the shot that we'll be using in this workflow tutorial (don't forget, you can download it and follow along—see page xii) with a Canon EOS 5D Mark IV, using a Canon 24–70mm f/2.8 lens. I took it in aperture priority mode at f/11, 1/15 of a second shutter speed, and at 100 ISO. Once I'm done with the shoot and back in my hotel, the very first thing I do is back up my photos to a portable 2-terabyte external hard drive (so I have one copy on my memory card and a second copy on that external drive). If I have a decent Internet connection, I also save my Lightroom Picks to Dropbox, so I have a cloud backup, too. At the right here, I swung the camera over from my shooting position to catch a photo of my brother Jeff. He has nothing to do with the tutorial; I just wanted to show you my awesome bro. :)

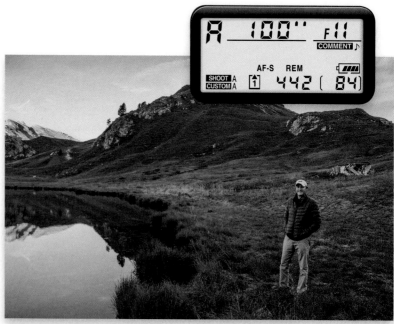

Once I get back from my trip (or if I have enough time while I'm on the trip), I import the images into Lightroom. By the way, of course, I'll always be importing to an external hard drive, whether I'm home or on the road (where I carry a lightweight WD Elements 2-terabyte external drive. Why this one? I liked that, since it was so light and small, it wouldn't take up a bunch of room in my bag, but more importantly, it was on sale for around $70).

Workflow Step One: Importing Your Images

Step One:

When I'm ready to import the images from my shoot into Lightroom, I plug my memory card reader into my computer and it brings up Lightroom's Import window (seen here). At the top, from left to right, you can see I'm importing from my memory card, then at the top center, I click on Copy (so I'm making a copy of the images on the memory card), and on the far right, it shows where I'm copying them to (Scott's External Hard Drive). If I see a shot where it's so messed up I can actually see it's messed up in the thumbnail (like one that's terribly out of focus), I turn off the checkbox for that thumbnail, since I would just wind up deleting it later anyway.

Step Two:

Over in the right side Panels area, under File Handling, I choose Minimal (the fast-loading thumbnail option) because I want to see my images in the Library module quickly. Next, I never want to import duplicates, so I always leave that checkbox turned on. I also pick a simple, descriptive name for the files (like "Dolomites," in this case), in the File naming section, and then I have Lightroom sequentially number them, starting with "-1." Lastly, in the Apply During Import section, from the Metadata pop-up menu, I apply my copyright metadata information to each photo as it's imported (see Chapter 3 for how to create a copyright template). It's a pretty simple and straightforward importing process. Now, I just hit the Import button and we're off and running!

Workflow Step Two: Sorting Your Images

Okay, your photos are in Lightroom, and it's time to start the process of finding our best shots. I use the SLIM system (we looked at this in Chapter 2) for my shoot organization, so we'll be creating a collection set, finding our Picks, then finding our Selects and sorting those into their own collections inside our collection set. Here's the exact process I use for all my shoots:

Step One:

At this point, your images have been imported, but we haven't done anything with them yet. So, in the Library module, go to the Collections panel (in the left side Panels area), click on the + (plus sign) button on the right side of the panel header, and choose **Create Collection Set** from the pop-up menu (as seen here). When the Create Collection Set dialog appears, give your new collection set a very descriptive name (I named mine "Dolomites with Jeff"), then in the Location section, choose the collection set you want this new set to appear inside (I put this inside my Landscape collection set), and then click the Create button.

Step Two:

We're going to create a new collection inside our Dolomites collection set for all the images from the shoot (I do this for every shoot). So, press **Command-A (PC: Ctrl-A)** to select all the photos you just imported, then press **Command-N (PC: Ctrl-N)** to bring up the Create Collection dialog (seen here). Name your collection "Full Shoot," and for Location, choose that collection set you just created in the previous step (in this case, it's Dolomites with Jeff). In the Options section, the Include Selected Photos checkbox should be turned on by default, but if it's not, turn it on (and leave the other options off), then click the Create button.

Step Three:
Now it's time to find our "keepers" from the shoot. So, click on the thumbnail for the first image you imported, then press **Shift-Tab** to hide all the panels (or press the letter **F** on your keyboard if you want to do this part in Full Screen view). Then, start moving through your images. If you see an image you like, press the letter **P** to mark it as a Pick (you'll see "Flag as Pick" appear right onscreen, as seen here. If you're in Full Screen view, you'll just see a tiny, white pick flag appear at the bottom center instead). Press the **Right Arrow key** on your keyboard to move to the next image, continuing through the rest of your images, marking the good shots as Picks, and just ignoring them and moving on if they're not.

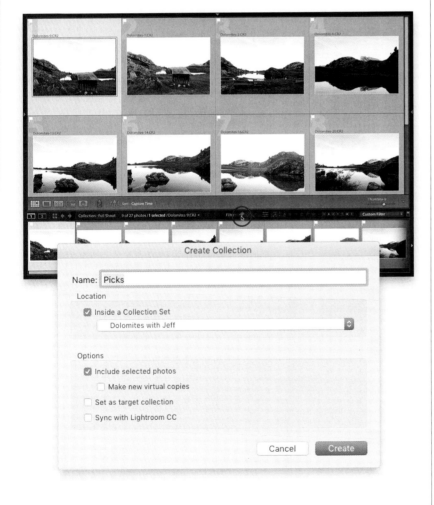

Step Four:
Now, let's turn on a filter that just shows our Picks (after all, this is what this is all about—separating our Picks from the rest of the shoot). Make sure the Filmstrip along the bottom is visible, and near the top center, to the right of Filter, click twice on the white Pick flag (shown circled here in red) to filter your images, so only the Picks are showing. *Note:* If you don't see three Pick flags to the right of Filter, just click directly on the word Filter to have them slide out. Now, press Command-A (PC: Ctrl-A) to select all your Picks, press Command-N (PC: Ctrl-N) to create a new collection, name this new collection "Picks," turn on the Inside a Collection Set checkbox, and from the pop-up menu, choose the Dolomites with Jeff collection set. Make sure the Include Selected Photos checkbox is turned on, and click the Create button. This saves your Picks in their own collection inside your Dolomites with Jeff collection set. So, to recap: at this point, we have a Dolomites with Jeff collection set, and inside it, we now have two collections: Full Shoot and Picks.

Continued

Step Five:

It's time to narrow things down even further, and take our time now, as we get down to the final images we'll be tweaking, and then maybe sharing online or printing, etc. In the Collections panel, click on the Picks collection we just created, then click on the first image (the one up in the top-left corner of the Preview area), and now let's go find the very best shots from our shoot—our "Selects." I do the same Shift-Tab routine to hide the panels, but since all these images already have a Pick flag, I tag my best of these images with a 5-star rating. So, as I come to an image I really like—one of the best images from this shoot—I press the number **5** on my keyboard, and it applies a 5-star rating (as seen here, where it says "Set Rating to 5" onscreen).

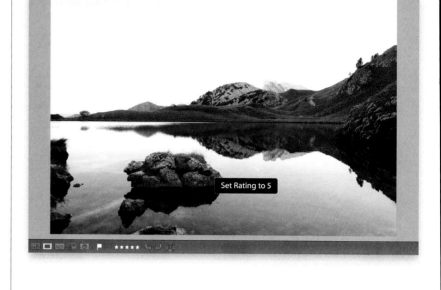

Step Six:

Go through your Picks collection, using the Right Arrow key on your keyboard, until you've tagged your very best shots as Selects (5 stars). When you're done, turn on the filter, so we just see the 5-star images in our Picks collection, by going to the top of the Filmstrip and clicking on the 5-star filter (shown circled here in red). Now, just your very best images from the shoot are visible.

Step Seven:
Press Command-A (PC: Ctrl-A) to select all your 5-star images, then press Command-N (PC: Ctrl-N) to create a new collection, name it "Selects," and then save this new collection inside the Dolomites with Jeff collection set. That's the process. We have a Dolomites with Jeff collection set, and inside it, we now have three collections: Full Shoot, Picks, and Selects.

Step Eight:
If you look in my Collections panel here, you'll see how this organization looks (and it should look familiar with what you learned back in Chapter 2). Inside my Landscape collection set, you'll see the Dolomites with Jeff collection set, and inside that, you'll see three collections:

(1) Full Shoot

(2) Picks

(3) Selects

The only images I would actually be tweaking, cropping, editing, or sharing would be the ones inside that Selects collection. That's how I sort and organize every shoot, whether it's a wedding, travel, portrait, or sports shoot, or whathaveya.

Workflow Step Three: Editing Your Selects

Now that you've whittled things down to the images you're going to tweak, let's get to work. Here, I'm going to take you through how I'd edit one of my Selects from start to finish, starting with the RAW, out-of-the-camera photo.

Step One:

Here's the original RAW image in the Develop module (download this image from the book's companion webpage, mentioned in the book's introduction). It has lots of work that needs to be done, starting with the fact that I didn't have an ND (neutral density) gradient filter with me, so the sky is overexposed and kind of washed out. The foreground is a bit backlit and in the shadows, and we've got some jet contrails in the sky, a few weeds that need pruning, and well…let's just say the image needs some TLC. I start by applying a color profile to the RAW photo. In this case, I applied the Adobe Vivid profile, but you can see in the before/after it didn't do that much to the image, but that profile will help down the road.

Step Two:

I'm going to start in the Basic panel by doing a simple technique—one that I've been using that works like a charm for dealing with washed-out skies in situations like this. I simply lower the Exposure amount until the sky looks pretty good, and then I deal with the foreground being in shadows, which is often easier to fix than a messed-up sky. So, that's what I did here—I dragged the Exposure down to –1.55 (as seen here). You can see what it did for the sky (versus how it looked in Step One), but it also made our foreground fairly dark. We can deal with that. Also, just so you can see the difference the color profile really makes, go back and switch the profile to Adobe Color. Ahhhh, big difference, right? Okay, switch it back to Adobe Vivid.

Step Three:

Now, let's expand the tonal range by setting our white and black points (well, by having Lightroom do it for us). Press-and-hold the Shift key and double-click directly on the word "Whites," then on "Blacks," and it sets the white and black points for you automatically. There are plenty of deep shadows in this image, so it didn't do that much with the Blacks slider, but it did kick up the Whites to +36.

Step Four:

To bring out detail in the hills and grass, drag the Shadows slider to the right until it looks good to you (in this case, I dragged it over to +86, opening up those shadow areas quite a bit). I went a bit farther than I needed to because I know I'll lose some of that when I increase the Contrast in the next step.

Continued

Step Five:

Let's kick up the Contrast a bit to make the brightest parts of the image brighter and the darker parts darker. I kick this up quite a bit usually, but in this case, I could only take it to +50 without the foreground getting too dark again, but that's still a pretty decent amount. Also, to enhance the definition in the sky, I'm going to pull back on the Highlights a bit, lowering them to around –40. That makes quite a difference in the sky.

Step Six:

Next, to bring out some details in the mountains and in the grass, I would add some Clarity (in this case, I dragged the slider to the right to +23), and to make the colors a bit more "colorful," I increased the Vibrance amount just a little (to +6, as seen here).

Step Seven:

Now let's get rid of some of the more distracting contrails in the sky (we can't get rid of them all because some are pretty large, like that one going horizontally across the center of the sky, and Lightroom just isn't cut out for this level of retouching—it would be a bit of a sticky retouch, even in Photoshop). Get the Spot Removal tool **(Q)** from the toolbox in the top of the right side Panels area (shown circled here), and start by painting a stroke over that contrail near the top-left corner (as you see here).

Step Eight:

There are a few more you can get rid of, and once the sky looks pretty decent, then you can move on to getting rid of some of that grass sticking up on the left side (as shown here). You might have to reposition the sample area a bit on those weeds (well, I did anyway) by clicking-and-dragging the sample area over to the left to find a better area. Be patient, and make your brush size just a little larger than the contrail or piece grass you want to remove, and don't be afraid to drag the sample area to a new spot if it looks funky (we looked at using the Spot Removal tool in Chapter 8).

Continued

Step Nine:

Next, let's enhance that sky a bit more by adding an ND gradient effect. Get the Graduated Filter tool **(M)** from the toolbox near the top of the right side Panels area (we looked at this tool in Chapter 6), double-click on the world "Effect" in the options below to zero all the sliders out, and then drag the Exposure slider to the left quite a bit to darken the exposure (here, I dragged it over to –0.89). Now, press-and-hold the Shift key (to keep it straight), then click-and-drag the tool from the top center of the image to just past the water's edge to darken the sky and have it graduate slowly down to transparent (as seen here). If you think the sky needs to be a little richer in color, you can crank up the Contrast at bit (that's what I did here, increasing it to 35 just in the areas affected by the Graduated Filter adjustment).

Step 10:

When we dragged the Graduated Filter down to the water's edge in the previous step, besides just darkening the sky, of course it darkened that rocky hill on the left, as well. Normally, we'd switch to the Erase brush and carefully paint away that area, but since we have the much more accurate and infinitely faster Range Mask feature now, we'll use that instead. So, go under Range Mask (at the bottom of the Graduated Filter options), and choose **Color**. Now, click on the eyedropper, and then click it on the color we want to keep (we can press-and-hold the Shift key to add up to a total of five color samplers). In this case, I tried clicking the eyedropper in a few places, but it kind of trashed the sky, so instead, I clicked-and-dragged over a range of colors (as seen here), and it perfectly masked the hills, removing the darkening immediately. Ya gotta love that!

Step 11:

Now we've just got to sharpen this puppy, and we're good to go. So, head down to the Detail panel and, in the Sharpening section, drag the Amount slider over a bit until it looks good to you (remember, to really see the effects of the sharpening, click on the exclamation point warning icon in the top left of the panel, and it'll zoom you in to a 1:1 actual size view. We looked at sharpening in Chapter 8). Here, I cranked the Amount to 70, but I wouldn't go much more than that—if you feel you want more sharpening, you can raise the Radius amount to 1.1, but that should do it. Okay, I think we're looking pretty decent. Let's see a before and after (below).

Step 12:

Press the letter **Y** on your keyboard to see a side-by-side before and after of where you started and where you wound up. If you decide you want to see a little more detail in the hills, you could take the Adjustment Brush **(K)**, zero all the sliders out, increase the Exposure amount to around +0.50, and use a small brush to paint over the hills in the background, but instead I just increased the Shadows slider by +10 (going from +86 to +96). Also, I thought the overall image now looked at little too colorful, so I went back and lowered the Vibrance amount from +6 to –3). That's my pretty typical start-to-finish workflow .

Workflow Step Four: Getting Client Feedback

If you're working for a client, or for a magazine or blog, or for a company's social media team, you might want to share some of the final images for feedback or advice on which image they want to use. Here's how I would create a quick online gallery, where they can mark which images are their favorites and even send direct feedback that you can view right within Lightroom.

Step One:

Once your images look okay, now it's time to share this Selects collection with your clients (if you're not doing client work, you can do this to share a collection with friends or family). In the Library module, make sure you have Sync with Lightroom CC turned on (click on the Lightroom nameplate in the upper-left corner to check; we looked at doing this in Chapter 14), then go to your Selects collection set in the Collections panel, and click the little sync checkbox to its left (it's circled here in red). By the way, if you want to change the name of this collection before your client sees it, Right-click on the collection's name and choose **Rename** (I renamed it "Dolomites Selects," as seen in the next step, only because I'm sharing this with a client).

Step Two:

Now that you've synced this collection, you can view it on the web (from any web browser), by going under the Library module's Help menu and choosing **View Your Synced Collections on the Web**. That will bring you to a private webpage created for you at lightroom.adobe.com, where you can sign-in with your Adobe username and password to see a list of your synced collections. When you see Dolomites Selects, click on it to see your Selects collection on the web. At this point, only you can see these images, so to share them, click on the Share button near the top center (as shown here).

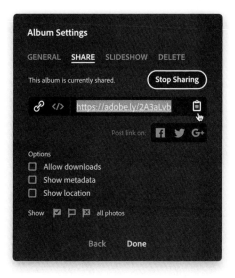

Step Three:

This brings up a Share Options dialog, asking you how you want to share these images. Choose Share This Album, and in the next dialog, click the Share This Album button (yeah, it asks you the same thing twice). You'll then see the Album Settings dialog you see here, and that web address you see highlighted is the address where people can see your Selects collection. Click on the little clipboard button to the right to copy that address into memory, so you can easily paste it into a text message or email to your client (or friends). There are a few more options here, but if you want to learn more, head back to Chapter 14.

Step Four:

When your client clicks that link, it'll launch their web browser, where they'll see your Dolomites Selects collection (and only that collection), and if they click on any of the thumbnails, they can see an image larger (as seen here). But, that's pretty much all they can do—view your images. If you want them to give you feedback (mark images or send you comments), they'll need to have an Adobe username and password (it's free). I usually either just create one for them or give them a "house account" I created for my clients to use. When they click on the little heart icon (to "like" an image) or the comment icon, both in the bottom left, the Activity panel will slide out from the right (seen here), and it will prompt them to log in to "like" an image or add a comment. If they do like a photo, or add a comment, you'll see a little yellow comment icon appear with your Selects collection in Lightroom on your computer. To see the comment(s), scroll down to the Library module's Comments panel in the right side Panels area (seen here), where you can then comment back and forth, just like a text message. Now I can see which image they want to go with, and the one I'll be using to make a large-sized print for them.

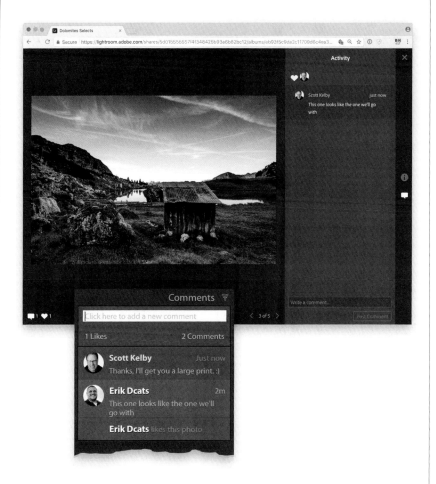

Workflow Step Five: Printing the Image

Okay, we've sorted and organized our images, we've edited the Selects, and our client has given us feedback on which image they want to use. Now, I'm going to make them a large-sized print, which is typically what I would do, even though I don't generally tell the client they're getting a big print—I do it as my way of saying thanks.

Step One:

Click on the image you want to print, then go to the Print module and, in the Template Browser, click on whichever template you want to use (I chose a preset I created earlier for the image you see here). The default page setup for this template is US Letter (8x11"), so I had to click the Page Setup button (at the bottom of the left side Panels area) and choose a larger size. When the dialog appears, choose the printer, paper size, and orientation, then click OK to apply these settings. You might need to tweak the margins a bit after choosing a new page size, since it doesn't automatically adjust everything.

Step Two:

Now it's time to print the image (this is covered in-depth back in Chapter 12). Scroll down to the Print Job panel (in the right side Panels area), and from the Print To pop-up menu at the top, choose **Printer**. Then, for Print Resolution, since I'm printing to a color inkjet printer, I can leave it at 240 ppi. Make sure the Print Sharpening checkbox is turned on, choose the amount of sharpening from the pop-up menu on the right (I generally choose High), and then choose the type of paper you'll be printing on from the Media Type pop-up menu (I chose Matte here). If your printer supports 16-bit printing, then you can turn on the 16 Bit Output checkbox. Then, in the Color Management section, choose your Profile and set your rendering Intent (again, covered in Chapter 12). I chose Relative here.

Step Three:
Now, click the Printer button at the bottom of the right side Panels area, and the Print dialog appears (the one shown here is from a Mac, but the Windows print dialog has the same basic features, just in a different layout). Your options will vary depending on your printer, but you'll want to make sure your printer's color management is turned off and you'll want to choose the type of paper you're printing to.

Step Four:
Let's print a proof. Click the Print button at the bottom of the right side Panels area, sit back, and wait for that puppy to roll out of the printer. Chances are your print is going to be darker than what you see on your super-bright, backlit computer screen. If so, turn on the Print Adjustment checkbox (at the bottom of the Print Job panel), drag the Brightness slider to the right a bit, and then make another test print to compare to your screen. It might take a couple of test prints to get it right, but once you know how much brighter to make it, remember that setting for other prints on the same type of paper (you can adjust the contrast the same way). However, if there's a color problem, like the image looks too red, or too blue, etc., then you'll need to jump back to the Develop module, go to the HSL panel, and lower the Saturation for that color, then make another test print. There you have it—my workflow, from beginning to end. Remember, this workflow stuff is at the very end of the book for a reason: because it only makes sense after you've read the rest of the book. So, if anything didn't make sense, make sure you go back and reference the chapters I gave you here, so you can learn about anything you might have skipped over or didn't think you'd need.

Other Ways You Can Continue Learning With Me

If this way of learning Lightroom resonated with you, and now you want to learn more about Lightroom (or Photoshop), or even just how to take better photos, I've got you totally covered! Here's a little bit about another book that I've written, using the same style and feel that I've written this book in, as well as some other cool resources. Hope you find these helpful.

Photoshop for Lightroom Users

As you saw a couple times here in the book, there are things that Lightroom still can't do and times when you'll need to jump over to Photoshop, so I created a book for Lightroom users to teach just those things photographers need to do over in Photoshop, without duplicating things we can already do in Lightroom. So, you're not going to learn all of Photoshop, just the stuff for photographers that you can't do here in Lightroom.

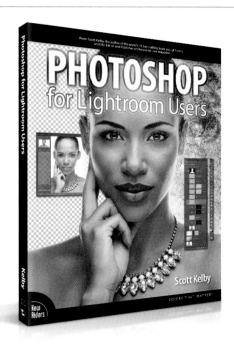

My Site: LightroomKillerTips.com

It's the #1 Lightroom blog on the planet, and it's where I post Lightroom tips, tutorials, and techniques most weekdays, along with Lightroom expert Rob Sylvan. We answer a lot of questions, do fun giveaways and contests, have free preset downloads, and it's just a really great community of Lightroom users. Go to LightroomKillerTips.com and bookmark it (or follow the RSS feed, if you like). There's nothing to sign up for or register—just come and hang out. You'll dig it.

Our Full-Length Online Training Classes on Lightroom

My full-time job is CEO at KelbyOne.com, where we teach tens of thousands of photographers all over the world how to become absolute sharks in Lightroom. We've got more than 50 full-length, in-depth online courses on Lightroom from the best-known Lightroom instructors in the world, including Matt Kloskowski, Serge Ramelli, Terry White, Lightroom Mobile Product Manager Josh Haftel, and yours truly (among others). Besides Lightroom, we've got literally hundreds of courses on everything from lighting to Photoshop, from posing to landscape photography, and everything in between, from instructors you know and trust. It's super-affordable (starting at just $10 a month), and you can be a monthly member or an annual KelbyOne Pro plan member, but either way, you'll be amazed at how fast you get really, really good! The full scoop is at KelbyOne.com.

Come Learn from Me Live

I'm out on the road doing live full-day Lightroom seminars all over the US, Canada, and in the UK, so if you get a chance, I hope you'll come out and spend the day with me. You can find my current seminar tour schedule (upcoming cities and dates) at KelbyOneLive.com, and I hope to meet you in person at one of my seminars this year!

Index

The Adobe Photoshop Lightroom Classic CC Book for Digital Photographers

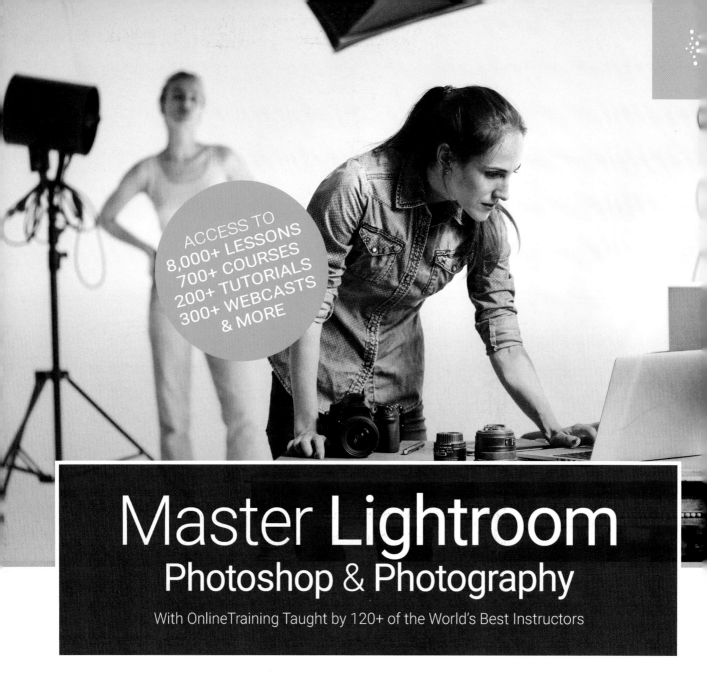

ACCESS TO
8,000+ LESSONS
700+ COURSES
200+ TUTORIALS
300+ WEBCASTS
& MORE

Master **Lightroom**
Photoshop & Photography

With OnlineTraining Taught by 120+ of the World's Best Instructors

Scott Kelby

Lindsay Adler

Joe McNally